M/B	Market to book ratio
MCC	Marginal cost of capital
MIRR	Modified internal rate of return
N	Calculator key denoting number of periods
n	(1) Life of a project (periods or years)
	(2) Number of shares outstanding
MVA	Market value added
NAL	Net advantage to leasing
NOPAT	Net operating profit after taxes
NPV	Net present value
NWC	Net working capital
P	(1) Price of a share of stock; P_0 = price of stock today
	(2) Price per unit of output
	(3) Probability of occurrence
P/E	Price/earnings ratio
PI	Profitability index
PMT	(1) Annuity payment
	(2) Payment key on calculators
PV	Present value
Q	Unit sales
r	Correlation coefficient
ROA	Return on assets
ROE	Return on equity
RP	Risk premium
	RP_M Market risk premium
S	(1) Dollar sales
	(2) Total market value of equity
SML	Security Market Line
Σ	Summation sign (capital sigma)
σ	Standard deviation (lowercase sigma)
T	Tax rate
t	Time
TIE	Times-interest-earned ratio
V	(1) Value
	(2) Variable cost per unit
V_L	Total market value of a levered firm
V_U	Total market value of an unlevered firm
w	Proportion or weight
	w_d Weight of debt
	w_{ps} Weight of preferred stock
	w_{ce} Weight of common equity
WACC	Weighted average cost of capital
YTC	Yield to call
YTM	Yield to maturity

Ninth Edition

FINANCIAL MANAGEMENT

THEORY AND PRACTICE

Ninth Edition

FINANCIAL MANAGEMENT

THEORY AND PRACTICE

EUGENE F. BRIGHAM
University of Florida

LOUIS C. GAPENSKI
University of Florida

MICHAEL C. EHRHARDT
University of Tennessee

The Dryden Press
Harcourt Brace College Publishers

Fort Worth   Philadelphia   San Diego   New York   Orlando   Austin   San Antonio
Toronto   Montreal   London   Sydney   Tokyo

Publisher	George Provol
Executive Editor	Mike Reynolds
Senior Developmental Editor	Anita Fallon
Project Manager	Becky Dodson
Production Manager	Anne Dunigan
Product Manager	Lisé Johnson
Art Director	Jeanette Barber
Project Management	Elm Street Publishing Services, Inc.
Compositor	The Clarinda Company
Text Type	10/12 Clearface
Cover Image	© PhotoDisc Signature Series

Requests for permission to make copies of any part of the work should be mailed to: Permissions Department, Harcourt Brace & Company, 6277 Sea Harbor Drive, Orlando, Florida 32887-6777.

Portions of this work were published in previous editions.

Address for Editorial Correspondence
The Dryden Press, 301 Commerce Street, Suite 3700, Fort Worth, TX 76102

Address for Orders
The Dryden Press, 6277 Sea Harbor Drive, Orlando, FL 32887
1-800-782-4479, or 1-800-433-0001 (in Florida)

ISBN 0-03-024399-8

Library of Congress Catalog Card Number: 98-71656

Printed in the United States of America

9 0 1 2 3 4 5 6 7   032   9 8 7 6 5 4

The Dryden Press
Harcourt Brace College Publishers

THE DRYDEN PRESS SERIES IN FINANCE

Amling and Droms
Investment Fundamentals

Berry and Young
Managing Investments: A Case Approach

Besley and Brigham
Principles of Finance

Boone, Kurtz, and Hearth
Planning Your Financial Future

Brigham
Brigham's Interactive Guide to Finance
CD-ROM

Brigham, Gapenski, and Daves
Intermediate Financial Management
Sixth Edition

Brigham, Gapenski, and Ehrhardt
Financial Management: Theory and Practice
Ninth Edition

Brigham, Gapenski, and Klein
1999 Cases in Financial Management:
Dryden Request

Brigham and Houston
Fundamentals of Financial Management
Eighth Edition

Brigham and Houston
Fundamentals of Financial Management:
Concise Second Edition

Chance
An Introduction to Derivatives
Fourth Edition

Clark, Gerlach, and Olson
Restructuring Corporate America

Cooley
Advances in Business Financial Management:
A Collection of Readings
Second Edition

Dickerson, Campsey, and Brigham
Introduction to Financial Management
Fourth Edition

Eaker, Fabozzi, and Grant
International Corporate Finance

Gardner, Mills, and Cooperman
Managing Financial Institutions: An Asset/Liability Approach
Fourth Edition

Gitman and Joehnk
Personal Financial Planning
Eighth Edition

Greenbaum and Thakor
Contemporary Financial Intermediation

Harrington and Eades
Case Studies in Financial Decision Making
Third Edition

Hayes and Meerschwam
Financial Institutions: Contemporary Cases in the
Financial Services Industry

Hearth and Zaima
Contemporary Investments:
Security and Portfolio Analysis
Second Edition

Johnson
Issues and Readings in Managerial Finance
Fourth Edition

Kidwell, Peterson, and Blackwell
Financial Institutions, Markets, and Money
Sixth Edition

Koch and MacDonald
Bank Management
Fourth Edition

Leahigh
Pocket Guide to Finance

Maness and Zietlow
Short-Term Financial Management

Martin, Cox, and MacMinn
The Theory of Finance: Evidence and Applications

Mayes and Shank
Financial Analysis with Lotus 1-2-3 for Windows

Mayes and Shank
Financial Analysis with Microsoft Excel

Mayo
Financial Institutions, Investments, and Management:
An Introduction
Sixth Edition

Mayo
Investments: An Introduction
Fifth Edition

Osteryoung, Newman, and Davies
Small Firm Finance: An Entrepreneurial Analysis

Reilly and Brown
Investment Analysis and Portfolio Management
Fifth Edition

Reilly and Norton
Investments
Fifth Edition

Sears and Trennepohl
Investment Management

Seitz and Ellison
Capital Budgeting and Long-Term Financing Decisions
Third Edition

Siegel and Siegel
Futures Markets

Smith and Spudeck
Interest Rates: Principles and Applications

Stickney and Brown
Financial Reporting and Statement Analysis:
A Strategic Perspective
Fourth Edition

Weston, Besley, and Brigham
Essentials of Managerial Finance
Eleventh Edition

PREFACE

For more information about this text be sure to visit the *Financial Management* web site at *http://www.dryden. com/finance.*

When we wrote the first edition of *Financial Management: Theory and Practice* more than 20 years ago, we had four goals: (1) to create a text that would help students make better financial decisions; (2) to provide a book that could be used in the introductory MBA course, but one that was complete enough for use as a reference text in follow-on case courses and after graduation; (3) to motivate students by demonstrating that finance is both interesting and relevant; and (4) to make the book clear enough so that students could go through the material without wasting time trying to figure out what we were saying.

As the title indicates, the book combines theory and practical applications. An understanding of finance theory is absolutely essential if one is to develop and implement effective financial strategies. Similarly, it is essential to have a working knowledge of the financial environment. Therefore, the book begins with basic concepts, including background on the economic and financial environment, financial statement analysis, risk analysis, and the valuation process. With this background, one can understand how specific techniques and decision rules can be used to help maximize the value of the firm. This structure has three important advantages:

1. Financial management is designed to help maximize the value of a firm. Value is determined, in the long run, by results as revealed in financial statements. Therefore, financial managers focus on how current decisions affect future financial statements. Our early coverage of financial statements thus helps students see what financial management is all about and how the effects of particular financial decisions are transmitted to various parts of the firm. Also, most financial decisions today are analyzed using spreadsheets, and if an instructor plans to emphasize spreadsheets in the course, financial statements provide an excellent starting point to illustrate the usefulness of spreadsheets.

2. Giving students an early exposure to risk analysis, discounted cash flow techniques, valuation procedures, and EVA/MVA permits us to use and reinforce these key concepts throughout the book.

3. Students, even those who do not plan to major in finance, generally enjoy working with stock and bond valuation models, rates of return, and the like. Since a student's ability to learn a subject is a function of his or her interest and motivation, and since *Financial Management* covers security markets and prices early on, the book's organization is sound from a pedagogic standpoint.

People familiar with past editions will note that a new coauthor, Mike Ehrhardt of the University of Tennessee, has been added. We (Brigham and Gapenski) wanted to add a coauthor, and when we read Mike's book, *The Search for Value,* which was commissioned by the Financial Management Association and published by the Harvard Business School Press, we thought, "This is the one!" Mike brings a wealth of experience to *Financial Management* as a teacher of the introductory MBA finance course, as a financial researcher, and as a consultant with various businesses. Mike's contributions are reflected throughout the text.

INTENDED MARKET AND USE

Financial Management is designed primarily for use in the introductory MBA finance course and then as a reference text in follow-on case courses and after graduation. There is enough material for two terms, especially if supplemented with cases and/or selected readings. The book can also be used as an undergraduate introductory text with exceptionally good students or when the introductory course is taught over two terms.

MAJOR CHANGES IN THE NINTH EDITION

As in every revision, we updated and clarified sections throughout the text. In addition, we always make a few major changes. In this edition, there were two major changes:

1. **Identification of core material.** Over the years, financial researchers have developed new theories, the financial markets have spawned many new types of securities, consulting firms have developed new and useful ways of thinking about financial practices, computers have facilitated new and better ways of analyzing decisions, and business has become increasingly global. All of this has led to the danger that textbooks and instructors will overwhelm students with more material than they can digest. New material must be added to the text because without it students would be obsolete even before they graduate. At the same time, if we try to cover too much, students will not learn much about anything.

   With this in mind, we reviewed every chapter to identify core topics that are essential to the introductory finance course, topics that are important but not essential, and topics that no longer warrant coverage. The core topics are now covered in the basic chapters, while important but not essential material is covered in appendix-like sections of chapters called "Extensions." This breakdown makes it easier for instructors to customize the package of material assigned so as to meet the specific needs of their students and to ensure the best fit of the introductory course into the overall business and finance curricula.

2. **New material.** Financial managers are becoming concerned with increasing shareholders' value and with the key role cash flows — as opposed to accounting profits — play in that process. Therefore, we beefed up our focus on cash flow, and especially free cash flow. Moreover, the role of incentives in value maximization is receiving increasing attention. Because people operate best if they are evaluated and rewarded on the basis of rational and relevant criteria, and because the recently developed concepts of EVA and MVA are particularly useful performance measures, we now spend more time on EVA and MVA. Finally, we increased our coverage of options and derivatives and their use in managing risks and thereby increasing value.

OTHER CHANGES IN THE NINTH EDITION

The entire book has been reviewed for completeness, ease of exposition, and currency. Hundreds of small changes have been made to keep the text up-to-date. Particular emphasis has been placed on updating the real-world examples and including the latest changes in the financial environment and in financial theory. Some examples of changes include the following:

The *Financial Management* web site address is *http://www.dryden.com/finance;* visit it often!

1. **Linkage with the World Wide Web.** All of us are aware of the rapid growth of the World Wide Web, and we recognize the almost limitless opportunities it will provide for financial education in the years ahead. With this in mind, The Dryden Press has developed what we think is a tremendous web site, one that will be of immense help to both instructors and students who use *Financial Management.*

   The web site address is *http://www.dryden.com/finance.* This ever-evolving web site is both a teaching and learning tool, with separate areas for students and instructors. Students visiting the site can access archived news summaries, use our database of financial research links, test their understanding with self-grading chapter quizzes, and more. Instructors will have access to NewsWire — recent article summaries from major business publications, along with discussion questions and references to the text. Instructors will also be able to download selected ancillaries, obtain sample teaching material, and share ideas with others who are using this textbook. Undoubtedly, improvements will continue over time.

We have also incorporated links to the web within the text, and a new feature that both students and professors will like is a set of marginal note references entitled, "On the WWW." These notes direct readers to sites on the web that are relevant to the subject being covered at that point in the text. These references are found throughout the book.

2. **Free cash flow valuation models.** In the eighth edition, we presented only the discounted dividend model for valuing corporations. That model is appropriate in certain situations, but it is inadequate when dealing with companies that do not pay dividends, when divisions as opposed to entire companies are being analyzed, when used with privately owned firms, or when takeover targets are being analyzed and the acquirer plans to make structural changes in the company's operations. To fill this void, we added a section on free cash flow valuation techniques to Chapter 9, "Stock Valuation," and we develop this discussion further in the chapters on capital budgeting, long-term financial planning, mergers, and bankruptcy.

3. **Splitting the financial statements and analysis chapters.** In the eighth edition, we had one long chapter on financial statements and their analysis. In this edition, we split the material into two new chapters, the first covering statements per se and the second their analysis. This provided two benefits. First, we wanted to increase our discussion of free cash flows, and the split made that feasible. Second, more and more students are taking the first finance course without a good accounting background, and the new chapter enabled us to present more foundation material. Third, because Chapter 3 now focuses exclusively on the analysis of financial statements, instructors who so choose can delay covering this material until later in the course, when financial statement analysis can be used to tie together in a "capstone" sense all of the topics previously covered.

4. **Solving discounted cash flow problems with spreadsheets.** In the eighth edition, we showed three approaches for solving time value of money problems: (a) a numerical approach with regular calculators, (b) the tabular approach, and (c) the use of financial calculators. We retained these three approaches in Chapter 7, "Discounted Cash Flow Analysis," but because managers are increasingly using spreadsheets to evaluate financial problems, we also show how to solve DCF problems using Microsoft *Excel* and other computer spreadsheets.

5. **Revised discussion of the cost of capital.** We significantly reworked and simplified Chapter 10, which covers the cost of capital. Our earlier discussion was unnecessarily complicated, with too much time spent on stock flotation costs and the resulting break points, even though established firms rarely issue new stock. We now emphasize the need to adjust the corporate cost of capital to account for differential project risk, and we show how firms make these risk adjustments.

6. **Increased coverage of multinational financial management.** We made several changes in this edition to strengthen our international coverage. First, we revised the multinational financial management chapter to incorporate the key topics of interest rate and purchasing power parity. Second, we expanded our coverage of international capital structures and capital budgeting, and we included new material on the European monetary system and the proposed common currency. And third, to better integrate international material with regular domestic financial management, we added new multinational illustrations and boxes throughout the book. These add a multinational dimension to sections previously discussed only in a domestic context.

Andy Naranjo, an international expert at the University of Florida, and Subu Venkataraman, who deals with international issues at Morgan Stanley, gave us many suggestions for the boxes, and they also helped us integrate international topics throughout the text.

7. **Real options and decision trees.** Chapter 13, "Risk Analysis and Real Options," now contains additional material on real, or strategic, options, as well as an expanded section on decision trees and their use in evaluating real options. We also streamlined and shortened the discussion of the optimal capital budget to reflect changes made in Chapter 10.

8. **Long-term financial planning.** In Chapter 14, we improved the development of projected financial statements for use in financial forecasting. It is now much easier to analyze the effects of alternative operating policies on a firm's value.

THE INSTRUCTIONAL PACKAGE: AN INTEGRATED APPROACH TO LEARNING

Financial Management includes a broad range of ancillary materials designed both to enhance students' learning and to make it easier for instructors to prepare for and conduct classes. The ancillaries are described here:

1. **Instructor's Manual.** This comprehensive manual contains answers to all text questions and problems, plus detailed solutions to the integrated cases. A computerized version of the IM is packaged with the print version to assist instructors with class preparation.

2. **PowerPoint Lecture Presentation.** This ancillary, prepared in Microsoft *PowerPoint,* covers all the essential issues presented in the chapter. Graphs, tables, lists, and calculations are developed sequentially, much as one might develop them on a blackboard. However, the slides are crisper, clearer, and more colorful, and color coding is used to tie together elements of a given slide. The new slide show is more polished than anything previously available. Based on our end-of-course evaluations, students overwhelmingly like the slides and recommend that we continue using them as an integral part of our lectures. The slides were initially developed with the assistance of Dr. Larry Wolken of Texas A&M University.

   When we first began using the slide show, we were concerned that we would lack flexibility in the classroom, because while one can navigate easily from slide to slide, one cannot change the slides themselves in the classroom. Our fears were unfounded. First, because we had spent a great deal of time designing the slides, our examples and materials turned out to be appropriate in most lecture situations. Second, when we used the slides in class, we found that we could easily depart from them by going to the blackboard, which also added variety and spontaneity. Now the slides provide the backbone of our lectures, but we spice them up by going to the blackboard to address current events, to present alternative examples, and to help answer questions.

3. **Blueprints.** As technological advances led lectures away from the blackboard, it became increasingly important to provide students with a hard copy of the lecture materials. Students must have hard copies if they are to focus on the lecture yet still develop a complete and useful set of notes. With this in mind, we concluded that *Blueprints* would be most useful if it actually consisted of copies of the slides. So, each chapter of *Blueprints* begins with the case itself and is then followed by copies of each slide, along with space for notes and comments.

   Blueprints has several other advantages. First, it offers flexibility for presenting alternative examples and discussing current events. Since *Blueprints* provides students with an almost complete set of notes, it is less necessary for instructors to lecture on every single topic in class. Second, space for notes is provided beside each slide, and since our discussion in class is tied directly to the slides, students can place their notes next to (or on) the relevant slide. This enables students to develop a better set of notes.

PowerPoint slides can be downloaded, with proper access, from the *Financial Management* web site *http://www.dryden.com/finance.*

When teaching this course, we use a "course pack" that consists of our syllabus, a 10- to 12-page calculator tutorial (taken from the *Technology Supplement* described below), some old exams, and *Blueprints*. Such a package can be provided by The Dryden Press to bookstores; for further information contact your local Dryden Press sales representative.

4. **Test Bank.** Although some instructors do not like multiple-choice questions, they do provide a useful means for testing students in many situations. If they are used, it is critically important that questions be both unambiguous and consistent with the lectures and assigned readings. To meet this need, we developed a large *Test Bank* containing more than 1,200 class-tested questions and problems. It is available both in book form and on diskette. A number of new and thoroughly class-tested conceptual questions and problems, which vary in level of difficulty, have been added to *Financial Management's Test Bank*. Information regarding the topics, degree of difficulty, and the correct answers, along with complete solutions for all numerical problems, is provided with each question.

   The *Test Bank* is available in book form and in Dryden's computerized test bank form (EXAMaster+). This software has many features that make test preparation, scoring, and grade recording easy. For example, EXAMaster+ allows automatic conversion of multiple-choice questions and problems into free-response questions. The sequence of test questions can be altered to make different versions of a given test, and the software makes it easy to add to or edit the existing test items or to compile a test which covers specific topics.

5. **Student Spreadsheet Applications Disk.** A diskette containing *Excel* spreadsheet models for the computer-related end-of-chapter problems is packaged with the textbook.

6. **Transparencies.** A set of more than 200 transparency acetates, designed to accompany the Mini Cases for use as lecture illustrations, is available from The Dryden Press.

Available via the *Financial Management* web site *http://www.dryden.com/finance/fincase.*

7. **Cases in Financial Management: Dryden Request.** More than 80 cases written by Eugene F. Brigham, Louis C. Gapenski, and Linda Klein are now available via the World Wide Web, with new cases to be added every year. The *Cases in Financial Management: Dryden Request* series is a customized case database which allows instructors to select cases and create their own customized casebooks. These cases can be used as supplements to illustrate the various topics covered in the textbook. Many of the cases come in directed and nondirected versions (that is, with and without guidance questions), and most of the cases have accompanying spreadsheet models. The models are not essential for working the cases, but they do reduce number crunching and thus leave more time for students to consider conceptual issues. The models also show students quite clearly the usefulness of computers for helping to make better financial decisions. Cases that we have found particularly useful for the different chapters are listed in the end-of-chapter references.

   All of the cases can be previewed *and* downloaded from the Dryden Press Finance Case web site *http://www.dryden.com/finance/fincase* with proper access. Case solutions and spreadsheet models can also be downloaded. For professorial access, contact your Dryden Press sales representative.

Real-company data available on the *Financial Management* web site *http://www.dryden.com/finance.*

8. **Data Disk.** In the textbook itself we incorporate many real-company examples to show how the concepts apply to actual companies. However, several professors involved in a focus group suggested that we should go one step further and provide instructors with real-company data. Although most introductory students do not have time to do much computer work, this may change in the not-so-distant future. In any event, we have put together a set of financial statement data from

several companies, along with a set of key economic statistics, including interest rates and stock market indexes, and made it available on the web.

9. **Technology Supplement.** The *Technology Supplement* contains tutorials for five commonly used financial calculators and for Microsoft *Excel, Lotus 1-2-3,* and *PowerPoint.* The calculator tutorials cover everything a student needs to know about calculators to work the problems in the text, and we provide them as a part of our course pack. These tutorials are generally about 12 typewritten pages. Some students are intimidated by the rather large manuals that accompany the calculators, and they find our brief, course-specific tutorials far easier to use. The spreadsheet tutorials are useful if students are asked to work cases, and the *PowerPoint* tutorial is useful to students who must make presentations or to instructors who want to make slides for their lectures.

10. **Video Package: Integrating Print and Video Technologies.** Brand-new videos feature financial concepts explained in terms of how companies do business today. Companies featured include Southwest Airlines, Pier 1 Imports, Kmart, Paradigm Simulations, Cadillac, and Marriott International.

    These videos are based on chapter opening vignettes and serve to capture students' attention for further discussion. For instance, how has Kmart managed its dividend policy while losing market value (Chapter 17)? Another case looks at how Southwest Airlines grew from one plane to its current fleet (Chapter 14).

    Although the videos, vignettes, and integrated cases are related to one another, instructors do not have to assign one in order to use another. Each stands on its own. There are many different classroom settings and course objectives, and our video format will not meet all needs. However, many instructors will find these videos extremely useful, and The Dryden Press will provide them to adopting instructors upon request.

Now available through the *Financial Management* web site *http://www.dryden.com/ finance.*

11. **Finance NewsWire.** One of the problems inherent in textbooks is keeping them current in a constantly changing world. When Orange County goes bankrupt or Baring Bank collapses or Procter & Gamble loses $200 million, it would be useful to relate these events to the textbook. Fortunately, the advent of the World Wide Web can help us keep up-to-date. Adopters of *Financial Management* will have access to a portion of the Dryden Press web site, where they will be provided with summaries of recent articles in *The Wall Street Journal, Business Week,* or some other major business publication, along with discussion questions and references to the text. This will facilitate incorporating late-breaking news into classroom discussions. One can also use the accompanying questions for quizzes and/or exams.

12. **Study Guide.** This supplement, which can be purchased by students, outlines the key section of each chapter and provides students with a set of questions and problems similar to those in the text and in the *Test Bank,* but with worked-out solutions. Instructors seldom use the *Study Guide* themselves, but some students find it extremely useful. Therefore, we recommend that instructors ask their bookstores to have copies available. Our bookstores generally have to reorder the *Study Guide,* which attests to its popularity with students.

The Dryden Press will provide complimentary supplements or supplement packages to those adopters qualified under Dryden's adoption policy. Please contact your sales representative to learn how you may qualify. If, as an adopter or potential user, you receive supplements you do not need, please return them to your sales representative or send them to the following address: Attn: Returns Department, Troy Warehouse, 465 South Lincoln Drive, Troy, MO 63379.

ACKNOWLEDGMENTS

This book reflects the efforts of a great many people over a number of years. First, we would like to thank the following people who helped with the Ninth Edition:

Sadhana M. Alangar	Wayne State University
G. Michael Boyd	Stetson University
Tina Galloway	University of Miami
Ilhan Meric	Rider University
Lawrence C. Wolken	Texas A&M University
Thomas V. Wright	Webster University
Zhong-guo Zhou	California State University, Fullerton

Second, earlier versions of individual chapters or entire sections were sent to professors and professionals doing research on specific topics. We are grateful for the insights provided by:

Edward I. Altman	New York University
Mary Schary Amram	Analysis Group Economics
Nasser Arshadi	University of Missouri
Abdul Aziz	Humboldt State University
William Beranek	University of Georgia
Gordon R. Bonner	University of Delaware
Ben S. Branch	Bank of New England and University of Massachusetts
David T. Brown	University of Florida
E. Bruce Frederickson	Syracuse University
Myron Gordon	University of Toronto
Hal Heaton	Brigham Young University
John Helmuth	Rochester Institute of Technology
Hugh Hunter	Eastern Washington University
James E. Jackson	Oklahoma State University
Vahan Janjigian	Northeastern University
Keith H. Johnson	University of Kentucky
Robert Kieschnick	George Mason University
Richard LeCompte	Wichita State University
Ilene Levin	University of Minnesota–Duluth
James T. Lindley	University of South Mississippi
R. Daniel Pace	Valparaiso University
Ralph A. Pope	California State University–Sacramento
Allen Rappaport	University of Northern Iowa
Fiona Robertson	Seattle University
James Schallheim	University of Utah
G. Bennett Stewart	Stern, Stewart, and Company
Robert Strong	University of Maine at Orono
Eugene Swinnerton	University of Detroit–Mercy
Robert Taggart	Boston College
Jonathan Tiemann	Wells Fargo Nikko Investment Advisors
Sheridan Titman	Boston College
Alan L. Tucker	Temple University
David Vang	University of St. Thomas
Gary R. Wells	Idaho State University
David Ziebart	University of Illinois at Urbana

In addition, we would like to thank the following people, whose reviews and comments on prior editions and companion books have contributed to this edition: Mike Adler, Syed Ahmad, Ed Altman, Bruce Anderson, Ron Anderson, Bob Angell, Vince Apilado, Henry Arnold, Bob Aubey, Gil Babcock, Peter Bacon, Kent Baker, Tom Bankston, Les Barenbaum, Charles Barngrover, Bill Beedles, Moshe Ben-Horim, Bill Beranek, Tom Berry, Bill Bertin, Tom Berry, Roger Bey, Dalton Bigbee, John Bildersee, Russ Boisjoly, Keith Boles, Geof Booth, Kenneth Boudreaux, Helen Bowers, Oswald Bowlin, Don Boyd, G. Michael Boyd, Pat Boyer, Joe Brandt, Elizabeth Brannigan, Greg Brauer, Mary Broske, Dave Brown, Kate Brown, Bill Brueggeman, Kirt Butler, Robert Button, Bill Campsey, Bob Carleson, Severin Carlson, David Cary, Steve Celec, Don Chance, Antony Chang, Susan Chaplinsky, Jay Choi, S. K. Choudhury, Lal Chugh, Maclyn Clouse, Margaret Considine, Phil Cooley, Joe Copeland, David Cordell, John Cotner, Charles Cox, David Crary, John Crockett, Roy Crum, Brent Dalrymple, Bill Damon, Joel Dauten, Steve Dawson, Sankar De, Miles Delano, Fred Dellva, Anand Desai, Bernard Dill, Greg Dimkoff, Les Dlabay, Mark Dorfman, Gene Drycimski, Dean Dudley, David Durst, Ed Dyl, Dick Edelman, Charles Edwards, John Ellis, Dave Ewert, John Ezzell, Richard Fendler, Michael Ferri, Jim Filkins, John Finnerty, Susan Fischer, Steven Flint, Russ Fogler, Dan French, Michael Garlington, Jim Garvin, Adam Gehr, Jim Gentry, Philip Glasgo, Rudyard Goode, Walt Goulet, Bernie Grablowsky, Theoharry Grammatikos, Ed Grossnickle, John Groth, Alan Grunewald, Manak Gupta, Sam Hadaway, Don Hakala, Sally Hamilton, Gerald Hamsmith, William Hardin, John Harris, Paul Hastings, Bob Haugen, Steve Hawke, Del Hawley, Robert Hehre, George Hettenhouse, Hans Heymann, Kendall Hill, Roger Hill, Tom Hindelang, Linda Hittle, Ralph Hocking, J. Ronald Hoffmeister, Jim Horrigan, John Houston, John Howe, Keith Howe, Steve Isberg, Jim Jackson, Kose John, Craig Johnson, Keith Johnson, Ramon Johnson, Ray Jones, Manuel Jose, Gus Kalogeras, Mike Keenan, Bill Kennedy, Joe Kiernan, Rick Kish, Linda Klein, Don Knight, Dorothy Koehl, Jaroslaw Komarynsky, Duncan Kretovich, Harold Krogh, Charles Kroncke, Joan Lamm, P. Lange, Howard Lanser, Martin Laurence, Ed Lawrence, Wayne Lee, Jim LePage, Jules Levine, John Lewis, Chuck Linke, Bill Lloyd, Susan Long, Judy Maese, Bob Magee, Ileen Malitz, Phil Malone, Terry Maness, Chris Manning, Terry Martell, D. J. Masson, John Mathys, John McAlhany, Andy McCollough, Bill McDaniel, Robin McLaughlin, Tom McCue, Jamshid Mehran, Larry Merville, Rick Meyer, Jim Millar, Ed Miller, John Mitchell, Carol Moerdyk, Bob Moore, Barry Morris, Gene Morris, Fred Morrissey, Chris Muscarella, David Nachman, Tim Nantell, Don Nast, Bill Nelson, Bob Nelson, Bob Niendorf, Tom O'Brien, Dennis O'Connor, John O'Donnell, Jim Olsen, Robert Olsen, Coleen Pantalone, Jim Pappas, Stephen Parrish, Glenn Petry, Jim Pettijohn, Rich Pettit, Dick Pettway, Hugo Phillips, John Pinkerton, Gerald Pogue, R. Potter, Franklin Potts, R. Powell, Chris Prestopino, Jerry Prock, Howard Puckett, Herbert Quigley, George Racette, Bob Radcliffe, Bill Rentz, Ken Riener, Charles Rini, John Ritchie, Pietra Rivoli, Antonio Rodriguez, E. M. Roussakis, Dexter Rowell, Jim Sachlis, Abdul Sadik, Thomas Scampini, Kevin Scanlon, Frederick Schadler, Mary Jane Scheuer, Carl Schweser, John Settle, Alan Severn, Sol Shalit, Frederic Shipley, Dilip Shome, Ron Shrieves, Neil Sicherman, J. B. Silvers, Clay Singleton, Joe Sinkey, Stacy Sirmans, Jaye Smith, Steve Smith, Don Sorenson, David Speairs, Ken Stanly, Ed Stendardi, Alan Stephens, Don Stevens, Jerry Stevens, Glen Strasburg, Philip Swensen, Ernie Swift, Paul Swink, Gary Tallman, Dennis Tanner, Russ Taussig, Richard Teweles, Ted Teweles, Andrew Thompson, George Trivoli, George Tsetsekos, Mel Tysseland, David Upton, Howard Van Auken, Pretorious Van den Dool, Pieter Vanderburg, Paul Vanderheiden, Jim Verbrugge, Patrick Vincent, Steve Vinson, Susan Visscher, John Wachowicz, Mike Walker, Sam Weaver, Kuo Chiang Wei, Bill Welch, Fred Weston, Norm Williams, Tony Wingler, Ed Wolfe, Don Woods, Michael Yonan, Dennis Zocco, and Kent Zumwalt.

Special thanks are due to Fred Weston, Myron Gordon, Merton Miller, and Franco Modigliani, who have done much to help develop the field of financial management and who provided us with instruction and inspiration; to Roy Crum, who coauthored the multinational finance chapter; to Larry Wolken, who offered his hard work and advice for the development of the *Lecture Presentation Software;* to Dana Aberwald Clark, Susan Ball, Mary Alice Hanebury, and Kay Mangan, who helped us develop the spreadsheet models; to Dana Aberwald Clark, who helped with the ancillaries; and to Susan Purcell and Tina Goforth, who provided both word processing and editorial support.

Both our colleagues and our students at the Universities of Florida and Tennessee gave us many useful suggestions, and the Dryden Press and Elm Street Publishing Services staffs — especially Anita Fallon, Sue Nodine, Lisé Johnson, and Mike Reynolds — helped greatly with all phases of text development, production, and marketing.

ERRORS IN THE TEXT

At this point, authors generally say something like this: "We appreciate all the help we received from the people listed above, but any remaining errors are, of course, our own responsibility." And in many books, there are plenty of remaining errors. Having experienced difficulties with errors ourselves, both as students and as instructors, we resolved to avoid this problem in *Financial Management*. As a result of our error detection procedures, we are convinced that the book is relatively free of mistakes.

Partly because of our confidence that few such errors remain, but primarily because we want very much to detect any errors that may have slipped by to correct them in subsequent printings, we decided to offer a reward of $10 per error to the first person who reports it to us. For purposes of this reward, errors are defined as misspelled words, nonrounding numerical errors, incorrect statements, and any other error that inhibits comprehension. Typesetting problems, such as irregular spacing and differences in opinion regarding grammatical or punctuation conventions, do not qualify for this reward. Given the ever-changing nature of the World Wide Web, changes in web addresses also do not qualify as errors. Finally, any qualifying error that has follow-through effects is counted as two errors only. Please report any errors to Mike Ehrhardt at the address given below.

CONCLUSION

Finance is, in a real sense, the cornerstone of the free enterprise system. Good financial management is therefore vitally important to the economic health of business firms, hence to the nation and the world. Because of its importance, financial management should be thoroughly understood, but this is easier said than done. The field is relatively complex, and it is undergoing constant change in response to shifts in economic conditions. All of this makes financial management stimulating and exciting, but also challenging and sometimes perplexing. We sincerely hope that the ninth edition of *Financial Management* will help you understand the financial problems faced by businesses today, as well as the best ways to solve those problems.

Eugene F. Brigham
Louis C. Gapenski
College of Business Administration
University of Florida
Gainesville, Florida 32611-7167

Michael C. Ehrhardt
College of Business Administration
University of Tennessee
Knoxville, Tennessee 37996-0540
e-mail:ehrhardt@utk.edu

July 1998

Brief Contents

PREFACE   vii

PART I   Introduction to Financial Management   1
CHAPTER 1   AN OVERVIEW OF FINANCIAL MANAGEMENT   3
CHAPTER 2   FINANCIAL STATEMENTS, CASH FLOW, AND TAXES   31
CHAPTER 3   ANALYSIS OF FINANCIAL STATEMENTS   71
   EXTENSIONS   109
CHAPTER 4   THE FINANCIAL ENVIRONMENT: MARKETS, INSTITUTIONS, AND INTEREST RATES   113

PART II   Fundamental Concepts   155
CHAPTER 5   RISK AND RETURN: THE BASICS   157
CHAPTER 6   RISK AND RETURN: EXTENSIONS   201
   EXTENSIONS   231
CHAPTER 7   TIME VALUE OF MONEY   235
   EXTENSIONS   282

PART III   Securities and Their Valuation   283
CHAPTER 8   BONDS AND THEIR VALUATION   285
CHAPTER 9   STOCKS AND THEIR VALUATION   323

PART IV   Strategic Investment Decisions   371
CHAPTER 10   THE COST OF CAPITAL   373
   EXTENSIONS   405
CHAPTER 11   THE BASICS OF CAPITAL BUDGETING   421
CHAPTER 12   CASH FLOW ESTIMATION AND OTHER TOPICS IN CAPITAL BUDGETING   459
CHAPTER 13   RISK ANALYSIS AND REAL OPTIONS   495
   EXTENSIONS   534

PART V   Strategic Financing Decisions   539
CHAPTER 14   LONG-TERM FINANCIAL PLANNING   541
CHAPTER 15   CAPITAL STRUCTURE DECISIONS: THE BASICS   579
CHAPTER 16   CAPITAL STRUCTURE DECISIONS: EXTENSIONS   621
CHAPTER 17   DISTRIBUTION TO SHAREHOLDERS: DIVIDENDS AND REPURCHASES   659

PART VI   Tactical Financing Decisions   695
CHAPTER 18   ISSUING SECURITIES, REFUNDING OPERATIONS, AND OTHER TOPICS   697
CHAPTER 19   LEASE FINANCING   735
   EXTENSIONS   759
CHAPTER 20   HYBRID FINANCING: PREFERRED STOCK, WARRANTS, AND CONVERTIBLES   763
   EXTENSIONS   786

PART VII   Working Capital Management   789
CHAPTER 21   CURRENT ASSET MANAGEMENT   791
CHAPTER 22   SHORT-TERM FINANCING   835
   EXTENSIONS   862
CHAPTER 23   WORKING CAPITAL MANAGEMENT: EXTENSIONS   867

PART VIII   SPECIAL TOPICS   905
CHAPTER 24   DERIVATIVES AND RISK MANAGEMENT   907
             EXTENSIONS   944
CHAPTER 25   BANKRUPTCY, REORGANIZATION, AND LIQUIDATION   951
             EXTENSIONS   978
CHAPTER 26   MERGERS, LBOS, DIVESTITURES, AND HOLDING
             COMPANIES   985
CHAPTER 27   MULTINATIONAL FINANCIAL MANAGEMENT   1027
CHAPTER 28   PENSION PLAN MANAGEMENT   1059

APPENDIXES
APPENDIX A   MATHEMATICAL TABLES   A-1
APPENDIX B   SOLUTIONS TO SELF-TEST PROBLEMS   A-11
APPENDIX C   ANSWERS TO END-OF-CHAPTER PROBLEMS   A-45
APPENDIX D   SELECTED EQUATIONS AND DATA   A-53

INDEX   A-65

CONTENTS

PREFACE   vii

PART I   INTRODUCTION TO FINANCIAL MANAGEMENT   1

CHAPTER 1   AN OVERVIEW OF FINANCIAL MANAGEMENT   3

Career Opportunities in Finance   4   Financial Management in the 1990s   6
Box: McDonald's Looks Overseas   7   The Financial Staff's Responsibilities   8
Alternative Forms of Business Organization   9   Finance in the Organizational
Structure of the Firm   12   The Goals of the Corporation   13   *Box:* Are CEOs
Overpaid?   17   Business Ethics and Social Responsibility   18   Agency
Relationships   20   Organization of the Book   25   Summary   26

CHAPTER 2   FINANCIAL STATEMENTS, CASH FLOW, AND TAXES   31

A Brief History of Accounting and Financial Statements   32   Financial Statements
and Reports   33   The Balance Sheet   34   The Income Statement   36   Statement
of Retained Earnings   38   *Box:* Sherlock Holmes, or Corporate Enemy Number 1?
39   Statement of Cash Flows   39   Modifying Accounting Data for Managerial
Decisions   42   MVA and EVA   46   *Box:* Economic Value Added (EVA) — Today's
Hottest Financial Idea   48   The Federal Income Tax System   50
Box: Tax Havens   58   Depreciation   59   Summary   59

CHAPTER 3   ANALYSIS OF FINANCIAL STATEMENTS   71

Ratio Analysis   72   Liquidity Ratios   72   Asset Management Ratios   74   Debt
Management Ratios   77   Profitability Ratios   81   *Box:* International Accounting:
Differences Create Headaches for Investors   82   Market Value Ratios   84   Trend
Analysis   85   The Value of Operations: Using the Ratios to Guide Managers   86
Tying the Ratios Together: The DuPont Chart and Equation   86   Comparative
Ratios and "Benchmarking"   91   *Box:* ROE Is Soaring to Record Heights   92
Uses and Limitations of Ratio Analysis   94   Looking Beyond the Numbers   95
Box: Financial Analysis in the Small Firm   96   Summary   97   Extensions   109

CHAPTER 4   THE FINANCIAL ENVIRONMENT: MARKETS, INSTITUTIONS,
AND INTEREST RATES   113

The Financial Markets   114   Financial Institutions   118   The Stock Market   123
Box: An Expensive Beer for the NASD   125   The Cost of Money   126   Interest Rate
Levels   127   The Determinants of Market Interest Rates   131   *Box:* A New, Truly
Riskless Treasury Bond   135   Investing Overseas   137   The Term Structure of
Interest Rates   137   *Box:* Measuring Country Risk   138   What Determines the
Shape of the Yield Curve?   140   Other Factors That Influence Interest Rate Levels
144   Interest Rate Levels and Stock Prices   146   Interest Rates and Business
Decisions   146   Summary   148

PART II   FUNDAMENTAL CONCEPTS   155

CHAPTER 5   RISK AND RETURN: THE BASICS   157

Investment Returns   158   Stand-Alone Risk   160   Risk in a Portfolio Context
169   *Box:* The Trade-Off between Risk and Return   170   *Box:* The Benefits of
Diversifying Overseas   179   The Relationship between Risk and Rates of Return

184   Physical Assets versus Securities   189   Some Concerns about Beta and the CAPM   190   Volatility versus Risk   191   Summary   192

CHAPTER 6   RISK AND RETURN: EXTENSIONS   201

Measuring Portfolio Risk   202   Efficient Portfolios   206   Choosing the Optimal Portfolio   209   The Capital Asset Pricing Model   212   The Capital Market Line 213   Calculating Beta Coefficients   216   Empirical Tests of the CAPM   220 Arbitrage Pricing Theory   223   Summary   226   Extensions   231

CHAPTER 7   TIME VALUE OF MONEY   235

Time Lines   236   Future Value   237   Present Value   244   Solving for Interest Rate and Time   247   Future Value of an Annuity   250   Present Value of an Annuity   254   Perpetuities   257   Uneven Cash Flow Streams   258   Semiannual and Other Compounding Periods   261   Comparison of Different Types of Interest Rates   266   Fractional Time Periods   268   Amortized Loans   269   Summary 271   Extensions   282

PART III   SECURITIES AND THEIR VALUATION   283

CHAPTER 8   BONDS AND THEIR VALUATION   285

Who Issues Bonds?   286   Key Characteristics of Bonds   287   Bond Valuation 291   Bond Yields   298   *Box:* Drinking Your Coupons   301   Bonds with Semiannual Coupons   301   Assessing the Riskiness of a Bond   302   Default Risk 306   *Box:* Santa Fe Bonds Finally Mature after 114 Years   313   Bond Markets   314 Summary   316

CHAPTER 9   STOCKS AND THEIR VALUATION   323

Legal Rights and Privileges of Common Stockholders   324   Types of Common Stock 325   The Market for Common Stock   326   *Box:* A Wild Initial Day of Trading   327 Common Stock Valuation   330   Valuing the Entire Corporation   342   Stock Market Equilibrium   349   *Box:* Run-Ups before Deals: Chicanery or Coincidence? 355   Actual Stock Prices and Returns   355   *Box:* Investing in Emerging Markets 358   Preferred Stock   361   Summary   362

PART IV   STRATEGIC INVESTMENT DECISIONS   371

CHAPTER 10   THE COST OF CAPITAL   373

The Weighted Average Cost of Capital   374   Cost of Debt, $k_d(1-T)$ 376 Cost of Preferred Stock, k_{ps} 377   Cost of Common Stock, k_s 378   Composite, or Weighted Average, Cost of Capital, WACC   382   Factors That Affect the Weighted Average Cost of Capital   383   *Box:* WACC Estimates for Some Large U.S. Corporations   384   *Box:* Global Variations in the Cost of Capital   385 Adjusting the Cost of Capital for Risk   386   Estimating Project Risk   387 Using the CAPM to Estimate a Project's Risk-Adjusted Cost of Capital   388 Techniques for Measuring Beta Risk   391   The Cost of Depreciation and Other Types of Internally Generated Funds   392   *Box:* The Cost of Equity Capital for Small Firms   394   Some Problem Areas in Cost of Capital   395 Four Mistakes to Avoid   396   Summary   397   Extensions   405

CHAPTER 11   THE BASICS OF CAPITAL BUDGETING   421

Importance of Capital Budgeting   422   Generating Ideas for Capital Projects   423
Project Classifications   424   Similarities between Capital Budgeting and Security
Valuation   425   Capital Budgeting Decision Rules   426   Comparison of the NPV
and IRR Methods   433   Modified Internal Rate of Return (MIRR)   440
Profitability Index   442   Conclusions on Capital Budgeting Methods   442
Business Practices   444   The Post-Audit   445   *Box:* Capital Budgeting in the
Small Firm   446   Using Capital Budgeting Techniques in Other Contexts   448
Summary   449

CHAPTER 12   CASH FLOW ESTIMATION AND OTHER TOPICS IN
CAPITAL BUDGETING   459

Estimating Cash Flows   460   Identifying the Relevant Cash Flows   461   Tax
Effects   464   Evaluating Capital Budgeting Projects   468   Example of Cash Flow
Analysis: Expansion Project   468   *Box:* GE Bets on Europe   473   Example of Cash
Flow Analysis: Replacement Project   473   Cash Flow Estimation Bias   476
Option Value   477   Comparing Projects with Unequal Lives   479   Abandonment
Value   482   Adjusting for Inflation   484   Summary   486

CHAPTER 13   RISK ANALYSIS AND REAL OPTIONS   495

Introduction to Project Risk Analysis   496   Techniques for Measuring Stand-Alone
Risk   497   *Box:* Coca-Cola Takes on the High-Risk, High-Return Markets of Asia
501   Should Firms Diversify to Reduce Corporate Risk?   505   Market Risk and
Divisional Betas   505   *Box:* High-Tech CFOs   506   Our View of Project Risk
Analysis   509   Risky Cash Outflows   512   Introduction to Real Options   513
Identifying Optimal Responses to Changing Conditions: Decision Trees   514
Determining the Value of Real Options   517   Real Options and Financial
Management   519   The Optimal Capital Budget   521   Establishing the Optimal
Capital Budget in Practice   523   Summary   524   Extensions   534

PART V   STRATEGIC FINANCING DECISIONS   539

CHAPTER 14   LONG-TERM FINANCIAL PLANNING   541

Strategic Plans   542   Operating Plans   544   The Financial Plan   546   Sales
Forecasts   546   Financial Statement Forecasting: The Percent of Sales Method
549   The AFN Formula   559   Forecasting Financial Requirements When the
Balance Sheet Ratios Are Subject to Change   563   Other Techniques for Forecasting
Financial Statements   565   Computerized Financial Planning Models   567
Summary   568

CHAPTER 15   CAPITAL STRUCTURE DECISIONS: THE BASICS   579

Business and Financial Risk   580   Capital Structure Theory   589   Setting the
Target Capital Structure When Cash Flows Are Perpetuities   595   Some
Considerations in the Capital Structure Decision   605   An Approach to Setting the
Target Capital Structure   609   Some Additional Insights into Capital Structure
Decisions   611   Summary   612

CHAPTER 16   CAPITAL STRUCTURE DECISIONS: EXTENSIONS   621

Capital Structure Theory: The Modigliani-Miller Models   622   The Hamada Model:
Introducing Market Risk   630   Capital Structure Theory: The Miller Model   632

Criticisms of the MM and Miller Models   635   Capital Structure Theory: The Trade-Off Models   636   Capital Structure Theory: The Signaling Model   641   Capital Structure Theory: Our View   645   Variations in Capital Structures   647   Book Weights versus Market Weights   649   Summary   651

CHAPTER 17   DISTRIBUTIONS TO SHAREHOLDERS: DIVIDENDS AND REPURCHASES   659

Dividends versus Capital Gains: What Do Investors Prefer?   660   Other Dividend Policy Issues   664   Dividend Stability   666   Establishing the Dividend Policy in Practice   668   Changing Dividend Policies   675   Dividend Reinvestment Plans   676   Summary of Factors Influencing Dividend Policy   678   Overview of the Dividend Policy Decision   679   Stock Dividends and Stock Splits   681   Stock Repurchases   683   *Box:* Stock Repurchases: An Easy Way to Boost Stock Prices?   685   *Box:* Share Repurchases Are Less Common Overseas   687   Summary   687

PART VI   TACTICAL FINANCING DECISIONS   695

CHAPTER 18   ISSUING SECURITIES, REFUNDING OPERATIONS, AND OTHER TOPICS   697

The Decision to Go Public   698   The Decision to List   700   Procedures for Selling New Common Stock   701   Advantages and Disadvantages of Financing with Common Stock   704   Securities Regulations and the Investment Banking Process   705   Recent Innovations in Types of Bonds   713   Advantages and Disadvantages of Long-Term Debt   719   Factors That Influence Long-Term Financing Decisions   719   Refunding Operations   723   Summary   728

CHAPTER 19   LEASE FINANCING   735

The Two Parties to Leasing   736   Types of Leases   736   Tax Effects   738   Financial Statement Effects   740   Evaluation by the Lessee   742   Evaluation by the Lessor   746   Other Issues in Lease Analysis   749   Other Reasons for Leasing   751   Summary   753   Extensions   759

CHAPTER 20   HYBRID FINANCING: PREFERRED STOCK, WARRANTS, AND CONVERTIBLES   763

Preferred Stock   764   Warrants   767   Convertibles   773   A Final Comparison of Warrants and Convertibles   779   Other Topics in Hybrid Financing   780   Summary   780   Extensions   786

PART VII   WORKING CAPITAL MANAGEMENT   789

CHAPTER 21   CURRENT ASSET MANAGEMENT   791

Working Capital Terminology   792   Alternative Current Asset Investment Policies   793   *Box:* EVA and Working Capital   795   The Concept of Zero Working Capital   795   Cash Management   796   *Box:* American Standard Embraces Demand Flow Management   797   The Cash Budget   798   Cash Management Techniques   803   Marketable Securities   806   Inventory   807   Inventory Costs   809   Inventory Control Systems   810   *Box:* Keeping Inventory Lean   812   Receivables Management   814   Credit Policy   818   Setting the Credit Period and Standards   819   Setting the Collection Policy   820   Cash Discounts   820   Other Factors Influencing Credit Policy   821   Summary   821

CHAPTER 22   SHORT-TERM FINANCING   835

Alternative Current Asset Financing Policies   835   Advantages and Disadvantages of Short-Term Financing   838   Sources of Short-Term Financing   839   Accruals   839   Accounts Payable (Trade Credit)   840   Short-Term Bank Loans   845   The Cost of Bank Loans   848   *Box:* The Travails of Jamesway   850   Choosing a Bank   852   Commercial Paper   854   Use of Security in Short-Term Financing   854   Summary   855   Extensions   862

CHAPTER 23   WORKING CAPITAL MANAGEMENT: EXTENSIONS   867

The Cash Conversion Cycle   868   Setting the Target Cash Balance   871   Accounting for Inventory   876   The Economic Ordering Quantity (EOQ) Model   877   EOQ Model Extensions   883   The Payments Pattern Approach to Monitoring Receivables   888   Analyzing Proposed Changes in Credit Policy   893   Summary   895

PART VIII   SPECIAL TOPICS   905

CHAPTER 24   DERIVATIVES AND RISK MANAGEMENT   907

Reasons to Manage Risk   908   Background on Derivatives   910   *Box:* Orange County Blues   912   Options   913   Introduction to Option Pricing Models   918   The Black-Scholes Option Pricing Model (OPM)   920   Other Types of Derivatives   924   Risk Management   929   Fundamentals of Risk Management   929   *Box:* Microsoft's Goal: Manage Every Risk!   930   *Box:* Barings and Sumitomo Suffer Large Losses in the Derivative Markets   932   Using Derivatives to Reduce Risks   933   Summary   939   Extensions   944

CHAPTER 25   BANKRUPTCY, REORGANIZATION, AND LIQUIDATION   951

Financial Distress and Its Consequences   952   Issues Facing a Firm in Financial Distress   954   Settlements without Going through Formal Bankruptcy   955   Federal Bankruptcy Law   958   Reorganization in Bankruptcy   959   Liquidation in Bankruptcy   967   Other Motivations for Bankruptcy   971   Some Criticisms of Bankruptcy Laws   971   Other Topics in Bankruptcy   972   Summary   972   Extensions   978

CHAPTER 26   MERGERS, LBOs, DIVESTITURES, AND HOLDING COMPANIES   985

Rationale for Mergers   986   Types of Mergers   989   Level of Merger Activity   989   Hostile versus Friendly Takeovers   991   Merger Regulation   993   Merger Analysis   995   *Box:* When You Merge You Combine More Than Just Financial Statements   1001   Structuring the Takeover Bid   1001   Accounting Treatment for Mergers   1002   Analysis for a "True Consolidation"   1006   The Role of Investment Bankers   1007   Who Wins: The Empirical Evidence   1010   Corporate Alliances   1011   Leveraged Buyouts   1012   Divestitures   1013   *Box:* Governments Are Divesting State-Owned Businesses to Spur Economic Efficiency   1014   Holding Companies   1016   *Box:* Merging as a Means of Exiting a Closely Held Business   1018   Summary   1019

CHAPTER 27   MULTINATIONAL FINANCIAL MANAGEMENT   1027

Multinational, or Global, Corporations   1028   Multinational versus Domestic Financial Management   1031   Exchange Rates   1032   The International Monetary

System   1035   Trading in Foreign Exchange   1038   Interest Rate Parity   1040
Purchasing Power Parity   1041   *Box:* Hungry for a Big Mac? Go to China!   1042
Inflation, Interest Rates, and Exchange Rates   1043   International Money and
Capital Markets   1044   Multinational Capital Budgeting   1047   International
Capital Structures   1049   Multinational Working Capital Management   1051
Summary   1053

CHAPTER 28   PENSION PLAN MANAGEMENT   1059

The Role and Scope of Pension Plan Management   1060   Three Types of Pension
Plans   1061   Key Terms and Concepts   1063   Pension Fund Mathematics: Defined
Benefit Plans   1067   Risks Inherent in Pension Plans   1068   Illustration of a
Defined Benefit versus a Defined Contribution Plan   1072   Defined Benefit versus
Defined Contribution Plans: The Employee Choice   1074   Developing a Plan
Strategy   1075   Pension Fund Investment Performance   1077   "Tapping" Pension
Fund Assets   1080   Retiree Health Benefits   1081   Summary   1082

APPENDIXES

APPENDIX A   MATHEMATICAL TABLES   A-1

APPENDIX B   SOLUTIONS TO SELF-TEST PROBLEMS   A-11

APPENDIX C   ANSWERS TO END-OF-CHAPTER PROBLEMS   A-45

APPENDIX D   SELECTED EQUATIONS AND DATA   A-53

INDEX   A-65

INTRODUCTION TO FINANCIAL MANAGEMENT

I

CHAPTER 1
AN OVERVIEW OF
FINANCIAL MANAGEMENT

CHAPTER 2
FINANCIAL STATEMENTS,
CASH FLOW, AND TAXES

CHAPTER 3
ANALYSIS OF FINANCIAL
STATEMENTS

CHAPTER 4
THE FINANCIAL
ENVIRONMENT: MARKETS,
INSTITUTIONS, AND
INTEREST RATES

The 110-story twin towers were developed to promote international commerce by centralizing the activities of private firms and public agencies involved in world trade. The towers are part of a complex that includes the World Financial Center, the headquarters of Merrill Lynch, Dow Jones, and the American Express Company.

©John Lawrence/Tony Stone Images

AN OVERVIEW OF FINANCIAL MANAGEMENT

*F*or many companies, the decision would have been both easy and positive. However, Ben and Jerry's Homemade Inc. has always taken pride in doing things differently. Faced with declining profits, the company was offered an opportunity to sell its premium ice cream in the lucrative Japanese market. However, Ben and Jerry's turned down the business because the Japanese firm that would have distributed their product had failed to develop a reputation for promoting social causes. Robert Holland, Jr., Ben and Jerry's CEO at the time, commented that, "The only reason to take the opportunity was to make money." Clearly, Holland, who resigned from the company in late 1996, thought there was more to running a business than just making money.

The company's cofounders, Ben Cohen and Jerry Greenfield, opened the first Ben and Jerry's ice cream shop in 1978 in a vacant Vermont gas station with just $12,000 of capital plus a commitment to run the business in a manner consistent with their underlying values. Even though it was more expensive, the company only bought milk and cream from small local farms in Vermont. In addition, 7.5 percent of the company's before-tax income was donated to charity, and each of the company's 700 employees received three free pints of ice cream each day. Moreover, the company had a policy of restricting the CEO's compensation to just seven times the salary of the company's lowest paid worker.

Until recently, Ben and Jerry's philosophy and commitment to social causes had not hindered its ability to make a lot of money. The company's stock grew by leaps and bounds up through the early 1990s, and its 1995 sales exceeded $150 million. However, in recent years the stock price fell from $33 to $10 a share. Part of the problem was increased competition in the premium ice cream market, along with a leveling off of sales in that market. Other problems include production inefficiencies and a slow, haphazard product development strategy.

The company lost money for the first time in 1994, and as a result, Cohen stepped down as CEO. Then Holland, a former consultant for McKinsey & Co. with a reputation as a turnaround specialist, was tapped as Cohen's replacement. To get Holland, though, the company had to abandon its old pay policy, and he was paid $326,000 in 1995, more than 14 times what an ice cream scooper made. Holland immediately took steps to improve the company's bottom line. As a result, sales increased, the company began making money, and its stock price climbed 70 percent, to $17, by mid-1996. Nevertheless, the recent decision not to enter the Japanese market demonstrates that the company has not abandoned its social consciousness.

All of this suggests that, in the future, Holland's successor will have to continue balancing the need for stronger financial performance against the desire to maintain the company's founding values. As you will see throughout the book, many of today's companies face challenges similar to those of Ben and Jerry's. Every day, corporations struggle with decisions such as these: Does it make sense to shift production overseas? What is the appropriate level of compensation for senior management? In general, how do we balance social concerns against the need to create value for our shareholders?

Visit http://www.dryden. com/finance to see the web site accompanying this text. This ever-evolving site, for students and instructors, is a tool for teaching, learning, financial research, and job searches.

The purpose of this chapter is to give you an idea of what financial management is all about. After you finish the chapter, you should have a reasonably good idea of what finance majors might do after graduation. You should also have a better understanding of (1) some of the forces that will affect financial management in the future; (2) the place of finance in a firm's organization; (3) the relationships between financial managers and their counterparts in the accounting, marketing, production, and personnel departments; (4) the goals of a firm; and (5) the way financial managers can contribute to the attainment of these goals.

CAREER OPPORTUNITIES IN FINANCE

Finance consists of three interrelated areas: (1) *money and capital markets,* which deals with securities markets and financial institutions; (2) *investments,* which focuses on the decisions made by both individual and institutional investors as they choose securities for their investment portfolios; and (3) *financial management,* or "business finance," which involves decisions within firms. The career opportunities within each field are many and varied, but financial managers must have a knowledge of all three areas if they are to do their jobs well.

Capital Markets and Institutions

Many finance majors go to work for financial institutions, including banks, insurance companies, mutual funds, and investment banking firms. For success here, one needs a knowledge of valuation techniques, the factors that cause interest rates to rise and fall, the regulations to which financial institutions are subject, and the various types of financial instruments (mortgages, auto loans, certificates of deposit, and so on). One also needs a general knowledge of all aspects of business administration, because the management of a financial institution involves accounting, marketing, personnel, and computer systems, as well as financial management. An ability to communicate, both orally and in writing, is important, and "people skills," or the ability to get others to do their jobs well, are critical.

One common entry-level job in this area is a bank officer trainee, where one goes into bank operations and learns about the business, from tellers' work, to cash management, to making loans. One could expect to spend a year or so being rotated among these different areas, after which he or she would settle into a department, often as an assistant manager in a branch. Alternatively, one might become a specialist in some area such as real estate, and be authorized to make loans going into millions of dollars, or in the management of trusts, estates, and pension funds. Similar career paths are available with insurance companies, investment companies, credit unions, and consumer loan companies.

Consult http://www.cob.ohio-state. edu/dept/fin/osujobs.htm for an excellent site containing information on a variety of business career areas, listings of current jobs, and a variety of other reference materials.

Investments

Finance graduates who go into investments often work for a brokerage house such as Merrill Lynch, either in sales or as a security analyst. Others work for banks, mutual funds, or insurance companies in the management of their investment portfolios; for financial consulting firms advising individual investors or pension funds on how to invest their capital; or for an investment banker, whose primary function is to help businesses raise new capital. The three main functions in the investments area are sales, the analysis of individual securities, and determining the optimal mix of securities for a given investor.

Financial Management

Financial management is the broadest of the three areas, and the one with the greatest number of job opportunities. Financial management is important in all types of businesses, including banks and other financial institutions, as well as industrial and retail firms. Financial management is also important in governmental operations, from schools to hospitals to highway departments. The job opportunities in financial management range from making decisions regarding plant expansions to choosing what types of securities to issue when financing expansion. Financial managers also have the responsibility for deciding the credit terms under which customers may buy, how much inventory the firm should carry, how much cash to keep on hand, whether to acquire other firms (merger analysis), and how much of the firm's earnings to plow back into the business versus pay out as dividends.

Regardless of which area a finance major goes into, he or she will need a knowledge of all three areas. For example, a bank lending officer cannot do his or her job well without a good understanding of financial management, because he or she must be able to judge how well a business is being operated. The same thing holds true for Merrill Lynch's security analysts and stockbrokers, who must have an understanding of general financial principles if they are to give their customers intelligent advice. Similarly, corporate financial managers need to know what their bankers are thinking about, and they also need to know how investors judge a firm's performance and thus determine its stock price. So, if you decide to make finance your career, you will need to know something about all three areas.

But suppose you do not plan to major in finance. Is the subject still important to you? Absolutely, for two reasons: (1) You need a knowledge of finance to make many personal decisions, ranging from investing for your retirement to deciding whether to lease versus buy a car. (2) Virtually all important business decisions have financial implications, so important decisions are generally made by teams from the accounting, finance, legal, marketing, personnel, and production departments. Therefore, if you want to succeed in the business arena, you must be highly competent in your own area, say, marketing, but you must also have a familiarity with the other business disciplines, including finance.

Since there are financial implications in virtually all business decisions, nonfinancial executives simply must know enough finance to work these implications into their own specialized analyses.[1] Because of this, every student of business, regardless of his or her major, should be concerned with financial management.

SELF-TEST QUESTIONS

What are the three main areas of finance?

If you have definite plans to go into one area, why is it necessary that you know something about the other areas?

Why is it necessary for business students who do not plan to major in finance to understand the basics of finance?

---

[1] It is an interesting fact that the course "Financial Management for Nonfinancial Executives" has the highest enrollment in most executive development programs.

FINANCIAL MANAGEMENT IN THE 1990s

When financial management emerged as a separate field of study in the early 1900s, the emphasis was on the legal aspects of mergers, the formation of new firms, and the various types of securities firms could issue to raise capital. During the Depression of the 1930s, the emphasis shifted to bankruptcy and reorganization, to corporate liquidity, and to the regulation of security markets. During the 1940s and early 1950s, finance continued to be taught as a descriptive, institutional subject, viewed more from the standpoint of an outsider rather than from that of a manager. However, a movement toward theoretical analysis began during the late 1950s, and the focus shifted to managerial decisions regarding the choice of assets and liabilities with the goal of maximizing the value of the firm. The focus on value maximization has received an increasing emphasis throughout the 1990s as more and more companies are implementing compensation plans that link managers' and employees' bonuses to value creation. Shareholder activism also is on the rise, as pension and mutual fund portfolio managers are buying large amounts of stock in companies and then putting pressure on the companies to take actions that benefit shareholders.

In addition to the focus on shareholder value maximization, two other trends have become increasingly important in recent years: (1) the globalization of business and (2) the increased use of information technology. These trends will undoubtedly continue in the years ahead.

Globalization of Business

Many companies today rely to a large and increasing extent on overseas operations. Table 1-1 summarizes the percentage of overseas revenues and profits for ten well-known corporations. Very clearly, these ten "American" companies are really international concerns.

Four factors have led to increased globalization of businesses: (1) Improvements in transportation and communications, which lowered shipping costs and made interna-

TABLE 1-1	Percentage of Revenue and Net Income from Overseas Operations for Ten Well-Known Corporations	
COMPANY	PERCENTAGE OF REVENUE ORIGINATED OVERSEAS	PERCENTAGE OF NET INCOME GENERATED OVERSEAS
Citicorp	59.3	57.9
Coca-Cola	70.5	68.7
Exxon	77.8	76.5
Ford Motor	30.5	14.0
General Electric	25.5	13.4
General Motors	29.0	53.9
IBM	62.8	85.4
McDonald's	54.3	56.3
Merck	32.1	26.3
Walt Disney	20.9	1.8

SOURCE: *Forbes* Magazine's 1995 Ranking of the Top 100 U.S. Multinationals.

MCDONALD'S LOOKS OVERSEAS

As Table 1-1 demonstrates, many large corporations are truly global enterprises. For example, consider McDonald's Corp. As of mid-1996, the company owned, operated, or licensed more than 17,000 eateries, and nearly 7,000 of them were located in 84 overseas nations. Moreover, McDonald's has been growing much faster overseas than at home in the United States.

This trend will undoubtedly continue, as demonstrated by the firm's plans for operations in China. It currently has two restaurants in China, but it plans to have 500 by the year 2000.

Not surprisingly, McDonald's overall financial performance is heavily influenced by its overseas business. Because markets are less saturated and competition is less keen, its international profit margins are higher than they are in the United States. As a result, McDonald's disclosed in a recent report that even though its domestic revenues were only up a lackluster 4 percent, it had a healthy overall increase in earnings because revenues generated outside the United States rose by 15 percent.

tional trade more feasible. (2) The increasing political clout of consumers, who desire low-cost, high-quality products, has helped lower trade barriers designed to protect inefficient, high-cost domestic manufacturers. (3) As technology has advanced, the cost of developing new products has increased. These rising costs have led to joint ventures between such companies as General Motors and Toyota, and to global operations for many firms as they seek to expand markets and thus spread development costs over higher unit sales. (4) In a world populated with multinational firms able to shift production to wherever costs are lowest, a firm whose manufacturing operations are restricted to one country cannot compete unless costs in its home country happen to be low, a condition that does not necessarily exist for many U.S. corporations. As a result of these four factors, survival requires that most manufacturers produce and sell globally.

Service companies, including banks, advertising agencies, and accounting firms, are also being forced to "go global," because global service firms can better serve their multinational clients. There will, of course, always be some purely domestic companies, but the most dynamic growth, and the best employment opportunities, are often with companies that operate worldwide.

Even businesses that operate exclusively in the United States are not immune to the effects of globalization. For example, the costs to a homebuilder in rural Nebraska are affected by interest rates and lumber prices, both of which are determined by worldwide supply and demand conditions. Furthermore, demand for the homebuilder's houses are influenced by interest rates and by conditions in the local farm economy, which depend to a large extent on foreign demand for wheat. To operate efficiently, the Nebraska builder must be able to forecast the demand for houses, and that demand depends on worldwide events. So, at least some knowledge of global economic conditions is important to virtually everyone, not just to those involved with businesses that operate internationally.

Information Technology

The 21st century will see continued advances in computer and communications technology, and this will continue to revolutionize the way financial decisions are made. Companies are linking networks of personal computers to one another, to the firms' own mainframe computers, to the Internet and the World Wide Web, and to their customers' and suppliers' computers. Thus, financial managers are increasingly able to share information and to have "face-to-face" meetings with distant colleagues through video teleconferencing. The ability to access and analyze data on a real-time basis also means that quantitative analysis is becoming more important, and "gut feel" no longer sufficient, in business decisions. As a result, the next generation of financial managers will need stronger computer and quantitative skills than were required in the past.

SELF-TEST
QUESTIONS

What are two key trends to look for in the 1990s and beyond?

How has financial management changed from the early 1900s to the 1990s?

How might a person become better prepared for a career in financial management?

THE FINANCIAL STAFF'S RESPONSIBILITIES

The financial staff's task is to acquire and then help employ resources so as to maximize the value of the firm. Here are some specific activities:

1. **Forecasting and planning.** The financial staff generally coordinates the planning process. This means they must interact with people from other departments as they look ahead and lay plans to shape the firm's future.

2. **Major investment and financing decisions.** A successful firm usually has rapid growth in sales, which requires investments in plant, equipment, and inventory. The financial staff must help determine the optimal sales growth rate, and also help decide what specific assets to acquire and the best way to finance those assets. For example, should the firm finance with debt, equity, or some combination of the two, and if debt is used, how much should be long term and how much should be short term?

3. **Coordination and control.** The financial staff must interact with other personnel to ensure that the firm is operated as efficiently as possible. All business decisions have financial implications, and all managers—financial and otherwise—need to take this into account. For example, marketing decisions affect sales growth, which in turn influences investment requirements. Thus, marketing decision makers must take account of how their actions affect and are affected by such factors as the availability of funds, inventory policies, and plant capacity utilization.

4. **Dealing with the financial markets.** The financial staff must deal with the money and capital markets. As we shall see in Chapter 4, each firm affects and is affected by the general financial markets where funds are raised, where the firm's securities are traded, and where investors either make or lose money.

5. **Risk management.** All businesses face risks, including natural disasters such as fires and floods, uncertainties in commodity and security prices, volatile interest rates, and fluctuating foreign exchange rates. However, many of these risks can be reduced by purchasing insurance or by hedging in the derivatives markets. The financial staff is responsible for the firm's overall risk management program, including identifying the risks that should be hedged and then hedging them in the most efficient manner.

In summary, people working in financial management make decisions regarding which assets their firms should acquire, how those assets should be financed, and how the firm should manage its existing resources. If these responsibilities are performed optimally, this will help to maximize the values of firms, and it will also contribute to the welfare of consumers and employees.

S E L F - T E S T
Q U E S T I O N

What are five specific activities with which finance people are involved?

ALTERNATIVE FORMS OF BUSINESS ORGANIZATION

There are three main forms of business organization: (1) sole proprietorships, (2) partnerships, and (3) corporations. In terms of numbers, about 80 percent of businesses are operated as sole proprietorships, while most of the remainder are divided equally between partnerships and corporations. Based on dollar value of sales, however, about 80 percent of all business is conducted by corporations, about 13 percent by sole proprietorships, and about 7 percent by partnerships and hybrids. Because most business is conducted by corporations, we will concentrate on them in this book. However, it is important to understand the differences among the various forms.

Sole Proprietorship

A **sole proprietorship** is an unincorporated business owned by one individual. Going into business as a sole proprietor is easy—one merely begins business operations. However, even the smallest businesses normally must be licensed by a governmental unit.

The proprietorship has three important advantages: (1) It is easily and inexpensively formed, (2) it is subject to few government regulations, and (3) the business avoids corporate income taxes.

The proprietorship also has three important limitations: (1) It is difficult for a proprietorship to obtain large sums of capital; (2) the proprietor has unlimited personal liability for the business's debts, which can result in losses that exceed the money he or she invested in the company; and (3) the life of a business organized as a proprietorship is limited to the life of the individual who created it. For these three reasons, sole proprietorships are used primarily for small-business operations. However, businesses are frequently started as proprietorships and then converted to corporations when their growth causes the disadvantages of being a proprietorship to outweigh the advantages.

Partnership

A **partnership** exists whenever two or more persons associate to conduct a noncorporate business. Partnerships may operate under different degrees of formality, ranging from informal, oral understandings to formal agreements filed with the secretary of the state in which the partnership was formed. The major advantage of a partnership is its low cost and ease of formation. The disadvantages are similar to those associated with proprietorships: (1) unlimited liability, (2) limited life of the organization, (3) difficulty transferring ownership, and (4) difficulty raising large amounts of capital. The tax treatment of a partnership is similar to that for proprietorships, but this is often an advantage, as we demonstrate in Chapter 2.

Regarding liability, the partners can potentially lose all of their personal assets, even assets not invested in the business, because under partnership law, each partner is liable for the business's debts. Therefore, if any partner is unable to meet his or her pro rata liability in the event the partnership goes bankrupt, the remaining partners must make good on the unsatisfied claims, drawing on their personal assets to the extent necessary. The partners of the national accounting firm Laventhol and Horwath, a huge partnership which went bankrupt as a result of suits filed by investors who relied on faulty audit statements, learned all about the perils of doing business as a partnership. Thus, a Texas partner who audits a business which goes under can bring ruin to a millionaire New York partner who never went near the client company.

The first three disadvantages—unlimited liability, impermanence of the organization, and difficulty of transferring ownership—lead to the fourth, the difficulty partnerships have in attracting substantial amounts of capital. This is generally not a problem for a slow-growing business, but if a business's products or services really catch on, and if it needs to raise large amounts of capital to capitalize on its opportunities, the difficulty in attracting capital becomes a real drawback. Thus, growth companies such as Hewlett-Packard and Microsoft generally begin life as a proprietorship or partnership, but at some point their founders find it necessary to convert to a corporation.

Corporation

A **corporation** is a legal entity created by a state, and it is separate and distinct from its owners and managers. This separateness gives the corporation three major advantages: (1) *Unlimited life.* A corporation can continue after its original owners and managers are deceased. (2) *Easy transferability of ownership interest.* Ownership interests can be divided into shares of stock, which, in turn, can be transferred far more easily than can proprietorship or partnership interests. (3) *Limited liability.* Losses are limited to the actual funds invested. To illustrate limited liability, suppose you invested $10,000 in a partnership which then went bankrupt owing $1 million. Because the owners are liable for the debts of a partnership, you could be assessed for a share of the company's debt, and you could be held liable for the entire $1 million if your partners could not pay their shares. Thus, an investor in a partnership is exposed to unlimited liability. On the other hand, if you invested $10,000 in the stock of a corporation which then went bankrupt, your potential loss on the investment would be limited to your $10,000 investment.[2] These three factors—unlimited life, easy transferability of ownership interest, and limited liability—make it much easier for corporations than for proprietorships or partnerships to raise money in the capital markets.

The corporate form offers significant advantages over proprietorships and partnerships, but it also has two disadvantages: (1) Corporate earnings may be subject to double taxation—the earnings of the corporation are taxed at the corporate level, and then any earnings paid out as dividends are taxed again as income to the stockholders. (2) Setting up a corporation, and filing the many required state and federal reports, is more complex and time-consuming than for a proprietorship or a partnership.

A proprietorship or a partnership can commence operations without much paperwork, but setting up a corporation requires that the incorporators prepare a charter and a set of bylaws. Although personal computer software that creates charters and bylaws is now available, a lawyer is required if the fledgling corporation has any nonstandard features. The *charter* includes the following information: (1) name of the proposed corporation, (2) types of activities it will pursue, (3) amount of capital stock, (4) number of directors, and (5) names and addresses of directors. The charter is filed with the secretary of the state in which the firm will be incorporated, and when it is

---

[2]In the case of small corporations, the limited liability feature is often a fiction, because bankers and other lenders frequently require personal guarantees from the stockholders of small, weak businesses.

approved, the corporation is officially in existence.[3] Then, after the corporation is in operation, quarterly and annual employment, financial, and tax reports must be filed with state and federal authorities.

The *bylaws* are a set of rules drawn up by the founders of the corporation. Included are such points as (1) how directors are to be elected (all elected each year, or perhaps one-third each year for three-year terms); (2) whether the existing stockholders will have the first right to buy any new shares the firm issues; and (3) procedures for changing the bylaws themselves, should conditions require it.

The value of any business other than a very small one will probably be maximized if it is organized as a corporation because:

1. Limited liability reduces the risks borne by investors, and, other things held constant, *the lower the firm's risk, the higher its value.*

2. A firm's value is dependent on its *growth opportunities,* which in turn are dependent on the firm's ability to attract capital. Since corporations can attract capital more easily than can unincorporated businesses, they are better able to take advantage of growth opportunities.

3. The value of an asset also depends on its *liquidity,* which means the ease of selling the asset and converting it to cash at a "fair market value." Since an investment in the stock of a corporation is much more liquid than a similar investment in a proprietorship or partnership, this too enhances the value of a corporation.

As we will see later in the chapter, most firms are managed with value maximization in mind, and this, in turn, has caused most large businesses to be organized as corporations.

Hybrid Forms of Organization

Although the three basic types of organization—proprietorships, partnerships, and corporations—dominate the business scene, several hybrid forms are gaining popularity. For example, there are some specialized types of partnerships that have somewhat different characteristics than the "plain vanilla" kind. First, it is possible to limit the liabilities of some of the partners by establishing a **limited partnership,** wherein certain partners are designated **general partners** and others **limited partners.** In a limited partnership, the limited partners are liable only for the amount of their investment in the partnership, while the general partners have unlimited liability. However, the limited partners typically have no control, which rests solely with the general partners, and their returns are likewise limited. Limited partnerships are common in real estate, oil, and equipment leasing ventures, but they are not widely used in general business situations because no one partner is usually willing to be the general partner and thus accept the majority of the business's risk, while would-be limited partners are unwilling to give up all control.

The **limited liability partnership (LLP),** sometimes called a **limited liability company (LLC),** is a relatively new type of partnership that is now permitted in many states. In both regular and limited partnerships, at least one partner is liable for the debts of the partnership. However, in an LLP, all partners enjoy limited liability with regard to the business's liabilities, and, in that regard, they are similar to shareholders

---

[3]Note that more than 60 percent of major U.S. corporations are chartered in Delaware, which has, over the years, provided a favorable legal environment for corporations. It is not necessary for a firm to be headquartered, or even to conduct operations, in its state of incorporation.

in a corporation. In effect, the LLP form of organization combines the limited liability advantage of a corporation with the tax advantages of a partnership. Of course, those who do business with an LLP as opposed to a regular partnership are aware of the situation, which increases the risk faced by lenders, customers, and others who deal with the LLP.

There are also several different types of corporations. One type that is common among professionals such as doctors, lawyers, and accountants is the **professional corporation (PC),** or in some states, the **professional association (PA).** All 50 states have statutes that prescribe the requirements for such corporations, which provide most of the benefits of incorporation but do not relieve the participants of professional (malpractice) liability. Indeed, the primary motivation behind the professional corporation was to provide a way for groups of professionals to incorporate and thus avoid certain types of unlimited liability, yet still be held responsible for professional liability.

Finally, note that if certain requirements are met, particularly with regard to size and number of stockholders, one (or more) individuals can establish a corporation but elect to be taxed as if the business were a proprietorship or partnership. Such firms, which differ not in organizational form but only in how their owners are taxed, are called **S corporations.** Although S corporations are similar in many ways to limited liability partnerships, LLPs frequently offer more flexibility and benefits to their owners—so many that large numbers of S corporation businesses are converting to this relatively new organizational form.

S E L F - T E S T
Q U E S T I O N S

What are the key differences between sole proprietorships, partnerships, and corporations?

Explain why the value of any business other than a very small one will probably be maximized if it is organized as a corporation.

Identify the hybrid forms of organization discussed in the text, and explain the differences among them.

FINANCE IN THE ORGANIZATIONAL STRUCTURE OF THE FIRM

Organizational structures vary from firm to firm, but Figure 1-1 presents a fairly typical picture of the role of finance within a corporation. The chief financial officer (CFO) generally has the title of vice-president: finance, and he or she reports to the president. The financial vice-president's key subordinates are the treasurer and the controller. In most firms the treasurer has direct responsibility for managing the firm's cash and marketable securities, for planning its capital structure, for selling stocks and bonds to raise capital, for overseeing the corporate pension plan, and for managing risk. The treasurer also supervises the credit manager, the inventory manager, the director of capital budgeting (who analyzes decisions related to investments in fixed assets), and the risk manager. The controller is typically responsible for the activities of the accounting and tax departments.

S E L F - T E S T
Q U E S T I O N

Identify the two primary subordinates who report to the firm's chief financial officer, and indicate the primary responsibilities of each.

FIGURE 1-1   Role of Finance in a Typical Business Organization

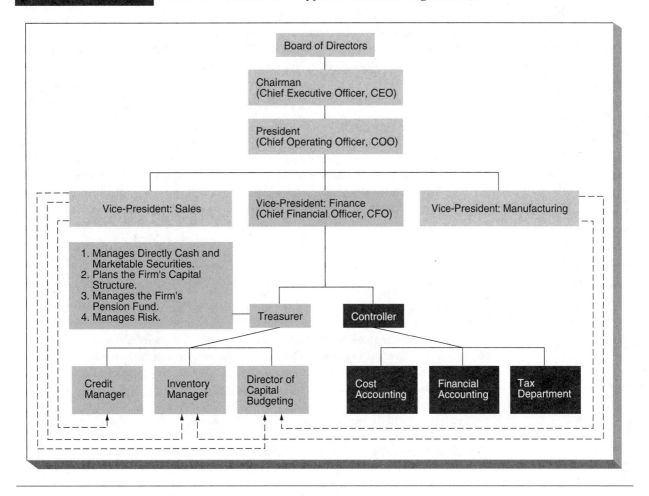

THE GOALS OF THE CORPORATION

Shareholders are the owners of a corporation, and they purchase stocks because they want to earn a good return on their investment without undue risk exposure. In most cases, shareholders elect directors, who then hire managers to run the corporation on a day-to-day basis. Since managers are supposed to be working on behalf of shareholders, it follows that they should pursue policies which enhance shareholder value. Consequently, throughout this book we operate on the assumption that management's primary goal is **stockholder wealth maximization,** which translates into *maximizing the price of the firm's common stock*. Firms do, of course, have other objectives—in particular, the managers who make the actual decisions are interested in their own personal satisfaction, in their employees' welfare, and in the good of the community and of society at large. Still, for the reasons set forth in the following sections, *stock price maximization is the most important goal for most corporations.*

Stock Price Maximization and Social Welfare

If a firm attempts to maximize its stock price, is this good or bad for society? In general, it is good. Aside from such illegal actions as attempting to form monopolies, violating safety codes, and failing to meet pollution requirements, *the same actions that maximize stock prices also benefit society.* Here are some of the reasons:

1. **To a large extent, the owners of stock *are* society.** Seventy-five years ago this was not true, because most stock ownership was concentrated in the hands of a relatively small segment of society, comprised of the wealthiest individuals. Since then, there has been explosive growth in pension funds, life insurance companies, and mutual funds. These institutions now own more than 60 percent of all stock. In addition, more than 43 percent of all U.S. adults now own stock individually, as compared with only 22 percent in 1990. Moreover, most people with a retirement plan have an indirect ownership interest in stocks. Thus, most members of society now have an important stake in the stock market, either directly or indirectly. Therefore, when a manager takes actions to maximize the stock price, this potentially improves the quality of life for millions of ordinary citizens.

2. **Consumers benefit.** Stock price maximization requires efficient, low-cost businesses that produce high-quality goods and services at the lowest possible cost. This means that companies must develop products and services that consumers want and need, which leads to new technology and new products. Also, companies that maximize their stock price must generate growth in sales by creating value for customers in the form of efficient and courteous service, adequate stocks of merchandise, and well-located business establishments.

   People sometimes argue that firms, in their efforts to raise profits and stock prices, increase product prices and gouge the public. In a reasonably competitive economy, which we have, prices are constrained by competition and consumer resistance. If a firm raises its prices beyond reasonable levels, it will simply lose its market share. Even giant firms such as General Motors lose business to Japanese and German firms, as well as to Ford and Chrysler, if they set prices above the level necessary to cover production costs plus a "normal" profit. Of course, firms *want* to earn more, and they constantly try to cut costs, develop new products (and so on), and thereby earn above-normal profits. Note, though, that if they are indeed successful and do earn above-normal profits, those very profits will attract competition, which will eventually drive prices down; so again, the main long-term beneficiary is the consumer.

3. **Employees benefit.** There are cases in which a stock increases when a company announces plans to lay off employees, but viewed over time this is the exception rather than the rule. In general, companies that successfully increase stock prices also grow and add more employees, thus benefiting society. Note too that many governments across the world, including U.S. federal and state governments, are privatizing some of their state-owned activities by selling these operations to investors. Perhaps not surprisingly, the sales and cash flows of recently privatized companies generally improve. Moreover, studies show that these newly privatized companies tend to grow and thus require more employees when they are managed with the goal of stock price maximization.

   Each year *Fortune* magazine conducts a survey of managers, analysts, and other knowledgeable people to determine the most admired companies. One of *Fortune*'s key criteria is companies' ability to attract, develop, and retain talented people. The results consistently show that there is a high correlation among a company's being admired, its ability to satisfy employees, and its creation of value for shareholders. Employees find that it is both fun and financially rewarding to work for successful companies. So, successful companies get the cream of the employee crop, and skilled, motivated employees are one of the keys to corporate success.

Managerial Actions to Maximize Shareholder Wealth

What types of actions can managers take to maximize a firm's stock price? To answer this question, we first need to ask, "What determines stock prices?" In a nutshell, it is *a company's ability to generate cash flows now and in the future.*

While we will address this issue in detail in Chapter 9, we can lay out three basic facts here: (1) Any financial asset, including a company's stock, is valuable only to the extent that it generates cash flows; (2) the timing of cash flows matters — cash received sooner is better, because it can be reinvested in the company to produce additional income or else be returned to investors; and (3) investors generally are averse to risk, so all else equal, they will pay more for a stock whose cash flows are relatively certain than for one whose cash flows are more risky. Because of these three facts, managers can enhance their firms' stock prices by increasing the size of the expected cash flows, by speeding up their receipt, and by reducing their riskiness.

Three factors primarily determine cash flows: (1) unit sales, (2) after-tax operating margins, and (3) capital requirements. The first factor has two parts, the *current level of sales* and the *expected future growth rate in sales.* Managers can increase sales, hence cash flows, by truly understanding their customers and then providing the goods and services that customers want. Some companies may luck into a situation that creates rapid sales growth, but the unfortunate reality is that market saturation and competition will, in the long term, cause their sales growth rate to decline to a level that is limited by population growth and inflation. Therefore, managers must constantly strive to create new products, services, and brand identities that cannot be easily replicated by competitors, and thus to extend the period of high growth for as long as possible.

The second determinant of cash flows is the amount of after-tax profit that the company can keep after it has paid its employees and suppliers. One possible way to increase operating profit is to charge higher prices. However, in a competitive economy such as ours, higher prices can be charged only for products that meet the needs of customers better than competitors' products.

Another way to increase operating profit is to reduce direct expenses such as labor and materials. However, and paradoxically, sometimes companies can create even higher profit by spending *more* on labor and materials. For example, choosing the lowest-cost supplier might result in using poor materials that lead to costly production problems. Therefore, managers should understand *supply chain management,* which often means developing long-term relationships with suppliers. Similarly, increasing employee training adds to costs, but it often pays off through increased productivity and reduced turnover. Therefore, the *human resources staff* can have a huge impact on operating profits.

The third factor affecting cash flows is the amount of money a company must invest in plant and equipment. In short, it takes cash to create cash. For example, as a part of their normal operations, most companies have funds tied up in inventory, machines, buildings, and so forth. But each dollar of cash tied up in operating assets is a dollar that the company must "rent" from investors and pay for by paying interest or dividends. Therefore, reducing asset requirements tends to increase cash flows, which increases the stock price. For example, companies that successfully implement *just-in-time* inventory systems generally increase their cash flows, because they have less cash tied up in inventory.

As these examples indicate, there are many ways to improve cash flows. All of them require the active participation of many departments, such as marketing, engineering, and logistics. One of the financial manager's roles is to show these other managers how their actions affect the company's ability to generate cash flow.

Financial managers also must decide *how to finance the firm:* What mix of debt and equity should be used, and what specific types of debt and equity securities should be issued? Also, what percentage of current earnings should be retained and reinvested rather than paid out as dividends; this is the **dividend policy decision.**

Each of these investment and financing decisions is likely to affect the level, timing, and riskiness of the firm's cash flows, and, therefore, the price of its stock. Naturally, managers should make investment and financing decisions designed to maximize the firm's stock price.

Although managerial actions affect stock prices, stocks are also influenced by such external factors as legal constraints, the general level of economic activity, tax laws, interest rates, and conditions in the stock market as diagrammed in Figure 1-2. Working within the set of external constraints shown in the box at the extreme left, management makes a set of long-run strategic policy decisions which chart a future course for the firm. These policy decisions, along with the general level of economic activity and the level of corporate income taxes, influence expected cash flows, their timing, their eventual payment to stockholders, and their perceived riskiness. These factors all affect the price of the stock, but so does another factor, conditions in the stock market as a whole.

Does It Make Sense to Try to Maximize Earnings per Share?

In arguing that managers should take steps to maximize the firm's stock price, we have indicated that managers should focus on increasing cash flows both now and in the future. We have said nothing about maximizing **profit** or **earnings per share (EPS).** Although today most analysts rely primarily on cash flow to assess performance, atten-

---

FIGURE 1-2   **Summary of Major Factors Affecting Stock Prices**

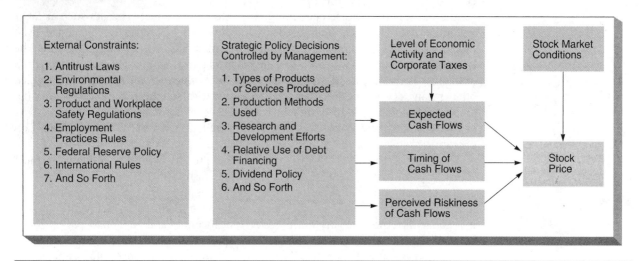

ARE CEOs OVERPAID?

At first glance the number is hard to believe: $203 million. That's what Disney's chief, Michael Eisner, received as compensation in 1993. This happened in a year when Disney's net income fell 63 percent, partly in response to losses at EuroDisney. In fact, Eisner's compensation was not that much less than Disney's 1993 net income, which totaled $229.8 million. A cynic might think, "If someone reduced net income by 63 percent and still earned $203 million, how much would the company pay if earnings actually rose?"

What is interesting is that Eisner's compensation received little or no resistance from the company's shareholders. Why? During his tenure as Disney's CEO, Eisner has made shareholders rich. Disney's market value has skyrocketed from $2.2 billion in 1984, when he took over as CEO, to more than $40 billion by mid-1996. If you had invested $1,000 in Disney stock in 1984, and reinvested all of your dividends, your investment would be worth nearly $30,000 today.

Eisner's record haul came largely in the form of stock options. His salary and bonus in 1993 totaled only $750,000, but he exercised long-term stock options worth more than $202 million. Clearly, those stock options provided Eisner with a significant incentive to raise the company's stock price, and he delivered.

Concerns about "excessive compensation" are most likely to arise when CEOs receive exorbitant levels of pay at the same time the firm's stock price is underperforming the market. Even in these instances, the issues may not be all that straightforward. The stock price may fall for reasons having nothing to do with the CEO—indeed, you could argue that CEOs probably work especially hard when the company's fortunes are declining. Also, you need to look at the long-run track record of the CEO and the firm. In Disney's case, the company's performance over time has been outstanding, even though during the year in which Eisner exercised his options and had a reported income of $203 million, the company's performance was lackluster.

Some critics argue that although performance incentives are appropriate as a method of compensation, the overall level of CEO compensation is still too high. Would Eisner have been unwilling to take the job if he had been offered only half as many stock options? Would he have put forth less effort, and would the stock price not have gone up as much? It is hard to say.

Eisner's compensation was extraordinary, but it was largely a one-time payment. The typical CEO of a large corporation generally receives annual compensation of less than $1 million. Although this certainly is respectable, it pales compared with the salaries sports stars and other entertainers receive. For example, it has been estimated that director Steven Spielberg earned more than $165 million in 1994, while the preschool icon Barney the Dinosaur earned $59 million for his creators in 1993 and another $25 million in 1994. More recently, Michael Jordan just signed a $25 million one-year contract to play basketball, 20-year-old Tiger Woods quit school to play golf for about $50 million, and actors Jim Carrey and Sylvester Stallone have signed deals which earn them $20 million per picture.

tion still is paid to accounting measures, especially EPS. The accounting performance measures are appealing (1) because they are easy to use and understand; (2) because they are calculated on the basis of (more or less) standardized accounting principles, which reflect the accounting profession's efforts to measure financial performance on a consistent basis both across firms and over time; and (3) because net income is supposed to reflect the firm's potential for producing cash flows over time. Nevertheless, as we will see in the next chapter, there are important differences between earnings and cash flows. Moreover, a firm's stock price is affected by both its performance this year and its expected performance in the future.

Even though cash flows ultimately determine stockholder value, financial managers cannot ignore EPS, because earnings announcements send messages to investors. Say, for example, a manager makes a decision that will greatly improve future cash flows and thus raise the stock price, yet the short-run effect will be a reduction in this year's EPS. Such a decision might be a change in inventory accounting policy which increases the reported cost of goods sold, hence lowers profits, but which also increases cash flow because it reduces taxes. In this case, it makes sense for the manager to make the change because it speeds cash flow, even though it reduces profits for this year. Note, though, that management must communicate the reason for the earnings decline or else the company's stock price would probably decline after the earnings announcement.

S E L F - T E S T
Q U E S T I O N S

What is management's primary goal?

How does stock price maximization benefit society?

What three basic factors determine the price of a stock?

What three factors determine cash flows?

Is profit maximization an appropriate goal for financial managers?

Should financial managers concentrate strictly on cash flow and ignore the impact of their decisions on EPS?

BUSINESS ETHICS AND SOCIAL RESPONSIBILITY

Is the goal of maximizing stock prices consistent or inconsistent with high standards of ethical behavior and social responsibility? It is definitely *consistent*. Many socially responsible firms have created enormous value for their owners, and many unethical firms now are bankrupt.

Business Ethics

The word *ethics* is defined in Webster's dictionary as "standards of conduct or moral behavior." **Business ethics** can be thought of as a company's attitude and conduct toward its employees, customers, community, and stockholders. High standards of ethical behavior demand that a firm treat each party that it deals with in a fair and honest manner. A firm's commitment to business ethics can be measured by the tendency of the firm and its employees to adhere to laws and regulations relating to such factors as product safety and quality, fair employment practices, fair marketing and selling practices, the use of confidential information for personal gain, community involvement, bribery, and illegal payments to obtain business.

There are many instances of firms engaging in unethical behavior. For example, in recent years the employees of several prominent Wall Street investment banking houses have been sentenced to prison for illegally using insider information on proposed mergers for their own personal gain, and E. F. Hutton, a large brokerage firm, lost its independence through a forced merger after it was convicted of cheating its banks out of millions of dollars in a check kiting scheme. Drexel Burnham Lambert, one of the largest investment banking firms, went bankrupt, and its "junk bond king," Michael Milken, who had earned $550 million in just one year, was sentenced to ten years in prison plus charged a huge fine for securities-law violations. Another investment bank, Salomon Brothers, was implicated in a Treasury bond scandal which resulted in the firing of its chairman and other top officers.

These cases received a lot of notoriety, but the results of a recent study indicate that the executives of most major firms in the United States believe that firms do try to maintain high ethical standards in all of their business dealings. Furthermore, most executives believe that there is a positive correlation between ethics and long-run profitability. For example, Chase Bank suggested that ethical behavior has increased its profitability because such behavior helped it (1) avoid fines and legal expenses, (2) build public trust, (3) attract business from customers who appreciate and support its policies, (4) attract and keep employees of the highest caliber, and (5) support the economic viability of the communities in which it operates.

Most firms today have in place strong codes of ethical behavior, and they also conduct training programs designed to ensure that employees understand the correct behavior in different business situations. However, it is imperative that top management—the chairman, president, and vice-presidents—be openly committed to ethical behavior, and that they communicate this commitment through their own personal actions as well as through company policies, directives, and punishment/ reward systems.

When conflicts arise between profits and ethics, sometimes the ethical considerations are so strong that they clearly dominate. However, in many cases the choice between ethics and profits is not clear cut. For example, suppose Norfolk Southern's managers know that its coal trains are polluting the air along its routes, but the amount of pollution is within legal limits and preventive actions would be costly. Are the managers ethically bound to reduce pollution? Similarly, suppose a medical products company's own research indicates that one of its new products may cause problems. However, the evidence is relatively weak, other evidence regarding benefits to patients is strong, and independent government tests show no adverse effects. Should the company make the potential problem known to the public? If it does release the negative (but questionable) information, this will hurt sales and profits, and possibly keep some patients who would benefit from the new product from using it. There are no obvious answers to questions such as these, but companies must deal with them on a regular basis, and a failure to handle the situation properly can lead to huge product liability suits and even to bankruptcy.

Social Responsibility

Another issue that deserves consideration is **social responsibility:** Should businesses operate strictly in their stockholders' best interests, or are firms also responsible for the welfare of their employees, customers, and the communities in which they operate? Certainly firms have an ethical responsibility to provide a safe working environment, to avoid polluting the air or water, and to produce safe products. However, socially responsible actions have costs, and not all businesses would voluntarily incur all such costs. If some firms act in a socially responsible manner while others do not, then the socially responsible firms will be at a disadvantage in attracting capital. To illustrate, suppose all firms in a given industry have close to **"normal" profits** and **rates of return on investment,** that is, close to the average for all firms and just sufficient to attract capital. If one company attempts to exercise social responsibility, it will have to raise prices to cover the added costs. If other firms in its industry do not follow suit, their costs and prices will be lower. The socially responsible firm will not be able to compete, and it will be forced to abandon its efforts. Thus, any voluntary socially responsible acts that raise costs will be difficult, if not impossible, in industries that are subject to keen competition.

What about oligopolistic firms with profits above normal levels—cannot such firms devote resources to social projects? Undoubtedly they can, and many large, successful firms do engage in community projects, employee benefit programs, and the like to a greater degree than would appear to be called for by pure profit or wealth maximization goals.[4] Furthermore, many such firms contribute large sums to charities. Still, publicly owned firms are constrained by capital market forces. To illustrate, suppose a saver who has funds to invest is considering two alternative firms. One devotes a substantial part of its resources to social actions, while the other concentrates on profits and stock prices. Many investors would shun the socially oriented firm, thus putting it at a disadvantage in the capital market. After all, why should the stockholders of one corporation subsidize society to a greater extent than those of other businesses? For

---

[4]Even firms like these often find it necessary to justify such projects at stockholder meetings by stating that these programs will contribute to long-run profit maximization.

this reason, even highly profitable firms (unless they are closely held rather than publicly owned) are generally constrained against taking unilateral cost-increasing social actions.

Does all this mean that firms should not exercise social responsibility? Not at all. But it does mean that most significant cost-increasing actions will have to be put on a *mandatory* rather than a voluntary basis to ensure that the burden falls uniformly on all businesses. Thus, such social benefit programs as fair hiring practices, minority training, product safety, pollution abatement, and antitrust actions are most likely to be effective if realistic rules are established initially and then enforced by government agencies. Of course, it is critical that industry and government cooperate in establishing the rules of corporate behavior, and that the costs as well as the benefits of such actions be estimated accurately and then taken into account.

In spite of the fact that many socially responsible actions must be mandated by government, in recent years numerous firms have voluntarily taken such actions, especially in the area of environmental protection, because they helped sales. For example, many detergent manufacturers now use recycled paper for their containers, and food companies are packaging more and more products in materials that consumers can recycle or that are biodegradable. To illustrate, McDonald's replaced its Styrofoam boxes, which take years to break down in landfills, with paper wrappers that are less bulky and decompose more rapidly. Some companies, such as The Body Shop and Ben & Jerry's, go to great lengths to be socially responsible. According to the president of The Body Shop, the role of business is to promote the public good, not just the good of the firm's shareholders. Furthermore, she argues that it is impossible to separate business from social responsibility. Finally, for some firms socially responsible actions may not de facto be costly—the companies heavily advertise their actions, and many consumers prefer to buy from socially responsible companies rather than from those that shun social responsibility.

SELF-TEST
QUESTIONS

How would you define "business ethics"?

Is "being ethical" good for profits in the long run? In the short run?

What would happen if one firm attempted to employ costly socially responsible programs but its competitors did not follow suit?

AGENCY RELATIONSHIPS

Managers are empowered by the owners of the firm—the shareholders—to make decisions. However, managers may have personal goals that compete with shareholder wealth maximization, and such potential conflicts of interest are dealt with under *agency theory.*

An *agency relationship* arises whenever one or more individuals, called *principals,* (1) hires another individual or organization, called an *agent,* to perform some service and (2) then delegates decision-making authority to that agent. Within the financial management context, the primary agency relationships are those (1) between stockholders and managers and (2) between managers and debtholders.[5]

---

[5]The classic work on the application of agency theory to financial management is Michael C. Jensen and William H. Meckling, "Theory of the Firm, Managerial Behavior, Agency Costs, and Ownership Structure," *Journal of Financial Economics,* October 1976, 305–360.

Agency Conflict I: Stockholders versus Managers

A potential **agency problem** arises whenever the manager of a firm owns less than 100 percent of the firm's common stock. If the firm is a proprietorship managed by its owner, the owner-manager will presumably operate so as to maximize his or her own welfare, with welfare measured in the form of increased personal wealth, more leisure, or perquisites.[6] However, if the owner-manager incorporates and then sells some of the stock to outsiders, a potential conflict of interests immediately arises. Now the owner-manager may decide to lead a more relaxed lifestyle and not work as strenuously to maximize shareholder wealth, because less of this wealth will accrue to him or her. Also, the owner-manager may decide to consume more perquisites, because some of these costs will be borne by the outside shareholders. In essence, the fact that the owner-manager will neither gain all the benefits of the wealth created by his or her efforts nor bear all of the costs of perquisites will increase the incentive to take actions that are not in the best interests of other shareholders.

In most large corporations, potential agency conflicts are important, because large firms' managers generally own only a small percentage of the stock. In this situation, shareholder wealth maximization could take a back seat to any number of conflicting managerial goals. For example, people have argued that some managers' primary goal seems to be to maximize the size of their firms.[7] By creating a large, rapidly growing firm, managers (1) increase their job security, because a hostile takeover is less likely; (2) increase their own power, status, and salaries; and (3) create more opportunities for their lower- and middle-level managers. Furthermore, since the managers of most large firms own only a small percentage of the stock, it has been argued that they have a voracious appetite for salaries and perquisites, and that they generously contribute corporate dollars to their favorite charities because they get the glory but outside stockholders bear the cost.

Obviously, managers can be encouraged to act in the stockholders' best interests through a set of incentives, constraints, and punishments. However, these tools are most effective if shareholders can observe all of the actions taken by managers. A potential *moral hazard* problem, wherein agents take unobserved actions in their own behalf, arises, because it is virtually impossible for shareholders to monitor all managerial actions. In general, to reduce both agency conflicts and the moral hazard problem, stockholders must incur *agency costs,* which include all costs borne by shareholders to encourage managers to maximize the firm's stock price rather than act in their own self-interests. There are three major categories of agency costs: (1) expenditures to monitor managerial actions, such as audit costs; (2) expenditures to structure the organization in a way that will limit undesirable managerial behavior, such as appointing outside investors to the board of directors; and (3) opportunity costs which are incurred when shareholder-imposed restrictions, such as requirements for stockholder votes on certain issues, limit the ability of managers to take timely actions that would enhance shareholder wealth.

In the absence of any type of shareholder effort to affect managerial behavior, and hence with zero agency costs, there will almost certainly be some loss of shareholder wealth due to improper managerial actions. Conversely, agency costs would be very high if shareholders attempted to ensure that every managerial action coincided exactly with shareholder interests. Thus, the optimal amount of agency costs to be borne by

---

[6]*Perquisites* are executive fringe benefits such as luxurious offices, executive assistants, expense accounts, limousines, corporate jets, generous retirement plans, and the like.

[7]See J. R. Wildsmith, *Managerial Theories of the Firm* (New York: Dunellen, 1974).

shareholders should be viewed like any other investment decision—agency costs should be incurred as long as each dollar spent returns more than a dollar in shareholder wealth.

There are two extreme positions regarding how to deal with shareholder-manager agency conflicts. At one extreme, if a firm's managers were compensated solely on the basis of stock price changes, agency costs would be low because managers would have a great deal of incentive to maximize shareholder wealth. However, it would be difficult if not impossible to hire competent managers under these terms, because the firm's earnings stream would be affected by economic events that were not under managerial control. At the other extreme, stockholders could monitor every managerial action, but this would be costly and inefficient. The optimal solution lies somewhere in the middle, where executive compensation is tied to performance but some monitoring is also done. Some specific mechanisms used to motivate managers to act in shareholders' best interests include (1) managerial compensation plans, (2) direct intervention by shareholders, (3) the threat of firing, and (4) the threat of takeover.

1. **Managerial compensation.** Managers obviously must be compensated, and the structure of the compensation package can and should be designed to meet two primary objectives: (a) to attract and retain able managers and (b) to align managers' actions as closely as possible with the interests of stockholders, who are primarily interested in stock price maximization. Different companies follow different compensation practices, but a typical senior executive's compensation is structured in three parts: (a) a specified annual salary, which is necessary to meet living expenses; (b) a cash or stock bonus paid at the end of the year, which depends on the company's profitability during the year; and (c) options to buy stock, or actual shares of stock, which reward the executive for long-term performance.

   Managers are more likely to focus on maximizing stock prices if they are themselves large shareholders. Often, companies grant senior managers **performance shares,** where the executive receives a number of shares dependent upon the company's actual performance and the executive's continued service. For example, in 1991 Coca-Cola granted one million shares of stock worth $81 million to its CEO, Roberto Goizueta. The award was based on Coke's performance under Goizueta's leadership, but it also stipulated that Goizueta would receive the shares only if he stayed with the company for the remainder of his career.

   Most large corporations also provide **executive stock options,** which allow managers to purchase stock at some future time at a given price. Obviously, a manager who has an option to buy, say, 10,000 shares of stock at a price of $10 during the next five years will have an incentive to help raise the stock's value to an amount greater than $10.

   The number of performance shares or options awarded is generally based on objective criteria. Years ago, the primary criteria were accounting measures such as earnings per share (EPS) and return on equity (ROE). Today, though, the focus is more on the market value of the firm's shares or, better yet, on the performance of its shares relative to other stocks in its industry.

   A relatively new measure of managerial performance, *economic value added (EVA),* is being used by more and more firms to tie executive compensation to stockholder wealth maximization. EVA is a way to measure a firm's true profitability. The cost of debt capital (interest expense) is deducted when accountants calculate net income, but no cost is deducted to account for the cost of common equity. Therefore, in an economic sense, net income overstates "true" income. EVA overcomes this flaw in conventional accounting.

EVA is found by taking the after-tax operating profit and subtracting the annual cost of *all* the capital a firm uses. The higher its EVA, the more wealth the firm is creating for its shareholders. There is a higher correlation between EVA and stock prices than between accounting measures such as earnings per share and stock prices, so compensation based on EVA provides managers with better incentives to maximize shareholder wealth. EVA and its companion measure, market value added (MVA), will be discussed in depth in Chapter 2.

Various procedures are used to structure compensation programs, and good programs are relatively complicated. Still, it has been thoroughly established that a well-designed compensation program can do wonders to improve a company's financial performance.

2. **Direct intervention by shareholders.** Years ago most stock was owned by individuals, but today the majority is owned by institutional investors such as insurance companies, pension funds, and mutual funds. Therefore, the institutional money managers have the clout, if they choose to use it, to exercise considerable influence over most firms' operations. First, they can talk with a firm's management and make suggestions regarding how the business should be run. In effect, institutional investors act as lobbyists for the body of stockholders. Second, any shareholder who has owned at least $1,000 of a company's stock for one year can sponsor a proposal which must be voted on at the annual stockholders' meeting, even if the proposal is opposed by management. Although shareholder-sponsored proposals are nonbinding and are limited to issues outside of day-to-day operations, the results of such votes are clearly heard by top management.

Why are institutions now taking such an interest in the management of companies they own? The primary reason is that they no longer have an easy exit from the market. Their portfolios are so big that if they decided to dump a stock in a hurry, the stock's price would take a free-fall. Rather than throwing up their hands and selling the stock, many institutional investors have decided to stay and work with management. Also, there has been considerable pressure on pension fund managers from the Department of Labor, which supervises pension fund investment practices under the Employee Retirement Income Security Act (ERISA). Under ERISA, pension fund managers are required to vote in the best interests of the funds' beneficiaries, which often means voting against corporate management. Finally, the Securities and Exchange Commission (SEC) has been expanding the number of issues that shareholders can address in shareholder-sponsored proposals. In its latest move, the SEC ruled that executive compensation is a permissible topic for proposals. In the past, executive compensation was classified as a matter of "ordinary business," hence not addressable in shareholder proposals. Similarly, the SEC recently forced several companies to allow shareholders to vote on "golden parachute" executive retirement packages, which are contract provisions that give a corporate executive a large severance payment if the company is taken over by another company and the executive loses his or her job.

The most fundamental change that institutional investors are lobbying for is a more independent board of directors—institutional investors see a management-controlled board as the weak link in the chain of managerial accountability to shareholders. Too often, according to most experts on corporate control, the directors are in management's hip pocket, which is why institutional investors are pressing for truly independent boards. In fact, many institutional investors would like to see an outside director installed as chairman of the board, as was done recently by General Motors, because they do not trust an inside chairman to serve the shareholders first and his or her management's interests second.

3. **The threat of firing.** Until recently, the probability of a large firm's management being ousted by its stockholders was so remote that it posed little threat. This situation existed because the shares of most firms were so widely distributed, and management's control over the voting mechanism so strong, that it was almost impossible for dissident stockholders to get the votes needed to overthrow a management team. However, as noted above, that situation is changing.

Consider the case of Baltimore Bancorp. Recently its chairman, Harry L. Robinson, spurned a friendly $17-per-share takeover offer from rival First Maryland Bancorp. Dismayed stockholders saw the stock price drop to $5 a share, and, led by a Baltimore businessman, they revolted. A slate of dissident directors was nominated, and they lined up the support of T. Rowe Price, a Baltimore mutual fund management company that held about 9 percent of the stock. At Baltimore Bancorp's next annual meeting, shareholders elected the dissident directors, who won all six of the board seats that were up for election. Then the board ousted Robinson, and a new management team was put in place.

For every obvious case of shareholders' directly ousting current management, there have been dozens of indirect ousters. For example, the CEOs or other top executives at American Express, Goodyear, General Motors, Kodak, and AT&T all resigned recently amid speculation that their departures were due to their companies' poor performance. More and more, the reasons for executive departures are shifting from "poor health" and "personal reasons" to "at the request of the board."

4. **The threat of takeovers. Hostile takeovers** (when management does not want the firm to be taken over) are most likely to occur when a firm's stock is undervalued relative to its potential because of poor management. In a hostile takeover, the managers of the acquired firm are generally fired, and any who manage to stay on lose status and authority. Thus, managers have a strong incentive to take actions designed to maximize stock prices. In the words of one company president, "If you want to keep your job, don't let your stock sell at a bargain price."

Agency Conflict II: Stockholders versus Creditors

In addition to conflicts between stockholders and managers, there can also be conflicts between stockholders (through managers) and creditors. Creditors have a claim on part of the firm's earnings stream for payment of interest and principal on the debt, and they have a claim on the firm's assets in the event of bankruptcy. However, stockholders have control (through the managers) of decisions that affect the riskiness of the firm. Creditors lend funds at rates that are based on (1) the riskiness of the firm's existing assets, (2) expectations concerning the riskiness of future asset additions, (3) the firm's existing capital structure (that is, the amount of debt financing used), and (4) expectations concerning future capital structure decisions. These are the primary determinants of the riskiness of a firm's cash flows, hence the safety of its debt issues.

Now suppose stockholders, acting through management, cause a firm to sell some relatively safe assets and invest the proceeds in a large new project that is far riskier than the firm's old assets. This increased risk will cause the required rate of return on the firm's debt to increase, and that will cause the value of the outstanding debt to fall. If the risky project is successful, all the benefits go to the stockholders, because creditors' returns are fixed at the old, low-risk rate. However, if the project is unsuccessful, the bondholders may have to share in the losses. From the stockholders' point of view, this amounts to a game of "heads I win, tails you lose," which is obviously not good for the creditors. Similarly, suppose its managers borrow additional funds and use the proceeds to repurchase some of the firm's outstanding stock in an effort to "leverage up" stockholders' return on equity. The value of the debt will probably decrease, because now there will be more debt backed by an unchanged amount of cash flow and assets. In both the riskier asset and the increased leverage situations, stockholders tend to gain at the expense of creditors.

Can and should stockholders, through their managers/agents, try to expropriate wealth from creditors? In general, the answer is no, for there is no room for unethical behavior in the business world. Indeed, creditors attempt to protect themselves against stockholders by placing restrictive covenants in debt agreements. Moreover, if creditors perceive that a firm's managers are trying to take advantage of them, they will either refuse to deal further with it or else will charge a higher than normal interest rate to compensate for the risk of possible exploitation. Thus, firms which deal unfairly with creditors either lose access to the debt markets or are saddled with high interest rates and restrictive covenants, all of which are detrimental to shareholders.

In view of all this, it follows that to best serve their shareholders in the long run, managers must play fairly with creditors. Managers, as agents of both shareholders and creditors, must act in a manner that is fairly balanced between the interests of the two classes of security holders. Similarly, because of other constraints and sanctions, management actions which would expropriate wealth from any of the firm's other *stakeholders,* including its employees, customers, suppliers, and community, will ultimately be to the detriment of its shareholders. In our society, stock price maximization requires fair treatment for all parties whose economic positions are affected by managerial decisions.

S E L F - T E S T
Q U E S T I O N S

What are agency costs, and who bears them?

What are some mechanisms that encourage managers to act in the best interests of stockholders? To not take advantage of bondholders?

Why should managers not take actions that are unfair to any of the firm's stakeholders?

ORGANIZATION OF THE BOOK

The primary goal of all managers should be to maximize the value of the firm. To achieve this goal, managers must have a general understanding of how businesses are organized, how financial markets operate, how interest rates are determined, how the tax system operates, and how accounting data are used to evaluate a business's performance. In addition, managers must have a good understanding of such fundamental concepts as time value of money, risk measurement, asset valuation, and evaluation of specific investment opportunities. This background information is essential for anyone involved with the kinds of decisions that affect the value of a firm's securities.

The organization of this book reflects these considerations, so Part I presents some background material in four chapters. Chapter 1 discusses the goals of the firm and the "philosophy" of financial management. Chapter 2 describes the key financial statements, discusses what they are designed to do, and then explains how our tax system affects earnings, cash flows, stock prices, and managerial decisions. Chapter 3 shows how financial statements are analyzed, and Chapter 4 discusses how financial markets operate and how interest rates are determined.

Part II considers two of the most fundamental concepts in financial management— risk and the time value of money. First, Chapters 5 and 6 explain how risk is measured and how it affects security prices and rates of return. Next, Chapter 7 discusses the time value of money and its effects on asset values and rates of return.

Part III covers issues related to financial assets, primarily stocks and bonds. Chapter 8 focuses on bonds, and Chapter 9 considers stocks. Both chapters describe the relevant institutional details, then explain how risk and time value jointly determine stock and bond prices.

Part IV, "Strategic Investment Decisions," applies the concepts covered in earlier chapters to decisions related to long-term, fixed asset investments. First, Chapter 10 explains how to measure the cost of the funds used to acquire fixed assets, or the cost of capital. Next, Chapter 11 shows how this information is used to evaluate potential capital investments by answering this question: Can we expect a project to provide a higher rate of return than the cost of the funds used to finance it? Only if the expected return exceeds the cost of capital will accepting a project increase stockholders' wealth. Chapter 12 goes into more detail on capital budgeting decisions, including replacement projects versus expansion projects, the effects of inflation, and the like. Finally, Chapter 13 shows how projects' riskiness is taken into account, and how the total capital budget should be determined.

Part V discusses strategic financing decisions, or how money should be raised. Since these decisions involve resource requirements, we begin with an explanation of financial planning in Chapter 14. Then, Chapters 15 and 16 examine capital structure theory, or the issue of how much debt versus equity the firm should use. Finally, Chapter 17 considers the firm's distribution policy; that is, how much net income should be retained for reinvestment versus being paid out, either as a dividend or as a share repurchase?

Part VI discusses some of the tactics involved in financing decisions. Chapter 18 describes how companies issue securities and how they refinance debt; Chapter 19 covers leasing; and Chapter 20 explains hybrid financing, including preferred stock, warrants, and convertible securities.

In Part VII, our focus shifts from long-term, strategic decisions to short-term, day-to-day operating decisions. Chapter 21 explains how companies manage their current assets, especially inventories and accounts receivables. Chapter 22 addresses the ways companies use short-term credit to support daily operations. Chapter 23 provides a treatment of some more advanced issues in the area of working capital management.

Finally, in Part VIII, we address several special topics which draw upon the earlier chapters. Included are derivatives, risk management, bankruptcy, mergers, multinational financial management, and pension plan management.

It is worth noting that instructors may cover the chapters in a different sequence from the order in the book. The chapters are written to a large extent in a modular, self-contained manner, so such reordering should present no major difficulties.

SUMMARY

This chapter has provided an overview of financial management. The key concepts covered are listed below.

- Finance consists of three interrelated areas: (1) **capital markets and institutions,** (2) **investments,** and (3) **financial management.**

- In recent years the two most important trends in finance have been the **increased globalization of business** and the growing use of **computers and information technology.** These trends are likely to continue in the future.

- The **financial staff's** task is to **obtain** and **use funds** so as to **maximize the value of the firm.**

- The three main forms of business organization are the **sole proprietorship,** the **partnership,** and the **corporation.**

- Although each form of organization offers advantages and disadvantages, **most business is conducted by corporations because this organizational form maximizes larger firms' values.**

- The primary goal of management should be to **maximize stockholders' wealth,** and this means **maximizing the firm's stock price.** Actions which maximize stock prices also increase social welfare.

- Three factors determine cash flows: (1) **sales,** (2) the **after-tax operating profit margin,** and (3) **capital requirements.**

- The **price of a firm's stock** depends on the **cash flows paid to shareholders,** the **timing of the cash flows,** and their **riskiness.** The level and riskiness of cash flows are affected by the **financial environment** as well as by **investment, financing,** and **dividend policy decisions** made by financial managers.

- An **agency problem** is a potential conflict of interests that can arise between a principal and an agent. Two important agency relationships are (1) those between the owners of the firm and its management and (2) those between the managers, acting for stockholders, and the debtholders.

- There are a number of ways to **motivate managers to act in the best interests of stockholders,** including (1) properly structured **managerial compensation,** (2) **direct intervention by stockholders,** (3) the **threat of firing,** and (4) the **threat of takeovers.**

Questions

1-1   Define each of the following terms:
a. Sole proprietorship; partnership; corporation
b. Limited partnership; limited liability partnership; professional corporation
c. Stockholder wealth maximization
d. Social responsibility; business ethics
e. Normal profits; normal rate of return
f. Agency problem
g. Economic value added (EVA)
h. Performance shares; executive stock options
i. Hostile takeover
j. Profit maximization
k. Earnings per share
l. Dividend policy

1-2   What are the three principal forms of business organization? What are the advantages and disadvantages of each?

1-3   Would the "normal" rate of return on investment be the same in all industries? Would "normal" rates of return change over time? Explain.

1-4   Would the role of the financial manager be likely to increase or decrease in importance relative to other executives if the rate of inflation increased? Explain.

1-5   Should stockholder wealth maximization be thought of as a long-term or a short-term goal — for example, if one action would probably increase the firm's earnings per share (EPS) from a current level of $41 to $51 in 6 months and then to $61 in 5 years, but another action would probably keep the EPS at $41 for several years but then increase it to $81 in 5 years, which action would be better? Can you think of some specific corporate actions which might have these general tendencies?

1-6   Drawing on your background in accounting, can you think of any accounting procedure differences that might make it difficult to compare the relative performance of different firms?

1-7   Would the management of a firm in an oligopolistic or in a competitive industry be more likely to engage in what might be called "socially conscious" practices? Explain your reasoning.

1-8   What is the difference between stock price maximization and profit maximization? Under what conditions might profit maximization not lead to stock price maximization?

1-9   If you were the president of a large, publicly owned corporation, would you make decisions to maximize stockholders' welfare or your own personal interests? What are some actions stockholders could take to ensure that management's interests and those of stockholders coincided? What are some other factors that might influence management's actions?

1-10   The president of International Microchips Inc. (IMI) made this statement in the company's annual report: "IMI's primary goal is to increase the value of the common stockholders' equity over time." Later on in the report, the following announcements were made:
   a.   The company contributed $2 million to the symphony orchestra in Seattle, its headquarters city.
   b.   The company is spending $600 million to open a new plant in Venezuela. No revenues will be produced by the plant for 4 years, so earnings will be depressed during this period versus what they would have been had the decision not been made to open the new plant.
   c.   The company is increasing its relative use of debt. Whereas assets were formerly financed with 30 percent debt and 70 percent equity, henceforth the financing mix will be 45/55.
   d.   The company uses a great deal of electricity in its manufacturing operations, and it generates most of this power itself. Plans are to utilize nuclear fuel rather than coal to produce electricity in the future.
   e.   The company has been paying out half of its earnings as dividends and retaining the other half. Henceforth, it will pay out only 40 percent as dividends.
   Discuss how each of these actions would be reacted to by IMI's stockholders, customers, and labor force, and then how each action might affect IMI's stock price.

1-11   Assume that you are serving on the board of directors of a medium-sized corporation and that you are responsible for establishing the compensation policies of senior management. You believe that the company's CEO is very talented, but your concern is that she is always looking for a better job and may want to boost the company's short-run performance (perhaps at the expense of long-run profitability) to make herself more marketable to other corporations. What effect would these concerns have on the compensation policy you put in place?

1-12   If the overall stock market is extremely volatile, and if many analysts foresee the possibility of a stock market crash, how might these factors influence the way corporations choose to compensate their senior executives?

1-13   Teacher's Insurance and Annuity Association–College Retirement Equity Fund (TIAA–CREF) is the largest institutional shareholder in the United States, controlling $125 billion in pension funds. Traditionally, TIAA–CREF has acted as a passive investor. However, TIAA–CREF announced a tough new corporate governance policy beginning October 5, 1993.
   In a statement mailed to all 1,500 companies in which it invests, TIAA–CREF outlined a policy designed to improve corporate performance, including a goal of higher stock prices for the $52 billion in stock assets it holds, and to encourage corporate boards to have a majority of independent (outside) directors. TIAA–CREF wants to see management more accountable to shareholder interests, as evidenced by its statement that the fund will vote against any director "where companies don't have an effective, independent board which can challenge the CEO."
   Historically, TIAA–CREF did not quickly sell poor-performing stocks. In addition, the fund invested a large part of its assets to match performance of the major market indexes, locking TIAA–CREF into ownership of certain companies. Further complicating the problem, TIAA–CREF owns stakes of from 1 percent to 10 percent in several companies, and selling such large blocks of stock would depress their prices.
   Common stock ownership confers a right to sponsor initiatives to shareholders regarding the corporation. A corresponding voting right exists for shareholders.
   a.   Is TIAA–CREF an ordinary shareholder?
   b.   Due to its asset size, TIAA–CREF assumes large positions with which it plans to actively vote. However, who owns TIAA–CREF?
   c.   Should the investment managers of a fund like TIAA–CREF determine the voting practices of the fund's shares, or should the voting rights be passed on to TIAA–CREF's stakeholders?

MINI CASE

Suppose you went home for a quick visit early in the term, and, over the course of the weekend, your brother, who received his MBA three years ago, asked you to tell him about the courses you are taking. After you told him that financial management was one of the courses, he asked you the following questions:

a. What kinds of career opportunities are open to finance majors?

b. What are the most important financial management issues of the 1990s?

c. What are the primary responsibilities of a corporate financial staff?

d. (1) What are the alternative forms of business organization?

    (2) What are their advantages and disadvantages?

e. What is the primary goal of the corporation?

    (1) Do firms have any responsibilities to society at large?

    (2) Is stock price maximization good or bad for society?

    (3) Should firms behave ethically?

f. What factors affect stock prices?

g. What determines cash flows?

h. What factors affect the level and riskiness of cash flows?

i. What is an agency relationship?

    (1) What agency relationships exist within a corporation?

    (2) What mechanisms exist to influence managers to act in shareholders' best interests?

    (3) Should shareholders (through managers) take actions that are detrimental to bondholders?

Selected Additional References

For alternative views on firms' goals and objectives, see the following articles:

Cornell, Bradford, and Alan C. Shapiro, "Corporate Stakeholders and Corporate Finance," *Financial Management,* Spring 1987, 5–14.

Donaldson, Gordon, "Financial Goals: Management versus Stockholders," *Harvard Business Review,* May–June 1963, 116–129.

Meckling, William H., and Michael C. Jensen, "Reflections on the Corporation as a Social Invention," *Midland Corporate Finance Journal,* Fall 1983, 6–15.

Seitz, Neil, "Shareholder Goals, Firm Goals and Firm Financing Decisions," *Financial Management,* Autumn 1982, 20–26.

The following articles extend our discussion of agency relationships:

Barnea, Amir, Robert A. Haugen, and Lemma W. Senbet, "Market Imperfections, Agency Problems, and Capital Structure: A Review," *Financial Management,* Summer 1981, 7–22.

Hand, John H., William P. Lloyd, and Robert B. Rogow, "Agency Relationships in the Close Corporation," *Financial Management,* Spring 1982, 25–30.

For a general review of academic finance, together with an extensive bibliography of key research articles, see

Brennan, Michael J., "Corporate Finance Over the Past 25 Years," *Financial Management,* Summer 1995, 9–22.

Cooley, Philip L., and J. Louis Heck, "Significant Contributions to Finance Literature," *Financial Management,* Tenth Anniversary Issue 1981, 23–33.

For more information on managerial compensation, see

Cooley, Philip L., and Charles E. Edwards, "Ownership Effects on Managerial Salaries in Small Business," *Financial Management,* Winter 1982, 5–9.

Hudson, Carl D., John S. Jahera, Jr., and William P. Lloyd, "Further Evidence on the Relationship between Ownership and Performance," *Financial Review,* May 1992, 227–239.

Lambert, Richard A., and David F. Larker, "Executive Compensation, Corporate Decision-Making and Shareholder Wealth: A Review of the Evidence," *Midland Corporate Finance Journal,*

Winter 1985, 6–22. The Winter 1985 issue of the *Midland Corporate Finance Journal* contains several other articles pertaining to executive compensation.

Long, Michael S., "The Incentives Behind the Adoption of Executive Stock Option Plans in U.S. Corporations," *Financial Management,* Autumn 1992, 12–21.

Sridharan, Uma V., "CEO Influence and Executive Compensation," *Financial Review,* February 1996, 51–66.

"Stern Stewart Roundtable on Management Incentive Compensation and Shareholder Value," *Journal of Applied Corporate Finance,* Summer 1992, 110–130.

Stern, Joel M., G. Bennett Stewart III, and Donald H. Chew, "The EVA® Financial Management System," *Journal of Applied Corporate Finance,* Summer 1995, 32–46.

For more information on the role of corporate directors, see

"Corporate Governance: The Role of Boards of Directors in Takeover Bids and Defenses," *Journal of Applied Corporate Finance,* Summer 1989, 6–35.

FINANCIAL STATEMENTS, CASH FLOW, AND TAXES

If you were a small investor who knew a little about finance and accounting, could you compete successfully against large institutional investors with armies of analysts, high-powered computers, and state-of-the-art trading strategies?

The answer, according to one Wall Street legend, is a resounding yes! Peter Lynch, who had an outstanding track record as manager of the $10 billion Fidelity Magellan fund and who went on to become the best-selling author of One Up on Wall Street *and* Beating the Street, *has long argued that small investors can beat the market by using common sense and information available to all of us as we go about our day-to-day lives.*

For example, a college student may be more adept at scouting out the new and interesting products which will become tomorrow's success stories than is an investment banker who works 75 hours a week in a New York office. Parents of young children are likely to know which baby foods will succeed, or which diapers are best. Couch potatoes may have the best feel for which tortilla chips have the brightest future, or whether a new remote control is worth its price.

The trick is to find a product which will boom, yet whose manufacturer's stock is undervalued. If this sounds too easy, you are right. Lynch argues that once you have discovered a good product, there is still much homework to be done. This involves combing through the vast amount of financial information that is regularly provided by companies. It also requires taking a closer and more critical look at how the company conducts its business—Lynch refers to this as "kicking the tires."

To illustrate his point, Lynch relates his experience with Dunkin' Donuts. As a consumer, Lynch was impressed with the quality of the product. This impression led him to take a closer look at the company's financial statements and operations. He liked what he saw, and Dunkin' Donuts became one of the best investments in his portfolio.

This chapter discusses what financial statements are, and the next one explains how they are analyzed. Once you have identified a good product as a possible investment, the principles discussed in these chapters will help you "do your homework."

One of the best sources for financial statements is produced free by the government. It is the EDGAR Database, and its site is http://www.sec.gov/edgarhp.htm.

A manager's primary goal is to maximize the value of his or her firm's stock. Value is based on the stream of earnings and cash flows the firm will generate in the future. But how does an investor go about estimating future earnings and cash flows, and how does a manager decide which actions are most likely to increase future earnings and cash flows? The answers to both questions lie in a study of the financial statements which publicly traded firms must provide to investors. Here "investors" include both institutions (banks, insurance companies, pension funds, and the like) and individuals. Thus, this chapter begins with a discussion of what the basic financial statements are, how they are used, and what kinds of financial information users need.

In theory, the value of any business asset—whether it is a *financial asset* such as a stock or a bond, or a *real (physical) asset* such as land, buildings, and equipment—depends on the usable, after-tax cash flows the asset is expected to produce. However, investors are also interested in reported accounting profits, which differ from cash flows. Therefore, the chapter also explains the difference between accounting income and cash flow. Finally, since it is *after-tax* income and cash flows that are important, the chapter provides an overview of the federal income tax system.

Much of the material in this chapter reviews concepts covered in basic accounting courses. However, the information is important enough to go over again—accounting is used to "keep score," and if a firm's managers do not know the score, they cannot tell how their actions will affect the stock's price. If you took midterm exams but were not told how you were doing, you would have a difficult time improving your grades. The same thing holds in business. If a firm's managers—whether they are in marketing, personnel, production, or finance—do not understand financial statements, they will not be able to judge the effects of their actions. Although only accountants need to know how to *make* financial statements, everyone involved with business needs to know how to *interpret* them.

A BRIEF HISTORY OF ACCOUNTING AND FINANCIAL STATEMENTS

Financial statements are pieces of paper with numbers written on them, but it is important to also think about the real assets that underlie the numbers. If you understand how and why accounting began, and how financial statements are used, you can better visualize why accounting information is so important.

Thousands of years ago, individuals (or families) were self-contained in the sense that they gathered their own food, made their own clothes, and built their own shelters. Then specialization began—some people became good at making pots, others at making arrowheads, others at making clothing, and so on.

As specialization began, so did trading, initially in the form of barter. At first, each artisan worked alone, and trade was strictly local. Eventually, though, master craftsmen set up small factories and employed workers, money (in the form of clamshells) began to be used, and trade expanded beyond the local area. As these developments occurred, a primitive form of banking began, with wealthy merchants lending profits from past dealings to enterprising factory owners who needed capital to expand or to young traders who needed money to buy wagons, ships, and merchandise.

When the first loans were made, lenders could physically inspect borrowers' assets and judge the likelihood of a loan being repaid. Eventually, though, lending became more complex—borrowers were developing larger factories, traders were acquiring fleets of ships and wagons, and loans were being made to develop distant mines and trading posts. At that point, lenders could no longer personally inspect the assets that backed their loans, and they needed some way of summarizing borrowers' assets. Also, some investments were made on a share-of-the-profits basis, and this meant that profits (or income) had to be determined. At the same time, factory owners and large merchants needed reports to see how effectively their own enterprises were being run, and governments needed information for use in assessing taxes. For all these reasons, a need arose for financial statements, for accountants to prepare those statements, and for auditors to verify the accuracy of the accountants' work.

The economic system has grown enormously since its beginning, and accounting has become more complex. However, the original reasons for financial statements still apply: Bankers and other investors need accounting information to make intelligent decisions, managers need it to operate their businesses efficiently, and taxing authorities need it to assess taxes in a reasonable way.

It should be intuitively clear that it is not easy to translate physical assets into numbers, which is what accountants do when they construct financial statements. The numbers shown on balance sheets generally represent the historical costs of assets. However, inventories may be spoiled, obsolete, or even missing; fixed assets such as machinery and buildings may have higher or lower values than their historical costs; and accounts receivable may be uncollectable. Also, some liabilities such as obligations to pay retirees' medical costs may not even show up on the balance sheet. Similarly, some costs reported on the income statement may be understated, as would be true if a plant with a useful life of 10 years were being depreciated over 40 years. When you examine a set of financial statements, you should keep in mind that a physical reality lies behind the numbers, and you should also realize that the translation from physical assets to "correct" numbers is far from precise.

We should also note that the traditional financial statements as prepared by accountants are designed more for use by creditors such as banks than for corporate managers and equity (stock) analysts. As a result, finance people today are modifying traditional accounting statements to make them more useful to managers and security analysts. The modified statements are based on standard accounting data, but they show things in a different and in some respects more useful way.

FINANCIAL STATEMENTS AND REPORTS

For an excellent example of a complete 1996 annual report on the web, see J.P. Morgan's at http://www.jpmorgan. com/CorpInfo/FinancialInfor mation/AnnualReport/1996/ contents.html. The complete report is also available in Adobe Acrobat format from this site.

Of the various reports corporations issue to their stockholders, the **annual report** is probably the most important. Two types of information are given in this report. First, there is a verbal section, often presented as a letter from the chairman, that describes the firm's operating results during the past year and discusses new developments that will affect future operations. Second, the annual report presents four basic financial statements — the *balance sheet,* the *income statement,* the *statement of retained earnings,* and the *statement of cash flows.* Taken together, these statements give an accounting picture of the firm's operations and financial position. Detailed data are provided for the two or three most recent years, along with historical summaries of key operating statistics for the past five or ten years.[1]

The quantitative and verbal information are equally important. The financial statements report *what has actually happened* to assets, earnings, and dividends over the past few years, whereas the verbal statements attempt to explain why things turned out the way they did.

For illustrative purposes, we use data on MicroDrive Inc., a producer of disk drives for microcomputers. Formed in 1982, MicroDrive has grown steadily and has earned a reputation for being one of the best firms in the microcomputer components industry. MicroDrive's earnings dropped a bit in 1998, to $113.5 million versus $118 million in 1997. Management reported that the decline resulted from a three-month strike that kept the firm from fully utilizing a new plant that had been financed mostly with debt.

---

[1]Firms also provide quarterly reports, but these are much less comprehensive. In addition, larger firms file even more detailed statements, giving breakdowns for each major division or subsidiary, with the Securities and Exchange Commission (SEC). These reports, called *10-K reports,* are made available to stockholders upon request to a company's corporate secretary. Finally, many larger firms also publish *statistical supplements,* which give financial statement data and key ratios going back 10 to 20 years, and their reports are available on the World Wide Web.

However, management went on to paint a more optimistic picture for the future, stating that full operations had been resumed, that several new products had been introduced, and that 1999 profits were expected to rise sharply. Of course, the profit increase may not occur, and analysts should compare management's past statements with subsequent results when judging the credibility of the projected improvement. In any event, *the information contained in an annual report is used by investors to help form expectations about future earnings and dividends.* Therefore, the annual report is obviously of great interest to investors.

SELF-TEST
QUESTIONS

What is the annual report, and what two types of information are given in it?

Why is the annual report of great interest to investors?

What four types of financial statements are typically included in the annual report?

THE BALANCE SHEET

The left-hand side of MicroDrive's year-end 1998 and 1997 **balance sheets,** which are given in Table 2-1, shows the firm's assets, while the right-hand side shows the liabilities and equity, or the claims against these assets. The assets are listed in order of their "liquidity," or the length of time it typically takes to convert them to cash. The claims are listed in the order in which they must be paid: Accounts payable must generally be paid within 30 days, notes payable within 90 days, and so on, down to the stockholders' equity accounts, which represent ownership and need never be "paid off."

Some additional points about the balance sheet are worth noting:

1. **Cash versus other assets.** Although the assets are all stated in terms of dollars, only cash represents actual money. Note, though, that some types of marketable securities have a very short time until maturity and can also be converted very quickly

| TABLE 2-1 | MicroDrive Inc.: December 31 Balance Sheets (Millions of Dollars) |

ASSETS	1998	1997	LIABILITIES AND EQUITY	1998	1997
Cash and equivalents	$ 10	$ 15	Accounts payable	$ 60	$ 30
Short-term investments	0	65	Notes payable	110	60
Accounts receivable	375	315	Accruals	140	130
Inventories	615	415	Total current liabilities	$ 310	$ 220
Total current assets	$1,000	$810	Long-term bonds	754	580
Net plant and equipment	1,000	870	Total debt	$1,064	$ 800
			Preferred stock (400,000 shares)	40	40
			Common stock (50,000,000 shares)	130	130
			Retained earnings	766	710
			Total common equity	$ 896	$ 840
Total assets	$2,000	$1,680	Total liabilities and equity	$2,000	$1,680

NOTE: The bonds have a sinking fund requirement of $20 million a year. Sinking funds are discussed in Chapter 8, but in brief, a sinking fund simply involves the repayment of long-term debt. Thus, MicroDrive was required to pay off $20 million of its mortgage bonds during 1998. The current portion of the long-term debt is included in notes payable here, although in a more detailed balance sheet it would be shown as a separate item under current liabilities.

into cash at prices close to their book values. These securities are called "cash equivalents," and they are included with cash. Other types of marketable securities have a longer time until maturity, and their market values are less predictable. These securities are classified as "short-term investments." Receivables are bills others owe MicroDrive, while inventories show the dollars the company has invested in raw materials, work-in-process, and finished goods available for sale. Finally, net plant and equipment reflect the amount of money MicroDrive paid for its fixed assets when it acquired those assets in the past, less accumulated depreciation.

With $10 million of cash, MicroDrive can write checks for a total of $10 million (versus current liabilities of $310 million due within a year). The noncash assets should produce cash over time, but they do not represent cash in hand, and the amount of cash they would bring if they were sold today could be higher or lower than the values at which they are carried on the books.

2. **Liabilities versus stockholders' equity.** The claims against assets are of two types — liabilities (or money the company owes) and the stockholders' ownership position.[2] The **common stockholders' equity,** or **net worth,** is a residual. For example, at the end of 1998,

$$\text{Assets} \quad - \quad \text{Liabilities} \quad - \text{Preferred stock} \quad = \quad \begin{matrix}\text{Common}\\\text{stockholders' equity.}\end{matrix}$$

$$\$2,000,000,000 \quad - \quad \$1,064,000,000 \quad - \quad \$40,000,000 \quad = \quad \$896,000,000.$$

Suppose assets decline in value — for example, suppose some of the accounts receivable are written off as bad debts. Liabilities and preferred stock remain constant, so the value of the common stockholders' equity must decline. Therefore, the risk of asset value fluctuations is borne by the common stockholders. Note, though, that if asset values rise (perhaps because of inflation), these benefits will accrue exclusively to the common stockholders.

3. **Preferred versus common stock.** As we will see in Chapter 20, preferred stock is a hybrid, or a cross between common stock and debt. In the event of bankruptcy, preferred stock ranks below debt but above common stock. Also, the preferred dividend is fixed, so preferred stockholders do not benefit if the company's earnings grow. Finally, many firms do not use any preferred stock, and those that do generally do not use much of it. Therefore, when the term "equity" is used in finance, we generally mean "common equity" unless the word "total" is included.

4. **Breakdown of the common equity accounts.** The common equity section is divided into two accounts — "common stock" and "retained earnings." The **retained earnings** account is built up over time as the firm "reinvests" a part of its earnings rather than paying all earnings out as dividends. The common stock account increases if the firm issues stock to raise capital, as discussed in Chapter 9.

The breakdown of the common equity accounts is important for some purposes but not for others. For example, a potential stockholder would want to know whether the company actually earned the funds reported in its equity accounts or

---

[2]One could divide liabilities into (1) debts owed to someone and (2) other items, such as deferred taxes, reserves, and so on. Because we do not make this distinction, the terms *debt* and *liabilities* are used synonymously. It should be noted that firms occasionally set up reserves for certain contingencies, such as the potential costs involved in a lawsuit currently in the courts. These reserves represent an accounting transfer from retained earnings to the reserve account. If the company wins the suit, retained earnings will be credited, and the reserve will be eliminated. If it loses, a loss will be recorded, cash will be reduced, and the reserve will be eliminated.

whether the funds came mainly from selling stock. A potential creditor, on the other hand, would be more interested in the total equity the owners have in the firm than in the source of the equity. In the remainder of this chapter, we generally aggregate the common stock and retained earnings accounts and call this sum *common equity* or *net worth*.

5. **Inventory accounting.** MicroDrive uses the FIFO (first-in, first-out) method to determine the inventory value shown on its balance sheet ($615 million). It could have used the LIFO (last-in, first-out) method. During a period of rising prices, by taking out old, low-cost inventory and leaving in new, high-cost items, FIFO will produce a higher balance sheet inventory value but a lower cost of goods sold on the income statement. (This is strictly accounting; companies actually use older items first.) Since MicroDrive uses FIFO, and since inflation has been occurring, (a) its balance sheet inventories are higher than they would have been had it used LIFO, (b) its cost of goods sold is lower than it would have been under LIFO, and (c) its reported profits are therefore higher. In MicroDrive's case, if the company had elected to switch to LIFO in 1998, its balance sheet figure for inventories would have been $585,000,000 rather than $615,000,000, and its earnings (which will be discussed in the next section) would have been reduced by $18,000,000. Thus, the inventory valuation method can have a significant effect on financial statements. This is important when an analyst is comparing different companies.

6. **Depreciation methods.** Most companies prepare two sets of financial statements — one for tax purposes and one for reporting to stockholders. Generally, they use the most accelerated depreciation method permitted under the law for tax purposes, but they use straight line, which results in a lower depreciation charge, for stockholder reporting. However, MicroDrive has elected to use rapid depreciation for both stockholder reporting and tax purposes. Had MicroDrive elected to use straight line depreciation for stockholder reporting, its 1998 depreciation expense would have been $25,000,000 less, so the $1 billion shown for "net plant" on its balance sheet, hence its retained earnings, would have been $25,000,000 higher. With less depreciation, its net income would also have been higher.

7. **The time dimension.** The balance sheet may be thought of as a snapshot of the firm's financial position *at a point in time* — for example, on December 31, 1997. Thus, on December 31, 1997, MicroDrive had $15 million of cash and equivalents, but this account had been reduced to $10 million by the end of 1998. The balance sheet changes every day as inventories are increased or decreased, as fixed assets are added or retired, as bank loans are increased or decreased, and so on. Companies whose businesses are seasonal have especially large changes in their balance sheets. For example, most retailers have high inventories and low receivables just before Christmas but low inventories and high accounts receivable just after Christmas. Therefore, firms' balance sheets change over the year, depending on when the statement is constructed.

S E L F - T E S T
Q U E S T I O N S

What is the balance sheet, and what information does it provide?

How is the order of the information shown on the balance sheet determined?

Why might a company's December 31 balance sheet differ from its June 30 balance sheet?

THE INCOME STATEMENT

Table 2-2 gives the 1998 and 1997 **income statements** for MicroDrive. Net sales are shown at the top of each statement, after which various costs, including income taxes,

TABLE 2-2	MicroDrive Inc.: Income Statements for Years Ending December 31 (Millions of Dollars, Except for Per-Share Data)

	1998	1997
Net sales	$3,000.0	$2,850.0
Costs excluding depreciation	2,616.2	2,497.0
Depreciation	100.0	90.0
Total operating costs	$2,716.2	$2,587.0
Earnings before interest and taxes (EBIT)	$ 283.8	$ 263.0
Less interest	88.0	60.0
Earnings before taxes (EBT)	$ 195.8	$ 203.0
Taxes (40%)	78.3	81.0
Net income before preferred dividends	$ 117.5	$ 122.0
Preferred dividends	4.0	4.0
Net income available to common stockholders	$ 113.5	$ 118.0
Common dividends	$ 57.5	$ 53.0
Addition to retained earnings	$ 56.0	$ 65.0
Per-share data:		
Common stock price	$23.00	$26.00
Earnings per share (EPS)[a]	$ 2.27	$ 2.36
Dividends per share (DPS)[a]	$ 1.15	$ 1.06
Book value per share (BVPS)[a]	$17.92	$16.80

[a]There are 50,000,000 shares of common stock outstanding. Note that EPS is based on earnings after preferred dividends—that is, on net income available to common stockholders. Calculations of EPS, DPS, and BVPS for 1998 are as follows:

$$\text{EPS} = \frac{\text{Net income}}{\text{Common shares outstanding}} = \frac{\$113,500,000}{50,000,000} = \$2.27.$$

$$\text{DPS} = \frac{\text{Dividends paid to common stockholders}}{\text{Common shares outstanding}} = \frac{\$57,500,000}{50,000,000} = \$1.15.$$

$$\text{BVPS} = \frac{\text{Total common equity}}{\text{Common shares outstanding}} = \frac{\$896,000,000}{50,000,000} = \$17.92.$$

are subtracted to obtain the net income available to common stockholders. A report on earnings and dividends per share is given at the bottom of the statement. Earnings per share (EPS) is called "the bottom line," denoting that of all the items on the income statement, EPS is the most important. MicroDrive earned $2.27 per share in 1998, down from $2.36 in 1997, but it still raised the dividend from $1.06 to $1.15.

While the balance sheet can be thought of as a snapshot in time, the income statement reports on operations *over a period of time,* for example, during the calendar year 1998. During 1998 MicroDrive had sales of $3 billion, and its net income available to common stockholders was $113.5 million. Income statements can cover any period of time, but they are usually prepared monthly, quarterly, or annually. Of course, sales, costs, and profits will be larger the longer the reporting period, and the sum of the last 12 monthly (or 4 quarterly) income statements should equal the values shown on the annual income statement.

For planning and control purposes, management generally forecasts monthly (or perhaps quarterly) income statements, and it then compares actual results to the forecasted statements. If revenues are below and costs above the forecasted levels, then management should take corrective steps before the problem becomes too serious.

What is an income statement, and what information does it provide?

Why is earnings per share called "the bottom line"?

Regarding the time period reported, how does the income statement differ from the balance sheet?

STATEMENT OF RETAINED EARNINGS

Changes in retained earnings between balance sheet dates are reported in the **statement of retained earnings.** Table 2-3 shows that MicroDrive earned $113.5 million during 1998, paid out $57.5 million in common dividends, and plowed $56 million back into the business. Thus, the balance sheet item "Retained earnings" increased from $710 million at the end of 1997 to $766 million at the end of 1998.

Note that "Retained earnings" represents a *claim against assets,* not assets per se. Moreover, firms retain earnings primarily to expand the business, and this means investing in plant and equipment, in inventories, and so on, *not* piling up cash in a bank account. Changes in retained earnings occur because common stockholders allow the firm to reinvest funds that otherwise could be distributed as dividends. *Thus, retained earnings as reported on the balance sheet do not represent cash and are not "available" for the payment of dividends or anything else.*[3]

What is the statement of retained earnings, and what information does it provide?

Why do changes in retained earnings occur?

Explain why the following statement is true: "Retained earnings as reported on the balance sheet do not represent cash and are not 'available' for the payment of dividends or anything else."

---

[3]The amount reported in the retained earnings account is *not* an indication of the amount of cash the firm has. Cash (as of the balance sheet date) is found in the cash account—an asset account. A positive number in the retained earnings account indicates only that in the past the firm has earned some income, but its dividends have been less than its earnings. Even though a company reports record earnings and shows an increase in the retained earnings account, it still may be short of cash.

The same situation holds for individuals. You might own a new BMW (no loan), lots of clothes, and an expensive stereo, hence have a high net worth, but if you had only 23 cents in your pocket plus $5 in your checking account, you would still be short of cash.

TABLE 2-3   MicroDrive Inc.: Statement of Retained Earnings for Year Ending December 31, 1998 (Millions of Dollars)

Balance of retained earnings, December 31, 1997	$710.0
Add: Net income, 1998	113.5
Less: Dividends to common stockholders	(57.5)[a]
Balance of retained earnings, December 31, 1998	$766.0

[a]Here, and throughout the book, parentheses are used to denote negative numbers.

SHERLOCK HOLMES, OR CORPORATE ENEMY NUMBER 1?

Is there more than meets the eye when it comes to looking at financial statements? One American University accounting professor certainly thinks so. His name is Howard Schilit, and he is recognized as a leading "forensic" accountant. As an independent consultant, Schilit works as a detective to search for the truth among the financial statements that companies make available to the public. *Business Week* has labeled Schilit the "Sherlock Holmes of Accounting." Many of the companies that he has targeted would characterize his work less charitably.

Schilit pores over financial statements and looks for cases where companies adopt accounting practices which overstate their true positions. These practices, which are generally legal and even consistent with generally accepted accounting principles (GAAP), are frequently referred to as "window dressing." In many instances, companies have considerable latitude in deciding how to account for various activities in their financial statements. Schilit objects, however, when he believes these statements result in an inaccurate picture of a company's financial health.

Business Week also reported that in a recent one-year period, Schilit investigated 39 companies and wrote negative reports on 24 of them. During this time, the average price of those 24 companies' stocks fell by 31 percent. Schilit has particularly targeted firms which recently went public (issued shares of stock to the public for the first time). These firms are often under pressure to quickly demonstrate strong performance, so they are tempted to use accounting gimmicks to boost profits.

Consider Kendall Square Research Corporation, which went public in 1992 at a price of $10 per share. Within the first year, its stock price more than doubled, to $22 a share, and its revenues increased from less than $1 million to nearly $21 million. Fidelity Investments, a large institutional investor, hired Schilit to see if this was too good to be true. Schilit concluded that it was. His report, along with a later report by the company's independent auditor, led to a dramatic restatement of the company's financial statements. The company ended up reporting a large loss for 1993, and in early 1994, its stock price fell to just over $2 per share. In an additional blow to investors, the company was delisted by the National Association of Securities Dealers (NASDAQ).

SOURCE: Adapted from "The Sherlock Holmes of Accounting," *Business Week*, September 5, 1994, 48–52.

STATEMENT OF CASH FLOWS

Even if a company reports a large net income during a year, the *amount of cash* reported on its year-end balance sheet may be the same or even lower than its beginning cash. The reason is that its net income can be used in a variety of ways, not just kept as cash in the bank. For example, the firm may use its net income to pay dividends, to increase inventories, to finance accounts receivable, to invest in fixed assets, to reduce debt, or to buy back common stock. Indeed, the company's cash position as reported on its balance sheet is affected by a great many factors, including the following:

1. **Net income.** Other things held constant, a positive net income will lead to more cash in the bank. However, as we discuss below, other things generally are not held constant.

2. **Noncash adjustments to net income.** To calculate cash flow, it is necessary to adjust net income to reflect noncash revenues and expenses, such as depreciation and deferred taxes. For most companies, the most significant noncash adjustment is due to depreciation. To see this more clearly, recall from accounting that depreciation is an annual charge against income which reflects the estimated dollar cost of capital equipment used up in the production process. For example, suppose a machine with a life of five years and a zero expected salvage value was purchased in 1997 for $100,000 and placed into service in 1998. This $100,000 cost would not be expensed in 1997. Rather, it would be written off over the machine's five-year depreciable life. If depreciation expense were not taken, profits would be overstated, and taxes would

be too high. Therefore, an annual depreciation charge is deducted from sales revenues, along with such other costs as labor and raw materials, to determine income. Note, though, that the $100,000 was actually spent back in 1997. Therefore, the depreciation charged against income in 1998 and subsequent years is not a cash outlay, as are labor or raw material charges. *Since depreciation is a noncash charge, it must be added back to net income when calculating the firm's cash flow.*

3. **Changes in working capital.** Increases in current assets other than cash, such as inventories and accounts receivable, decrease cash, whereas decreases in these accounts increase cash. For example, if inventories are to increase, the firm must use some of its cash to buy the additional inventory. Conversely, if inventories decrease, this generally means the firm is selling inventories and not replacing all of them, hence generating cash. On the other hand, if payables increase, the firm has received additional credit from its suppliers, which saves cash, but if payables decrease, this means it has used cash to pay off its suppliers. Therefore, increases in current liabilities such as accounts payable increase cash, whereas decreases in current liabilities decrease it.

4. **Fixed assets.** If a company invests in fixed assets, this will reduce its cash position. On the other hand, the sale of fixed assets will increase cash.

5. **Security transactions.** If a company issues stock or bonds during the year, the funds raised will increase its cash position. On the other hand, if the company uses cash to buy back outstanding stock or to pay off debt, or pays dividends to its shareholders, this will reduce cash.

Each of the above factors is reflected in the **statement of cash flows,** which summarizes the changes in a company's cash position. The statement separates activities into three categories:

1. *Operating activities,* which includes net income, depreciation, and changes in current assets and liabilities other than cash and short-term debt.

2. *Investing activities,* which includes investments in or sales of fixed assets.

3. *Financing activities,* which includes raising cash by issuing short-term debt, long-term debt, or stock. Also, since dividends paid and cash used to buy back outstanding stock or bonds reduce the company's cash, such transactions are included here.

Accounting texts explain how to prepare the statement of cash flows, but the statement is used to help answer questions such as these: Is the firm generating enough cash to purchase the additional assets required for growth? Is the firm generating any extra cash that can be used to repay debt or to invest in new products? Such information is useful both for managers and investors, so the statement of cash flows is an important part of the annual report. Financial managers generally use this statement, along with the cash budget, when forecasting their companies' cash positions. This issue is considered in more detail in Chapter 14.

Table 2-4 shows MicroDrive's statement of cash flows as it would appear in the company's annual report. The top section shows cash generated by and used in operations—for MicroDrive, operations provided net cash flows of *minus* $2.5 million. The sum of net income plus noncash adjustments is called **net cash flow.** For MicroDrive, the only noncash charge is depreciation, so its net cash flow is $117.5 + $100 = $217.5 million. Although net cash flow is positive, the net increase in working capital (current assets minus current liabilities) is so large that MicroDrive actually has a *negative* $2.5 million net cash flow from operations. This subtotal, the minus $2.5 million net cash

TABLE 2-4	MicroDrive Inc.: Statement of Cash Flows for 1998 (Millions of Dollars)

	CASH PROVIDED
Operating Activities	
Net income	$117.5
Adjustments:	
Noncash adjustments:	
Depreciation[a]	100.0
Due to changes in working capital:[b]	
Increase in accounts receivable	(60.0)
Increase in inventories	(200.0)
Increase in accounts payable	30.0
Increase in accruals	10.0
Net cash provided by operating activities	($ 2.5)
Long-Term Investing Activities	
Cash used to acquire fixed assets[c]	($230.0)
Financing Activities	
Sale of short-term investments	$ 65.0
Increase in notes payable	50.0
Increase in bonds outstanding	174.0
Payment of dividends	(61.5)
Net cash provided by financing activities	227.5
Summary	
Net change in cash	($ 5.0)
Cash at beginning of year	15.0
Cash at end of year	$ 10.0

[a]Depreciation is a noncash expense that was deducted when calculating net income. It must be added back to show the correct cash flow from operations.

[b]An increase in a current asset *decreases* cash. An increase in a current liability *increases* cash. For example, inventories increased by $200 million, so that reduced cash by a like amount.

[c]The net increase in fixed assets is $130 million; however, this net amount is after a deduction for the year's depreciation expense. Depreciation expense should be added back to show the increase in gross fixed assets. From the company's income statement, we see that the 1998 depreciation expense is $100 million; thus, expenditures on fixed assets were actually $230 million.

flow provided by operating activities, is in many respects the most important figure in any of the financial statements. Profits as reported on the income statement can be "doctored" by such tactics as depreciating assets too slowly, not recognizing bad debts promptly, and the like. However, it is far more difficult to simultaneously doctor profits and the working capital accounts. Therefore, it is not uncommon for a company to have positive net income up until the day it declares bankruptcy. In such cases, however, the net cash flow from operations almost always begins to deteriorate years earlier, and analysts who keep an eye on cash flow could predict trouble. Therefore, if you ever are analyzing a company and are pressed for time, look first at the trend in net cash flow provided by operating activities, because it will tell you more than any other number.

The second section shows long-term fixed-asset investing activities. MicroDrive purchased fixed assets totaling $230 million; this was the only long-term investment it made during 1998.

The third section, financing activities, includes borrowing from banks (notes payable), selling new bonds, and paying dividends on common and preferred stock. MicroDrive raised $289 million by borrowing and by selling short-term investments, but it paid $61.5 million in preferred and common dividends, so its net inflow of funds from financing activities was $227.5 million.

When all of these sources and uses of cash are totaled, we see that MicroDrive's cash outflows exceeded its cash inflows by $5 million during 1998; that is, its net change in cash was a *negative* $5 million.

MicroDrive's statement of cash flows should be worrisome to its managers and to outside analysts. The company had a $2.5 million cash shortfall from operations, it spent an additional $230 million on new fixed assets, and it paid out another $61.5 million in dividends. It covered these cash outlays by borrowing heavily and by selling off $65 million of short-term investments. Obviously, this situation cannot continue year after year, so something will have to be done. In Chapter 3, we will consider some of the actions MicroDrive's financial staff might recommend to ease the cash flow problem.

SELF-TEST
QUESTION

What is the statement of cash flows, and what types of questions does it answer?

MODIFYING ACCOUNTING DATA FOR MANAGERIAL DECISIONS

Thus far in the chapter we have focused on financial statements as they are prepared by accountants and presented in the annual report. However, these statements are designed more for use by creditors and tax collectors than for managers and equity (stock) analysts. Therefore, certain modifications are used for corporate decision making and stock valuation purposes. In the following sections we discuss how financial analysts combine stock prices and accounting data to evaluate and reward managerial performance.

Operating Assets and Operating Capital

Different firms have different financial structures, different tax situations, and different amounts of nonoperating assets such as marketable securities. These differences affect traditional accounting measures such as the rate of return on equity, and they can cause two firms, or two divisions within a single firm, that actually have similar operations to appear to be operated with different efficiency. This is important, because if managerial compensation systems are to function properly, operating managers must be judged and compensated for those things that are under their control, not on the basis of things outside their control. Therefore, to judge managerial performance, we need to compare managers' ability to generate *operating income* (or *EBIT*) with the *operating assets* under their control.

The first step in modifying the traditional accounting framework is to divide total assets into two categories, **operating assets,** which consist of the cash, accounts receivable, inventories, and fixed assets necessary to operate the business, and **nonoperating assets,** which would include marketable securities, investments in subsidiaries, land held for future use, and the like. Moreover, operating assets are further divided into **working capital** and **plant and equipment.** Obviously, if a manager can generate a given amount of profits and cash flows with a relatively small investment in operating assets, that reduces the amount of capital investors must put up and thus increases the rate of return on that capital.

The primary source of capital for business is **investors** — stockholders, bondholders, and lenders such as banks. Investors must be paid for the use of their money, with payment coming as interest in the case of debt and as dividends plus capital gains in the case of stock. So, if a company acquires more assets than it actually needs, and thus raises too much capital, then its capital costs will be unnecessarily high.

Must all of the capital used to acquire assets be obtained from investors? The answer is no, because some of the funds will come from suppliers and be reported as **accounts payable,** while other funds will come as **accrued wages and accrued taxes,** which amount to short-term loans from workers and tax authorities. Generally, both accounts payable and accruals are "free" in the sense that no explicit fee is charged for their use.[4] Therefore, if a firm needs $100 million of current assets, but it has $10 million of accounts payable and another $10 million of accrued wages and taxes, then its **investor-supplied capital** would be only $80 million.

Those current assets used in operations are called **operating working capital,** and operating working capital less accounts payable and accruals is called **net operating working capital.** Therefore, net operating working capital is the working capital acquired with investor-supplied funds.[5] Here is a workable definition in equation form:

$$\text{Net operating working capital} = \text{All current assets that do not pay interest} \quad \textbf{(2-1)} \\ - \text{All current liabilities that do not charge interest.}$$

Now think about how these concepts can be used in practice. First, all companies must carry some cash to "grease the wheels" of their operations. Companies continuously cash checks from customers and write checks to suppliers, employees, and so on. Because inflows and outflows do not coincide perfectly, a company must keep some cash in its bank account. In other words, some cash is required to conduct operations. The same is true for most other current assets, such as inventory and accounts receivable, which are required for normal operations. However, any short-term securities the firm holds generally result from investment decisions made by the treasurer, and they are not used in the core operations. Therefore, short-term investments are normally excluded when calculating net operating working capital.[6]

---

[4]Actually, as we discuss in Chapter 22, there may be a cost to some accounts payable. Ordinarily, though, trade credit is free to well-run firms.

[5]Note that the term "capital" can be given two meanings. First, when accountants use the term "capital," they typically mean the sum of long-term debt, preferred stock, and common equity, or perhaps those items plus interest-bearing short-term debt. However, when economists use the term, they generally mean assets used in production, as in "labor plus capital." If all funds were raised from long-term sources, and if all assets were operating assets, then money capital would equal operating assets, and the accountants' capital would always equal the economists' capital. When you encounter the term "capital" in the business and financial literature, it can mean either asset capital or money capital. For example, in Coca-Cola's operating manuals, which explain to its employees how Coke wants the company to be operated, capital means "assets financed by investor-supplied capital." However, in most accounting and finance textbooks, and in the traditional finance literature, "capital" means investor-supplied capital, not assets. It might be easier if we picked one meaning and then used it consistently in this book. However, that would be misleading, because both meanings are encountered in practice. Therefore, we shall use the term "capital" in both ways. However, you should be able to figure out which definition is implied from the context in which the term is used.

[6]If the marketable securities are held as a substitute for cash, and therefore reduce the cash requirements, then they may be classified as part of operating working capital. Generally, though, large holdings of marketable securities are held as a reserve for some contingency or else a temporary "parking place" for funds prior to an acquisition, a major capital investment program, or the like.

Some current liabilities—especially accounts payable and accruals—arise in the normal course of operations. Moreover, each dollar of these current liabilities is a dollar that the company does not have to raise from investors to acquire current assets. Therefore, when finding the net operating working capital, we deduct these current liabilities from the operating current assets. Other current liabilities that charge interest, such as notes payable to banks, are treated as investor-supplied capital and thus are not deducted when calculating net working capital.

We can apply these definitions to MicroDrive, using the balance sheet data given back in Table 2-1. Here is the net operating working capital for 1998:

$$\text{Net operating working capital} = (\text{Cash} + \text{Accounts receivable} + \text{Inventories})$$
$$- (\text{Accounts payable} + \text{Accruals})$$

$$= (\$10 + \$375 + \$615) - (\$60 + \$140)$$
$$= \$800 \text{ million.}$$

MicroDrive's total operating capital for 1998 was

$$\text{Total operating capital} = (\text{Net operating working capital}) + (\text{Net fixed assets}) \quad \textbf{(2-2)}$$

$$= \$800 + \$1,000$$
$$= \$1,800 \text{ million.}$$

Now note that MicroDrive's net operating working capital at year-end 1997 was

$$\text{Net operating working capital} = (\$15 + \$315 + \$415) - (\$30 + \$130)$$
$$= \$585 \text{ million,}$$

and, with $870 million of fixed assets included, its total operating capital was

$$\text{Total operating capital} = \$585 + \$870$$
$$= \$1,455 \text{ million.}$$

Therefore, MicroDrive increased its operating capital to $1,800 from $1,455 million, or by $345 million, during 1998. Furthermore, most of this increase went into working capital, which rose from $585 to $800 million, or by $215 million. This 37 percent increase in net operating working capital, when sales only rose by about 5 percent (from $2,850 to $3,000 million), should set off warning bells in your head: What caused MicroDrive to tie up so much additional cash in working capital? We will address this question in detail later in the chapter.

Net Operating Profit after Taxes (NOPAT)

If two companies have different amounts of debt, hence different interest charges, they could have identical operating performances but different net incomes—the one with more debt would have a lower net income. Net income is certainly important, but as the example below shows, net income does not always reflect the true performance of a company's operations or the effectiveness of its operating managers and employees. A better measurement for comparing managers' performance is **net operating profit after taxes,** or **NOPAT,** which is the amount of profit a company would generate if it had no debt and held no financial assets. NOPAT is defined as follows:[7]

---

[7]For firms with a more complicated tax situation, it is better to define NOPAT as follows: NOPAT = (Net income before preferred dividends) + (Net interest expense)(1 − Tax rate). Also, if firms are able to defer paying some of their taxes, perhaps by the use of accelerated depreciation, then NOPAT should be adjusted to reflect the taxes that the company actually paid on its operating income. The Copeland and Stewart books listed in the references at the end of the chapter explain in detail these and other adjustments.

$$NOPAT = EBIT(1 - Tax\ rate). \qquad \textbf{(2-3)}$$

Using data from the income statements of Table 2-2, MicroDrive's 1998 NOPAT was

$$NOPAT = \$283.8(1 - 0.4) = \$283.8(0.6) = \$170.3\ million.$$

In 1998 MicroDrive generated an after-tax profit of $170.3 million from its operations. This was actually a little better than the 1997 NOPAT of $263(0.6) = $157.8 million. However, the income statements in Table 2-2 show that MicroDrive's earnings per share declined from 1997 to 1998. This decrease in EPS was caused by an increase in interest expense, and not by a decrease in operating profit. See Table 2-2. Moreover, the balance sheets in Table 2-1 show that debt increased from 1997 to 1998. But why did MicroDrive increase its debt? MicroDrive's investment in operating capital increased dramatically from 1997 to 1998, and that increase was financed primarily with debt.

Free Cash Flow

Earlier in the chapter we defined net cash flow as being equal to net income plus noncash adjustments, typically net income plus depreciation. Note, though, that cash flows cannot be maintained over time unless depreciating fixed assets are replaced, so management is not completely free to use cash flows however it chooses. Therefore, we now define another term, **free cash flow,** which is the cash flow actually available for distribution to investors *after the company has made all the investments in fixed assets and working capital necessary to sustain ongoing operations.*

When you studied income statements in accounting, the emphasis probably was on the firm's net income, which is its **accounting profit.** However, we began this chapter by telling you that the value of a company's operations is determined by the stream of cash flows that the operations will generate now and in the future. As the statement of cash flows shows, accounting profit and cash flow can be quite different.

To be more specific, the value of a company's operations depends on all the future expected **free cash flows (FCF),** defined as after-tax operating profit minus the amount of investment in working capital and fixed assets necessary to sustain the business. Thus, free cash flow represents the cash that is actually available for distribution to investors. Therefore, the way for managers to make their companies more valuable is to increase their free cash flow.

Calculating Free Cash Flow

As shown earlier in the chapter, MicroDrive had a 1998 NOPAT of $170.3 million. Its **operating cash flow** is NOPAT plus any noncash adjustments as shown on the statement of cash flows. For MicroDrive, where depreciation is the only noncash charge, the 1998 operating cash flow is

$$Operating\ cash\ flow = NOPAT + Depreciation \qquad \textbf{(2-4)}$$

$$= \$170.3 + \$100$$

$$= \$270.3\ million.$$

As shown earlier in the chapter, MicroDrive had $1,455 million of operating assets, or operating capital, at the end of 1997, but $1,800 million at the end of 1998. Therefore, during 1998, it made a **net investment in operating capital** of

Net investment in operating capital = $1,800 − $1,455 = $345 million.

Fixed assets rose from $870 to $1,000 million, or by $130 million. However, Micro-Drive took $100 million of depreciation, so its gross investment in fixed assets was $130 + $100 = $230 million for the year. With this background, we find the **gross investment in operating capital** as follows:

$$\text{Gross investment} = \text{Net investment} + \text{Depreciation}$$
$$= \$345 + \$100 = \$445 \text{ million.}$$

MicroDrive's free cash flow in 1998 was

$$\text{FCF} = \text{Operating cash flow} - \text{Gross investment in operating capital} \qquad \textbf{(2-5)}$$
$$= \$270.3 - \$445$$
$$= -\$174.7 \text{ million.}$$

An algebraically equivalent equation is

$$\text{FCF} = \text{NOPAT} - \text{Net investment in operating capital} \qquad \textbf{(2-5a)}$$
$$= \$170.3 - \$345$$
$$= -\$174.7 \text{ million.}$$

Equations 2-5 and 2-5a are equivalent because depreciation is added to both NOPAT and net investment.

Even though MicroDrive had a positive NOPAT, its very high investment in operating capital resulted in a negative free cash flow. Since free cash flow is what is available for distribution to investors, not only was there nothing for investors, but investors actually had to provide *more* money to MicroDrive to keep the business going. Investors provided most of the required new money as debt.

Is a negative free cash flow always bad? The answer is, "Not necessarily. It depends on why the free cash flow was negative." If FCF was negative because NOPAT was negative, this is a bad sign, because the company probably is experiencing operating problems. Exceptions to this might be startup companies, or companies that are incurring significant current expenses to launch a new product line. Also, many high-growth companies have positive NOPAT but negative free cash flow due to investments in operating assets needed to support growth. There is nothing wrong with profitable growth, even if it causes negative cash flows in the short term.

SELF-TEST
QUESTIONS

What is net operating working capital? Why does it exclude most short-term investments and also notes payable?

What is total operating capital? Why is it important for managers to calculate a company's capital requirements?

What is NOPAT? Why might it be a better performance measure than net income?

What is free cash flow? Why is free cash flow the most important determinant of a firm's value?

MVA AND EVA

Neither traditional accounting data nor the modified data as discussed in the preceding section deal with stock prices. Since the primary goal of management is to maximize the firm's stock price, we need to bring stock prices into the picture. Financial analysts have therefore developed two new performance measures, MVA, or Market

Value Added, and EVA, or Economic Value Added. These concepts are discussed in this section.[8]

Market Value Added (MVA)

The primary goal of most firms is to maximize shareholders' wealth. This goal obviously benefits shareholders, but it also ensures that scarce resources are allocated efficiently, which benefits the economy. Shareholder wealth is maximized by maximizing the *difference* between the market value of the firm's equity and the amount of equity capital that was supplied by shareholders. This difference is called the **Market Value Added (MVA):**

$$MVA = \text{Market value of equity} - \text{Equity capital supplied by shareholders}$$
$$= (\text{Shares outstanding})(\text{Stock price}) - \text{Total common equity.} \qquad \text{(2-6)}$$

To illustrate, consider Coca-Cola. In 1996, its total market equity value was $131 billion, while its balance sheet showed that stockholders had put up only $6 billion. Thus, Coca-Cola's MVA was $131 − $6 = $125 billion. This $125 billion represents the difference between the money that Coca-Cola's stockholders have invested in the corporation since its founding—including retained earnings—versus the cash they could get if they sold the business. By maximizing this spread, management maximizes the wealth of its shareholders.

Economic Value Added (EVA)

Whereas MVA measures the effects of managerial actions since the very inception of a company, **Economic Value Added (EVA)** focuses on managerial effectiveness in a given year. The basic formula for EVA is as follows:

$$EVA = \text{Net operating profit after taxes, or NOPAT}$$
$$- \text{After-tax dollar cost of capital used to support operations}$$

$$= EBIT(1 - \text{Corporate tax rate})$$
$$- (\text{Operating capital})(\text{After-tax percentage cost of capital}). \qquad \text{(2-7)}$$

Operating capital is the amount of interest-bearing debt, preferred stock, and common equity used to acquire the company's net operating assets, that is, net operating working capital plus net plant and equipment. Operating assets equals capital used to buy operating assets. EVA is an estimate of a business's true economic profit for the year, and it differs sharply from accounting profit.[9] EVA represents the residual income that remains after the cost of *all* capital, including equity capital, has been deducted, whereas accounting profit is determined without imposing a charge for equity capital. As we will discuss more completely in Chapter 10, equity capital has a cost, because funds provided by shareholders could have been invested elsewhere where they would have earned a return. Shareholders give up the opportunity to invest funds elsewhere when they provide capital to the firm. The return they could earn elsewhere in investments of equal risk represents the cost of equity capital. This cost is an *opportunity cost* rather than an *accounting cost,* but it is quite real nevertheless.

Notice that when calculating EVA we do not add back depreciation. Although it is not a cash expense, depreciation is a cost, and it is therefore deducted when determining

---

[8]The concepts of EVA and MVA were developed by Joel Stern and Bennett Stewart, co-founders of the consulting firm Stern Stewart & Company. Stern Stewart copyrighted the terms "EVA" and "MVA," so other consulting firms have given other names to these values. Still, EVA and MVA are the terms most commonly used in practice.

[9]The most important reason EVA differs from accounting profit is that the cost of equity capital is deducted when EVA is calculated. Other factors that could lead to differences include adjustments that might be made to depreciation, to research and development costs, to inventory valuations, and so on. See G. Bennett Stewart III, *The Quest for Value* (New York: HarperCollins Publishers Inc., 1991).

ECONOMIC VALUE ADDED (EVA)—TODAY'S HOTTEST FINANCIAL IDEA

According to *Fortune* magazine, "Economic Value Added (EVA)" is today's hottest financial idea. Developed and popularized by the consulting firm Stern Stewart & Co., EVA helps managers ensure that a given business unit is adding to stockholder value, while investors can use it to spot stocks that are likely to increase in value.

What exactly is EVA? EVA is a way to measure an operation's true profitability. The cost of debt capital (interest expense) is deducted when accountants calculate net income, but no cost is deducted to account for the cost of common equity. Therefore, in an economic sense, net income overstates "true" income. EVA overcomes this flaw in conventional accounting.

EVA is found by taking the after-tax operating profit and subtracting the annual cost of *all* the capital a firm uses. Such highly successful giants as Coca-Cola, AT&T, Quaker Oats, Briggs & Stratton, and CSX have jumped on the EVA bandwagon and attribute much of their success to its use. According to AT&T financial executive William H. Kurtz, EVA played a major role in AT&T's decision to acquire McCaw Cellular. In addition, AT&T made EVA the primary measure of its business unit managers' performance. Quaker Oats's CEO William Smithburg said, "EVA makes managers act like shareholders. It's the true corporate faith for the 1990s."

Surprisingly, many corporate executives have no idea how much capital they are using or what that capital costs. The cost of debt capital

is easy to determine because it shows up in financial statements as interest expense; however, the cost of equity capital, which is actually much larger than the cost of debt capital, does not appear in financial statements. As a result, managers often regard equity as free capital, even though it actually has a high cost. So, until a management team determines its cost of capital, it cannot know whether it is covering all costs and thereby adding value to the firm.

Although EVA is perhaps the most widely discussed concept in finance today, it is not completely new; the need to earn more than the cost of capital is actually one of the oldest ideas in business. However, the idea is often lost because of a misguided focus on conventional accounting.

John Snow, the chief executive officer who introduced the EVA concept to CSX Corporation in 1988, notes that CSX has lots of capital tied up in its fleets of locomotives, containers, trailers, and railcars, and in its tracks and rights-of-way, and that CSX's effectiveness in using that capital determines its market value. Snow's stiffest challenge has been in the fast-growing, but low-margin, intermodal business, where trains rush freight to waiting trucks or ships. In 1988, CSX Intermodal lost $70 million after all capital costs were considered—thus, its EVA was a negative $70 million. The division was told that it must break even by 1993 or be sold. Intermodal's employees realized what would happen to their jobs if the division were sold, so they worked hard and were able to increase freight volume by 25 percent even as they reduced capital by selling off containers, trailers, and locomo-

tives. Wall Street has also noticed the improvement. CSX's stock price was $28 when Snow introduced the EVA concept in 1988, but it had climbed to $82.50 by 1993.

Briggs & Stratton, a maker of gasoline engines, tells a similar success story. When EVA was introduced in 1990, management was earning a return of only 7.7 percent on capital versus a cost of 12 percent. Drastic changes were made, the return on capital was pushed up over its cost, and, as a result, the stock price quadrupled in four years.

Coca-Cola formally introduced the EVA concept to its managers after Roberto Goizueta took over as CEO in 1981. Since then, Coke has restructured its business, sharply lowered its average cost of capital, and increased its EVA even more sharply. As a result, its stock price increased from $3 to $57.

One of EVA's greatest virtues is its direct link to stock prices. AT&T found an almost perfect correlation between its EVA and its stock price. Moreover, security analysts have found that stock prices track EVA far more closely than other factors such as earnings per share, operating margin, or return on equity. This correlation occurs because EVA is what investors really care about, namely, the net cash return on their capital. Therefore, more and more security analysts are calculating companies' EVAs and using them to help identify good buys in the stock market.

SOURCES: "The Real Key to Creating Wealth," *Fortune,* September 20, 1993, 38–44; "America's Best Wealth Creators," *Fortune,* November 28, 1994, 143–162; "Creating Shareholder Wealth," *Fortune,* December 11, 1995.

both net income and EVA. Our calculation of EVA assumes that the true economic depreciation of the company's fixed assets exactly equals the depreciation used for accounting and tax purposes. If this were not the case, adjustments would have to be made to obtain a more accurate measure of EVA.

EVA provides a good measure of the extent to which the firm has added to shareholder value. Therefore, if managers focus on EVA, this will help to ensure that they operate in a manner that is consistent with maximizing shareholder wealth. Note too that EVA can be determined for divisions as well as for the company as a whole, so it provides a useful basis for determining managerial compensation at all levels. As a result of all this, EVA is being used by an increasing number of firms as the primary basis for determining managerial compensation.

Table 2-5 shows how MicroDrive's MVA and EVA are calculated. The stock price was $23 per share at year-end 1998, down from $26 per share at the end of 1997; its percentage after-tax cost of capital was 10.8 percent in 1997 and 11.0 percent in 1998, and its tax rate was 40 percent. Other data in Table 2-5 were given in the basic financial statements provided earlier in the chapter. Note first that the lower stock price and the higher book value of equity (due to retaining earnings during 1998) combined to reduce the MVA. The 1998 MVA is still positive, but $460 − $254 = $206 million of stockholders' value was lost during 1998.

EVA for 1997 was just barely positive, and in 1998 it was negative. Operating income (NOPAT) rose, but EVA still declined, primarily because the amount of capital rose more sharply than NOPAT—by about 24 percent versus 8 percent—and the cost of this increased capital pulled EVA down.

Recall also that net income fell somewhat from 1997 to 1998, but not nearly so dramatically as the decline in EVA. Net income does not reflect the amount of equity capital employed, but EVA does. Because of this omission, net income is not as useful as EVA either for setting corporate goals or for measuring managerial performance.

We will have more to say about both MVA and EVA later in the book, but we can close this section with two observations. First, there is a relationship between MVA and EVA, but it is not a direct one. If a company has a history of negative EVAs, then its MVA will probably be negative, and vice versa if it has a history of positive EVAs. How-

TABLE 2-5	MVA and EVA for MicroDrive (Millions of Dollars)	

	1998	**1997**
MVA Calculation		
Price per share	$23.0	$26.0
Number of shares (millions)	50	50
Market value of equity	$1,150.0	$1,300.0
Book value of equity	$896.0	$840.0
MVA = Market value − Book value	$254.0	$460.0
EVA Calculation		
EBIT	$283.8	$263.0
Tax rate	40%	40%
NOPAT = EBIT (1 − T)	$170.3	$157.8
Total investor-supplied operating capital[a]	$1,800.0	$1,455.0
After-tax cost of capital (%)	11.0%	10.8%
Dollar cost of capital	$198.0	$157.1
EVA = NOPAT − Capital cost	($27.7)	$0.70

[a]Investor-supplied operating capital equals the sum of notes payable, long-term debt, preferred stock, and common equity less short-term investments. For MicroDrive, it could also be calculated as total liabilities and equity minus accounts payable, accruals, and short-term investments.

ever, the stock price, which is the key ingredient in the MVA calculation, depends more on expected future performance than on historical performance. Therefore, a company with a history of negative EVAs could have a positive MVA, provided investors expect a turnaround in the future.

The second observation is that when EVAs or MVAs are used to evaluate managerial performance as part of an incentive compensation program, EVA is the measure that is typically used. The reasons are (1) EVA shows the value added during a given year, whereas MVA reflects performance over the company's entire life, perhaps even including times before the current managers were born, and (2) EVA can be applied to individual divisions or other units of a large corporation, whereas MVA must be applied to the entire corporation. For these reasons, MVA is used primarily to evaluate top corporate officers over periods of five to ten years, or longer.

<table>
<tr><td>SELF-TEST
QUESTIONS</td><td>Define the terms "Market Value Added (MVA)" and "Economic Value Added (EVA)."
How does EVA differ from accounting profit?</td></tr>
</table>

THE FEDERAL INCOME TAX SYSTEM

The values of stocks, bonds, and mortgages, as well as assets such as plants or even entire firms, depend on the cash flows produced by the assets. Cash flows consist of *usable* income plus any depreciation, and usable income means income *after taxes*.

Our tax laws can be changed by Congress, and in recent years changes have occurred frequently. Indeed, a major change has occurred, on average, every three to four years since 1913, when our federal income tax system began. Further, certain parts of our tax system are tied to the rate of inflation, so changes occur automatically each year, depending on the rate of inflation during the previous year. Therefore, although this section will give you a good background on the basic nature of our tax system, you should consult current rate schedules and other data published by the Internal Revenue Service (available in U.S. post offices) before you file your personal or business tax returns.

Currently (1998), federal income tax rates for individuals go up to 39.6 percent, and, when Social Security, Medicare, and state and city income taxes are included, the marginal tax rate on an individual's income can easily exceed 50 percent. Business income is also taxed heavily. The income from partnerships and proprietorships is reported by the individual owners as personal income and, consequently, is taxed at federal-plus-state rates going up to 50 percent or more. Corporate profits are subject to federal income tax rates of up to 39 percent, plus state income taxes. Furthermore, corporations pay taxes and then distribute after-tax income to their stockholders as dividends, which are also taxed. So, corporate income is really subject to double taxation. *Because of the magnitude of the tax bite, taxes play a critical role in many financial decisions.*

As this text is being written, a Republican Congress and a Democratic administration continue to debate the merits of different changes in the tax laws. Even in the unlikely event that no explicit changes are made in the tax laws, changes will still occur because certain aspects of the tax calculation are tied to the inflation rate. Thus, by the time you read this chapter, tax rates and other factors will almost certainly be different from those we provide. Still, if you understand this section, you will understand the basics of our tax system, and you will know how to operate under the revised tax code.

Taxes are so complicated that university law schools offer master's degrees in taxation to lawyers, many of whom are also CPAs. In a field complicated enough to warrant such detailed study, only the highlights can be covered in a book such as this. This is really enough, though, because managers and investors should and do rely on tax specialists rather than trusting their own limited knowledge. Still, it is important to know the basic elements of the tax system as a starting point for discussions with tax experts.

Individual Income Taxes

Individuals pay taxes on wages and salaries, on investment income (dividends, interest, and profits from the sale of securities), and on the profits of proprietorships and partnerships. Our tax rates are **progressive**—that is, the higher one's income, the larger the percentage paid in taxes. Table 2-6 gives the tax rates for single individuals and married couples filing joint returns under the rate schedules that were in effect in April 1998.

1. **Taxable income** is defined as gross income less a set of exemptions and deductions which are spelled out in the instructions to the tax forms individuals must file. When filing a tax return in 1998 for the tax year 1997, each taxpayer received an exemption of $2,650 for each dependent, including the taxpayer, which reduces taxable income. However, this exemption is indexed to rise with inflation, and the exemption is phased out (taken away) for high-income taxpayers. Also, certain expenses including mortgage interest paid, state and local income taxes paid, and charitable contributions can be deducted and thus be used to reduce taxable income, but again, high-income taxpayers lose most of these deductions.

2. The **marginal tax rate** is defined as the tax rate on the last unit of income. Marginal rates, which are shown in the third column of Table 2-6, begin at 15 percent and rise to 39.6 percent. Note, though, that when consideration is given to the phase-out of exemptions and deductions, to Social Security and Medicare taxes, and to state taxes, the marginal tax rate can actually exceed 50 percent.

3. One can calculate **average tax rates** from the data in Table 2-6. For example, if Jill Smith, a single individual, had taxable income of $35,000, her tax bill would be $3,697.50 + ($35,000 − $24,650)(0.28) = $3,697.50 + $2,898.00 = $6,595.50. Her *average tax rate* would be $6,595.50/$35,000 = 18.8% versus a *marginal rate* of 28 percent. If Jill received a raise of $1,000, bringing her income to $36,000, she would have to pay $280 of it as taxes, so her after-tax raise would be $720. In addition, her Social Security and Medicare taxes would increase by $76.50, which would cut her net raise to $643.50.

4. As indicated in the notes to the table, the tax code indexes tax brackets to inflation to avoid the **bracket creep** that occurred several years ago and that in reality raised tax rates substantially.[10]

Taxes on Dividend and Interest Income.   Most dividend and interest income received by individuals is added to their other income and thus is taxed at rates going up to

---

[10]For example, if you were single and had a taxable income of $24,650, your tax bill would be $3,697.50. Now suppose inflation caused prices to double and your income, being tied to a cost-of-living index, rose to $49,300. Because our tax rates are progressive, if tax brackets were not indexed, your taxes would jump to $10,599.50. Your after-tax income would thus increase from $20,952.50 to $38,700.50, but, because prices have doubled, your real income would *decline* from $20,952.50 to $19,350.25 (calculated as one-half of $38,700.50). You would be in a higher tax bracket, so you would be paying a higher percentage of your real income in taxes. If this happened to everyone, and if Congress failed to change tax rates sufficiently, real disposable incomes would decline because the federal government would be taking a larger share of the national product. This is called the federal government's "inflation dividend." However, since tax brackets are now indexed, if your income doubled due to inflation, your tax bill would also double, but your after-tax real income would remain constant at $20,952.50. Bracket creep was a real problem until the 1980s, but indexing put an end to it. A change in the way the Consumer Price Index is calculated would affect real income tax rates.

| TABLE 2-6 | Individual Tax Rates for 1997 Tax Year |

SINGLE INDIVIDUALS

If Your Taxable Income Is	You Pay This Amount on the Base of the Bracket	Plus This Percentage on the Excess over the Base	Average Tax Rate at Top of Bracket
Up to $24,650	$ 0	15.0%	15.0%
$24,650–$59,750	3,697.50	28.0	22.6
$59,750–$124,650	13,525.50	31.0	27.0
$124,650–$271,050	33,644.50	36.0	31.9
Over $271,050	86,348.50	39.6	39.6

MARRIED COUPLES FILING JOINT RETURNS

If Your Taxable Income Is	You Pay This Amount on the Base of the Bracket	Plus This Percentage on the Excess over the Base	Average Tax Rate at Top of Bracket
Up to $41,200	$ 0	15.0%	15.0%
$41,200–$99,600	6,180.00	28.0	22.6
$99,600–$151,750	22,532.00	31.0	25.5
$151,750–$271,050	38,698.50	36.0	30.1
Over $271,050	81,646.50	39.6	39.6

NOTES:

a. These are the tax rates for the 1997 tax year. The income ranges at which each tax rate takes effect, as well as the ranges for the additional taxes discussed below, are indexed with inflation each year, so they will change from those shown in the table.

b. The average tax rate approaches 39.6 percent as taxable income rises without limit. At $1 million of taxable income, the average tax rates for single individuals and married couples filing joint returns are 37.5 percent and 37.0 percent, respectively, while at $10 million they are 39.4 and 39.3 percent.

c. In 1997, a *personal exemption* of $2,650 per person or dependent could be deducted from gross income to determine taxable income. Thus, a husband and wife with two children would have a 1997 exemption of $4 \times \$2,650 = \$10,600$. The amount of the exemption is scheduled to increase with inflation. However, if the gross income exceeds certain limits ($181,800 for joint returns and $121,200 for single individuals in 1997), the exemption is phased out, and this has the effect of raising the effective tax rate on incomes over the specified limit by about 0.5 percent per family member, or 2.0 percent for a family of four. In addition, taxpayers can claim *itemized deductions* for charitable contributions and certain other items, but these deductions are reduced if the gross income exceeds $121,200 (for both single individuals and joint returns), and this raises the effective tax rate for high-income taxpayers by another 1 percent or so. The combined effect of the loss of exemptions and the reduction of itemized deductions is about 3 percent, so the marginal federal tax rate for high-income individuals goes up to about 42.6 percent.

In addition, there is the Social Security tax, which amounts to 6.2 percent (12.4 percent for a self-employed person) on up to $65,400 of earned income, plus a 1.45 percent Medicare payroll tax (2.9 percent for self-employed individuals) on *all* earned income. Finally, older high-income taxpayers who receive Social Security payments must pay taxes on 85 percent of their Social Security receipts, up from 50 percent in 1994. All of this pushes the effective tax rate up even further.

about 50 percent.[11] Since corporations pay dividends out of earnings that have already been taxed, there is *double taxation* of corporate income—income is first taxed at the corporate rate, and when what is left is paid out as dividends, it is taxed again at the personal rate.

---

[11]You do not pay Social Security and Medicare taxes on interest, dividends, and capital gains, only on earned income, but state taxes are often imposed on dividends, interest, and capital gains.

It should be noted that under U.S. tax laws, interest on most state and local government bonds, called *municipals* or *"munis,"* is not subject to federal income taxes. Thus, investors get to keep all of the interest received from most municipal bonds but only a fraction of the interest received from bonds issued by corporations or by the U.S. government. This means that a lower-yielding muni can provide the same after-tax return as a higher-yielding corporate bond. For example, a taxpayer in the 39.6 percent marginal tax bracket who could buy a muni that yielded 5.5 percent would have to receive a before-tax yield of 9.11 percent on a corporate or U.S. Treasury bond to have the same after-tax income:

$$\frac{\text{Equivalent pre-tax yield}}{\text{on taxable bond}} = \frac{\text{Yield on muni}}{1 - \text{Marginal tax rate}}$$

$$= \frac{5.5\%}{1 - 0.396} = 9.11\%.$$

If we know the yield on the taxable bond, we can use the following equation to find the equivalent yield on a muni:

$$\text{Equivalent yield on muni} = \left(\begin{array}{c}\text{Pre-tax yield} \\ \text{on taxable} \\ \text{bond}\end{array}\right)(1 - \text{Marginal tax rate})$$

$$= 9.11\% \ (1 - 0.396) = 9.11\%(0.604) = 5.5\%.$$

The exemption from federal taxes stems from the separation of federal and state powers, and its primary effect is to help state and local governments borrow at lower rates than they otherwise could.

Munis always yield less than corporate bonds with similar risk, maturity, and liquidity. Because of this, it would make no sense for someone in a zero or very low tax bracket to buy munis. Therefore, most munis are owned by high-bracket investors.

Capital Gains versus Ordinary Income.   Assets such as stocks, bonds, and real estate are defined as *capital assets*. If you buy a capital asset and later sell it for more than your purchase price, the profit is called a **capital gain;** if you suffer a loss, it is called a **capital loss.** An asset sold within one year of the time it was purchased produces a *short-term gain or loss*, one held for more than a year but less than 18 months produces an *intermediate-term gain or loss*, and one held for 18 months or longer produces a *long-term gain or loss*. Thus, if you buy 100 shares of Disney stock for $42 per share and sell it for $52 per share, you make a capital gain of $100 \times \$10$, or $1,000. However, if you sell the stock for $32 per share, you will have a $1,000 capital loss. Depending on how long you held the stock, you will have a short-term, intermediate-term, or long-term gain or loss. If you sell the stock for exactly $42 per share, you make neither a gain nor a loss; you simply get your $4,200 back, and no tax is due.

Short-term capital gains are added to such ordinary income as wages, dividends, and interest and then are taxed at the same rate as ordinary income. However, intermediate- and long-term gains are taxed differently. The rate on intermediate-term gains is capped at 28 percent, and the top rate on long-term gains is 20 percent. Thus, if in 1997 you were in the 39.6 percent tax bracket, any short-term gains you earned would be taxed just like ordinary income, but your intermediate- and long-term gains would be taxed at 28 and 20 percent, respectively. Thus, capital gains on assets held for more than 12 months are better than ordinary income for many people because the tax bite is smaller.[12]

---

[12]The tax code governing capital gains is very complex, and we have illustrated only the most common provision. For example, property purchased after December 31, 2000, and held for more than five years will be taxed at a maximum rate of 18 percent. Also, certain portions of some types of capital gains are taxed at a rate of 10 percent, which falls to an 8 percent rate if the property is held for more than five years.

Capital gains tax rates have varied over time, but they have generally been lower than rates on ordinary income. The reason is simple — Congress wants the economy to grow, for growth we need investment in productive assets, and low capital gains tax rates encourage investment. To see why, suppose you owned a company that earned $1 million after corporate taxes. Because it is your company, you could have it pay out the entire $1 million profit as dividends, or you could have it retain and reinvest all or part of the income to expand the business. If it paid dividends, they would be taxable to you at a rate of 39.6 percent. However, if the company reinvests its income, that reinvestment should cause the company's earnings and stock price to increase. Then, if you wait for 18 months and then sell some of your stock at a now-higher price, you will have earned capital gains, but they will be taxed at only 20 percent. Further, you can postpone the capital gains tax indefinitely by simply not selling the stock.

It should be clear that a lower tax rate on capital gains will encourage investment. The owners of small businesses will want to reinvest income to get capital gains, as will stockholders in large corporations. Individuals with money to invest will understand the tax advantages associated with investing in newly formed companies versus buying bonds, so new ventures will have an easier time attracting equity capital. All in all, lower capital gains tax rates stimulate capital formation and investment.[13]

Corporate Income Taxes

The corporate tax structure, shown in Table 2-7, is relatively simple. To illustrate, if a firm had $65,000 of taxable income, its tax bill would be

$$\text{Taxes} = \$7,500 + 0.25(\$15,000)$$
$$= \$7,500 + \$3,750 = \$11,250,$$

and its average tax rate would be $11,250/$65,000 = 17.3\%$. Note that corporate income above $18,333,333 has an average and marginal tax rate of 35 percent.[14]

Interest and Dividend Income Received by a Corporation.   Interest income received by a corporation is taxed as ordinary income at regular corporate tax rates. *However, 70 percent of the dividends received by one corporation from another is excluded from*

---

[13]A total of 50 percent of any capital gains on the newly issued stock of certain small companies is excluded from taxation, provided the small-company stock is held for five years or longer. The remaining 50 percent of the gain is taxed at a rate of 20 percent. Thus, if one bought newly issued stock from a qualifying small company and held it for at least five years, any capital gains would be taxed at a maximum rate of 10 percent. This provision was designed to help small businesses obtain equity capital.

[14]Prior to 1987, many large, profitable corporations such as General Electric and Boeing paid no income taxes. The reasons for this were as follows: (1) expenses, especially depreciation, were defined differently for calculating taxable income than for reporting earnings to stockholders, so some companies reported positive profits to stockholders but losses — hence no taxes — to the Internal Revenue Service; and (2) some companies which did have tax liabilities used various tax credits to offset taxes that would otherwise have been payable. This situation was effectively eliminated in 1987.

The principal method used to eliminate this situation is the Alternative Minimum Tax (AMT). Under the AMT, both corporate and individual taxpayers must figure their taxes in two ways, the "regular" way and the AMT way, and then pay the higher of the two. The AMT is calculated as follows: (1) Figure your regular taxes. (2) Take your taxable income under the regular method and then add back certain items, especially income on certain municipal bonds, depreciation in excess of straight line depreciation, certain research and drilling costs, itemized or standard deductions (for individuals), and a number of other items. (3) The income determined in (2) is defined as AMT income, and it must then be multiplied by the AMT tax rate to determine the tax due under the AMT system. An individual or corporation must then pay the higher of the regular tax or the AMT tax. In 1997, there were two AMT tax rates for individuals (26 percent and 28 percent, depending on the level of AMT income and filing status). Most corporations have an AMT rate of 20 percent. However, there is no AMT for very small companies, defined as those that have had average sales of less than $5 million for the last three years beginning 1994 and whose average sales continue to be less than $7.5 million.

TABLE 2-7   Corporate Tax Rates as of January 1998

If a Corporation's Taxable Income Is	It Pays This Amount on the Base of the Bracket	Plus This Percentage on the Excess over the Base	Average Tax Rate at Top of Bracket
Up to $50,000	$ 0	15%	15.0%
$50,000–$75,000	7,500	25	18.3
$75,000–$100,000	13,750	34	22.3
$100,000–$335,000	22,250	39	34.0
$335,000–$10,000,000	113,900	34	34.0
$10,000,000–$15,000,000	3,400,000	35	34.3
$15,000,000–$18,333,333	5,150,000	38	35.0
Over $18,333,333	6,416,667	35	35.0

taxable income, while the remaining 30 percent is taxed at the ordinary tax rate.[15] Thus, a corporation earning more than $18,333,333 and paying a 35 percent marginal tax rate would pay only $(0.30)(0.35) = 0.105 = 10.5\%$ of its dividend income as taxes, so its effective tax rate on dividends received would be 10.5 percent. If this firm had $10,000 in pre-tax dividend income, its after-tax dividend income would be $8,950:

$$\frac{\text{After-tax}}{\text{income}} = \text{Before-tax income} - \text{Taxes}$$

$$= \text{Before-tax income} - (\text{Before-tax income})(\text{Effective tax rate})$$
$$= \text{Before-tax income}(1 - \text{Effective tax rate})$$
$$= \$10,000\,[1 - (0.30)(0.35)]$$
$$= \$10,000(1 - 0.105) = \$10,000(0.895) = \$8,950.$$

If the corporation pays its own after-tax income out to its stockholders as dividends, the income is ultimately subjected to *triple taxation:* (1) the original corporation is first taxed, (2) the second corporation is then taxed on the dividends it received, and (3) the individuals who receive the final dividends are taxed again. This is the reason for the 70 percent exclusion on intercorporate dividends.

If a corporation has surplus funds that can be invested in marketable securities, the tax factor favors investment in stocks, which pay dividends, rather than in bonds, which pay interest. For example, suppose GE had $100,000 to invest, and it could buy either bonds that paid interest of $8,000 per year or preferred stock that paid dividends of $7,000. GE is in the 35 percent tax bracket; therefore, its tax on the interest, if it bought bonds, would be $0.35(\$8,000) = \$2,800$, and its after-tax income would be $5,200. If it bought preferred (or common) stock, its tax would be $0.35\,[(0.30)(\$7,000)] = \$735$, and its after-tax income would be $6,265. Other factors might

---

[15]The size of the dividend exclusion actually depends on the degree of ownership. Corporations that own less than 20 percent of the stock of the dividend-paying company can exclude 70 percent of the dividends received; firms that own more than 20 percent but less than 80 percent can exclude 80 percent of the dividends; and firms that own more than 80 percent can exclude the entire dividend payment. We will, in general, assume a 70 percent dividend exclusion.

lead GE to invest in bonds, but the tax factor certainly favors stock investments when the investor is a corporation.[16]

Interest and Dividends Paid by a Corporation.   A firm's operations can be financed with either debt or equity capital. If it uses debt, it must pay interest on this debt, whereas if it uses equity, it is expected to pay dividends to the equity investors (stockholders). The interest *paid by* a corporation is deducted from its operating income to obtain its taxable income. However, dividends paid are not deductible. Therefore, a firm needs $1 of pre-tax income to pay $1 of interest, but if it is in the 40 percent federal-plus-state tax bracket, it needs $1.67 of pre-tax income to pay $1 of dividends:

$$\frac{\text{Pre-tax income needed}}{\text{to pay \$1 of dividends}} = \frac{\$1}{1 - \text{Tax rate}} = \frac{\$1}{0.60} = \$1.67.$$

$$\text{Proof: After-tax income} = \$1.67 - \text{Tax} = \$1.67 - \$1.67(0.4)$$
$$= \$1.67(1 - 0.4) = \$1.00.$$

Table 2-8 shows the situation for a firm with $10 million of assets, sales of $5 million, and $1.5 million of earnings before interest and taxes (EBIT). As shown in Column 1, if the firm were financed entirely by bonds, and if it made interest payments of $1.5 million, its taxable income would be zero, taxes would be zero, and its investors would receive the entire $1.5 million. (The term *investors* includes both stockholders and bondholders.) However, as shown in Column 2, if the firm had no debt and was therefore financed only by stock, all of the $1.5 million of EBIT would be taxable income to the corporation, the tax would be $1,500,000(0.40) = $600,000, and investors would receive only $0.9 million versus $1.5 million under debt financ-

---

[16]This illustration demonstrates why corporations favor investing in lower-yielding preferred stocks over higher-yielding bonds. When tax consequences are considered, the yield on the preferred stock, $[1 - 0.35(0.30)](7.0\%) = 6.265\%$, is higher than the yield on the bond, $(1 - 0.35)(8.0\%) = 5.200\%$. Also, note that corporations are restricted in their use of borrowed funds to purchase other firms' preferred or common stocks. Without such restrictions, firms could engage in *tax arbitrage*, whereby the interest on borrowed funds reduces taxable income on a dollar-for-dollar basis, but taxable income is increased by only $0.30 per dollar of dividend income. Thus, current tax laws reduce the 70 percent dividend exclusion in proportion to the amount of borrowed funds used to purchase the stock.

TABLE 2-8   Cash Flows to Investors under Bond and Stock Financing: $10 Million of Assets

	USE BONDS (1)	USE STOCK (2)
Sales	$5,000,000	$5,000,000
Operating costs	3,500,000	3,500,000
Earnings before interest and taxes (EBIT)	$1,500,000	$1,500,000
Interest (15%)	1,500,000	0
Taxable income	$ 0	$1,500,000
Federal-plus-state taxes (40%)	0	$ 600,000
After-tax income	$ 0	$ 900,000
Income to investors	$1,500,000	$ 900,000
Rate of return on $10 million of assets	15.0%	9.0%

ing. The rate of return to investors on their $10 million investment is therefore much higher if debt is used.

Of course, it is generally not possible to finance exclusively with debt capital, and the risk of doing so would offset the benefits of the higher expected income. *Still, the fact that interest is a deductible expense has a profound effect on the way businesses are financed—our corporate tax system favors debt financing over equity financing.* This point is discussed in more detail in Chapters 10, 15, and 16.

Corporate Capital Gains.   Before 1987, corporate long-term capital gains were taxed at lower rates than corporate ordinary income, so the situation was similar for corporations and individuals. Under current law, however, corporations' capital gains are taxed at the same rates as their operating income.

Corporate Loss Carry-Back and Carry-Forward.   Ordinary corporate operating losses can be carried back **(carry-back)** to each of the preceding 2 years and forward **(carry-forward)** for the next 20 years and used to offset taxable income in those years. For example, an operating loss in 1999 could be carried back and used to reduce taxable income in 1998 and 1997, and forward, if necessary, and used in 2000, 2001, and so on, to the year 2019. The loss is typically applied first to the earliest year, then to the next earliest year, and so on, until losses have been used up or the 20-year carry-forward limit has been reached.

To illustrate, suppose Apex Corporation had $2 million of *pre-tax* profits (taxable income) in 1997 and 1998, and then, in 1999, Apex lost $12 million. Also, assume that Apex's federal-plus-state tax rate is 40 percent. As shown in Table 2-9, the company would use the carry-back feature to recompute its taxes for 1997, using $2 million of the 1999 operating losses to reduce the 1997 pre-tax profit to zero. This would permit it to recover the taxes paid in 1997. Therefore, in 1999 Apex would receive a refund of its 1997 taxes because of the loss experienced in 1999. Because $10 million of the unrecovered losses would still be available, Apex would repeat this procedure for 1998. Thus, in 1999 the company would pay zero taxes for 1999 and also would receive a refund for taxes paid in 1997 and 1998. Apex would still have $8 million of unrecovered losses to carry forward, subject to the 20-year limit. This $8 million could be used until the entire $12 million loss had been used to offset taxable income. The purpose of permit-

TABLE 2-9	Apex Corporation: Calculation of Loss Carry-Back and Carry-Forward for 1997 and 1998 Using a $12 Million 1999 Loss	
	1997	**1998**
Original taxable income	$2,000,000	$2,000,000
Carry-back credit	− 2,000,000	− 2,000,000
Adjusted profit	$ 0	$ 0
Taxes previously paid (40%)	800,000	800,000
Difference = Tax refund	$ 800,000	$ 800,000
Total refund check received in 1999: $800,000 + $800,000 = $1,600,000.		
Amount of loss carry-forward available for use in 2000–2019:		
1999 loss		$12,000,000
Carry-back losses used		$ 4,000,000
Carry-forward losses still available		$ 8,000,000

TAX HAVENS

Many multinational corporations have found an interesting but controversial way to reduce their tax burdens: By shifting some of their operations to countries with low or nonexistent taxes. Over the years, several countries have passed tax laws which make the countries *tax havens* designed to attract foreign investment. Notable examples include the Bahamas, the Grand Caymans, and the Netherlands Antilles.

Rupert Murdoch, chairman of global media giant News Corporation, has in some years paid virtually no taxes on his U.S. businesses, despite the fact that these businesses represent roughly 70 percent of his total operating profit. How has Murdoch been able to reduce his tax burden? By shifting profits to a News Corp. subsidiary which is incorporated in the Netherlands Antilles. As Murdoch puts it, "Moving assets around like that is one of the advantages of being global."

While activities such as Murdoch's are legal, some have questioned their ethics. Clearly, shareholders want corporations to take legal steps to reduce taxes. Indeed, many argue that managers have a fiduciary responsibility to take such actions whenever they are cost effective. Moreover, citizens of the various tax havens benefit from foreign investment. Who loses? Obviously, the United States loses tax revenue whenever a domestic corporation establishes a subsidiary in a tax haven. Ultimately, this loss of tax revenue either reduces services or raises the tax burden on other corporations and individuals. Nevertheless, even the U.S. government is itself somewhat ambivalent about the establishment of off-shore subsidiaries — it does not like to lose tax revenues, but it does like to encourage foreign investment.

ting this loss treatment is to avoid penalizing corporations whose incomes fluctuate substantially from year to year.

Improper Accumulation to Avoid Payment of Dividends.   Corporations could refrain from paying dividends and thus permit their stockholders to avoid personal income taxes on dividends. To prevent this, the Tax Code contains an **improper accumulation** provision which states that earnings accumulated by a corporation are subject to penalty rates *if the purpose of the accumulation is to enable stockholders to avoid personal income taxes*. A cumulative total of $250,000 (the balance sheet item "retained earnings") is by law exempted from the improper accumulation tax for most corporations. This is a benefit primarily to small corporations.

The improper accumulation penalty applies only if the retained earnings in excess of $250,000 are *shown by the IRS to be unnecessary to meet the reasonable needs of the business*. A great many companies do indeed have legitimate reasons for retaining more than $250,000 of earnings. For example, earnings may be retained and used to pay off debt, to finance growth, or to provide the corporation with a cushion against possible cash drains caused by losses. How much a firm should properly accumulate for uncertain contingencies is a matter of judgment. We shall consider this matter again in Chapter 17, which deals with corporate dividend policy.

Consolidated Corporate Tax Returns.   If a corporation owns 80 percent or more of another corporation's stock, it can aggregate income and file one consolidated tax return; thus, the losses of one company can be used to offset the profits of another. (Similarly, one division's losses can be used to offset another division's profits.) No business ever wants to incur losses (you can go broke losing $1 to save 35¢ in taxes), but tax offsets do help make it feasible for large, multidivisional corporations to undertake risky new ventures or ventures that will suffer losses during a developmental period.

Taxation of Small Businesses: S Corporations

The Tax Code permits small businesses that meet certain restrictions as spelled out in the code to be set up as corporations and thus receive the benefits of the corporate form of organization — especially limited liability — yet still be taxed as proprietorships or partnerships rather than as corporations. These corporations are called **S corporations.** ("Regular" corporations are called C corporations.) If a corporation elects S corporation status for tax purposes, all of the business's income is reported as personal income by its stockholders, on a pro rata basis, and thus is taxed at the rates that apply to individuals. This is an important benefit to the owners of small corporations in which all or most of the income earned each year will be distributed as dividends, because then the income is taxed only once, at the individual level.

Explain what is meant by the statement: "Our tax rates are progressive."

Are tax rates progressive for all income ranges?

Explain the difference between marginal tax rates and average tax rates.

What are capital gains and losses, and how do they differ from ordinary income?

How does the federal income tax system treat corporate dividends received by a corporation versus those received by an individual? Why is this distinction made?

What is the difference in the tax treatment of interest and dividends paid by a corporation? Does this difference favor debt or equity financing?

Briefly explain how tax loss carry-back and carry-forward procedures work.

What is a "municipal bond," and how are these bonds taxed?

DEPRECIATION

Depreciation plays an important role in income tax calculations—the larger the depreciation, the lower the taxable income, the lower the tax bill, and the higher the cash flow from operations. Congress specifies, in the Tax Code, both the life over which assets can be depreciated for tax purposes and the methods of depreciation which can be used. We will discuss in detail how depreciation is calculated, and how it affects income and cash flows, when we take up capital budgeting in Chapters 11, 12, and 13.

SUMMARY

The primary purposes of this chapter are (1) to describe the basic financial statements, (2) to present some background information on cash flows, and (3) to provide an overview of the federal income tax system. The key concepts covered are listed below.

- The four basic statements contained in the **annual report** are the balance sheet, the income statement, the statement of retained earnings, and the statement of cash flows. Investors use the information provided in these statements to form expectations about the future levels of earnings and dividends, and about the firm's riskiness.

- The **balance sheet** shows assets on the left-hand side and liabilities and equity, or claims against assets, on the right-hand side. The balance sheet may be thought of as a snapshot of the firm's financial position at a particular point in time.

- The **income statement** reports the results of operations over a period of time, and it shows earnings per share as its "bottom line."

- The **statement of retained earnings** shows the change in retained earnings between the balance sheet dates. Retained earnings represent a claim against assets, not assets per se.

- A firm's **statement of cash flows** reports the impact of operating, investing, and financing activities on cash flows over an accounting period.

- **Net cash flow** differs from **accounting profit** because some of the revenues and expenses reflected in accounting profits may not have been received or paid out in cash during the year. Depreciation is typically the largest noncash item, so net cash flow is often expressed as net income plus depreciation. Investors are at least as interested in a firm's projected net cash flow as in reported earnings because it is cash, not paper profit, that is paid out as dividends and plowed back into the business to produce growth.

- **Net operating working capital** is defined as the difference between those current assets that earn no interest (generally, all except marketable securities) and those current liabilities on which no interest is charged (generally, accounts payable and accruals). Thus, net working capital is the net amount of short-term operating assets that must be financed by investors if the company is to conduct its normal operations.

- **Net operating assets** is defined as the sum of net working capital plus net plant and equipment. It is the net amount of assets that a company needs to conduct its normal operations. Operating assets are also equal to the amount of money that investors have provided to support operations. The terms **net operating assets** and **operating capital** (or just **capital**) are often used interchangeably. Every dollar tied up in operating capital is a dollar that has a cost to the company.

- **NOPAT** is net operating profit after taxes. It is the after-tax profit a company would have if it had no debt and no investments in financial assets. Since it excludes the effects of financial decisions, it is a better measure of operating performance than is net income.

- **Operating cash flow** arises from normal operations, and it is the difference between cash revenues and cash costs, including taxes on operating income. Operating cash flow differs from net cash flow because operating cash flow does not include either interest income or interest expense.

- **Free cash flow (FCF)** is the amount of cash flow remaining after a company makes the asset investments necessary to support operations. In other words, FCF is the amount of cash flow available for distribution to investors, *so the value of a company is directly related to its ability to generate free cash flow.*

- **Market Value Added (MVA)** represents the difference between the market value of a firm's stock and the amount of equity its investors have supplied.

- **Economic Value Added (EVA)** is the difference between after-tax operating profit and the total cost of capital, including the cost of equity capital. EVA is an estimate of the value created by management during the year, and it differs substantially from accounting profit because no charge for the use of equity capital is reflected in accounting profit.

- The value of any asset depends on the stream of **after-tax cash flows** it produces. Tax rates and other aspects of our tax system are changed by Congress every year or so.

- In the United States, tax rates are **progressive**—the higher one's income, the larger the percentage paid in taxes.

- Assets such as stocks, bonds, and real estate are defined as **capital assets.** If a capital asset is sold for more than its cost, the profit is called a **capital gain.** If the asset is sold for a loss, it is called a **capital loss.** Assets held for over a year provide **long-term** gains or losses.

- Corporate income paid out as dividends is subject to **double taxation:** the income is first taxed at the corporate level, and then shareholders must pay personal taxes on their dividends.

- Interest income received by a corporation is taxed as **ordinary income;** however, 70 percent of the dividends received by one corporation from another are excluded from **taxable income.** The reason for this exclusion is that corporate dividend income is ultimately subjected to **triple taxation.**

- Because interest paid by a corporation is a **deductible** expense while dividends are not, our tax system favors debt over equity financing.

- Ordinary corporate operating losses can be **carried back** to each of the preceding 2 years and **forward** for the next 20 years and used to offset taxable income in those years.

- **S corporations** are small businesses which have the limited-liability benefits of the corporate form of organization yet are taxed as a partnership or a proprietorship.

Questions

2-1   Define each of the following terms:
a. Annual report; balance sheet; income statement
b. Common stockholders' equity, or net worth; retained earnings
c. Statement of retained earnings; statement of cash flows
d. Depreciation; inventory valuation methods
e. Net operating working capital; operating capital
f. Accounting profit; net cash flow; operating cash flow; NOPAT; free cash flow
g. Market Value Added; Economic Value Added
h. Progressive tax; taxable income
i. Marginal and average tax rates
j. Bracket creep
k. Capital gain or loss
l. Tax loss carry-back and carry-forward
m. Improper accumulation
n. S corporation

2-2   What four statements are contained in most annual reports?

2-3   If a "typical" firm reports $20 million of retained earnings on its balance sheet, could its directors declare a $20 million cash dividend without any qualms whatsoever?

2-4   Explain the following statement: "While the balance sheet can be thought of as a snapshot of the firm's financial position *at a point in time,* the income statement reports on operations *over a period of time.*"

2-5   Differentiate between accounting income and net cash flow. Why might these two numbers differ?

2-6   Differentiate between operating cash flow and net cash flow. Why might these two numbers differ?

2-7   What do the numbers on financial statements actually represent?

2-8   Who are some of the basic users of financial statements, and how do they use them?

2-9   What is operating capital, and why is it important?

2-10   Explain the difference between NOPAT and net income. Which is a better measure of the performance of a company's operations?

2-11   What is free cash flow? Why is it the most important measure of cash flow?

2-12   In what way does the Tax Code discourage corporations from paying high dividends to their shareholders?

2-13   What does *double taxation of corporate income* mean?

2-14   If you were starting a business, what tax considerations might cause you to prefer to set it up as a proprietorship or a partnership rather than as a corporation?

2-15   Explain how the federal income tax structure affects the choice of financing (use of debt versus equity) of U.S. business firms.

2-16   For someone planning to start a new business, is the average or the marginal tax rate more relevant?

Self-Test Problems   (Solutions Appear in Appendix B)

ST-1
Net Income, Cash Flow, and EVA

Last year Rattner Robotics had $5,000,000 in operating income (EBIT). The company had a Net depreciation expense of $1,000,000 and an interest expense of $1,000,000; its corporate tax rate was 40 percent. The company has $14,000,000 in non-interest-earning current assets and $4,000,000 in non-interest-bearing current liabilities; it has $15,000,000 in net plant and equipment. It estimates that it has an after-tax cost of capital of 10 percent. Assume that Rattner's only noncash item was depreciation.

a. What was the company's net income for the year?
b. What was the company's net cash flow?
c. What was the company's net operating profit after taxes (NOPAT)?
d. What was the company's operating cash flow?
e. If capital in the previous year was $24,000,000, what was the company's free cash flow (FCF) for the year?
f. What was the company's Economic Value Added (EVA)?

ST-2
Effect of Form of Organization on Taxes

Mary Henderson is planning to start a new business, MH Enterprises, and she must decide whether to incorporate or to do business as a sole proprietorship. Under either form, Henderson will initially own 100 percent of the firm, and tax considerations are important to her. She plans to finance the firm's expected growth by drawing a salary just sufficient for her family living expenses, which she estimates will be about $40,000, and by retaining all other income in the business. Assume that as a married woman with one child, she files a joint return. She has income tax exemptions of $3 \times \$2,650 = \$7,950$, and she estimates that her itemized deductions for each of the 3 years will be $9,700. She expects MH Enterprises to grow and to earn income of $52,700 in 1999, $90,000 in 2000, and $150,000 in 2001. Which form of business organization will allow Henderson to pay the lowest taxes (and retain the most income) during the period from 1999 to 2001? Assume that the tax rates given in the chapter are applicable for all future years. (Social Security taxes would also have to be paid, but ignore them.)

Problems

Note: By the time this book is published, Congress might have changed rates and/or other provisions of current tax law—as noted in the chapter, such changes occur fairly often. Work all problems on the assumption that the information in the chapter is applicable.

2-1
Income Statement

Little Books Inc. recently reported net income of $3 million. Its operating income (EBIT) was $6 million, and the company pays a 40 percent tax rate. What was the company's interest expense for the year? [Hint: Divide $3 million by $(1 - T) = 0.6$ to find taxable income.]

2-2
Net Cash Flow

Kendall Corners Inc. recently reported net income of $3.1 million. The company's depreciation expense was $500,000. What is the company's approximate net cash flow?

2-3
After-Tax Yield

An investor recently purchased a corporate bond which yields 9 percent. The investor is in the 36 percent tax bracket. What is the bond's after-tax yield?

2-4
Personal Taxes

Joe and Jane Keller are a married couple who file a joint income tax return. The couple's taxable income was $97,000. How much federal taxes did they owe? Use the tax tables given in the chapter.

2-5
After-Tax Yield

Corporate bonds issued by Johnson Corporation currently yield 8 percent. Municipal bonds of equal risk currently yield 6 percent. At what tax rate would an investor be indifferent between these two bonds?

2-6
Corporate Tax Liability

The Talley Corporation had a 1998 taxable income of $365,000 from operations after all operating costs but before (1) interest charges of $50,000, (2) dividends received of $15,000, (3) dividends paid of $25,000, and (4) income taxes. What is the firm's income tax liability and its after-tax income? What are the company's marginal and average tax rates on taxable income?

2-7
Corporate Tax Liability

The Wendt Corporation had $10.5 million of taxable income from operations in 1998.
a. What is the company's federal income tax bill for the year?
b. Assume the firm receives an additional $1 million of interest income from some bonds it owns. What is the tax on this interest income?
c. Now assume that Wendt does not receive the interest income but does receive an additional $1 million as dividends on some stock it owns. What is the tax on this dividend income?

2-8
After-Tax Yield

The Shrieves Corporation has $10,000 which it plans to invest in marketable securities. It is choosing between AT&T bonds, which yield 7.5 percent, state of Florida muni bonds, which yield 5 percent, and AT&T preferred stock, with a dividend yield of 6 percent. Shrieves' corporate tax rate is 35 percent, and 70 percent of the dividends received are tax exempt. Assuming that the investments are equally risky and that Shrieves chooses strictly on the basis of after-tax returns, which security should be selected? What is the after-tax rate of return on the highest-yielding security?

2-9
After-Tax Yield

Your personal tax rate is 36 percent. You can invest in either corporate bonds which yield 9 percent or municipal bonds (of equal risk) which yield 7 percent. Which investment should you choose? (Ignore state income taxes.)

2-10
Cash Flow

The Klaven Corporation has operating income (EBIT) of $750,000. The company's depreciation expense is $200,000. Klaven is 100 percent equity financed, and it faces a 40 percent tax rate. What is the company's net income? What is its net cash flow? What is its operating cash flow?

2-11
Balance Sheet

Which of the following actions will, all else equal, increase the amount of cash on a company's balance sheet?
a. The company issues $2 million in new common stock.
b. The company invests $3 million in new plant and equipment.
c. The company generates negative net income and negative net cash flow during the year.
d. The company increases the dividend paid on its common stock.

2-12
Financial Statements

The Smythe-Davidson Corporation just issued its annual report. The current year's balance sheet and income statement as they appeared in the annual report are given below. Answer the questions that follow based on information given in the financial statements.

SMYTHE-DAVIDSON CORPORATION: BALANCE SHEET AS OF DECEMBER 31, 1998 (MILLIONS OF DOLLARS)

Assets		Liabilities and Equity	
Cash and equivalents	$ 15	Accounts payable	$ 120
Accounts receivable	515	Notes payable	220
Inventories	880	Accruals	280
Total current assets	$1,410	Total current liabilities	$ 620
Net plant and equipment	2,590	Long-term bonds	1,520
		Total debt	$2,140
		Preferred stock (800,000 shares)	80
		Common stock (100 million shares)	260
		Retained earnings	1,520
		Common equity	$1,780
Total assets	$4,000	Total liabilities and equity	$4,000

SMYTHE-DAVIDSON CORPORATION: INCOME STATEMENT FOR YEAR ENDING DECEMBER 31, 1998 (MILLIONS OF DOLLARS)

Sales	$6,250
Operating costs excluding depreciation	5,230
Depreciation	220
EBIT	$ 800
Less: Interest	180
EBT	$ 620
Taxes (40%)	248
Net income before preferred dividends	372
Preferred dividends	8
Net income available to common stockholders	$ 364
Common dividends paid	$ 146
Earnings per share	$3.64

a. Assume that all of the firm's revenues were received in cash during the year and that all costs except depreciation were paid in cash during the year. What is the firm's net cash flow available to common stockholders for the year? How is this number different from the accounting profit reported by the firm?

b. Construct the firm's Statement of Retained Earnings for December 31, 1998.

c. How much money has the firm reinvested in itself over the years instead of paying out dividends?

d. At the present time, how large a check could the firm write without it bouncing?

e. How much money must the firm pay its current creditors within the next year?

2-13
Income and Cash Flow Analysis

The Menendez Corporation expects to have sales of $12 million in 1999. Costs other than depreciation are expected to be 75 percent of sales, and depreciation is expected to be $1.5 million. All sales revenues will be collected in cash, and costs other than depreciation must be paid for during the year. Menendez's federal-plus-state tax rate is 40 percent.

a. Set up an income statement. What is Menendez's expected net cash flow?

b. Suppose Congress changed the tax laws so that Menendez's depreciation expenses doubled. No changes in operations occurred. What would happen to reported profit and to net cash flow?

c. Now suppose that Congress, instead of doubling Menendez's depreciation, reduced it by 50 percent. How would profit and net cash flow be affected?

d. If this were your company, would you prefer Congress to cause your depreciation expense to be doubled or halved? Why?

e. In the situation in which depreciation doubled, would this possibly have an adverse effect on the company's stock price and on its ability to borrow money?

2-14
Income Statement

Last year Martin Motors reported the following income statement:

Sales	$2,000,000
Cost of goods sold	1,200,000
Depreciation	500,000
Total operating costs	$1,700,000
Operating income (EBIT)	$ 300,000
Interest expense	100,000
Taxable income (EBT)	$ 200,000
Taxes (40%)	80,000
Net income	$ 120,000

The company's CEO, Joe Lawrence, was unhappy with the firm's performance. This year, he would like to see net income doubled to $240,000. Depreciation, interest expense, and tax rate will all remain constant, and the cost of goods sold will also remain at 60 percent of sales. How much sales revenue must the company generate to achieve the CEO's net income target?

2-15
Free Cash Flow

You have just obtained financial information for the past 2 years for Powell Panther Corporation. Answer the following questions.

POWELL PANTHER CORPORATION: INCOME STATEMENTS FOR YEAR ENDING DECEMBER 31 (MILLIONS OF DOLLARS)

	1998	1997
Sales	$1,200.0	$1,000.0
Operating costs excluding depreciation	1,020.0	850.0
Depreciation	30.0	25.0
Earnings before interest and taxes	$ 150.0	$ 125.0
Less interest	21.7	20.2
Earnings before taxes	$ 128.3	$ 104.8
Taxes (40%)	51.3	41.9
Net income available to common stockholders	$ 77.0	$ 62.9
Common dividends	60.5	4.4

POWELL PANTHER CORPORATION: BALANCE SHEETS AS OF DECEMBER 31 (MILLIONS OF DOLLARS)

	1998	1997
Assets		
Cash and equivalents	$ 12.0	$ 10.0
Short-term investments	0.0	0.0
Accounts receivable	180.0	150.0
Inventories	180.0	200.0
Total current assets	$372.0	$360.0
Net plant and equipment	300.0	250.0
Total assets	$672.0	$610.0
Liabilities and Equity		
Accounts payable	$108.0	$ 90.0
Notes payable	67.0	51.5
Accruals	72.0	60.0
Total current liabilities	$247.0	$201.5
Long-term bonds	150.0	150.0
Total debt	$397.0	351.5
Common stock (50 million shares)	50.0	50.0
Retained earnings	225.0	208.5
Common equity	$275.0	$258.5
Total liabilities and equity	$672.0	$610.0

a. What is the net operating profit after taxes (NOPAT) for 1998?
b. What are the amounts of net operating working capital for 1997 and 1998?
c. What are the amounts of total operating capital for 1997 and 1998?
d. What is the free cash flow for 1998?
e. How can you explain the large increase in dividends in 1998?

2-16
Loss Carry-Back, Carry-Forward

The Herrmann Company has made $150,000 before taxes during each of the last 15 years, and it expects to make $150,000 a year before taxes in the future. However, in 1998 the firm incurred a loss of $650,000. The firm will claim a tax credit at the time it files its 1998 income tax return, and it will receive a check from the U.S. Treasury. Show how it calculates this credit, and then indicate the firm's tax liability for each of the next 5 years. Assume a 40 percent tax rate on *all* income to ease the calculations.

2-17
Loss Carry-Back, Carry-Forward

The projected taxable income of the McAlhany Corporation, formed in 1999, is indicated in the table below. (Losses are shown in parentheses.) What is the corporate tax liability for each year? Assume a constant federal-plus-state tax rate of 40 percent.

YEAR	TAXABLE INCOME
1999	($ 95,000,000)
2000	70,000,000
2001	55,000,000
2002	80,000,000
2003	(150,000,000)

2-18
Form of Organization

Susan Visscher has operated her small restaurant as a sole proprietorship for several years, but projected changes in her business's income have led her to consider incorporating. Visscher is married and has two children. Her family's only income, an annual salary of $52,000, is from operating the business. (The business actually earns more than $52,000, but Susan reinvests the additional earnings in the business.) She itemizes deductions, and she is able to deduct $8,600. These deductions, combined with her four personal exemptions for 4 × $2,650 = $10,600, give her a taxable income of $52,000 − $8,600 − $10,600. (Assume the personal exemption remains at $2,650.) Of course, her actual taxable income, if she does not incorporate, would be higher by the amount of reinvested income. Visscher estimates that her business earnings before salary and taxes for the period 1999 to 2001 will be:

YEAR	EARNINGS BEFORE SALARY AND TAXES
1999	$ 70,000
2000	95,000
2001	110,000

a. What would her total taxes (corporate plus personal) be in each year under
   (1) A non-S corporate form of organization? (1999 tax = $7,620.)
   (2) A proprietorship? (1999 tax = $8,868.)
b. Should Visscher incorporate? Discuss.

2-19
Personal Taxes

Mary Jarvis, a single individual, has this situation for the year 1998: salary of $82,000; dividend income of $12,000; interest on Disney bonds of $5,000; interest on state of Florida municipal bonds of $10,000; proceeds of $22,000 from the sale of Disney stock purchased in 1984 at a cost of $9,000; and proceeds of $22,000 from the November 1998 sale of Disney stock purchased in October 1998 at a cost of $21,000. Jarvis gets one exemption ($2,650), and she has allowable itemized deductions of $4,900; these amounts will be deducted from her gross income to determine her taxable income.
a. What is Jarvis's federal tax liability for 1998?
b. What are her marginal and average tax rates?
c. If she had $5,000 to invest and was offered a choice of either state of Florida bonds with a yield of 6 percent or more Disney bonds with a yield of 8 percent, which should she choose, and why?
d. At what marginal tax rate would Jarvis be indifferent in her choice between the Florida and Disney bonds?

Spreadsheet Problem

Work the problem in this section only if you are using the computer problem diskette.

2-20
Form of Organization

The problem requires you to rework Problem 2-18, using the data given below. Use File C2 on the computer problem diskette.
a. Suppose Visscher decides to pay out (1) 50 percent or (2) 100 percent of the after-salary corporate income in each year as dividends. Would such dividend policy changes affect her decision about whether or not to incorporate?
b. Suppose business improves, and actual earnings before salary and taxes in each year are twice the original estimate. Assume that if Visscher chooses to incorporate she will continue to receive a salary of $52,000, and to reinvest additional earnings in the business. (No dividends would be paid.) What would be the effect of this increase in business income on Visscher's decision to incorporate or not incorporate?

MINI CASE

Donna Jamison, a 1993 graduate of the University of Florida with four years of banking experience, was recently brought in as assistant to the chairman of the board of Computron Industries, a manufacturer of electronic calculators.

The company doubled its plant capacity, opened new sales offices outside its home territory, and launched an expensive advertising campaign. Computron's results were not satisfactory, to put it mildly. Its board of directors, which consisted of its president and vice-president plus its major stockholders (who were all local business people) was most upset when directors learned how the expansion was going. Suppliers were being paid late and were unhappy, and the bank was complaining about the deteriorating situation and threatening to cut off credit. As a result, Al Watkins, Computron's president, was informed that changes would have to be made, and quickly, or he would be fired. Also, at the board's insistence Donna Jamison was brought in and given the job of assistant to Fred Campo, a retired banker who was Computron's chairman and largest stockholder. Campo agreed to give up a few of his golfing days and to help nurse the company back to health, with Jamison's help.

Jamison began by gathering financial statements and other data.

BALANCE SHEETS

	1998	1997
Assets		
Cash	$ 7,282	$ 9,000
Short-term investments	0	48,600
Accounts receivable	632,160	351,200
Inventories	1,287,360	715,200
Total current assets	$1,926,802	$1,124,000
Gross fixed assets	1,202,950	491,000
Less accumulated depreciation	263,160	146,200
Net fixed assets	$ 939,790	$ 344,800
Total assets	$2,866,592	$1,468,800
Liabilities and Equity		
Accounts payable	$ 524,160	$ 145,600
Notes payable	720,000	200,000
Accruals	489,600	136,000
Total current liabilities	$1,733,760	$ 481,600
Long-term debt	1,000,000	323,432
Common stock (100,000 shares)	460,000	460,000
Retained earnings	(327,168)	203,768
Total equity	$ 132,832	$ 663,768
Total liabilities and equity	$2,866,592	$1,468,800

INCOME STATEMENTS

	1998	1997
Sales	$5,834,400	$3,432,000
Cost of goods sold	5,728,000	2,864,000
Other expenses	680,000	340,000
Depreciation	116,960	18,900
Total operating costs	$6,524,960	$3,222,900
EBIT	($ 690,560)	$ 209,100
Interest expense	176,000	62,500
EBT	($ 866,560)	$ 146,600
Taxes (40%)	(346,624)	58,640
Net income	($ 519,936)	$ 87,960
EPS	($ 5.199)	$ 0.880
DPS	$ 0.110	$ 0.220
Book value per share	$ 1.328	$ 6.638
Stock price	$ 2.25	$ 8.50
Shares outstanding	100,000	100,000
Tax rate	40.00%	40.00%
Lease payments	40,000	40,000
Sinking fund payments	0	0

STATEMENT OF RETAINED EARNINGS, 1998

Balance of retained earnings, 12/31/97	$ 203,768
Add: Net income, 1998	(519,936)
Less: Dividends paid	(11,000)
Balance of retained earnings, 12/31/98	($ 327,168)

STATEMENT OF CASH FLOWS, 1998

Operating Activities

Net Income	($ 519,936)
Adjustments:	
Noncash adjustments:	
Depreciation	116,960
Changes in working capital:	
Change in accounts receivable	(280,960)
Change in inventories	(572,160)
Change in accounts payable	378,560
Change in accruals	353,600
Net cash provided by operating activities	($ 523,936)
Long-Term Investing Activities	
Cash used to acquire fixed assets	($ 711,950)
Financing Activities	
Change in short-term investments	$ 48,600
Change in notes payable	520,000
Change in long-term debt	676,568
Payment of cash dividends	(11,000)
Net cash provided by financing activities	$1,234,168
Sum: Net change in cash	(1,718)
Plus: Cash at beginning of year	$ 9,000
Cash at end of year	$ 7,282

Assume that you are Jamison's assistant, and you must help her answer the following questions for Campo. (Note: We will continue with this case in Chapter 3, and you will feel more comfortable with the analysis there, but answering these questions will help prepare you for Chapter 3. Provide clear explanations, not just yes or no answers!)

a. What effect did the expansion have on sales, net operating profit after taxes (NOPAT), net operating working capital, capital, and net income?

b. What effect did the expansion have on net cash flow, operating cash flow, and free cash flow?

c. Jamison also has asked you to estimate Computron's EVA. She estimates that the after-tax cost of capital was 11 percent in 1997 and 13 percent in 1998.

d. Looking at Computron's stock price today, would you conclude that the expansion increased or decreased MVA?

e. Computron purchases materials on 30-day terms, meaning that it is supposed to pay for purchases within 30 days of receipt. Judging from its 1998 balance sheet, do you think Computron pays suppliers on time? Explain. If not, what problems might this lead to?

f. Computron spends money for labor, materials, and fixed assets (depreciation) to make products, and still more money to sell those products. Then, it makes sales which result in receivables, which eventually result in cash inflows. Does it appear that Computron's sales price exceeds its costs per unit sold? How does this affect the cash balance?

g. Suppose Computron's sales manager told the sales staff to start offering 60-day credit terms rather than the 30-day terms now being offered. Computron's competitors react by offering similar terms, so sales remain constant. What effect would this have on the cash account? How would the cash account be affected if sales doubled as a result of the credit policy change?

h. Can you imagine a situation in which the sales price exceeds the cost of producing and selling a unit of output, yet a dramatic increase in sales volume causes the cash balance to decline?

i. In general, could a company like Computron increase sales without a corresponding increase in inventory and other assets? Would the asset increase occur before the increase in sales, and, if so, how would that affect the cash account and the statement of cash flows?

j. Did Computron finance its expansion program with internally generated funds (additions to retained earnings plus depreciation) or with external capital? How does the choice of financing affect the company's financial strength?

k. Refer to the income statements and the statement of cash flows. Suppose Computron broke even in 1998 in the sense that sales revenues equaled total operating costs plus interest charges. Would the asset expansion have caused the company to experience a cash shortage which required it to raise external capital?

l. If Computron started depreciating fixed assets over 7 years rather than 10 years, would that affect (1) the physical stock of assets, (2) the balance sheet account for fixed assets, (3) the company's reported net income, and (4) its cash position? Assume the same depreciation method is used for stockholder reporting and for tax calculations, and the accounting change has no effect on assets' physical lives.

m. Explain how (1) inventory valuation methods, (2) the accounting policy regarding expensing versus capitalizing research and development, and (3) the policy with regard to funding future retirement plan costs (retirement pay and retirees' health benefits) could affect the financial statements.

n. Computron's stock sells for $2.25 per share even though the company had large losses. Does the positive stock price indicate that some investors are irrational?

o. Computron followed the standard practice of paying dividends on a quarterly basis. It paid a dividend during the first two quarters of 1998, then eliminated the dividend when management realized that a loss would be incurred for the year. The dividend was cut before the losses were announced, and at that point the stock price fell from $8.50 to $3.50. Why would an $0.11, or even a $0.22, dividend reduction lead to a $5.00 stock price reduction?

p. Explain how earnings per share, dividends per share, and book value per share are calculated, and what they mean. Why does the market price per share *not* equal the book value per share?

q. How much new money did Computron borrow from its bank during 1998? How much additional credit did its suppliers extend? Its employees and the taxing authorities?

r. If you were Computron's banker, or the credit manager of one of its suppliers, would you be worried about your job? If you were a current Computron employee, a retiree, or a stockholder, should you be concerned?

s. The 1998 income statement shows negative taxes, that is, a tax credit. How much taxes would the company have had to pay in the past to actually get this credit? If taxes paid within the last 2 years had been less than $346,624, what would have happened? Would this have affected the statement of cash flows and the ending cash balance?

t. Working with Jamison has required you to put in a lot of overtime, so you have had very little time to spend on your private finances. It's now April 1, and you have only two weeks left to file your income tax return. You have managed to get all the information together that you will need to complete your return. Computron paid you a salary of $45,000, and you received $3,000 in dividends from common stock that you own. You are single, so your personal exemption is $2,650, and your itemized deductions are $4,550.

   (1) On the basis of the information above and the 1998 individual tax rate schedule, what is your tax liability?

   (2) What are your marginal and average tax rates?

u. Assume that a corporation has $100,000 of taxable income from operations plus $5,000 of interest income and $10,000 of dividend income. What is the company's tax liability?

v. Assume that after paying your personal income tax as calculated in Part t, you have $5,000 to invest. You have narrowed your investment choices down to California bonds with a yield of 7 percent or equally risky Exxon bonds with a yield of 10 percent. Which one should you choose and why? At what marginal tax rate would you be indifferent to the choice between California and Exxon bonds?

Selected Additional References

The effects of alternative accounting policies on financial statements are discussed in the invest-ment textbooks referenced in Chapter 5 and also in the many excellent texts on financial state-ment analysis. For example, see

Fraser, Lyn M., *Understanding Financial Statements* (Englewood Cliffs, N.J.: Prentice-Hall, 1992).

Gibson, Charles H., and Patricia A. Frishkoff, *Financial Statement Analysis* (Boston: Kent, 1986).

Hawkins, David E., *Corporate Financial Reporting and Analysis* (Homewood, Ill.: Irwin, 1986).

For an excellent treatment of the relationship between free cash flows and the value of a com-pany, see

Copeland, Tom, Tim Koller, and Jack Murrin, *Valuation: Measuring and Managing the Value of Companies* (New York: John Wiley & Sons, Inc., 1992).

Stewart, G. Bennett, *The Quest for Value* (New York: Harper Collins, 1991). Stewart is a found-ing partner of the consulting firm Stern Stewart & Co.

The following articles provide additional information on the effect of corporate taxes on busi-ness behavior:

Angell, Robert J., and Tony Wingler, "A Note on Expensing versus Depreciating under the Accel-erated Cost Recovery System," *Financial Management*, Winter 1982, 34–35.

Comiskey, Eugene E., and James R. Hasselback, "Analyzing the Profit and Tax Relationship," *Financial Management*, Winter 1973, 57–62.

McCarty, Daniel E., and William R. McDaniel, "A Note on Expensing versus Depreciating under the Accelerated Cost Recovery System: Comment," *Financial Management*, Summer 1983, 37–39.

For a good reference guide to tax issues, see

Federal Tax Course (Englewood Cliffs, N.J.: Prentice-Hall, published annually).

ANALYSIS OF FINANCIAL STATEMENTS

*S*unbeam Corporation, maker of toasters, blenders, and other consumer products, took on too much debt in the 1980s, and that debt forced it into bankruptcy. These problems were cleared up in 1990, and from 1990 to 1994 the company experienced strong growth in earnings. However, business dropped in 1995, and the 1995 profit margin shrunk to 4 percent from 9 percent in 1994. At the same time, sales stagnated, and the return on equity dropped to a paltry 5.4 percent. As a result, Sunbeam's stock, which sold for $26 a share in 1994, fell to $12 in 1996.

Superstar money managers Michael Price and Michael Steinhardt had taken control of the company while Sunbeam was in bankruptcy, and in 1996 they held 42 percent of its shares. Needless to say, Price and Steinhardt were disappointed with the company's 1996 performance. As a result, they fired Sunbeam's CEO and brought in a turnaround specialist, "Chain Saw" Al Dunlap, to straighten things out.

Dunlap earned his nickname as a result of his actions at other troubled companies, most recently Scott Paper. During his 18-month tenure at Scott, Dunlap dramatically cut costs and eliminated more than 11,000 jobs. As a result, Scott's stock rose sharply, and Dunlap was able to sell the company to Kimberly Clark at a price which increased Scott's value by $6.5 billion. For his efforts, he received incentive compensation to the tune of $100 million.

The day Dunlap's appointment at Sunbeam was announced, its stock jumped 49 percent, from $12½ to $18⅝, thereby raising the company's market value by nearly $500 million. Obviously, Sunbeam's stockholders thought Dunlap could do with it what he had done with Scott Paper. Quickly, he fired a number of top managers and announced plans to cut the work force in half. In addition, he announced plans to reduce corporate overhead by 60 percent and to sell off any part of the company that cannot be made profitable.

While the market's response to Dunlap's appointment was enthusiastic, some skeptics doubt that he will be able to turn Sunbeam around quickly. To restore profitability, Dunlap will have to boost sales by improving products, developing innovative new products, and expanding into new markets. Cost cuts alone won't do it.

As you study this chapter, think about Sunbeam. An analysis of any firm's financial statements can highlight its shortcomings, and that information can then be used to improve performance. In addition, financial statement analysis can be used to forecast how such strategic decisions as the sale of a division, a major marketing program, or expanding a plant are likely to affect future financial performance. Chain Saw Al will undoubtedly use such studies in the months ahead as he attempts to improve Sunbeam's performance — his next $100 million depends on it.

The primary goal of financial management is to maximize the stock price, not such accounting measures such as net income or EPS. However, accounting data do influence stock prices, and to understand why a company is performing the way it is and to plan how to improve it, one needs to evaluate the information reported in the financial statements. Chapter 2 described the primary statements and showed how they change as a firm's operations undergo change. Now, in Chapter 3, we show how financial statements are used by managers to improve performance, by lenders to evaluate the likelihood of collecting on loans, and by stockholders to forecast earnings, dividends, and stock prices.

If management is to maximize a firm's value, it must take advantage of the firm's strengths and, simultaneously, correct its weaknesses. Financial statement analysis helps by (1) comparing the firm's performance with that of other firms in the same industry and (2) evaluating trends in operations over time. These studies help management identify deficiencies and then take actions to improve performance. In this chapter, we focus on how financial managers (and investors) evaluate the current financial position. Then, in the remaining chapters, we examine the types of actions managements can take to improve performance and thus increase their stock prices.

This chapter should, for the most part, be a review of concepts you learned in accounting. However, accounting focuses on how financial statements are *made,* whereas our focus is on how they are *used* by management to improve the firm's performance and by investors when they set values on the firm's stock and bonds.

RATIO ANALYSIS

Financial statements report both on a firm's position at a point in time (the balance sheet) and on its operations over some past period (the income statement and statement of cash flows). However, the real value of financial statements lies in the fact that they can be used to help predict future earnings and dividends. From an investor's standpoint, *predicting the future is what financial statement analysis is all about,* while from management's standpoint, *financial statement analysis is useful both to help anticipate future conditions and, more important, as a starting point for planning actions that will affect the future course of events.*

Financial ratios are designed to help one evaluate a financial statement. For example, Firm A might have debt of $5,248,760 and interest charges of $419,900, while Firm B might have debt of $52,647,980 and interest charges of $3,948,600. Which company is stronger? The burden of these debts, and the companies' ability to repay them, can best be evaluated (1) by comparing each firm's debt to its assets and (2) by comparing the interest it must pay to the income it has available for payment of interest. Such comparisons are made by *ratio analysis.*

In the paragraphs which follow, we will calculate the financial ratios for MicroDrive Inc., using data from the balance sheets and income statements given in Tables 2-1 and 2-2 back in Chapter 2. We will also evaluate the ratios in relation to the industry averages. Note that all dollar amounts in the ratio calculations are in millions.

LIQUIDITY RATIOS

A **liquid asset** is one that trades in an active market and hence can be quickly converted to cash at the going market price, and a firm's "liquidity position" deals with this question: Will the firm be able to pay off its debts as they come due over the next year or so? As shown in Table 2-1 in Chapter 2, MicroDrive has debts totaling $310 million that must be paid off within the coming year. Will it have trouble satisfying those obligations? A full liquidity analysis requires the use of cash budgets, but by relating the amount of cash and other current assets to current obligations, ratio analysis provides a quick, easy-to-use measure of liquidity. Two commonly used **liquidity ratios** are discussed in this section.

Ability to Meet Short-Term Obligations: The Current Ratio

Current assets normally include cash, marketable securities, accounts receivable, and inventories. Current liabilities consist of accounts payable, short-term notes payable, current maturities of long-term debt, accrued taxes, and other accrued expenses (principally wages). The **current ratio** is calculated by dividing current assets by current liabilities:

$$\text{Current ratio} = \frac{\text{Current assets}}{\text{Current liabilities}}$$

$$= \frac{\$1,000}{\$310} = 3.2 \text{ times.}$$

Industry average $= 4.2$ times.

MicroDrive has a lower current ratio than the average for its industry. Is this good or bad? Sometimes the answer depends on who is asking the question. For example, suppose a supplier is trying to decide whether to extend credit to MicroDrive. In general, creditors like to see a high current ratio. If a company is getting into financial difficulty, it will begin paying its bills (accounts payable) more slowly, borrowing from its bank, and so on. If current liabilities are rising faster than current assets, the current ratio will fall, and this could spell trouble. Because the current ratio provides the best single indicator of the extent to which the claims of short-term creditors are covered by assets that are expected to be converted to cash fairly quickly, it is the most commonly used measure of short-term solvency.

MicroDrive's current ratio is well below the average for its industry, 4.2, so its liquidity position is relatively weak. Still, since current assets are scheduled to be converted to cash in the near future, it is highly probable that they could be liquidated at close to their stated value. With a current ratio of 3.2, MicroDrive could liquidate current assets at only 31 percent of book value and still pay off current creditors in full.[1]

Now consider the current ratio from the perspective of a shareholder. A high current ratio could mean that the company has a lot of money tied up in nonproductive assets, such as excess cash or marketable securities, or in inventory. In fact, it was Chrysler's buildup of marketable securities that led to a recent confrontation between Chrysler's management and Kirk Kerkorian, who owned 15 percent of Chrysler's stock. Kerkorian and Lee Iacocca, Chrysler's former CEO, said that a better use of the cash would be to reinvest the money in the company's operations or else return it to shareholders. Chrysler's management disagreed, arguing that the funds were needed to weather possible future economic downturns. Although the situation was not resolved to the complete satisfaction of Kerkorian and Iacocca, Chrysler did reduce its security holdings, and its stock rose.

Although industry average figures are discussed later in some detail, it should be noted that an industry average is not a magic number that all firms should strive to maintain — in fact, some very well-managed firms will be above the average while other good firms will be below it. However, if a firm's ratios are far removed from the

---

[1] 1/3.2 = 0.31, or 31 percent. Note that 0.31($1,000) = $310, the amount of current liabilities.

averages for its industry, this is a red flag, and analysts should be concerned about why the variance occurs. For example, suppose a low current ratio could be traced to low inventories. Is this a competitive advantage resulting from the firm's mastery of just-in-time inventory management, or is it an Achilles heel that is causing the firm to miss shipments and lose sales? Ratio analysis doesn't answer such questions, but it does point to areas of potential concern.

Quick, or Acid Test, Ratio

The **quick,** or **acid test, ratio** is calculated by deducting inventories from current assets and then dividing the remainder by current liabilities:

$$\text{Quick, or acid test, ratio} = \frac{\text{Current assets} - \text{Inventories}}{\text{Current liabilities}}$$

$$= \frac{\$385}{\$310} = 1.2 \text{ times.}$$

$$\text{Industry average} = 2.1 \text{ times.}$$

Inventories are typically the least liquid of a firm's current assets, hence those on which losses are most likely to occur in the event of liquidation. Therefore, a measure of the firm's ability to pay off short-term obligations without relying on the sale of inventories is important.

The industry average quick ratio is 2.1, so MicroDrive's 1.2 ratio is low in comparison with other firms in its industry. Still, if the accounts receivable can be collected, the company can pay off its current liabilities without having to liquidate its inventory.

S E L F - T E S T
Q U E S T I O N S

Identify two ratios that are used to analyze a firm's liquidity position, and write out their equations.

What are the characteristics of a liquid asset? Give some examples.

Which current asset is typically the least liquid?

ASSET MANAGEMENT RATIOS

The second group of ratios, the **asset management ratios,** measure how effectively the firm is managing its assets. These ratios are designed to answer this question: Does the total amount of each type of asset as reported on the balance sheet seem reasonable, too high, or too low in view of current and projected sales levels? If a company has excessive investments in assets, then its capital costs will be unduly high, and its stock price will suffer. On the other hand, if a company does not have enough assets, it will lose sales, which will hurt free cash flow and the stock price. Therefore, it is important to have the *right* amount invested in assets. Ratios which analyze the different types of assets are described in this section.

Evaluating Inventories: The Inventory Turnover Ratio

The **inventory turnover ratio** is defined as sales divided by inventories:

$$\text{Inventory turnover ratio} = \frac{\text{Sales}}{\text{Inventories}}$$

$$= \frac{\$3,000}{\$615} = 4.9 \text{ times.}$$

$$\text{Industry average} = 9.0 \text{ times.}$$

As a rough approximation, each item of MicroDrive's inventory is sold out and restocked, or "turned over," 4.9 times per year. "Turnover" is a term that originated many years ago with the old Yankee peddler, who would load up his wagon with goods, then go off on his route to peddle his wares. The merchandise was called "working capital" because it was what he actually sold, or "turned over," to produce his profits, whereas his "turnover" was the number of trips he took each year. Annual sales divided by inventory equaled turnover, or trips per year. If he made 10 trips per year, stocked 100 pans, and made a gross profit of $5 per pan, his annual gross profit would be (100)($5)(10) = $5,000. If he went faster and made 20 trips per year, his gross profit would double, other things held constant. So, his turnover directly affected his profits.

MicroDrive's turnover of 4.9 times is much lower than the industry average of 9 times. This suggests that MicroDrive has too much inventory. Excess inventory is, of course, unproductive, and it represents an investment with a low or zero rate of return. MicroDrive's low inventory turnover ratio also makes us question the current ratio. With such a low turnover, we must wonder whether the firm is actually holding damaged or obsolete goods not worth their stated value.[2]

Note that sales occur over the entire year, whereas the inventory figure is for one point in time. For this reason, it would be better to use an average inventory measure.[3] If the firm's business is highly seasonal, or if there has been a strong upward or downward sales trend during the year, it is essential to make some such adjustment. To maintain comparability with industry averages, however, we did not use the average inventory figure.

Evaluating Receivables: The Days Sales Outstanding

Days sales outstanding (DSO), also called the "average collection period" (ACP), is used to appraise accounts receivable, and it is calculated by dividing accounts receivable by average daily sales to find the number of days' sales that are tied up in receivables. Thus, the DSO represents the average length of time that the firm must wait after making a sale before receiving cash, or the average collection period. MicroDrive has 45 days sales outstanding, well above the 36-day industry average.[4]

$$\text{DSO} = \frac{\text{Days sales outstanding}}{} = \frac{\text{Receivables}}{\text{Average sales per day}} = \frac{\text{Receivables}}{\text{Annual sales}/360}$$

$$= \frac{\$375}{\$3,000/360} = \frac{\$375}{\$8.333} = 45 \text{ days.}$$

$$\text{Industry average} = 36 \text{ days.}$$

---

[2]A problem arises calculating and analyzing the inventory turnover ratio. Sales are stated at market prices, so if inventories are carried at cost, as they generally are, the calculated turnover overstates the true turnover ratio. Therefore, it would be more appropriate to use cost of goods sold in place of sales in the formula's numerator. However, established compilers of financial ratio statistics such as Dun & Bradstreet use the ratio of sales to inventories carried at cost. To develop a figure that can be compared with those published by Dun & Bradstreet and similar organizations, it is necessary to measure inventory turnover with sales in the numerator, as we do here.

[3]Preferably, the average inventory value should be calculated by summing the monthly figures during the year and dividing by 12. If monthly data are not available, one can add the beginning and ending figures and divide by 2. Both methods adjust for growth but not for seasonal effects.

[4]Note that by convention the financial community generally uses 360 rather than 365 as the number of days in the year. Also, it would be better to use *average* receivables, either an average of the monthly figures or (beginning receivables + ending receivables)/2 = ($315 + $375)/2 = $345 in the formula. Had the annual average receivables been used, MicroDrive's DSO would have been $345.00/$8.333 = 41 days. The 41-day figure is the more accurate one, but because the industry average was based on year-end receivables, we used 45 days for our comparison. The DSO is discussed further in Chapters 21 and 23.

The DSO can also be evaluated by comparison with the terms on which the firm sells its goods. For example, MicroDrive's sales terms call for payment within 30 days, so the fact that 45 days' sales, not 30 days', are outstanding indicates that customers, on the average, are not paying their bills on time. This deprives MicroDrive of funds which it could use to reduce debt or invest in productive assets. Moreover, in some instances the fact that a customer is paying its bills late may signal that the customer is in financial trouble, in which case MicroDrive may have a hard time ever collecting the account. Therefore, if the trend in DSO is up, but the credit policy has not been changed, this would be strong evidence that steps should be taken to expedite the collection of accounts receivable.

Evaluating Fixed Assets: The Fixed Assets Turnover Ratio

The **fixed assets turnover ratio** measures how effectively the firm uses its plant and equipment, and it is calculated by dividing sales by net fixed assets:

$$\text{Fixed assets turnover ratio} = \frac{\text{Sales}}{\text{Net fixed assets}}$$

$$= \frac{\$3,000}{\$1,000} = 3.0 \text{ times.}$$

$$\text{Industry average} = 3.0 \text{ times.}$$

MicroDrive's ratio of 3.0 times is equal to the industry average, indicating that the firm is using its fixed assets about as intensively as are other firms in its industry. Therefore, MicroDrive seems to have about the right amount of fixed assets in relation to other firms.

A potential problem exists when interpreting the fixed assets turnover ratio. Recall from accounting that fixed assets reflect the historical costs of the assets. Inflation has caused the value of many assets that were purchased in the past to be seriously understated. Therefore, if we were comparing an old firm which had acquired many of its fixed assets years ago at low prices with a new company which had acquired its fixed assets only recently, we probably would find that the old firm had the higher fixed assets turnover ratio. However, this would be more reflective of the difficulty accountants have in dealing with inflation than of any inefficiency on the part of the new firm. The accounting profession is trying to devise ways of making financial statements reflect current values rather than historical values. If balance sheets were actually stated on a current value basis, this would help us make better comparisons, but today the problem still exists. Since financial analysts typically do not have the data necessary to make adjustments, they simply recognize that a problem exists and deal with it judgmentally. In MicroDrive's case, the issue is not a serious one because all firms in the industry have been expanding at about the same rate, hence the balance sheets of the comparison firms are reasonably comparable.[5]

Evaluating Total Assets: The Total Assets Turnover Ratio

The **total assets turnover ratio** measures the turnover of all the firm's assets; it is calculated by dividing sales by total assets:

---

[5]See FASB #33, *Financial Reporting and Changing Prices* (September 1979), for a discussion of the effects of inflation on financial statements.

$$\text{Total assets turnover ratio} = \frac{\text{Sales}}{\text{Total assets}}$$

$$= \frac{\$3,000}{\$2,000} = 1.5 \text{ times.}$$

$$\text{Industry average} = 1.8 \text{ times.}$$

MicroDrive's ratio is somewhat below the industry average, indicating that the company is not generating a sufficient volume of business given its total asset investment. Sales should be increased, some assets should be disposed of, or a combination of these steps should be taken.

Linking Asset Management and Free Cash Flow: The Operating Capital Requirement Ratio

A fundamental question for managers is, "How much must the company invest in operating assets in order to support a given level of sales?" Recall from Chapter 2 that operating assets, or operating capital, is the sum of net operating working capital plus net fixed assets, and it equals the funds investors have provided to support operations. The **operating capital requirement ratio** measures the relationship between operating capital and sales:

$$\text{Operating capital requirement ratio} = \frac{\text{Operating capital}}{\text{Sales}}$$

$$= \frac{\$1,800}{\$3,000} = 60.0\%.$$

$$\text{Industry average} = 50.3\%.$$

This means that MicroDrive requires 60 cents of operating capital for every dollar of sales, versus only 50 cents for the average company in its industry. If MicroDrive could reduce its investment in operating capital without lowering sales, its capital costs would decline, its return on capital would increase, and its stock price would rise.

S E L F - T E S T
Q U E S T I O N S

Identify five ratios that are used to measure how effectively a firm is managing its assets, and write out their equations.

What potential problem might arise with the inventory turnover ratio?

What potential problem might arise when comparing different firms' fixed assets turnover ratios?

Why does the operating capital requirement ratio affect the stock price?

DEBT MANAGEMENT RATIOS

The extent to which a firm uses debt financing, or its **financial leverage,** has three important implications: (1) By raising funds through debt, stockholders can maintain control of a firm while limiting their investment. (2) Creditors look to the equity, or owner-supplied funds, to provide a margin of safety, so if the stockholders have provided only a small proportion of the total financing, the risks of the enterprise are borne mainly by its creditors. (3) If the firm earns more on investments financed with borrowed funds than it pays in interest, the return on the owners' capital is magnified, or "leveraged."

To understand better how financial leverage affects risk and return, consider Table 3-1. Here we analyze two companies that are identical except for the way they are

TABLE 3-1	Effects of Financial Leverage on Stockholders' Returns

FIRM U (UNLEVERAGED)

Current assets	$ 50	Debt	$ 0
Fixed assets	50	Common equity	100
Total assets	$100	Total liabilities and equity	$100

	EXPECTED CONDITIONS (1)	BAD CONDITIONS (2)
Sales	$100.00	$82.50
Operating costs	70.00	80.00
Operating income (EBIT)	$ 30.00	$ 2.50
Interest	0.00	0.00
Earnings before taxes (EBT)	$ 30.00	$ 2.50
Taxes (40%)	12.00	1.00
Net income (NI)	$18.00	$ 1.50
$ROE_U = NI/Common\ equity = NI/\$100 =$	18.00%	1.50%

FIRM L (LEVERAGED)

Current assets	$ 50	Debt (interest = 15%)	$ 50
Fixed assets	50	Common equity	50
Total assets	$100	Total liabilities and equity	$100

	EXPECTED CONDITIONS (1)	BAD CONDITIONS (2)
Sales	$100.00	$82.50
Operating costs	70.00	80.00
Operating income (EBIT)	$ 30.00	$ 2.50
Interest (15%)	7.50	7.50
Earnings before taxes (EBT)	$ 22.50	($ 5.00)
Taxes (40%)	9.00	(2.00)
Net income (NI)	$ 13.50	($ 3.00)
$ROE_L = NI/Common\ equity = NI/\$50 =$	27.00%	(6.00%)

financed. Firm U (for "unleveraged") has no debt, whereas Firm L (for "leveraged") is financed half with equity and half with debt that costs 15 percent. Both companies have $100 of assets and $100 of sales, and their expected operating income (also called earnings before interest and taxes, or EBIT) is $30. Thus, both firms *expect* to earn $30, before taxes, on their assets. Of course, things could turn out badly, in which case EBIT would be lower, and in the second column of the table, we show EBIT declining from $30 to $2.50 under bad conditions.

Even though both companies' assets produce the same expected EBIT, under normal conditions Firm L will provide its stockholders with a return on equity of 27 percent versus only 18 percent for Firm U. This difference is caused by Firm L's use of debt, which raises the expected rate of return to stockholders for two reasons: (1) Since interest is deductible, the use of debt lowers the tax bill and leaves more operating income available to its investors. (2) If the expected rate of return on assets (EBIT/Total assets) exceeds the interest rate on debt, as it generally does, then a company can use debt to acquire assets, pay the interest on the debt, and have something left over as a "bonus" for its stockholders. For our hypothetical firms, these two effects combine to push Firm L's expected rate of return on equity up far above that of Firm U. *Thus, debt can be used to "leverage up" the rate of return on equity.*

However, financial leverage can cut both ways. As we show in Column 2, if sales are lower and costs are higher than were expected, the return on assets will also be lower than was expected. Under these conditions, the leveraged firm's return on equity falls especially sharply, and losses occur. For example, under the "bad conditions" in Table 3-1, the debt-free firm still shows a profit, but Firm L shows a loss and thus has a negative return on equity. This occurs because Firm L needs cash to service its debt, while Firm U does not. Firm U, because of its strong balance sheet, could ride out the recession and be ready for the next boom. Firm L, on the other hand, must pay interest of $7.50 regardless of its level of sales. Since in a recession its operations do not generate enough income to meet the interest payments, cash would be depleted, and the firm probably would need to raise additional funds. Because it would be running a loss, Firm L would have a hard time selling stock to raise capital. Moreover, its losses would cause lenders to raise the interest rate, increasing L's problems still further. As a result, Firm L just might not survive to enjoy the next boom.

We see, then, that firms with relatively high debt ratios have higher expected returns when the economy is normal, but they can also suffer losses when the economy goes into a recession. Thus, firms with low debt ratios are less risky, but they also forego the opportunity to leverage up their return on equity. The prospects of high returns are desirable, but investors are averse to risk. *Therefore, decisions about the use of debt require firms to balance higher expected returns against increased risk.* Determining the optimal amount of debt for a given firm is a complicated process, and we defer a discussion of this topic until Chapters 15 and 16. For now, we will simply look at two procedures analysts use to examine the firm's debt: (1) check the balance sheet to determine the extent to which borrowed funds have been used to finance assets, and (2) review the income statement to see the extent to which fixed charges are covered by operating profits.

How the Firm Is Financed: Total Debt to Total Assets

The ratio of total debt to total assets, generally called the **debt ratio,** measures the percentage of funds provided by creditors:

$$\text{Debt ratio} = \frac{\text{Total debt}}{\text{Total assets}}$$

$$= \frac{\$310 + \$754}{\$2,000} = \frac{\$1,064}{\$2,000} = 53.2\%.$$

Industry average $= 40.0\%$.

Total debt includes both current liabilities and long-term debt. Creditors prefer low debt ratios because the lower the ratio, the greater the creditors' protection against losses in the event of bankruptcy. Stockholders, on the other hand, like the fact that leverage magnifies expected earnings.

MicroDrive's debt ratio is 53.2 percent, which means that its creditors have supplied more than half of its total financing. As we will discuss in Chapters 15 and 16, a variety of factors determine a company's optimal debt ratio. Even within the same industry, optimal debt ratios may differ considerably. Nevertheless, the fact that MicroDrive's debt ratio exceeds the industry average raises a red flag and may make it costly for MicroDrive to borrow additional funds without first raising more equity capital. Creditors may be reluctant to lend the firm more money, and management would probably be subjecting the firm to the risk of bankruptcy if it sought to increase the debt ratio by borrowing additional funds.[6]

Ability to Pay Interest: Times Interest Earned

The **times-interest-earned (TIE) ratio** is determined by dividing earnings before interest and taxes (EBIT in Table 2-2) by the interest charges:

$$\text{Times-interest-earned (TIE) ratio} = \frac{\text{EBIT}}{\text{Interest charges}}$$

$$= \frac{\$283.8}{\$88} = 3.2 \text{ times.}$$

Industry average = 6.0 times.

The TIE ratio measures the extent to which operating income can decline before the firm is unable to meet its annual interest costs. Failure to meet this obligation can bring legal action by the firm's creditors, possibly resulting in bankruptcy. Note that earnings before interest and taxes, rather than net income, is used in the numerator. Because interest is paid with pre-tax dollars, the full amount of EBIT is available to pay interest.

MicroDrive's interest is covered 3.2 times. Since the industry average is 6 times, MicroDrive has a relatively low margin of safety. Thus, the TIE ratio reinforces our conclusion based on the debt ratio that MicroDrive would face difficulties if it attempted to borrow additional funds.

Ability to Service Debt: The Fixed Charge Coverage Ratio

The **fixed charge coverage ratio** is similar to the times-interest-earned ratio, but it is more inclusive because it recognizes that many firms lease assets and also must make sinking fund payments.[7] Leasing is widespread in certain industries, making this ratio preferable to the times-interest-earned ratio for many purposes. MicroDrive's annual lease payments are $28 million, and it must make an annual $20 million sinking fund payment to help retire its debt. Because sinking fund payments must be paid with after-tax dollars, whereas interest and lease payments are paid with pre-tax dollars, the sinking fund payment must be "grossed up" by dividing by (1 − Tax rate) to find the before-tax income required to pay taxes and still have enough left to make the sinking fund payment.[8]

---

[6]The ratio of debt to equity is also used in financial analysis. The debt-to-assets (D/A) and debt-to-equity (D/E) ratios are simply transformations of each other:

$$D/E = \frac{D/A}{1 - D/A}, \text{ and } D/A = \frac{D/E}{1 + D/E}.$$

[7]A sinking fund is a required annual payment designed to reduce the balance of a bond or preferred stock issue. It is similar to the principal reduction part of a home loan payment. Sinking funds are discussed in Chapter 8.

[8]Note that $20/0.6 = $33.33. Therefore, if the company had pre-tax income of $33.33, it could pay taxes at a 40 percent rate and have exactly $20 left with which to make the sinking fund payment. Thus, a $20 sinking fund payment requires $20/0.6 = $33.33 of pre-tax income. Dividing by (1 − T) is called "grossing up" an after-tax value to find the corresponding pre-tax value.

Fixed charges include interest, annual long-term lease obligations, and sinking fund payments, and the fixed charge coverage ratio is defined as follows:

$$\begin{array}{l} \text{Fixed charge} \\ \text{coverage ratio} \end{array} = \frac{\text{EBIT} + \text{Lease payments}}{\underset{\text{charges}}{\text{Interest}} + \underset{\text{payments}}{\text{Lease}} + \dfrac{\text{Sinking fund payments}}{(1 - \text{Tax rate})}}$$

$$= \frac{\$283.8 + \$28}{\$88 + \$28 + \dfrac{\$20}{0.6}} = 2.1 \text{ times.}$$

Industry average $= 5.5$ times.

MicroDrive's fixed charges are covered only 2.1 times, versus an industry average of 5.5 times. Again, this indicates that the firm is weaker than average, and this reinforces the argument that MicroDrive would probably encounter difficulties if it attempted to increase its debt.

SELF-TEST QUESTIONS

How does the use of financial leverage affect current stockholders' control?

How do taxes influence a firm's willingness to finance with debt?

In what way does the decision to use debt involve a risk-versus-return trade-off?

Explain the following statement: "Analysts look at both balance sheet and income statement ratios when appraising a firm's financial condition."

Name three ratios that are used to measure the extent to which a firm uses financial leverage, and write out their equations.

PROFITABILITY RATIOS

Profitability is the net result of a number of policies and decisions. The ratios examined thus far provide useful clues as to the effectiveness of a firm's operations, but the **profitability ratios** show the combined effects of liquidity, asset management, and debt on operating results.

Profit Margin on Sales

The **profit margin on sales,** calculated by dividing net income by sales, gives the profit per dollar of sales:

$$\begin{array}{l} \text{Profit margin} \\ \text{on sales} \end{array} = \frac{\begin{array}{c}\text{Net income available to}\\\text{common stockholders}\end{array}}{\text{Sales}}$$

$$= \frac{\$113.5}{\$3,000} = 3.8\%.$$

Industry average $= 5.0\%$.

MicroDrive's profit margin is below the industry average of 5 percent. This sub-par result occurs because costs are too high. High costs generally occur because of inefficient operations, but MicroDrive's low profit margin also results from its heavy use of debt. Recall that net income is income *after interest*. Therefore, if two firms have identical operations in the sense that their sales, operating costs, and EBIT are the same, but if one firm uses more debt than the other, then it will have higher interest charges. Those interest charges will pull its net income down, and since sales are constant, the result will be a relatively low profit margin. In such a case, the low profit margin would

INTERNATIONAL ACCOUNTING: DIFFERENCES CREATE HEADACHES FOR INVESTORS

You must be a good financial detective to analyze financial statements, especially if the company operates overseas. Despite attempts to standardize accounting practices, there are many differences in the way financial information is reported in different countries, and these differences create headaches for investors trying to make cross-border company comparisons.

A study by three Rider College accounting professors demonstrated that huge differences can exist. The professors constructed a computer model to evaluate the net income of a hypothetical but typical company operating in different countries. Applying the standard accounting practices of each country, the hypothetical company would have reported net income of $34,600 in the United States, $250,000 in the United Kingdom, $240,000 in Australia, and $10,402 in Germany.

Such variances occur for a number of reasons. In most countries, including the United States, an asset's balance sheet value is reported at original cost less any accumulated depreciation. However, in some countries, asset values are adjusted to more accurately reflect current market values. Also, inventory valuation methods vary from country to country, as does the treatment of goodwill. Other differences arise from the treatment of leases, research and development costs, and pension plans.

Differences in accounting practices arise from a variety of legal, historical, cultural, and economic factors. For example, in Germany and Japan large banks are the key source of both debt and equity capital, whereas in the United States public capital markets are most important. As a result, U.S. corporations disclose a great deal of information to the public, while German and Japanese corporations use very conservative accounting practices which appeal to the banks.

not indicate an operating problem, just a difference in financing strategies, and the firm with the low profit margin might well end up with a higher rate of return on its stockholders' investment due to its use of financial leverage. We will see exactly how profit margins and the use of debt interact to affect stockholder returns shortly.

Basic Earning Power (BEP)

The **basic earning power (BEP) ratio** is calculated by dividing earnings before interest and taxes (EBIT) by total assets:

$$\text{Basic earning power ratio (BEP)} = \frac{\text{EBIT}}{\text{Total assets}}$$

$$= \frac{\$283.8}{\$2,000} = 14.2\%.$$

$$\text{Industry average} = 17.2\%.$$

This ratio shows the raw earning power of the firm's assets, before the influence of taxes and leverage, and it is useful for comparing firms with different tax situations and different degrees of financial leverage. Because of its low turnover ratios and its high operating capital requirement ratio, MicroDrive is not getting as high a return on its assets as is the average computer company.[9]

Operating Profit Margin after Taxes

How profitable are MicroDrive's operations? That is the question answered by the **operating profit margin** after taxes:

---

[9]Notice that EBIT is earned throughout the year, whereas the total assets figure is an end-of-the-year number. Therefore, it would be conceptually better to calculate this ratio as EBIT/Average assets = EBIT/[(Beginning assets + Ending assets)/2]. We have not made this adjustment because the published ratios used for comparative purposes do not include it. However, when we construct our own comparative ratios, we do make the adjustment. Incidentally, the same adjustment would also be appropriate for two of the following ratios, ROA and ROE.

$$\text{Operating profit margin after taxes} = \frac{\text{NOPAT}}{\text{Sales}}$$

$$= \frac{\$170.3}{\$3,000} = 5.7\%.$$

Industry average = 5.7%.

Recall that NOPAT is net operating profit after taxes, and it is calculated as EBIT$(1 - T) =$ $\$283.8(0.6) = \$170.3$. Therefore, after operating costs and taxes, MicroDrive generates about 5.7 cents for every dollar of sales, which is approximately equal to the industry average.

Return on Total Assets

The ratio of net income to total assets measures the **return on total assets (ROA)** after interest and taxes:

$$\frac{\text{Return on}}{\text{total assets}} = \text{ROA} = \frac{\text{Net income available to common stockholders}}{\text{Total assets}}$$

$$= \frac{\$113.5}{\$2,000} = 5.7\%.$$

Industry average = 9.0%.

MicroDrive's 5.7 percent return is well below the 9 percent average for the industry. This low return results from (1) the company's low basic earning power plus (2) its high interest costs which result from its above-average use of debt, both of which cause its net income to be relatively low.

Return on Common Equity

The ratio of net income to common equity measures the **return on common equity (ROE),** or the *rate of return on stockholders' investment:*

$$\frac{\text{Return on}}{\text{common equity}} = \text{ROE} = \frac{\text{Net income available to common stockholders}}{\text{Common equity}}$$

$$= \frac{\$113.5}{\$896} = 12.7\%.$$

Industry average = 15.0%.

MicroDrive's 12.7 percent return is below the 15 percent industry average, but not as far below as the return on total assets. This somewhat better result is due to the company's greater use of debt, a point that is analyzed in detail later in the chapter.

SELF-TEST
QUESTIONS

Identify and write out the equations for five ratios that show the combined effects of liquidity, asset management, and debt management on profitability.

Why is the basic earning power ratio useful? The ratio of NOPAT/Sales?

What does ROE measure? Does using debt lower ROE?

Why does the use of debt lower the ROA?

MARKET VALUE RATIOS

A final group of ratios, the **market value ratios,** relates the firm's stock price to its earnings and book value per share. These ratios give management an indication of what investors think of the company's past performance and future prospects. If the liquidity, asset management, debt management, and profitability ratios are all good, then the market value ratios will be high, and the stock price will probably be as high as can be expected.

Price/Earnings Ratio

The **price/earnings (P/E) ratio** shows how much investors are willing to pay per dollar of reported profits. MicroDrive's stock sells for $23, so with an EPS of $2.27 its P/E ratio is 10.1:

$$\text{Price/earnings (P/E) ratio} = \frac{\text{Price per share}}{\text{Earnings per share}}$$

$$= \frac{\$23.00}{\$2.27} = 10.1 \text{ times.}$$

$$\text{Industry average} = 12.5 \text{ times.}$$

As we will see in Chapter 9, P/E ratios are higher for firms with strong growth prospects, other things held constant, but they are lower for riskier firms. Since MicroDrive's P/E ratio is below the average for other computer components companies, this suggests that the company is regarded as being somewhat riskier than most, as having poorer growth prospects, or both.

Market/Book Ratio

The ratio of a stock's market price to its book value gives another indication of how investors regard the company. Companies with relatively high rates of return on equity generally sell at higher multiples of book value than those with low returns. First, we find MicroDrive's book value per share:

$$\text{Book value per share} = \frac{\text{Common equity}}{\text{Shares outstanding}}$$

$$= \frac{\$896}{50} = \$17.92.$$

Now we divide the market price per share by the book value to get a **market/book (M/B) ratio** of 1.3 times:

$$\text{Market/book ratio} = \text{M/B} = \frac{\text{Market price per share}}{\text{Book value per share}}$$

$$= \frac{\$23.00}{\$17.92} = 1.3 \text{ times.}$$

$$\text{Industry average} = 1.7 \text{ times.}$$

Investors are willing to pay less for a dollar of MicroDrive's book value than for one of an average computer components company.

The average company followed by the *Value Line Investment Survey* had a market/book ratio of about 3.0 during 1997. Since M/B ratios typically exceed 1.0, this means that investors are willing to pay more for stocks than their accounting book values. This situation occurs primarily because asset values, as reported by accountants on corporate balance sheets, do not reflect either inflation or "goodwill." Thus, assets purchased years ago at preinflation prices are carried at their original costs, even though inflation might have caused their actual values to rise substantially, and going concerns have a value greater than their historical costs.

If a company earns a low rate of return on its assets, then its M/B ratio will be relatively low versus an average company. Thus, some airlines, which have not fared well in recent years, sell at M/B ratios below 1.0, while very successful firms such as Microsoft (which makes the operating systems for virtually all PCs) achieve high rates of return on their assets, and their market values are well in excess of their book values. In early 1998, Microsoft's book value per share was $8.20 versus a market price of $158, so its market/book ratio was $158/$8.20 = 19.3 times.

Describe the ratios that relate a firm's stock price to its earnings and book value per share, and write out their equations.

How do market value ratios reflect what investors think about a stock's risk and expected rate of return?

What does the price/earnings (P/E) ratio show? If one firm's P/E ratio is lower than that of another firm, name two factors that might explain the difference.

How is book value per share calculated? Explain how inflation and "goodwill" cause book values to deviate from market values.

TREND ANALYSIS

It is important to analyze trends in ratios as well as their absolute levels, for trends give clues as to whether the financial situation is likely to improve or to deteriorate. To do a **trend analysis,** one simply plots a ratio over time, as shown in Figure 3-1. This graph shows that MicroDrive's rate of return on common equity has been declining since

---

FIGURE 3-1   Rate of Return on Common Equity, 1994–1998

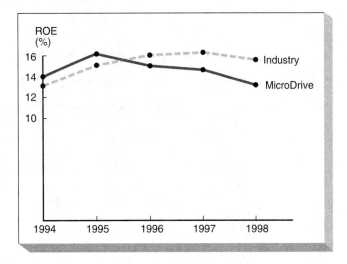

1995, even though the industry average has been relatively stable. All the other ratios could be analyzed similarly.

Common size analysis and **percent change analysis** are two other techniques that can be used to identify trends in financial statements. Common size analysis is also useful in comparative analysis, and some sources of industry data, such as Robert Morris Associates, are presented only in common size form. The Extension at the end of this chapter explains these two techniques.

How does one do a trend analysis?

What important information does a trend analysis provide?

THE VALUE OF OPERATIONS: USING THE RATIOS TO GUIDE MANAGERS

Table 3-2 summarizes MicroDrive's ratios, and the last two entries show that Micro-Drive's market value ratios are lower than those of its average competitor. What is causing this? Recall from Chapter 2 that the size and riskiness of a company's current and expected future free cash flows determine the value of its operations. Therefore, investors must expect MicroDrive's future free cash flows to grow more slowly or else to be riskier than those of its competitors.

Figure 3-2 shows how free cash flows are affected by the after-tax operating profit margin and the capital requirement ratio. A low after-tax operating profit margin will drag down free cash flows, but MicroDrive has an after-tax operating profit margin that is similar to that of other firms in its industry, as shown in Table 3-2. However, Micro-Drive has a very high capital requirement ratio, which lowers its free cash flow. Even if its free cash flows were no riskier than those of its peers, and even if its sales were projected to grow as fast as those of its competitors, its free cash flows would still lag because it ties up too much money in operating assets. Note that MicroDrive had a negative free cash flow in 1998, but its market value was positive. Investors thus expect free cash flow to improve in the future.

How do the operating profit margin and capital requirement ratios affect the value of a company's operations?

TYING THE RATIOS TOGETHER: THE DU PONT CHART AND EQUATION

Figure 3-3, which is called a modified **Du Pont chart** because that company's managers developed the general approach, shows how the return on equity is affected by asset turnover, the profit margin, and leverage. The left-hand side of the chart develops the *profit margin on sales*. The various expense items are listed and then summed to obtain MicroDrive's total costs, which are subtracted from sales to obtain the company's net income. When we divide net income by sales to get the profit margin, we find that 3.8 percent of each sales dollar is left over for stockholders. If the profit margin is low or trending down, as it is here, one can examine the individual expense items to identify and then correct problems.

The right-hand side of Figure 3-3 lists the various categories of assets, totals them, and then divides sales by total assets to find the number of times MicroDrive "turns its assets over" each year. The company's total assets turnover ratio is 1.5 times.

TABLE 3-2   MicroDrive Inc.: Summary of Financial Ratios (Millions of Dollars)

RATIO	FORMULA FOR CALCULATION	CALCULATION	RATIO	INDUSTRY AVERAGE	COMMENT
Liquidity					
Current	$\dfrac{\text{Current assets}}{\text{Current liabilities}}$	$\dfrac{\$1,000}{\$310}$	= 3.2×	4.2×	Poor
Quick, or acid, test	$\dfrac{\text{Current assets} - \text{Inventories}}{\text{Current liabilities}}$	$\dfrac{\$385}{\$310}$	= 1.2×	2.1×	Poor
Asset Management					
Inventory turnover	$\dfrac{\text{Sales}}{\text{Inventories}}$	$\dfrac{\$3,000}{\$615}$	= 4.9×	9.0×	Poor
Days sales outstanding (DSO)	$\dfrac{\text{Receivables}}{\text{Annual sales}/360}$	$\dfrac{\$375}{\$8.333}$	= 45 days	36 days	Poor
Fixed assets turnover	$\dfrac{\text{Sales}}{\text{Net fixed assets}}$	$\dfrac{\$3,000}{\$1,000}$	= 3.0×	3.0×	OK
Total assets turnover	$\dfrac{\text{Sales}}{\text{Total assets}}$	$\dfrac{\$3,000}{\$2,000}$	= 1.5×	1.8×	Somewhat low
Capital requirement	$\dfrac{\text{Operating capital}}{\text{Sales}}$	$\dfrac{\$1,800}{\$3,000}$	= 60.0%	50.3%	Poor
Debt Management					
Total debt to total assets	$\dfrac{\text{Total debt}}{\text{Total assets}}$	$\dfrac{\$1,064}{\$2,000}$	= 53.2%	40.0%	High (risky)
Times-interest-earned (TIE)	$\dfrac{\text{Earnings before interest and taxes (EBIT)}}{\text{Interest charges}}$	$\dfrac{\$283.8}{\$88}$	= 3.2×	6.0×	Low (risky)
Fixed charge coverage	$\dfrac{\text{Earnings before interest and taxes} + \text{Lease payments}}{\text{Interest charges} + \text{Lease payments} + \dfrac{\text{SF payments}}{(1-T)}}$	$\dfrac{\$311.8}{\$149.3}$	= 2.1×	5.5×	Low (risky)
Profitability					
Operating profit margin after taxes	$\dfrac{\text{NOPAT}}{\text{Sales}} = \dfrac{\text{EBIT}(1-T)}{\text{Sales}}$	$\dfrac{\$170.3}{\$3,000}$	= 5.7%	5.7%	OK
Profit margin on sales	$\dfrac{\text{Net income available to common stockholders}}{\text{Sales}}$	$\dfrac{\$113.5}{\$3,000}$	= 3.8%	5.0%	Poor
Basic earning power (BEP)	$\dfrac{\text{Earnings before interest and taxes (EBIT)}}{\text{Total assets}}$	$\dfrac{\$283.8}{\$2,000}$	= 14.2%	17.2%	Poor
Return on total assets (ROA)	$\dfrac{\text{Net income available to common stockholders}}{\text{Total assets}}$	$\dfrac{\$113.5}{\$2,000}$	= 5.7%	9.0%	Poor
Return on common equity (ROE)	$\dfrac{\text{Net income available to common stockholders}}{\text{Common equity}}$	$\dfrac{\$113.5}{\$896}$	= 12.7%	15.0%	Poor
Market Value					
Price/earnings (P/E)	$\dfrac{\text{Price per share}}{\text{Earnings per share}}$	$\dfrac{\$23.00}{\$2.27}$	= 10.1×	12.5×	Low
Market/book (M/B)	$\dfrac{\text{Market price per share}}{\text{Book value per share}}$	$\dfrac{\$23.00}{\$17.92}$	= 1.3×	1.7×	Low

FIGURE 3-2   Explaining the Market Value of MicroDrive Inc. (Millions of Dollars)

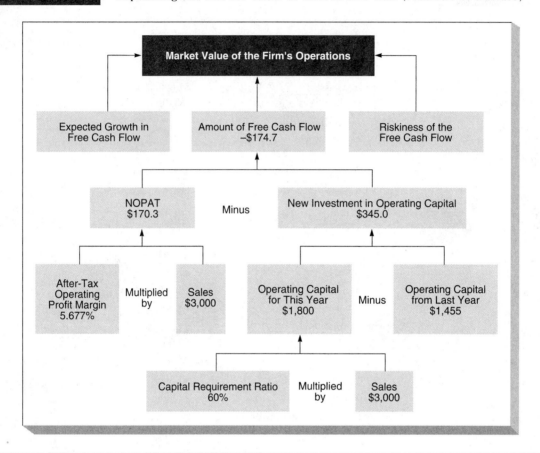

The profit margin times the total assets turnover is called the **Du Pont equation,** and it gives the rate of return on assets (ROA):

$$ROA = \text{Profit margin} \times \text{Total assets turnover}$$

$$= \frac{\text{Net income}}{\text{Sales}} \times \frac{\text{Sales}}{\text{Total assets}} \tag{3-1}$$

$$= 3.8\% \times 1.5 = 5.7\%.$$

MicroDrive made 3.8 percent, or 3.8 cents, on each dollar of sales, and assets were "turned over" 1.5 times during the year. Therefore, the company earned a return of 5.7 percent on its assets; see the upper left section of Figure 3-3.

If the company were financed only with common equity, the rate of return on assets (ROA) and the return on equity (ROE) would be the same, because the total assets would equal the common equity:

$$ROA = \frac{\text{Net income}}{\text{Total assets}} = \frac{\text{Net income}}{\text{Common equity}} = ROE.$$

This equality holds if and only if Total assets = Common equity, that is, if the company uses no debt. MicroDrive does use debt, so its common equity is less than its total assets. Therefore, the return to the common stockholders (ROE) must be greater than

| FIGURE 3-3 | Modified Du Pont Chart for MicroDrive Inc. (Millions of Dollars) |

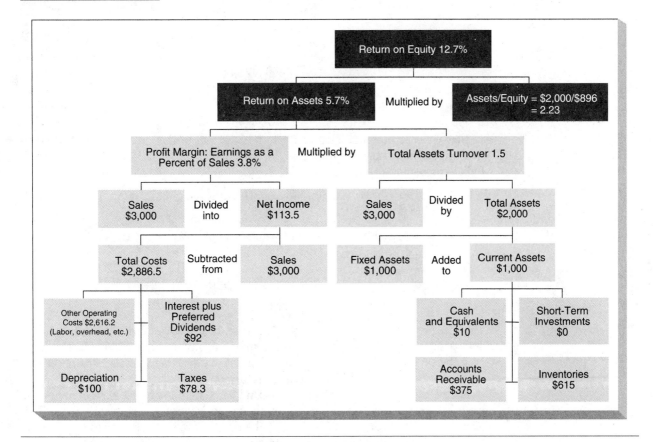

the ROA of 5.7 percent. Specifically, the rate of return on assets (ROA) can be multiplied by the **equity multiplier,** which is the ratio of assets to common equity:

$$\text{Equity multiplier} = \frac{\text{Total assets}}{\text{Common equity}}$$

$$= \frac{\$2,000}{\$896} = 2.23.$$

Note that firms which use a large amount of debt financing (more leverage) will necessarily have a high equity multiplier—the more the debt, the less the equity, hence the higher the equity multiplier. For example, if a firm has $100 of assets and is financed with $80, or 80 percent debt then its equity will be $20, and its equity multiplier will be $100/$20 = 5. Had it used only $20 of debt, then its equity would have been $80, and its equity multiplier would have been only $100/$80 = 1.25.[10]

---

[10]Expressed algebraically,

$$\text{Debt ratio} = \frac{D}{A} = \frac{A-E}{A} = \frac{A}{A} - \frac{E}{A} = 1 - \frac{1}{\text{Equity multiplier}}.$$

Here D is debt, E is equity, A is total assets, and A/E is the equity multiplier. This equation ignores preferred stock.

The firm's return on equity (ROE) depends on its ROA and its use of leverage:[11]

$$ROE = ROA \times \text{Equity multiplier}$$

$$= \frac{\text{Net income}}{\text{Total assets}} \times \frac{\text{Total assets}}{\text{Common equity}} \qquad \text{(3-2)}$$

$$= 5.7\% \times \$2,000/\$896$$

$$= 5.7\% \times 2.23$$

$$= 12.7\%.$$

Now we can combine Equations 3-1 and 3-2 to form the *Extended Du Pont equation,* which shows how the profit margin, the assets turnover ratio, and the equity multiplier combine to determine the ROE:

$$ROE = (\text{Profit margin}) (\text{Total assets turnover}) (\text{Equity multiplier})$$

$$= \frac{\text{Net income}}{\text{Sales}} \times \frac{\text{Sales}}{\text{Total assets}} \times \frac{\text{Total assets}}{\text{Common equity}}. \qquad \text{(3-3)}$$

For MicroDrive, we have

$$ROE = (3.8\%) (1.5) (2.23)$$

$$= 12.7\%.$$

The 12.7 percent rate of return could, of course, be calculated directly: both Sales and Total assets cancel, leaving Net income/Common equity = \$113.5/\$896 = 12.7%. However, the Du Pont equation shows how the profit margin, the total assets turnover, and the use of debt interact to determine the return on equity.[12]

MicroDrive's management can use the Du Pont system to analyze ways of improving performance. Focusing on the left, or "profit margin," side of its modified Du Pont chart, MicroDrive's marketing people can study the effects of raising sales prices (or lowering them to increase volume), of moving into new products or markets with higher margins, and so on. The company's cost accountants can study various expense items and, working with engineers, purchasing agents, and other operating personnel, seek ways to hold down costs. On the "turnover" side, MicroDrive's financial analysts, working with both production and marketing people, can investigate ways to reduce the investment in various types of assets. At the same time, the treasury staff can analyze the effects of alternative financing strategies, seeking to hold down interest expense and the risk of debt while still using leverage to increase the rate of return on equity.

As a result of such an analysis, Ellen Jackson, MicroDrive's president, recently announced a series of moves designed to cut operating costs by more than 20 percent per year. Jackson also announced that the company intends to concentrate its capital in

---

[11]Note that we could also find the ROE by "grossing up" the ROA, that is, by dividing the ROA by the common equity fraction: ROE = ROA/Equity fraction = 5.7%/0.448 = 12.7%. The two procedures are algebraically equivalent.

[12]Another ratio that is frequently used is the following:

$$\text{Rate of return on investors' capital} = \frac{\text{Net income} + \text{Interest}}{\text{Debt} + \text{Equity}}.$$

The numerator shows the dollar returns to investors, the denominator shows the total amount of money investors have put up, and the ratio itself shows the rate of return on all investors' capital. This ratio is especially important for public utilities, where regulators are concerned about the companies' using their monopoly positions to earn excessive returns on investors' capital. In fact, regulators try to set utility prices (service rates) at levels that will cause the return on investors' capital to equal a company's cost of capital as defined in Chapter 10.

markets where profit margins are reasonably high, and that if competition increases in certain of its product markets, MicroDrive will withdraw from those markets. Micro-Drive is seeking a high return on equity, and Jackson recognizes that if competition drives profit margins too low in a particular market, it will be impossible to earn high returns on the capital invested to serve that market. Therefore, if it is to achieve a high ROE, MicroDrive may have to develop new products and shift capital into new areas. The company's future depends on this type of analysis, and the Du Pont system can help it achieve success.

Jackson herself and MicroDrive's other executives have a strong incentive for improving the company's financial performance, because their compensation is based to a large extent on how well the company does. MicroDrive's executives receive a salary which is sufficient to cover their living costs, but their compensation package also includes "performance shares" which will be awarded if and only if the company meets or exceeds target levels for earnings and the stock price. These target levels are based on MicroDrive's performance relative to other high-tech companies. So, if Micro-Drive does well, then Jackson and the other executives—and the stockholders—will also do well. But if things deteriorate, Jackson could be looking for a new job.

SELF-TEST QUESTIONS	
	Explain how the extended Du Pont equation and chart can be used to reveal the basic determinants of ROE.
	What is the equity multiplier?
	How can management use the Du Pont system to analyze ways of improving the firm's performance?

COMPARATIVE RATIOS AND "BENCHMARKING"

Ratio analysis involves comparisons, because a company's ratios are compared with those of other firms in the same industry, that is, with industry average figures. How-ever, like most firms, MicroDrive's managers go one step further—they also compare their ratios with those of a smaller set of leading computer companies. This technique is called **benchmarking,** and the companies used for the comparison are called *bench-mark companies*. For example, MicroDrive benchmarks against Apex Systems, Cablenet, Carter Controls, BMR Corporation, Magnetic Sciences, and Luxor Corpora-tion. MicroDrive's management considers these to be the best-managed companies with operations similar to its own. Here is the comparison of MicroDrive's ROE versus those of the benchmark firms:

	ROE
Cablenet	28%
Carter	26
BMR	22
Magnetic Sciences	19
Luxor	16
MicroDrive	**13**
Apex	9

Similar comparisons are made for the other key ratios, and this procedure allows man-agement to see, on a company-by-company basis, how it stacks up against its major competitors.

ROE IS SOARING TO RECORD HEIGHTS

Historically, the average ROE for U.S. corporations has ranged from 10 percent to 13 percent. However, during the last few years ROEs have risen sharply, and in early 1996 the average for the *Fortune* 500 was about 15 percent. Even more incredible, the average ROE for the 30 companies in the Dow Jones Industrial Average was a startling 20.5 percent.

What explains these high ROEs? To answer this question, *Fortune*'s writers used the Du Pont equation to analyze the companies. They noted that ROE can rise for one of three reasons: higher profit margins, greater efficiency in the use of assets (as measured by the total assets turnover ratio), or increased leverage (as measured by the equity multiplier). According to *Fortune,* each of

these factors contributed to the increase in ROE. Write-offs associated with corporate restructurings, along with stock buy-back programs, reduced common equity and thereby increased the equity multiplier. At the same time, asset turnover increased as firms became more efficient in their use of assets. For example, as we will discuss more fully in Chapter 21, many companies adopted just-in-time inventory systems, which reduced the amount of inventory needed to support a given level of sales. This increased inventory turnover and thus total assets turnover.

However, the most important reason for the rise in ROE was a truly dramatic increase in profit margins. Profit margins were relatively constant from 1960 through 1989, but during the 1990s, sales increased at a much faster rate than costs, causing

profit margins to soar. Indeed, widening margins explain over half of the recent increase in ROEs.

Are ROEs likely to remain at their current high levels? Probably not, according to *Fortune*. Much of the recent increase in margins can be attributed to aggressive cost-cutting, but as firms continue to cut costs and improve efficiencies, there is less room for improvement. Also, part of the increase in ROE occurred because the economy was relatively strong for a number of years. Once the economy turns down, the average ROE will probably decline as well. Finally, high rates of return will attract new capital and rising capacity, which will lead to price-cutting. So eventually rates of return should fall to a level more consistent with "normal" profits.

Many companies also benchmark various parts of their overall operation against top companies, whether they are in the same industry or not. For example, MicroDrive has a division that sells hard drives directly to consumers through catalogs and the Internet. This division's shipping department benchmarks against L.L. Bean, even though they are in different industries, because L.L. Bean's shipping department is one of the best. MicroDrive wants its own shippers to strive to match L.L. Bean's record for on-time shipments.

Comparative ratios are available from a number of sources. One useful set is compiled by Dun & Bradstreet (D&B), which provides various ratios for a large number of industries; nine of these ratios are shown for a small sample of industries in Table 3-3. Useful ratios can also be found in the *Annual Statement Studies* published by Robert Morris Associates, which is the national association of bank loan officers. The U.S. Commerce Department's *Quarterly Financial Report,* which is found in most libraries, gives a set of ratios for manufacturing firms by industry group and size of firm. Trade associations and individual firms' credit departments also compile industry average financial ratios. Finally, financial statement data for thousands of publicly owned corporations are available on magnetic tapes and CDs, and since brokerage houses, banks, and other financial institutions have access to these data, security analysts can and do generate comparative ratios tailored to their specific needs.

Each of the data-supplying organizations uses a somewhat different set of ratios designed for its own purposes. For example, D&B deals mainly with small firms, many of which are proprietorships, and it sells its services primarily to banks and other lenders. Therefore, D&B is concerned largely with the creditor's viewpoint, and its ratios emphasize current assets and liabilities, not market value ratios. So, when you select a comparative data source, you should be sure that your emphasis is similar to that of the

| TABLE 3-3 | Dun & Bradstreet Ratios for Selected Industries: Upper Quartile, Median, and Lower Quartile[a] |

SIC CODES, LINE OF BUSINESS, AND NUMBER OF CONCERNS REPORTING	QUICK RATIO	CURRENT RATIO	TOTAL LIABILITIES TO NET WORTH	DAYS SALES OUTSTANDING	NET SALES TO INVENTORY	TOTAL ASSETS TO NET SALES	RETURN ON NET SALES	RETURN ON TOTAL ASSETS	RETURN ON NET WORTH
	×	×	%	DAYS	×	%	%	%	%
2879	2.3	4.7	24.2	22.7	8.8	58.8	4.2	6.4	8.1
Agricultural chemicals	1.1	2.0	67.7	54.4	6.2	75.8	2.0	2.6	3.9
(45)	0.6	1.1	159.1	78.6	3.4	108.9	−1.5	−1.5	−2.6
3724	1.8	3.3	42.5	47.8	11.6	49.3	7.3	13.2	25.5
Aircraft parts, including	1.1	2.0	90.4	61.0	6.2	75.9	2.8	3.7	10.4
engines (62)	0.7	1.5	260.1	70.5	4.0	96.8	0.2	−0.1	0.2
2051	1.8	2.9	33.8	19.7	53.7	25.5	5.4	15.1	45.4
Bakery products	1.0	1.6	99.7	24.1	35.6	33.4	2.9	7.4	16.5
(116)	0.6	0.9	184.9	30.3	20.4	49.0	0.8	2.8	3.4
2086	1.7	3.3	27.5	22.3	25.1	33.9	5.6	12.4	24.8
Beverages	0.9	1.6	61.2	29.2	17.6	47.8	2.5	5.2	14.1
(91)	0.5	1.1	145.0	42.7	12.6	65.0	0.2	0.8	4.9
3312	1.7	2.6	52.5	34.0	19.1	32.6	7.6	15.5	47.3
Blast furnaces and steel	1.0	1.8	135.8	43.4	8.5	57.0	4.7	8.4	21.0
mills (244)	0.7	1.3	318.0	57.0	6.2	86.8	1.8	2.8	8.3
2731	2.3	4.9	23.6	36.3	9.6	43.2	11.5	17.6	35.2
Book publishing	1.2	2.3	83.9	59.5	4.9	65.2	5.1	5.9	16.1
(317)	0.7	1.5	188.9	92.2	2.8	103.1	1.1	1.4	4.0

[a]The median and quartile ratios can be illustrated by an example. The median quick ratio for agricultural chemical manufacturers, as shown in this table, is 1.1. To obtain this figure, the ratios of current assets less inventories to current debt for each of the 45 concerns were arranged in a graduated series, with the largest ratio at the top and the smallest at the bottom. The median ratio of 1.1 is the ratio halfway between the top and the bottom. The ratio of 2.3, representing the upper quartile, is one-quarter of the way down from the top (or halfway between the top and the median). The ratio 0.6, representing the lower quartile, is one-quarter of the way up from the bottom (or halfway between the median and the bottom). SIC codes are "Standard Industrial Classification" codes used by the U.S. government to classify companies.

SOURCE: Industry Norms and Key Business Ratios, 1995–96 Edition, Dun & Bradstreet Credit Services.

agency whose ratios you plan to use. Additionally, there are often definitional differences in the ratios presented by different sources, so before using a source, be sure to verify the exact definitions of the ratios to ensure consistency with your own work.

SELF-TEST QUESTIONS

Differentiate between trend analysis and comparative ratio analysis.

Why is it useful to conduct comparative ratio analysis?

What is benchmarking, and how does it differ from comparative ratio analysis?

USES AND LIMITATIONS OF RATIO ANALYSIS

As noted earlier, ratio analysis is used by three main groups: (1) *managers,* who employ ratios to help analyze, control, and thus improve their firms' operations; (2) *credit analysts,* such as bank loan officers or bond rating analysts, who analyze ratios to help ascertain a company's ability to pay its debts; and (3) *stock analysts,* who are interested in a company's efficiency, risk, and growth prospects. In later chapters we will look more closely at the basic factors which underlie each ratio, and at that point you will understand better how to interpret and use ratios. Note, though, that while ratio analysis can provide useful information concerning a company's operations and financial condition, it does have limitations that necessitate care and judgment. Some potential problems are listed below:

1. Many large firms operate different divisions in different industries, and for such companies it is difficult to develop a meaningful set of industry averages for comparative purposes. Therefore, ratio analysis is more useful for small, narrowly focused firms than for large, multidivisional ones.

2. Most firms want to be better than average, so merely attaining average performance is not necessarily good. As a target for high-level performance, it is best to focus on the industry leaders' ratios. Benchmarking helps in this regard.

3. Inflation may distort firms' balance sheets, causing reported values to be substantially different from "true" values. Further, since inflation affects both depreciation charges and inventory costs, profits are also affected. Thus, a ratio analysis for one firm over time, or a comparative analysis of firms of different ages, must be interpreted with judgment.

4. Seasonal factors can also distort a ratio analysis. For example, the inventory turnover ratio for a food processor will be radically different if the balance sheet figure used for inventory is the one just before versus just after the close of the canning season. This problem can be minimized by using monthly averages for inventory (and receivables) when calculating turnover ratios.

5. Firms sometimes employ **"window dressing" techniques** to make their financial statements look stronger. To illustrate, a Chicago builder borrowed on a two-year basis on December 29, 1998, held the proceeds of the loan as cash for a few days, and then paid off the loan ahead of time on January 2, 1999. This improved his current and quick ratios, and made his year-end 1998 balance sheet look good. However, the improvement was strictly window dressing, because a few days later the balance sheet was back at the old level.

6. Different accounting practices can distort comparisons. As noted earlier, inventory valuation and depreciation methods can affect financial statements and thus distort comparisons among firms. Also, if one firm leases a substantial amount of its productive equipment, then its assets may appear low relative to sales because leased assets often do not appear on the balance sheet. At the same time, the liability associated with the lease obligation may not be shown as a debt. Therefore, leasing can artificially improve both the turnover and the debt ratios. However, the accounting profession has taken steps to reduce this problem.

7. It is difficult to generalize about whether a particular ratio is "good" or "bad." For example, a high current ratio may indicate a strong liquidity position, which is good, or excessive cash, which is bad (because excess cash in the bank is a non-earning asset). Similarly, a high fixed assets turnover ratio may denote either a firm that uses its assets efficiently or one that is undercapitalized and cannot afford to buy enough assets.

8. A firm may have some ratios that look "good" and others that look "bad," making it difficult to tell whether the company is, on balance, strong or weak. However, statistical procedures can be used to analyze the *net effects* of a set of ratios. Many banks and other lending organizations use discriminant analysis, a statistical technique, to analyze potential borrowers' financial ratios, and on the basis of this analysis, classify companies according to their probability of getting into financial trouble. See the Extensions section to Chapter 25 for a description of discriminant analysis and its application to bankruptcy prediction.

Ratio analysis is useful, but analysts should be aware of these problems and make adjustments as necessary. Ratio analysis conducted in a mechanical, unthinking manner is dangerous, but used intelligently and with good judgment, it can provide useful insights into a firm's operations. Your judgment in interpreting a set of ratios is bound to be weak at this point, but it will improve as you go through the remainder of the book.

SELF-TEST QUESTIONS

List three types of ratios users. Would these different types of users emphasize the same or different types of ratios?

List several potential problems with ratio analysis.

LOOKING BEYOND THE NUMBERS

Hopefully, working through this chapter has given you a better understanding of how to analyze financial statements and interpret accounting numbers. These are important skills when making business decisions, when evaluating performance, and when forecasting likely future developments.

While it is important to understand and interpret financial statements, sound financial analysis involves more than just calculating and interpreting numbers. Good analysts recognize that certain qualitative factors must also be considered. These factors, as summarized by the American Association of Individual Investors (AAII), are as follows:

1. *Are the company's revenues tied to one key customer?* If so, the company's performance may dramatically decline if the customer goes elsewhere. On the other hand, if the relationship is firmly entrenched, this might actually stabilize sales.

2. *To what extent are the company's revenues tied to one key product?* Companies that rely on a single product may be more efficient and more focused, but a lack of diversification increases risk. If revenues come from several different products, the overall bottom line will be less affected by a drop in the demand for any one product.

3. *To what extent does the company rely on a single supplier?* Depending on a single supplier may lead to unanticipated shortages, which is something that investors and potential creditors need to assess.

4. *What percentage of the company's business is generated overseas?* Companies with a large percentage of overseas business are often able to realize higher growth and larger profit margins. However, firms with overseas operations find that earnings from these operations are strongly affected by changes in the value of the local currency. Thus, fluctuations in currency markets create additional risks for firms with large overseas operations.

5. *Competition.* Generally, increased competition lowers prices and profit margins. In forecasting future performance, it is important to assess both the likely actions of the current competition and the likelihood of new competitors in the future.

FINANCIAL ANALYSIS
IN THE SMALL FIRM

Financial ratio analysis is especially useful for small businesses, and readily available sources provide comparative data by size of firm. For example, Robert Morris Associates provides comparative ratios for a number of small-firm classes, down to a size range of zero to $250,000 in annual sales. Nevertheless, analyzing a small firm's statements presents some unique problems. We examine here some of those problems from the standpoint of a bank loan officer, one of the most frequent users of ratio analysis.

When evaluating a small-business loan applicant, a banker is essentially making a prediction about the company's ability to repay its debt. In making this prediction, the banker will be especially concerned about indicators of liquidity and about continuing prospects for profitability. Bankers like to do business with a new customer if it appears that loans can be paid off on time and that the company will remain in business and therefore continue to be a customer for some years to come. Thus, both short-run and long-run viability are of interest to the banker. Note too that the banker's perceptions about the business are important to the owner-manager, because the bank will probably be the firm's primary source of funds.

The first problem the banker is likely to encounter is that, unlike the bank's bigger customers, the small firm may not have audited financial statements. Further, the statements that are available may have been produced on an irregular basis (for example, in some months or quarters but not in others). If the firm is young, it may have historical financial statements for only one year, or perhaps none at all. Also, the financial statements may not have been produced by a reputable accounting firm but by the owner's brother-in-law.

The poor quality of its financial data may therefore be a hinderance for a small business that is attempting to establish a banking relationship. This could keep the firm from getting credit even though it is really on solid financial ground. Therefore, it is in the owner's interest to make sure that the firm's financial data are credible, even if it is more expensive to do so. Furthermore, if the banker is uncomfortable with the data, the firm's management should also be uncomfortable: Because many managerial decisions depend on the numbers in the firm's accounting statements, those numbers should be as accurate as possible.

For a given set of financial ratios, a small firm may be riskier than a larger one. Small firms often produce a single product, rely heavily on a single customer, or both. For example, several years ago a company called Yard Man Inc. manufactured and sold lawn equipment. Most of Yard Man's sales were to Sears, so most of its revenues and profits were due to its Sears account. When Sears decided to drop Yard Man as a supplier, the company was left without its most important customer. Yard Man is no longer in business. Because large firms typically have a broad customer base, they are not as exposed to the sudden loss of a large portion of their business.

A similar danger applies to a single-product company. Just as the loss of a key customer can be disastrous for a small business, so can a shift in the tides of consumer interest in a particular fad. For example, Coleco manufactured and sold the extremely popular Cabbage Patch dolls. The phenomenal popularity of the dolls was a great boon for Coleco. However, the public is fickle — one can never predict when such a fad will die out, leaving the company with a great deal of capacity to make a product that no one will buy, and with a large amount of overvalued inventory. Exactly that situation hit Coleco, and it was forced into bankruptcy.

Extending credit to a small company, especially to a small owner-managed company, often involves yet another risk that is less of a problem for larger firms — dependence on a single key individual whose unexpected death could cause the company to fail. Similarly, if the company is family owned and managed, there is typically one key decision maker, even though several other family members may be involved in helping to manage the company.

In the case of a family business, the loss of the top person may not wipe out the company, but it often creates the equally serious problem of who will assume the leadership role. The loss of a key family member is often a highly emotional event, and it is not at all unusual for it to be followed by an ugly and protracted struggle for control of the business. It is in the family's interest, and certainly in the creditors' interests, to see that a plan of management succession is clearly specified before trouble arises. If no good succession plan is in place, often the firm will be forced to carry "key person insurance," payable to the bank and used to retire the loan in the event of the key person's death.

In summary, to determine the creditworthiness of a small firm, the financial analyst must "look beyond the ratios" and analyze the viability of the firm's products, customers, management, and market. Still, ratio analysis is the first step in a sound credit analysis.

6. *Future prospects.* Does the company invest heavily in research and development? If so, its future prospects may depend critically on the success of new products in the pipeline. For example, the market's assessment of a computer company depends on what next year's products look like. Likewise, investors in pharmaceutical companies are interested in knowing whether the company has developed any "breakthrough" drugs that may be marketable in the years ahead.

7. *Legal and regulatory environment.* Changes in laws and regulations have important implications for many industries. For example, when forecasting the future of tobacco companies, it is crucial that an analyst factor in the effects of proposed regulations and pending or likely lawsuits. Likewise, when assessing banks, telecommunications firms, and electric utilities, analysts need to forecast both the way in which these industries will be regulated in the years ahead and the ability of individual firms to respond to changes in regulation.

<table>
<tr><td>S E L F - T E S T
Q U E S T I O N</td><td>What are some qualitative factors analysts should consider when evaluating a company's likely future financial performance?</td></tr>
</table>

SUMMARY

The primary purpose of this chapter was to discuss techniques used by investors and managers to analyze financial statements. The key concepts covered are listed below.

- **Financial statement analysis** generally begins with the calculation of a set of **financial ratios** designed to reveal the relative strengths and weaknesses of a company as compared with other companies in the same industry, and to show whether its financial position has been improving or deteriorating over time.

- **Liquidity ratios** show the relationship of a firm's current assets to its current liabilities, and thus its ability to meet maturing debts.

- Two commonly used liquidity ratios are the **current ratio** and the **quick,** or **acid test, ratio.**

- **Asset management ratios** measure how effectively a firm is managing its assets.

- Asset management ratios include **inventory turnover, days sales outstanding, fixed assets turnover, total assets turnover,** and **operating capital requirements.**

- **Debt management ratios** reveal (1) the extent to which the firm is financed with debt and (2) its likelihood of defaulting on its debt obligations.

- Debt management ratios include the **debt ratio, times-interest-earned ratio,** and **fixed charge coverage ratio.**

- **Profitability ratios** show the combined effects of liquidity, asset management, and debt management on operating results.

- Profitability ratios include the **operating profit margin after taxes,** the **profit margin on sales,** the **basic earning power ratio,** the **return on total assets,** and the **return on common equity.**

- **Market value ratios** relate the firm's stock price to its earnings and book value per share, and they give management an indication of what investors think of the company's past performance and future prospects.

- The key market value ratios are the **price/earnings ratio** and the **market/book ratio.**

- **Trend analysis,** where one plots a ratio over time, is important, because it reveals whether the firm's ratios are improving or deteriorating over time.

- The **Du Pont system** is designed to show how the profit margin on sales, the assets turnover ratio, and the use of debt interact to determine the rate of return on equity. Management can use the Du Pont system to analyze ways of improving the firm's performance.

- **Benchmarking** is the process of comparing a particular company with a group of exceptionally well-managed companies.

- In analyzing a small firm's financial position, ratio analysis is a useful starting point. However, the analyst must also (1) examine the quality of the financial data, (2) ensure that the firm is sufficiently diversified to withstand shifts in customers' buying habits, and (3) determine whether the firm has a plan for the succession of its management.

Ratio analysis has limitations, but used with care and judgment, it can be very helpful.

Questions

3-1   Define each of the following terms:
a. Liquidity ratios: current ratio; quick, or acid test, ratio
b. Asset management ratios: inventory turnover ratio; days sales outstanding (DSO); fixed assets turnover ratio; total assets turnover ratio; operating capital requirement ratio
c. Financial leverage: debt ratio; times-interest-earned (TIE) ratio; fixed charge coverage ratio
d. Profitability ratios: operating profit margin after taxes; profit margin on sales; basic earning power (BEP) ratio; return on total assets (ROA); return on common equity (ROE)
e. Market value ratios: price/earnings (P/E) ratio; market/book (M/B) ratio; book value per share
f. Trend analysis; comparative ratio analysis; benchmarking
g. Du Pont chart; Du Pont equation
h. "Window dressing"; seasonal effects on ratios

3-2   Financial ratio analysis is conducted by four groups of analysts: managers, equity investors, long-term creditors, and short-term creditors. What is the primary emphasis of each of these groups in evaluating ratios?

3-3   Why would the inventory turnover ratio be more important when analyzing a grocery chain than an insurance company?

3-4   Over the past year, M. D. Ryngaert & Co. has realized an increase in its current ratio and a drop in its total assets turnover ratio. However, the company's sales, quick ratio, and fixed assets turnover ratio have remained constant. What explains these changes?

3-5   Profit margins and turnover ratios vary from one industry to another. What differences would you expect to find between a grocery chain such as Safeway and a steel company? Think particularly about the turnover ratios, the profit margin, and the Du Pont equation.

3-6   How does inflation distort ratio analysis comparisons, both for one company over time (trend analysis) and when different companies are compared? Are only balance sheet items or both balance sheet and income statement items affected?

3-7   If a firm's ROE is low and management wants to improve it, explain how using more debt might help.

3-8   How might (a) seasonal factors and (b) different growth rates distort a comparative ratio analysis? Give some examples. How might these problems be alleviated?

3-9   Why is it sometimes misleading to compare a company's financial ratios with other firms which operate in the same industry?

3-10 Indicate the effects of the transactions listed in the following table on total current assets, current ratio, and net income. Use (+) to indicate an increase, (−) to indicate a decrease, and (0) to indicate either no effect or an indeterminate effect. Be prepared to state any necessary assumptions, and assume an initial current ratio of more than 1.0. (Note: A good accounting background is necessary to answer some of these questions; if yours is not strong, just answer the questions you can handle.)

		TOTAL CURRENT ASSETS	CURRENT RATIO	EFFECT ON NET INCOME
a.	Cash is acquired through issuance of additional common stock.	____	____	____
b.	Merchandise is sold for cash.	____	____	____
c.	Federal income tax due for the previous year is paid.	____	____	____
d.	A fixed asset is sold for less than book value.	____	____	____
e.	A fixed asset is sold for more than book value.	____	____	____
f.	Merchandise is sold on credit.	____	____	____
g.	Payment is made to trade creditors for previous purchases.	____	____	____
h.	A cash dividend is declared and paid.	____	____	____
i.	Cash is obtained through short-term bank loans.	____	____	____
j.	Short-term notes receivable are sold at a discount.	____	____	____
k.	Marketable securities are sold below cost.	____	____	____
l.	Advances are made to employees.	____	____	____
m.	Current operating expenses are paid.	____	____	____
n.	Short-term promissory notes are issued to trade creditors in exchange for past due accounts payable.	____	____	____
o.	Ten-year notes are issued to pay off accounts payable.	____	____	____
p.	A fully depreciated asset is retired.	____	____	____
q.	Accounts receivable are collected.	____	____	____
r.	Equipment is purchased with short-term notes.	____	____	____
s.	Merchandise is purchased on credit.	____	____	____
t.	The estimated taxes payable are increased.	____	____	____

Self-Test Problems   (Solutions Appear in Appendix B)

ST-1
Debt Ratio

K. Billingsworth & Co. had earnings per share of $4 last year, and it paid a $2 dividend. Total retained earnings increased by $12 million during the year, while book value per share at year-end was $40. Billingsworth has no preferred stock, and no new common stock was issued during the year. If Billingsworth's year-end debt (which equals its total liabilities) was $120 million, what was the company's year-end debt/assets ratio?

ST-2
Ratio Analysis

The following data apply to A.L. Kaiser & Company (millions of dollars):

Cash and marketable securities	$100.00
Fixed assets	$283.50
Sales	$1,000.00
Net income	$50.00
Quick ratio	2.0×
Current ratio	3.0×
DSO	40 days
ROE	12%

Kaiser has no preferred stock—only common equity, current liabilities, and long-term debt.

a. Find Kaiser's (1) accounts receivable (A/R), (2) current liabilities, (3) current assets, (4) total assets, (5) ROA, (6) common equity, and (7) long-term debt.

b. In Part a, you should have found Kaiser's accounts receivable (A/R) = $111.1 million. If Kaiser could reduce its DSO from 40 days to 30 days while holding other things constant, how much cash would it generate? If this cash were used to buy back common stock (at book value), thus reducing the amount of common equity, how would this affect (1) the ROE, (2) the ROA, and (3) the total debt/total assets ratio?

Problems

3-1
Liquidity Ratios

Ace Industries has current assets equal to $3 million. The company's current ratio is 1.5, and its quick ratio is 1.0. What is the firm's level of current liabilities? What is the firm's level of inventories?

3-2
Days Sales Outstanding

Baker Brothers has a DSO of 40 days. The company's average daily sales are $20,000. What is the level of its accounts receivable? Assume there are 360 days in a year.

3-3
Debt Ratio

Bartley Barstools has an equity multiplier of 2.4. The company's assets are financed with some combination of long-term debt and common equity. What is the company's debt ratio?

3-4
Du Pont Analysis

Doublewide Dealers has an ROA of 10 percent, a 2 percent profit margin, and a return on equity equal to 15 percent. What is the company's total assets turnover? What is the firm's equity multiplier?

3-5
Ratio Calculations

Assume you are given the following relationships for the Brauer Corporation:

Sales/total assets	1.5×
Return on assets (ROA)	3%
Return on equity (ROE)	5%

Calculate Brauer's profit margin and debt ratio.

3-6
Liquidity Ratios

The Petry Company has $1,312,500 in current assets and $525,000 in current liabilities. Its initial inventory level is $375,000, and it will raise funds as additional notes payable and use them to increase inventory. How much can Petry's short-term debt (notes payable) increase without pushing its current ratio below 2.0? What will be the firm's quick ratio after Petry has raised the maximum amount of short-term funds?

3-7
Ratio Calculations

The Kretovich Company had a quick ratio of 1.4, a current ratio of 3.0, an inventory turnover of 6 times, total current assets of $810,000, and cash and marketable securities of $120,000. What were Kretovich's annual sales and its DSO?

3-8
Times-Interest-Earned Ratio

The H.R. Pickett Corporation has $500,000 of debt outstanding, and it pays an interest rate of 10 percent annually. Pickett's annual sales are $2 million, its average tax rate is 30 percent, and its net profit margin on sales is 5 percent. If the company does not maintain a TIE ratio of at least 5 times, its bank will refuse to renew the loan, and bankruptcy will result. What is Pickett's TIE ratio?

3-9
Return on Equity

Midwest Packaging's ROE last year was only 3 percent, but its management has developed a new operating plan designed to improve things. The new plan calls for a total debt ratio of 60 percent, which will result in interest charges of $300,000 per year. Management projects an EBIT of $1,000,000 on sales of $10,000,000, and it expects to have a total assets turnover ratio of 2.0. Under these conditions, the tax rate will be 34 percent. If the changes are made, what return on equity will the company earn?

3-10
Return on Equity

Central City Construction Company, which is just being formed, needs $1 million of assets, and it expects to have a basic earning power ratio of 20 percent. Central City will own no securities, so all of its income will be operating income. If it chooses to, Central City can finance up to 50 percent of its assets with debt, which will have an 8 percent interest rate. Assuming a 40 percent federal-plus-state tax rate on all taxable income, what is the *difference* between its expected ROE if Central City finances with 50 percent debt versus its expected ROE if it finances entirely with common stock?

3-11
Conceptual: Return on Equity

Which of the following statements is most correct? (Hint: Work Problem 3-10 before answering 3-11, and consider the solution setup for 3-10 as you think about 3-11.)

a. If a firm's expected basic earning power (BEP) is constant for all of its assets and exceeds the interest rate on its debt, then adding assets and financing them with debt will raise the firm's expected rate of return on common equity (ROE).

b. The higher its tax rate, the lower a firm's BEP ratio will be, other things held constant.

c. The higher the interest rate on its debt, the lower a firm's BEP ratio will be, other things held constant.

d. The higher its debt ratio, the lower a firm's BEP ratio will be, other things held constant.

e. Statement a is false, but b, c, and d are all true.

3-12
Return on Equity

Lloyd and Daughters Inc. has sales of $200,000, a net income of $15,000, and the following balance sheet:

Cash	$ 10,000	Accounts payable	$ 30,000
Receivables	50,000	Other current liabilities	20,000
Inventories	150,000	Long-term debt	50,000
Net fixed assets	90,000	Common equity	200,000
Total assets	$300,000	Total liabilities and equity	$300,000

a. The company's new owner thinks that inventories are excessive and can be lowered to the point where the current ratio is equal to the industry average, 2.5×, without affecting either sales or net income. If inventories are sold off and not replaced so as to reduce the current ratio to 2.5×, if the funds generated are used to reduce common equity (stock can be repurchased at book value), and if no other changes occur, by how much will the ROE change?

b. Now suppose we wanted to take this problem and modify it for use on an exam, that is, to create a new problem which you have not seen to test your knowledge of this type of problem. How would your answer change if (1) We doubled all the dollar amounts? (2) We stated that the target current ratio was 3×? (3) We stated that the target was to achieve an inventory turnover ratio of 2× rather than a current ratio of 2.5×? (Hint: Compare the ROE obtained with an inventory turnover ratio of 2× to the original ROE obtained before any changes are considered.) (4) We said that the company had 10,000 shares of stock outstanding, and we asked how much the change in Part a would increase EPS? (5) What would your answer to (4) be if we changed the original problem to state that the stock was selling for twice book value, so common equity would not be reduced on a dollar-for-dollar basis?

c. Now explain how we could have set the problem up to have you focus on changing accounts receivable, or fixed assets, or using the funds generated to retire debt (we would give you the interest rate on outstanding debt), or how the original problem could have stated that the company needed *more* inventories and it would finance them with new common equity or with new debt.

3-13
Ratio Analysis

Data for Barry Computer Company and its industry averages follow.

a. Calculate the indicated ratios for Barry.

b. Construct the extended Du Pont equation for both Barry and the industry.

c. Outline Barry's strengths and weaknesses as revealed by your analysis.

d. Suppose Barry had doubled its sales as well as its inventories, accounts receivable, and common equity during 1998. How would that information affect the validity of your ratio analysis? (Hint: Think about averages and the effects of rapid growth on ratios if averages are not used. No calculations are needed.)

BARRY COMPUTER COMPANY: BALANCE SHEET AS OF DECEMBER 31, 1998 (IN THOUSANDS)

Cash	$ 77,500	Accounts payable	$129,000
Receivables	336,000	Notes payable	84,000
Inventories	241,500	Other current liabilities	117,000
Total current assets	$655,000	Total current liabilities	$330,000
Net fixed assets	292,500	Long-term debt	256,500
		Common equity	361,000
Total assets	$947,500	Total liabilities and equity	$947,500

BARRY COMPUTER COMPANY: INCOME STATEMENT FOR YEAR ENDED DECEMBER 31, 1998 (IN THOUSANDS)

Sales		$1,607,500
Cost of goods sold		
Materials	$717,000	
Labor	453,000	
Heat, light, and power	68,000	
Indirect labor	113,000	
Depreciation	41,500	1,392,500
Gross profit		$ 215,000
Selling expenses		115,000
General and administrative expenses		30,000
Earnings before interest and taxes (EBIT)		$ 70,000
Interest expense		24,500
Earnings before taxes (EBT)		$ 45,500
Federal and state income taxes (40%)		18,200
Net income		$ 27,300

RATIO	BARRY	INDUSTRY AVERAGE
Current assets/current liabilities	_____	2.0×
Days sales outstanding	_____	35 days
Sales/inventory	_____	6.7×
Sales/fixed assets	_____	12.1×
Sales/total assets	_____	3.0×
Operating capital/sales	_____	24.0%
After-tax EBIT/sales	_____	1.7%
Net income/sales	_____	1.2%
Net income/total assets	_____	3.6%
Net income/common equity	_____	9.0%
Total debt/total assets	_____	60.0%

3-14
Balance Sheet Analysis

Complete the balance sheet and sales information in the table that follows for Hoffmeister Industries using the following financial data:

Debt ratio: 50%
Quick ratio: 0.80×
Total assets turnover: 1.5×
Days sales outstanding: 36 days
Gross profit margin on sales: (Sales − Cost of goods sold)/Sales = 25%
Inventory turnover ratio: 5×

BALANCE SHEET

Cash	___	Accounts payable	___
Accounts receivable	___	Long-term debt	60,000
Inventories	___	Common stock	___
Fixed assets	___	Retained earnings	97,500
Total assets	$300,000	Total liabilities and equity	___
Sales	___	Cost of goods sold	___

3-15
Du Pont Analysis

The Ferri Furniture Company, a manufacturer and wholesaler of high-quality home furnishings, has been experiencing low profitability in recent years. As a result, the board of directors has replaced the president of the firm with a new president, Helen Adams, who has asked you to make an analysis of the firm's financial position using the Du Pont chart. The most recent industry average ratios, and Ferri's financial statements, are as follows:

INDUSTRY AVERAGE RATIOS

Current ratio	2×	Sales/fixed assets	6×
Debt/total assets	30%	Sales/total assets	3×
Times-interest-earned	7×	Profit margin on sales	3%
Sales/inventory	10×	Return on total assets	9%
Days sales outstanding	24 days	Return on common equity	12.9%

FERRI FURNITURE COMPANY: BALANCE SHEET AS OF DECEMBER 31, 1998 (MILLIONS OF DOLLARS)

Cash	$ 45	Accounts payable	$ 45
Marketable securities	33	Notes payable	45
Net receivables	66	Other current liabilities	21
Inventories	159	Total current liabilities	$111
Total current assets	$303	Long-term debt	24
		Total liabilities	$135
Gross fixed assets	225		
Less depreciation	78	Common stock	114
Net fixed assets	$147	Retained earnings	201
		Total stockholders' equity	$315
Total assets	$450	Total liabilities and equity	$450

FERRI FURNITURE COMPANY: INCOME STATEMENT FOR YEAR ENDED DECEMBER 31, 1998 (MILLIONS OF DOLLARS)

Net sales	$795.0
Cost of goods sold	660.0
Gross profit	$135.0
Selling expenses	73.5
Depreciation expense	12.0
Earnings before interest and taxes	$ 49.5
Interest expense	4.5
Earnings before taxes (EBT)	45.0
Taxes (40%)	18.0
Net income	$ 27.0

a. Calculate those ratios that you think would be useful in this analysis.
b. Construct an extended Du Pont equation for Ferri, and compare the company's ratios to the industry average ratios.
c. Do the balance sheet accounts or the income statement figures seem to be primarily responsible for the low profits?
d. Which specific accounts seem to be most out of line in relation to other firms in the industry?
e. If Ferri had a pronounced seasonal sales pattern, or if it grew rapidly during the year, how might that affect the validity of your ratio analysis? How might you correct for such potential problems?

3-16

Ratio Analysis

The Corrigan Corporation's forecasted 1999 financial statements follow, along with some industry average ratios.
a. Calculate Corrigan's 1999 forecasted ratios, compare them with the industry average data, and comment briefly on Corrigan's projected strengths and weaknesses.
b. What do you think would happen to Corrigan's ratios if the company initiated cost-cutting measures that allowed it to hold lower levels of inventory and substantially decreased the cost of goods sold? No calculations are necessary. Think about which ratios would be affected by changes in these two accounts.

CORRIGAN CORPORATION: FORECASTED BALANCE SHEET AS OF DECEMBER 31, 1999

Cash	$ 72,000
Accounts receivable	439,000
Inventories	894,000
Total current assets	$1,405,000
Land and building	238,000
Machinery	132,000
Other fixed assets	61,000
Total assets	$1,836,000
Accounts and notes payable	$ 432,000
Accruals	170,000
Total current liabilities	$602,000
Long-term debt	404,290
Common stock	575,000
Retained earnings	254,710
Total liabilities and equity	$1,836,000

CORRIGAN CORPORATION: FORECASTED INCOME STATEMENT FOR 1999

Sales	$4,290,000
Cost of goods sold	3,580,000
Gross operating profit	$ 710,000
General administrative and selling expenses	236,320
Depreciation	159,000
Miscellaneous	134,000
Earnings before taxes (EBT)	$ 180,680
Taxes (40%)	72,272
Net income	$ 108,408

Per-Share Data

EPS	$4.71
Cash dividends	$0.95
P/E ratio	5×
Market price (average)	$23.57
Number of shares outstanding	23,000

INDUSTRY FINANCIAL RATIOS (1999)[a]

Quick ratio	1.0×
Current ratio	2.7×
Inventory turnover[b]	7.0×
Days sales outstanding	32 days
Fixed assets turnover[b]	13.0×
Total assets turnover[b]	2.6×
Return on assets	9.1%
Return on equity	18.2%
Debt ratio	50.0%
Profit margin on sales	3.5%
P/E ratio	6.0×

[a]Industry average ratios have been constant for the past 4 years.
[b]Based on year-end balance sheet figures.

Spreadsheet Problem

Work the problem in this section only if you are using the computer problem diskette.

3-17
Ratio Analysis

Use the model in the File C3 to solve this problem.

a. Refer back to Problem 3-16. Suppose Corrigan Corporation is considering installing a new computer system which would provide tighter control of inventories, accounts receivable, and accounts payable. If the new system is installed, the following data are projected (rather than the data given in Problem 3-16) for the indicated balance sheet and income statement accounts:

Accounts receivable	$ 395,000
Inventories	700,000
Other fixed assets	150,000
Accounts and notes payable	275,000
Accruals	120,000
Cost of goods sold	3,450,000
Administrative and selling expenses	248,775
P/E ratio	6×

How do these changes affect the projected ratios and the comparison with the industry averages? (Note that any changes to the income statement will change the amount of retained earnings; therefore, the model is set up to calculate 1999 retained earnings as 1998 retained earnings plus net income minus dividends paid. The model also adjusts the cash balance so that the balance sheet balances.)

b. If the new computer were even more efficient than Corrigan's management had estimated, and thus caused the cost of goods sold to decrease by $125,000 from the projections in Part a, what effect would that have on the company's financial position?

c. If the new computer were less efficient than Corrigan's management had estimated, and caused the cost of goods sold to increase by $125,000 from the projections in Part a, what effect would that have on the company's financial position?

d. Change, one by one, the other items in Part a to see how each change affects the ratio analysis. Then think about, and write a paragraph describing, how computer models like this one can be used to help make better decisions about the purchase of such things as a new computer system.

MINI CASE

The first part of the case, presented in Chapter 2, discussed the situation that Computron Industries was in after an expansion program. Thus far, sales have not been up to the forecasted level, costs have been higher than were projected, and a large loss occurred in 1998, rather than the expected profit. As a result, its managers, directors, and investors are concerned about the firm's survival.

Donna Jamison was brought in as assistant to Fred Campo, Computron's chairman, who had the task of getting the company back into a sound financial position. Computron's 1997 and 1998 balance sheets and income statements, together with projections for 1999, are shown in the following tables. Also, the tables show the 1997 and 1998 financial ratios, along with industry average data. The 1999 projected financial statement data represent Jamison's and Campo's best guess for 1999 results, assuming that some new financing is arranged to get the company "over the hump."

	1999E	1998	1997
BALANCE SHEETS			
Assets			
Cash	$ 14,000	$ 7,282	$ 9,000
Short-term investments	71,632	0	48,600
Accounts receivable	878,000	632,160	351,200
Inventories	1,716,480	1,287,360	715,200
Total current assets	$2,680,112	$1,926,802	$1,124,000
Gross fixed assets	1,197,160	1,202,950	491,000
Less accumulated depreciation	380,120	263,160	146,200
Net fixed assets	$ 817,040	$ 939,790	$ 344,800
Total assets	$3,497,152	$2,866,592	$1,468,800
Liabilities and Equity			
Accounts payable	$ 436,800	$ 524,160	$ 145,600
Notes payable	600,000	720,000	200,000
Accruals	408,000	489,600	136,000
Total current liabilities	$1,444,800	$1,733,760	$ 481,600
Long-term debt	500,000	1,000,000	323,432
Common stock	1,680,936	460,000	460,000
Retained earnings	(128,584)	(327,168)	203,768
Total equity	$1,552,352	$ 132,832	$ 663,768
Total liabilities and equity	$3,497,152	$2,866,592	$1,468,800

NOTE: "E" indicates estimated. The 1999 data are forecasts.

	1999E	1998	1997
INCOME STATEMENTS			
Sales	$7,035,600	$5,834,400	$3,432,000
Cost of goods sold	5,728,000	5,728,000	2,864,000
Other expenses	680,000	680,000	340,000
Depreciation	116,960	116,960	18,900
Total operating costs	$6,524,960	$6,524,960	$3,222,900
EBIT	$ 510,640	($ 690,560)	$ 209,100
Interest expense	88,000	176,000	62,500
EBT	$ 422,640	($ 866,560)	$ 146,600
Taxes (40%)	169,056	(346,624)	58,640
Net income	$ 253,584	($ 519,936)	$ 87,960
EPS	$1.014	($5.199)	$0.880
DPS	$0.220	$0.110	$0.220
Book value per share	$6.209	$1.328	$6.638
Stock price	$12.17	$2.25	$8.50
Shares outstanding	250,000	100,000	100,000
Tax rate	40.00%	40.00%	40.00%
Lease payments	40,000	40,000	40,000
Sinking fund payments	0	0	0

NOTE: "E" indicates estimated. The 1999 data are forecasts.

	1999E	1998	1997	INDUSTRY AVERAGE
RATIO ANALYSIS				
Current		1.1×	2.3×	2.7×
Quick		0.4×	0.8×	1.0×
Inventory turnover		4.5×	4.8×	6.1×
Days sales outstanding (DSO)		39.0	36.8	32.0
Fixed assets turnover		6.2×	10.0×	7.0×
Total assets turnover		2.0×	2.3×	2.6×
Operating capital requirement		31.8%	33.2%	29.5%
Debt ratio		95.4%	54.8%	50.0%
TIE		−3.9×	3.3×	6.2×
Fixed charge coverage		−3.0×	2.4×	5.1×
Operating profit margin after taxes		−7.1%	3.7%	4.3%
Profit margin		−8.9%	2.6%	3.5%
Basic earning power		−24.1%	14.2%	19.1%
ROA		−18.1%	6.0%	9.1%
ROE		−391.4%	13.3%	18.2%
Price/earnings		−0.4×	9.7×	14.2×
Market/book		1.7×	1.3×	2.4×
Book value per share		$1.33	$6.64	n.a.

NOTE: "E" indicates estimated. The 1999 data are forecasts.

Jamison examined monthly data for 1998 (not given in the case), and she detected an improving pattern during the year. Monthly sales were rising, costs were falling, and large losses in the early months had turned to a small profit by December. Thus, the annual data looked somewhat worse than final monthly data. Also, it appears to be taking longer for the advertising program to get the message across, for the new sales offices to generate sales, and for the new manufacturing facilities to operate efficiently. In other words, the lags between spending money and deriving benefits were longer than Computron's managers had anticipated. For these reasons, Jamison and Campo see hope for the company—provided it can survive in the short run.

Jamison must prepare an analysis of where the company is now, what it must do to regain its financial health, and what actions should be taken. Your assignment is to help her answer the following questions. Provide clear explanations, not yes or no answers.

a. Why are ratios useful? What are the five major categories of ratios?
b. Calculate the 1999 current and quick ratios based on the projected balance sheet and income statement data. What can you say about the company's liquidity position in 1997, 1998, and as projected for 1999? We often think of ratios as being useful (1) to managers to help run the business, (2) to bankers for credit analysis, and (3) to stockholders for stock valuation. Would these different types of analysts have an equal interest in the liquidity ratios?
c. Calculate the 1999 inventory turnover, days sales outstanding (DSO), fixed assets turnover, operating capital requirement, and total assets turnover. How does Computron's utilization of assets stack up against other firms in its industry?
d. Calculate the 1999 debt, times-interest-earned, and fixed charge coverage ratios. How does Computron compare with the industry with respect to financial leverage? What can you conclude from these ratios?
e. Calculate the 1999 operating profit margin after taxes, profit margin, basic earning power (BEP), return on assets (ROA), and return on equity (ROE). What can you say about these ratios?
f. Calculate the 1999 price/earnings ratio and market/book ratio. Do these ratios indicate that investors are expected to have a high or low opinion of the company?
g. Use the extended Du Pont equation to provide a summary and overview of Computron's financial condition as projected for 1999. What are the firm's major strengths and weaknesses?
h. Use the following simplified 1999 balance sheet to show, in general terms, how an improvement in the DSO would tend to affect the stock price. For example, if the company could improve its collection procedures and thereby lower its DSO from 44.9 days to the 32-day industry average without affecting sales, how would that change "ripple through" the financial statements (shown in thousands below) and influence the stock price?

Accounts receivable	$ 878	Debt	$1,945
Other current assets	1,802		
Net fixed assets	817	Equity	1,552
Total assets	$3,497	Liabilities plus equity	$3,497

i. Does it appear that inventories could be adjusted, and, if so, how should that adjustment affect Computron's profitability and stock price?
j. In 1998, the company paid its suppliers much later than the due dates, and it was not maintaining financial ratios at levels called for in its bank loan agreements. Therefore, suppliers could cut the company off, and its bank could refuse to renew the loan when it comes due in 90 days. On the basis of data provided, would you, as a credit manager, continue to sell to Computron on credit? (You could demand cash on delivery, that is, sell on terms of COD, but that might cause Computron to stop buying from your company.) Similarly, if you were the bank loan officer, would you recommend renewing the loan or demand its repayment? Would your actions be influenced if, in early 1999, Computron showed you its 1999 projections plus proof that it was going to raise over $1.2 million of new equity capital?
k. In hindsight, what should Computron have done back in 1997?
l. What are some potential problems and limitations of financial ratio analysis?
m. What are some qualitative factors analysts should consider when evaluating a company's likely future financial performance?

Selected Additional References and Cases

The effects of alternative accounting policies on both financial statements and ratios based on these statements are discussed in the investment textbooks referenced in Chapter 5, and also in the many excellent texts on financial statement analysis. For example, see

Fraser, Lyn M., *Understanding Financial Statements* (Englewood Cliffs, N.J.: Prentice-Hall, 1992).

Gibson, Charles H., and Patricia A. Frishkoff, *Financial Statement Analysis* (Boston: Kent, 1986).

Hawkins, David F., *Corporate Financial Reporting and Analysis* (Homewood, Ill.: Irwin, 1986).

For further information on the relative usefulness of various financial ratios, see

Chen, Kung H., and Thomas A. Shimerda, "An Empirical Analysis of Useful Financial Ratios," *Financial Management*, Spring 1981, 51–60.

Considerable work has been done to establish the relationship between bond ratings and financial ratios. For one example, see

Belkaoui, Ahmed, *Industrial Bonds and the Rating Process* (London: Quorum Books, 1983).

For sources of ratios and common size statements, see the following:

Dun & Bradstreet, *Key Business Ratios* (New York: Updated annually).

Financial Research Associates, *Financial Studies of the Small Business* (Arlington, Va.: Updated annually).

Robert Morris Associates, *Annual Statement Studies* (Philadelphia: Updated annually).

The following cases from the Cases in Financial Management: Dryden Request *series focus on financial analysis:*

Case 35, "Mark X Company (A)," which illustrates the use of ratio analysis in the evaluation of a firm's existing and potential financial positions.

Case 36, "Garden State Container Corporation," which is similar in content to Case 35.

Case 36A, "Safe Packaging Corporation," which updates Case 36.

EXTENSIONS

Common Size Analysis and Percent Change Analysis

Common Size Analysis. In a *common size analysis,* all income statement items are divided by sales, and all balance sheet items are divided by total assets. Thus, a common size income statement shows each item as a percentage of sales, and a common size balance sheet shows each item as a percentage of total assets. The advantage of common size analysis is that it facilitates comparisons of balance sheets and income statements over time and across companies.

Table 3E-1 contains MicroDrive's 1997 and 1998 common size income statements, along with the composite statement for the industry. (Note: Rounding may cause addition/subtraction differences in Tables 3E-1 and 3E-2.) MicroDrive's operating costs are slightly above average, as are its interest expenses, but its taxes are relatively low because of its low EBIT. The net effect of all these forces is a relatively low profit margin.

Table 3E-2 shows MicroDrive's common size balance sheets, along with the industry average. Its accounts receivable are significantly higher than the industry average, its inventories are significantly higher, and it uses far more fixed charge capital (debt and preferred) than the average firm.

Percentage Change Analysis. A final technique used to help analyze a firm's financial statements is *percentage change analysis.* In this type of analysis, growth rates are calculated for all income statement items and balance sheet accounts. To illustrate, Table 3E-3 contains MicroDrive's income statement percentage change analysis for 1998. Sales increased at a 5.3 percent rate during 1998, while total operating costs increased at a slower 5.0 percent rate, leading to 7.9 percent growth in EBIT. The fact that sales increased faster than operating costs is positive, but this "good news" was offset by a 46.7 percent increase in interest expense. The significant growth in interest expense caused growth in both earnings before taxes and net income to be negative. Thus, the percentage change analysis points out that the decrease in reported income in 1998 resulted almost exclusively from an increase in interest expense. This conclusion could be reached by analyzing dollar amounts, but percentage change analysis simplifies the task. The same type of analysis applied to the balance sheets would show that assets grew at a 19.0 percent rate, largely because inventories grew at a whopping 48.2 percent rate. With only a 5.3 percent growth in sales, the extreme growth in inventories should be of great concern to MicroDrive's managers.

| TABLE 3E-1 | MicroDrive Inc.: Common Size Income Statements |

	1997	1998	1998 INDUSTRY COMPOSITE
Net sales	100.0%	100.0%	100.0%
Costs excluding depreciation	87.6	87.2	87.6
Depreciation	3.2	3.3	2.8
Total operating costs	90.8%	90.5%	90.4%
Earnings before interest and taxes (EBIT)	9.2%	9.5%	9.6%
Less interest	2.1	2.9	1.3
Earnings before taxes (EBT)	7.1%	6.5%	8.3%
Taxes (40%)	2.8	2.6	3.3
Net income before preferred dividends	4.3%	3.9%	5.0%
Preferred dividends	0.1	0.1	0.0
Net income available to common stockholders (profit margin)	4.1%	3.8%	5.0%

| TABLE 3E-2 | MicroDrive Inc.: Common Size Balance Sheets |

	1997	1998	1998 INDUSTRY COMPOSITE
Assets			
Cash and marketable securities	4.8%	0.5%	3.2%
Accounts receivable	18.8	18.8	17.8
Inventories	24.7	30.8	19.8
Total current assets	48.2%	50.0%	40.8%
Net plant and equipment	51.8	50.0	59.2
Total assets	100.0%	100.0%	100.0%
Liabilities and Equity			
Accounts payable	1.8%	3.0%	1.8%
Notes payable	3.6	5.5	4.4
Accruals	7.7	7.0	3.6
Total current liabilities	13.1%	15.5%	9.8%
Long-term bonds	34.5	37.7	30.2
Total debt	47.6%	53.2%	40.0%
Preferred equity	2.4	2.0	0.0
Common equity	50.0	44.8	60.0
Total liabilities and equity	100.0%	100.0%	100.0%

| TABLE 3E-3 | MicroDrive Inc.: Income Statement Percentage Change Analysis (Millions of Dollars, except for Per-Share Data) |

	1997	1998	PERCENT CHANGE
Net sales	$2,850	$3,000.0	5.3%
Costs excluding depreciation	$2,497	$2,616.2	4.8%
Depreciation	90	100.0	11.1
Total operating costs	$2,587	$2,716.2	5.0%
Earnings before interest and taxes (EBIT)	$ 263	$ 283.8	7.9%
Less interest	60	88.0	46.7
Earnings before taxes (EBT)	$ 203	$ 195.8	(3.5%)
Taxes (40%)	81	78.3	(3.3)
Net income before preferred dividends	$122	$ 117.5	(3.7%)
Preferred dividends	4	4.0	0
Net income available to common stockholders	$ 118	$ 113.5	(3.8%)
Common dividends	$53	$57.5	8.5%
Addition to retained earnings	$65	$56.0	(13.8%)
Per-share data:			
Common stock price	$24.00	$ 23.00	(4.2%)
Earnings per share (EPS)	$ 2.36	$ 2.27	(3.8%)
Dividends per share (DPS)	$ 1.06	$ 1.15	8.5%

The conclusions reached in common size and percentage change analyses generally parallel those derived from ratio analysis. However, occasionally a serious deficiency is highlighted by only one of the three analyticalses techniques. Also, it is often useful to have all three and to drive home to management, in slightly different ways, the need to take corrective actions. Thus, a thorough financial statement analysis will include ratio, percentage change, and common size analyses, as well as a Du Pont analysis.

The Financial Environment: Markets, Institutions, and Interest Rates

*F*inancial managers and investors do not operate in a vacuum—they make decisions within a complex financial environment. This environment includes financial markets and institutions, tax and regulatory policies, and the state of the economy, both in the United States and around the world. The environment both dictates the available financial alternatives and affects the outcomes of various decisions. Therefore, it is crucial that financial managers and investors have a good understanding of the environment in which they operate.

Good financial decisions require an understanding of the current and future direction of the economy, interest rates, and the stock market—but trying to figure out what is going to happen is no trivial matter. One tool analysts use to forecast the future direction of the economy and interest rates is the yield curve, a graph that shows the relationship between short-term and long-term interest rates. Studies indicate that if long-term rates are considerably higher than short-term rates, future inflation and interest rates are likely to increase. On the other hand, if long-term rates are lower than short-term rates, this suggests that an economic downturn is coming.

Management's assessment of future inflation has a profound effect on financing decisions. If management is convinced that inflation will not be a problem, it will probably rely on short-term funds to raise new capital. However, if inflation seems likely to accelerate, this suggests that interest rates will rise, so management will be inclined to "lock in" current rates by using long-term debt. For example, JCPenney recently issued $600 million of long-term debt in three parts: $200 million matured in 12 years and had a cost of 7.38 percent, $200 million had a 20-year maturity and cost 7.65 percent, and $200 million matured in 30 years and had a cost of 6.90 percent. The 30-year portion also gives investors an option to sell the bonds back to the company if interest rates rise, which explains the lower cost of these bonds.

In a press release, Penney indicated that it planned to use the $600 million to pay off some of its outstanding short-term debt. At the time of the Penney issue, its short-term debt had a cost of 5.5 percent. Why would it issue long-term debt at more than 7 percent to pay off short-term debt that cost only 5.5 percent? Clearly, Penney was afraid interest rates would rise in the future, which would drive up the cost of funds when it comes time to roll over, or replace, the short-term debt. By locking in long-term rates, the company protected itself against an increase in interest rates. Of course, if rates remain at current levels or decline, Penney's decision will turn out to be a mistake. We will find out in the years ahead if Penney made a good decision.

Financial managers need to understand the environment and markets within which businesses operate. Therefore, this chapter describes the markets where capital is raised, securities are traded, and stock prices are established, as well as the institutions which operate in these markets. In the process, we shall also explore the principal factors that determine the level of interest rates in the economy.

THE FINANCIAL MARKETS

The Federal Reserve's Board of Governors provides much data and information related to financial markets. See their home page at http://www.bog.frb.fed.us for links to financial data.

Businesses, individuals, and governments often need to raise capital. For example, suppose Carolina Power & Light (CP&L) forecasts an increase in the demand for electricity in North Carolina, and the company decides to build a new power plant. Because CP&L almost certainly will not have the $2 billion or so necessary to pay for the plant, the company will have to raise this capital in the financial markets. Or suppose Mr. Fong, the proprietor of a San Francisco hardware store, decides to expand into appliances. Where will he get the money to buy the initial inventory of TV sets, washers, and freezers? Similarly, if the Johnson family wants to buy a home that costs $100,000, but they have only $20,000 in savings, how can they raise the additional $80,000? If the city of New York wants to borrow $200 million to finance a new sewer plant, or the federal government needs money to pay off maturing bonds, they too need access to the capital markets.

On the other hand, some individuals and firms have incomes which are greater than their current expenditures, so they have funds available to invest. For example, Carol Hawk has an income of $36,000, but her expenses are only $30,000, and in 1998 Ford Motor Company had accumulated more than $19 billion of excess cash, which it needs to invest.

Types of Markets

People and organizations seeking to borrow money are brought together with those with surplus funds in the *financial markets*. Note that "markets" is plural—there are a great many different financial markets in a developed economy such as ours. Each market deals with a somewhat different type of instrument in terms of the instrument's maturity and the assets backing it. Also, different markets serve different types of customers, or operate in different parts of the country. Here are some of the major types of markets:

1. **Physical asset markets** (also called "tangible" or "real" asset markets) are those for such products as wheat, autos, real estate, computers, and machinery. **Financial asset markets,** on the other hand, deal with stocks, bonds, notes, mortgages, and other **financial instruments.** All of these instruments are simply pieces of paper with contractual provisions that entitle their owners to specific rights and claims on real assets. For example, a corporate bond issued by IBM entitles its owner to a specific claim on the cash flows produced by IBM's physical assets, and a share of IBM stock entitles its owner to a different set of claims on IBM's cash flows. Unlike these conventional financial instruments, the contractual provisions of **derivative security** are not direct claims on either real assets or their cash flows. Instead, derivatives are claims whose value depends on what happens to the value of some other asset. Futures and options are two important types of derivatives, and their values depend on what happens to the prices of other assets, say, IBM stock, Japanese yen, or pork bellies. Therefore, the value of a derivative security is *derived* from the value of an underlying real asset.

2. **Spot markets** and **futures markets** are terms that refer to whether the assets are being bought or sold for "on-the-spot" delivery (literally, within a few days) or for delivery at some future date, such as six months or a year into the future.

3. **Money markets** are the markets for short-term, highly liquid debt securities. The New York and London money markets have long been the world's largest, but Tokyo is rising rapidly. **Capital markets** are the markets for long-term debt and corporate stocks. The New York Stock Exchange, where the stocks of the largest U.S. corporations are traded, is a prime example of a capital market. There is no hard and fast rule on this, but when describing debt markets, "short term" generally means less than one year, "intermediate term" means one to five years, and "long term" means more than five years.

4. **Mortgage markets** deal with loans secured by residential, commercial, and industrial real estate, or farmland, while **consumer credit markets** involve loans on autos and appliances, as well as loans for education, vacations, and so on.

5. **World, national, regional,** and **local markets** also exist. Thus, depending on an organization's size and scope of operations, it may be able to borrow all around the world, or it may be confined to a strictly local, even neighborhood, market.

6. **Primary markets** are the markets in which corporations raise new capital. If Microsoft were to sell a new issue of common stock to raise capital, this would be a primary market transaction. The corporation selling the newly created stock receives the proceeds from the sale in a primary market transaction. **Secondary markets** are markets in which existing, already outstanding, securities are traded among investors. Thus, if Jane Doe decided to buy 1,000 shares of AT&T stock, the purchase would occur in the secondary market. The New York Stock Exchange is a secondary market, since it deals in outstanding, as opposed to newly issued, stocks and bonds. Secondary markets also exist for mortgages, various other types of loans, and other financial assets. The corporations whose securities are being traded are not involved in secondary market transactions and, thus, do not receive any funds from such a sale.

7. **Private markets,** where transactions are worked out directly between two parties, are differentiated from **public markets,** where standardized contracts are traded on organized exchanges. Bank loans and private placements of debt with insurance companies are examples of private market transactions. Since these transactions are private, they may be structured in any manner that appeals to the two parties. By contrast, securities that are issued in public markets (for example, common stock and corporate bonds) are ultimately held by a large number of individuals. Public securities must have fairly standardized contractual features, both to appeal to a broad range of investors and also because public investors cannot afford the time to study unique, nonstandardized contracts. Their diverse ownership and trading activity also ensures that public securities are relatively liquid. Private market securities are, therefore, more tailor-made but less liquid, whereas public market securities are more liquid but subject to greater standardization.

Other classifications could be made, but this breakdown is sufficient to show that there are many types of financial markets. Also, note that the distinctions among markets are often blurred and unimportant, except as a general point of reference. For example, it makes little difference if a firm borrows for 11, 12, or 13 months, hence, whether we have a "money" or "capital" market transaction. You should recognize the big differences among types of markets, but don't get hung up trying to distinguish them at the boundaries.

A healthy economy is dependent on efficient transfers of funds from people who are net savers to firms and individuals who need capital. Without efficient transfers, the economy simply could not function: Carolina Power & Light could not raise capital, so Raleigh's citizens would have no electricity; the Johnson family would not have adequate housing; Carol Hawk would have no place to invest her savings; and so on. Obviously, the level of employment and productivity, hence our standard of living, would be much lower. Therefore, it is absolutely essential that our financial markets function efficiently — not only quickly, but also at a low cost.[1]

Table 4-1 gives a listing of the most important instruments traded in the various financial markets. The instruments are arranged from top to bottom in ascending order of typical length of maturity. As we go through the book, we will look in much more detail at many of the instruments listed in Table 4-1. For example, we will see that there are many varieties of corporate bonds, ranging from "plain vanilla" bonds to bonds that are convertible into common stocks to bonds whose interest payments vary depending on the inflation rate. Still, the table gives an idea of the characteristics and costs of the instruments traded in the major financial markets.

Recent Trends

Financial markets have experienced tremendous change during the 1980s and 1990s. Technological advances in computers and telecommunications, along with the globalization of banking and commerce, have led to deregulation, and this has increased competition throughout the world. The result is a much more efficient, internationally linked market, but one that is far more complex than we had a few years ago. While these developments have been largely positive, they have also created problems for policy makers. At a recent conference, Federal Reserve Board Chairman Alan Greenspan stated that modern financial markets "expose national economies to shocks from new and unexpected sources, and with little if any lag." He went on to say that central banks must develop new ways to evaluate and limit risks to the financial system. Large amounts of capital move quickly around the world in response to changes in interest and exchange rates, and these movements can disrupt local institutions and economies. The Southeast Asia crisis of 1998 is a good example.

With globalization has come the need for greater cooperation among regulators at the international level, but the task is not easy. Factors that complicate coordination include (1) the differing structures of the various nations' banking and securities industries, (2) the trend in Europe toward financial service conglomerates, and (3) a reluctance on the part of individual countries to give up control over their national monetary policies. Still, regulators are unanimous about the need to close the gaps in the supervision of worldwide markets.

Another important trend in recent years has been the increased use of **derivatives.** A derivative is any security whose value is *derived* from the price of some other "underlying" asset. An option to buy IBM stock is a derivative, as is a contract to buy Japanese yen six months from now. The value of the IBM option depends on the price performance of IBM's stock, which depends on the expected future free cash flows of IBM's operations. The value of the Japanese yen "future" depends on the exchange rate between yen and dollars, which depends on economic activities in the two economies. The market for derivatives has grown faster than any other market in recent years, primarily because corporations use them to hedge various risks.

---

[1]As the countries of the former Soviet Union and other Eastern European nations move toward capitalism, just as much attention must be paid to the establishment of cost-efficient financial markets as to electrical power, transportation, communications, and other infrastructure systems. Economic efficiency is simply impossible without a good system for allocating capital within the economy.

			SECURITY CHARACTERISTICS		
INSTRUMENT (1)	**MARKET** (2)	**MAJOR PARTICIPANTS** (3)	**RISKINESS** (4)	**ORIGINAL MATURITY** (5)	**INTEREST RATE ON 9/19/97**[a] (6)
U.S. Treasury bills	Money	Sold by U.S. Treasury to finance federal expenditures	Default-free	91 days to 1 year	5.0%
Banker's acceptances	Money	A firm's promise to pay, guaranteed by a bank	Low degree of risk if guaranteed by a strong bank	Up to 180 days	5.5
Commercial paper	Money	Issued by financially secure firms to large investors	Low default risk	Up to 270 days	5.5
Negotiable certificates of deposit (CDs)	Money	Issued by major money-center commercial banks to large investors	Default risk depends on the strength of the issuing bank	Up to 1 year	5.6
Money market mutual funds	Money	Invest in Treasury bills, CDs, and commercial paper; held by individuals and businesses	Low degree of risk	No specific maturity (instant liquidity)	5.1
Eurodollar market time deposits	Money	Issued by banks outside U.S.	Default risk depends on the strength of the issuing bank	Up to 1 year	5.6
Consumer credit loans	Money	Issued by banks/credit unions/finance companies to individuals	Risk is variable	Variable	Variable
U.S. Treasury notes and bonds	Capital	Issued by U.S. government	No default risk, but price will decline if interest rates rise	2 to 30 years	6.5
Mortgages	Capital	Borrowings from commercial banks and S&Ls by individuals and businesses	Risk is variable	Up to 30 years	7.4
State and local government bonds	Capital	Issued by state and local governments to individuals and institutional investors	Riskier than U.S. government securities, but exempt from most taxes	Up to 30 years	5.4
Corporate bonds	Capital	Issued by corporations to individuals and institutional investors	Riskier than U.S. government securities, but less risky than preferred and common stocks; varying degree of risk depending on strength of issuer	Up to 40 years[b]	7.2
Leases	Capital	Similar to debt in that firms can lease assets rather than borrow and then buy the assets	Risk similar to corporate bonds	Generally 3 to 20 years	Similar to bond yields
Preferred stocks	Capital	Issued by corporations to individuals and institutional investors	Riskier than corporate bonds, but less risky than common stock	Unlimited	6 to 8
Common stocks[c]	Capital	Issued by corporations to individuals and institutional investors	Risky	Unlimited	10 to 15

[a]The yield reported on money market mutual funds is from *The Wall Street Journal*. Most other data are from the *Federal Reserve Statistical Release*. Money market rates assume a 3-month maturity. The corporate bond rate is for AAA-rated bonds.

[b]Just recently, a few corporations have issued 100-year bonds; however, the majority have issued bonds with maturities less than 40 years.

[c]Common stocks are expected to provide a "return" in the form of dividends and capital gains rather than interest. Of course, if you buy a stock, your *actual* return may be considerably higher or lower than your *expected* return.

Derivatives can be used either to reduce risks or as speculative investments, which increase risk. As an example of a risk-reducing usage, suppose an importer's net income tends to fall whenever the dollar falls relative to the yen, because that would increase the cost of imports from Japan. That company could reduce its risk by purchasing derivatives which increase in value whenever the dollar declines. This would be called a *hedging operation,* and its purpose would be to reduce risk exposure. Speculation, on the other hand, is done in the hope of high returns, but it raises risk exposure. For example, Procter & Gamble recently disclosed that it lost $150 million on derivative investments, and Orange County (California) went bankrupt as a result of speculation with derivatives.

How has the introduction of derivative products influenced the financial markets? The size and complexity of derivatives transactions concern regulators, academics, and members of Congress. Fed Chairman Greenspan noted that, in theory, derivatives should allow companies to manage risk better, but he stated that it is not clear whether recent innovations have "increased or decreased the inherent stability of the financial system." The use of derivatives will be discussed more fully in Chapter 24.

Another major trend involves stock ownership patterns. The number of individuals who have a stake in the stock market is increasing, but the percentage of corporate shares owned by individuals is decreasing. How can these two statements both be true? The answer has to do with institutional versus individual ownership of shares. More than 43 percent of all U.S. adults now have investments in the stock market, compared with only 22 percent in 1990. However, more than 60 percent of all stock now is owned by pension funds, mutual funds, and life insurance companies. Thus, more and more individuals are investing in the market, but they are doing so indirectly, through retirement plans and mutual funds. In any event, the performance of the stock market now has a greater impact on the U.S. population than ever before. Also, the direct ownership of stocks is being concentrated in institutions, with professional portfolio managers making the investment decisions and controlling the votes. Note too that if a fund holds a high percentage of a given corporation's shares, it would probably severely depress the stock's price if it tried to sell out. Thus, to some extent, the larger institutions are "locked into" many of the shares they own. This has led to a phenomenon called **relationship investing,** where portfolio managers think of themselves as large, active, long-term investors. Rather than being passive investors who "vote with their feet," they are taking a much more active role in trying to force managers to behave in a manner that is in the best interests of shareholders.

SELF-TEST QUESTIONS

Distinguish between physical asset markets and financial asset markets.

What is the difference between spot and futures markets?

Distinguish between money and capital markets.

What is the difference between primary and secondary markets?

Differentiate between private and public markets.

Why are financial markets essential for a healthy economy?

What are derivatives, and why are they used?

What is "relationship investing"?

FINANCIAL INSTITUTIONS

Transfers of capital between savers and those who need capital take place in the three different ways diagrammed in Figure 4-1:

FIGURE 4-1   Diagram of the Capital Formation Process

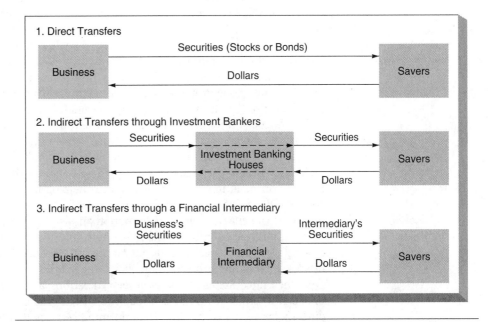

1. *Direct transfers* of money and securities, as shown in the top section, occur when a business sells its stocks or bonds directly to savers, without going through any type of financial institution. The business delivers its securities to savers, who in turn give the firm the money it needs.

2. As shown in the middle section, transfers may also go through an *investment banking house* such as Merrill Lynch, which serves as a middleman and facilitates the issuance of securities. The company sells its stocks or bonds to the investment bank, which, in turn, sells these same securities to savers. The businesses' securities and the savers' money merely "pass through" the investment banking house. However, the investment bank does buy and hold the securities for a period of time, so it is taking a risk—it may not be able to resell them to savers for as much as it paid. Because new securities are involved and the corporation receives the proceeds of the sale, this is a primary market transaction.

3. Transfers can also be made through a *financial intermediary* such as a bank or mutual fund. Here the intermediary obtains funds from savers and gives the savers in exchange its own securities. The intermediary then uses this money to purchase and then hold a business's securities. For example, a saver might give dollars to a bank, receiving from it a certificate of deposit, and then the bank might lend the money to a small business in the form of a mortgage loan. Thus, intermediaries literally create new forms of capital—in this case, certificates of deposit, which are both safer and more liquid than mortgages and thus are better securities for most savers to hold. The existence of intermediaries greatly increases the efficiency of our money and capital markets.

In our example, we assume that the entity needing capital is a business, and specifically a corporation, but it is easy to visualize the demander of capital as a home purchaser, a government unit, and so on.

Direct transfers of funds from savers to businesses are possible and do occur on occasion, but it is generally more efficient for a business to enlist the services of an **investment banking house.** Merrill Lynch, Salomon Smith Barney, Morgan Stanley, and Goldman Sachs are examples of financial service corporations which offer investment banking services. Such organizations (1) help corporations design securities with features that are currently attractive to investors, (2) buy these securities from the corporation, and (3) resell them to savers. Although the securities are sold twice, this process is really one primary market transaction, with the investment banker acting as a facilitator to help transfer capital from savers to businesses.

The **financial intermediaries** shown in the third section of Figure 4-1 do more than simply transfer money and securities between firms and savers—they literally create new financial products. Since the intermediaries are generally large, they gain economies of scale in analyzing the creditworthiness of potential borrowers, in processing and collecting loans, and in pooling risks and thus helping individual savers diversify, that is, "not put all their financial eggs in one basket." Further, a system of specialized intermediaries can enable savings to do more than just draw interest. For example, individuals can put money into banks and get both interest income and a convenient way of making payments (checking), or put money into life insurance companies and get both interest income and protection for their beneficiaries.

In the United States and other developed nations, a set of specialized, highly efficient financial intermediaries has evolved. The situation is changing rapidly, however, and different types of institutions are performing services that were formerly reserved for others, causing institutional distinctions to become blurred. Still, there is a degree of institutional identity, and here are the major classes of intermediaries:

1. *Commercial banks,* the traditional "department stores of finance," serve a wide variety of savers and borrowers. Historically, commercial banks were the major institutions which handled checking accounts and through which the Federal Reserve System expanded or contracted the money supply. Today, however, several other institutions also provide checking services and significantly influence the money supply. Conversely, commercial banks are providing an ever-widening range of services, including stock brokerage services and insurance.

    Note that commercial banks are quite different from investment banks. Commercial banks lend money, whereas investment banks help companies raise capital from other parties. Prior to 1933, commercial banks offered investment banking services, but the Glass-Steagall Act, which was passed in 1933, prohibited commercial banks from engaging in investment banking. Thus, the Morgan Bank was broken up into two separate organizations, one of which is now the Morgan Guaranty Trust Company, a commercial bank, while the other is Morgan Stanley Dean Witter, a major investment banking house. Note also that Japanese and European banks can offer both commercial and investment banking services. This hinders U.S. banks in global competition, so efforts are being made to get the Glass-Steagall Act repealed or modified.

2. *Savings and loan associations (S&Ls),* which have traditionally served individual savers and residential and commercial mortgage borrowers, take the funds of many small savers and then lend this money to home buyers and other types of borrowers. Because the savers obtain a degree of liquidity that would be absent if they made the mortgage loans directly, perhaps the most significant economic function of the S&Ls is to "create liquidity" which would otherwise be lacking. Also, the S&Ls have more expertise in analyzing credit, setting up loans, and making collections than individual savers, so they reduce the costs and increase the availability of

real estate loans. Finally, the S&Ls hold large, diversified portfolios of loans and other assets and thus spread risks in a manner that would be impossible if small savers were making mortgage loans directly. Because of these factors, savers benefit by being able to invest in more liquid, better managed, and less risky assets, whereas borrowers benefit by being able to obtain more capital, and at a lower cost, than would otherwise be possible.

In the 1980s, the S&L industry experienced severe problems when (a) short-term interest rates paid on savings accounts rose well above the returns being earned on the existing mortgages held by S&Ls and (b) commercial real estate suffered a severe slump, resulting in high mortgage default rates. Together, these events forced many S&Ls to either merge with stronger institutions or close their doors.

3. *Mutual savings banks,* which are similar to S&Ls, operate primarily in the northeastern states, accept savings primarily from individuals, and lend mainly on a long-term basis to home buyers and consumers.

4. *Credit unions* are cooperative associations whose members are supposed to have a common bond, such as being employees of the same firm. Members' savings are loaned only to other members, generally for auto purchases, home improvement loans, and home mortgages. Credit unions are often the cheapest source of funds available to individual borrowers.

5. *Life insurance companies* take savings in the form of premiums; invest these funds in stocks, bonds, real estate, and mortgages; and finally make payments to the beneficiaries of the insured parties. In recent years, life insurance companies have also offered a variety of tax-deferred savings plans designed to provide benefits to the participants when they retire.

6. *Mutual funds* are corporations which accept money from savers and then use these funds to buy stocks, long-term bonds, or short-term debt instruments issued by businesses or government units. These organizations pool funds and thus reduce risks by diversification. They also achieve economies of scale in analyzing securities, managing portfolios, and buying and selling securities. Different funds are designed to meet the objectives of different types of savers. Hence, there are bond funds for those who desire safety, stock funds for savers who are willing to accept significant risks in the hope of higher returns, and still other funds that are used as interest-bearing checking accounts (the **money market funds**). There are literally thousands of different mutual funds with dozens of different goals and purposes.

Mutual funds have grown more rapidly than any other institution in recent years, in large part because of a change in the way corporations provide for employees' retirement. Before the 1980s, most corporations said, in effect, "Come work for us, and when you retire, we will give you a retirement income based on the salary you were earning during the last five years before you retired." The company was then responsible for setting aside funds each year to make sure that it had the money available to pay the agreed-upon retirement benefits. That situation is changing rapidly. Today, new employees are likely to be told, "Come work for us, and we will give you some money each payday which you can invest for your future retirement. You can't get the money until you retire (without paying a huge tax penalty), but if you invest wisely, you can retire in comfort." Most employees know they don't know how to invest wisely, so they turn their retirement funds over to a mutual fund. Hence, mutual funds are growing rapidly. Excellent information on the objectives and past performance of the various funds are provided in publications such as *Value Line Investment Survey* and *Morningstar Mutual Funds,* which are available in most libraries.

7. *Pension funds* are retirement plans funded by corporations or government agencies for their workers and administered generally by the trust departments of commercial banks or by life insurance companies. Pension funds invest primarily in bonds, stocks, mortgages, and real estate.

Changes in the structure of pension plans over the last decade have had a profound impact on both individuals and financial markets. Historically, most large corporations and governmental units used *defined benefit* plans to provide for their employees' retirement. In a defined benefit plan, the employer guarantees the level of benefits the employee will receive when he or she retires, and it is the employer's responsibility to invest funds to ensure that it can meet its obligations when its employees retire. Under defined benefit plans, employees have little or no say about how the money in the pension plan is invested—this decision is made by the corporate employer. Note that employers, not employees, bear the risk that investments held by the plan will not perform well.

In recent years many companies (including virtually all new companies, especially those in the rapidly growing high-tech sector) have begun to use *defined contribution* plans, under which employers make specified, or defined, payments into the plan. Then, when the employee retires, his or her pension benefits are determined by the amount of assets in the plan. Therefore, in a defined contribution plan the employee bears the risks inherent in investments, and the employee has the responsibility for making investment decisions.

The most common type of defined contribution plan is the *401(k)* plan, named after the section in the federal act which established the legal basis for the plan. Governmental units, including universities, can use *403(b)* plans, which operate essentially like 401(k) plans. In all of these plans, employees must choose from among a set of investment alternatives. Typically, the employer agrees to make some "defined contribution" to the plan, and the employee can also make a supplemental payment. Then, the employer contracts with an insurance company plus one or more mutual fund companies, and then employees must choose among investments ranging from "guaranteed investment contracts" to government bond funds to domestic corporate bond and stock funds to international stock and bond funds. Under most plans, the employees can, within certain limits, shift their investments from category to category. Thus, if someone thinks the stock market is currently overvalued, he or she can tell the mutual fund to move the money from a stock fund to a money market fund. Similarly, employees can gradually shift from 100 percent stock to a mix of stocks and bonds as they grow older.

This change in the structure of pension plans has had two extremely important effects. First, individuals must now make the primary investment decisions for their pension plans. Since such decisions can mean the difference between a comfortable retirement and living on the street, it is important that those covered by defined contribution plans understand the fundamentals of investing. Second, whereas defined benefit plan managers typically invest in individual stocks and bonds, most individuals invest 401(k) money through mutual funds. Since 401(k) defined contribution plans are growing rapidly, the result is rapid growth in the mutual fund industry. This, in turn, has implications for the security markets, and for businesses that need to attract capital.

Financial institutions have historically been heavily regulated, with the primary purpose of this regulation being to ensure the safety of the institutions and thus to protect investors. However, these regulations—which have taken the form of prohibitions on nationwide branch banking, restrictions on the types of assets the institutions can buy, ceilings on the interest rates they can pay, and limitations on the types of services they can provide—have tended to impede the free flow of capital and thus have hurt the efficiency of our capital markets. Recognizing this fact, Congress has authorized some major changes, and more are on the horizon.

The result of the ongoing regulatory changes has been a blurring of the distinctions between the different types of institutions. Indeed, the trend in the United States today is toward huge **financial service corporations,** which own banks, S&Ls, investment banking houses, insurance companies, pension plan operations, and mutual funds, and which have branches across the country and even around the world. Examples of financial service corporations, most of which started in one area but have now diversified to cover most of the financial spectrum, include Transamerica, Merrill Lynch, American Express, Citicorp, Fidelity, and BankAmerica.

<table>
<tr><td>SELF-TEST
QUESTIONS</td><td>Identify three different ways capital is transferred between savers and borrowers.

What is the difference between a commercial bank and an investment bank?

Distinguish between investment banking houses and financial intermediaries.

List the major types of intermediaries and briefly describe the function of each.</td></tr>
</table>

THE STOCK MARKET

As noted earlier, secondary markets are those in which outstanding, previously issued securities are traded. By far the most active secondary market, and the most important one to financial managers, is the *stock market*. Here the prices of firms' stocks are established. Since the primary goal of financial management is to maximize the firm's stock price, a knowledge of the stock market is important to anyone involved in managing a business.

The Stock Exchanges

There are two basic types of stock markets: (1) *organized exchanges,* which include the New York Stock Exchange (NYSE), the American Stock Exchange (AMEX), and several regional exchanges, and (2) the less formal *over-the-counter market*. Since the organized exchanges have actual physical market locations and are easier to describe and understand, we consider them first.

The **organized security exchanges** are tangible physical entities. Each of the larger ones occupies its own building, has a limited number of members, and has an elected governing body—its board of governors. Members are said to have "seats" on the exchange, although everybody stands up. These seats, which are bought and sold, give the holder the right to trade on the exchange. There are more than 1,300 seats on the New York Stock Exchange, and recently NYSE seats were selling for about $1.5 million.

Most of the larger investment banking houses operate *brokerage departments,* and they own seats on the exchanges and designate one or more of their officers as members. The exchanges are open on all normal working days, with the members meeting in a large room equipped with telephones and other electronic equipment that enable each member to communicate with his or her firm's offices throughout the country.

Like other markets, security exchanges facilitate communication between buyers and sellers. For example, Merrill Lynch (the largest brokerage firm) might receive an order in its Atlanta office from a customer who wants to buy 100 shares of AT&T stock. Simultaneously, Salomon's Denver office might receive an order from a customer wishing to sell 100 shares of AT&T. Each broker communicates by wire with the firm's representative on the NYSE. Other brokers throughout the country are also communicating with their own exchange members. The exchange members with *sell orders* offer the shares for sale, and they are bid for by the members with *buy orders*. Thus, the exchanges operate as *auction markets*.[2]

The Over-the-Counter Market

In contrast to the organized security exchanges, the **over-the-counter market** is a nebulous, intangible organization. An explanation of the term "over-the-counter" will help clarify exactly what this market is. As noted above, the exchanges operate as auction markets—buy and sell orders come in more or less simultaneously, and exchange members match these orders. If a stock is traded less frequently, perhaps because it is the stock of a new or a small firm, few buy and sell orders come in, and matching them within a reasonable length of time would be difficult. To avoid this problem, some brokerage firms maintain an inventory of such stocks—they buy when individual investors want to sell and sell when investors want to buy. At one time, the inventory of securities was kept in a safe, and the stocks, when bought and sold, were literally passed over the counter.

Today, the over-the-counter market is defined to include all facilities that are needed to conduct security transactions not conducted on the organized exchanges. These facilities consist of (1) the relatively few *dealers* who hold inventories of over-the-counter securities and who are said to "make a market" in these securities; (2) the thousands of brokers who act as *agents* in bringing the dealers together with investors; and (3) the computers, terminals, and electronic networks that provide a communications link between dealers and brokers. The dealers who make a market in a particular stock continuously quote a price at which they are willing to buy the stock (the *bid price*) and a price at which they will sell shares (the *asked price*). Each dealer's prices, which are adjusted as supply and demand conditions change, can be read off computer screens all across the country. The *spread* between bid and asked prices represents the dealer's markup, or profit.

---

[2]The NYSE is actually a modified auction market, wherein people (through their brokers) bid for stocks. Originally—about 200 years ago—brokers would literally shout, "I have 100 shares of Erie for sale; how much am I offered?" and then sell to the highest bidder. If a broker had a buy order, he or she would shout, "I want to buy 100 shares of Erie; who'll sell at the best price?" The same general situation still exists, although the exchanges now have members known as *specialists* who facilitate the trading process by keeping an inventory of shares of the stocks in which they specialize. If a buy order comes in at a time when no sell order arrives, the specialist will sell off some inventory. Similarly, if a sell order comes in, the specialist will buy and add to inventory. The specialist sets a *bid price* (the price the specialist will pay for the stock) and an *asked price* (the price at which shares will be sold out of inventory). The bid and asked prices are set at levels designed to keep the inventory in balance. If many buy orders start coming in because of favorable developments or sell orders come in because of unfavorable events, the specialist will raise or lower prices to keep supply and demand in balance. Bid prices are lower than asked prices, with the difference, or *spread,* representing the specialist's profit margin.

Special facilities are available to help institutional investors such as mutual funds or pension funds sell large blocks of stock without depressing their prices. In essence, brokerage houses which cater to institutional clients will purchase blocks (defined as 10,000 or more shares) and then resell the stock to other institutions or individuals. Also, when a firm has a major announcement which is likely to cause its stock price to change sharply, it will ask the exchanges to halt trading in its stock until the announcement has been made and digested by investors. Thus, when Texaco announced that it planned to acquire Getty Oil, trading was halted for one day in both Texaco and Getty stocks.

**AN EXPENSIVE BEER
FOR THE NASD**

A few summers ago, two professors met for a beer at an academic conference. During their conversation, the professors, William Christie of Vanderbilt University and Paul Schultz of Ohio State University, decided it would be interesting to see how prices are set for NASDAQ stocks. The results of their study were startling to many, and they produced a real firestorm in the investment community.

When looking through data on the bid/asked spreads set by NASDAQ market makers, Christie and Schultz found that the market makers routinely avoided posting quotes which had "odd-eighth fractions," that is, $\frac{1}{8}$, $\frac{3}{8}$, $\frac{5}{8}$, and $\frac{7}{8}$. For example, if a market maker were to use odd-eighth quotes,

he might offer to buy a stock for $10\frac{1}{2}$ a share or sell it for $10\frac{5}{8}$, thus providing a "spread," or profit, of $\frac{1}{8}$ point ($10\frac{5}{8} - 10\frac{1}{2} = \frac{1}{8}$). The spread between the two prices is the market maker's compensation for providing a market and taking the risk associated with holding an inventory of a given stock. Note that if he or she avoided odd-eighths fractions, then the sell price would be $10\frac{3}{4}$ (which is $10\frac{6}{8}$), so the spread would be $10\frac{6}{8} - 10\frac{1}{2} = \frac{1}{4}$, or twice as high as if he or she made an odd-eighths quote.

What amazed Christie and Schultz was the fact that this practice was so widespread—even for widely followed stocks such as Apple Computer and Lotus Development. The professors concluded that the evidence strongly suggested that there was tacit collusion among NASDAQ

dealers designed to keep spreads artificially high.

The National Association of Securities Dealers (NASD) originally denied the accusations, and then tried to provide a justification for the practice.

The publicity surrounding the study led the Securities and Exchange Commission (SEC) to investigate. Without admitting guilt, the NASD recently settled with the SEC, and, as part of the agreement, the dealers agreed to spend $100 million during the next five years to improve their enforcement practices—which explains why the professors' beers turned out to be so expensive for the NASD!

SOURCE: William Christie, "An Expensive Beer for the N.A.S.D.," *The New York Times,* August 25, 1996, Sec. 3, 12.

Brokers and dealers who make up the over-the-counter market are members of a self-regulating body known as the *National Association of Securities Dealers (NASD),* which licenses brokers and oversees trading practices. The computerized trading network used by NASD is known as the NASD Automated Quotation System (NASDAQ), and *The Wall Street Journal* and other newspapers provide information on NASDAQ transactions.

In terms of numbers of issues, the majority of stocks are traded over the counter, and trading volume is greater on NASDAQ stocks than on the NYSE. However, because the stocks of most large companies are listed on the exchanges, about half of the dollar volume of stock trading takes place on the exchanges. In recent years, many large companies—including Microsoft, Intel, MCI, and Apple—have elected to remain NASDAQ stocks, so the over-the-counter market is growing faster than the exchanges.

Some Trends in Security Trading Procedures

From the NYSE's inception in 1792 until the 1970s, the vast majority of all stock trading occurred on the Exchange and was conducted by member firms. The NYSE established a set of minimum brokerage commission rates, and no member firm could charge a commission lower than the set rate. This was a monopoly, pure and simple. However, on May 1, 1975, the Securities and Exchange Commission (SEC), with strong prodding from the Antitrust Division of the Justice Department, forced the NYSE to abandon its fixed commissions. Commission rates declined dramatically, falling in some cases as much as 95 percent from former levels.

These changes were a boon to the investing public, but not to the brokerage industry. Several "full-service" brokerage houses went bankrupt, and others were forced to merge with stronger firms. The number of brokerage houses has declined from literally thousands in the 1960s to a much smaller number of large, strong, nationwide companies, many of which are units of diversified financial service corporations. Deregulation has also spawned a number of "discount brokers," some of which are affiliated with commercial banks or mutual fund investment companies.[3]

There has also been a rise in "third market" activities, where large financial institutions trade both listed and unlisted stocks among themselves on a 24-hour basis. Buyers and sellers in this market are located all around the globe — New York, San Francisco, Tokyo, Singapore, Zurich, and London — and this makes the 24-hour trading day a necessity. The exchanges have resisted extending their trading hours because it would inconvenience members, but competition will eventually force all major exchanges to operate around the clock. Today, institutional investors, and even some individuals, can trade by computer at any time, day or night.

SELF-TEST QUESTIONS | What are the two basic types of stock markets, and how do they differ?
How has deregulation changed security trading procedures?

THE COST OF MONEY

Capital in a free economy is allocated through the price system. *The interest rate is the price paid to borrow debt capital. With equity capital, investors expect to receive dividends and capital gains, and these are the components whose sum is the cost of equity money.* The factors which affect the supply of and the demand for investment capital, hence the cost of money, are discussed in this section.

The four most fundamental factors affecting the cost of money are (1) **production opportunities**, (2) **time preferences for consumption**, (3) **risk**, and (4) **inflation**. To see how these factors operate, visualize an isolated island community where the people live on fish. They have a stock of fishing gear which permits them to survive reasonably well, but they would like to have more fish. Now suppose Mr. Crusoe had a bright idea for a new type of fishnet that would enable him to double his daily catch. However, it would take him a year to perfect his design, to build his net, and to learn how to use it efficiently, and Mr. Crusoe would probably starve before he could put his new net into operation. Therefore, he might suggest to Ms. Robinson, Mr. Friday, and several others that if they would give him one fish each day for a year, he would return two fish a day during all of the next year. If someone accepted the offer, then the fish which Ms. Robinson or one of the others gave to Mr. Crusoe would constitute *savings;* these savings would be *invested* in the fishnet; and the extra fish the net produced would constitute a *return on the investment.*

Obviously, the more productive Mr. Crusoe thought the new fishnet would be, the more he could afford to offer potential investors for their savings. In this example, we assume that Mr. Crusoe thought he would be able to pay, and thus he offered, a 100 percent rate of return — he offered to give back two fish for every one he received. He might have tried to attract savings for less — for example, he might have decided to offer only 1.5 fish next year for every one he received this year, which would represent a 50 percent rate of return to Ms. Robinson and the other potential savers.

How attractive Mr. Crusoe's offer appeared to a potential saver would depend in large part on the saver's *time preference for consumption.* For example, Ms. Robinson

---

[3]Full-service brokers give investors information on different stocks and make recommendations as to which stocks to buy. Discount brokers do not give advice — they merely execute orders. Some brokerage houses (institutional houses) cater primarily to institutional investors such as pension funds and insurance companies, while others cater to individual investors and are called "retail houses." Large firms such as Merrill Lynch generally have both retail and institutional brokerage operations.

might be thinking of retirement, and she might be willing to trade fish today for fish in the future on a one-for-one basis. On the other hand, Mr. Friday might have a wife and several young children and need his current fish, so he might be unwilling to "lend" a fish today for anything less than three fish next year. Mr. Friday would be said to have a high time preference for current consumption and Ms. Robinson a low time preference. Note also that if the entire population were living right at the subsistence level, time preferences for current consumption would necessarily be high, aggregate savings would be low, interest rates would be high, and capital formation would be difficult.

The *risk* inherent in the fishnet project, and thus in Mr. Crusoe's ability to repay the loan, would also affect the return investors would require: the higher the perceived risk, the higher the required rate of return. Also, in a more complex society there are many businesses like Mr. Crusoe's, many goods other than fish, and many savers like Ms. Robinson and Mr. Friday. Therefore, people use money as a medium of exchange rather than barter with fish. When money is used, its value in the future, which is affected by *inflation*, comes into play: the higher the expected rate of inflation, the larger the required return. We discuss this point in detail later in the chapter.

Thus, we see that the interest rate paid to savers depends in a basic way (1) on the rate of return producers expect to earn on invested capital, (2) on savers' time preferences for current versus future consumption, (3) on the riskiness of the loan, and (4) on the expected future rate of inflation. Producers' expected returns on their business investments set an upper limit on how much they can pay for savings, while consumers' time preferences for consumption establish how much consumption they are willing to defer, hence how much they will save at different rates of interest offered by producers.[4] Higher risk and higher inflation also lead to higher interest rates.

SELF-TEST
QUESTIONS

What is the price paid to borrow money called?

What is the "price" of equity capital?

What four fundamental factors affect the cost of money?

INTEREST RATE LEVELS

Capital is allocated among borrowers by interest rates: Firms with the most profitable investment opportunities are willing and able to pay the most for capital, so they tend to attract it away from inefficient firms or from those whose products are not in demand. Of course, our economy is not completely free in the sense of being influenced only by market forces. For example, the federal government has agencies which help designated individuals or groups obtain credit on favorable terms. Among those eligible for this kind of assistance are small businesses, certain minorities, and firms willing to build plants in areas with high unemployment. Still, most capital in the U.S. economy is allocated through the price system.

Figure 4-2 shows how supply and demand interact to determine interest rates in two capital markets. Markets A and B represent two of the many capital markets in existence. The going interest rate, which can be designated as either k or i, but for purposes of our discussion is designated as k, is initially 10 percent for the low-risk securities in

---

[4]The term "producers" is really too narrow. A better word might be "borrowers," which would include corporations, home purchasers, people borrowing to go to college, or even people borrowing to buy autos or to pay for vacations. Also, the wealth of a society and its demographics influence its people's ability to save and thus their time preferences for current versus future consumption.

FIGURE 4-2   Interest Rates as a Function of Supply and Demand for Funds

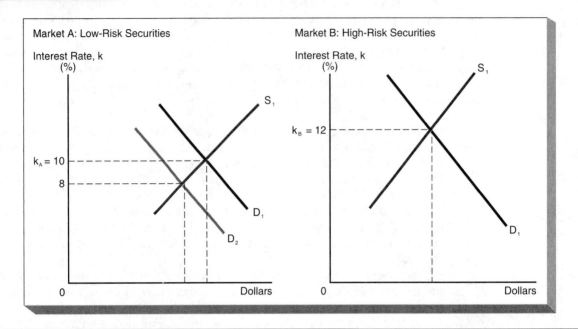

Market A.[5] Borrowers whose credit is strong enough to borrow in Market A can obtain funds at a cost of 10 percent, and investors who want to put their money to work without much risk can obtain a 10 percent return. Riskier borrowers must obtain higher-cost funds in Market B. Investors who are more willing to take risks invest in Market B, expecting to earn a 12 percent return but also realizing that they might actually receive much less.

If the demand for funds declines, as it typically does during business recessions, the demand curves will shift to the left, as shown in Curve D_2 in Market A. The market-clearing, or equilibrium, interest rate in this example declines to 8 percent. Similarly, you should be able to visualize what would happen if the Federal Reserve tightened credit: The supply curve, S_1, would shift to the left, and this would raise interest rates and lower the level of borrowing in the economy.

Capital markets are interdependent. For example, if Markets A and B were in equilibrium before the demand shift to D_2 in Market A, then investors were willing to accept the higher risk in Market B in exchange for a *risk premium* of 12% − 10% = 2%. After the shift to D_2, the risk premium would initially increase to 12% − 8% = 4%. Immediately, though, this much larger premium would induce some of the lenders in Market A to shift to Market B, which would, in turn, cause the supply curve in Market A to shift to the left (or up) and that in Market B to shift to the right. The transfer of capital between markets would raise the interest rate in Market A and lower it in Market B, thus bringing the risk premium back closer to the original 2 percent.

There are many capital markets in the United States. U.S. firms also invest and raise capital throughout the world, and foreigners both borrow and lend in the United States. There are markets for home loans; farm loans; business loans; federal, state, and local gov-

[5]The letter "k" is the traditional symbol for interest rates, but "i" is used frequently today because this term corresponds to the interest rate key on most financial calculators. Therefore, in Chapter 7, when we discuss calculators, the term "i" will be used for interest rate.

ernment loans; and consumer loans. Within each category, there are regional markets as well as different types of submarkets. For example, in real estate there are separate markets for first and second mortgages and for loans on single-family homes, apartments, office buildings, shopping centers, vacant land, and so on. Within the business sector there are dozens of types of debt and also several different markets for common stocks.

There is a price for each type of capital, and these prices change over time as shifts occur in supply and demand conditions. Figure 4-3 shows how long- and short-term interest rates to business borrowers have varied since the late 1950s. Notice that short-term interest rates are especially prone to rise during booms and then fall during recessions. (The shaded areas of the chart indicate recessions.) When the economy is expanding, firms need capital, and this demand for capital pushes rates up. Also, inflationary pressures are strongest during business booms, and that also exerts upward pressure on rates. Conditions are reversed during recessions such as the one in 1991 and 1992. Slack business reduces the demand for credit, the rate of inflation falls, and the result is a drop in interest rates. Furthermore, the Federal Reserve often lowers rates during recessions to help stimulate the economy.

These tendencies do not hold exactly — the period from 1984 to 1989 is a case in point. The price of oil fell dramatically in 1985 and 1986, reducing inflationary pressures on other prices and easing fears of serious long-term inflation. Earlier, these fears had pushed

FIGURE 4-3   Long- and Short-Term Interest Rates, 1959–1997

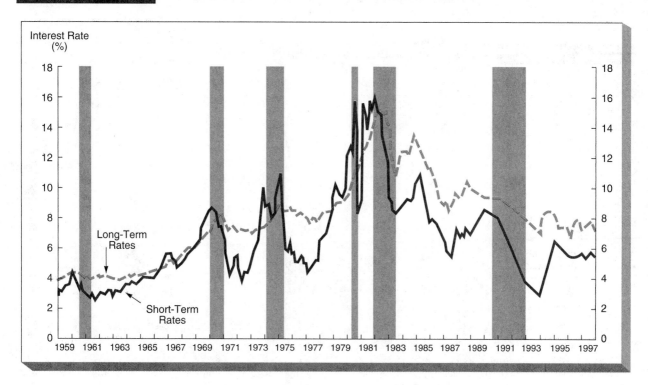

NOTES:

a. The shaded areas designate business recessions.

b. Short-term rates are measured by four- to six-month loans to very large, strong corporations, and long-term rates are measured by AAA corporate bonds.

SOURCE: *Federal Reserve Bulletin.*

interest rates to record levels. The economy from 1984 to 1987 was fairly strong, but declining fears about inflation more than offset the normal tendency of interest rates to rise during good economic times, and the net result was lower interest rates.[6]

The relationship between inflation and long-term interest rates is highlighted in Figure 4-4, which plots rates of inflation along with long-term interest rates. In the late 1950s and early 1960s, inflation averaged 1 percent per year, and interest rates on high-quality, long-term bonds averaged 5 percent. Then the Vietnam War heated up, leading to an increase in inflation, and interest rates began an upward climb. When the war ended in the early 1970s, inflation dipped a bit, but then the 1973 Arab oil embargo led to rising oil prices, much higher inflation rates, and sharply higher interest rates.

Inflation peaked at about 13 percent in 1980, but interest rates continued to increase into 1981 and 1982, and they remained quite high until 1985, because people were afraid inflation would start to climb again. Thus, the "inflationary psychology" created during the 1970s persisted to the mid-1980s.

Gradually, though, people began to realize that the Federal Reserve was serious about keeping inflation down, that global competition was keeping U.S. auto producers and other corporations from raising prices as they had in the past, and that constraints on corporate price increases were diminishing labor unions' ability to push through

---

[6]Short-term rates are responsive to current economic conditions, whereas long-term rates primarily reflect long-run expectations for inflation. As a result, short-term rates are sometimes above and sometimes below long-term rates. The relationship between long-term and short-term rates is called the *term structure of interest rates*, and it is discussed later in the chapter.

FIGURE 4-4   Relationship between Annual Inflation Rates and Long-Term Interest Rates, 1959–1997

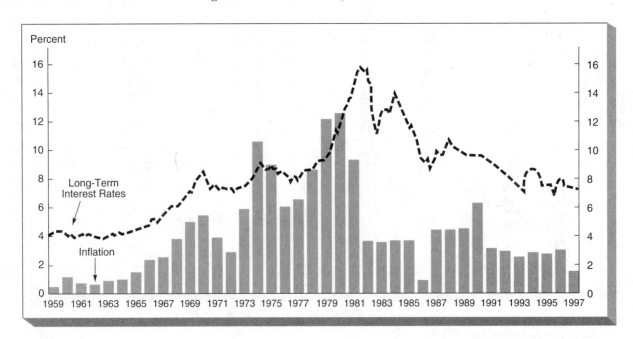

NOTES:

a. Interest rates are those on AAA long-term corporate bonds.

b. Inflation is measured as the annual rate of change in the Consumer Price Index (CPI).

SOURCE: *Federal Reserve Bulletin.*

cost-increasing wage hikes. As these realizations set in, interest rates declined, and the "current real rate of interest," which is the difference between the current interest rate and the current inflation rate, declined as shown in Figure 4-4.

In recent years, inflation has been running at less than 3 percent a year. However, long-term interest rates have been volatile, because investors are not sure if inflation is truly under control or is getting ready to jump back to the higher levels of the 1980s. In the years ahead, we can be sure that the level of interest rates will vary (1) with changes in the current rate of inflation and (2) with changes in expectations about future inflation.

<table>
<tr><td>

S E L F - T E S T
Q U E S T I O N S

</td><td>

How are interest rates used to allocate capital among firms?

What happens to market-clearing, or equilibrium, interest rates in a capital market when the demand for funds declines? When the supply of funds increases?

Why does the price of capital change during booms and recessions?

How does risk affect interest rates?

</td></tr>
</table>

THE DETERMINANTS OF MARKET INTEREST RATES

In general, the quoted (or nominal) interest rate on a debt security, k, is composed of a real risk-free rate of interest, k*, plus several premiums that reflect inflation, the riskiness of the security, and the security's marketability (or liquidity). This relationship can be expressed as follows:

$$\text{Quoted interest rate} = k = k^* + IP + DRP + LP + MRP$$
$$= k_{RF} \quad + DRP + LP + MRP. \tag{4-1}$$

Here

k = the quoted, or nominal, rate of interest on a given security.[7] There are many different securities, hence many different quoted interest rates.

k^* = the real risk-free rate of interest. k^* is pronounced "k-star," and it is the rate that would exist on a riskless security if zero inflation were expected.

k_{RF} = $k^* + IP$, and it is the quoted risk-free rate of interest on a security such as a U.S. Treasury bill, which is very liquid and also free of most risks. Note that k_{RF} includes the premium for expected inflation, because $k_{RF} = k^* + IP$.

IP = inflation premium. IP is equal to the average expected inflation rate over the life of the security. The expected future inflation rate is not necessarily equal to the current inflation rate, so IP is not necessarily equal to current inflation as reported in Figure 4-4.

DRP = default risk premium. This premium reflects the possibility that the issuer will not pay interest or principal at the stated time and in the stated amount. DRP is zero for U.S. Treasury securities, but it rises as the riskiness of issuers increases.

LP = liquidity, or marketability, premium. This is a premium charged by lenders to reflect the fact that some securities cannot be converted to cash on short notice at a "reasonable" price. LP is very low for Treasury securities and for securities

---

[7]The term *nominal* as it is used here means the *stated* rate as opposed to the *real* rate, which is adjusted to remove inflation effects. If you bought a ten-year Treasury bond in January 1997, the quoted, or nominal, rate would be about 6.5 percent, but if inflation averages 3 percent over the next ten years, the real rate would be about 6.5% − 3% = 3.5%.

issued by large, strong firms, but it is relatively high on securities issued by very small firms.

MRP = maturity risk premium. As we will explain later, longer-term bonds, even Treasury bonds, are exposed to a significant risk of price declines, and a maturity risk premium is charged by lenders to reflect this risk.

As noted above, since $k_{RF} = k^* + IP$, we can rewrite Equation 4-1 as follows:

$$\text{Nominal, or quoted, rate} = k = k_{RF} + DRP + LP + MRP.$$

We discuss the components whose sum makes up the quoted, or nominal, rate on a given security in the following sections.

The Real Risk-Free Rate of Interest, k*

The **real risk-free rate of interest, k*,** is defined as the interest rate that would exist on a riskless security if no inflation were expected, and it may be thought of as the rate of interest on *short-term* U.S. Treasury securities in an inflation-free world. The real risk-free rate is not static—it changes over time depending on economic conditions, especially (1) on the rate of return corporations and other borrowers expect to earn on productive assets and (2) on people's time preferences for current versus future consumption. Borrowers' expected returns on real asset investments set an upper limit on how much they can afford to pay for borrowed funds, while savers' time preferences for consumption establish how much consumption they are willing to defer, hence the amount of funds they will lend at different interest rates. The real risk-free rate on long-term securities can be measured by the market yield on indexed U.S. Treasury bonds, and it has averaged about 3.5 percent in recent years.[8] Indexed bonds are discussed in a box later in the chapter.

The Nominal, or Quoted, Risk-Free Rate of Interest, k_RF

The **nominal,** or **quoted, risk-free rate, k_RF,** is the real risk-free rate plus a premium for expected inflation: $k_{RF} = k^* + IP$. To be strictly correct, the risk-free rate should mean the interest rate on a totally risk-free security—one that has no risk of default, no maturity risk, no liquidity risk, and no risk of loss if the actual rate of inflation exceeds the expected rate. There is no such security, hence there is no observable truly risk-free rate. However, U.S. Treasury bills (T-bills), which are short-term securities issued by the U.S. government, are free of most risks. Indexed Treasury bonds are also essentially risk free, but they provide a real as opposed to a nominal return, so they cannot be used to measure the nominal risk-free rate.

If the term "risk-free rate" is used without either the modifier "real" or the modifier "nominal," people generally mean the quoted (nominal) rate, and we will follow that convention in this book. Therefore, when we use the term "risk-free rate, k_RF," we mean the nominal risk-free rate, which includes an inflation premium equal to the average expected inflation rate over the life of the security. In general, we use the T-bill rate to approximate the short-term risk-free rate, and the T-bond rate to approximate

---

[8]The real rate of interest as discussed here is different from the *current* real rate as discussed in connection with Figure 4-4. The current real rate is the current interest rate minus the current (or latest past) inflation rate, while the real rate, without the word "current," is the current interest rate minus the *expected future* inflation rate. For example, suppose the current quoted rate for short-term Treasury bills is 6 percent, inflation during the latest year was 3 percent, and inflation expected for the coming year is 5 percent. Then the *current* real rate would be 6% − 3% = 3%, but the *expected* real rate would be 6% − 5% = 1%. In the press, the term "real rate" generally means the current real rate, but in economics and finance, hence in this book unless otherwise noted, the real rate means the one based on *expected* inflation rates.

the long-term risk-free rate. So, whenever you see the term "risk-free rate," assume that we are referring either to the quoted U.S. T-bill rate or to the quoted T-bond rate.

Inflation Premium (IP)

Inflation has a major impact on interest rates because it erodes the purchasing power of the dollar and lowers the real rate of return on investments. To illustrate, suppose you saved $1,000 and invested it in a Treasury bill that matures in one year and pays a 5 percent interest rate. At the end of the year, you will receive $1,050 — your original $1,000 plus $50 of interest. Now suppose the inflation rate during the year is 10 percent, and it affects all items equally. If gas had cost $1 per gallon at the beginning of the year, it would cost $1.10 at the end of the year. Therefore, your $1,000 would have bought $1,000/$1 = 1,000 gallons at the beginning of the year, but only $1,050/$1.10 = 955 gallons at the end. In *real terms*, you would be worse off — you would receive $50 of interest, but it would not be sufficient to offset inflation. You would thus be better off buying 1,000 gallons of gas (or some other storable asset such as land, timber, apartment buildings, wheat, or gold) than buying the Treasury bill.

Investors are well aware of all this, so when they lend money, they build in an **inflation premium (IP)** equal to the average expected inflation rate over the life of the security. As discussed previously, for a short-term, default-free U.S. Treasury bill, the actual interest rate charged, $k_{T\text{-bill}}$, would be the real risk-free rate, k^*, plus the inflation premium (IP):

$$k_{T\text{-bill}} = k_{RF} = k^* + IP.$$

Therefore, if the real risk-free rate of interest were $k^* = 3\%$, and if inflation were expected to be 4 percent (and hence $IP = 4\%$) during the next year, then the quoted rate of interest on one-year T-bills would be 7 percent. In September 1997, the expected one-year inflation rate was about 2.9 percent, and the yield on one-year T-bills was about 5.3 percent. This implies that the real risk-free rate on short-term securities at that time was 2.4 percent.

It is important to note that the inflation rate built into interest rates is the *inflation rate expected in the future*, not the rate experienced in the past. Thus, the latest reported figures might show an annual inflation rate of 3 percent, but that is for a past period. If people on the average expect a 6 percent inflation rate in the future, then 6 percent would be built into the current interest rate. Note also that the inflation rate reflected in the quoted interest rate on any security is the *average rate of inflation expected over the security's life*. Thus, the inflation rate built into a 1-year bond is the expected inflation rate for the next year, but the inflation rate built into a 30-year bond is the average rate of inflation expected over the next 30 years.[9]

Expectations for future inflation are closely, but not perfectly, correlated with rates experienced in the recent past. Therefore, if the inflation rate reported for last month increased, people would tend to raise their expectations for future inflation, and this change in expectations would cause an increase in interest rates.

Germany, Japan, and Switzerland have had lower inflation rates than the United States, hence their interest rates have generally been lower than ours. Italy and most

---

[9]To be theoretically precise, we should use a *geometric average*. Also, since millions of investors are active in the market, it is impossible to determine exactly the consensus expected inflation rate. Survey data are available, however, which give us a reasonably good idea of what investors expect over the next few years. For example, in 1980 the University of Michigan's Survey Research Center reported that people expected inflation during the next year to be 11.9 percent and that the average rate of inflation expected over the next five to ten years was 10.5 percent. Those expectations led to record-high interest rates. However, the economy cooled in 1981 and 1982, and, as Figure 4-4 showed, actual inflation dropped sharply after 1980. This led to gradual reductions in the *expected future* inflation rate. In September 1997, as we write this, the expected future inflation rate is about 2.9 percent. As inflationary expectations change, so do quoted market interest rates.

South American countries have experienced high inflation, and that is reflected in their interest rates.

Default Risk Premium (DRP)

The risk that a borrower will *default* on a loan, which means not pay the interest or principal, also affects the market interest rate on a security: the greater the default risk, the higher the interest rate. Treasury securities have no default risk, hence they carry the lowest interest rates on taxable securities in the United States. For corporate bonds, the higher the bond's rating, the lower its default risk, and, consequently, the lower its interest rate.[10] Here are some representative interest rates on long-term bonds during September 1997:

	RATE	DRP
U.S. Treasury	6.5%	—
AAA	7.2	0.7%
AA	7.3	0.8
A	7.4	0.9
BBB	7.7	1.2
BB+	8.4	1.9

The difference between the quoted interest rate on a T-bond and that on a corporate bond with similar maturity, liquidity, and other features is the **default risk premium (DRP).** Therefore, if the bonds listed above were otherwise similar, the default risk premium would be DRP = 7.2% − 6.5% = 0.7% for AAA corporate bonds, 7.3% − 6.5% = 0.8% for AA, 7.4% − 6.5% = 0.9% for A corporate bonds, and so forth. Default risk premiums vary somewhat over time, but the September 1997 figures are representative of levels in recent years.

Liquidity Premium (LP)

A "liquid" asset can be converted to cash quickly and at a "fair market value." Financial assets are generally more liquid than real assets. Because liquidity is desirable, investors include **liquidity premiums (LP)** when market rates of securities are established. Although it is difficult to accurately measure liquidity premiums, a differential of at least two and probably four or five percentage points exists between the least liquid and the most liquid financial assets of similar default risk and maturity.

Maturity Risk Premium (MRP)

U.S. Treasury securities are free of default risk in the sense that one can be virtually certain that the federal government will pay interest on its bonds and will also pay them off when they mature. Therefore, the default risk premium on Treasury securities is essentially zero. Further, active markets exist for Treasury securities, so their liquidity premiums are also close to zero. Thus, as a first approximation, the rate of interest on a Treasury bond should be the risk-free rate, k_{RF}, which is equal to the real risk-free rate, k^*, plus an inflation premium, IP. However, an adjustment is needed for long-term Treasury bonds. The prices of long-term bonds decline sharply whenever interest rates

---

[10]Bond ratings, and bonds' riskiness in general, are discussed in detail in Chapter 8. For now, merely note that bonds rated AAA are judged to have less default risk than bonds rated AA, while AA bonds are less risky than A bonds, and so on. Ratings are designated AAA or Aaa, AA or Aa, and so forth, depending on the rating agency. In this book, the designations are used interchangeably.

A NEW, TRULY RISKLESS TREASURY BOND

Investors who purchase bonds must constantly worry about inflation. If inflation turns out to be greater than expected, bonds will provide a lower-than-expected real return. To protect themselves against expected increases in inflation, investors build an inflation risk premium into their required rate of return. This raises borrowers' costs.

In January 1997, inflation was running below 3 percent a year, yet long-term Treasury rates were about 6.7 percent. A considerable portion of the 6.7 percent rate was attributed to the market's fear that inflation will rise in the years ahead. Therefore, long-term rates should decline if investors can be convinced that inflation is under control. Indeed, the actions taken by the Federal Reserve in recent years have been designed primarily to convince the bond market that the Fed was not going to tolerate rising inflation.

In order to provide investors with an inflation-protected bond, and also to reduce the cost of debt to the government, on January 29, 1997, the U.S. Treasury issued $7 billion of 10-year inflation-indexed bonds. The bonds will pay an interest rate of 3.375 percent, plus an additional amount sufficient to offset inflation, at the end of each year. For example, if inflation as measured by the CPI during the year ending January 28, 1998, turns out to be 3.00 percent, then the holder of one of these bonds would receive two benefits. First, he or she would receive $33.75 of interest, which is 3.375 percent of the bond's initial stated, or "par," value of $1,000. Second, the stated value of the bond would be increased by the inflation rate, to $1,000(1.03) = $1,030, causing the holder's wealth to rise by another $30. Thus, the total return during the first year would be $33.75 of interest plus $30 of capital appreciation, or $63.75 in total, and the total rate of return would be $63.75/$1,000 = 6.375%.

Interest during the second year would be figured as the coupon rate of 3.375 percent times the inflation-adjusted par value, or 0.03375($1,030) = $34.76. Thus, the cash income provided by the bond would rise by exactly enough to cover inflation, producing a real, inflation-adjusted rate of 3.375 percent. Further, since the principal would also rise by the inflation rate, it too would be protected from inflation.

This same adjustment process will continue each year until the bonds mature in January 2007, at which time they will pay the adjusted maturity value, which would be $1,343.92 if inflation continues at the rate of 3 percent per year.

The 3.375 percent rate was set at the auction—interested investors notified the Treasury of how many bonds they were willing to buy at different interest rates. Obviously, potential buyers would buy more bonds if the rate were set relatively high, fewer at a lower rate. Thus Mr. X might indicate that he would buy $1 million of the bonds if the rate was set at 3 percent, $2 million if the rate was 3.5 percent, $3 million at 4 percent, and so on. When the bidding was closed, the Treasury determined that to sell the entire issue, the coupon rate would have to be set at 3.375 percent—that was the lowest rate that would clear the market.

Federal Reserve Board Chairman Greenspan lobbied in favor of the indexed bonds on the grounds that they would help him and the Fed make better estimates of investors' expectations about inflation. He did not explain his reasoning (to our knowledge), but it might have gone something like this:

- We know that interest rates in general are determined as follows:

$$k = k^* + IP + MRP + DRP + LP.$$

- For Treasury bonds, DRP and LP are essentially zero, so for a 10-year bond the rate is

$$k = k^* + IP + MRP.$$

The reason the MRP is not zero is that if inflation increases, interest rates will rise and the price of the bonds will decline. Therefore, "regular" 10-year bonds are exposed to maturity risk, hence a maturity risk premium is built into their market interest rate.

- The indexed bonds are protected against inflation—if inflation increases, then so will their dollar returns, and as a result, their price will not decline in real terms. Therefore, indexed bonds should have no MRP, hence their market return is

$$k_{RF} = k^* + 0 + 0 = k^*.$$

In other words, the market rate on indexed bonds is the real rate.

- The difference between the yield on a regular 10-year bond and that on an indexed bond is the sum of the 10-year bonds' IP and MRP. Assume that the yield on regular 10-year bonds was 6.725 percent when the indexed bonds were issued, and the indexed bonds' yield was 3.375 percent. The difference, 3.35 percent, is the average expected inflation rate over the next 10 years plus the MRP for ten-year bonds.

- The 10-year MRP is about 1.0 percent, and it has been relatively stable in recent years. Therefore, the expected rate of inflation in January 1997 was about 3.35% − 1.00% = 2.35%.

The interest received and the increase in principal are taxed each year as interest income, even though cash from the appreciation will not be received until the bond matures. Therefore, these bonds are especially suitable for individual retirement accounts (IRAs), which are not taxed until funds are withdrawn.

SOURCE: "Inflation Notes Will Offer Fed Forecast Tool," *The Wall Street Journal,* February 3, 1997, C1.

rise, and since interest rates can and do occasionally rise, all long-term bonds, even Treasury bonds, have an element of risk called **interest rate risk.** As a general rule, the bonds of any organization, from the U.S. government to Continental Airlines, have more interest rate risk the longer the maturity of the bond.[11] Therefore, a **maturity risk premium (MRP),** which is higher the longer the years to maturity, must be included in the required interest rate.

The effect of maturity risk premiums is to raise interest rates on long-term bonds relative to those on short-term bonds. This premium, like the others, is difficult to measure, but (1) it varies somewhat over time, rising when interest rates are more volatile and uncertain, then falling when interest rates are more stable, and (2) in recent years, the maturity risk premium on 30-year T-bonds appears to have generally been in the range of one or two percentage points.[12]

We should mention that although long-term bonds are heavily exposed to interest rate risk, short-term bills are heavily exposed to **reinvestment rate risk.** When short-term bills mature and the funds are reinvested, or "rolled over," a decline in interest rates would necessitate reinvestment at a lower rate, and this would result in a decline in interest income. To illustrate, suppose you had $100,000 invested in one-year T-bills, and you lived on the income. In 1981, short-term rates were about 15 percent, so your income would have been about $15,000. However, your income would have declined to about $9,000 by 1983, and to just $5,300 by 1997. Had you invested your money in long-term T-bonds, your income (but not the value of the principal) would have been stable.[13] Thus, although "investing short" preserves one's principal, the interest income provided by short-term T-bills is less stable than the interest income on long-term bonds.

SELF-TEST
QUESTIONS

Write out an equation for the nominal interest rate on any debt security.

Distinguish between the *real* risk-free rate, k^*, and the *nominal,* or *quoted,* risk-free rate, k_{RF}.

How is inflation dealt with when interest rates are determined by investors in the financial markets?

Does the interest rate on a T-bond include a default risk premium? Explain.

Distinguish between liquid and illiquid assets, and identify some assets that are liquid and some that are illiquid.

Briefly explain the following statement: "Although long-term bonds are heavily exposed to interest rate risk, short-term bills are heavily exposed to reinvestment rate risk. The maturity risk premium reflects the net effects of these two opposing forces."

---

[11]For example, if someone had bought a 30-year Treasury bond for $1,000 in 1972, when the long-term interest rate was 7 percent, and held it until 1981, when long-term T-bond rates were about 14.5 percent, the value of the bond would have declined to about $514. That would represent a loss of almost half the invested capital, and it demonstrates that long-term bonds, even U.S. Treasury bonds, are not riskless. However, had the investor purchased short-term T-bills in 1972 and reinvested the principal each time the bills matured, he or she would still have had $1,000 in 1981. This point will be discussed in detail in Chapter 8.

[12]The MRP for long-term bonds has averaged 1.5 percent over the last 70 years. See *Stocks, Bonds, Bills, and Inflation: 1997 Yearbook* (Chicago: Ibbotson Associates, 1997).

[13]Long-term bonds also have some reinvestment rate risk. If one is saving and investing for some future purpose, say, to buy a house or for retirement, then to actually earn the quoted rate on a long-term bond, the interest payments must be reinvested at the quoted rate. However, if interest rates fall, the interest payments must be reinvested at a lower rate; thus, the realized return would be less than the quoted rate. Note, though, that reinvestment rate risk is lower on a long-term bond than on a short-term bond because only the interest payments (rather than interest plus principal) on the long-term bond are exposed to reinvestment rate risk. Zero coupon bonds, which are discussed in Chapter 18, are completely free of reinvestment rate risk during their life.

INVESTING OVERSEAS

In addition to inflation and liquidity, investors should consider other risk factors before investing overseas. First there is **country risk,** which refers to the risk that arises from investing or doing business in a particular country. See the box on the next page. This risk depends on the country's economic, political, and social environment. Countries with stable economic, social, political, and regulatory systems provide a safer climate for investment, and therefore less country risk, than less stable nations. Examples of country risk include the risk associated with changes in tax rates, regulations, currency conversion, and exchange rates. Country risk also includes the risk that property will be expropriated without adequate compensation, as well as new host country stipulations about local production, sourcing or hiring practices, and damage or destruction of facilities due to internal strife.

A second thing to keep in mind when investing overseas is that more often than not the security will be denominated in a currency other than the dollar, which means that the value of your investment will depend on what happens to exchange rates. This is known as **exchange rate risk.** For example, if a U.S. investor purchases a Japanese bond, interest will probably be paid in Japanese yen, which must then be converted into dollars if the investor wants to spend his or her money in the United States. If the yen weakens relative to the dollar, then it will buy fewer dollars, hence the investor will receive fewer dollars when it comes time to convert. Alternatively, if the yen strengthens relative to the dollar, the investor will earn higher dollar returns. It therefore follows that the effective rate of return on a foreign investment will depend on both the performance of the foreign security and on what happens to exchange rates over the life of the investment.

In Chapter 27, we will discuss exchange rates in considerably more detail. However, at this point we should mention two factors which can lead to exchange rate fluctuations. First, changes in relative inflation will lead to changes in exchange rates. If expected inflation increases more within some foreign country than in the United States, the value of that country's currency is likely to fall. Second, an increase in country risk will also cause that country's currency to fall. Consequently, inflation risk, country risk, and exchange rate risk are all interrelated.

SELF-TEST QUESTIONS

What is country risk?

Identify two factors which can cause exchange rates to fluctuate.

THE TERM STRUCTURE OF INTEREST RATES

A study of Figure 4-3 reveals that at certain times such as 1997, short-term interest rates were lower than long-term rates, whereas at times during 1980 and 1981, short-term rates were higher than long-term rates. The relationship between long- and short-term rates, which is known as the **term structure of interest rates,** is important to corporate treasurers, who must decide whether to borrow by issuing long- or short-term debt, and to investors, who must decide whether to buy long- or short-term bonds. Thus, it is important to understand (1) how long- and short-term rates are related to each other and (2) what causes shifts in their relative positions.

To begin, we can look up in a source such as *The Wall Street Journal* or the web the interest rates on Treasury bonds of various maturities at a given point in time.[14] For

---

[14]The Federal Reserve provides a daily update on bond yields at http://www.bog.fed.us/releases/H15/update.

MEASURING COUNTRY RISK

Various forecasting services measure the level of country risk in different countries and provide indexes that measure factors such as each country's expected economic performance, access to world capital markets, political stability, and level of internal conflict. Country risk analysts use sophisticated models to measure it, thus providing corporate managers and overseas investors with a way to judge both the relative and absolute risk of investing in a given country. A sample of recent country risk estimates compiled by *Euromoney* are presented in the following table. The higher the country's score, the lower its estimated country risk. The maximum possible score is 100.

The countries with the least country risk all have strong, market-based economies, ready access to worldwide capital markets, relatively little social unrest, and a stable political climate. Luxembourg's top ranking may surprise many, but this ranking is the result of the country's strong economic performance and its status as a tax haven for foreign investment. Some may also be surprised that the United States was not ranked number one. Even though the U.S. economy has been quite strong in recent years, the economies of some other countries have been even stronger (e.g., Luxembourg, Switzerland, and Singapore). Also, the United States typically does not receive the highest

ranking with respect to political risk—this likely stems from the ongoing uncertainty about whether there will be major shifts in tax and regulatory policies within the United States. Note, though, that there is really not much difference between 98.55 and 97.17—none of the top five countries have much country risk.

Arguably, there are fewer surprises when looking at the bottom five. Each of these countries has considerable social and political unrest, and none have embraced a market-based economic system. Clearly, an investment in any of these countries is a risky proposition.

Top Five Countries (Least Amount of Country Risk)

RANK	COUNTRY	TOTAL SCORE (MAXIMUM POSSIBLE = 100)
1	Luxembourg	98.55
2	Switzerland	98.45
3	Singapore	98.38
4	Japan	97.19
5	United States	97.17

Bottom Five Countries (Greatest Amount of Country Risk)

RANK	COUNTRY	TOTAL SCORE (MINIMUM POSSIBLE = 0)
174	Cuba	11.72
175	North Korea	8.02
176	Surinam	6.80
177	Iraq	5.50
178	Afghanistan	5.07

example, the tabular section of Figure 4-5 presents interest rates for different maturities on two dates. The set of data for a given date, when plotted on a graph such as that in Figure 4-5, is called the **yield curve** for that date. The yield curve changes both in position and in slope over time. In March 1980, all rates were relatively high, and short-term rates were higher than long-term rates, causing the yield curve to be *downward sloping*. However, by October 1997, all rates had fallen, and short-term rates were lower than long-term rates, so the yield curve at that time was *upward sloping*. Had we drawn the yield

FIGURE 4-5   U.S. Treasury Bond Interest Rates on Different Dates

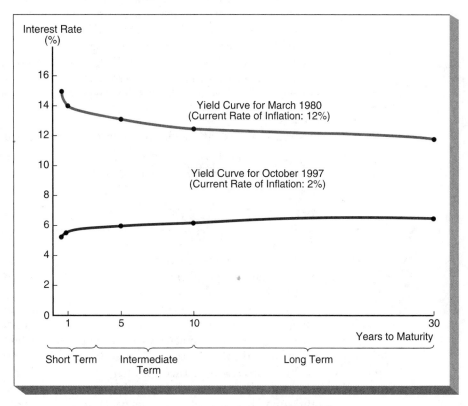

	INTEREST RATE	
TERM TO MATURITY	MARCH 1980	OCTOBER 1997
6 months	15.0%	5.3%
1 year	14.0	5.5
5 years	13.5	5.9
10 years	12.8	6.1
30 years	12.3	6.4

curve during January 1982, it would have been essentially horizontal, for long-term and short-term bonds on that date had about the same rate of interest. (See Figure 4-3.)

Figure 4-5 shows yield curves for U.S. Treasury securities, but we could have constructed them for corporate bonds. For example, we could have developed a yield curve for AT&T, Exxon, Continental Airlines, or any other company that borrows money over a range of maturities. Had we constructed such curves and plotted them on Figure 4-5, the corporate yield curves would have been above those for Treasury securities because the corporate yields would include default risk premiums. However, the corporates would have had the same general shape as the Treasury curves. Also, the riskier the corporation, the higher its yield curve, so Continental, which is in a relatively weak financial position, would have had a yield curve substantially higher than that of Exxon, which has a top bond rating.

Historically, in most years long-term rates have been above short-term rates, so the yield curve normally slopes upward. For this reason, people often call an upward-sloping yield curve a **"normal" yield curve** and a yield curve which slopes downward an **inverted,** or **"abnormal," yield curve.** Thus, in Figure 4-5 the yield curve for March 1980 was inverted, but the one for October 1997 was normal. We explain in detail in the next section why an upward slope is the normal situation, but briefly, the reason is that short-term securities have less interest rate risk than longer-term securities, hence smaller MRPs. Therefore, short-term rates are normally lower than long-term rates.

SELF - TEST
QUESTIONS

What is a yield curve, and what information would you need to draw this curve?

Distinguish between the shapes of a "normal" yield curve and an "abnormal" yield curve, and explain when each might exist.

WHAT DETERMINES THE SHAPE OF THE YIELD CURVE?[15]

The shape of the yield curve depends on two key factors: (1) expectations about future inflation and (2) perceptions about the relative riskiness of securities with different maturities.

Some academics and practitioners contend that this second factor — relative maturities — is considerably less important than expectations about future rates. They argue that the market is dominated by large bond traders who buy and sell securities of different maturities each day, that these traders focus only on short-term returns, and that they are less concerned with risk. According to this view, a bond trader is just as willing to buy a 30-year bond to pick up a short-term profit as he would be to buy a three-month security. Strict proponents of this view argue that the shape of the yield curve is therefore determined only by market expectations about future interest rates. This position has been called the *pure expectations theory* of the term structure of interest rates.

A majority of academics and practitioners would argue, however, that risks associated with changing rates do matter, and, moreover, that the market views long-term securities as riskier than short-term securities. This view is often referred to as the *liquidity preference theory*. The rationales for each of these theories are described below.

Expectations Theory

The **expectations theory,** sometimes referred to as the *pure expectations theory,* states that the yield curve depends only on expectations about future interest rates. To begin, the expectations theory holds that long-term interest rates are a weighted average of current and expected future short-term interest rates. For example, if one-year Treasury bills currently yield 7 percent, but one-year bills are expected to yield 7.5 percent a year from now, investors will expect to earn an average of 7.25 percent over the next two years:[16]

$$\frac{7\% + 7.5\%}{2} = 7.25\%.$$

---

[15]This section is relatively technical, but instructors can omit it without loss of continuity.

[16]Technically, we should be using geometric averages rather than arithmetic averages, but the differences are not material in this example. For a discussion of this point, see Robert C. Radcliffe, *Investment: Concepts, Analysis, and Strategy,* 5th ed. (Reading, MA: Addison-Wesley, 1997), Chapter 5.

According to the expectations theory, this implies that a two-year Treasury note purchased today should also yield 7.25 percent. Similarly, if 10-year bonds yield 9 percent today, and if 5-year bonds are expected to yield 7.5 percent 10 years from now, then an investor with a 15-year horizon will expect to earn 9 percent for 10 years and 7.5 percent for 5 years, for an average return of 8.5 percent over the 15 years:

$$\frac{9\% + 9\% + \cdots + 9\% + 7.5\% + \cdots + 7.5\%}{15} = \frac{10(9\%) + 5(7.5\%)}{15} = 8.5\%.$$

Consequently, a 15-year bond should yield this same return, 8.5 percent.

To understand the logic behind this averaging process, ask yourself what would happen if long-term yields were *not* an average of expected short-term yields. For example, suppose two-year bonds yielded only 7 percent, not the 7.25 percent calculated above. Bond traders would be able to earn a profit by adopting the following strategy:

1. Borrow money for two years at a cost of 7 percent.
2. Invest the money in a series of one-year bonds. The expected return over the two-year period would be $(7.0 + 7.5)/2 = 7.25\%$.

In this case, bond traders would rush to borrow money (demand funds) in the two-year market and invest (or supply funds) in the one-year market. Recall from Figure 4-2 that an increase in the demand for funds raises interest rates, whereas an increase in the supply of funds reduces interest rates. Therefore, bond traders' actions would push up the two-year yield but reduce the yield on one-year bonds. The net effect would be to bring about a market equilibrium in which two-year rates were a weighted average of expected future one-year rates.

The pure expectations theory assumes that investors establish bond prices and interest rates strictly on the basis of expectations for interest rates. This means that they are indifferent with respect to maturity in the sense that they do not view long-term bonds as being riskier than short-term bonds. Therefore, according to the pure expectations theory, the maturity risk premium (MRP) is equal to zero.

Moreover, according to the pure expectations theory, k_t, the nominal interest rate on Treasury securities is determined as the sum of the real risk-free rate, k^*, plus an inflation premium, IP. Therefore, the nominal rate on a U.S. Treasury bond that matures in t years would be found as follows:

$$k_t = k^* + IP_t.$$

Here IP_t is found as the average inflation rate over the t years until the bond matures. The real risk-free rate tends to be fairly constant over time, so changes in interest rates are driven largely by changes in expected inflation. Note also that under the pure expectations theory, the MRP is assumed to be zero, and for Treasury securities the default risk premium (DRP) and liquidity premium (LP) are also zero.

To illustrate the pure expectations theory, suppose that in late December 1998 the real risk-free rate of interest was expected to remain constant at 3 percent ($k^* = 3\%$). Also, assume that the expected inflation rates for the next three years were as follows:

	EXPECTED ANNUAL (1-YEAR) INFLATION RATE	EXPECTED AVERAGE INFLATION RATE FROM 1998 TO INDICATED YEAR
1999	3%	3%/1 = 3.0%
2000	5%	(3% + 5%)/2 = 4.0%
2001	7%	(3% + 5% + 7%)/3 = 5.0%

Given these expectations, the following pattern of interest rates should exist:

	REAL RISK-FREE RATE (k*)		INFLATION PREMIUM, WHICH IS EQUAL TO THE AVERAGE EXPECTED INFLATION RATE (IP_t)		NOMINAL TREASURY BOND RATE FOR EACH MATURITY (k_{T-BOND})
1-year bond:	3%	+	3.0%	=	6.0%
2-year bond:	3%	+	4.0%	=	7.0%
3-year bond:	3%	+	5.0%	=	8.0%

Had the pattern of expected inflation rates been reversed, with inflation expected to fall from 7 percent to 5 percent and then to 3 percent, the following situation would have existed:

	REAL RISK-FREE RATE		AVERAGE EXPECTED INFLATION RATE		TREASURY BOND RATE FOR EACH MATURITY
1-year bond	3%	+	7.0%	=	10.0%
2-year bond	3%	+	6.0%	=	9.0%
3-year bond	3%	+	5.0%	=	8.0%

These hypothetical data are plotted in Figure 4-6. As you can see, an upward-sloping yield curve occurs when interest rates are expected to increase in the future. This increase could be due to an increase in expected inflation (as is the case in the example above) or to an expected increase in the real risk-free rate. By contrast, a downward-sloping yield curve occurs when interest rates are expected to decline.

In practice, we can never actually observe the marginal investor's expected inflation rate or the real risk-free rate. However, if the pure expectations theory were correct, we could "back out" of the yield curve the bond market's best guess about future interest rates. If, for example, you observe that Treasury securities with one- and two-year maturities yield 7 percent and 8 percent, respectively, this information could be used to calculate the market's forecast of what one-year rates will yield one year from now. If the pure expectations theory is correct, the rate on two-year bonds is the average of the current one-year rate and the one-year rate expected a year from now. Since the current one-year rate is 7 percent, this implies that the one-year rate one year from now is expected to be 9 percent:

$$2\text{-year yield} = 8\% = \frac{7\% + X\%}{2}$$

$$X = 16\% - 7\% = 9\% = 1\text{-year yield expected next year.}$$

Liquidity Preference Theory

The pure expectations theory assumes that the maturity risk premium (MRP) is zero. However, convincing evidence suggests that there is a positive maturity risk premium—investors require higher rates of return on longer-term bonds, other things held constant.

This has given rise to the **liquidity preference theory,** which states that long-term bonds normally yield more than short-term bonds for two reasons: (1) Investors generally prefer to hold short-term securities because such securities are more liquid in the sense that they can be converted to cash with little danger of loss of principal. Investors will, therefore, generally accept lower yields on short-term securities, and this leads to relatively low short-term rates. (2) Borrowers, on the other hand, gener-

| **FIGURE 4-6** | Hypothetical Example of the Term Structure of Interest Rates |

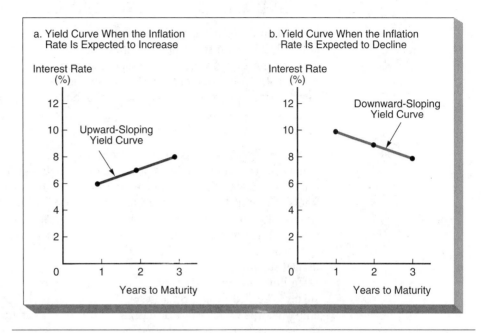

ally prefer long-term debt because short-term debt exposes them to the risk of having to repay the debt under adverse conditions. Accordingly, borrowers are willing to pay a higher rate, other things held constant, for long-term funds than for short-term funds, and this also leads to relatively low short-term rates. Thus, lender and borrower preferences both operate to cause short-term rates to be lower than long-term rates. Taken together, these two sets of preferences imply that under normal conditions (1) a positive maturity risk premium (MRP) exists and (2) the MRP increases with years to maturity, causing the yield curve to be upward sloping.

It is important to understand that the liquidity preference theory does not imply that expectations do not matter. Indeed, most proponents of the liquidity preference theory would agree that expectations about future interest rates are the most important factor explaining the shape of the yield curve. However, they reject the *pure* expectations theory. Since evidence suggests that there is a positive maturity risk premium, both expectations and liquidity preferences seem to affect interest rates. As a result, when the slope of the yield curve changes, this could imply either that the market now thinks rates are going to be different in the future versus what it previously thought, that the maturity risk premium has changed, or that both events have occurred.[17]

SELF-TEST
QUESTIONS

What are the two primary factors that explain the shape of the yield curve?

Why might the yield curve slope *downward* at a particular point in time?

[17]Some analysts subscribe to another theory, the *market segmentation theory,* which argues that long- and short-term bonds trade in separate markets and that there is little or no connection between the yields on short- and long-term bonds. Proponents of this theory suggest that the yield curve is explained by the relative supply and demand of long- and short-term securities — if the demand for long-term capital is strong relative to the supply of such capital, while the reverse holds in the short-term market, then the yield curve will be upward sloping. While supply and demand conditions are clearly important, most researchers today argue that the actions of bond traders, who buy and sell bonds of different maturities all day, arbitrage away any yield differentials caused by market imperfections and thus ensure that markets are not highly segmented.

OTHER FACTORS THAT INFLUENCE INTEREST RATE LEVELS

In addition to inflationary expectations and liquidity preferences, several other factors also influence both the general level of interest rates and the shape of the yield curve. The four most important are (1) Federal Reserve policy; (2) the level of the federal budget deficit; (3) international factors, including the foreign trade balance and interest rates in other countries; and (4) the level of business activity.

Federal Reserve Policy

As you probably learned in your economics courses, (1) the money supply has a major effect on both the level of economic activity and the inflation rate, and (2) in the United States, the Federal Reserve Board controls the money supply. If the Fed wants to stimulate the economy, as it did in 1995, it increases growth in the money supply. The initial effect of such an action is to cause interest rates to decline. However, a larger money supply may also lead to an increase in the expected inflation rate, which could push interest rates up. The reverse holds if the Fed tightens the money supply.

To illustrate, in 1981 inflation was quite high, so the Fed tightened up the money supply. The Fed deals primarily in the short-term end of the market, so this tightening had the direct effect of pushing short-term rates up sharply. At the same time, the very fact that the Fed was taking strong action to reduce inflation led to a decline in expectations for long-run inflation, which led to a decline in long-term bond yields.

In 1991, the situation was just the reverse. To combat the recession, the Fed took steps to reduce interest rates. Short-term rates fell, and long-term rates also dropped, but not as sharply. These lower rates benefitted heavily indebted businesses and individual borrowers, and home mortgage refinancings put additional billions of dollars into consumers' pockets. Savers, of course, lost out, but the net effect of lower interest rates was a stronger economy. Lower rates encourage businesses to borrow for investment, stimulate the housing market, and bring down the value of the dollar relative to other currencies, which helps U.S. exporters and thus lowers the trade deficit.

During periods when the Fed is actively intervening in the markets, the yield curve may be temporarily distorted. Short-term rates will be temporarily "too low" if the Fed is easing credit, and "too high" if it is tightening credit. Long-term rates are not affected as much by Fed intervention. For example, the fear of rising inflation led the Federal Reserve to increase short-term interest rates six times during 1994. While short-term rates rose by nearly 4 percentage points, long-term rates increased by only 1.5 percentage points.

Federal Deficits

If the federal government spends more than it takes in from tax revenues, it runs a deficit, and that deficit must be covered either by borrowing or by printing money (increasing the money supply). If the government borrows, this added demand for funds pushes up interest rates. If it prints money, this increases expectations for future inflation, which also drives up interest rates. Thus, the larger the federal deficit, other things held constant, the higher the level of interest rates. Whether long- or short-term rates are more affected depends on how the deficit is financed, so we cannot state, in general, how deficits will affect the slope of the yield curve.

International Factors

Businesses and individuals in the United States buy from and sell to people and firms in other countries. If we buy more than we sell (that is, if we import more than we export), we are said to be running a *foreign trade deficit*. When trade deficits occur, they must be financed, and the main source of financing is debt. In other words, if we import $200 billion of goods but export only $100 billion, we run a trade deficit of $100 billion, and we would probably borrow the $100 billion.[18] Therefore, the larger our trade deficit, the more we must borrow, and as we increase our borrowing, this drives up interest rates. Also, the foreigners who hold U.S. debt are willing to continue doing so if and only if the rate paid on this debt is competitive with interest rates in other countries. Therefore, if the Federal Reserve attempts to lower interest rates in the United States, causing our rates to fall below rates abroad, then foreigners will sell U.S. bonds, those sales will depress bond prices, and the result will be higher U.S. rates.

The United States has been running annual trade deficits since the mid-1970s, and the cumulative effect of these deficits is that the United States has become the largest debtor nation of all time. As a result, our interest rates are very much influenced by interest rates in other countries around the world (higher rates abroad lead to higher U.S. rates). Because of all this, U.S. corporate treasurers — and anyone else who is affected by interest rates — must keep up with developments in the world economy.

Business Activity

Figure 4-3, presented earlier, can be examined to see how business conditions influence interest rates. Here are the key points revealed by the graph:

1. Because inflation increased from 1959 to 1981, the general tendency during that period was toward higher interest rates. However, since the 1981 peak, the trend has generally been downward.

2. Until 1966, short-term rates were almost always below long-term rates. Thus, in those years the yield curve was almost always "normal" in the sense that it was upward sloping.

3. The shaded areas in the graph represent recessions, during which (1) both the demand for money and the rate of inflation tend to fall and (2) the Federal Reserve tends to increase the money supply in an effort to stimulate the economy. As a result, there is a tendency for interest rates to decline during recessions. Currently, in January 1998, we are in a period of relatively stable, but slow, growth. The Fed is reluctant to lower interest rates because it is afraid that action would speed up the economy too much and lead to higher inflation. At the same time, the Fed does not want to raise rates, because that might drive the economy into a recession. Therefore, interest rates are currently relatively stable.

4. During recessions, short-term rates decline more sharply than long-term rates. This occurs because (1) the Fed operates mainly in the short-term sector, so its intervention has the strongest effect there, and (2) long-term rates reflect the average expected inflation rate over the next 20 to 30 years, and this expectation generally does not change much, even when the current inflation rate is low because of a recession or high because of a boom. So, short-term rates are more volatile than long-term rates.

---

[18]The deficit could also be financed by selling assets, including gold, corporate stocks, entire companies, and real estate. The United States has financed its massive trade deficits by all of these means in recent years, but the primary method has been by borrowing from foreigners.

SELF-TEST
QUESTIONS

Other than inflationary expectations and liquidity preferences, name some additional factors which influence interest rates, and explain the effects of each.

How does the Fed stimulate the economy? How does the Fed affect interest rates?

Does the Fed have complete control over U.S. interest rates; that is, can it set rates at any level it chooses?

INTEREST RATE LEVELS AND STOCK PRICES

Interest rates have two effects on corporate profits: (1) Because interest is a cost, the higher the interest rate, the lower a firm's profits, other things held constant. (2) Interest rates affect the level of economic activity, and economic activity affects corporate profits. Interest rates obviously affect stock prices because of their effects on profits, but perhaps even more important, they have an effect due to competition in the marketplace between stocks and bonds: *If interest rates rise sharply, investors can get higher returns in the bond market, which induces them to sell stocks and to transfer funds from the stock market to the bond market.* Selling stocks in response to rising interest rates obviously depresses stock prices. Of course, the reverse occurs if interest rates decline. Indeed, the bull market of December 1991, when the Dow Jones Industrial Index rose 10 percent in less than a month, was caused almost entirely by a sharp drop in long-term interest rates.

The experience of Kansas City Power, the electric utility serving western Missouri and eastern Kansas, can be used to illustrate the effects of interest rates on stock prices. In 1983, the firm's stock sold for $9.50 per share, and, since the firm paid a $1.17 dividend, the dividend yield was $1.17/$9.50 = 12.3%. Kansas City Power's bonds at the time also yielded about 12.3 percent. Thus, if someone had saved $100,000 and invested it in either the stock or the bonds, his or her annual income would have been about $12,300. (The investor might also have expected the stock price to grow over time, providing some capital gains, but that point is not relevant to this example.)

By late 1997, interest rates were lower, and Kansas City Power's bonds were yielding less than 8 percent. If the stock still yielded 12.3 percent, investors would be much more inclined to invest in the stock than in the bonds. Thus, investment money would flow into the stock rather than the bonds, and the stock price would be bid up. Indeed, this is exactly what happened. Kansas City Power's stock sold for $29 in late 1997, a gain of 205 percent over the period. The dividend increased from $1.17 to $1.62, or by 38 percent versus the 205 percent stock price increase. Thus, the major factor in the stock price rise was not the growth in dividends but, rather, the fact that interest rates had fallen. The $29 stock price produced a dividend yield of $1.62/$29 = 5.6%, which was in line with the firm's current bond yield.

SELF-TEST
QUESTION

In what two ways do changes in interest rates affect stock prices?

INTEREST RATES AND BUSINESS DECISIONS

The yield curve for October 1997, shown earlier in Figure 4-5, indicates how much the U.S. government had to pay in 1997 to borrow money for one year, five years, ten years, and so on. A business borrower would have had to pay somewhat more, but assume for the moment that we are back in October 1997 and that the yield curve for that year also applies to your company. Now suppose your company has decided (1) to build a new plant with a 30-year life which will cost $1 million and (2) to raise the $1 million by selling an issue of debt (or borrowing) rather than by selling stock. If you borrowed in 1997 on a short-term basis—say, for one year—your interest cost for that year would be only 5.5 percent, or $55,000. On the other hand, if you used long-term (30-year) financing, your cost would be 6.4 percent, or $64,000. Therefore, at first glance, it would seem that you should use short-term debt.

However, this could prove to be a horrible mistake. If you use short-term debt, you will have to renew your loan every year, and the rate charged on each new loan will reflect the then-current short-term rate. Interest rates could return to their March 1980 levels, in which case you would be paying 14 percent, or $140,000, per year. These high interest payments would cut into, and perhaps eliminate, your profits. Your reduced profitability could easily increase your firm's risk to the point where its bond rating would be lowered, causing lenders to increase the risk premium built into the interest rate they charge. That would force you to pay an even higher rate, which would further reduce your profitability, worry lenders even more, and make them reluctant to renew your loan. If your lenders refused to renew the loan and demanded its repayment, as they would have every right to do, you might have to sell assets at a loss, which could lead to bankruptcy.

On the other hand, if you used long-term financing in 1997, your interest costs would remain constant at $64,000 per year, so an increase in interest rates in the economy would not hurt you. You might even be able to buy up some of your bankrupt competitors at bargain prices—bankruptcies increase dramatically when interest rates rise, primarily because many firms do use too much short-term debt.

Does all this suggest that firms should always avoid short-term debt? Not necessarily. If inflation falls over the next few years, so will interest rates. If you had borrowed on a long-term basis for 6.4 percent in October 1997, your company would be at a major disadvantage if it was locked into 6.4 percent debt while its competitors (who used short-term debt in 1997 and thus rode interest rates down in subsequent years) had a borrowing cost of only 3 or 4 percent.

Financing decisions would be easy if we could develop accurate forecasts of future interest rates. Unfortunately, predicting interest rates with consistent accuracy is somewhere between difficult and impossible—people who make a living by selling interest rate forecasts say it is difficult, but many others say it is impossible.

Even if it is difficult to predict future interest rate *levels,* it is easy to predict that interest rates will *fluctuate*—they always have, and they always will. This being the case, sound financial policy calls for using a mix of long- and short-term debt, as well as equity, to position the firm so that it can survive in any interest rate environment. Further, the optimal financial policy depends in an important way on the nature of the firm's assets—the easier it is to sell off assets to generate cash, the more feasible it is to use large amounts of short-term debt. This makes it more feasible for a firm to finance its current assets than its fixed assets with short-term debt. We will return to this issue later in the book, when we discuss working capital policy.

Changes in interest rates also have implications for savers. For example, if you had a 401(k) plan—and someday you probably will—you would probably want to invest some of your money in a bond mutual fund. You could choose a fund that had an average maturity of 25 years, 10 years, 5 years, or 1 year. How would your choice affect your investment results, hence your retirement income? First, the annual interest income earned by the plan would be affected. For example, if the yield curve were upward sloping, as it normally is, you would earn more interest if you chose a fund that held long-term bonds. Note, though, that if you chose a long-term fund and interest rates then rose, the market value of the bonds in the fund would decline. For example, as we will see in Chapter 8, if you had $100,000 in a fund whose average bond had a maturity of

25 years and a coupon rate of 6 percent, and if interest rates then rose from 6 percent to 10 percent, the market value of your fund would decline from $100,000 to about $64,000. Of course, if rates declined, your fund would increase in value. In any event, your choice of maturity would have a major effect on your investment performance, hence your future income.

If short-term interest rates are lower than long-term rates, why might a borrower still choose to finance with long-term debt?

Explain the following statement: "Financing with short-term debt will probably increase a firm's expected profits but also increase its risk."

SUMMARY

In this chapter, we discussed the nature of financial markets, the types of institutions that operate in these markets, how interest rates are determined, and some of the ways in which interest rates affect business decisions. The key concepts covered are listed below.

- There are many different types of **financial markets.** Each market serves a different region or deals with a different type of security.

- **Physical asset markets,** also called tangible or real asset markets, are those for such products as wheat, autos, and real estate.

- **Financial asset markets** deal with stocks, bonds, notes, mortgages, and other claims on real assets.

- **Spot markets** and **futures markets** are terms that refer to whether the assets are being bought or sold for "on-the-spot" delivery or for delivery at some future date.

- **Money markets** are the markets for debt securities with maturities of less than one year.

- **Capital markets** are the markets for long-term debt and corporate stocks.

- **Primary markets** are the markets in which corporations raise new capital.

- **Secondary markets** are markets in which existing, already outstanding, securities are traded among investors.

- Securities firms have been busy developing new financial products called **derivatives,** which are securities whose value is derived from the price of some other "underlying" asset.

- Transfers of capital between borrowers and savers take place (1) by **direct transfers** of money and securities; (2) by transfers through **investment banking houses,** which act as middlemen; and (3) by transfers through **financial intermediaries,** which create new securities.

- Among the major classes of intermediaries are **commercial banks, savings and loan associations, mutual savings banks, credit unions, pension funds, life insurance companies,** and **mutual funds.**

- One result of ongoing regulatory changes has been a blurring of the distinctions between the different financial institutions. The trend in the United States has been toward **financial service corporations** which offer a wide range of financial services, including investment banking, brokerage operations, insurance, and commercial banking.

- The **stock market** is an especially important market because this is where stock prices (which are used to "grade" managers' performances) are established.

- There are two basic types of stock markets—the **organized exchanges** and the **over-the-counter market.**

- Capital is allocated through the price system—a price must be paid to "rent" money. Lenders charge **interest** on funds they lend, while equity investors receive **dividends** and **capital gains** in return for letting firms use their money.

- Four fundamental factors affect the cost of money: (1) **production opportunities,** (2) **time preferences for consumption,** (3) **risk,** and (4) **inflation.**

- The **risk-free rate of interest, k_{RF},** is defined as the real risk-free rate, k^*, plus an inflation premium, IP, hence $k_{RF} = k^* + IP$.

- The **nominal** (or **quoted**) **interest rate** on a debt security, **k,** is composed of the real risk-free rate, k^*, plus premiums that reflect inflation (IP), default risk (DRP), liquidity (LP), and maturity risk (MRP):

$$k = k^* + IP + DRP + LP + MRP.$$

- If the **real risk-free rate of interest and the various premiums were constant over time,** interest rates would be stable. However, both the real rate and the premiums—especially the premium for expected inflation—**do change over time, causing market interest rates to change.** Also, Federal Reserve intervention to increase or decrease the money supply, as well as international currency flows, lead to fluctuations in interest rates.

- The relationship between the interest rates on securities and the securities' maturities is known as the **term structure of interest rates,** and the **yield curve** is a graph of this relationship.

- The shape of the yield curve depends on two key factors: (1) **expectations about future inflation** and (2) **perceptions about the relative riskiness of securities with different maturities.**

- The yield curve is normally **upward sloping**—this is called a **normal yield curve.** However, the curve can slope downward (an **inverted yield curve**) if the inflation rate is expected to decline.

- A number of theories have been proposed to explain the shape of the yield curve at any point in time. These theories include the **expectations theory** and the **liquidity preference theory.**

- **Interest rate levels have a profound effect on stock prices.** Higher interest rates (1) slow down the economy, (2) increase interest expenses and thus lower corporate profits, and (3) cause investors to sell stocks and transfer funds to the bond market. Thus, higher interest rates depress stock prices.

- Because interest rate levels are difficult if not impossible to predict, **sound financial policy** calls for using a mix of short- and long-term debt, and also for positioning the firm to survive in any future interest rate environment.

Questions

4-1   Define each of the following terms:
   a. Money market; capital market
   b. Primary market; secondary market
   c. Private markets; public markets
   d. Derivatives
   e. Investment banker; financial service corporation

    f. Financial intermediary

    g. Mutual fund; money market fund

    h. Organized security exchanges; over-the-counter market

    i. Production opportunities; time preferences for consumption

    j. Real risk-free rate of interest, k^*; nominal risk-free rate of interest, k_{RF}

    k. Inflation premium (IP)

    l. Default risk premium (DRP)

    m. Liquidity; liquidity premium (LP)

    n. Interest rate risk; maturity risk premium (MRP)

    o. Reinvestment rate risk

    p. Term structure of interest rates; yield curve

    q. "Normal" yield curve; inverted ("abnormal") yield curve

    r. Expectations theory

    s. Liquidity preference theory

    t. Foreign trade deficit

4-2   What are financial intermediaries, and what economic functions do they perform?

4-3   Suppose interest rates on residential mortgages of equal risk were 7 percent in California and 9 percent in New York. Could this differential persist? What forces might tend to equalize rates? Would differentials in borrowing costs for businesses of equal risk located in California and New York be more or less likely to exist than differentials in residential mortgage rates? Would differentials in the cost of money for New York and California firms be more likely to exist if the firms being compared were very large or if they were very small? What are the implications of all this for the pressure now being put on Congress to permit banks to engage in nationwide branching?

4-4   What would happen to the standard of living in the United States if people lost faith in the safety of our financial institutions? Why?

4-5   How does a cost-efficient capital market help to reduce the prices of goods and services?

4-6   Which fluctuate more, long-term or short-term interest rates? Why?

4-7   Suppose you believe that the economy is just entering a recession. Your firm must raise capital immediately, and debt will be used. Should you borrow on a long-term or a short-term basis? Why?

4-8   Suppose the population of Area Y is relatively young while that of Area O is relatively old, but everything else about the two areas is equal.

    a. Would interest rates likely be the same or different in the two areas? Explain.

    b. Would a trend toward nationwide branching by banks and savings and loans, and the development of nationwide diversified financial corporations, affect your answer to Part a?

4-9   Suppose a new process was developed which could be used to make oil out of seawater. The equipment required is quite expensive, but it would, in time, lead to very low prices for gasoline, electricity, and other types of energy. What effect would this have on interest rates?

4-10   Suppose a new and much more liberal Congress and administration were elected, and their first order of business was to take away the independence of the Federal Reserve System, and to force the Fed to greatly expand the money supply. What effect would this have

    a. On the level and slope of the yield curve immediately after the announcement?

    b. On the level and slope of the yield curve that would exist two or three years in the future?

4-11   It is a fact that the federal government (1) encouraged the development of the savings and loan industry; (2) virtually forced the industry to make long-term, fixed-interest-rate mortgages; and (3) forced the savings and loans to obtain most of their capital as deposits that were withdrawable on demand.

    a. Would the savings and loans have higher profits in a world with a "normal" or an inverted yield curve?

    b. Would the savings and loan industry be better off if the individual institutions sold their mortgages to federal agencies and then collected servicing fees or if the institutions held the mortgages that they originated?

4-12   Suppose interest rates on Treasury bonds rose from 7 to 14 percent as a result of higher interest rates in Europe. What effect would this have on the price of an average company's common stock?

Self-Test Problem   (Solution Appears in Appendix B)

ST-1

Inflation Rates

Assume that it is now January 1, 1999. The rate of inflation is expected to be 4 percent throughout 1999. However, increased government deficits and renewed vigor in the economy are then expected to push inflation rates higher. Investors expect the inflation rate to be 5 percent in 2000,

6 percent in 2001, and 7 percent in 2002. The real risk-free rate, k*, is expected to remain at 2 percent over the next 5 years. Assume that no maturity risk premiums are required on bonds with 5 years or less to maturity. The current interest rate on 5-year T-bonds is 8 percent.
a. What is the average expected inflation rate over the next 4 years?
b. What should be the prevailing interest rate on 4-year T-bonds?
c. What is the implied expected inflation rate in 2003, or Year 5, given that Treasury bonds which mature in that year yield 8 percent?

Problems

4-1
Expected Rate of Interest

The real risk-free rate of interest is 3 percent. Inflation is expected to be 2 percent this year and 4 percent during the next 2 years. Assume that the maturity risk premium is zero. What is the yield on 2-year Treasury securities? What is the yield on 3-year Treasury securities?

4-2
Default Risk Premium

A Treasury bond which matures in 10 years has a yield of 6 percent. A 10-year corporate bond has a yield of 8 percent. Assume that the liquidity premium on the corporate bond is 0.5 percent. What is the default risk premium on the corporate bond?

4-3
Expected Rate of Interest

One-year Treasury securities yield 5 percent. The market anticipates that 1 year from now, 1-year Treasury securities will yield 6 percent. If the pure expectations hypothesis is correct, what should be the yield today for 2-year Treasury securities?

4-4
Maturity Risk Premium

The real risk-free rate is 3 percent, and inflation is expected to be 3 percent for the next 2 years. A 2-year Treasury security yields 6.2 percent. What is the maturity risk premium for the 2-year security?

4-5
Expected Rate of Interest

Interest rates on 1-year Treasury securities are currently 5.6 percent, while 2-year Treasury securities are yielding 6 percent. If the pure expectations theory is correct, what does the market believe will be the yield on 1-year securities 1 year from now?

4-6
Expected Rate of Interest

Interest rates on 4-year Treasury securities are currently 7 percent, while interest rates on 6-year Treasury securities are currently 7.5 percent. If the pure expectations theory is correct, what does the market believe that 2-year securities will be yielding 4 years from now?

4-7
Expected Rate of Interest

The real risk-free rate is 3 percent. Inflation is expected to be 3 percent this year, 4 percent next year, and then 3.5 percent thereafter. The maturity risk premium is estimated to be $0.0005 \times (t - 1)$, where t = number of years to maturity. What is the nominal interest rate on a 7-year Treasury bill?

4-8
Expected Rate of Interest

Suppose the annual yield on a 2-year Treasury bond is 4.5 percent, while that on a 1-year bond is 3 percent. k* is 1 percent, and the maturity risk premium is zero.
a. Using the expectations theory, forecast the interest rate on a 1-year bond during the second year. (Hint: Under the expectations theory, the yield on a 2-year bond is equal to the average yield on 1-year bonds in Years 1 and 2.)
b. What is the expected inflation rate in Year 1? Year 2?

4-9
Expected Rate of Interest

Assume that the real risk-free rate is 2 percent and that the maturity risk premium is zero. If the nominal rate of interest on 1-year bonds is 5 percent and that on comparable-risk 2-year bonds is 7 percent, what is the 1-year interest rate that is expected for Year 2? What inflation rate is expected during Year 2? Comment on why the average interest rate during the 2-year period differs from the 1-year interest rate expected for Year 2.

4-10
Maturity Risk Premium

Assume that the real risk-free rate, k*, is 3 percent and that inflation is expected to be 8 percent in Year 1, 5 percent in Year 2, and 4 percent thereafter. Assume also that all Treasury bonds are highly liquid and free of default risk. If 2-year and 5-year Treasury bonds both yield 10 percent, what is the difference in the maturity risk premiums (MRPs) on the two bonds; that is, what is MRP_5 minus MRP_2?

4-11
Interest Rates

Due to a recession, the inflation rate expected for the coming year is only 3 percent. However, the inflation rate in Year 2 and thereafter is expected to be constant at some level above 3 percent. Assume that the real risk-free rate is k* = 2% for all maturities and that the expectations theory fully explains the yield curve, so there are no maturity premiums. If 3-year Treasury bonds yield 2 percentage points more than 1-year bonds, what inflation rate is expected after Year 1?

4-12
Yield Curves

Suppose you and most other investors expect the inflation rate to be 7 percent next year, to fall to 5 percent during the following year, and then to remain at a rate of 3 percent thereafter. Assume that the real risk-free rate, k*, will remain at 2 percent and that maturity risk premiums on Treasury securities rise from zero on very short-term bonds (those that mature in a few days) to a level of 0.2 percentage point for 1-year securities. Furthermore, maturity risk premiums increase 0.2 percentage point for each year to maturity, up to a limit of 1.0 percentage point on 5-year or longer-term T-bonds.

a. Calculate the interest rate on 1-, 2-, 3-, 4-, 5-, 10-, and 20-year Treasury securities, and plot the yield curve.

b. Now suppose Exxon, an AAA-rated company, had bonds with the same maturities as the Treasury bonds. As an approximation, plot an Exxon yield curve on the same graph with the Treasury bond yield curve. (Hint: Think about the default risk premium on Exxon's long-term versus its short-term bonds.)

c. Now plot the approximate yield curve of Long Island Lighting Company, a risky nuclear utility.

4-13
Yield Curves

The following yields on U.S. Treasury securities were taken from *The Wall Street Journal* in September 1997:

TERM	RATE
6 months	5.5%
1 year	5.6
2 years	5.8
3 years	5.9
4 years	6.0
5 years	6.0
10 years	6.3
20 years	6.5
30 years	6.4

Plot a yield curve based on these data.

4-14
Inflation and Interest Rates

In late 1980, the U.S. Commerce Department released new figures which showed that inflation was running at an annual rate of close to 15 percent. At the time, the prime rate of interest was 21 percent, a record high. However, many investors expected the new Reagan administration to be more effective in controlling inflation than the Carter administration had been. Moreover, many observers believed that the extremely high interest rates and generally tight credit, which resulted from the Federal Reserve System's attempts to curb the inflation rate, would shortly bring about a recession, which, in turn, would lead to a decline in the inflation rate and also in the interest rate. Assume that at the beginning of 1981, the expected inflation rate for 1981 was 13 percent; for 1982, 9 percent; for 1983, 7 percent; and for 1984 and thereafter, 6 percent.

a. What was the average expected inflation rate over the 5-year period 1981–1985? (Use the arithmetic average.)

b. What average *nominal* interest rate would, over the 5-year period, be expected to produce a 2 percent real risk-free rate of return on 5-year Treasury securities?

c. Assuming a real risk-free rate of 2 percent and a maturity risk premium which starts at 0.1 percent and increases by 0.1 percent each year, estimate the interest rate in January 1981 on bonds that mature in 1, 2, 5, 10, and 20 years, and draw a yield curve based on these data.

d. Describe the general economic conditions that could be expected to produce an upward-sloping yield curve.

e. If the consensus among investors in early 1981 had been that the expected inflation rate for every future year was 10 percent (that is, $I_t = I_{t+1} = 10\%$ for t = 1 to ∞), what do you think the yield curve would have looked like? Consider all the factors that are likely to affect the curve. Does your answer here make you question the yield curve you drew in Part c?

MINI CASE

Assume that you recently graduated with a degree in finance and have just reported to work as an investment advisor at the brokerage firm of Balik and Kiefer Inc. Your first assignment is to explain the nature of the U.S. financial markets to Michelle DellaTorre, a professional tennis player who has just come to the United States from Chile. DellaTorre is a highly ranked tennis player who expects to invest substantial amounts of money through Balik and Kiefer. She is also very bright, and, therefore, she would like to understand in general terms what will happen to her money. Your boss has developed the following set of questions which you must ask and answer to explain the U.S. financial system to DellaTorre.

a. What is a market? How are physical asset markets differentiated from financial markets?

b. Differentiate between money markets and capital markets.

c. Differentiate between a primary market and a secondary market. If Apple Computer decided to issue additional common stock, and DellaTorre purchased 100 shares of this stock from Merrill Lynch, the underwriter, would this transaction be a primary market transaction or a secondary market transaction? Would it make a difference if DellaTorre purchased previously outstanding Apple stock in the over-the-counter market?

d. Describe the three primary ways in which capital is transferred between savers and borrowers.

e. Securities can be traded on organized exchanges or in the over-the-counter market. Define each of these markets, and describe how stocks are traded in each of them.

f. What do we call the price that a borrower must pay for debt capital? What is the price of equity capital? What are the four most fundamental factors that affect the cost of money, or the general level of interest rates, in the economy?

g. What is the real risk-free rate of interest (k^*) and the nominal risk-free rate (k_{RF})? How are these two rates measured?

h. Define the terms inflation premium (IP), default risk premium (DRP), liquidity premium (LP), and maturity risk premium (MRP). Which of these premiums is included when determining the interest rate on (1) short-term U.S. Treasury securities, (2) long-term U.S. Treasury securities, (3) short-term corporate securities, and (4) long-term corporate securities? Explain how the premiums would vary over time and among the different securities listed above.

i. DellaTorre is also interested in investing in countries other than the United States. Describe the various types of risks that arise when investing overseas.

j. What is the term structure of interest rates? What is a yield curve? At any given time, how would the yield curve facing an AAA-rated company compare with the yield curve for U.S. Treasury securities? At any given time, how would the yield curve facing a BB-rated company compare with the yield curve for U.S. Treasury securities? Draw a graph to illustrate your answer.

k. Two main theories have been advanced to explain the shape of the yield curve: (1) the expectations theory and (2) the liquidity preference theory. Briefly describe each of these theories. Do economists regard one as being "true"?

l. Suppose most investors expect the inflation rate to be 5 percent next year, 6 percent the following year, and 8 percent thereafter. The real risk-free rate is 3 percent. The maturity risk premium is zero for bonds that mature in 1 year or less, 0.1 percent for 2-year bonds, and then the MRP increases by 0.1 percent per year thereafter for 20 years, after which it is stable. What is the interest rate on 1-year, 10-year, and 20-year Treasury bonds? Draw a yield curve with these data. Is your yield curve consistent with the expectations theory or with the liquidity preference theory?

Selected Additional References

Textbooks which focus on interest rates and financial markets include

Fabozzi, Frank J., *Bond Markets: Analysis and Strategies* (Englewood Cliffs, N.J.: Prentice-Hall, 1992).

Johnson, Hazel J., *Financial Institutions and Markets: A Global Perspective* (New York: McGraw-Hill, 1993).

Kidwell, David S., Richard Peterson, and David Blackwell, *Financial Institutions, Markets, and Money* (Fort Worth, Tex.: Dryden Press, 1993).

Kohn, Mier, *Money, Banking, and Financial Markets* (Fort Worth, Tex.: Dryden Press, 1993).

Livingston, Miles, *Money and Capital Markets* (Cambridge, Mass.: Blackwell, 1996).

Smith, Stephen D., and Raymond E. Spudeck, *Interest Rates: Theory and Application* (Fort Worth, Tex.: Dryden Press, 1993).

For current empirical data and a forecast of monetary conditions, see the most recent edition of this annual publication:

Salomon Brothers, *Supply and Demand for Credit* (New York).

The classic works on term structure theories include the following:

Culbertson, John M., "The Term Structure of Interest Rates," *Quarterly Journal of Economics,* November 1957, 489–504.

Fisher, Irving, "Appreciation and Interest," *Publications of the American Economic Association,* August 1986, 23–29 and 91–92.

Hicks, J. R., *Value and Capital* (London: Oxford University Press, 1946).

Lutz, F. A., "The Structure of Interest Rates," *Quarterly Journal of Economics,* November 1940, 36–63.

Modigliani, Franco, and Richard Sutch, "Innovations in Interest Rate Policy," *American Economic Review,* May 1966, 178–197.

For additional information on financial institutions, see

Greenbaum, Stuart I., and Anjan V. Thakor, *Contemporary Financial Intermediation* (Fort Worth, Tex.: Dryden Press, 1995).

Kaufman, George G., *The U.S. Financial System* (Englewood Cliffs, N.J.: Prentice-Hall, 1995).

CHAPTER 5
RISK AND RETURN:
THE BASICS

CHAPTER 6
RISK AND RETURN:
EXTENSIONS

CHAPTER 7
TIME VALUE OF MONEY

The Transamerica pyramid, built in 1972, has become a modern landmark of San Francisco. The building's design caused a storm of public protest when it was made public in 1969, but according to the results of a 1995 survey, it is one of the 20 most recognizable graphic icons of the century. William L. Pereira, who chose the pyramidal configuration both to allow more light to reach the street level than a conventional-shaped building and to make a statement of architectural sculpture, designed it.

©Kerrick James/The PhotoFile

RISK AND RETURN: THE BASICS

If someone had invested $1,000 in a portfolio of large-company stocks in 1925 and then reinvested all dividends received, their investment would have grown to $1,371,000 by 1996. Over the same time period, a portfolio of small-company stocks would have grown even more, to $4,496,000. But if instead they had invested in long-term government bonds, the value of their portfolio would have been only $34,000, and a measly $13,500 if the funds were in short-term bonds.

Given these numbers, why would anyone invest in bonds? The answer is, "Because bonds are less risky." While common stocks have over the past 71 years produced considerably higher returns, (1) we cannot be sure that the past is prologue to the future, and (2) stock values are more likely to experience sharp declines than bonds, so one has a greater chance of losing money on a stock investment. This is especially true if someone is investing with a relatively short time horizon, say, three years or less. For example, in 1990 the average small-company stock lost 21.6 percent of its value, and large-company stocks lost 3.2 percent. Bonds, though, provided positive returns that year, as they almost always do.

Of course, some stocks are riskier than others, and even in years when the overall stock market is up, many individual stocks go down. Therefore, putting all your money into one stock is extremely risky. According to a recent Business Week *article, the single best weapon against risk is diversification: "By spreading your money around, you're not tied to the fickleness of a given market, stock, or industry. . . . Correlation, in portfolio-manager speak, helps you diversify properly because it describes how closely two investments track each other. If they move in tandem, they're likely to suffer from the same bad news. So, you should combine assets with low correlations."*

U.S. investors tend to think of "the stock market" as the U.S. stock market. However, U.S. stocks amount to only about 35 percent of the value of all stocks. Foreign markets have been quite profitable, and they are not perfectly correlated with U.S. markets. Therefore, global diversification offers U.S. investors an opportunity to raise returns and at the same time reduce risk. However, foreign investing brings some risks of its own, most notably "exchange rate risk," which is the danger that exchange rate shifts will decrease the number of dollars a foreign currency will buy.

Although the central thrust of the Business Week *article was on ways to measure and then reduce risk, it did point out that some newly created instruments which are actually extremely risky have been marketed as low-risk investments to naive investors. For example, several mutual funds have advertised that their portfolios "contain only securities backed by the U.S. government," but they failed to highlight that the funds themselves are using financial leverage, are investing in "derivatives," or are taking some other action which boosts current yields but exposes investors to huge risks.*

When you finish this chapter, you should understand what risk is, how it is measured, and what actions can be taken to minimize it or at least ensure that you are adequately compensated for bearing it.

In this chapter, we will examine how investment risk is measured and how it affects investment returns. We start from the basic premise that investors like returns and dislike risk. Therefore, people will invest in riskier assets only if they expect to receive above average returns. We will define precisely what the term *risk* means as it relates to investments, examine procedures managers use to measure risk, and discuss the relationship between risk and return. Chapter 6 goes on to study risk in more depth. Then, in Chapters 8 and 9, we extend these relationships to show how risk and return interact to determine stock and bond prices. Business executives should understand these concepts and think about them as they plan the actions which will shape their firms' futures.[1]

As you will see, risk can be measured in different ways, and different conclusions about an asset's riskiness can be reached depending on the measure used. This can be confusing, but it will help if you remember the following:

1. All financial assets are expected to produce *cash flows,* and the riskiness of an asset is judged in terms of the riskiness of its cash flows.

2. The riskiness of an asset can be considered in two ways: (1) on a *stand-alone basis,* where the asset's cash flows are analyzed by themselves, or (2) in a *portfolio context,* where the cash flows from a number of assets are combined and then the consolidated cash flows are analyzed.[2] There is an important difference between standalone and portfolio risk, and an asset which has a great deal of risk if held by itself may be much less risky if it is held as part of a larger portfolio.

3. In a portfolio context, a stock's risk can be divided into two components: (1) a *diversifiable risk component,* which can be diversified away and hence is of little concern to diversified investors, and (2) a *market risk component,* which reflects the risk of a general stock market decline and which cannot be eliminated by diversification, hence *does* concern investors. Only market risk is *relevant* — diversifiable risk is irrelevant to most investors because it can be eliminated.

4. An asset with a high degree of relevant (market) risk must provide a relatively high expected rate of return to attract investors. Investors in general are *averse to risk,* so they will not buy risky assets unless those assets have high expected returns.

5. In this chapter, we focus on *financial assets* such as stocks and bonds, but the concepts discussed here also apply to *physical assets* such as machines, trucks, or even whole plants. We apply risk analysis to physical assets in Chapter 13.

INVESTMENT RETURNS

With most investments, an individual or business spends money today with the expectation of earning even more money in the future. The concept of *return* provides investors with a convenient way of expressing the financial performance of an investment. To illustrate, suppose you buy ten shares of a stock for $1,000. The stock pays no

---

[1]This chapter presents all of the risk and return concepts needed to understand the material presented in the remaining chapters. However, Chapter 5 does not go into depth on the theoretical foundations of risk and return, so you may want to read (or your instructor may assign) Chapter 6 to provide you with a more in-depth understanding of these concepts.

[2]A *portfolio* is a collection of investment securities. If you owned some General Motors stock, some Exxon stock, and some IBM stock, you would be holding a three-stock portfolio. Because diversification lowers risk, most stocks are held in portfolios.

dividends, but at the end of one year, you sell the stock for $1,100. What is the return on your $1,000 investment?

One way of expressing an investment return is in *dollar terms*. The dollar return is simply the total dollars received from the investment less the amount invested:

$$\text{Dollar return} = \text{Amount received} - \text{Amount invested}$$

$$= \$1,100 - \$1,000$$

$$= \$100.$$

If, at the end of the year, you had sold the stock for only $900, your dollar return would have been −$100.

Although expressing returns in dollars is easy, two problems arise: (1) To make a meaningful judgment about the adequacy of the return, you need to know the scale (size) of the investment; a $100 return on a $100 investment is a very good return (assuming the investment is held for one year), but a $100 return on a $10,000 investment would be a poor return. (2) You also need to know the timing of the return; a $100 return on a $100 investment is a very good return if it occurs after one year, but the same dollar return after 20 years would not be very good.

The solution to the scale and timing problems of dollar returns is to express investment results as *rates of return,* or *percentage returns.* For example, the rate of return on the one-year stock investment, when $1,100 is received after one year, is 10 percent:

$$\text{Rate of return} = \frac{\text{Amount received} - \text{Amount invested}}{\text{Amount invested}}$$

$$= \frac{\text{Dollar return}}{\text{Amount invested}} = \frac{\$100}{\$1,000}$$

$$= 0.10 = 10\%.$$

The rate of return calculation "standardizes" the return by considering the return per unit of investment. In this example, the return of 0.10, or 10 percent, indicates that each dollar invested will earn 0.10($1.00) = $0.10. If the rate of return had been negative, this would indicate that the original investment was not even recovered. For example, selling the stock for only $900 results in a −10 percent rate of return, which means that each dollar invested lost 10 cents.

Note also that a $10 return on a $100 investment produces a 10 percent rate of return, while a $10 return on a $1,000 investment results in a rate of return of only 1 percent. Thus, the percentage return takes account of the size of the investment.

Expressing rates of return on an annual basis, which is typically done in practice, solves the timing problem. A $10 return after one year on a $100 investment results in a 10 percent annual rate of return, while a $10 return after five years yields only a 1.9 percent annual rate of return. We will discuss all this in detail in Chapter 7, which deals with the time value of money.

Although we illustrated return concepts with one outflow and one inflow, in later chapters we demonstrate that rate of return concepts can easily be applied in situations where multiple cash flows occur over time. For example, when Intel makes an investment in new chip-making technology, the investment is made and the resulting inflows occur over a number of years. For now, it is sufficient to recognize that the rate of return solves the two major problems associated with dollar returns, hence the rate of return is the most common measure of investment performance.

SELF-TEST
QUESTIONS
Differentiate between dollar return and rate of return.

Why is the rate of return superior to the dollar return?

Is the rate of return an application of time value analysis? Explain.

STAND-ALONE RISK

Risk is defined in *Webster's* as "a hazard; a peril; exposure to loss or injury." Thus, risk refers to the chance that some unfavorable event will occur. If you engage in skydiving, you are taking a chance with your life—skydiving is risky. If you bet on the horses, you are risking your money. If you invest in speculative stocks (or, really, *any* stock), you are taking a risk in the hope of making an appreciable return.

An asset's risk can be analyzed in two ways: (1) on a stand-alone basis, where the asset is considered in isolation, and (2) on a portfolio basis, where the asset is held as one of a number of assets in a portfolio. Thus, an asset's **stand-alone risk** is the risk an investor would face if he or she held only this one asset. Most assets are held in portfolios, but it is necessary to understand stand-alone risk in order to understand risk in a portfolio context.

To illustrate the riskiness of financial assets, suppose an investor buys $100,000 of short-term Treasury bills with an expected return of 5 percent. In this case, the rate of return on the investment, 5 percent, can be estimated quite precisely, and the investment is defined as being essentially *risk free*. However, if the $100,000 were invested in the stock of a company just being organized to prospect for oil in the mid-Atlantic, then the investment's return could not be estimated precisely. One might analyze the situation and conclude that the *expected* rate of return, in a statistical sense, is 20 percent, but the investor should also recognize that the *actual* rate of return could range from, say, +1,000 percent to −100 percent. Because there is a significant danger of actually earning much less than the expected return, the stock would be relatively risky.

No investment will be undertaken unless the expected rate of return is high enough to compensate the investor for the perceived risk of the investment. In our example, it is clear that few if any investors would be willing to buy the oil company's stock if its expected return were the same as that of the T-bill.

Naturally, a risky investment might not actually produce its expected rate of return—if assets always produced their expected returns, they would not be risky.

Investment risk, then, is related to the probability of actually earning less than the expected return—the greater the chance of a low or negative return, the riskier the investment. However, risk can be defined more precisely, and it is useful to do so.

Probability Distributions

An event's *probability* is defined as the chance that the event will occur. For example, a weather forecaster might state, "There is a 40 percent chance of rain today and a 60 percent chance of no rain." If all possible events, or outcomes, are listed, and if a probability is assigned to each event, the listing is called a **probability distribution.** For our weather forecast, we could set up the following probability distribution:

OUTCOME (1)	PROBABILITY (2)	(3)
Rain	0.4 =	40%
No rain	0.6 =	60
	1.0 =	100%

The possible outcomes are listed in Column 1, while the probabilities of these outcomes, expressed both as decimals and as percentages, are given in Columns 2 and 3. Notice that the probabilities must sum to 1.0, or 100 percent.

Probabilities can also be assigned to the possible outcomes (or returns) from an investment. If you buy a bond, you expect to receive interest on the bond, and those interest payments will provide you with a rate of return on your investment. The possible outcomes from this investment are (1) that the issuer will make the required payments or (2) that the issuer will default on the payments. The higher the probability of default, the riskier the bond, and the higher the risk, the higher the required rate of return. If you invest in a stock instead of buying a bond, you will again expect to earn a return on your money. A stock's return will come from dividends plus capital gains, which result if you sell the stock for more than you paid for it. Again, the riskier the stock—which means the higher the probability that the firm will fail to pay the expected dividends or that the stock price will decline rather than increase as you expected—the higher the expected return must be to induce you to make the investment.

With this in mind, consider the possible rates of return (dividend yield plus capital gain or loss) that you might earn next year on a $10,000 investment in the stock of either Martin Products Inc. or U.S. Electric Company. Martin manufactures and distributes computer terminals and equipment for the rapidly growing data transmission industry. Because it faces intense competition, its new products may or may not be competitive in the marketplace, so its future earnings cannot be predicted very well. Indeed, some new company could develop better products and literally bankrupt Martin. U.S. Electric, on the other hand, supplies an essential service, and because it has city franchises which protect it from competition, its sales and profits are relatively stable and predictable.

The rate of return probability distributions for the two companies are shown in Table 5-1. There is a 30 percent chance of strong demand, in which case both companies will have high earnings, pay high dividends, and enjoy capital gains. There is a 40 percent probability of normal demand and moderate returns, and there is a 30 percent probability of weak demand, which will mean low earnings and dividends as well as capital losses. Notice, however, that Martin Products' rate of return could vary far more widely than that of U.S. Electric. There is a fairly high probability that the value of Martin's stock will drop substantially, resulting in a 70 percent loss, while there is no chance of a loss for U.S. Electric.[3]

Expected Rate of Return

If we multiply each possible outcome by its probability of occurrence and then sum these products, as in Table 5-2, we have a *weighted average* of outcomes. The weights are the probabilities, and the weighted average is the **expected rate of return, $\hat{k}$,** called "k-hat."[4] The expected rates of return for both Martin Products and U.S. Electric are shown in Table 5-2 to be 15 percent. This type of table is known as a *payoff matrix*.

---

[3]It is, of course, completely unrealistic to think that any stock has no chance of a loss. Only in hypothetical examples could this occur. To illustrate, the price of Columbia Gas's stock dropped from $34.50 to $20.00 in just three hours on June 19, 1991. All investors were reminded that any stock is exposed to some risk of loss, and those investors who bought Columbia Gas on June 18 learned that lesson the hard way.

[4]In Chapters 8 and 9, we will use k_d and k_s to signify the returns on bonds and stocks, respectively. However, this distinction is unnecessary in this chapter, so we just use the general term, k, to signify the expected return on an investment.

TABLE 5-1	Probability Distributions for Two Stocks

		RATE OF RETURN ON STOCK IF THIS DEMAND OCCURS	
DEMAND FOR THE COMPANY'S PRODUCTS	PROBABILITY OF THIS DEMAND OCCURRING	MARTIN PRODUCTS	U.S. ELECTRIC
Strong	0.3	100%	20%
Normal	0.4	15	15
Weak	0.3	(70)	10
	1.0		

TABLE 5-2	Calculation of Expected Rates of Return: Payoff Matrix

		MARTIN PRODUCTS		U.S. ELECTRIC	
DEMAND FOR THE COMPANY'S PRODUCTS (1)	PROBABILITY OF THIS DEMAND OCCURRING (2)	RATE OF RETURN IF THIS DEMAND OCCURS (3)	PRODUCT: (2) × (3) = (4)	RATE OF RETURN IF THIS DEMAND OCCURS (5)	PRODUCT: (2) × (5) = (6)
Strong	0.3	100%	30%	20%	6%
Normal	0.4	15	6	15	6
Weak	0.3	(70)	(21)	10	3
	1.0		$\hat{k} = 15\%$		$\hat{k} = 15\%$

The expected rate of return calculation can also be expressed as an equation which does the same thing as the payoff matrix table:[5]

$$\text{Expected rate of return} = \hat{k} = P_1 k_1 + P_2 k_2 + \cdots + P_n k_n$$

$$= \sum_{i=1}^{n} P_i k_i. \tag{5-1}$$

Here k_i is the ith possible outcome, P_i is the probability of the ith outcome, and n is the number of possible outcomes. Thus, $\hat{k}$ is a weighted average of the possible outcomes (the k_i values), with each outcome's weight being its probability of occurrence. Using the data for Martin Products, we obtain its expected rate of return as follows:

$$\hat{k} = P_1(k_1) + P_2(k_2) + P_3(k_3)$$

$$= 0.3(100\%) + 0.4(15\%) + 0.3(-70\%)$$

$$= 15\%.$$

---

[5]The second form of the equation is simply a shorthand expression in which sigma (Σ) means "sum up," or add the values of n factors. If $i = 1$, then $P_i k_i = P_1 k_1$; if $i = 2$, then $P_i k_i = P_2 k_2$; and so on until $i = n$, the last possible outcome. The symbol $\sum_{i=1}^{n}$ simply says, "Go through the following process: First, let $i = 1$ and find the first product; then let $i = 2$ and find the second product; then continue until each individual product up to $i = n$ has been found, and then add these individual products to find the expected rate of return."

U.S. Electric's expected rate of return is also 15 percent:

$$\hat{k} = 0.3(20\%) + 0.4(15\%) + 0.3(10\%)$$

$$= 15\%.$$

We can graph the rates of return to obtain a picture of the variability of possible outcomes; this is shown in the Figure 5-1 bar charts. The height of each bar signifies the probability that a given outcome will occur. The range of probable returns for Martin Products is from −70 to +100 percent, with an expected return of 15 percent. The expected return for U.S. Electric is also 15 percent, but its range is much narrower.

Thus far, we have assumed that only three situations can exist: strong, normal, and weak demand. Actually, of course, demand could range from a deep depression to a fantastic boom, and there are an unlimited number of possibilities in between. Suppose we had the time and patience to assign a probability to each possible level of demand (with the sum of the probabilities still equaling 1.0) and to assign a rate of return to each stock for each level of demand. We would have a table similar to Table 5-1, except that it would have many more entries in each column. This table could be used to calculate expected rates of return as shown previously, and the probabilities and outcomes could be approximated by continuous curves such as those presented in Figure 5-2. Here we have changed the assumptions so that there is essentially a zero probability that Martin Products' return will be less than −70 percent or more than 100 percent, or that

| FIGURE 5-1 | Probability Distributions of Martin Products' and U.S. Electric's Rates of Return |

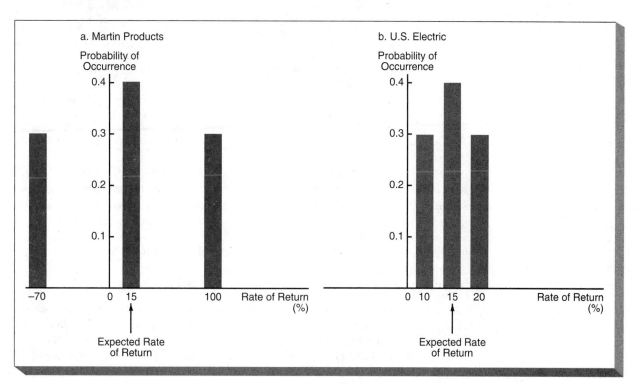

| FIGURE 5-2 | Continuous Probability Distributions of Martin Products' and U.S. Electric's Rates of Return |

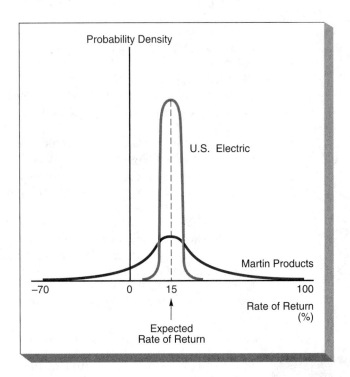

NOTE: The assumptions regarding the probabilities of various outcomes have been changed from those in Figure 5-1. There the probability of obtaining exactly 15 percent was 40 percent; here it is *much smaller* because there are many possible outcomes instead of just three. With continuous distributions, it is more appropriate to ask what the probability is of obtaining at least some specified rate of return than to ask what the probability is of obtaining exactly that rate. This topic is covered in detail in statistics courses.

U.S. Electric's return will be less than 10 percent or more than 20 percent, but virtually any return within these limits is possible.

The tighter, or more peaked, the probability distribution, the more likely it is that the actual outcome will be close to the expected value, and, consequently, the less likely it is that the actual return will end up far below the expected return. Thus, the tighter the probability distribution, the lower the risk assigned to a stock. Since U.S. Electric has a relatively tight probability distribution, its *actual return* is likely to be closer to its 15 percent *expected return* than is that of Martin Products.

Measuring Stand-Alone Risk: The Standard Deviation

To be most useful, any measure of risk should have a definite value — we need a measure of the tightness of the probability distribution. One such measure is the **standard deviation,** the symbol for which is σ, pronounced "sigma." The smaller the standard deviation, the tighter the probability distribution, and, accordingly, the lower the riskiness of the stock. To calculate the standard deviation, we proceed as shown in Table 5-3, taking the following steps:

TABLE 5-3	Calculating Martin Products' Standard Deviation

$k_i - \hat{k}$ (1)	$(k_i - \hat{k})^2$ (2)	$(k_i - \hat{k})^2 P_i$ (3)
$100 - 15 = 85$	7,225	$(7,225)(0.3) = 2,167.5$
$15 - 15 = 0$	0	$(0)(0.4) = 0.0$
$-70 - 15 = -85$	7,225	$(7,225)(0.3) = 2,167.5$
		Variance $= \sigma^2 = 4,335.0$

$$\text{Standard deviation} = \sigma = \sqrt{\sigma^2} = \sqrt{4,335} = 65.84\%.$$

1. Calculate the expected rate of return:

$$\text{Expected rate of return} = \hat{k} = \sum_{i=1}^{n} P_i k_i.$$

For Martin, we previously found $\hat{k} = 15\%$.

2. Subtract the expected rate of return ($\hat{k}$) from each possible outcome (k_i) to obtain a set of deviations about $\hat{k}$ as shown in Column 1 of Table 5-3:

$$\text{Deviation}_i = k_i - \hat{k}.$$

3. Square each deviation, then multiply the result by the probability of occurrence for its related outcome, and then sum these products to obtain the **variance** of the probability distribution as shown in Columns 2 and 3 of the table:

$$\text{Variance} = \sigma^2 = \sum_{i=1}^{n} (k_i - \hat{k})^2 P_i. \tag{5-2}$$

4. Finally, find the square root of the variance to obtain the standard deviation:

$$\text{Standard deviation} = \sigma = \sqrt{\sum_{i=1}^{n} (k_i - \hat{k})^2 P_i}. \tag{5-3}$$

Thus, the standard deviation is a weighted average of the deviations from the expected value, and it provides an idea of how far above or below the expected value the actual value is likely to be. Martin's standard deviation is seen in Table 5-3 to be $\sigma = 65.84\%$. Using these same procedures, we find U.S. Electric's standard deviation to be 3.87 percent. Martin Products has a far larger standard deviation, which indicates a far greater variation of returns and thus a much greater chance that the actual return will be far below the expected return. Therefore, Martin Products is a much riskier investment than U.S. Electric when held alone.

Recall from statistics that a normal probability distribution looks like a bell curve. Both distributions in Figure 5-2 are approximately normal. If a probability distribution is normal, the *actual* return will be within ±1 standard deviation of the *expected* return 68.26 percent of the time. Figure 5-3 illustrates this point, and it also shows the situation for ±2σ and ±3σ. For Martin Products, $\hat{k} = 15\%$ and $\sigma = 65.84\%$, whereas $\hat{k} = 15\%$ and $\sigma = 3.87\%$ for U.S. Electric. Thus, if the two distributions were normal, there would be a 68.26 percent probability that Martin's actual return would be in the range of 15 ± 65.84 percent, or from −50.84 to 80.84 percent. For U.S. Electric, the 68.26 percent range is 15 ± 3.87 percent, or from 11.13 to 18.87 percent. With such a small σ, there is only a small probability that U.S. Electric's return would be significantly less

Wilshire Associates provides a download site for returns on various stock indexes such as the Wilshire 5000 and the Wilshire 4500. Wilshire's home page can be found at http://www.wilshire.com. The returns data, which can be downloaded onto your computer, are accessed through the Products menu.

FIGURE 5-3   Probability Ranges for a Normal Distribution

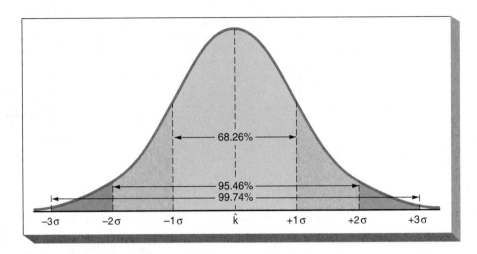

NOTES:

a. The area under the normal curve always equals 1.0, or 100 percent. *Thus, the areas under any pair of normal curves drawn on the same scale, whether they are peaked or flat, must be equal.*

b. Half of the area under a normal curve is to the left of the mean, indicating that there is a 50 percent probability that the actual outcome will be less than the mean, and half is to the right of $\hat{k}$, indicating a 50 percent probability that it will be greater than the mean.

c. Of the area under the curve, 68.26 percent is within $\pm 1\sigma$ of the mean, indicating that the probability is 68.26 percent that the actual outcome will be within the range $\hat{k} - 1\sigma$ to $\hat{k} + 1\sigma$.

d. Procedures exist for finding the probability of other ranges. These procedures are covered in statistics courses.

e. For a normal distribution, the larger the value of σ, the greater the probability that the actual outcome will vary widely from, and hence perhaps be far below, the expected, or most likely, outcome. *Since the probability of having the actual result turn out to be far below the expected result is one definition of risk, and since σ measures this probability, we can use σ as a measure of risk.* This definition may not be a good one, however, if we are dealing with an asset held in a diversified portfolio. This point is covered later in the chapter.

than expected, so the stock is not very risky. For the average firm listed on the New York Stock Exchange, σ has generally been about 35 percent in recent years.[6]

Measuring Stand-Alone Risk: The Coefficient of Variation

If a choice must be made between two investments which have the same expected rate of return but different standard deviations, most people would choose the one with the lower

---

[6]In the example, we described the procedure for finding the mean and standard deviation when the data are in the form of a known probability distribution. If only sample returns data over some past period are available, the standard deviation of returns can be estimated using this formula:

$$\text{Estimated } \sigma = S = \sqrt{\frac{\sum_{t=1}^{n} (\bar{k}_t - \bar{k}_{Avg})^2}{n - 1}}. \tag{5-3a}$$

Here $\bar{k}_t$ ("k bar t") denotes the past realized rate of return in Period t, and $\bar{k}_{Avg}$ is the average annual return earned during the last n years. Here is an example:

YEAR	k_t
1995	15%
1996	−5
1997	20

(footnote continues)

standard deviation and, therefore, the lower risk. Similarly, given a choice between two investments with the same risk (standard deviation) but different expected rates of return, investors would generally prefer the investment with the higher expected return. To most people, this is common sense — return is "good," risk is "bad," and, consequently, investors want as much return and as little risk as possible. But how do we choose between two investments when one has the higher expected rate of return but the other has the lower standard deviation? To help answer this question, we use another measure of risk, the **coefficient of variation (CV)**, which is the standard deviation divided by the expected return:

$$\text{Coefficient of variation} = CV = \frac{\sigma}{\hat{k}}. \tag{5-4}$$

The coefficient of variation shows the risk per unit of return, and it provides a more meaningful basis for comparison when the expected returns on two alternatives are not the same. Since U.S. Electric and Martin Products have the same expected return, the coefficient of variation is not really useful in this case. The firm with the larger standard deviation, Martin, must have the larger coefficient of variation when the means are equal. In fact, the coefficient of variation for Martin is 65.84/15 = 4.39 and that for U.S. Electric is 3.87/15 = 0.26. Thus, Martin is almost 17 times riskier than U.S. Electric on the basis of this criterion.

For a case where the coefficient of variation is necessary, consider Projects X and Y, which have different expected rates of return and different standard deviations. The situation with Projects X and Y is graphed in Figure 5-4. Project X has a 60 percent expected rate of return and a 15 percent standard deviation, while Project Y has an 8 percent expected return but only a 3 percent standard deviation. Is Project X riskier, on a relative basis, because it has the larger standard deviation? If we calculate the coefficients of variation for these two projects, we find that Project X has a coefficient of variation of 15%/60% = 0.25, and Project Y has a coefficient of variation of 3%/8% = 0.375. Thus, we see that Project Y actually has more risk per unit of return than Project X, in spite of the fact that X's standard deviation is larger. Therefore, even though Project Y has the lower standard deviation, according to the coefficient of variation it is riskier than Project X.

Project Y has the smaller standard deviation, hence the more peaked probability distribution, but it is clear from the graph that the chances of a really low return are higher for Y than for X because X's expected return is so high. Because the coefficient of variation captures the effects of both risk and return, it is a better measure for evaluating risk in situations where investments have substantially different expected returns.

Footnote 6, *continued*

$$\bar{k}_{Avg} = \frac{(15 - 5 + 20)}{3} = 10.0\%$$

$$\text{Estimated } \sigma \text{ (or S)} = \sqrt{\frac{(15 - 10)^2 + (-5 - 10)^2 + (20 - 10)^2}{3 - 1}}$$

$$= \sqrt{\frac{350}{2}} = 13.2\%.$$

The historical σ is often used as an estimate of the future σ. Much less often, and generally incorrectly, $\bar{k}_{Avg}$ for some relatively short past period, such as ten years, is used as an estimate of $\hat{k}$, the expected future return. Because past variability is likely to be repeated, σ may be a good estimate of future risk, but it is much less reasonable to expect that the past *level* of return over a relatively short period (which could have been as high as +100% or as low as −50%) is the best expectation of what investors think will happen in the future.

Equation 5-3a is built into all financial calculators, and it is very easy to use. We simply enter the rates of return and press the key marked S (or S_x) to get the standard deviation. Note, though, that calculators have no built-in formula for finding σ where probabilistic data are involved; there you must go through the process outlined in Table 5-3 and Equation 5-3.

| FIGURE 5-4 | Comparison of Probability Distributions and Rates of Return for Projects X and Y |

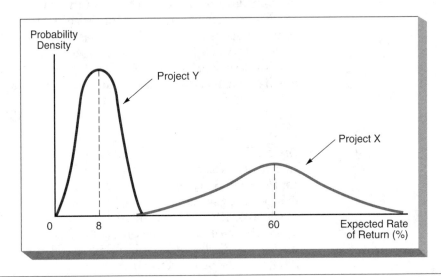

Risk Aversion and Required Returns

Suppose you have worked hard and saved $1 million, which you now plan to invest. You can buy a 5 percent U.S. Treasury note, and at the end of one year you will have a sure $1.05 million, which is your original investment plus $50,000 in interest. Alternatively, you can buy stock in R&D Enterprises. If R&D's research programs are successful, your stock will increase in value to $2.1 million. However, if the research is a failure, the value of your stock will go to zero, and you will be penniless. You regard R&D's chances of success or failure as being 50-50, so the expected value of the stock investment is 0.5($0) + 0.5($2,100,000) = $1,050,000. Subtracting the $1 million cost of the stock leaves an expected profit of $50,000, or an expected (but risky) 5 percent rate of return:

$$\text{Expected rate of return} = \frac{\text{Expected ending value} - \text{Cost}}{\text{Cost}}$$

$$= \frac{\$1,050,000 - \$1,000,000}{\$1,000,000}$$

$$= \frac{\$50,000}{\$1,000,000} = 5\%.$$

Thus, you have a choice between a sure $50,000 profit (representing a 5 percent rate of return) on the Treasury note and a risky expected $50,000 profit (also representing a 5 percent expected rate of return) on the R&D Enterprises stock. Which one would you choose? *If you choose the less risky investment, you are risk averse. Most investors are indeed risk averse, and certainly the average investor is risk averse with regard to his or her "serious money." Because this is a well-documented fact, we shall assume* **risk aversion** *throughout the remainder of the book.*

What are the implications of risk aversion for security prices and rates of return? The answer is that, other things held constant, the higher a security's risk, the lower its price and the higher its required return. To see how risk aversion affects security prices, consider again U.S. Electric and Martin Products. Suppose each stock sold for $100 per share and each had an expected dividend of $15. Neither had any expected capital gain, so both had an expected rate of return of 15 percent. Investors are averse to risk, so under these conditions there would be a general preference for U.S. Electric. People with money to invest would bid for U.S. Electric rather than Martin stock, and Martin's stockholders would start selling their stock and using the money to buy U.S. Electric stock. Buying pressure would drive up the price of U.S. Electric's stock, and selling pressure would simultaneously cause Martin's price to decline.

These price changes, in turn, would cause changes in the expected rates of return on the two securities. Suppose, for example, that U.S. Electric's stock price was bid up from $100 to $150, whereas Martin's stock price declined from $100 to $75. This would cause U.S. Electric's expected return to fall to 10 percent, while Martin's expected return would rise to 20 percent. The difference in expected returns, 20% − 10% = 10%, is a **risk premium, RP,** which represents the additional compensation investors require for assuming the higher risk of Martin stock.

This example demonstrates a very important principle: *In a market dominated by risk-averse investors, riskier securities must have higher expected returns, as estimated by the marginal investor, than less risky securities. If this situation does not hold, buying and selling in the market will force it to occur.* We will consider the question of how much higher the returns on risky securities must be later in the chapter, after we see how diversification affects the way risk should be measured.

<table>
<tr><td>S E L F - T E S T
Q U E S T I O N S</td><td>What does "investment risk" mean?

Set up an illustrative probability distribution for an investment.

What is a payoff matrix?

Which of the two stocks graphed in Figure 5-2 is less risky? Why?

How does one calculate the standard deviation?

Which is a better measure of risk if assets have different expected returns: (1) the standard deviation or (2) the coefficient of variation? Explain.

Explain the following statement: "Most investors are risk averse."

How does risk aversion affect rates of return?</td></tr>
</table>

RISK IN A PORTFOLIO CONTEXT

In the preceding section, we considered the riskiness of assets held in isolation. Now we analyze the riskiness of assets held in portfolios. As we shall see, an asset held as part of a portfolio is less risky than the same asset held in isolation. Accordingly, most financial assets are held as parts of portfolios. Banks, pension funds, insurance companies, mutual funds, and other financial institutions are required by law to hold diversified portfolios. Even individual investors—at least those whose security holdings constitute a significant part of their total wealth—generally hold portfolios, not the stock of only one firm. This being the case, from an investor's standpoint the fact that a particular stock goes up or down is not very important; *what is important is the return on his or her portfolio, and the portfolio's risk. Logically, then, the risk and return of an individual security should be analyzed in terms of how that security affects the risk and return of the portfolio in which it is held.*

To illustrate, Payco American is a collection agency company which operates nationwide through 37 offices. The company is not well known, its stock is not very liquid, its earnings have fluctuated quite a bit in the past, and it doesn't pay a dividend. All this suggests that Payco is risky, and that its required rate of return, k, should be relatively high. However, Payco's required rate of return in 1998, and all other years, was quite low in relation to those of most other companies. This indicates that investors regard

THE TRADE-OFF BETWEEN RISK AND RETURN

Ibbotson Associates' *Annual Yearbook* documents the historical trade-off between risk and return for different classes of investments. As the table shows, those assets that produced the highest average returns also had the highest standard deviations and the widest ranges of returns. For example, small-company stocks had the highest average annual return, 17.7 percent, but their standard deviation of returns, 34.1 percent, was also the highest. By contrast, U.S. Treasury bills had the lowest standard deviation, 3.3 percent, but they also had the lowest average return, 3.8 percent.

When deciding among alternative investments, one needs to be aware of the trade-off between risk and return. While there is certainly no guarantee that history will repeat itself, past returns observed over a long period are a good starting point for estimating investments' returns in the future. Likewise, the standard deviations of past returns provide useful insights into the risks of different investments. For T-bills, however, the standard deviation needs to be interpreted carefully. Note that the table shows that Treasury bills have a positive standard deviation, which indicates some risk. However, if you invested in a one-year Treasury bill and held it for the full year, your realized return would be the same regardless of what happened to the economy that year, and thus the standard deviation of your return would be zero. So, why does the table show a 3.3 percent standard deviation for T-bills, which indicates a nonzero risk? In fact, a T-bill is riskless *if you hold it for one year,* but if you invest in a rolling portfolio of one-year T-bills and hold it for a number of years, your investment income will vary depending on what happens to the level of interest rates in each year. So, while you can be sure of the return you will earn on a T-bill in a given year, you cannot be sure of the return you will earn on a portfolio of T-bills over a period of time.

SOURCE: *Stocks, Bonds, Bills, and Inflation: 1997 Yearbook* (Chicago: Ibbotson Associates, 1997), Table 2-1, 33.

Payco as being a low-risk company in spite of its uncertain profits. The reason for this counterintuitive fact has to do with diversification and its effect on risk. Payco's earnings rise during recessions, whereas most other companies' earnings tend to decline when the economy slumps. Therefore, adding Payco to a portfolio of "normal" stocks tends to stabilize returns on the entire portfolio.

Portfolio Returns

The **expected return on a portfolio, $\hat{k}_p$,** is simply the weighted average of the expected returns on the individual assets in the portfolio, with the weights being the fraction of the total portfolio invested in each asset:

$$\hat{k}_p = w_1\hat{k}_1 + w_2\hat{k}_2 + \cdots + w_n\hat{k}_n$$

$$= \sum_{i=1}^{n} w_i\hat{k}_i.$$

(5-5)

Summary Statistics of Annual Total Returns, 1926–1996

	Average Return	Standard Deviation	Distribution
Large-company stocks	12.7%	20.3%	
Small-company stocks[a]	17.7	34.1	
Long-term corporate bonds	6.0	8.7	
Long-term government	5.4	9.2	
Intermediate-term government	5.4	5.8	
U.S. Treasury bills	3.8	3.3	
Inflation	3.2	4.5	

−90%   0%   90%

[a]The small-company total return in 1933 was 142.9 percent.

SOURCE: *Stocks, Bonds, Bills, and Inflation: 1997 Yearbook* (Chicago: Ibbotson Associates, 1997).

Here the $\hat{k}_i$'s are the expected returns on the individual stocks, the w_i's are the weights, and there are n stocks in the portfolio. Note (1) that w_i is the fraction of the portfolio's dollar value invested in Stock i (that is, the value of the investment in Stock i divided by the total value of the portfolio) and (2) that the w_i's must sum to 1.0.

Assume that in August 1998, a security analyst estimated that the following returns could be expected on the stocks of four large companies:

	EXPECTED RETURN, $\hat{k}$
Microsoft	14%
General Electric	13
Arctic Oil	20
Citicorp	18

If we formed a $100,000 portfolio, investing $25,000 in each stock, the expected portfolio return would be 16.25%:

$$\hat{k}_p = w_1\hat{k}_1 + w_2\hat{k}_2 + w_3\hat{k}_3 + w_4\hat{k}_4$$

$$= 0.25(14\%) + 0.25(13\%) + 0.25(20\%) + 0.25(18\%)$$

$$= 16.25\%.$$

Of course, after the fact and a year later, the actual **realized rates of return, k̄,** on the individual stocks — the $\bar{k}_i$, or "k-bar," values — will almost certainly differ from their expected values, so $\bar{k}_p$ will be different from $\hat{k}_p = 16.25\%$. For example, Microsoft's stock might double in price and provide a return of +100%, whereas Citicorp might have a terrible year, fall sharply, and have a return of −75%. Note, though, that those two events would be somewhat offsetting, so the portfolio's return might still be close to its expected return, even though the individual stocks' actual returns were far from their expected returns.

Portfolio Risk

As we just saw, the expected return on a portfolio is simply the weighted average of the expected returns on the individual assets in the portfolio. However, unlike returns, the riskiness of a portfolio, σ_p, is generally *not* the weighted average of the standard deviations of the individual assets in the portfolio; the portfolio's standard deviation will be *smaller* than the weighted average of the assets' σ's. In fact, it is theoretically possible to combine stocks which are individually quite risky as measured by their standard deviations and to form a portfolio which is completely riskless, with $\sigma_p = 0$.

To illustrate the effect of combining assets, consider the situation in Figure 5-5. The bottom section gives data on rates of return for Stocks W and M individually, and also for a portfolio invested 50 percent in each stock. The three top graphs show plots of the data in a time series format, and the lower graphs show the probability distributions of returns, assuming that the future is expected to be like the past. The two stocks would be quite risky if they were held in isolation, but when they are combined to form Portfolio WM, they are not risky at all. (Note: These stocks are called W and M because the graphs of their returns in Figure 5-5 resemble a W and an M.)

The reason Stocks W and M can be combined to form a riskless portfolio is that their returns move countercyclically to each other — when W's returns fall, those of M rise, and vice versa. The tendency of two variables to move together is called **correlation,** and the **correlation coefficient, r,** measures this tendency.[7] In statistical terms, we say that the returns on Stocks W and M are *perfectly negatively correlated,* with r = −1.0.

The opposite of perfect negative correlation, with r = −1.0, is *perfect positive correlation,* with r = +1.0. Returns on two perfectly positively correlated stocks (M and M′) would move up and down together, and a portfolio consisting of two such stocks would be exactly as risky as the individual stocks. This point is illustrated in Figure 5-6, where we see that the portfolio's standard deviation is equal to that of the individual stocks. *Thus, diversification does nothing to reduce risk if the portfolio consists of perfectly positively correlated stocks.*

Figures 5-5 and 5-6 demonstrate that when stocks are perfectly negatively correlated (r = −1.0), all risk can be diversified away, but when stocks are perfectly positively cor-

---

[7]The *correlation coefficient, r,* can range from +1.0, denoting that the two variables move up and down in perfect synchronization, to −1.0, denoting that the variables always move in exactly opposite directions. A correlation coefficient of zero indicates that the two variables are not related to each other — that is, changes in one variable are *independent* of changes in the other.

It is easy to calculate correlation coefficients with a financial calculator. Simply enter the returns on the two stocks and then press a key labeled "r." For W and M, r = −1.0.

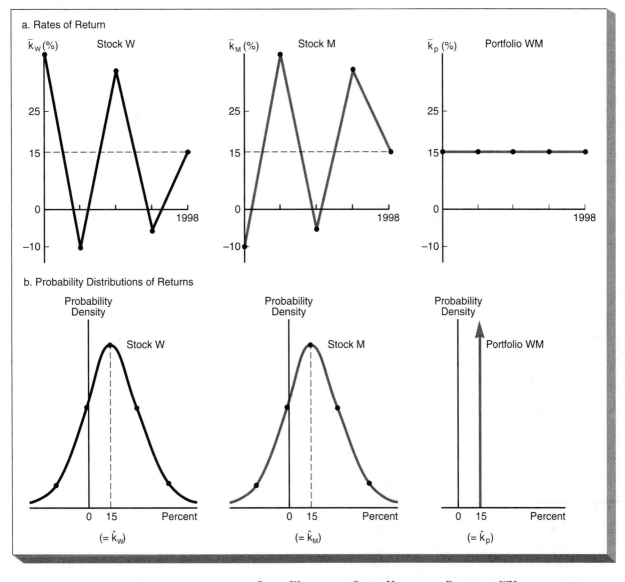

FIGURE 5-5 Rate of Return Distributions for Two Perfectly Negatively Correlated Stocks (r = −1.0) and for Portfolio WM

Year	Stock W ($\bar{k}_W$)	Stock M ($\bar{k}_M$)	Portfolio WM ($\bar{k}_p$)
1994	40.0%	(10.0%)	15.0%
1995	(10.0)	40.0	15.0
1996	35.0	(5.0)	15.0
1997	(5.0)	35.0	15.0
1998	15.0	15.0%	15.0%
Average return	15.0%	15.0%	15.0%
Standard deviation	22.6%	22.6%	00.0%

FIGURE 5-6   Rate of Return Distributions for Two Perfectly Positively Correlated Stocks (r = +1.0) and for Portfolio MM′

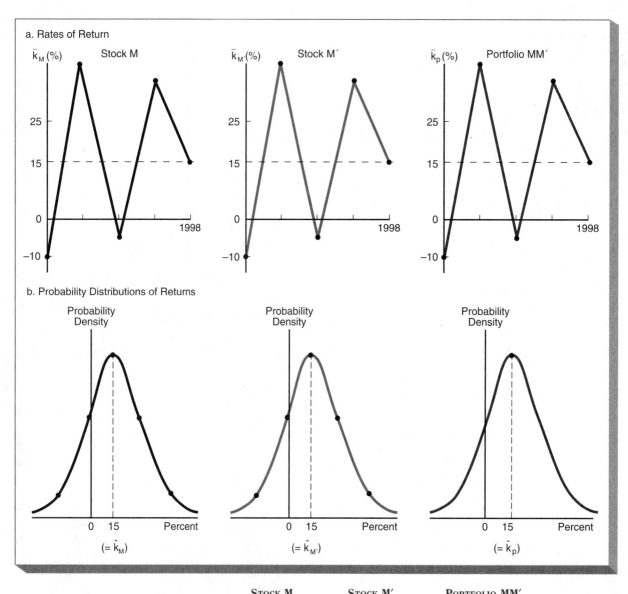

a. Rates of Return

b. Probability Distributions of Returns

YEAR	STOCK M ($\bar{k}_M$)	STOCK M′ ($\bar{k}_{M'}$)	PORTFOLIO MM′ ($\bar{k}_p$)
1994	(10.0%)	(10.0%)	(10.0%)
1995	40.0	40.0	40.0
1996	(5.0)	(5.0)	(5.0)
1997	35.0	35.0	35.0
1998	15.0	15.0	15.0
Average return	15.0%	15.0%	15.0%
Standard deviation	22.6%	22.6%	22.6%

related (r = +1.0), diversification does no good whatsoever. In reality, most stocks are positively correlated, but not perfectly so. On average, the correlation coefficient for the returns on two randomly selected stocks would be about +0.6, and for most pairs of stocks, r would lie in the range of +0.5 to +0.7. *Under such conditions, combining stocks into portfolios reduces risk but does not eliminate it completely.* Figure 5-7 illustrates this point with two stocks whose correlation coefficient is r = +0.67. The portfolio's average return is 15 percent, which is exactly the same as the average return for each of the two stocks, but its standard deviation is 20.6 percent, which is less than the standard deviation of either stock. Thus, the portfolio's risk is *not* an average of the risks of its individual stocks—diversification has reduced, but not eliminated, risk.

From these two-stock portfolio examples, we have seen that in one extreme case (r = −1.0), risk can be completely eliminated, while in the other extreme case (r = +1.0), diversification does nothing to limit risk. Between these extremes, combining two stocks into a portfolio reduces, but does not eliminate, the riskiness inherent in the individual stocks.

What would happen if we included more than two stocks in the portfolio? *As a rule, the riskiness of a portfolio will decline as the number of stocks in the portfolio increases.* If we added enough partially correlated stocks, could we completely eliminate risk? In general, the answer is no, but the extent to which adding stocks to a portfolio reduces its risk depends on the *degree of correlation* among the stocks: The smaller the positive correlation coefficients, the lower the risk in a large portfolio. If we could find a set of stocks whose correlations were zero or negative, all risk could be eliminated. *In the real world, where correlations among individual stocks are generally positive but less than +1.0, some, but not all, risk can be eliminated.*

To test your understanding, would you expect to find higher correlations between the returns on two companies in the same or in different industries? For example, would the correlation of returns on Ford's and General Motors' stocks be higher, or would the correlation coefficient be higher between either Ford or GM and AT&T, and how would those correlations affect the risk of portfolios containing them?

Here is the answer. Ford's and GM's returns have a correlation coefficient of about 0.9 because both are affected by auto sales. However, their correlation is only about 0.6 with AT&T. A two-stock portfolio consisting of Ford and GM would be less well diversified than a two-stock portfolio consisting of Ford or GM, plus AT&T. Thus, to minimize risk, portfolios should be diversified across industries.

Before leaving this section we should reiterate one point. In the real world, it is *impossible* to find stocks like W and M, whose returns are expected to be perfectly negatively correlated. *Therefore, it is impossible to form completely riskless stock portfolios.* Diversification can reduce risk, but it cannot eliminate it. The real world is closer to the situation depicted in Figure 5-7.

Diversifiable Risk versus Market Risk

As noted earlier, it is difficult if not impossible to find stocks whose expected returns are not positively correlated—most stocks tend to do well when the national economy is strong and badly when it is weak.[8] Thus, even very large portfolios end up with a sub-

---

[8]It is not too hard to find a few stocks that happened to have risen because of a particular set of circumstances in the past while most other stocks were declining, but it is much harder to find stocks that could logically be *expected* to go up in the future when other stocks are falling. Payco American, the collection agency discussed earlier, may be one of those rare exceptions.

Note, though, that *derivative* securities, which are discussed in detail in Chapter 24, have been created to help reduce the riskiness of stock portfolios. Derivatives can be designed to have negative correlation with a given stock or with a market index.

| FIGURE 5-7 | Rate of Return Distributions for Two Partially Correlated Stocks (r = +0.67) and for Portfolio WY |

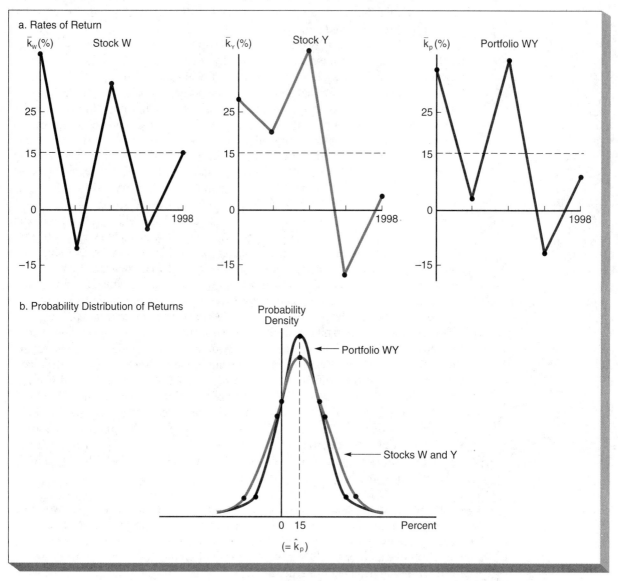

YEAR	STOCK W $(\bar{k}_W)$	STOCK Y $(\bar{k}_Y)$	PORTFOLIO WY $(\bar{k}_p)$
1994	40.0%	28.0%	34.0%
1995	(10.0)	20.0	5.0
1996	35.0	41.0	38.0
1997	(5.0)	(17.0)	(11.0)
1998	15.0	3.0	9.0
Average return	15.0%	15.0%	15.0%
Standard deviation	22.6%	22.6%	20.6%

stantial amount of risk, but not as much risk as if all the money were invested in only one stock.

To see more precisely how portfolio size affects portfolio risk, consider Figure 5-8, which shows how portfolio risk is affected by forming larger and larger portfolios of randomly selected New York Stock Exchange stocks. Standard deviations are plotted for an average one-stock portfolio, an average two-stock portfolio, and so on, up to a portfolio consisting of all 2,000-plus common stocks that were listed on the NYSE at the time the data were graphed. The graph illustrates that, in general, the riskiness of a portfolio consisting of large-company stocks tends to decline and to approach some limit as the size of the portfolio increases. According to data accumulated in recent years, σ_1, the standard deviation of a one-stock portfolio (or an average stock), is approximately 35 percent. A portfolio consisting of all stocks, which is called the **market portfolio,** would have a standard deviation, σ_M, of about 20.4 percent, which is shown as the horizontal dashed line in Figure 5-8.

Thus, almost half of the riskiness inherent in an average individual stock can be eliminated if the stock is held in a reasonably well-diversified portfolio, which is one containing 40 or more stocks. Some risk always remains, however, so it is virtually

FIGURE 5-8   Effects of Portfolio Size on Portfolio Risk for Average Stocks

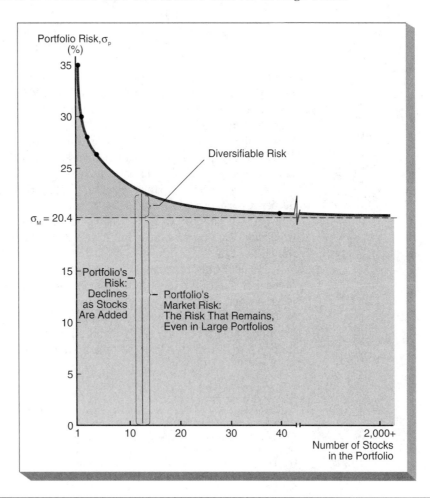

impossible to diversify away the effects of broad stock market movements that affect almost all stocks.

That part of the risk of a stock which *can* be eliminated is called *diversifiable risk,* while that part which *cannot* be eliminated is called *market risk.*[9] The fact that a large part of the riskiness of any individual stock can be eliminated by holding it in a large portfolio is vitally important.

Diversifiable risk is caused by such random events as lawsuits, strikes, successful and unsuccessful marketing programs, winning or losing a major contract, and other events that are unique to a particular firm. Since these events are random, their effects on a portfolio can be eliminated by diversification—bad events in one firm will be off-set by good events in another. **Market risk,** on the other hand, stems from factors which systematically affect most firms: war, inflation, recessions, and high interest rates. Since most stocks tend to be negatively affected by these factors, market risk cannot be eliminated by diversification.

We know that investors demand a premium for bearing risk; that is, the higher the riskiness of a security, the higher its expected return must be to induce investors to buy (or to hold) it. However, if investors are primarily concerned with the riskiness of their *portfolios* rather than the risk of the individual securities in the portfolio, how should the riskiness of an individual stock be measured? One answer is provided by the **Capital Asset Pricing Model (CAPM),** an important tool used to analyze the relationship between risk and rates of return.[10] The primary conclusion of the CAPM is this: *The relevant riskiness of an individual stock is its contribution to the riskiness of a well-diversified portfolio.* In other words, the riskiness of General Electric's stock to a doctor who has a portfolio of 40 stocks or to a trust officer managing a 150-stock portfolio is the contribution the GE stock makes to the portfolio's riskiness. The stock might be quite risky if held by itself, but if half of its risk can be eliminated by diversification, then its **relevant risk,** which is its *contribution to the portfolio's risk,* is much smaller than its stand-alone risk.

A simple example will help make this point clear. Suppose you are offered the chance to flip a coin once; if a head comes up, you win $20,000, but if it comes up tails, you lose $16,000. This is a good bet—the expected return is 0.5($20,000) + 0.5(-$16,000) = $2,000. However, it is a highly risky proposition, because you have a 50 percent chance of losing $16,000. Thus, you might well refuse to make the bet. Alternatively, suppose you were offered the chance to flip a coin 100 times, and you would win $200 for each head but lose $160 for each tail. It is possible that you would flip all heads and win $20,000, and it is also possible that you would flip all tails and lose $16,000, but the chances are very high that you would actually flip about 50 heads and about 50 tails, winning a net of about $2,000. Although each individual flip is a risky bet, collectively you have a low-risk proposition because most of the risk has been diversified away. This is the idea behind holding portfolios of stocks rather than just one stock, except that with stocks all of the risk cannot be eliminated by diversification—those risks related to broad, systematic changes in the stock market will remain.

---

[9]Diversifiable risk is also known as *company-specific,* or *unsystematic,* risk. Market risk is also known as *nondiversifiable,* or *systematic,* or *beta,* risk; it is the risk that remains after diversification.

[10]Indeed, the 1990 Nobel Prize was awarded to the developers of the CAPM, Professors Harry Markowitz and William F. Sharpe. The CAPM is a relatively complex subject, and only its basic elements are presented in this chapter. For a more detailed discussion, see Chapter 6.

The basic concepts of the CAPM were developed specifically for common stocks, and, therefore, the theory is examined first in this context. However, it has become common practice to extend CAPM concepts to capital budgeting and to speak of firms as having "portfolios of tangible assets and projects." In Chapter 13, we discuss the implications of the CAPM for capital budgeting and corporate diversification.

THE BENEFITS OF DIVERSIFYING OVERSEAS

The size of the global stock market has grown steadily over the last several decades, and it passed the $15 trillion mark during 1995. U.S. stocks account for approximately 41 percent of this total, whereas the Japanese and European markets constitute roughly 25 and 26 percent, respectively. The rest of the world makes up the remaining 8 percent. Although the U.S. equity market has long been the world's biggest, its share of the world total has decreased steadily over time.

The expanding universe of securities available internationally suggests the possibility of achieving a better risk-return trade-off than could be obtained by investing solely in U.S. securities. So, investing overseas might lower risk without sacrificing expected returns. The potential benefits of diversification are due to the facts that the correlation between the returns on U.S. and international securities is fairly low, and returns in developing nations are often quite high.

Figure 5-8, presented earlier, demonstrated that an investor can significantly reduce the risk of his or her portfolio by holding a large number of stocks. The figure accompanying this box suggests that investors may be able to reduce risk even further by holding a large portfolio of stocks from all around the world, because returns on domestic and international stocks are not perfectly correlated.

Despite the apparent benefits from investing overseas, the typical U.S. investor still dedicates less than 10 percent of his or her portfolio to foreign stocks—even though foreign stocks represent roughly 60 percent of the worldwide equity market. Researchers and practitioners alike have struggled to understand this reluctance to invest overseas. One explanation is that investors prefer domestic stocks because they have lower transaction costs. However, this explanation is not completely convincing, given that recent studies have found that investors buy and sell their overseas stocks more fre-

quently than they trade their domestic stocks. Other explanations for the domestic bias could be the additional risks from investing overseas (for example, exchange rate risk) or the fact that the typical U.S. investor is uninformed about international investments and/or views international investments as being extremely risky or uncertain. More recently, other analysts have argued that as world capital markets have become more integrated, the correlation of returns between different countries has increased, hence that the benefits from international diversification have declined.

Whatever the reason for the current reluctance to hold international assets, it is likely that in the years ahead U.S. investors will allocate more and more of their portfolios to overseas investments.

SOURCE: Kenneth Kasa, "Measuring the Gains from International Portfolio Diversification," *Federal Reserve Bank of San Francisco Weekly Letter,* Number 94-14, April 8, 1994.

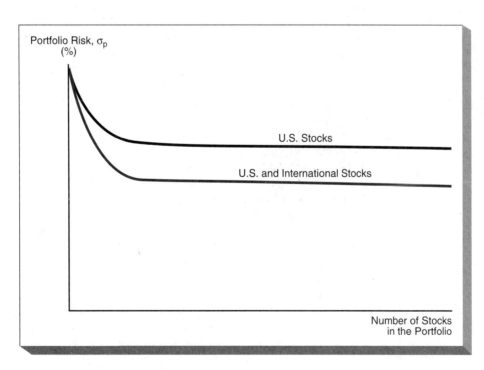

Are all stocks equally risky in the sense that adding them to a well-diversified portfolio would have the same effect on the portfolio's riskiness? The answer is no. Different stocks will affect the portfolio differently, so different securities have different degrees of relevant risk. How can the relevant risk of an individual stock be measured? As we have seen, all risk except that related to broad market movements can, and presumably will, be diversified away. After all, why accept risk that can be easily eliminated? *The risk that remains after diversifying is market risk, or the risk that is inherent in the market, and it can be measured by the degree to which a given stock tends to move up or down with the market.* In the next section, we develop a measure of a stock's market risk, and then, in a later section, we introduce a method for determining the required rate of return on a stock, given its market risk.

The Concept of Beta

The tendency of a stock to move up and down with the market is reflected in its **beta coefficient, b.** Beta is a key element of the CAPM. An *average-risk stock* is defined as one that tends to move up and down in step with the general market as measured by some index such as the Dow Jones Industrials, the S&P 500, or the New York Stock Exchange Index. Such a stock will, *by definition,* have a beta, b, of 1.0, which indicates that, in general, if the market moves up by 10 percent, the stock will also move up by 10 percent, while if the market falls by 10 percent, the stock will likewise fall by 10 percent. A portfolio of such b = 1.0 stocks will move up and down with the broad market averages, and it will be just as risky as the averages.

If b = 0.5, the stock is only half as volatile as the market—it will rise and fall only half as much—and a portfolio of such stocks will be half as risky as a portfolio of b = 1.0 stocks. On the other hand, if b = 2.0, the stock is twice as volatile as an average stock, so a portfolio of such stocks will be twice as risky as an average portfolio. The value of such a portfolio could double—or halve—in a short time, and if you held such a portfolio, you could quickly go from millionaire to pauper.

Figure 5-9 graphs the relative volatility of three stocks. The data below the graph assume that in 1996 the "market," defined as a portfolio consisting of all stocks, had a total return (dividend yield plus capital gains yield) of $k_M = 10\%$, and Stocks H, A, and L (for High, Average, and Low risk) also all had returns of 10 percent. In 1997, the market went up sharply, and the return on the market portfolio was $\bar{k}_M = 20\%$. Returns on the three stocks also went up: H soared to 30 percent; A went up to 20 percent, the same as the market; and L only went up to 15 percent. Now, suppose that the market dropped in 1998, and the market return was $\bar{k}_M = -10\%$. The three stocks' returns also fell, H plunging to −30 percent, A falling to −10 percent, and L going down only to $\bar{k}_L = 0\%$. Thus, the three stocks all moved in the same direction as the market, but H was by far the most volatile; A was just as volatile as the market; and L was less volatile.

Beta measures a stock's volatility relative to an average stock, which by definition has b = 1.0, and a stock's beta can be calculated by plotting a line like those in Figure 5-9. The slopes of the lines show how each stock moves in response to a movement in the general market—*indeed, the slope coefficient of such a "regression line" is defined as a beta coefficient.* (Procedures for actually calculating betas are described in Chapter 6.) Betas for literally thousands of companies are calculated and published by Merrill Lynch, *Value Line,* and numerous other organizations, and the beta coefficients of some well-known companies are shown in Table 5-4. Most stocks have betas in the range of 0.50 to 1.50, and the average for all stocks is 1.0 by definition.

FIGURE 5-9   Relative Volatility of Stocks H, A, and L

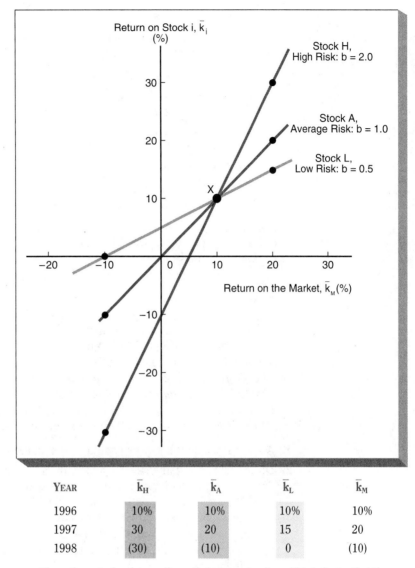

YEAR	$\overline{k}_H$	$\overline{k}_A$	$\overline{k}_L$	$\overline{k}_M$
1996	10%	10%	10%	10%
1997	30	20	15	20
1998	(30)	(10)	0	(10)

NOTE: These three stocks plot exactly on their regression lines. This indicates that they are exposed only to market risk. Mutual funds which concentrate on stocks with betas of 2, 1, and 0.5 would have patterns similar to those shown in the graph.

Theoretically, it is possible for a stock to have a negative beta. In this case, the stock's returns would tend to rise whenever the returns on other stocks fall. In practice, we have never seen a stock with a negative beta. For example, *Value Line* follows more than 1,700 stocks, and not one has a negative beta. Keep in mind, though, that a stock in a given year may move counter to the overall market, even though the stock's beta is positive. If a stock has a positive beta, we would *expect* its return to increase whenever the overall stock market rises. However, company-specific factors may cause the stock's realized return to decline, even though the market's return is positive.

| TABLE 5-4 | Ilustrative List of Beta Coefficients |

STOCK	BETA
America Online	2.10
Bally Entertainment	1.55
Microsoft Corp.	1.20
General Electric	1.15
Procter & Gamble	1.05
Coca-Cola	1.00
Heinz	0.90
IBM	0.90
Energen Corp.[a]	0.70
Empire District Electric	0.55

[a]Energen is a gas distribution company. It has a monopoly in much of Alabama, and its rates are adjusted every three months so as to keep its profits relatively constant.

SOURCE: *Value Line,* August 16, 1996.

If a stock whose beta is greater than 1.0 is added to a b = 1.0 portfolio, then the portfolio's beta, and consequently its riskiness, will increase. Conversely, if a stock whose beta is less than 1.0 is added to a b = 1.0 portfolio, the portfolio's beta and risk will decline. *Thus, since a stock's beta measures its contribution to the riskiness of a portfolio, beta is the theoretically correct measure of the stock's riskiness.*

The preceding analysis of risk in a portfolio context is part of the Capital Asset Pricing Model (CAPM), and we can summarize our discussion to this point as follows:

1. A stock's risk consists of two components, market risk and diversifiable risk.

2. Diversifiable risk can be eliminated by diversification, and most investors do indeed diversify, either by holding large portfolios or by purchasing shares in a mutual fund. We are left, then, with market risk, which is caused by general movements in the stock market and which reflects the fact that most stocks are systematically affected by events like war, recessions, and inflation. Market risk is the only relevant risk to a rational, diversified investor because such an investor would eliminate diversifiable risk.

3. Investors must be compensated for bearing risk—the greater the riskiness of a stock, the higher its required return. However, compensation is required only for risk which cannot be eliminated by diversification. If risk premiums existed on stocks due to diversifiable risk, well-diversified investors would start buying those securities (which would not be especially risky to such investors) and bid up their prices, and the stocks' final (equilibrium) expected returns would reflect only non-diversifiable market risk.

If this point is not clear, an example may help clarify it. Suppose half of Stock A's risk is market risk (it occurs because Stock A moves up and down with the market), while the other half of A's risk is diversifiable. You hold only Stock A, so you are exposed to all of its risk. As compensation for bearing so much risk, you want a risk premium of 8 percent over the 10 percent T-bond rate. Thus, your required return is $k_A = 10\% + 8\% = 18\%$. But suppose other investors, including your professor, are well diversified; they also hold Stock A, but they have eliminated its diversifiable risk and thus are exposed to only half as much risk as you. Therefore, their risk premium will be only half as large as yours, and their required rate of return will be $k_A = 10\% + 4\% = 14\%$.

If the stock were yielding more than 14 percent in the market, diversified investors, including your professor, would buy it. If it were yielding 18 percent, you would be willing to buy it. However, well-diversified investors would have bid its price up and its yield down, hence you could not buy it at a price low enough to provide you with an 18 percent return. In the end, you would have to accept a 14 percent return or else keep your money in the bank. Thus, risk premiums in a market populated by diversified investors can reflect only market risk.

4. The market risk of a stock is measured by its beta coefficient, which is an index of the stock's relative volatility. Some benchmark betas follow:

    $b = 0.5$: Stock is only half as volatile, or risky, as an average stock.

    $b = 1.0$: Stock is of average risk.

    $b = 2.0$: Stock is twice as risky as an average stock.

5. *Since a stock's beta coefficient shows how the stock would affect the riskiness of a diversified portfolio, beta is the most relevant measure of any stock's risk.*

Portfolio Beta Coefficients

A portfolio consisting of low-beta securities will itself have a low beta, because the beta of a portfolio is a weighted average of the individual securities' betas:

$$b_p = w_1 b_1 + w_2 b_2 + \cdots + w_n b_n$$

$$= \sum_{i=1}^{n} w_i b_i. \tag{5-6}$$

Here b_p is the beta of the portfolio, and it shows how volatile the portfolio is in relation to the market; w_i is the fraction of the portfolio invested in the ith stock; and b_i is the beta coefficient of the ith stock. For example, if an investor holds a $100,000 portfolio consisting of $33,333.33 invested in each of three stocks, and if each of the stocks has a beta of 0.7, then the portfolio's beta will be $b_p = 0.7$:

$$b_p = 0.3333(0.7) + 0.3333(0.7) + 0.3333(0.7) = 0.7.$$

Such a portfolio will be less risky than the market, so it should experience relatively narrow price swings and have relatively small rate-of-return fluctuations. In terms of Figure 5-9, the slope of its regression line would be 0.7, which is less than that for a portfolio of average stocks.

Now suppose one of the existing stocks is sold and replaced by a stock with $b_i = 2.0$. This action will increase the beta of the portfolio from $b_{p1} = 0.7$ to $b_{p2} = 1.13$:

$$b_{p2} = 0.3333(0.7) + 0.3333(0.7) + 0.3333(2.0)$$

$$= 1.13.$$

Had a stock with $b_i = 0.2$ been added, the portfolio beta would have declined from 0.7 to 0.53. Adding a low-beta stock, therefore, would reduce the riskiness of the portfolio. In general, adding new stocks to a portfolio can change the riskiness of that portfolio.

S E L F - T E S T
Q U E S T I O N S

Explain the following statement: "An asset held as part of a portfolio is generally less risky than the same asset held in isolation."

What is meant by *perfect positive correlation, perfect negative correlation,* and *zero correlation?*

In general, can the riskiness of a portfolio be reduced to zero by increasing the number of stocks in the portfolio? Explain.

What is an average-risk stock? What will be its beta?

Why is beta the theoretically correct measure of a stock's riskiness?

If you plotted the returns on a particular stock versus those on the Dow Jones Index over the past five years, what would the slope of the regression line you obtained indicate about the stock's market risk?

THE RELATIONSHIP BETWEEN RISK AND RATES OF RETURN

In the preceding section, we saw that under the CAPM theory, beta is the appropriate measure of a stock's relevant risk. However, for a given level of risk as measured by beta, what rate of return will investors require to compensate them for bearing that risk? To begin, let us define the following terms:

$\hat{k}_i$ = *expected* rate of return on the ith stock.

k_i = *required* rate of return on the ith stock. Note that if $\hat{k}_i$ is less than k_i, you would not purchase this stock, or you would sell it if you owned it. If $\hat{k}_i$ were greater than k_i, you would want to buy the stock, because it looks like a bargain. You would be indifferent if $\hat{k}_i = k_i$.

$\bar{k}$ = realized, after-the-fact return. One obviously does not know $\bar{k}$ at the time he or she is considering the purchase of a stock.

k_{RF} = risk-free rate of return. In this context, k_{RF} is generally measured by the return on a long-term U.S. Treasury bond.

b_i = beta coefficient of the ith stock. The beta of an average stock is $b_A = 1.0$.

k_M = required rate of return on a portfolio consisting of all stocks, which is called the *market portfolio*. k_M is also the required rate of return on an average ($b_A = 1.0$) stock. So, $k_M = k_A$.

$RP_M = (k_M - k_{RF})$ = risk premium on "the market," and also on an average ($b = 1.0$) stock. This is the additional return over the risk-free rate required to compensate an average investor for assuming an average amount of risk. Average risk means a stock whose beta = $b_A = 1.0$.

$RP_i = (k_M - k_{RF})b_i = (RP_M)b_i$ = risk premium on the ith stock. A stock's risk premium will be less than, equal to, or greater than the premium on an average stock, RP_M, depending on whether its beta is less than, equal to, or greater than 1.0. If $b_i = b_A = 1.0$, then $RP_i = RP_M$.

The **market risk premium, RP$_M$,** shows the premium investors require for bearing the risk of an average stock, and it depends on the degree of risk aversion that investors on average have.[11] Let us assume that at the current time, Treasury bonds yield k_{RF} = 6% and an average share of stock has a required return of k_M = 11%. Therefore, the market risk premium is 5 percent:

$$RP_M = k_M - k_{RF} = 11\% - 6\% = 5\%.$$

It follows that if one stock were twice as risky as another, its risk premium would be twice as high, while if its risk were only half as much, its risk premium would be half as large. Further, we can measure a stock's relative riskiness by its beta coefficient. If we know the market risk premium, RP$_M$, and the stock's risk as measured by its beta coefficient, b_i, we can find the stock's risk premium as the product $(RP_M)b_i$. For example, if b_i = 0.5 and RP$_M$ = 5%, then RP$_i$ is 2.5 percent:

$$\text{Risk premium for Stock i} = RP_i = (RP_M)b_i \qquad \textbf{(5-7)}$$
$$= (5\%)(0.5)$$
$$= 2.5\%.$$

As the discussion in Chapter 4 implied, the required return for any investment can be expressed in general terms as

$$\text{Required return} = \text{Risk-free return} + \text{Premium for risk.}$$

Here the risk-free return already includes a premium for expected inflation, and we assume that the assets under consideration have similar maturities and liquidity. Under these conditions, the required return for Stock i can be written as follows:

$$\text{SML Equation:} \quad \begin{array}{c}\text{Required return}\\\text{on Stock i}\end{array} = \begin{array}{c}\text{Risk-free}\\\text{rate}\end{array} + \left(\begin{array}{c}\text{Market risk}\\\text{premium}\end{array}\right)\left(\begin{array}{c}\text{Stock i's}\\\text{beta}\end{array}\right)$$

$$k_i = k_{RF} + (k_M - k_{RF})b_i \qquad \textbf{(5-8)}$$
$$= k_{RF} + (RP_M)b_i$$
$$= 6\% + (11\% - 6\%)(0.5)$$
$$= 6\% + 5\%(0.5)$$
$$= 8.5\%.$$

Equation 5-8 is called the **Security Market Line (SML) equation.**

If some other Stock j were riskier than Stock i and had b_j = 2.0, then its required rate of return would be 16 percent:

$$k_j = 6\% + (5\%)2.0 = 16\%.$$

An average stock, with b = 1.0, would have a required return of 11 percent, the same as the market return:

$$k_A = 6\% + (5\%)1.0 = 11\% = k_M.$$

---

[11]It should be noted that the risk premium of an average stock, $k_M - k_{RF}$, cannot be measured with great precision because it is impossible to obtain precise values for the expected future return on the market, k_M. However, empirical studies suggest that where long-term U.S. Treasury bonds are used to measure k_{RF} and where k_M is an estimate of the expected return on the S&P 400 Industrial Stocks, the market risk premium varies somewhat from year to year, and it has generally ranged from 4 to 8 percent during the last 20 years.

FIGURE 5-10   The Security Market Line (SML)

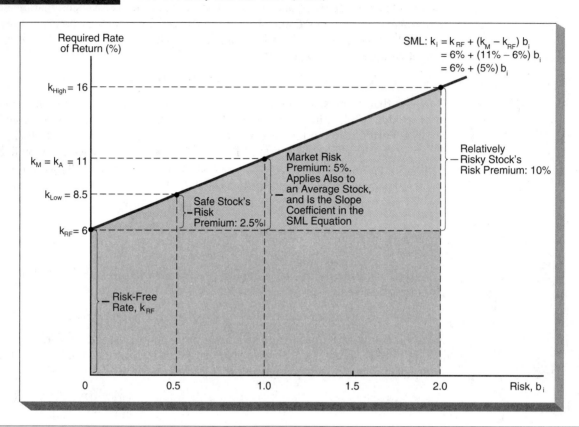

As noted above, Equation 5-8 is called the *Security Market Line (SML)* equation, and it is often expressed in graph form, as in Figure 5-10, which shows the SML when $k_{RF} = 6\%$ and $k_M = 11\%$. Note the following points:

1. Required rates of return are shown on the vertical axis, while risk as measured by beta is shown on the horizontal axis. This graph is quite different from the one shown in Figure 5-9, where historical returns on stocks were plotted on the vertical axis and returns on the market index were shown on the horizontal axis. The slopes of the three lines in Figure 5-9 were used to calculate the three stocks' betas, and those betas were then plotted as points on the horizontal axis of Figure 5-10.

2. Riskless securities have $b_i = 0$; therefore, k_{RF} appears as the vertical axis intercept in Figure 5-10. If we could construct a portfolio which had a beta of zero, it would have an expected return equal to the risk-free rate.

3. The slope of the SML shows how much the required return increases as risk increases. Thus, the slope of the SML reflects the degree of risk aversion in the economy—the greater the average investor's aversion to risk, then (1) the steeper the slope of the SML, (2) the greater the risk premium for all stocks, and (3) the higher the required rate of return on all stocks.[12]

_____

[12]Students sometimes confuse beta with the slope of the SML. This is a mistake. The slope of any straight line is equal to the "rise" divided by the "run," or $(Y_1 - Y_0)/(X_1 - X_0)$. Consider Figure 5-10. If we let $Y = k$ and $X = $ beta, and we go from the origin to $b = 1.0$, we see that the slope is $(k_M - k_{RF})/(b_M - b_{RF}) = (11\% - 6\%)/(1 - 0) = 5\%$. Thus, the slope of the SML is equal to $(k_M - k_{RF})$, the market risk premium. In Figure 5-10, $k_i = 6\% + 5\%b_i$, so a doubling of beta (for example, from 1.0 to 2.0) would produce a 5 percentage point increase in k_i.

4. The values we worked out for stocks with $b_i = 0.5$, $b_i = 1.0$, and $b_i = 2.0$ agree with the values shown on the graph for k_{Low}, k_A, and k_{High}.

Both the Security Market Line and a company's position on it change over time due to changes in interest rates, investors' aversion to risk, and individual companies' betas. Such changes are discussed in the following sections.

The Impact of Inflation

As we learned in Chapter 4, interest amounts to "rent" on borrowed money, or the price of money. Thus, k_{RF} is the price of money to a riskless borrower. We also learned that the risk-free rate as measured by the rate on U.S. Treasury securities is called the *nominal*, or *quoted, rate,* and it consists of two elements: (1) a *real inflation-free rate of return, k*,* and (2) an *inflation premium, IP,* equal to the anticipated rate of inflation.[13] Thus, $k_{RF} = k* + IP$. The real rate on long-term Treasury bonds has historically ranged from 2 to 4 percent, with a mean of about 3 percent. Therefore, if no inflation were expected, long-term Treasury bonds would yield about 3 percent. However, as the expected rate of inflation increases, a premium must be added to the real risk-free rate to compensate investors for the loss of purchasing power that results from inflation. Therefore, the 6 percent k_{RF} shown in Figure 5-10 might be thought of as consisting of a 3 percent real risk-free rate of return plus a 3 percent inflation premium: $k_{RF} = k* + IP = 3\% + 3\% = 6\%$.

If the expected inflation rate rose by 2 percent, to $3\% + 2\% = 5\%$, this would cause k_{RF} to rise to 8 percent. Such a change is shown in Figure 5-11. Notice that under the CAPM, the increase in k_{RF} leads to an *equal* increase in the rate of return on all risky assets, because the same inflation premium is built into the required rate of return of both riskless and risky assets.[14] For example, the rate of return on an average stock, k_M, increases from 11 to 13 percent. Other risky securities' returns also rise by two percentage points.

Changes in Risk Aversion

The slope of the Security Market Line reflects the extent to which investors are averse to risk—the steeper the slope of the line, the greater the average investor's risk aversion. Suppose investors were indifferent to risk; that is, they were not risk averse. If k_{RF} were 6 percent, then risky assets would also have a required return of 6 percent, because if there were no risk aversion, there would be no risk premium, and the SML would graph as a horizontal line. As risk aversion increases, so does the risk premium, and this causes the slope of the SML to become steeper.

Figure 5-12 illustrates an increase in risk aversion. The market risk premium rises from 5 to 7.5 percent, causing k_M to rise from $k_{M1} = 11\%$ to $k_{M2} = 13.5\%$. The returns on other risky assets also rise, and the effect of this shift in risk aversion is more pronounced on riskier securities. For example, the required return on a stock with $b_i = 0.5$

---

[13]Long-term Treasury bonds also contain a maturity risk premium, MRP. Here we include the MRP in k* to simplify the discussion.

[14]Recall that the inflation premium for any asset is equal to the average expected rate of inflation over the asset's life. Thus, in this analysis we must assume either that all securities plotted on the SML graph have the same life or else that the expected rate of future inflation is constant.

It should also be noted that k_{RF} in a CAPM analysis can be proxied by either a long-term rate (the T-bond rate) or a short-term rate (the T-bill rate). Traditionally, the T-bill rate was used, but in recent years there has been a movement toward use of the T-bond rate because there is a closer relationship between T-bond yields and stocks than between T-bill yields and stocks. See *Stocks, Bonds, Bills, and Inflation: 1997 Yearbook* (Chicago: Ibbotson Associates, 1997) for a discussion.

FIGURE 5-11   Shift in the SML Caused by an Increase in Inflation

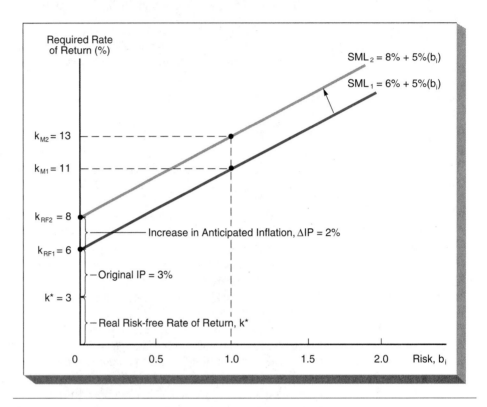

increases by only 1.25 percentage points, from 8.5 to 9.75 percent, whereas that on a stock with $b_i = 1.5$ increases by 3.75 percentage points, from 13.5 to 17.25 percent.

Changes in a Stock's Beta Coefficient

As we shall see later in the book, a firm can influence its market risk, hence its beta, through changes in the composition of its assets and also through its use of debt. A company's beta can also change as a result of external factors such as increased competition in its industry, the expiration of basic patents, and the like. When such changes occur, the required rate of return also changes. For example, consider MicroDrive Inc., with a beta of 1.40. Now suppose some action occurred which caused MicroDrive's beta to increase from 1.40 to 2.00. If the conditions depicted in Figure 5-10 held, Micro-Drive's required rate of return would increase from 13 to 16 percent:

$$k_1 = k_{RF} + (k_M - k_{RF})b_i$$
$$= 6\% + (11\% - 6\%)1.40$$
$$= 13\%$$

to

$$k_2 = 6\% + (11\% - 6\%)2.0$$
$$= 16\%.$$

As we shall see in Chapter 9, this change would have a dramatic impact on MicroDrive's stock.

| FIGURE 5-12 | Shift in the SML Caused by Increased Risk Aversion |

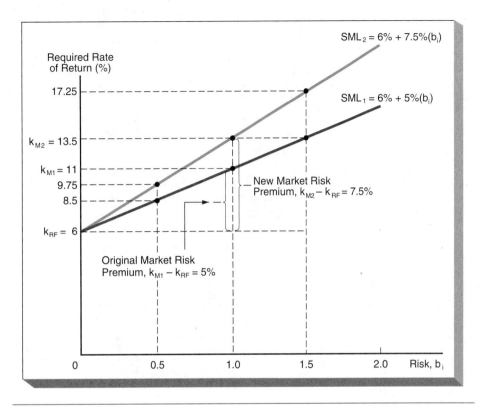

SELF-TEST
QUESTIONS

Differentiate among the expected rate of return ($\hat{k}$), the required rate of return (k), and the realized, after-the-fact return ($\bar{k}$) on a stock. Which would have to be larger to get you to buy the stock, $\hat{k}$ or k? Would $\hat{k}$, k, and $\bar{k}$ typically be the same or different?

What are the differences between the relative volatility graph (Figure 5-9), where "betas are made," and the SML graph (Figure 5-10), where "betas are used"? Discuss both how the graphs are constructed and the information they convey.

What happens to the SML graph in Figure 5-10 when inflation increases or decreases?

What happens to the SML graph when risk aversion increases or decreases?

What would the SML look like if investors were indifferent to risk, that is, had zero risk aversion?

How can a firm influence its market risk as reflected in its beta?

PHYSICAL ASSETS VERSUS SECURITIES

In a book on financial management for business firms, why do we spend so much time discussing the riskiness of stocks? Why not begin by looking at the riskiness of such business assets as plant and equipment? *The reason is that, for a management whose primary goal is stock price maximization, the overriding consideration is the riskiness of the firm's stock, and the relevant risk of any physical asset must be measured in terms of its effect on the stock's risk as seen by investors.* For example, suppose

Goodyear Tire Company is considering a major investment in a new product, recapped tires. Sales of recaps, hence earnings on the new operation, are highly uncertain, so on a stand-alone basis the new venture appears to be quite risky. However, suppose returns in the recap business are negatively correlated with Goodyear's regular operations—when times are good and people have plenty of money, they buy new tires, but when times are bad, they tend to buy more recaps. Therefore, returns would be high on regular operations and low on the recap division during good times, but the opposite would occur during recessions. The result might be a pattern like that shown earlier in Figure 5-5 for Stocks W and M. Thus, what appears to be a risky investment when viewed on a stand-alone basis might not be very risky when viewed within the context of the company as a whole.

This analysis can be extended to the corporation's stockholders. Because Goodyear's stock is owned by diversified stockholders, the real issue each time management makes an asset investment is this: *How will this investment affect the risk of our stockholders?* Again, the stand-alone risk of an individual project may look quite high, but viewed in the context of the project's effect on stockholders' risk, it may not be very large. We will address this issue again in Chapters 10 and 13, where we examine the effects of capital budgeting on companies' beta coefficients and thus on stockholders' risks.

SELF-TEST
QUESTIONS

Explain the following statement: "The stand-alone risk of an individual project may be quite high, but viewed in the context of the project's effect on stockholders, its true risk may not be very large."

How would the correlation between returns on a project and returns on the firm's other assets affect the project's risk?

SOME CONCERNS ABOUT BETA AND THE CAPM

The Capital Asset Pricing Model (CAPM) is more than just an abstract theory described in textbooks—it is also widely used by analysts, investors, and corporations. However, despite the CAPM's intuitive appeal, a number of recent studies have raised concerns about its validity. In particular, a study by Eugene Fama of the University of Chicago and Kenneth French of Yale found no relationship between stocks' historical returns and their market betas.

If beta does not determine returns, what does? Fama and French found two variables that are consistently related to stock returns: (1) the firm's size and (2) its market/book ratio. After adjusting for other factors, they found that smaller firms have provided relatively high returns, and that returns are higher on stocks with low market/book ratios. However, they found no relationship between a stock's beta and its return.

As an alternative to the traditional CAPM, researchers and practitioners have begun to look to more general multi-beta models that extend the CAPM and address its shortcomings. The multi-beta model is an attractive generalization of the traditional CAPM model's insight that market risk—risk that cannot be diversified away—underlies the pricing of assets. In a multi-beta model, risk is measured relative to a set of factors that determine the behavior of asset returns, whereas the CAPM gauges risk only relative to the market return. It is important to note that the risky factors in multi-beta models are all nondiversifiable sources of risk.

Practitioners and academicians have long recognized the limitations of the CAPM, and they are constantly looking for ways to improve it. The multi-beta model is a potential step in that direction. Although the CAPM represents a significant step forward in security pricing theory, it does have some deficiencies when applied in practice, hence estimates of k_i found through use of the SML may be subject to considerable error.[15]

SELF-TEST
QUESTION | Are there any reasons to question the validity of the CAPM? Explain.

VOLATILITY VERSUS RISK

Before closing this chapter, we should note that earnings volatility does not necessarily imply risk. For example, suppose a company's sales and earnings fluctuate widely from month to month, from year to year, or in some other manner. Does this imply that the company is risky in either a stand-alone or portfolio sense? If the fluctuations follow seasonal or cyclical patterns, as for an ice cream distributor or a steel company, they can be predicted, hence volatility would not signify much in the way of risk. If the ice cream company's earnings dropped about as much as they normally do this winter, this would not concern investors, so the company's stock price would not be affected. Similarly, if a steel company's earnings fell during a recession, this would not be a surprise, so the company's stock price would not fall nearly as much as its earnings. *Therefore, earnings volatility does not necessarily imply investment risk.*

Now consider some other company, say, Wal-Mart. In 1995 Wal-Mart's earnings declined for the first time in its history. That decline worried investors—they were concerned that Wal-Mart's era of rapid growth had ended. The result was that Wal-Mart's stock price suffered a larger percentage decline than its earnings. *Now we conclude that while a downturn in earnings does not necessarily imply risk, it could, depending on what caused the downturn.*

Now let's consider stock price volatility as opposed to earnings volatility. Is stock price volatility more likely to imply risk than earnings volatility? The answer is a loud yes! Stock prices vary primarily because investors are uncertain about the future, especially about future earnings. So, if you see a company whose stock price fluctuates relatively widely (which will result in a high beta), you can bet that its future earnings are relatively unpredictable. Thus, biotech companies have less predictable earnings than electric utilities. Therefore, biotechs' stock prices are volatile, and these companies have relatively high betas.

To conclude, keep two points in mind: (1) *Earnings volatility does not necessarily signify risk*—you have to think about the cause of the volatility before reaching any conclusion as to whether earnings volatility indicates risk. (2) *Stock price volatility does signify risk* (except for stocks that are negatively correlated with the market, which are few and far between, if they exist at all).

SELF-TEST
QUESTIONS | Does earnings volatility necessarily imply risk? Explain.

Is stock price volatility more likely to imply risk than earnings volatility? Explain.

---

[15]Chapter 6 contains more information about the CAPM as well as one of the multi-beta models.

SUMMARY

The primary goals of this chapter were (1) to show how risk is measured in financial analysis and (2) to explain how risk affects rates of return. The key concepts covered are listed below.

- **Return** measures the financial performance of an investment. It can be expressed either in **dollar terms** or as a **percentage rate of return**.

- **Risk** can be defined as the chance that some unfavorable event will occur.

- The riskiness of an asset's cash flows can be considered on a **stand-alone basis** (each asset by itself) or in a **portfolio context,** where the investment is combined with other assets and its risk is reduced through **diversification.**

- Most rational investors hold **portfolios of assets,** and they are more concerned with the riskiness of their portfolios than with the riskiness of individual assets.

- The **expected return** on an investment is the mean value of its probability distribution of returns.

- The **greater the probability** that the actual return will be far below the expected return, the **greater the stand-alone risk** associated with an asset.

- The average investor is **risk averse,** which means that he or she must be compensated for holding risky assets. Therefore, riskier assets have higher required returns than less risky assets.

- An asset's risk consists of (1) **diversifiable risk,** which can be eliminated by diversification, plus (2) **market risk,** which cannot be eliminated by diversification.

- The **relevant risk** of an individual asset is its contribution to the riskiness of a well-diversified **portfolio,** which is the asset's **market risk.** Since market risk cannot be eliminated by diversification, investors must be compensated for bearing it.

- A stock's **beta coefficient, b,** is a measure of its market risk. Beta measures the extent to which the stock's returns move relative to the market.

- A **high-beta stock** is more volatile than an average stock, while a **low-beta stock** is less volatile than an average stock. An **average stock** has $b = 1.0$.

- The **beta of a portfolio** is a **weighted average** of the betas of the individual securities in the portfolio.

- The **Security Market Line (SML)** equation shows the relationship between a security's market risk and its required rate of return. The return required for any security is equal to the **risk-free rate** plus the **market risk premium** times the **security's beta:** $k_i = k_{RF} + (k_M - k_{RF})b_i$.

- The expected rate of return on a stock as seen by the marginal investor is generally equal to its required return—otherwise, prices will adjust to force an equality. However, a number of things can happen to cause the required rate of return to change: (1) the **risk-free rate can change** because of changes in anticipated inflation, (2) **a stock's beta can change,** and (3) **investors' aversion to risk can change.**

- Because returns on assets in different countries are not perfectly correlated, **global diversification** may result in lower risk for multinational companies and globally diversified portfolios.

In Chapters 8 and 9, we will see how a security's rate of return affects its value. Then, in the remainder of the book, we will examine the ways in which a firm's management can influence a stock's riskiness and hence its price.

Questions

5-1 Define the following terms, using graphs or equations to illustrate your answers wherever feasible:
a. Stand-alone risk; risk; probability distribution
b. Expected rate of return, $\hat{k}$
c. Continuous probability distribution
d. Standard deviation, σ; variance, σ^2; coefficient of variation, CV
e. Risk aversion; realized rate of return, $\bar{k}$
f. Risk premium for Stock i, RP_i; market risk premium, RP_M
g. Capital Asset Pricing Model (CAPM)
h. Expected return on a portfolio, $\hat{k}_p$; market portfolio
i. Correlation coefficient, r; correlation
j. Market risk; diversifiable risk; relevant risk
k. Beta coefficient, b; average stock's beta, b_A
l. Security Market Line (SML); SML equation
m. Slope of SML as a measure of risk aversion

5-2 The probability distribution of a less risky expected return is more peaked than that of a riskier return. What shape would the probability distribution have for (a) completely certain returns and (b) completely uncertain returns?

5-3 Security A has an expected return of 7 percent, a standard deviation of expected returns of 35 percent, a correlation coefficient with the market of –0.3, and a beta coefficient of –1.5. Security B has an expected return of 12 percent, a standard deviation of returns of 10 percent, a correlation with the market of 0.7, and a beta coefficient of 1.0. Which security is riskier? Why?

5-4 Suppose you owned a portfolio consisting of $250,000 worth of long-term U.S. government bonds.
a. Would your portfolio be riskless?
b. Now suppose you hold a portfolio consisting of $250,000 worth of 30-day Treasury bills. Every 30 days your bills mature, and you reinvest the principal ($250,000) in a new batch of bills. Assume that you live on the investment income from your portfolio and that you want to maintain a constant standard of living. Is your portfolio truly riskless?
c. Can you think of any asset that would be completely riskless? Could someone develop such an asset? Explain.

5-5 A life insurance policy is a financial asset. The premiums paid represent the investment's cost.
a. How would you calculate the expected return on a life insurance policy?
b. Suppose the owner of a life insurance policy has no other financial assets—the person's only other asset is "human capital," or lifetime earnings capacity. What is the correlation coefficient between returns on the insurance policy and returns on the policyholder's human capital?
c. Life insurance companies have to pay administrative costs and sales representatives' commissions; hence, the expected rate of return on insurance premiums is generally low, or even negative. Use the portfolio concept to explain why people buy life insurance in spite of negative expected returns.

5-6 If investors' aversion to risk increased, would the risk premium on a high-beta stock increase more or less than that on a low-beta stock? Explain.

5-7 If a company's beta were to double, would its expected return double?

5-8 Is it possible to construct a portfolio of stocks which has an expected return equal to the risk-free rate?

Self-Test Problems   (Solutions Appear in Appendix B)

ST-1
Realized Rates of Return

Stocks A and B have the following historical returns:

YEAR	STOCK A'S RETURNS, k_A	STOCK B'S RETURNS, k_B
1994	(10.00%)	(3.00%)
1995	18.50	21.29
1996	38.67	44.25
1997	14.33	3.67
1998	33.00	28.30

a. Calculate the average rate of return for each stock during the period 1994 through 1998. Assume that someone held a portfolio consisting of 50 percent of Stock A and 50 percent of Stock B. What would have been the realized rate of return on the portfolio in each year from 1994 through 1998? What would have been the average return on the portfolio during this period?

b. Now calculate the standard deviation of returns for each stock and for the portfolio. Use Equation 5-3a in Footnote 6.

c. Looking at the annual returns data on the two stocks, would you guess that the correlation coefficient between returns on the two stocks is closer to 0.9 or to −0.9?

d. If you added more stocks at random to the portfolio, which of the following is the most accurate statement of what would happen to σ_p?

   (1) σ_p would remain constant.

   (2) σ_p would decline to somewhere in the vicinity of 21 percent.

   (3) σ_p would decline to zero if enough stocks were included.

ST-2
Beta and Required Rate of Return

ECRI Corporation is a holding company with four main subsidiaries. The percentage of its business coming from each of the subsidiaries, and their respective betas, are as follows:

SUBSIDIARY	PERCENTAGE OF BUSINESS	BETA
Electric utility	60%	0.70
Cable company	25	0.90
Real estate	10	1.30
International/special projects	5	1.50

a. What is the holding company's beta?

b. Assume that the risk-free rate is 6 percent and the market risk premium is 5 percent. What is the holding company's required rate of return?

c. ECRI is considering a change in its strategic focus; it will reduce its reliance on the electric utility subsidiary, so the percentage of its business from this subsidiary will be 50 percent. At the same time, ECRI will increase its reliance on the international/special projects division, so the percentage of its business from that subsidiary will rise to 15 percent. What will be the shareholders' required rate of return if they adopt these changes?

Problems

5-1
Expected Return

A stock's expected return has the following distribution:

DEMAND FOR THE COMPANY'S PRODUCTS	PROBABILITY OF THIS DEMAND OCCURRING	RATE OF RETURN IF THIS DEMAND OCCURS
Weak	0.1	(50%)
Below average	0.2	(5)
Average	0.4	16
Above average	0.2	25
Strong	0.1	60
	1.0	

Calculate the stock's expected return, standard deviation, and coefficient of variation.

5-2
Portfolio Beta

An individual has $35,000 invested in a stock which has a beta of 0.8 and $40,000 invested in a stock with a beta of 1.4. If these are the only two investments in her portfolio, what is her portfolio's beta?

5-3
Expected and Required Rates of Return

Assume that the risk-free rate is 5 percent and the market risk premium is 6 percent. What is the expected return for the overall stock market? What is the required rate of return on a stock that has a beta of 1.2?

5-4
Required Rate of Return

Assume that the risk-free rate is 6 percent and the expected return on the market is 13 percent. What is the required rate of return on a stock that has a beta of 0.7?

5-5
Expected Returns

The market and Stock J have the following probability distributions:

PROBABILITY	k_M	k_J
0.3	15%	20%
0.4	9	5
0.3	18	12

a. Calculate the expected rates of return for the market and Stock J.
b. Calculate the standard deviations for the market and Stock J.
c. Calculate the coefficients of variation for the market and Stock J.

5-6
Expected Returns

Stocks X and Y have the following probability distributions of expected future returns:

PROBABILITY	X	Y
0.1	(10%)	(35%)
0.2	2	0
0.4	12	20
0.2	20	25
0.1	38	45

a. Calculate the expected rate of return, $\hat{k}$, for Stock Y. ($\hat{k}_X = 12\%$.)
b. Calculate the standard deviation of expected returns for Stock X. (That for Stock Y is 20.35 percent.) Now calculate the coefficient of variation for Stock Y. Is it possible that most investors might regard Stock Y as being *less* risky than Stock X? Explain.

5-7
Required Rate of Return

Suppose $k_{RF} = 5\%$, $k_M = 10\%$, and $k_A = 12\%$.
a. Calculate Stock A's beta.
b. If Stock A's beta were 2.0, what would be A's new required rate of return?

5-8
Required Rate of Return

Suppose $k_{RF} = 9\%$, $k_M = 14\%$, and $b_i = 1.3$.
a. What is k_i, the required rate of return on Stock i?
b. Now suppose k_{RF} (1) increases to 10 percent or (2) decreases to 8 percent. The slope of the SML remains constant. How would this affect k_M and k_i?
c. Now assume k_{RF} remains at 9 percent but k_M (1) increases to 16 percent or (2) falls to 13 percent. The slope of the SML does not remain constant. How would these changes affect k_i?

5-9
Portfolio Beta

Suppose you hold a diversified portfolio consisting of a $7,500 investment in each of 20 different common stocks. The portfolio beta is equal to 1.12. Now, suppose you have decided to sell one of the stocks in your portfolio with a beta equal to 1.0 for $7,500 and to use these proceeds to buy another stock for your portfolio. Assume the new stock's beta is equal to 1.75. Calculate your portfolio's new beta.

5-10
Portfolio Required Return

Suppose you are the money manager of a $4 million investment fund. The fund consists of 4 stocks with the following investments and betas:

STOCK	INVESTMENT	BETA
A	$ 400,000	1.50
B	600,000	(0.50)
C	1,000,000	1.25
D	2,000,000	0.75

If the market required rate of return is 14 percent and the risk-free rate is 6 percent, what is the fund's required rate of return?

5-11
Portfolio Beta

You have a $2 million portfolio consisting of a $100,000 investment in each of 20 different stocks. The portfolio has a beta equal to 1.1. You are considering selling $100,000 worth of one stock which has a beta equal to 0.9 and using the proceeds to purchase another stock which has a beta equal to 1.4. What will be the new beta of your portfolio following this transaction?

5-12
Required Rate of Return

Stock R has a beta of 1.5, Stock S has a beta of 0.75, the expected rate of return on an average stock is 13 percent, and the risk-free rate of return is 7 percent. By how much does the required return on the riskier stock exceed the required return on the less risky stock?

5-13
Expected Returns

Suppose you won the Florida lottery and were offered (1) $0.5 million or (2) a gamble in which you would get $1 million if a head were flipped but zero if a tail came up.
a. What is the expected value of the gamble?
b. Would you take the sure $0.5 million or the gamble?
c. If you choose the sure $0.5 million, are you a risk averter or a risk seeker?
d. Suppose you actually take the sure $0.5 million. You can invest it in either a U.S. Treasury bond that will return $537,500 at the end of a year or a common stock that has a 50-50 chance of being either worthless or worth $1,150,000 at the end of the year.
   (1) What is the expected dollar profit on the stock investment? (The expected profit on the T-bond investment is $37,500.)
   (2) What is the expected rate of return on the stock investment? (The expected rate of return on the T-bond investment is 7.5 percent.)
   (3) Would you invest in the bond or the stock?
   (4) Exactly how large would the expected profit (or the expected rate of return) have to be on the stock investment to make *you* invest in the stock, given the 7.5 percent return on the bond?
   (5) How might your decision be affected if, rather than buying one stock for $0.5 million, you could construct a portfolio consisting of 100 stocks with $5,000 invested in each? Each of these stocks has the same return characteristics as the one stock—that is, a 50-50 chance of being worth either zero or $11,500 at year-end. Would the correlation between returns on these stocks matter?

5-14
Security Market Line

The Kish Investment Fund, in which you plan to invest some money, has total capital of $500 million invested in 5 stocks:

STOCK	INVESTMENT	STOCK'S BETA COEFFICIENT
A	$160 million	0.5
B	120 million	2.0
C	80 million	4.0
D	80 million	1.0
E	60 million	3.0

The beta coefficient for a fund like Kish Investment can be found as a weighted average of the fund's investments. The current risk-free rate is 6 percent, whereas market returns have the following estimated probability distribution for the next period:

PROBABILITY	MARKET RETURN
0.1	7%
0.2	9
0.4	11
0.2	13
0.1	15

a. What is the estimated equation for the Security Market Line (SML)? (Hint: First determine the expected market return.)
b. Compute the fund's required rate of return for the next period.
c. Suppose Bridget Nelson, the president, receives a proposal for a new stock. The investment needed to take a position in the stock is $50 million, it will have an expected return of 15 percent, and its estimated beta coefficient is 2.0. Should the new stock be purchased? At what expected rate of return should the fund be indifferent to purchasing the stock?

5-15
Realized Rates of Return

Stocks A and B have the following historical returns:

YEAR	STOCK A'S RETURNS, k_A	STOCK B'S RETURNS, k_B
1994	(18.00%)	(14.50%)
1995	33.00	21.80
1996	15.00	30.50
1997	(0.50)	(7.60)
1998	27.00	26.30

a. Calculate the average rate of return for each stock during the period 1994 through 1998.
b. Assume that someone held a portfolio consisting of 50 percent of Stock A and 50 percent of Stock B. What would have been the realized rate of return on the portfolio in each year from 1994 through 1998? What would have been the average return on the portfolio during this period?
c. Calculate the standard deviation of returns for each stock and for the portfolio.
d. Calculate the coefficient of variation for each stock and for the portfolio.
e. If you are a risk-averse investor, would you prefer to hold Stock A, Stock B, or the portfolio? Why?

5-16
Financial Calculator Needed; Expected and Required Rates of Return

You have observed the following returns over time:

YEAR	STOCK X	STOCK Y	MARKET
1994	14%	13%	12%
1995	19	7	10
1996	−16	−5	−12
1997	3	1	1
1998	20	11	15

Assume that the risk-free rate is 6 percent and the market risk premium is 5 percent.
a. What are the betas of Stocks X and Y?
b. What are the required rates of return for Stocks X and Y?
c. What is the required rate of return for a portfolio consisting of 80 percent of Stock X and 20 percent of Stock Y?
d. If Stock X's expected return is 22 percent, is Stock X under- or overvalued?

Spreadsheet Problem

Work the problem in this section only if you are using the computer problem diskette.

5-17
Realized Rates of Return

Using the computerized model in File C5, rework Problem 5-15, assuming that a third stock, Stock C, is available for inclusion in the portfolio. Stock C has the following historical returns:

YEAR	STOCK C'S RETURNS, k_C
1994	32.00%
1995	(11.75)
1996	10.75
1997	32.25
1998	(6.75)

a. Calculate (or read from the computer screen) the average return, standard deviation, and coefficient of variation for Stock C.
b. Assume that the portfolio now consists of 33.33 percent of Stock A, 33.33 percent of Stock B, and 33.33 percent of Stock C. How does this affect the portfolio return, standard deviation, and coefficient of variation versus when 50 percent was invested in A and in B?
c. Make some other changes in the portfolio, making sure that the percentages sum to 100 percent. For example, enter 25 percent for Stock A, 25 percent for Stock B, and 50 percent for Stock C. (Note that the program will not allow you to enter a zero for the percentage in Stock C.) Notice that $\hat{k}_p$ remains constant and that σ_p changes. Why do these results occur?
d. In Problem 5-15, the standard deviation of the portfolio decreased only slightly, because Stocks A and B were highly positively correlated with one another. In this problem, the addition of Stock C causes the standard deviation of the portfolio to decline dramatically, even though $\sigma_C = \sigma_A = \sigma_B$. What does this indicate about the correlation between Stock C and Stocks A and B?
e. Would you prefer to hold the portfolio described in Problem 5-15 consisting only of Stocks A and B or a portfolio that also included Stock C? If others react similarly, how might this affect the stocks' prices and rates of return?

MINI CASE

Assume that you recently graduated with a major in finance, and you just landed a job as a financial planner with Merrill Finch Inc., a large financial services corporation. Your first assignment is to invest $100,000 for a client. Because the funds are to be invested in a business at the end of 1 year, you have been instructed to plan for a 1-year holding period. Further, your boss has restricted you to the following investment alternatives, shown with their probabilities and associated outcomes. (Disregard for now the items at the bottom of the data; you will fill in the blanks later.)

RETURNS ON ALTERNATIVE INVESTMENTS

				ESTIMATED RATE OF RETURN			
STATE OF THE ECONOMY	PROBABILITY	T-BILLS	HIGH TECH	COLLECTIONS	U.S. RUBBER	MARKET PORTFOLIO	2-STOCK PORTFOLIO
Recession	0.1	8.0%	(22.0%)	28.0%	10.0%*	(13.0%)	3.0%
Below average	0.2	8.0	(2.0)	14.7	(10.0)	1.0	
Average	0.4	8.0	20.0	0.0	7.0	15.0	10.0
Above average	0.2	8.0	35.0	(10.0)	45.0	29.0	
Boom	0.1	8.0	50.0	(20.0)	30.0	43.0	15.0
$\hat{k}$				1.7%	13.8%	15.0%	
σ		0.0		13.4	18.8	15.3	
CV				7.9	1.4	1.0	
b				−0.86	0.68		

*Note that the estimated returns of U.S. Rubber do not always move in the same direction as the overall economy. For example, when the economy is below average, consumers purchase fewer tires than they would if the economy was stronger. However, if the economy is in a flat-out recession, a large number of consumers who were planning to purchase a new car may choose to wait and instead purchase new tires for the car they currently own. Under these circumstances, we would expect U.S. Rubber's stock price to be higher if there is a recession than if the economy was just below average.

Merrill Finch's economic forecasting staff has developed probability estimates for the state of the economy, and its security analysts have developed a sophisticated computer program which was used to estimate the rate of return on each alternative under each state of the economy. High Tech Inc. is an electronics firm; Collections Inc. collects past-due debts; and U.S. Rubber manufactures tires and various other rubber and plastics products. Merrill Finch also maintains an "index fund" which owns a market-weighted fraction of all publicly traded stocks; you can invest in that fund, and thus obtain average stock market results. Given the situation as described, answer the following questions.

a. What are investment returns? What is the return on an investment that costs $1,000 and is sold after 1 year for $1,100?

b. (1) Why is the T-bill's return independent of the state of the economy? Do T-bills promise a completely risk-free return? (2) Why are High Tech's returns expected to move with the economy whereas Collections' are expected to move counter to the economy?

c. Calculate the expected rate of return on each alternative and fill in the blanks on the row for $\hat{k}$ in the table above.

d. You should recognize that basing a decision solely on expected returns is only appropriate for risk-neutral individuals. Since your client, like virtually everyone, is risk averse, the riskiness of each alternative is an important aspect of the decision. One possible measure of risk is the standard deviation of returns. (1) Calculate this value for each alternative, and fill in the blank on the row for σ in the table above. (2) What type of risk is measured by the standard deviation? (3) Draw a graph which shows *roughly* the shape of the probability distributions for High Tech, U.S. Rubber, and T-bills.

e. Suppose you suddenly remembered that the coefficient of variation (CV) is generally regarded as being a better measure of stand-alone risk than the standard deviation when the alternatives being considered have widely differing expected returns. Calculate the missing CVs, and fill in the blanks on the row for CV in the table above. Does the CV produce the same risk rankings as the standard deviation?

f. Suppose you created a 2-stock portfolio by investing $50,000 in High Tech and $50,000 in Collections. (1) Calculate the expected return ($\hat{k}_p$), the standard deviation (σ_p), and the coefficient of variation (CV_p) for this portfolio and fill in the appropriate blanks in the table above. (2) How does the riskiness of this 2-stock portfolio compare with the riskiness of the individual stocks if they were held in isolation?

g. Suppose an investor starts with a portfolio consisting of one randomly selected stock. What would happen (1) to the riskiness and (2) to the expected return of the portfolio as more and more randomly selected stocks were added to the portfolio? What is the implication for investors? Draw a graph of the two portfolios to illustrate your answer.

h. (1) Should portfolio effects impact the way investors think about the riskiness of individual stocks? (2) If you decided to hold a 1-stock portfolio, and consequently were exposed to more risk than diversified investors, could you expect to be compensated for all of your risk; that is, could you earn a risk premium on that part of your risk that you could have eliminated by diversifying?

i. The expected rates of return and the beta coefficients of the alternatives as supplied by Merrill Finch's computer program are as follows:

SECURITY	RETURN ($\hat{k}$)	RISK (BETA)
High Tech	17.4%	1.29
Market	15.0	1.00
U.S. Rubber	13.8	0.68
T-bills	8.0	0.00
Collections	1.7	(0.86)

(1) What is a beta coefficient, and how are betas used in risk analysis? (2) Do the expected returns appear to be related to each alternative's market risk? (3) Is it possible to choose among the alternatives on the basis of the information developed thus far? Use the data given at the start of the problem to construct a graph which shows how the T-bill's, High Tech's, and Collections' beta coefficients are calculated. Then discuss what betas measure and how they are used in risk analysis.

j. (1) Write out the Security Market Line (SML) equation, use it to calculate the required rate of return on each alternative, and then graph the relationship between the expected and required rates of return. (2) How do the expected rates of return compare with the required rates of return? (3) Does the fact that Collections has an expected return which is less than the T-bill rate make any sense? (4) What would be the market risk and the required return of a 50-50 portfolio of High Tech and Collections? Of High Tech and U.S. Rubber?

k. (1) Suppose investors raised their inflation expectations by 3 percentage points over current estimates as reflected in the 8 percent T-bill rate. What effect would higher inflation have on the SML and on the returns required on high- and low-risk securities? (2) Suppose instead that investors' risk aversion increased enough to cause the market risk premium to increase by 3 percentage points. (Inflation remains constant.) What effect would this have on the SML and on returns of high- and low-risk securities?

Selected Additional References and Cases

Probably the best sources of additional information on probability distributions and single-asset risk measures are statistics textbooks. For example, see

Kohler, Heinz, *Statistics for Business and Economics* (New York: HarperCollins, 1994).

Mendenhall, William, Richard L. Schaeffer, and Dennis D. Wackerly, *Mathematical Statistics with Applications* (Boston: PWS, 1996).

Probably the best place to find an extension of portfolio theory concepts is one of the investments textbooks. These are some good ones:

Francis, Jack C., *Investments: Analysis and Management* (New York: McGraw-Hill, 1991).

Radcliffe, Robert C., *Investment: Concepts, Analysis, and Strategy* (New York: HarperCollins, 1994).

Reilly, Frank K., and Keith C. Brown, *Investment Analysis and Portfolio Management* (Fort Worth, Tex.: Dryden Press, 1997).

Sharpe, William F., *Investments* (Englewood Cliffs, N.J.: Prentice-Hall, 1995).

Those who want to start at the beginning in studying portfolio theory should see

Markowitz, Harry M., "Portfolio Selection," *Journal of Finance,* March 1952, 77–91.

_____, "Foundations of Portfolio Theory," *Journal of Finance,* June 1991, 469–477.

The following case from the Cases in Financial Management: Dryden Request *series covers many of the concepts discussed in this chapter as well as concepts to be covered in Chapter 6:*

Case 2, "Peachtree Securities, Inc. (A)."

RISK AND RETURN: EXTENSIONS*

*O*ne of the most useful references for people working in investments and portfolio management is Stocks, Bonds, Bills, and Inflation, *published annually by Ibbotson Associates. The latest Ibbotson report presents a history of the total returns realized from 1926 through 1996 in the following six U.S. capital markets:*

1. *Small-company stocks, as represented by the smallest 20 percent of stocks (by market value) listed on the New York Stock Exchange.*

2. *Large-company stocks, as represented by the Standard and Poor's 500 Stock Composite Index (S&P 500).*

3. *Long-term corporate bonds, as represented by the Salomon Brothers long-term, high-grade corporate bond total return index.*

4. *Long-term government bonds, as represented by a U.S. Treasury bond with a 20-year maturity.*

5. *Intermediate-term government bonds, as represented by a U.S. Treasury bond with a five-year maturity.*

6. *U.S. Treasury bills, as represented by a bill with a maturity of approximately 30 days.*

A long-term perspective of capital market history reveals the general relationship between risk and return across different asset classes, as well as the relationship between nominal and real (inflation-adjusted) returns. By studying the past, one can make inferences about what is likely to happen in the future. Although the specific events that occurred from 1926 through 1996 will not be repeated, similar events, such as economic recessions and booms, will undoubtedly recur, and such events will probably affect future investment returns in much the same way as they did in the past.

The Ibbotson report presents historical data in many different formats, but perhaps the most widely used is the annual return data. For example, the 1997 Yearbook, *which contains data for 71 years (1926 through 1996), provides the following total return information, along with inflation data:*

INVESTMENT	AVERAGE ANNUAL RETURN	HIGHEST ANNUAL RETURN	LOWEST ANNUAL RETURN
Small-company stocks	17.7%	142.9%	−58.0%
Large-company stocks	12.7	54.0	−43.3
Long-term corporate bonds	6.0	43.8	−8.1
Long-term government bonds	5.4	40.4	−9.2
Intermediate-term government bonds	5.4	29.1	−2.3
U.S. Treasury bills	3.8	14.7	0.0
Inflation	3.2	18.2	−10.3

---

*This chapter may be omitted without loss of continuity.

The most striking feature of the historical data is the significant difference in risk and return characteristics among the investments. Although a portfolio of small-company stocks averaged a 17.7 percent annual return, the return on T-bills averaged only 3.8 percent. In fact, the return on T-bills barely kept pace with inflation, earning on average only 60 basis points (0.6 percentage point) above inflation. When taxes are considered, the real return on T-bills was negative. For example, an investor who paid only 20 percent in taxes would have an after-tax average return on T-bills of only 0.8(3.8%) ≈ 3.0%, which means a real loss of about 20 basis points per year.

Why do historical returns vary so widely among investments? The answer is simple: risk. To see this more clearly, note that an investor in small-company stocks would have lost 58 percent of the value of his or her portfolio in one of the past 71 years (to be precise, in 1937), while the worst pre-tax experience for an investor holding T-bills was to break even. In general, we see that a strong relationship exists between risk and return—the higher the risk, the higher the return. Although we have not quantified the riskiness of the listed investments, a numerical analysis would lead to the same conclusion—namely, to obtain higher returns, investors must accept greater risk.

I n Chapter 5 we presented the key elements of risk and return analysis. There we saw that much of the risk inherent in a stock can be eliminated by diversification, so rational investors should hold portfolios of stocks rather than just one stock. We also introduced the Capital Asset Pricing Model (CAPM), which links risk and required rates of return, using a stock's beta coefficient as the relevant measure of risk. In this chapter, we extend the Chapter 5 material by presenting an in-depth treatment of portfolio concepts and the CAPM. Additionally, we show how betas are actually calculated, and we discuss an alternative view of the risk/return relationship, the Arbitrage Pricing Theory (APT).

MEASURING PORTFOLIO RISK

In the preceding chapter, we examined portfolio risk at an intuitive level. We now describe how portfolio risk is actually measured and dealt with in practice. First, the riskiness of a portfolio, which may itself be continued as a single asset held in isolation, is measured by the standard deviation of its return distribution. Equation 6-1 is used to calculate this standard deviation:[1]

$$\text{Portfolio standard deviation} = \sigma_p = \sqrt{\sum_{i=1}^{n} (k_{pi} - \hat{k}_p)^2 P_i}. \tag{6-1}$$

Here σ_p is the portfolio's standard deviation; k_{pi} is the return on the portfolio under the *i*th state of the economy; $\hat{k}_p$ is the expected rate of return on the portfolio; P_i is the probability of occurrence of the *i*th state of the economy; and there are n economic states. This equation is exactly the same as the one for the standard deviation of a single asset, except that here the asset is a portfolio of assets (for example, a mutual fund).

[1]Other risk measures such as the coefficient of variation or semivariance could also be used to measure the risk of a portfolio, but since portfolio returns (1) are approximately normally distributed and (2) have reasonably similar expected values, these refinements are not necessary and hence are not used.

Covariance and the Correlation Coefficient

Two key concepts in portfolio analysis are (1) covariance and (2) the correlation coefficient. **Covariance** is a measure which combines the variance (or volatility) of a stock's returns with the tendency of those returns to move up or down at the same time other stocks move up or down. For example, the covariance between Stocks A and B tells us whether the returns of the two stocks tend to rise and fall together, and how large those movements tend to be. Equation 6-2 defines the covariance (Cov) between Stocks A and B:

$$\text{Covariance} = \text{Cov(AB)} = \sum_{i=1}^{n} (k_{Ai} - \hat{k}_A)(k_{Bi} - \hat{k}_B) P_i. \qquad \textbf{(6-2)}$$

The first term in parentheses after the Σ is the deviation of Stock A's return from its expected value under the *i*th state of the economy; the second term is Stock B's deviation under the same state; and P_i is the probability of the *i*th state occurring. Before going through an example, note these points:

1. If the returns on A and B tend to move together, the terms in parentheses will both be positive or both be negative for each state of the economy; that is, if k_{Ai} is above its expected value, $\hat{k}_A$, then k_{Bi} generally will be above $\hat{k}_B$, and vice versa. Therefore, if the returns move together, the terms in parentheses will both be positive or both be negative, hence the product $(k_{Ai} - \hat{k}_A)(k_{Bi} - \hat{k}_B)$ will be positive, while if the returns move counter to one another, the products will tend to be negative. However, if the two stocks' returns fluctuate randomly, then the products will sometimes be positive and sometimes be negative, and the sum of the products will be close to zero because the positives and negatives will tend to cancel out. Therefore, if Stocks A and B tend to move together, their covariance, Cov(AB), will be positive, while if they tend to move counter to one another, Cov(AB) will be negative. If they fluctuate randomly, Cov(AB) could be either positive or negative, but, in either event, it will be close to zero.

2. If the return on either A or B is highly uncertain, then it will have a high standard deviation, its deviations as shown in the parenthetical terms will tend to be large, the products will tend to be large, and the absolute size of Cov(AB) will also tend to be large. However, Cov(AB) will be small, even if σ_A and/or σ_B is large, if A and B move randomly, because the plus and minus terms will cancel out.

3. If either stock has a zero standard deviation, hence is riskless, then all of its deviations $(k_i - \hat{k})$ will be zero, and Cov(AB) also will be zero. Similarly, if one asset is not completely riskless, but it has a relatively low risk, then its deviations will tend to be small, and this, too, will produce a small Cov(AB).

4. Therefore, Cov(AB) will be large and positive if two assets have large standard deviations and tend to move together; it will be large and negative for two high σ assets which move counter to one another; and it will be small if the two assets' returns move randomly, rather than up or down with one another, or if either of the assets has a small standard deviation.

To illustrate the calculation process, first look at Table 6-1, which presents the probability distributions of the rates of return on four stocks, and at Figure 6-1, which plots scatter diagrams between returns on several pairs of the stocks. We can use Equation 6-2 to calculate the covariance between Stocks F and G as follows:

| TABLE 6-1 | Probability Distributions of Stocks E, F, G, and H |

PROBABILITY OF OCCURRENCE	RATE OF RETURN DISTRIBUTION			
	E	F	G	H
0.1	10.0%	6.0%	14.0%	2.0%
0.2	10.0	8.0	12.0	6.0
0.4	10.0	10.0	10.0	9.0
0.2	10.0	12.0	8.0	15.0
0.1	10.0	14.0	6.0	20.0
$\hat{k} =$	10.0%	10.0%	10.0%	10.0%
$\sigma =$	0.0%	2.2%	2.2%	5.0%

$$\text{Cov(FG)} = \sum_{i=1}^{5} (k_{Fi} - \hat{k}_F)(k_{Gi} - \hat{k}_G)P_i$$

$$= (6 - 10)(14 - 10)(0.1) + (8 - 10)(12 - 10)(0.2)$$
$$+ (10 - 10)(10 - 10)(0.4) + (12 - 10)(8 - 10)(0.2)$$
$$+ (14 - 10)(6 - 10)(0.1)$$

$$= -4.8.$$

The negative sign indicates that the rates of return on Stocks F and G tend to move in opposite directions, which is consistent with the pattern shown in Panel b of Figure 6-1.

If we calculated the covariance between Stocks F and H, we would find Cov(FH) = +10.8, indicating that these assets tend to move together, as indicated by the positive slope in Panel c. A zero covariance, as between Stocks E and F, indicates that there is no relationship between the variables; that is, the variables are independent. (E's return is always 10 percent, so $\sigma_E = 0\%$, and the covariance of E with any asset must be zero.)

It is difficult to interpret the magnitude of the covariance term, so a related statistic, the **correlation coefficient,** is generally used to measure the degree of comovement between two variables. The correlation coefficient standardizes the covariance by dividing by a product term, which facilitates comparisons by putting things on a similar scale. The correlation coefficient, r, is calculated as follows for variables A and B:

$$\text{Correlation coefficient(AB)} = r_{AB} = \frac{\text{Cov(AB)}}{\sigma_A \sigma_B}. \qquad (6\text{-}3)$$

The sign of the correlation coefficient is the same as the sign of the covariance, so a positive sign means that the variables move together, a negative sign indicates that they move in opposite directions, and if r is close to zero, they move independently of one another. Moreover, the standardization process confines the correlation coefficient to values between −1.0 and +1.0. Finally, note that Equation 6-3 can be solved to find the covariance:

$$\text{Cov(AB)} = r_{AB}\sigma_A\sigma_B. \qquad (6\text{-}3a)$$

FIGURE 6-1   Scatter Diagrams

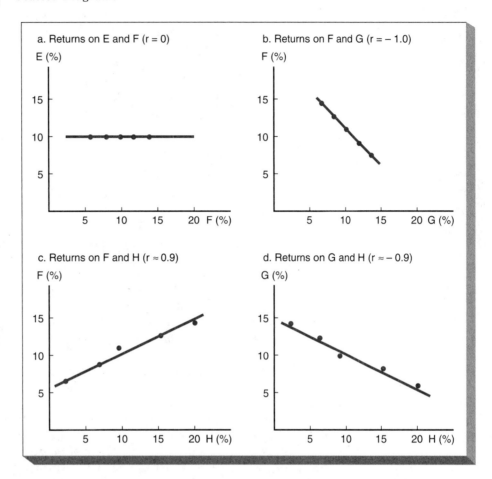

a. Returns on E and F (r = 0)

b. Returns on F and G (r = − 1.0)

c. Returns on F and H (r ≈ 0.9)

d. Returns on G and H (r ≈ − 0.9)

NOTES:

a. The lines shown in each graph are called *regression lines;* they will be discussed in detail in a later section.

b. These graphs are drawn as if each point had an equal probability of occurrence.

Using Equation 6-3, we find the correlation coefficient between Stocks F and G to be −1.0 (except for a rounding error):

$$r_{FG} = \frac{-4.8}{(2.2)(2.2)} \approx -1.0.$$

These two stocks are said to be perfectly negatively correlated. As Panel b of Figure 6-1 shows, the regression line for these two assets' rates of return is negatively sloped, and all points lie exactly on the line. Whenever the points are all on the regression line, r must be equal to 1.0 if the line slopes up and to −1.0 if the line slopes down.

The correlation coefficient between Stocks F and H is +0.9. Thus, there is a strong positive relationship—their regression line is upward sloping, but all points in Panel c are not exactly on the line. Generally, the closer the points are to the regression line, the higher the absolute value of the correlation coefficient.

The Two-Asset Case

Under the assumption that the distributions of returns on the individual securities are normal, a complicated looking but operationally simple equation can be used to determine the riskiness of a two-asset portfolio:[2]

$$\text{Portfolio SD} = \sigma_p = \sqrt{x^2\sigma_A^2 + (1-x)^2\sigma_B^2 + 2x(1-x)r_{AB}\sigma_A\sigma_B}. \qquad (6\text{-}4)$$

Here x is the fraction of the portfolio invested in Security A, so $(1-x)$ is the fraction invested in Security B. We illustrate the equation in the next section.

S E L F - T E S T
Q U E S T I O N S

How is the riskiness of a portfolio measured?

What does the correlation coefficient measure?

EFFICIENT PORTFOLIOS

One important use of portfolio risk concepts is to select **efficient portfolios,** defined as those portfolios that provide the highest expected return for any degree of risk, or the lowest degree of risk for any expected return. To illustrate the concept, assume that two securities, A and B, are available, and we can allocate our funds between them in any proportion. Suppose Security A has an expected rate of return of $\hat{k}_A = 5\%$ and a standard deviation of returns $\sigma_A = 4\%$, while $\hat{k}_B = 8\%$ and $\sigma_B = 10\%$. Our first task is to determine the set of *attainable* portfolios, and then from this attainable set to select the *efficient* subset.

To construct the attainable set, we need data on the degree of correlation between the two securities' expected returns, r_{AB}. Let us work with three different assumed degrees of correlation, $r_{AB} = +1.0$, $r_{AB} = 0$, and $r_{AB} = -1.0$, and use them to develop the portfolios' expected returns, $\hat{k}_p$, and standard deviations, σ_p. (Of course, only one correlation can exist; our example simply shows three alternative situations that might exist.)

To calculate k_p, we use a modified version of Equation 5-5 from Chapter 5, substituting the given values for $\hat{k}_A$ and $\hat{k}_B$, and then solving for k_p at different values of x. For example, when x equals 0.75, then $\hat{k}_p = 5.75\%$:

$$\hat{k}_p = x\hat{k}_A + (1-x)\hat{k}_B$$

$$= 0.75(5\%) + 0.25(8\%) = 5.75\%. \qquad (5\text{-}5a)$$

Other values of $\hat{k}_p$ were found similarly, and they are shown in the $\hat{k}_p$ column of Table 6-2.

Next, we use Equation 6-4 to find σ_p. Substitute the given values for σ_A, σ_B, and r_{AB}, and then solve for σ_p at different values of x. For example, in the case where $r_{AB} = 0$ and x = 0.75, then $\sigma_p = 3.9\%$:

$$\sigma_p = \sqrt{x^2\sigma_A^2 + (1-x)^2\sigma_B^2 + 2x(1-x)r_{AB}\sigma_A\sigma_B}$$

$$= \sqrt{(0.5625)(16) + (0.0625)(100) + 2(0.75)(0.25)(0)(4)(10)}$$

$$= \sqrt{9.00 + 6.25} = \sqrt{15.25} = 3.9\%.$$

---

[2]Equation 6-4 is derived from Equation 6-1 in standard statistics books. Notice that if x = 1, all of the portfolio is invested in Security A, and Equation 6-4 reduces to σ_A:

$$\sigma_p = \sqrt{\sigma_A^2} = \sigma_A.$$

The portfolio contains but a single asset, so the risk of the portfolio and that of the asset are identical. Equation 6-4 could be expanded to include any number of assets by adding additional terms, but we shall not do so here.

| TABLE 6-2 | | $\hat{k}_p$ and σ_p under Various Assumptions | | | | |

PROPORTION OF PORTFOLIO IN SECURITY A (VALUE OF x)	PROPORTION OF PORTFOLIO IN SECURITY B (VALUE OF $1 - x$)	$\hat{k}_p$	σ_p		
			CASE I ($r_{AB} = +1.0$)	CASE II ($r_{AB} = 0$)	CASE III ($r_{AB} = -1.0$)
1.00	0.00	5.00%	4.0%	4.0%	4.0%
0.75	0.25	5.75	5.5	3.9	0.5
0.50	0.50	6.50	7.0	5.4	3.0
0.25	0.75	7.25	8.5	7.6	6.5
0.00	1.00	8.00	10.0	10.0	10.0

Table 6-2 gives $\hat{k}_p$ and σ_p values for x = 1.00, 0.75, 0.50, 0.25, and 0.00, and Figure 6-2 plots $\hat{k}_p$, σ_p, and the attainable set of portfolios for each correlation. In both the table and the graphs, note the following points:

1. The three graphs across the top row of Figure 6-2 designate Case I, where the two assets are perfectly positively correlated, that is, $r_{AB} = +1.0$. The three graphs in the middle row are for the zero correlation case, and the three in the bottom row are for perfect negative correlation.

2. All three cases are more theoretical than realistic because we would rarely encounter $r_{AB} = -1.0$, 0.0, or +1.0. Generally, in the real world, r_{AB} would be in the range of +0.5 to +0.7 for most stocks. Case II (zero correlation) produces graphs which, pictorially, most closely resemble real-world examples.

3. The left column of graphs shows how the *expected portfolio* returns vary with different combinations of A and B. We see that these graphs are identical in each of the three cases: The portfolio return, $\hat{k}_p$, is a linear function of x, and it does not depend on the correlation coefficients. This is also seen from the single $\hat{k}_p$ column in Table 6-2.

4. The middle column of graphs shows how risk is affected by the portfolio mix. Starting from the top, we see that portfolio risk, σ_p, increases linearly in Case I, where $r_{AB} = +1.0$; it is nonlinear in Case II; and Case III shows that risk can be completely diversified away if $r_{AB} = -1.0$. Thus σ_p, unlike $\hat{k}_p$, *does* depend on correlation.

5. Note that in both Cases II and III someone holding only Stock A could sell some A, buy some B, and both increase his or her expected return and also lower risk.

6. The right column of graphs shows the attainable, or feasible set of portfolios constructed with different mixes of Securities A and B. Unlike the other columns, which plotted return and risk versus the portfolio's composition, each of the three graphs here were plotted from pairs of k_p and σ_p as shown in Table 6-2. For example, Point A in the upper right graph is the point $\hat{k}_p$ = 5%, σ_p = 4% from the Case I data. All other points on the curves were plotted similarly. With only two securities in the portfolio, the attainable set is a curve or line, and we can achieve each risk/return combination on the relevant curve by some allocation of our investment funds between Securities A and B.

7. Are all combinations on the attainable set equally good? The answer is no: Only that part of the attainable set from Y to B in Cases II and III is defined to be efficient. The part from A to Y is inefficient because for any degree of risk on the line segment AY,

FIGURE 6-2   Illustrations of Portfolio Returns, Risk, and the Attainable Set of Portfolios

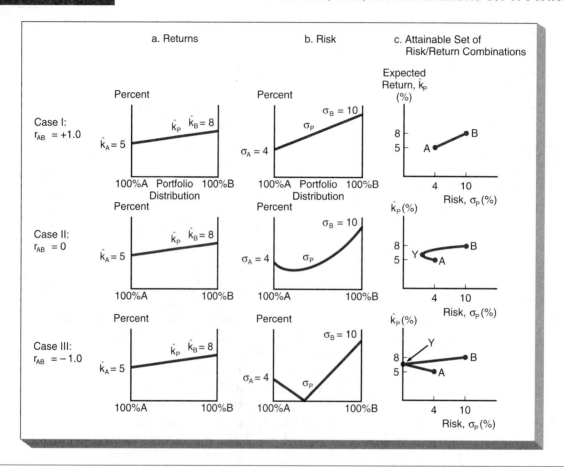

a higher return can be found on segment YB. Thus, no rational investor would hold a portfolio that lay on segment AY. In Case I, however, the entire feasible set is efficient—here no combination of the securities can be ruled out.

From these examples we see that in one extreme case (r = −1.0), risk can be completely eliminated, while in the other extreme case (r = +1.0), diversification does no good whatever. In between these extremes, combining two stocks into a portfolio reduces but does not eliminate the riskiness inherent in the individual stocks.[3]

SELF-TEST
QUESTIONS

What is meant by the term "attainable, or feasible, set"?

Within the attainable set, which portfolios are "efficient"?

---

[3]If we differentiate Equation 6-4, set the derivative equal to zero, and then solve for x, we obtain the fraction of the portfolio that should be invested in Security A if we wish to form the least-risky portfolio. Here is the equation:

$$\text{Minimum risk portfolio: } x = \frac{\sigma_B(\sigma_B - r_{AB}\sigma_A)}{\sigma_A^2 + \sigma_B^2 - 2r_{AB}\sigma_A\sigma_B}.$$

As a rule, we limit x to the range 0 to +1.0; that is, if the solution value is x > 1.0, set x = 1.0, and if x is negative, set x = 0. A negative x would imply short sales, and x > 1.0 would imply borrowing. (See Footnote 7 for a definition of a short sale.)

FIGURE 6-3	The Efficient Set of Investments

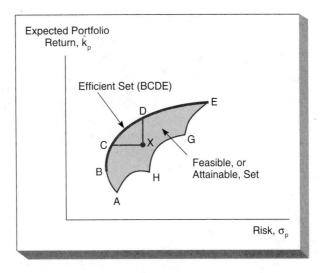

CHOOSING THE OPTIMAL PORTFOLIO

With only two assets, the feasible set of portfolios is a line or curve as shown in the third column of graphs back in Figure 6-2. However, if we were to increase the number of assets, we would obtain an area such as the shaded area in Figure 6-3. The points A, H, G, and E represent single securities (or portfolios containing only one security). All the other points in the shaded area and its boundaries, which comprise the feasible set, represent portfolios of two or more securities. Each point in this area represents a particular portfolio with a risk of σ_p and an expected return of $\hat{k}_p$. For example, point X represents one such portfolio's risk and expected return, as do B, C, and D.

Given the full set of potential portfolios that could be constructed from the available assets, which portfolio should actually be held? This choice involves two separate decisions: (1) determining the efficient set of portfolios and (2) choosing from the efficient set the single portfolio that is best for the specific investor.

The Efficient Frontier

In Figure 6-3, the boundary line BCDE defines the efficient set of portfolios, which is also called the **efficient frontier.**[4] Portfolios to the left of the efficient set are not possible because they lie outside the attainable set. Portfolios to the right of the boundary line (interior portfolios) are inefficient because some other portfolio would provide either a higher return for the same degree of risk or a lower risk for the same rate of return. For example, Portfolio X is dominated by Portfolios C and D.

---

[4]A computational procedure for determining the efficient set of portfolios was developed by Harry Markowitz and first reported in his article "Portfolio Selection," *Journal of Finance,* March 1952. In this article, Markowitz developed the basic concepts of portfolio theory, and he later won the Nobel Prize in economics for his work.

Risk/Return Indifference Curves

Given the efficient set of portfolios, which specific portfolio should an investor choose? To determine the optimal portfolio for a particular investor, we must know the investor's attitude toward risk as reflected in his or her risk/return trade-off function, or **indifference curve**.

An investor's risk/return trade-off function is based on the standard economic concepts of utility theory and indifference curves, which are illustrated in Figure 6-4. The curves labeled I_Y and I_Z represent the indifference curves of Individuals Y and Z. Ms. Y is indifferent with regard to the riskless 5 percent portfolio, a portfolio with an expected return of 6 percent but a risk of $\sigma_p = 1.4\%$, and so on. Mr. Z is indifferent between a riskless 5 percent return, an expected 6 percent return with risk of $\sigma_p = 3.3\%$, and so on.

Notice that Ms. Y requires a higher expected rate of return to compensate for any given amount of risk; thus, Ms. Y is said to be more **risk averse** than Mr. Z. Her higher risk aversion causes Ms. Y to require a higher **risk premium**—defined here as the difference between the 5 percent riskless return and the expected return required to compensate for any specific amount of risk—than does Mr. Z. Thus, Ms. Y requires a risk premium (RP_Y) of 2.5 percent to compensate for a risk of $\sigma_p = 3.3\%$, while Mr. Z's risk premium for this degree of risk is only $RP_Z = 1.0\%$. *As a generalization, the steeper the slope of an investor's indifference curve, the more risk averse the investor.* Thus, Ms. Y is more risk averse than Mr. Z.

FIGURE 6-4   Risk/Return Indifference Curves

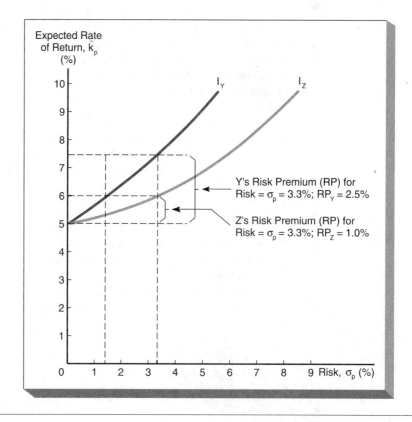

FIGURE 6-5   Selecting the Optimal Portfolio of Risky Assets

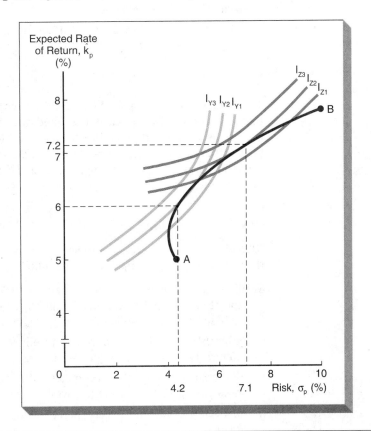

Each individual has a "map" of indifference curves; the indifference maps for Ms. Y and Mr. Z are shown in Figure 6-5. The higher curves denote a greater level of satisfaction (or utility). Thus, I_{Z2} is better than I_{Z1} because, for any level of risk, Mr. Z has a higher expected return, hence greater utility. An infinite number of indifference curves could be drawn in the map for each individual, and each individual has a unique map.

The Optimal Portfolio for an Investor

Figure 6-5 also shows the feasible set of portfolios for the two-asset case, under the assumption that $r_{AB} = 0$, as it was developed in Figure 6-2. The optimal portfolio for each investor is found at the tangency point between the efficient set of portfolios and one of the investor's indifference curves. This tangency point marks the highest level of satisfaction the investor can attain. Ms. Y, who is more risk averse than Mr. Z, chooses a portfolio with a lower expected return (about 6 percent) but a riskiness of only $\sigma_p = 4.2\%$. Mr. Z picks a portfolio that provides an expected return of about 7.2 percent, but it has a risk of about $\sigma_p = 7.1\%$. Ms. Y's portfolio is more heavily weighted with the less risky security, while Mr. Z's portfolio contains a larger proportion of the more risky security.[5]

---

[5]Ms. Y's portfolio would contain 67 percent of Security A and 33 percent of Security B, whereas Mr. Z's portfolio would consist of 27 percent of Security A and 73 percent of Security B. These percentages can be determined with Equation 5-5a by simply seeing what percentage of the two securities is consistent with $k_p = 6.0\%$ and 7.2%. For example, $x(5\%) + (1 - x)(8\%) = 7.2\%$, and solving for x, we obtain $x = 0.27$ and $(1 - x) = 0.73$.

What is the efficient frontier?

What are indifference curves?

Conceptually, how does an investor choose his or her optimal portfolio?

THE CAPITAL ASSET PRICING MODEL

The **Capital Asset Pricing Model (CAPM),** which was introduced in Chapter 5, specifies the relationship between risk and required rates of return on assets when they are held in well-diversified portfolios. In Chapter 5, we focused on the Security Market Line, because that is the "bottom line" of the CAPM. In this chapter, we expand on that discussion by presenting the assumptions behind the CAPM and by showing how the SML was developed.

Basic Assumptions of the CAPM

As in all financial theories, a number of assumptions were made in the development of the CAPM; they are summarized in the following list:[6]

1. All investors focus on a single holding period, and they seek to maximize the expected utility of their terminal wealth by choosing among alternative portfolios on the basis of each portfolio's expected return and standard deviation.

2. All investors can borrow or lend an unlimited amount at a given risk-free rate of interest, k_{RF}, and there are no restrictions on short sales of any asset.[7]

3. All investors have identical estimates of the expected returns, variances, and covariances among all assets; that is, investors have homogeneous expectations.

4. All assets are perfectly divisible and perfectly liquid (that is, marketable at the going price).

5. There are no transactions costs.

6. There are no taxes.

7. All investors are price takers (that is, all investors assume that their own buying and selling activity will not affect stock prices).

8. The quantities of all assets are given and fixed.

Theoretical extensions in the literature have relaxed some of these assumptions, and in general these extensions have led to conclusions that are reasonably consistent with the basic theory. However, even the extensions contain assumptions which are both strong and unrealistic, so the validity of the model can only be established through empirical tests. More will be said later about the empirical validity of the CAPM, but first we must discuss its basic properties and conclusions.

---

[6]The CAPM was originated by William F. Sharpe in his article "Capital Asset Prices: A Theory of Market Equilibrium under Conditions of Risk," which appeared in the September 1964 issue of the *Journal of Finance*. Note that Professor Sharpe won the Nobel Prize in economics for his capital asset pricing work. The assumptions inherent in Sharpe's model were spelled out by Michael C. Jensen in "Capital Markets: Theory and Evidence," *Bell Journal of Economics and Management Science*, Autumn 1972, 357–398.

[7]In a *short sale*, one borrows a stock and then sells it, expecting to buy it back later (at a lower price) in order to repay the person from whom the stock was borrowed. If you sell short and the stock price rises, you lose, but you win if the price declines.

| What are the key assumptions of the CAPM?

In what sense are these assumptions unrealistic? Explain.

THE CAPITAL MARKET LINE

Figure 6-5 showed the set of portfolio opportunities for the two-asset case, and it illustrated how indifference curves can be used to select the optimal portfolio from the feasible set. In Figure 6-6, we show a similar diagram for the many-asset case, but here we also include a risk-free asset with a return k_{RF}. The riskless asset by definition has zero risk, hence $\sigma = 0\%$, so it is plotted on the vertical axis.

The figure shows both the feasible set of portfolios of risky assets (the shaded area) and a set of indifference curves (I_1, I_2, I_3) for a particular investor. Point N, where indifference curve I_1 is tangent to the efficient set, represents a possible portfolio choice; it is the point on the efficient set of risky portfolios where the investor obtains the highest possible return for a given amount of risk, σ_p, and the smallest degree of risk for a given expected return, $\hat{k}_p$.

However, the investor can do better than Portfolio N—he or she can reach a higher indifference curve. In addition to the feasible set of risky portfolios, we now have a risk-free asset that provides a riskless return, k_{RF}. Given the risk-free asset, investors can create new portfolios that combine the risk-free asset with a portfolio of risky assets. This enables them to achieve any combination of risk and return on the straight line connecting k_{RF} with M, the point of tangency between that straight

---

FIGURE 6-6. Investor Equilibrium: Combining the Risk-Free Asset
with the Market Portfolio

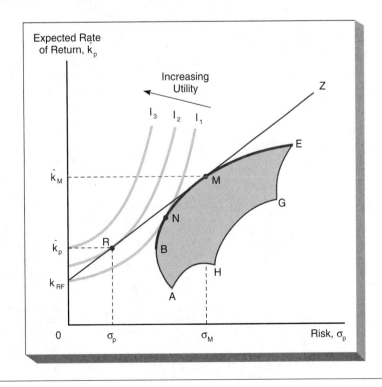

line and the efficient frontier of risky asset portfolios.[8] Some portfolios on the line $k_{RF}MZ$ will be preferred to most risky portfolios on the efficient frontier BNME, so the points on the line $k_{RF}MZ$ now represent the best attainable combinations of risk and return.

Given the new opportunities along line $k_{RF}MZ$, our investor will move from Point N to Point R, which is on his or her highest attainable risk/return indifference curve. Note that any point on the old efficient frontier BNME (except the point of tangency M) is dominated by some point along the line $k_{RF}MZ$. In general, since investors can include both the risk-free security and a fraction of the risky portfolio, M, in a portfolio, it will be possible to move to a point such as R. In addition, if the investor can borrow as well as lend (lending is equivalent to buying risk-free debt securities) at the riskless rate, k_{RF}, it is possible to move out on the line segment MZ, and one would do so if his or her indifference curve were tangent to $k_{RF}MZ$ to the right of Point M.[9]

All investors should hold portfolios lying on the line $k_{RF}MZ$ under the conditions assumed in the CAPM. This implies that they should hold portfolios that are combinations of the risk-free security and the risky portfolio M. Thus, the addition of the risk-free asset totally changes the efficient set: The efficient set now lies along line $k_{RF}MZ$ rather than along the curve BNME. Also, note that if the capital market is to be in equilibrium, M must be a portfolio that contains every risky asset in exact proportion to that asset's fraction of the total market value of all assets; that is, if Security i is x percent of the total market value of all securities, x percent of the market portfolio M must consist of Security i. (In other words, M is the market-value-weighted portfolio of *all* risky assets in the economy.) Thus, all investors should hold portfolios which lie on the line $k_{RF}MZ$, with the particular location of a given individual's portfolio being determined by the point at which his or her indifference curve is tangent to the line.

---

[8]The risk/return combinations between a risk-free asset and a risky asset (a single stock or a portfolio of stocks) will always be linear. To see this, consider the following equations, which were developed earlier, for return, $\hat{k}_p$, and risk, σ_p, for any combination x and $(1-x)$:

$$\hat{k}_p = xk_{RF} + (1-x)\hat{k}_M, \tag{5-5a}$$

and

$$\sigma_p = \sqrt{x^2\sigma_{RF}^2 + (1-x)^2\sigma_M^2 + 2x(1-x)r_{RF/M}\sigma_{RF}\sigma_M}. \tag{6-4a}$$

Equation 5-5a is linear. From Equation 6-4a, we know that k_{RF} is the risk-free asset, so $\sigma_{RF} = 0$; hence, σ_{RF}^2 is also zero. Using this information, we can simplify Equation 6-4a as follows:

$$\sigma_p = \sqrt{(1-x)^2\sigma_M^2} = (1-x)\sigma_M. \tag{6-4b}$$

Thus, σ_p is also linear when a riskless asset is combined with a portfolio of risky assets.

If expected returns as measured by $\hat{k}_p$ and risk as measured by σ_p are both linear functions of x, then the relationship between $\hat{k}_p$ and σ_p, when graphed as in Figure 6-6, must also be linear. For example, if 100 percent of the portfolio is invested in k_{RF} with a return of 8 percent, the portfolio return will be 8 percent and σ_p will be 0. If 100 percent is invested in M, with $k_M = 12\%$ and $\sigma_M = 10\%$, then $\sigma_p = 1.0(10\%) = 10\%$, and $\hat{k}_p = 0(8\%) + 1.0(12\%) = 12\%$. If 50 percent of the portfolio is invested in M and 50 percent in the risk-free asset, then $\sigma_p = 0.5(10\%) = 5\%$, and $\hat{k}_p = 0.5(8\%) + 0.5(12\%) = 10\%$. Plotting these points will reveal the linear relationship given as $k_{RF}MZ$ in Figure 6-6.

[9]An investor who is highly averse to risk will have a steep indifference curve and will end up holding only the riskless asset, or perhaps at a point such as R, holding some of the risky market portfolio and some of the riskless asset. An investor only slightly averse to risk will have a relatively flat indifference curve, which will cause him or her to move out beyond M toward Z, borrowing to do so. This investor might buy stocks on *margin*, which means borrowing and using the stocks as collateral. If individuals' borrowing rates are higher than k_{RF}, then the line $k_{RF}MZ$ will tilt down (that is, be less steep) beyond M. This condition would invalidate the basic CAPM, or at least require it to be modified. Therefore, the assumption of being able to borrow or lend at the same rate is crucial to CAPM theory.

The line $k_{RF}MZ$ in Figure 6-6 is called the **Capital Market Line (CML).** It has an intercept of k_{RF} and a slope of $(\hat{k}_M - k_{RF})/\sigma_M$.[10] Therefore, the equation for the Capital Market Line may be expressed as follows:

$$\text{CML:} \hat{k}_P = k_{RF} + \left(\frac{\hat{k}_M - k_{RF}}{\sigma_M}\right)\sigma_p. \tag{6-5}$$

The expected rate of return *on an efficient portfolio* is equal to the riskless rate plus a risk premium that is equal to $(\hat{k}_M - k_{RF})/\sigma_M$ multiplied by the portfolio's standard deviation, σ_p. Thus, the CML specifies a linear relationship between expected return and risk, with the slope of the CML being equal to the expected return on the market portfolio of risky stocks, $\hat{k}_M$, minus the risk-free rate, k_{RF}, which is called the **market risk premium,** all divided by the standard deviation of returns on the market portfolio, σ_M:

$$\text{Slope of the CML} = (\hat{k}_M - k_{RF})/\sigma_M.$$

For example, suppose $k_{RF} = 10\%$, $\hat{k}_M = 15\%$, and $\sigma_M = 15\%$. Then, the slope of the CML would be $(15\% - 10\%)/15\% = 0.33$, and if a particular portfolio had $\sigma_p = 10\%$, then its $\hat{k}_p$ would be

$$\hat{k}_p = 10\% + 0.33(10\%) = 13.3\%.$$

A riskier portfolio with $\sigma_p = 20\%$ would have $\hat{k}_p = 10\% + 0.33(20\%) = 16.6\%$.

The CML is graphed in Figure 6-7. It is a straight line with an intercept at k_{RF} and a slope equal to the market risk premium $(\hat{k}_M - k_{RF})$ divided by σ_M. The slope of the CML reflects the aggregate attitude of investors toward risk.

In Chapter 5 we saw that the standard deviation (σ_i) of an individual stock should not be used to measure its riskiness, because some of the risk as reflected in σ_i can be eliminated by diversification. Therefore, since its beta reflects risk after taking diversification benefits into account, beta rather than σ_i is used to measure individual stocks' riskiness to investors. The relationship between individual stocks' riskiness and their required returns is set forth in the Security Market Line (SML), so in an SML graph such as that given back in Figure 5-10, we show beta on the horizontal axis. We discuss how betas are calculated in the next section.

Note that an efficient portfolio is one that is well diversified, hence all of its unsystematic risk has been eliminated and its only remaining risk is market risk. Therefore, unlike individual stocks, the riskiness of an efficient portfolio is measured by its standard deviation, σ_p. The CML equation specifies the relationship between risk and return for such efficient portfolios, that is, for portfolios that lie on the CML, and in the CML equation and graph, risk is measured by the portfolio standard deviation. For an individual stock, the relevant (market) risk is measured by its beta coefficient, b, and the relationship between risk and return is specified by the Security Market Line (SML) equation. Be sure to keep in mind the distinction between the SML and the CML—and why that distinction exists.

SELF-TEST QUESTIONS

Draw a graph which shows the feasible set of risky assets, the efficient frontier, the risk-free asset, and the CML.

Write out the equation for the CML and explain its meaning.

What is the difference between CML and the SML?

---

[10]Recall that the slope of any line is measured as $\Delta Y/\Delta X$, or the change in height associated with a given change in horizontal distance. k_{RF} is at 0 on the horizontal axis, so $\Delta X = \sigma_M - 0 = \sigma_M$. The vertical axis difference associated with a change from k_{RF} to $\hat{k}_M$ is $\hat{k}_M - k_{RF}$. Therefore, slope = $\Delta Y/\Delta X = (\hat{k}_M - k_{RF})/\sigma_M$.

| FIGURE 6-7 | The Capital Market Line (CML) |

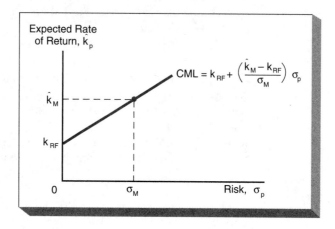

NOTE: We did not draw it in, but you can visualize the shaded space shown in Figure 6-6 in this graph, and the CML as the line formed by connecting k_{RF} with the tangent to the shaded space.

CALCULATING BETA COEFFICIENTS

As we noted back in Chapter 5 and also in the preceding section, the relevant measure of risk for use in the Security Market Line (SML) equation is the stock's beta coefficient, which measures the volatility of a stock relative to that of a portfolio containing all stocks. In this section, we show how betas are calculated and used, and in the process we explain in more detail the difference between diversifiable risk and market risk.

The market risk of a given stock can be measured by its tendency to move with the general market. The procedure for determining market risk is illustrated in Figure 6-8 and explained in the following paragraphs.[11] First, however, familiarize yourself with the definitions of the terms used in Figure 6-8:

$\bar{k}_J$ = historical (realized) rate of return on Stock J. (Recall that $\hat{k}_J$ and k_J are defined as Stock J's expected and required returns, respectively.)

$\bar{k}_M$ = historical (realized) rate of return on the market.

a_J = vertical axis intercept term for Stock J.

b_J = slope, or beta coefficient, for Stock J.

e_J = random error, reflecting the difference between the actual return on Stock J in a given year and the return as predicted by the regression line.

The historical returns on Stock J are given in the lower section of Figure 6-8, along with historical returns on the market, $\bar{k}_M$. Notice that when returns on the market are high, returns on Stock J likewise tend to be high, and when the market is down, Stock J's returns are low. This general relationship is expressed more precisely in the regression line shown in Figure 6-8.

---

[11]It should be noted that beta analysis in practice is somewhat more difficult than our discussion makes it sound. We will see this in Chapter 10.

FIGURE 6-8   Calculating Beta Coefficients

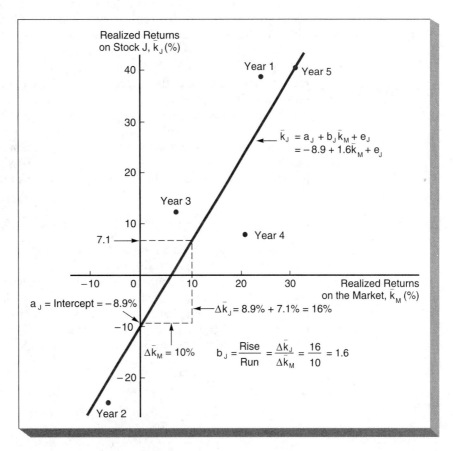

YEAR	STOCK J ($\bar{k}_J$)	MARKET ($\bar{k}_M$)
1	38.6%	23.8%
2	(24.7)	(7.2)
3	12.3	6.6
4	8.2	20.5
5	40.1	30.6
Average $\bar{k}$ =	14.9%	14.9%
σ_k =	26.5%	15.1%

Recall that the equation $Y = a + bX + e$ is the standard form of a simple linear regression. It states that the dependent variable, Y, is equal to a constant, a, plus b times X, where X is the "independent" variable, plus a random error term. Thus, the rate of return on Stock J during a given time period depends on what happens to the general stock market, which is measured by $\bar{k}_M$, plus the effects of random events which affect Stock J but do not affect most other stocks.

In general, the regression equation is obtained by ordinary least squares regression analysis, using either a calculator with statistical functions or a computer with a regression software package such as a spreadsheet's regression function. The plot of the regression equation is called the **regression line.** In his 1964 article which set forth the CAPM, Sharpe called the regression line the stock's **characteristic line.** Thus, a stock's beta is the slope of its characteristic line.

To illustrate the regression process, assume that we have drawn the regression line in Figure 6-8 "by hand" without the benefit of a financial calculator or spreadsheet regression function. Once the regression, or characteristic, line has been drawn, we can estimate its intercept and slope, the a and b values in $Y = a + bX$. The intercept, a, is simply the point where the line cuts the vertical axis. The slope coefficient, b, can be estimated by the "rise over run" method. This involves calculating the amount by which $\bar{k}_J$ increases for a given increase in $\bar{k}_M$. For example, we observe (in Figure 6-8) that $\bar{k}_J$ increases from -8.9 to $+7.1$ percent (the rise) as $\bar{k}_M$ increases from 0.0 to 10.0 percent (the run). Thus, b, the beta coefficient, can be measured as follows:

$$b_J = \frac{\text{Rise}}{\text{Run}} = \frac{\Delta Y}{\Delta X} = \frac{7.1\% - (-8.9\%)}{10.0\% - 0.0\%} = \frac{16.0\%}{10.0\%} = 1.6.$$

Note that rise over run is a ratio, and it would be the same if measured using any two arbitrarily selected points on the line.

Although the "by eye" approach is useful for visualizing what the beta concept is all about, an in-depth understanding and efficient application of the concept require the use of statistics. Basic statistics courses demonstrate that the following equation can be used to calculate the slope of any simple linear regression line, and this formula is also programmed into the statistical functions on calculators and computers:

$$b_J = \frac{\text{Covariance between Stock J and the market}}{\text{Variance of market returns}} = \frac{\text{Cov}(k_J, k_M)}{\sigma_M^2}$$

$$= \frac{r_{JM}\sigma_J\sigma_M}{\sigma_M^2} = r_{JM}\left(\frac{\sigma_J}{\sigma_M}\right).$$

Thus, a stock's beta, hence its market risk, depends on (1) its correlation with the stock market as a whole, r_{JM}, and (2) its own variability, σ_J, relative to the variability of the market, σ_M. In the Figure 6-8 example, $r_{JM} = 0.91$, $\sigma_J = 26.5\%$, and $\sigma_M = 15.1\%$. Therefore, $b_J = 0.91(26.5\%/15.1\%) = 0.91(1.755) = 1.60$.

Now that we have plotted Stock J's historical rates of return and estimated its beta coefficient, we can note the following points:

1. The *predicted future* returns on Stock J are assumed to bear a linear relationship of the following form to those of the market:

$$\text{Predicted future rate of return} = \hat{k}_J = a_J + b_J\hat{k}_M + e_J$$

$$= -8.9\% + 1.6\hat{k}_M + e_J. \tag{6-6}$$

Here we assume that the historical relationship between Stock J and the market as a whole, as given by its characteristic line, will continue on into the future.[12]

---

[12]The characteristic line equation is also called the *Market Model.* The Market Model asserts that the relationship between returns on individual stocks and returns on the market is linear and can be expressed by Equation 6-6. The Capital Asset Pricing Model (CAPM), on the other hand, states that, in equilibrium, returns on individual stocks can be expressed by the Security Market Line, Equation 5-8. The two models require different assumptions, so the acceptance of one model does not necessarily imply acceptance of the other. We will use the Market Model, or characteristic line, only to estimate betas for use in the Security Market Line of the CAPM. For more information on the Market Model and the differences between the two models, see Robert C. Radcliffe, *Investment: Concepts, Analysis, Strategy* (Glenview, Ill.: Scott, Foresman, 1996).

2. In addition to general market movements, each firm also faces events that are unique to it and thus are independent of the general economic climate. Such events cause the returns on Firm J's stock to move somewhat independently of those for the market as a whole, and these random events are accounted for by the random error term, e_J. Before the fact, the expected value of the error term is zero; after the fact, it is generally either positive or negative. This component of total risk is the stock's **diversifiable, or company-specific, risk,** and rational investors will eliminate its effects by holding diversified portfolios of stocks.

3. The regression coefficient, b (the beta coefficient), is a market sensitivity index; it measures the relative volatility of a given stock versus the average stock, or "the market." The tendency of an individual stock to move with the market constitutes a risk, because the market does fluctuate, and these fluctuations cannot be diversified away. This part of total risk is the stock's **market, or nondiversifiable, risk.** Even well-diversified portfolios contain some market risk.

4. The relationship between a stock's total risk, market risk, and diversifiable risk can be expressed as follows:

$$\text{Total risk} = \text{Variance} = \text{Market risk} + \text{Diversifiable risk}$$

$$\sigma_J^2 \quad = \quad b_J^2 \sigma_M^2 \quad + \quad \sigma_{e_J}^2.$$

Here σ_J^2 is the variance (or total risk) of Stock J, σ_M^2 is the variance of the market, b_J is Stock J's beta coefficient, and $\sigma_{e_J}^2$ is the variance of Stock J's regression error term.

5. If in Figure 6-8 all the points had plotted exactly on the regression line, then the variance of the error term, $\sigma_{e_J}^2$, would have been zero, and all of the stock's total risk would have been market risk. On the other hand, if the points were widely scattered about the regression line, much of the stock's total risk would be diversifiable. The shares of a large, well-diversified mutual fund would plot very close to the regression line, as would those of a broadly diversified firm such as GE.

6. If the stock market never fluctuated, then stocks would have no market risk. Of course, the market does fluctuate, so market risk is present—even if you hold an extremely well-diversified portfolio, you will still suffer losses if the market falls. In recent years, the standard deviation of annual market returns, σ_M, has been about 18 percent. However, on a single day, October 19, 1987, the market lost about 25 percent of its value.

7. Beta is a measure of relative market risk, but the *actual* market risk of Stock J is $b_J^2 \sigma_M^2$. Market risk can also be expressed in standard deviation form, $b_J \sigma_M$, so Stock J's market risk is $b_J \sigma_M = 1.6(15.1\%) = 24.2\%$, while its total risk is $\sigma_J = 26.5\%$. The higher a stock's beta, the higher its market risk. If beta were zero, the stock would have no market risk, while if beta were 1.0, the stock would be exactly as risky as the market—assuming the stock is held in a diversified portfolio—and the stock's market risk would be σ_M.

8. The diversifiable risk can and should be eliminated by diversification, so the *relevant* risk is market risk, not total risk. If Stock J had b = 0.5, then the stock's relevant risk would be $b_J \sigma_M = 0.5(15.1\%) = 7.55\%$. A portfolio of such low-beta stocks would have a standard deviation of expected returns of $\sigma_p = 7.55\%$, or one-half the standard deviation of expected returns on a portfolio of average (b = 1.0) stocks. Had Stock J been a high-beta stock (b = 2.0), then its relevant risk would have been $b_J \sigma_M = 2.0(15.1\%) = 30.2\%$. A portfolio of b = 2.0 stocks would have $\sigma_p = 30.2\%$, so such a portfolio would be twice as risky as a portfolio of average stocks.

9. A stock's risk premium depends only on its market risk, not its total risk: $RP_J = (k_M - k_{RF})b_J$. Mr. S might own only Stock J, and hence be concerned with its total risk and seek a return based on that risk. However, if other investors hold well-diversified portfolios, they would face less risk from Stock J. Therefore, if Stock J offered a return high enough to satisfy Mr. S, it would represent a bargain for other investors, who would then buy it, pushing its price up and its yield down in the process. Since most financial assets are held by diversified investors, and since any given security can have only one price and hence only one rate of return, market action drives each stock's risk premium to the level specified by its relevant, or market, risk.

S E L F - T E S T
Q U E S T I O N S

Explain the meaning and significance of a stock's beta coefficient. Illustrate your explanation by drawing, on one graph, the characteristic lines for stocks with low, average, and high risk. (Hint: Let your three characteristic lines intersect at $\bar{k}_i = \bar{k}_M = 9\%$, the assumed risk-free rate.)

How are stand-alone risk, market risk, and diversifiable risk related?

EMPIRICAL TESTS OF THE CAPM

As noted earlier, the CAPM was developed on the basis of a set of assumptions. If those assumptions were all true, then the CAPM would have to be true. However, since the assumptions are not completely correct, the basic SML equation, $k_i = k_{RF} + (k_M - k_{RF})b_i$, might or might not represent an accurate description of how investors behave and of how rates of return are established in the marketplace. For example, if many investors are not fully diversified, hence have not eliminated all diversifiable risk from their portfolios, then (1) beta would not be an adequate measure of risk and (2) the SML would not fully explain how required returns are set. Also, if the interest rate that investors must pay to borrow money is greater than the risk-free rate (that is, if the borrowing rate is greater than the lending rate), then the CML would not continue in a straight line beyond Point M as it does in Figure 6-6, and this too would invalidate the SML. And, of course, taxes and brokerage costs do exist, and their presence could also distort the CAPM relationships.

For all these reasons, it is entirely possible that the CAPM is not completely valid, in which case the SML will not produce accurate estimates of k_i. Therefore, the CAPM must be tested empirically and validated before it can be used with real confidence. The literature dealing with empirical tests of the CAPM is quite extensive, so we can give here only a synopsis of some of the key work.

Tests of the Stability of Beta Coefficients

According to the CAPM, the beta used to estimate a stock's market risk should reflect investors' estimates of the stock's *future* volatility in relation to that of the market. Obviously, we do not know now how a stock will be related to the market in the future, nor do we know how the average investor views this expected future relative volatility. All we have are data on past volatility, which we can use to plot the characteristic line and to calculate *historical betas*. If historical betas have been stable over time, then there would seem to be reason for investors to use past betas as estimators of future volatility. For example, if Stock J's beta had been stable in the past, then its historical b_J would probably be a good proxy for its *ex ante*, or expected, beta. By "stable" we mean that if b_J were calculated with data from the period of say, 1994 to 1998, then this same beta (approximately) should be found from 1999 to 2003.

Robert Levy, Marshall Blume, and others have studied the question of beta stability in depth.[13] Levy calculated betas for individual securities, as well as for portfolios of securities, over a range of time intervals. He concluded (1) that the betas of individual stocks are unstable, hence that past betas for *individual securities* are *not* good estimators of their future risk, but (2) that betas of portfolios of ten or more randomly selected stocks are reasonably stable, hence that past *portfolio* betas are good estimators of future portfolio volatility. In effect, the errors in individual securities' betas tend to offset one another in a portfolio. The work of Blume and others supports this position.

The conclusion that follows from the beta stability studies is that the CAPM is a better concept for structuring investment portfolios than it is for estimating the cost of capital for individual securities. We will return to this issue in Chapter 10, when we discuss cost of capital estimation procedures.

Tests of the CAPM Based on the Slope of the SML

As we noted in Chapter 5, the CAPM states that a linear relationship exists between a security's required rate of return and its beta. Further, when the SML is graphed, the vertical axis intercept should be k_{RF}, and the required rate of return for a stock (or portfolio) with $b = 1.0$ should be k_M, the required rate of return on the market. Various researchers have attempted to test the validity of the CAPM by calculating betas and realized rates of return, plotting these values in graphs such as that in Figure 6-9, and then observing whether or not (1) the intercept is equal to k_{RF}, (2) the regression line is linear, and (3) the line passes through the point $b = 1.0$, k_M. Monthly historical rates of return are generally used for stocks, and both 30-day Treasury bill rates and long-term Treasury bond rates have been used to estimate the value of k_{RF}. Also, most of the studies actually analyzed portfolios rather than individual securities because security betas are so unstable.

Before discussing the results of the tests, it is critical to recognize that although the CAPM is an ex ante, or forward-looking model, the data used to test it are entirely historical. This presents a problem, for there is no reason to believe that *realized* rates of return over past holding periods are necessarily equal to the rates of return people *expect* in the future. Also, historical betas may or may not reflect expected future risk. This lack of ex ante data makes it extremely difficult to test the CAPM, but for what it is worth, here is a summary of the key results:

1. The evidence generally shows a significant positive relationship between realized returns and systematic risk. However, the slope of the relationship is usually less than that predicted by the CAPM.

2. The relationship between risk and return appears to be linear. Empirical studies give no evidence of significant curvature in the risk/return relationship.

3. Tests that attempt to assess the relative importance of market and company-specific risk do not yield conclusive results. The CAPM implies that company-specific risk should not be relevant, yet both kinds of risk appear to be positively related to security returns; that is, higher returns seem to be required to compensate for diversifiable as well as market risk. However, it may be that the observed relationships reflect statistical problems rather than the true nature of capital markets.

---

[13]See Robert A. Levy, "On the Short-Term Stationarity of Beta Coefficients," *Financial Analysts Journal,* November-December 1971, 55–62, and Marshall E. Blume, "Betas and Their Regression Tendencies," *Journal of Finance,* June 1975, 785–796.

FIGURE 6-9   Tests of the CAPM

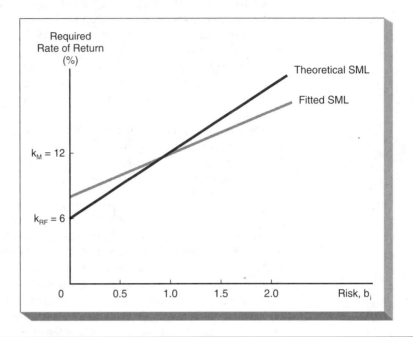

4. Richard Roll has questioned whether it is even conceptually possible to test the CAPM.[14] Roll showed that the linear relationship which prior researchers had observed in graphs like Figure 6-9 resulted from the mathematical properties of the models being tested, hence that a finding of linearity proved nothing whatsoever about the validity of the CAPM. Roll's work did not disprove the CAPM, but he did show that it is virtually impossible to prove that investors behave in accordance with its predictions.

5. If the CAPM were completely valid, it should apply to all financial assets, including bonds. In fact, when bonds are introduced into the analysis, they *do not* plot on the SML. This is worrisome, to say the least.

The Fama–French Study

As we discussed in Chapter 5, a recent study by Eugene F. Fama and Kenneth R. French of the University of Chicago seriously challenges the CAPM. Fama and French examined the relationships between betas and returns on thousands of stocks over the past 50 years. According to the CAPM, high-beta stocks should provide higher returns than low-beta stocks. However, the Fama–French study revealed no relationship between historical betas and historical returns—low-beta stocks provided about the same returns as high-beta stocks.

It will take more research to decide whether the Fama–French study truly invalidates the CAPM. The CAPM is purely an expectational model, and as such, its logic is sound. But we only have historical data, not expectational data, available for testing. So,

---

[14]See Richard Roll, "A Critique of the Asset Pricing Theory's Tests," *Journal of Financial Economics,* March 1977, 129–176.

the fact that no relationship is found between historical betas and historical returns does not convince us that the CAPM concept is wrong.

Current Status of the CAPM

The CAPM is extremely appealing at an intellectual level: It is logical and rational, and once someone works through and understands the theory, his or her reaction is usually to accept it without question. However, doubts begin to arise when one thinks about the assumptions upon which the model is based, and these doubts are as much reinforced as reduced by the empirical tests. Our own views as to the current status of the CAPM are as follows:

1. The CAPM framework, with its focus on market as opposed to stand-alone risk, is clearly a useful way to think about the riskiness of assets. Thus, as a conceptual model, the CAPM is of truly fundamental importance.

2. When applied in practice, the CAPM appears to provide neat, precise answers to important questions about risk and required rates of return. However, the answers are less clear than they seem. The simple truth is that we do not know precisely how to measure any of the inputs required to implement the CAPM. These inputs should all be ex ante, yet only ex post data are available. Further, as we shall see in Chapter 10, historical data on $\bar{k}_M$, k_{RF}, and betas vary greatly depending on the time period studied and the methods used to estimate them. Thus, although the CAPM appears precise, estimates of k_i found through its use are subject to potentially large errors.

3. Because the CAPM is logical in the sense that it represents the way risk-averse people ought to behave, the model is a useful conceptual tool.

4. It is appropriate to think about many financial problems in a CAPM framework. However, it is important to recognize the limitations of the CAPM when using it in practice. We will elaborate on this point in Chapters 10 and 13.

SELF-TEST
QUESTIONS

What are the two major types of tests that have been performed to test the validity of the CAPM? (Hint: Beta stability and slope of the SML.)

Are there any reasons to question the validity of the CAPM? Explain.

ARBITRAGE PRICING THEORY

The CAPM is a single-factor model. That is, it specifies risk as a function of only one factor, the security's beta coefficient. Perhaps the risk/return relationship is more complex, with a stock's required return a function of more than one factor. For example, what if investors, because personal tax rates on capital gains are lower than those on dividends, value capital gains more highly than dividends? Then, if two stocks had the same market risk, the stock paying the higher dividend would have the higher required rate of return. In that case, required returns would be a function of two factors, market risk and dividend policy.

Further, what if many factors were required to specify the equilibrium risk/return relationship rather than just one or two? Stephen Ross has proposed an approach called the **Arbitrage Pricing Theory (APT).**[15] The APT can include any number of risk factors,

---

[15]See Stephen A. Ross, "The Arbitrage Theory of Capital Asset Pricing," *Journal of Economic Theory,* December 1976, 341–360.

so the required return could be a function of two, three, four, or more factors. We should note at the outset that the APT is based on complex mathematical and statistical theory which goes far beyond the scope of this text. Also, although the APT model is widely discussed in academic literature, practical usage to date has been limited. However, usage may increase, so students should at least have an intuitive idea of what the APT is all about.

The SML states that each stock's required return is equal to the risk-free rate plus the product of the market risk premium times the stock's beta coefficient:

$$k_i = k_{RF} + (k_M - k_{RF})b_i. \tag{6-7}$$

The realized return, $\overline{k}_i$, which will generally be different from the required return, can be expressed as follows:

$$\overline{k}_i = \hat{k}_i + (\overline{k}_M - \hat{k}_M)b_i + e_i. \tag{6-8}$$

Thus, the realized return, $\overline{k}_i$, will be equal to the expected return, $\hat{k}_i$, plus a positive or negative increment, $(\overline{k}_M - \hat{k}_M)b_i$, which depends jointly on the stock's beta and whether the market did better or worse than was expected, plus a random error term, e_i.

The market's realized return, $\overline{k}_M$, is in turn determined by a number of factors, including domestic economic activity as measured by gross domestic product (GDP), the strength of the world economy, the level of inflation, changes in tax laws, and so forth. Further, different groups of stocks are affected in different ways by these fundamental factors. So, rather than specifying a stock's return as a function of one factor (return on the market), one could specify required and realized returns on individual stocks as a function of various fundamental economic factors. If this were done, we would transform Equation 6-8 into 6-9:

$$\overline{k}_i = \hat{k}_i + (\overline{F}_1 - \hat{F}_1)b_{i1} + \cdots + (\overline{F}_j - \hat{F}_j)b_{ij} + e_i. \tag{6-9}$$

Here

$\overline{k}_i$ = realized rate of return on Stock i.

$\hat{k}_i$ = expected rate of return on Stock i.

$\overline{F}_j$ = realized value of economic Factor j.

$\hat{F}_j$ = expected value of Factor j.

b_{ij} = sensitivity of Stock i to economic Factor j.

e_i = effect of unique events on the realized return of Stock i.

Equation 6-9 shows that the realized return on any stock is equal to (1) the stock's expected return, (2) increases or decreases which depend on unexpected changes in fundamental economic factors times the sensitivity of the stock to these changes, and (3) a random term which reflects changes unique to the firm or industry.

Certain stocks or groups of stocks are most sensitive to Factor 1, others to Factor 2, and so forth, and every portfolio's returns depend on what happened to the different fundamental factors. Theoretically, one could construct a portfolio such that (1) the portfolio was riskless and (2) the net investment in it was zero (some stocks would be sold short, with the proceeds from the short sales being used to buy the stocks held long). Such a zero investment portfolio must have a zero expected return, or else arbitrage operations would occur, which, in turn, would cause the prices of the underlying assets to change until the portfolio's expected return was zero. Using some complex mathematics and a set of assumptions including the possibility of short sales, the APT equivalent of the CAPM's Security Market Line can be developed from Equation 6-9:[16]

$$k_i = k_{RF} + (k_1 - k_{RF})b_{i1} + \cdots + (k_j - k_{RF})b_{ij}. \qquad \textbf{(6-10)}$$

Here k_j is the required rate of return on a portfolio that is sensitive only to the jth economic factor ($b_j = 1.0$) and has zero sensitivity to all other factors. Thus, for example, $(k_2 - k_{RF})$ is the risk premium on a portfolio with $b_2 = 1.0$ and all other $b_j = 0.0$. Note that Equation 6-10 is identical in form to the SML, but it permits a stock's required return to be a function of multiple factors.

To illustrate the APT concept, assume that all stocks' returns depend on only three risk factors: inflation, industrial production, and the aggregate degree of risk aversion (the cost of bearing risk, which we assume is reflected in the spread between the yields on Treasury and low-grade bonds). Further, suppose (1) the risk-free rate is 8.0 percent; (2) the required rate of return is 13 percent on a portfolio with unit sensitivity ($b = 1.0$) to inflation and zero sensitivities ($b = 0.0$) to industrial production and degree of risk aversion; (3) the required return is 10 percent on a portfolio with unit sensitivity to industrial production and zero sensitivities to inflation and degree of risk aversion; and (4) the required return is 6 percent on a portfolio (the risk-bearing portfolio) with unit sensitivity to the degree of risk aversion and zero sensitivities to inflation and industrial production. Finally, assume that Stock i has factor sensitivities (betas) of 0.9 to the inflation portfolio, 1.2 to the industrial production portfolio, and −0.7 to the risk-bearing portfolio. Stock i's required rate of return, according to the APT, would be 16.3 percent:

$$k_i = 8\% + (13\% - 8\%)0.9 + (10\% - 8\%)1.2 + (6\% - 8\%)(-0.7)$$

$$= 16.3\%.$$

Note that if the required rate of return on the market was 15.0 percent and Stock i had a CAPM beta of 1.1, then its required rate of return, according to the SML, would be 15.7 percent:

$$k_i = 8\% + (15\% - 8\%)1.1 = 15.7\%.$$

The primary theoretical advantage of the APT is that it permits several economic factors to influence individual stock returns, whereas the CAPM assumes that the impact of all factors, except those unique to the firm, can be captured in a single measure, the volatility of the stock with respect to the market portfolio. Also, the APT requires fewer assumptions than the CAPM and hence is a more general theory. Finally, the APT does not assume that all investors hold the market portfolio, a CAPM requirement that clearly is not met in practice.

However, the APT faces several major hurdles in implementation, the most severe being that the APT does not identify the relevant factors. Thus, APT does not tell us what factors influence returns, nor does it even indicate how many factors should appear in the model. There is some empirical evidence that only three or four factors are relevant: perhaps inflation, industrial production, the spread between low- and high-grade bonds, and the term structure of interest rates, but no one knows for sure.

The APT's proponents argue that it is not actually necessary to identify the relevant factors. Researchers use a complex statistical procedure called **factor analysis** to

---

[16]See Thomas E. Copeland and J. Fred Weston, *Financial Theory and Corporate Policy* (Reading, Mass.: Addison-Wesley, 1988).

develop the APT parameters. Basically, they start with hundreds, or even thousands, of stocks and then create several different portfolios, where the returns on each portfolio are not highly correlated with returns on the other portfolios. Thus, each portfolio is apparently more heavily influenced by one of the unknown factors than are the other portfolios. Then, the required rate of return on each portfolio becomes the estimate for that unknown economic factor, shown as k_j in Equation 6-10. The sensitivities of each individual stock's returns to the returns on that portfolio are the factor sensitivities (betas). Unfortunately, the results of factor analysis are not easily interpreted, hence it does not provide significant insights into the underlying economic determinants of risk.

The APT is in an early stage of development, and there are still many unanswered questions. Nevertheless, the basic premise of the APT—that returns can be a function of several factors rather than just one—has considerable intuitive appeal. If the factors can be identified, and if the theory can be satisfactorily explained to practitioners, then the APT might replace the CAPM as the primary model describing the relationship between risk and return. Currently, though, CAPM rules.

SELF-TEST QUESTIONS

What is the primary difference between the APT and the CAPM?

What are some disadvantages of the APT?

SUMMARY

Chapter 6 completes our discussion of risk and return for traded securities. The primary goal of this chapter was to extend your knowledge of risk and return concepts. The key concepts covered are listed below:

- The **feasible set** of portfolios represents all portfolios that can be constructed from a given set of assets.

- An **efficient portfolio** is one that offers the most return for a given amount of risk, or the least risk for a given amount of return.

- The **optimal portfolio** for an investor is defined by the tangency point between the **efficient set** of portfolios and the investor's highest **indifference curve.**

- The **Capital Asset Pricing Model (CAPM)** describes the relationship between market risk and required rates of return.

- The CAPM is based on an extensive set of **assumptions.**

- The **Capital Market Line (CML)** describes the risk/return relationship for efficient portfolios; that is, for portfolios that consist of a mix of the market portfolio and a riskless asset.

- The **Security Market Line (SML)** is an integral part of the CAPM, and it describes the risk/return relationship for individual assets. The required rate of return for any Stock i is equal to the **risk-free rate** plus the **market risk premium** times the stock's **beta coefficient:** $k_i = k_{RF} + (k_M - k_{RF})b_i$.

- Stock i's **beta coefficient, b_i,** is a measure of the stock's **market risk.** Beta measures the **volatility** of returns on a security **relative to returns on the market,** which is the portfolio of all risky assets.

- The beta coefficient is measured by the slope of the stock's **characteristic line,** which is found by regressing historical returns on the stock versus historical returns on the market.

- Although the CAPM provides a convenient framework for thinking about risk and return issues, it *cannot be proven empirically*, and its parameters are very difficult to estimate. Thus, the CAPM should be used with caution.

- Deficiencies in the CAPM have motivated theorists to seek other risk/return equilibrium models, and the **Arbitrage Pricing Theory (APT)** is one important new model.

In the next three chapters, we will see how a security's required rate of return affects its value. Then, in most of the remainder of the book, we will examine the ways in which a firm's management can influence a stock's riskiness and hence its price.

Questions

6-1   Define the following terms, using graphs or equations to illustrate your answers wherever feasible:
   a. Portfolio
   b. Feasible set
   c. Efficient portfolio
   d. Efficient frontier
   e. Indifference curve
   f. Optimal portfolio
   g. Capital Asset Pricing Model (CAPM)
   h. Capital Market Line (CML)
   i. Characteristic line
   j. Beta coefficient, b; average stock's beta, $b_A = b_M$
   k. Arbitrage Pricing Theory (APT)

6-2   Security A has an expected rate of return of 6 percent, a standard deviation of expected returns of 30 percent, a correlation coefficient with the market of −0.25, and a beta coefficient of −0.5. Security B has an expected return of 11 percent, a standard deviation of returns of 10 percent, a correlation with the market of 0.75, and a beta coefficient of 0.5. Which security is more risky? Why?

Self-Test Problem   (Solution Appears in Appendix B)

ST-1
Risk and Return

You are planning to invest $200,000. Two securities, A and B, are available, and you can invest in either of them or in a portfolio with some of each. You estimate that the following probability distributions of returns are applicable for A and B:

SECURITY A		SECURITY B	
P_A	k_A	P_B	k_B
0.1	−10%	0.1	−30%
0.2	5	0.2	0
0.4	15	0.4	20
0.2	25	0.2	40
0.1	40	0.1	70
	$\hat{k}_A = ?$		$\hat{k}_B = 20.0\%$
	$\sigma_A = ?$		$\sigma_B = 25.7\%$

a. The expected return for Security B is $\hat{k}_B = 20\%$, and $\sigma_B = 25.7\%$. Find $\hat{k}_A$ and σ_A.
b. Use the equation in Footnote 3 to find the value of w_A that produces the minimum risk portfolio. Assume $r_{AB} = -0.5$ for Parts b and c.
c. Construct a table giving $\hat{k}_p$ and σ_p for portfolios with $w_A = 1.00$, 0.75, 0.50, 0.25, 0.0, and the minimum risk value of w_A. (Hint: For $w_A = 0.75$, $\hat{k}_p = 16.25\%$ and $\sigma_p = 8.5\%$; for $w_A = 0.5$, $\hat{k}_p = 17.5\%$ and $\sigma_p = 11.1\%$; for $w_A = 0.25$, $\hat{k}_p = 18.75\%$ and $\sigma_p = 17.9\%$.)
d. Graph the feasible set of portfolios and identify the efficient frontier of the feasible set.
e. Suppose your risk/return trade-off function, or indifference curve, is tangent to the efficient set at the point where $\hat{k}_p = 18\%$. Use this information, plus the graph constructed in Part d, to locate (approximately) your optimal portfolio. Draw in a reasonable indifference curve, indicate the percentage of your funds invested in each security, and determine the optimal portfolio's σ_p and $\hat{k}_p$. (Hint: Estimate σ_p and $\hat{k}_p$ graphically, and then use the equation for $\hat{k}_p$ to determine w_A.)

f. Now suppose a riskless asset with a return $k_{RF} = 10\%$ becomes available. How would this change the investment opportunity set? Explain why the efficient frontier becomes linear.

g. Given the indifference curve in Part e, would you change your portfolio? If so, how? (Hint: Assume the indifference curves are parallel.)

h. What are the beta coefficients of Stocks A and B? [Hints: (1) Recognize that $k_i = k_{RF} + b_i(k_M - k_{RF})$ and solve for b_i and (2) assume that your preferences match those of most other investors.]

Problems

6-1
Characteristic Line and
Security Market Line

You are given the following set of data:

HISTORICAL RATES OF RETURN

YEAR	NYSE	STOCK X
1	(26.5%)	(14.0%)
2	37.2	23.0
3	23.8	17.5
4	(7.2)	2.0
5	6.6	8.1
6	20.5	19.4
7	30.6	18.2

a. Use a calculator with a linear regression function (or a spreadsheet) to determine Stock X's beta coefficient, or plot these data points on a scatter diagram, draw in the regression line, and then estimate the value of the beta coefficient.

b. Determine the arithmetic average rates of return for Stock X and the NYSE over the period given. Calculate the standard deviations of returns for both Stock X and the NYSE.

c. Assuming (1) that the situation during Years 1 to 7 is expected to hold true in the future (that is, $\hat{k}_X = \bar{k}_X$; $k_M = \bar{k}_M$; and both σ_X and b_X in the future will equal their past values), and (2) that Stock X is in equilibrium (that is, it plots on the Security Market Line), what is the risk-free rate?

d. Plot the Security Market Line.

e. Suppose you hold a large, well-diversified portfolio and are considering adding to the portfolio either Stock X or another stock, Stock Y, that has the same beta as Stock X but a higher standard deviation of returns. Stocks X and Y have the same expected returns; that is, $\hat{k}_X = \hat{k}_Y = 10.6\%$. Which stock should you choose?

6-2
Characteristic Line

You are given the following set of data:

HISTORICAL RATES OF RETURN

YEAR	NYSE	STOCK Y
1	4.0%	3.0%
2	14.3	18.2
3	19.0	9.1
4	(14.7)	(6.0)
5	(26.5)	(15.3)
6	37.2	33.1
7	23.8	6.1
8	(7.2)	3.2
9	6.6	14.8
10	20.5	24.1
11	30.6	18.0
	Mean = 9.8%	9.8%
	σ = 19.6%	13.8%

a. Construct a scatter diagram showing the relationship between returns on Stock Y and the market, and then draw a freehand approximation of the regression line. What is the approximate value of the beta coefficient? If you have a calculator with a linear regression function or a spreadsheet, check the approximate value of beta obtained from the graph.

b. Give a verbal interpretation of what the regression line and the beta coefficient show about Stock Y's volatility and relative riskiness as compared with those of other stocks.

c. Suppose the scatter of points had been more spread out, but the regression line was exactly where your present graph shows it. How would this affect (1) the firm's risk if the stock is held in a one-asset portfolio and (2) the actual risk premium on the stock if the CAPM holds exactly?

d. Suppose the regression line had been downward sloping and the beta coefficient had been negative. What would this imply about (1) Stock Y's relative riskiness, (2) its correlation with the market, and (3) its probable risk premium?

e. Construct an illustrative probability distribution graph of returns on portfolios consisting of (1) only Stock Y, (2) 1 percent each of 100 stocks with beta coefficients similar to that of Stock Y, and (3) all stocks (that is, the distribution of returns on the market). Use as the expected rate of return the arithmetic mean as given previously for both Stock Y and the market and assume that the distributions are normal. Are the expected returns "reasonable"; that is, is it reasonable that $k_Y = k_M = 9.8\%$?

6-3
SML and CML Comparison

The beta coefficient of an asset can be expressed as a function of the asset's correlation with the market as follows:

$$b_i = \frac{r_{iM}\sigma_i}{\sigma_M}.$$

a. Substitute this expression for beta into the Security Market Line (SML), Equation 5-8. This results in an alternative form of the SML.

b. Compare your answer to Part a with the Capital Market Line (CML), Equation 6-5. What similarities are observed? What conclusions can be drawn?

MINI CASE

To begin, briefly review the Chapter 5 Mini Case. Then, extend your knowledge of risk and return by answering the following questions:

a. What is the Capital Asset Pricing Model (CAPM)? What are the assumptions that underlie the model?

b. Construct a reasonable, but hypothetical, graph which shows risk, as measured by portfolio standard deviation, on the X axis and expected rate of return on the Y axis. Now add an illustrative feasible (or attainable) set of portfolios, and show what portion of the feasible set is efficient. What makes a particular portfolio efficient? Don't worry about specific values when constructing the graph—merely illustrate how things look with "reasonable" data.

c. Now add a set of indifference curves to the graph created for Part b. What do these curves represent? What is the optimal portfolio for this investor? Finally, add a second set of indifference curves which leads to the selection of a different optimal portfolio. Why do the two investors choose different portfolios?

d. Now add the risk-free asset. What impact does this have on the efficient frontier?

e. Write out the equation for the Capital Market Line (CML) and draw it on the graph. Interpret the CML. Now add a set of indifference curves, and illustrate how an investor's optimal portfolio is some combination of the risky portfolio and the risk-free asset. What is the composition of the risky portfolio?

f. What is a characteristic line? How is this line used to estimate a stock's beta coefficient? Write out and explain the formula that relates total risk, market risk, and diversifiable risk.

g. What are two potential tests that can be conducted to verify the CAPM? What are the results of such tests? What is Roll's critique of CAPM tests?

h. Briefly explain the difference between the CAPM and the Arbitrage Pricing Theory (APT).

i. What is the current status of the APT?

Selected Additional References and Cases

Probably the best place to find more information on CAPM and APT concepts is one of the investments textbooks. These are some good recent ones:

Francis, Jack C., *Investments: Analysis and Management* (New York: McGraw-Hill, 1991).

Radcliffe, Robert C., *Investment: Concepts, Analysis, and Strategy* (Glenview, Ill.: Scott, Foresman, 1996).

Reilly, Frank K., and Keith C. Brown, *Investment Analysis and Portfolio Management* (Fort Worth, Tex.: Dryden Press, 1997).

Sharpe, William F., *Investments* (Englewood Cliffs, N.J.: Prentice-Hall, 1995).

For a thorough discussion of beta stability, see

Kolb, Robert W., and Ricardo J. Rodriguez, "The Regression Tendencies of Betas: A Reappraisal," *The Financial Review*, May 1989, 319–334.

———, "Is the Distribution of Betas Stationary?" *Journal of Financial Research*, Winter 1990, 279–283.

Those who want to start at the beginning in studying portfolio theory and the CAPM should see

Lintner, John, "Security Prices, Risk, and Maximal Gains from Diversification," *Journal of Finance*, December 1965, 587–616.

Markowitz, Harry M., "Portfolio Selection," *Journal of Finance*, March 1952, 77–91.

Mossin, Jan, "Security Pricing and Investment Criteria in Competitive Markets," *American Economic Review*, December 1969, 749–756.

Sharpe, William F., "Capital Asset Prices: A Theory of Market Equilibrium under Conditions of Risk," *Journal of Finance*, September 1964, 425–442.

———, "Capital Asset Prices with and without Negative Holdings," *Journal of Finance*, June 1991, 489–509.

Literally thousands of articles providing theoretical extensions and tests of the CAPM theory have appeared in finance journals. Some of the more important earlier papers are contained in a book compiled by Jensen:

Jensen, Michael C., ed., *Studies in the Theory of Capital Markets* (New York: Praeger, 1972).

For one challenge to the CAPM, see

Wallace, Anise, "Is Beta Dead?" *Institutional Investor*, July 1980, 23–30.

For a recent article supporting a positive link between market risk and return, see

Marston, Felicia, and Robert S. Hanes, "Risk and Return: A Revisit Using Expected Returns," *Financial Review*, February 1993, 117–137.

For additional discussion of Arbitrage Pricing Theory, see

Bower, Dorothy H., Richard S. Bower, and Dennis E. Logue, "A Primer on Arbitrage Pricing Theory," *Midland Corporate Finance Journal*, Fall 1984, 31–40.

Bubnys, Edward L., "Simulating and Forecasting Utility Stock Returns: Arbitrage Pricing Theory vs. Capital Asset Pricing Model," *The Financial Review*, February 1990, 1–23.

Goldenberg, David H., and Ashok J. Robin, "The Arbitrage Pricing Theory and Cost-of-Capital Estimation: The Case of Electric Utilities," *Journal of Financial Research*, Fall 1991, 181–196.

Robin, Ashok, and Ravi Shukla, "The Magnitude of Pricing Errors in the Arbitrage Pricing Theory," *Journal of Financial Research*, Spring 1991, 65–82.

Additional references concerning the use of the CAPM are given in Chapter 8.

The following case from the Cases in Financial Management: Dryden Request *series covers many of the concepts discussed in this chapter:*

Case 2, "Peachtree Securities, Inc. (A)."

EXTENSIONS

Continuous Probability Distributions

In Chapter 5, we illustrated risk/return concepts using discrete distributions, and we assumed that only three states of the economy could exist. In reality, however, the state of the economy can range from a deep recession to a fantastic boom, and there are an infinite number of possibilities in between. It is inconvenient to work with a large number of outcomes using discrete distributions, but it is relatively easy to deal with such situations with **continuous distributions** since they can be completely specified by only two or three summary statistics such as the mean (or expected value), standard deviation, and a measure of skewness. In the past, financial managers did not have the tools necessary to use continuous distributions in practical risk analyses. Now, however, firms have access to computers and powerful software packages, such as the *Interactive Financial Planning System (IFPS)* and spreadsheet add-ins, which can process continuous distributions. Thus, if financial risk analysis is computerized, as is increasingly the case, it is often preferable to use continuous distributions to express the distribution of outcomes.[1]

Uniform Distribution.   One continuous distribution that is often used in financial models is the **uniform distribution,** in which each possible outcome has the same probability of occurrence as any other outcome; hence, there is no clustering of values. Figure 6E-1 shows two uniform distributions.

Distribution A of Figure 6E-1 has a range of −5 to +15 percent. Therefore, the absolute size of the range is 20 units. Since the entire area under the density function must equal 1.00, the height of the distribution, h, must be 0.05: $20h = 1.0$, so $h = 1/20 = 0.05$. We can use this information to find the probability of different outcomes. For example, suppose we want to find the probability that the rate of return will be less than zero. The probability is the area under the density function from −5 to 0 percent; that is, the shaded area:

Area = (Right point − Left point)(Height of distribution)

$$= [0 - (-5)][0.05] = 0.25 = 25\%.$$

Similarly, the probability of a rate of return between 5 and 15 is 50 percent:

Probability = Area = $(15 - 5)(0.05) = 0.50 = 50\%$.

The expected rate of return is the midpoint of the range, or 5 percent, for both distributions in Figure 6E-1. Since there is a smaller probability of the actual return falling very far below the expected return in Distribution B, Distribution B depicts a less risky situation in the stand-alone risk sense.

Triangular Distribution.   Another useful continuous distribution is the **triangular distribution.** This type of distribution, which is illustrated in Figure 6E-2, has a clustering of values around the most likely outcome, and the probability of occurrence declines in each direction from the most likely outcome. Distribution C has a range of −5 to +15 percent and a most likely return of +10 percent. Distribution D has a most likely return of 5 percent, but its range is only from 0 to +10 percent. Note that Distribution C is skewed to the left, while Distribution D is symmetric. The expected rate of return for Distribution C is 6.67 percent, whereas that of D is only 5 percent.[2] However, it is obvious by inspection that Distribution C is riskier; its dispersion about the mean is greater than that for Distribution D, and it has a significant chance of actual losses, whereas losses are not possible in Distribution D.

Normal Distribution.   Because it is discussed so much in statistics courses, is so easy to use, and conforms well to so many real-world situations, the most commonly used continuous distribution is the **normal distribution.** It is symmetric about the expected value, and its tails extend out to plus and minus infinity. Figure 6E-3 is a normal distribution with an expected, or mean (μ, pronounced "mu"), rate of return of 10 percent and a standard deviation (σ, or sigma) of 5 percent. Approximately 68.3 percent of the area under any normal curve lies within $\pm 1\sigma$ of its mean, 95.5 percent lies within $\pm 2\sigma$, and 99.7 percent lies within $\pm 3\sigma$. Therefore, the probability of actually achieving a rate of return within the range of 5 to 15 percent ($\mu \pm 1\sigma$) is 68.3 percent, and so forth. Obviously, the smaller the standard deviation, the smaller the probability of the actual outcome deviating very much from the expected value, and hence the smaller the total risk of the investment.

If we want to find the probability that an outcome will fall between 7.5 and 12.5 percent, we must calculate the area

---

[1]Computerized risk analysis techniques are discussed in detail in Chapter 13.

[2]Note that the most likely outcome equals the expected outcome only when the distribution is symmetric. If the distribution is skewed to the left, the expected outcome falls to the left of the most likely outcome, and vice versa. Also, note that the expected outcome of a triangular distribution is found by using this equation:

(Lower limit + Most likely outcome + Upper limit)/3.

Thus, the expected rate of return for Distribution C is $(-5\% + 10\% + 15\%)/3 = 6.67\%$.

Uniform Probability Distributions

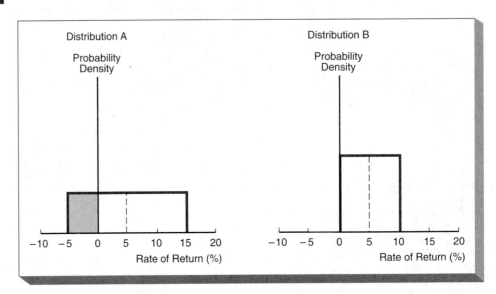

NOTE: The expected rate of return for both distributions is $\hat{k} = 5\%$.

Triangular Probability Distributions

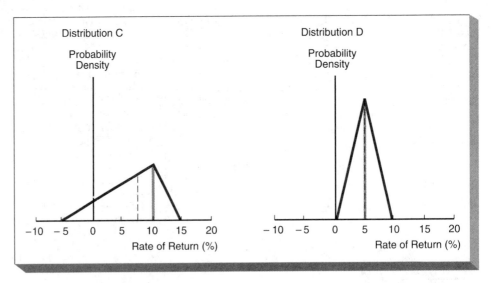

NOTE: The most likely rate of return is 10 percent for Distribution C and 5 percent for Distribution D; the expected rates of return are $\hat{k}_C = 6.67\%$ and $\hat{k}_D = 5\%$.

FIGURE 6E-3   Normal Probability Distribution

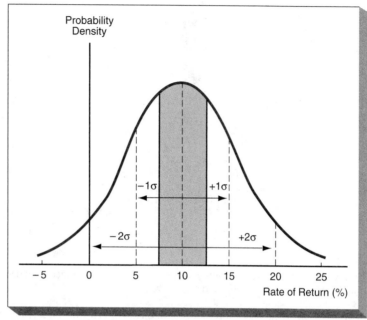

NOTE: The most likely and expected rate of return is 10 percent.

beneath the curve between these points, or the shaded area in Figure 6E-3. This area can be determined by integration or, more easily, by the use of statistical tables of the area under the normal curve.[3] To use the tables, we first use the following formula to standardize the distribution:

$$z = \frac{x - \mu}{\sigma}. \qquad \text{(6E-1)}$$

Here z is the standardized variable, or the number of standard deviations from the mean; x is the outcome of interest; and μ and σ are the mean and standard deviation of the distribution, respectively.[4] In our example, we are interested in the probability that an outcome will fall between 7.5 and 12.5 percent. Since the mean of the distribution is 10, and it is between the two points of interest, we must evaluate and

then combine two probabilities, one to the left and one to the right of the mean. We first normalize these points by using Equation 6E-1:

$$z_{Left} = \frac{7.5 - 10}{5} = -0.5; \quad z_{Right} = \frac{12.5 - 10}{5} = +0.5.$$

The areas associated with these z values as found in Table 6E-1 are 0.1915 and 0.1915.[5] This means that the probability is 0.1915 that the actual outcome will fall between 7.5 and 10 percent and also 0.1915 that it will fall between 10 and 12.5 percent. Thus, the probability that the outcome will fall between 7.5 and 12.5 percent is 0.1915 + 0.1915 = 0.3830, or 38.3 percent.

Suppose we are interested in determining the probability that the actual outcome will be less than zero. We first deter-

---

[3]The equation for the normal curve is tedious to integrate, thus making the use of tables much more convenient. The equation for the normal curve is

$$f(x) = \frac{1}{\sqrt{2\pi\sigma^2}} e^{-(x-\mu)^2/2\sigma^2}$$

where π and e are mathematical constants; μ and σ denote the expected value, or mean, and standard deviation of the probability distribution, respectively; and x is any possible outcome.

[4]Note that if the point of interest is 1σ away from the mean, then $x - \mu = \sigma$, so $z = \sigma/\sigma = 1.0$. Thus, when z = 1.0, the point of interest is 1σ away from the mean; when z = 2, the deviation is 2σ; and so forth.

[5]Note that the negative sign on z_{Left} is ignored. Since the normal curve is symmetric around the mean, the minus sign merely indicates that the point of interest lies to the left of the mean.

TABLE 6E-1	Area Under the Normal Curve

z	AREA FROM THE MEAN TO THE POINT OF INTEREST
0.0	0.0000
0.5	0.1915
1.0	0.3413
1.5	0.4332
2.0	0.4773
2.5	0.4938
3.0	0.4987

NOTE: Here z is the number of standard deviations from the mean. Some area tables are set up to indicate the area to the left or right of the indicated z values, but in our table, we indicate the area between the mean and the z value. Thus, the area from the mean to either z = +0.5 or −0.5 is 0.1915, or 19.15 percent of the total area or probability. A more complete set of values can be found in Table A-5 at the end of the book.

mine that the probability is 0.4773 that the outcome will be between 0 and 10 percent and then observe that the probability of an outcome less than the mean, 10, is 0.5000. Thus, the probability of an outcome less than zero is 0.5000 − 0.4773 = 0.0227, or 2.27 percent.

Using Continuous Distributions. Continuous distributions are generally used in financial analysis in the following manner:

1. Someone with a good knowledge of a particular situation is asked to specify the most applicable type of distribution and its parameters. For example, a company's marketing manager might be asked to supply this information for sales of a given product, or an engineer might be asked to estimate the construction costs of a capital project.

2. A financial analyst could then use these input data to help evaluate the riskiness of a given decision. For example, the analyst might conclude that the probability is 50 percent, that the actual rate of return on a project will be between 5 and 10 percent, that the probability of a loss (negative rate of return) on the project is 15 percent, or that the probability of a return greater than 10 percent is 25 percent. Generally, such an analysis would be done by using a computer program. We shall return to this topic in Chapter 13.

In theory, we should use the specific distribution that best represents the true situation. Sometimes the true distribution is known, but with most financial data, it is not known. For example, we might think that interest rates could range from 8 to 15 percent next year, with a most likely value of 10 percent. This suggests a triangular distribution. Or we might think that interest rates next year can best be represented by a normal distribution, with a mean of 10 percent and a standard deviation of 2.5 percent. The point is, there is simply no type of distribution that is always "best"; you need to be familiar with different types of distributions and their properties, and then you must select the best distribution for the problem at hand.

TIME VALUE OF MONEY

*W*ill *you be able to retire? Your reaction to this question is probably, "First things first! I'm worried about getting a job, not retiring!" But an awareness of the retirement situation could help you land a job because (1) this is an important issue today, (2) employers prefer to hire people who know the issues, and (3) professors often test students on the time value of money with problems related to saving for some future purpose, including retirement. So read on.*

A recent Fortune *article began with some interesting facts: (1) The U.S. savings rate is the lowest of any industrial nation. (2) The ratio of U.S. workers to retirees, which was 17 to 1 in 1950, is now down to 3.2 to 1, and it will decline to less than 2 to 1 after the year 2000. (3) With so few people paying into the Social Security system, and so many drawing funds out, Social Security may soon be in serious trouble. The article concluded that even people making $85,000 per year will have trouble maintaining a reasonable standard of living after they retire, and many of today's college students will have to support their parents.*

If Ms. Jones, who earns $85,000, retires in 1999, expects to live for another 20 years after retirement, and needs 80 percent of her pre-retirement income, she would require $68,000 during 1999. However, if inflation amounts to 5 percent per year, her income requirement would increase to $110,765 in 10 years and to $180,424 in 20 years. If inflation were 7 percent, her Year 20 requirement would jump to $263,139! How much wealth would Ms. Jones need at retirement to maintain her standard of living, and how much would she have to save during each working year to accumulate that wealth?

The answer depends on a number of factors, including the rate she could earn on savings, the inflation rate, and when her savings program began. Also, the answer would depend on how much she will get from Social Security and from her corporate retirement plan, if she has one. (She should not count on much from Social Security unless she is really down and out.) Note, too, that her plans could be upset if the inflation rate increased, if the return on her savings changed, or if she lived beyond 20 years.

Fortune and other organizations have done studies relating to the retirement issue, using the tools and techniques described in this chapter. The general conclusion is that most Americans have been putting their heads in the sand—many of us have been ignoring what is almost certainly going to be a huge personal and social problem. But if you study this chapter carefully, you can avoid the trap that seems to be catching so many people.

---

*I*n Chapter 1, we saw that the primary goal of financial management is to maximize the value of the firm's stock. We also saw that stock values depend in part on the timing of the cash flows investors expect to receive from an investment—a dollar expected soon is worth more than a dollar expected in the distant future. Therefore, it is essential for financial managers to have a clear understanding of the time value of money and its impact on the value of the firm. These concepts are discussed in this chapter, where we show how the timing of cash flows affects asset values and rates of return.

The principles of time value analysis have many applications, ranging from setting up schedules for paying off loans to decisions about whether to acquire new equipment. *In fact, of all the concepts used in finance, none is more important than the time value of money, also called discounted cash flow (DCF) analysis.* Since this concept is used throughout the remainder of the book, it is vital that you understand the material in this chapter before you move on to other topics.[1]

TIME LINES

Suppose you are planning a trip to Europe in three years. You would like to begin saving for it now, by investing $1,000 that your rich great-aunt gave you for your birthday. If you put the money in a bank account that pays 5 percent interest, how much will you have in this account when you start your trip in three years? Drawing a **time line** is the first step in answering this type of question. Time lines are used to visualize what is happening in a particular problem and then to help set up the problem for solution. To illustrate the time line concept, consider the following diagram:

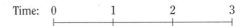

Time 0 is today; Time 1 is one period from today, or the end of Period 1; Time 2 is two periods from today, or the end of Period 2; and so on. Thus, the numbers above the tick marks represent end-of-period values. Often the periods are years, but other time intervals such as semiannual periods, quarters, months, or even days can be used. If each period on the time line represents a year, the interval from the 0 tick mark to the tick mark 1 would be Year 1, the interval from 1 to 2 would be Year 2, and so on. Note that each tick mark corresponds to the end of one period as well as the beginning of the next period. In other words, the tick mark at Time 1 represents the *end* of Year 1, and it also represents the *beginning* of Year 2 because Year 1 has just passed.

Cash flows are placed directly below the tick marks, and interest rates are shown directly above the time line. Unknown cash flows, which you are trying to find in the analysis, are indicated by a symbol such as FV, which stands for "future value." Now consider the following time line:

Here the interest rate for each of the three periods is 5 percent; a single amount (or lump sum) cash **outflow** is made at Time 0; and the future value at Time 3 value is an unknown **inflow.** Since the initial $1,000 is an outflow (you give $1,000 to the bank), it has a minus sign. Since the future value is an inflow, it does not have a minus sign, which implies a plus sign. Note that no cash flows occur at Times 1 and 2. Note also that we do not show dollar signs on time lines to reduce clutter.

---

[1]This chapter, and indeed the entire book, is written on the assumption that students have financial calculators. As a result, procedures for obtaining financial calculator solutions are set forth in each of the major sections, along with procedures for obtaining solutions by using regular calculators or tables. It is highly desirable for each student to obtain a financial calculator and to learn how to use it, because financial calculators and computers—and not clumsy, rounded, and incomplete tables—are used exclusively in businesses.

Now consider a different situation, where a $1,000 cash outflow is made today, and we will receive an unknown amount at the end of Time 2:

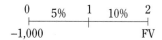

Here the interest rate is 5 percent during the first period, but it rises to 10 percent during the second period. If the interest rate is constant in all periods, we show it only in the first period, but if it changes, we show all the relevant rates on the time line.

Time lines are essential when you are first learning time value concepts, but even experts use time lines to analyze complex problems. We will be using time lines throughout the book, and you should get into the habit of using them when you work problems.

S E L F - T E S T
Q U E S T I O N

Draw a three-year time line to illustrate the following situation: (1) An outflow of $10,000 occurs at Time 0. (2) Inflows of $5,000 then occur at the end of Years 1, 2, and 3. (3) The interest rate during all three years is 23.375 percent.

FUTURE VALUE

A dollar in hand today is worth more than a dollar to be received in the future because, if you had it now, you could invest it, earn interest, and end up with more than one dollar in the future. The process of going from today's values, or present values (PVs), to future values (FVs) is called **compounding.** To illustrate, suppose you deposit $100 in a bank that pays 5 percent interest each year. How much would you have at the end of one year? To begin, we define the following terms:

PV = present value, or beginning amount, in your account. Here PV = $100.

i = interest rate the bank pays on the account per year. The interest earned is based on the balance at the beginning of each year, and we assume that it is paid at the end of the year. Here i = 5%, or, expressed as a decimal, i = 0.05. Throughout this chapter, we designate the interest rate as i (or I) because that symbol is used on most financial calculators. Note, though, that in later chapters we use the symbol k to denote interest rates because k is used more often in the financial literature.

INT = dollars of interest you earn during the year = Beginning amount × i. Here INT = $100(0.05) = $5.

FV_n = future value, or ending amount, of your account at the end of n years. Whereas PV is the value now, or the *present value,* FV_n is the value n years into the *future,* after the interest earned has been added to the account.

n = number of periods involved in the analysis. Here n = 1.

In our example, n = 1, so FV_n can be calculated as follows:

$$FV_n = FV_1 = PV + INT$$

$$= PV + PV(i)$$

$$= PV(1 + i).$$

$$= \$100(1 + 0.05) = \$100(1.05) = \$105.$$

Thus, the **future value (FV)** at the end of one year, FV_1, equals the present value multiplied by 1 plus the interest rate, so you will have $105 after one year.

What would you end up with if you left your $100 in the account for five years? Here is a time line set up to show the amount at the end of each year:

	0	5%	1	2	3	4	5
Initial deposit:	−100		FV$_1$ = ?	FV$_2$ = ?	FV$_3$ = ?	FV$_4$ = ?	FV$_5$ = ?
Interest earned:			5.00	5.25	5.51	5.79	6.08
Amount at the end of each period = FV$_n$:			105.00	110.25	115.76	121.55	127.63

Note the following points: (1) You start by depositing $100 in the account—this is shown as an outflow at t = 0. (2) You earn $100(0.05) = $5 of interest during the first year, so the amount at the end of Year 1 (or t = 1) is $100 + $5 = $105. (3) You start the second year with $105, earn $5.25 on the now larger amount, and end the second year with $110.25. Your interest during Year 2, $5.25, is higher than the first year's interest, $5, because you earned $5(0.05) = $0.25 interest on the first year's interest. (4) This process continues, and because the beginning balance is higher in each succeeding year, the annual interest earned increases. (5) The total interest earned, $27.63, is reflected in the final balance at t = 5, $127.63.

Note that the value at the end of Year 2, $110.25, is equal to

$$FV_2 = FV_1(1 + i)$$
$$= PV(1 + i)(1 + i)$$
$$= PV(1 + i)^2$$
$$= \$100(1.05)^2 = \$110.25.$$

Continuing, the balance at the end of Year 3 is

$$FV_3 = FV_2(1 + i)$$
$$= PV(1 + i)^3$$
$$= \$100(1.05)^3 = \$115.76,$$

and

$$FV_5 = \$100(1.05)^5 = \$127.63.$$

In general, the future value of an initial lump sum at the end of n years can be found by applying Equation 7-1:

$$FV_n = PV(1 + i)^n. \tag{7-1}$$

Equation 7-1 and most other time value of money equations can be solved in four ways: numerically with a regular calculator, with interest tables, with a financial calculator, or with a computer spreadsheet program. Most advanced work in financial management will be done with a financial calculator or on a computer, but when learning basic concepts it is best to work through all of the other methods.

Numerical Solution

One can use a regular calculator and either multiply (1 + i) by itself n − 1 times or else use the exponential function to raise (1 + i) to the nth power. With most calculators, you would enter 1 + i = 1.05 and multiply it by itself four times, or else enter 1.05, then press the y^x (exponential) function key, and then enter 5. In either case, your answer would be 1.2763 (if you set your calculator to display four decimal places), which you would multiply by $100 to get the final answer, $127.6282, which would be rounded to $127.63.

| TABLE 7-1 | Future Value Interest Factors: $FVIF_{i,n} = (1 + i)^n$ |

PERIOD (n)	4%	5%	6%
1	1.0400	1.0500	1.0600
2	1.0816	1.1025	1.1236
3	1.1249	1.1576	1.1910
4	1.1699	1.2155	1.2625
5	1.2167	1.2763	1.3382
6	1.2653	1.3401	1.4185

In certain problems, it is extremely difficult to arrive at a solution using a regular calculator. We will tell you this when we have such a problem, and in these cases we will not show a numerical solution. Also, at times we show the numerical solution just below the time line, as a part of the diagram, rather than in a separate section.

Interest Tables (Tabular Solution)

The **Future Value Interest Factor for i and n (FVIF$_{i,n}$)** is defined as $(1 + i)^n$, and these factors can be found by using a regular calculator as discussed above and then put into tables. Table 7-1 is illustrative, while Table A-3 in Appendix A at the back of the book contains FVIF$_{i,n}$ values for a wide range of i and n values.

Since $(1 + i)^n = FVIF_{i,n}$, Equation 7-1 can be rewritten as follows:

$$FV_n = PV(FVIF_{i,n}). \qquad \text{(7-1a)}$$

To illustrate, the FVIF for our five-year, 5 percent interest problem can be found in Table 7-1 by looking down the first column to Period 5, and then looking across that row to the 5 percent column, where we see that $FVIF_{5\%,5} = 1.2763$. Then, the value of $100 after five years is found as follows:

$$FV_n = PV(FVIF_{i,n})$$
$$= \$100(1.2763) = \$127.63.$$

Before financial calculators became readily available (in the 1980s), such tables were used extensively, but they are rarely used today in the real world.

Financial Calculator Solution

Equation 7-1 and a number of other equations have been programmed directly into financial calculators, and these calculators can be used to find future values. Note that calculators have five keys which correspond to the five most commonly used time value of money variables:

Here

    N = the number of periods. Some calculators use n rather than N.

    I = interest rate per period. Some calculators use i or I/YR rather than I.

PV = present value.

PMT = payment. This key is used only if the cash flows involve a series of equal, or constant, payments (an annuity). If there are no periodic payments in a particular problem, then PMT = 0.

FV = future value.

On some financial calculators, these keys are actually buttons on the face of the calculator, while on others they are shown on a screen after going into the time value of money (TVM) menu.

In this chapter, we will deal with equations which involve only four of the variables at any one time—three of the variables will be known, and the calculator will then solve for the fourth (unknown) variable. In the next chapter, when we deal with bonds, we will use all five variables in the bond valuation equation.[2]

To find the future value of $100 after five years at 5 percent using a financial calculator, note that we must solve Equation 7-1:

$$FV_n = PV(1 + i)^n. \tag{7-1}$$

The equation has four variables, FV_n, PV, i, and n. If we know any three, we can solve for the fourth. In our example, we enter N = 5, I = 5, PV = 100, and PMT = 0. Then, when we press the FV key, we get the answer, FV = 127.63 (rounded to two decimal places).[3]

Many financial calculators require that all cash flows be designated as either inflows or outflows, with outflows being entered as negative numbers. In our illustration, you deposit, or put in, the initial amount (which is an outflow to you) and you take out, or receive, the ending amount (which is an inflow to you). If your calculator requires that you follow this sign convention, the PV would be entered as −100. If you entered 100, then the FV would appear as −127.63. Also, (1) enter the −100 by keying in 100 and then pressing the "change sign" or +/− key, and (2) on some calculators you are required to press a "Compute" key before pressing the FV key.

Sometimes the convention of changing signs can be confusing. For example, if you have $100 in the bank now and want to find out how much you will have after five years if your account pays 5 percent interest, the calculator will give you a negative answer, in this case −127.63, because the calculator assumes you are going to withdraw the funds. This sign convention should cause you no problem.

We should also note that financial calculators permit you to specify the number of decimal places that are displayed. Twelve significant digits are actually used in the calculations, but we generally use two places for answers when working with dollars or

---

[2]The equation programmed into the calculators actually has five variables, one for each key. In this chapter, the value of one of the variables is always zero. It is a good idea to get into the habit of inputting a zero for the unused variable (whose value is automatically set equal to zero when you clear the calculator's memory); if you forget to clear your calculator, inputting a zero will help you avoid trouble. Note also that we have prepared a *Technology Supplement* which provides instructions on the leading calculators for using all the functions necessary for this book. Calculator manuals go into a lot of detail on things we never do; hence they are longer and more complex than they need to be for our purposes. See the Preface for information on obtaining the *Technology Supplement*.

[3]Here we assume that compounding occurs once each year. Most calculators have a setting which can be used to designate the number of compounding periods per year. For example, the HP-10B comes preset with payments at 12 per year. You would need to change it to 1 per year to get FV = 127.63. With the HP-10B, you would do this by typing 1, pressing the gold key, and then pressing the P/YR key.

percentages and four places when working with decimals. The nature of the problem dictates how many decimal places should be displayed.

Spreadsheet Solution

Spreadsheet programs are ideally suited for solving time value of money problems.[4] With very little effort, the spreadsheet itself becomes a time line. Here is how the problem would look in a spreadsheet:

	A	B	C	D	E	F	G
1	Interest rate	0.05					
2	Time	0	1	2	3	4	5
3	Cash flow	−100					
4	Future value		105.00	110.25	115.76	121.55	**127.63**

Cell B1 shows the interest rate, entered as a decimal number, 0.05. Row 2 shows the periods for the time line. With *Microsoft Excel,* you could enter **0** in Cell B2, then the formula **=B2+1** in Cell C2, and then copy this formula into Cells D2 through G2 to produce the time periods shown on Row 2. Note that if your time line had many years, say, 50, you would simply copy the formula across more columns. Other procedures could also be used to enter the periods.

Row 3 shows the cash flows. In this case, there is only one cash flow, shown in Cell B3. Row 4 shows the future value of this cash flow at the end of each year. Cell C4 contains the formula for Equation 7-1. The formula could be written as **=−$B$3*(1+.05)^C2**, but we wrote it as **=−$B$3*(1+$B$1)^C2**, which gives us the flexibility to change the interest rate in Cell B1 to see how the future value changes with changes in interest rates. Note that the formula has a minus sign for the PV (which is in Cell B3) to account for the minus sign of the cash flow. This formula was then copied into Cells D4 through G4. As Cell G4 shows, the value of $100 at the end of five years when compounded at 5 percent per year is $127.63.

Comparing the Four Procedures

The first step in solving any time value problem is to understand the verbal description of the problem well enough to diagram it on a time line. Woody Allen said that 90 percent of success is just showing up. With time value problems, 90 percent of success is correctly setting up the time line.

After you diagram the problem on a time line, your next step is to pick an approach to solve the problem. Which of the four approaches should you use — numerical, tabular,

---

[4]In this section, and in other sections and chapters, we discuss spreadsheet solutions to various financial problems. We generally use *Microsoft Excel* in our work, and we illustrate spreadsheet applications with *Excel* examples. If a reader is not familiar with spreadsheets and has no interest in them, then these sections can be omitted. Note also that the first spreadsheet program, *Visicalc,* was invented by Dan Bricklin, a Harvard MBA student who wanted to calculate answers for a business case. For those who are not familiar with spreadsheets but want to learn something about them, our *Technology Supplement* provides brief tutorials for several popular spreadsheet programs. See our Preface for information on how to obtain the *Technology Supplement.*

financial calculator, or spreadsheet? In general, you should use the easiest approach. But which is easiest? The answer depends on the particular situation.

First, we would never recommend the tabular approach—it went out when calculators were invented some 20 years ago. Second, all business students should know Equation 7-1 by heart and should also know how to use a financial calculator. So, for simple problems such as finding the future value of a single payment, it is probably easiest and quickest to use either the numerical approach or a financial calculator.

For problems with more than a couple of cash flows, the numerical approach is usually too time consuming, so here either the calculator or spreadsheet approaches would generally be used. Calculators are portable and quick to set up, but if many calculations of the same type must be done, or if inputs such as the interest rate must be changed to see the effects of changes in variables, the spreadsheet approach may be more efficient. If the problem has many irregular cash flows, or if you want to analyze many scenarios with different cash flows, then the spreadsheet approach is the most efficient. The important thing is that you understand the various approaches well enough to make a rational choice, given the nature of the problem and the equipment you have available.

Problem Format

To help you understand the various types of time value problems, we generally use a standard format. First, we state the problem in words. Next, we diagram the problem on a time line. Then, beneath the time line, we show the equation that must be solved. Finally, we present four alternative approaches for solving the equation to obtain the answer: (1) use a regular calculator to obtain a numerical solution, (2) use the tables, (3) use a financial calculator, or (4) use a spreadsheet program. For some of the very easy problems, we will not show a spreadsheet solution, and for some difficult problems, we will not show numerical or tabular solutions because they are simply too inefficient.

To illustrate the format, consider the five-year, 5 percent example:

Time Line:

0	5%	1	2	3	4	5
−100						FV = ?

Equation:

$$FV_n = PV(1 + i)^n = \$100(1.05)^5.$$

1. Numerical Solution:

0	5%	1	2	3	4	5
100 × 1.05		× 1.05	× 1.05	× 1.05	× 1.05	= 127.63
		105.00	110.25	115.76	121.55	

Using a regular calculator, raise 1.05 to the 5th power and multiply by $100 to get $FV_5 = \$127.63$.

2. Tabular Solution:

Look up $FVIF_{5\%,5}$ in Table 7-1 or Table A-3 at the end of the book, and then multiply by $100:

$$FV_5 = \$100(FVIF_{5\%,5}) = \$100(1.2763) = \$127.63.$$

3. Financial Calculator Solution:

	Inputs:	5	5	−100	0	
		N	I	PV	PMT	FV
	Output:					= 127.63

Note that the calculator diagram tells you to input N = 5, I = 5, PV = −100, and PMT = 0, and then to press the FV key to get the answer, 127.63. Interest rates are entered as percentages (5), not decimals (0.05). Also, note that in this particular problem, the PMT key does not come into play, as no constant series of payments is involved.[5] Finally, you should recognize that small rounding differences will often occur among the various solution methods because tables use fewer significant digits (4) than do calculators (12), and also because rounding sometimes is done at intermediate steps in long problems.

4. Spreadsheet Solution:

	A	B	C	D	E	F	G
1	Interest rate	0.05					
2	Time	0	1	2	3	4	5
3	Cash flow	−100					
4	Future value		105.00	110.25	115.76	121.55	**127.63**

Cell G4 contains the formula for Equation 7-1: **=−$B$3*(1+$B$1)^G2** or **=−B$3*(1+.05)^G2**. You could also enter, in Cell G4 (or G5) the *Excel* FV function **=FV(5%,5,0,−100,0)**, where the first argument is the interest rate, the second is the number of periods, the third is the annual payments (which are zero because there are no annuity payments), the fourth is the present value or initial payment, and the fifth indicates that the $127.63 is paid at the end rather than the beginning of the year. Note that the interest rate must be written as either 0.05 or 5%, not 5 as in a financial calculator. You could also use the *Excel* function wizard to create the FV formula. Place the pointer on Cell G4 (or G5), and click on the function wizard. Then, at the prompts enter B1, 0.05, or 5% for rate, 5 for nper or number of periods, 0 for pmt, −100 for pv to show the initial payment, and 0 for type to indicate that payments occur at the end rather than at the beginning of the period. Then press "Finish" to obtain the FV, 127.63. With the function, you could use only Columns A and B.

Graphic View of the Compounding Process: Growth

Figure 7-1 shows how $1 (or any other lump sum) grows over time at various interest rates. The data used to plot the curves could be obtained from Table A-3, or it could be generated with a calculator or computer. The higher the rate of interest, the faster the rate of growth. The interest rate is, in fact, a growth rate: If a sum is deposited and earns 5 percent interest, then the funds on deposit will grow at a rate of 5 percent per period. Note also that time value concepts can be applied to anything that is growing — sales, population, earnings per share, or whatever.

---

[5]We input PMT = 0, but if you cleared the calculator before you started, the PMT register would already have been set to 0.

FIGURE 7-1   Relationships among Future Value, Growth, Interest Rates, and Time

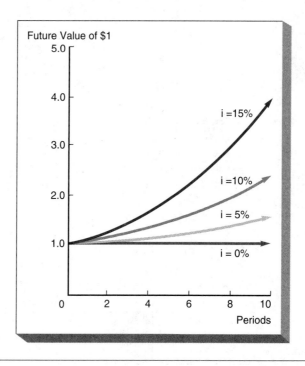

Explain what is meant by the following statement: "A dollar in hand today is worth more than a dollar to be received next year."

What is compounding? Explain why earning "interest on interest" is called "compound interest."

Set up a time line that shows the following situation: (1) Your initial deposit is $100. (2) The account pays 5 percent interest annually. (3) You want to know how much money you will have at the end of three years.

Write out an equation which you could use to solve the preceding problem.

What are the five TVM (time value of money) input keys on a financial calculator? List them (horizontally) in the proper order.

PRESENT VALUE

Suppose you have some extra cash, and you have a chance to buy a low-risk security which will pay $127.63 at the end of five years. Your local bank is currently offering 5 percent interest on five-year certificates of deposit (CDs), and you regard the security as being exactly as safe as a CD. The 5 percent rate is defined as your **opportunity cost rate,** or the rate of return you could earn on an alternative investment of similar risk. How much should you be willing to pay for the security?

From the future value example presented in the previous section, we saw that an initial amount of $100 invested at 5 percent per year would be worth $127.63 at the end of five years. As we will see in a moment, you should be indifferent to the choice between $100 today and $127.63 at the end of five years. The $100 is defined as the **present value,** or **PV,** of $127.63 due in five years when the opportunity cost rate is 5 percent. If the price of the security were less than $100, you should buy it, because its price would then be less than the $100 you would have to spend on a similar-risk alternative to end up with \$127.63 after five years. Conversely, if the security cost more than \$100, you should not buy it, because you would have to invest only \$100 in a similar-risk alternative to end up with \$127.63 after five years. If the price were exactly \$100, then you should be indifferent—you could either buy the security or turn it down. Therefore, \$100 is defined as the security's **fair,** or **equilibrium, value.**

In general, *the present value of a cash flow due n years in the future is the amount which, if it were on hand today, would grow to equal the future amount.* Since \$100 would grow to \$127.63 in five years at a 5 percent interest rate, \$100 is the present value of \$127.63 due in five years when the opportunity cost rate is 5 percent.

Finding present values is called **discounting,** and it is simply the reverse of compounding—if you know the PV, you can compound to find the FV, while if you know the FV, you can discount to find the PV. When discounting, you would follow these steps:

Time Line:

Equation:

To develop the discounting equation, we begin with the future value equation, Equation 7-1:

$$FV_n = PV(1 + i)^n = PV(FVIF_{i,n}).$$ **(7-1)**

Next, we solve for PV in several equivalent forms:

$$PV = \frac{FV_n}{(1 + i)^n} = FV_n\left(\frac{1}{1+i}\right)^n = FV_n(PVIF_{i,n}).$$ **(7-2)**

The last form of Equation 7-2 recognizes that the interest factor $PVIF_{i,n}$ is equal to the term in parentheses in the second version of the equation.

1. Numerical Solution:

Divide \$127.63 by 1.05 five times, or by $(1.05)^5$, to find PV = \$100.

2. Tabular Solution:

The term in parentheses in Equation 7-2 is called the **Present Value Interest Factor for i and n,** or **PVIF_{i,n},** and Table A-1 in Appendix A contains present value interest factors for selected values of i and n. The value of $PVIF_{i,n}$ for i = 5% and n = 5 is 0.7835, so the present value of \$127.63 to be received after five years when the appropriate interest rate is 5 percent is \$100:

$$PV = \$127.63(PVIF_{5\%,5}) = \$127.63(0.7835) = \$100.$$

3. Financial Calculator Solution:

Inputs:	5	5		0	127.63
	N	I	PV	PMT	FV
Output:			= −100		

Enter N = 5, I = 5, PMT = 0, and FV = 127.63, and then press PV to get PV = –100. This is the easy way!

4. Spreadsheet Solution

	A	B	C	D	E	F	G
1	Interest rate	0.05					
2	Time	0	1	2	3	4	5
3	Cash flow			0	0	0	0	127.63
4	Present value	**100**					

You could enter the spreadsheet version of Equation 7-2 in Cell B4, **=127.63/(1+0.05)^5**, but you could also use the built-in spreadsheet PV function. In *Excel,* the easiest formula is **=NPV(0.05,C3:G3)**. You must enter zeros in C3:F3. This would find the present value of each number in the range of cells from C3 to G3, discounted at 5 percent, then show their sum in Cell B4. *Excel* provides other formulas, and you could use the function wizard to access them. In this simple example, there is only one number in the range, 127.63 in Cell G3. However, many finance problems involve cash flows in many different years, and the NPV function is an efficient way to find the present value in such cases. Also, note that the interest rate in the formula is an actual number; it could be shown as a cell reference, as 0.05, or as 5%, but not as 5, the way it is entered in a financial calculator.

Graphic View of the Discounting Process

Figure 7-2 shows how the present value of $1 (or any other sum) to be received in the future diminishes as the years to receipt and the interest rate increase.

FIGURE 7-2   Relationships among Present Value, Interest Rates, and Time

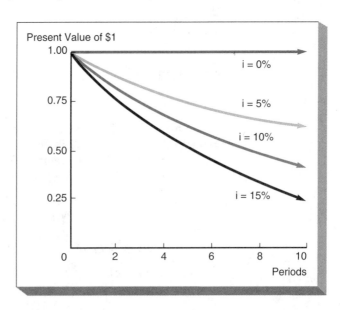

Again, the data used to plot the curves could be obtained either with a calculator or from Table A-1, and the graph shows (1) that the present value of a sum to be received at some future date decreases and approaches zero as the payment date is extended further into the future, and (2) that the rate of decrease is greater the higher the interest (discount) rate. At relatively high interest rates, funds due in the future are worth very little today, and even at a relatively low discount rate, the present value of a sum due in the very distant future is quite small. For example, at a 20 percent discount rate, $1 million due in 100 years is worth approximately 1 cent today. (However, 1 cent would grow to almost $1 million in 100 years at 20 percent.)

S E L F - T E S T
Q U E S T I O N S

What is meant by the term "opportunity cost rate"?

What is discounting? How is it related to compounding?

How does the present value of an amount to be received in the future change as the time is extended and the interest rate increased?

SOLVING FOR INTEREST RATE AND TIME

At this point, you should realize that compounding and discounting are related, and that we have been dealing with one equation in two different forms:

FV Form:

$$FV_n = PV(1 + i)^n. \tag{7-1}$$

PV Form:

$$PV = \frac{FV_n}{(1 + i)^n} = FV_n \left(\frac{1}{1 + i}\right)^n. \tag{7-2}$$

There are four variables in these equations—PV, FV, i, and n—and if you know the values of any three, you (or your financial calculator) can find the value of the fourth. Thus far, we have always given you the interest rate (i) and the number of years (n), plus either the PV or the FV. In many situations, though, you will need to solve for either i or n, as we discuss below.

Solving for i

Suppose you can buy a security for $78.35 which will pay you $100 after five years. Here we know PV, FV, and n, and you want to find i, the interest rate you would earn on the investment. Such problems are solved as follows:

Time Line:

```
  0     i = ?   1         2         3         4         5
  |--------------|---------|---------|---------|---------|
-78.35                                                  100
```

Equation:

$$FV_n = PV(1 + i)^n \tag{7-1}$$

$$\$100 = \$78.35(1 + i)^5. \text{ Solve for i.}$$

1. Numerical Solution:

Use Equation 7-1 to solve for i:

$$\$100 = \$78.35(1 + i)^5$$

$$\frac{\$100}{\$78.35} = (1 + i)^5$$

$$(1 + i)^5 = 1.276$$

$$1 + i = (1.276)^{(1/5)}$$

$$1 + i = 1.050$$

$$i = 0.05 = 5\%.$$

Therefore, the interest rate is 5 percent.

2. Tabular Solution:

$$FV_n = PV(1 + i)^n = PV(FVIF_{i,n})$$

$$\$100 = \$78.35(FVIF_{i,5})$$

$$FVIF_{i,5} = \$100/\$78.35 = 1.2763.$$

Find the value of the FVIF as shown above, and then look across the Period 5 row in Table A-3 until you find FVIF = 1.2763. This value is in the 5% column, so the interest rate at which $78.35 grows to $100 over five years is 5 percent. This procedure can be used only if the interest rate is in the table; therefore, it will not work for fractional interest rates or where n is not a whole number. Approximation procedures can be used, but they are laborious and inexact.

3. Financial Calculator Solution:

Inputs: 5   −78.35   0   100

                  N   I   PV   PMT   FV

Output: = 5.0

Enter N = 5, PV = −78.35, PMT = 0, and FV = 100, and then press I to get I = 5%. This procedure can be used for any interest rate or for any value of n, including fractional values.

4. Spreadsheet Solution:

	A	B	C	D	E	F	G
1	Time	0	1	2	3	4	5
2	Cash flow	−78.35	0	0	0	0	100
3	Interest rate	5%					

Most spreadsheets have a built-in function to find the interest rate. In *Excel,* you could enter the formula **=IRR(B2:G2)** in Cell B3, either by looking up the formula in a manual or by following the steps in the function wizard. At any rate, the formula calculates the internal rate of return, or IRR, and its argument is the range of the cash flows. We will have more to say about the IRR in Chapter 11, but for now think of it as a way to find the interest rate that makes 78.35 grow to 100 in five years. *Excel* also has other ways that could be used to find the 5 percent, but for this problem the IRR function is easiest to apply.

Solving for n

Suppose you know that a security will provide a return of 5 percent per year, that it will cost $78.35, and that you will receive $100 at maturity, but you do not know when the security matures. Thus, you know PV, FV, and i, but you do not know n, the number of periods. Here is the situation:

Time Line:

Equation:

$$FV_n = PV(1 + i)^n \tag{7-1}$$

$100 = \$78.35(1.05)^n$. Solve for n.

1. Numerical Solution:

Use Equation 7-1 to solve for n:

$$\$100 = \$78.35 \ (1 + 0.05)^n.$$

Transform to

$$\$100/\$78.35 = 1.276 = (1 + 0.05)^n.$$

Take the natural log of both sides, and then solve for n:

$$n \ LN(1.05) = LN(1.276)$$

$$n = LN(1.276)/LN(1.05)$$

Find the logs with a calculator, and complete the solution:

$$n = 0.2437/0.0488$$

$$= 4.9955 \approx 5.0.$$

Therefore, 5 is the number of years it takes for $78.35 to grow to $100 if the interest rate is 5 percent.

2. Tabular Solution:

$$FV_n = PV(1 + i)^n = PV(FVIF_{i,n})$$

$$\$100 = \$78.35(FVIF_{5\%,n})$$

$$FVIF_{5\%,n} = \$100/\$78.35 = 1.2763.$$

Now look down the 5% column in Table A-3 until you find FVIF = 1.2763. This value is in Row 5, which indicates that it takes five years for $78.35 to grow to $100 at a 5 percent interest rate.

3. Financial Calculator Solution:

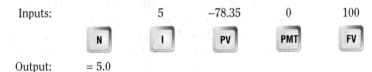

Inputs: 5   −78.35   0   100

N   I   PV   PMT   FV

Output: = 5.0

Enter I = 5, PV = −78.35, PMT = 0, and FV = 100, and then press N to get N = 5.

4. Spreadsheet Solution:

To solve this problem with a spreadsheet, you could enter the formula = **78.35*(1.05)^B2** in Cell B4 and then use the goal-seeking function on the Tools menu to find a value for B2 that causes the value in B4 to equal 100. The value is 5.00.

SELF-TEST QUESTIONS

Assuming that you are given PV, FV, and the interest rate, i, write out an equation that can be used to determine the time period, n.

Explain how a financial calculator can be used to solve for i and n.

FUTURE VALUE OF AN ANNUITY

An **annuity** is a series of equal payments made at fixed intervals for a specified number of periods. For example, $100 at the end of each of the next three years is a three-year annuity. The payments are given the symbol PMT, and they can occur at either the beginning or the end of each period. If the payments occur at the *end* of each period, as they typically do, the annuity is called an **ordinary, or deferred, annuity.** Payments on mortgages, car loans, and student loans are typically set up as ordinary annuities. If payments are made at the *beginning* of each period, the annuity is an **annuity due.** Rental payments for an apartment, life insurance premiums, and lottery payoffs are typically set up as annuities due. Since ordinary annuities are more common in finance, when the term "annuity" is used in this book, you should assume that the payments occur at the end of each period unless otherwise noted.

Ordinary Annuities

An ordinary, or deferred, annuity consists of a series of equal payments made at the *end* of each period. If you deposit $100 at the end of each year for three years in a savings account that pays 5 percent interest per year, how much will you have at the end of three years? To answer this question, we must find the future value of the annuity, **FVA$_n$**. Each payment is compounded out to the end of Period n, and the sum of the compounded payments is the future value of the annuity, FVA$_n$.

Time Line:

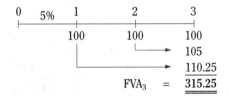

Here we show the regular time line as the top portion of the diagram, but we also show how each cash flow is compounded to produce the value FVA$_n$ in the lower portion of the diagram.

Equation:

$$FVA_n = PMT(1 + i)^{n-1} + PMT(1 + i)^{n-2} + PMT(1 + i)^{n-3} + \cdots + PMT(1 + i)^0$$

$$= PMT \sum_{t=1}^{n} (1 + i)^{n-t}$$

$$= PMT\left(\frac{(1 + i)^n - 1}{i}\right)$$ **(7-3)**

$$= PMT(FVIFA_{i,n}).$$

The first line of Equation 7-3 represents the application of Equation 7-1 to each individual payment of the annuity. In other words, each term is the compounded amount of a single payment, with the superscript in each term indicating the number of periods during which the payment earns interest. For example, because the first annuity payment was made at the end of Period 1, interest would be earned in Periods 2 through n only, so compounding would be for n − 1 periods rather than n periods. Compounding for the second payment would be for Period 3 through Period n, or n − 2 periods, and so on. The last payment is made at the end of the annuity's life, so there is no time for interest to be earned.

The second line of Equation 7-3 is just a shorthand version of the first form, but the third line is different—it is found by applying the algebra of geometric progressions. This form of Equation 7-3 is especially useful when the required values of i and n are not in the tables and no financial calculator is available. Finally, the fourth line shows the payment multiplied by the **Future Value Interest Factor for an Annuity (FVIFA$_{i,n}$),** which is the tabular approach.

1. Numerical Solution:

The lower section of the time line shows the numerical solution, which involves using the first line of Equation 7-3. The future value of each cash flow is found, and those FVs are summed to find the FV of the annuity, $315.25. If a long annuity were being evaluated, this process would be quite tedious, and in that case you probably would use the form of Equation 7-3 found on the third line:

$$FVA_n = PMT \left(\frac{(1 + i)^n - 1}{i}\right)$$

$$= \$100\left(\frac{(1 + 0.05)^3 - 1}{0.05}\right) = \$100(3.1525) = \$315.25.$$ **(7-3)**

2. Tabular Solution:

The fourth line of Equation 7-3 shows the FVIFA$_{i,n}$, which is calculated as the term in parentheses in the third line of Equation 7-3. FVIFAs have been calculated for various combinations of i and n, and Table A-4 in Appendix A contains a set of FVIFA factors. To find the answer to the three-year, $100 annuity problem, first refer to Table A-4 and look down the 5% column to the third period; the FVIFA is 3.1525. Thus, the future value of the $100 annuity is $315.25:

$$FVA_n = PMT(FVIFA_{i,n})$$

$$FVA_3 = \$100(FVIFA_{5\%,3}) = \$100(3.1525) = \$315.25.$$ **(7-3)**

3. Financial Calculator Solution:

Inputs: 3   5   0   −100

N   I   PV   PMT   FV

Output: = 315.25

Note that in annuity problems, the PMT key is used in conjunction with the N and I keys, plus either the PV or the FV key, depending on whether you are trying to find the PV or the FV of the annuity. In our example, you want the FV, so press the FV key to get the answer, $315.25. Since there is no initial payment, we input PV = 0.

4. Spreadsheet Solution:

	A	B	C	D	E
1	Interest rate	0.05			
2	Time	0	1	2	3
3	Cash flow		100	100	100
4	Future value				**315.25**

Most spreadsheets have a built-in function to find the future value of an annuity. In *Excel*, the formula in Cell E4 would be **=FV(0.05,3, − 100).** Like the financial calculator approach, the payment is entered as a negative number to show that it is a cash outflow. Unlike with a financial calculator, you must enter the interest rate as a number. You can format this number as 0.05 or as 5%, but you cannot enter it as 5, the way you would with a financial calculator. Note that it isn't even necessary to show the time line, since the FV function doesn't require you to input a range of cash flows. Still, the time line is useful to help visualize the problem. Also, you could use the function wizard to develop the equation.

Annuities Due

Had the three $100 payments in the previous example been made at the *beginning* of each year, the annuity would have been an *annuity due*. On the time line, each payment would be shifted to the left one year; therefore, each payment would be compounded for one extra year.

Time Line:

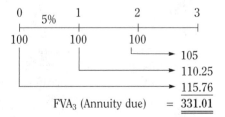

Again, the time line is shown at the top of the diagram, and the values as calculated with a regular calculator are shown under Year 3. The payments occur earlier, so more interest is earned. Therefore, the future value of the annuity due is larger—$331.01 versus $315.25 for the ordinary annuity.

Equation:

$$FVA_n(Due) = PMT(1 + i)^n + PMT(1 + i)^{n-1} + PMT(1 + i)^{n-2} + \cdots + PMT(1 + i)$$

$$= PMT \sum_{t=1}^{n} (1 + i)^{n+1-t}$$

$$= PMT\left(\frac{(1 + i)^n - 1}{i}\right)(1 + i) \qquad (7\text{-}3a)$$

$$= PMT(FVIFA_{i,n})(1 + i).$$

The only difference between Equation 7-3a for annuities due and Equation 7-3 for ordinary annuities is that every term in Equation 7-3a is compounded for one extra period, reflecting the fact that each payment for an annuity due occurs one period earlier than for a corresponding ordinary annuity.

1. Numerical Solution:

The lower section of the time line shows the numerical solution using the first line of Equation 7-3a. The future value of each cash flow is found, and those FVs are summed to find the FV of the annuity, $331.01. Because this process is quite tedious for long annuities, you probably would use the third line of Equation 7-3a:

$$FVA_n(Due) = PMT \left(\frac{(1 + i)^n - 1}{i}\right)(1 + i) \qquad (7\text{-}3a)$$

$$= \$100\left(\frac{(1 + 0.05)^3 - 1}{0.05}\right)(1 + 0.05) = \$100(3.1525)(1.05) = \$331.01.$$

2. Tabular Solution:

The fourth line of Equation 7-3a shows how the $FVIFA_{i,n}$ for an ordinary annuity can be used to find the value of an annuity due. In an annuity due, each payment is compounded for one additional period, so the future value of the entire annuity is equal to the future value of an ordinary annuity compounded for one additional period. Here is the tabular solution:

$$FVA_n (Due) = PMT(FVIFA_{i,n})(1 + i) \qquad (7\text{-}3a)$$

$$= \$100(3.1525)(1.05) = \$331.01.$$

3. Financial Calculator Solution:

Most financial calculators have a switch, or key, marked "DUE" or "BEG" that permits you to switch from end-of-period payments (ordinary annuity) to beginning-of-period payments (annuity due). When the beginning mode is activated, the display will normally show the word "BEGIN." Thus, to deal with annuities due, switch your calculator to "BEGIN" and proceed as before:

Inputs:	3	5	0	−100	
	N	I	PV	PMT	FV
Output:					= 331.01

Enter N = 3, I = 5, PV = 0, PMT = −100, and then press FV to get the answer, $331.01. *Since most problems specify end-of-period cash flows, you should always switch your calculator back to "END" mode after you work an annuity due problem.*

4. Spreadsheet Solution:

For the annuity due, the spreadsheet formula is **=FV(0.05,3,−100,0,1),** developed using the function wizard. The solution value is $331.01. The fourth term in the formula, 0, means that no extra payment is made at t = 0, and the last term, 1, tells the computer that this is an annuity due. As in the case of an ordinary annuity, there is no need to enter the time line in the spreadsheet, but time lines do reduce the odds of making an error, especially for complicated problems.

What is the difference between an ordinary annuity and an annuity due?

How do you modify the equation for determining the value of an ordinary annuity to find the value of an annuity due?

Which annuity has the greater *future* value: an ordinary annuity or an annuity due? Why?

Explain how financial calculators can be used to solve future value of annuity problems.

PRESENT VALUE OF AN ANNUITY

Suppose you were offered the following alternatives: (1) a three-year annuity with payments of $100 or (2) a lump sum payment today. You have no need for the money during the next three years, so if you accept the annuity, you would deposit the payments in a bank account that pays 5 percent interest per year. Similarly, the lump sum payment would be deposited into a bank account. How large must the lump sum payment today be to make it equivalent to the annuity?

Ordinary Annuities

If the payments come at the end of each year, then the annuity is an ordinary annuity, and it would be set up as follows:

Time Line:

```
            0    5%    1        2        3
            |----------|--------|--------|
                      100      100      100
   95.24  ◄───────────┘        |        |
   90.70  ◄────────────────────┘        |
   86.38  ◄─────────────────────────────┘
PVA₃  =  272.32
```

The regular time line is shown at the top of the diagram, and the numerical solution values are shown in the left column. The PV of the annuity, **PVA$_n$,** is $272.32.

Equation:

The general equation used to find the PV of an ordinary annuity is shown below:

$$PVA_n = PMT\left(\frac{1}{1+i}\right)^1 + PMT\left(\frac{1}{1+i}\right)^2 + \cdots + PMT\left(\frac{1}{1+i}\right)^n$$

$$= PMT \sum_{t=1}^{n}\left(\frac{1}{1+i}\right)^t$$

$$= PMT\left(\frac{1 - \dfrac{1}{(1+i)^n}}{i}\right)$$

$$= PMT(PVIFA_{i,n}).$$

(7-4)

1. Numerical Solution:

The lower section of the time line shows the numerical solution, $272.32, calculated by using the first line of Equation 7-4, where the present value of each cash flow is found and then summed to find the PV of the annuity. If the annuity has many payments, it is easier to use the third line of Equation 7-4:

$$PVA_n = PMT\left(\frac{1 - \dfrac{1}{(1+i)^n}}{i}\right)$$

$$= \$100\left(\frac{1 - \dfrac{1}{(1+0.05)^3}}{0.05}\right) = \$100(2.7232) = \$272.32.$$

2. Tabular Solution:

The fourth line of Equation 7-4 shows how to use the $PVIFA_{i,n}$ to find the PV of an annuity. $PVIFA_{i,n}$ for different values of i and n are shown in Table A-2 at the back of the book. To find the answer to the three-year, $100 annuity problem, simply refer to Table A-2 and look down the 5% column to the third period. The PVIFA is 2.7232, so the present value of the $100 annuity is $272.32:

$$PVA_n = PMT(PVIFA_{i,n})$$
$$PVA_3 = \$100(PVIFA_{5\%,3}) = \$100(2.7232) = \$272.32.$$

3. Financial Calculator Solution:

Inputs: 3   5   −100   0

 [N]   [I]   [PV]   [PMT]   [FV]

Output: = 272.32

Enter N = 3, I = 5, PMT = −100, and FV = 0, and then press the PV key to find the PV, $272.32.

4. Spreadsheet Solution:

	A	B	C	D	E
1	Interest rate	0.05			
2	Time	0	1	2	3
3	Cash flow		100	100	100
4	Present value	**$272.32**			

There are two ways to solve this problem. One is to enter the NPV formula in Cell B4, **=NPV(0.05,C3:E3)**. This will find the present value of each cash flow in Cells C3 through E3, and then add them together. The second way is to enter the PV annuity function in Cell B4, **=PV(0.05,3,−100)**. The NPV function could be used even if the cash flows were not the same. The PV function requires that the cash flows be constant. In this example, both methods result in a value of $272.32.

One especially important application of the annuity concept relates to loans with constant payments, such as mortgages and auto loans. With such loans, called *amor-*

tized loans, the amount borrowed is the present value of an ordinary annuity, and the payments constitute the annuity stream. We will examine constant payment loans in more depth in a later section of this chapter.

Annuities Due

Had the three $100 payments in the preceding example been made at the beginning of each year, the annuity would have been an *annuity due.* Each payment would be shifted to the left one year, so each payment would be discounted for one less year. Here is the time line setup:

Time Line:

$$\text{PVA}_3 \text{ (Annuity due)} = \underline{285.94}$$

Again, we find the PV of each cash flow and then sum these PVs to find the PV of the annuity due. This procedure is illustrated in the lower section of the time line diagram. Since the cash flows occur sooner, the PV of the annuity due exceeds that of the ordinary annuity, $285.94 versus $272.32.

Equation:

$$\text{PVA}_n(\text{Due}) = \text{PMT}\left(\frac{1}{1+i}\right)^0 + \text{PMT}\left(\frac{1}{1+i}\right)^1 + \cdots + \text{PMT}\left(\frac{1}{1+i}\right)^{n-1}$$

$$= \text{PMT} \sum_{t=1}^{n} \left(\frac{1}{1+i}\right)^{t-1} \tag{7-4a}$$

$$= \text{PMT}\left(\frac{1 - \dfrac{1}{(1+i)^n}}{i}\right)(1+i)$$

$$= \text{PMT}(\text{PVIFA}_{i,n})(1+i).$$

1. Numerical Solution:

The lower section of the time line shows the numerical solution, $285.94, calculated by using the first line of Equation 7-4a, where the present value of each cash flow is found and then summed to find the PV of the annuity due. If the annuity has many payments, it is easier to use the third line of Equation 7-4a:

$$\text{PVA}_n(\text{Due}) = \text{PMT}\left(\frac{1 - \dfrac{1}{(1+i)^n}}{i}\right)(1+i) \tag{7-4a}$$

$$= \$100\left(\frac{1 - \dfrac{1}{(1+0.05)^3}}{0.05}\right)(1+0.05) = \$100(2.7232)(1+0.05) = \$285.94.$$

2. Tabular Solution:

The fourth line of Equation 7-4a gives the tabular formula for the PV of an annuity due. Since the payments of an annuity due come in faster, an annuity due is more valuable than an ordinary annuity. This higher value is found by multiplying the PV of an ordinary annuity by $(1 + i)$:

$$PVA_n(Due) = PMT(PVIFA_{i,n})(1 + i) \qquad \textbf{(7-4a)}$$

$$= \$100(2.7232)(1.05) = \$285.94.$$

3. Financial Calculator Solution:

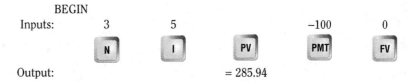

BEGIN
Inputs: 3   5   −100   0

Output: = 285.94

Switch to the beginning-of-period mode, and then enter N = 3, I = 5, PMT = −100, and FV = 0, and then press PV to get the answer, $285.94. *Again, since most problems deal with end-of-period cash flows, don't forget to switch your calculator back to the "END" mode.*

4. Spreadsheet Solution:

For the case of an annuity due, the spreadsheet formula is **=PV(0.05,3,−100,0,1)**. This would give a present value of $285.94. The fourth term in the formula, 0, means that you are not making any additional payments at t = 0, and the last term, 1, tells the computer that this is an annuity due. It is not necessary to enter the time line in the spreadsheet, although the time line may make the problem easier to visualize.

S E L F - T E S T
Q U E S T I O N S

Which annuity has the greater present value: an ordinary annuity or an annuity due? Why?

Explain how financial calculators can be used to find the present value of annuities.

PERPETUITIES

Most annuities call for payments to be made over some finite period of time — for example, $100 per year for three years. However, some annuities go on indefinitely, or perpetually, and these annuities are called **perpetuities.** The present value of a perpetuity is found by applying Equation 7-5:[6]

$$PV(Perpetuity) = \frac{Payment}{Interest\ rate} = \frac{PMT}{i}. \qquad \textbf{(7-5)}$$

Perpetuities can be illustrated by some British securities issued after the Napoleonic Wars. In 1815, the British government sold a huge bond issue and used the proceeds to pay off many smaller issues that had been floated in prior years to pay for the wars. Since the purpose of the bonds was to consolidate past debts, the bonds were called **consols.** Suppose each consol promised to pay $100 per year in perpetuity. (Actually, interest was stated in pounds.) What would each bond be worth if the opportunity cost rate, or discount rate, was 5 percent? The answer is $2,000:

$$PV\ (Perpetuity) = \frac{\$100}{0.05} = \$2,000\ if\ i = 5\%.$$

Suppose the interest rate rose to 10 percent; what would happen to the consol's value? The value would drop to $1,000:

$$PV\ (Perpetuity) = \frac{\$100}{0.10} = \$1,000\ at\ i = 10\%.$$

---

[6]The derivation of Equation 7-5 is given in Appendix 4A of Eugene F. Brigham and Louis C. Gapenski, *Intermediate Financial Management,* 5th ed. (Forth Worth, Tex.: Dryden Press, 1996).

We see that the value of a perpetuity changes dramatically when interest rates change. Perpetuities are discussed further in Chapter 9.

SELF-TEST
QUESTIONS

What happens to the value of a perpetuity when interest rates increase? What happens when interest rates decrease? Why do these changes occur?

UNEVEN CASH FLOW STREAMS

The definition of an annuity includes the words *constant payment*—in other words, annuities involve payments that are equal in every period. Although many financial decisions do involve constant payments, other important decisions involve uneven, or nonconstant, cash flows; for example, common stocks typically pay an increasing stream of dividends over time, and fixed asset investments such as new equipment normally do not generate constant cash flows. Consequently, it is necessary to extend our time value discussion to include **uneven cash flow streams.**

Throughout the book, we will follow convention and reserve the term **payment (PMT)** for annuity situations where the cash flows are equal amounts, and we will use the term **cash flow (CF)** to denote uneven cash flows. Financial calculators are set up to follow this convention, so if you are dealing with uneven cash flows, you will need to use the "cash flow register."

Present Value of an Uneven Cash Flow Stream

The PV of an uneven cash flow stream is found as the sum of the PVs of the individual cash flows of the stream. For example, suppose we must find the PV of the following cash flow stream, discounted at 6 percent:

0		1	2	3	4	5	6	7
	6%							
PV = ?		100	200	200	200	200	0	1,000

The PV will be found by applying this general present value equation:

$$PV = CF_1\left(\frac{1}{1+i}\right)^1 + CF_2\left(\frac{1}{1+i}\right)^2 + \cdots + CF_n\left(\frac{1}{1+i}\right)^n$$

$$= \sum_{t=1}^{n} CF_t\left(\frac{1}{1+i}\right)^t = \sum_{t=1}^{n} CF_t(PVIF_{i,t}).$$

(7-6)

We could find the PV of each individual cash flow using the numerical, tabular, or financial calculator methods, and then sum these values to find the present value of the stream. Here is what the process would look like:

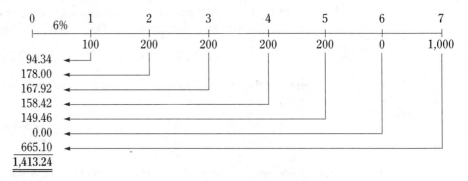

0		1	2	3	4	5	6	7
	6%							
		100	200	200	200	200	0	1,000

94.34
178.00
167.92
158.42
149.46
0.00
665.10
1,413.24

All we did was to apply Equation 7-6, show the individual PVs in the left column of the diagram, and then sum these individual PVs to find the PV of the entire stream.

The present value of a cash flow stream can always be found by summing the present values of the individual cash flows as shown above. However, cash flow regularities within the stream may allow the use of shortcuts. For example, notice that Cash Flows 2 through 5 represent an annuity. We can use that fact to solve the problem in a slightly different manner:

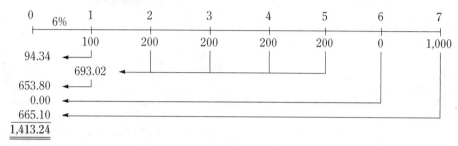

Cash flows during Years 2 to 5 represent an ordinary annuity, and we find its PV at Year 1 (one period before the first payment). This PV ($693.02) must then be discounted back one more period to get its Year 0 value, $653.80.

Problems involving uneven cash flows can be solved in one step with most financial calculators. First, you input the individual cash flows, in chronological order, into the cash flow register. Cash flows are usually designated CF_0, CF_1, CF_2, CF_3, and so on. Next, you enter the interest rate, I. At this point, you have substituted in all the known values of Equation 7-6, so you only need to press the NPV key to find the present value of the stream. The calculator has been programmed to find the PV of each cash flow and then to sum these values to find the PV of the entire stream. To input the cash flows for this problem, enter 0 (because $CF_0 = 0$), 100, 200, 200, 200, 200, 0, 1000 in that order into the cash flow register, enter I = 6, and then press NPV to obtain the answer, $1,413.19. This answer differs slightly from the long-form solution because of rounding differences.

Two points should be noted. First, when dealing with the cash flow register, the calculator uses the term "NPV" rather than "PV." The N stands for "net," so NPV is the abbreviation for "Net Present Value," which is simply the net present value of a series of positive and negative cash flows. Our example has no negative cash flows, but if it did, we would simply input them with negative signs.[7]

The second point to note is that annuities can be entered into the cash flow register more efficiently by using the N_j key. (On some calculators, you are prompted to enter the number of times the cash flow occurs, and on still other calculators, the procedures for inputting data, as we discuss next, may be different. You should consult your calculator manual or our *Technology Supplement* to determine the appropriate steps for your specific calculator.) In this illustration, you would enter $CF_0 = 0$, $CF_1 = 100$, $CF_2 = 200$, $N_j = 4$ (which tells the calculator that the 200 occurs 4 times), $CF_6 = 0$, and $CF_7 = 1000$. Then enter I = 6 and press the NPV key, and 1,413.19 will appear in the display. Also, note that amounts entered into the cash flow register remain in the register until they are cleared. Thus, if you had previously worked a problem with eight cash flows, and then moved to a problem with only four cash flows, the calculator

---

[7]To input negative numbers, type in the positive number, then press the +/− key to change the sign to negative. If you begin by typing the minus sign, you make the mistake of subtracting the negative number from the last number that was entered in the calculator.

would simply add the cash flows from the second problem to those of the first problem. Therefore, you must be sure to clear the cash flow register before starting a new problem.

Spreadsheets are especially useful for solving problems with uneven cash flows. Just as with financial calculators, you must enter the cash flows in the spreadsheet:

	A	B	C	D	E	F	G	H	I
1	Interest rate	0.06							
2	Time	0	1	2	3	4	5	6	7
3	Cash flow		100	200	200	200	200	0	1,000
4	Present value	1,413.19							

One of the advantages of spreadsheets over financial calculators is that you can see the cash flows, which makes it easy to spot any typing errors. The formula in Cell B4 is the now familiar NPV function, =**NPV(B1,C3:I3)**, entered using the function wizard with the B1 cell reference for the interest rate.

Future Value of an Uneven Cash Flow Stream

The future value of an uneven cash flow stream (sometimes called the **terminal value**) is found by compounding each payment to the end of the stream and then summing the future values:

$$FV_n = CF_1(1+i)^{n-1} + CF_2(1+i)^{n-2} + \cdots + CF_n(1+i)^{n-t}$$

$$= \sum_{t=1}^{n} CF_t(1+i)^{n-t} = \sum_{t=1}^{n} CF_t(FVIF_{i,n-t}).$$

(7-7)

The future value of our illustrative uneven cash flow stream is $2,124.92:

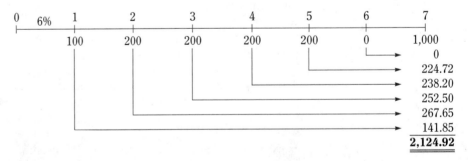

Some financial calculators have a net future value (NFV) key which, after the cash flows and interest rate have been entered, can be used to obtain the future value of an uneven cash flow stream. In any event, it is easy enough to compound the individual cash flows to the terminal year and then sum them to find the FV of the stream. Also, we are generally more interested in the present value of an asset's cash flow stream than in the future value because the present value represents today's value, which is used to find the fair value of the asset. Finally, note that the cash flow stream's net present value can be used to find its net future value: NFV = NPV $(1 + i)^n$. Thus, in our example, you could find the PV of the stream, then find the FV of that PV, compounded for n periods at i percent. In the illustrative problem, find

PV = 1,413.19 using the cash flow register and I = 6%. Then enter N = 7, I = 6, PV = −1,413.19, and PMT = 0, and then press FV to find FV = 2,124.92, which equals the NFV shown on the time line above.

Solving for i with Uneven Cash Flow Streams

It is relatively easy to solve for i numerically or with the tables when the cash flows are lump sums or annuities. However, it is *extremely difficult* to solve for i if the cash flows are uneven, because then you would have to go through many tedious trial-and-error calculations. With a spreadsheet program or a financial calculator, though, it is easy to find the value of i. For example, with a financial calculator input the CF values into the cash flow register and then press the IRR key. IRR stands for "internal rate of return," which is the percentage return on an investment. We will defer further discussion of this calculation for now, but we will take it up later, in our discussion of capital budgeting methods in Chapter 11.[8]

Give two examples of financial decisions that would typically involve uneven cash flows. (Hint: Think about a bond or a stock which you plan to hold for five years.)

What is meant by the term "terminal value"?

SEMIANNUAL AND OTHER COMPOUNDING PERIODS

In all of our examples thus far, we have assumed that interest is compounded once a year, or annually. This is called **annual compounding.** Suppose, however, that you put $100 into a bank which states that it pays a 6 percent annual interest rate but that interest is credited each six months. This is called **semiannual compounding.** How much would you have accumulated at the end of one year, two years, or some other period under semiannual compounding? Note that virtually all bonds pay interest semiannually, most stocks pay dividends quarterly, and most mortgages, student loans, and auto loans require monthly payments. Therefore, it is essential that you understand how to deal with nonannual compounding.

To illustrate semiannual compounding, assume that $100 is placed into an account at an interest rate of 6 percent and left there for three years. First, consider again what would happen under *annual* compounding:

1. Time Line, Equation, and Numerical Solution:

$$\text{FV}_n = \text{PV}(1 + i)^n = \$100(1.06)^3$$
$$= \$119.10.$$

2. Tabular Solution:

$$\text{FV}_3 = \$100(\text{FVIF}_{6\%,3}) = \$100(1.1910) = \$119.10.$$

---

[8]To obtain an IRR solution, at least one of the cash flows must have a negative sign, indicating that it is an investment. Since none of the CFs in our example were negative, the cash flow stream has no IRR. However, had we input a cost for CF_0, say, −$1,000, we could have obtained an IRR, which would be the rate of return earned on the $1,000 investment. Here IRR = 13.96%.

3. Financial Calculator Solution:

Inputs: 3   6   −100   0

Output: = 119.10

4. Spreadsheet Solution:

A spreadsheet could be developed as we did earlier in the chapter in our discussion of future value. Rows would be set up to show the interest rate (6 percent), time (t = 0 through t = 3), and cash flow (−100 at t = 0). Then the future value at t = 3, 119.10, could be determined with an *Excel* formula.

The above calculations are for *annual* compounding, but our bank account pays interest *semiannually,* which is more frequent than once a year. Whenever payments occur more frequently than once a year, or when interest is stated to be compounded more than once a year, then you must convert the stated interest rate to a "periodic rate" and the number of years to "number of periods," as follows:

Periodic rate = Stated rate/Number of payments per year.

Number of periods = Number of years × Periods per year.

In our example, where we must find the value of $100 after three years when the stated interest rate is 6 percent, compounded semiannually (or twice a year), you would begin by making the following conversions:

Periodic rate = 6%/2 = 3%.

Periods = N = 3 × 2 = 6.

In this situation, the investment will earn 3 percent every six months over six periods, not 6 percent per year for three years. As we shall see, there is a significant difference between these two procedures.

You should make the conversions as your first step when working on such a problem *because calculations must be done using the appropriate number of periods and periodic rate, not the number of years and stated rate.* Periodic rates and number of periods, not yearly rates and number of years, should normally be shown on time lines and entered into your calculator whenever you are dealing with nonannual compounding.[9]

With this background, we can now find the value of $100 after three years if it is held in an account that pays a stated rate of 6 percent, but with semiannual compounding. Here is the time line:

Time Line:

1. Equation and Numerical Solution:

$$FV_n = PV(1 + i)^n = \$100(1.03)^6$$

$$= \$100(1.1941) = \$119.41.$$

---

[9]With some financial calculators, you can enter the annual (nominal) rate and the number of compounding periods rather than make the conversion we recommend. We prefer making the conversion because it is easier to see the problem setup in a time line, and also because it is easy to forget to readjust your calculator after you change its settings and to then make an error on the next problem because of the incorrect setting.

Here i = rate per period = annual rate/compounding periods per year = 6%/2 = 3%, and n = the total number of periods = years × periods per year = 3 × 2 = 6.

2. Tabular Solution:

$$FV_6 = \$100(FVIF_{3\%,6}) = \$100(1.1941) = \$119.41.$$

Look up FVIF for 3%, 6 periods in Table A-3 and complete the arithmetic.

3. Financial Calculator Solution:

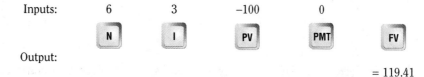

Inputs: 6   3   −100   0

Output:
= 119.41

Enter N = years × periods per year = 3 × 2 = 6, I = annual rate/periods per year = 6/2 = 3, PV = −100, and PMT = 0. Then press FV to find the answer, $119.41.

4. Spreadsheet Solution:

The spreadsheet developed to find the future value of a lump sum under semiannual compounding would look like the one for annual compounding, with two changes: The interest rate would be halved, and the time line would show twice as many periods. The future value under semiannual compounding, $119.41, would be larger than $119.10, the future value under annual compounding, because interest on interest is being earned more frequently.

Throughout the world economy, different compounding periods are used for different types of investments. For example, bank accounts generally pay interest daily; most bonds pay interest semiannually; and stocks generally pay dividends quarterly.[10] If we are to properly compare securities with different compounding periods, we need to put them on a common basis. This requires us to distinguish between **nominal, or quoted, interest rates** and **effective, or equivalent, annual rates.**[11]

The nominal, or quoted, or stated, interest rate in our example is 6 percent. *The effective (or equivalent) annual rate (EAR, also called EFF%) is defined as that rate which would produce the same ending (future) value if annual compounding had been used.* In our example, the effective annual rate is the once-a-year rate which would produce an FV of $119.41 at the end of Year 3. Here is a time line of the situation:

```
 0 EAR (or EFF%) 1              2            3 Years
 |               |              |            |
-100                                        119.41
```

Our task now is to find the effective annual rate, EAR or EFF%, that is equivalent to 6 percent with semiannual compounding.

---

[10]Some banks and savings and loans even pay interest compounded *continuously.* Continuous compounding is discussed in the Extensions section of this chapter.

[11]The term *nominal rate* as it is used here has a different meaning than the way it was used in Chapter 4. There, nominal interest rates referred to stated market rates as opposed to real (zero inflation) rates. In this chapter, the term *nominal rate* means the stated, or quoted, annual rate as opposed to the effective annual rate. In both cases, though, *nominal* means *stated,* or *quoted,* as opposed to some adjusted rate.

We can determine the effective annual rate, given the nominal rate and the number of compounding periods per year, by solving this equation:

$$\text{Effective annual rate} = \text{EAR (or EFF\%)} = \left(1 + \frac{i_{\text{Nom}}}{m}\right)^m - 1.0. \qquad \textbf{(7-8)}$$

Here i_{Nom} is the nominal, or quoted, interest rate, and m is the number of compounding periods per year. For example, to find the effective annual rate if the nominal rate is 6 percent and semiannual compounding is used, we have[12]

$$\text{Effective annual rate} = \text{EAR (or EFF\%)} = \left(1 + \frac{0.06}{2}\right)^2 - 1.0$$

$$= (1.03)^2 - 1.0$$

$$= 1.0609 - 1.0 = 0.0609 = 6.09\%.$$

The points made about semiannual compounding can be generalized: When compounding occurs more frequently than once a year, we can use a modified version of Equation 7-1 to find the future value of any lump sum:

$$\text{Annual compounding: } FV_n = PV(1 + i)^n. \qquad \textbf{(7-1)}$$

$$\text{More frequent compounding: } FV_n = PV\left(1 + \frac{i_{\text{Nom}}}{m}\right)^{mn}. \qquad \textbf{(7-9)}$$

Here i_{Nom} is the nominal, or quoted, rate, m is the number of times compounding occurs per year, and n is the number of years. For example, when banks pay daily interest, the value of m is set at 365 and Equation 7-9 is applied.[13]

To illustrate the effect of compounding monthly rather than annually, consider the interest rate charged on credit cards. Many banks charge 1.5 percent per month, and, in their advertising, they state that the **Annual Percentage Rate (APR)** is $1.5 \times 12 = 18$ percent. However, the "true" rate is the effective annual rate of 19.6 percent:

$$\text{Effective annual rate} = \text{EAR (or EFF\%)} = \left(1 + \frac{0.18}{12}\right)^{12} - 1$$

$$= (1.015)^{12} - 1.0$$

$$= 0.196 = 19.6\%.$$

Semiannual and other compounding periods can also be used for discounting, and for both lump sums and annuities. First, consider the case where we want to find the PV of an ordinary annuity of $100 per year for three years when the interest rate is 8 percent, *compounded annually:*

Time Line:

```
      0    8%    1          2          3
      ├─────────┼──────────┼──────────┤
   PV = ?      100        100        100
```

---

[12]Most financial calculators are programmed to find the EAR or, given the EAR, to find the nominal rate. This is called "interest rate conversion," and you simply enter the nominal rate and the number of compounding periods per year and then press the EFF% key to find the effective annual rate.

[13]To illustrate, the future value of $1 invested at 10 percent for 1 year under daily compounding is $1.1052:

$$FV_n = \$1\left(1 + \frac{0.10}{365}\right)^{365(1)} = \$1(1.105156) = \$1.1052.$$

Note also that banks sometimes use 360 as the number of days per year for this and other calculations.

1. Numerical Solution:

Find the PV of each cash flow and sum them. The PV of the annuity is $257.71.

2. Tabular Solution:

$$PVA_n = PMT(PVIFA_{i,n})$$
$$= \$100(PVIFA_{8\%,3}) = \$100(2.5771) = \$257.71.$$

3. Financial Calculator Solution:

Inputs: 3   8   100   0

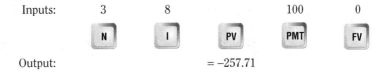

Output: = −257.71

4. Spreadsheet Solution:

A spreadsheet could be developed as we did earlier in the chapter in our discussion of the present value of an annuity. Rows would be set up to show the interest rate (8 percent), time (t = 0 through t = 3), and cash flows (100 at t = 1 through t = 3). Then the present value of the annuity, 257.71, could be determined using the *Excel* PV function.

Now, let's change the situation to *semiannual compounding,* where the annuity calls for payments of $50 each six months rather than $100 per year, and the rate is 8 percent, compounded semiannually. Here is the time line:

Time Line:

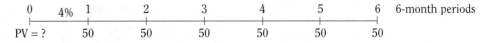

1. Numerical Solution:

Find the PV of each cash flow by discounting at 4 percent. Treat each tick mark on the time line as a period, so there are six periods. The PV of the annuity turns out to be $262.11 versus $257.71 under annual compounding.

2. Tabular Solution:

$$PVA_n = PMT(PVIFA_{i,n})$$
$$= \$50(PVIFA_{4\%,6}) = \$50(5.2421) = \$262.11.$$

3. Financial Calculator Solution:

Inputs: 6   4   50   0

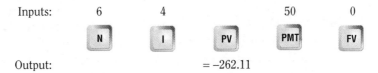

Output: = −262.11

4. Spreadsheet Solution:

The spreadsheet developed to find the present value of an annuity under semiannual compounding would look like the one for annual compounding, but the interest rate and annuity payment would be halved, and the time line would have twice as many periods.

The annuity value with semiannual compounding is 262.11, which is greater than the annual annuity value. The reason is that the semiannual payments come in sooner, so the $50 semiannual annuity is more valuable than the $100 annual annuity.

SELF-TEST
QUESTIONS

What changes must you make in your calculations to determine the future value of an amount that is being compounded at 8 percent semiannually versus one being compounded annually at 8 percent?

Why is semiannual compounding better than annual compounding from a saver's standpoint? What about a borrower's standpoint?

Define the terms "annual percentage rate," "effective (or equivalent) annual rate," and "nominal interest rate."

How does the term "nominal rate" as used in this chapter differ from the term as it was used in Chapter 4?

COMPARISON OF DIFFERENT TYPES OF INTEREST RATES

People in finance often work with three types of interest rates: nominal rates, i_{Nom}; periodic rates, i_{PER}; and effective annual rates, EAR or EFF%. Therefore, it is essential that you understand what each one is and when it should be used.

1. **Nominal, or quoted, rate.** This is the rate that is quoted by banks, brokers, and other financial institutions. So, if you talk with a banker, broker, mortgage lender, auto finance company, or student loan officer about rates, the nominal rate is the one he or she will normally quote you. However, to be meaningful, the quoted nominal rate must also include the number of compounding periods per year. For example, a bank might offer 8.5 percent, compounded quarterly, on CDs, or a mutual fund might offer 8 percent, compounded monthly, on its money market account.

   The nominal rate is also called the Annual Percentage Rate (APR). If a credit card issuer quotes an APR rate of 18 percent, monthly, this means an interest rate of $18/12 = 1.5$ percent per month.

   Nominal rates can be compared with one another, *but only if the instruments being compared use the same number of compounding periods per year.* Thus, you could compare the quoted yields on two bonds if they both pay interest semi-annually. However, to compare an 8.5 percent, annual payment CD with an 8 per-cent, daily payment money market fund, we would need to put both instruments on an *effective (or equivalent) annual rate (EAR)* basis as discussed later in this section.

   Note that the nominal rate is never shown on a time line, and it is never used as an input in a financial calculator (unless compounding occurs only once a year, in which case i_{Nom} = periodic rate = EAR). If more frequent compounding occurs, you should use the periodic rate as discussed below.

2. **Periodic rate, i_{PER}.** This is the rate charged by a lender or paid by a borrower each period. It can be a rate per year, per six-month period, per quarter, per month, per day, or per any other time interval. For example, a bank might charge 1.5 percent per month on its credit card loans, or a finance company might charge 3 percent per quarter on consumer loans. We find the periodic rate as follows:

$$\text{Periodic rate, } i_{PER} = i_{Nom}/m, \tag{7-10}$$

which implies that

$$\text{Nominal annual rate} = i_{Nom} = (\text{Periodic rate})(m). \qquad \textbf{(7-11)}$$

Here i_{Nom} is the nominal annual rate and m is the number of compounding periods per year. To illustrate, consider a finance company loan at 3 percent per quarter:

$$\text{Nominal annual rate} = i_{Nom} = (\text{Periodic rate})(m) = (3\%)(4) = 12\%,$$

or

$$\text{Periodic rate} = i_{Nom}/m = 12\%/4 = 3\% \text{ per quarter.}$$

If there is only one payment per year, or if interest is added only once a year, then m = 1, and the periodic rate is equal to the nominal rate.

The periodic rate is the rate that is generally shown on time lines and used in calculations.[14] To illustrate use of the periodic rate, suppose you make the following eight quarterly payments of $100 each into an account which pays a nominal rate of 12 percent, compounded quarterly. How much would you have after two years?

Time Line and Equation:

$$FVA_n = \sum_{t=1}^{n} PMT(1 + i)^{n-t} = \sum_{t=1}^{8} \$100(1.03)^{8-t}.$$

1. Numerical Solution:

Compound each $100 payment at 12/4 = 3 percent for the appropriate number of periods, and then sum these individual FVs to find the FV of the payment stream, $889.23.

2. Tabular Solution:

Look up FVIFA for 3%, 8 periods, in Table A-4, and complete the arithmetic:

$$FVA_n = PMT(FVIFA_{i,n})$$

$$= \$100(FVIFA_{3\%,8}) = \$100(8.8923) = \$889.23.$$

---

[14]The only exception is in situations where (1) annuities are involved and (2) the payment periods do not correspond to the compounding periods. If an annuity is involved and if its payment periods do not correspond to the compounding periods—for example, if you are making quarterly payments into a bank account to build up a specified future sum, but the bank pays interest on a daily basis—then the calculations are more complicated. For such problems, one can proceed in two alternative ways. (1) Determine the periodic (daily) interest rate by dividing the nominal rate by 360 (or 365 if the bank uses a 365-day year), then compound each payment over the exact number of days from the payment date to the terminal point, and then sum the compounded payments to find the future value of the annuity. This is what would generally be done in the real world, because with a computer, it would be a simple process. (2) Calculate the EAR based on daily compounding, then find the corresponding nominal rate based on quarterly compounding (because the annuity payments are made quarterly), then find the quarterly periodic rate, and then use that rate with standard annuity procedures. The second procedure is faster with a calculator, but hard to explain and generally not used in practice given the ready availability of computers.

3. Financial Calculator Solution:

Inputs: 8   3   0   −100

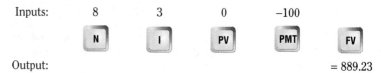

Output: = 889.23

Input N = 2 × 4 = 8, I = 12/4 = 3, PV = 0, and PMT = −100, and then press the FV key to get FV = $889.23.

4. Spreadsheet Solution:

A spreadsheet could be developed as we did earlier in the chapter in our discussion of the future value of an annuity. Rows would be set up to show the interest rate, time, cash flow, and future value of the annuity. The interest rate used in the spreadsheet would be the periodic interest rate (i_{Nom}/m) and the number of time periods shown would be (m)(n).

3. **Effective (or equivalent) annual rate (EAR).** This is the annual rate which produces the same result as if we had compounded at a given periodic rate m times per year. The EAR is found as follows:

$$\text{EAR (or EFF\%)} = \left(1 + \frac{i_{Nom}}{m}\right)^m - 1.0. \qquad \textbf{(7-8)}$$

You could also use the interest conversion feature of a financial calculator.

In the EAR equation, i_{Nom}/m is the periodic rate, and m is the number of periods per year. For example, suppose you could borrow using either a credit card which charges 1 percent per month or a bank loan with a 12 percent quoted nominal interest rate that is compounded quarterly. Which should you choose? To answer this question, the cost rate of each alternative must be expressed as an EAR:

$$\text{Credit card loan: EAR} = (1 + 0.01)^{12} - 1.0 = (1.01)^{12} - 1.0$$

$$= 1.126825 - 1.0 = 0.126825 = 12.6825\%.$$

$$\text{Bank loan: EAR} = (1 + 0.03)^4 - 1.0 = (1.03)^4 - 1.0$$

$$= 1.125509 - 1.0 = 0.125509 = 12.5509\%.$$

Thus, the credit card loan is slightly more costly than the bank loan. This result should have been intuitive to you—both loans have the same 12 percent nominal rate, yet you would have to make monthly payments on the credit card versus quarterly payments under the bank loan.

The EAR rate generally is not used in calculations. Rather, it is used to compare the effective cost or rate of return on loans or investments when payment periods differ, as in the credit card versus bank loan example.

SELF-TEST
QUESTIONS

Define the nominal (or quoted) rate, the periodic rate, and the effective annual rate.

How are the nominal rate, the periodic rate, and the effective annual rate related?

What is the one situation where all three of these rates will be the same?

Which rate should generally be shown on time lines and used in calculations?

FRACTIONAL TIME PERIODS

In all the examples used thus far in the chapter, we have assumed that payments occur at either the beginning or the end of periods, but not at some date *within* a period.

However, we often encounter situations that require compounding or discounting over fractional periods. For example, suppose you deposited $100 in a bank that pays 10 percent interest, interest added annually. How much would be in your account after nine months, or 75 percent of the way through the year? The answer is $100; since interest is added only at the end of the year, no interest would have been added after only nine months. Years ago, before computers made daily compounding easy, banks really did compound interest annually, but today they generally credit interest daily.

Now let's ask a more realistic question: If a bank adds interest to your account daily, that is, uses daily compounding, and the nominal rate is 10 percent with a 360-day year, how much will be in your account after nine months? The answer is $107.79:[15]

$$\text{Periodic rate} = i_{PER} = 0.10/360 = 0.00027778 \text{ per day.}$$

$$\text{Number of days} = 0.75(360) = 270.$$

$$\text{Ending amount} = \$100(1.00027778)^{270} = \$107.79.$$

Now suppose you borrow $100 from a bank which charges 10 percent per year "simple interest," which means annual rather than daily compounding, but you borrow the $100 for only 270 days. How much interest will you have to pay for the use of $100 for 270 days? Here we would calculate a daily interest rate, i_{PER}, as above, but multiply by 270 rather than use it as an exponent:

$$\text{Interest owed} = \$100(0.00027778)(270) = \$7.50 \text{ interest charged.}$$

You would owe the bank a total of $107.50 after 270 days. This is the procedure most banks actually use to calculate interest on loans.

Finally, let's consider a somewhat different situation. Say an Internet access firm had 100 customers at the end of 1997, and its customer base is expected to grow steadily at the rate of 10 percent per year. What is the estimated customer base nine months into the new year? This problem would be set up exactly like the bank account with daily compounding, and the estimate would be 107.79 customers, rounded to 108.[16]

The most important thing in problems like these, as in all time value problems, is to be careful! Think about what is involved in a logical, systematic manner, draw a time line if it would help you visualize the situation, and then apply the appropriate equations.

AMORTIZED LOANS

One of the most important applications of compound interest involves loans that are paid off in installments over time. Included are automobile loans, home mortgage loans, student loans, and most business loans other than very short-term loans and long-term bonds. If a loan is to be repaid in equal periodic amounts (monthly, quarterly, or annually), it is said to be an **amortized loan.**[17]

To illustrate, suppose a firm borrows $1,000, and the loan is to be repaid in three equal payments at the end of each of the next three years. (In this case, there is only

---

[15]Here we assumed a 360-day year, and we also assumed that the nine months all have 30 days. In real-world calculations, the bank's computer (and many financial calculators) would have a built-in calendar, and if you input the beginning and ending dates, the computer or calculator would tell you the exact number of days, taking account of 30-day months, 31-day months, and 28- or 29-day months.

[16]If the number of customers truly is growing *steadily*, then you could use continuous compounding as described in the Extension section to this chapter.

[17]The word *amortized* comes from the Latin *mors,* meaning "death," so an amortized loan is one that is "killed off" over time.

one payment per year, so years = periods and the stated rate = periodic rate.) The lender charges a 6 percent interest rate on the loan balance that is outstanding at the beginning of each year. The first task is to determine the amount the firm must repay each year, or the constant annual payment. To find this amount, recognize that the $1,000 represents the present value of an annuity of PMT dollars per year for three years, discounted at 6 percent:

Time Line and Equation:

$$
\begin{array}{ccccccc}
0 & 6\% & 1 & & 2 & & 3 \\
\vdash & & \dashv & & \dashv & & \dashv \\
1{,}000 & & \text{PMT} & & \text{PMT} & & \text{PMT}
\end{array}
$$

$$PV = \frac{PMT}{(1+i)^1} + \frac{PMT}{(1+i)^2} + \frac{PMT}{(1+i)^3} = \sum_{t=1}^{3} \frac{PMT}{(1+i)^t}$$

$$\$1{,}000 = \sum_{t=1}^{3} \frac{PMT}{(1.06)^t}.$$

Here we know everything except PMT, so we can solve the equation for PMT.

1. Numerical Solution:

You could follow the trial-and-error procedure, inserting values for PMT in the equation until you found a value that "worked" and caused the right side of the equation to equal $1,000. This would be a tedious process, but you would eventually find PMT = $374.11.

2. Tabular Solution:

Substitute in known values and look up PVIFA for 6%, 3 periods in Table A-2:

$$PVA_n = PMT(PVIFA_{i,n})$$

$$\$1{,}000 = PMT(PVIFA_{6\%,3}) = PMT(2.6730)$$

$$PMT = \$1{,}000/2.6730 = \$374.11.$$

3. Financial Calculator Solution:

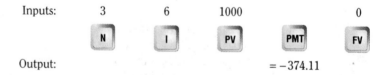

Inputs: 3   6   1000   0

N   I   PV   PMT   FV

Output: = −374.11

Enter N = 3, I = 6, PV = 1000, and FV = 0, and then press the PMT key to find PMT = −$374.11.

4. Spreadsheet Solution:

The spreadsheet is ideal for developing amortization tables. The setup is similar to Table 7-2, but you would want to include "input" cells for the interest rate, principal value, and the length of the loan. This would make the spreadsheet flexible in the sense that the loan terms could be changed and a new amortization table would be recalculated instantly. Then use the function wizard to find the payment. If you had I = 6% in B1, N = 3 in B2, and PV = 1000 in B3, then the function = PMT(B1, B2, B3) would find the payment, $374.11.

TABLE 7-2		Loan Amortization Schedule, 6 Percent Interest Rate			

YEAR	BEGINNING AMOUNT (1)	PAYMENT (2)	INTEREST[a] (3)	REPAYMENT OF PRINCIPAL[b] (2) − (3) = (4)	REMAINING BALANCE (1) − (4) = (5)
1	$1,000.00	$ 374.11	$ 60.00	$ 314.11	$685.89
2	685.89	374.11	41.15	332.96	352.93
3	352.93	374.11	21.18	352.93	0.00
		$1,122.33	$122.33	$1,000.00	

[a]Interest is calculated by multiplying the loan balance at the beginning of the year by the interest rate. Therefore, interest in Year 1 is $1,000(0.06) = $60; in Year 2 it is $685.89(0.06) = $41.15; and in Year 3 it is $352.93(0.06) = $21.18.

[b]Repayment of principal is equal to the payment of $374.11 minus the interest charge for each year.

The firm must pay the lender $374.11 at the end of each of the next three years, and the percentage cost to the borrower, which is also the rate of return to the lender, will be 6 percent. Each payment consists partly of interest and partly of repayment of principal. This breakdown is given in the **amortization schedule** shown in Table 7-2. The interest component is largest in the first year, and it declines as the outstanding balance of the loan decreases. For tax purposes, a business borrower or homeowner reports the interest component shown in Column 3 as a deductible cost each year, while the lender reports this same amount as taxable income.

Financial calculators are programmed to calculate amortization tables — you simply enter the input data, and then press one key to get each entry in Table 7-2. If you have a financial calculator, it is worthwhile to read the appropriate section of the calculator manual and learn how to use its amortization feature. With a spreadsheet such as *Excel* or *Lotus,* it is easy to set up and print out a full amortization schedule.

S E L F - T E S T
Q U E S T I O N S

To construct an amortization schedule, how do you determine the periodic payment?

How do you determine the amount of each payment that goes to interest and to principal?

SUMMARY

Financial decisions often involve situations in which someone pays money at one point in time and receives money at some later time. Dollars that are paid or received at two different points in time are different, and this difference is recognized and accounted for by *time value of money (TVM) analysis.* We summarize below the types of TVM analysis and the key concepts covered in this chapter, using the data shown in Figure 7-3 to illustrate the various points. Refer to the figure constantly, and try to find in it an example of the points covered as you go through this summary.

- **Compounding** is the process of determining the **future value (FV)** of a cash flow or a series of cash flows. The compounded amount, or future value, is equal to the beginning amount plus the interest earned.

- Future value: $FV_n = PV(1 + i)^n = PV(FVIF_{i,n}).$
  (single payment)

FIGURE 7-3   Illustration for Chapter Summary
(i = 4%, Annual Compounding)

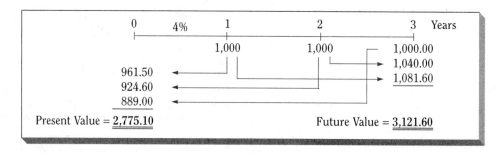

Example $1,000 compounded for 1 year at 4 percent:

$$FV_1 = \$1,000(1.04)^1 = \$1,040.$$

- **Discounting** is the process of finding the **present value (PV)** of a future cash flow or a series of cash flows; discounting is the reciprocal of compounding.

- Present value: $PV = \dfrac{FV_n}{(1 + i)^n} = FV_n\left(\dfrac{1}{1 + i}\right)^n = FV_n(PVIF_{i,n}).$
  (single payment)

Example: $1,000 discounted back for 2 years at 4 percent:

$$PV = \frac{\$1,000}{(1.04)^2} = \$1,000\left(\frac{1}{1.04}\right)^2 = \$1,000(0.9246) = \$924.60.$$

- An **annuity** is defined as a series of equal periodic payments (PMT) for a specified number of periods.
- Future value:
  (annuity)

$$FVA_n = PMT(1 + i)^{n-1} + PMT(1 + i)^{n-2} + PMT(1 + i)^{n-3} + \cdots + PMT(1 + i)^0$$

$$= PMT \sum_{t=1}^{n} (1 + i)^{n-t}$$

$$= PMT \left(\frac{(1 + i)^n - 1}{i}\right)$$

$$= PMT(FVIFA_{i,n}).$$

Example: FVA of 3 payments of $1,000 when i = 4%:

$$FVA_3 = \$1,000(3.1216) = \$3,121.60.$$

- Present value: $PVA_n = \dfrac{PMT}{(1 + i)^1} + \dfrac{PMT}{(1 + i)^2} + \cdots + \dfrac{PMT}{(1 + i)^n}$
  (annuity)

$$= PMT \sum_{t=1}^{n} \left[\frac{1}{1 + i}\right]^t = PMT \left(\frac{1 - \dfrac{1}{(1 + i)^n}}{i}\right)$$

$$= PMT(PVIFA_{i,n}).$$

Example: PVA of 3 payments of $1,000 when i = 4% per period:

$$PVA_3 = \$1,000(2.7751) = \$2,775.10.$$

- An annuity whose payments occur at the *end* of each period is called an **ordinary annuity.** The formulas above are for ordinary annuities.

- If each payment occurs at the *beginning* of the period rather than at the end, then we have an **annuity due.** In Figure 7-3, the payments would be shown at Years 0, 1, and 2 rather than at Years 1, 2, and 3. The PV of each payment would be larger, because each payment would be discounted back one year less, so the PV of the annuity would also be larger. Similarly, the FV of the annuity due would also be larger because each payment would be compounded for an extra year. The following formulas can be used to convert the PV and FV of an ordinary annuity to an annuity due:

$$PVA \text{ (annuity due)} = PVA \text{ of an ordinary annuity} \times (1 + i), \text{ and}$$

$$FVA \text{ (annuity due)} = FVA \text{ of an ordinary annuity} \times (1 + i).$$

Example: PVA of 3 beginning-of-year payments of $1,000 when i = 4%:

$$PVA \text{ (annuity due)} = \$1,000(2.7751)(1.04) = \$2,886.10.$$

Example: FVA of 3 beginning-of-year payments of $1,000 when i = 4%:

$$FVA \text{ (annuity due)} = \$1,000(3.1216)(1.04) = \$3,246.46.$$

- If the time line in Figure 7-3 were extended out forever so that the $1,000 payments went on forever, we would have a **perpetuity** whose value could be found as follows:

$$\text{Value of perpetuity} = \frac{PMT}{i} = \frac{\$1,000}{0.04} = \$25,000.$$

- If the cash flows in Figure 7-3 were unequal, we could not use the annuity formulas. To find the PV or FV of an uneven series, find the PV or FV of each individual cash flow and then sum them. Note, though, that if some of the cash flows constitute an annuity, then the annuity formula can be used to calculate the present value of that part of the cash flow stream.

- **Financial calculators** have built-in programs which perform all of the operations discussed in this chapter. It would be useful for you to buy such a calculator and to learn how to use it.

- **Spreadsheet programs** are especially useful for problems with many uneven cash flows. They also are very useful if you want to solve a problem repeatedly with different inputs.

- TVM calculations generally involve equations which have four variables, and if you know three of the values, you (or your calculator) can solve for the fourth.

- If you know the cash flows and the PV (or FV) of a cash flow stream, you can **determine the interest rate.** For example, in the Figure 7-3 illustration, if you were given the information that a loan called for 3 payments of $1,000 each, and that the loan had a value today of PV = $2,775.10, then you could find the interest rate that caused the sum of the PVs of the payments to equal $2,775.10. Since we are dealing with an annuity, you could proceed as follows:
  a. With a financial calculator, enter N = 3, PV = 2,775.10, PMT = –1,000, FV = 0, and then press the I key to find I = 4%.
  b. To use the tables, first recognize that $PVA_n = \$2,775.10 = \$1,000(PVIFA_{i,3})$. Then solve for $PVIFA_{i,3}$:

$$PVIFA_{i,3} = \$2,775.10/\$1,000 = 2.7751.$$

Look up 2.7751 in Table A-2, in the third row. It is in the 4% column, so the interest rate must be 4 percent. If the factor did not appear in the table, this would indicate that the interest rate was not a whole number. In that case, you could not use this procedure to find the exact rate. In practice, though, this is not a problem, because in business people use financial calculators or computers to find interest rates.

- Thus far in the summary, we have assumed that payments are made, and interest is earned, annually. However, many contracts call for more frequent payments; for example, mortgage and auto loans call for monthly payments, and most bonds pay interest semiannually. Similarly, most banks compute interest daily. When compounding occurs more frequently than once a year, this fact must be recognized. We can use the Figure 7-3 example to illustrate semiannual compounding. First, recognize that the 4 percent stated rate is a nominal rate which must be converted to a periodic rate, and the number of years must be converted to periods:

$$i_{PER} = \text{Stated rate/Periods per year} = 4\%/2 = 2\%.$$

$$\text{Periods} = \text{Years} \times \text{Periods per year} = 3 \times 2 = 6.$$

The periodic rate and number of periods would be used for calculations and shown on time lines.

If the $1,000 per-year payments were actually payable as $500 each 6 months, you would simply redraw Figure 7-3 to show 6 payments of $500 each, but you would also use a **periodic interest rate** of $4\%/2 = 2\%$ for determining the PV or FV of the payments.

- If we are comparing the costs of loans which require payments more than once a year, or the rates of return on investments which pay interest more frequently, then the comparisons should be based on **equivalent** (or **effective**) rates of return using this formula:

$$\text{Effective annual rate} = \text{EAR (or EFF\%)} = \left(1 + \frac{i_{Nom}}{m}\right)^m - 1.0.$$

For semiannual compounding, the effective annual rate is 4.04 percent:

$$\left(1 + \frac{0.04}{2}\right)^2 - 1.0 = (1.02)^2 - 1.0 = 1.0404 - 1.0 = 0.0404 = 4.04\%.$$

- The general equation for finding the future value for any number of compounding periods per year is:

$$FV_n = PV\left(1 + \frac{i_{Nom}}{m}\right)^{mn},$$

where

i_{Nom} = quoted interest rate.

   m = number of compounding periods per year.

   n = number of years.

- An **amortized loan** is one that is paid off in equal payments over a specified period. An **amortization schedule** shows how much of each payment constitutes interest, how much is used to reduce the principal, and the unpaid balance at each point in time.

The concepts covered in this chapter will be used throughout the remainder of the book. For example, in Chapters 8 and 9, we will apply present value concepts to the process of valuing bonds and stocks, and we will see that the market prices of securities are established by determining the present values of the cash flows they are expected to provide. In later chapters, the same basic concepts are applied to corporate decisions involving expenditures on capital assets, to the types of capital that should be used to pay for assets, to leasing decisions, and so forth.

Questions

7-1 Define each of the following terms:
a. PV; i; INT; FV_n; PVA_n; FVA_n; PMT; m; i_{Nom}
b. $FVIF_{i,n}$; $PVIF_{i,n}$; $FVIFA_{i,n}$; $PVIFA_{i,n}$
c. Opportunity cost rate
d. Annuity; lump sum payment; cash flow; uneven cash flow stream
e. Ordinary (deferred) annuity; annuity due
f. Perpetuity; consol
g. Outflow; inflow; time line
h. Compounding; discounting
i. Annual, semiannual, quarterly, monthly, and daily compounding
j. Effective annual rate (EAR); nominal (quoted) interest rate; APR; periodic rate
k. Amortization schedule; principal component versus interest component of a payment; amortized loan
l. Terminal value

7-2 What is an *opportunity cost rate?* How is this rate used in discounted cash flow analysis, and where is it shown on a time line? Is the opportunity rate a single number which is used in all situations?

7-3 An *annuity* is defined as a series of payments of a fixed amount for a specific number of periods. Thus, $100 a year for 10 years is an annuity, but $100 in Year 1, $200 in Year 2, and $400 in Years 3 through 10 does *not* constitute an annuity. However, the second series *contains* an annuity. Is this statement true or false?

7-4 If a firm's earnings per share grew from $1 to $2 over a 10-year period, the *total growth* would be 100 percent, but the *annual growth rate* would be *less than* 10 percent. True or false? Explain.

7-5 Would you rather have a savings account that pays 5 percent interest compounded semiannually or one that pays 5 percent interest compounded daily? Explain.

7-6 To find the present value of an uneven series of cash flows, you must find the PVs of the individual cash flows and then sum them. Annuity procedures can never be of use, even if some of the cash flows constitute an annuity (for example, $100 each for Years 3, 4, 5, and 6), because the entire series is not an annuity. Is this statement true or false? Explain.

7-7 The present value of a perpetuity is equal to the payment on the annuity, PMT, divided by the interest rate, i: PV = PMT/i. What is the *sum,* or future value, of a perpetuity of PMT dollars per year? (Hint: The answer is infinity, but explain why.)

Self-Test Problems (Solutions Appear in Appendix B)

ST-1
Future Value

Assume that it is now January 1, 1999. On January 1, 2000, you will deposit $1,000 into a savings account that pays 8 percent.
a. If the bank compounds interest annually, how much will you have in your account on January 1, 2003?
b. What would your January 1, 2003, balance be if the bank used quarterly compounding rather than annual compounding?
c. Suppose you deposited the $1,000 in 4 payments of $250 each on January 1 of 2000, 2001, 2002, and 2003. How much would you have in your account on January 1, 2003, based on 8 percent annual compounding?
d. Suppose you deposited 4 equal payments in your account on January 1 of 2000, 2001, 2002, and 2003. Assuming an 8 percent interest rate, how large would each of your payments have to be for you to obtain the same ending balance as you calculated in Part a?

ST-2
Time Value of Money

Assume that it is now January 1, 1999, and you will need $1,000 on January 1, 2003. Your bank compounds interest at an 8 percent annual rate.

a. How much must you deposit on January 1, 2000, to have a balance of $1,000 on January 1, 2003?

b. If you want to make equal payments on each January 1 from 2000 through 2003 to accumulate the $1,000, how large must each of the 4 payments be?

c. If your father were to offer either to make the payments calculated in Part b ($221.92) or to give you a lump sum of $750 on January 1, 2000, which would you choose?

d. If you have only $750 on January 1, 2000, what interest rate, compounded annually, would you have to earn to have the necessary $1,000 on January 1, 2003?

e. Suppose you can deposit only $186.29 each January 1 from 2000 through 2003, but you still need $1,000 on January 1, 2003. What interest rate, with annual compounding, must you seek out to achieve your goal?

f. To help you reach your $1,000 goal, your father offers to give you $400 on January 1, 2000. You will get a part-time job and make 6 additional payments of equal amounts each 6 months thereafter. If all of this money is deposited in a bank which pays 8 percent, compounded semi-annually, how large must each of the 6 payments be?

g. What is the effective annual rate being paid by the bank in Part f?

h. *Reinvestment rate risk* was defined in Chapter 4 as being the risk that maturing securities (and coupon payments on bonds) will have to be reinvested at a lower rate of interest than they were previously earning. Is there a reinvestment rate risk involved in the preceding analysis? If so, how might this risk be eliminated?

ST-3
Effective Annual Rates

Bank A pays 8 percent interest, compounded quarterly, on its money market account. The managers of Bank B want its money market account to equal Bank A's effective annual rate, but interest is to be compounded on a monthly basis. What nominal, or quoted, rate must Bank B set?

Problems

7-1
Present and Future Values for Different Periods

Find the following values, *using the equations,* and then work the problems using a financial calculator or the tables to check your answers. Disregard rounding differences. (Hint: If you are using a financial calculator, you can enter the known values and then press the appropriate key to find the unknown variable. Then, without clearing the TVM register, you can "override" the variable which changes by simply entering a new value for it and then pressing the key for the unknown variable to obtain the second answer. This procedure can be used in Parts b and d, and in many other situations, to see how changes in input variables affect the output variable.)

a. An initial $500 compounded for 1 year at 6 percent.

b. An initial $500 compounded for 2 years at 6 percent.

c. The present value of $500 due in 1 year at a discount rate of 6 percent.

d. The present value of $500 due in 2 years at a discount rate of 6 percent.

7-2
Present and Future Values for Different Interest Rates

Use the tables or a financial calculator to find the following values. See the hint for Problem 7-1.

a. An initial $500 compounded for 10 years at 6 percent.

b. An initial $500 compounded for 10 years at 12 percent.

c. The present value of $500 due in 10 years at a 6 percent discount rate.

d. The present value of $1,552.90 due in 10 years at a 12 percent discount rate and at a 6 percent rate. Give a verbal definition of the term *present value,* and illustrate it using a time line with data from this problem. As a part of your answer, explain why present values are dependent upon interest rates.

7-3
Time for a Lump Sum to Double

To the closest year, how long will it take $200 to double if it is deposited and earns the following rates? [Notes: (1) See the hint for Problem 7-1. (2) This problem cannot be solved exactly with some financial calculators. For example, if you enter PV = −200, PMT = 0, FV = 400, and I = 7 in an HP-12C, and then press the N key, you will get 11 years for Part a. The correct answer is 10.2448 years, which rounds to 10, but the calculator rounds up. However, the HP-10B and HP-17B give the correct answer. You should look up FVIF = 400/200 = 2 in the tables for Parts a, b, and c, but figure out Part d.]

a. 7 percent.

b. 10 percent.

c. 18 percent.

d. 100 percent.

7-4
Future Value of an Annuity

Find the *future value* of the following annuities. The first payment in these annuities is made at the *end* of Year 1; that is, they are *ordinary annuities*. (Note: See the hint to Problem 7-1. Also, note that you can leave values in the TVM register, switch to "BEG," press FV, and find the FV of the annuity due.)

a. $400 per year for 10 years at 10 percent.
b. $200 per year for 5 years at 5 percent.
c. $400 per year for 5 years at 0 percent.
d. Now rework Parts a, b, and c assuming that payments are made at the *beginning* of each year; that is, they are *annuities due*.

7-5
Present Value of an Annuity

Find the *present value* of the following *ordinary annuities* (see note to Problem 7-4):

a. $400 per year for 10 years at 10 percent.
b. $200 per year for 5 years at 5 percent.
c. $400 per year for 5 years at 0 percent.
d. Now rework Parts a, b, and c assuming that payments are made at the *beginning* of each year; that is, they are *annuities due*.

7-6
Uneven Cash Flow Stream

a. Find the present values of the following cash flow streams. The appropriate interest rate is 8 percent. (Hint: It is fairly easy to work this problem dealing with the individual cash flows. However, if you have a financial calculator, read the section of the manual which describes how to enter cash flows such as the ones in this problem. This will take a little time, but the investment will pay huge dividends throughout the course. Note, if you do work with the cash flow register, then you must enter $CF_0 = 0$.)

YEAR	CASH STREAM A	CASH STREAM B
1	$100	$300
2	400	400
3	400	400
4	400	400
5	300	100

b. What is the value of each cash flow stream at a 0 percent interest rate?

7-7
Effective Rate of Interest

Find the interest rates, or rates of return, on each of the following:

a. You *borrow* $700 and promise to pay back $749 at the end of 1 year.
b. You *lend* $700 and receive a promise to be paid $749 at the end of 1 year.
c. You borrow $85,000 and promise to pay back $201,229 at the end of 10 years.
d. You borrow $9,000 and promise to make payments of $2,684.80 per year for 5 years.

7-8
Future Value for Various
Compounding Periods

Find the amount to which $500 will grow under each of the following conditions:

a. 12 percent compounded annually for 5 years.
b. 12 percent compounded semiannually for 5 years.
c. 12 percent compounded quarterly for 5 years.
d. 12 percent compounded monthly for 5 years.

7-9
Present Value for Various
Compounding Periods

Find the present value of $500 due in the future under each of the following conditions:

a. 12 percent nominal rate, semiannual compounding, discounted back 5 years.
b. 12 percent nominal rate, quarterly compounding, discounted back 5 years.
c. 12 percent nominal rate, monthly compounding, discounted back 1 year.

7-10
Future Value of an Annuity for
Various Compounding Periods

Find the future values of the following ordinary annuities:

a. FV of $400 each 6 months for 5 years at a nominal rate of 12 percent, compounded semi-annually.
b. FV of $200 each 3 months for 5 years at a nominal rate of 12 percent, compounded quarterly.
c. The annuities described in Parts a and b have the same amount of money paid into them during the 5-year period and both earn interest at the same nominal rate, yet the annuity in Part b earns $101.60 more than the one in Part a over the 5 years. Why does this occur?

7-11
Effective versus
Nominal Interest Rates

Universal Bank pays 7 percent interest, compounded annually, on time deposits. Regional Bank pays 6 percent interest, compounded quarterly.

a. Based on effective interest rates, in which bank would you prefer to deposit your money?
b. Could your choice of banks be influenced by the fact that you might want to withdraw your funds during the year as opposed to at the end of the year? In answering this question, assume that funds must be left on deposit during the entire compounding period in order for you to receive any interest.

7-12
Amortization Schedule

a. Set up an amortization schedule for a $25,000 loan to be repaid in equal installments at the end of each of the next 5 years. The interest rate is 10 percent.

b. How large must each annual payment be if the loan is for $50,000? Assume that the interest rate remains at 10 percent and that the loan is paid off over 5 years.

c. How large must each payment be if the loan is for $50,000, the interest rate is 10 percent, and the loan is paid off in equal installments at the end of each of the next 10 years? This loan is for the same amount as the loan in Part b, but the payments are spread out over twice as many periods. Why are these payments not half as large as the payments on the loan in Part b?

7-13
Effective Rates of Return

Assume that AT&T's pension fund managers are considering two alternative securities as investments: (1) Security Z (for zero intermediate-year cash flows), which costs $422.41 today, pays nothing during its 10-year life, and then pays $1,000 after 10 years or (2) Security B, which has a cost today of $1,000 and which pays $80 at the end of each of the next 9 years and then $1,080 at the end of Year 10.

a. What is the rate of return on each security?

b. Assume that the interest rate AT&T's pension fund managers can earn on the fund's money falls to 6 percent immediately after the securities are purchased and is expected to remain at that level for the next 10 years. What would the price of each security change to, what would the fund's profit be on each security, and what would be the percentage profit (profit divided by cost) for each security?

c. Assuming that the cash flows for each security had to be reinvested at the new 6 percent market interest rate, (1) what would be the value attributable to each security at the end of 10 years and (2) what "actual, after-the-fact" rate of return would the fund have earned on each security? (Hint: The "actual" rate of return is found as the interest rate which causes the PV of the compounded Year 10 amount to equal the original cost of the security.)

d. Now assume all the facts as given in Parts b and c except assume that the interest rate *rose* to 12 percent rather than fell to 6 percent. What would happen to the profit figures as developed in Part b and to the "actual" rates of return as determined in Part c? Explain your results.

7-14
Required Annuity Payments

A father is planning a savings program to put his daughter through college. His daughter is now 13 years old. She plans to enroll at the university in 5 years, and it should take her 4 years to complete her education. Currently, the cost per year (for everything—food, clothing, tuition, books, transportation, and so forth) is $12,500, but a 5 percent inflation rate in these costs is forecasted. The daughter recently received $7,500 from her grandfather's estate; this money, which is invested in a bank account paying 8 percent interest, compounded annually, will be used to help meet the costs of the daughter's education. The rest of the costs will be met by money the father will deposit in the savings account. He will make 6 equal deposits to the account—one in each year from now until his daughter starts college. These deposits will begin today and will also earn 8 percent interest.

a. What will be the present value of the cost of 4 years of education at the time the daughter becomes 18? [Hint: Calculate the future value of the cost (at 5%) for each year of her education, then discount three of these costs back (at 8%) to the year in which she turns 18, then sum the four costs.]

b. What will be the value of the $7,500 which the daughter received from her grandfather's estate when she starts college at age 18? (Hint: Compound for 5 years at 8%.)

c. If the father is planning to make the first of 6 deposits today, how large must each deposit be for him to be able to put his daughter through college?

7-15
Present Value Comparison

Which amount is worth more at 14 percent: $1,000 in hand today or $2,000 due in 6 years?

7-16
Growth Rates

Hanebury Corporation's 1999 sales were $12 million. Sales were $6 million 5 years earlier (in 1994).

a. To the nearest percentage point, at what rate have sales been growing?

b. Suppose someone calculated the sales growth for Hanebury Corporation in Part a as follows: "Sales doubled in 5 years. This represents a growth of 100 percent in 5 years, so, dividing 100 percent by 5, we find the growth rate to be 20 percent per year." Explain what is wrong with this calculation.

7-17
Expected Rate of Return

Washington-Pacific invests $4 million to clear a tract of land and to set out some young pine trees. The trees will mature in 10 years, at which time Washington-Pacific plans to sell the forest at an expected price of $8 million. What is Washington-Pacific's expected rate of return?

7-18
Effective Rate of Interest

Your broker offers to sell you a note for $13,250 that will pay $2,345.05 per year for 10 years. If you buy the note, what rate of interest (to the closest percent) will you be earning?

7-19
Effective Rate of Interest

A mortgage company offers to lend you $85,000; the loan calls for payments of $8,273.59 per year for 30 years. What interest rate is the mortgage company charging you?

7-20
Required Lump Sum Payment

To complete your last year in business school and then go through law school, you will need $10,000 per year for 4 years, starting next year (that is, you will need to withdraw the first $10,000 one year from today). Your rich uncle offers to put you through school, and he will deposit in a bank paying 7 percent interest a sum of money that is sufficient to provide the four payments of $10,000 each. His deposit will be made today.
a. How large must the deposit be?
b. How much will be in the account immediately after you make the first withdrawal? After the last withdrawal?

7-21
Repaying a Loan

While Mary Corens was a student at the University of Florida, she borrowed $12,000 in student loans at an annual interest rate of 9 percent. If Mary repays $1,500 per year, how long, to the nearest year, will it take her to repay the loan?

7-22
Reaching a Financial Goal

You need to accumulate $10,000. To do so, you plan to make deposits of $1,250 per year, with the first payment being made a year from today, in a bank account which pays 12 percent annual interest. Your last deposit will be less than $1,250 if less is needed to round out to $10,000. How many years will it take you to reach your $10,000 goal, and how large will the last deposit be?

7-23
Present Value of a Perpetuity

What is the present value of a perpetuity of $100 per year if the appropriate discount rate is 7 percent? If interest rates in general were to double and the appropriate discount rate rose to 14 percent, what would happen to the present value of the perpetuity?

7-24
PV and Effective Annual Rate

Assume that you inherited some money. A friend of yours is working as an unpaid intern at a local brokerage firm, and her boss is selling some securities which call for four payments, $50 at the end of each of the next 3 years, plus a payment of $1,050 at the end of Year 4. Your friend says she can get you some of these securities at a cost of $900 each. Your money is now invested in a bank that pays an 8 percent nominal (quoted) interest rate but with quarterly compounding. You regard the securities as being just as safe, and as liquid, as your bank deposit, so your required effective annual rate of return on the securities is the same as that on your bank deposit. You must calculate the value of the securities to decide whether they are a good investment. What is their present value to you?

7-25
Loan Amortization

Assume that your aunt sold her house on December 31 and that she took a mortgage in the amount of $10,000 as part of the payment. The mortgage has a quoted (or nominal) interest rate of 10 percent, but it calls for payments every 6 months, beginning on June 30, and the mortgage is to be amortized over 10 years. Now, 1 year later, your aunt must inform the IRS and the person who bought the house of the interest that was included in the two payments made during the year. (This interest will be income to your aunt and a deduction to the buyer of the house.) To the closest dollar, what is the total amount of interest that was paid during the first year?

7-26
Loan Amortization

Your company is planning to borrow $1,000,000 on a 5-year, 15%, annual payment, fully amortized term loan. What fraction of the payment made at the end of the second year will represent repayment of principal?

7-27
Nonannual Compounding

a. It is now January 1, 1999. You plan to make 5 deposits of $100 each, one every 6 months, with the first payment being made *today*. If the bank pays a nominal interest rate of 12 percent but uses semiannual compounding, how much will be in your account after 10 years?
b. You must make a payment of $1,432.02 ten years from today. To prepare for this payment, you will make 5 equal deposits, beginning today and for the next 4 quarters, in a bank that pays a nominal interest rate of 12 percent, quarterly compounding. How large must each of the 5 payments be?

7-28
Nominal Rate of Return

Anne Lockwood, manager of Oaks Mall Jewelry, wants to sell on credit, giving customers 3 months in which to pay. However, Anne will have to borrow from her bank to carry the accounts payable. The bank will charge a nominal 15 percent, but with monthly compounding. Anne wants to quote a nominal rate to her customers (all of whom are expected to pay on time) which will exactly cover her financing costs. What nominal annual rate should she quote to her credit customers?

7-29
Required Annuity Payments

Assume that your father is now 50 years old, that he plans to retire in 10 years, and that he expects to live for 25 years after he retires, that is, until he is 85. He wants a fixed retirement income that has the same purchasing power at the time he retires as $40,000 has today (he realizes that the real value of his retirement income will decline year by year after he retires). His retirement income will begin the day he retires, 10 years from today, and he will then get 24 additional annual payments. Inflation is expected to be 5 percent per year from today forward; he currently has $100,000 saved up; and he expects to earn a return on his savings of 8 percent per year, annual compounding. To the nearest dollar, how much must he save during each of the next 10 years (with deposits being made at the end of each year) to meet his retirement goal?

Spreadsheet Problem

Work the problem in this section only if you are using the computer problem diskette.

7-30
Loan Amortization

Use the computerized model in File C7 to solve this problem. Set up an amortization schedule for a $30,000 loan to be repaid in equal installments at the end of each of the next 20 years at an interest rate of 10 percent.
a. What is the annual payment?
b. Set up an amortization schedule for a $60,000 loan to be repaid in 20 equal annual installments at an interest rate of 10 percent. What is the annual payment?
c. Set up an amortization schedule for a $60,000 loan to be repaid in 20 equal annual installments at an interest rate of 20 percent. What is the annual payment?

MINI CASE

Assume that you are nearing graduation and that you have applied for a job with a local bank. As part of the bank's evaluation process, you have been asked to take an examination which covers several financial analysis techniques. The first section of the test addresses discounted cash flow analysis. See how you would do by answering the following questions.
a. Draw time lines for (a) a $100 lump sum cash flow at the end of Year 2, (b) an ordinary annuity of $100 per year for 3 years, and (c) an uneven cash flow stream of −$50, $100, $75, and $50 at the end of Years 0 through 3.
b. (1) What is the future value of an initial $100 after 3 years if it is invested in an account paying 10 percent annual interest?
   (2) What is the present value of $100 to be received in 3 years if the appropriate interest rate is 10 percent?
c. We sometimes need to find how long it will take a sum of money (or anything else) to grow to some specified amount. For example, if a company's sales are growing at a rate of 20 percent per year, how long will it take sales to double?
d. What is the difference between an ordinary annuity and an annuity due? What type of annuity is shown below? How would you change it to the other type of annuity?

e. (1) What is the future value of a 3-year ordinary annuity of $100 if the appropriate interest rate is 10 percent?
   (2) What is the present value of the annuity?
   (3) What would the future and present values be if the annuity were an annuity due?
f. What is the present value of the following uneven cash flow stream? The appropriate interest rate is 10 percent, compounded annually.

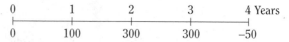

g. What annual interest rate will cause $100 to grow to $125.97 in 3 years?
h. (1) Will the future value be larger or smaller if we compound an initial amount more often than annually, for example, every 6 months, or *semiannually*, holding the stated interest rate constant? Why?
   (2) Define (a) the stated, or quoted, or nominal rate (i_{Nom}), (b) the periodic rate (i_{Per}), and (c) the effective annual rate (EAR).
   (3) What is the effective annual rate for a nominal rate of 10 percent, compounded semiannually? Compounded quarterly? Compounded daily?
   (4) What is the future value of $100 after 3 years under 10 percent semiannual compounding? Quarterly compounding?

i. Will the effective annual rate ever be equal to the nominal (quoted) rate?
j. (1) What is the value at the end of Year 3 of the following cash flow stream if the quoted interest rate is 10 percent, compounded semiannually?

	0	1	2	3 Years
	0	100	100	100

   (2) What is the PV of the same stream?
   (3) Is the stream an annuity?
   (4) An important rule is that you should *never* show a nominal rate on a time line or use it in calculations unless what condition holds? (Hint: Think of annual compounding, when $i_{Nom} = EAR = i_{Per}$.) What would be wrong with your answer to Questions j (1) and j (2) if you used the nominal rate (10%) rather than the periodic rate ($i_{Nom}/2 = 10\%/2 = 5\%$)?

k. (1) Construct an amortization schedule for a $1,000, 10 percent annual rate loan with 3 equal installments.
   (2) What is the annual interest expense for the borrower, and the annual interest income for the lender, during Year 2?

l. Suppose on January 1, 1999, you deposit $100 in an account that pays a nominal, or quoted, interest rate of 11.33463 percent, with interest added (compounded) daily. How much will you have in your account on October 1, or after 9 months?

m. Now suppose you leave your money in the bank for 21 months. Thus, on January 1, 1999, you deposit $100 in an account that pays a 12 percent effective annual interest rate. How much will be in your account on October 1, 2000?

n. Suppose someone offered to sell you a note calling for the payment of $1,000 fifteen months from today. They offer to sell it to you for $850. You have $850 in a bank time deposit which pays a 6.76649 percent nominal rate with daily compounding, which is a 7 percent effective annual interest rate, and you plan to leave the money in the bank unless you buy the note. The note is not risky—you are sure it will be paid on schedule. Should you buy the note? Check the decision in three ways: (1) by comparing your future value if you buy the note versus leaving your money in the bank, (2) by comparing the PV of the note with your current bank account, and (3) by comparing the EAR on the note versus that of the bank account.

o. Suppose the note discussed in Part n had a cost of $850, but called for 5 quarterly payments of $190 each, with the first payment due in 3 months rather than $1,000 at the end of 15 months. Would it be a good investment for you?

Selected Additional References

For a more complete discussion of the mathematics of finance, see

Atkins, Allen B., and Edward A. Dyl, "The Lotto Jackpot: The Lump Sum versus the Annuity," *Financial Practice and Education,* Fall/Winter 1995, 107–111.

Cissell, Robert, Helen Cissell, and David C. Flaspohler, *Mathematics of Finance* (Boston: Houghton Mifflin, 1978).

Lindley, James T., "Compounding Issues Revisited," *Financial Practice and Education,* Fall 1993, 127–129.

To learn more about using financial calculators, see the manual which came with your calculator. For example, see

Hewlett-Packard, *HP-10B Business Calculator Owner's Manual,* June 1990.

White, Mark A., *Financial Analysis with an Electronic Calculator,* 2nd edition (Chicago: Irwin, 1995).

———, "Financial Problem Solving with an Electronic Calculator: Texas Instruments' BA II Plus," *Financial Practice and Education,* Fall 1993, 123–126.

EXTENSIONS

Continuous Compounding and Discounting

In Chapter 7 we dealt only with situations where interest is added at discrete intervals — annually, semiannually, monthly, and so forth. In some instances, though, it is possible to have instantaneous, or *continuous,* growth. In this extension, we discuss present value and future value calculations when the interest rate is compounded continuously.

Continuous Compounding.   The relationship between discrete and **continuous compounding** is illustrated in Figure 7E-1. Panel a shows the annual compounding case, where interest is added once a year; Panel b shows the situation when compounding occurs twice a year; and Panel c shows interest being earned continuously. As the graphs show, the more frequent the compounding period, the larger the final compounded amount because interest is earned on interest more often.

Equation 7-9 in the chapter can be applied to any number of compounding periods per year:

More frequent compounding: $FV_n = PV \left(1 + \dfrac{i_{Nom}}{m}\right)^{mn}$.   **(7-9)**

To illustrate, let PV = $100, i = 10%, and n = 5. At various compounding periods per year, we obtain the following future values at the end of five years:

Annual: $FV_5 = \$100 \left(1 + \dfrac{0.10}{1}\right)^{1(5)} = \$100(1.10)^5$
$$= \$161.05.$$

Semiannual: $FV_5 = \$100 \left(1 + \dfrac{0.10}{2}\right)^{2(5)} = \$100(1.05)^{10}$
$$= \$162.89.$$

Monthly: $FV_5 = \$100 \left(1 + \dfrac{0.10}{12}\right)^{12(5)} = \$100(1.0083)^{60}$
$$= \$164.53.$$

Daily: $FV_5 = \$100 \left(1 + \dfrac{0.10}{365}\right)^{365(5)} = \$164.86.$

We could keep going, compounding every hour, every minute, every second, and so on. At the limit, we could compound every instant, or *continuously.* The equation for continuous compounding is

$$FV_n = PV(e^{in}). \qquad \text{(7E-1)}$$

Here e is the value 2.7183. . . . If $100 is invested for five years at 10 percent compounded continuously, then FV_5 is calculated as follows:[1]

Continuous: $FV_5 = \$100[e^{0.10(5)}] = \$100(2.7183 . . .)^{0.5}$
$$= \$164.87.$$

Continuous Discounting.   Equation 7E-1 can be transformed into Equation 7E-2 and used to determine present values under continuous discounting:

$$PV = \dfrac{FV_n}{e^{in}} = FV_n(e^{-in}). \qquad \text{(7E-2)}$$

Thus, if $1,649 is due in ten years, and if the appropriate *continuous* discount rate, i, is 5 percent, then the present value of this future payment is

$$PV = \dfrac{\$1,649}{(2.7183 . . .)^{0.5}} = \dfrac{\$1,649}{1.649} = \$1,000.$$

---

[1]Calculators with exponential functions can be used to evaluate Equation 7E-1. For example, with an HP-10B you would type .5, then press the e^x key to get 1.6487, and then multiply by $100 to get $164.87.

FIGURE 7E-1   Annual, Semiannual, and Continuous Compounding: Future Value with i = 25%

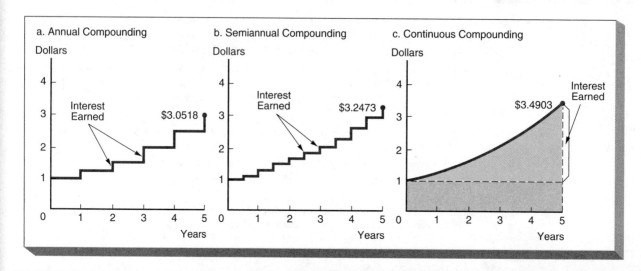

CHAPTER 8
BONDS AND THEIR VALUATION

CHAPTER 9
STOCKS AND THEIR VALUATION

Sitting on two city blocks and rising one-quarter mile above the ground, the Sears Tower's 110 stories comprise some 4.5 million gross square feet of office and commercial space. Sears Roebuck and Co. sold the building in 1994 as part of a corporate downsizing. The new owner is AEW Partnership L.P., and the Tower's tenants include heavyweights AT&T Co., IBM, and Eastman Kodak.

© Frank Cezus/FPG International

BONDS AND THEIR VALUATION

*I*nterest rates plunged in 1993, and corporate borrowers scrambled to lock in low rates by selling long-term bonds. The outer limit for most long-term bonds had been 40 years—investors were unwilling to assume that companies could repay debts due farther in the future, so maturities had been limited to 40 years to avoid prohibitive risk premiums.

When interest rates took this nosedive, investors found many of their old, high-yielding bonds either maturing or being called, and they were forced to reinvest their money at new, much lower interest rates. This caused their incomes to plunge. This held true for individual retirees and pension funds, both of which invest heavily in the bond market.

How can investors protect themselves against a drop in rates? And how can a corporate borrower lock in a low rate and thus be protected against a later rise in interest rates? The answer, in both cases, is to use longer-term bonds.

Recognizing all this, a large pension fund approached Morgan Stanley & Co., a leading investment banking firm, and asked about the availability of extremely long-term bonds. This fund wanted to lengthen the average maturity of its portfolio, and 100-year bonds would do the trick. However, almost no 100-year bonds existed; two railroads had sold such bonds in the 1800s, but the dollar amounts were too small to make much difference to a large fund. Morgan Stanley seized the opportunity and immediately began to call clients who might be interested in issuing long-term bonds to lock in the low current rates. Within a week, Disney had agreed to sell $150 million worth of 7.5 percent, 100-year bonds, buyers were clamoring for them, and the offering "flew out the window."

Soon after the Disney issue, Coca-Cola announced its own 100-year issue, which was also well received. The quick sellout of these issues provided clear evidence that at least some investors have an interest in holding 100-year bonds. But others have their doubts. According to Glenn Murphy, chief investment officer of Travelers Asset Management, the Disney issue will ultimately be a "historic artifact, a curiosity." And William Gross, head of fixed-income investment at Pacific Investment Management, noting the ups and downs of entertainment companies, stated, "It's crazy. Look at the path of Coney Island over the last 50 years and see what happens to amusement parks."

Even if Disney continues to do well and pays interest and principal as they come due, these bonds could still produce headaches for investors. A relatively small 1 percentage point increase in interest rates would cause the value of the Disney bond to fall from its $1,000 offering price to $882, and if long-term interest rates return to the level they were ten years ago, the bond's value would drop to just $538.

Since the Disney and Coke issues, there has been a slow but steady stream of these "century bonds"—Bell South Telecommunications, Columbia/HCA Healthcare Corporation, and the Port Authority of New York and New Jersey are examples. However, not all issues have been successful. Late in 1995, News America Finance Inc. issued $600 million in 50-year bonds and $150 million in 100-year bonds. In both cases, the company's lead underwriter, Goldman Sachs, had a hard time finding interested buyers.

Arguably, the fact that the company's credit quality was considerably weaker than the prior issuers of 100-year bonds made the News America bonds a tough sell. Describing this issue, one analyst, Stephen Clark of Technical Data, stated, "This is a borderline-junk credit for a company in an industry that is changing dramatically. Super long debt is usually issued by companies known for their stability and the staying power of their products, like Coca-Cola or Disney."

If you had some extra money, would you be willing to invest in Disney's bonds? How might the terms on the Disney bonds affect the company's stock price? If you were running a business and needed debt capital, might Disney's decision to use 100-year debt affect the way you thought about financing your own company? When you finish this chapter, you should at least know how to think about these questions.

I f you skim through *The Wall Street Journal,* you will see references to a wide variety of bonds. This variety may seem confusing, but there are actually just a few character-istics which distinguish the various types of bonds. Also, you should note that any bond can be valued using the principles discussed in Chapter 7.

While bonds are often viewed as relatively safe investments, one can certainly lose money on them. Indeed, "riskless" long-term U.S. Treasury bonds declined by more than 20 percent during 1994, and "safe" Mexican government bonds declined by 25 per-cent in just one day, December 27, 1994. Investors who had regarded bonds as being riskless, or at least fairly safe, learned a sad lesson. However, it is also possible to rack up impressive gains in the bond market. In 1995, U.S. Treasury bonds produced a 17.4 percent total return, and corporate bonds did even better—their total return was nearly 21 percent.

In this chapter, we will discuss the types of bonds companies and government agen-cies issue, the terms that are contained in bond contracts, and the types of risks to which both bond investors and issuers are exposed.

WHO ISSUES BONDS?

A **bond** is a long-term contract under which a borrower agrees to make payments of interest and principal, on specific dates, to the holders of the bond. For example, on January 2, 1999, MicroDrive Inc. borrowed $50 million by selling 50,000 individual bonds for $1,000 each. MicroDrive received the $50 million, and in exchange it promised to make annual interest payments and to repay the $50 million on a specified maturity date.

Investors have many choices when investing in bonds, but bonds are classified into four main types: Treasury, corporate, municipal, and foreign. Each type differs with respect to expected return and degree of risk.

Treasury bonds, sometimes referred to as government bonds, are issued by the fed-eral government.[1] It is reasonable to assume that the federal government will make

---

[1]The U.S. Treasury actually issues three types of securities: "bills," "notes," and "bonds." A bond makes an equal payment every six months until it matures, at which time it makes an additional lump sum payment. If the maturity at the time of issue is less than ten years, the security is rather arbitrarily called a note rather than a bond. A bill (or "T-bill") is a security with a maturity of 52 weeks or less at the time of issue, and it makes no payments at all until it matures. T-bills are sold at a discount (that is, at a price below their matu-rity value), and the differential between the issue price and the maturity value constitutes interest.

good on its promised payments, so these bonds have no default risk. However, Treasury bond prices decline when interest rates rise, so they are not free of all risks.

Corporate bonds, as the name implies, are issued by corporations. Unlike Treasury bonds, corporate bonds are exposed to default risk—if the issuing company gets into trouble, it may be unable to make the promised interest and principal payments. Different corporate bonds have different levels of default risk, depending on the issuing company's characteristics and on the terms of the specific bond. Default risk often is referred to as "credit risk," and, as we saw in Chapter 4, the larger the default or credit risk, the higher the interest rate the issuer must pay.

Municipal bonds, or "munis," are issued by state and local governments. Like corporate bonds, munis have default risk. However, munis offer one major advantage over all other bonds: As we discussed in Chapter 2, the interest earned on most municipal bonds is exempt from federal taxes, and also from state taxes if the holder is a resident of the issuing state. Consequently, municipal bonds carry interest rates that are considerably lower than those on corporate bonds with the same default risk.

Foreign bonds are issued by foreign governments or foreign corporations. Foreign corporate bonds are, of course, exposed to default risk, and so are some foreign government bonds. An additional risk exists if the bonds are denominated in a currency other than that of the investor's home currency. For example, if a U.S. investor purchases a corporate bond denominated in Japanese yen, and the yen subsequently falls relative to the dollar, then the investor will lose money, even if the company does not default on its bonds.

SELF-TEST QUESTIONS	What is a bond?
	What are the four main types of bonds?
	Why are U.S. Treasury bonds not riskless?
	To what extra type of risk are investors of foreign bonds exposed?

KEY CHARACTERISTICS OF BONDS

Although all bonds have some common characteristics, they do not always have the same contractual features. For example, most corporate bonds have provisions for early repayment (call features), but these provisions can be quite different for different bonds. Differences in contractual provisions, and in the underlying strength of the companies backing the bonds, lead to major differences in bonds' risks, prices, and expected returns. To understand bonds, it is important for you to understand the following terms.

Par Value

The **par value** is the stated face value of the bond; for illustrative purposes we generally assume a par value of $1,000, although any multiple of $1,000 (for example, $5,000) can be used. The par value generally represents the amount of money the firm borrows and promises to repay on the maturity date.

Coupon Interest Rate

MicroDrive's bonds require the company to pay a fixed number of dollars of interest each year (or, more typically, each six months). When this **coupon payment,** as it is called, is divided by the par value, the result is the **coupon interest rate.** For example,

MicroDrive's bonds have a $1,000 par value, and they pay $100 in interest each year. The bond's coupon interest is $100, so its coupon interest rate is $100/$1,000 = 10%. The $100 is the yearly "rent" on the $1,000 loan. This payment, which is fixed at the time the bond is issued, remains in force during the life of the bond.[2] Typically, at the time a bond is issued, its coupon payment is set at a level which will enable the bond to be issued at or near its par value.

In some cases, a bond's coupon payment may vary over time. For these **floating rate,** or *indexed,* **bonds,** the payment rate is set for, say, the initial six-month period, after which it is adjusted every six months based on some market rate. Some corporate issues have been tied to the Treasury bond rate, while other issues have been tied to other rates. Many additional provisions can be included in floating rate issues; for example, some are convertible to fixed rate debt, whereas others have upper and lower limits ("caps" and "floors") on how high or low the yield can go.

Floating rate debt is popular with investors who are worried about the risk of rising interest rates, since the payment received increases whenever market rates rise. This causes the market value of the debt to be stabilized, and it also provides lenders such as banks with income which is better geared to their own obligations. (Banks' deposit costs rise with interest rates, so the income on floating rate loans rises just when banks' deposit costs are rising.) Moreover, floating rate debt appeals to corporations that want to issue long-term debt without committing themselves to paying a historically high interest rate for the entire life of the loan. Of course, if interest rates move even higher after a floating rate bond has been issued, the borrower would have been better off issuing conventional, fixed rate debt.

Some bonds pay no coupons at all, but are offered at a substantial discount below their par values and hence provide capital appreciation rather than interest income. These securities are called **zero coupon bonds** *("zeros").* Other bonds pay some coupon interest, but not enough to be issued at par. In general, any bond originally offered at a price significantly below its par value is called an **original issue discount bond (OID).** Corporations first used zeros in a major way in 1981. In recent years IBM, Alcoa, JCPenney, ITT, Cities Service, GMAC, Martin-Marietta, and many other companies have used zeros to raise billions of dollars. Some of the details associated with issuing or investing in zero coupon bonds are discussed more fully in Chapter 18.

Maturity Date

Bonds generally have a specified **maturity date** on which the par value must be repaid. MicroDrive's bonds, which were issued on January 2, 1999, will mature on January 1, 2014; thus, they had a 15-year maturity at the time they were issued. Most bonds have **original maturities** (the maturity at the time the bond is issued) ranging from 10 to 40 years, but any maturity is legally permissible. Of course, the effective maturity of a bond declines each year after it has been issued. Thus, MicroDrive's bonds had a 15-year original maturity, but in 2000, a year later, they will have a 14-year maturity, and so on.

---

[2]At one time, most bonds literally had a number of small (1/2- by 2-inch), dated coupons attached to them, and on each interest payment date, the owner would clip off the coupon for that date and either cash it at his or her bank or mail it to the company's paying agent, who would then mail back a check for the interest. A 30-year, semiannual bond would start with 60 coupons, whereas a 5-year annual payment bond would start with only 5 coupons. Today, new bonds must be *registered*—no physical coupons are involved, and interest checks are mailed automatically to the registered owners of the bonds. Even so, people continue to use the terms *coupon* and *coupon interest rate* when discussing registered bonds.

Provisions to Call (or Redeem) Bonds

Most corporate bonds contain a **call provision,** which gives the issuing corporation the right to call the bonds for redemption.[3] The call provision generally states that the company must pay the bondholders an amount greater than the par value if they are called. The additional sum, which is termed a *call premium,* is typically set equal to one year's interest if the bonds are called during the first year, and the premium declines at a constant rate of INT/N each year thereafter, where INT = annual interest and N = original maturity in years. For example, the call premium on a $1,000 par value, ten-year, 10 percent bond would generally be $100 if it were called during the first year, $90 during the second year (calculated by reducing the $100, or 10 percent, premium by one-tenth), and so on. However, bonds are often not callable until several years (generally five to ten) after they were issued. This is known as a *deferred call,* and the bonds are said to have *call protection.*

Suppose a company sold bonds when interest rates were relatively high. Provided the issue is callable, the company could sell a new issue of low-yielding securities if and when interest rates drop. It could then use the proceeds of the new issue to retire the high-rate issue and thus reduce its interest expense. This process is called a *refunding operation,* and it is discussed in greater detail in Chapter 18.

A call provision is valuable to the firm but potentially detrimental to investors. If interest rates go up, the company will not call the bond, and the investor will be stuck with the original coupon rate on the bond, even though interest rates in the economy have risen sharply. However, if interest rates fall, the company *will* call the bond and pay off investors, who will then have to reinvest the proceeds at the current market interest rate, which is lower than the rate investors were getting on the original bond. In other words, the investor loses when interest rates go up, but doesn't reap the gains when rates fall. To induce an investor to take this type of risk, a new issue of callable bonds must provide a higher interest rate than an otherwise similar issue of non-callable bonds. For example, on August 30, 1997, Pacific Timber Company sold a bond issue yielding 9.5 percent; these bonds were callable immediately. On the same day, Northwest Milling Company sold an issue with similar risk and maturity which yielded 9.2 percent; its bonds were noncallable for ten years. Investors were willing to accept a 0.3 percent lower interest rate on Northwest's bonds for the assurance that the 9.2 percent interest rate would be earned for at least ten years. Pacific, on the other hand, had to incur a 0.3 percent higher annual interest rate to obtain the option of calling the bonds in the event of a subsequent decline in interest rates.

Bonds that are **redeemable at par** at the holder's option protect the holder against a rise in interest rates. If rates rise, the price of fixed-rate bonds declines. However, if holders have the option of turning their bonds in and having them redeemed at par, they are protected against rising rates. Examples of such debt include Transamerica's $50 million issue of 25-year, 8½ percent bonds. The bonds are not callable by the company, but holders can turn them in for redemption at par five years after the date of issue. If interest rates have risen, holders will turn in the bonds and reinvest the proceeds at a higher rate. This feature enabled Transamerica to sell the bonds with an 8½ percent coupon at a time when other similarly rated bonds had yields of 9 percent.

In late 1988, the corporate bond markets were sent into turmoil by the leveraged buyout of RJR Nabisco. RJR's bonds dropped in value by 20 percent within days of the LBO announcement, and the prices of many other corporate bonds also plunged, because

---

[3]Most municipal bonds also contain call provisions. Although the U.S. Treasury no longer issues callable bonds, some past Treasury issues were callable.

investors feared that a boom in LBOs would load up many companies with excessive debt, leading to lower bond ratings and declining bond prices. All this led to a resurgence of concern about *event risk,* which is the risk that some sudden action, such as an LBO, will occur and increase the credit risk of the company, hence lower the firm's bond rating and the value of its outstanding bonds. Investors' concern over event risk meant that those firms deemed most likely to face events that could harm bondholders suddenly had to pay dearly to raise new debt capital, if they could raise it at all. In an attempt to control debt costs, a new type of protective covenant was devised to minimize event risk. This covenant, called a *super poison put,* enables a bondholder to turn in, or "put" a bond back to the issuer at par in the event of a takeover, merger, or major recapitalization.

Poison puts had actually been around since 1986, when the leveraged buyout trend took off. However, the earlier puts proved to be almost worthless because they allowed investors to "put" their bonds back to the issuer at par value only in the event of an *unfriendly* takeover. But since almost all takeovers are eventually approved by the target firm's board, mergers that started as hostile generally ended as friendly. Also, the earlier poison puts failed to protect investors from voluntary recapitalizations, in which a company loads up on debt to pay a big, one-time dividend to stockholders or to buy back its own stock. The "super" poison puts that were used following the RJR buyout announcement protected against both of these actions. This is a good illustration of how quickly the financial community reacts to changes in the marketplace.

Sinking Funds

Some bonds include a **sinking fund provision** designed to facilitate the orderly retirement of the issue. Typically, the sinking fund requires the firm to retire a portion of the bonds each year. On rare occasions the firm may be required to deposit money with a trustee, who invests the funds and then uses the accumulated sum to retire the bonds when they mature. Usually, though, the sinking fund is used to buy back a certain percentage of the issue each year. A failure to meet the sinking fund requirement causes the bond issue to be thrown into default, which may force the company into bankruptcy. Obviously, a sinking fund can constitute a significant cash drain on the firm.

In most cases, the firm is given the right to handle the sinking fund in either of two ways:

1. The company can call in for redemption (at par value) a certain percentage of the bonds each year; for example, it might be able to call 5 percent of the total original amount of the issue at a price of $1,000 per bond. The bonds are numbered serially, and those called for redemption are determined by a lottery administered by the trustee.

2. The company may buy the required number of bonds on the open market.

The firm will choose the least-cost method. If interest rates have risen, causing bond prices to fall, it will buy bonds in the open market at a discount; if interest rates have fallen, it will call the bonds. Note that a call for sinking fund purposes is quite different from a refunding call as discussed above. A sinking fund call typically requires no call premium,[4] but only a small percentage of the issue is normally callable in any one year.

Although sinking funds are designed to protect bondholders by ensuring that an issue is retired in an orderly fashion, you should recognize that sinking funds at times work to the detriment of bondholders. For example, suppose a bond carries a 10 percent interest rate, but yields on similar bonds have fallen to 7.5 percent. A sinking fund call at par would require an investor to give up a bond that pays $100 of interest and then to reinvest in a bond that pays only $75 per year. This obviously harms those

---

[4]Some sinking funds require the issuer to pay a call premium.

bondholders whose bonds are called. On balance, however, bonds that have a sinking fund are regarded as being safer than those without such a provision, so at the time they are issued sinking fund bonds have lower coupon rates than otherwise similar bonds without sinking funds.

Other Features

Several other types of bonds are used sufficiently often to warrant mention. First, **convertible bonds** are bonds that are convertible into shares of common stock, at a fixed price, at the option of the bondholder. Convertibles have a lower coupon rate than nonconvertible debt, but they offer investors a chance for capital gains in exchange for the lower coupon rate. Bonds issued with **warrants** are similar to convertibles. Warrants are options which permit the holder to buy stock for a stated price, thereby providing a capital gain if the price of the stock rises. Bonds that are issued with warrants, like convertibles, carry lower coupon rates than straight bonds. Convertibles and warrants are discussed in Chapter 20.

Another type of bond is an **income bond,** which pays interest only if the interest is earned. These securities cannot bankrupt a company, but from an investor's standpoint they are riskier than "regular" bonds. Yet another bond is the **indexed,** or **purchasing power, bond,** which is popular in Brazil, Israel, and a few other countries plagued by high rates of inflation. Indexed bonds were also issued by the U.S. Treasury in 1997. The interest rate paid on these bonds is based on the consumer price index, so the interest paid rises automatically when the inflation rate rises, thus protecting the bondholders against inflation.

SELF-TEST QUESTIONS

Define floating rate bonds and zero coupon bonds.

What are the two ways a sinking fund can be handled? Which method will be chosen by the firm if interest rates have risen? If interest rates have fallen?

What is the difference between a call for sinking fund purposes and a refunding call?

Are securities that provide for a sinking fund regarded as being riskier than those without this type of provision? Explain.

Why is a call provision advantageous to a bond issuer? When will the issuer initiate a refunding call? Why?

Define convertible bonds, bonds with warrants, income bonds, and indexed bonds.

Why do bonds with warrants and convertible bonds have lower coupons than similarly rated bonds that do not have these features?

What problem was solved by the introduction of long-term floating rate debt, and how is the rate on such bonds determined?

BOND VALUATION

The value of any financial asset—a stock, a bond, a lease, or even a physical asset such as an apartment building or a piece of machinery—is simply the present value of the cash flows the asset is expected to produce.

The cash flows from a specific bond depend on its contractual features as described above. For a standard coupon-bearing bond such as the one issued by MicroDrive, the cash flows consist of interest payments (10 percent) during the 15-year life of the bond, plus a return of the principal amount borrowed (generally the $1,000 par value) when the bond matures. In the case of a floating rate bond, the interest payments depend on the level of interest rates over time. In the case of a zero coupon bond, there are no interest payments, only the return of principal when the bond matures. For a "regular" bond, here is the situation:

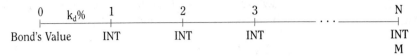

Here

k_d = the bond's market rate of interest = 10%. This is the discount rate that is used to calculate the present value of the bond's cash flows. Note that k_d is *not* the coupon interest rate, and it is equal to the coupon rate only if (as in this case) the bond is selling at par. Generally, the coupon rate is set at k_d when the bond is issued, so most bonds sell at par, hence have k_d = coupon rate only at the time of issue. Thereafter, interest rates as measured by k_d will fluctuate, but the coupon rate is fixed, so k_d will equal the coupon rate only by chance. We used the term "i" or "I" to designate the interest rate in Chapter 7 because those terms are used on financial calculators, but "k," with the subscript "d" to designate the rate on a debt security, is normally used in finance.[5]

N = the number of years before the bond matures = 15. Note that N declines each year after the bond has been issued, so a bond that had a maturity of 15 years when it was issued (original maturity = 15) will have N = 14 after one year, N = 13 after two years, and so on. Note also that at this point we assume that the bond pays interest once a year, or annually, so N is measured in years. Later on, we will deal with semiannual payment bonds, which pay interest each six months.

INT = dollars of interest paid each year = Coupon rate × Par value = 0.10($1,000) = $100. In calculator terminology, INT = PMT = 100. If the bond had been a semiannual payment bond, the payment would have been $50 each six months. The payment would be zero if MicroDrive had issued zero coupon bonds, and it would vary if the bond was a "floater."

M = the par, or maturity, value of the bond = $1,000. This amount must be paid off at maturity.

We can now redraw the time line to show the numerical values for all variables except the bond's value:

```
0      10%    1         2         3                    15
|-------+-----|---------|---------|-------- · · · ------|
Bond's Value   100       100       100                 100
                                                      1,000
                                                      ─────
                                                      1,100
```

The following general equation, written in several forms, can be solved to find the value of any bond:

$$\text{Bond's value} = V_B = \frac{\text{INT}}{(1 + k_d)^1} + \frac{\text{INT}}{(1 + k_d)^2} + \cdots + \frac{\text{INT}}{(1 + k_d)^N} + \frac{M}{(1 + k_d)^N}$$

$$(8\text{-}1)$$

$$= \sum_{t=1}^{N} \frac{\text{INT}}{(1 + k_d)^t} + \frac{M}{(1 + k_d)^N}$$

---

[5]The appropriate interest rate on debt securities was discussed in Chapter 4. The bond's riskiness, liquidity, and years to maturity, as well as supply and demand conditions in the capital markets, all influence the interest rate on bonds.

$$= \text{INT}\left(\frac{1 - \frac{1}{(1+k_d)^N}}{k_d}\right) + \frac{M}{(1+k_d)^N}$$

$$= \text{INT}(\text{PVIFA}_{k_d,N}) + M(\text{PVIF}_{k_d,N}).$$

Inserting values for our particular bond, we have

$$V_B = \sum_{t=1}^{15} \frac{\$100}{(1.10)^t} + \frac{\$1,000}{(1.10)^{15}}$$

$$= \$100\left(\frac{1 - \frac{1}{(1.1)^{15}}}{0.1}\right) + \frac{\$1,000}{(1.1)^{15}}$$

$$= \$100(\text{PVIFA}_{10\%,15}) + \$1,000(\text{PVIF}_{10\%,15}).$$

Notice that the cash flows consist of an annuity of N years plus a lump sum payment at the end of Year N, and this fact is reflected in Equation 8-1. Further, Equation 8-1 can be solved by the four procedures discussed in Chapter 7: (1) numerically, (2) using the tables, (3) with a financial calculator, and (4) with a spreadsheet.

Numerical Solution:

Simply discount each cash flow back to the present and sum these PVs to find the bond's value; see Figure 8-1 for an example. This procedure is not very efficient, especially if the bond has many years to maturity. Alternatively, you could use the formula in the third row of Equation 8-1 with a simple or scientific calculator, although this would still be somewhat cumbersome.

FIGURE 8-1   **Time Line for MicroDrive Inc.'s Bonds, 10% Interest Rate**

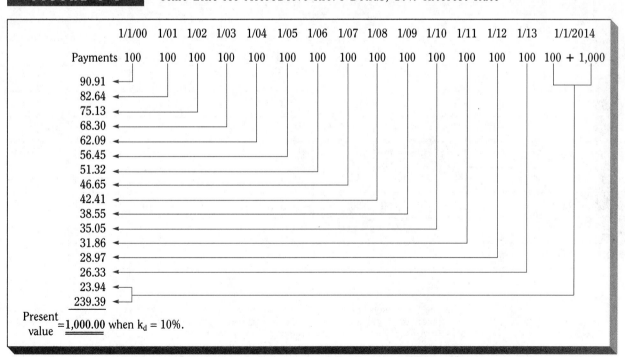

Tabular Solution:

Simply look up the appropriate PVIFA and PVIF values in Tables A-1 and A-2 at the end of the book, insert them into the equation, and complete the arithmetic:

$$V_B = \$100(7.6061) + \$1,000(0.2394)$$
$$= \$760.61 + \$239.40 \approx \$1,000.$$

There is a one cent rounding difference, which results from the fact that the tables only go to four decimal places.

Financial Calculator Solution:

In Chapter 7, we worked problems where only four of the five time value of money (TVM) keys were used, but all five keys are used with bonds. Here is the setup:

Inputs:	15	10		100	1000
	N	I	PV	PMT	FV
Output:			= −1,000		

Simply input N = 15, I = k = 10, INT = PMT = 100, M = FV = 1000, and then press the PV key to find the value of the bond, $1,000. Since the PV is an outflow to the investor, it is shown with a negative sign. The calculator is programmed to solve Equation 8-1: It finds the PV of an annuity of $100 per year for 15 years, discounted at 10 percent, then it finds the PV of the $1,000 maturity payment, and then it adds these two PVs to find the value of the bond.[6]

Spreadsheet Solution:

	A	B	C	D	E	F	G	H	I	J	K	L	M	N	O	P	Q
1	Spreadsheet for bond value calculation																
2				Going rate, or yield													
3	Coupon rate	10%				10%											
4																	
5	Time	0	1	2	3	4	5	6	7	8	9	10	11	12	13	14	15
6	Interest Pmt		100	100	100	100	100	100	100	100	100	100	100	100	100	100	100
7	Maturity Pmt																1000
8	Total CF		100	100	100	100	100	100	100	100	100	100	100	100	100	100	1100
9																	
10	PV of CF	1000															

---

[6]The bond prices quoted by brokers are calculated as described. However, if you bought a bond between interest payment dates, you would have to pay the basic price plus accrued interest. Thus, if you purchased a MicroDrive bond six months after it was issued, your broker would send you an invoice stating that you must pay $1,000 as the basic price of the bond plus $50 interest, representing one-half the annual interest of $100. The seller of the bond would receive $1,050. If you bought the bond the day before its interest payment date, you would pay $1,000 + (364/365)($100) = $1,099.73. Of course, you would receive an interest payment of

The formula in Cell B10 is: **=NPV(F3,C8:Q8)**, where NPV is the *Excel* function, F3 designates the interest rate at which cash flows are discounted, and C8:Q8 specifies the range containing the cash flows. The formula produces a value of $1,000. By changing the interest rate in F3, we can instantly find the value of the bond at any other discount rate.

Excel and other spreadsheet software packages also provide specialized functions for bond prices. For example, in *Excel* you could use the function wizard to enter this formula:

$$=PRICE(Date(1999,1,2),Date(2014,1,2,),10\%,10\%,100,1,0).$$

The first two arguments in the function give the current and maturity dates. The next argument is the bond's coupon rate, followed by the current market interest rate, or yield. The fifth argument, 100, is the redemption value of the bond at maturity, expressed as a percent of the face value. The sixth argument is the number of payments per year, and the last one, 0, tells the program to use the U.S. convention for counting days, which is to assume 30 days per month and 360 days per year. This function produces the value 100, which is the current price expressed as a percent of the bond's par value, which is $1,000. Therefore, you can multiply $1,000 by 100 percent to get the current price, which is $1,000. This function is useful when the values of many bonds in a portfolio must be calculated, and it is essential if bonds are being evaluated between coupon payment dates.

Changes in Bond Values over Time

At the time a coupon bond is issued, the coupon is generally set at a level that will cause the market price of the bond to equal its par value. If a lower coupon were set, investors would not be willing to pay $1,000 for the bond, while if a higher coupon were set, investors would clamor for the bond and bid its price up over $1,000. Investment bankers can judge quite precisely the coupon rate that will cause a bond to sell at its $1,000 par value.

A bond that has just been issued is known as a *new issue.* (Investment bankers classify a bond as a new issue for about one month after it has first been issued.) Once the bond has been on the market for a while, it is classified as an *outstanding bond,* also called a *seasoned issue.* Newly issued bonds generally sell very close to par, but the prices of seasoned bonds often vary widely from par. Except for floating rate bonds, coupon payments are constant, so when interest rates change, a bond with a $100 coupon that sold at par when it was issued will sell for more or less than $1,000 thereafter.

MicroDrive's bonds with a 10 percent coupon rate were originally issued at par. If k_d remained constant at 10 percent, what would the value of the bond be one year after it was issued? Now the term to maturity is only 14 years — that is, $N = 14$. With a financial calculator, just override $N = 15$ with $N = 14$, press the PV key, and you find a value of $1,000. If we continued, setting $N = 13$, $N = 12$, and so forth, we would see that the value of the bond will remain at $1,000 as long as the going interest rate remains constant at the coupon rate, 10 percent.

Now suppose interest rates in the economy fell after the MicroDrive bonds were issued, and, as a result, k_d *fell below the coupon rate,* decreasing from 10 to 5 percent.

$100 at the end of the next day. See Self-Test Problem 1 for a detailed discussion of bond quotations between interest payment dates.

Throughout the chapter, we assume that bonds are being evaluated immediately after an interest payment date. The more expensive financial calculators such as the HP-17B have a built-in calendar which permits the calculation of exact values between interest payment dates, and, of course, the same thing can be done with spreadsheets.

Both the coupon interest payments and the maturity value remain constant, but now 5 percent values for PVIF and PVIFA would have to be used in Equation 8-1. The value of the bond at the end of the first year would rise to $1,494.96:

$$V_B = \$100(\text{PVIFA}_{5\%,14}) + \$1,000(\text{PVIF}_{5\%,14})$$

$$= \$100(9.8986) + \$1,000(0.5051)$$

$$= \$989.86 + \$505.10$$

$$= \$1,494.96.$$

With a financial calculator, just change $k_d = I$ from 10 to 5, and then press the PV key to get the answer, $1,494.93. Thus, if k_d fell *below* the coupon rate, the bond would sell above par, or at a *premium*.

The arithmetic of the bond value increase should be clear, but what is the logic behind it? The fact that k_d has fallen to 5 percent means that if you had $1,000 to invest, you could buy new bonds like MicroDrive's (every day some 10 to 12 companies sell new bonds), except that these new bonds would pay $50 of interest each year rather than $100. Naturally, you would prefer $100 to $50, so you would be willing to pay more than $1,000 for a MicroDrive bond to obtain its higher coupons. All investors would react similarly, and as a result, MicroDrive's bonds would be bid up in price to $1,494.93, at which point they would provide the same rate of return to a potential investor as the new bonds, 5 percent.

Assuming that interest rates remain constant at 5 percent for the next 14 years, what would happen to the value of a MicroDrive bond? It would fall gradually from $1,494.93 at present to $1,000 at maturity, when MicroDrive will redeem each bond for $1,000. This point can be illustrated by calculating the value of the bond 1 year later, when it has 13 years remaining to maturity. With a financial calculator, merely input the values for N, I, PMT, and FV, now using N = 13, and press the PV key to find the value of the bond, $1,469.68. Thus, the value of the bond will have fallen from $1,494.93 to $1,469.68, or by $25.25. If you were to calculate the value of the bond at other future dates, the price would continue to fall as the maturity date approached.

Notice that if you purchased the bond at a price of $1,494.93 and then sold it one year later with k_d still at 5 percent, you would have a capital loss of $25.25, or a total return of $100.00 − $25.25 = $74.75. Your percentage rate of return would consist of an *interest yield* (also called a *current yield*) plus a *capital gains yield*, calculated as follows:

$$\text{Interest, or current, yield} = \quad \$100/\$1,494.93 \quad = \quad 0.0669 = \quad 6.69\%$$

$$\text{Capital gains yield} = - \$25.25/\$1,494.93 \; = -0.0169 = \underline{-1.69\%}$$

$$\text{Total rate of return, or yield} = \quad \$74.75/\$1,494.93 \; = \quad 0.0500 = \underline{\underline{5.00\%}}$$

Had interest rates risen from 10 to 15 percent during the first year after issue rather than fallen, you would enter N = 14, I = 15, PMT = 100, and FV = 1000, and then press the PV key to find the value of the bond, $713.78. In this case, the bond would sell at a *discount* of $286.22 below its par value:

$$\text{Discount} = \text{Price} - \text{Par value} = \$713.78 - \$1,000.00$$

$$= -\$286.22.$$

The total expected future return on the bond would again consist of a current yield and a capital gains yield, but now the capital gains yield would be *positive*. The total return would be 15 percent. To see this, calculate the price of the bond with 13 years left to maturity, assuming that interest rates remain at 15 percent. With a calculator, enter N = 13, I = 15, PMT = 100, and FV = 1000, and then press PV to obtain the bond's value, $720.84.

Notice that the capital gain for the year is the difference between the bond's value at Year 2 (with 13 years remaining) and the bond's value at Year 1 (with 14 years remaining), or $720.84 − $713.78 = $7.06. The interest yield, capital gains yield, and total rate of return are calculated as follows:

$$\text{Interest, or current, yield} = \$100/\$713.78 = 0.1401 = 14.01\%$$

$$\text{Capital gains yield} = \$7.06/\$713.78 = 0.0099 = \underline{0.99\%}$$

$$\text{Total rate of return, or yield} = \$107.06/\$713.78 = 0.1500 = \underline{15.00\%}$$

Figure 8-2 graphs the value of the bond over time, assuming that interest rates in the economy (1) remain constant at 10 percent, (2) fall to 5 percent and then remain constant at that level, or (3) rise to 15 percent and remain constant at that level. Of course, if interest rates do *not* remain constant, then the price of the bond will fluctuate. However, regardless of what future interest rates do, the bond's price will approach

---

FIGURE 8-2   Time Path of the Value of a 10% Coupon, $1,000 Par Value Bond When Interest Rates Are 5%, 10%, and 15%

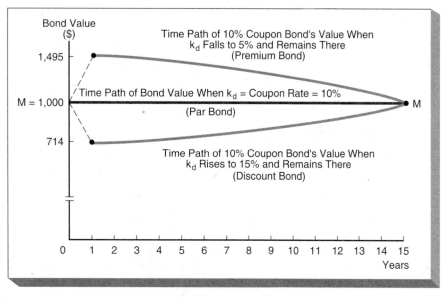

YEAR	$k_d = 5\%$	$k_d = 10\%$	$k_d = 15\%$
0	—	$1,000	—
1	$1,494.93	1,000	$713.78
.	.	.	.
.	.	.	.
.	.	.	.
15	1,000	1,000	1,000

NOTE: The curves for 5% and 15% have a slight bow.

$1,000 as it nears the maturity date (barring bankruptcy, in which case the bond's value might fall dramatically).

Figure 8-2 illustrates the following key points:

1. Whenever the going rate of interest, k_d, is equal to the coupon rate, a *fixed-rate* bond will sell at its par value. Normally, the coupon rate is set equal to the going rate when a bond is issued, causing it to sell at par initially.

2. Interest rates do change over time, but the coupon rate remains fixed after the bond has been issued. Whenever the going rate of interest *rises above* the coupon rate, a fixed-rate bond's price will fall *below* its par value. Such a bond is called a **discount bond.**

3. Whenever the going rate of interest *falls below* the coupon rate, a fixed-rate bond's price will rise *above* its par value. Such a bond is called a **premium bond.**

4. Thus, an *increase* in interest rates will cause the prices of outstanding bonds to *fall,* whereas a *decrease* in rates will cause bond prices to *rise.*

5. The market value of a bond will always approach its par value as its maturity date approaches, provided the firm does not go bankrupt.

These points are very important, for they show that bondholders may suffer capital losses or make capital gains, depending on whether interest rates rise or fall after the bond was purchased. And, as we saw in Chapter 4, interest rates do indeed change over time.

S E L F - T E S T
Q U E S T I O N S

What is meant by the terms "new issue" and "seasoned issue"?

Explain, verbally, the following equation:

$$V_B = \sum_{t=1}^{N} \frac{INT}{(1 + k_d)^t} + \frac{M}{(1 + k_d)^N}.$$

Explain what happens to the price of a fixed-rate bond if (1) interest rates rise above the bond's coupon rate or (2) interest rates fall below the bond's coupon rate.

What is a "discount bond"? A "premium bond"?

Why do the prices of fixed-rate bonds fall if expectations for inflation rise?

BOND YIELDS

If you examine the bond market table of *The Wall Street Journal* or a price sheet put out by a bond dealer, you will typically see information regarding each bond's maturity date, price, and coupon interest rate. You will also see the bond's reported yield. Unlike the coupon interest rate, which is fixed, the bond's yield varies from day to day depending on current market conditions. Moreover, the yield can be calculated in three different ways, and three "answers" can be obtained. These different yields are described in the following sections.

Yield to Maturity

Suppose you were offered a 14-year, 10 percent annual coupon, $1,000 par value bond at a price of $1,494.93. What rate of interest would you earn on your investment if you bought the bond and held it to maturity? This rate is called the bond's **yield to maturity (YTM),** and it is the interest rate generally discussed by investors when they talk about rates of return. The yield to maturity is generally the same as the market rate of interest, k_d, and to find it, all you need to do is solve Equation 8-1 for k_d:

$$V_B = \$1,494.93 = \frac{\$100}{(1 + k_d)^1} + \cdots + \frac{\$100}{(1 + k_d)^{14}} + \frac{\$1,000}{(1 + k_d)^{14}}.$$

You could substitute values for k_d until you find a value that "works" and forces the sum of the PVs on the right side of the equal sign to equal $1,494.93. Alternatively, you could substitute values of k_d into the third form of Equation 8-1 until you find a value that works.

Finding k_d = YTM by trial-and-error would be a tedious, time-consuming process, but as you might guess, it is easy with a financial calculator.[7] Here is the setup:

Inputs: 14   −1494.93   100   1000

[N]   [I]   [PV]   [PMT]   [FV]

Output: = 5

Simply enter N = 14, PV = −1494.93, PMT = 100, and FV = 1000, and then press the I key. The answer, 5 percent, will then appear.

The yield to maturity is identical to the total rate of return discussed in the preceding section. The yield to maturity can also be viewed as the bond's *promised rate of return*, which is the return that investors will receive if all the promised payments are made. However, the yield to maturity equals the *expected rate of return* only if (1) the probability of default is zero and (2) the bond cannot be called. If there is some default risk, or if the bond may be called, then there is some probability that the promised payments to maturity will not be received, in which case the calculated yield to maturity will differ from the expected return.

The YTM for a bond that sells at par consists entirely of an interest yield, but if the bond sells at a price other than its par value, the YTM will consist of the interest yield plus a positive or negative capital gains yield. Note also that a bond's yield to maturity changes whenever interest rates in the economy change, and this is almost daily. One who purchases a bond and holds it until it matures will receive the YTM that existed on the purchase date, but the bond's calculated YTM will change frequently between the purchase date and the maturity date.[8]

Yield to Call

If you purchased a bond that was callable and the company called it, you would not have the option of holding it until it matured. Therefore, the yield to maturity would not be

---

[7]A few years ago, bond traders all had specialized tables called *bond tables* that gave yields on bonds of different maturities selling at different premiums and discounts. Because calculators are so much more efficient (and accurate), bond tables are no longer used.

Most spreadsheets have specialized functions to find yields on bonds. For example, in *Excel* you could enter the formula: =YIELD(current date, maturity date, coupon rate, current price, redemption price as a percent of par value, number of payments per year, indicator for the convention to use when counting the days in the month). The spreadsheet would then produce the yield on the bond.

Also, one could use the compound interest tables at the back of this book (Tables A-1 and A-2) to find PVIF factors which force the following equation to an equality:

$$V_B = \$1,494.93 = \$100(PVIFA_{k_d,14}) + \$1,000(PVIF_{k_d,14}).$$

Factors for 5 percent would "work," indicating that 5 percent is the bond's YTM. This procedure can be used only if the YTM works out to a whole number percentage.

[8]We assume here that the investor will spend all coupon payments and the principal payment as soon as the payments are received. If instead the investor plans to reinvest some of these payments, the total return will not equal the original YTM. We discuss this in more detail later in the chapter.

earned. For example, if MicroDrive's 10 percent coupon bonds were callable, and if interest rates fell from 10 percent to 5 percent, then the company could call in the 10 percent bonds, replace them with 5 percent bonds, and save $100 − $50 = $50 interest per bond per year. This would be beneficial to the company, but not to its bondholders.

If current interest rates are well below an outstanding bond's coupon rate, then a callable bond is likely to be called, and investors will estimate its most likely rate of return as the **yield to call (YTC)** rather than as the yield to maturity. To calculate the YTC, solve this equation for k_d:

$$\text{Price of bond} = \sum_{t=1}^{N} \frac{\text{INT}}{(1 + k_d)^t} + \frac{\text{Call price}}{(1 + k_d)^N}. \tag{8-2}$$

Here N is the number of years until the company can call the bond; call price is the price the company must pay in order to call the bond (it is often set equal to the par value plus one year's interest); and k_d is the YTC.

To illustrate, suppose MicroDrive's bonds had a provision that permitted the company, if it desired, to call the bonds ten years after the issue date at a price of $1,100. Suppose further that interest rates had fallen, and one year after issuance the going interest rate had declined, causing the price of the bonds to rise to $1,494.93. Here is the time line and the setup for finding the bond's YTC with a financial calculator:

The YTC is 4.21 percent—this is the return you would earn if you bought the bond at a price of $1,494.93 and it was called nine years from today. (The bond could not be called until ten years after issuance, and one year has gone by, so there are nine years left until the first call date.)

Do you think MicroDrive *will* call the bonds when they become callable? MicroDrive's action would depend on what the going interest rate is when the bonds become callable. If the going rate remains at $k_d = 5\%$, then MicroDrive could save 10% − 5% = 5%, or $50 per bond per year, by calling them and replacing the 10 percent bonds with a new 5 percent issue. There would be costs to the company to refund the issue, but the interest savings would probably be worth the cost, so MicroDrive would probably refund the bonds. Therefore, you would probably earn YTC = 4.21% rather than YTM = 5% if you bought the bonds under the indicated conditions.

The analysis used to decide whether or not to call a bond is covered in detail in Chapter 18. In the balance of this chapter, we assume that bonds are not callable unless otherwise noted, but some of the end-of-chapter problems deal with yield to call.

Current Yield

If you examine brokerage house reports on bonds, you will often see reference to a bond's **current yield.** The current yield is the annual interest payment divided by the bond's current price. For example, if MicroDrive's 10 percent coupon bonds were currently selling at $985, their current yield would be 10.15 percent ($100/$985).

DRINKING YOUR COUPONS
Chateau Teyssier, an English vineyard, was seeking cash to purchase some additional vines and to modernize its production facilities. Their solution? With the assistance of a leading underwriter, Matrix Securities, the vineyard recently issued 375 bonds, each costing 2,650 British pounds. The issue raised nearly 1 million pounds, which is roughly $1.5 million.

What makes these bonds interesting is that, instead of getting paid with something boring like money, the bonds pay their investors with wine. Each June until 2002, when the bonds mature, investors will receive their "coupons." Between 1997 and 2001, each bond will provide six cases of the vineyard's rose or claret. Starting in 1998 and continuing through maturity in 2002, investors will also receive four cases

of its prestigious Saint Emilion Grand Cru. Then, in 2002, they will get their money back.

The bonds are not without risk. The vineyard's owner, Jonathan Malthus, acknowledges that the quality of the wine, "is at the mercy of the gods."

SOURCE: Steven Irvine, "My Wine Is My Bond, and I Drink My Coupons," *Euromoney,* July 1996, 7. Used with permission.

Unlike the yield to maturity, the current yield does not generally represent the return that investors should expect from holding the bond. The current yield provides information about the cash income a bond will generate in a given year, but since it does not take account of capital gains or losses that will be realized if the bond is held until maturity (or call), it does not provide an accurate measure of the total expected return.

The fact that the current yield does not provide an accurate measure of the total return can be illustrated with a zero coupon bond. Since zeros pay no annual income, they always have a current yield of zero. This indicates that the bond will not provide any cash interest income, but since it will appreciate in value over time, its total return clearly exceeds zero.

SELF-TEST
QUESTIONS

Describe the difference between the yield to maturity and the yield to call.

How does a bond's current yield differ from its total return?

Could the current yield exceed the total return?

BONDS WITH SEMIANNUAL COUPONS

Although some bonds pay interest annually, the vast majority actually pay interest semiannually. To evaluate semiannual payment bonds, we must modify Equation 8-1 as follows:

1. Divide the annual coupon interest payment by 2 to determine the amount of interest paid each six months.

2. Multiply the years to maturity, N, by 2 to determine the number of semiannual periods.

3. Divide the nominal (quoted) interest rate, k_d, by 2 to determine the periodic (semiannual) interest rate.

After making these changes, we have the following equation for finding the value of a bond that pays interest semiannually:

$$V_B = \sum_{t=1}^{2N} \frac{INT/2}{(1 + k_d/2)^t} + \frac{M}{(1 + k_d/2)^{2N}}. \qquad \text{(8-1a)}$$

To illustrate, assume now that MicroDrive's bonds pay $50 interest each six months rather than $100 at the end of each year. Thus, each interest payment is only half as large, but there are twice as many of them. The coupon rate is thus "10 percent, semi-annual payments." This is the nominal, or quoted, rate.[9]

When the going (nominal) rate of interest is 5 percent with semiannual compounding, the value of this 15-year bond is found as follows:

Inputs: 30   2.5   50   1000

N   I   PV   PMT   FV

Output: = –1,523.26

Enter N = 30, k = I = 2.5, PMT = 50, FV = 1000, and then press the PV key to obtain the bond's value, $1,523.26. The value with semiannual interest payments is slightly larger than $1,518.98, the value when interest is paid annually. This higher value occurs because interest payments are received somewhat faster under semiannual compounding.

Describe how the annual bond valuation formula is changed to evaluate semiannual coupon bonds. Then write out the revised formula.

ASSESSING THE RISKINESS OF A BOND

Interest Rate Risk

As we saw in Chapter 4, interest rates go up and down over time, and an increase in interest rates leads to a decline in the value of an outstanding bond. This risk of a decline in bond values due to rising interest rates is called **interest rate risk.** To illustrate, suppose you bought some 10 percent MicroDrive bonds at a price of $1,000, and interest rates in the following year rose to 15 percent. As we saw above, the price of the bonds would fall to $713.78, so you would have a loss of $286.22 per bond.[10] Interest rates can and do rise, and rising rates cause a loss of value for bondholders. Thus, people or firms who invest in bonds are exposed to risk from changing interest rates.

One's exposure to interest rate risk is higher on bonds with long maturities than on those maturing in the near future.[11] This point can be demonstrated by showing how

---

[9]In this situation, the nominal coupon rate of "10 percent, semiannually," is the rate that bond dealers, corporate treasurers, and investors generally would discuss. Of course, the *effective annual rate* would be higher than 10 percent at the time the bond was issued:

$$EAR = EFF\% = \left(1 + \frac{k_{Nom}}{m}\right)^m - 1 = \left(1 + \frac{0.10}{2}\right)^2 - 1 = (1.05)^2 - 1 = 10.25\%.$$

Note also that 10 percent with annual payments is different than 10 percent with semiannual payments. Thus, we have assumed an increase in effective rates in this section from the situation in the preceding section, where we assumed 10 percent with annual payments.

[10]You would have an *accounting* (and tax) loss only if you sold the bond; if you held it to maturity, you would not have such a loss. However, even if you did not sell, you would still have suffered a *real economic loss in an opportunity cost sense* because you would have lost the opportunity to invest at 15 percent and would be stuck with a 10 percent bond in a 15 percent market. In an economic sense, "paper losses" are just as bad as realized accounting losses.

[11]Actually, a bond's maturity and coupon rate both affect interest rate risk. Low coupons mean that most of the bond's return will come from repayment of principal, whereas on a high coupon bond with the same maturity, more of the cash flows will come in during the early years due to the relatively large coupon payments. A measurement called "duration," which finds the average number of years the bond's PV of cash flows remain outstanding, has been developed to combine maturity and coupons. A zero coupon bond, which has no interest payments and whose payments all come at maturity, has a duration equal to the bond's maturity. Coupon bonds all have durations that are shorter than maturity, and the higher the coupon rate, the shorter the duration. Bonds with longer duration are exposed to more interest rate risk. The Extensions section of Chapter 24 provides a discussion of duration.

the value of a 1-year bond with a 10 percent annual coupon fluctuates with changes in k_d, and then comparing these changes with those on a 14-year bond as calculated previously. The 1-year bond's values at different interest rates are shown below:

Value at k_d = 5%:

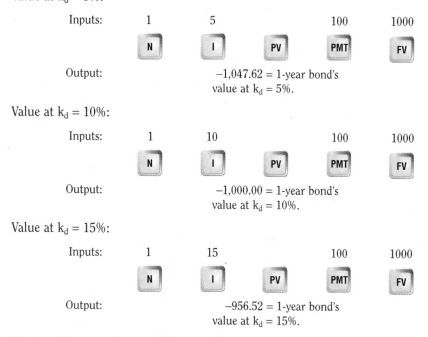

Inputs: 1   5   100   1000
          N   I   PV   PMT   FV

Output: −1,047.62 = 1-year bond's
                     value at k_d = 5%.

Value at k_d = 10%:

Inputs: 1   10   100   1000
          N   I   PV   PMT   FV

Output: −1,000.00 = 1-year bond's
                     value at k_d = 10%.

Value at k_d = 15%:

Inputs: 1   15   100   1000
          N   I   PV   PMT   FV

Output: −956.52 = 1-year bond's
                     value at k_d = 15%.

You would obtain the first value with a financial calculator by entering N = 1, I = 5, PMT = 100, and FV = 1000, and then pressing PV to get −$1,047.62. With everything still in your calculator, enter I = 10 to override the old I = 5, and press PV to find the bond's value at k_d = I = 10; it is −$1,000. Then enter I = 15 and press the PV key to find the last bond value, −$956.52. Disregard the minus signs—the calculator shows a negative PV if the PMT and FV are inputted as positive numbers.

The values of the 1-year and 14-year bonds at several current market interest rates are summarized and plotted in Figure 8-3. Notice how much more sensitive the price of the 14-year bond is to changes in interest rates. At a 10 percent interest rate, both the 14-year and the 1-year bonds are valued at $1,000. When rates rise to 15 percent, the 14-year bond falls to $713.78, but the 1-year bond only falls to $956.52.

For bonds with similar coupons, this differential sensitivity to changes in interest rates always holds true—the longer the maturity of the bond, the more its price changes in response to a given change in interest rates. Thus, even if the risk of default on two bonds is exactly the same, the one with the longer maturity is typically exposed to more risk from a rise in interest rates.[12]

The logical explanation for this difference in interest rate risk is simple. Suppose you bought a 14-year bond that yielded 10 percent, or $100 a year. Now suppose interest rates on comparable-risk bonds rose to 15 percent. You would be stuck with only $100 of interest for the next 14 years. On the other hand, had you bought a 1-year bond, you would have a low return for only 1 year. At the end of the year, you would get your

[12]If a 10-year bond were plotted in Figure 8-3, its curve would lie between those of the 14-year bond and the 1-year bond. The curve of a 1-month bond would be almost horizontal, indicating that its price would change very little in response to an interest rate change, but a 100-year bond (or a perpetuity) would have a very steep slope. Also, zero coupon bond prices are quite sensitive to interest rate changes, and the longer the maturity of the zero, the greater its price sensitivity. Therefore, a 30-year zero coupon bond would have a huge amount of interest rate risk.

| FIGURE 8-3 | Value of Long- and Short-Term 10% Annual Coupon Bonds at Different Market Interest Rates |

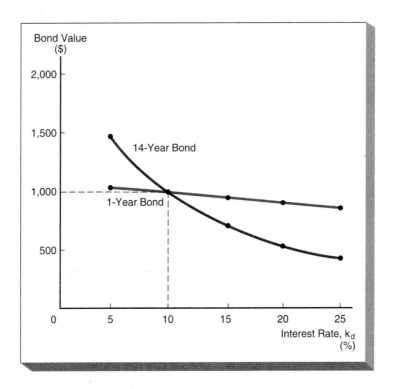

	VALUE OF	
CURRENT MARKET INTEREST RATE, k_d	1-YEAR BOND	14-YEAR BOND
5%	$1,047.62	$1,494.93
10	1,000.00	1,000.00
15	956.52	713.78
20	916.67	538.94
25	880.00	426.39

NOTE: Bond values were calculated using a financial calculator assuming annual, or once-a-year, compounding.

$1,000 back, and you could then reinvest it and receive 15 percent, or $150 per year, for the next 13 years. Thus, interest rate risk reflects the length of time one is committed to a given investment.

As we just saw, the prices of long-term bonds are more sensitive to changes in interest rates than are short-term bonds. To induce an investor to take this extra risk, long-term bonds must have a higher expected rate of return than short-term bonds. This additional return is the maturity risk premium (MRP), which we discussed in Chapter 4. Therefore, one might expect to see higher yields on long-term than on short-term bonds. Does this actually happen? Generally, the answer is yes. Recall from Chapter 4 that the yield curve usually is upward sloping, which is consistent with the idea that longer maturity bonds must have a higher expected rate of return to compensate for their higher risk.

Reinvestment Rate Risk

As we saw in the preceding section, an *increase* in interest rates will hurt bond-holders because it will lead to a decline in the value of a bond portfolio. But can a *decrease* in interest rates also hurt bondholders? The answer is yes, because if interest rates fall, a bondholder will probably suffer a reduction in his or her income. For example, consider a retiree who has a portfolio of bonds and lives off the income they produce. The bonds, on average, have a coupon rate of 10 percent. Now suppose interest rates decline to 5 percent. Many of the bonds will be called, and as calls occur, the bondholder will have to replace 10 percent bonds with 5 percent bonds. Even bonds that are not callable will mature, and when they do, they will have to be replaced with lower-yielding bonds. Thus, our retiree will suffer a reduction of income.

The risk of an income decline due to a drop in interest rates is called **reinvestment rate risk,** and its importance has been demonstrated to all bondholders in recent years as a result of the sharp drop in rates since the mid-1980s. Reinvestment rate risk is obviously high on callable bonds. It is also high on short maturity bonds, because the shorter the maturity of a bond, the fewer the years when the relatively high old interest rate will be earned, and the sooner the funds will have to be reinvested at the new low rate. Thus, retirees whose primary holdings were short-term securities, such as bank CDs and short-term bonds, were hurt badly by the recent decline in rates, but holders of long-term bonds are still enjoying their old high rates.

Comparing Interest Rate and Reinvestment Rate Risk

Notice that interest rate risk relates to the *value* of the bonds in a portfolio, while reinvestment rate risk relates to the *income* the portfolio produces. If you hold long-term bonds, you will face interest rate risk; that is, the value of your bonds will decline if interest rates rise. However, you will not face much reinvestment rate risk, so your income will be stable. On the other hand, if you hold short-term bonds, you will not be exposed to much interest rate risk, so the value of your portfolio will be stable, but you will be exposed to reinvestment rate risk, and your income will decline if interest rates fall.

We see, then, that no fixed-rate bond can be considered totally riskless—even most Treasury bonds are exposed to both interest rate and reinvestment rate risk.[13] One can minimize interest rate risk by holding short-term bonds or minimize reinvestment rate risk by holding long-term bonds, but the actions that lower one type of risk increase the other. Bond portfolio managers try to balance these two risks, but some risk generally remains in any bond.

<table>
<tr><td>S E L F - T E S T
Q U E S T I O N S</td><td>Differentiate between interest rate risk and reinvestment rate risk.

To which type of risk are holders of long-term bonds more exposed? Short-term bondholders?</td></tr>
</table>

---

[13]Note, though, that indexed Treasury bonds are essentially riskless, but they pay a relatively low real rate. Also, risks have not disappeared—they are simply transferred from bondholders to taxpayers.

DEFAULT RISK

Another important risk associated with bonds is default risk. If the issuer defaults, investors receive less than the promised return on the bond. Therefore, investors need to assess a bond's default risk before making a purchase. Recall from Chapter 4 that the quoted interest rate includes a default risk premium—the greater the default risk, the higher the bond's yield to maturity. The default risk on Treasury securities is zero, but default risk can be substantial for corporate and municipal bonds.

Suppose two bonds have the same promised stream of cash flows, coupon rate, maturity, liquidity, and inflation exposure, but different levels of default risk. Investors will naturally pay less for the bond with the greater chance of default. As a result, bonds with higher default risk will have higher interest rates: $k_d = k^* + IP + DRP + LP + MRP$.

If its default risk changes, this will affect the price of a bond. For example, if the default risk of the MicroDrive bonds increases, the bonds' price will fall and the yield to maturity (YTM = k_d) will increase.

In this section we consider some issues related to default risk. First, we show that corporations and municipalities can use different provisions in their bond contracts to influence the default risk of their bonds. Second, we discuss bond ratings, which are used to measure default risk. Third, we describe the "junk bond market," which is the market for bonds with a relatively high probability of default.

Bond Contract Provisions That Influence Default Risk

Default risk is affected by both the financial strength of the issuer and the terms of the bond contract, especially whether collateral has been pledged to secure the bond. Several types of contract provisions are discussed below.

Bond Indentures.   An **indenture** is a legal document that spells out the rights of both bondholders and the issuing corporation, and a **trustee** is an official (usually a bank) who represents the bondholders and makes sure the terms of the indenture are carried out. The indenture may be several hundred pages in length, and it will include **restrictive covenants** that cover such points as the conditions under which the issuer can pay off the bonds prior to maturity, the level at which the issuer's times-interest-earned ratio must be maintained if the company is to issue additional debt, and restrictions against the payment of dividends unless earnings meet certain specifications.

The trustee is responsible for monitoring the covenants and for taking appropriate action if a violation does occur. What constitutes "appropriate action" varies with the circumstances. It might be that to insist on immediate compliance would result in bankruptcy and possibly large losses on the bonds. In such a case, the trustee might decide that the bondholders would be better served by giving the company a chance to work out its problems and thus avoid forcing it into bankruptcy.

The Securities and Exchange Commission (1) approves indentures and (2) makes sure that all indenture provisions are met before allowing a company to sell new securities to the public. Also, it should be noted that the indentures of many larger corporations were actually written in the 1930s or 1940s, and that many issues of new bonds sold since then were covered by the same indenture. The interest rates on the bonds, and perhaps also the maturities, varied depending on market conditions at the time of each issue, but bondholders' protection as spelled out in the indenture was the same for all bonds of the same type. A firm will have different indentures for each of the major types of bonds it issues. For example, one indenture will cover its first mortgage bonds, another its debentures, and a third its convertible bonds.

Mortgage Bonds.   Under a **mortgage bond,** the corporation pledges certain assets as security for the bond. To illustrate, in 1996, Billingham Corporation needed $10 million to build a major regional distribution center. Bonds in the amount of $4 million, secured by a *first mortgage* on the property, were issued. (The remaining $6 million was financed with equity capital.) If Billingham defaults on the bonds, the bondholders can foreclose on the property and sell it to satisfy their claims.

If Billingham chose to, it could issue *second mortgage bonds* secured by the same $10 million of assets. In the event of liquidation, the holders of these second mortgage bonds would have a claim against the property, but only after the first mortgage bondholders had been paid off in full. Thus, second mortgages are sometimes called *junior mortgages,* because they are junior in priority to the claims of *senior mortgages,* or *first mortgage bonds.*

All mortgage bonds are subject to an indenture. The indentures of many major corporations were written 20, 30, 40, or more years ago. These indentures are generally "open ended," meaning that new bonds can be issued from time to time under the existing indenture. However, the amount of new bonds that can be issued is virtually always limited to a specified percentage of the firm's total "bondable property," which generally includes all land, plant, and equipment.

For example, Savannah Electric Company can issue first mortgage bonds totaling up to 60 percent of its fixed assets. If its fixed assets totaled $1 billion, and if it had $500 million of first mortgage bonds outstanding, it could, by the property test, issue another $100 million of bonds (60% of $1 billion = $600 million).

At times, Savannah Electric has been unable to issue any new first mortgage bonds because of another indenture provision: its times-interest-earned (TIE) ratio was below 2.5, the minimum coverage that it must have if it sells new bonds. Thus, although Savannah Electric passed the property test, it failed the coverage test, so it could not issue first mortgage bonds. Savannah Electric then had to finance with junior bonds. Since first mortgage bonds would have carried lower rates of interest than junior long-term debt, this restriction was a costly one.

Savannah Electric's neighbor, Georgia Power Company, has more flexibility under its indenture—its interest coverage requirement is only 2.0. In hearings before the Georgia Public Service Commission, it was suggested that Savannah Electric should change its indenture coverage to 2.0 so that it could issue more first mortgage bonds. However, this was simply not possible—the holders of the outstanding bonds would have to approve the change, and it is inconceivable that they would vote for a change that would seriously weaken their position.

Debentures.   A **debenture** is an unsecured bond, and as such it provides no lien against specific property as security for the obligation. Debenture holders are, therefore, general creditors whose claims are protected by property not otherwise pledged. In practice, the use of debentures depends both on the nature of the firm's assets and on its general credit strength. An extremely strong company such as AT&T will tend to use debentures; it simply does not need to put up property as security for its debt. Debentures are also issued by weak companies which have already pledged most of their assets as collateral for mortgage loans. In this latter case, the debentures are relatively risky, and they will bear a high interest rate.

Subordinated Debentures.   The term *subordinate* means "below," or "inferior to," and, in the event of bankruptcy, subordinated debt has claims on assets only after senior debt has been paid off. **Subordinated debentures** may be subordinated either to designated notes payable (usually bank loans) or to all other debt. In the event of liquidation or reorganization, holders of subordinated debentures cannot be paid until all senior debt, as named in the debentures' indenture, has been paid. Precisely how subordination works, and how it strengthens the position of senior debtholders, is explained in detail in Chapter 25.

Development Bonds.   Some companies may be in a position to benefit from the sale of either **development bonds** or **pollution control bonds**. State and local governments may set up both *industrial development agencies* and *pollution control agencies*. These agencies are allowed, under certain circumstances, to sell **tax-exempt bonds**, then to make the proceeds available to corporations for specific uses deemed (by Congress) to be in the public interest. Thus, an industrial development agency in Florida might sell bonds to provide funds for a paper company to build a plant in the Florida Panhandle, where unemployment is high. Similarly, a Detroit pollution control agency might sell bonds to provide Ford with funds to be used to purchase pollution control equipment. In both cases, the income from the bonds would be tax exempt to the holders, so the bonds would sell at relatively low interest rates. Note, however, that these bonds are guaranteed by the corporation that will use the funds, not by a governmental unit, so their rating reflects the credit strength of the corporation using the funds.

Municipal Bond Insurance.   Municipalities can have their bonds insured, in which an insurance company guarantees to pay the coupon and principal payments should the issuer default. This reduces risk to investors, who will thus accept a lower coupon rate for an insured bond vis-à-vis an uninsured one. Even though the municipality must pay a fee to get its bonds insured, its savings due to the lower coupon rate often makes insurance cost-effective. Keep in mind that the insurers are private companies, and the value added by the insurance depends on the creditworthiness of the insurer. However, the larger ones are strong companies, and their own ratings are AAA. Therefore, the bonds they insure are also rated AAA, regardless of the credit strength of the municipal issuer. Bond ratings are discussed in the next section.

Bond Ratings

Since the early 1900s, bonds have been assigned quality ratings that reflect their probability of going into default. The three major rating agencies are Moody's Investors Service (Moody's), Standard & Poor's Corporation (S&P), and Fitch Investors Service. Moody's and S&P rating designations are shown in Table 8-1.[14] The triple- and double-A bonds are extremely safe. Single-A and triple-B bonds are also strong enough to be called **investment grade bonds**, and they are the lowest-rated bonds that many banks

---

[14] In the discussion to follow, reference to the S&P code is intended to imply the Moody's and Fitch's codes as well. Thus, triple-B bonds mean both BBB and Baa bonds; double-B bonds mean both BB and Ba bonds; and so on.

| **TABLE 8-1** | Moody's and S&P Bond Ratings |

	INVESTMENT GRADE				**JUNK BONDS**			
Moody's	Aaa	Aa	A	Baa	Ba	B	Caa	C
S&P	AAA	AA	A	BBB	BB	B	CCC	D

NOTE: Both Moody's and S&P use "modifiers" for bonds rated below triple-A. S&P uses a plus and minus system; thus, A+ designates the strongest A-rated bonds and A– the weakest. Moody's uses a 1, 2, or 3 designation, with 1 denoting the strongest and 3 the weakest; thus, within the double-A category, Aa1 is the best, Aa2 is average, and Aa3 is the weakest.

and other institutional investors are permitted by law to hold. Double-B and lower bonds are speculative, or **junk bonds**. These bonds have a significant probability of going into default. A later section discusses junk bonds in more detail.

Bond Rating Criteria.   Bond ratings are based on both qualitative and quantitative factors, some of which are listed below:

1. **Ratios:** How strong are the debt ratio, the times-interest-earned ratio, the fixed charge coverage ratio, the current ratio, and other ratios? The better the ratios, the higher the bond's rating.

2. **Mortgage provisions:** Is the bond secured by a mortgage? If it is, and if the property has a high value in relation to the amount of bonded debt, the bond's rating is enhanced.

3. **Subordination provisions:** Is the bond subordinated to other debt? If so, it will be rated at least one notch below the rating it would have if it were not subordinated. Conversely, a bond with other debt subordinated to it will have a somewhat higher rating.

4. **Guarantee provisions:** Some bonds are guaranteed by other firms. If a weak company's debt is guaranteed by a strong company (usually the weak company's parent), the bond will be given the strong company's rating.

5. **Sinking fund:** Does the bond have a sinking fund to ensure systematic repayment? This feature is a plus factor to the rating agencies.

6. **Maturity:** Other things the same, a bond with a shorter maturity will be judged less risky than a longer-term bond, and this will be reflected in the ratings.

7. **Stability:** Are the issuer's sales and earnings stable?

8. **Regulation:** Is the issuer regulated, and could an adverse regulatory climate cause the company's economic position to decline? Regulation is especially important for utilities, railroads, and telephone companies.

9. **Antitrust:** Are any antitrust actions pending against the firm that could erode its position?

10. **Overseas operations:** What percentage of the firm's sales, assets, and profits are from overseas operations, and what is the political climate in the host countries?

11. **Environmental factors:** Is the firm likely to face heavy expenditures for pollution control equipment?

12. **Product liability:** Are the firm's products safe? The tobacco companies today are under pressure, and so are their bond ratings.

13. **Pension liabilities:** Does the firm have unfunded pension liabilities that could pose a future problem?

14. **Labor unrest:** Are there potential labor problems on the horizon that could weaken the firm's position? As this is written, a number of airlines face this problem, and it has caused their ratings to be lowered.

15. **Accounting policies:** If a firm uses relatively conservative accounting policies, its reported earnings will be of "higher quality" than if it uses less conservative procedures. Thus, conservative accounting policies are a plus factor in bond ratings.

Representatives of the rating agencies have consistently stated that no precise formula is used to set a firm's rating; all the factors listed, plus others, are taken into account, but not in a mathematically precise manner. Statistical studies have borne out this contention, for researchers who have tried to predict bond ratings on the basis of quantitative data have had only limited success, indicating that the agencies use subjective judgment when establishing a firm's rating.[15]

Importance of Bond Ratings.   Bond ratings are important both to firms and to investors. First, because a bond's rating is an indicator of its default risk, the rating has a direct, measurable influence on the bond's interest rate and the firm's cost of debt. Second, most bonds are purchased by institutional investors rather than individuals, and many institutions are restricted to investment-grade securities. Thus, if a firm's bonds fall below BBB, it will have a difficult time selling new bonds, because many potential purchasers will not be allowed to buy them.

As a result of their higher risk and more restricted market, lower-grade bonds have higher required rates of return, k_d, than high-grade bonds. Figure 8-4 illustrates this point. In each of the years shown on the graph, U.S. government bonds have had the lowest yields, AAAs have been next, and BBB bonds have had the highest yields. The figure also shows that the gaps between yields on the three types of bonds vary over time, indicating that the cost differentials, or risk premiums, fluctuate from year to year. This point is highlighted in Figure 8-5, which gives the yields on the three types of bonds and the risk premiums for AAA and BBB bonds in June 1963 and September 1997.[16] Note first that the risk-free rate, or vertical axis intercept, rose more than 2 percentage points from 1963 to 1997, primarily reflecting the increase in realized and anticipated inflation. Second, the slope of the line has increased since 1963, indicating an increase in investors' risk aversion. Thus, the penalty for having a low credit rating varies over time. Occasionally, as in 1963, the penalty is quite small, but at other times it is large. These slope differences reflect investors' aversion to risk.

Changes in Ratings.   Changes in a firm's bond rating affect both its ability to borrow long-term capital and the cost of that capital. Rating agencies review outstanding bonds on a periodic basis, occasionally upgrading or downgrading a bond as a result of its issuer's changed circumstances. For example, the September 4, 1996, issue of *Standard & Poor's CreditWeek* reported that Tribune Co.'s senior debt had been downgraded from A+ to A. This downgrading reflected the higher debt burden the company will have in 1997 following its acquisition of Renaissance Communications Corp. While the Renaissance acquisition bolsters Tribune's business position and diversifies its advertising market exposure, it was paid for by borrowing and thus increased Tribune's debt ratio. In the same issue, *CreditWeek* upgraded the subordinated debt of Specialty Equipment Companies, which provides McDonald's with ice cream machines and grills, from B– to B, to reflect Specialty's improving financial ratios.

Junk Bonds

Prior to the 1980s, fixed-income investors such as pension funds and insurance companies were generally unwilling to buy risky bonds, so it was almost impossible for

---

[15]See Ahmed Belkaoui, *Industrial Bonds and the Rating Process* (London: Quorum Books, 1983).

[16]The term *risk premium* ought to reflect only the difference in expected (and required) returns between two securities that results from differences in their risk. However, the differences between *yields to maturity* on different types of bonds consist of (1) a true risk premium; (2) a liquidity premium, which reflects the fact that U.S. Treasury bonds are more readily marketable than most corporate bonds; (3) a call premium, because most Treasury bonds are not callable whereas corporate bonds are; and (4) an expected loss differential, which reflects the probability of loss on the corporate bonds. As an example of the last point, suppose the yield to maturity on a BBB bond was 8 percent versus 7 percent on government bonds, but there was a 5 percent probability of total default loss on the corporate bond. In this case, the expected return on the BBB bond would be 0.95(8%) + 0.05(0%) = 7.6%, and the risk premium would be 0.6 percent, not the full 1 percentage point difference in "promised" yields to maturity. Because of all these points, the risk premiums given in Figure 8-5 overstate somewhat the true (but unmeasurable) theoretical risk premiums.

FIGURE 8-4   Yields on Selected Long-Term Bonds, 1959–1997

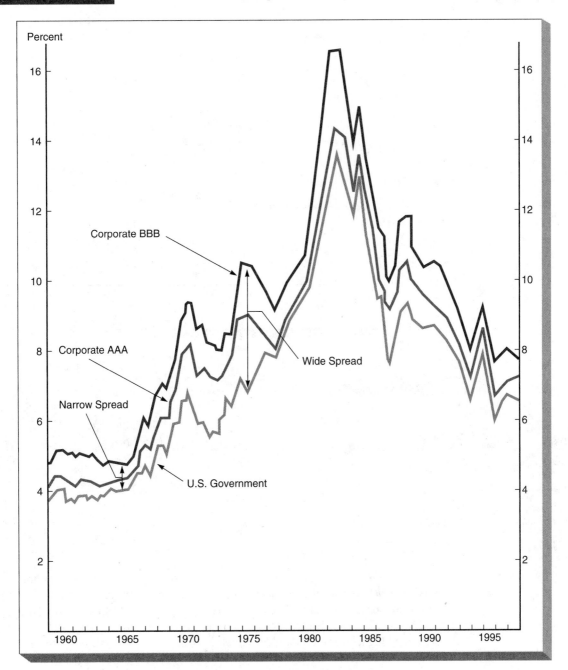

SOURCES: Federal Reserve Board, *Historical Chart Book,* 1983, and *Federal Reserve Bulletin,* various issues.

risky companies to raise capital in the public bond markets. Then, in the late 1970s, Michael Milken of the investment banking firm Drexel Burnham Lambert, relying on historical studies which showed that risky bonds yielded more than enough to compensate for their risk, began to convince institutional investors of the merits of purchasing risky debt. Thus was born the "junk bond," a high-risk, high-yield bond issued

| FIGURE 8-5 | Relationship between Bond Ratings and Bond Yields, 1963 and 1997 |

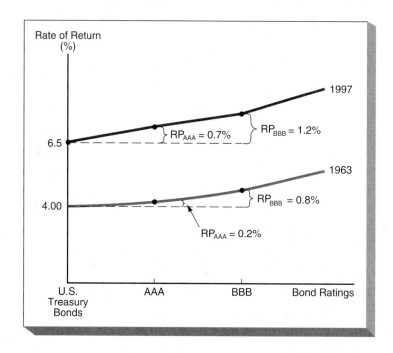

	LONG-TERM GOVERNMENT BONDS (DEFAULT-FREE) (1)	AAA CORPORATE BONDS (2)	BBB CORPORATE BONDS (3)	RISK PREMIUMS	
				AAA (4) = (2) − (1)	BBB (5) = (3) − (1)
June 1963	4.0%	4.2%	4.8%	0.2%	0.8%
September 1997	6.5	7.2	7.7	0.7	1.2

RP$_{AAA}$ = risk premium on AAA bonds.
RP$_{BBB}$ = risk premium on BBB bonds.

SOURCES: *Federal Reserve Bulletin,* December 1963, and *Federal Reserve Statistical Release,* October 1997.

to finance a leveraged buyout, a merger, or a troubled company.[17] For example, Public Service of New Hampshire financed construction of its troubled Seabrook nuclear plant with junk bonds, and junk bonds were used by Ted Turner to finance the development of CNN and Turner Broadcasting. In junk bond deals, the debt ratio is generally extremely high, so the bondholders must bear as much risk as stockholders normally would. The bonds' yields reflect this fact—a promised return of 25 percent per annum was required to sell the Public Service of New Hampshire bonds.

The emergence of junk bonds as an important type of debt is another example of how the investment banking industry adjusts to and facilitates new developments in capital markets. In the 1980s, mergers and takeovers increased dramatically. People

---

[17]Another type of junk bond is one that was highly rated when it was issued but whose rating has fallen because its issuer corporation has fallen on hard times. Such bonds are called "fallen angels."

SANTA FE BONDS FINALLY MATURE AFTER 114 YEARS

In 1995, Santa Fe Pacific Company made the final payment on some outstanding bonds that were originally issued in 1881! While the bonds were paid off in full, their history has been anything but routine.

Since the bonds were issued in 1881, investors have seen Santa Fe go through two bankruptcy reorganizations, two depressions, several recessions, two world wars, and the collapse of the gold standard. Through it all, the company remained intact, although ironically it did agree to be acquired by Burlington Northern just prior to the bonds' maturity.

When the bonds were issued by the Santa Fe railroad company in 1881, they had a 6 percent coupon. After a promising start, competition in the railroad business, along with the Depression of 1893, dealt a crippling one-two punch to the com-

pany's fortunes. After two bankruptcy reorganizations — and two new management teams — the company got back on its feet, and in 1895 it replaced the original bonds with new 100-year bonds. The new bonds, sanctioned by the Bankruptcy Court, matured in 1995 and carried a 4 percent coupon. However, they also had a wrinkle that was in effect until 1900 — the company could skip the coupon payment if, in management's opinion, earnings were not sufficiently high to service the debt. After 1900, the company could no longer just ignore the coupon, but it did have the option of deferring the payments if management deemed deferral necessary. In the late 1890s, Santa Fe did skip the interest, and the bonds sold at an all-time low of $285 (28.5% of par) in 1896. The bonds reached a peak in 1946, when they sold for $1,312.50 in the strong, low interest rate economy after World War II.

Interestingly, the bonds' principal payment was originally pegged to the price of gold, meaning that the principal received at maturity would increase if the price of gold increased. This type of contract was declared invalid in 1933 by President Roosevelt and Congress, and the decision was upheld by the Supreme Court in a 5-4 vote. If just one Supreme Court justice had gone the other way, then, due to an increase in the price of gold, the bonds would have been worth $18,626 rather than $1,000 when they matured in 1995!

In many ways, the saga of the Santa Fe bonds is a testament to the stability of the U.S. financial system. On the other hand, it signifies the many types of risks that investors face when they purchase long-term bonds. Investors in the 100-year bonds recently issued by Disney and Coca-Cola, among others, should perhaps take note.

---

like T. Boone Pickens and Henry Kravitz thought that certain old-line, established companies were run inefficiently and were financed too conservatively, and they wanted to take these companies over and restructure them. Michael Milken and his staff at Drexel Burnham Lambert began an active campaign to persuade certain institutions (often S&Ls) to purchase high-yield bonds. Milken developed expertise in putting together deals that were attractive to the institutions yet apparently feasible in the sense that projected cash flows were sufficient to meet the projected interest payments. The fact that interest on the bonds was tax deductible, combined with the much higher debt ratios of the restructured firms, also increased after-tax cash flows and helped make the deals appear feasible.

The development of junk bond financing has done much to reshape the U.S. financial scene. The existence of these securities led directly to the loss of independence of Gulf Oil and hundreds of other companies, and it led to major shake-ups in such companies as CBS, Union Carbide, and USX (formerly U.S. Steel). It also caused Drexel Burnham Lambert to leap from essentially nowhere in the 1970s to become the most profitable investment banking firm during the 1980s.

The phenomenal growth of the junk bond market was impressive, but controversial. In 1989, Drexel Burnham was forced into bankruptcy, and "junk bond king" Michael Milken, who had earned $500 million two years earlier, was sent to jail. These events led to the collapse of the junk bond market in the early 1990s. Since then, however, the junk bond market has rebounded, and junk bonds are here to stay as an important form of corporate financing.

Differentiate between mortgage bonds and debentures.

Name the major rating agencies, and list some factors that affect bond ratings.

Why are bond ratings important both to firms and to investors?

For what purposes have junk bonds typically been used?

BOND MARKETS

Corporate bonds are traded primarily in the over-the-counter market. Most bonds are owned by and traded among the large financial institutions (for example, life insurance companies, mutual funds, and pension funds, all of which deal in very large blocks of securities), and it is relatively easy for the over-the-counter bond dealers to arrange the transfer of large blocks of bonds among the relatively few holders of the bonds. It would be much more difficult to conduct similar operations in the stock market among the literally millions of large and small stockholders, so a higher percentage of stocks trade on the exchanges.

Information on bond trades in the over-the-counter market is not published, but a representative group of bonds is listed and traded on the bond division of the NYSE. Figure 8-6 gives a section of the bond market page of *The Wall Street Journal* for trading on September 19, 1997. A total of 246 issues were traded on that date, but we show only the bonds of Cleveland Electric Company. Note that Cleveland Electric had three different bonds that were traded on September 19; the company actually had more than ten bond issues outstanding, but most of them did not trade on that date.

The bonds of Cleveland Electric and other companies can have various denominations, but for convenience we generally think of each bond as having a par value of $1,000 — this is how much per bond the company borrowed and how much it must someday repay. However, since other denominations are possible, for trading and reporting purposes bonds are quoted as percentages of par. Looking at the first bond listed in the data in Figure 8-6, we see that there is an 8¾ just after the company's name; this indicates that the bond is of the series which pays 8¾ percent interest, or 0.0875($1,000) = $87.50 of interest per year. The 8¾ percent is the bond's *coupon rate.* The Cleveland Electric bonds, and all the others listed in the *Journal,* pay interest semi-annually, so all rates are nominal, not EAR rates. The 05 which comes next indicates

---

FIGURE 8-6   NYSE Bond Market Transactions, September 19, 1997

	CORPORATION BONDS			
	VOLUME $13,781,000			
BONDS	CUR YLD	VOL	CLOSE	NET CHG.
ClevEl 8¾05	8.6	15	102	+½
ClevEl 9¼09	8.9	51	103¾	· · ·
ClevEl 8⅜12	8.3	34	101⅛	−¼

SOURCE: *The Wall Street Journal,* September 22, 1997, C17.

that this bond matures and must be repaid in the year 2005; it is not shown in the figure, but this bond was issued in 1970, so it had a 35-year original maturity. The 8.6 in the second column is the bond's current yield: Current yield = $87.50/$1,020 = 8.58%, rounded to 8.6 percent. The 15 in the third column indicates that 15 of these bonds were traded on September 19, 1997. Since the price shown in the fourth column is expressed as a percentage of par, the bond closed at 102 percent, which translates to $1,020, a $5 increase from the previous day.

Coupon rates are generally set at levels which reflect the "going rate of interest" on the day a bond is issued. If the rates were set lower, investors simply would not buy the bonds at the $1,000 par value, so the company could not borrow the money it needed. Thus, bonds generally sell at their par values on the day they are issued, but bond prices fluctuate thereafter as interest rates change.

As shown in Figure 8-7, the Cleveland bonds initially sold at par, rose above par in the early 1970s when interest rates dipped below 8.75 percent, hit a low in 1981, and rose thereafter. The increase resulted from (1) the general decline in interest rates and (2) the fact that bonds approach their par values as their maturity approaches.

S E L F - T E S T
Q U E S T I O N S

Why do most bond trades occur in the over-the-counter market?

If a bond issue is to be sold at par, how will its coupon rate be determined?

FIGURE 8-7   Cleveland Electric 8.75%, 35-Year Bond:
Market Value as Interest Rates Change

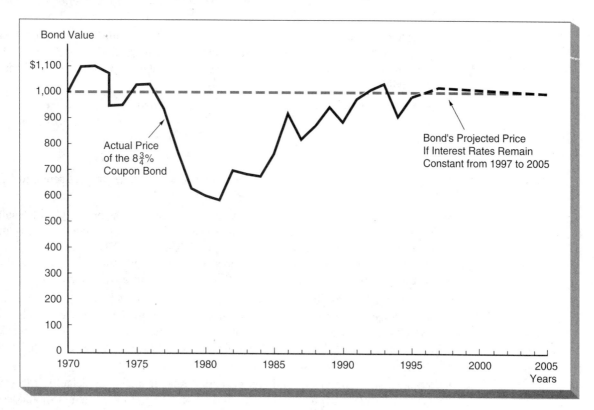

NOTE: The line from 1997 to 2005 appears linear, but it actually has a slight curve.

SUMMARY

This chapter described the different types of bonds governments and corporations issue, explained how bond prices are established, and discussed how investors go about estimating the rates of return they can expect to earn. The key concepts covered are summarized below.

- A **bond** is a long-term promissory note issued by a business or governmental unit. The issuer receives money in exchange for promising to make interest payments and to repay the principal on a specified future date.

- Some recent innovations in long-term financing include **zero coupon bonds,** which pay no annual interest but which are issued at a discount; **floating rate debt,** whose interest payments fluctuate with changes in the general level of interest rates; and **junk bonds,** which are high-risk, high-yield instruments issued by firms which use a great deal of financial leverage.

- A **call provision** gives the issuing corporation the right to redeem the bonds prior to maturity under specified terms, usually at a price greater than the maturity value (the difference is a **call premium**). A firm will typically call a bond if interest rates fall substantially below the coupon rate.

- A **redeemable bond** gives the investor the right to sell the bond back to the issuing company at a previously specified price. This is a useful feature (for investors) if interest rates rise or if the company engages in unanticipated risky activities.

- A **sinking fund** is a provision which requires the corporation to retire a portion of the bond issue each year. The purpose of the sinking fund is to provide for the orderly retirement of the issue. A sinking fund typically requires no call premium.

- The **value of a bond** is found as the present value of an **annuity** (the interest payments) plus the present value of a lump sum (the **principal**). The bond is evaluated at the appropriate periodic interest rate over the number of periods for which interest payments are made.

- The equation used to find the value of an annual coupon bond is:

$$V_B = \sum_{t=1}^{N} \frac{INT}{(1 + k_d)^t} + \frac{M}{(1 + k_d)^N}.$$

An adjustment to the formula must be made if the bond pays interest **semiannually:** divide INT and k_d by 2, and multiply N by 2.

- The return earned on a bond held to maturity is defined as the bond's **yield to maturity (YTM)**. If the bond can be redeemed before maturity, it is **callable**, and the return investors receive if it is called is defined as the **yield to call (YTC)**. The YTC is found as the present value of the interest payments received while the bond is outstanding plus the present value of the call price (the par value plus a call premium).

- The longer the maturity of a bond, the more its price will change in response to a given change in interest rates; this is called **interest rate risk**. However, bonds with short maturities expose investors to high **reinvestment rate risk**, which is the risk that income from a bond portfolio will decline because cash flows received from bonds will be rolled over at lower interest rates.

- Corporate and municipal bonds have **default risk**. If an issuer defaults, investors receive less than the promised return on the bond. Therefore, investors should evaluate a bond's default risk before making a purchase.

- There are many different types of bonds with different sets of features. These include **convertible bonds, bonds with warrants, income bonds, purchasing power (indexed) bonds, mortgage bonds, debentures, subordinated debentures, junk bonds, development bonds,** and **insured municipal bonds**. The return required on each type of bond is determined by the bond's riskiness.

- Bonds are assigned **ratings** which reflect the probability of their going into default. The highest rating is AAA, and they go down to D. The higher a bond's rating, the lower its risk and its interest rate.

Questions

8-1 Define each of the following terms:
a. Bond; Treasury bond; corporate bond; municipal bond; foreign bond
b. Par value; maturity date
c. Coupon payment; coupon interest rate
d. Floating rate bond; zero coupon bond; original issue discount bond (OID)
e. Call provision; redeemable bond; sinking fund
f. Convertible bond; warrant; income bond; indexed, or purchasing power, bond
g. Premium bond; discount bond
h. Current yield (on a bond); yield to maturity (YTM); yield to call (YTC)
i. Reinvestment risk; interest rate risk
j. Default risk
k. Indentures; mortgage bond; debenture; subordinated debenture
l. Development bond; municipal bond insurance
m. Junk bond; investment-grade bond

8-2 Is it true that the following equation can be used to find the value of an N-year bond that pays interest once a year?

$$V_B = \sum_{t=1}^{N} \frac{\text{Annual interest}}{(1 + k_d)^t} + \frac{\text{Par value}}{(1 + k_d)^N}.$$

8-3 "The values of outstanding bonds change whenever the going rate of interest changes. In general, short-term interest rates are more volatile than long-term interest rates. Therefore, short-term bond prices are more sensitive to interest rate changes than are long-term bond prices." Is this statement true or false? Explain.

8-4 The rate of return you would get if you bought a bond and held it to its maturity date is called the bond's yield to maturity. If interest rates in the economy rise after a bond has been issued, what will happen to the bond's price and to its YTM? Does the length of time to maturity affect the extent to which a given change in interest rates will affect the bond's price?

8-5 If you buy a *callable* bond and interest rates decline, will the value of your bond rise by as much as it would have risen if the bond had not been callable? Explain.

8-6 A sinking fund can be set up in one of two ways:
(1) The corporation makes annual payments to the trustee, who invests the proceeds in securities (frequently government bonds) and uses the accumulated total to retire the bond issue at maturity.
(2) The trustee uses the annual payments to retire a portion of the issue each year, either calling a given percentage of the issue by a lottery and paying a specified price per bond or buying bonds on the open market, whichever is cheaper.
Discuss the advantages and disadvantages of each procedure from the viewpoint of both the firm and its bondholders.

8-7 Indicate whether each of the following actions will increase or decrease a bond's yield to maturity:
a. A bond's price increases.
b. The company's bonds are downgraded by the rating agencies.
c. A change in the bankruptcy code makes it more difficult for bondholders to receive payments in the event a firm declares bankruptcy.

d. The economy enters a recession.

e. The bonds become subordinated to another debt issue.

Self-Test Problems (Solutions Appear in Appendix B)

ST-1
Bond Valuation

The Pennington Corporation issued a new series of bonds on January 1, 1975. The bonds were sold at par ($1,000), have a 12 percent coupon, and mature in 30 years, on December 31, 2004. Coupon payments are made semiannually (on June 30 and December 31).

a. What was the YTM of Pennington's bonds on January 1, 1975?

b. What was the price of the bond on January 1, 1980, 5 years later, assuming that the level of interest rates had fallen to 10 percent?

c. Find the current yield and capital gains yield on the bond on January 1, 1980, given the price as determined in Part b.

d. On July 1, 1998, Pennington's bonds sold for $916.42. What was the YTM at that date?

e. What were the current yield and capital gains yield on July 1, 1998?

f. Now, assume that you purchased an outstanding Pennington bond on March 1, 1998, when the going rate of interest was 15.5 percent. How large a check must you have written to complete the transaction? This is a hard question! (Hint: $PVIFA_{7.75\%,13} = 8.0136$ and $PVIF_{7.75\%,13} = 0.3789$.)

ST-2
Sinking Fund

The Vancouver Development Company has just sold a $100 million, 10-year, 12 percent bond issue. A sinking fund will retire the issue over its life. Sinking fund payments are of equal amounts and will be made *semiannually,* and the proceeds will be used to retire bonds as the payments are made. Bonds can be called at par for sinking fund purposes, or the funds paid into the sinking fund can be used to buy bonds in the open market.

a. How large must each semiannual sinking fund payment be?

b. What will happen, under the conditions of the problem thus far, to the company's debt service requirements per year for this issue over time?

c. Now suppose Vancouver Development set up its sinking fund so that *equal annual amounts,* payable at the end of each year, are paid into a sinking fund trust held by a bank, with the proceeds being used to buy government bonds that pay 9 percent interest. The payments, plus accumulated interest, must total $100 million at the end of 10 years, and the proceeds will be used to retire the bonds at that time. How large must the annual sinking fund payment be now?

d. What are the annual cash requirements for covering bond service costs under the trusteeship arrangement described in Part c? (Note: Interest must be paid on Vancouver's outstanding bonds but not on bonds that have been retired.)

e. What would have to happen to interest rates to cause the company to buy bonds on the open market rather than call them under the original sinking fund plan?

Problems

8-1
Bond Valuation

Callaghan Motors' bonds have 10 years remaining to maturity. Interest is paid annually, the bonds have a $1,000 par value, and the coupon interest rate is 8 percent. The bonds have a yield to maturity of 9 percent. What is the current market price of these bonds?

8-2
Yield to Maturity;
Financial Calculator Needed

Wilson Wonders' bonds have 12 years remaining to maturity. Interest is paid annually, the bonds have a $1,000 par value, and the coupon interest rate is 10 percent. The bonds sell at a price of $850. What is their yield to maturity?

8-3
Yield to Maturity and Call;
Financial Calculator Needed

Thatcher Corporation's bonds will mature in 10 years. The bonds have a face value of $1,000 and an 8 percent coupon rate, paid semiannually. The price of the bonds is $1,100. The bonds are callable in 5 years at a call price of $1,050. What is the yield to maturity? What is the yield to call?

8-4
Current Yield

Heath Foods' bonds have 7 years remaining to maturity. The bonds have a face value of $1,000 and a yield to maturity of 8 percent. They pay interest annually and have a 9 percent coupon rate. What is their current yield?

8-5
Bond Valuation;
Financial Calculator Needed

Nungesser Corporation has issued bonds which have a 9 percent coupon rate, payable semiannually. The bonds mature in 8 years, have a face value of $1,000, and a yield to maturity of 8.5 percent. What is the price of the bonds?

8-6
Bond Valuation

The Garraty Company has two bond issues outstanding. Both bonds pay $100 annual interest plus $1,000 at maturity. Bond L has a maturity of 15 years, and Bond S a maturity of 1 year.

a. What will be the value of each of these bonds when the going rate of interest is (1) 5 percent, (2) 8 percent, and (3) 12 percent? Assume that there is only one more interest payment to be made on Bond S.

b. Why does the longer-term (15-year) bond fluctuate more when interest rates change than does the shorter-term bond (1-year)?

8-7
Yield to Maturity

The Heymann Company's bonds have 4 years remaining to maturity. Interest is paid annually; the bonds have a $1,000 par value; and the coupon interest rate is 9 percent.
a. What is the yield to maturity at a current market price of (1) $829 or (2) $1,104?
b. Would you pay $829 for one of these bonds if you thought that the appropriate rate of interest was 12 percent—that is, if $k_d = 12\%$? Explain your answer.

8-8
Yield to Call

Six years ago, The Singleton Company sold a 20-year bond issue with a 14 percent annual coupon rate and a 9 percent call premium. Today, Singleton called the bonds. The bonds originally were sold at their face value of $1,000. Compute the realized rate of return for investors who purchased the bonds when they were issued and who surrender them today in exchange for the call price.

8-9
Bond Yields;
Financial Calculator Needed

A 10-year, 12 percent semiannual coupon bond, with a par value of $1,000, may be called in 4 years at a call price of $1,060. The bond sells for $1,100. (Assume that the bond has just been issued.)
a. What is the bond's yield to maturity?
b. What is the bond's current yield?
c. What is the bond's capital gain or loss yield?
d. What is the bond's yield to call?

8-10
Yield to Maturity;
Financial Calculator Needed

You just purchased a bond which matures in 5 years. The bond has a face value of $1,000, and has an 8 percent annual coupon. The bond has a current yield of 8.21 percent. What is the bond's yield to maturity?

8-11
Current Yield;
Financial Calculator Needed

A bond which matures in 7 years sells for $1,020. The bond has a face value of $1,000 and a yield to maturity of 10.5883 percent. The bond pays coupons semiannually. What is the bond's current yield?

8-12
Nominal Interest Rate

Lloyd Corporation's 14 percent coupon rate, semiannual payment, $1,000 par value bonds, which mature in 30 years, are callable 5 years from now at a price of $1,050. The bonds sell at a price of $1,353.54, and the yield curve is flat. Assuming that interest rates in the economy are expected to remain at their current level, what is the best estimate of Lloyd's nominal interest rate on new bonds?

8-13
Bond Valuation

Suppose Ford Motor Company sold an issue of bonds with a 10-year maturity, a $1,000 par value, a 10 percent coupon rate, and semiannual interest payments.

a. Two years after the bonds were issued, the going rate of interest on bonds such as these fell to 6 percent. At what price would the bonds sell?
b. Suppose that, 2 years after the initial offering, the going interest rate had risen to 12 percent. At what price would the bonds sell?
c. Suppose that the conditions in Part a existed—that is, interest rates fell to 6 percent 2 years after the issue date. Suppose further that the interest rate remained at 6 percent for the next 8 years. What would happen to the price of the Ford Motor Company bonds over time?

8-14
Bond Reporting

Look up the prices of American Telephone & Telegraph's (AT&T) bonds in *The Wall Street Journal* (or some other newspaper which provides this information).
a. If AT&T were to sell a new issue of $1,000 par value long-term bonds, approximately what coupon interest rate would it have to set on the bonds if it wanted to bring them out at par?
b. If you had $10,000 and wanted to invest it in AT&T, what return would you expect to get if you bought AT&T's bonds?

8-15
Discount Bond Valuation

Assume that in February 1969 the Los Angeles Airport authority issued a series of 3.4 percent, 30-year bonds. Interest rates rose substantially in the years following the issue, and as they did, the price of the bonds declined. In February 1982, 13 years later, the price of the bonds had dropped from $1,000 to $650. In answering the following questions, assume that the bond requires annual interest payments.
a. Each bond originally sold at its $1,000 par value. What was the yield to maturity of these bonds when they were issued?
b. Calculate the yield to maturity in February 1982.
c. Assume that interest rates stabilized at the 1982 level and stayed there for the remainder of the life of the bonds. What would have been the bonds' price in February 1997, when they had 2 years remaining to maturity?
d. What will the price of the bonds be the day before they mature in 1999? (Disregard the last interest payment.)

e. In 1982, the Los Angeles Airport bonds were classified as "discount bonds." What happens to the price of a discount bond as it approaches maturity? Is there a "built-in capital gain" on such bonds?

f. The coupon interest payment divided by the market price of a bond is called the bond's *current yield*. Using the answers to Parts b and c, what would have been the current yield of a Los Angeles Airport bond (1) in February 1982 and (2) in February 1997? What would have been its capital gains yields and total yields (total yield equals yield to maturity) on those same two dates?

8-16
Yield to Call

It is now January 1, 1999, and you are considering the purchase of an outstanding Racette Corporation bond that was issued on January 1, 1997. The Racette bond has a 9.5 percent annual coupon and a 30-year original maturity (it matures on December 31, 2026). There is a 5-year call protection (until December 31, 2001), after which time the bond can be called at 109 (that is, at 109 percent of par, or $1,090). Interest rates have declined since the bond was issued, and the bond is now selling at 116.575 percent of par, or $1,165.75. You want to determine both the yield to maturity and the yield to call for this bond. (Note: The yield to call considers the effect of a call provision on the bond's probable yield. In the calculation, we assume that the bond will be outstanding until the call date, at which time it will be called. Thus, the investor will have received interest payments for the call-protected period and then will receive the call price — in this case, $1,090 — on the call date.)

a. What is the yield to maturity in 1999 for the Racette bond? What is its yield to call?

b. If you bought this bond, which return do you think you would actually earn? Explain your reasoning.

c. Suppose the bond had sold at a discount. Would the yield to maturity or the yield to call have been more relevant?

8-17
Interest Rate Sensitivity;
Financial Calculator Needed

A bond trader purchased each of the following bonds at a yield to maturity of 8 percent. Immediately after she purchased the bonds, interest rates fell to 7 percent. What is the percentage change in the price of each bond after the decline in interest rates? Fill in the following table:

	PRICE @ 8%	PRICE @ 7%	PERCENTAGE CHANGE
10-year, 10% annual coupon	_____	_____	_____
10-year zero	_____	_____	_____
5-year zero	_____	_____	_____
30-year zero	_____	_____	_____
$100 perpetuity	_____	_____	_____

8-18
Bond Valuation;
Financial Calculator Needed

An investor has two bonds in his portfolio. Each bond matures in 4 years, has a face value of $1,000, and has a yield to maturity equal to 9.6 percent. One bond, Bond C, pays an annual coupon of 10 percent, the other bond, Bond Z, is a zero coupon bond.

a. Assuming that the yield to maturity of each bond remains at 9.6 percent over the next 4 years, what will be the price of each of the bonds at the following time periods? Fill in the following table:

t	PRICE OF BOND C	PRICE OF BOND Z
0	_____	_____
1	_____	_____
2	_____	_____
3	_____	_____
4	_____	_____

b. Plot the time path of the prices for each of the two bonds.

Spreadsheet Problem

Work this problem only if you are using the computer problem diskette.

8-19
Yield to Call

Use the computerized model in File C8 to solve this problem.

a. Refer back to Problem 8-16. Suppose that on January 1, 2000, the Racette bond is selling for $1,200. What does this indicate about the level of interest rates in 2000 as compared with interest rates a year earlier? What will be the yield to maturity and the yield to call on the Racette bond on this date? Note that the bond now has 27 years remaining until maturity and 2 years until it can be called. Which rate should an investor expect to receive if he or she buys the bond on this date?

b. Suppose that instead of increasing the price, the Racette bond falls to $800 on January 1, 2000. What will be the yield to maturity and the yield to call on this date? Which rate should an investor expect to receive?

MINI CASE

Robert Balik and Carol Kiefer are vice-presidents of Mutual of Chicago Insurance Company and codirectors of the company's pension fund management division. A major new client, the California League of Cities, has requested that Mutual of Chicago present an investment seminar to the mayors of the represented cities, and Balik and Kiefer, who will make the actual presentation, have asked you to help them by answering the following questions. Because the Walt Disney Company operates in one of the league's cities, you are to work Disney into the presentation. (See the vignette which opened the chapter for information on Disney.)

a. What are the key features of a bond?

b. What are call provisions and sinking fund provisions? Do these provisions make bonds more or less risky?

c. How is the value of any asset whose value is based on expected future cash flows determined?

d. How is the value of a bond determined? What is the value of a 10-year, $1,000 par value bond with a 10 percent annual coupon if its required rate of return is 10 percent?

e. (1) What would be the value of the bond described in Part d if, just after it had been issued, the expected inflation rate rose by 3 percentage points, causing investors to require a 13 percent return? Would we now have a discount or a premium bond? (If you do not have a financial calculator, $PVIF_{13\%,10} = 0.2946$; $PVIFA_{13\%,10} = 5.4262$.)

   (2) What would happen to the bond's value if inflation fell, and k_d declined to 7 percent? Would we now have a premium or a discount bond?

   (3) What would happen to the value of the 10-year bond over time if the required rate of return remained at 13 percent, or if it remained at 7 percent? (Hint: With a financial calculator, enter PMT, I, FV, and N, and then change (override) N to see what happens to the PV as the bond approaches maturity.)

f. (1) What is the yield to maturity on a 10-year, 9 percent, annual coupon, $1,000 par value bond that sells for $887.00? That sells for $1,134.20? What does the fact that a bond sells at a discount or at a premium tell you about the relationship between k_d and the bond's coupon rate?

   (2) What are the total return, the current yield, and the capital gains yield for the discount bond? (Assume the bond is held to maturity and the company does not default on the bond.)

g. What is *interest rate (or price) risk?* Which bond has more interest rate risk, an annual payment 1-year bond or a 10-year bond? Why?

h. What is *reinvestment rate risk?* Which has more reinvestment rate risk, a 1-year bond or a 10-year bond?

i. How does the equation for valuing a bond change if semiannual payments are made? Find the value of a 10-year, semiannual payment, 10 percent coupon bond if nominal $k_d = 13\%$. (Hint: $PVIF_{6.5\%,20} = 0.2838$ and $PVIFA_{6.5\%,20} = 11.0185$.)

j. Suppose you could buy, for $1,000, either a 10 percent, 10-year, annual payment bond or a 10 percent, 10-year, semiannual payment bond. They are equally risky. Which would you prefer? If $1,000 is the proper price for the semiannual bond, what is the equilibrium price for the annual payment bond?

k. Suppose a 10-year, 10 percent, semiannual coupon bond with a par value of $1,000 is currently selling for $1,135.90, producing a nominal yield to maturity of 8 percent. However, the bond can be called after 5 years for a price of $1,050.

   (1) What is the bond's *nominal yield to call (YTC)?*

   (2) If you bought this bond, do you think you would be more likely to earn the YTM or the YTC? Why?

l. Disney's bonds were issued with a yield to maturity of 7.5 percent. Does the yield to maturity represent the promised or expected return on the bond?

m. Disney's bonds were rated AA– by S&P. Would you consider these bonds investment grade or junk bonds?

n. What factors determine a company's bond rating?

Selected Additional References and Cases

Many investment textbooks cover bond valuation models in depth and detail. Some of the better ones are listed in the Chapter 5 references.

For some recent works on valuation, see

Bey, Roger P., and J. Markham Collins, "The Relationship between Before- and After-Tax Yields on Financial Assets," *The Financial Review,* August 1988, 313–343.

Taylor, Richard W., "The Valuation of Semiannual Bonds between Interest Payment Dates," *The Financial Review,* August 1988, 365–368.

Tse, K. S. Maurice, and Mark A. White, "The Valuation of Semiannual Bonds between Interest Payment Dates: A Correction," *Financial Review,* November 1990, 659–662.

The following cases in the Cases in Financial Management: Dryden Request *series cover many of the valuation concepts contained in Chapter 8.*

Case 3, "Peachtree Securities, Inc. (B);" Case 43, "Swan Davis;" Case 49, "Beatrice Peabody;" and Case 56, "Laura Henderson."

STOCKS AND THEIR VALUATION

A $1,000 investment in Disney in 1970 would have grown to $50,000 by 1996, and the same $1,000 investment in Wal-Mart would have done even better—it would have been worth $700,000! However, as any seasoned investor can tell you, stocks can also fall. For example, if at the start of 1997 you had put $1,000 in Westbridge Capital, a previously high-flying NYSE medical company, you would have ended the year with just $42.

All boats rise with the tide, but the same does not hold for the stock market—regardless of the trend, some individual stocks make huge gains while others experience losses. For example, the Dow Jones Industrial Average rose 23 percent in 1997, but IBM gained 38 percent while Eastman Kodak lost 24 percent. These are both large, relatively stable companies—price swings were even larger for smaller companies.

By virtually any measure, the stock market has performed extraordinarily well in recent years. As of early 1998, the Dow Jones Industrial Average was just over 8400, up nearly 31 percent in the latest 12 months. To put this in perspective, the Dow reached 1000 in 1965, then took another 22 years to hit 2000, then eight more years to double to 4000 in 1995. Then the market really began to climb—it took just over two years to double again to 8000.

The recent bull market greatly enhanced the wealth of many people, making it possible for them to take early retirement, to buy expensive homes, and to finance large expenditures such as college tuition. Encouraged by this performance, an increasing number of investors have flocked to the market, and today more than 50 million Americans own stock. Moreover, a rising stock market makes it easier and cheaper for corporations to raise equity capital, which sets the stage for continued economic growth.

Some observers, however, are concerned that many investors do not seem to recognize that the stock market is also risky. There is no guarantee that the market will continue to rise, and even in bull markets some stocks decline. Federal Reserve Board Chairman Alan Greenspan made the comment that investors may be pushing stock prices up due to "irrational exuberance." If he is right, the market is due for a fall.

While it is difficult to predict prices with precision, we are not completely in the dark when it comes to valuing stocks and determining those most appropriate for a given investor. After studying this chapter, you should have a reasonably good understanding of the factors that influence stock prices. Then, with that knowledge—and a little luck—you might be able to find the next Disney or Wal-Mart, and avoid being a victim of "irrational exuberance."

In Chapter 8 we examined bonds. In this chapter, we take up two other important securities, common and preferred stocks. The value of a stock is determined using the time value of money concepts presented in Chapter 7. However, valuing any asset requires a knowledge of the asset's characteristics, so we begin with some background information on common stock.

LEGAL RIGHTS AND PRIVILEGES OF COMMON STOCKHOLDERS

The common stockholders are the *owners* of a corporation, and as such they have certain rights and privileges as discussed in this section.

Control of the Firm

Its common stockholders have the right to elect a firm's directors, who, in turn, elect the officers who manage the business. In a small firm, the major stockholder typically assumes the positions of president and chairperson of the board of directors. In a large, publicly owned firm, the managers typically have some stock, but their personal holdings are generally insufficient to give them voting control. Thus, the managements of most publicly owned firms can be removed by the stockholders if they decide the management team is not effective.

State and federal laws stipulate how stockholder control is to be exercised. First, corporations must hold an election of directors periodically, usually once a year, with the vote taken at the annual meeting. Typically, one-third of the directors are elected each year for a three-year term. Each share of stock has one vote; thus, the owner of 1,000 shares has 1,000 votes for each director.[1] Stockholders can appear at the annual meeting and vote in person, but typically they transfer their right to vote to a second party by means of a **proxy.** Management always solicits stockholders' proxies and usually gets them. However, if earnings are poor and stockholders are dissatisfied, an outside group may solicit the proxies in an effort to overthrow management and take control of the business. This is known as a **proxy fight.**

The question of control has become a central issue in recent years. The frequency of proxy fights has increased, as have attempts by one corporation to take over another by purchasing a majority of the outstanding stock. This latter action is called a **takeover.** Some well-known examples of recent takeover battles include KKR's acquisition of RJR Nabisco, Chevron's acquisition of Gulf Oil, and IBM's fight to take over Lotus Development.

Managers who do not have majority control (more than 50 percent of their firms' stock) are very much concerned about proxy fights and takeovers, and many of them attempt to get stockholder approval for changes in their corporate charters that would make takeovers more difficult. For example, a number of companies have gotten their stockholders to agree (1) to elect only one-third of the directors each year (rather than electing all directors each year), (2) to require 75 percent of the stockholders (rather than 50 percent) to approve a merger, and (3) to vote in a "poison pill" provision which would allow the stockholders of a firm that is taken over by another firm to buy shares in the second firm at a reduced price. The poison pill makes the acquisition unattractive and, thus, wards off hostile takeover attempts. Managements seeking such changes generally cite a fear that the firm will be picked up at a bargain price, but it often appears that managers' concerns about their own positions might be an even more important consideration.

Management moves to make takeovers more difficult have been countered by stockholders, especially large institutional stockholders, who do not want to see barriers

---

[1]In the situation described, a 1,000-share stockholder could cast 1,000 votes for each of three directors if there were three contested seats on the board. An alternative procedure that may be prescribed in the corporate charter calls for *cumulative voting*. Here the 1,000-share stockholder would get 3,000 votes if there were three vacancies, and he or she could cast all of them for one director. Cumulative voting helps small groups to get representation on the board.

erected to protect incompetent managers. To illustrate, the California Public Employees Retirement System (Calpers), which is one of the largest institutional investors, announced plans recently to conduct a proxy fight with several corporations whose financial performances were poor in Calpers' judgment. Calpers wants companies to give outside (nonmanagement) directors more clout and to force managers to be more responsive to stockholder complaints.

Prior to 1993, SEC rules prohibited large investors such as Calpers from getting together to force corporate managers to institute policy changes. However, the SEC changed its rules in 1993, and now large investors can work together to force management changes. This ruling helps keep managers focused on stockholder concerns, which means the maximization of stock prices.

The Preemptive Right

Common stockholders often have the right, called the **preemptive right,** to purchase any new shares sold by the firm. In some states, the preemptive right is automatically included in every corporate charter; in others, it is necessary to insert it specifically into the charter.

The purpose of the preemptive right is twofold. First, it enables current stockholders to maintain control. If it were not for this safeguard, the management of a corporation could issue a large number of additional shares and purchase these shares itself. Management could thereby seize control of the corporation and frustrate the will of the current stockholders.

The second, and by far the more important, reason for the preemptive right is to protect stockholders against a dilution of value. For example, suppose 1,000 shares of common stock, each with a price of $100, were outstanding, making the total market value of the firm $100,000. If an additional 1,000 shares were sold at $50 a share, or for $50,000, this would raise the total market value to $150,000. When total market value is divided by new total shares outstanding, a value of $75 a share is obtained. The old stockholders thus lose $25 per share, and the new stockholders have an instant profit of $25 per share. Thus, selling common stock at a price below the market value would dilute its price and transfer wealth from the present stockholders to those who were allowed to purchase the new shares. The preemptive right prevents such occurrences.

SELF-TEST QUESTIONS

Identify some actions that companies have taken to make takeovers more difficult.

What are the two primary reasons for the existence of the preemptive right?

TYPES OF COMMON STOCK

Although most firms have only one type of common stock, in some instances **classified stock** is used to meet the special needs of the company. Generally, when special classifications of stock are used, one type is designated *Class A,* another *Class B,* and so on. Small, new companies seeking funds from outside sources frequently use different types of common stock. For example, when Genetic Concepts went public recently, its Class A stock was sold to the public, and it received a dividend, but this stock had no voting rights for five years. Its Class B stock, which was retained by the organizers of the company, had full voting rights for five years, but the legal terms stated that dividends could not be paid on the Class B stock until the company had established its earning power by building up retained earnings to a designated level. The use of classified stock thus enabled the public to take a position in a conservatively financed growth company without sacrificing income, while the founders retained absolute control during the crucial early stages of the firm's development. At the same time, outside investors were protected against excessive withdrawals of funds by the original owners. As is often the case in such situations, the Class B stock was called **founders' shares.**

Note that "Class A," "Class B," and so on, have no standard meanings. Most firms have no classified shares, but a firm that does could designate its Class B shares as founders' shares and its Class A shares as those sold to the public, while another could reverse these designations. Still other firms could use stock classifications for entirely different purposes. For example, when General Motors acquired Hughes Aircraft for $5 billion, it paid in part with a new Class H common, GMH, which had limited voting rights and whose dividends were tied to Hughes's performance as a GM subsidiary. The reasons for the new stock were reported to be (1) that GM wanted to limit voting privileges on the new classified stock because of management's concern about a possible takeover and (2) that Hughes employees wanted to be rewarded more directly on Hughes's own performance than would have been possible through regular GM stock.

GM's deal posed a problem for the NYSE, which had a rule against listing any company's common stock if the company had any nonvoting common stock outstanding. GM made it clear that it was willing to delist if the NYSE did not change its rules. The NYSE concluded that such arrangements as GM had made were logical and were likely to be made by other companies in the future, so it changed its rules to accommodate GM. In reality, though, the NYSE had little choice. In recent years, the over-the-counter (OTC) market has proven that it can provide a deep, liquid market for common stocks, and the defection of GM would have hurt the NYSE much more than GM.

As these examples illustrate, the right to vote is often a distinguishing characteristic between different classes of stock. Suppose two classes of stock differ in but one respect: One class has voting rights but the other does not. As you would expect, the stock with voting rights would be more valuable, typically by some two to four percentage points. Thus, if the stock with no voting rights sold for $100, then the one with voting rights would probably sell for $102 to $104.

<table>
<tr><td>SELF-TEST
QUESTION</td><td>What are some reasons a company might use classified stock?</td></tr>
</table>

THE MARKET FOR COMMON STOCK

Some companies are so small that their common stocks are not actively traded; they are owned by only a few people, usually the companies' managers. Such firms are said to be **privately owned,** or **closely held, corporations,** and their stock is called **closely held stock.** In contrast, the stocks of most larger companies are owned by a large number of investors, most of whom are not active in management. Such companies are called **publicly owned corporations,** and their stock is called **publicly held stock.**

As we saw in Chapter 4, the stocks of smaller publicly owned firms are not listed on an exchange; they trade in the **over-the-counter (OTC) market,** and the companies and their stocks are said to be **unlisted.** However, larger publicly owned companies generally apply for listing on an **organized security exchange,** and they and their stocks are said to be **listed.** Often companies are first listed on a regional exchange such as the Pacific Coast or Midwest Exchange. Then, as they grow, they move up to the American Stock Exchange (AMEX). Finally, if they grow large enough, they are listed on the "Big Board," the New York Stock Exchange (NYSE). About 7,000 stocks are traded in the OTC market, but in terms of market value of both outstanding shares and daily transactions, the NYSE and the OTC markets are equally important.

A recent study found that institutional investors owned more than 60 percent of all publicly held common stocks. Included are pension funds, mutual funds, foreign

A WILD INITIAL DAY OF TRADING

It took General Dynamics, a major defense contractor, 43 years to get the value of its stock to $2.7 billion. Netscape Communications accomplished the same feat in about one minute in August 1995, when technology-crazed investors had their first chance to buy Netscape's stock on the open market. Never mind that Netscape had never earned a profit or that it had been giving away its primary product free on the Internet.

Netscape produces *Netscape Navigator,* a "web browser" program that enables users to view information on the World Wide Web, the graphical interface portion of the Internet. The company was founded in April 1994 by James Clark, a noted Silicon Valley pioneer, and Marc Andreesen, a 24-year-old techie from the University of Illinois. The IPO (initial public offering) created a nest egg of $565 million for Mr. Clark, who owned 9.7 million shares of Netscape's stock. Mr. Andreesen's gain of $58 million, while not on par with Mr. Clark's, was not bad for 16 months' work.

How did this all happen? Until August 1995, Netscape had been a privately owned company, with most of the stock owned by four investors: Clark, Andreesen, James Barksdale, who was brought in from McCaw Cellular to be Netscape's president and chief executive officer, and John Doerr, a Silicon Valley venture capitalist. (A venture capitalist is an investor who makes equity investments in startup firms.) To support development of its *Netscape Navigator* and related software, the company needed additional capital, and its best means of raising new funds was to sell common stock to the public. So, on August 8, 1995, the company raised $140 million by selling 5 million shares of common stock at a price of $28 per share.

Original plans called for issuing 3.5 million shares at $14 per share, but demand was so great during the weeks prior to the sale that both the amount and price were increased. Still, investor demand for the stock was so great that the company could have sold 100 million shares. This pent-up demand caused a near panic on August 9, the first day the shares were publicly traded. Lucky investors who got stock for $28 saw it open at $71 per share on the over-the-counter market, be bid up to $75, and then drop back to end the day at $58.

Netscape's stock continues to attract attention. First, the stock had a 2-for-1 split in 1996, so its adjusted IPO price was $14 rather than $28. Its price range during 1997 was $23 to $59, and its latest close was $21. Netscape is currently in a fierce battle with Microsoft to be the dominant Internet browser company. Those who remain bullish on the stock point to the vast growth potential of Internet-related products, as more and more people throughout the world begin surfing the information superhighway. Bears argue, however, that Netscape's stock was wildly overvalued—they are skeptical about both the profit potential of Internet-related products and Netscape's ability to compete with that 800-pound gorilla named Microsoft.

investors, insurance companies, and brokerage firms. These institutions buy and sell relatively actively, however, so they account for about 75 percent of all transactions. Thus, institutional investors have a heavy influence on the prices of individual stocks.

Types of Stock Market Transactions

We can classify stock market transactions into three distinct types:

1. **Trading in the outstanding shares of established, publicly owned companies: the secondary market.** MicroDrive Inc., the company we analyzed in earlier chapters, has 50 million shares of stock outstanding. If the owner of 100 shares sells his or her stock, the trade is said to have occurred in the **secondary market.** Thus, the market for outstanding shares, or *used shares,* is the secondary market. The company receives no new money when sales occur in this market.

2. **Additional shares sold by established, publicly owned companies: the primary market.** If MicroDrive decides to issue an additional 1 million shares to raise new equity capital, this transaction is said to occur in the **primary market.**[2]

---

[2]MicroDrive has 60 million shares authorized but only 50 million outstanding; thus, it has 10 million authorized but unissued shares. If it had no authorized but unissued shares, management could increase the authorized shares by obtaining stockholders' approval, which would generally be granted without any arguments.

3. **Initial public offerings by privately held firms: the IPO market.** Several years ago, the Coors Brewing Company, which was owned by the Coors family at the time, decided to sell some stock to raise capital needed for a major expansion program.[3] This type of transaction is called **going public**—whenever stock in a closely held corporation is offered to the public for the first time, the company is said to be going public. The market for stock that is just being offered to the public is called the **initial public offering (IPO) market.**

IPOs have received a lot of attention in recent years, primarily because a number of "hot" issues have realized spectacular gains—often in the first few minutes of trading. Consider the IPO of Boston Rotisserie Chicken, which has since been renamed Boston Market. The company's underwriter, Merrill Lynch, set an offering price of $20 a share. However, because of intense demand for the issue, the stock's price rose 75 percent within the first two hours of trading. By the end of the first day, the stock price had risen by 143 percent, and the company's end-of-the-day market value was $800 million—which was particularly startling, given that the company had recently reported a $5 million loss on sales of only $8.3 million. More recently, shares of the trendy restaurant chain Planet Hollywood rose nearly 50 percent in its first day of trading, and when Netscape first hit the market, its stock price hit $70 a share versus an offering price of only $28 a share.

Table 9-1 lists the largest, the best performing, and the worst performing IPOs of 1997, and it shows how they performed from their offering dates through year-end 1997. As the table shows, not all IPOs are as well received as were Netscape and Boston Chicken. Moreover, even if you are able to identify a "hot" issue, it is often difficult to purchase shares in the initial offering. These deals are generally *oversubscribed,* which means that the demand for shares at the offering price exceeds the number of shares issued. In such instances, investment bankers favor large institutional investors (who are their best customers), and small investors find it hard, if not impossible, to get in on the ground floor. They can buy the stock in the after-market, but evidence suggests that if you do not get in on the ground floor, the average IPO underperforms the overall market over the longer run.[4]

Before you conclude that it isn't fair to let the best customers have the stock in an initial offering, think about what it takes to become a best customer. Best customers are usually investors who have done lots of business in the past with the investment banking firm's brokerage department. In other words, they have paid large sums as commissions in the past, and they are expected to continue doing so in the future. As is so often true, there is no free lunch—most of the investors who get in on the ground floor of an IPO have in fact paid for this privilege. See Chapter 18 for a more detailed discussion of investment banking.

It is important to recognize that firms can go public without raising any additional capital. For example, the Ford Motor Company was once owned exclusively by the Ford family. When Henry Ford died, he left a substantial part of his stock to the Ford Foundation. When the Foundation later sold some of this stock to the general public, the Ford Motor Company went public, even though the company raised no capital in the transaction.

---

[3]The stock Coors offered to the public was designated Class B, and it was nonvoting. The Coors family retained the founders' shares, called Class A stock, which carried full voting privileges. The company was large enough to obtain an NYSE listing, but at that time the Exchange had a requirement that listed common stocks must have full voting rights, which precluded Coors from obtaining an NYSE listing.

[4]See Jay R. Ritter, "The Long-Run Performance of Initial Public Offerings," *Journal of Finance,* March 1991, Vol. 46, No. 1, 3–27.

| TABLE 9-1 | | Initial Public Offerings of 1997—And How They Performed | | | | |

ISSUER	OFFERING DATE	GLOBAL AMOUNT (MILLIONS)	OFFERING PRICE	U.S. AMOUNT (MILLIONS)	12/31/97 PRICE	PERCENT CHANGE[a]
The Biggest						
Telstra Corp.	11/17/97	$9,732.0	$47.45	$499.8	$41.75	+49.6%[b]
France Telecom	10/17/97	6,608.8	31.69	836.1	36.00	+13.6
China Telecom	10/16/97	3,965.0	30.50	423.6	33.56	+10.0
Electricidade de Portugal	6/16/97	2,113.7	25.84	303.6	38.75	+50.0
Santa Fe International	6/9/97	997.5	28.50	798.0	40.75	+43.0
Unibanco Holdings	5/21/97	963.6	33.75	695.9	32.19	−4.6
CIT Group Holdings	11/13/97	850.5	27.00	850.5	32.25	+19.4
Galileo International	7/24/97	784.0	24.50	548.8	27.63	+12.8
Magyar Tavkozlesi	11/13/97	773.8	18.65	313.4	26.00	+39.4
Polo Ralph Lauren	6/11/97	767.0	26.00	611.0	24.25	−6.7

ISSUER	OFFERING DATE	OFFERING PRICE	12/31/97 PRICE	PERCENT CHANGE[a]
The Best Performers				
Rambus	5/13/97	$12.00	$45.75	+281.2%
LHS Group	5/15/97	16.00	59.75	+273.4
Complete Business Solutions	3/5/97	12.00	43.50	+262.5
Star Telecommunications	6/12/97	9.00	32.13	+256.9
Friede Goldman International	7/21/97	17.00	29.88	+251.5[c]
DAOU Systems	2/13/97	9.00	31.25	+247.2
Crystal Systems Solutions	1/31/97	7.50	25.50	+240.0
Amazon.com	5/15/97	18.00	60.25	+234.7
Transcrypt International	1/22/97	8.00	24.88	+210.9
Radiant Systems	2/13/97	9.50	28.50	+200.0
The Worst Performers				
DTM Corp.	5/2/97	$ 8.00	$1.38	−82.8%
DSI Toys	5/29/97	8.00	1.88	−76.5
Axiom	7/7/97	12.00	4.00	−66.7
Ionica Group	7/18/97	19.57	6.63	−66.1
National Auto Finance Co.	1/29/97	8.50	3.00	−64.7
Children's Place Retail Stores	9/18/97	14.00	5.13	−63.4
Colonial Downs Holdings	3/18/97	9.50	3.50	−63.1
Qualix Group	2/12/97	8.00	2.97	−62.9
Celerity Systems	11/4/97	7.50	3.00	−60.0
Big Dog Holdings	9/26/97	14.00	5.63	−59.8

NOTE: Best and worst performers exclude deals of $10 million or less
[a]Offer through year end
[b]Return calculated from $27.91 offer price of the deal's first installment
[c]Adjusted for stock split
SOURCE: "1997 Initial Public Offerings—And How They Performed," *The Wall Street Journal*, January 2, 1998, R4. © 1997 Dow Jones & Company, Inc. All Rights Reserved Worldwide.

Differentiate between a closely held corporation and a publicly owned corporation.

Differentiate between a listed stock and an unlisted stock.

Differentiate between primary and secondary markets.

What is an IPO?

COMMON STOCK VALUATION

Common stock represents an ownership interest in a corporation, but to the typical investor, a share of common stock is simply a piece of paper characterized by two features:

1. It entitles its owner to dividends, but only if the company has earnings out of which dividends can be paid, and only if management chooses to pay dividends rather than retaining and reinvesting all the earnings. Whereas a bond contains a *promise* to pay interest, common stock provides no such promise — if you own a stock, you may *expect* a dividend, but your expectations may not in fact be met. To illustrate, Long Island Lighting Company (LILCO) had paid dividends on its common stock for more than 50 years, and people expected those dividends to continue. However, when the company encountered severe problems a few years ago, it stopped paying dividends. Note, though, that LILCO continued to pay interest on its bonds; if it had not, then it would have been declared bankrupt, and the bondholders could potentially have taken over the company.

2. Stock can be sold at some future date, hopefully at a price greater than the purchase price. If the stock is actually sold at a price above its purchase price, the investor will receive a *capital gain*. Generally, at the time people buy common stocks, they do expect to receive capital gains; otherwise, they would not buy the stocks. However, after the fact, one can end up with capital losses rather than capital gains. LILCO's stock price dropped from $17.50 to $3.75 in one year, so the *expected* capital gain on that stock turned out to be a huge *actual* capital loss.

Definitions of Terms Used in Stock Valuation Models

Common stocks provide an expected future cash flow stream, and a stock's value is found in the same manner as the values of other financial assets — namely, as the present value of the expected future cash flow stream. The expected cash flows consist of two elements: (1) the dividends expected in each year and (2) the price investors expect to receive when they sell the stock. The expected final stock price includes the return of the original investment plus an expected capital gain.

We saw in Chapter 1 that managers seek to maximize the values of their firms' stocks. A manager's actions affect both the stream of income to investors and the riskiness of that stream. Therefore, managers need to know how alternative actions are likely to affect stock prices. At this point we develop some models to help show how the value of a share of stock is determined. We begin by defining the following terms:

D_t = dividend the stockholder *expects* to receive at the end of Year t. D_0 is the most recent dividend, which has already been paid; D_1 is the first dividend expected, and it will be paid at the end of this year; D_2 is the dividend expected at the end of two years; and so forth. D_1 represents the first cash flow a new purchaser of the stock will receive. Note that D_0, the dividend which has just been paid, is known with certainty. However, all future dividends are expected values, so the estimate of D_t may differ among investors.[5]

P_0 = actual **market price** of the stock today.

$\hat{P}_t$ = expected price of the stock at the end of each Year t (pronounced "P hat t"). $\hat{P}_0$ is the **intrinsic**, or *theoretical*, **value** of the stock today as seen by the particular investor doing the analysis; $\hat{P}_1$ is the price expected at the end of one year; and so on. Note that $\hat{P}_0$ is the intrinsic value of the stock today based on a particular investor's estimate of the stock's expected dividend stream and the riskiness of that stream. Hence, whereas the market price P_0 is fixed and is identical for all investors, $\hat{P}_0$ could differ among investors depending on how optimistic they are regarding the company. The caret, or "hat," is used to indicate that $\hat{P}_t$ is an estimated value. $\hat{P}_0$, the individual investor's estimate of the intrinsic value today, could be above or below P_0, the current stock price, but an investor would buy the stock only if his or her estimate of $\hat{P}_0$ were equal to or greater than P_0.

Since there are many investors in the market, there can be many values for $\hat{P}_0$. However, we can think of a group of "average," or "marginal," investors whose actions actually determine the market price. For these marginal investors, P_0 must equal $\hat{P}_0$; otherwise, a disequilibrium would exist, and buying and selling in the market would change P_0 until $P_0 = \hat{P}_0$ for a marginal investor.

g = expected **growth rate** in dividends as predicted by a marginal investor. If dividends are expected to grow at a constant rate, g is also equal to the expected rate of growth in earnings and in the stock's price. Different investors may use different g's to evaluate a firm's stock, but the market price, P_0, is set on the basis of the g estimated by marginal investors.

k_s = minimum acceptable, or **required rate of return,** on the stock, considering both its riskiness and the returns available on other investments. Again, this term generally relates to marginal investors. The determinants of k_s include the real rate of return, expected inflation, and risk premiums, as discussed in Chapter 5.

$\hat{k}_s$ = **expected rate of return** which an investor who buys the stock expects to receive. $\hat{k}_s$ (pronounced "k hat s") could be above or below k_s, but one would buy the stock only if $\hat{k}_s$ were equal to or greater than k_s.

$\bar{k}_s$ = **actual,** or **realized,** *after-the-fact* **rate of return,** pronounced "k bar s." You may *expect* to obtain a return of $\hat{k}_s = 15$ percent if you buy Exxon stock today, but if the market goes down, you may end up next year with an actual realized return that is much lower, perhaps even negative.

D_1/P_0 = expected **dividend yield** on the stock during the coming year. If the stock is expected to pay a dividend of $D_1 = \$1$ during the next 12 months, and if its current price is $P_0 = \$10$, then the expected dividend yield is $\$1/\$10 = 0.10 = 10\%$.

---

[5]Stocks generally pay dividends quarterly, so theoretically we should evaluate them on a quarterly basis. However, in stock valuation, most analysts work on an annual basis because the data generally are not precise enough to warrant refinement to a quarterly model. For additional information on the quarterly model, see Charles M. Linke and J. Kenton Zumwalt, "Estimation Biases in Discounted Cash Flow Analysis of Equity Capital Cost in Rate Regulation," *Financial Management,* Autumn 1984, 15–21.

$\dfrac{\hat{P}_1 - P_0}{P_0}$ = expected **capital gains yield** on the stock during the coming year. If the stock sells for $10 today, and if it is expected to rise to $10.50 at the end of one year, then the expected capital gain is $\hat{P}_1 - P_0 = \$10.50 - \$10.00 = \$0.50$, and the expected capital gains yield is $\$0.50/\$10 = 0.05 = 5\%$.

Expected total return = $\hat{k}_s$ = expected dividend yield (D_1/P_0) plus expected capital gains yield $[(\hat{P}_1 - P_0)/P_0]$. In our example, the **expected total return** = $\hat{k}_s$ = 10% + 5% = 15%.

Expected Dividends as the Basis for Stock Values

In our discussion of bonds in Chapter 8, we found the value of a bond as the present value of interest payments over the life of the bond plus the present value of the bond's maturity (or par) value:

$$V_B = \frac{INT}{(1 + k_d)^1} + \frac{INT}{(1 + k_d)^2} + \cdots + \frac{INT}{(1 + k_d)^N} + \frac{M}{(1 + k_d)^N}.$$

Stock prices are likewise determined as the present value of a stream of cash flows, and the basic stock valuation equation is similar to the bond valuation equation. What are the cash flows that corporations provide to their stockholders? First, think of yourself as an investor who buys a stock with the intention of holding it (in your family) forever. In this case, all that you (and your heirs) will receive is a stream of dividends, and the value of the stock today is calculated as the present value of an infinite stream of dividends:

$$\text{Value of stock} = \hat{P}_0 = \text{PV of expected future dividends}$$

$$= \frac{D_1}{(1 + k_s)^1} + \frac{D_2}{(1 + k_s)^2} + \cdots + \frac{D_\infty}{(1 + k_s)^\infty}$$

$$= \sum_{t=1}^{\infty} \frac{D_t}{(1 + k_s)^t}. \tag{9-1}$$

What about the more typical case, where you expect to hold the stock for a finite period and then sell it—what will be the value of $\hat{P}_0$ in this case? Unless the company is likely to be liquidated and thus to disappear, *the value of the stock is again determined by Equation 9-1*. To see this, recognize that for any individual investor, the expected cash flows consist of expected dividends plus the expected sale price of the stock. However, the sale price the current investor receives will depend on the dividends some future investor expects. Therefore, for all present and future investors in total, expected cash flows must be based on expected future dividends. Put another way, unless a firm is liquidated or sold to another concern, the cash flows it provides to its stockholders will consist only of a stream of dividends. Therefore, the value of a share of its stock must be established as the present value of that expected dividend stream.

The general validity of Equation 9-1 can also be confirmed by asking the following question: Suppose I buy a stock and expect to hold it for one year. I will receive dividends during the year plus the value $\hat{P}_1$ when I sell out at the end of the year. But what will determine the value of $\hat{P}_1$? The answer is that it will be determined as the present value of the dividends expected during Year 2 plus the stock price at the end of that year, which, in turn, will be determined as the present value of another set of future dividends and an even more distant stock price. This process can be continued ad infinitum, and the ultimate result is Equation 9-1.[6]

Equation 9-1 is a generalized stock valuation model in the sense that the time pattern of D_t can be anything: D_t can be rising, falling, or constant, it can be fluctuating randomly, or it can even be zero for several years, and Equation 9-1 will still hold. Often, however, the projected stream of dividends is expected to follow a systematic pattern, in which case we can develop a simplified (that is, easier to evaluate) version of the stock valuation model expressed in Equation 9-1. In the following sections, we consider the cases of zero growth, constant growth, and nonconstant growth.

Stock Values with Zero Growth

Suppose dividends are not expected to grow at all but to remain constant. Here we have a **zero growth stock,** for which the dividends expected in future years are equal to some constant amount—that is, $D_1 = D_2 = D_3$ and so on. Therefore, we can drop the subscripts on D and rewrite Equation 9-1 as follows:

$$\hat{P}_0 = \frac{D}{(1 + k_s)^1} + \frac{D}{(1 + k_s)^2} + \cdots + \frac{D}{(1 + k_s)^\infty}. \qquad \text{(9-1a)}$$

As we noted in Chapter 7 in connection with the British consol bond, a security that is expected to pay a constant amount each year forever is called a perpetuity. *Therefore, a zero growth stock is a perpetuity.*

Although a zero growth stock is expected to provide a constant stream of dividends into the indefinite future, each dividend has a smaller present value than the preceding one, and as the years get very large, the present value of the future dividends approaches zero. To illustrate, suppose D = \$1.15 and k_s = 13.4%. We can rewrite Equation 9-1a as follows:

$$\hat{P}_0 = \frac{\$1.15}{(1.134)^1} + \frac{\$1.15}{(1.134)^2} + \frac{\$1.15}{(1.134)^3} + \cdots + \frac{\$1.15}{(1.134)^{50}} + \cdots + \frac{\$1.15}{(1.134)^{100}} + \cdots$$

$$= \quad \$1.01 \quad + \quad \$0.89 \quad + \quad \$0.79 \quad + \cdots + \quad \$0.002 \quad + \cdots + \$0.000004 + \cdots$$

We can also show the zero growth stock in graph form, as in Figure 9-1. The horizontal line shows the constant dividend stream, D_t = \$1.15. The descending step function curve shows the present value of each future dividend. If we extended the analysis on out to infinity and then summed the present values of all the future dividends, the sum would be equal to the value of the stock.

As we saw in Chapter 7, the value of any perpetuity is simply the payment divided by the discount rate, so the value of a zero growth stock reduces to this formula:

$$\hat{P}_0 = \frac{D}{k_s}. \qquad \text{(9-2)}$$

---

[6]We should note that investors periodically lose sight of the long-run nature of stocks as investments and forget that in order to sell a stock at a profit, one must find a buyer who will pay the higher price. If you analyzed a stock's value in accordance with Equation 9-1, concluded that the stock's market price exceeded a reasonable value, and then bought the stock anyway, then you would be following the "bigger fool" theory of investment—you think that you may be a fool to buy the stock at its excessive price, but you also think that when you get ready to sell it, you can find someone who is an even bigger fool. The bigger fool theory was widely followed in the summer of 1987, just before the stock market lost more than one-third of its value in the October 1987 crash. Many people think it is back in vogue now, in 1998.

FIGURE 9-1　Present Values of Dividends of a Zero Growth Stock (Perpetuity)

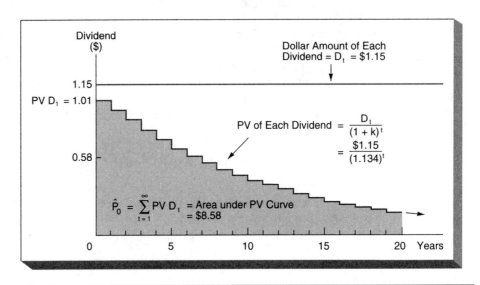

Therefore, the value of our illustrative stock is $8.58:

$$\hat{P}_0 = \frac{\$1.15}{0.134} = \$8.58.$$

If you extended Figure 9-1 on out forever and then added up the present value of each individual dividend, you would end up with the intrinsic value of the stock, $8.58.[7] The actual market price of the stock, P_0, could be greater than, less than, or equal to $8.58, depending on other investors' perceptions of the dividend pattern and riskiness of the stock.

We could transpose the $\hat{P}_0$ and the k_s in Equation 9-2 and solve for k_s to produce Equation 9-3:

$$\hat{k}_s = \frac{D}{P_0}. \tag{9-3}$$

We could then look up the price of the stock and the latest dividend, P_0 and D, in the newspaper, and D/P_0 would be the rate of return we could expect to earn if we bought the stock. Since we are dealing with an *expected rate of return,* we put a "hat" on the k value. Thus, if we bought the stock at a price of $8.58 and expected to receive a constant dividend of $1.15, our expected rate of return would be

$$\hat{k}_s = \frac{\$1.15}{\$8.58} = 0.134 = 13.4\%.$$

----

[7]If you think that having a stock pay dividends forever is unrealistic, then think of it as lasting only for 50 years. Here you would have an annuity of $1.15 per year for 50 years discounted at 13.4 percent. Enter N = 50, I = 13.4, and PMT = 1.15, and then press PV to find the value of the annuity. It is $8.57, which differs by only a penny from that of the perpetuity. Thus, the dividends from Years 51 to infinity contribute almost nothing to the value of the stock.

Normal, or Constant, Growth

Although the zero growth model is applicable to a few companies, the earnings and dividends of most companies are expected to increase over time. Expected growth rates vary from company to company, but dividend growth on average is expected to continue in the foreseeable future at about the same rate as that of the nominal gross domestic product (real GDP plus inflation). On this basis, one might expect the dividend of an average, or "normal," company to grow at a rate of 6 to 8 percent a year. Thus, if a **normal,** or **constant, growth** company's last dividend, which has already been paid, was D_0, its dividend in any future Year t may be forecasted as $D_t = D_0(1 + g)^t$, where g is the constant expected rate of growth. For example, if MicroDrive just paid a dividend of $1.15 (that is, $D_0 = \$1.15$), and if investors expect an 8 percent growth rate, then the estimated dividend one year hence would be $D_1 = \$1.15(1.08) = \$1.24$; D_2 would be $1.34; and the estimated dividend five years hence would be

$$D_t = D_0(1 + g)^t = \$1.15(1.08)^5 = \$1.69.$$

Using this method for estimating future dividends, we can determine the current stock value, $\hat{P}_0$, using Equation 9-1 as set forth previously—in other words, we can find the expected future cash flow stream (the dividends), then calculate the present value of each dividend payment, and finally sum these present values to find the value of the stock. Thus, the intrinsic value of the stock is equal to the present value of its expected future dividends.

If g is constant, Equation 9-1 may be rewritten as follows:[8]

$$\hat{P}_0 = \frac{D_0(1 + g)^1}{(1 + k_s)^1} + \frac{D_0(1 + g)^2}{(1 + k_s)^2} + \cdots + \frac{D_0(1 + g)^\infty}{(1 + k_s)^\infty}$$

$$= D_0 \sum_{t=1}^{\infty} \frac{(1 + g)^t}{(1 + k_s)^t}$$

$$= \frac{D_0(1 + g)}{k_s - g} = \frac{D_1}{k_s - g}. \tag{9-4}$$

Inserting values into Equation 9-4, we find the value of our illustrative stock to be $23.00:

$$\hat{P}_0 = \frac{\$1.15(1.08)}{0.134 - 0.08} = \frac{\$1.242}{0.054} = \$23.00.$$

The **constant growth model** as set forth in the last term of Equation 9-4 is often called the Gordon Model, after Myron J. Gordon, who did much to develop and popularize it.

Note that Equation 9-4 is sufficiently general to encompass the zero growth case described earlier: If growth is zero, this is simply a special case of constant growth, and Equation 9-4 is equal to Equation 9-2. Note also that a necessary condition for the derivation of Equation 9-4 is that k_s be greater than g. Look back at the second form of Equation 9-4. If g is larger than k_s, then $(1 + g)^t/(1 + k_s)^t$ must always be greater than one. In this case, Equation 9-4 is the sum of an infinite number of terms, with each term being a number larger than one. Therefore, if the constant g were greater than k_s, the resulting stock price would be infinite! Since no company is worth an infinite price, it is impossible to have a constant growth rate that is greater than k_s. *So, if you try to*

---

[8]The last form of Equation 9-4 is derived in Appendix 4A of Eugene F. Brigham and Louis C. Gapenski, *Intermediate Financial Management,* 5th ed. (Fort Worth, Tex.: Dryden Press, 1996). In essence, Equation 9-4 is the sum of a geometric progression, and the final result is the solution value of the progression.

FIGURE 9-2   Present Values of Dividends of a Constant Growth Stock:
$D_0 = \$1.15$, $g = 8\%$, $k_s = 13.4\%$

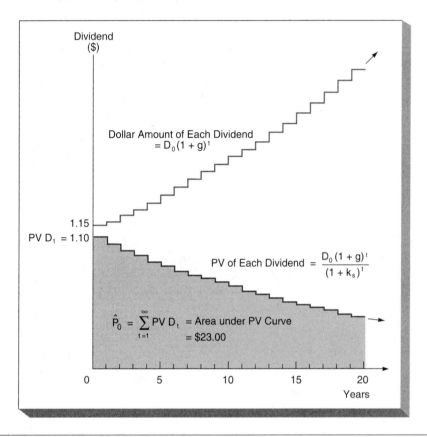

use the constant growth model in a situation where g is greater than k_s, you will violate laws of economics and mathematics, and your results will be both wrong and meaningless.

The concept underlying the valuation process for a constant growth stock is graphed in Figure 9-2. Dividends are growing at the rate $g = 8\%$, but because $k_s > g$, the present value of each future dividend is declining. For example, the dividend in Year 1 is $D_1 = D_0(1 + g)^1 = \$1.15(1.08) = \$1.242$. However, the present value of this dividend, discounted at 13.4 percent, is $PV(D_1) = \$1.242/(1.134)^1 = \$1.095$. The dividend expected in Year 2 grows to $\$1.242(1.08) = \$1.341$, but the present value of this dividend falls to $\$1.04$. Continuing, $D_3 = \$1.449$ and $PV(D_3) = \$0.993$, and so on. Thus, the expected dividends are growing, but the present value of each successive dividend is declining, because the dividend growth rate (8%) is less than the rate used for discounting the dividends to the present (13.4%).

If we summed the present values of each future dividend, this summation would be the value of the stock, $\hat{P}_0$. When g is a constant, this summation is equal to $D_1/(k_s - g)$, as shown in Equation 9-4. Therefore, if we extended the lower step function curve in Figure 9-2 on out to infinity and added up the present values of each future dividend, the summation would be identical to the value given by Equation 9-4, $\$23.00$.

Growth in dividends occurs primarily as a result of growth in *earnings per share (EPS)*. Earnings growth, in turn, results from a number of factors, including (1) inflation, (2) the amount of earnings the company retains and reinvests, and (3) the rate of return the company earns on its equity (ROE). Regarding inflation, if output (in units) is stable, but both sales prices and input costs rise at the inflation rate, then EPS will also grow at the inflation rate. Even without inflation, EPS will also grow as a result of the reinvestment, or plowback, of earnings. If the firm's earnings are not all paid out as dividends (that is, if some fraction of earnings is retained), the dollars of investment behind each share will rise over time, and that should lead to growth in earnings and dividends.

Even though a stock's value is derived from expected dividends, this does not necessarily mean that corporations can increase their stock prices by simply raising the current dividend. Shareholders care about *all* dividends, both current and those expected in the future. Moreover, there is a trade-off between current dividends and future dividends. Companies that pay high current dividends have less money to retain and reinvest in the business, and that lowers the rate of growth in earnings and dividends. So, the issue is this: Do shareholders prefer higher current dividends at the cost of a slower rate of growth in dividends, the reverse, or are stockholders indifferent? As we will see in Chapter 17, there is no simple answer to this question. Shareholders prefer to have the company retain earnings, hence pay less current dividends, if it has highly profitable investment opportunities, but they want the company to pay earnings out if its investment opportunities are poor. Taxes also play a role, as dividends and capital gains are taxed differently, so dividend policy affects investors' taxes. We will consider dividend policy in detail in Chapter 17.

Do Stock Prices Reflect Long-Term or Short-Term Events?

Managers often complain that the stock market is shortsighted and that it cares only about next quarter's performance. Let's use the constant growth model to test this assertion. MicroDrive's most recent dividend was $1.15, and it is expected to grow at a rate of 8 percent per year. Since we know the growth rate, we can forecast the dividends for each of the next five years and then find their present values:

$$PV = \frac{D_0(1+g)^1}{(1+k_s)^1} + \frac{D_0(1+g)^2}{(1+k_s)^2} + \frac{D_0(1+g)^3}{(1+k_s)^3} + \frac{D_0(1+g)^4}{(1+k_s)^4} + \frac{D_0(1+g)^5}{(1+k_s)^5}$$

$$= \frac{\$1.15(1.08)^1}{(1.134)^1} + \frac{\$1.15(1.08)^2}{(1.134)^2} + \frac{\$1.15(1.08)^3}{(1.134)^3} + \frac{\$1.15(1.08)^4}{(1.134)^4} + \frac{\$1.15(1.08)^5}{(1.134)^5}$$

$$= \frac{\$1.242}{(1.134)^1} + \frac{\$1.341}{(1.134)^2} + \frac{\$1.449}{(1.134)^3} + \frac{\$1.565}{(1.134)^4} + \frac{\$1.690}{(1.134)^5}$$

$$= 1.095 + 1.043 + 0.993 + 0.946 + 0.901$$

$$\approx \$5.00.$$

Recall that MicroDrive's stock price is $23.00. Therefore, only $5.00, or 22 percent, of the $23.00 stock price is attributable to short-term cash flows. This means that MicroDrive's managers will have a bigger impact on the stock price if they work to increase long-term cash flows rather than focus on short-term flows. This situation holds for most companies. Indeed, a number of professors and consulting firms have used actual company data to show that more than 80 percent of a typical company's stock price is due to cash flows expected more than five years in the future.

This brings up an interesting question. If most of a stock's value is due to long-term cash flows, why do managers and analysts focus so much attention on quarterly earnings? Part of the answer lies in the information conveyed by short-term earnings. For example, if actual quarterly earnings are lower than expected, not because of fundamental problems but only because a company has increased its R&D expenditures, studies have shown that the stock price probably won't decline and may actually increase. This makes sense, because R&D should increase future cash flows. On the other hand, if quarterly earnings are lower than expected because customers don't like the company's new products, then this new information will have negative implications for future values of g, the long-term growth rate. As we show later in this chapter, even small changes in g can lead to large changes in stock prices. Therefore, while the quarterly earnings itself might not be terribly important, the information they convey about future prospects can be terribly important.

Another reason many managers focus on short-term earnings is that some firms pay managerial bonuses on the basis of current earnings rather than stock prices (which reflect future earnings). For these managers, the concern with quarterly earnings is not due to their effect on stock prices — it's due to current earnings' effect on bonuses.[9]

Expected Rate of Return on a Constant Growth Stock

We can solve Equation 9-4 for k_s, again using the hat to denote that we are dealing with an expected rate of return:[10]

$$
\begin{array}{c}
\text{Expected rate} \\
\text{of return}
\end{array} =
\begin{array}{c}
\text{Expected} \\
\text{dividend} \\
\text{yield}
\end{array} +
\begin{array}{c}
\text{Expected growth} \\
\text{rate, or capital} \\
\text{gains yield}
\end{array}
$$

$$
\hat{k}_s = \frac{D_1}{P_0} + g. \tag{9-5}
$$

Thus, if you buy a stock for a price $P_0 = \$23$, and if you expect the stock to pay a dividend $D_1 = \$1.242$ one year from now and to grow at a constant rate $g = 8\%$ in the future, then your expected rate of return will be 13.4 percent:

$$
\hat{k}_s = \frac{\$1.242}{\$23} + 8\% = 5.4\% + 8\% = 13.4\%.
$$

In this form, we see that $\hat{k}_s$ is the *expected total return* and that it consists of an *expected dividend yield,* $D_1/P_0 = 5.4\%$, plus an *expected growth rate or capital gains yield,* $g = 8\%$.

Suppose this analysis had been conducted on January 1, 1999, so $P_0 = \$23$ is the January 1, 1999, stock price, and $D_1 = \$1.242$ is the dividend expected at the end of 1999. What is the expected stock price at the end of 1999? We would again apply Equation 9-4, but this time we would use the year-end dividend, $D_2 = D_1(1 + g) = \$1.242(1.08) = \$1.3414$:

$$
\hat{P}_{12/31/99} = \frac{D_{2000}}{k_s - g} = \frac{\$1.3414}{0.134 - 0.08} = \$24.84.
$$

Now, notice that $24.84 is 8 percent greater than P_0, the $23 price on January 1, 1999:

$$
\$23(1.08) = \$24.84.
$$

---

[9]Many apparent puzzles in finance can be explained either by managerial compensation systems or by peculiar features of the Tax Code. So, if you can't explain a firm's behavior in terms of economic logic, look to bonuses or taxes as possible explanations.

[10]The k_s value in Equation 9-4 is a *required* rate of return, but when we transform to obtain Equation 9-5, we are finding an *expected* rate of return. The transformation requires that $k_s = \hat{k}_s$, which holds if the stock market is in equilibrium, a condition that will be discussed later in the chapter.

Thus, we would expect to make a capital gain of $24.84 - $23.00 = $1.84 during 1999, which would provide a capital gains yield of 8 percent:

$$\text{Capital gains yield}_{1999} = \frac{\text{Capital gain}}{\text{Beginning price}} = \frac{\$1.84}{\$23.00} = 0.08 = 8\%.$$

We could extend the analysis on out, and in each future year the expected capital gains yield would always equal g, the expected dividend growth rate.

Continuing, the dividend yield in 2000 could be estimated as follows:

$$\text{Dividend yield}_{2000} = \frac{D_{2000}}{\hat{P}_{12/31/99}} = \frac{\$1.3414}{\$24.84} = 0.054 = 5.4\%.$$

The dividend yield for 2001 could also be calculated, and again it would be 5.4 percent. Thus, *for a constant growth stock,* the following conditions must hold:

1. The dividend is expected to grow forever at a constant rate, g.
2. The stock price is expected to grow at that same rate.
3. The expected dividend yield is a constant.
4. The expected capital gains yield is also a constant, and it is equal to g.
5. The expected total return, $\hat{k}_s$, is equal to the expected dividend yield plus the expected growth rate: $\hat{k}_s$ = dividend yield + g.

The term *expected* should be clarified — it means expected in a probabilistic sense, as the statistically expected outcome. Thus, if we say the growth rate is expected to remain constant at 8 percent, we mean that the best prediction for the growth rate in any future year is 8 percent, not that we literally expect the growth rate to be exactly 8 percent in each future year. In this sense, the constant growth assumption is reasonable for many large, mature companies.

Supernormal, or Nonconstant, Growth

Firms typically go through *life cycles.* During the early part of their lives, their growth is much faster than that of the economy as a whole; then they match the economy's growth; and finally their growth is slower than that of the economy.[11] Automobile manufacturers in the 1920s and computer software firms such as Microsoft in the 1990s are examples of firms in the early part of the cycle; these firms are called **supernormal,** or **nonconstant, growth** firms. Figure 9-3 illustrates nonconstant growth and also compares it with normal growth, zero growth, and negative growth.[12]

---

[11]The concept of life cycles could be broadened to *product cycle,* which would include both small startup companies and large companies like Procter & Gamble, which periodically introduce new products that give sales and earnings a boost. We should also mention *business cycles,* which alternately depress and boost sales and profits. The growth rate just after a major new product has been introduced, or just after a firm emerges from the depths of a recession, is likely to be much higher than the "expected long-run average growth rate," which is the proper number for a DCF analysis.

[12]A negative growth rate indicates a declining company. A mining company whose profits are falling because of a declining ore body is an example. Someone buying such a company would expect its earnings, and consequently its dividends and stock price, to decline each year, and this would lead to capital losses rather than capital gains. Obviously, a declining company's stock price will be relatively low, and its dividend yield must be high enough to offset the expected capital loss and still produce a competitive total return. Students sometimes argue that they would not be willing to buy a stock whose price was expected to decline. However, if the annual dividends are large enough to *more than offset* the falling stock price, the stock could still provide a good return.

FIGURE 9-3   Illustrative Dividend Growth Rates

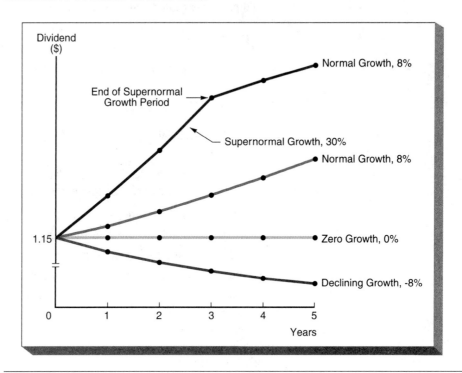

In the figure, the dividends of the supernormal growth firm are expected to grow at a 30 percent rate for three years, after which the growth rate is expected to fall to 8 percent, the assumed average for the economy. The value of this firm, like any other, is the present value of its expected future dividends as determined by Equation 9-1. In the case in which D_t is growing at a constant rate, we simplified Equation 9-1 to $\hat{P}_0 = D_1/(k_s - g)$. In the supernormal case, however, the expected growth rate is not a constant—it declines at the end of the period of supernormal growth.

To find the value of such a stock, or of any nonconstant growth stock when the growth rate will eventually stabilize, we proceed in three steps:

1. Find the PV of the dividends during the period of nonconstant growth.

2. Find the price of the stock at the end of the nonconstant growth period, at which point it has become a constant growth stock, and discount this price back to the present.

3. Add these two components to find the intrinsic value of the stock, $\hat{P}_0$.

Figure 9-4 can be used to illustrate the process for valuing nonconstant growth stocks, assuming the following five facts exist:

k_s = stockholders' required rate of return = 13.4%. This rate is used to discount the cash flows.

N = years of supernormal growth = 3.

g_s = rate of growth in both earnings and dividends during the supernormal growth period = 30%. (Note: The growth rate during the supernormal growth period

FIGURE 9-4   Process for Finding the Value of a Supernormal Growth Stock

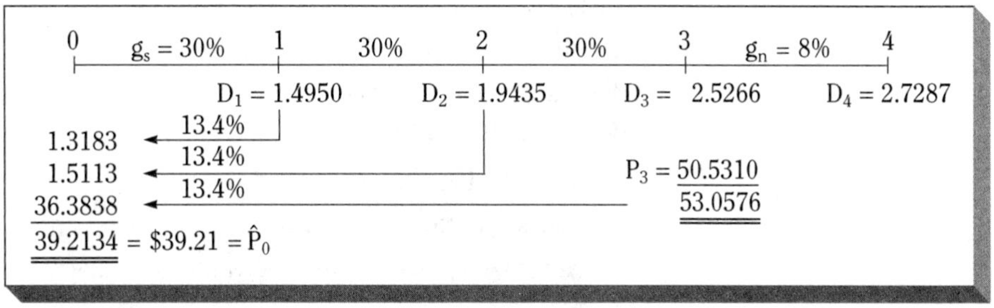

NOTES TO FIGURE 9-4:

Step 1. Calculate the dividends expected at the end of each year during the supernormal growth period. Calculate the first dividend, $D_1 = D_0(1 + g_s) = \$1.15(1.30) = \$1.4950$. Here g_s is the growth rate during the three-year supernormal growth period, 30 percent. Show the $1.4950 on the time line as the cash flow at Time 1. Then, calculate $D_2 = D_1(1 + g_s) = \$1.4950(1.30) = \$1.9435$, and then $D_3 = D_2(1 + g_s) = \$1.9435(1.30) = \$2.5266$. Show these values on the time line as the cash flows at Time 2 and Time 3. Note that D_0 is used only to calculate D_1.

Step 2. The price of the stock is the PV of dividends from Time 1 to infinity, so in theory we could project each future dividend, with the normal growth rate, $g_n = 8\%$, used to calculate D_4 and subsequent dividends. However, we know that after D_3 has been paid, which is at Time 3, the stock becomes a constant growth stock. Therefore, we can use the constant growth formula to find $\hat{P}_3$, which is the PV of the dividends from Time 4 to infinity as evaluated at Time 3.

First, we determine $D_4 = \$2.5266(1.08) = \$2.7287$ for use in the formula, and then we calculate $\hat{P}_3$ as follows:

$$\hat{P}_3 = \frac{D_4}{k_s - g_n} = \frac{\$2.7287}{0.134 - 0.08} = \$50.5310.$$

We show this $50.5310 on the time line as a second cash flow at Time 3. The $50.5310 is a Time 3 cash flow in the sense that the owner of the stock could sell it for $50.5310 at Time 3 and also in the sense that $50.5310 is the present value of the dividend cash flows from Time 4 to infinity. Note that the *total cash flow* at Time 3 consists of the sum of $D_3 + \hat{P}_3 = \$2.5266 + \$50.5310 = \$53.0576$.

Step 3. Now that the cash flows have been placed on the time line, we can discount each cash flow at the required rate of return, $k_s = 13.4\%$. We could discount each flow by dividing by $(1.134)^t$, where $t = 1$ for Time 1, $t = 2$ for Time 2, and $t = 3$ for Time 3. This produces the PVs shown to the left below the time line, and the sum of the PVs is the value of the supernormal growth stock, $39.21.

With a financial calculator, you can find the PV of the cash flows as shown on the time line with the cash flow (CFLO) register of your calculator. Enter 0 for CF_0 because you get no cash flow at Time 0, $CF_1 = 1.495$, $CF_2 = 1.9435$, and $CF_3 = 2.5266 + 50.531 = 53.0576$. Then enter $I = 13.4$, and press the NPV key to find the value of the stock, $39.21.

---

could vary from year to year. Also, there could be several different supernormal growth periods, e.g., 30% for three years, then 20% for three years, and then a constant 8%.) This rate is shown directly on the time line.

g_n = rate of normal, constant growth after the supernormal period = 8%. This rate is also shown on the time line, between Periods 3 and 4.

D_0 = last dividend the company paid = $1.15.

The valuation process as diagrammed in Figure 9-4 is explained in the steps set forth below the time line. The value of the supernormal growth stock is calculated to be $39.21.

Explain the following statement: "Whereas a bond contains a promise to pay interest, common stock typically provides an expectation of but no promise of dividends plus capital gains."

Are stock values based more on current earnings or long-term earnings forecasts?

What are the two parts of a stock's expected total return?

Write out and explain the valuation model for a zero growth stock.

Write out and explain the valuation model for a constant growth stock.

How does one calculate the capital gains yield and the dividend yield of a stock?

Explain how one would find the value of a supernormal growth stock.

VALUING THE ENTIRE CORPORATION

In the previous section, we presented several equations for valuing a firm's common stock. These equations had one common element: They all assumed that the firm is currently paying a dividend. But consider the situation of a startup company formed to develop and market a new product. Such a company generally expects to have low sales during its first few years as it develops and begins to market its product. Then, if the product catches on, sales will grow rapidly for several years. For example, Compaq Computer had just three employees when it was founded in 1982. Its first year was devoted to product development, so 1982 sales were zero. In early 1983, however, Compaq introduced its personal computer, and its 1983 sales hit $111 million, a record first-year volume for any new firm. Two years later, Compaq was included in *Fortune's* 500 largest U.S. industrial firms. Obviously, Compaq was more successful than most new businesses, but growth rates of 100, 500, or even 1,000 percent are not uncommon during firms' early years.

Growing sales require additional assets—Compaq could not have grown as it did without increasing its assets. Moreover, asset growth must be financed by increasing some liability and/or equity account. Small firms can often obtain some bank credit, but they must maintain a reasonable balance between debt and equity. Thus, additional bank borrowings require increases in equity, but small firms have limited access to the stock market. Moreover, even if they can sell stock, their owners are often reluctant to do so for fear of losing voting control. Therefore, the best source of equity for most small businesses is from retaining earnings, so most small firms pay no dividends during their rapid growth years. Eventually, most successful firms do pay dividends, with dividends growing rapidly at first but then slowing down as the firm approaches maturity.

Although most larger firms do pay a dividend, some firms, even highly profitable ones such as Microsoft, have never paid a dividend. How can the value of such a company be determined? Similarly, suppose you start a business, and someone offers to buy it from you. How could you determine its value, or that of any privately held business? Or suppose you work for a company with a number of divisions. How could you determine the value of one particular division which the company wants to sell? In none of these cases could you use the dividend growth model. However, you could use the **total company,** or **corporate, valuation model.**

The Corporate Value Model

Tables 9-2 and 9-3 contain the actual 1998 and projected 1999 to 2002 financial statements for MagnaVision Inc., which produces optical systems for use in medical photography. (See Chapter 14 for more details on how to project financial statements.)

TABLE 9-2	MagnaVision Inc.: Income Statements (Millions of Dollars Except for Per Share Data)				
	ACTUAL	**PROJECTED**			
	1998	**1999**	**2000[b]**	**2001**	**2002**
Net sales	$700.0	$850.0	$1,000.0	$1,100.0	$1,155.0
Costs (except depreciation)	$599.0	$734.0	$ 911.0	$ 935.0	$ 982.0
Depreciation	28.0	31.0	34.0	36.0	38.0
Total operating costs	$627.0	$765.0	$ 945.0	$ 971.0	$1,020.0
Earnings before interest and taxes (EBIT)	$ 73.0	$ 85.0	$ 55.0	$ 129.0	$ 135.0
Less: Net interest[a]	13.0	15.0	16.0	17.0	19.0
Earnings before taxes	$ 60.0	$ 70.0	$ 39.0	$ 112.0	$ 116.0
Taxes (40%)	24.0	28.0	15.6	44.8	46.4
Net income before preferred dividends	$ 36.0	$ 42.0	$ 23.4	$ 67.2	$ 69.6
Preferred dividends	6.0	7.0	7.4	8.0	8.3
Net income available for common dividends	$ 30.0	$ 35.0	$ 16.0	$ 59.2	$ 61.3
Common dividends	—	—	—	$ 44.2	$ 45.3
Addition to retained earnings	$ 30.0	$ 35.0	$ 16.0	$ 15.0	$ 16.0
Number of shares	100	100	100	100	100
Dividends per share	—	—	—	$0.442	$0.453

NOTES:

[a]"Net interest" is interest paid on debt less interest earned on marketable securities. Both items could be shown separately on the income statements, but for this example we combine them and show net interest.

[b]Net income is projected to decline in 2000. This is due to a projected cost for a one-time marketing program in that year.

Growth has been rapid in the past, but the market is becoming saturated, so the sales growth rate is expected to decline from 21 percent in 1999 to a sustainable rate of 5 percent in 2002 and beyond. Profit margins are expected to improve as the production process becomes more efficient and because MagnaVision will no longer be incurring marketing costs associated with the introduction of a major product. All items on the financial statements are projected to grow at a 5 percent rate after the year 2002. Notice that the company does not pay a dividend, but it is expected to start paying out about 75 percent of its earnings beginning in 2001. (Chapter 17 explains in more detail how companies decide how much to pay out in dividends.)

In Chapters 1 and 2 we explained that a firm's value is determined by its ability to generate cash flow, both now and in the future. Therefore, MagnaVision's value can be calculated as the present value of its expected future free cash flows (FCF) from operations, discounted at its cost of capital, k_c, plus the value of its nonoperating assets. Here is the equation for the value of operations, or the firm's value as a going concern:

$$\text{Value of operations} = V_{op} = \text{PV of expected future free cash flow}$$

$$= \frac{FCF_1}{(1 + k_c)^1} + \frac{FCF_2}{(1 + k_c)^2} + \cdots + \frac{FCF_\infty}{(1 + k_c)^\infty} \qquad \textbf{(9-6)}$$

$$= \sum_{t=1}^{\infty} \frac{FCF_t}{(1 + k_c)^t}.$$

TABLE 9-3	MagnaVision Inc.: Balance Sheets (Millions of Dollars)				

| | ACTUAL | PROJECTED | | | |
	1998	1999	2000	2001	2002
Assets					
Cash	$ 17.0	$ 20.0	$ 22.0	$ 23.0	$ 24.0
Marketable securities[a]	63.0	70.0	80.0	84.0	88.0
Accounts receivable	85.0	100.0	110.0	116.0	121.0
Inventories	170.0	200.0	220.0	231.0	243.0
Total current assets	$ 335.0	$ 390.0	$ 432.0	$ 454.0	$ 476.0
Net plant and equipment	279.0	310.0	341.0	358.0	376.0
Total assets	$ 614.0	$ 700.0	$ 773.0	$ 812.0	$ 852.0
Liabilities and Equity					
Accounts payable	$ 17.0	$ 20.0	$ 22.0	$ 23.0	$ 24.0
Notes payable	123.0	140.0	160.0	168.0	176.0
Accruals	43.0	50.0	55.0	58.0	61.0
Total current liabilities	$ 183.0	$ 210.0	$ 237.0	$ 249.0	$ 261.0
Long-term bonds	$ 124.0	$ 140.0	$ 160.0	$ 168.0	$ 176.0
Preferred stock	62.0	70.0	80.0	84.0	88.0
Common stock[b]	200.0	200.0	200.0	200.0	200.0
Retained earnings	45.0	80.0	96.0	111.0	127.0
Common equity	$ 245.0	$ 280.0	$ 296.0	$ 311.0	$ 327.0
Total liabilities and equity	$ 614.0	$ 700.0	$ 773.0	$ 812.0	$ 852.0

NOTES:

[a]All assets except marketable securities are operating assets required to support sales. The marketable securities are financial assets not required in operations.

[b]Par plus paid-in capital.

In Chapter 10 we explain how to estimate the cost of capital, but for now just assume that MagnaVision's cost of capital is 10.84 percent. To find its going concern value, we use an approach similar to the nonconstant dividend growth model, proceeding as follows:

1. Assume that the firm will experience nonconstant growth for N years, after which it will grow at some constant rate.

2. Calculate the expected free cash flow for each of the N nonconstant growth years, and find the PV of these cash flows.

3. Recognize that after Year N growth will be constant, so we can use the constant growth formula to find the firm's value at Year N. This "terminal value" is the sum of the PVs for N + 1 and all subsequent years, discounted back to Year N. Then, the Year N value must be discounted back to the present to find its PV at Year 0.

4. Now sum all the PVs, those of the annual free cash flows during the nonconstant period plus the PV of the terminal value, to find the firm's value of operations. This going concern value, when added to the value of the nonoperating assets, is the total value of the firm.

TABLE 9-4	Calculating MagnaVision's Expected Free Cash Flow (Millions of Dollars)				

| | ACTUAL 1998 | PROJECTED | | | |
		1999	2000	2001	2002
Calculation of Free Cash Flow					
1. Required net operating working capital	$212.00	$250.00	$275.00	$289.00	$303.00
2. Required net plant and equipment	279.00	310.00	341.00	358.00	376.00
3. Required net operating assets	$491.00	$560.00	$616.00	$647.00	$679.00
4. Required net new investment in operating assets = change in net operating assets from previous year		69.00	56.00	31.00	32.00
5. NOPAT [Net operating profit after taxes = EBIT × (1 – Tax rate)]		$ 51.00	$ 33.00	$ 77.40	$ 81.00
6. Less: Required investment in operating assets		69.00	56.00	31.00	32.00
7. Free cash flow		($ 18.00)	($ 23.00)	$ 46.40	$ 49.00

NOTE: NOPAT declines in 2000 because of a marketing expenditure projected for that year. See Note b in Table 9-2.

Table 9-4 calculates free cash flow for each year, using procedures discussed in Chapter 2. Line 1, with data for 1998 from the balance sheets in Table 9-3, shows the required net operating working capital, or operating current assets minus operating current liabilities, for 1998:

$$\begin{matrix} \text{Required net} \\ \text{operating} \\ \text{working capital} \end{matrix} = \begin{pmatrix} \text{Cash +} \\ \text{Accounts receivable} \\ \text{+ Inventories} \end{pmatrix} - \begin{pmatrix} \text{Accounts} \\ \text{payable +} \\ \text{Accruals} \end{pmatrix}$$

$$= (\$17.00 + \$85.00 + \$170.00) - (\$17.00 + \$43.00)$$

$$= \$212.00.$$

Line 2 shows required net plant and equipment, and Line 3, which is the sum of Lines 1 and 2, shows the required net operating assets, sometimes called net operating capital. For 1998, net operating capital is $212 + $279 = $491 million.

Line 4 shows the required net annual addition to operating assets, found as the change in net operating assets from the previous year. For 1999, the required net investment in operating assets is $560 – $491 = $69 million.

Line 5 shows NOPAT, or net operating profit after taxes. Note that EBIT is operating earnings *before* taxes, while NOPAT is operating earnings *after* taxes. Therefore, NOPAT = EBIT(1 – T). With 1999 EBIT of $85 as shown in Table 9-2 and a tax rate of 40 percent, NOPAT as projected for 1999 is $51 million:

$$\text{NOPAT} = \text{EBIT}(1 - T) = \$85(1.0 - 0.4) = \$51 \text{ million.}$$

Although MagnaVision's operating assets are projected to produce $51 million of after-tax profits in 1999, the company must invest $69 million in new assets in 1999. Therefore, the free cash flow for 1999, shown on Line 7, is a negative $18 million:

$$\text{Free cash flow (FCF)} = \$51 - \$69 = -\$18.00 \text{ million.}$$

This negative free cash flow in the early years is typical for young, high-growth companies. Even though net operating profit after taxes (NOPAT) is positive in all years, free cash flow is negative because of the need to invest in operating assets. The negative free cash flow means the company will have to obtain new funds from investors, and the balance sheets in Table 9-3 show that notes payable, long-term bonds, and preferred stock all increase from 1998 to 1999. Stockholders will also help fund MagnaVision's growth—they will receive no dividends until 2001, so all of the net income from 1998 to 2001 will be reinvested. However, as growth slows, free cash flow will become positive, and MagnaVision plans to use some of its FCF to pay dividends beginning in 2001.[13]

A variant of the constant growth dividend model (Equation 9-4) is shown below as Equation 9-7. This equation can be used to find the value of MagnaVision's operations once its free cash flows stabilize and begin to grow at a constant rate:

$$V_{\text{op(at time N)}} = \sum_{t=N+1}^{\infty} \frac{FCF_t}{(1 + k_c)^{t-N}}$$

$$= \frac{FCF_N(1 + g)}{k_c - g} = \frac{FCF_{N+1}}{k_c - g}.$$

(9-7)

Based on a 10.84 percent cost of capital, a $49 million free cash flow in 2002, and a 5 percent growth rate, the value of MagnaVision's operations as of December 31, 2002, is forecasted to be $880.99 million:

$$V_{\text{op(12/31/02)}} = \frac{FCF_{12/31/02}(1 + g)}{k_c - g} = \frac{FCF_{12/31/03}}{k_c - g}$$

(9-7a)

$$= \frac{\$49(1 + 0.05)}{0.1084 - 0.05} = \frac{\$51.45}{0.1084 - 0.05} = \$880.99.$$

This $880.99 million figure is called the company's **terminal, or horizon, value,** because it is the value at the end of the forecast period. Moreover, this is the amount that MagnaVision could expect to receive if it sold its operating assets on December 31, 2002.

Figure 9-5 shows the free cash flow for each year during the nonconstant growth period, along with the value of operations in 2002, at the end of the nonconstant growth period. To find the value of operations as of "today," December 31, 1998, we find the PV of each annual cash flow in Figure 9-5, discounting at the 10.84 percent cost of

---

[13]MagnaVision plans to increase its debt and preferred stock each year so as to maintain a constant capital structure. We discuss capital structure in detail in Chapters 14, 15, and 16.

FIGURE 9-5   Process for Finding the Value of Operations
for a Nonconstant Growth Company

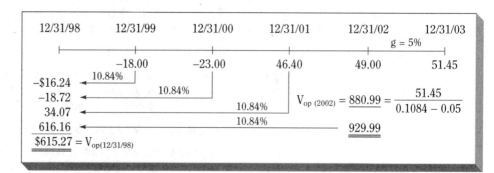

capital. The sum of the PVs is approximately $615 million, and it represents an estimate of the price MagnaVision could expect to receive if it sold its operating assets today, December 31, 1998.

The total value of any company is the value of its operations plus the value of its nonoperating assets. As the December 31, 1998, balance sheet in Table 9-3 shows, MagnaVision had $63 million of marketable securities on that date. Unlike operating assets, we do not have to calculate a present value for marketable securities because short-term financial assets as reported on the balance sheet are at, or close to, their market value. Therefore, MagnaVision's total value on December 31, 1998, is $615.27 + $63.00 = $678.27 million.

If the company's total value on December 31, 1998, is $678.27 million, what is the value of its common equity? First, note that notes payable and long-term debt total $123 + $124 = $247 million, and these securities have the first claim on assets and income. (Accounts payable and accruals were netted out earlier.) Next, the preferred stock has a claim of $62 million, and it also ranks above the common. Therefore, the value left for common stockholders is $678.27 − $247 − $62 = $369.27 million.

Figure 9-6 is a bar chart which analyzes the sources of MagnaVision's value. The left bar shows the company's total value as the sum of its nonoperating assets plus its going concern value. Next, what is the claim of each class of investors on that total value? This breakdown is shown in the middle bar. Debtholders have the highest priority claim, and MagnaVision owes $123 million on notes payable and $124 million on long-term bonds, for a total of $247 million. The preferred stockholders have the next claim, $62 million. The remainder of the value belongs to the common equity, and it

FIGURE 9-6   MagnaVision's Value as of December 31, 1998

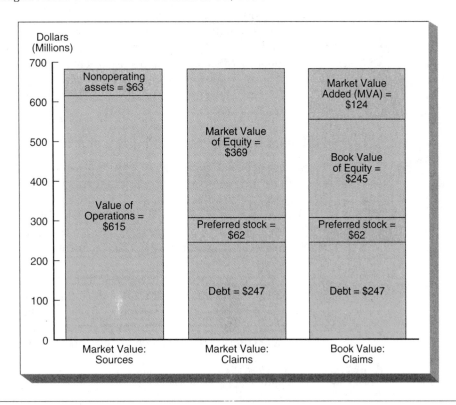

TABLE 9-5	Finding the Value of MagnaVision's Stock (Millions of Dollars Except for Per Share Data)	
	1. Value of operations (net of payables and accruals)	$615.27
	2. Plus value of nonoperating assets	63.00
	3. Total market value of the firm	$678.27
	4. Less: Value of debt	247.00
	Value of preferred stock	62.00
	5. Value of common equity	$369.27
	6. Divide by number of shares	100
	7. Value per share	$3.69

amounts to $678.27 − $247.00 − $62.00 = $369.27 million.[14] Finally, the bar on the right side of Figure 9-6 divides the market value of the equity into the book value, which represents the actual investment stockholders have made, and the additional market value added (MVA) by management.

Table 9-5 summarizes the calculations used to find MagnaVision's stock value. There are 100 million shares outstanding, and their total value is $369.27 million. Therefore, the value of a single share is $3.69 ($369.27/100 = $3.69).

The Dividend Growth Model Applied to MagnaVision

MagnaVision has not yet begun to pay dividends. However, as shown in Table 9-2, a cash dividend of $0.442 per share is forecasted for 2001, the dividend is expected to grow by about 2.5 percent in 2002, and then dividends are expected to grow at a constant 5 percent rate thereafter. In Chapter 10 we explain how to estimate each component cost of capital; for now we simply assume that the firm's cost of equity is 14 percent. In this situation, we can apply the nonconstant dividend growth model as developed earlier in the chapter. Figure 9-7 shows that the value of MagnaVision's stock, based on this model, is $3.70 per share, which is identical to the value found using the total corporate model except for rounding errors.

Comparing the Total Company and Dividend Growth Models

Since the total company and dividend growth models give the same answer, does it matter which model you choose? In general, it does. For example, if you were a financial analyst estimating the values of mature companies whose dividends are expected to grow steadily in the future, it would probably be more efficient to use the dividend growth model. Here you would only need to estimate the growth rate in dividends, not the entire set of pro forma financial statements. Chapter 10 explains some techniques for estimating growth rates.

However, if a company is paying a dividend but is still in the high-growth stage of its life cycle, you would need to project the future financial statements before you could make a reasonable estimate of future dividends. Then, since you would have already estimated future financial statements, it would be a toss-up as to whether the total company model or the dividend growth model would be easier to apply. Intel, which

---

[14]Rather than subtracting the book values of debt and preferred stock, it would be better to subtract their market values. In most cases, including this one, the book values of fixed income securities are close to their market values, and when this is true, one can simply work with book values.

| FIGURE 9-7 | Using the DCF Dividend Model to Find MagnaVision's Stock Value |

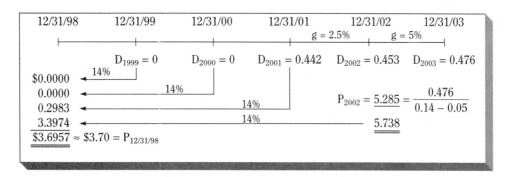

pays a dividend of 12 cents versus earnings of about $5, is an example of a company to which you could apply either model.

Now suppose you were trying to estimate the value of a company that has never paid a dividend, such as Microsoft, or a new firm that is about to go public, or a division which GE or some other large company is planning to sell. In all of these situations, you would have no choice: You would have to estimate future financial statements and use the total company valuation model.

Actually, even if a company is paying steady dividends, much can be learned from the corporate value model, so many analysts today use it for all types of valuations. The process of projecting the future financial statements can reveal quite a bit about the company's operations and financing needs. Also, such an analysis can provide insights into actions that might be taken to increase the company's value. This is called *value-based management,* and we discuss it in more detail in Chapter 14.

SELF-TEST
QUESTIONS

Write out the equation for the corporate value model, and explain what it does.

What is the terminal, or horizon, value?

What conditions are necessary if one is to use the dividend growth model? When is it essential to use the corporate value model?

Why might someone use the corporate model even though the dividend model could be used?

STOCK MARKET EQUILIBRIUM

Recall from Chapter 5 that the required return on Stock X, k_X, can be found using the Security Market Line (SML) equation as it was developed in our discussion of the Capital Asset Pricing Model (CAPM):

$$k_X = k_{RF} + (k_M - k_{RF}) b_X.$$

If the risk-free rate of return is 8 percent, the required return on an average stock is 12 percent, and Stock X has a beta of 2, then the marginal investor will require a return of 16 percent on Stock X, calculated as follows:

$$k_X = 8\% + (12\% - 8\%) 2.0$$

$$= 16\%.$$

This 16 percent required return is shown as the point on the SML in Figure 9-8 associated with beta = 2.0.

FIGURE 9-8   Expected and Required Returns on Stock X

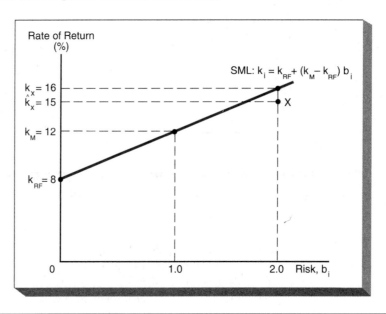

The **marginal investor** will want to buy Stock X if its expected rate of return is more than 16 percent, will want to sell it if the expected rate of return is less than 16 percent, and will be indifferent, hence will hold but not buy or sell, if the expected return is exactly 16 percent. Now suppose the investor's portfolio contains Stock X, and he or she analyzes the stock's prospects and concludes that its earnings, dividends, and price can be expected to grow at a constant rate of 5 percent per year. The last dividend was $D_0 = \$2.8571$, so the next expected dividend is

$$D_1 = \$2.8571(1.05) = \$3.$$

Our marginal investor observes that the present price of the stock, P_0, is $30. Should he or she purchase more of Stock X, sell it, or maintain the present position?

The investor can calculate Stock X's *expected rate of return* as follows:

$$\hat{k}_X = \frac{D_1}{P_0} + g = \frac{\$3}{\$30} + 5\% = 15\%.$$

This value is plotted on Figure 9-8 as Point X, which is below the SML. Because the expected rate of return is less than the required return, this investor would want to sell the stock, as would most other holders. However, few people would want to buy at the $30 price, so the present owners would be unable to find buyers unless they cut the price of the stock. Thus, the price would decline, and this decline would continue until the stock's price reached $27.27. At that point, the security would be in **equilibrium,** defined as the price at which the expected rate of return, 16 percent, is equal to the required rate of return:

$$\hat{k}_X = \frac{\$3}{\$27.27} + 5\% = 11\% + 5\% = 16\% = k_X.$$

Had the stock initially sold for less than $27.27, say, at $25, events would have been reversed. Investors would have wanted to buy the stock because its expected rate of return exceeded its required rate of return, and buy orders would have driven the price up to $27.27.

To summarize, in equilibrium two related conditions must hold:

1. A stock's expected rate of return as seen by the marginal investor must equal its required rate of return: $\hat{k}_i = k_i$.

2. The actual market price must equal the intrinsic value as estimated by the marginal investor: $P_0 = \hat{P}_0$.

Of course, some individual investors might believe that $\hat{k}_i > k$ and $\hat{P}_0 > P_0$, hence would invest most of their funds in the stock, while others might have an opposite view and would sell all of their shares. However, it is the marginal investor who establishes the actual market price, and for this investor, we must have $\hat{k}_i = k_i$ and $P_0 = \hat{P}_0$. If these conditions do not hold, trading will occur until they do hold.

Changes in Equilibrium Stock Prices

Stock prices are not constant—they undergo violent changes at times. For example, on October 19, 1987, the Dow Jones average dropped 508 points, and the average stock lost about 23 percent of its value on that one day. Some individual stocks lost more than 70 percent of their value. Many investors (and companies) were wiped out, and a number of suicides occurred. On a brighter note, the Dow Jones average has increased by more than 100 points on a number of days during the 1990s. But what goes up often comes down. The Dow dropped 554 points on October 27, 1997, wiping out more than $600 billion of wealth. This was the largest ever single-day point drop, and the 12th worst percentage loss (7.18 percent). On the next day, however, the Dow increased by 337 points, a record single-day increase. At the risk of understatement, the stock market is quite volatile!

To see how such changes can occur, assume that Stock X is in equilibrium, selling at a price of $27.27 per share. If all expectations were exactly met, during the next year the price would gradually rise to $28.63, or by 5 percent. However, many different events could occur to cause a change in the equilibrium price. To illustrate, consider again the inputs used to develop Stock X's price of $27.27, along with some new inputs:

	VARIABLE VALUE	
	ORIGINAL	NEW
Risk-free rate, k_{RF}	8%	7%
Market risk premium, $k_M - k_{RF}$	4%	3%
Stock X's beta coefficient, b_X	2.0	1.0
Stock X's expected growth rate, g_X	5%	6%
D_0	$2.8571	$2.8571
Price of Stock X	$27.27	?

Now give yourself a test: How would the change in each variable, by itself, affect the price, and what is your guess as to the new stock price?

Every change, taken alone, would lead to an *increase* in the price. The first three changes all lower k_X, which declines from 16 to 10 percent:

$$\text{Original } k_X = 8\% + 4\%(2.0) = 16\%.$$

$$\text{New } k_X = 7\% + 3\%(1.0) = 10\%.$$

Using these values together with the new g value, we find that $\hat{P}_0$ rises from \$27.27 to \$75.71.[15]

$$\text{Original } \hat{P}_0 = \frac{\$2.8571(1.05)}{0.16 - 0.05} = \frac{\$3}{0.11} = \$27.27.$$

$$\text{New } \hat{P}_0 = \frac{\$2.8571(1.06)}{0.10 - 0.06} = \frac{\$3.0285}{0.04} = \$75.71.$$

At the new price, the expected and required rates of return will be equal:[16]

$$\hat{k}_X = \frac{\$3.0285}{\$75.71} + 6\% = 10\% = k_X.$$

As this example illustrates, even small changes in the size or riskiness of expected future dividends can cause large changes in stock prices. What might cause investors to change their expectations about future dividends? It could be new information about the specific company, such as preliminary results for an R&D program, initial sales of a new product, or the discovery of harmful side effects from the use of an existing product. Or, new information that will affect many companies could arrive, such as a tightening of interest rates by the Federal Reserve. Given the existence of computers and telecommunications networks, new information hits the market on an almost continuous basis, and it causes frequent and sometimes large changes in stock prices. In other words, *ready availability of information causes stock prices to be volatile!*

If a stock's price is stable, that probably means that little new information is arriving. But if you think it's risky to invest in a volatile stock, imagine how risky it would be to invest in a stock which rarely released new information about its sales or operations. It may be bad to see your stock's price jump around, but it would be a lot worse to see a stable quoted price most of the time but then to see huge moves on the rare days when new information was released. Fortunately, in our economy timely information is readily available. Evidence suggests that stocks, especially those of large companies, adjust rapidly to new information. Consequently, equilibrium ordinarily exists for any given stock, and required and expected returns are generally equal. Stock prices certainly change, sometimes violently and rapidly, but this simply reflects changing conditions and expectations. There are, of course, times when a stock appears to react for several months to favorable or unfavorable developments, but this does not signify a long adjustment period; rather, it simply indicates that as more new pieces of information about the situation become available, the market adjusts to them. The ability of the market to adjust to new information is discussed in the next section.

The Efficient Markets Hypothesis

A body of theory called the **Efficient Markets Hypothesis (EMH)** holds (1) that stocks are always in equilibrium and (2) that it is impossible for an investor to consistently "beat the market." Essentially, those who believe in the EMH note that there are 100,000 or so full-time, highly trained, professional analysts and traders operating in

---

[15]A price change of this magnitude is by no means rare. The prices of *many* stocks double or halve during a year. For example, during 1996, TSR, a software firm, increased in value by 967 percent. On the other hand, Best Products, a catalog retailer, fell by 99.7 percent.

[16]It should be obvious by now that *actual realized* rates of return are not necessarily equal to expected and required returns. Thus, an investor might have *expected* to receive a return of 15 percent if he or she had bought TSR or Best Products stock in 1996, but, after the fact, the realized return on TSR was far above 15 percent, whereas that on Best Products was far below.

the market, while there are fewer than 3,000 major stocks. Therefore, if each analyst followed 30 stocks (which is about right, as analysts tend to specialize in the stocks in a specific industry), there would on average be 1,000 analysts following each stock. Further, these analysts work for organizations such as Citibank, Merrill Lynch, Prudential Insurance, and the like, which have billions of dollars available with which to take advantage of bargains. In addition, as a result of SEC disclosure requirements and electronic information networks, as new information about a stock becomes available, these 1,000 analysts generally receive and evaluate it at about the same time. Therefore, the price of a stock will adjust almost immediately to any new development.

Levels of Market Efficiency

If markets are efficient, stock prices will rapidly reflect all available information. This raises an important question: What types of information are available and, therefore, incorporated into stock prices? Financial theorists have discussed three forms, or levels, of market efficiency.

Weak-Form Efficiency.   The **weak form** of the EMH states that all information contained in past price movements is fully reflected in current market prices. If this were true, then information about recent trends in stock prices would be of no use in selecting stocks — the fact that a stock has risen for the past three days, for example, would give us no useful clues as to what it will do today or tomorrow. People who believe that weak-form efficiency exists also believe that "tape watchers" and "chartists" are wasting their time.[17]

For example, after studying the past history of the stock market, a chartist might "discover" the following pattern: If a stock falls three consecutive days, its price typically rises 10 percent the following day. The technician would then conclude that investors could make money by purchasing a stock whose price has fallen three consecutive days.

But if this pattern truly existed, wouldn't other investors also discover it, and if so, why would anyone be willing to sell a stock after it had fallen three consecutive days if they know the stock's price is expected to increase by 10 percent the next day? In other words, if a stock is selling at $40 per share after falling three consecutive days, why would investors sell the stock if they expected it to rise to $44 per share one day later? Those who believe in weak-form efficiency argue that if the stock would really rise to $44 per share tomorrow, its price *today* would actually rise to somewhere near $44 per share immediately, thereby eliminating the trading opportunity. Consequently, weak-form efficiency implies that any information that comes from past stock prices is rapidly incorporated into the current stock price.

Semistrong-Form Efficiency.   The **semistrong form** of the EMH states that current market prices reflect all *publicly available* information. Therefore, if semistrong-form efficiency exists, it would do no good to pore over annual reports or other published data, because market prices would have adjusted to any good or bad news contained in such reports back when the news came out. With semistrong-form efficiency, investors should expect to earn the returns predicted by the SML, but they should not expect to do any better unless they have good luck or information that is not publicly available. However, insiders (for example, the presidents of companies) who have information

---

[17]Tape watchers are people who watch the NYSE tape, while chartists plot past patterns of stock price movements. Both are called "technicians," and both believe that they can tell if something is happening to the stock that will cause its price to move up or down in the near future.

which is not publicly available can earn abnormal returns (returns higher than those predicted by the SML) even under semistrong-form efficiency.

Another implication of semistrong-form efficiency is that whenever information is released to the public, stock prices will respond only if the information is different from what had been expected. If, for example, a company announces a 30 percent increase in earnings, and if that increase is about what analysts had been expecting, the announcement should have little or no effect on the company's stock price. On the other hand, the stock price would fall if analysts had expected earnings to increase by more than 30 percent, but it would rise if they had expected a smaller increase.

Strong-Form Efficiency.   The **strong form** of the EMH states that current market prices reflect all pertinent information, whether publicly available or privately held. If this form holds, even insiders would find it impossible to earn abnormal returns in the stock market.[18]

Many empirical studies have been conducted to test for the three forms of market efficiency. Most of these studies suggest that the stock market is indeed highly efficient in the weak form and reasonably efficient in the semistrong form, at least for the larger and more widely followed stocks. However, the strong-form EMH does not hold, so abnormal profits can be made by those who possess inside information.

Implications of Market Efficiency

What bearing does the EMH have on financial decisions? Since stock prices do seem to reflect public information, most stocks appear to be fairly valued. This does not mean that new developments could not cause a stock's price to soar or to plummet, but it does mean that stocks in general are neither overvalued nor undervalued—they are fairly priced and in equilibrium. However, there are certainly cases in which corporate insiders have information not known to outsiders.

If the EMH is correct, it is a waste of time for most of us to analyze stocks by looking for those that are undervalued. If stock prices already reflect all publicly available information, and hence are fairly priced, one can "beat the market" only by luck, and it is difficult, if not impossible, for anyone to consistently outperform the market averages. Empirical tests have shown that the EMH is, in its weak and semistrong forms, valid. However, people such as corporate officers who have inside information can do better than the averages, and individuals and organizations that are especially good at digging out information on small, new companies also seem to do consistently well. Also, some investors may be able to analyze and react more quickly than others to releases of new information, and these investors may have an advantage over others. However, the buy-sell actions of those investors quickly bring market prices into equilibrium. Therefore, it is generally safe to assume that $\hat{k} = k$, that $\hat{P}_0 = P_0$, and that stocks plot on the SML.[19]

---

[18]Several cases of illegal insider trading have made the news headlines. These cases involved employees of several major investment banking houses and even an employee of the SEC. In the most famous case, Ivan Boesky admitted to making $50 million by purchasing the stock of firms he knew were about to be acquired. He went to jail, and he had to pay a large fine, but he helped disprove the strong-form EMH.

[19]Market efficiency also has important implications for managerial decisions, especially those pertaining to common stock issues, stock repurchases, and tender offers. Stocks appear to be fairly valued, so decisions based on the premise that a stock is undervalued or overvalued must be approached with caution. However, managers do have better information about their own companies than outsiders, and this information can legally be used to the companies' (but not the managers') advantage.

We should also note that some Wall Street pros have consistently beaten the market over many years, which is inconsistent with the EMH. An interesting article in the April 3, 1995, issue of *Fortune* (Terence P. Paré, "Yes, You Can Beat the Market") argued strongly against the EMH. Paré suggested that each stock has

RUN-UPS BEFORE DEALS: CHICANERY OR COINCIDENCE?

Most studies find that markets are not strong-form efficient—the market can be beaten by those with access to inside information. Inside information is particularly valuable when it comes to corporate takeovers.

An article in *Business Week* claimed that one out of every three big mergers in 1994 was preceded by suspicious insider trading. For example, the day before American Home Products launched a $95 per share hostile takeover bid for American Cyanamid, there was heavy trading in Cyanamid, and its stock price jumped from $60⅝ to $63 a share. The article went on to document a number of similar cases, all with sharp run-ups in the target firms' stock prices just before merger announcements.

The Securities and Exchange Commission (SEC), which is responsible for policing insider trading, regularly investigates such cases to determine whether there was any illegal insider trading. To be sure, some preannouncement run-ups are undoubtedly legitimate—perhaps a large number of buy orders just randomly came in, or, more likely, perhaps some market professionals guessed correctly that a merger was likely. However, there are cases in which the evidence strongly suggests information was "leaked" prior to the takeover. Harry C. Johnson, chairman and president of Red Eagle Resources Corporation, which was recently acquired by Lomak Petroleum, put it best after he saw the stock price of his company rise 16 percent the day before the deal was announced: "When there are a lot of people involved in a deal, you have to believe in the tooth fairy to think there can't be leakage."

SOURCE: Adapted from "Insider Trading," *Business Week*, December 12, 1994.

S E L F - T E S T
Q U E S T I O N S

For a stock to be in equilibrium, what two conditions must hold?

What is the Efficient Markets Hypothesis (EMH)?

What is the difference among the three forms of the EMH: (1) weak form, (2) semistrong form, and (3) strong form?

What are the implications of the EMH for financial decisions?

ACTUAL STOCK PRICES AND RETURNS

Our discussion thus far has focused on *expected* stock prices and *expected* rates of return. Anyone who has ever invested in the stock market knows that there can be, and there generally are, large differences between *expected* and *realized* prices and returns.

We can use IBM to illustrate this point. In early 1991, IBM's stock price was about $120 per share. Its 1990 dividend, D_0, was $4.84, but analysts expected the dividend to grow at a constant rate of about 8 percent in the future. Thus, an average investor who bought IBM at a price of $120 expected to earn about 12.4 percent:

$$\hat{k}_s = \begin{array}{c} \text{Expected dividend} \\ \text{yield} \end{array} + \begin{array}{c} \text{Expected growth rate, which is also} \\ \text{the expected capital gains yield} \end{array}$$

$$= \frac{D_0(1+g)}{P_0} + g = \frac{\$5.23}{\$120} + 8\%$$

$$= 4.4\% + 8.0\% = 12.4\%.$$

---

a fundamental value, but when good or bad news about it is announced, most investors fail to interpret this news correctly. As a result, stocks are generally priced above or below their long-term values.

Think of a graph with stock price on the vertical axis and years on the horizontal axis. A stock's fundamental value might be moving up steadily over time as it retains and reinvests earnings. However, its actual price might fluctuate about the intrinsic value line, overreacting to good or bad news and indicating departures from equilibrium. Successful value investors, according to the article, use fundamental analysis to identify stocks' intrinsic values, and then they buy stocks that are undervalued and sell those that are overvalued.

Paré's argument implies that the market is systematically out of equilibrium and that investors can act on this knowledge to beat the market. That position may turn out to be correct, but it may also be that the superior performance Paré noted simply demonstrates that some people are better at obtaining and interpreting information than others, or have been lucky in the past.

FIGURE 9-9   S&P 500 Index, 1967–1997

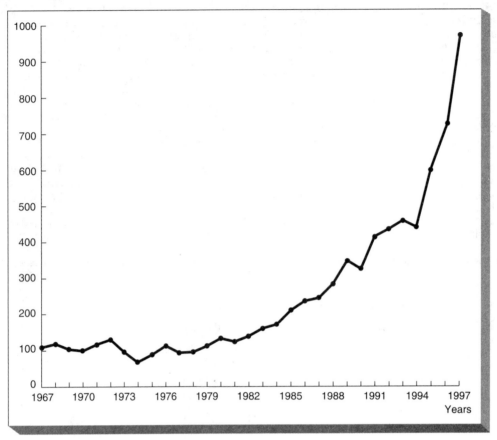

SOURCE: Data taken from various issues of *The Wall Street Journal,* "Stock Market Data Bank" section.

In fact, things did not work out as expected. IBM's share of the computer market in 1991 was weaker than had been predicted, so IBM's earnings did not grow as fast as expected, and its dividend remained at $4.84. So, rather than growing, IBM's stock price declined, and it closed on December 31, 1991, at $89, down $31 for the year. Thus, on a beginning-of-the-year investment of $120, the annual return on IBM for 1991 was −21.8 percent:

$$\bar{k}_s = \text{Actual dividend yield} + \text{Actual capital gains yield}$$

$$= \frac{\$4.84}{\$120} + \frac{-\$31}{\$120} = 4.0\% - 25.8\% = -21.8\%.$$

Many other stocks performed similarly to IBM, or worse, in 1991.

By contrast, IBM's realized returns in recent years have been higher than expected. IBM's shareholders enjoyed a total return of roughly 25 percent in 1995, 67 percent in 1996, and 38 percent in 1997. A turnaround of the company's fortunes, combined with a strong overall market, led to these better-than-expected results.

Figure 9-9 shows how the market value of a portfolio of stocks has moved in recent years, and Figure 9-10 shows how total realized returns on the portfolio have varied from year to year. The market trend has been strongly up, but it has gone up in some

FIGURE 9-10   S&P 500 Index, Total Returns:
Dividend Yield + Capital Gain or Loss, 1967–1997

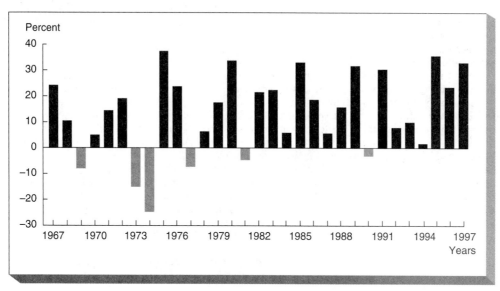

SOURCE: *Stocks, Bonds, Bills, and Inflation: 1998 Yearbook* (Chicago: Ibbotson Associates, 1998).

years and down in others, and the stocks of individual companies have likewise gone up and down.[20] We know from theory that expected returns, as estimated by a marginal investor, are always positive, but in some years, as Figure 9-10 shows, actual returns are negative. Of course, even in bad years some individual companies do well, so "the name of the game" in security analysis is to pick the winners. Financial managers attempt to take actions which will put their companies into the winners' column, but they don't always succeed. In subsequent chapters, we will examine the actions that managers can take to increase the odds of their firms doing relatively well in the marketplace.

Investing in International Stocks

As noted in Chapter 5, the U.S. stock market amounts to only 35 percent of the world stock market, and this is prompting many U.S. investors to hold at least some foreign stocks. Analysts have long touted the benefits of investing overseas, arguing that foreign stocks both improve diversification and provide good growth opportunities. For example, after the U.S. stock market rose an average of 17.5 percent a year during the 1980s, many analysts thought that the U.S. market in the 1990s was due for a correction, and they suggested that investors should increase their holdings of foreign stocks.

To the surprise of many, however, U.S. stocks have outperformed foreign stocks thus far in the 1990s — they have gained about 15 percent a year versus only 3 percent for foreign

---

[20]If we constructed graphs like Figures 9-9 and 9-10 for individual stocks rather than for a large portfolio, far greater variability would be shown. Also, if we constructed a graph like Figure 9-10 for bonds, it would have the same general shape, but the bars would be somewhat smaller, indicating that gains and losses on bonds are generally smaller than those on stocks. Above-average bond returns occur in years when interest rates decline, and losses on bonds occur only when interest rates rise sharply.

INVESTING IN EMERGING MARKETS

Given the possibilities of better diversification and higher returns, U.S. investors have been putting more and more money into foreign stocks. While many investors limit their foreign holdings to developed countries such as Japan, Germany, Canada, and the United Kingdom, others have broadened their portfolios to include emerging markets such as South Korea, Mexico, Singapore, Taiwan, and Russia.

Emerging markets provide opportunities for larger returns, but they also entail greater risks. For example, Russian stocks rose more than 150 percent in the first half of 1996,

as it became apparent that Boris Yeltsin would be reelected president. By contrast, if you had invested in Taiwanese stocks, you would have lost 30 percent in 1995—a year in which most stock markets performed extremely well.

Stocks in emerging markets are intriguing for two reasons. First, developing nations have the greatest potential for growth. Second, while stock returns in developed countries often move in sync with one another, stocks in emerging markets march to their own drummers. Therefore, the correlation between U.S. stocks and those in emerging markets are generally lower than between U.S. stocks and those of other developed

countries. Thus, correlation data suggest that emerging markets improve the diversification of U.S. investors' portfolios. (Recall from Chapter 5 that the lower the correlation, the better the diversification.)

On the other hand, stocks in emerging markets are often extremely risky, they are less liquid, they involve higher transaction costs, and most U.S. investors do not have ready access to information on the companies involved. To reduce these problems, mutual fund companies have created *country funds,* which invest in "baskets of stocks," for many emerging nations.

stocks. Figure 9-11 shows how stocks in different countries performed in 1997. In each case, the lower number in the white box indicates how stocks in that country performed in terms of its local currency, while the upper number shows how the country's stocks performed in terms of the U.S. dollar. For example, in 1997 Australian stocks rose by 9.5 percent, but the Australian dollar declined more than 19 percent versus the U.S. dollar. Therefore, if U.S. investors had bought Australian stocks, they would have made 9.5 percent in Australian dollar terms, but those Australian dollars would have bought 19 percent fewer dollars, so the effective return would have been −10.3 percent. So, the results of foreign investments depend in part on what happens to the exchange rate. Indeed, when you invest overseas, you are making two bets: (1) that foreign stocks will increase in their local markets and (2) that the currencies in which you will be paid will rise relative to the dollar.

Despite the fact that U.S. stocks have outperformed foreign stocks in recent years, this by no means suggests that investors should avoid foreign stocks. Foreign investments still improve diversification, and it is inevitable that there will be years when foreign stocks outperform domestic stocks. When this occurs, U.S. investors will be glad they put some of their eggs in overseas markets.

Stock Market Reporting

Figure 9-12, taken from a daily newspaper, is a section of the stock market page for stocks listed on the NYSE. For each stock, the NYSE report provides specific data on the trading that took place the prior day. Similar information is available for stocks listed on the other exchanges as well as for the larger stocks traded over the counter.

Stocks are listed alphabetically, from AAR Industries to Zweig; the data in Figure 9-12 were taken from the top of the listing. We examine the data for Abbott Laboratories, AbbotLab, shown about three-fourths down the table. The two columns on the left show the highest and lowest prices at which the stocks have sold during the past year; Abbott Labs has traded in the range from $68^{15}/_{16}$ to $47^{3}/_{8}$ during the preceding 52 weeks. The figure just to the right of the company's ticker symbol is the dividend; Abbott Labs had a current indicated annual dividend rate of $1.08 per share and a dividend yield (which is the current dividend divided by the closing stock price) of 1.7 per-

FIGURE 9-11 1997 Performance of the Dow Jones World Stock Indexes

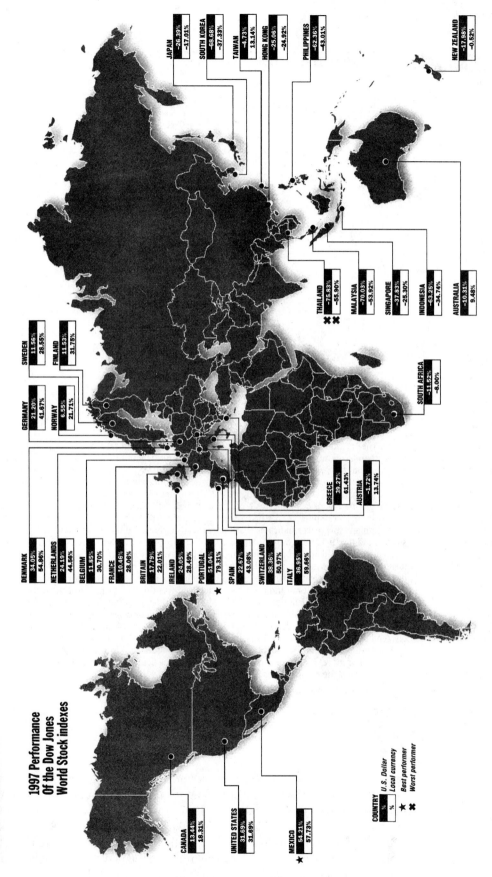

1997 Performance
Of the Dow Jones
World Stock indexes

SOURCE: "1997 Performance of the Dow Jones World Stock Indexes," *The Wall Street Journal*, January 2, 1998, R10. © 1997 Dow Jones & Company, Inc. All Rights Reserved Worldwide.

FIGURE 9-12 Stock Market Transactions, September 19, 1997

Quotations as of 5 p.m. Eastern Time
Friday, September 19, 1997

	52 Weeks Hi	52 Weeks Lo	Stock	Sym	Div	Yld %	PE	Vol 100s	Hi	Lo	Close	Net Chg
			-A-A-A-									
	38 7/16	22 5/8	AAR	AIR	.48	1.4	23	816	33 15/16	33 1/2	33 15/16	...
▲	26 1/4	15 1/2	ABM Indus	ABM	.40	1.5	23	120	26 1/2	26	26 5/16	+ 3/16
n	24 7/16	18 3/8	ABN AMRO ADR	AAN	.25p	...	...	832	20 5/8	20 1/4	20 7/16	− 1/4
	10 7/8	9 3/4	ACM Gvt Fd	ACG	.90a	8.3	...	733	10 7/8	10 3/4	10 13/16	...
	8	6 7/8	ACM OppFd	AOF	.63	8.1	...	148	7 15/16	7 13/16	7 13/16	− 1/16
	10 1/8	8 3/4	ACM SecFd	GSF	.90	8.9	...	998	10 1/8	10	10 1/16	...
	7	6 1/4	ACM SpctmFd	SI	.57	8.8	...	437	6 9/16	6 1/2	6 1/2	...
	14 7/8	11 3/8	ACM MgmdInc	ADF	1.35	9.2	...	379	14 5/8	14 9/16	14 5/8	...
	10 5/16	9 1/4	ACM MgdIncFd	AMF	.90	8.8	...	588	10 3/16	10 1/8	10 3/16	− 1/16
	14	12 1/4	ACM MuniSec	AMU	.90	6.5	...	49	14	13 7/8	13 15/16	+ 1/16
	27 7/16	16 3/8	♣ACX Tch A	ACX		...	dd	168	26 15/16	26 7/16	26 3/4	− 1/8
s	42 1/8	18 1/8	♣AES Cp	AES		...	45	4173	41 15/16	41 9/16	41 15/16	+ 3/16
	57 7/8	34	♣AFLAC	AFL	.46	.8	13	2408	56 3/16	55 3/8	55 5/8	− 1/2
	36 5/16	22 7/8	AGCO Cp	AG	.04	.1	14	2383	34 1/2	34 1/8	34 5/16	+ 1/8
	22	18 3/8	AGL Res	ATG	1.08	5.6	14	1047	19 7/16	19 1/16	19 1/8	− 3/8
	20 1/4	11 1/2	AgSvcAm	ASV		...	20	421	19 1/4	19	19 1/8	− 1/8
n▲	25 9/16	25	AICI CapTr pf		.35p	...	...	362	25 5/8	25 7/16	25 9/16	...
	20 3/8	13 1/4	AJL PepsTr	AJP	1.44	9.1	...	483	15 13/16	15 9/16	15 3/4	+ 1/8
	24 3/4	20 1/4	♣AMLI Resdntl	AML	1.72	7.5	19	616	23 9/16	22 7/8	23	− 11/16
	55 9/16	32 7/8	♣AMP	AMP	1.04	1.9	46	5827	55 1/8	54 3/16	55 1/16	+ 1/16
	118 1/2	78 1/4	AMR	AMR		...	10	12045	118	114 3/16	116 1/4	+ 1 13/16
	50 3/4	40 7/8	♣ARCO Chm	RCM	2.80	6.3	18	432	45 1/8	44 3/4	44 3/4	− 5/8
▼	41	28 13/16	ASA	ASA	1.20	4.2	...	720	29 3/16	28 11/16	28 11/16	− 5/16
s	45 1/16	30 3/4	AT&T	T	1.32	3.0	14	59865	44 3/16	43 3/8	44	− 3/16
	35 1/8	27 5/8	AXA-UAP ADR	AXA	.65p	...	...	363	33 3/4	33	33 1/2	+ 1/16
s	40 3/4	10 1/2	AamesFnl	AAM	.13	.8	11	8132	17 1/8	16 3/8	16 1/2	− 1/2
n	26 1/8	24 1/2	AbbeyNtl		2.19	8.4	...	49	26 1/8	25 15/16	26	...
	68 15/16	47 3/8	AbbotLab	ABT	1.08	1.7	25	14249	64 15/16	63 9/16	64 7/16	+ 11/16
n▲	27 1/16	12 1/2	Abercrombie A	ANF		...	...	806	27 5/16	26 11/16	27 1/4	+ 7/16
	21	12 5/8	Abitibi g	ABY	.40	...	...	444	17 13/16	17 5/8	17 13/16	+ 3/16
	24 3/4	17 3/8	♣AcceptIns	AIF		...	12	327	24 3/16	23 15/16	24 1/8	− 1/16
▲	31	15 3/4	AccuStaff	ASI		...	53	5743	31 3/8	30 3/4	31 1/8	+ 5/8
▲	89 3/4	46 7/8	ACE Ltd	ACL	.88	1.0	13	1733	93 3/8	91 11/16	92 9/16	+ 3 9/16
	10 3/8	6 1/8	AcmeElec	ACE		...	cc	179	7 3/16	7 1/16	7 1/16	...
	21 5/8	13	AcmeMetals	AMI		...	dd	215	16 15/16	16 1/2	16 11/16	− 1/16
n	24 5/8	14	ACNielsen	ART		...	...	2022	24	23 3/16	23 5/8	+ 3/8

NOTES: The "pf" following the stock name of the AICI Captr listing tells us that this one is a preferred stock rather than a common stock. A "▲" preceding the columns containing a stock's 52-week high and low prices indicates that the price hit a new 52-week high, whereas a "▼" indicates a new 52-week low. An "x" preceding the columns containing the 52-week high and low prices indicates that the stock went ex-dividend that day; this means that someone who buys the stock will not receive the next dividend. An "s" preceding the 52-week high and low prices indicates that the stock was split within the past 52 weeks. (See Chapter 17 for a discussion of stock splits.) AT&T had a stock split during the past 52-week period. An "n" preceding the 52-week high and low prices indicates that the stock is newly issued within the past 52 weeks. There were five stocks in Figure 9-12 that were newly issued within the past 52 weeks. Those companies whose listings are underlined have had large changes in volume compared with average trading volume. An "a" following the dividend column indicates an extra dividend in addition to the regular dividend, while an "f" following the dividend column indicates that the annual dividend was increased on the last declaration date. An "e" following the dividend column indicates that a dividend was declared or paid in the preceding 12 months, but there is no regular dividend rate. A "j" following the dividend column indicates the dividend paid this year; however, at the last dividend meeting a dividend was omitted or deferred. An "m" following the dividend column indicates that the dividend was reduced when the Board last declared the dividend. A "p" following the dividend column indicates that this is an initial dividend and that no yield is calculated. A "dd" in the PE column indicates a loss in the most recent four quarters, and a "cc" in the PE column indicates that the P/E ratio is 100 or more. Finally, a "club" appearing before the company name indicates that *Journal* readers can obtain a copy of the company's annual report.

SOURCE: *The Wall Street Journal,* September 22, 1997, C3.

cent. Next comes the ratio of the stock's price to its last 12 months' earnings (the P/E ratio), followed by the volume of trading for the day: 1,424,900 shares of Abbott Labs stock were traded on September 19, 1997. Following the volume come the high and low prices for the day, and then the closing price. On September 19, Abbott Labs traded as high as $\$64\frac{15}{16}$ and as low as $\$63\frac{9}{16}$, while the last trade was at $\$64\frac{7}{16}$. The last column gives the change from the closing price on the previous day. Abbott Labs' closing price was up $\frac{11}{16}$ from the previous day's closing price.

If a stock is *not* in equilibrium, explain how financial markets adjust to bring it into equilibrium.

Explain why expected, required, and realized returns are often different.

What are the key benefits of adding foreign stocks to a portfolio?

When a U.S. investor purchases foreign stocks, what two things is he or she hoping will happen?

PREFERRED STOCK[21]

Preferred stock is a *hybrid*—it is similar to bonds in some respects and to common stock in others. The hybrid nature of preferred stock becomes apparent when we try to classify it in relation to bonds and common stock. Like bonds, preferred stock has a par value and a fixed amount of dividends which must be paid before dividends can be paid on the common stock. However, if the preferred dividend is not earned, the directors can omit (or "pass") it without throwing the company into bankruptcy. So, although preferred stock has a fixed payment like bonds, a failure to make this payment will not lead to bankruptcy.

As noted above, preferred stocks entitle their owners to regular, fixed dividend payments. If the payments last forever, the issue is a perpetuity whose value, V_{ps}, is found as follows:

$$V_{ps} = \frac{D_{ps}}{k_{ps}}. \qquad (9\text{-}8)$$

V_{ps} is the value of the preferred stock, D_{ps} is the preferred dividend, and k_{ps} is the required rate of return. MicroDrive has preferred stock outstanding which pays a dividend of $10 per year. If the required rate of return on this preferred stock is 10 percent, its value is $100, found by solving Equation 9-8 as follows:

$$V_{ps} = \frac{\$10.00}{0.10} = \$100.00.$$

If we know the current price of a preferred stock and its dividend, we can solve for the rate of return:

$$k_{ps} = \frac{D_{ps}}{V_{ps}}. \qquad (9\text{-}8a)$$

Some preferred stocks have a stated maturity date, say, 50 years. If MicroDrive's preferred matured in 50 years, paid a $10 annual dividend, and had a required return of 8 percent, then we could find its price as follows: Enter N = 50, I = 8, PMT = 10, and FV = 100. Then press PV to find the price, V_{ps} = $124.47. If k = I = 10%, change I = 8 to I = 10, and find P = V_{ps} = PV = $100. If you know the price of a share of preferred stock, you can solve for I to find the expected rate of return, $\hat{k}_{ps}$.

Most preferred stock pays dividends quarterly. This is true for MicroDrive, so we could find the effective rate of return on its preferred stock (perpetual or maturing) as follows:

$$\text{EFF\%} = \text{EAR}_{ps} = \left(1 + \frac{k_{Nom}}{m}\right)^m - 1 = \left(1 + \frac{0.10}{4}\right)^4 - 1 = 10.38\%.$$

If an investor wanted to compare the returns on MicroDrive's bonds and its preferred stock, it would be best to convert the nominal rates on each security to effective rates and then compare these "equivalent annual rates."

---

[21]Additional information on preferred stock is provided in Chapter 20.

SELF-TEST
QUESTIONS

Explain the following statement: "Preferred stock is a hybrid security."

Is the equation used to value preferred stock more like the one used to evaluate a bond or the one used to evaluate a "normal" common stock?

SUMMARY

Corporate decisions should be analyzed in terms of how alternative courses of action are likely to affect a firm's value. However, it is necessary to know how stock prices are established before attempting to measure how a given decision will affect a specific firm's value. This chapter showed how stock values are determined, and also how investors go about estimating the rates of return they expect to earn. The key concepts covered are summarized below.

- A **proxy** is a document which gives one person the power to act for another person, typically the power to vote shares of common stock. A **proxy fight** occurs when an outside group solicits stockholders' proxies in an effort to vote a new management team into office.

- A **takeover** occurs when a person or group succeeds in ousting a firm's management and taking control of the company.

- Stockholders often have the right to purchase any additional shares sold by the firm. This right, called the **preemptive right,** protects the control of the present stock-holders and prevents dilution of their stock's value.

- Although most firms have only one type of common stock, in some instances **classified stock** is used to meet the special needs of the company. One type of classified stock is **founders' shares.** This is stock owned by the firm's founders that carries sole voting rights but restricted dividends for a specified number of years.

- A **closely held corporation** is one that is owned by a few individuals who are typically associated with the firm's management.

- A **publicly owned corporation** is one that is owned by a relatively large number of individuals who are not actively involved in its management.

- Whenever stock in a closely held corporation is offered to the public for the first time, the company is said to be **going public.** The market for stock that is just being offered to the public is called the **initial public offering (IPO) market.**

- The **value of a share of stock** is calculated as the **present value of the stream of dividends** the stock is expected to provide in the future.

- The equation used to find the **value of a constant growth stock** is:

$$\hat{P}_0 = \frac{D_1}{k_s - g}.$$

- The **total rate of return** from a stock consists of a **dividend yield** plus a **capital gains yield.** For a constant growth firm, both the expected dividend yield and the expected capital gains yield are constant.

- The equation for $\hat{k}_s$, the **expected rate of return on a constant growth stock,** can be expressed as follows:

$$\hat{k}_s = \frac{D_1}{P_0} + g.$$

- A **zero growth stock** is one whose future dividends are not expected to grow at all, while a **supernormal growth stock** is one whose earnings and dividends are expected to grow much faster than the economy as a whole over some specified time period and then to grow at the "normal" rate.

- To find the **present value of a supernormal growth stock,** (1) find the dividends expected during the supernormal growth period, (2) find the price of the stock at the end of the supernormal growth period, (3) discount the dividends and the projected price back to the present, and (4) sum these PVs to find the current value of the stock, $\hat{P}_0$.

- The **corporate value model** can be used to find the value of a company that does not pay dividends. The value of the company's operations is the present value of all expected future free cash flows, discounted at the company's overall cost of capital. The total value of the corporation is equal to the value of operations plus the value of any nonoperating assets, such as marketable securities. The value of common stock is the value of the corporation minus the value of its debt and preferred stock.

- The **Efficient Markets Hypothesis (EMH)** holds (1) that stocks are always in equilibrium and (2) that it is impossible for an investor who does not have inside information to consistently "beat the market." Therefore, according to the EMH, stocks are always fairly valued ($\hat{P}_0 = P_0$), the required return on a stock is equal to its expected return ($k = \hat{k}$), and all stocks' expected returns plot on the SML.

- Differences can and do exist between expected and realized returns in the stock and bond markets—only for short-term, risk-free assets are expected and actual (or realized) returns equal.

- When U.S. investors purchase foreign stocks, they hope (1) that the stock prices will increase in the local market and (2) that the foreign currencies will rise relative to the U.S. dollar.

- **Preferred stock** is a hybrid security having some characteristics of debt and some of equity.

- Most preferred stocks are **perpetuities,** and the value of a share of perpetual preferred stock is found as the dividend divided by the required rate of return:

$$V_{ps} = \frac{D_{ps}}{k_{ps}}.$$

- **Preferred stock scheduled to mature** is evaluated with a formula that is identical in form to the bond value formula.

Questions

9-1   Define each of the following terms:
  a. Proxy; proxy fight; takeover
  b. Preemptive right
  c. Classified stock; founders' shares
  d. Closely held corporation; publicly owned corporation
  e. Over-the-counter (OTC) market; organized security exchange
  f. Secondary market; primary market
  g. Going public; initial public offering (IPO) market
  h. Intrinsic value ($\hat{P}_0$); market price (P_0)
  i. Required rate of return, k_s; expected rate of return, $\hat{k}_s$; actual, or realized, rate of return, $\bar{k}_s$
  j. Capital gains yield; dividend yield; expected total return
  k. Zero growth stock
  l. Normal, or constant, growth; supernormal, or nonconstant, growth
  m. Corporate value model
  n. Equilibrium

o. Efficient Markets Hypothesis (EMH); three forms of EMH
p. Preferred stock

9-2 Two investors are evaluating AT&T's stock for possible purchase. They agree on the expected value of D_1 and also on the expected future dividend growth rate. Further, they agree on the riskiness of the stock. However, one investor normally holds stocks for 2 years, while the other normally holds stocks for 10 years. On the basis of the type of analysis done in this chapter, they should both be willing to pay the same price for AT&T's stock. True or false? Explain.

9-3 A bond that pays interest forever and has no maturity date is a perpetual bond. In what respect is a perpetual bond similar to a no-growth common stock, and to a share of preferred stock?

9-4 If you bought a share of common stock, you would typically expect to receive dividends plus capital gains. Would you expect the distribution between dividend yield and capital gains to be influenced by the firm's decision to pay more dividends rather than to retain and reinvest more of its earnings?

9-5 Is it true that the following expression can be used to find the value of a constant growth stock?

$$\hat{P}_0 = \frac{D_0}{k_s + g}.$$

9-6 It is frequently stated that the primary purpose of the preemptive right is to allow individuals to maintain their proportionate share of the ownership and control of a corporation.
a. How important do you suppose this consideration is for the average stockholder of a firm whose shares are traded on the New York or American Stock Exchanges?
b. Is the preemptive right likely to be of more importance to stockholders of publicly owned or closely held firms? Explain.

Self-Test Problems (Solutions Appear in Appendix B)

ST-1
Stock Growth Rates and Valuation

You are considering buying the stocks of two companies that operate in the same industry; they have very similar characteristics except for their dividend payout policies. Both companies are expected to earn $6 per share this year. However, Company D (for "dividend") is expected to pay out all of its earnings as dividends, while Company G (for "growth") is expected to pay out only one-third of its earnings, or $2 per share. D's stock price is $40. G and D are equally risky. Which of the following is most likely to be true?
a. Company G will have a faster growth rate than Company D. Therefore, G's stock price should be greater than $40.
b. Although G's growth rate should exceed D's, D's current dividend exceeds that of G, and this should cause D's price to exceed G's.
c. An investor in Stock D will get his or her money back faster because D pays out more of its earnings as dividends. Thus, in a sense, D is like a short-term bond, and G is like a long-term bond. Therefore, if economic shifts cause k_d and k_s to increase, and if the expected streams of dividends from D and G remain constant, both Stocks D and G will decline, but D's price should decline further.
d. D's expected and required rate of return is $\hat{k}_s = k_s = 15\%$. G's expected return will be higher because of its higher expected growth rate.
e. If we observe that G's price is also $40, the best estimate of G's growth rate is 10 percent.

ST-2
Constant Growth Stock Valuation

Ewald Company's current stock price is $36, and its last dividend was $2.40. In view of Ewald's strong financial position and its consequent low risk, its required rate of return is only 12 percent. If dividends are expected to grow at a constant rate, g, in the future, and if k_s is expected to remain at 12 percent, what is Ewald's expected stock price 5 years from now?

ST-3
Supernormal Growth Stock Valuation

Snyder Computer Chips Inc. is experiencing a period of rapid growth. Earnings and dividends are expected to grow at a rate of 15 percent during the next 2 years, at 13 percent in the third year, and at a constant rate of 6 percent thereafter. Snyder's last dividend was $1.15, and the required rate of return on the stock is 12 percent.
a. Calculate the value of the stock today.
b. Calculate $\hat{P}_1$ and $\hat{P}_2$.
c. Calculate the dividend yield and capital gains yield for Years 1, 2, and 3.

ST-4
Corporate Valuation

Watkins Inc. has never paid a dividend, and when it might begin paying dividends is unknown. Its current free cash flow is $100,000, and this FCF is expected to grow at a constant 7 percent rate. The overall cost of capital is $k_c = 11\%$. Watkins currently holds $325,000 of nonoperating marketable securities. Its long-term debt is $1,000,000, but it has never issued preferred stock.

a. Calculate Watkins' value of operations.
b. Calculate the company's total value.
c. Calculate the value of its common equity.

Problems

9-1
DPS Calculation

Warr Corporation just paid a dividend of $1.50 a share (i.e., $D_0 = \$1.50$). The dividend is expected to grow 5 percent a year for the next 3 years, and then 10 percent a year thereafter. What is the expected dividend per share for each of the next 5 years?

9-2
Constant Growth Valuation

Thomas Brothers is expected to pay a $0.50 per share dividend at the end of the year (i.e., $D_1 = \$0.50$). The dividend is expected to grow at a constant rate of 7 percent a year. The required rate of return on the stock, k_s, is 15 percent. What is the value per share of the company's stock?

9-3
Constant Growth Valuation

Harrison Clothiers' stock currently sells for $20 a share. The stock just paid a dividend of $1.00 a share (i.e., $D_0 = \$1.00$). The dividend is expected to grow at a constant rate of 10 percent a year. What stock price is expected 1 year from now? What is the required rate of return on the company's stock?

9-4
Preferred Stock Valuation

Fee Founders has preferred stock outstanding which pays a dividend of $5 at the end of each year. The preferred stock sells for $60 a share. What is the preferred stock's required rate of return?

9-5
Corporate Valuation

EMC Corporation has never paid a dividend. Its current free cash flow is $400,000 and is expected to grow at a constant rate of 5 percent. The overall cost of capital is $k_c = 12\%$. Calculate EMC's value of operations.

9-6
Supernormal Growth Valuation

A company currently pays a dividend of $2 per share, $D_0 = 2$. It is estimated that the company's dividend will grow at a rate of 20 percent per year for the next 2 years, then the dividend will grow at a constant rate of 7 percent thereafter. The company's stock has a beta equal to 1.2, the risk-free rate is 7.5 percent, and the market risk premium is 4 percent. What would you estimate is the stock's current price?

9-7
Constant Growth Rate, g

A stock is trading at $80 per share. The stock is expected to have a year-end dividend of $4 per share ($D_1 = 4$) which is expected to grow at some constant rate g throughout time. The stock's required rate of return is 14 percent. If you are an analyst who believes in efficient markets, what would be your forecast of g?

9-8
Constant Growth Valuation

You are considering an investment in the common stock of Keller Corp. The stock is expected to pay a dividend of $2 a share at the end of the year ($D_1 = \$2.00$). The stock has a beta equal to 0.9. The risk-free rate is 5.6 percent, and the market risk premium is 6 percent. The stock's dividend is expected to grow at some constant rate g. The stock currently sells for $25 a share. Assuming the market is in equilibrium, what does the market believe will be the stock price at the end of 3 years? (That is, what is $\hat{P}_3$?)

9-9
Preferred Stock Rate of Return

What will be the nominal rate of return on a preferred stock with a $100 par value, a stated dividend of 8 percent of par, and a current market price of (a) $60, (b) $80, (c) $100, and (d) $140?

9-10
Declining Growth
Stock Valuation

Martell Mining Company's ore reserves are being depleted, so its sales are falling. Also, its pit is getting deeper each year, so its costs are rising. As a result, the company's earnings and dividends are declining at the constant rate of 5 percent per year. If $D_0 = \$5$ and $k_s = 15\%$, what is the value of Martell Mining's stock?

9-11
Rates of Return and Equilibrium

The beta coefficient for Stock C is $b_C = 0.4$, whereas that for Stock D is $b_D = -0.5$. (Stock D's beta is negative, indicating that its rate of return rises whenever returns on most other stocks fall. There are very few negative beta stocks, although collection agency stocks are sometimes cited as an example.)
a. If the risk-free rate is 9 percent and the expected rate of return on an average stock is 13 percent, what are the required rates of return on Stocks C and D?
b. For Stock C, suppose the current price, P_0, is $25; the next expected dividend, D_1, is $1.50; and the stock's expected constant growth rate is 4 percent. Is the stock in equilibrium? Explain, and describe what will happen if the stock is not in equilibrium.

9-12
Supernormal Growth
Stock Valuation

Assume that the average firm in your company's industry is expected to grow at a constant rate of 6 percent and its dividend yield is 7 percent. Your company is about as risky as the average firm in the industry, but it has just successfully completed some R&D work which leads you to expect that its earnings and dividends will grow at a rate of 50 percent $[D_1 = D_0(1 + g) = D_0(1.50)]$ this year and 25 percent the following year, after which growth should match the 6 percent industry average rate. The last dividend paid (D_0) was $1. What is the value per share of your firm's stock?

9-13
Supernormal Growth Stock Valuation

Microtech Corporation is expanding rapidly, and it currently needs to retain all of its earnings, hence it does not pay any dividends. However, investors expect Microtech to begin paying dividends, with the first dividend of $1.00 coming 3 years from today. The dividend should grow rapidly—at a rate of 50 percent per year—during Years 4 and 5. After Year 5, the company should grow at a constant rate of 8 percent per year. If the required return on the stock is 15 percent, what is the value of the stock today?

9-14
Corporate Valuation

Brooks Enterprises has never paid a dividend. Free cash flow is projected to be $80,000 and $100,000 for the next 2 years, respectively, and after the second year it is expected to grow at a constant rate of 8 percent. The company's weighted average cost of capital is $k_c = 12\%$.

a. What is the terminal, or horizon, value of operations? (Hint: Find the value of all free cash flows beyond Year 2 discounted back to Year 2.)

b. Calculate the value of Brooks' operations.

9-15
Preferred Stock Valuation

Ezzell Corporation issued preferred stock with a stated dividend of 10 percent of par. Preferred stock of this type currently yields 8 percent, and the par value is $100. Assume dividends are paid annually.

a. What is the value of Ezzell's preferred stock?

b. Suppose interest rate levels rise to the point where the preferred stock now yields 12 percent. What would be the value of Ezzell's preferred stock?

9-16
Constant Growth Stock Valuation

Your broker offers to sell you some shares of Bahnsen & Co. common stock that paid a dividend of $2 *yesterday*. You expect the dividend to grow at the rate of 5 percent per year for the next 3 years, and, if you buy the stock, you plan to hold it for 3 years and then sell it.

a. Find the expected dividend for each of the next 3 years; that is, calculate D_1, D_2, and D_3. Note that $D_0 = \$2$.

b. Given that the appropriate discount rate is 12 percent and that the first of these dividend payments will occur 1 year from now, find the present value of the dividend stream; that is, calculate the PV of D_1, D_2, and D_3, and then sum these PVs.

c. You expect the price of the stock 3 years from now to be $34.73; that is, you expect $\hat{P}_3$ to equal $34.73. Discounted at a 12 percent rate, what is the present value of this expected future stock price? In other words, calculate the PV of $34.73.

d. If you plan to buy the stock, hold it for 3 years, and then sell it for $34.73, what is the most you should pay for it?

e. Use Equation 9-4 to calculate the present value of this stock. Assume that $g = 5\%$, and it is constant.

f. Is the value of this stock dependent upon how long you plan to hold it? In other words, if your planned holding period were 2 years or 5 years rather than 3 years, would this affect the value of the stock today, $\hat{P}_0$?

9-17
Return on Common Stock

You buy a share of The Ludwig Corporation stock for $21.40. You expect it to pay dividends of $1.07, $1.1449, and $1.2250 in Years 1, 2, and 3, respectively, and you expect to sell it at a price of $26.22 at the end of 3 years.

a. Calculate the growth rate in dividends.

b. Calculate the expected dividend yield.

c. Assuming that the calculated growth rate is expected to continue, you can add the dividend yield to the expected growth rate to get the expected total rate of return. What is this stock's expected total rate of return?

9-18
Constant Growth Stock Valuation

Investors require a 15 percent rate of return on Levine Company's stock ($k_s = 15\%$).

a. What will be Levine's stock value if the previous dividend was $D_0 = \$2$ and if investors expect dividends to grow at a constant compound annual rate of (1) −5 percent, (2) 0 percent, (3) 5 percent, and (4) 10 percent?

b. Using data from Part a, what is the Gordon (constant growth) model value for Levine's stock if the required rate of return is 15 percent and the expected growth rate is (1) 15 percent or (2) 20 percent? Are these reasonable results? Explain.

c. Is it reasonable to expect that a constant growth stock would have $g > k_s$?

9-19
Stock Reporting

Look up the prices of American Telephone & Telegraph's (AT&T) stock in *The Wall Street Journal* (or some other newspaper which provides this information).

a. What was the stock's price range during the last year?
b. What is AT&T's current dividend? What is its dividend yield?
c. What change occurred in AT&T's stock price the day the newspaper was published?
d. If you had $10,000 and wanted to invest it in AT&T, what return would you expect to get if you bought AT&T's stock? (Hint: Think about capital gains when you answer this question.)

9-20
Supernormal Growth
Stock Valuation

It is now January 1, 1999. Wayne-Martin Electric Inc. (WME) has just developed a solar panel capable of generating 200 percent more electricity than any solar panel currently on the market. As a result, WME is expected to experience a 15 percent annual growth rate for the next 5 years. By the end of 5 years, other firms will have developed comparable technology, and WME's growth rate will slow to 5 percent per year indefinitely. Stockholders require a return of 12 percent on WME's stock. The most recent annual dividend (D_0), which was paid yesterday, was $1.75 per share.

a. Calculate WME's expected dividends for 1999, 2000, 2001, 2002, and 2003.
b. Calculate the value of the stock today, $\hat{P}_0$. Proceed by finding the present value of the dividends expected at the end of 1999, 2000, 2001, 2002, and 2003 plus the present value of the stock price which should exist at the end of 2003. The year-end 2003 stock price can be found by using the constant growth equation. Notice that to find the December 31, 2003, price, you use the dividend expected in 2004, which is 5 percent greater than the 2003 dividend.
c. Calculate the expected dividend yield, D_1/P_0, the capital gains yield expected in 1999, and the expected total return (dividend yield plus capital gains yield) for 1999. (Assume that $\hat{P}_0 = P_0$, and recognize that the capital gains yield is equal to the total return minus the dividend yield.) Also calculate these same three yields for 2004.
d. How might an investor's tax situation affect his or her decision to purchase stocks of companies in the early stages of their lives, when they are growing rapidly, versus stocks of older, more mature firms? When does WME's stock become "mature" in this example?
e. Suppose your boss tells you she believes that WME's annual growth rate will be only 12 percent during the next 5 years and that the firm's normal growth rate will be only 4 percent. Without doing any calculations, what general effect would these growth-rate changes have on the price of WME's stock?
f. Suppose your boss also tells you that she regards WME as being quite risky and that she believes the required rate of return should be 14 percent, not 12 percent. Again, without doing any calculations, how would the higher required rate of return affect the price of the stock, its capital gains yield, and its dividend yield?

9-21
Supernormal Growth
Stock Valuation

Taussig Technologies Corporation (TTC) has been growing at a rate of 20 percent per year in recent years. This same growth rate is expected to last for another 2 years.

a. If $D_0 = \$1.60$, $k = 10\%$, and $g_n = 6\%$, what is TTC's stock worth today? What are its expected dividend yield and capital gains yield at this time?
b. Now assume that TTC's period of supernormal growth is to last another 5 years rather than 2 years. How would this affect its price, dividend yield, and capital gains yield? Answer in words only.
c. What will be TTC's dividend yield and capital gains yield once its period of supernormal growth ends? (Hint: These values will be the same regardless of whether you examine the case of 2 or 5 years of supernormal growth; the calculations are very easy.)
d. Of what interest to investors is the changing relationship between dividend yield and capital gains yield over time?

9-22
Free Cash Flow

Use the following income statements and balance sheets to calculate Garnet Inc.'s free cash flow for 1999.

GARNET INC.	1999	1998
INCOME STATEMENT:		
Net sales	$ 530.0	$ 530.0
Costs (except depreciation)	400.0	380.0
Depreciation	30.0	25.0
Total operating costs	$ 430.0	$ 405.0

Earnings before interest and taxes (EBIT)	100.0	95.0
Less interest	23.0	21.0
Earnings before taxes	77.0	74.0
Taxes (40%)	30.8	29.6
Net income	$ 46.2	$ 44.4

BALANCE SHEET:

Assets

Cash	$ 28.0	$ 27.0
Marketable securities	69.0	66.0
Accounts receivable	84.0	80.0
Inventories	112.0	106.0
Total current assets	$ 293.0	$ 279.0
Net plant and equipment	281.0	265.0
Total assets	$ 574.0	$ 544.0

Liabilities and Equity

Accounts payable	$ 56.0	$ 52.0
Notes payable	138.0	130.0
Accruals	28.0	28.0
Total current liabilities	$ 222.0	$ 210.0
Long-term bonds	$ 173.0	$ 164.0
Common stock	100.0	100.0
Retained earnings	79.0	70.0
Common equity	$ 179.0	$ 170.0
Total liabilities and equity	$ 574.0	$ 544.0

9-23
Corporate Valuation

Dozier Corporation is a fast-growing supplier of office products. Analysts project the following free cash flows (FCFs) during the next 3 years, after which FCF is expected to grow at a constant 7 percent rate. Dozier's cost of capital is $k_c = 13\%$.

Time	1	2	3
Free cash flow ($ millions)	−$20	$30	$40

a. What is Dozier's terminal, or horizon, value? (Hint: Find the value of all free cash flows beyond Year 3 discounted back to Year 3.)
b. What is the current value of operations for Dozier?
c. Suppose Dozier has $10 million in marketable securities, $100 million in debt, and 10 million shares of stock. What is the price per share?

9-24
Equilibrium Stock Price

The risk-free rate of return, k_{RF}, is 11 percent; the required rate of return on the market, k_M, is 14 percent; and Upton Company's stock has a beta coefficient of 1.5.
a. If the dividend expected during the coming year, D_1, is $2.25, and if g = a constant 5%, at what price should Upton's stock sell?
b. Now, suppose the Federal Reserve Board increases the money supply, causing the risk-free rate to drop to 9 percent and k_M to fall to 12 percent. What would this do to the price of the stock?
c. In addition to the change in Part b, suppose investors' risk aversion declines; this fact, combined with the decline in k_{RF}, causes k_M to fall to 11 percent. At what price would Upton's stock sell?
d. Now, suppose Upton has a change in management. The new group institutes policies that increase the expected constant growth rate to 6 percent. Also, the new management stabilizes sales and profits, and thus causes the beta coefficient to decline from 1.5 to 1.3. Assume that k_{RF} and k_M are equal to the values in Part c. After all these changes, what is Upton's new equilibrium price? (Note: D_1 goes to $2.27.)

9-25
Beta Coefficients

Suppose Chance Chemical Company's management conducts a study and concludes that if Chance expanded its consumer products division (which is less risky than its primary business, industrial chemicals), the firm's beta would decline from 1.2 to 0.9. However, consumer products have a somewhat lower profit margin, and this would cause Chance's constant growth rate in earnings and dividends to fall from 7 to 5 percent.

a. Should management make the change? Assume the following: $k_M = 12\%$; $k_{RF} = 9\%$; $D_0 = \$2$.

b. Assume all the facts as given above except the change in the beta coefficient. How low would the beta have to fall to cause the expansion to be a good one? (Hint: Set $\hat{P}_0$ under the new policy equal to $\hat{P}_0$ under the old one, and find the new beta that will produce this equality.)

Spreadsheet Problem

Work the problem in this section only if you are using the computer problem diskette.

9-26
Supernormal Growth
Stock Valuation

Use the model in File C9 to solve this problem.

a. Refer back to Problem 9-20. Rework Part e, using the computerized model to determine what WME's expected dividends and stock price would be under the conditions given.

b. Suppose your boss tells you that she regards WME as being quite risky and that she believes the required rate of return should be higher than the 12 percent originally specified. Rework the problem under the conditions given in Part e, except change the required rate of return to (1) 13 percent, (2) 15 percent, and (3) 20 percent to determine the effects of the higher required rates of return on WME's stock price.

MINI CASE

Robert Balik and Carol Kiefer are senior vice-presidents of the Mutual of Chicago Insurance Company. They are co-directors of the company's pension fund management division, with Balik having responsibility for fixed income securities (primarily bonds) and Kiefer being responsible for equity investments. A major new client, the California League of Cities, has requested that Mutual of Chicago present an investment seminar to the mayors of the represented cities, and Balik and Kiefer, who will make the actual presentation, have asked you to help them.

To illustrate the common stock valuation process, Balik and Kiefer have asked you to analyze the Bon Temps Company, an employment agency that supplies word processor operators and computer programmers to businesses with temporarily heavy workloads. You are to answer the following questions.

a. Describe briefly the legal rights and privileges of common stockholders.

b. (1) Write out a formula that can be used to value any stock, regardless of its dividend pattern.

(2) What is a constant growth stock? How are constant growth stocks valued?

(3) What happens if a company has a constant g which exceeds its k_s? Will many stocks have expected $g > k_s$ in the short run (i.e., for the next few years)? In the long run (i.e., forever)?

c. Assume that Bon Temps has a beta coefficient of 1.2, that the risk-free rate (the yield on T-bonds) is 7 percent, and that the required rate of return on the market is 12 percent. What is the required rate of return on the firm's stock?

d. Assume that Bon Temps is a constant growth company whose last dividend (D_0, which was paid yesterday) was $2.00 and whose dividend is expected to grow indefinitely at a 6 percent rate.

(1) What is the firm's expected dividend stream over the next 3 years?

(2) What is the firm's current stock price?

(3) What is the stock's expected value 1 year from now?

(4) What are the expected dividend yield, the capital gains yield, and the total return during the first year?

e. Now assume that the stock is currently selling at $30.29. What is the expected rate of return on the stock?

f. What would the stock price be if its dividends were expected to have zero growth?

g. Now assume that Bon Temps is expected to experience supernormal growth of 30 percent for the next 3 years, then to return to its long-run constant growth rate of 6 percent. What is the stock's value under these conditions? What is its expected dividend yield and capital gains yield in Year 1? In Year 4?

h. Is the stock price based more on long-term or short-term expectations? Answer this by finding the percentage of Bon Temps current stock price based on dividends expected more than 3 years in the future.

i. Suppose Bon Temps is expected to experience zero growth during the first 3 years and then to resume its steady-state growth of 6 percent in the fourth year. What is the stock's value now? What is its expected dividend yield and its capital gains yield in Year 1? In Year 4?

j. Finally, assume that Bon Temps' earnings and dividends are expected to decline by a constant 6 percent per year, that is, $g = -6\%$. Why would anyone be willing to buy such a stock, and at what price should it sell? What would be the dividend yield and capital gains yield in each year?

k. Bon Temps embarks on an aggressive expansion that requires additional capital. Management decides to finance the expansion by borrowing $40 million and by halting dividend payments to increase retained earnings. The projected free cash flows for the next 3 years are -$5 million, $10 million, and $20 million. After the third year, free cash flow is projected to grow at a constant 6 percent. The overall cost of capital is $k_c = 10\%$. What is the value of Bon Temps' operations? If it has 10 million shares of stock and $40 million total debt, what is the price per share?

l. What does market equilibrium mean?

m. If equilibrium does not exist, how will it be established?

n. What is the Efficient Markets Hypothesis, what are its three forms, and what are its implications?

o. Phyfe Company recently issued preferred stock. It pays an annual dividend of $5, and the issue price was $50 per share. What is the expected return to an investor on this preferred stock?

Selected Additional References and Cases

Many investment textbooks cover stock valuation models in depth and detail. Some of the better ones are listed in the Chapter 5 references.

The seminal work on stock valuation models is

Williams, John Burr, *The Theory of Investment Value* (Cambridge, Mass.: Harvard University Press, 1938).

The following classic articles extend J. B. Williams' works:

Durand, David, "Growth Stocks and the Petersburg Paradox," *Journal of Finance,* September 1957, 348–363.

Gordon, Myron J., and Eli Shapiro, "Capital Equipment Analysis: The Required Rate of Profit," *Management Science,* October 1956, 102–110.

For some recent works on valuation, see

Bey, Roger P., and J. Markham Collins, "The Relationship between Before- and After-Tax Yields on Financial Assets," *The Financial Review,* August 1988, 313–343.

Brooks, Robert, and Billy Helms, "An N-Stage, Fractional Period, Quarterly Dividend Discount Model," *Financial Review,* November 1990, 651–657.

Copeland, Tom, Tim Koller, and Jack Murrin, *Valuation: Measuring and Managing the Value of Companies,* 2nd ed. (New York: John Wiley & Sons, Inc., 1994).

The following cases in the Cases in Financial Management: Dryden Request *series cover many of the valuation concepts contained in Chapter 9.*

Case 3, "Peachtree Securities, Inc. (B);" Case 43, "Swan-Davis;" Case 49, Beatrice Peabody;" and Case 56, "Laura Henderson."

STRATEGIC INVESTMENT DECISIONS

IV

CHAPTER 10
THE COST OF CAPITAL

CHAPTER 11
THE BASICS OF CAPITAL
BUDGETING

CHAPTER 12
CASH FLOW ESTIMATION
AND OTHER TOPICS IN
CAPITAL BUDGETING

CHAPTER 13
RISK ANALYSIS AND REAL
OPTIONS

Edward Lloyd opened a coffee
shop in the late 1860s, and it
developed into a reliable
source of shipping
information. Soon ship
owners and captains from all
over London became
subscribers to Lloyd's, and its
new business of underwriting
ship journeys became
formalized. Moving five times
over two centuries, Richard
Rogers designed the current
home of Lloyd's, which
opened in 1986 with an
underwriting area of 200,000
square feet.

© Index Stock

THE COST OF CAPITAL

*W*hat company is America's top wealth creator? According to a recent Fortune article, the winner is Coca-Cola. Investors have entrusted $10.8 billion to Coke's managers, who then caused that investment to grow to $135.7 billion. The difference between the $135.7 billion market value and the $10.8 billion Coke's investors provided is called its Market Value Added, or MVA. Thus, Coke's managers have, since the company's inception, added a stunning $124.9 billion to their shareholders' wealth. General Electric, Microsoft, Intel, and Merck are next on Fortune's list of top MVA creators.

Is there any way to pick a company today that is likely to be a superior wealth creator in the future? Fortune reported that Steven Einhorn, research chief at Goldman Sachs, along with other top analysts, uses a tool called Economic Value Added, or EVA, to evaluate companies, while companies themselves use EVA to measure their performance and to determine managerial bonuses.

Exactly what is EVA? Developed by the consulting firm Stern Stewart & Company, EVA is designed to measure a corporation's true profitability for a given year, and it is calculated as after-tax operating profits less the annual cost of all the capital the firm uses.

The idea behind EVA is simple — firms are truly profitable and create value if and only if their income exceeds the cost of all the capital they use to finance operations. The conventional measure of performance, net income, takes into account the cost of debt, which shows up on financial statements as interest expense, but it does not reflect the cost of equity. Therefore, a firm can report positive net income yet still be unprofitable in an economic sense if its net income is less than its cost of equity. EVA corrects this flaw by recognizing that to properly measure a firm's performance, it is necessary to account for the cost of equity capital.

Managers create EVA by developing, implementing, and nurturing projects that generate returns greater than their costs of capital. On average, Coke's projects earned 36 percent, which greatly exceeded its 9.7 percent cost of capital. As a result, Coke had an EVA of $2.4 billion, which is outstanding. On the other hand, RJR Nabisco's average project earned a meager 6.2 percent, much less than its 9.8 percent cost of capital, so its EVA was a negative $1.2 billion. EVA represents value added during a single year, and MVA represents total value created since the company's inception, so there is an obvious correlation between EVA and MVA. Therefore, given RJR's negative EVA, it is not surprising that its lifetime MVA was a negative $12.0 billion. Note, though, that EVA for a given year could be negative, yet a company could still have a positive MVA because it had performed well in prior years.

In this chapter, we explain how a company can measure its cost of capital and then use that cost of capital to help make various decisions. As you go through the chapter, think about Coca-Cola and RJR Nabisco, and the role the cost of capital plays in creating or destroying wealth.

SOURCE: Richard Teitelbaum, "America's Greatest Wealth Creators," *Fortune,* November 10, 1997, 265–276.

Managers make decisions every day that involve trade-offs between cash flow now and cash flow later. For example, a production manager must evaluate the trade-off between the negative cash flow caused by reconfiguring an assembly line and the future positive cash flows due to lower labor costs. A CEO must determine whether the negative cash flow of building a factory to manufacture a new product is justified by the expected positive future cash flows of the product. These are examples of **capital budgeting.**

Chapter 11 explains in detail the techniques used in capital budgeting, but the key to understanding the process is to recognize (1) that investors provide managers with the necessary funds, or **capital,** to undertake projects, and (2) managers, if they are good stewards of the money entrusted to them, invest only in projects that produce rates of return at least as high as the returns investors could get elsewhere. The return investors could get elsewhere is their **opportunity cost of capital,** also called their **required rate of return.**

Although the most important use of the cost of capital is in capital budgeting, it is also used for other purposes. For example, the cost of capital is a key factor in decisions relating to the use of debt versus equity capital. It is also important in the regulation of electric, gas, and telephone companies. These utilities are natural monopolies in the sense that one firm can supply service at a lower cost than could two or more firms. Since it has a monopoly, your electric or telephone company could, if it were unregulated, exploit you. Therefore, regulators (1) determine the cost of the capital investors have provided the utility and (2) then set rates designed to permit the company to earn its cost of capital, no more and no less.

THE WEIGHTED AVERAGE COST OF CAPITAL

Ohio State has a web site with video clips of business professionals discussing various topics of interest in finance. The site can be found at http://www.cob.ohio-state.edu/~fin/clips.htm. The two video clips relevant to capital budgeting come from Steve Walsh, assistant treasurer of JCPenney: "How We Do Capital Budgeting" and "On the Cost of Capital and Debt." Be forewarned that these files are quite large and are best downloaded using a rapid Internet link.

The corporate valuation model in Chapter 9 explained how to find the value of a firm's operations. Recall that we estimated future free cash flows from operations, discounted them at the firm's overall cost of capital, and then summed the PVs to find the firm's value as a going concern. Capital budgeting is a similar process, except it focuses on proposed new projects rather than on the firm's existing assets.

What precisely do the terms "cost of capital" and "overall cost of capital" mean? To begin, note that it is possible to finance a firm entirely with common equity. However, most firms employ several types of capital, called **capital components,** with common and preferred stock, along with debt, being the three most frequently used types.[1] All capital components have one feature in common: The investors who provided the funds expect to receive a return on their investment.

If a firm's only investors were common stockholders, then the cost of capital used in capital budgeting would be the required rate of return on equity. However, most firms employ different types of capital, and, due to differences in risk, these different securities have different required rates of return. The required rate of return on each capital component is called its **component cost,** and the cost of capital used to analyze capital budgeting decisions should be a *weighted average* of the various components' costs. We call this weighted average just that, the **weighted average cost of capital,** or **WACC.**

Most firms set target percentages for the different financing sources. For example, National Computer Corporation (NCC) plans to raise 30 percent of its required capital

---

[1]There may actually be many variations within these three capital components, such as voting and nonvoting common stock, short-term and long-term debt, secured and unsecured debt, and so forth. There are also hybrid securities, such as convertible bonds, bonds with warrants, and lease financing. We discuss all these variations in later chapters.

as debt, 10 percent as preferred stock, and 60 percent as common equity. This is called its **target capital structure.** We discuss how targets are established in Chapters 15 and 16, but for now simply accept NCC's 30/10/60 percentages as given.

Although NCC and other firms try to stay close to their target capital structures, they frequently deviate from them in the short run for several reasons. First, market conditions may be more favorable in one market than another at a particular time. For example, if the stock market is extremely strong, a company may decide that it is a good time to issue common stock. The second, and probably more important, reason for deviations relates to flotation costs, which are the costs that a firm must incur to issue securities. The Extension at the end of this chapter discusses flotation costs in detail, but note that these costs are to a large extent fixed, so they become prohibitively high if small amounts of capital are raised. Thus, it is inefficient and expensive to issue relatively small amounts of debt, preferred stock, and common stock. Therefore, companies tend to finance with common stock one year, with debt the next, and with preferred the following year, thus fluctuating around their target capital structure rather than staying right on it all the time.

This situation can cause managers to make a serious error in their capital budgeting. To illustrate, assume that NCC is currently at its target capital structure, and it is now considering how to raise capital to finance next year's projects. NCC could raise a combination of debt and equity, but to minimize flotation costs it will raise either debt or equity, but not both. Let's suppose it decides to issue debt, at a cost of 11 percent. The argument is sometimes made that the cost of capital this year is 11 percent, because only debt at 11 percent will be used. However, this is incorrect. If NCC finances this year's projects with debt, it will move away from its target capital structure. Then, as expansion occurs in the future, it will at some point find it necessary to raise additional equity.

Now suppose NCC borrows heavily at 11 percent during 1999, using up its debt capacity in the process, to finance projects which yield 12 percent. In 2000, it has new projects available that yield 13 percent, well above the return on the 1999 projects. However, because it used up its debt capacity in 1999, it must issue equity, which costs 14.7 percent. Therefore, the company might reject these 13 percent projects because they would have to be financed with 14.7 percent money.

However, this entire capital budgeting process would be incorrect. Why should a company accept 12 percent projects one year and then reject 13 percent projects the next? Notice also that if NCC had reversed the order of its financing, raising equity in 1999 and debt in 2000, it would have reversed its capital budgeting decisions, rejecting all projects in 1999 and accepting them all in 2000. Does it make sense to accept or reject projects just because of the more or less arbitrary sequence in which capital is raised? The answer is *no. To avoid such errors, managers should view companies as ongoing concerns, and calculate their costs of capital as weighted averages of the various types of funds they use, regardless of the specific source of financing employed in a particular year.*

The following sections discuss each of the component costs in more detail, and then we show how to combine them to calculate the weighted average cost of capital.

<table>
<tr><td>

S E L F - T E S T
Q U E S T I O N S

</td><td>

What are the three major capital components?

What is a component cost?

What is a target capital structure?

Why should the cost of capital used in capital budgeting be calculated as a weighted average of the various types of funds the firm generally uses rather than the cost of the specific financing used to fund a particular project?

</td></tr>
</table>

COST OF DEBT, $k_d(1 - T)$

The first step in estimating the cost of debt is to determine the rate of return debtholders require, or k_d. Although estimating k_d is conceptually straightforward, some problems arise in practice. Companies use both fixed and floating rate debt, straight and convertible debt, and debt with and without sinking funds, and each form has a somewhat different cost.

It is unlikely that the financial manager will know at the start of a planning period the exact types and amounts of debt that will be used during the period: The type or types used will depend on the specific assets to be financed and on capital market conditions as they develop over time. Even so, the financial manager does know what types of debt are typical for his or her firm. For example, NCC typically issues commercial paper to raise short-term money to finance working capital, and it issues 30-year bonds to raise long-term debt used to help finance its capital budgeting projects. Since the WACC is used primarily in capital budgeting, NCC's treasurer uses the cost of 30-year bonds in her WACC estimate.

Assume that it is January 1999, and NCC's financial staff is estimating WACC for the coming year. How should they calculate the component cost of debt? Most financial managers would begin by discussing current and prospective interest rates with their firms' investment bankers. Assume that NCC's bankers stated that a new 30-year, noncallable, straight bond issue would require an 11 percent coupon rate with semiannual payments, and that it would be offered to the public at its $1,000 par value. Therefore, k_d is equal to 11 percent.[2]

Note that the 11 percent is the cost of **new, or marginal, debt,** and it will probably not be the same as the average rate on NCC's previously issued debt, which is called the **historical, or embedded, rate.** The embedded cost is important for some decisions but not for others. For example, the average cost of all the capital raised in the past and still outstanding is used by regulators when they determine the rate of return a public utility should be allowed to earn. However, in financial management the WACC is used primarily to make investment decisions, and these decisions hinge on projects' returns versus the cost of new, or marginal, capital. *Thus, for our purposes, the relevant cost is the marginal cost of new debt to be raised during the planning period.*

Suppose NCC had issued debt in the past, and its bonds are publicly traded. The financial staff could use the market price of the bonds to find their yield to maturity (or yield to call if the bonds sell at a premium and are likely to be called). The YTM (or YTC) is the rate of return the existing bondholders expect to receive, and it is also a good estimate of k_d, the rate of return that new bondholders would require.

If NCC had no publicly traded debt, its staff could look at yields on publicly traded debt of similar firms. This too should provide a reasonable estimate of k_d.

The required return to investors, k_d, is not equal to the company's cost of debt because, since interest payments are deductible, the government in effect pays part of the total cost. As a result, the cost of debt to the firm is less than the rate of return required by debtholders.

The **after-tax cost of debt, $k_d(1 - T)$,** is used to calculate the weighted average cost of capital, and it is the interest rate on debt, k_d, less the tax savings that result because

---

[2]The effective annual rate is $(1 + 0.11/2)^2 - 1 = 11.3\%$, but NCC and most other companies use nominal rates for all component costs.

interest is deductible. This is the same as k_d multiplied by $(1 - T)$, where T is the firm's marginal tax rate:[3]

$$\text{After-tax component cost of debt} = \text{Interest rate} - \text{Tax savings}$$

$$= \quad k_d \quad - \quad k_d T$$

$$= k_d(1 - T). \qquad \textbf{(10-1)}$$

Therefore, if NCC can borrow at an interest rate of 11 percent, and if it has a marginal federal-plus-state tax rate of 40 percent, then its after-tax cost of debt is 6.6 percent:

$$k_d(1 - T) = 11\%(1.0 - 0.4)$$

$$= 11\%(0.6)$$

$$= 6.6\%.$$

Why is the after-tax cost of debt rather than the before-tax cost used to calculate the weighted average cost of capital?

Is the relevant cost of debt the interest rate on already *outstanding* debt or that on *new* debt? Why?

COST OF PREFERRED STOCK, k_{ps}

A number of firms, including NCC, use preferred stock as part of their permanent financing mix. Preferred dividends are not tax deductible. Therefore, the company bears their full cost, and *no tax adjustment is used when calculating the cost of preferred stock*. Note too that while some preferreds are issued without a stated maturity date, today most have a sinking fund which effectively limits their life. Finally, although it is not mandatory that preferred dividends be paid, firms generally have every intention of doing so, because otherwise (1) they cannot pay dividends on their common stock, (2) they will find it difficult to raise additional funds in the capital markets, and (3) in some cases preferred stockholders can take control of the firm.

The component **cost of preferred stock** used to calculate the weighted average cost of capital, $\mathbf{k_{ps}}$, is the preferred dividend, D_{ps}, divided by the net issuing price, P_n, which is the price the firm receives after deducting flotation costs:

$$\text{Component cost of preferred stock} = k_{ps} = \frac{D_{ps}}{P_n}. \qquad \textbf{(10-2)}$$

For example, NCC has preferred stock that pays a $10 dividend per share and sells for $100 per share in the market. If NCC issued new shares of preferred, it would incur an

---

[3]The federal tax rate for most corporations is 35 percent. However, most corporations are also subject to state income taxes, so the marginal tax rate on most corporate income is about 40 percent. For illustrative purposes, we assume that the effective federal-plus-state tax rate on marginal income is 40 percent. Also, note that the cost of debt is considered in isolation. The effect of debt on the cost of equity, as well as on future increments of debt, is ignored when the weighted cost of a combination of debt and equity is calculated in this chapter, but it will be treated in Chapters 15 and 16. Finally, the tax rate is *zero* for a firm with losses. Therefore, for a company that does not pay taxes, the cost of debt is not reduced; that is, in Equation 10-1, the tax rate equals zero, so the after-tax cost of debt is equal to the interest rate.

It should also be noted that we have ignored flotation costs (the costs incurred for new issuances) on debt. The reason is that the vast majority of debt (more than 99 percent) is privately placed, hence has no flotation cost. Also, the adjustment for flotation costs usually has a very small impact on the cost of debt. See the Extension at the end of this chapter for more details.

underwriting (or flotation) cost of 2.5 percent, or $2.50 per share, so it would net $97.50 per share. Therefore, NCC's cost of preferred stock is 10.3 percent:

$$k_{ps} = \$10/\$97.50 = 10.3\%.$$

Does the component cost of preferred stock include or exclude flotation costs? Explain.

Why is no tax adjustment made to the cost of preferred stock?

COST OF COMMON STOCK, k_s

Companies can raise common equity in two ways:[4] (1) by issuing new shares and (2) by retaining earnings. If new shares are issued, what rate of return must the company earn to satisfy the new stockholders? In Chapter 9, we saw that investors require a return of k_s. However, a company must earn more than k_s to provide this rate of return to investors, because it will incur flotation costs to issue new stock. In addition, an increase in the supply of stock will put pressure on the price of the stock, forcing the company to sell the new stock at a lower price than existed before the new issue was announced.

The combined effects of flotation costs and price pressure inhibit companies from issuing additional common stock. Mature corporations almost never issue new common stock in "regular" offerings to the public. A few do issue shares through new-stock dividend reinvestment plans, quite a few sell stock to their employees, and companies occasionally issue stock to finance huge projects or mergers. The Extension to this chapter discusses the effects of issuing stock on the cost of capital, but for the remainder of the chapter we assume that the companies in our examples, like most, do not plan to issue new shares.

Does new equity capital raised by retaining earnings have a cost? The answer is a resounding yes. If some of its earnings are retained, then the firm's stockholders will incur an *opportunity cost*—the earnings could have been paid out as dividends (or used to repurchase stock), in which case stockholders could then have reinvested the money in stocks, bonds, real estate, and so on. *Thus, the firm should earn on its reinvested earnings at least as much as its stockholders themselves could earn on alternative investments of equivalent risk.*

What rate of return can stockholders expect to earn on equivalent-risk investments? The answer is k_s, because they could earn that return by simply buying the stock of the firm in question or that of a similar firm. *Therefore, k_s is the cost of common equity raised by retaining earnings.* If a company cannot earn at least k_s on reinvested earnings, then it should pass those earnings on to its stockholders and let them invest the money themselves in assets that do provide k_s.

---

[4]New stock can be sold to the public, to existing stockholders through dividend reinvestment plans, and to employees through various option and purchase plans. It could also be argued that companies can raise equity in another way—by making investments in projects that are expected to earn more than their cost of capital. In the next chapter, we refer to such projects as "positive NPV projects," which means that the PV of their cash flows exceeds the investment outlay necessary to take them on. It could be argued that a positive NPV increases the value of the common equity, and in that sense generates new equity. That situation undoubtedly does apply at times. However, the more typical situation is that investors already expect the company to produce positive NPV projects, hence when the company actually finds and invests in one, this has already been reflected in the stock price. Still, if a company does come up with a large, unexpected, and extraordinarily profitable project, the very discovery of that project may increase the market value of its equity, increase its ability to use debt financing, and in that sense provide new equity capital.

Whereas debt and preferred stock are contractual obligations which have easily determined costs, it is more difficult to estimate k_s. However, we can employ the principles developed in Chapters 5, 6, and 9 to produce reasonably good cost of equity estimates. Three methods are typically used: (1) the Capital Asset Pricing Model (CAPM), (2) the bond-yield-plus-risk-premium approach, and (3) the discounted cash flow (DCF) method. These methods are not mutually exclusive—no one dominates the others, and all are subject to error when used in practice. Therefore, when faced with the task of estimating a company's cost of equity, we generally use all three methods and then choose among them on the basis of our confidence in the data used for each in the specific case at hand.

The CAPM Approach

To estimate the cost of common stock using the Capital Asset Pricing Model (CAPM) as developed in Chapter 5, we proceed as follows:

Step 1. Estimate the risk-free rate, k_{RF}, generally taken to be the yield on a long-term U.S. Treasury bond.

Step 2. Estimate the stock's beta coefficient, b_i, and use it as an index of the stock's risk. The i signifies the *i*th company's beta.

Step 3. Estimate the current expected rate of return on the market, or on an "average" stock, k_M.[5]

Step 4. Substitute the preceding values into the CAPM equation to estimate the required rate of return on the stock in question:

$$k_s = k_{RF} + (k_M - k_{RF})b_i. \tag{10-3}$$

Equation 10-3 shows that the CAPM estimate of k_s begins with the risk-free rate, k_{RF}, to which is added a risk premium set equal to the risk premium on an average stock, $k_M - k_{RF}$, scaled up or down to reflect the particular stock's risk as measured by its beta coefficient.

To illustrate the CAPM approach for NCC, assume that $k_{RF} = 8\%$, $k_M = 14\%$, and $b_i = 1.1$, indicating that NCC is somewhat riskier than average. Therefore, NCC's cost of equity is

$$k_s = 8\% + (6\%)(1.1)$$

$$= 8\% + 6.6\%$$

$$= 14.6\%.$$

If NCC had been an average stock, with $b = 1.0$, then its cost of equity would have been 14 percent:

$$k_s = k_M = 8\% + (6\%)(1.0) = 14\%.$$

It should be noted that although the CAPM approach appears to yield an accurate, precise estimate of k_s, there are actually several problems with it. First, as we saw in Chapter 5, if a firm's stockholders are not well diversified, they may be concerned with *stand-alone risk* in addition to market risk. In that case, the firm's true investment risk would not be measured by its beta, and the CAPM procedure would understate the correct value of k_s. Further, even if the CAPM method is valid, it is hard to obtain

---

[5]Many analysts actually estimate k_M, the expected market return, as the sum of the current risk-free rate and the market risk premium. See the Extension section for a more detailed discussion of ways to estimate the risk premium.

correct estimates of the inputs required to make it operational because (1) there is controversy about whether to use long-term or short-term Treasury yields for k_{RF}, (2) it is hard to estimate the beta that investors expect the company to have in the future, and (3) it is difficult to estimate the market risk premium. See the Extension section for a more detailed discussion of these issues.

Bond-Yield-plus-Risk-Premium Approach

Analysts who do not have complete confidence in the CAPM often use a subjective, ad hoc procedure to estimate a firm's cost of common equity: they simply add a judgmental risk premium of 3 to 5 percentage points to the interest rate on the firm's own long-term debt. It is logical to think that firms with risky, low-rated, and consequently high-interest-rate debt will also have risky, high-cost equity, and the procedure of basing the cost of equity on a readily observable debt cost utilizes this logic. For example, if an extremely strong firm such as Southern Bell had bonds which yielded 8 percent, its cost of equity might be estimated as follows:

$$k_s = \text{Bond yield} + \text{Risk premium} = 8\% + 4\% = 12\%.$$

The bonds of NCC, a riskier company, have a yield of 11 percent, making its estimated cost of equity 15 percent:

$$k_s = 11\% + 4\% = 15\%.$$

Because the 4 percent risk premium is a judgmental estimate, the estimated value of k_s is also judgmental. Empirical work in recent years suggests that the risk premium over a firm's own bond yield has generally ranged from 4 to 7 percentage points, so this method is not likely to produce a precise cost of equity—about all it can do is get us "into the right ballpark." Table 10E-3 in the Extension section provides some information on risk premiums.

Dividend-Yield-plus-Growth-Rate, or Discounted Cash Flow (DCF), Approach

In Chapter 9, we saw that both the price and the expected rate of return on a share of common stock depend, ultimately, on the dividends expected on the stock:

$$P_0 = \frac{D_1}{(1 + k_s)^1} + \frac{D_2}{(1 + k_s)^2} + \cdots$$

$$= \sum_{t=1}^{\infty} \frac{D_t}{(1 + k_s)^t}. \tag{10-4}$$

Here P_0 is the current price of the stock; D_t is the dividend expected to be paid at the end of Year t; and k_s is the required rate of return. If dividends are expected to grow at a constant rate, then, as we saw in Chapter 9, Equation 10-4 reduces to this important formula:

$$P_0 = \frac{D_1}{k_s - g}. \tag{10-5}$$

We can solve for k_s to obtain the required rate of return on common equity, which, for the marginal investor, is also equal to the expected rate of return:

$$k_s = \hat{k}_s = \frac{D_1}{P_0} + \text{Expected g.} \tag{10-6}$$

Thus, investors expect to receive a dividend yield, D_1/P_0, plus a capital gain, g, for a total expected return of $\hat{k}_s$, and in equilibrium this expected return is also equal to the required return, k_s. This method of estimating the cost of equity is called the *discounted cash flow, or DCF, method.* Henceforth, we will assume that equilibrium exists, hence $\hat{k} = k$, so we can use the terms k_s and $\hat{k}_s$ interchangeably.

It is easy to determine the dividend yield, but it is difficult to establish the proper growth rate. If past growth rates in earnings and dividends have been relatively stable, and if investors appear to be projecting a continuation of past trends, then g may be based on the firm's historic growth rate. *However, if the company's past growth has been abnormally high or low, either because of its own unique situation or because of general economic fluctuations, then investors will not project the past growth rate into the future.* In this case, g must be estimated in some other manner.

Security analysts regularly make earnings and dividend growth forecasts, looking at such factors as projected sales, profit margins, and competitive factors. For example, *Value Line,* which is available in most libraries, provides growth rate forecasts for 1,700 companies, and Merrill Lynch, Salomon Smith Barney, and other organizations make similar forecasts. Therefore, someone making a cost of equity estimate can obtain several analysts' forecasts, average them, use the average as a proxy for the growth expectations of investors in general, and then combine this g with the current dividend yield to estimate $\hat{k}_s$ as follows:

$$\hat{k}_s = \frac{D_1}{P_0} + \text{Growth rate as projected by security analysts.}$$

Again, note that this estimate of $\hat{k}_s$ is based on the assumption that g is expected to remain constant in the future.[6]

Another method for estimating g is called the **retention growth rate method.** Here we first forecast the firm's average future dividend payout ratio and its complement, the *retention rate,* and then multiply the retention rate by the company's expected future rate of return on equity (ROE):

$$g = (\text{Retention rate})(\text{ROE}) = (1.0 - \text{Payout rate})(\text{ROE}). \tag{10-7}$$

Security analysts often use this procedure when they estimate growth rates. For example, suppose NCC is expected to have a constant ROE of 14.5 percent, and it is expected to pay out 52 percent of its earnings and to retain 48 percent. In this case, its forecasted growth rate would be $g = (0.48)(14.5\%) = 7.0\%$.

To illustrate the DCF approach, suppose NCC's stock sells for $32; its next expected dividend is $2.40; and its expected growth rate is 7 percent. NCC's expected and required rate of return, hence its cost of common stock, would then be 14.5 percent:

$$\hat{k}_s = k_s = \frac{\$2.40}{\$32.00} + 7.0\%$$

$$= 7.5\% + 7.0\%$$

$$= 14.5\%.$$

---

[6]Analysts' growth rate forecasts are usually for five years into the future, and the rates provided represent the average growth rate over that five-year horizon. Studies have shown that analysts' forecasts represent the best source of growth rate data for DCF cost of capital estimates. See Robert Harris, "Using Analysts' Growth Rate Forecasts to Estimate Shareholder Required Rates of Return," *Financial Management,* Spring 1986.

Note also that two organizations—IBES and Zacks—collect the forecasts of leading analysts for most larger companies, average these forecasts, and then publish the averages. The IBES and Zacks data are available over the Internet through on-line computer data services.

This 14.5 percent is the minimum rate of return that management must expect to earn to justify retaining earnings and plowing them back into the business rather than paying them out to stockholders as dividends. Put another way, since investors have an *opportunity* to earn 14.5 percent if earnings are paid to them as dividends, then the company's *opportunity cost* of equity from retained earnings is 14.5 percent.

Comparison of the CAPM, Risk Premium, and DCF Methods

We have discussed three methods for estimating the required rate of return on common stock—CAPM, bond-yield-plus-risk-premium, and DCF. For NCC, the CAPM estimate is 14.6 percent, the bond-yield-plus-risk-premium estimate is 15.0 percent, and the DCF estimate is 14.5 percent. The overall average is 14.7 percent. In our view, there is sufficient consistency in the results to warrant the use of 14.7 percent as our estimate of the cost of common stock for NCC. If the methods produced widely varied estimates, then the financial analyst would have to use his or her judgment as to the relative merits of each estimate and then choose the estimate which seemed most reasonable under the circumstances.

People experienced in estimating equity capital costs recognize that both careful analysis and sound judgment are required. It would be nice to pretend that judgment is unnecessary and to specify an easy, precise way of determining the exact cost of equity capital. Unfortunately, this is not possible—finance is in large part a matter of judgment, and we simply must face that fact.

<table>
<tr><td>

SELF-TEST
QUESTIONS

</td><td>

What are the two sources of equity capital?

Why do most established firms not issue additional shares of common stock?

Explain why there is a cost for retained earnings; that is, why is retained earnings not free capital?

What three approaches are used to estimate the cost of common stock?

Identify some problems with the CAPM approach.

What is the reasoning behind the bond-yield-plus-risk-premium approach?

Which of the two components of the constant growth DCF formula, the dividend yield or the growth rate, is more difficult to estimate? Why?

How can the expected growth rate be estimated?

</td></tr>
</table>

COMPOSITE, OR WEIGHTED AVERAGE, COST OF CAPITAL, WACC

As we shall see in Chapters 15 and 16, each firm has an optimal capital structure, defined as that mix of debt, preferred, and common equity that causes its stock price to be maximized. Therefore, a value-maximizing firm will establish a *target (optimal) capital structure* and then raise new capital in a manner that will keep the actual capital structure on target over time. In this chapter, we assume that the firm has identified its optimal capital structure, that it uses this optimum as the target, and that it finances so as to remain constantly on target. How the target is established will be examined in Chapters 15 and 16.

The target proportions of debt, preferred stock, and common equity, along with the component costs of capital, are used to calculate the firm's *weighted average cost of capital, WACC*. To illustrate, suppose NCC has a target capital structure calling for 30 percent debt, 10 percent preferred stock, and 60 percent common equity. Its before-tax cost of debt, k_d, is 11 percent; its after-tax cost of debt is $k_d(1 - T) = 11\%(0.6) = 6.6\%$; its cost of preferred stock, k_{ps}, is 10.3 percent; its cost of common equity, k_s, is 14.7 percent; its marginal tax rate is 40 percent, and all of its new equity will come from retained earnings. Now we can calculate NCC's weighted average cost of capital, WACC, as follows:

$$\text{WACC} = w_d k_d (1 - T) + w_{ps} k_{ps} + w_{ce} k_s \qquad \textbf{(10-8)}$$

$$= 0.3(11.0\%)(0.6) + 0.1(10.3\%) + 0.6(14.7\%)$$

$$= 11.8\%.$$

Here w_d, w_{ps}, and w_{ce} are the weights used for debt, preferred, and common equity, respectively.

Every dollar of new capital that NCC obtains will, on average, consist of 30 cents of debt with an after-tax cost of 6.6 percent, 10 cents of preferred stock with a cost of 10.3 percent, and 60 cents of common equity with a cost of 14.7 percent. The average cost of each whole dollar, the WACC, is 11.8 percent.

Two points should be noted. First, the WACC is the weighted average cost of each new, or *marginal,* dollar of capital — it is not the average cost of all dollars raised in the past. We are primarily interested in obtaining a cost of capital for use in capital budgeting, and for this purpose the cost of the new money that will be invested is the relevant cost. On average, each of these new dollars will consist of some debt, some preferred, and some common equity.

Second, the percentage capital components, called weights, could be based on (1) accounting values as shown on the balance sheet (book values), (2) current market values of the capital components, or (3) management's target capital structure, which is presumably an estimate of the firm's optimal capital structure. *The correct weights are those based on the firm's target capital structure, since this is the best estimate of how the firm will, on average, raise money in the future.*

SELF-TEST QUESTIONS | How does one calculate the weighted average cost of capital? Write out the equation. On what should the weights be based?

FACTORS THAT AFFECT THE WEIGHTED AVERAGE COST OF CAPITAL

The cost of capital is affected by a variety of factors. Some are beyond the firm's control, but others are influenced by its financing and investment policies.

Factors the Firm Cannot Control

The two most important factors which are beyond a firm's direct control are (1) the level of interest rates and (2) taxes.

The Level of Interest Rates.   If interest rates in the economy rise, the cost of debt increases because firms will have to pay bondholders a higher interest rate to obtain debt capital. Also, recall from our discussion of the CAPM that higher interest rates also increase the costs of common and preferred equity capital. During the early 1990s, interest rates in the United States declined significantly. This reduced the cost of both debt and equity capital for all firms, which encouraged additional investment. Our lower interest rates also enabled U.S. firms to compete more effectively with German and Japanese firms, which in the past had enjoyed relatively low costs of capital.

WACC ESTIMATES FOR SOME LARGE U.S. CORPORATIONS

As noted in Chapter 2, the New York consulting firm of Stern Stewart & Company regularly estimates EVAs and MVAs for large U.S. corporations. To obtain these estimates, Stern Stewart must calculate a WACC for each company. The table below presents some recent WACC estimates as calculated by Stern Stewart for a sample of corporations, along with their debt-to-total-capital ratios.

These estimates suggest that a typical company has a WACC some-where in the 9 percent to 15 percent range and that the WACC varies considerably depending on (1) the company's risk and (2) the amount of debt it uses. Companies in riskier businesses, such as Intel and Motorola, presumably have higher costs of common equity. Moreover, they tend not to use as much debt. These two factors, in combination, result in higher WACCs than those of companies that operate in more stable businesses, such as Wal-Mart, Heinz, and BellSouth. We will discuss the effects of capital structure on WACC in more detail in Chapters 15 and 16.

Note, though, that riskier companies also have the potential for producing higher returns, and what really matters to shareholders is whether a company is able to generate returns in excess of its cost of capital, thus obtaining a positive EVA.

SOURCE: "Who Are the Real Wealth Creators?" *Fortune*, December 9, 1996, 107.

COMPANY	WACC	BOOK VALUE DEBT RATIO
Intel	14.5%	3%
General Electric	13.5	7
Walt Disney	12.3	33
Coca-Cola	12.0	14
Motorola	11.6	15
AT&T	9.9	39
H.J. Heinz	9.8	47
BellSouth	9.5	33
Exxon	9.4	18
Wal-Mart	9.4	43

Tax Rates.   Tax rates, which are largely beyond the control of an individual firm (although firms do lobby for more favorable tax treatment), have an important effect on the cost of capital. Tax rates are used in the calculation of the cost of debt as used in the WACC, and there are other less apparent ways in which tax policy affects the cost of capital. For example, lowering the capital gains tax rate relative to the rate on ordinary income would make stocks more attractive, which would reduce the cost of equity relative to that of debt. That would, as we will see in Chapters 15 and 16, lead to a change in a firm's optimal capital structure (toward less debt and more equity).

Factors the Firm Can Control

A firm can affect its cost of capital through (1) its capital structure policy, (2) its dividend policy, and (3) its investment (capital budgeting) policy.

Capital Structure Policy.   In this chapter, we assume that a firm has a given target capital structure, and we use weights based on that target structure to calculate the WACC. It is clear, though, that a firm can change its capital structure, and such a change can affect its cost of capital. The after-tax cost of debt is lower than the cost of equity. Therefore, if the firm decides to use more debt and less common equity, this change in the weights in the WACC equation will tend to lower the WACC. However, an increase in the

GLOBAL VARIATIONS IN THE COST OF CAPITAL

For U.S. firms to be competitive with foreign companies, they must have costs of capital which are similar to those of their international competitors. In the past, many experts argued that U.S. firms were at a disadvantage. In particular, Japanese firms enjoyed lower costs of capital, which lowered their total costs and thus made it harder for U.S. firms to compete.

Recent events, however, have considerably narrowed cost of capital differences between U.S. and Japanese firms. After-tax real interest rates, once much higher in the United States, are now roughly the same, so the cost of debt financing is now similar in the two countries. Likewise, the U.S. stock market has outperformed the Japanese market in recent years, making it easier and cheaper for U.S. firms to raise equity capital.

As capital markets become increasingly integrated, cross-country differences in the cost of capital are likely to disappear. Today, most large corporations raise capital throughout the world, hence we are moving toward one global capital market rather than distinct capital markets in each country. Although government policies and market conditions can affect the cost of capital within a given country, this primarily affects smaller firms that do not have access to global capital markets, and even these differences are becoming less important as time goes by. What matters most is the risk of the individual firm, not the market in which it raises capital.

SOURCE: "Better Buys Abroad," *Forbes*, January 16, 1995, 69. Reprinted by permission of *Forbes* magazine. ©Forbes Inc., 1994.

use of debt will increase the riskiness of both the debt and the equity, and increases in component costs will tend to offset the effects of the change in the weights. In Chapters 15 and 16, we will discuss this in more depth, and we will demonstrate that a firm's optimal capital structure is the one which minimizes its cost of capital.

Dividend Policy.   As we shall see in Chapter 17, the percentage of earnings paid out in dividends may affect a stock's required rate of return, k_s. Also, if a firm's payout ratio is so high that it must issue new stock to fund its capital budget, this will force it to incur flotation costs, and this too will affect its cost of capital. This second point is discussed in detail in the Extension to this chapter and also in Chapter 17.

Investment Policy.   When we estimate the cost of capital, we use as the starting point the required rates of return on the firm's outstanding stock and bonds. Those cost rates reflect the riskiness of the firm's existing assets. Therefore, we have implicitly been assuming that new capital will be invested in assets of the same type and with the same degree of risk as is embedded in the existing assets. This assumption is generally correct, as most firms do invest in assets similar to those it currently uses. However, it would be incorrect if the firm dramatically changed its investment policy. For example, if a firm invests in an entirely new line of business, its marginal cost of capital should reflect the riskiness of that new business. To illustrate, ITT Corporation recently sold its finance company and purchased Caesar's World, a casino gambling firm. This dramatic shift in corporate focus almost certainly affected ITT's cost of capital. Likewise, Disney's purchase of the ABC television network changed the nature and risk of its assets in a way that might also influence its cost of capital. The effect of investment policy on capital costs is discussed in detail in the next section and in Chapter 13.

SELF-TEST QUESTIONS

What two factors which affect the cost of capital are generally beyond the firm's control?

What three policies under the firm's control are likely to affect its cost of capital?

Explain how a change in interest rates would affect each component of the weighted average cost of capital.

FIGURE 10-1   Risk and the Cost of Capital

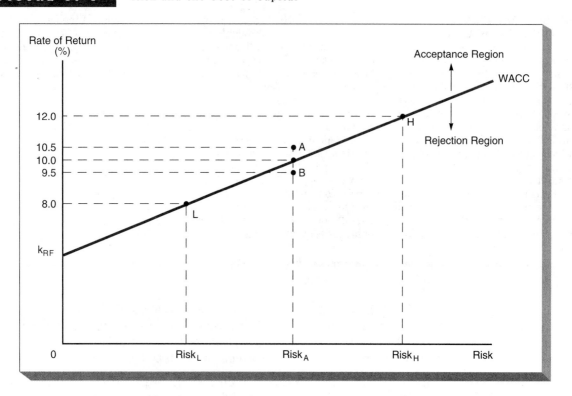

ADJUSTING THE COST OF CAPITAL FOR RISK

As noted earlier, the cost of capital is a key element in the capital budgeting process. As you will see in the next three chapters, a project should be accepted if and only if its estimated return exceeds its cost of capital. For this reason, the cost of capital is sometimes referred to as a "hurdle rate"—project returns must "jump the hurdle" to be accepted.

As we saw in Chapter 5, investors require higher returns for riskier investments. Consequently, a company that is raising capital to take on risky projects will have a higher cost of capital than a company that is financing safer projects. Figure 10-1 illustrates the trade-off between risk and the cost of capital. Firm L is a low-risk business with a WACC of 8 percent, whereas Firm H is exposed to high risks and has a WACC of 12 percent. Thus, Firm L will accept one of its typical projects only if its expected return is above 8 percent. The corresponding hurdle rate for Firm H's typical project is 12 percent.

It is important to remember that the cost of capital values presented in Figure 10-1 represent the overall, or composite, WACCs for each firm and, thus, only represent the hurdle rate of a "typical" project for each firm. Different projects generally have different risks. Moreover, the hurdle rate for each project should reflect the risk of the project itself, not necessarily the risk associated with the firm's average project as reflected in its composite WACC. For example, assume that Firms L and H are both considering the same Project A. This project has more risk than a typical Firm L project but less risk than a typical Firm H project. As shown in Figure 10-1, Project A has a 10.5 percent expected return. At first, we might be tempted to conclude that Firm L should accept Project A because its 10.5 percent return is above its 8 percent WACC, while Firm H should turn the project down because its return is less than Firm H's 12 percent WACC. However, this would be wrong. The relevant hurdle rate is the *project's WACC,* which is 10 percent, as read from the WACC line in Figure 10-1. Since the project's return exceeds its 10 percent cost, *both* firms should accept Project A.

Next, consider Project B. It has the same risk as Project A, but its expected return is 9.5 percent versus its 10 percent hurdle rate. Both firms should reject Project B. However, if they based their decisions on their overall WACCs rather than on Project B's own risk-adjusted cost of capital, Firm L would accept Project B because its return is above Firm L's 8 percent WACC. Note, though, that if Firm L's managers accept Project B, they would reduce their shareholders' wealth, because the project's return is not high enough to justify its risk. Applying a specific hurdle rate to each project ensures that every project will be evaluated properly.

Continuing, if a company has different divisional costs of capital, then it would be incorrect to use the company's overall cost of capital to find the NPV of all the company's projects. For example, consider Starlight Sandwich Shops, a company with two divisions — a bakery operation and a chain of cafes. The bakery division is low risk and has a 10 percent cost of capital. The cafe division is riskier and has a 14 percent cost of capital. Each division is approximately the same size, so Starlight's overall cost of capital is 12 percent. The bakery manager has a project with an 11 percent expected rate of return, and the cafe division manager has a project with a 13 percent expected return. Should these projects be accepted or rejected? Starlight can create value if it accepts the bakery's project, since its rate of return is greater than its cost of capital (11% > 10%), but the cafe project's rate of return is less than its cost of capital (13% < 14%), so it should be rejected. However, if one simply compared the two projects' returns with Starlight's 12 percent overall cost of capital, then the bakery's value-adding project would be rejected while the cafe's value-destroying project would be accepted.

S E L F - T E S T Q U E S T I O N S

Why is the cost of capital sometimes referred to as a "hurdle rate"?

How should firms evaluate projects with different risks?

Should all divisions within a firm use the firm's composite WACC when considering capital budgeting projects? Explain.

ESTIMATING PROJECT RISK

Although it is intuitively clear that riskier projects have a higher cost of capital, it is difficult to actually estimate project risk. First, note that three separate and distinct types of risk can be identified:

1. **Stand-alone risk** is the project's risk disregarding the fact that it is but one asset within the firm's portfolio of assets and that the firm is but one stock in a typical investor's portfolio of stocks. Stand-alone risk is measured by the variability of the project's expected returns.

2. **Corporate, or within-firm, risk** is the project's risk to the corporation, giving consideration to the fact that the project represents only one of the firm's portfolio of assets, hence that some of its risk effects will be diversified away. Corporate risk is measured by the project's impact on uncertainty about the firm's future earnings.

3. **Market, or beta, risk** is the riskiness of the project as seen by a well-diversified stockholder who recognizes that the project is only one of the firm's assets and that the firm's stock is but one part of the investor's total portfolio. Market risk is measured by the project's effect on the firm's beta coefficient.

Taking on a project with a high degree of either stand-alone or corporate risk will not necessarily affect the firm's beta. However, if the project has highly uncertain returns, and if those returns are highly correlated with returns on the firm's other assets and with most other assets in the economy, then the project will have a high degree of all types of risk. For example, suppose General Motors decides to undertake a major expansion to build electric autos. GM is not sure how its technology will work on a mass production basis, so there are great risks in the venture—its stand-alone risk is high. Management also estimates that the project will do best if the economy is strong, for then people will have more money to spend on the new autos. This means that the project will tend to do well if GM's other divisions do well and will tend to do badly if other divisions do badly. This being the case, the project will also have high corporate risk. Finally, since GM's profits are highly correlated with those of most other firms, the project's beta will also be high. Thus, this project will be risky under all three definitions of risk.

Of the three measures, market risk is theoretically the most relevant because of its direct effect on stock prices. Unfortunately, the market risk for a project is also the most difficult to estimate. In practice, most decision makers consider all three risk measures in a judgmental manner, and then they classify projects into subjective risk categories. Then, using the composite WACC as a starting point, **risk-adjusted costs of capital** are developed for each category. For example, a firm might establish three risk classes—high, average, and low—then assign average-risk projects the average (composite) cost of capital, higher-risk projects an above-average cost, and lower-risk projects a below-average cost. Thus, if a company's composite WACC estimate were 10 percent, its managers might use 10 percent to evaluate average-risk projects, 12 percent for high-risk projects, and 8 percent for low-risk projects. While this approach is better than not risk adjusting at all, these risk adjustments are necessarily subjective and somewhat arbitrary. Unfortunately, given the data, there is no completely satisfactory way to specify exactly how much higher or lower we should go in setting risk-adjusted costs of capital.

SELF-TEST QUESTIONS

What are the three types of project risk?

Which type of project risk is theoretically the most relevant? Why?

Describe one procedure firms can use when developing costs of capital for projects with differing degrees of risk.

USING THE CAPM TO ESTIMATE A PROJECT'S RISK-ADJUSTED COST OF CAPITAL

Many firms use the CAPM to estimate the cost of capital for specific projects or divisions. To begin, recall from Chapter 5 that the Security Market Line equation expresses the risk/return relationship as follows:

$$k_s = k_{RF} + (k_M - k_{RF})b_i.$$

As an example, consider the case of Huron Steel Company, an integrated steel producer operating in the Great Lakes region. For simplicity, assume that Huron uses only equity capital, so its cost of equity is also its corporate cost of capital, or WACC. Huron's beta = b = 1.1; k_{RF} = 8%; and k_M = 12%. Thus, Huron's cost of equity is 12.4 percent:

$$k_s = 8\% + (12\% - 8\%)1.1$$
$$= 8\% + (4\%)1.1$$
$$= 12.4\%.$$

This suggests that investors should be willing to give Huron money to invest in average-risk projects if the company expects to earn 12.4 percent or more on this money. Here again, by average risk we mean projects having risk similar to the firm's existing assets. *Therefore, as a first approximation, Huron should invest in capital projects if and only if these projects have an expected return of 12.4 percent or more.*[7] Huron should use 12.4 percent as its discount rate to determine the NPV of an average-risk project.

Suppose, however, that taking on a particular project would cause a change in Huron's beta coefficient, which, in turn, would change the company's cost of equity. For example, suppose Huron is considering the construction of a fleet of barges to haul iron ore, and barge operations have betas of 1.5 rather than 1.1. Since the firm itself may be regarded as a "portfolio of assets," and since the beta of any portfolio is a weighted average of the betas of its individual assets, taking on the barge project would cause the overall corporate beta to rise to somewhere between the original beta of 1.1 and the barge project's beta of 1.5. The exact value of the new beta would depend on the relative size of the investment in barge operations versus Huron's other assets. If 80 percent of Huron's total funds ended up in basic steel operations with a beta of 1.1 and 20 percent in barge operations with a beta of 1.5, the new corporate beta would be 1.18:

$$\text{New beta} = 0.8(1.1) + 0.2(1.5)$$

$$= 1.18.$$

This increase in Huron's beta coefficient would cause its stock price to decline *unless the increased beta were offset by a higher expected rate of return.* Specifically, taking on the new project would cause the overall corporate cost of capital to rise from the original 12.4 percent to 12.72 percent:

$$k_s = 8\% + (4\%)1.18$$

$$= 12.72\%.$$

Therefore, to keep the barge investment from lowering the value of the firm, Huron's overall expected rate of return must also rise from 12.4 to 12.72 percent.

If investments in basic steel must earn 12.4 percent, how much must Huron expect to earn on the barge investment to cause the new overall expected rate of return to equal 12.72 percent? We know that if Huron undertakes the barge investment, it will have 80 percent of its assets invested in basic steel projects earning 12.4 percent and 20 percent in barge operations earning "X" percent, and the average required rate of return will be 12.72 percent. Therefore,

$$0.8(12.4\%) + 0.2X = 12.72\%$$

$$0.2X = 2.8\%$$

$$X = 14\%.$$

Since X = 14%, we see that the barge project must have an expected return of at least 14 percent if the corporation is to earn its new cost of capital.

In summary, if Huron takes on the barge project, its corporate beta will rise from 1.1 to 1.18, its cost of capital will rise from 12.4 to 12.72 percent, and the barge

---

[7]To simplify things somewhat, we assume that the firm uses only equity capital. If debt is used, the cost of capital used must be a weighted average of the costs of debt and equity.

FIGURE 10-2   Using the Security Market Line Concept in Capital Budgeting

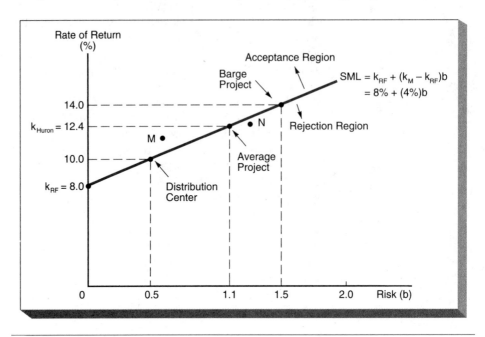

investment must earn 14 percent if the company is to earn its new overall cost of capital.

This line of reasoning leads to the conclusion that if the beta coefficient for each project, b_p, could be determined, then a **project cost of capital, $k_{Project}$**, for each individual project could be found as follows:

$$k_{Project} = k_{RF} + (k_M - k_{RF})b_p.$$

Thus, for basic steel projects with $b = 1.1$, Huron should use 12.4 percent as the cost of capital. The barge project, with $b = 1.5$, should be evaluated at a 14 percent cost of capital:

$$k_{Barge} = 8\% + (4\%)1.5$$

$$= 8\% + 6\%$$

$$= 14\%.$$

On the other hand, a low-risk project, such as a new distribution center with a beta of only 0.5, would have a cost of capital of 10 percent:

$$k_{Center} = 8\% + (4\%)0.5$$

$$= 10\%.$$

Figure 10-2 gives a graphic summary of these concepts as applied to Huron Steel. Note the following points:

1. The SML is the same Security Market Line that we developed in Chapter 5. It shows how investors are willing to make trade-offs between risk as measured by beta and expected returns. The higher the beta risk, the higher the rate of return needed to

compensate investors for bearing this risk. The SML specifies the nature of this relationship.

2. Huron Steel initially has a beta of 1.1, so its required rate of return on average-risk investments is 12.4 percent.

3. High-risk investments such as the barge line require higher rates of return, whereas low-risk investments such as the distribution center require lower rates of return. If Huron concentrates its new investments in either high- or low-risk projects as opposed to average-risk projects, its corporate beta will rise or fall from the current value of 1.1. Consequently, Huron's required rate of return on common stock will change from its current value of 12.4 percent.

4. If the expected rate of return on a given capital project lies *above* the SML, the expected rate of return on the project is more than enough to compensate for its risk, and the project should be accepted. Conversely, if the project's rate of return lies *below* the SML, it should be rejected. Thus, Project M in Figure 10-2 is acceptable, whereas Project N should be rejected. N has a higher expected return than M, but the differential is not enough to offset its much higher risk.

5. For simplicity, the Huron Steel illustration is based on the assumption that the company used no debt financing, which allows us to use the SML to plot the company's cost of capital. The basic concepts presented in the Huron illustration also hold for companies that use debt financing. The discount rate applied in capital budgeting is the firm's weighted average cost of capital. When debt financing is used, the project's cost of equity must be combined with the cost of debt to obtain the project's overall cost of capital.

SELF-TEST
QUESTIONS

What is meant by the term "average-risk project"? Based on the CAPM, how would one find the cost of capital for such a project, for a low-risk project, and for a high-risk project?

Complete the following sentence: An increase in a company's beta coefficient would cause its stock price to decline unless its expected rate of return . . .

Explain why you should accept a given capital project if its expected rate of return lies above the SML. What if the expected rate of return lies on the SML? Below the SML?

TECHNIQUES FOR MEASURING BETA RISK

In Chapter 6 we discussed the estimation of betas for stocks, and we indicated the difficulties in estimating beta. The estimation of project betas is much more difficult, and more fraught with uncertainty. However, two approaches have been used to estimate individual assets' betas—the pure play method and the accounting beta method.

The Pure Play Method

In the **pure play method,** the company tries to find several single-product companies in the same line of business as the project being evaluated, and it then averages those companies' betas to determine the cost of capital for its own project. For example, suppose Huron could find three existing single-product firms that operate barges, and suppose also that Huron's management believes its barge project would be subject to the same risks as those firms. Huron could then determine the betas of those firms, average them, and use this average beta as a proxy for the barge project's beta.[8]

The pure play approach can only be used for major assets such as whole divisions, and even then it is frequently difficult to implement because it is often impossible to find pure play proxy firms. However, when IBM was considering going into personal computers, it was able to obtain data on Apple Computer and several other essentially pure play personal computer companies. This is often the case when a firm considers a major investment outside its primary field.

The Accounting Beta Method

As noted above, it may be impossible to find single-product, publicly traded firms suitable for the pure play approach. If that is the case, we may be able to use the **accounting beta method.** Betas normally are found as described in Chapter 6—by regressing the returns of a particular company's *stock* against returns on a *stock market index*. However, we could run a regression of the company's *accounting return on assets* against the *average return on assets* for a large sample of companies, such as those included in the S&P 500. Betas determined in this way (that is, by using accounting data rather than stock market data) are called *accounting betas*.

Accounting betas for a totally new project can be calculated only after the project has been accepted, placed in operation, and begun to generate output and accounting results—too late for the capital budgeting decision. However, to the extent management thinks a given project is similar to other projects the firm has undertaken in the past, some other project's accounting beta can be used as a proxy for that of the project in question. In practice, accounting betas are normally calculated for divisions or other large units, not for single assets, and divisional betas are then used for the division's projects.

S E L F - T E S T
Q U E S T I O N   Describe the pure play and the accounting beta methods for estimating individual projects' betas.

THE COST OF DEPRECIATION AND OTHER TYPES OF INTERNALLY GENERATED FUNDS

For many firms, depreciation is the largest source of funds as shown in their statement of cash flows, and these depreciation-generated funds are available to support the capital budget. How should depreciation be handled?

First, note that a good approximation to the firm's internally generated cash flow is found as follows:

$$\text{Internal cash flow} = \text{Net income} - \text{Cash dividends} + \text{Depreciation}$$

$$= \text{Retained earnings} + \text{Depreciation}.$$

This approximation is accurate if the firm does not liquidate assets and if its policies regarding working capital are stable. If the firm sells off fixed assets, liquidates inventory, accelerates the collection of receivables, or stretches out its payables, these actions will affect its internal cash flows. Still, for most firms the equation is reasonably accurate.

---

[8]If the pure play firms employ different capital structures than that of Huron, this fact must be dealt with by adjusting the beta coefficients. See Chapter 13 for a discussion of this aspect of the pure play method.

Internally generated cash can be used however management chooses—to retire debt, to pay more dividends, or to invest in operating assets. If the funds are to be reinvested, do they have a cost, and if so, what is that cost? As we have already seen, the cost of the first element of internal funds, retained earnings, is k_s, the required rate of return on the stock. But what about the second element, depreciation? What is its cost? Here is the thought process used to develop the cost of depreciation funds:

1. First, the existence of depreciation means that fixed assets are wearing out and becoming obsolete, and that their value as reported on the balance sheet has declined. Thus, if the firm is to continue operating, some or all of the depreciation-generated funds must be reinvested in fixed assets.

2. Still, the firm has the *opportunity* to distribute the depreciation-generated funds to its investors—it is not forced to reinvest those funds. Indeed, if the firm cannot earn at least as much as investors themselves could earn, it should pay the funds out even though this would mean contracting in size.

3. The firm could distribute the depreciation-generated funds to its common or preferred stockholders, or its bondholders, or it could give some to each group. However, if it passed along all the depreciation funds to stockholders, the debt ratio would increase, while this ratio would decrease if all of the funds were used to retire debt.

4. The capital used to buy the depreciating assets was provided by all its investors, common stockholders, preferred stockholders, and bondholders. If it were distributed entirely to common stockholders, the debt ratio would rise, the riskiness of the bonds would rise, and the now higher risk would cause the value of the bonds to decline. Bondholders obviously would not like this, so to prevent it from occurring debt contracts contain clauses that de facto prevent companies from distributing depreciation flows except on a pro rata basis to all of its investors. (Actually, the clauses generally stipulate that the debt ratio will not be allowed to rise above some specified level without restrictions being imposed, and that distributions to common stockholders must be made from earnings under most circumstances.)

5. The effective result of all this is that depreciation cash flows, if they are to be distributed rather than reinvested, must be distributed on a pro rata basis to common stockholders, preferred stockholders, and bondholders.

6. Since depreciation-generated funds—if they are not reinvested in the company—must be distributed to all the firm's investors, the cost of depreciation funds should reflect the opportunity costs of all three groups. As we have already seen, the common stockholders' opportunity cost is k_s, that of the preferred stockholders is k_{ps}, and that of bondholders is k_d, with an after-tax cost of $k_d(1 - T)$.

7. The average opportunity cost should be based on the same capital structure weights that were used to calculate the WACC.

8. Finally, if both the component costs and the weights of the depreciation cash flows are the same as those used to calculate the basic WACC, then the opportunity cost of depreciation funds must be the same as the basic WACC. Similar reasoning would apply to other types of internally generated funds, such as funds made available from the sale of fixed assets or inventories.

Our conclusion from all this is that so long as the firm (1) obtains its new common equity as retained earnings rather than by issuing new common stock, (2) does not change its target capital structure, and (3) invests in assets that have about the same

THE COST OF EQUITY CAPITAL FOR SMALL FIRMS

The three equity cost-estimating techniques discussed in this chapter (DCF, bond-yield-plus-risk-premium, and CAPM) have serious limitations when applied to small firms. Consider first the constant growth model, $k_s = D_1/P_0 + g$. Imagine a small, rapidly growing firm, such as Bio-Technology General (BTG), which will not in the foreseeable future pay dividends. For firms like this, the constant growth model is simply not applicable. In fact, it is difficult to imagine any dividend model that would be of practical benefit for such a firm because of the difficulty of estimating dividends and growth rates.

The second method, which calls for adding a risk premium of 3 to 5 percent to the firm's cost of debt, can be used for some small firms, but problems arise if the firm does not have a publicly traded bond outstanding. BTG, for example, has no public debt outstanding, so we would have trouble using the bond-yield-plus-risk-premium approach for BTG.

The third approach, the CAPM, is often not usable, because if the firm's stock is not publicly traded, then we cannot calculate its beta. For the privately owned firm, we might use the "pure play" CAPM technique, which involves finding a publicly owned firm in the same line of business, estimating that firm's beta, and then using that beta as a replacement for the one of the small business in question.

To illustrate the pure play approach, again consider BTG. The firm is not publicly traded, so we cannot estimate its beta. However, data are available on more established firms, such as Genentech and Genetic Industries, so we could use their betas as representative of the biological and genetic engineering industry. Of course, these firms' betas would have to be subjectively modified to reflect their larger sizes and more established positions, as well as to take account of the differ-ences in the nature of their products and their capital structures as compared to those of BTG. Still, as long as there are public companies in similar lines of business available for comparison, their betas can be used to help estimate the cost of capital of a firm whose equity is not publicly traded. Note also that a "liquidity premium" as discussed in Chapter 4 would also have to be added to reflect the illiquidity of the small, nonpublic firm's stock.

Flotation Costs for Small Issues

When external equity capital is raised, flotation costs increase the cost of equity capital above that of internal funds. These flotation costs are especially significant for smaller firms, and they can substantially affect capital budgeting decisions involving external equity funds. To illustrate this point, consider a firm that is expected to pay constant dividends forever, hence its growth rate is zero. In this case, if F is the percentage flotation cost, then the cost of equity capital is $k_e = D_1/[P_0(1 - F)]$. The higher the flotation cost, the higher the cost of external equity.

How big is F? Small debt and equity issues have considerably higher flotation costs than large issues. For example, a non-IPO issue of common stock which raises more than $100 million in capital would have a flotation cost of about 3.5 percent. For a firm that is expected to provide a constant 15 percent dividend yield (that is, $D_1/P_0 = 15\%$), the cost of equity would be 15%/(1 − 0.04), or 15.6 percent. However, a similar but smaller firm which raises less than $10 million would have a flotation cost of about 13 percent, which would result in a flotation-adjusted cost of equity capital of 15%/(1 − 0.13) = 17.2 percent, or 1.6 percentage points higher. This differential would be even larger if an IPO were involved. Therefore, it is clear that a small firm would have to earn considerably more on the same proj-ect than a large firm. Small firms are therefore at a substantial disadvantage because of flotation cost effects.

The Small-Firm Effect

A number of researchers have observed that portfolios of small firms' stocks have earned consistently higher average returns than those of large firms' stocks; this is called the "small-firm effect." On the surface, it would seem to be advantageous to the small firm to provide average returns in the stock market that are higher than those of large firms. In reality, however, this is bad news—what the small-firm effect means is that the capital market demands higher returns on stocks of small firms than on the stocks of otherwise similar large firms. Therefore, the basic cost of equity capital is higher for small firms. This compounds the high flotation cost problem noted above.

It may be argued that the stocks of small firms are riskier than those of large firms, and that accounts for the differences in returns. It is true that academic research usually finds that betas are higher for small firms than for large ones. However, the returns for small firms are still larger even after adjusting for the effects of their higher risks as reflected in their beta coefficients.

The small-firm effect is an anomaly in the sense that it is not consistent with the CAPM theory. Still, higher returns reflect a higher cost of capital, so we must conclude that small firms do have higher capital costs than otherwise similar large firms. The manager of a small firm should take this factor into account when estimating his or her firm's cost of equity capital. In general, the cost of equity appears to be about four percentage points higher for small firms (those with market values of less than $20 million) than for large New York Stock Exchange firms with similar risk characteristics.

risk as its existing assets, then the WACC as we calculated it can be used for capital budgeting purposes. Note, though, as we discussed earlier, the corporate WACC must be adjusted to reflect risk for projects whose risks differ from those of the firm's average project.

SELF-TEST
QUESTION
| Why is the WACC the appropriate opportunity cost for depreciation and other types of internally generated funds?

SOME PROBLEM AREAS IN COST OF CAPITAL

A number of difficult issues relating to the cost of capital either have not been mentioned or were glossed over in this chapter. These topics are covered in advanced finance courses, but they deserve some mention now both to alert you to potential dangers and to provide you with a preview of some of the matters dealt with in advanced courses.

1. **Privately owned firms.** Our discussion of the cost of equity was related to publicly owned corporations, and we have concentrated on the rate of return required by public stockholders. However, there is a serious question about how one should measure the cost of equity for a firm whose stock is not traded. Tax issues are also especially important in these cases. As a general rule, the same principles of cost of capital estimation apply to both privately held and publicly owned firms, but the problems of obtaining input data are somewhat different for each.

2. **Small businesses.** Small businesses are generally privately owned, making it difficult to estimate their cost of equity. The box entitled "The Cost of Equity Capital for Small Firms" discusses this issue.

3. **Measurement problems.** One cannot overemphasize the practical difficulties encountered when estimating the cost of equity. It is very difficult to obtain good input data for the CAPM, for g in the formula $k_s = D_1/P_0 + g$, and for the risk premium in the formula $k_s =$ Bond yield + Risk premium. As a result, we can never be sure just how accurate our estimated cost of capital is.

4. **Costs of capital for projects of differing riskiness.** As we will see in Chapter 13, it is difficult to measure projects' risks, hence to assign risk-adjusted discount rates to capital budgeting projects of differing degrees of riskiness.

5. **Capital structure weights.** In this chapter, we have simply taken as given the target capital structure and used this target to obtain the weights used to calculate WACC. As we shall see in Chapters 15 and 16, establishing the target capital structure is a major task in itself.

Although this list of problems may appear formidable, the state of the art in cost of capital estimation is really not in bad shape. The procedures outlined in this chapter can be used to obtain cost of capital estimates that are sufficiently accurate for practical purposes, and the problems listed here merely indicate the desirability of refinements. The refinements are not unimportant, but the problems we have identified do not invalidate the usefulness of the procedures outlined in the chapter.

SELF-TEST
QUESTION
| Identify some problem areas in cost of capital analysis. Do these problems invalidate the cost of capital procedures discussed in the chapter?

FOUR MISTAKES TO AVOID

We often see managers and students make the following mistakes when estimating the cost of capital. Although we have discussed these errors previously at separate places in the chapter, they are worth repeating here:

1. **Use the current cost of debt.** Don't use the coupon rate on a firm's existing debt as the pre-tax cost of debt. The relevant pre-tax cost of debt is the interest rate the firm would pay if it issued debt today.

2. **When applying the CAPM method, never use the historical average return on stocks with the current risk-free rate.** The historical average return on common stocks has been about 12.7 percent, the historical return on long-term Treasury bonds about 5.2 percent, and the difference between them, which is the **historical risk premium,** is 7.5 percent. The **current risk premium** is found as the difference between an estimate of the current expected rate of return on common stocks and the current expected yield on T-bonds. To illustrate, suppose an estimate of the future return on common stock is 14.0 percent, and the current rate on long-term T-bonds is 6.9 percent. This implies a current market risk premium of 14.0% − 6.9% = 7.1%. A case could be made for using either the historical or the current risk premium, but it would be wrong to take the *historical* rate of return on the market, 12.5 percent, subtract from it the *current* 6.9 percent rate on T-bonds, and then use 12.5% − 6.9% = 5.6% as the risk premium.

3. **Use the target capital structure to determine the weights for the WACC.** If you are an outside analyst and do not know the target weights, it is better to estimate weights based on the current market values of the capital components than their book values. This is especially true for equity. For example, the stock of an average U.S. firm in 1998 had a market value that was about four times its book value, and in general, stocks' market values are rarely close to their book values. If the company's debt is not publicly traded, then it is reasonable to use the book value of debt to estimate the weights, since book and market values of debt, especially short-term debt, are usually close to one another. To summarize, if you don't know the target weights, then use market values rather than book values to obtain the weights used to calculate WACC.

4. **Always remember that capital components are funds that come from investors.** If it's not from an investor, then it's not a capital component. Sometimes the argument is made that accounts payable and accruals are sources of funding and should be included in the calculation of the WACC. However, these accounts are due to operating relationships with suppliers and employees, and they are deducted when determining the investment requirement for a project. Therefore, they should not be included in the WACC. Of course, they are not ignored in either corporate valuation or capital budgeting. As we showed in Chapters 2 and 9, current liabilities do affect free cash flow, hence have an effect on corporate valuation. Moreover, in Chapter 12 we show that the same is true for capital budgeting, namely, that current liabilities affect the cash flows of a project, but not its WACC.[9]

---

[9]The same reasoning could be applied to other items on the balance sheet, such as deferred taxes. The existence of deferred taxes means that the government has collected less in taxes than a company would owe if the same depreciation and amortization rates were used for taxes as for stockholder reporting. In this sense, the government is "making a loan to the company." However, the deferred tax account is not a source of funds from investors, hence it is not considered to be a capital component. Moreover, the cash flows that are used in capital budgeting and in corporate valuation reflect the actual taxes that the company must pay, not the "normalized" taxes it might report on its income statement. In other words, the correct adjustment for the deferred tax account is made in the cash flows, not in the WACC.

SELF-TEST
QUESTION| What are four common mistakes people make when estimating the WACC?

SUMMARY

This chapter showed how the weighted average cost of capital is developed for use in capital budgeting. The key concepts covered are listed below.

- The cost of capital used in capital budgeting is a **weighted average** of the types of capital the firm uses, typically debt, preferred stock, and common equity.

- The **component cost of debt** is the **after-tax** cost of new debt. It is found by multiplying the cost of new debt by $(1 - T)$, where T is the firm's marginal tax rate: $k_d(1 - T)$.

- The **component cost of preferred stock** is calculated as the preferred dividend divided by the net issuing price, where the net issuing price is the price the firm receives after deducting flotation costs: $k_{ps} = D_{ps}/P_n$.

- The **cost of common equity**, k_s, is also called the **cost of common stock.** It is the rate of return required by the firm's stockholders, and it can be estimated by three methods: (1) the **CAPM approach,** (2) the **bond-yield-plus-risk-premium approach,** and (3) the **dividend-yield-plus-growth-rate, or DCF, approach.**

- To use the **CAPM approach,** one (1) estimates the firm's beta, (2) multiplies this beta by the market risk premium to determine the firm's risk premium, and (3) adds the firm's risk premium to the risk-free rate to obtain the firm's cost of common stock: $k_s = k_{RF} + (k_M - k_{RF})b_i$.

- The best proxy for the **risk-free rate** is the yield on long-term T-bonds.

- The **bond-yield-plus-risk-premium approach** calls for adding a risk premium of from 3 to 5 percentage points to the firm's interest rate on long-term debt: k_s = Bond yield + RP.

- To use the **dividend-yield-plus-growth-rate approach,** which is also called the **discounted cash flow (DCF) approach,** one adds the firm's expected growth rate to its expected dividend yield: $k_s = D_1/P_0 + g$.

- The growth rate can be estimated from historical earnings and dividends or by use of the **retention growth model, g = (1.0-Payout Rate) (ROE),** or it can be based on analysts' forecasts.

- Each firm has a **target capital structure,** defined as that mix of debt, preferred stock, and common equity which minimizes its **weighted average cost of capital (WACC):**

$$WACC = w_d k_d (1 - T) + w_{ps} k_{ps} + w_{ce} k_s.$$

- **Various factors affect a firm's cost of capital.** Some of these factors are determined by the financial environment, but the firm influences others through its financing, investment, and dividend policies.

- The three equity cost-estimating techniques discussed in this chapter have **serious limitations** when applied to small firms, thus increasing the need for the small-business manager to use judgment.

- Stock offerings of less than $1 million have an average flotation cost of 21 percent, while the average flotation cost on large common stock offerings is about 4 percent. As a result, a small firm would have to earn considerably more on the same project than a large firm. Also, the capital market demands higher returns on stocks of small firms than on otherwise similar stocks of large firms — this is called the **small-firm effect.**

- Ideally, the **cost of capital** for each project should reflect the risk of the project itself, not necessarily the risks associated with the firm's average project as reflected in its composite WACC.

- **Failing to adjust for differences in project risk** would lead a firm to accept too many value-destroying risky projects and reject too many value-adding safe ones. Over time, the firm would become more risky, its WACC would increase, and its shareholder value would suffer.

- A project's **stand-alone risk** is the risk the project would have if it were the firm's only asset and if stockholders held only that one stock. Stand-alone risk is measured by the variability of the asset's expected returns.

- **Corporate,** or **within-firm, risk** reflects the effects of a project on the firm's risk, and it is measured by the project's effect on the firm's earnings variability.

- **Market,** or **beta, risk** reflects the effects of a project on the riskiness of stockholders, assuming they hold diversified portfolios. Market risk is measured by the project's effect on the firm's beta coefficient.

- Most decision makers consider all three risk measures in a judgmental manner and then classify projects into subjective risk categories. Using the composite WACC as a starting point, risk-adjusted costs of capital are developed for each category. The **risk-adjusted cost of capital** is the cost of capital appropriate for a given project, given the riskiness of that project. The greater the risk, the higher the cost of capital.

- As an alternative to the judgmental approaches, firms can use the **CAPM** to estimate the cost of capital for specific projects or divisions. However, estimating betas for projects is difficult.

- The **pure play** and **accounting beta methods** can sometimes be used to estimate betas for large projects or for divisions.

The cost of capital as developed in this chapter is used in the following chapters to evaluate capital budgeting projects. In addition, we will extend the concepts developed here in Chapters 15 and 16, where we consider the effect of the capital structure on the cost of capital.

Questions

10-1 Define each of the following terms:
a. Weighted average cost of capital, WACC
b. After-tax cost of debt, $k_d(1 - T)$
c. Cost of preferred stock, k_{ps}
d. Cost of common equity or cost of common stock, k_s
e. Target capital structure

10-2 In what sense is the WACC an average cost? A marginal cost?

10-3 How would each of the following affect a firm's cost of debt, $k_d(1 - T)$; its cost of equity, k_s; and its weighted average cost of capital, WACC? Indicate by a plus (+), a minus (−), or a zero (0) if the factor would raise, lower, or have an indeterminate effect on the item in question. Assume other things are held constant. Be prepared to justify your answer, but recognize that several of the parts probably have no single correct answer; these questions are designed to stimulate thought and discussion.

	EFFECT ON		
	$k_d(1-T)$	k_s	WACC
a. The corporate tax rate is lowered.	_____	_____	_____
b. The Federal Reserve tightens credit.	_____	_____	_____
c. The firm uses more debt.	_____	_____	_____
d. The dividend payout ratio is increased.	_____	_____	_____
e. The firm doubles the amount of capital it raises during the year.	_____	_____	_____
f. The firm expands into a risky new area.	_____	_____	_____
g. The firm merges with another firm whose earnings are countercyclical to those of the first firm and to the stock market.	_____	_____	_____
h. The stock market falls drastically, and our firm's stock price falls along with the rest.	_____	_____	_____
i. Investors become more risk averse.	_____	_____	_____
j. The firm is an electric utility with a large investment in nuclear plants. Several states propose a ban on nuclear power generation.	_____	_____	_____

10-4 Distinguish between beta (or market) risk, within-firm (or corporate) risk, and stand-alone risk for a potential project. Of the three measures, which is theoretically the most relevant, and why?

10-5 Suppose a firm estimates its cost of capital for the coming year to be 10 percent. What might be reasonable costs of capital for average-risk, high-risk, and low-risk projects?

Self-Test Problem (Solution Appears in Appendix B)

ST-1
WACC
Longstreet Communications Inc. (LCI) has the following capital structure, which it considers to be optimal:

Debt	25%
Preferred stock	15
Common stock	60
Total capital	100%

LCI's tax rate is 40 percent and investors expect earnings and dividends to grow at a constant rate of 9 percent in the future. LCI paid a dividend of $3.60 per share last year (D_0), and its stock currently sells at a price of $60 per share. Treasury bonds yield 11 percent; an average stock has a 14 percent expected rate of return; and LCI's beta is 1.51. These terms would apply to new security offerings:

Preferred: New preferred could be sold to the public at a price of $100 per share, with a dividend of $11. Flotation costs of $5 per share would be incurred.

Debt: Debt could be sold at an interest rate of 12 percent.

a. Find the component costs of debt, preferred stock, and common stock. Assume LCI does not have to issue any additional shares of common stock.
b. What is the WACC?

Problems

10-1
Cost of Equity
David Ortiz Motors has a target capital structure of 40 percent debt and 60 percent equity. The yield to maturity on the company's outstanding bonds is 9 percent, and the company's tax rate is

40 percent. Ortiz's CFO has calculated the company's WACC as 9.96 percent. What is the company's cost of equity capital?

10-2
Cost of Preferred Stock

Tunney Industries can issue perpetual preferred stock at a price of $50 a share. The issue is expected to pay a constant annual dividend of $3.80 a share. The flotation cost on the issue is estimated to be 5 percent. What is the company's cost of preferred stock, k_{ps}?

10-3
Cost of Equity

Javits & Sons' common stock is currently trading at $30 a share. The stock is expected to pay a dividend of $3.00 a share at the end of the year ($D_1 = \$3.00$), and the dividend is expected to grow at a constant rate of 5 percent a year. What is the cost of common equity?

10-4
After-Tax Cost of Debt

Calculate the after-tax cost of debt under each of the following conditions:
a. Interest rate, 13 percent; tax rate, 0 percent.
b. Interest rate, 13 percent; tax rate, 20 percent.
c. Interest rate, 13 percent; tax rate, 35 percent.

10-5
After-Tax Cost of Debt

The Heuser Company's currently outstanding 10 percent coupon bonds have a yield to maturity of 12 percent. Heuser believes it could issue at par new bonds that would provide a similar yield to maturity. If its marginal tax rate is 35 percent, what is Heuser's after-tax cost of debt?

10-6
Cost of Preferred Stock

Trivoli Industries plans to issue some $100 par preferred stock with an 11 percent dividend. The stock is selling on the market for $97.00, and Trivoli must pay flotation costs of 5 percent of the market price. What is the cost of the preferred stock for Trivoli?

10-7
After-Tax Cost of Debt

A company's 6 percent coupon rate, semiannual payment, $1,000 par value bond which matures in 30 years sells at a price of $515.16. The company's federal-plus-state tax rate is 40 percent. What is the firm's component cost of debt for purposes of calculating the WACC? (Hint: Base your answer on the *nominal* rate.)

10-8
Cost of Equity

The earnings, dividends, and stock price of Carpetto Technologies Inc. are expected to grow at 7 percent per year in the future. Carpetto's common stock sells for $23 per share, its last dividend was $2.00, and the company will pay a dividend of $2.14 at the end of the current year.
a. Using the discounted cash flow approach, what is its cost of equity?
b. If the firm's beta is 1.6, the risk-free rate is 9 percent, and the expected return on the market is 13 percent, what will be the firm's cost of equity using the CAPM approach?
c. If the firm's bonds earn a return of 12 percent, what will k_s be using the bond-yield-plus-risk-premium approach? (Hint: Use the midpoint of the risk premium range.)
d. On the basis of the results of Parts a through c, what would you estimate Carpetto's cost of equity to be?

10-9
Cost of Equity

The Bouchard Company's EPS was $6.50 in 1998 and $4.42 in 1993. The company pays out 40 percent of its earnings as dividends, and the stock sells for $36.
a. Calculate the past growth rate in earnings. (Hint: This is a 5-year growth period.)
b. Calculate the *next* expected dividend per share, D_1. ($D_0 = 0.4(\$6.50) = \$2.60$.) Assume that the past growth rate will continue.
c. What is the cost of equity, k_s, for the Bouchard Company?

10-10
Calculation of g and EPS

Sidman Products' stock is currently selling for $60 a share. The firm is expected to earn $5.40 per share this year and to pay a year-end dividend of $3.60.
a. If investors require a 9 percent return, what rate of growth must be expected for Sidman?
b. If Sidman reinvests earnings in projects whose average return is equal to the stock's expected rate of return, what will be next year's EPS? [Hint: $g = b(ROE)$, where b = fraction of earnings reinvested.]

10-11
WACC Estimation

On January 1, the total market value of the Tysseland Company was $60 million. During the year, the company plans to raise and invest $30 million in new projects. The firm's present market value capital structure, shown below, is considered to be optimal. Assume that there is no short-term debt.

Debt	$30,000,000
Common equity	30,000,000
Total capital	$60,000,000

New bonds will have an 8 percent coupon rate, and they will be sold at par. Common stock is currently selling at $30 a share. Stockholders' required rate of return is estimated to be 12 percent, consisting of a dividend yield of 4 percent and an expected constant growth rate of 8 percent.

(The next expected dividend is $1.20, so $1.20/$30 = 4%.) The marginal corporate tax rate is 40 percent.

a. To maintain the present capital structure, how much of the new investment must be financed by common equity?

b. Assume that there is sufficient cash flow such that Tysseland can maintain its target capital structure without issuing additional shares of equity. What is the WACC?

c. Suppose now that there is not enough internal cash flow and the firm must issue new shares of stock. Qualitatively speaking, what will happen to the WACC?

10-12
WACC Estimation

The following tabulation gives earnings per share figures for Pappas Manufacturing during the preceding 10 years. The firm's common stock, 140,000 shares outstanding, is now selling for $50 a share, and the expected dividend for the coming year (1999) is 50 percent of EPS for the year. Investors expect past trends to continue, so g may be based on the historical earnings growth rate.

YEAR	EPS
1989	$2.00
1990	2.16
1991	2.33
1992	2.52
1993	2.72
1994	2.94
1995	3.18
1996	3.43
1997	3.70
1998	4.00

The current interest rate on new debt is 8 percent. The firm's marginal federal-plus-state tax rate is 40 percent. The firm's market value capital structure, considered to be optimal, is as follows:

Debt	$ 3,000,000
Common equity	7,000,000
Total capital	$10,000,000

a. Calculate the firm's after-tax cost of new debt and of common equity, assuming new equity comes only from reinvested cash flow. Calculate the cost of equity, assuming constant growth; that is, $\hat{k}_s = D_1/P_0 + g = k_s$.

b. Find the firm's WACC, assuming no new common stock is sold.

10-13
Market Value Capital Structure

Suppose the Schoof Company has this *book value* balance sheet:

Current assets	$30,000,000	Current liabilities	$10,000,000
Fixed assets	50,000,000	Long-term debt	30,000,000
		Common equity	
		Common stock (1 million shares)	1,000,000
		Retained earnings	39,000,000
Total assets	$80,000,000	Total claims	$80,000,000

The current liabilities consist entirely of notes payable to banks, and the interest rate on this debt is 10 percent, the same as the rate on new bank loans. The long-term debt consists of 30,000 bonds, each of which has a par value of $1,000, carries an annual coupon interest rate of 6 percent, and matures in 20 years. The going rate of interest on new long-term debt, k_d, is 10 percent, and this is the present yield to maturity on the bonds. The common stock sells at a price of $60 per share. Calculate the firm's market value capital structure.

10-14
Cost of Equity
Estimation Methods

You have just estimated the cost of equity for Shrieves Shipping Company using all three estimation techniques. The results are summarized in the following table:

METHOD	k_s ESTIMATE
CAPM	12.1%
DCF	14.0
Bond-yield-plus-risk-premium	15.4

The inconsistency of the results is worrisome, but you must still develop your equity cost estimate. What factors might you consider as you attempt to place confidence in the above estimates?

10-15
WACC Estimation

A summary of the balance sheet of Travellers Inn Inc. (TII), a company which was formed by
merging a number of regional motel chains and which hopes to rival Holiday Inn on the national
scene, is shown in the table:

TRAVELLERS INN: DECEMBER 31, 1998 (MILLIONS OF DOLLARS)

Cash	$ 10	Accounts payable	$ 10
Accounts receivable	20	Accruals	10
Inventories	20	Short-term debt	5
Current assets	$ 50	Current liabilities	$ 25
Net fixed assets	50	Long-term debt	30
		Preferred stock	5
		Common equity	
		Common stock	$ 10
		Retained earnings	30
		Total common equity	$ 40
Total assets	$100	Total liabilities and equity	$100

These facts are also given for TII:
(1) Short-term debt consists of bank loans which currently cost 10 percent, with interest
payable quarterly. These loans are used to finance receivables and inventories on a seasonal
basis, so in the off-season, bank loans are zero.
(2) The long-term debt consists of 20-year, semiannual payment mortgage bonds with a coupon
rate of 8 percent. Currently, these bonds provide a yield to investors of $k_d = 12\%$. If new
bonds were sold, they would yield investors 12 percent.
(3) TII's perpetual preferred stock has a $100 par value, pays a quarterly dividend of $2, and has
a yield to investors of 11 percent. New perpetual preferred would have to provide the same
yield to investors, and the company would incur a 5 percent flotation cost to sell it.
(4) The company has 4 million shares of common stock outstanding. $P_0 = \$20$, but the stock has
recently traded in a range of $17 to $23. $D_0 = \$1$ and $EPS_0 = \$2$. ROE based on average equity
was 24 percent in 1998, but management expects to increase this return on equity to 30 percent; however, security analysts are not aware of management's optimism in this regard.
(5) Betas, as reported by security analysts, range from 1.3 to 1.7; the T-bond rate is 10 percent;
and k_M is estimated by various brokerage houses to be in the range of 14.5 to 15.5 percent.
Brokerage house reports forecast growth rates in the range of 10 to 15 percent over the foreseeable future. However, some analysts do not explicitly forecast growth rates, but they indicate to their clients that they expect TII's historical trends as shown in the table below to
continue.
(6) At a recent conference, TII's financial vice-president polled some pension fund investment
managers on the minimum rate of return they would have to expect on TII's common to
make them willing to buy the common rather than TII bonds, when the bonds yielded 12
percent. The responses suggested a risk premium over TII bonds of 4 to 6 percentage points.
(7) TII is in the 40 percent federal-plus-state tax bracket.
(8) TII's principal investment banker, Henry, Kaufman & Company, predicts a decline in interest rates, with k_d falling to 10 percent and the T-bond rate to 8 percent, although Henry,

Kaufman & Company acknowledges that an increase in the expected inflation rate could lead to an increase rather than a decrease in rates.

(9) Here is the historical record of EPS and DPS:

YEAR	EPS[a]	DPS[a]	YEAR	EPS[a]	DPS[a]
1984	$0.09	$0.00	1992	$0.78	$0.00
1985	−0.20	0.00	1993	0.80	0.00
1986	0.40	0.00	1994	1.20	0.20
1987	0.52	0.00	1995	0.95	0.40
1988	0.10	0.00	1996	1.30	0.60
1989	0.57	0.00	1997	1.60	0.80
1990	0.61	0.00	1998	2.00	1.00
1991	0.70	0.00			

[a]Adjusted for a 2:1 stock split in 1988, a 3:1 split in 1996, and 10 percent stock dividends in 1985 and 1993.

Assume that you are a recently hired financial analyst, and your boss, the treasurer, has asked you to estimate the company's WACC; assume no new equity will be issued. Your cost of capital should be appropriate for use in evaluating projects which are in the same risk class as the firm's average assets now on books.

MINI CASE

During the last few years, Cox Technologies has been too constrained by the high cost of capital to make many capital investments. Recently, though, capital costs have been declining, and the company has decided to look seriously at a major expansion program that had been proposed by the marketing department. Assume that you are an assistant to Jerry Lee, the financial vice-president. Your first task is to estimate Cox's cost of capital. Lee has provided you with the following data, which he believes may be relevant to your task:

(1) The firm's tax rate is 40 percent.

(2) The current price of Cox's 12 percent coupon, semiannual payment, noncallable bonds with 15 years remaining to maturity is $1,153.72. Cox does not use short-term interest-bearing debt on a permanent basis. New bonds would be privately placed with no flotation cost.

(3) The current price of the firm's 10 percent, $100 par value, quarterly dividend, perpetual preferred stock is $113.10. Cox would incur flotation costs of $2.00 per share on a new issue.

(4) Cox's common stock is currently selling at $50 per share. Its last dividend (D_0) was $4.19, and dividends are expected to grow at a constant rate of 5 percent in the foreseeable future. Cox's beta is 1.2, the yield on T-bonds is 7 percent, and the market risk premium is estimated to be 6 percent. For the bond-yield-plus-risk-premium approach, the firm uses a 4 percentage point risk premium.

(5) Cox's target capital structure is 30 percent long-term debt, 10 percent preferred stock, and 60 percent common equity.

To structure the task somewhat, Lee has asked you to answer the following questions.

a. (1) What sources of capital should be included when you estimate Cox's weighted average cost of capital (WACC)?

(2) Should the component costs be figured on a before-tax or an after-tax basis?

(3) Should the costs be historical (embedded) costs or new (marginal) costs?

b. What is the market interest rate on Cox's debt and its component cost of debt?

c. (1) What is the firm's cost of preferred stock?

(2) Cox's preferred stock is riskier to investors than its debt, yet the preferred's yield to investors is lower than the yield to maturity on the debt. Does this suggest that you have made a mistake? (Hint: Think about taxes.)

d. (1) What are the two primary ways companies raise common equity?

(2) Why is there a cost associated with reinvested earnings?

(3) Cox doesn't plan to issue new shares of common stock. Using the CAPM approach, what is Cox's estimated cost of equity?

   e. (1) What is the estimated cost of equity using the discounted cash flow (DCF) approach?
      (2) Suppose the firm has historically earned 15 percent on equity (ROE) and retained 35 percent of earnings, and investors expect this situation to continue in the future. How could you use this information to estimate the future dividend growth rate, and what growth rate would you get? Is this consistent with the 5 percent growth rate given earlier?
      (3) Could the DCF method be applied if the growth rate was not constant? How?
   f. What is the cost of equity based on the bond-yield-plus-risk-premium method?
   g. What is your final estimate for the cost of equity, k_s?
   h. What is Cox's weighted average cost of capital (WACC)?
   i. What are four common mistakes in estimating the WACC that Cox should avoid?
   j. What are the three types of risk, and which is most relevant for estimating the cost of capital?
   k. What are two ways to estimate divisional betas?
   l. Should Cox use the same cost of capital for all projects? How might it adjust the cost of capital for different projects?

Selected Additional References and Cases

For a comprehensive treatment of the cost of capital, see

Ehrhardt, Michael C., *The Search for Value: Measuring the Company's Cost of Capital* (Boston: Harvard Business School Press, 1994).

The following articles provide some valuable insights into the CAPM approach to estimating the cost of equity:

Beaver, William H., Paul Kettler, and Myron Scholes, "The Association between Market Determined and Accounting Determined Risk Measures," *Accounting Review,* October 1970, 654–682.

Bowman, Robert G., "The Theoretical Relationship between Systematic Risk and Financial (Accounting) Variables," *Journal of Finance,* June 1979, 617–630.

Chen, Carl R., "Time-Series Analysis of Beta Stationarity and Its Determinants: A Case of Public Utilities," *Financial Management,* Autumn 1982, 64–70.

Cooley, Philip L., "A Review of the Use of Beta in Regulatory Proceedings," *Financial Management,* Winter 1981, 75–81.

The weighted average cost of capital as described in this chapter is widely used in both industry and academic circles. It has been criticized on several counts, but to date it has withstood the challenges. See the following articles:

Arditti, Fred D., and Haim Levy, "The Weighted Average Cost of Capital as a Cutoff Rate: A Critical Examination of the Classical Textbook Weighted Average," *Financial Management,* Fall 1977, 24–34.

Beranek, William, "The Weighted Average Cost of Capital and Shareholder Wealth Maximization," *Journal of Financial and Quantitative Analysis,* March 1977, 17–32.

Boudreaux, Kenneth J., and Hugh W. Long; John R. Ezzell and R. Burr Porter; Moshe Ben Horim; and Alan C. Shapiro, "The Weighted Average Cost of Capital: A Discussion," *Financial Management,* Summer 1979, 7–23.

Reilly, Raymond R., and William E. Wacker, "On the Weighted Average Cost of Capital," *Journal of Financial and Quantitative Analysis,* January 1973, 123–126.

Some other works that are relevant include the following:

Alberts, W. W., and Stephen H. Archer, "Some Evidence on the Effect of Company Size on the Cost of Equity Capital," *Journal of Financial and Quantitative Analysis,* March 1973, 229–242.

Amihud, Yakov, and Haim Mendelson, "Liquidity and Cost of Capital: Implications for Corporate Management," *Journal of Applied Corporate Finance,* Fall 1989, 65–73.

Brigham, Eugene F., Dilip K. Shome, and Steve R. Vinson, "The Risk Premium Approach to Measuring a Utility's Cost of Equity," *Financial Management,* Spring 1985, 33–45.

Chen, Andrew, "Recent Developments in the Cost of Debt Capital," *Journal of Finance*, June 1978, 863–883.

Harris, Robert S., "Using Analysts' Growth Forecasts to Estimate Shareholder Required Rates of Return," *Financial Management*, Spring 1986, 58–67.

Harris, Robert S., and Felecia C. Marston, "Estimating Shareholder Risk Premia Using Analysts' Growth Forecasts," *Financial Management*, Summer 1992, 63–70.

Myers, Stewart C., "Interactions of Corporate Financing and Investments Decisions—Implications for Capital Budgeting," *Journal of Finance*, March 1974, 1–25.

Nantell, Timothy J., and C. Robert Carlson, "The Cost of Capital as a Weighted Average," *Journal of Finance*, December 1975, 1343–1355.

Siegal, Jeremy J., "The Application of DCF Methodology for Determining the Cost of Equity Capital," *Financial Management*, Spring 1985, 46–53.

Taggart, Robert A., Jr., "Consistent Valuation and Cost of Capital Expressions with Corporate and Personal Taxes," *Financial Management*, Autumn 1991, 8–20.

Timme, Stephen G., and Peter C. Eisemann, "On the Use of Consensus Forecasts of Growth in the Constant Growth Model: The Case of Electric Utilities," *Financial Management*, Winter 1989, 23–35.

For some insights into the cost of capital techniques used by major firms, see

Gitman, Lawrence J., and Vincent A. Mercurio, "Cost of Capital Techniques Used by Major U.S. Firms: Survey and Analysis of Fortune's 1000," *Financial Management*, Winter 1982, 21–29.

Additional references on the cost of capital are cited in Chapters 6, 12, and 13.

The following cases in the Cases in Financial Management: Dryden Request *series cover concepts related to the cost of capital:*

Case 4A, "West Coast Semiconductor;" Case 4B, "Ace Repair;" Case 4C, "Premier Paint & Body;" Case 6, "Randolph Corporation;" and Case 57, "Auto Hut."

EXTENSIONS

Flotation Costs and the Marginal Cost of Capital Schedule

As we noted earlier in the chapter, most debt is privately placed, and most equity is raised internally as retained earnings. In these cases, there are no flotation costs, hence the component costs of debt and equity should be estimated as discussed in the chapter. But if companies issue debt or new stock to the public, then the issue of flotation costs can become important. In the following sections, we explain how to estimate the component costs of publicly issued debt and stock, and we show how these new component costs affect the marginal cost of capital.

Axis Goods Inc., a retailer of trendy sportswear, has a target capital structure of 45 percent debt, 2 percent preferred stock, and 53 percent common stock. Its common stock sells for $23, the next expected dividend is $1.24, and the expected constant growth rate is 8 percent. Based on the constant growth DCF model, Axis' cost of common equity is $k_s = 13.4\%$ when the equity is raised as retained earnings. Axis' cost of preferred stock is 10.3 percent, based on the method discussed in the chapter, which incorporates flotation costs. In the following sections, we examine the effects of flotation costs on the component costs of debt and common stock, and on the marginal cost of capital.

Flotation Costs and the Component Cost of Debt.   Axis can issue a 30-year, $1,000 par value bond with an interest rate of 10 percent, paid annually. Here, T = 40%, so the after-tax component cost of debt is $k_d(1.0 - 0.4)10\% = 6.0\%$. However, if Axis must incur flotation costs, F, of 1 percent of the value of the issue, then this formula must be used to find the after-tax cost of debt:

$$M(1 - F) = \sum_{t=1}^{N} \frac{INT(1 - T)}{(1 + k_d)^t} + \frac{M}{(1 + k_d)^N}.$$

Here M is the bond's maturity value, F is the flotation percentage, N is the bond's maturity, T is the firm's tax rate, INT is the dollars of interest per period, and k_d is the after-tax cost of debt adjusted for flotation. With a financial calculator, enter N = 30, PV = −990, PMT = 60, and FV = 1000. Solving for I, we find I = $k_d(1 - T)$ = 6.07%, which is the after-tax component cost of debt. Notice that the 6.07 percent theoretically correct after-tax cost of debt is quite close to the original 6.00 percent after-tax cost, so in this instance adjusting for flotation doesn't make much difference.

However, the flotation adjustment would be higher if F were larger or the bond's life were shorter. For example, if F was 10 percent rather than 1 percent, then the flotation-adjusted $k_d(1 - T)$ would have been 6.79 percent. With N at 1 year rather than 30 years, and F still equal to 1 percent, then $k_d(1 - T) =$ 7.07%. Finally, if $F = 10\%$ and $N = 1$, then $k_d(1 - T) = 17.78\%$, in which case the differential would be far too high to ignore.

Strictly speaking, the after-tax cost of debt should reflect the *expected* cost of debt. While Axis' bonds have a promised return of 10 percent, there is some chance of default, so its bondholders' expected return (and consequently Axis' cost) is a bit less than 10 percent. However, for a relatively strong company such as Axis, this difference is quite small. Note too that, as we saw earlier, flotation costs raise the true costs of debt, while default possibilities lower the true cost. Since these two factors have opposite effects, ignoring both of them is, to some extent, a situation where "two wrongs make a right." Therefore, if F is relatively low, N is relatively long, and the risk of default is not very high (as is typically true when firms issue debt to the public), then the unadjusted $k_d(1 - T)$ is generally a good approximation of the cost of debt. Also, as we shall see in subsequent chapters, the cost of capital is used to discount capital budgeting cash flows, those cash flows are generally uncertain (hence measured with a large amount of error), and it is generally not terribly important to measure one number (the cost of capital) out to four-decimal-place accuracy when some other number in the equation (the cash flows to be discounted) is subject to extremely large errors. For this reason, few people in the real world spend a lot of time worrying about flotation adjustments, except when they are high.

Cost of Newly Issued Common Stock, or External Equity, k_e.

The **cost of new common equity, k_e,** or external equity, is higher than the cost of retained earnings, k_s, because of flotation costs involved in issuing new common stock. What rate of return must be earned on funds raised by selling stock to make issuing new stock worthwhile? To put it another way, what is the cost of new common stock?

The answer, for a constant growth stock, is found by applying this formula:[1]

$$k_e = \frac{D_1}{P_0(1 - F)} + g. \qquad (10E\text{-}1)$$

Here F is the percentage **flotation cost** incurred in selling the new stock, so $P_0(1 - F)$ is the net price per share received by the company.

Assuming that Axis has a flotation cost of 10 percent, its cost of new outside equity is computed as follows:

$$k_e = \frac{\$1.24}{\$23(1 - 0.10)} + 8.0\%$$

$$= \frac{\$1.24}{\$20.70} + 8.0\%$$

$$= 6.0\% + 8.0\% = 14.0\%.$$

Investors require a return of $k_s = 13.4\%$ on the stock. However, because of flotation costs the company must earn *more* than 13.4 percent on the net funds obtained by selling stock if investors are to receive a 13.4 percent return on the money they put up. Specifically, if the firm earns 14 percent on funds obtained by issuing new stock, then earnings per share will remain at the previously expected level, the firm's expected dividend can be maintained, and, as a result, the price per share will not decline. If the firm earns less than 14 percent, then earnings, dividends, and growth will fall below expectations, causing the stock price to decline. If the firm earns more than 14 percent, the stock price will rise.[2]

---

[1]Equation 10E-1 is derived as follows:

Step 1. The old stockholders expect the firm to pay a stream of dividends, D_t, which will be derived from existing assets with a per-share value of P_0. New investors will likewise expect to receive the same stream of dividends, but the funds available to invest in assets will be less than P_0 because of flotation costs. For new investors to receive their expected dividend stream *without impairing the D_t stream of the old investors,* the new funds obtained from the sale of stock must be invested at a return high enough to provide a dividend stream whose present value is equal to the net price the firm will receive:

$$P_n = P_0(1 - F) = \sum_{t=1}^{\infty} \frac{D_t}{(1 + k_e)^t}. \qquad (10E\text{-}2)$$

Here D_t is the dividend stream to new (and old) stockholders, and k_e is the cost of new outside equity.

Step 2. When growth is constant, Equation 10E-2 reduces to

$$P_n = P_0(1 - F) = \frac{D_1}{k_e - g}. \qquad (10E\text{-}2a)$$

Step 3. Equation 10E-2a can be rearranged to produce Equation 10E-1:

$$k_e = \frac{D_1}{P_0(1 - F)} + g.$$

[2]On occasion it is useful to use another equation to calculate the cost of external equity:

$$k_e = \frac{\text{Dividend yield}}{(1 - F)} + g = \frac{D_1/P_0}{(1 - F)} + g. \qquad (10E\text{-}1a)$$

Equation 10E-1a is derived algebraically from Equation 10E-1, and it is useful when information on dividend yields, but not on dollar dividends and stock prices, is available.

The reason for the flotation adjustment can be made clear by a simple example. Suppose Weaver Candy Company has $100,000 of assets and no debt, it earns a 15 percent return (or $15,000) on its assets, and it pays all earnings out as dividends, so its growth rate is zero. The company has 1,000 shares of stock outstanding, so EPS = DPS = $15, and P_0 = $100. Weaver's cost of equity is thus k_s = $15/$100 + 0 = 15%. Now suppose Weaver can get a return of 15 percent on new assets. Should it sell new stock to acquire new assets? If it sold 1,000 new shares of stock to the public for $100 per share, but incurred a 10 percent flotation cost on the issue, it would net $100 − 0.10($100) = $90 per share, or $90,000 in total. It would then invest this $90,000 and earn 15 percent, or $13,500. Its new total earnings would be $15,000 from the old assets plus $13,500 from the new assets, or $28,500 in total, but it would now have 2,000 shares of stock outstanding. Therefore, its EPS and DPS would decline from $15 to $14.25:

$$\text{New EPS and DPS} = \frac{\$28,500}{2,000} = \$14.25.$$

Because its EPS and DPS would fall, the stock price also would fall, from P_0 = $100 to P_1 = $14.25/0.15 = $95.00. This result occurs because while investors put up $100 per share, the company received and invested only $90 per share. Thus, we see that the $90 must earn more than 15 percent to provide investors with a 15 percent return on the $100 they put up. Put another way, dollars raised by selling new stock must "work harder" than dollars raised by retaining earnings.

Now suppose Weaver earned a return of k_e based on Equation 10E-1 on the $90,000 of new assets:

$$k_e = \frac{D_1}{P_0(1 - F)} + g$$

$$= \frac{\$15}{\$100(0.90)} + 0 = 16.667\%.$$

Here is the new situation:

$$\text{New total earnings} = \$15,000 + \$90,000(0.16667)$$
$$= \$15,000 + \$15,000$$
$$= \$30,000.$$

$$\text{New EPS and DPS} = \$30,000/2,000 = \$15.$$
$$\text{New price} = \$15/0.15 = \$100 = \text{Original price.}$$

Thus, if the return on the new assets is equal to k_e as calculated by Equation 10E-1, then EPS, DPS, and the stock price will all remain constant. If the return on the new assets exceeds k_e, then EPS, DPS, and P_0 will rise. This confirms the fact that because of flotation costs, the cost of external equity exceeds the cost of equity raised internally from retained earnings.

How Much Does It Cost to Raise External Capital? A recent study by four professors provides some insights into how much it costs U.S. corporations to raise external capital. Using information from the Securities Data Company, they found the average flotation cost for debt and equity issued in the 1990s as presented in Table 10E-1.

The common stock flotation costs are for non-IPOs. Costs associated with IPOs are even higher—flotation costs are about 17 percent of gross proceeds for common equity if the amount raised is less than $10 million and about 6 percent if more than $500 million is raised. The data include both utility and nonutility companies. If utilities were excluded, flotation costs would be somewhat higher.

Marginal Cost of Capital, MCC. The *marginal cost* of any item is the cost of another unit of that item. For example, the marginal cost of labor is the cost of adding one additional worker. The marginal cost of labor may be $25 per person if 10 workers are added but $35 per person if the firm tries to hire 100 new workers, because it will be harder to

TABLE 10E-1   Average Flotation Costs for Debt and Equity

Amount of Capital Raised (Millions of Dollars)	Average Flotation Cost for Common Stock (% of Total Capital Raised)	Average Flotation Cost for New Debt (% of Total Capital Raised)
2–9.99	13.28	4.39
10–19.99	8.72	2.76
20–39.99	6.93	2.42
40–59.99	5.87	1.32
60–79.99	5.18	2.34
80–99.99	4.73	2.16
100–199.99	4.22	2.31
200–499.99	3.47	2.19
500 and up	3.15	1.64

SOURCE: Inmoo Lee, Scott Lochhead, Jay Ritter, and Quanshui Zhao, "The Costs of Raising Capital," *The Journal of Financial Research*, Vol. XIX, No. 1, Spring 1996, 59–74. Reprinted with permission.

find 100 people willing and able to do the work. The same concept applies to capital. As the firm tries to attract more new dollars, the cost of each dollar will at some point rise. *Thus, the* **marginal cost of capital (MCC)** *is defined as the cost of the last dollar of new capital the firm raises, and the marginal cost rises as more and more capital is raised during a given period.*

We can use Axis Goods to illustrate the marginal cost of capital concept. The company's target capital structure and other data follow:

Long-term debt	$ 754,000,000	45%
Preferred stock	40,000,000	2
Common equity	896,000,000	53
Total capital	$1,690,000,000	100%

$k_d = 10\%$.

$k_{ps} = 10.3\%$.

$T = 40\%$.

$P_0 = \$23$.

$g = 8\%$, and it is expected to remain constant.

$D_0 = \$1.15 =$ dividends per share in the *last* period. D_0 has already been paid, so someone who purchased this stock today would *not* receive D_0 — rather, he or she would receive D_1, the *next* dividend.

$D_1 = D_0(1 + g) = \$1.15(1.08) = \$1.24$.

$k_s = D_1/P_0 + g = (\$1.24/\$23) + 0.08 = 0.054 + 0.08 = 0.134$
$= 13.4\%$.

On the basis of these data, the weighted average cost of capital, WACC, is 10 percent:

$$\text{WACC} = \begin{pmatrix}\text{Fraction}\\\text{of}\\\text{debt}\end{pmatrix}\begin{pmatrix}\text{Interest}\\\text{rate}\end{pmatrix}(1 - T)$$
$$+ \begin{pmatrix}\text{Fraction}\\\text{of}\\\text{preferred}\\\text{stock}\end{pmatrix}\begin{pmatrix}\text{Cost}\\\text{of}\\\text{preferred}\\\text{stock}\end{pmatrix}$$
$$+ \begin{pmatrix}\text{Fraction of}\\\text{common}\\\text{equity}\end{pmatrix}\begin{pmatrix}\text{Cost}\\\text{of}\\\text{equity}\end{pmatrix}$$
$$= (0.45)(10\%)(0.6) + (0.02)(10.3\%) + (0.53)(13.4\%)$$
$$= 2.7\% + 0.2\% + 7.1\%$$
$$= 10.0\%.$$

Note that short-term debt is not included in the capital structure. Axis uses its cost of capital in the capital budgeting process, which involves long-term assets, and it finances those assets with long-term capital. Thus, current liabilities do not enter the calculation. We discuss this point in more detail in Chapters 15 and 16.[3]

As long as Axis keeps its capital structure on target, and as long as its debt has an after-tax cost of 6 percent, its preferred stock a cost of 10.3 percent, and its common equity a cost of 13.4 percent, then its weighted average cost of capital will be WACC = 10%. Each dollar the firm raises will consist of some long-term debt, some preferred stock, and some common equity, and the cost of the whole dollar will be 10 percent.

A graph which shows how the WACC changes as more and more new capital is raised during a given year is called the **marginal cost of capital schedule.** The graph shown in Figure 10E-1 is Axis MCC schedule. Here the dots represent dollars raised. Because each dollar of new capital has a cost of 10 percent, the marginal cost of capital (MCC) for Axis is constant at 10 percent under the assumptions we have used thus far.[4]

The New Equity Break Point. Could Axis raise an unlimited amount of new capital at the 10 percent cost? The answer is no. As a practical matter, as a company raises larger and larger sums during a given time period, the costs of debt, preferred stock, and common equity begin to rise, and as this occurs, the weighted average cost of each new dollar also rises. Thus, just as corporations cannot hire unlimited numbers of workers at a constant wage, they cannot raise unlimited amounts of capital at a constant cost. At some point, the cost of each new dollar will increase.

Where will this point occur for Axis? As a first step to determining the point at which the MCC begins to rise, recognize that although the company's balance sheet shows total long-term capital of $1,690,000,000, all of this capital was raised in the past, and it has been invested in assets which are being used in operations. New (or marginal) capital presumably will be raised so as to maintain the 45/2/53 debt/preferred/common relationship. Therefore, if Axis wants to raise $1,000,000 in new capital, it should obtain $450,000 of debt, $20,000 of preferred stock, and $530,000 of common equity. The new common equity could come from two sources: (1) retained earnings, defined as that part of this year's profits which management decides to retain in the business rather than use for dividends (but not earnings retained in the past, for these have already been invested in plant, equipment, inventories, and so on); or (2) proceeds from the sale of new common stock.

The debt will have an interest rate of 10 percent and an after-tax cost of 6 percent, and the preferred stock will have a cost of 10.3 percent. *The cost of common equity will be $k_s = 13.4\%$ as long as the equity is obtained as retained earnings, but it will jump to $k_e = 14\%$ once the company uses up all of its retained earnings and is thus forced to sell new common stock.*

---

[3]Also see Eugene F. Brigham and Louis C. Gapenski, *Intermediate Financial Management*, 5th ed., Chapter 6.

[4]Axis' MCC schedule in Figure 10E-1 would be different (higher) if the company used any capital structure other than 45 percent debt, 2 percent preferred, and 53 percent common equity. This point will be developed in Chapters 15 and 16. As a general rule, a different MCC schedule exists for every possible capital structure, and the optimal structure is the one that produces the lowest MCC schedule.

FIGURE 10E-1   Marginal Cost of Capital (MCC) Schedule for Axis Goods Inc.

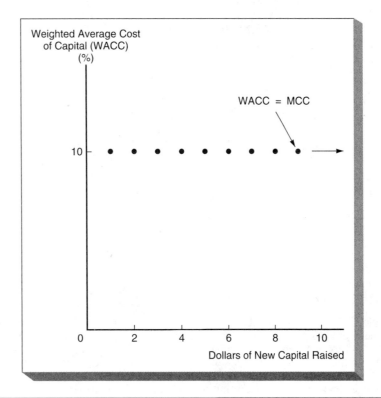

Axis' weighted average cost of capital, when it uses new retained earnings (earnings retained this year, not in the past) and also when it uses new common stock, is shown in Table 10E-2. We see that the weighted average cost of each dollar is 10 percent as long as retained earnings are used, but the WACC jumps to 10.3 percent as soon as the firm exhausts its retained earnings and is forced to sell new common stock.

How much new capital can Axis raise before it exhausts its retained earnings and is forced to sell new common stock; that is, where will an increase in the MCC schedule occur? We find this point as follows:[5]

1. Assume that the company expects to have total earnings of $137.8 million in 1998. Further, it has a target payout ratio of 45 percent, so it plans to pay out 45 percent of its earnings as dividends. Thus, the retained earnings for the year are projected to be $137.8(1.0 − 0.45) = $75.8 million.

2. We know that Axis expects to have $75.8 million of retained earnings for the year. We also know that if the company is to remain at its optimal capital structure, it must raise each dollar as 45 cents of debt, 2 cents of preferred, and 53 cents of common equity. Therefore, each 53 cents of retained earnings will support $1 of capital, and the $75.8 million of retained earnings will not be exhausted, hence

the WACC will not rise, until $75.8 million of retained earnings, plus some additional amount of debt and preferred stock, have been used up.

3. We now want to know how much *total new capital* — debt, preferred stock, and retained earnings — can be raised before the $75.8 million of retained earnings is exhausted and Axis is forced to sell new common stock. In effect, we are seeking some amount of capital, X, which is called a **break point (BP)** and which represents the total financing that can be done before Axis is forced to sell new common stock.

4. We know that 53 percent, or 0.53, of X, the total capital raised, will be retained earnings, whereas 47 percent will be debt plus preferred. We also know that retained earnings will amount to $75.8 million. Therefore,

$$\text{Retained earnings} = 0.53X = \$75,800,000.$$

5. Solving for X, which is the *retained earnings break point,* we obtain $BP_{RE} = \$143$ million:

$$X = BP_{RE} = \frac{\text{Retained earnings}}{\text{Equity fraction}} = \frac{\$75,800,000}{0.53}$$

$$= \$143,018,868 \approx 143 \text{ million.}$$

---

[5]The numbers in this set of calculations are rounded. Since the inputs are estimates, it makes little sense to carry estimates out to very many decimal places — this is "spurious accuracy."

TABLE 10E-2	Axis' WACC Using New Retained Earnings and New Common Stock

I. WACC when Equity Is from New Retained Earnings

	WEIGHT	×	COMPONENT COST	=	PRODUCT
Debt	0.45		6.0%		2.7%
Preferred stock	0.02		10.3		0.2
Common equity (Retained earnings)	0.53		13.4		7.1
	1.00				$WACC_1 = 10.0\%$

II. WACC when Equity Is from Sale of New Common Stock

	WEIGHT	×	COMPONENT COST	=	PRODUCT
Debt	0.45		6.0%		2.7%
Preferred stock	0.02		10.3		0.2
Common equity (New common stock)	0.53		14.0		7.4
	1.00				$WACC_2 = 10.3\%$

6. Thus, given $75.8 million of retained earnings, Axis can raise a total of $143 million, consisting of 0.53 ($143 million) = $75.8 million of retained earnings plus 0.02($143 million) = $2.9 million of preferred stock plus 0.45($143 million) = $64.3 million of new debt supported by these new retained earnings, without altering its capital structure (dollars in millions):

New debt supported by retained earnings	$64.3	45%
Preferred stock supported by retained earnings	2.9	2
Retained earnings	75.8	53
Total capital supported by retained earnings, or break point for retained earnings	$143.0	100%

7. The value of X, or BP_{RE} = $143 million, is defined as the *retained earnings break point,* and it is the amount of total capital at which a break, or jump, occurs in the MCC schedule.

Figure 10E-2 graphs Axis' marginal cost of capital schedule with the retained earnings break point. Each dollar has a weighted average cost of 10 percent until the company has raised a total of $143 million. This $143 million will consist of $64.3 million of new debt with an after-tax cost of 6 percent, $2.9 million of preferred stock with a cost of 10.3 percent, and $75.8 million of retained earnings with a cost of 13.4 percent. However, if Axis raises one dollar over $143 million, each new dollar will contain 53 cents of equity *obtained by selling new common equity at a cost of 14 percent;* therefore, WACC jumps from 10 percent to 10.3 percent, as calculated back in Table 10E-2.

Note that we don't really think the MCC jumps by precisely 0.3 percent when we raise $1 over $143 million. Thus, Figure 10E-2 should be regarded as an approximation rather than as a precise representation of reality.

The MCC Schedule beyond the Break Point.   There is a jump, or break, in Axis' MCC schedule at $143 million of new capital. Could there be other breaks in the schedule? Yes, there could. The cost of capital could also rise due to increases in the cost of debt or the cost of preferred stock, or as a result of further increases in flotation costs as the firm issues more and more common stock. Some people have asserted that the costs of capital components other than common stock should not rise. Their argument is that as long as the capital structure does not change, and presuming that the firm uses new capital to invest in projects with the same expected return and degree of risk as its existing projects, investors should be willing to invest unlimited amounts of additional capital at the same rate. However, this argument is not borne out in empirical studies. In practice, the demand curve for securities is downward sloping, so the more securities issued during a given period, (1) the lower the price received for the securities and (2) the higher the required rate of return. Therefore, the more new financing required, the higher the firm's WACC.

As a result of all this, firms face increasing MCC schedules, such as the one shown in Figure 10E-2. Here we have identified a specific retained earnings break point, but because of estimation difficulties, we have not attempted to identify precisely any additional break points. Moreover, we have (1) shown the MCC schedule to be upward sloping, reflecting a positive relationship between capital raised and capital costs, and (2) we indicate our inability to measure these costs precisely by using a band of costs rather than a single line. Note that this band exists over the whole range of capital raised — our component costs are only estimates, these estimates become more uncertain as the firm requires more and more capital, and thus the band widens as the amount of new capital raised increases.

Using the MCC in Capital Budgeting.   As noted at the outset of the chapter, the cost of capital is a key element in the

FIGURE 10E-2   Marginal Cost of Capital Schedule beyond the Break Point for Axis Goods Inc.

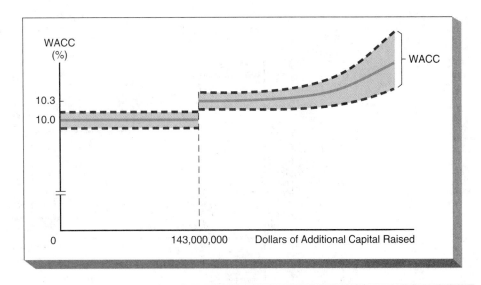

capital budgeting process. In essence, capital budgeting consists of these steps:

1. Identify the set of available investment opportunities.
2. Estimate the future cash flows associated with each project.
3. Find the present value of each future cash flow, discounted at the cost of the capital used to finance the project, and sum these PVs to obtain the total PV of each project.
4. Compare each project's PV with its cost, and accept a project if the PV of its future cash inflows exceeds the cost of the project.

An issue that arises is picking the appropriate point on the marginal cost of capital schedule for use in capital budgeting. As we have seen, every dollar raised by Axis Goods Inc. is a weighted average which consists of 45 cents of debt, 2 cents of preferred stock, and 53 cents of common equity (with the equity coming from retained earnings until they have been used up, and then from the issuance of new common stock). Further, we saw that the WACC is constant for a while, but after the firm has exhausted its least expensive sources of capital, the WACC begins to rise. Thus, the firm has an *MCC schedule* which shows its WACC at different amounts of capital raised; Figure 10E-2 gave Axis' MCC schedule.

Since its cost of capital depends on how much capital the firm raises, just which cost rate should we use in capital budgeting? Put another way, which of the WACC numbers shown in Figure 10E-2 should be used to evaluate an average-risk project? We could use 10.0 percent, 10.3 percent, or some higher number, but which one *should* we use? The answer is based on the concept of marginal analysis as developed in economics. In economics, you learned that firms should expand output to the point where marginal revenue is equal to marginal cost. At that point,

the last unit of output exactly covers its cost—further expansion would reduce profits, while the firm would forgo profits at any lower production rate. Therefore, the firm should expand to the point where its marginal revenue equals its marginal cost.

This same type of analysis is applied in capital budgeting. We have already developed the marginal cost curve—it is the MCC schedule. Now we need to develop a schedule that is analogous to the marginal revenue schedule. This is the **Investment Opportunity Schedule (IOS),** which shows the rate of return expected on each potential investment opportunity. As you will see in the next chapter, rates of return on capital projects are found in essentially the same way as rates of returns on stocks and bonds. Thus, we can calculate an expected rate of return on each potential project, and we can then plot those returns on the same graph that shows our marginal cost of capital. Figure 10E-3 gives such a graph for Axis. Projects A, B, and C all have expected rates of return which exceed the cost of the capital that will be used to finance them, but the expected return on Project D is less than its cost of capital. Therefore, Projects A, B, and C should be accepted, and Project D should be rejected.

The WACC at the point where the Investment Opportunity Schedule intersects the MCC curve is defined as "the corporate cost of capital"—this point reflects the marginal cost of capital to the corporation. In our Figure 10E-3 example, Axis' corporate cost of capital is WACC = 10.3%.

Estimating Inputs for the CAPM and DCF Methods

As we noted in the chapter, it is difficult to estimate the inputs for the CAPM and DCF approaches. The following sections provide guidance in making these estimates.

FIGURE 10E-3   Combining the MCC and IOS Schedules to Determine the Optimal Capital Budget

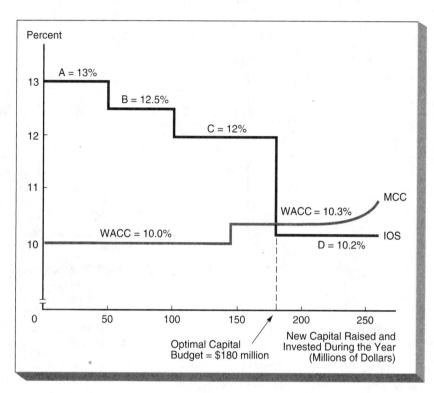

PROJECT	COST (IN MILLIONS)	RATE OF RETURN
A	$50	13.0%
B	50	12.5
C	80	12.0
D	80	10.2

Estimating Inputs for the CAPM. Under the CAPM we assume that the cost of equity is equal to the risk-free rate plus a risk premium that is equal to the stock's beta coefficient times the market risk premium as set forth in the Security Market Line (SML) equation:

$$k_s = \text{Risk-free rate} + \text{Risk premium}$$
$$= k_{RF} + (k_M - k_{RF})b_i.$$

We obtain estimates of (1) the risk-free rate, k_{RF}, (2) the firm's beta, b_i, and (3) the required rate of return on the market, k_M, and then estimate the required rate of return on the firm's stock, k_s. This required return is a measure of the cost of retained earnings.

Estimating the Risk-Free Rate. The starting point for the CAPM cost of equity estimate is k_{RF}, the risk-free rate. There is really no such thing as a truly riskless asset in the U.S. economy. Treasury securities are essentially free of default risk, but long-term T-bonds will suffer capital losses if

interest rates rise, and a portfolio of short-term T-bills will provide a volatile earnings stream because the rate earned on T-bills varies over time.

Since we cannot in practice find a truly riskless rate upon which to base the CAPM, what rate should we use? Our preference—and this preference is shared by most practitioners—is to use the rate on long-term Treasury bonds. Here are our reasons:

1. Capital market rates include a real, riskless rate (generally thought to vary from 2 to 4 percent) plus a premium for inflation which reflects the expected inflation rate over the life of the security, be it 30 days or 40 years. The expected rate of inflation is likely to be relatively high during booms and low during recessions. Therefore, during booms T-bill rates tend to be high to reflect the high current inflation rate, whereas in recessions T-bill rates are generally low. T-bond rates, on the other hand, reflect expected inflation rates over a long period, so they are far less volatile than T-bill rates.

2. Common stocks are long-term securities, and although a particular stockholder may not have a long investment horizon, most stockholders do invest on a long-term basis. Therefore, it is reasonable to think that stock returns embody long-term inflation expectations similar to those reflected in bonds rather than the short-term expectations in bills. Therefore, the cost of equity should be more highly correlated with T-bond rates than with T-bill rates.

3. Treasury bill rates are also subject to more random disturbances than are Treasury bond rates. For example, bills are used by the Federal Reserve System to control the money supply, and bills are used by foreign governments, firms, and individuals as a temporary safe haven for money. Thus, if the Fed decides to stimulate the economy, it drives down the bill rate, and the same thing happens if trouble erupts somewhere in the world and money flows into the United States seeking safety. T-bond rates are also influenced by Fed actions and by international money flows, but not to the same extent as T-bill rates. This is another reason why T-bill rates are more volatile than T-bond rates and, most experts agree, more volatile than k_s.

4. T-bills are essentially free of interest rate risk, but they are exposed to a relatively high degree of reinvestment rate risk. Long-term investors such as pension funds and life insurance companies are as concerned about reinvestment rate risk as interest rate risk. Therefore, most long-term investors would feel equally exposed to risk if they held bills or bonds.

5. When the CAPM is used to estimate a particular firm's cost of equity over time, bond rates produce more reasonable results. For example, when T-bill rates were low in 1977 and 1978, the CAPM produced a cost of equity estimate for Texas Utilities of about 11 percent. T-bill rates then shot up in 1979 and 1980, and the T-bill-based CAPM estimate more than doubled, to 23 percent. The company's bond yields, meanwhile, only rose from 9 to 14 percent. Neither we nor the company's management believed that the cost of equity rose by 12 full percentage points at a time when the cost of long-term debt was rising by only 5 percentage points. CAPM estimates based on T-bond yields produced much more reasonable results.[6]

6. In theory, the CAPM is supposed to measure the expected return over a particular holding period. When it is used to estimate the cost of equity for a project, the theoretically correct holding period to use for the CAPM is the life of the project. Since many projects have long lives, the holding period for the CAPM also should be long. Therefore, the rate on a long-term T-bond is a logical choice for the risk-free rate.

In light of the preceding discussion, we believe that the cost of common equity is more closely related to Treasury bond rates than to T-bill rates. This leads us to favor T-bonds as the base rate, or k_{RF}, in a CAPM cost of equity analysis. T-bond rates can be found in *The Wall Street Journal* or the *Federal Reserve Bulletin*. Generally, we use the yield on a 20-year T-bond as the proxy for the risk-free rate. Assuming that this rate was 8.0 percent in January 1999, we would use this as our estimate for k_{RF} in a January 1999 CAPM cost of equity estimate.

Estimating the Market Risk Premium. The market risk premium, $RP_M = k_M - k_{RF}$, can be estimated on the basis of (1) ex post, or historical, data or (2) ex ante, or forward-looking, data.

Ex Post Risk Premium. A very complete and accurate ex post risk premium study, updated annually, is available from Ibbotson Associates, who examine market data over long periods of time to find the average annual rates of return on stocks, T-bills, T-bonds, and a set of high-grade corporate bonds.[7] For example, Table 10E-3 summarizes some results from their 1997 study, which covers the period 1926–1996.

Note that common stocks provided the highest average return over the 71-year period, while Treasury bills gave the lowest. T-bills barely covered inflation versus a substantial real return for common stocks. However, the superior returns on stocks had its cost—stocks were by far the riskiest of the investments listed as judged by the standard deviation, and they would also rank as riskiest in a CAPM framework. To further illustrate the risk differentials, we note that the range of annual returns on stocks was from −43.3 to 54.0 percent, while the range on T-bills was only 0.0 to 14.7 percent. The Ibbotson study provides strong empirical support for the premise that higher returns can be obtained only by bearing greater risk.

Table 10E-3 also reports the risk premiums, or differences, among the various securities. For example, Ibbotson found the average risk premium of stocks over T-bonds to be 7.5 percentage points.[8] However, these premiums have large

---

[6]All of this can be illustrated by a true but not-very-funny story. A particular state public utility commission hired a professor who used T-bill rates as the base rate in his CAPM analysis to estimate the cost of capital for the state's utilities. Each utility's cost of capital in turn was built into its electric, gas, or telephone rates. Therefore, the lower the cost of capital, the lower the utility service rates, and the less political heat the commission faced. This particular commission was very politically sensitive—so much so that one of its staff members admitted privately that the commission had selected its cost of capital expert on the basis of who could produce the lowest number.

The commission hired the professor in 1978, when T-bill rates, and thus his CAPM cost of equity estimates based on the T-bill rate, were very low. But the rate cases did not come up until 1979, and by then, the bill rate had gone through the roof. As a result, the professor's cost of equity estimates were even higher than the companies were asking permission to earn! At that point, the commission rejected the CAPM approach and sent the professor home.

[7]See *Stocks, Bonds, Bills and Inflation: 1996 Yearbook* (Chicago: Ibbotson Associates, 1997). Also, note that Ibbotson now recommends using the T-bond rate as the proxy for the risk-free rate when using the CAPM. Before 1988, Ibbotson recommended that T-bills be used.

[8]It is worth noting that Ibbotson Associates calculates average returns in two ways: (1) by taking each of the 71 annual holding period returns and deriving the arithmetic average of these annual returns and (2) by finding the compound annual rate of return over the whole period, which amounts to a geometric average. The stocks over T-bonds risk premium as measured by arithmetic averages is 1.8 percentage points higher than the geometric mean risk premium. This leads to the question of which average to use. The arithmetic average is most consistent with the standard CAPM; under the CAPM, investors are supposed to be concerned with returns during the next period (say, one year) and to focus on the expected return and the standard deviation of this return.

TABLE 10E-3	Selected Ibbotson Associates Data, 1926–1996		
		ARITHMETIC MEAN	**STANDARD DEVIATION**
Average Rates of Return			
Common stocks		12.7%	20.3%
Long-term corporate bonds		6.0	8.7
Long-term government bonds		5.4	9.2
Treasury bills		3.8	3.3
Inflation rate		3.2	4.5
Risk Premiums			
Common stocks over T-bills		8.9%	Not reported
Common stocks over T-bonds		7.5	Not reported
T-bonds over T-bills		1.4	Not reported

standard deviations, so one must use them with caution. Although not reported, we estimate the standard deviation of the stocks over T-bonds premium to be more than 20 percent. Also, it should be noted that the choice of the beginning and ending periods can have a major impact on the calculated risk premiums. Ibbotson Associates used the longest period available to them, but had their data begun some years earlier or later, or ended earlier, their results would have been seriously affected. Indeed, over many periods their data would indicate *negative* risk premiums, which would lead to the conclusion that Treasury securities have a higher required return than common stocks, which is contrary to both financial theory and common sense. All this suggests that historical risk premiums should be approached with caution. As one businessman muttered after listening to a professor give a lecture on the CAPM, "Beware of academicians bearing gifts!"

Ex Ante Risk Premiums. The ex post approach to risk premiums used by Ibbotson Associates assumes that investors expect future results, on average, to equal past results. However, as we noted, the estimated risk premium varies greatly depending on the period selected, and, in any event, investors today probably expect results in the future to be different from those achieved during the Great Depression of the 1930s, the World War II years of the 1940s, and the peaceful boom years of the 1950s, all of which are included (and given equal weight with more recent results) in the Ibbotson data. The questionable assumption that future expectations are equal to past realizations, together with the sometimes nonsensical results obtained in historical risk premium studies, has led to a search for ex ante risk premiums.

The most common approach to ex ante premiums is to use the discounted cash flow (DCF) model to estimate the expected market rate of return, $\hat{k}_M = k_M$, then to calculate RP_M as $k_M - k_{RF}$, and finally to use this estimate of RP_M in the SML. This procedure recognizes that if markets are in equilibrium, the expected rate of return on the market is also its required rate of return, so when we estimate $\hat{k}_M$, we are also estimating k_M:

$$\text{Expected rate of return} = \hat{k}_M = \frac{D_1}{P_0} + g = k_{RF} + RP_M = k_M = \text{Required rate of return}.$$

Since D_1 for the market as measured by the S&P 500 or some other index can be predicted quite accurately, and since the current market value of the index (used for P_0) is also known, the major task is to estimate g, the average expected long-term growth rate for the market index. Even here, however, the estimation task is simplified because one can reasonably assume a constant long-term growth rate for a portfolio of mature stocks such as those in the S&P 500.

Financial services companies such as *Value Line* publish, on a regular basis, a forecast based on DCF methodology for the expected rate of return on the market, $\hat{k}_M$. One can subtract the current T-bond rate from such a market forecast to obtain an estimate of the current market risk premium, RP_M. To illustrate, assume that *Value Line's* reported expected return on the market in January 1999 was 14.0 percent. The T-bond rate, as mentioned earlier, is assumed to be 8.0 percent. Thus, *Value Line's* implied market risk premium over T-bonds would be 6.0 percentage points.

Two potential problems arise when we attempt to use data from organizations such as *Value Line*. First, what we really want is *investors'* expectations, not those of security analysts. However, this is probably not a major problem, since several studies have proved beyond much doubt that investors, on average, form their own expectations on the basis of professional analysts' forecasts. The second problem is that there are a number of securities firms besides *Value Line*, and, at any given time, different analysts' forecasts of future market returns are somewhat different. This suggests that it would be most appropriate to obtain a number of forecasts of $\hat{k}_M$ and then to use the average value to estimate RP_M for use in the SML. Several services (including Zacks and Institutional Brokers Estimate System, or IBES) publish data on the forecasts of essentially all widely followed analysts, so one can use the Zacks or IBES aggregate growth rate forecast, along with an aggregate dividend yield, to develop a consensus RP_M forecast and thus avoid potential bias from the use of only one organization's estimate. However, we have followed the forecasts of several of the larger organizations over a period of several years, and we have rarely found their $\hat{k}_M$ estimates to differ by more than ±0.3 percentage point from one another. Therefore, for present purposes, the assumed *Value Line* $\hat{k}_M = k_M = 14.0\%$ and $RP_M = 6.0$ percentage points may be considered to be a "reasonable" proxy for the expectations of the marginal investor. Note, though, that ex ante risk premiums are not stable: they vary over time. Therefore, when using the CAPM to estimate the cost of equity, it is best to use a current estimate of the ex ante RP_M.

Estimating Beta. The last parameter needed for a CAPM cost of equity estimate is the beta coefficient. Recall from Chapter 6 that a stock's beta is a measure of its volatility relative to that of an average stock, and that betas are generally estimated from the stock's characteristic line by running a linear regression between past returns on the stock in question and past returns on some market index. We define betas developed in this manner as **historical betas.**

Note, however, that historical betas show how risky a stock was *in the past*, whereas investors are interested in *future* risk. It may be that a given company appeared to be quite safe in the past, but that things have changed, and its future risk is judged to be higher than its past risk, or vice versa. AT&T is a good example. AT&T was among the bluest of the blue chips when it owned the regional telephone companies, but investors now recognize that AT&T as it exists today faces far more intense competition than it ever faced in the past. Chrysler, on the other hand, was practically bankrupt a few years ago, but it now appears to be reasonably healthy. Therefore, one would think that Chrysler's risk had declined while AT&T's had increased.

Now consider the use of beta as a measure of a company's risk. If we use its historical beta in a CAPM framework to measure a firm's cost of equity, we are implicitly assuming that the company's future risk is the same as its past risk. This would be a troublesome assumption for a company like Chrysler or AT&T today. But what about most companies in most years? As a general rule, is future risk sufficiently similar to past risk to warrant the use of historical betas in a CAPM analysis? For individual firms, past risk is often *not* a good predictor of future risk, and historical betas of individual firms are often not very stable.

Since historical betas may not be good predictors of future risk, researchers have sought ways to improve them. This has led to the development of two different types of betas: (1) adjusted betas and (2) fundamental betas. **Adjusted betas** grew largely out of the work of Marshall E. Blume, who showed that true betas tend to move toward 1.0 over time.[9] Therefore, one can begin with a firm's pure historical statistical beta, make an adjustment for the expected future movement toward 1.0,

and produce an adjusted beta which will, on average, be a better predictor of the future beta than would the unadjusted historical beta. *Value Line* publishes betas based on approximately this formula:

Adjusted beta = 0.33 (Historical beta) + 0.67(1.0).

Consider American Camping Corporation, a retailer of supplies for outdoor activities. ACC's historical beta is 1.2. Therefore, its adjusted beta is:

Adjusted beta = 0.33(1.2) + 0.67(1.0) = 1.1.

Other researchers have extended the adjustment process to include such fundamental risk variables as financial leverage, sales volatility, and the like. The end product here is a **fundamental beta.**[10] These betas are constantly adjusted to reflect changes in a firm's operations and capital structure, whereas with historical betas (including adjusted ones), such changes might not be reflected until several years after the company's "true" beta had changed.

Adjusted betas are obviously heavily dependent on unadjusted historical betas, and so are fundamental betas as they are actually calculated. Therefore, the plain old historical beta, calculated as the slope of the characteristic line, is important even if one goes on to develop a more exotic version. With this in mind, it should be noted that several different sets of data can be used to calculate historical betas, and the different data sets produce different results. Here are some points to note:

1. Betas can be based on historical periods of different lengths. For example, data for the past one, two, three, and so on, years may be used. Most people who calculate betas today use five years of data, but this choice is arbitrary, and different lengths of time usually alter significantly the calculated beta for a given company.[11]

2. Returns may be calculated on holding periods of different lengths—a day, a week, a month, a quarter, a year, and so on. For example, if it has been decided to analyze data on NYSE stocks over a five-year period, then we might obtain $52(5) = 260$ weekly returns on each stock and on the market index. We could also use $12(5) = 60$ monthly returns, or $1(5) = 5$ annual returns. The set of returns on each stock, however large the set turns out to be, would then be regressed on the corresponding market returns to obtain the stock's beta. In statistical analysis, it is generally better to have more rather than fewer observations, because using more observations generally leads to greater statistical confidence. This suggests the use of weekly returns, and, say, five years of data, for a sample size of 260, or even daily returns for a still larger sample size. However, the shorter the holding period, the more likely the data are to exhibit

---

[9]See Marshall E. Blume, "Betas and Their Regression Tendencies," *Journal of Finance,* June 1975, 785–796.

[10]See Barr Rosenberg and James Guy, "Beta and Investment Fundamentals," *Financial Analysts Journal,* May–June 1976, 60–72. Rosenberg, a professor at the University of California at Berkeley, later set up a company which calculates fundamental betas by a proprietary procedure and then sells them to institutional investors.

[11]A commercial provider of betas once told the authors that his firm, and others, did not know what the right period was, but they all decided to use five years in order to reduce the apparent differences between various services' betas, because large differences reduced everyone's credibility!

TABLE 10E-4	Beta Coefficients for Five Companies		
		MERRILL LYNCH	**VALUE LINE**
	Chrysler	1.26	1.20
	Polaroid	0.86	0.90
	IBM	0.89	0.95
	Mobil	0.64	0.70
	Southwestern Public Service	0.51	0.65

random "noise." Also, the greater the number of years of data, the more likely it is that the company's basic risk position has changed (for example, see the preceding comments on Chrysler and AT&T). Thus, the choice of both the number of years of data and the length of the holding period for calculating rates of return involves trade-offs between a desire to have many observations versus a desire to rely on recent and consequently more relevant data.

3. The value used to represent "the market" is also an important consideration, as the index used can have a significant effect on the calculated beta. Many analysts today use the New York Stock Exchange Composite Index (based on more than 2,000 common stocks, weighted by the value of each company), but others use the S&P 500 Index or some other group, including one (the Wilshire Index) with more than 5,000 stocks. In theory, the broader the index, the better the beta. Indeed, the index should really include returns on all stocks, bonds, leases, private businesses, real estate, and even "human capital." As a practical matter, however, we cannot get accurate returns data on most other types of assets, so measurement problems largely restrict us to stock indexes.

The bottom line of all this is that one can calculate betas in many different ways and, depending on the method used, different betas, hence different costs of capital, will result. To illustrate this point, consider Table 10E-4, which contains the beta coefficients for five well-known companies as reported in 1996 by Merrill Lynch and *Value Line*. Merrill Lynch uses the S&P 500 as the market index, while *Value Line* uses the New York Stock Exchange Composite Index. Further, *Value Line* betas are adjusted, while the Merrill Lynch betas listed in Table 10E-4 are pure historical betas. Merrill Lynch uses five years of monthly returns, or 60 observations; *Value Line* uses 260 weekly observations.

Where does this leave financial managers regarding the proper beta? They must "pay their money and take their choice." Some managers calculate their own betas, using whichever procedure seems most appropriate under the circumstances. Others use betas calculated by organizations such as Merrill Lynch or *Value Line*, perhaps using one service or perhaps averaging the betas of several services. The choice is a matter of judgment and data availability, for there is no "right" beta. Generally, though, the betas derived from different sources will, for a given company, be reasonably close together. If they are not, then our confidence in the CAPM cost of capital estimate will be diminished.

Illustration of the CAPM Approach. We are now in a position to estimate American Camping's cost of equity from retained earnings by the CAPM method. We use as the risk-free rate the assumed T-bond rate in January 1999, which is 8.0 percent, and *Value Line's* assumed estimate of the expected return on the market, $\hat{k}_M = k_M = 14.0\%$. Thus, we can write the SML equation for January 1999 as follows:

$$k_s = k_{RF} + (k_M - k_{RF})b_i$$
$$= 8.0\% + (14.0\% - 8.0\%)b_i = 8.0\% + (6.0\%)b_i.$$

Therefore, if we know a company's beta, we can insert it into the SML equation and estimate the company's cost of stock, k_s. We have two estimates of ACC's beta, an adjusted beta of 1.1 and an unadjusted beta of 1.2. Using the adjusted beta, we obtain $k_{ACC} = 14.6\%$:

$$k_{ACC} = 8.0\% + (6.0\%)1.1 = 14.6\%.$$

Using the unadjusted beta, we obtain 15.2 percent. Therefore, on the basis of this CAPM analysis, ACC's cost of common stock falls in the range of 14.6 to 15.2 percent.

Rather than using single values, we could have developed high and low estimates for the risk-free rate and for the market risk premium. Then, by combining all of the low estimators and all of the high estimators, we could have estimated the extreme low and high values of ACC's cost of common stock. Obviously, this range would have been greater than 14.6 to 15.2 percent.

Estimating Inputs for the DCF Approach.

Three inputs are required by the DCF approach: the current stock price, the current dividend, and the expected growth in dividends. Of these inputs, the growth rate is by far the most difficult to estimate. The following sections describe the most commonly used approaches for estimating the growth rate: (1) historical growth rates, (2) the retention growth model, and (3) analysts' forecasts.

Historical Growth Rates. First, if earnings and dividend growth rates have been relatively stable in the past, and if investors expect these trends to continue, then the past realized growth rate may be used as an estimate of the expected future growth rate. To illustrate, consider Figure 10E-4, which gives EPS and DPS data from 1984 to 1998 for ACC, along with a plot of these data on a semilog scale. Note these points:

FIGURE 10E-4 American Camping Corporation: Semilog Plot of EPS and DPS, 1984–1998

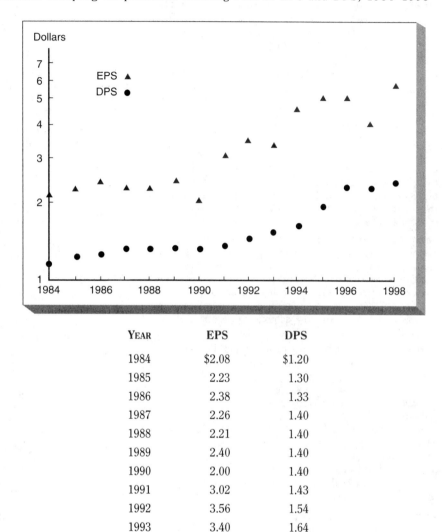

YEAR	EPS	DPS
1984	$2.08	$1.20
1985	2.23	1.30
1986	2.38	1.33
1987	2.26	1.40
1988	2.21	1.40
1989	2.40	1.40
1990	2.00	1.40
1991	3.02	1.43
1992	3.56	1.54
1993	3.40	1.64
1994	4.65	1.72
1995	5.12	1.95
1996	5.14	2.20
1997	4.05	2.20
1998	5.73	2.30

1. **Time period.** We show 15 years of data in Figure 10E-4, but we could have used 25 years, 5 years, or 10 years. There is no rule as to the appropriate number of years to analyze when calculating historical growth rates. However, the period chosen should reflect, to the extent possible, conditions similar to those expected in the future.

2. **Compound growth rate, point-to-point.** The easiest historical growth rate to calculate is the compound rate between two dates. For example, EPS grew at an annual rate of 7.5 percent from 1984 to 1998, and DPS grew at a 4.8 percent rate during this same period.[12] Note that the point-to-point growth rate could change radically if we used two different

[12]To obtain g_{EPS} using a financial calculator, enter −2.08 as PV, 5.73 as FV, 14 as N (because, with 15 data points, we have 14 growth periods: 1998 − 1984 = 14), and then press I to obtain the growth rate, 7.5 percent.

points. For example, if we calculated the five-year EPS growth rate from 1992 to 1997, we would obtain 2.6 percent, but the five-year rate one year later, from 1993 to 1998, is 11.0 percent. This radical change occurs because the point-to-point rate is extremely sensitive to the beginning and ending years chosen.

3. **Compound growth rate, average-to-average.** To alleviate the problem of beginning and ending year sensitivity, some analysts use an average-to-average calculation. For example, to calculate ACC's EPS growth rate over the period 1992 to 1997, *Value Line*'s analysts would (1) get the average EPS over the years 1991 to 1993 and use this value ($3.33) as the beginning year, (2) get the average EPS over the years 1996 to 1998 and use this value ($4.97) as the ending year, and (3) calculate a growth rate of 8.3 percent based on these data. This procedure is superior to the simple point-to-point calculation for purposes of estimating g.

4. **Least squares regression.** A third way, and in our view the best way, to estimate historical growth rates is by log-linear least squares regression. The regression method gives consideration to all data points in the series; thus, it is the least likely to be biased by a randomly high or low beginning or ending year. The only practical way to estimate a least squares growth rate is with a computer or a financial calculator.[13]

5. **Earnings versus dividends.** If earnings and dividends are growing at the same rate, there is no problem, but if these two growth rates are unequal, we do have a problem. First, the DCF model requires the expected *dividend* growth rate. However, if EPS and DPS are growing at different rates, something is going to have to change—these two series cannot indefinitely grow at two different rates. There is no rule for handling differences in historical g_{EPS} and g_{DPS}, and where they differ, this simply demonstrates yet another problem with using historical growth as a proxy for expected future growth. Like many aspects of finance, judgment is required when estimating growth rates.

Table 10E-5 summarizes the historical growth rates we have just discussed. It is obvious that one can take a given set of historical data and, depending on the years and the calculation method used, obtain a large number of quite different growth rates. Now recall our purpose in making these calculations: We are seeking the future dividend growth rate that investors expect, and we reasoned that, if past growth rates have been stable, then investors might base future expectations on past trends. This is a reasonable proposition, but, unfortunately, one rarely finds much historical stability. Therefore, the use of historical growth rates in a DCF analysis must be applied with judgment, and also be used (if at all) in conjunction with other growth estimation methods as discussed next.

Retention Growth Model. Another method for estimating the growth rate is to use the *retention growth model:*

$$g = b(r). \qquad \text{(10E-3)}$$

Here r is the expected future return on equity (ROE), and b is the fraction of its earnings that a firm is expected to retain (1 − Payout ratio).[14] Equation 10E-3 produces a constant growth rate, but when we use it we are, by implication, making four important assumptions: (1) We expect the payout rate, and thus the retention rate, b = 1 − Payout, to remain constant; (2) we expect the return on equity on new investment, r, to equal the firm's current ROE, which implies that we expect the return on equity to remain constant; (3) the firm is not expected to issue new common stock, or, if it does, we expect this new stock to be sold at a price equal to its book value; and (4) future projects are expected to have the same degree of risk as the firm's existing assets.

ACC has had an average return on equity of about 15 percent over the past 15 years. The ROE has been relatively steady, but even so it has ranged from a low of 11.0 percent to a high of 17.6 percent. In addition, ACC's dividend payout rate has averaged 0.52 over the past 15 years, so its retention rate, b, has averaged 1.0 − 0.52 = 0.48. Using Equation 10E-3, we estimate g to be 7.2 percent:

$$g = 0.48(15\%) = 7.2\%.$$

This figure, together with the historical EPS and DPS growth rates examined earlier, might lead us to conclude that American Camping's expected growth rate is in the range of 6.5 to 7.5 percent. Therefore, if we forecasted ACC's next annual dividend to be $2.40, and if its current stock price is $32, then its dividend yield would be $D_1/P_0 = \$2.40/\$32 = 0.075$ or 7.5%,

---

[13]Log-linear regression is a standard time-series linear regression in which the data for the dependent (Y) variable are plotted as natural logarithms. The slope of the regression line is then the average annual growth rate, assuming continuous compounding. In a standard time-series linear regression of EPS or DPS, the slope of the regression line is the average annual dollar change. To find the EPS growth rate with a financial calculator, use the regression routine, entering years as the X variable and ln EPS as the Y variable. Obtain the slope coefficient of the regression, b, which is the annual growth rate assuming continuous compounding. Then find e^b, which produces the value 1 + g, where g is the effective annual growth rate. For example, using the EPS data in Figure 10E-4, we obtain a slope coefficient of b = 0.07607, then find EXP (0.07607) $= e^{0.07607} = 1.07903$, so g = 7.903%. The exact regression procedures are calculator specific, but with an HP-17B, one would enter the years and the EPS and DPS data, specify an exponential model (EXP), find the slope coefficient m, go into the math menu and press the exponential key (EXP = e^x) to find 1 + g, and subtract 1.0 to obtain the growth rate. With an HP-10B, one would enter the EPS or DPS data, convert to natural logs (LN), complete the regression and determine the slope coefficient (m), convert to e^x, and then subtract 1.0 to obtain the growth rate. Other calculators require somewhat different procedures. Also, note that the same procedures can be used with a spreadsheet program to find the growth rate—input each value of EPS, run a regression, then find = EXP(regression coefficient), which is 1 + g. Finally, note that these procedures can be used to find the growth rate of any variable that changes over time, not just EPS or DPS.

[14]Since there are more terms for which symbols are needed than there are letters in the alphabet, some letters are used to denote several different things. This is one of those instances, and b is standard notation for both the beta coefficient and the retention rate. Note also that the retention rate is the complement of the payout rate, that is, Retention rate = (1 − Payout rate).

TABLE 10E-5   American Camping Corporation: Historical Growth Rates

Method (Period)	EPS	DPS	Average
Point-to-point (1993–1998)	11.0%	7.0%	9.0%
Point-to-point (1984–1998)	7.5	4.8	6.2
Average-to-average (1992–1997)	8.3	7.7	8.0
Average-to-average (1985–1997)	6.9	4.7	5.8
Least squares regression (1993–1998)	6.6	7.6	7.1
Least squares regression (1984–1998)	7.9	4.6	6.3

and its DCF cost of capital would be in the range of 14.0 to 15.0 percent:

$$\hat{k}_{ACC} = D_1/P_0 + g.$$

Lower end: $k_{ACC} = \hat{k}_{ACC} = 7.5\% + 6.5\% = 14.0\%.$

Upper end: $k_{ACC} = \hat{k}_{ACC} = 7.5\% + 7.5\% = 15.0\%.$

This is reasonably close to the 14.6 to 15.2 percent range found by use of the CAPM method.

Analysts' Forecasts. A third technique calls for using security analysts' forecasts. Analysts publish growth rate estimates for most of the larger publicly owned companies. For example, *Value Line* provides such forecasts on 1,700 companies, and all of the larger brokerage houses provide similar forecasts. Further, several companies compile analysts' forecasts on a regular basis and provide summary information such as the median and range of forecasts on widely followed companies. These growth rate summaries, such as the one compiled by Lynch, Jones & Ryan in its Institutional Brokers Estimate System (IBES), can be ordered for a fee and obtained either in hardcopy format or as on-line computer data.

However, these forecasts often involve nonconstant growth. For example, in January 1999, some analysts were forecasting that ACC would have a 10.4 percent annual growth rate in earnings and dividends over the next five years, or from 1999 through 2003, and they were forecasting a steady-state growth rate beyond 2003 of 6.5 percent. On the basis of the current $32 market price and a D_1 of $2.40, we can use the nonconstant growth stock valuation approach developed in Chapter 9 to find the expected rate of return. However, obtaining the solution is no trivial matter—we used a spreadsheet model and found $\hat{k}_s = k_s$ to be 15.0 percent.

As an alternative, a nonconstant growth forecast can be used to develop a proxy constant growth rate. Computer simulations indicate that dividends beyond Year 50 contribute very little to the value of any stock—the present value of dividends beyond Year 50 is virtually zero, so for practical purposes, we can ignore anything beyond 50 years. If we consider only a 50-year horizon, we can develop a weighted average growth rate and use it as a constant growth rate for cost of capital purposes. In the ACC case, we assumed a growth rate of 10.4 percent for 5 years followed by a growth rate of 6.5 percent for 45 years, which produces an average growth rate of 0.10(10.4%) + 0.90(6.5%) = 6.9%. This constant growth proxy results in $k_s = \hat{k}_s = 14.4\%$:

$$k_s = \hat{k}_s = \frac{\$2.40}{\$32} + 6.9\%$$

$$= 7.5\% + 6.9\% = 14.4\%.$$

These nonconstant growth DCF calculations suggest a range for k_s of 14.4 to 15.0 percent.

THE BASICS OF
CAPITAL BUDGETING

Just a few years ago, Chrysler was in trouble. Its stock price had plummeted, its bonds had been downgraded, and its future looked bleak. But what a difference a few years can make! Chrysler's stock, which sold for $6 a share in the early 1990s, passed $36 a share in 1997, after the company's directors declared a two-for-one split and raised the dividend. Moreover, Chrysler's debt rating has improved to investment grade, and the company continues to report strong earnings.

How did the "Chrysler Miracle" come about? First, Chrysler developed a new concept for designing and producing new models. Whereas most other companies have separate design and manufacturing teams, Chrysler combined its two groups into an integrated "platform team." This new approach cut both design time and manufacturing costs, and the result was world leadership in profits per vehicle. Second, because Chrysler was not as well capitalized as its rivals, a shortage of resources forced it to limit model offerings, which turned out to be a blessing in disguise. And third, Chrysler has concentrated on the North American market, which has been stronger than the European and Asian markets.

Chrysler hired a new chief executive officer in 1992, Robert Eaton, former head of GM's European operations. Eaton is given high marks by most industry watchers, but Chrysler's comeback really began much earlier, under the regime of retired chairman Lee Iacocca. The real test of Eaton's managerial skills will be seen in how Chrysler fares in coming years.

Eaton and his team face some big, important decisions. The company has accumulated more than $8 billion in cash, despite the fact that its capital spending now exceeds $4 billion per year, double the amount spent in 1992. Management plans to use most of this cash for capital expenditures, arguing that to maintain its momentum, new cars must be designed, manufacturing plants must be modernized and expanded, and R&D efforts on electric cars and other innovative products must be continued.

Despite its strong performance, Chrysler recently had to fight off an attack from its largest shareholder, Kirk Kerkorian, who had been pressuring the company to return much of its cash to shareholders—either through higher dividends or stock repurchases. To rebuff Kerkorian's efforts to take over the company, Chrysler was forced to repurchase some of its stock and also to increase the dividend.

In a nutshell, Eaton and Kerkorian disagreed about whether Chrysler's anticipated investments would be able to earn greater returns than what shareholders could earn elsewhere on other investments of equal risk. If it can, then management would be correct to retain and reinvest most of its cash. If not, Kerkorian will turn out to have been right.

In the years ahead, each of Chrysler's investment decisions will require careful analysis, much of it based on the techniques described in this chapter. As you read this chapter, think about how Chrysler—or any other company—could use capital budgeting analysis to make better investment decisions.

In the last chapter, we discussed the cost of capital. Now we turn to investment decisions involving fixed assets, or *capital budgeting*. Here the term *capital* refers to long-term assets used in production, while a *budget* is a plan which details projected inflows and outflows during some future period. Thus, the *capital budget* is an outline of planned investments in fixed assets, and **capital budgeting** is the whole process of analyzing projects and deciding which ones to include in the capital budget.

Our coverage of capital budgeting is divided into three chapters. This chapter gives an overview and explains the basic techniques used in capital budgeting analysis. Chapter 12 goes on to explain how cash flows are estimated, and then Chapter 13 discusses how risk is dealt with in capital budgeting.

IMPORTANCE OF CAPITAL BUDGETING

A number of factors combine to make capital budgeting perhaps the most important function financial managers and their staffs must perform. First, since the results of capital budgeting decisions continue for many years, investments in fixed assets cause the firm to lose some of its flexibility. For example, the purchase of an asset with an economic life of ten years "locks in" the firm for a ten-year period. Further, because asset expansion is based on expected future sales, a decision to buy an asset that is expected to last ten years requires a ten-year sales forecast. Finally, a firm's capital budgeting decisions define its strategic direction, because moves into new products, services, or markets must be preceded by capital expenditures.

An erroneous forecast of asset requirements can have serious consequences. If the firm invests too much, it will incur unnecessarily high depreciation and other expenses. On the other hand, if it does not invest enough, two problems may arise. First, its equipment may not be sufficiently modern to enable it to produce competitively. Second, if it has inadequate capacity, it may lose market share to rival firms, and regaining lost customers requires heavy selling expenses, price reductions, or product improvements, all of which are costly.

Timing is also important—capital assets must be available when they are needed. Edward Ford, executive vice-president of Western Design, a decorative tile company, gave the authors an illustration of the importance of capital budgeting. His firm tried to operate near capacity most of the time. During a four-year period, Western experienced intermittent spurts in the demand for its products, which forced it to turn away orders. After these sharp increases in demand, Western would add capacity by renting an additional building, then purchasing and installing the appropriate equipment. It would take six to eight months to get the additional capacity ready, but by then demand had dried up—other firms with available capacity had already taken an increased share of the market. Once Western began to properly forecast demand and plan its capacity requirements a year or so in advance, it was able to maintain and even increase its market share.

Effective capital budgeting can improve both the timing and the quality of asset acquisitions. If a firm forecasts its needs for capital assets in advance, it can purchase and install the assets before they are needed. Unfortunately, many firms do not order capital goods until existing assets are approaching full-capacity usage. If sales increase because of an increase in general market demand, all firms in the industry will tend to order capital goods at about the same time. This results in backlogs, long waiting times for machinery, a deterioration in the quality of the capital equipment, and an increase in costs. The firm that foresees its needs and purchases capital assets during slack periods can avoid these problems. Note, though, that if a firm forecasts an increase in demand and then expands to meet the anticipated demand, but sales do not increase, it will be saddled with excess capacity and high costs, which can lead to losses or even bankruptcy. Thus, an accurate sales forecast is critical.

Capital budgeting typically involves substantial expenditures, and before a firm can spend a large amount of money, it must have the funds lined up—large amounts of money are not available automatically. Therefore, a firm contemplating a major capital expenditure program should plan its financing far enough in advance to be sure funds are available.

S E L F - T E S T Q U E S T I O N S	Why are capital budgeting decisions so important? Why is the sales forecast a key element in a capital budgeting decision?

GENERATING IDEAS FOR CAPITAL PROJECTS

The same general concepts that are used in security valuation are also involved in capital budgeting. However, whereas a set of stocks and bonds exists in the securities market, and investors select from this set, *capital budgeting projects are created by the firm.* For example, a sales representative may report that customers are asking for a particular product that the company does not now produce. The sales manager then discusses the idea with the marketing research group to determine the size of the market for the proposed product. If it appears that a significant market does exist, cost accountants and engineers will be asked to estimate production costs. If they conclude that the product can be produced and sold at a sufficient profit, the project will be undertaken.

A firm's growth, and even its ability to remain competitive and to survive, depends on a constant flow of ideas for new products, for ways to make existing products better, and for ways to operate at a lower cost. Accordingly, a well-managed firm will go to great lengths to develop good capital budgeting proposals. For example, the executive vice-president of one very successful corporation indicated that his company takes the following steps to generate projects:

> Our R&D department is constantly searching for new products and for ways to improve existing products. In addition, our executive committee, which consists of senior executives in marketing, production, and finance, identifies the products and markets in which our company should compete, and the committee sets long-run targets for each division. These targets, which are spelled out in the corporation's **strategic business plan,** provide a general guide to the operating executives who must meet them. The operating executives then seek new products, set expansion plans for existing products, and look for ways to reduce production and distribution costs. Since bonuses and promotions are based on each unit's ability to meet or exceed its targets, these economic incentives encourage our operating executives to seek out profitable investment opportunities.
>
> While our senior executives are judged and rewarded on the basis of how well their units perform, people further down the line are given bonuses for suggestions which lead to profitable investments. Additionally, a percentage of our corporate profit is set aside for distribution to nonexecutive employees, and we have an Employees' Stock Ownership Plan (ESOP) to provide further incentives. Our objective is to encourage employees at all levels to keep an eye out for good ideas, including those that lead to capital investments.

If a firm has capable and imaginative executives and employees, and if its incentive system is working properly, many ideas for capital investment will be advanced. Some ideas will be good ones, but others will not. Therefore, procedures must be established for screening projects, the primary topic of this chapter.

S E L F - T E S T
Q U E S T I O N | What are some ways firms get ideas for capital projects?

PROJECT CLASSIFICATIONS

Analyzing capital expenditure proposals is not a costless operation—benefits can be gained, but analysis does have a cost. For certain types of projects, a relatively detailed analysis may be warranted; for others, simpler procedures should be used. Accordingly, firms generally categorize projects and then analyze those in each category somewhat differently:

1. **Replacement: maintenance of business.** One category consists of expenditures to replace worn-out or damaged equipment used in the production of profitable products. Replacement projects are necessary if the firm is to continue in business. The only issues here are (a) should this operation be continued and (b) should we continue to use the same production processes? The answers are usually yes, so maintenance decisions are normally made without going through an elaborate decision process.

2. **Replacement: cost reduction.** This category includes expenditures to replace serviceable but obsolete equipment. The purpose here is to lower the costs of labor, materials, and other inputs such as electricity. These decisions are discretionary, and a fairly detailed analysis is generally required.

3. **Expansion of existing products or markets.** Expenditures to increase output of existing products, or to expand retail outlets or distribution facilities in markets now being served, are included here. These decisions are more complex because they require an explicit forecast of growth in demand. Mistakes are more likely, so a more detailed analysis is required. Also, the go/no-go decision is generally made at a higher level within the firm.

4. **Expansion into new products or markets.** These are investments to produce a new product or to expand into a geographic area not currently being served. These projects involve strategic decisions that could change the fundamental nature of the business, and they normally require the expenditure of large sums of money with delayed paybacks. Invariably, a detailed analysis is required, and the final decision is generally made at the very top—by the board of directors as a part of the firm's strategic plan.

5. **Safety and/or environmental projects.** Expenditures necessary to comply with government orders, labor agreements, or insurance policy terms fall into this category. These expenditures are called *mandatory investments,* and they often involve *non-revenue-producing projects.* How they are handled depends on their size, with small ones being treated much like the Category 1 projects described above.

6. **Research and development.** For many firms, R&D constitutes the largest and most important type of capital expenditure. Although these expenditures can, conceptually, be analyzed in the same way as tangible asset investments, the cash flows they produce are often too uncertain to warrant a standard DCF analysis. What happens, generally, is that managers think in subjective DCF terms about R&D expenditures, then appropriate a certain amount of money to conduct research on a given project or set of projects. Since R&D results are almost always highly uncertain, and since continuing to fund a project will depend on results at earlier stages, the decision tree analysis discussed in Chapter 13 is often used.

7. **Other.** This catch-all includes office buildings, parking lots, executive aircraft, and so on. How they are handled varies among companies.

In general, relatively simple calculations, and only a few supporting documents, are required for replacement decisions, especially maintenance-type investments in profitable plants. A more detailed analysis is required for cost-reduction replacements, for expansion of existing product lines, and especially for investments in new products or areas. Also, within each category projects are broken down by their dollar costs: Larger investments require increasingly detailed analysis and approval at a higher level within the firm. Thus, whereas a plant manager may be authorized to approve maintenance expenditures up to $10,000 on the basis of a relatively unsophisticated analysis, the full board of directors may have to approve decisions which involve either amounts over $1 million or expansions into new products or markets. Hard data are generally lacking for new-product decisions, so here judgments, as opposed to detailed cost data, are especially important.

S E L F - T E S T
Q U E S T I O N

Identify the major project classification categories, and explain how they are used.

SIMILARITIES BETWEEN CAPITAL BUDGETING AND SECURITY VALUATION

Once a potential capital budgeting project has been identified, its evaluation involves the same steps that are used in security analysis:

1. First, the cost of the project must be determined. This is similar to finding the price that must be paid for a stock or bond.

2. Next, management estimates the expected cash flows from the project, including the salvage value of the asset at the end of its expected life. This is similar to estimating the future dividend or interest payment stream on a stock or bond.

3. Third, the riskiness of the projected cash flows must be estimated. This requires information about the probability distribution (uncertainty) of the cash flows.

4. Given the project's riskiness, management determines the cost of capital at which the cash flows should be discounted.

5. Next, the expected cash flows are put on a present value basis to obtain an estimate of the asset's value to the firm. This is equivalent to finding the present value of a stock's expected future dividends.

6. Finally, the present value of the expected cash flows is compared with the required outlay, or cost. If the PV of the cash flows exceeds the cost, the project should be accepted. Otherwise, it should be rejected. (Alternatively, if the expected rate of return on the project exceeds its cost of capital, the project is accepted.)

If an individual investor identifies and invests in a stock or bond whose market price is less than its true value, the investor's wealth will increase. Similarly, if a firm identifies (or creates) an investment opportunity with a present value greater than its cost, the value of the firm will increase. Thus, there is a direct link between capital budgeting and stock values: The more effective the firm's capital budgeting procedures, the higher its stock price.

S E L F - T E S T
Q U E S T I O N

List the six steps in the capital budgeting process, and compare them with the steps in security valuation.

| FIGURE 11-1 | Net Cash Flows for Projects S and L |

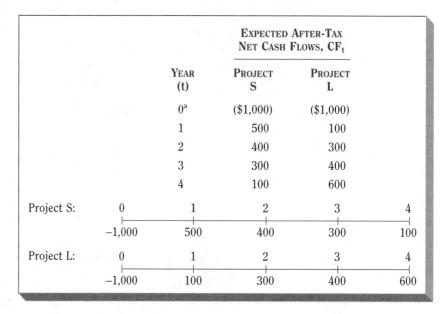

YEAR (t)	EXPECTED AFTER-TAX NET CASH FLOWS, CF_t	
	PROJECT S	PROJECT L
0[a]	($1,000)	($1,000)
1	500	100
2	400	300
3	300	400
4	100	600

Project S:

0	1	2	3	4
−1,000	500	400	300	100

Project L:

0	1	2	3	4
−1,000	100	300	400	600

[a]CF_0 represents the net investment outlay, or initial cost.

CAPITAL BUDGETING DECISION RULES

Six key methods are used to rank projects and to decide whether or not they should be accepted for inclusion in the capital budget: (1) payback, (2) discounted payback, (3) net present value (NPV), (4) internal rate of return (IRR), (5) modified internal rate of return (MIRR), and (6) profitability index (PI). We will explain how each ranking criterion is calculated, and then we will evaluate how well each performs in terms of identifying those projects which will maximize the firm's stock price.

We use the cash flow data shown in Figure 11-1 for Projects S and L to illustrate each method. Also we assume that the projects are equally risky. Note that the cash flows, CF_t, are expected values, and that they have been adjusted to reflect taxes, depreciation, and salvage values. Further, since many projects require an investment in both fixed assets and net operating working capital, the investment outlays shown as CF_0 include these cash flows.[1] Finally, we assume that all cash flows occur at the end of the designated year. Incidentally, the S stands for *short* and the L for *long:* Project S is a short-term project in the sense that its cash inflows come in sooner than L's.

Payback Period

The **payback period,** defined as the expected number of years required to recover the original investment, was the first formal method used to evaluate capital budgeting

---

[1]The most difficult part of the capital budgeting process is estimating the cash flows. For simplicity, the net cash flows are treated as a given in this chapter, which allows us to focus on the capital budgeting decision rules. However, in Chapter 12 we discuss cash flow estimation in detail, and you will see that the relevant cash flows are the project's free cash flows, as defined in Chapter 2. Also, recall from Chapter 2 that net operating working capital is equal to current assets (except for short-term financial investments) minus accounts payable and accruals.

FIGURE 11-2   Payback Period for Projects S and L

Project S:	0	1	2	3	4
Net cash flow	−1,000	500	400	300	100
Cumulative NCF	−1,000	−500	−100	200	300

Project L:	0	1	2	3	4
Net cash flow	−1,000	100	300	400	600
Cumulative NCF	−1,000	−900	−600	−200	400

projects. The payback calculation is diagrammed in Figure 11-2, and it is explained below for Project S.

1. Enter $CF_0 = -1000$ in your calculator. (You do not need to use the cash flow register; just have your display show −1,000.)
2. Now add $CF_1 = 500$ to find the cumulative cash flow at the end of Year 1. The result is −500.
3. Now add $CF_2 = 400$ to find the cumulative cash flow at the end of Year 2. This is −100.
4. Now add $CF_3 = 300$ to find the cumulative cash flow at the end of Year 3. This is +200.
5. We see that by the end of Year 3 the cumulative inflows have more than recovered the initial outflow. Thus, the payback occurred during the third year. If the $300 of inflows come in evenly during Year 3, then the exact payback period can be found as follows:

$$\text{Payback}_S = \text{Year before full recovery} + \frac{\text{Unrecovered cost at start of year}}{\text{Cash flow during year}}$$

$$= 2 + \frac{100}{300} = 2.33 \text{ years.}$$

Applying the same procedure to Project L, we find $\text{Payback}_L = 3.33$ years.

The shorter the payback period, the better. Therefore, if the firm required a payback of three years or less, Project S would be accepted but Project L would be rejected. If the projects were **mutually exclusive,** S would be ranked over L because S has the shorter payback. *Mutually exclusive* means that if one project is taken on, the other must be rejected. For example, the installation of a conveyor-belt system in a warehouse and the purchase of a fleet of forklifts for the same warehouse would be mutually exclusive projects—accepting one implies rejection of the other. **Independent projects** are projects whose cash flows are independent of one another.

Some firms use a variant of the regular payback, the **discounted payback period,** which is similar to the regular payback period except that the expected cash flows are discounted by the project's cost of capital. Thus, the discounted payback period is defined as the number of years required to recover the investment from *discounted* net cash flows. Figure 11-3 contains the discounted net cash flows for Projects S and L, assuming both projects have a cost of capital of 10 percent. To construct Figure 11-3, each cash inflow is divided by $(1 + k)^t = (1.10)^t$, where t is the year in which the cash flow occurs and k is the project's cost of capital. After three years, Project S will have generated $1,011 in discounted cash inflows. Since the cost is $1,000, the discounted

FIGURE 11-3   Projects S and L: Discounted Payback Period

Project S:	0	1	2	3	4
Net cash flow	−1,000	500	400	300	100
Discounted NCF (at 10%)	−1,000	455	331	225	68
Cumulative discounted NCF	−1,000	−545	−214	11	79
Project L:	0	1	2	3	4
Net cash flow	−1,000	100	300	400	600
Discounted NCF (at 10%)	−1,000	91	248	301	410
Cumulative discounted NCF	−1,000	−909	−661	−360	50

payback is just under three years, or, to be precise, $2 + (\$214/\$225) = 2.95$ years. Project L's discounted payback is 3.88 years:

$$\text{Discounted payback}_S = 2.0 + \$214/\$225 = 2.95 \text{ years.}$$

$$\text{Discounted payback}_L = 3.0 + \$360/\$410 = 3.88 \text{ years.}$$

For Projects S and L, the rankings are the same regardless of which payback method is used; that is, Project S is preferred to Project L, and Project S would still be selected if the firm were to require a discounted payback of three years or less. Often, however, the regular and the discounted paybacks produce conflicting rankings.

Note that the payback is a type of "breakeven" calculation in the sense that if cash flows come in at the expected rate until the payback year, then the project will break even. However, the regular payback does not take account of the cost of capital—no cost for the debt or equity used to undertake the project is reflected in the cash flows or the calculation. The discounted payback does take account of capital costs—it shows the breakeven year after covering debt and equity costs.

An important drawback of both the payback and discounted payback methods is that they ignore cash flows that are paid or received after the payback period. For example, consider two projects, X and Y, each of which requires an up-front cash outflow of $3,000, so $CF_0 = -\$3,000$. Assume that both projects have a cost of capital of 10 percent. Project X is expected to produce cash inflows of $1,000 each of the next four years, while Project Y will produce no cash flows the first four years but then generate a cash inflow of $1,000,000 five years from now. Common sense suggests that Project Y creates more value for the firm's shareholders, yet its payback and discounted payback make it look worse than Project X. Consequently, both payback methods have serious deficiencies. Therefore, we will not dwell on the finer points of payback analysis.[2]

Although the payback method has some serious faults as a ranking criterion, it does provide information on how long funds will be tied up in a project. Thus, the shorter the payback period, other things held constant, the greater the project's

---

[2]Another capital budgeting technique that was once used widely is the *accounting rate of return (ARR)*, which examines a project's contribution to the firm's net income. Although some companies still calculate an ARR, it really has no redeeming features, so we will not discuss it in this text. See Eugene F. Brigham and Louis C. Gapenski, *Intermediate Financial Management,* 5th ed., Chapter 7.

liquidity. Also, since cash flows expected in the distant future are generally riskier than near-term cash flows, the payback is often used as one indicator of a project's *riskiness.*

Net Present Value (NPV)

As the flaws in the payback were recognized, people began to search for ways to improve the effectiveness of project evaluations. One such method is the **net present value (NPV) method,** which relies on **discounted cash flow (DCF) techniques.** To implement this approach, we proceed as follows:

1. Find the present value of each cash flow, including both inflows and outflows, discounted at the project's cost of capital.
2. Sum these discounted cash flows; this sum is defined as the project's NPV.
3. If the NPV is positive, the project should be accepted, while if the NPV is negative, it should be rejected. If two projects with positive NPVs are mutually exclusive, the one with the higher NPV should be chosen.

The equation for the NPV is as follows:

$$NPV = CF_0 + \frac{CF_1}{(1+k)^1} + \frac{CF_2}{(1+k)^2} + \cdots + \frac{CF_n}{(1+k)^n}$$

$$= \sum_{t=0}^{n} \frac{CF_t}{(1+k)^t}. \qquad (11\text{-}1)$$

Here CF_t is the expected net cash flow at Period t, k is the project's cost of capital, and n is its life. Cash outflows (expenditures such as the cost of buying equipment or building factories) are treated as *negative* cash flows. For our Projects S and L, only CF_0 is negative, but for many large projects such as the Alaska Pipeline, an electric generating plant, or a new jet aircraft, outflows occur for several years before operations begin and cash flows turn positive.

At a 10 percent cost of capital, Project S's NPV is $78.82:

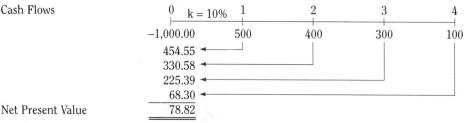

By a similar process, we find $NPV_L = \$49.18$. On this basis, both projects should be accepted if they are independent, but S should be chosen if they are mutually exclusive.

It is not hard to calculate the NPV as was done in the time line by using Equation 11-1 and a regular calculator, along with the interest rate tables or the PV formula. However, it is more efficient to use a financial calculator. Different calculators are set up somewhat differently, but they all have a section of memory called the "cash flow register" which is used for uneven cash flows such as those in Projects S and L (as opposed to equal annuity cash flows). A solution process for Equation 11-1 is literally programmed into financial calculators, and all you have to do is enter the cash flows (being sure to observe the signs), along with the value of k = I. At that point, you have (in your calculator) this equation:

$$NPV_S = -1,000 + \frac{500}{(1.10)^1} + \frac{400}{(1.10)^2} + \frac{300}{(1.10)^3} + \frac{100}{(1.10)^4}.$$

The equation has one unknown, NPV. Now all you need to do is to ask the calculator to solve the equation for you, which you do by pressing the NPV button (and, on some calculators, the "compute" button). The answer, 78.82, will appear on the screen.[3]

Most projects last for more than four years, and, as you will see in Chapter 12, most projects require many calculations to develop the estimated cash flows. Therefore, financial analysts generally use spreadsheets when dealing with capital budgeting projects. For Project S, this spreadsheet could be used (disregard for now Row 6; we discuss it in the next section):

	A	B	C	D	E	F
1	Project S					
2	k =	10%				
3	Time	0	1	2	3	4
4	Cash flow	−1,000	500	400	300	100
5	NPV =	$78.82				
6	IRR =					

---

[3]The *Technology Supplement* provided to instructors and available for copying by users explains this and other commonly used calculator applications. For those who do not have the *Supplement*, the steps for two popular calculators, the HP-10B and the HP-17B, are shown below. If you have another type of financial calculator, see its manual or the *Supplement*.

HP-10B

1. Clear the memory.
2. Enter CF_0 as follows: 1000 `+/−` `CFj`.
3. Enter CF_1 as follows: 500 `CFj`.
4. Repeat the process to enter the other cash flows. Note that CF 0, CF 1, and so forth, flash on the screen as you press the `CFj` button. If you hold the button down, CF 0 and so forth will remain on the screen until you release it.
5. Once the CFs have been entered, enter k = I = 10%: 10 `I/YR`.
6. Now that all of the inputs have been entered, you can press `■` `NPV` to get the answer, NPV = $78.82.
7. If a cash flow is repeated for several years, you can avoid having to enter the CFs for each year. For example, if the $500 cash flow for Year 1 had also been the CF for Years 2 through 10, making 10 of these $500 cash flows, then after entering 500 `CFj` the first time, you could enter 10 `■` `Nj`. This would automatically enter 10 CFs of 500.

HP-17B

1. Go to the cash flow (CFLO) menu, clear if FLOW(0) = ? does not appear on the screen.
2. Enter CF_0 as follows: 1000 `+/−` `INPUT`.
3. Enter CF_1 as follows: 500 `INPUT`.

(continues)

In *Excel*, the formula in Cell B5 is: **=B4+NPV(B2,C4:F4)**, and it results in a value of $78.82.[4] For a simple problem such as this, setting up a spreadsheet may not seem worth the trouble. However, in real-world problems there will be a number of rows above our cash flow line, starting with expected sales, then deducting various costs and taxes, and ending up with the cash flows shown on Row 4. Moreover, once a spreadsheet has been set up, it is easy to change input values to see what would happen if inputs are changed. For example, we could see what would happen if lower sales caused all cash flows to decline by $15, or if the cost of capital rose to 10.5 percent. It is easy to make such changes and then see the effects on NPV.

Rationale for the NPV Method

The rationale for the NPV method is straightforward. An NPV of zero signifies that the project's cash flows are just sufficient to repay the invested capital and to provide the required rate of return on that capital. If a project has a positive NPV, then it is generating more cash than is needed to service its debt and to provide the required return to shareholders, and this excess cash accrues solely to the firm's stockholders. Therefore, if a firm takes on a project with a positive NPV, the wealth of the stockholders is improved. In our example, shareholders' wealth would increase by $78.82 if the firm takes on Project S, but by only $49.18 if it takes on Project L. Viewed in this manner, it is easy to see why S is preferred to L, and it is also easy to see the logic of the NPV approach.[5]

There is also a direct relationship between NPV and EVA (economic value added) — NPV is equal to the present value of the project's future EVAs. Therefore, accepting positive NPV projects should result in a positive EVA for the company, and to a positive MVA (market value added, or the excess of the firm's market value over its book value). So, a reward system that compensates managers for producing positive EVA will lead to the use of NPV for making capital budgeting decisions.

Internal Rate of Return (IRR)

In Chapter 8 we presented procedures for finding the yield to maturity, or rate of return, on a bond — if you invest in a bond, hold it to maturity, and receive all of the promised cash flows, you will earn the YTM on the money you invested. Exactly the same concepts are employed in capital budgeting when the **internal rate of return**

---

4. Now the calculator will ask you if the 500 is for Period 1 only or if it is also used for several following periods. Since it is only used for Period 1, press **INPUT** to answer "1." Alternatively, you could press **EXIT** and then **#T?** to turn off the prompt for the remainder of the problem. For some problems, you will want to use the repeat feature.

5. Enter the remaining CFs, being sure to turn off the prompt or else to specify "1" for each entry.

6. Once the CFs have all been entered, press **EXIT** and then **CALC**.

7. Now enter k = I = 10% as follows: 10 **I%** .

8. Now press **NPV** to get the answer, NPV = $78.82.

[4]Note that you cannot enter the −$1,000 cost as part of the NPV range. It occurs at t = 0, but the *Excel* NPV function assumes that all cash flows in the designated range occur at the end of the periods.

[5]This description of the process is somewhat oversimplified. Both analysts and investors anticipate that firms will identify and accept positive NPV projects, and current stock prices reflect these expectations. Thus, stock prices react to announcements of new capital projects only to the extent that such projects were not already expected. In this sense, we may think of a firm's value as consisting of two parts: (1) the value of its existing assets and (2) the value of its "growth opportunities," or future projects with positive NPVs.

(IRR) method is used. The **IRR** is defined as that discount rate which equates the present value of a project's expected cash inflows to the present value of the project's costs:

$$PV(\text{Inflows}) = PV(\text{Investment costs}),$$

or, equivalently, the rate which forces the NPV to equal zero:

$$NPV = CF_0 + \frac{CF_1}{(1 + IRR)^1} + \frac{CF_2}{(1 + IRR)^2} + \cdots + \frac{CF_n}{(1 + IRR)^n}$$

$$= \sum_{t=0}^{n} \frac{CF_t}{(1 + IRR)^t} = 0. \tag{11-2}$$

For our Project S, here is the time line setup:

	0	IRR	1	2	3	4
Cash Flows	−1,000		500	400	300	100
Sum of PVs for CF$_{1-4}$	1,000					
Net Present Value	0					

$$NPV = -1,000 + \frac{500}{(1 + IRR)^1} + \frac{400}{(1 + IRR)^2} + \frac{300}{(1 + IRR)^3} + \frac{100}{(1 + IRR)^4} = 0.$$

Thus, we have an equation with one unknown, IRR, and we need to solve for IRR.

Although it is easy to find the NPV without a financial calculator, this is *not* true of the IRR. If the cash flows are constant from year to year, then we have an annuity, and we can use annuity factors as discussed in Chapter 7 to find the IRR. However, if the cash flows are not constant, as is generally the case in capital budgeting, then it is difficult to find the IRR without a financial calculator. Without a calculator, you must solve Equation 11-2 by trial-and-error—try some discount rate (or PVIF factor) and see if the equation solves to zero, and if it does not, try a different discount rate, and continue until you find the rate that forces the equation to equal zero. The discount rate that causes the equation (and the NPV) to equal zero is defined as the IRR. For a realistic project with a fairly long life, the trial-and-error approach is a tedious, time-consuming task.

Fortunately, it is easy to find IRRs with a financial calculator. You follow procedures almost identical to those used to find the NPV. First, you enter the cash flows as shown on the time line into the calculator's cash flow register. In effect, you have entered the cash flows into the equation shown below the time line. Note that we have one unknown, IRR, which is the discount rate that forces the equation to equal zero. The calculator has been programmed to solve for the IRR, and you activate this program by pressing the button labeled "IRR." Then the calculator solves for IRR and displays it on the screen. Here are the IRRs for Projects S and L as found with a financial calculator:[6]

$$IRR_S = 14.5\%$$

$$IRR_L = 11.8\%.$$

---

[6]To find the IRR with an HP-10B or HP-17B, repeat the steps given in Footnote 3. Then, with an HP-10B, press ■ **IRR/YR**, and, after a pause, 14.49, Project S's IRR, will appear. With the HP-17B, simply press **IRR%** to get the IRR. With both calculators, you would generally want to get both the NPV and the IRR after entering the input data, before clearing the cash flow register. The *Technology Supplement* explains how to find IRR with several other calculators.

It is also easy to find the IRR using the same spreadsheet we used for the NPV. With *Excel,* we simply enter this formula in Cell B6: **=IRR(B4:F4).** For Project S, the result is 14.5 percent.[7]

If both projects have a cost of capital, or **hurdle rate,** of 10 percent, then the internal rate of return rule indicates that if the projects are independent, both should be accepted—they are both expected to earn more than the cost of the capital needed to finance them. If they are mutually exclusive, S ranks higher and is the one that should be accepted. If the cost of capital is above 14.5 percent, both projects should be rejected.

Notice that the internal rate of return formula, Equation 11-2, is simply the NPV formula, Equation 11-1, solved for the particular discount rate that forces the NPV to equal zero. Thus, the same basic equation is used for both methods, but in the NPV method the discount rate, k, is specified and the NPV is found, whereas in the IRR method the NPV is specified to equal zero, and the interest rate that forces this equality (the IRR) is calculated.

Mathematically, the NPV and IRR methods will always lead to the same accept/reject decisions for independent projects, because for NPV to be positive, IRR must exceed k. However, NPV and IRR can give conflicting rankings for mutually exclusive projects. This point will be discussed in more detail shortly.

Rationale for the IRR Method

Why is the particular discount rate that equates a project's cost with the present value of its receipts (the IRR) so special? The reason is based on this logic: (1) The IRR on a project is its expected rate of return. (2) If the IRR exceeds the cost of the funds used to finance the project, a surplus remains after paying for the capital, and that surplus accrues to the firm's stockholders. (3) Therefore, taking on a project whose IRR exceeds its cost of capital increases shareholders' wealth. On the other hand, if the internal rate of return is less than the cost of capital, then taking on the project imposes a cost on current stockholders. It is this "breakeven" characteristic that makes the IRR useful in evaluating capital projects.

S E L F - T E S T
Q U E S T I O N S

What four capital budgeting ranking methods were discussed in this section?

Describe each method, and give the rationale for its use.

What two methods always lead to the same accept/reject decision for independent projects?

In what sense does the payback method convey information about risk and liquidity that is not conveyed by the DCF methods?

COMPARISON OF THE NPV AND IRR METHODS

In many respects the NPV method is better than IRR, so it is tempting to explain NPV only, to state that it should be used to select projects, and to go on to the next topic. However, the IRR method is familiar to many corporate executives, it is widely entrenched in industry, and it does have some virtues. Therefore, it is important for you to understand the IRR method but also to be able to explain why, at times, a project with a lower IRR may be preferable to one with a higher IRR.

---

[7]Note that the full range can be specified with the IRR formula, because *Excel*'s IRR function assumes that the first cash flow (the negative $1,000) occurs at $t = 0$. Note too that you can use the function wizard to find the IRR. This is convenient if you don't have the formula committed to memory.

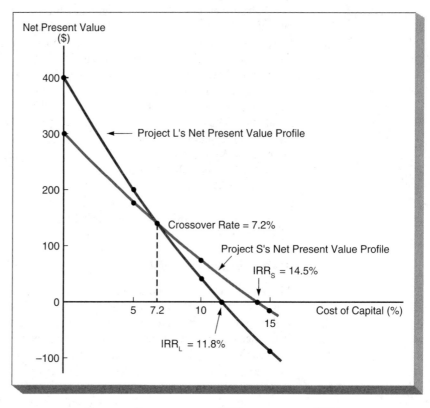

FIGURE 11-4   Net Present Value Profiles: NPVs of Projects S and L at Different Costs of Capital

DISCOUNT RATE	NPV$_S$	NPV$_L$
0%	$300.00	$400.00
5	180.42	206.50
10	78.82	49.18
15	(8.33)	(80.14)

NPV Profiles

A graph which plots a project's NPV against the discount rate is defined as the project's **net present value profile;** profiles for Projects L and S are shown in Figure 11-4. To construct NPV profiles, first note that at a zero discount rate, the NPV is simply the total of the project's undiscounted cash flows. Thus, at a zero discount rate NPV$_S$ = $300, and NPV$_L$ = $400. These values are plotted as the vertical axis intercepts in Figure 11-4. Next, we calculate the projects' NPVs at three discount rates, 5, 10, and 15 percent, and plot these values. The four points plotted on our graph for each project are shown at the bottom of the figure.[8]

---

[8]To calculate the points with a financial calculator, enter the cash flows in the cash flow register, enter I = 0, and press the NPV button to find the NPV at a zero cost of capital. Then enter I = 5 to override the zero, and press NPV to get the NPV at 5 percent. Repeat these steps for 10 and 15 percent. With a spreadsheet, you could use the Data Table command to quickly generate the data shown below the graph in Figure 11-4 and then have the spreadsheet create the graph shown in Figure 11-4.

Recall that the IRR is defined as the discount rate at which a project's NPV equals zero. Therefore, *the point where its net present value profile crosses the horizontal axis indicates a project's internal rate of return.* Since we calculated IRR_S and IRR_L in an earlier section, we can confirm the validity of the graph.

When we connect the data points, we have the net present value profiles.[9] NPV profiles can be very useful in project analysis, and we will use them often in the remainder of the chapter.

NPV Rankings Depend on the Cost of Capital

Figure 11-4 shows that the NPV profiles of both Project L and Project S decline as the discount rate increases. But notice in the figure that Project L has the higher NPV at low discount rates, while Project S has the higher NPV if the discount rate is greater than the 7.2 percent **crossover rate.** Notice also that Project L's NPV is "more sensitive" to changes in the discount rate than is NPV_S; that is, Project L's net present value profile has the steeper slope, indicating that a given change in k has a larger effect on NPV_L than on NPV_S.

To see why L has the greater sensitivity, recall first that the cash flows from S are received faster than those from L. In a payback sense, S is a short-term project, while L is a long-term project. Next, recall the equation for the NPV:

$$NPV = \frac{CF_0}{(1+k)^0} + \frac{CF_1}{(1+k)^1} + \cdots + \frac{CF_n}{(1+k)^n}.$$

The impact of an increase in the discount rate is much greater on distant than on near-term cash flows. To illustrate, consider the following:

$$\text{PV of \$100 due in 1 year @ } k = 5\%: \frac{\$100}{(1.05)^1} = \$95.24.$$

$$\text{PV of \$100 due in 1 year @ } k = 10\%: \frac{\$100}{(1.10)^1} = \$90.91.$$

$$\text{Percentage decline due to higher } k = \frac{\$95.24 - \$90.91}{\$95.24} = 4.5\%.$$

- -

$$\text{PV of \$100 due in 20 years @ } k = 5\%: \frac{\$100}{(1.05)^{20}} = \$37.69.$$

$$\text{PV of \$100 due in 20 years @ } k = 10\%: \frac{\$100}{(1.10)^{20}} = \$14.86.$$

$$\text{Percentage decline due to higher } k = \frac{\$37.69 - \$14.86}{\$37.69} = 60.6\%.$$

Thus, a doubling of the discount rate causes only a 4.5 percent decline in the PV of a Year 1 cash flow, but the same doubling of the discount rate causes the PV of a Year 20 cash flow to fall by more than 60 percent. Therefore, if a project has most of its cash flows coming in the early years, its NPV will not decline very much if the cost of capital increases, but a project whose cash flows come later will be severely penalized by higher capital costs. Accordingly, Project L, which has its largest cash flows in the later

---

[9]Notice that the NPV profiles are curved—they are *not* straight lines. NPV approaches the t = 0 cash flow (the cost of the project) as the discount rate increases without limit. The reason is that, at an infinitely high discount rate, the PV of the inflows would be zero, so NPV at ($k = \infty$) is simply CF_0, which in our example is −$1,000. We should also note that under certain conditions the NPV profiles can cross the horizontal axis several times, or never cross it. This point is discussed later in the chapter.

years, is hurt badly if the cost of capital is high, while Project S, which has relatively rapid cash flows, is affected less by high capital costs. Therefore, Project L's NPV profile has the steeper slope.

Independent Projects

If an *independent* project is being evaluated, then the NPV and IRR criteria always lead to the same accept/reject decision: if NPV says accept, IRR also says accept. To see why this is so, assume that Projects L and S are independent, and then look back at Figure 11-4 and notice (1) that the IRR criterion for acceptance for either project is that the project's cost of capital is less than (or to the left of) the IRR and (2) that whenever a project's cost of capital is less than its IRR, its NPV is positive. Thus, at any cost of capital less than 11.8 percent, Project L will be acceptable by both the NPV and the IRR criteria, while both methods reject the project if the cost of capital is greater than 11.8 percent. Project S—and all other independent projects under consideration—could be analyzed similarly, and it will always turn out that if the IRR method says accept, then so will the NPV method.

Mutually Exclusive Projects

Now assume that Projects S and L are *mutually exclusive* rather than independent. That is, we can choose either Project S or Project L, or we can reject both, but we cannot accept both projects. Notice in Figure 11-4 that as long as the cost of capital is *greater than* the crossover rate of 7.2 percent, then (1) NPV_S is larger than NPV_L, and (2) IRR_S exceeds IRR_L. Therefore, if k is *greater* than the crossover rate of 7.2 percent, the two methods both lead to the selection of Project S. However, if the cost of capital is *less than* the crossover rate, the NPV method ranks Project L higher, but the IRR method indicates that Project S is better. *Thus, a conflict exists if the cost of capital is less than the crossover rate.* NPV says choose mutually exclusive L, while IRR says take S. Which answer is correct? Logic suggests that the NPV method is better, because it selects the project which adds the most to shareholder wealth.[10]

There are two basic conditions which can cause NPV profiles to cross, and thus cause conflicts to arise between NPV and IRR: (1) when *project size (or scale) differences* exist, meaning that the cost of one project is larger than that of the other, or (2) when *timing differences* exist, meaning that the timing of cash flows from the two projects differs such that most of the cash flows from one project come in the early years while most of the cash flows from the other project come in the later years, as occurred with our Projects L and S.[11]

When either size or timing differences occur, the firm will have different amounts of funds to invest in the various years, depending on which of the two mutually exclusive projects it chooses. For example, if one project costs more than the other, then the firm will have more money at t = 0 to invest elsewhere if it selects the smaller project. Similarly, for projects of equal size, the one with the larger early cash inflows—in our example,

---

[10]The crossover rate is easy to calculate. Simply go back to Figure 11-1, where we set forth the two projects' cash flows, and calculate the difference in those flows in each year. The differences are $CF_S - CF_L = \$0, +\$400, +\$100, -\$100,$ and $-\$500$, respectively. Enter these values in the cash flow register of a financial calculator, press the IRR button, and the crossover rate, $7.17\% \approx 7.2\%$, appears. Be sure to enter $CF_0 = 0$ or else you will not get the correct answer.

[11]Of course, it is possible for mutually exclusive projects to differ with respect to both scale and timing. Also, if mutually exclusive projects have different lives (as opposed to different cash flow patterns over a common life), this introduces further complications, and for meaningful comparisons, some mutually exclusive projects must be evaluated over a common life. This point will be discussed in Chapter 12.

Project S—provides more funds for reinvestment in the early years. Given this situation, the rate of return at which differential cash flows can be invested is a critical issue.

The key to resolving conflicts between mutually exclusive projects is this: How useful is it to generate cash flows sooner rather than later? The value of early cash flows depends on the return we can earn on those cash flows, that is, the rate at which we can reinvest them. *The NPV method implicitly assumes that the rate at which cash flows can be reinvested is the cost of capital, whereas the IRR method assumes that the firm can reinvest at the IRR.* These assumptions are inherent in the mathematics of the discounting process. The cash flows may actually be withdrawn as dividends by the stockholders and spent on beer and pizza, but the NPV method still assumes that cash flows can be reinvested at the cost of capital, while the IRR method assumes reinvestment at the project's IRR.

Which is the better assumption—that cash flows can be reinvested at the cost of capital, or that they can be reinvested at the project's IRR? It can be demonstrated that generally the best assumption is that projects' cash flows are reinvested at the cost of capital.[12] Therefore, we conclude that *the best* **reinvestment rate assumption** *is the cost of capital, which is consistent with the NPV method.* This, in turn, leads us to prefer the NPV method, at least for a firm willing and able to obtain capital at a cost reasonably close to its current cost of capital.

We should reiterate that, when projects are independent, the NPV and IRR methods both lead to exactly the same accept/reject decision. However, *when evaluating mutually exclusive projects, especially those that differ in scale and/or timing, the NPV method should be used.*

Multiple IRRs

There is one other situation in which the IRR approach may not be usable—this is when projects have nonnormal cash flows. A project has *normal* cash flows if one or more cash outflows (costs) are followed by a series of cash inflows. If, however, a project calls for a large cash outflow either sometime during or at the end of its life, then the project has *nonnormal* cash flows. Projects with nonnormal cash flows can present unique difficulties when they are evaluated by the IRR method, with the most common problem being the existence of **multiple IRRs.**

When one solves Equation 11-2 to find the IRR for a project with nonnormal cash flows,

$$\sum_{t=0}^{n} \frac{CF_t}{(1 + IRR)^t} = 0, \qquad (11\text{-}2)$$

it is possible to obtain more than one value of IRR, which means that multiple IRRs occur. Notice that Equation 11-2 is a polynomial of degree n, so it has n different roots, or solutions. All except one of the roots are imaginary numbers when investments have normal cash flows (one or more cash outflows followed by cash inflows), so in the normal case, only one value of IRR appears. However, the possibility of multiple real roots, hence multiple IRRs, arises when the project has nonnormal cash flows (negative net cash flows occur during some year after the project has been placed in operation).

To illustrate this problem, suppose a firm is considering the expenditure of $1.6 million to develop a strip mine (Project M). The mine will produce a cash flow of $10 million at the end of Year 1. Then, at the end of Year 2, $10 million must be expended to

---

[12]Again, see Eugene F. Brigham and Louis C. Gapenski, *Intermediate Financial Management,* 5th ed., Chapter 7, for a discussion of this point.

restore the land to its original condition. Therefore, the project's expected net cash flows are as follows (in millions of dollars):

EXPECTED NET CASH FLOWS

YEAR 0	END OF YEAR 1	END OF YEAR 2
–$1.6	+$10	–$10

These values can be substituted into Equation 11-2 to derive the IRR for the investment:

$$\text{NPV} = \frac{-\$1.6 \text{ million}}{(1 + \text{IRR})^0} + \frac{\$10 \text{ million}}{(1 + \text{IRR})^1} + \frac{-\$10 \text{ million}}{(1 + \text{IRR})^2} = 0.$$

When solved, we find that NPV = 0 when IRR = 25% and also when IRR = 400%.[13] Therefore, the IRR of the investment is both 25 and 400 percent. This relationship is depicted graphically in Figure 11-5.[14] Note that no dilemma would arise if the NPV method were used; we would simply use Equation 11-1, find the NPV, and use this to evaluate the project. If Project M's cost of capital were 10 percent, then its NPV would be –$0.77 million, and the project would be rejected. If k were between 25 and 400 percent, the NPV would be positive.

One of the authors encountered another example of multiple internal rates of return when a major California bank *borrowed* funds from an insurance company and then used these funds (plus an initial investment of its own) to buy a number of jet engines, which it then leased to a major airline. The bank expected to receive positive net cash flows (lease payments plus tax savings minus interest on the insurance company loan) for a number of years, then several large negative cash flows as it repaid the insurance company loan, and, finally, a large inflow from the sale of the engines when the lease expired.[15]

The bank discovered two IRRs and wondered which was correct. It could not ignore the IRR and use the NPV method since the lease was already on the books,

---

[13]If you attempted to find the IRR of Project M with many financial calculators, you would get an error message. This same message would be given for all projects with multiple IRRs. However, as discussed below, financial calculators have a procedure where you key in guesses as to the IRR and then obtain the solutions. Also, you can still find Project M's IRRs by first calculating NPVs using several different values for k and then plotting the NPV profile. The intersections with the X-axis give a rough idea of the IRR values. Finally, you can use trial-and-error to find the exact values of k which force NPV = 0.

As noted above, that some calculators, including the HP-10B and 17B, can find the IRR. At the error message, key in a guess, store it, and repress the IRR key. With the HP-10B, type 10 ■ STO ■ IRR, and the answer, 25.00, appears. If you enter as your guess a cost of capital less than the one at which NPV in Figure 11-5 is maximized (about 100 percent), the lower IRR, 25 percent, is displayed. If you guess a high rate, say, 150, the higher IRR is shown.

The IRR function in spreadsheets also begins its trial-and-error search for a solution with an initial guess. If you omit the initial guess, the *Excel* default start point is 10 percent. Now suppose the values –1.6, +10, and –10 were in Cells A1:C1. You could use this *Excel* formula: **=IRR(A1:C1,10%)**, where 10 percent is the initial guess, and it would produce a result of 25 percent. If you used a guess of 150 percent, you would have this formula: **=IRR(A1:C1,150%)**, and it would produce a result of 400 percent.

[14]Does Figure 11-5 suggest that the firm should try to *raise* its cost of capital to about 100 percent in order to maximize the NPV of the project? Certainly not. The firm should seek to *minimize* its cost of capital; this will cause its stock price to be maximized. Actions taken to raise the cost of capital might make this particular project look good, but those actions would be terribly harmful to the firm's more numerous projects with normal cash flows. Only if the firm's cost of capital is high in spite of efforts to keep it down will the illustrative project have a positive NPV.

[15]The situation described here is a *leveraged lease*. See Chapter 19 for more on leases.

FIGURE 11-5   NPV Profile for Project M

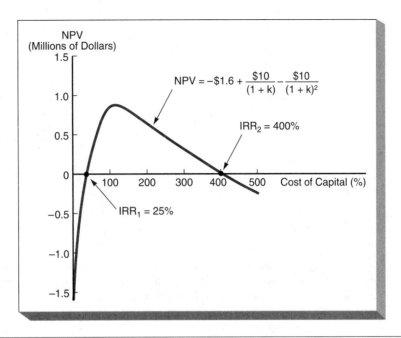

and the bank's senior loan committee, as well as Federal Reserve bank examiners, wanted to know the return on the lease. The bank's solution called for calculating and then using the "modified internal rate of return" as discussed in the next section.

The examples just presented illustrate one problem, multiple IRRs, that can arise when the IRR criterion is used with a project that has nonnormal cash flows. Use of the IRR method on projects having nonnormal cash flows could produce other problems such as no IRR or an IRR which leads to an incorrect accept/reject decision. In all such cases, the NPV criterion could be easily applied, and the NPV method leads to conceptually correct capital budgeting decisions.

SELF-TEST QUESTIONS

Describe how NPV profiles are constructed.

What is the crossover rate, and how does it affect the choice between mutually exclusive projects?

What two basic conditions can lead to conflicts between the NPV and IRR methods?

Why is the "reinvestment rate" considered to be the underlying cause of conflicts between the NPV and IRR methods?

If a conflict exists, should the capital budgeting decision be made on the basis of the NPV or the IRR ranking? Why?

Explain the difference between normal and nonnormal cash flows.

What is the "multiple IRR problem," and what condition is necessary for its occurrence?

MODIFIED INTERNAL RATE OF RETURN (MIRR)

In spite of a strong academic preference for NPV, surveys indicate that executives prefer IRR over NPV. Apparently, managers find it intuitively more appealing to evaluate investments in terms of percentage rates of return than dollars of NPV. Given this fact, can we devise a percentage evaluator that is better than the regular IRR? The answer is yes—we can modify the IRR and make it a better indicator of relative profitability, hence better for use in capital budgeting. The new measure is called the **modified IRR,** or **MIRR,** and it is defined as follows:

$$PV \text{ costs} = PV \text{ terminal value}$$

$$\sum_{t=0}^{n} \frac{COF_t}{(1+k)^t} = \frac{\sum_{t=0}^{n} CIF_t(1+k)^{n-t}}{(1+MIRR)^n}$$

$$PV \text{ costs} = \frac{TV}{(1+MIRR)^n}. \tag{11-2a}$$

Here COF refers to cash outflows (negative numbers), or the cost of the project, and CIF refers to cash inflows (positive numbers). The left term is simply the PV of the investment outlays when discounted at the cost of capital, and the numerator of the right term is the future value of the inflows, assuming that the cash inflows are reinvested at the cost of capital. The future value of the cash inflows is also called the *terminal value,* or *TV.* The discount rate that forces the PV of the TV to equal the PV of the costs is defined as the MIRR.[16]

If the investment costs are all incurred at $t = 0$, and if the first operating inflow occurs at $t = 1$, as is true for our illustrative Projects S and L as shown in Figure 11-1, then this equation may be used:

$$Cost = \frac{TV}{(1+MIRR)^n} = \frac{\sum_{t=1}^{n} CIF_t(1+k)^{n-t}}{(1+MIRR)^n}. \tag{11-2b}$$

We can illustrate the calculation with Project S:

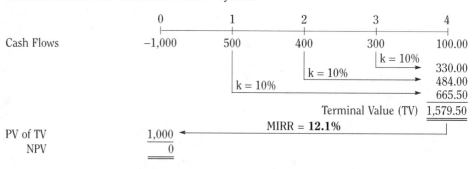

[16]There are several alternative definitions for the MIRR. The differences primarily relate to whether negative cash flows which occur after positive cash flows begin should be compounded and treated as part of the TV or discounted and treated as a cost. A related issue is whether negative and positive flows in a given year should be netted or treated separately. For a complete discussion, see William R. McDaniel, Daniel E. McCarty, and Kenneth A. Jessell, "Discounted Cash Flow with Explicit Reinvestment Rates: Tutorial and Extension," *The Financial Review,* August 1988, 369–385, and David M. Shull, "Interpreting Rates of Return: A Modified Rate of Return Approach," *Financial Practice and Education,* Fall 1993, 67–71.

Using the cash flows as set out on the time line, first find the terminal value by compounding each cash inflow at the 10 percent cost of capital. Then enter N = 4, PV = −1000, PMT = 0, FV = 1579.5, and then press the I button to find $MIRR_S$ = 12.1%. Similarly, we find $MIRR_L$ = 11.3%.[17]

The modified IRR has a significant advantage over the regular IRR. MIRR assumes that cash flows from all projects are reinvested at some explicit rate, generally the cost of capital, while the regular IRR assumes that the cash flows from each project are reinvested at the project's own IRR. Since reinvestment at the cost of capital (or some other explicit rate) is generally more correct, the modified IRR is a better indicator of a project's true profitability. The MIRR also solves the multiple IRR problem. To illustrate, with k = 10%, Project M (the strip mine project) has MIRR = 5.6% versus its 10 percent cost of capital, so it should be rejected. This is consistent with the decision based on the NPV method, because at k = 10%, NPV = −$0.77 million.

Is MIRR as good as NPV for choosing between mutually exclusive projects? If two projects are of equal size and have the same life, then NPV and MIRR will always lead to the same decision. Thus, for any set of projects like our Projects S and L, if NPV_S > NPV_L, then $MIRR_S$ > $MIRR_L$, and the kinds of conflicts we encountered between NPV and the regular IRR will not occur. Also, if the projects are of equal size, but differ in lives, the MIRR will always lead to the same decision as the NPV if the MIRRs are both calculated using as the terminal year the life of the longer project. (Just fill in zeros for the shorter project's missing cash flows.) However, if the projects differ in size, then conflicts can still occur. For example, if we were choosing between a large project and a small mutually exclusive one, then we might find NPV_L > NPV_S, but $MIRR_S$ > $MIRR_L$.

Our conclusion is that the MIRR is superior to the regular IRR as an indicator of a project's "true" rate of return, or "expected long-term rate of return," but the NPV method is still better for choosing among mutually exclusive projects because it provides a better indicator of how much each project will increase the value of the firm.

SELF-TEST
QUESTIONS

Describe how the modified IRR (MIRR) is calculated.

What is the primary difference between the MIRR and the regular IRR?

What advantages does the MIRR have over the regular IRR for making capital budgeting decisions?

What condition can cause the MIRR and NPV methods to produce conflicting rankings?

---

[17]With some calculators, including the HP-17B, you could enter the cash inflows in the cash flow register (being sure to enter CF_0 = 0), enter I = 10, and then press the NFV key to find TV = 1,579.50. The HP-10B does not have a NFV key, but you can still use the cash flow register to find TV. Enter the cash flows in the cash flow register (with CF_0 = 0), then enter I = 10, then press ■ NPV to find the PV of the inflows, which is 1,078.82. Now, with the regular time value keys, enter N = 4, I = 10, PV = −1078.82, PMT = 0, and press FV to find TV = 1,579.50. Similar procedures can be used with other financial calculators.

Most spreadsheets have a function for finding the MIRR. Refer back to our spreadsheet for Project S, with cash flows of −1,000, 500, 400, 300, and 100 in Cells B4:F4. You could use the *Excel* function wizard to set up the following formula: =MIRR(B4:F4,10%,10%). Here the first 10 percent is the cost of capital used for discounting, and the second one is the rate used for compounding, or the reinvestment rate. In our definition of the MIRR, we assume that reinvestment is at the cost of capital, so we enter 10 percent twice. The result is an MIRR of 12.1 percent.

PROFITABILITY INDEX

Another method used to evaluate projects is the **profitability index (PI),** or the *benefit/ cost ratio,* as it is sometimes called:

$$PI = \frac{PV \text{ benefits}}{PV \text{ costs}} = \frac{\sum_{t=0}^{n} \frac{CIF_t}{(1+k)^t}}{\sum_{t=0}^{n} \frac{COF_t}{(1+k)^t}}.$$
(11-3)

Here CIF_t represents the expected cash *inflows,* or benefits, and COF_t represents the expected cash *outflows,* or costs. The PI shows the *relative* profitability of any project, or the present value of benefits per present value dollar of costs. The PI for Project S, based on a 10 percent cost of capital, is 1.079:

$$PI_S = \frac{\$1,078.82}{\$1,000} = 1.079.$$

Thus, on a present value basis, Project S is expected to produce $1.079 for each $1 of investment. Project L, with a PI of 1.049, should produce $1.049 for each dollar invested.

A project is acceptable if its PI is greater than 1.0, and the higher the PI, the higher the project's ranking. Therefore, both S and L would be accepted by the PI criterion if they were independent, and S would be ranked ahead of L if they were mutually exclusive.

Mathematically, the NPV, IRR, MIRR, and PI methods will always lead to the same accept/reject decisions for *independent* projects: If a project's NPV is positive, its IRR and MIRR will always exceed k, and its PI will always be greater than 1.0. However, these methods can give conflicting rankings for *mutually exclusive* projects. This point is discussed in more detail in the next section.

SELF-TEST
QUESTION

Explain how the PI is calculated. Why might someone be interested in the PI?

CONCLUSIONS ON CAPITAL BUDGETING METHODS

We have discussed six capital budgeting decision methods, comparing the methods against one another and highlighting their relative strengths and weaknesses. In the process, we probably created the impression that "sophisticated" firms should use only one method in the decision process, NPV. However, virtually all capital budgeting decisions are analyzed by computer, so it is easy to calculate and list all the decision measures: payback and discounted payback, NPV, IRR, modified IRR (MIRR), and PI. In making the accept/reject decision, most large, sophisticated firms such as IBM, GE, and Royal Dutch Petroleum calculate and consider all of the measures, because each one provides decision makers with a somewhat different piece of relevant information.

Payback and discounted payback provide an indication of both the *risk* and the *liquidity* of a project—a long payback means (1) that the investment dollars will be locked up for many years, hence the project is relatively illiquid, and (2) that the project's cash flows must be forecast far out into the future, hence the project is probably risky. A good analogy for this is the bond valuation process. An investor should never compare the *yields* to maturity on two bonds without also considering their *terms* to maturity, because a bond's riskiness is significantly influenced by its maturity.

NPV is important because it gives a direct measure of the dollar benefit of the project to shareholders, so we regard NPV as the best single measure of *profitability*. IRR also measures profitability, but here it is expressed as a percentage rate of return, which many decision makers prefer. Further, IRR contains information concerning a project's "safety margin." To illustrate, consider the following two projects: Project S (for small) costs $10,000 at t = 0 and is expected to return $16,500 at the end of one year, while Project L (for large) costs $100,000 and has an expected payoff of $115,500 after one year. At a 10 percent cost of capital, both projects have an NPV of $5,000, so by the NPV rule we should be indifferent between them. However, Project S has a much larger margin for error. Even if its realized cash inflow were 39 percent below the $16,500 forecast, the firm would still recover its $10,000 investment. On the other hand, if Project L's inflows fell by only 13 percent from the forecasted $115,500, the firm would not recover its investment. Further, if no inflows were ever generated, the firm would lose only $10,000 with Project S but $100,000 if it took on Project L.

The NPV provides no information about either the "safety margin" inherent in the cash flow forecasts or the amount of capital at risk. However, the IRR does provide "safety margin" information—Project S's IRR is a whopping 65.0 percent, while Project L's IRR is only 15.5 percent. As a result, the realized return could fall substantially for Project S, and it would still make money. Finally, the modified IRR has all the virtues of the IRR, but (1) it incorporates a better reinvestment rate assumption, and (2) it avoids the multiple rate of return problem.

The PI measures profitability relative to the cost of a project—it shows the "bang per buck." Like the IRR, it gives an indication of the project's risk, for a high PI means that cash flows could fall quite a bit and the project would still be profitable.

The different measures provide different types of information to decision makers. Since it is easy to calculate all of them, all should be considered in the decision process. For any specific decision, more weight might be given to one measure than another, but it would be foolish to ignore the information provided by any of the methods.

Just as it would be foolish to ignore these capital budgeting methods, it would also be foolish to make decisions based *solely* on them. One cannot know at Time 0 the exact cost of future capital, or the exact future cash flows. These inputs are simply estimates, and if they turn out to be incorrect, then so will be the calculated NPVs and IRRs. *Thus, quantitative methods provide valuable information, but they should not be used as the sole criteria for accept/reject decisions* in the capital budgeting process. Rather, managers should use quantitative methods in the decision-making process but also consider the likelihood that actual results will differ from the forecasts. Qualitative factors, such as the chances of a tax increase, or a war, or a major product liability suit, should also be considered. *In summary, quantitative methods such as NPV and IRR should be considered as an aid to informed decisions but not as a substitute for sound managerial judgment.*

In this same vein, managers should ask sharp questions about any project that has a large NPV, a high IRR, or a high PI. In a perfectly competitive economy, there would be no positive NPV projects—all companies would have the same opportunities, and competition would quickly eliminate any positive NPV. Therefore, positive NPV projects must be predicated on some imperfection in the marketplace, and the longer the life of the project, the longer that imperfection must last. Therefore, managers should be able to identify the imperfection and explain why it will persist before accepting that a project will really have a positive NPV. Valid explanations might include patents or proprietary technology, which is how pharmaceutical and software firms create positive NPV projects. Hoechst's Allegra® allergy medicine and Microsoft's Windows 95® operating system are examples. Companies can also create positive NPV by being the first entrant into a new market or by creating new products that meet some previously unidentified consumer needs. The Post-it® notes invented by 3M and the fourth door on Chrysler's 1996 Caravans are examples. Similarly, Dell developed procedures for direct sales of microcomputers, and in the process created projects with enormous NPV. Also, companies such as Southwest Airlines have managed to train and motivate their workers better than their competitors, and this has led to positive NPV projects. In all of these cases, the companies developed some source of competitive advantage, and that advantage resulted in positive NPV projects.

This discussion suggests three things: (1) If you can't identify the reason a project has a positive projected NPV, then its actual NPV will probably not be positive. (2) Positive NPV projects don't just happen—they result from hard work to develop some competitive advantage. At the risk of oversimplification, the primary job of a manager is to find and develop areas of competitive advantage. (3) Some competitive advantages last longer than others, with their durability depending on competitors' ability to replicate them. Patents, the control of scarce resources, or large size in an industry where strong economies of scale exist can keep competitors at bay. Also, it is hard to develop competence in R&D or build a culture that motivates the workforce. However, it is relatively easy to replicate features on products. Chrysler's fourth door on the Caravan certainly created positive NPV in 1996, but competitors quickly introduced a fourth door on their own minivans. The bottom line is that managers should strive to develop nonreplicatible sources of competitive advantage, and if such an advantage cannot be demonstrated, then you should question projects with high NPV, especially if they have long lives.

SELF-TEST QUESTIONS	Describe the advantages and disadvantages of the six capital budgeting methods discussed in this chapter.
	Should capital budgeting decisions be made solely on the basis of a project's NPV?
	What are some possible reasons that a project might have a large NPV?

BUSINESS PRACTICES

Harold Bierman published a survey of the capital budgeting methods used by the Fortune 500 industrial companies; here is a summary of his findings:[18]

1. This 1993 study found that every single one of the responding firms used some type of DCF method. In 1955, a similar study reported that only 4 percent of large companies used a DCF method. Thus, large firms' usage of DCF methodology has increased dramatically since the 1950s.

2. The payback period was used by 84 percent of Bierman's surveyed companies. However, no company used it as the primary method, and most companies gave the greatest weight to a DCF method. In 1955, surveys similar to Bierman's found that payback was the most important method.

3. Currently, 99 percent of the Fortune 500 companies use IRR, while 85 percent use NPV. Thus, most firms actually use both methods.

4. Ninety-three percent of Bierman's companies calculate a weighted average cost of capital as part of their capital budgeting process. A few companies apparently use the same WACC for all projects, but 73 percent adjust the corporate WACC to

---

[18]Harold Bierman, "Capital Budgeting in 1993: A Survey," *Financial Management,* Autumn 1993, 24.

account for project risk, and 23 percent make adjustments to reflect divisional risk. We will cover risk analysis in Chapter 12.

5. An examination of surveys done by other authors led Bierman to conclude that there has been a strong trend toward the acceptance of academic recommendations, at least by large companies.

A second 1993 study, conducted by Joe Walker, Richard Burns, and Chad Denson (WBD), focused on small companies.[19] WBD began by noting the same trend toward the use of DCF that Bierman cited, but they reported that only 21 percent of small companies used DCF versus 100 percent for Bierman's large companies. WBD also noted that within their sample, the smaller the firm, the smaller the likelihood that DCF would be used. The focal point of the WBD study was *why* small companies use DCF so much less frequently than large firms. WBD actually based their questionnaire on our box entitled "Capital Budgeting in the Small Firm" on pages 446 and 447, and they concluded that the reasons given in that section do indeed explain why DCF is used infrequently by small firms. The three most frequently cited reasons, according to the survey, were (1) small firms' preoccupation with liquidity, which is best indicated by payback, (2) a lack of familiarity with DCF methods, and (3) a belief that for small projects DCF is not worth the effort.

The general conclusion one can reach from these studies is that large firms should and do use the procedures we recommend, and that managers of small firms, especially managers with aspirations for future growth, should at least understand DCF procedures well enough to make rational decisions about using or not using them. Moreover, as computer technology makes it easier and less expensive for small firms to use DCF methods, and as more and more of their competitors begin using these methods, survival will necessitate increased DCF usage.

<table>
<tr><td>S E L F - T E S T
Q U E S T I O N S</td><td>What were Bierman's findings from his survey of capital budgeting methods used by the Fortune 500 companies?

How did the WBD study's findings differ from Bierman's findings?

What general considerations can be reached from these studies?</td></tr>
</table>

THE POST-AUDIT

An important aspect of the capital budgeting process is the **post-audit,** which involves (1) comparing actual results with those predicted by the project's sponsors and (2) explaining why any differences occurred. For example, many firms require that the operating divisions send a monthly report for the first six months after a project goes into operation, and a quarterly report thereafter, until the project's results are up to expectations. From then on, reports on the operation are reviewed on a regular basis like those of other operations.

The post-audit has three main purposes:

1. **Improve forecasts.** When decision makers are forced to compare their projections with actual outcomes, there is a tendency for estimates to improve. Conscious or unconscious biases are observed and eliminated; new forecasting methods are sought as the need for them becomes apparent; and people simply tend to do

---

[19]Joe Walker, Richard Burns, and Chad Denson, "Why Small Manufacturing Firms Shun DCF," *Journal of Small Business Finance,* 1993, 233–249.

CAPITAL BUDGETING IN THE SMALL FIRM

The allocation of capital in small firms is as important as it is in large ones. In fact, given their lack of access to the capital markets, it is often more important in the small firm, because the funds necessary to correct a mistake may not be available. Also, large firms allocate capital to numerous projects, so a mistake on one can be offset by successes with others. Small firms do not have this luxury.

In spite of the importance of capital expenditures to small business, studies of the way decisions are made generally suggest that many small firms use "back-of-the-envelope" analysis, or perhaps no analysis at all. For example, when L. R. Runyon studied 214 firms with net worths of $500,000 to $1,000,000, he found that almost 70 percent relied upon payback or some other questionable criteria. Only 14 percent used a discounted cash flow analysis, and about 9 percent indicated that they used no formal analysis at all. Studies of larger firms, on the other hand, generally find that most analyze capital budgeting decisions using discounted cash flow techniques.

We are left with a puzzle. Capital budgeting is clearly important to small firms, yet these firms do not use the tools that have been developed to improve these decisions. Why does this situation exist? One argument is that managers of small firms are simply not well trained; they are unsophisticated. This argument suggests that the managers would use the more sophisticated techniques if they understood them better.

Another argument relates to the fact that management talent is a scarce resource in small firms. That is, even if the managers were exceptionally sophisticated, perhaps demands on them are such that they simply cannot take the time to use elaborate techniques to analyze proposed projects. In other words, small-business managers may be capable of doing careful discounted cash flow analysis, but it would be irrational for them to allocate the time required for such an analysis.

A third argument relates to the cost of analyzing capital projects. To some extent, these costs are fixed; the costs of analysis may be larger for bigger projects, but not by much. To the extent that these costs are indeed fixed, it may not be economical to incur them if the project itself is relatively small. This argument suggests that small firms with small projects may in some cases be making the sensible decision when they rely on management's "gut feeling."

Note also that a major part of the capital budgeting process in large firms involves lower-level analysts' marshalling facts needed by higher-level decision makers. This step is less necessary in the small firm. Thus, a cursory examination of a small firm's decision process might suggest that capital budgeting decisions are based on snap judgment, but if that judgment is exercised by someone with a total knowledge of the firm and its markets, it could represent a better decision than one based on an elaborate analysis by a lower-level employee in a large firm.

Also, as Runyon reported in his study of manufacturing firms, small firms tend to be cash oriented. They are concerned with basic survival, so they tend to look at expenditures from the standpoint of their near-term effects on cash. This cash and survival orientation leads firms to focus on a relatively short time horizon, and this, in turn, may lead to an emphasis on the payback method. The limitations of payback are well known, but in spite of those limitations, the technique is popular in small business, as it gives the firm a feel for when the cash committed to an investment will be recovered and thus available to repay loans or for new opportunities. Therefore, small firms that are cash oriented and have limited managerial resources may find the payback method appealing. It represents a compromise between the need for extensive analysis on the

---

everything better, including forecasting, if they know that their actions are being monitored.

2. **Improve operations.** Businesses are run by people, and people can perform at higher or lower levels of efficiency. When a divisional team has made a forecast about an investment, its members are, in a sense, putting their reputations on the line. If costs are above predicted levels, sales below expectations, and so on, executives in production, sales, and other areas will strive to improve operations and to bring results into line with forecasts. In a discussion related to this point, one executive made this statement: "You academicians worry only about making good decisions. In business, we also worry about making decisions good."

3. **Identify abandonment/termination opportunities.** Although the decision to undertake a project may be the correct one based on information at hand, things do not

one hand and the high costs of analysis on the other.

Small firms also face greater uncertainty in the cash flows they might generate beyond the immediate future. Large firms such as AT&T and General Motors have "staying power"—they can make an investment and then ride out business downturns or situations of excess capacity in an industry. Such periods are called "shakeouts," and it is the smaller firms that are generally shaken out. Therefore, most small-business managers are uncomfortable making forecasts beyond a few years. Since discounted cash flow techniques require explicit estimates of cash flows through the life of the project, small-business managers may not take seriously an analysis that hinges on "guesstimate" numbers which, if wrong, could lead to bankruptcy.

The Value of the Firm and Capital Budgeting

The single most appealing argument for the use of net present value in capital budgeting is that NPV gives an explicit measure of the effect the investment will have on the firm's value: if NPV is positive, the investment will increase the firm's value and make its owners wealthier. In small firms, however, the stock is often not traded in public markets, so its value cannot be observed. Also,

for reasons of control, many small-business owners and managers may not want to broaden ownership by going public.

It is difficult to argue for value-based techniques when the firm's value itself is unobservable. Furthermore, in a closely held firm, the objectives of the individual owner-manager may extend beyond the firm's monetary value. For example, the owner-manager may value the firm's reputation for quality and service and therefore may make an investment that would be rejected on purely economic grounds. In addition, the owner-manager may not hold a well-diversified investment portfolio but may instead have all of his or her eggs in this one basket. In that case, the manager would logically be sensitive to the firm's stand-alone risk, not just to its undiversifiable component. Thus, one project might be viewed as desirable because of its contribution to risk reduction in the firm as a whole, whereas another project with a low beta but high diversifiable risk might be unacceptable, even though in a CAPM framework it would be judged superior.

Another problem faced by a firm that is not publicly traded is that its cost of equity capital is not easily determined—the P_0 term in the cost of equity equation $k = D_1/P_0 + g$ is not observable, nor is its beta. Since a cost of capital estimate is required

to use either the NPV or the IRR method, a small firm in an industry of small firms may simply have no basis for estimating its cost of capital.

Conclusions

Small firms make less extensive use of DCF techniques than larger firms. This may be a rational decision resulting from a conscious or subconscious conclusion that the costs of sophisticated analyses outweigh their benefits; it may reflect nonmonetary goals of small businesses' owner-managers; or it may reflect difficulties in estimating the cost of capital, which is required for DCF analyses but not for payback. However, nonuse of DCF methods may also reflect a weakness in many small firms. We simply do not know. We do know that small businesses must do all they can to compete effectively with big business, and to the extent that a small business fails to use DCF methods because its manager is unsophisticated or uninformed, it may be putting itself at a serious competitive disadvantage.

SOURCE: L. R. Runyon, "Capital Expenditure Decision Making in Small Firms," *Journal of Business Research*, September 1983, 389–397. Reprinted with permission.

always turn out as expected. If initial operating results indicate that a project is not likely to achieve its expected profitability, it may be best for the firm to abandon rather than continue the project. Furthermore, most projects, at some point in their lives, lose their economic viability and should be terminated. Both the post-audit and a continuing review of ongoing operations help identify the optimal point for abandonment or termination of a project.

The post-audit is not a simple process—a number of factors can cause complications. First, we must recognize that each element of the cash flow forecast is subject to uncertainty, so a percentage of all projects undertaken by any reasonably aggressive firm will necessarily go awry. This fact must be considered when appraising the performances of the operating executives who submit capital expenditure requests. Second, projects sometimes fail to meet expectations for reasons beyond the control of the operating executives and for reasons that no one could realistically be expected to anticipate. For example, the 1997–1998 Asian financial crisis adversely affected many projects. Third, although some projects stand alone and permit ready identification of costs and revenues, the actual cost savings that result from projects such as a new computer system may be very hard to measure. Fourth, it is often hard to hand out blame or praise because the executives who were responsible for launching a given investment may have moved on by the time the results are known.

Because of these difficulties, some firms tend to play down the importance of the post-audit. However, the results of post-audits often conclude that (1) the actual NPVs of most cost reduction projects exceed their expected NPVs by a slight amount, (2) expansion projects generally fall short of their expected NPVs by a slight amount, and (3) new product and new market projects fall short by relatively large amounts. Thus, biases seem to exist, and companies that understand them can build in corrections and thus design better capital budgeting programs. In summary, our observations of businesses and governmental units suggest that the best-run and most successful organizations put great emphasis on post-audits. Accordingly, we regard the post-audit as being one of the most important elements in a good capital budgeting system.

SELF-TEST QUESTIONS

What is done in the post-audit?

Identify several purposes of the post-audit.

What are some factors which can cause complications in the post-audit?

USING CAPITAL BUDGETING TECHNIQUES IN OTHER CONTEXTS

The techniques developed in this chapter can help managers make a number of different types of decisions. One example is the use of these techniques when evaluating corporate mergers. Companies frequently decide to acquire other firms to obtain low-cost production facilities, to increase capacity, or to expand into new markets, and the analysis related to such mergers is conceptually similar to that related to regular capital budgeting. Thus, when AT&T decided to go into the cellular telephone business, it had the choice of building facilities from the ground up or acquiring an existing business. AT&T chose to acquire McCaw Cellular. In the analysis related to the merger, AT&T's managers used the techniques employed in regular capital budgeting analysis. We discuss merger analysis in detail in Chapter 26.

Managers also use capital budgeting techniques when deciding whether to downsize personnel or to sell off particular assets or divisions. Like capital budgeting, such an analysis requires an assessment of how the action will affect the firm's cash flows. In a downsizing, companies typically spend money (i.e., invest) in severance payments to employees who are no longer needed, but the companies then receive benefits in the form of lower future wage costs. When assets are sold, the pattern of cash flows is reversed from those in a typical capital budgeting decision—positive cash flows are realized at the outset, but the firm is sacrificing future cash flows that it would have received if it had continued to use the asset. So, when deciding whether it makes sense to shed assets, managers compare the cash received with the present value of the lost outflows. If the net present value is positive, the asset sale would increase shareholder value.

Most decisions should be based on whether they contribute to shareholder value, and that, in turn, can be determined by estimating the net present value of a set of cash flows. However, as you will see in the next chapter, the hardest part is coming up with reasonable estimates of those cash flows.

S E L F - T E S T
Q U E S T I O N

Give some examples of other decisions that can be analyzed with the capital budgeting techniques developed in this chapter.

SUMMARY

This chapter discussed the capital budgeting process. The key concepts covered are listed below.

- **Capital budgeting** is the process of analyzing potential long-term investments. Capital budgeting decisions are probably the most important ones financial managers must make.

- The **payback period** is defined as the number of years required to recover a project's cost. The regular payback method ignores cash flows beyond the payback period, and it does not consider the time value of money. The payback does, however, provide an indication of a project's risk and liquidity, because it shows how long the invested capital will be "at risk."

- The **discounted payback method** is similar to the regular payback method except that it discounts cash flows at the project's cost of capital. It considers the time value of money, but it ignores cash flows beyond the payback period.

- The **net present value (NPV) method** discounts all cash flows at the project's cost of capital and then sums those cash flows. The project is accepted if the NPV is positive.

- The **internal rate of return (IRR)** is defined as the discount rate which forces a project's NPV to equal zero. The project is accepted if the IRR is greater than the cost of capital.

- The NPV and IRR methods make the same accept/reject decisions for **independent projects,** but if projects are **mutually exclusive,** then ranking conflicts can arise. If conflicts arise, the NPV method should be used. The NPV and IRR methods are both superior to the payback, but NPV is superior to IRR.

- The NPV method assumes that cash flows will be reinvested at the firm's cost of capital, while the IRR method assumes reinvestment at the project's IRR. **Reinvestment at the cost of capital is generally a better assumption** in that it is closer to reality.

- The **modified IRR (MIRR) method** corrects some of the problems with the regular IRR. MIRR involves finding the **terminal value (TV)** of the cash inflows, compounded at the firm's cost of capital, and then determining the discount rate which forces the present value of the TV to equal the present value of the outflows.

- The **profitability index (PI)** shows the dollars of present value divided by the dollars of cost, so it measures relative profitability.

- Sophisticated managers consider all of the project evaluation measures because each measure provides a useful piece of information.

- The **post-audit** is a key element of capital budgeting. By comparing actual results with predicted results and then determining why differences occurred, decision makers can improve both their operations and their forecasts of projects' outcomes.

■ Small firms tend to use the payback method rather than a discounted cash flow method. This may be rational, because (1) the **cost** of conducting a DCF analysis **may outweigh the benefits** for the project being considered, (2) **the firm's cost of capital cannot be estimated accurately,** or (3) the small-business owner may be considering **nonmonetary goals.**

Although this chapter has presented the basic elements of the capital budgeting process, there are many other aspects of this crucial topic. Some of the more important ones are discussed in the following chapter.

Questions

11-1 Define each of the following terms:
a. The capital budget; capital budgeting; strategic business plan
b. Regular payback period; discounted payback period
c. Independent projects; mutually exclusive projects
d. DCF techniques; net present value (NPV) method
e. Internal rate of return (IRR) method
f. Modified internal rate of return (MIRR) method; profitability index
g. NPV profile; crossover rate
h. Nonnormal cash flow projects; normal cash flow projects; multiple IRRs
i. Project cost of capital, or discount rate
j. Reinvestment rate assumption
k. Post-audit

11-2 How is a project classification scheme (for example, replacement, expansion into new markets, and so forth) used in the capital budgeting process?

11-3 Explain why the NPV of a relatively long-term project, defined as one for which a high percentage of its cash flows are expected in the distant future, is more sensitive to changes in the cost of capital than is the NPV of a short-term project.

11-4 Explain why, if two mutually exclusive projects are being compared, the short-term project might have the higher ranking under the NPV criterion if the cost of capital is high, but the long-term project might be deemed better if the cost of capital is low. Would changes in the cost of capital ever cause a change in the IRR ranking of two such projects?

11-5 In what sense is a reinvestment rate assumption embodied in the NPV, IRR, and MIRR methods? What is the assumed reinvestment rate of each method?

11-6 "If a firm has no mutually exclusive projects, only independent ones, and it also has both a constant cost of capital and projects with normal cash flows in the sense that each project has one or more outflows followed by a stream of inflows, then the NPV and IRR methods will always lead to identical capital budgeting decisions." Discuss this statement. What does it imply about using the IRR method in lieu of the NPV method? If each of the assumptions made in the question were changed (one by one), how would these changes affect your answer?

11-7 Are there conditions under which a firm might be better off if it were to choose a machine with a rapid payback rather than one with a larger NPV?

11-8 A firm has $100 million available for capital expenditures. It is considering investing in one of two projects; each has a cost of $100 million. Project A has an IRR of 20 percent and an NPV of $9 million. It will be terminated at the end of 1 year at a profit of $20 million, resulting in an immediate increase in earnings per share (EPS). Project B, which cannot be postponed, has an IRR of 30 percent and an NPV of $50 million. However, the firm's short-run EPS will be reduced if it accepts Project B, because no revenues will be generated for several years.
a. Should the short-run effects on EPS influence the choice between the two projects?
b. How might situations like the one described here influence a firm's decision to use payback as a part of the capital budgeting process?

Self-Test Problem   (Solution Appears in Appendix B)

ST-1
Project Analysis

You are a financial analyst for the Hittle Company. The director of capital budgeting has asked you to analyze two proposed capital investments, Projects X and Y. Each project has a cost of

$10,000, and the cost of capital for each project is 12 percent. The projects' expected net cash flows are as follows:

	EXPECTED NET CASH FLOWS	
YEAR	PROJECT X	PROJECT Y
0	($10,000)	($10,000)
1	6,500	3,500
2	3,000	3,500
3	3,000	3,500
4	1,000	3,500

a. Calculate each project's payback period, net present value (NPV), internal rate of return (IRR), and modified internal rate of return (MIRR).
b. Which project or projects should be accepted if they are independent?
c. Which project should be accepted if they are mutually exclusive?
d. How might a change in the cost of capital produce a conflict between the NPV and IRR rankings of these two projects? Would this conflict exist if k were 5%? (Hint: Plot the NPV profiles.)
e. Why does the conflict exist?

Problems

11-1
Payback Period

Project K has a cost of $52,125, its expected net cash inflows are $12,000 per year for 8 years, and its cost of capital is 12 percent. What is the project's payback period (to the closest year)? (Hint: Begin by constructing a time line.)

11-2
NPV

Refer to Problem 11-1. What is the project's NPV?

11-3
IRR

Refer to Problem 11-1. What is the project's IRR?

11-4
Discounted Payback Period

Refer to Problem 11-1. What is the project's discounted payback period?

11-5
MIRR

Refer to Problem 11-1. What is the project's MIRR?

11-6
NPV

Your division is considering two investment projects, each of which requires an up-front expenditure of $15 million. You estimate that the investments will produce the following net cash flows:

YEAR	PROJECT A	PROJECT B
1	$ 5,000,000	$20,000,000
2	10,000,000	10,000,000
3	20,000,000	6,000,000

What are the two projects' net present values, assuming the cost of capital is 10 percent? 5 percent? 15 percent?

11-7
NPV; Financial Calculator Required

Northwest Utility Corporation has a cost of capital of 11.5 percent, and it has a project with the following net cash flows:

t	NET CASH FLOW
0	−$200
1	235
2	−65
3	300

What is the project's NPV?

11-8
NPVs, IRRs, and MIRRs for
Independent Projects

Edelman Engineering is considering including two pieces of equipment, a truck and an overhead pulley system, in this year's capital budget. The projects are independent. The cash outlay for the truck is $17,100, and that for the pulley system is $22,430. The firm's cost of capital is 14 percent. After-tax cash flows, including depreciation, are as follows:

YEAR	TRUCK	PULLEY
1	$5,100	$7,500
2	5,100	7,500
3	5,100	7,500
4	5,100	7,500
5	5,100	7,500

Calculate the IRR, the NPV, and the MIRR for each project, and indicate the correct accept/reject decision for each.

11-9
NPVs and IRRs for Mutually
Exclusive Projects

B. Davis Industries must choose between a gas-powered and an electric-powered forklift truck for moving materials in its factory. Since both forklifts perform the same function, the firm will choose only one. (They are mutually exclusive investments.) The electric-powered truck will cost more, but it will be less expensive to operate; it will cost $22,000, whereas the gas-powered truck will cost $17,500. The cost of capital that applies to both investments is 12 percent. The life for both types of truck is estimated to be 6 years, during which time the net cash flows for the electric-powered truck will be $6,290 per year and those for the gas-powered truck will be $5,000 per year. Annual net cash flows include depreciation expenses. Calculate the NPV and IRR for each type of truck, and decide which to recommend.

11-10
Capital Budgeting Methods

Project S has a cost of $10,000 and is expected to produce benefits (cash flows) of $3,000 per year for 5 years. Project L costs $25,000 and is expected to produce cash flows of $7,400 per year for 5 years. Calculate the two projects' NPVs, IRRs, MIRRs, and PIs, assuming a cost of capital of 12 percent. Which project would be selected, assuming they are mutually exclusive, using each ranking method? Which should actually be selected?

11-11
Present Value of Costs

The Costa Rican Coffee Company is evaluating the within-plant distribution system for its new roasting, grinding, and packing plant. The two alternatives are (1) a conveyor system with a high initial cost but low annual operating costs and (2) several forklift trucks, which cost less but have considerably higher operating costs. The decision to construct the plant has already been made, and the choice here will have no effect on the overall revenues of the project. The cost of capital for the plant is 9 percent, and the projects' expected net costs are listed below:

YEAR	EXPECTED NET CASH COSTS	
	CONVEYOR	FORKLIFT
0	($300,000)	($120,000)
1	(66,000)	(96,000)
2	(66,000)	(96,000)
3	(66,000)	(96,000)
4	(66,000)	(96,000)
5	(66,000)	(96,000)

a. What is the IRR of each alternative?
b. What is the present value of costs of each alternative? Which method should be chosen?

11-12
MIRR and NPV

Your company is considering two mutually exclusive projects, X and Y, whose costs and cash flows are shown below:

YEAR	X	Y
0	($1,000)	($1,000)
1	100	1,000
2	300	100
3	400	50
4	700	50

The projects are equally risky, and their cost of capital is 12 percent. You must make a recommendation, and you must base it on the modified IRR (MIRR). What is the MIRR of the better project?

11-13
NPV and IRR

A company is analyzing two mutually exclusive projects, S and L, whose cash flows are shown below:

	0	1	2	3	4
S	−1,000	900	250	10	10
L	−1,000	0	250	400	800

The company's cost of capital is 10 percent, and it can get an unlimited amount of capital at that cost. What is the *regular IRR* (not MIRR) of the *better* project? (Hint: Note that the better project may or may not be the one with the higher IRR.)

11-14
MIRR

Project X has a cost of $1,000 at t = 0, and it is expected to produce a uniform cash flow stream for 10 years, i.e., the CFs are the same in Years 1 through 10, and it has a regular IRR of 12 percent. The cost of capital for the project is 10 percent. What is the project's modified IRR (MIRR)?

11-15
NPV and IRR Analysis

After discovering a new gold vein in the Colorado mountains, CTC Mining Corporation must decide whether to mine the deposit. The most cost-effective method of mining gold is sulfuric acid extraction, a process that results in environmental damage. To go ahead with the extraction, CTC must spend $900,000 for new mining equipment and pay $165,000 for its installation. The gold mined will net the firm an estimated $350,000 each year over the 5-year life of the vein. CTC's cost of capital is 14 percent. For the purposes of this problem, assume that the cash inflows occur at the end of the year.
a. What is the NPV and IRR of this project?
b. Should this project be undertaken, ignoring environmental concerns?
c. How should environmental effects be considered when evaluating this, or any other, project? How might these effects change your decision in Part b?

11-16
NPV and IRR

John's Publishing Company, a new service that writes term papers for college students, provides 10-page term papers from a list of more than 500 topics. Each paper will cost $7.50 and is written by a graduate in the topic area. John's will pay $20,000 for the rights to all of the manuscripts. In addition, each author will receive $0.50 in royalties for every paper sold. Marketing expenses are estimated to be a total of $20,000 divided equally between Years 1 and 2, and John's cost of capital is 11 percent. Sales are expected as follows:

YEAR	VOLUME
1	10,000
2	7,000
3	3,000

a. What is the payback period for this investment? Its NPV? Its IRR?
b. What are the ethical implications of this investment?

11-17
NPV and IRR Analysis

Sharon Evans, who graduated from the local university 3 years ago with a degree in marketing, is manager of Ann Naylor's store in the Southwest Mall. Sharon's store has 5 years remaining on its lease. Rent is $2,000 per month, 60 payments remain, and the next payment is due in 1 month. The mall's owner plans to sell the property in a year and wants rents at that time to be high so the property will appear more valuable. Therefore, Sharon has been offered a "great deal" (owner's words) on a new 5-year lease. The new lease calls for zero rent for 9 months, then payments of $2,600 per month for the next 51 months. The lease cannot be broken, and Ann Naylor Corporation's cost of capital is 12 percent (or 1 percent per month). Sharon must make a decision. A good one could help her career and move her up in management, but a bad one could hurt her prospects for promotion.
a. Should Sharon accept the new lease? (Hint: Be sure to use 1 percent per month.)
b. Suppose Sharon decided to bargain with the mall's owner over the new lease payment. What new lease payment would make Sharon indifferent between the new and the old leases? (Hint: Find FV of the first 9 payments at t = 9, then treat this as the PV of a 51-period annuity whose payments represent the incremental rent during Months 10 to 60.)
c. Sharon is not sure of the 12 percent cost of capital—it could be higher or lower. At what *nominal cost* of capital would Sharon be indifferent between the two leases? (Hint: Calculate the differences between the two payment streams, and find the IRR of this difference stream.)

11-18
NPV and IRR Analysis

Cummings Products Company is considering two mutually exclusive investments. The projects' expected net cash flows are as follows:

	EXPECTED NET CASH FLOWS	
YEAR	PROJECT A	PROJECT B
0	($300)	($405)
1	(387)	134
2	(193)	134
3	(100)	134
4	600	134
5	600	134
6	850	134
7	(180)	0

a. Construct NPV profiles for Projects A and B.
b. What is each project's IRR?
c. If you were told that each project's cost of capital was 12 percent, which project should be selected? If the cost of capital was 18 percent, what would be the proper choice?
d. What is each project's MIRR at a cost of capital of 12 percent? At k = 18%? (Hint: Consider Period 7 as the end of Project B's life.)
e. What is the crossover rate, and what is its significance?

11-19
Timing Differences

The Ewert Exploration Company is considering two mutually exclusive plans for extracting oil on property for which it has mineral rights. Both plans call for the expenditure of $10,000,000 to drill development wells. Under Plan A, all the oil will be extracted in 1 year, producing a cash flow at t = 1 of $12,000,000, while under Plan B, cash flows will be $1,750,000 per year for 20 years.
a. What are the annual incremental cash flows that will be available to Ewert Exploration if it undertakes Plan B rather than Plan A? (Hint: Subtract Plan A's flows from B's.)
b. If the firm accepts Plan A, then invests the extra cash generated at the end of Year 1, what rate of return (reinvestment rate) would cause the cash flows from reinvestment to equal the cash flows from Plan B?
c. Suppose a company has a cost of capital of 10 percent. Is it logical to assume that it would take on all available independent projects (of average risk) with returns greater than 10 percent? Further, if all available projects with returns greater than 10 percent have been taken, would this mean that cash flows from past investments would have an opportunity cost of only 10 percent, because all the firm could do with these cash flows would be to replace money that has a cost of 10 percent? Finally, does this imply that the cost of capital is the correct rate to assume for the reinvestment of a project's cash flows?
d. Construct NPV profiles for Plans A and B, identify each project's IRR, and indicate the crossover rate of return.

11-20
Sale Differences

The Pinkerton Publishing Company is considering two mutually exclusive expansion plans. Plan A calls for the expenditure of $50 million on a large-scale, integrated plant which will provide an expected cash flow stream of $8 million per year for 20 years. Plan B calls for the expenditure of $15 million to build a somewhat less efficient, more labor-intensive plant which has an expected cash flow stream of $3.4 million per year for 20 years. The firm's cost of capital is 10 percent.
a. Calculate each project's NPV and IRR.
b. Set up a Project Δ by showing the cash flows that will exist if the firm goes with the large plant rather than the smaller plant. What are the NPV and the IRR for this Project Δ?
c. Graph the NPV profiles for Plan A, Plan B, and Project Δ.
d. Give a logical explanation, based on reinvestment rates and opportunity costs, as to why the NPV method is better than the IRR method when the firm's cost of capital is constant at some value such as 10 percent.

11-21
Multiple Rates of Return

The Ulmer Uranium Company is deciding whether or not it should open a strip mine, the net cost of which is $4.4 million. Net cash inflows are expected to be $27.7 million, all coming at the end of Year 1. The land must be returned to its natural state at a cost of $25 million, payable at the end of Year 2.
a. Plot the project's NPV profile.
b. Should the project be accepted if k = 8%? If k = 14%? Explain your reasoning.

c. Can you think of some other capital budgeting situations where negative cash flows during or at the end of the project's life might lead to multiple IRRs?

d. What is the project's MIRR at k = 8%? At k = 14%? Does the MIRR method lead to the same accept/reject decision as the NPV method?

11-22
Multiple Rates of Return

The Durst Development Company (DDC) has many excellent investment opportunities, but it has insufficient cash to undertake them all. Now DDC is offered the chance to borrow $2 million from the Rancho Palisades Retirement Fund at 10 percent, and the loan is to be repaid at the end of 1 year. Also, a "consulting fee" of $700,000 will be paid to Rancho Palisades' mayor at the end of 1 year for helping to arrange the credit. Of the $2 million received, $1 million will be used immediately to buy an old city-owned hotel and to convert it into a gambling casino. The other $1 million will be invested in other lucrative DDC projects that otherwise would have to be foregone because of a lack of capital. For 2 years, all cash generated by the casino will be plowed back into the casino project. At the end of the 2 years, the casino will be sold for $2 million.

Assuming that (1) the deal has been worked out in the sunshine and is completely legal and (2) cash from other DDC Company operations will be available to make the required payments at the end of Year 1, under what rate of return conditions should DDC accept the offer? Disregard taxes.

11-23
Present Value of Costs

The Aubey Coffee Company is evaluating the within-plant distribution system for its new roasting, grinding, and packing plant. The two alternatives are (1) a conveyor system with a high initial cost, but low annual operating costs, and (2) several forklift trucks, which cost less, but have considerably higher operating costs. The decision to construct the plant has already been made, and the choice here will have no effect on the overall revenues of the project. The cost of capital for the plant is 8 percent, and the projects' expected net costs are listed in the table:

	EXPECTED NET COST	
YEAR	CONVEYOR	FORKLIFT
0	($500,000)	($200,000)
1	(120,000)	(160,000)
2	(120,000)	(160,000)
3	(120,000)	(160,000)
4	(120,000)	(160,000)
5	(20,000)	(160,000)

a. What is the IRR of each alternative?

b. What is the present value of costs of each alternative? Which method should be chosen?

11-24
Payback, NPV, and MIRR

Your division is considering two investment projects, each of which requires an up-front expenditure of $25 million. You estimate that the cost of capital is 10 percent and that the investments will produce the following after-tax cash flows (in millions of dollars):

YEAR	PROJECT A	PROJECT B
1	5	20
2	10	10
3	15	8
4	20	6

a. What is the regular payback period for each of the projects?

b. What is the discounted payback period for each of the projects?

c. If the two projects are independent and the cost of capital is 10 percent, which project or projects should the firm undertake?

d. If the two projects are mutually exclusive and the cost of capital is 5 percent, which project should the firm undertake?

e. If the two projects are mutually exclusive and the cost of capital is 15 percent, which project should the firm undertake?

f. What is the crossover rate?

g. If the cost of capital is 10 percent, what is the modified IRR (MIRR) of each project?

Spreadsheet Problem

Work the problem in this section only if you are using the computer problem diskette.

11-25
Mutually Exclusive Projects

Use the model in File C11 to solve this problem. Midwest Manufacturing Company is considering two mutually exclusive investments. The projects' expected net cash flows are as follows:

EXPECTED NET CASH FLOW

YEAR	PROJECT A	PROJECT B
0	($300)	($405)
1	(387)	134
2	(193)	134
3	(100)	134
4	600	134
5	600	134
6	850	134
7	(180)	0

a. Construct NPV profiles for Projects A and B.
b. What is each project's IRR?
c. If you were told that each project's cost of capital is 10 percent, which project should be selected? If the cost of capital were 17 percent, what would the proper choice be?
d. What is each project's MIRR at a cost of capital of 10 percent? At k = 17%?
e. What is the crossover rate, and what is its significance?
f. The firm's management is confident of the projects' cash flows in Years 0 to 6 but is uncertain as to what the Year 7 cash flows will be for the two projects. Under a worst-case scenario, Project A's Year 7 cash flow will be –$300 and B's will be –$150, while under a best-case scenario, the cash flows will be –$70 and +$120 for Projects A and B, respectively. Answer Parts b through d using these new cash flows. Which project should be selected under each scenario?
g. Put the Year 7 cash flows back to –$180 for A and zero for B. Now change the cost of capital and observe what happens to NPV at k = 0%, 5%, 20%, and 400% (input as 4.0).

MINI CASE

Assume that you recently went to work for Axis Components Company, a supplier of auto repair parts used in the after-market with products from Chrysler, Ford, and other auto makers. Your boss, the chief financial officer (CFO), has just handed you the estimated cash flows for two proposed projects. Project L involves adding a new item to the firm's ignition system line; it would take some time to build up the market for this product, so the cash inflows would increase over time. Project S involves an add-on to an existing line, and its cash flows would decrease over time. Both projects have 3-year lives, because Axis is planning to introduce entirely new models after 3 years.

Here are the projects' net cash flows (in thousands of dollars):

EXPECTED NET CASH FLOW

YEAR	PROJECT L	PROJECT S
0	($100)	($100)
1	10	70
2	60	50
3	80	20

Depreciation, salvage values, net working capital requirements, and tax effects are all included in these cash flows.

The CFO also made subjective risk assessments of each project, and he concluded that both projects have risk characteristics which are similar to the firm's average project. Axis's weighted average cost of capital is 10 percent. You must now determine whether one or both of the projects should be accepted.

a. What is capital budgeting? Are there any similarities between a firm's capital budgeting decisions and an individual's investment decisions?

b. What is the difference between independent and mutually exclusive projects? Between projects with normal and nonnormal cash flows?

c. (1) What is the payback period? Find the paybacks for Projects L and S.
   (2) What is the rationale for the payback method? According to the payback criterion, which project or projects should be accepted if the firm's maximum acceptable payback is 2 years, and if Projects L and S are independent? If they are mutually exclusive?
   (3) What is the difference between the regular and discounted payback periods?
   (4) What is the main disadvantage of discounted payback? Is the payback method of any real usefulness in capital budgeting decisions?

d. (1) Define the term *net present value (NPV)*. What is each project's NPV?
   (2) What is the rationale behind the NPV method? According to NPV, which project or projects should be accepted if they are independent? Mutually exclusive?
   (3) Would the NPVs change if the cost of capital changed?

e. (1) Define the term *internal rate of return (IRR)*. What is each project's IRR?
   (2) How is the IRR on a project related to the YTM on a bond?
   (3) What is the logic behind the IRR method? According to IRR, which projects should be accepted if they are independent? Mutually exclusive?
   (4) Would the projects' IRRs change if the cost of capital changed?

f. (1) Draw NPV profiles for Projects L and S. At what discount rate do the profiles cross?
   (2) Look at your NPV profile graph without referring to the actual NPVs and IRRs. Which project or projects should be accepted if they are independent? Mutually exclusive? Explain. Are your answers correct at any cost of capital less than 23.6 percent?

g. (1) What is the underlying cause of ranking conflicts between NPV and IRR?
   (2) What is the "reinvestment rate assumption," and how does it affect the NPV versus IRR conflict?
   (3) Which method is the best? Why?

h. (1) Define the term *modified IRR (MIRR)*. Find the MIRRs for Projects L and S.
   (2) What are the MIRR's advantages and disadvantages vis-à-vis the regular IRR? What are the MIRR's advantages and disadvantages vis-à-vis the NPV?

i. As a separate project (Project P), the firm is considering sponsoring a pavilion at the upcoming World's Fair. The pavilion would cost $800,000, and it is expected to result in $5 million of incremental cash inflows during its 1 year of operation. However, it would then take another year, and $5 million of costs, to demolish the site and return it to its original condition. Thus, Project P's expected net cash flows look like this (in millions of dollars):

YEAR	NET CASH FLOWS
0	($0.8)
1	5.0
2	(5.0)

The project is estimated to be of average risk, so its cost of capital is 10 percent.
(1) What is Project P's NPV? What is its IRR? Its MIRR?
(2) Draw Project P's NPV profile. Does Project P have normal or nonnormal cash flows? Should this project be accepted?

Selected Additional References and Cases

For an in-depth treatment of capital budgeting techniques, see

Bierman, Harold, Jr., and Seymour Smidt, *The Capital Budgeting Decision* (New York: Macmillan, 1993).

Grant, Eugene L., William G. Ireson, and Richard S. Leavenworth, *Principles of Engineering Economy* (New York: John Wiley & Sons, 1990).

Levy, Haim, and Marshall Sarnat, *Capital Investment and Financial Decisions* (Englewood Cliffs, N.J.: Prentice-Hall, 1994).

Seitz, Neil E., and Mitch Ellison, *Capital Budgeting and Long-Term Financing Decisions* (Fort Worth, Tex.: Dryden Press, 1995).

For a discussion of strategic considerations in capital budgeting, see

Crum, Roy L., and Frans G. J. Derkinderen, eds., *Readings in Strategies for Corporate Investments* (New York: Pitman, 1981).

The following articles present interesting comparisons of four different approaches to finding NPV:

Brick, Ivan E., and Daniel G. Weaver, "A Comparison of Capital Budgeting Techniques in Identifying Profitable Investments," *Financial Management,* Winter 1984, 29–39.

Greenfield, Robert L., Maury R. Randall, and John C. Woods, "Financial Leverage and Use of the Net Present Value Investment Criterion," *Financial Management,* Autumn 1983, 40–44.

Five articles related directly to the topics in this chapter are

Bacon, Peter W., "The Evaluation of Mutually Exclusive Investments," *Financial Management,* Summer 1977, 55–58.

Chaney, Paul K., "Moral Hazard and Capital Budgeting," *Journal of Financial Research,* Summer 1989, 113–128.

Lewellen, Wilbur G., Howard P. Lanser, and John J. McConnell, "Payback Substitutes for Discounted Cash Flow," *Financial Management,* Summer 1973, 17–23.

Miller, Edward M., "Safety Margins and Capital Budgeting Criteria," *Managerial Finance,* Number 2/3, 1988, 1–8.

Woods, John C., and Maury R. Randall, "The Net Present Value of Future Investment Opportunities: Its Impact on Shareholder Wealth and Implications for Capital Budgeting Theory," *Financial Management,* Summer 1989, 85–92.

For five recent articles which discuss the capital budgeting methods actually used in practice, see

Kim, Suk H., Trevor Crick, and Seung H. Kim, "Do Executives Practice What Academics Preach?" *Management Accounting,* November 1986, 49–52.

Mukherjee, Tarun K., "Capital Budgeting Surveys: The Past and the Future," *Review of Business and Economic Research,* Spring 1987, 37–56.

————, "The Capital Budgeting Process of Large U.S. Firms: An Analysis of Capital Budgeting Manuals," *Managerial Finance,* Number 2/3, 1988, 28–35.

Ross, Marc, "Capital Budgeting Practices of Twelve Large Manufacturers," *Financial Management,* Winter 1986, 15–22.

Weaver, Samuel C., Donald Peters, Roger Cason, and Joe Daleiden, "Capital Budgeting," *Financial Management,* Spring 1989, 10–17.

Additional capital budgeting references are provided in Chapters 12 and 13.

For a case which focuses on capital budgeting decision methods, see

Case 11, "Chicago Valve Company," in the *Cases in Financial Management: Dryden Request* series.

CASH FLOW
ESTIMATION AND OTHER
TOPICS IN CAPITAL BUDGETING

Coca-Cola, Pepsi, and other established soft-drink companies have seen upstarts such as Snapple and Arizona Iced Tea pick up a significant share of their market. Coke and Pepsi are not exactly hurting—they remain by far the dominant players in the soft-drink industry. Still, these companies did not get where they are by rolling over for newcomers, and they are constantly investigating new products and markets.

Iced tea, lemonade, and other fruit drinks are becoming increasingly popular, so Coke and Pepsi are either in these markets or actively considering entry. Coke's product line includes Nestea Iced Tea, Minute Maid, Powerade, and Fruitopia. Pepsi has All Sport, and it has also entered into a partnership with Lipton Iced Tea. Quaker Oats, which makes Gatorade, acquired Snapple but then sold it at a loss.

Whenever these companies contemplate the development of a new product, they must conduct a capital budgeting analysis. Let's say, for example, that Coke is deciding whether to produce and market a new lemonade product. Here are some of the factors that it would have to consider:

1. *How many people would like the new product well enough to buy it, and how many units would each customer buy per year?*

2. *What share of the lemonade market could Coke expect to capture?*

3. *How important would price be; that is, would demand be greatly affected by a small change in price?*

4. *If Coke did go into the lemonade market, and if it were highly profitable, how long would it take Pepsi and other competitors to follow, and how badly would Coke's prices and sales be eroded?*

5. *How much would lemonade sales cut into the sales of Coke's other products?*

6. *How large an investment would be required to set up a plant to produce lemonade and then launch a marketing campaign?*

7. *What would the production and distribution costs per unit be?*

8. *If the product were successful in the United States, might this lead to a worldwide expansion, hence to additional profits?*

While Coke's track record has been impressive in recent years, this by no means guarantees that it would succeed in the lemonade market. Quaker Oats' $1.7 billion acquisition of Snapple illustrates many of the difficulties that arise when making investments in the beverage business—sales of Snapple declined in 1996, leading to the conclusion that Quaker Oats paid at least $1 billion too much for it.

As you study this chapter, think about the difficulties involved in forecasting each of the cash flow elements associated with new projects—unit sales, sales price, operating costs, and capital required to set up operations. The forecasting task is daunting, yet good cash flow forecasts are essential for good capital budgeting decisions. The principles and concepts discussed in this chapter can help you avoid the pitfalls that get companies into trouble.

The basic principles of capital budgeting were covered in Chapter 11. Now we examine some additional issues, including (1) the way cash flows are estimated, (2) replacement decisions, (3) mutually exclusive projects with unequal lives, and (4) the effects of inflation on capital budgeting analysis.

ESTIMATING CASH FLOWS

The most important, but also the most difficult, step in capital budgeting is estimating projects' cash flows—the investment outlays and the annual net cash inflows after a project goes into operation. Many variables are involved, and many individuals and departments participate in the process. For example, the forecasts of unit sales and sales prices are normally made by the marketing group, based on their knowledge of price elasticity, advertising effects, the state of the economy, competitors' reactions, and trends in consumers' tastes. Similarly, the capital outlays associated with a new product are generally obtained from the engineering and product development staffs, while operating costs are estimated by cost accountants, production experts, personnel specialists, purchasing agents, and so forth.

It is difficult to accurately forecast the costs and revenues associated with a large, complex project, so forecast errors can be quite large. For example, when several major oil companies decided to build the Alaska Pipeline, the original cost estimates were in the neighborhood of $700 million. However, the final cost was closer to $7 billion. Similar (or even worse) miscalculations are common in forecasts of product design costs, such as the costs to develop a new personal computer. Further, as difficult as plant and equipment costs are to estimate, sales revenues and operating costs over the project's life are even more uncertain. For example, several years ago, Federal Express developed an electronic delivery service system (ZapMail). It used the correct capital budgeting technique, NPV, but it incorrectly estimated the project's cash flows: Projected revenues were too high, projected costs were too low, and virtually no one was willing to pay the price required to cover the project's costs. As a result, cash flows failed to meet the forecasted levels, and Federal Express ended up losing about $200 million on the venture. This example demonstrates a basic truth—if cash flow estimates are not reasonably accurate, any analytical technique, no matter how sophisticated, can lead to poor decisions. Because of its financial strength, Federal Express was able to absorb losses on the project, but the ZapMail venture could have forced a weaker firm into bankruptcy.

The financial staff's role in the forecasting process includes (1) obtaining information from various departments, such as engineering and marketing, (2) ensuring that everyone involved with the forecast uses a consistent set of economic assumptions, and (3) making sure that no biases are inherent in the forecasts. This last point is extremely important, because managers often become emotionally involved with pet projects or develop empire-building complexes, both of which lead to cash flow forecasting biases that make bad projects look good—on paper.

It is almost impossible to overstate the problems one can encounter in cash flow forecasts. It is also difficult to overstate the importance of these forecasts. Still, observing the principles discussed in the next several sections will help minimize forecasting errors.

SELF-TEST
QUESTIONS

What is the most important step in a capital budgeting analysis?

What departments are involved in estimating a project's cash flows?

What is the financial staff's role in the forecasting process for capital projects?

IDENTIFYING THE RELEVANT CASH FLOWS

The starting point in any capital budgeting analysis is identifying the **relevant cash flows,** defined as the specific set of cash flows that should be considered in the decision at hand. Analysts often make errors in estimating cash flows, but two cardinal rules can help you avoid mistakes. First, capital budgeting decisions must be based on *cash flows,* not accounting income. Second, only *incremental cash flows* are relevant.

Recall from Chapter 2 that *free cash flow* is the cash flow available for distribution to investors. In a nutshell, the relevant cash flow for a project is the *additional* free cash flow that the company expects if it implements the project, that is, the cash flow above and beyond what the company could expect if it doesn't implement the project. The following sections discuss the relevant cash flows in more detail.

Project Cash Flow versus Accounting Income

We showed in Chapter 9 that a firm's value depends on its *free cash flows*. Similarly, the value of a project depends on its free cash flow. We illustrate the estimation of project cash flow later in the chapter with a comprehensive example, but it is important for you to understand the four major ways that project cash flow differs from accounting income.

Costs of Fixed Assets. Most projects require fixed assets, and the funds used to purchase these assets must come from investors, both stockholders and lenders. Asset purchases represent a *negative* project cash flow, because the funds come *from* investors. Even though the acquisition of fixed assets represents a cash outflow, accountants do not show the purchase of fixed assets as a deduction from accounting income. Instead, they deduct a depreciation expense each year throughout the life of the asset.

It is important to note that the full costs of fixed assets include any shipping and installation costs. When a firm acquires fixed assets, it often must incur substantial costs for shipping and installing the equipment. These charges are added to the price of the equipment when the project's cost is being determined. Also, the full cost of the equipment, including shipping and installation costs, is used as the *depreciable basis* when depreciation charges are being calculated. For example, if a company bought a computer with an invoice price of $100,000 and paid another $10,000 for shipping and installation, then the full cost of the computer (and its depreciable basis) would be $110,000. Note too that fixed assets can often be sold at the end of a project's life. If this is the case, then the after-tax cash proceeds represent a positive cash flow. We will illustrate both depreciation and cash flow from asset sales later in the chapter.

Noncash Charges. In calculating net income, accountants usually subtract some noncash charges, in particular, depreciation, from revenues. So, while accountants do not subtract the purchase price of fixed assets when calculating accounting income, they do subtract a charge each year for depreciation. Depreciation shelters income from taxation, and this has an impact on cash flow, but depreciation itself is not a cash flow. Therefore, depreciation must be added back when estimating a project's cash flow.

Changes in Net Operating Working Capital. Normally, additional inventories are required to support a new operation, and expanded sales also lead to additional accounts receivable. However, payables and accruals increase spontaneously as a result of the expansion, and this reduces the cash needed to finance inventories and receivables. The difference between the required increase in current assets and the spontaneous increase in current liabilities is the **change in net operating working capital.** If this change is positive, as it generally is for expansion projects, then additional financing, over and above the cost of the fixed assets, will be needed.

Toward the end of a project's life, inventories will be used but not replaced, and receivables will be collected without corresponding replacements. As these changes occur, the firm will receive cash inflows. In this manner, the investment in working capital will be returned by the end of the project's life.

Interest Expenses Are Not Included in Project Cash Flows. Recall from Chapter 11 that we discount each project's cash flows at its cost of capital, and that the cost of capital is a weighted average of the costs of debt and equity (WACC), adjusted for the project's risk. Moreover, the WACC is the rate of return necessary to satisfy all of the firm's investors — debtholders and stockholders. The discounting process *reduces* the cash flows to account for capital costs, both debt and equity costs. If interest charges were first deducted and then the resulting cash flows were discounted, this would result in a double counting of the cost of debt. *Therefore, you should not subtract interest expenses when finding a project's cash flows.*

Note that this procedure differs from that for calculating accounting income. Accountants attempt to measure the profit available just for stockholders, so interest expenses are subtracted. However, project cash flow is the cash flow available for all investor and bondholders, as well as stockholders, so interest expenses are not subtracted. All this is analogous to the procedures used in the corporate valuation model of Chapter 9, where the company's free cash flows are discounted at the WACC.[1]

Incremental Cash Flows

In evaluating a project, we focus on those cash flows that occur if and only if we accept the project. These cash flows, called **incremental cash flows,** represent the change in the firm's total cash flow that occurs as a direct result of accepting the project. Three special problems in determining incremental cash flows are discussed next.

Sunk Costs. A **sunk cost** is an outlay that has already been committed or that has already occurred, hence is not affected by the decision under consideration. Since sunk costs are not incremental costs, they should not be included in the analysis. To illustrate, in 1997, Northeast BankCorp was considering the establishment of a branch office in a newly developed section of Boston. To help with its evaluation, Northeast had, back in 1996, hired a consulting firm to perform a site analysis; the cost was $100,000, and this amount was expensed for tax purposes in 1996. Is this 1996 expenditure a relevant cost with respect to the 1997 capital budgeting decision? The answer

---

[1]An alternative approach to capital budgeting is to estimate the cash flows that are available for equity holders. These equity cash flows are defined as the project's cash flows minus all cash flows related to debt (i.e., the after-tax interest expense plus any change in debt due to new borrowing or principal repayment). Note that equity cash flows also differ from accounting income, because accounting income does not adjust for changes in debt. We could discount these equity cash flows at the cost of equity and compare this PV with the amount of equity invested in the project. This approach is analogous to the discounted dividend model in Chapter 9. Although this produces the same NPV as our approach, we do not recommend it because it is more complicated. In particular, the analyst must estimate the amounts of debt and equity that support the project in each year of its life.

is no—the $100,000 is a *sunk cost,* and it will not affect Northeast's future cash flows regardless of whether or not the new branch is built. It often turns out that a particular project has a negative NPV when all the associated costs, including sunk costs, are considered. However, on an incremental basis, the project may be a good one because the *incremental cash flows* are large enough to produce a positive NPV on the *incremental investment.*

Opportunity Costs.   A second potential problem relates to **opportunity costs,** which are cash flows that could be generated from an asset the firm already owns provided it is not used for the project in question. To illustrate, Northeast BankCorp already owns a piece of land that is suitable for the branch location. When evaluating the prospective branch, should the cost of the land be disregarded because no additional cash outlay would be required? The answer is no, because there is an *opportunity cost* inherent in the use of the property. In this case, the land could be sold to yield $150,000 after taxes. Use of the site for the branch would require forgoing this inflow, so the $150,000 must be charged as an opportunity cost against the project. Note that the proper land cost in this example is the $150,000 market-determined value, irrespective of whether Northeast originally paid $50,000 or $500,000 for the property. (What Northeast paid would, of course, have an effect on taxes, hence on the after-tax opportunity cost.)

Effects on Other Parts of the Firm: Externalities.   The third potential problem involves the effects of a project on other parts of the firm, which economists call **externalities.** For example, some of Northeast's customers who would use the new branch are already banking with Northeast's downtown office. The loans and deposits, hence profits, generated by these customers would not be new to the bank; rather, they would represent a transfer from the main office to the branch. Thus, the net income produced by these customers should not be treated as incremental income in the capital budgeting decision. On the other hand, having a suburban branch would help the bank attract new business to its downtown office, because some people like to be able to bank both close to home and close to work. In this case, the additional income that would actually flow to the downtown office should be attributed to the branch. Although they are often difficult to quantify, *externalities* (which can be either positive or negative) should be considered.

When a new project takes sales from an existing product, this is often called **cannibalization.** Naturally, firms do not like to cannibalize their existing products, but it often turns out that if they do not, someone else will. To illustrate, IBM for years refused to provide full support for its PC division because it did not want to steal sales from its highly profitable mainframe business. That turned out to be a huge strategic error, because it allowed Intel, Microsoft, Compaq, and others to become dominant forces in the computer industry. Therefore, when considering externalities, the full implications of the proposed new project should be taken into account.

Timing of Cash Flow

We must account properly for the timing of cash flows. Accounting income statements are for periods such as years or months, so they do not reflect exactly when during the period cash revenues or expenses occur. Because of the time value of money, capital budgeting cash flows should in theory be analyzed exactly as they occur. Of course, there must be a compromise between accuracy and feasibility. A time line with daily cash flows would in theory be most accurate, but daily cash flow estimates would be costly to construct, unwieldy to use, and probably no more accurate than annual cash flow estimates because we simply cannot forecast well enough to warrant this degree of detail. Therefore, in most cases, we simply assume that all cash flows occur at the end of every year. However, for some projects, it may be useful to assume that cash flows occur at mid-year, or even quarterly or monthly.

Why should companies use project cash flow rather than accounting income when finding the NPV of a project?

What are four ways that project cash flows differ from accounting income?

How do shipping and installation costs affect the costs of fixed assets and the depreciable basis?

What is the most common noncash charge that must be added back when finding project cash flows?

What is net operating working capital, and how is an increase in it dealt with in capital budgeting?

How does the company get back the dollars it invests in net operating working capital?

Explain what the following terms mean, and assess their relevance in capital budgeting: incremental cash flow, sunk cost, opportunity cost, externality, and cannibalization.

TAX EFFECTS

Taxes can have a major impact on cash flows, and in many cases tax effects will make or break a project. Therefore, it is critical that taxes be dealt with correctly. Our tax laws are extremely complex, and they are subject to interpretation and to change. The financial staff can get assistance from the firm's accountants and tax lawyers, but even so, it is necessary for financial analysts to have a working knowledge of the current tax laws and their effects on cash flows.

An Overview of Depreciation

Suppose Blockbuster Entertainment buys a computerized inventory system and uses it for five years, after which it is scrapped. The cost of the video rentals supported by the system must include a charge for the system, and this charge is called *depreciation*. Because depreciation reduces profits as calculated by accountants, the higher a firm's depreciation charges, the lower its reported net income. However, depreciation is not a cash charge, so higher depreciation levels do not reduce cash flows. Indeed, higher depreciation *increases* cash flows, because the higher a firm's depreciation, the lower its tax bill.

Companies often calculate depreciation one way when figuring taxes and another way when reporting income to investors: many use the *straight line* method for stockholder reporting (or "book" purposes), but they use the fastest rate permitted by law for tax purposes. Under the straight line method used for stockholder reporting, one normally takes the cost of the asset, subtracts its estimated salvage value, and divides the net amount by the asset's useful economic life. For an asset with a five-year life, which costs $100,000 and has a $12,500 salvage value, the annual straight line depreciation charge is ($100,000 − $12,500)/5 = $17,500. Note, however, as we discuss later in this section, that salvage value is *not* considered for tax depreciation purposes.

For tax purposes, Congress changes the permissible tax depreciation methods from time to time. Prior to 1954, the straight line method was required for tax purposes, but in 1954 *accelerated* methods (double-declining balance and sum-of-years'-digits) were permitted. Then, in 1981, the old accelerated methods were replaced by a simpler procedure known as the Accelerated Cost Recovery System (ACRS). The ACRS system was changed again in 1986 as a part of the Tax Reform Act, and it is now known as the *Modified Accelerated Cost Recovery System (MACRS);* a 1993 tax law made further changes in this area.

Note that U.S. tax laws are very complicated, and in this text we can only provide an overview of MACRS designed to give you a basic understanding of the impact of depreciation on capital budgeting decisions. Further, the tax laws change so often that the numbers we present may be outdated before the book is even published. Thus, when dealing with tax depreciation in real-world situations, current Internal Revenue Service (IRS) publications or individuals with expertise in tax matters should be consulted.

Calculating Tax Depreciation

For tax purposes, the entire cost of an asset is expensed over its depreciable life. Historically, an asset's depreciable life was determined by its estimated useful economic life; an asset was supposed to be fully depreciated at the same time that it reached the end of its useful economic life. However, MACRS totally abandoned that practice and set simple guidelines which created several classes of assets, each with a more-or-less arbitrarily prescribed life called a *recovery period* or *class life*. The MACRS class life bears only a rough relationship to the expected useful economic life.

A major effect of the MACRS system has been to shorten the depreciable lives of assets, thus giving businesses larger tax deductions and thereby increasing their cash flows available for investment. Table 12-1 describes the types of property that fit into the different class life groups, and Table 12-2 sets forth the MACRS recovery allowance percentages (depreciation rates) for selected classes of investment property.

Consider Table 12-1 first. The first column gives the MACRS class life, while the second column describes the types of assets which fall into each category. Property in the 27.5- and 39-year categories (real estate) must be depreciated by the straight line method, but 3-, 5-, 7-, and 10-year property (personal property) can be depreciated either on an accelerated basis using the rates shown in Table 12-2 or by the straight line method.[2]

As we saw earlier in the chapter, higher depreciation expenses result in lower taxes, hence higher cash flows. Therefore, since a firm has the choice of using the straight line rates or the accelerated rates shown in Table 12-2, most elect to use the accelerated rates.

The yearly recovery allowance, or depreciation expense, is determined by multiplying each asset's *depreciable basis* by the applicable recovery percentage shown in Table 12-2. Calculations are discussed in the following sections.

Half-Year Convention.   Under MACRS, the assumption is generally made that property is placed in service in the middle of the first year. Thus, for three-year class life property, the recovery period begins in the middle of the year the asset is placed in service and ends three years later. The effect of the *half-year convention* is to extend the

---

[2]As a benefit to very small companies, the Tax Code also permits companies to *expense,* which is equivalent to depreciating over one year, up to $17,500 of equipment. Thus, if a small company bought one asset worth up to $17,500, it could write the asset off in the year it was acquired. This is called "Section 179 expensing." We shall disregard this provision throughout the book.

| TABLE 12-1 | Class Lives for Different Types of Property |

CLASS	TYPE OF PROPERTY
3-year	Certain special manufacturing tools
5-year	Automobiles, light-duty trucks, computers, and certain special manufacturing equipment
7-year	Most industrial equipment, office furniture, and fixtures
10-year	Certain longer-lived types of equipment
27.5-year	Residential rental real property such as apartment buildings
39-year	All nonresidential real property, including commercial and industrial buildings

| TABLE 12-2 | Recovery Allowance Percentages for Personal Property |

OWNERSHIP YEAR	CLASS OF INVESTMENT			
	3-YEAR	5-YEAR	7-YEAR	10-YEAR
1	33%	20%	14%	10%
2	45	32	25	18
3	15	19	17	14
4	7	12	13	12
5		11	9	9
6		6	9	7
7			9	7
8			4	7
9				7
10				6
11				3
	100%	100%	100%	100%

NOTES:

a. We developed these recovery allowance percentages based on the 200 percent declining balance method prescribed by MACRS, with a switch to straight line depreciation at some point in the asset's life. For example, consider the 5-year recovery allowance percentages. The straight line percentage would be 20 percent per year, so the 200 percent declining balance multiplier is 2.0(20%) = 40% = 0.4. However, because the half-year convention applies, the MACRS percentage for Year 1 is 20 percent. For Year 2, there is 80 percent of the depreciable basis remaining to be depreciated, so the recovery allowance percentage is 0.40(80%) = 32%. In Year 3, 20% + 32% = 52% of the depreciation has been taken, leaving 48%, so the percentage is 0.4(48%) ≈ 19%. In Year 4, the percentage is 0.4(29%) ≈ 12%. After 4 years, straight line depreciation exceeds the declining balance depreciation, so a switch is made to straight line (this is permitted under the law). However, the half-year convention must also be applied at the end of the class life, and the remaining 17 percent of depreciation must be taken (amortized) over 1.5 years. Thus, the percentage in Year 5 is 17%/1.5 ≈ 11%, and in Year 6, 17% − 11% = 6%. Although the tax tables carry the allowance percentages out to two decimal places, we have rounded to the nearest whole number for ease of illustration.

b. Residential rental property (apartments) is depreciated over a 27.5-year life, whereas commercial and industrial structures are depreciated over 39 years. In both cases, straight line depreciation must be used. The depreciation allowance for the first year is based, pro rata, on the month the asset was placed in service, with the remainder of the first year's depreciation being taken in the 28th or 40th year.

recovery period out one more year, so three-year class life property is depreciated over four calendar years, five-year property is depreciated over six calendar years, and so on. This convention is incorporated into Table 12-2's recovery allowance percentages.[3]

Depreciable Basis.   The *depreciable basis* is a critical element of MACRS because each year's allowance (depreciation expense) depends jointly on the asset's depreciable basis and its MACRS class life. The depreciable basis under MACRS is equal to the purchase price of the asset plus any shipping and installation costs. The basis is *not* adjusted for *salvage value* (which is the estimated market value of the asset at the end of its useful life) regardless of whether accelerated or the alternate straight line method is used.

Sale of a Depreciable Asset.   If a depreciable asset is sold, the sale price (actual dollars received) minus the then-existing undepreciated book value is added to operating income and taxed at the firm's marginal tax rate. For example, suppose a firm buys a five-year class life asset for $100,000 and sells it at the end of the fourth year for $25,000. The asset's book value is equal to $100,000(0.11 + 0.06) = $100,000(0.17) = $17,000. Therefore, $25,000 − $17,000 = $8,000 is added to the firm's operating income and is taxed at the firm's marginal tax rate.

Depreciation Illustration.   Assume that Blockbuster Entertainment buys a $150,000 machine which falls into the MACRS five-year class life and places it into service on March 15, 1999. Blockbuster must pay an additional $30,000 for delivery and installation. Salvage value is not considered, so the machine's depreciable basis is $180,000. (Delivery and installation charges are included in the depreciable basis rather than expensed in the year incurred.) Each year's recovery allowance (tax depreciation expense) is determined by multiplying the depreciable basis by the applicable recovery allowance percentage. Thus, the depreciation expense for 1999 is 0.20($180,000) = $36,000, and for 2000 it is 0.32($180,000) = $57,600. Similarly, the depreciation expense is $34,200 for 2001, $21,600 for 2002, $19,800 for 2003, and $10,800 for 2004. The total depreciation expense over the six-year recovery period is $180,000, which is equal to the depreciable basis of the machine.

As noted above, most firms use straight line depreciation for stockholder reporting purposes but MACRS for tax purposes. *For these firms, for capital budgeting, MACRS should be used.* The reason is that, in capital budgeting, we are concerned with cash flows, not reported income. Since MACRS depreciation is used for taxes, this type of depreciation must be used to determine the taxes that will be assessed against a particular project. Only if the depreciation method used for tax purposes is also used for capital budgeting will the analysis produce accurate cash flow estimates.

S E L F - T E S T Q U E S T I O N S	What do the acronyms ACRS and MACRS stand for?
	Briefly describe the tax depreciation system under MACRS.
	How does the sale of a depreciable asset affect a firm's cash flows?

---

[3]The half-year convention also applies if the straight line alternative is used, with half of one year's depreciation taken in the first year, a full year's depreciation taken in each of the remaining years of the asset's class life, and the remaining half-year's depreciation taken in the year following the end of the class life. You should recognize that virtually all companies have computerized depreciation systems. Each asset's depreciation pattern is programmed into the system at the time of its acquisition, and the computer aggregates the depreciation allowances for all assets when the accountants close the books and prepare financial statements and tax returns.

EVALUATING CAPITAL BUDGETING PROJECTS

Up until this point, we have discussed several important aspects of cash flow analysis, but we have not seen how they affect capital budgeting decisions. Conceptually, these decisions are straightforward: A project creates value for the firm's shareholders if and only if the net present value of its incremental cash flows is positive. In practice, however, estimating these cash flows is quite difficult.

In general, the incremental cash flows from a project can be classified as follows:

1. *Initial investment outlay.* The initial investment includes the up-front cost of fixed assets associated with the project plus any increases in net working capital.
2. *Operating cash flows over the project's life.* These are the incremental cash inflows over the project's economic life. Annual operating cash flow equals after-tax operating income plus depreciation. Recall (a) that depreciation is added back because it is a noncash expense and (b) that financing costs (including interest expense) are not included because they are accounted for in the discounting process.
3. *Terminal year cash flows.* At the end of a project's life, some extra cash flows are frequently received. These include the salvage value of the fixed assets, adjusted for taxes if assets are not sold at their book value, plus the return of the net working capital.

For each year of the project's economic life, the *net cash flow* is determined as the sum of the cash flows from each of the three categories. These annual net cash flows, along with the project's cost of capital, are then plotted on a time line and used to calculate the project's NPV and IRR. This procedure is illustrated in the following section.

As we shall see below, the relevant cash flows are different for expansion projects than they are for the replacement of an existing asset.

SELF-TEST QUESTION | What three types of cash flows must be considered when evaluating a proposed project?

EXAMPLE OF CASH FLOW ANALYSIS: EXPANSION PROJECT

In this section, we tie things together by examining a capital budgeting decision that faces Regency Integrated Chips (RIC), a Minneapolis-based technology company. RIC's research and development department has developed a small microprocessor and sensor system specifically designed to control commercial landscape watering systems. Once programmed, the system would automatically sense the need for watering in each separate watering zone and then provide just the right amount of water to each zone. This project has now reached the stage where a decision must be made on whether to go forward with production.

Investment requirements for the project are itemized in Table 12-3. The firm would need a new plant, which could be built and made ready for production two years after the "go" decision is made. The plant would require a 25-acre site, and RIC currently has an option to purchase a suitable tract for $1.2 million; the option could be exercised in late 1999. Building construction would begin in early 2000 and would continue through 2001. The building, which according to a special tax ruling has a MACRS 31.5-year recovery period, would cost an estimated $8 million; a $4 million payment would

TABLE 12-3	Investment Outlays, 1999–2001				
FIXED ASSETS	**1999**	**2000**	**2001**	**TOTAL COSTS, 1999–2001**	**DEPRECIABLE BASIS**
Land	$1,200,000	$ 0	$ 0	$ 1,200,000	$ 0
Building	0	4,000,000	4,000,000	8,000,000	8,000,000
Equipment	0	0	10,000,000	10,000,000	10,000,000
Total fixed assets	$1,200,000	$4,000,000	$14,000,000	$19,200,000	
Net working capital[a]	0	0	6,600,000	6,600,000	
Total investment	$1,200,000	$4,000,000	$20,600,000	$25,800,000	

[a]12 percent of first year's sales, or 0.12($55,000,000) = $6,600,000.

be made on December 31, 2000, and the remaining $4 million would be paid on December 31, 2001.

The necessary equipment would be installed late in 2001 and would be paid for on December 31, 2001. The equipment has a MACRS five-year recovery period and would cost $9.5 million, plus another $500,000 for installation.

The project would also require an initial investment in net working capital equal to 12 percent of the estimated sales in the first year. The initial working capital investment would be made on December 31, 2001, and on December 31 of each following year net working capital would be increased by an amount equal to 12 percent of any sales increase expected during the coming year. The project's estimated economic life is six years. At that time, the land is expected to have a market value of $1.7 million, the building a value of $1.0 million, and the equipment a value of $2 million. The marketing vice-president believes that annual sales would be 25,000 units if the systems were priced at $2,200 each. (See Table 12-4.) The production department has estimated that variable manufacturing costs would total 65 percent of dollar sales, and that fixed overhead costs, excluding depreciation, would be $8 million for the first year of operations. Sales prices and fixed overhead costs, other than depreciation, are projected to increase with inflation, which is expected to average 6 percent per year over the six-year life of the project.

RIC's marginal federal-plus-state tax rate is 40 percent; its weighted average cost of capital is 11.5 percent; and the company's policy, for capital budgeting purposes, is to assume that cash flows occur at the end of each year. Since the plant would begin operations on January 1, 2002, the first operating cash flows would thus occur on December 31, 2002.

As one of the company's financial analysts, you have been assigned to conduct the capital budgeting analysis. For now, you may assume that the project has the same risk as the firm's existing assets, hence you may use the corporate cost of capital, 11.5 percent, for this project. Later on, we will examine additional information concerning the riskiness of the project, but at this point assume that the project is of average risk.

Analysis of the Cash Flows

The first step in the analysis is to summarize the investment outlays required for the project; this is done in Table 12-3. Note that the land cannot be depreciated, hence we show its depreciable basis to be $0. Also, since the project will require an

| TABLE 12-4 | Net Cash Flows, 2002–2007 |

	2002	2003	2004	2005	2006	2007
1. Unit sales	25,000	25,000	25,000	25,000	25,000	25,000
2. Sale price[a]	$ 2,200	$ 2,332	$ 2,472	$ 2,620	$ 2,777	$ 2,944
3. Net sales[a]	$55,000,000	$58,300,000	$61,800,000	$65,500,000	$69,425,000	$73,600,000
4. Variable costs[b]	35,750,000	37,895,000	40,170,000	42,575,000	45,126,250	47,840,000
5. Fixed costs (overhead)[a]	8,000,000	8,480,000	8,988,800	9,528,128	10,099,816	10,705,805
6. Depreciation (building)[c]	120,000	240,000	240,000	240,000	240,000	240,000
7. Depreciation (equipment)[c]	2,000,000	3,200,000	1,900,000	1,200,000	1,100,000	600,000
8. Earnings before taxes	$ 9,130,000	$ 8,485,000	$10,501,200	$11,956,872	$12,858,934	$14,214,195
9. Taxes (40%)	3,652,000	3,394,000	4,200,480	4,782,749	5,143,574	5,685,678
10. Projected net operating income	$ 5,478,000	$ 5,091,000	$ 6,300,720	$ 7,174,123	$ 7,715,360	$ 8,528,517
11. Add back noncash expenses[d]	2,120,000	3,440,000	2,140,000	1,440,000	1,340,000	840,000
12. Cash flow from operations[e]	$ 7,598,000	$ 8,531,000	$ 8,440,720	$ 8,614,123	$ 9,055,360	$ 9,368,517
13. Net working capital[f]	$ 6,996,000	$ 7,416,000	$ 7,860,000	$ 8,331,000	$ 8,832,000	$ 0
14. Investment in NWC[g]	(396,000)	(420,000)	(444,000)	(471,000)	(501,000)	8,832,000
15. Net salvage value[h]						5,972,000
16. Total projected cash flow[i]	$ 7,202,000	$ 8,111,000	$ 7,996,720	$ 8,143,123	$ 8,554,360	$24,172,517

[a]The 2002 estimates are increased by the assumed 6 percent inflation rate.
[b]65 percent of net sales.
[c]MACRS depreciation rates are as follows:

YEAR	1	2	3	4	5	6
Building	1.5%	3%	3%	3%	3%	3%
Equipment	20	32	19	12	11	6

These percentages are multiplied by each asset's depreciable basis to get the depreciation expense for each year. Note that the allowances have been rounded for ease of computation.
[d]In this case, depreciation on building and equipment.
[e]Net operating income plus noncash expenses.
[f]Net working capital is equal to 12 percent of the following year's net sales. For example, NWC in 2002 is equal to 12 percent of 2003 sales, or (0.12)($58,300,000) = $6,996,000.
[g]The investment in NWC is equal to the change in net working capital from the previous year. For example, the change in working capital for 2003 is equal to $7,416,000 − $6,996,000 = $420,000. This increase in NWC is a negative cash flow. The cumulative working capital investment is recovered when the project ends in 2007.
[h]See Table 12-5 for the net salvage value calculation.
[i]Row 16 is the sum of Rows 12, 14, and 15.

increase in net working capital during 2001, this is shown as an investment outlay for that year.

Having estimated the capital requirements, we must now forecast the operating cash flows that will occur once production begins; these are set forth in Table 12-4. The operating cash flows estimates are based on information provided by RIC's various departments. Note that the sales price and fixed costs are projected to increase each year by the 6 percent inflation rate, and since variable costs are 65 percent of dollar sales, they too will rise by 6 percent each year. The change in net working capital

(NWC) represents the additional investment required to support sales increases (12 percent of the next year's sales increase, which in this case results only from inflation) during 2002–2006, and the recovery of the cumulative net working capital investment in 2007. The depreciation amounts were obtained by multiplying each asset's depreciable basis by the MACRS recovery allowance rates set forth in Note c to Table 12-4.

The analysis also requires an estimate of the cash flows generated by salvage values; Table 12-5 summarizes this analysis. First, we compare the projected 2007 market values against the 2007 book values. The land cannot be depreciated, and its estimated 2007 salvage value is greater than the initial purchase price. Thus, RIC would have to pay taxes on the profit. The building's estimated salvage value is less than its book value — it will be sold at a loss for tax purposes. The loss will reduce the company's taxable income and thus generate a tax savings. In effect, the company has been depreciating the building too slowly, so it would write off the loss against ordinary income. On the other hand, the equipment will be sold for more than book value, so the company would have to pay ordinary taxes on the $2 million difference. In all cases, book value is the depreciable cost less accumulated depreciation. The total cash flow from the salvage values is merely the sum of the land, building, and equipment components.

Making the Decision

To summarize the data and get it ready for evaluation, we combine all the net cash flows on a time line as shown in Table 12-6. The table also shows the payback period, IRR, MIRR, and NPV (at the 11.5 percent cost of capital). The project appears to be acceptable using the NPV, IRR, or MIRR methods, and it would also be acceptable if RIC required a payback of six years or less. Note, however, that the analysis thus far has been based on the assumption that the project has the same

---

TABLE 12-5	After-Tax Salvage Values, 2007		
	LAND	BUILDING	EQUIPMENT
Salvage (ending market) value	$1,700,000	$1,000,000	$ 2,000,000
Initial cost	1,200,000	8,000,000	10,000,000
Depreciable basis (2001)	0	8,000,000	10,000,000
Book value (2007)[a]	1,200,000	6,680,000	0
Capital gains income	$ 500,000	$ 0	$ 0
Ordinary income (loss)[b]	0	(5,680,000)	2,000,000
Taxes[c]	200,000	(2,272,000)	800,000
Net salvage value (Salvage value – Taxes)	$1,500,000	$3,272,000	$ 1,200,000

Net cash flow from salvage value = $1,500,000 + $3,272,000 + $1,200,000 = $5,972,000.

[a]Book value for the building in 2007 equals depreciable cost minus accumulated MACRS depreciation of $1,320,000. The accumulated depreciation on the equipment is $10,000,000. See Table 12-4.

[b]Building: $1,000,000 market value – $6,680,000 book value = –$5,680,000 = depreciation shortfall, which is treated as an operating expense in 2007.
Equipment: $2,000,000 market value – $0 book value = $2,000,000 depreciation recapture, which is treated as ordinary income in 2007.

[c]Since corporate capital gains are now taxed at the ordinary income rate, all taxes are based on RIC's 40 percent marginal federal-plus-state rate. The table is set up to differentiate ordinary income from capital gains because Congress may some day reinstate differential tax rates on those two income sources.

TABLE 12-6	Time Line of Consolidated End-of-Year Net Cash Flows, 1999–2007

1999	2000	2001	2002	2003	2004	2005	2006	2007
($1,200,000)	($4,000,000)	($20,600,000)	$7,202,000	$8,111,000	$7,996,720	$8,143,123	$8,554,360	$24,172,517

IRR: 25.1% versus an 11.5% cost of capital.
MIRR: 17.9% versus an 11.5% cost of capital.
NPV: $12,075,384.
Payback period: 5.3 years from first outflow (1999).

degree of risk as the company's average project. If the project is riskier than an average project, then it would be necessary to increase the cost of capital, which in turn might cause the NPV to become negative and the IRR and MIRR to fall below k. In Chapter 13, we extend the evaluation of this project to include the necessary risk analysis. Note also that in practice we would do the analysis using a computer spreadsheet, and the information given in Tables 12-3 through 12-6 would all be generated in the spreadsheet.

We should emphasize that capital budgeting decisions are actually based on both quantitative factors such as the calculated NPV, IRR, and MIRR *plus* qualitative, subjective factors such as the firm's strategic long-run plans. Therefore, in actual practice the fact that a calculated NPV is positive does not necessarily mean the project will be accepted, or that a negative NPV automatically leads to rejection. Of course, if managers *knew for certain* that the calculated numbers were correct, they would follow the rules and accept all positive NPV projects. However, the cash flows and cost of capital estimates used to develop the NPV are based on a number of assumptions, and if those assumptions turn out to be incorrect, then the *actual* NPV can turn out to be quite different from the *forecasted* NPV. Moreover, different members of the management team are likely to think that different assumptions are best, hence disagree on projects' "true" NPVs.

Managers will discuss the assumptions used to generate a project's cash flows, and the NPV will be calculated based on different sets of assumptions. The effects of incorrect decisions will also be considered—if the required investment represents a large percentage of the firm's capital, and if the company would be bankrupted if the assumptions turn out to be incorrect, then that fact would enter the final decision. On the other hand, if a number of small, independent projects are involved, forecasting errors might be offsetting and thus not have serious adverse consequences.

As a result of all this, major capital budgeting decisions are based on quantitative information plus subjective, judgmental factors. We will discuss all this further in the next chapter, when we address the issue of risk.

SELF-TEST
QUESTIONS

What is an expansion project?

How does RIC account for inflation in the cash flow estimation process?

Why was it necessary to include changes in net working capital in the analysis?

Describe how depreciation tax effects were included in the Table 12-4 operating cash flows.

Explain the meaning of the negative taxes shown for the building in the net salvage value analysis in Table 12-5.

GE BETS ON EUROPE

The never-ending search for growing and profitable markets has led many U.S. companies to make large investments in foreign countries, especially the rapidly growing markets of Asia and Latin America. Recently, less attention has been paid to Europe as a result of Europe's relatively anemic growth rate, along with the perception, either fair or unfair, that the European market remains stodgy and overregulated, with limited profit potential.

This general attitude notwithstanding, one well-known company, General Electric, has been making huge bets on the European market—more than $10 billion since 1989. Half of this money has been used to invest in new plants and equipment, while the other half has been used to fund nearly 50 acqui-sitions. GE's European investments include satellite broadcasting, financial services, and power plants.

Companies that invest overseas face a large set of investment opportunities and have great opportunities for diversification. However, foreign investment exposes them to challenges and risks not faced in the U.S. market. Thus, the profitability of GE's European investments depends on a variety of factors, including the strength of the European economy, exchange rates, and whether European workers and suppliers feel comfortable dealing with GE.

So far, GE's gamble on Europe appears to be paying off. In its most recent fiscal year, GE reported profits of $1 billion from its European subsidiary—or about 15 percent of the company's total annual profit. GE has been particularly successful in its financing business. Other areas, including the consumer appliance business, have been considerably less profitable. Overall, though, GE has done well in Europe. Whether it can continue its success in the European market is an open question. However, nobody has questioned GE's resolve. This resolve is reflected in a recent comment to *Fortune* by Sumantra Ghoshal, a London business school professor: "Investing in Europe today requires guts. GE has guts."

SOURCE: "If Europe's Dead, Why Is GE Investing Billions There? At a Time When It's Fashionable to Belittle Europe's Slow Growth, Jack Welch Is Making a Mammoth, Contrarian Bet on the World's Most Mature Market," *Fortune*, September 9, 1996, 114. *Fortune*, © 1996 Time Inc. All rights reserved.

EXAMPLE OF CASH FLOW ANALYSIS: REPLACEMENT PROJECT

RIC's watering system project was used to show how an expansion project is analyzed. Companies also make **replacement decisions,** where cash flows from both the old and the new assets must be considered. Replacement analysis is illustrated with an example from RIC's research and development (R&D) division.

A lathe for trimming molded plastics was purchased 10 years ago at a cost of $7,500. The machine had an expected life of 15 years at the time it was purchased, and management originally estimated, and still believes, that the salvage value will be zero at the end of the 15-year life. The machine is being depreciated on a straight line basis; therefore, its annual depreciation charge is $500, and its present book value is $2,500.

The R&D manager reports that a new special-purpose machine can be purchased for $12,000 (including freight and installation), and, over its five-year life, it will reduce labor and raw materials usage sufficiently to cut annual operating costs from $7,000 to $4,000. This reduction in costs will cause before-tax profits to rise by $7,000 − $4,000 = $3,000 per year.

It is estimated that the new machine can be sold for $2,000 at the end of five years; this is its estimated salvage value. The old machine's actual current market value is $1,000, which is below its $2,500 book value. If the new machine is acquired, the old lathe will be sold to another company rather than exchanged for the new machine. The company's marginal federal-plus-state tax rate is 40 percent, and the replacement project is assumed to be of average risk. Net working capital requirements will also increase by $1,000 at the time of replacement. By an IRS ruling, the new machine falls into the three-year MACRS class, and, since the cash flows are of average risk, the project's cost of capital is 11.5 percent, the firm's average cost of capital. Should the replacement be made?

TABLE 12-7	Replacement Analysis Worksheet					
YEAR:	**0**	**1**	**2**	**3**	**4**	**5**
I. Investment Outlay						
1. Cost of new equipment	($12,000)					
2. Market value of old equipment	1,000					
3. Tax savings on sale of old equipment	600					
4. Increase in net working capital	(1,000)					
5. Total net investment	($11,400)					
II. Operating Inflows over the Project's Life						
6. After-tax decrease in costs		$1,800	$1,800	$1,800	$1,800	$1,800
7. Depreciation on new machine		$3,960	$5,400	$1,800	$ 840	$ 0
8. Depreciation on old machine		500	500	500	500	500
9. Change in depreciation (7 − 8)		$3,460	$4,900	$1,300	$ 340	($ 500)
10. Tax savings from depreciation (0.4 × 9)		1,384	1,960	520	136	(200)
11. Net operating cash flows (6 + 10)		$3,184	$3,760	$2,320	$1,936	$1,600
III. Terminal Year Cash Flows						
12. Estimated salvage value of new machine						$2,000
13. Tax on salvage value						(800)
14. Return of net working capital						1,000
15. Total termination cash flows						$2,200
IV. Net Cash Flows						
16. Net cash flow time line	($11,400)	$3,184	$3,760	$2,320	$1,936	$3,800
V. Results						

NPV: −$388.77.

IRR: 10.1% versus an 11.5% cost of capital.

MIRR: 10.7% versus an 11.5% cost of capital.

Payback period: 4.1 years.

Table 12-7 shows the worksheet format the company uses to analyze replacement projects. Each line is numbered, and a line-by-line description of the table follows.

Line 1. The top section of the table, Lines 1 through 5, sets forth the cash flows which occur at (approximately) t = 0, the time the investment is made. Line 1 shows the purchase price of the new machine, including installation and freight charges. Since it is an outflow, it is negative.

Line 2. Here we show the price received from the sale of the old equipment.

Line 3. Since the old equipment would be sold at less than book value, the sale would create a loss which would reduce the firm's taxable income, and thus its next quarterly income tax payment. The tax saving is equal to (Loss)(T) = ($1,500)(0.40) = $600, where T is the marginal corporate tax rate. The Tax Code defines this loss as an operating loss, because it reflects the fact that inadequate depreciation was taken on the old asset. If there had been a profit on the sale (that is, if the sale price had exceeded book value), Line 3 would have shown a tax liability, a cash outflow. In the actual case, the equipment would be sold at a loss, so no taxes would be paid, and the company would realize a tax savings of $600.[4]

Line 4. The investment in additional net working capital (new current asset requirements minus increases in accounts payable and accruals) is shown here. This investment will be recovered at the end of the project's life (see Line 14). No taxes are involved.

Line 5. Here we show the total net cash outflow at the time the replacement is made. The company writes a check for $12,000 to pay for the machine, and another $1,000 is invested in net working capital. However, these outlays are partially offset by proceeds from the sale of the old equipment and a reduced tax bill.

Line 6. Section II of the table shows the *incremental operating cash flows,* or benefits, that are expected if the replacement is made. The first of these benefits is the reduction in operating costs shown on Line 6. Cash flows increase because operating costs are reduced by $3,000. However, reduced costs also mean higher taxable income, hence higher income taxes. Here is the calculation:

Reduction in costs = Δ cost =	$3,000
Associated increase in taxes = $T(\Delta$ cost) = 0.4($3,000) =	1,200
Increase in net after-tax cash flows due to cost reduction = Δ NCF =	$1,800

Had the replacement resulted in an increase in sales in addition to the reduction in costs (that is, if the new machine had been both larger and more efficient), then this amount would also be reported on Line 6 (or a separate line could be added). Also, note that the $3,000 cost savings is constant over Years 1 through 5; had the annual savings been expected to change over time, this fact would have to be built into the analysis.

Line 7. The depreciable basis of the new machine, $12,000, is multiplied by the appropriate MACRS recovery allowance for three-year class property (see Table 12-2) to obtain the depreciation figures shown on Line 7. Note that if you summed across Line 7, the total would be $12,000, the depreciable basis.

Line 8. Line 8 shows the $500 straight line depreciation on the old machine.

Line 9. The depreciation expense on the old machine as shown on Line 8 can no longer be taken if the replacement is made, but the new machine's depreciation will be available. Therefore, the $500 depreciation on the old machine is subtracted from that on the new machine to show the net change in annual depreciation. The change is positive in Years 1 through 4 but negative in Year 5. The Year 5 negative change in annual depreciation signifies that the purchase of the replacement machine results in a *decrease* in depreciation expense during that year.

Line 10. The change in depreciation results in a tax reduction which is equal to the change in depreciation multiplied by the tax rate: Depreciation tax savings = T(Change in depreciation) = 0.40($3,460) = $1,384 for Year 1. Note that the relevant cash flow is the tax savings on the *net change* in depreciation, not just the depreciation on the new

---

[4]If the old asset were being exchanged for the new asset, rather than being sold to a third party, the tax consequences would be different. In an exchange of similar assets, no gain or loss is recognized. If the market value of the old asset is greater than its book value, the depreciable basis of the new asset is decreased by the excess amount. Conversely, if the market value of the old asset is less than its book value, the depreciable basis is increased by the shortfall.

equipment. Capital budgeting decisions are based on *incremental* cash flows, and since RIC will lose $500 of depreciation if it replaces the old machine, that fact must be taken into account.

Line 11.   Here we show the net operating cash flows over the project's five-year life. These flows are found by adding the after-tax cost savings to the depreciation tax savings, or Line 6 + Line 10.

Line 12.   Part III shows the cash flows associated with the termination of the project. To begin, Line 12 shows the estimated salvage value of the new machine at the end of its five-year life, $2,000.[5]

Line 13.   Since the book value of the new machine at the end of Year 5 is zero, the company will have to pay taxes of $2,000(0.4) = $800.

Line 14.   An investment of $1,000 in net working capital was shown as an outflow at t = 0. This investment, like the new machine's salvage value, will be recovered when the project is terminated at the end of Year 5. Accounts receivable will be collected, inventories will be drawn down and not replaced, and the result will be an inflow of $1,000 at t = 5.

Line 15.   Here we show the total cash flows resulting from terminating the project.

Line 16.   Part IV shows, on Line 16, the total net cash flows in a form suitable for capital budgeting evaluation. In effect, Line 16 is a "time line."

Part V of the table, "Results," shows the replacement project's NPV, IRR, MIRR, and payback. Because the project has average risk, a cost of capital of 11.5 percent is appropriate. At this cost of capital, the NPV is negative. Therefore, the project is not acceptable, hence the old lathe should not be replaced.

SELF-TEST
QUESTION

In a replacement analysis, incremental cash flows in a "new minus old" sense are evaluated. How does this type of analysis differ from that used to evaluate an expansion project?

CASH FLOW ESTIMATION BIAS

As noted at the beginning of the chapter, cash flow estimation is the most critical, and also the most difficult, part of the capital budgeting process. For most projects, cash flows must be forecasted many years into the future, and estimation errors are bound to occur.[6] Clearly, large errors can and do occur. However, large firms evaluate and accept many projects every year, and if the cash flow estimates are unbiased and the errors are random, estimation errors will tend to cancel each other out. Some projects will have NPV estimates that are too high and others will have estimates that are too low, but the average realized NPV on all the projects accepted should be relatively close to the aggregate NPV estimate.

---

[5]In this analysis, the salvage value of the old machine is zero. However, if the old machine was expected to have a positive salvage value at the end of five years, replacing the old machine now would eliminate this cash flow. Thus, the after-tax salvage value of the old machine would represent an opportunity cost to the firm, and it would be included as a Year 5 cash outflow in the terminal cash flow section of the worksheet.

[6]For a discussion of the cash flow estimation practices of some large firms, as well as some estimates of the inaccuracies involved, see Randolph A. Pohlman, Emmanuel S. Santiago, and F. Lynn Markel, "Cash Flow Estimation Practices of Large Firms," *Financial Management*, Summer 1988, 71–79.

Unfortunately, several studies indicate that capital budgeting cash flow forecasts are often biased—many managers tend to be overly optimistic, so revenues tend to be overstated and costs understated.[7] The end result is an upward bias in net operating cash flows and thus an upward bias in estimated NPVs. This is most likely to occur if managers are paid on the basis of the size of the company, hence are motivated to maximize size rather than to create wealth. Even when this is not the case, managers can become emotionally attached to their projects and thus fail to objectively assess projects' potential negative factors.

If a bias exists at a particular firm, then accepting a project with a zero estimated NPV will likely result in a loss, hence in a decrease in shareholders' wealth. Recognizing that biases may exist, senior managers at many firms now develop data on divisional managers' forecasting accuracies and then consider this information in the capital budgeting decision process. Some companies lower the cash flow estimates of managers whose track records suggest that their forecasts are too rosy, while other companies increase the cost of capital, or hurdle rate, applied to such project submissions.

The first step in identifying cash flow estimation bias, especially for projects that are estimated to be highly profitable, is to ask this question: What is the underlying cause of this project's high profitability? If the firm has some inherent advantage such as patent protection, unique marketing expertise, or a well-known brand name, then some of its projects may truly be extraordinarily profitable. However, in the long run above-normal profits generally attract competition and thus are eroded. If there is reason to believe that competition is likely to increase, and if division managers cannot identify any unique factor which would support a project's continued high profitability, then senior management should be concerned about estimation bias.

RIC's top management considered the possibility of estimation bias when they reviewed the watering system project. With an IRR of 25.1 percent and an MIRR of 17.9 percent versus a cost of capital of 11.5 percent, the project is clearly projected to earn above-normal profits. These high profits might attract other firms into the market, and new entry might cause the actual cash flows to fall far below those forecast in Table 12-4. However, RIC's management concluded that competitors would not be able to develop and produce a competing product within the next several years. Further, they noted that the unit sales forecasts were held constant over the life of the project, which is probably conservative. Finally, as we will see in Chapter 13, the project is actually quite risky, and the forecasted returns are not out of line in view of the risks involved.

SELF-TEST QUESTIONS

Why might cash flow estimation bias exist in the capital budgeting decision process? What can be done to counteract such a bias?

OPTION VALUE

Traditional discounted cash flow (DCF) analysis—where an asset's cash flows are estimated and then discounted to obtain the asset's NPV—has been the cornerstone of asset valuation since the 1950s. Accordingly, most of our discussion of capital budgeting focuses on DCF valuation techniques. However, in recent years a growing number of academics and practitioners have demonstrated that DCF valuation techniques do

---

[7]For a discussion of cash flow estimation bias, see Stephen W. Pruitt and Lawrence J. Gitman, "Capital Budgeting Forecast Biases: Evidence from the *Fortune* 500," *Financial Management*, Spring 1987, 46–51.

not always tell the complete story about a project's value and that rote use of these techniques can, at times, lead to incorrect capital budgeting decisions.[8]

DCF techniques were originally developed to value securities such as stocks and bonds. These securities are passive investments—once they have been purchased, most investors have no influence over the cash flows the assets produce. However, real assets are not passive investments—managerial actions can influence their results. Furthermore, investing in a new project often brings with it a potential increase in the firm's future opportunities. Opportunities are, in effect, **options**— the right but not the obligation to take some action in the future. As we discuss in detail in Chapter 24, options are valuable, so any project that expands the firm's set of opportunities has positive **option value.** Similarly, any project that reduces the set of future opportunities has negative option value. A project's impact on the firm's opportunities, or its option value, may not be captured by conventional NPV analysis. Therefore, option value should be considered separately.

To illustrate one type of option value created by projects, consider the situation facing McDonald's when it decided to build a restaurant in Moscow. The company had to get a whole series of permits, set up a supply system, find a site, and train a set of employees who were totally unfamiliar with operations like McDonald's. It would be impossible to justify building the new restaurant on the basis of an NPV analysis—the NPV would be hugely negative. However, McDonald's management felt that setting up the Moscow operation would give it experience in doing business in Russia, and, if the venture were successful, it would open the door to millions of potential new customers. Thus, the main value expected from the Moscow investment was in the form of an option, not the direct cash flows the Moscow restaurant would produce. Hundreds of other companies are setting up operations in China, Latin America, Africa, and other areas for the strategic options those investments provide, in spite of the negative NPVs produced by conventional NPV analysis.

Compaq Computer provides a somewhat different type of example. Compaq recently invested about $3 million in Intellon Corporation, a small startup company which is attempting to develop a commercially viable system which uses buildings' interior wiring for digital communications. Compaq could not justify its investment on the basis of an NPV analysis, but it wanted to be in on the ground floor if Intellon's technology turns out to be feasible for use in developing "intelligent buildings." Then, Compaq could supply the computers that would control the system. Compaq and hundreds of other companies are spending billions on "strategic investments" in smaller companies like Intellon, primarily for the option value these investments provide.

Another type of option that can add value is the ability to *abandon,* or discontinue, a project, either to cut losses or because the operation is more valuable to some other party and can be sold for more than the present value of the remaining cash flows. Often, capital budgeting analyses are conducted assuming a fixed life for each project. However, if a project can be abandoned, it may be less risky and have a higher expected value than is indicated by conventional fixed-life NPV analysis. We will discuss aban-

---

[8]For an excellent general discussion of the problems inherent in discounted cash flow valuation techniques as applied to capital budgeting, see Avinash K. Dixit and Robert S. Pindyck, "The Options Approach to Capital Investment," *Harvard Business Review,* May–June 1995, 105–115. For more information on the option value inherent in investment timing decisions, see Stephen A. Ross, "Uses, Abuses, and Alternatives to the Net-Present-Value Rule," *Financial Management,* Autumn 1995, 96–101. Also, the Spring 1987 issue of the *Midland Corporate Finance Journal* contains several interesting articles on the use of option concepts in capital budgeting.

donment options and their effects in more detail later in this chapter and again in Chapter 13.

It should also be noted that a conventional NPV analysis can, at times, overstate the value of a project. This occurs because accepting a certain type of project today "kills off" future opportunities. To illustrate, consider the situation recently faced by Royal Dutch Petroleum when it was deciding whether or not to open a newly discovered oil field. The exploratory work had already been done, so the company knew how much oil was in the field, and it also knew how much it would cost to get it out of the ground and how much it could earn on each barrel produced. The project had a positive NPV, hence conventional discounted cash flow analysis indicated that the field should be developed. However, a conventional analysis implicitly assumes that the project will be undertaken now or never, because the analysis provides only two possible choices—accept or reject.

Yet suppose oil prices turn out to be significantly higher five years from now. In that case, each barrel extracted and sold at today's prices would preclude selling that barrel in the future at a higher price. Therefore, the NPV of the project might be higher if Royal Dutch delayed taking it on rather than going forward today. By opening the oil field today, the company is, in effect, "exercising an option" and thus reducing its future opportunities. In such cases, a conventional NPV analysis may overstate the value of the project, so decision makers should insist on an NPV that is both positive and also large enough to offset the option value given up by not holding the oil field for future development. Indeed, some companies deliberately set hurdle rates that are above the calculated cost of capital when evaluating projects that contain such *timing options*. By doing so, they recognize that taking on the project today involves some loss of value due to extinguishing an implicit call option.

Our conclusion to all this is that the true values of projects which include embedded options may exceed those shown in a straightforward NPV calculation, while the NPVs of projects which limit future opportunities may be overstated. Therefore, managers should identify such options and take them into account in their capital budgeting decisions. Decision trees, which we discuss in Chapter 13, provide one method for formally dealing with options. Also, option pricing models, which we discuss in Chapter 24, can be used in certain situations. A great deal of work is going on in this area, and we expect to see more widespread use of option analysis as a supplement to discounted cash flow analysis in capital budgeting in the future. For now, you should recognize that as a result of embedded options some projects have more or less value than is indicated by their NPVs, and this value should, at a minimum, be subjectively considered when making capital budgeting decisions.

SELF-TEST QUESTIONS

How might option considerations cause a conventional NPV valuation to produce an incorrect decision recommendation for a project?

What actions can managers take to correct the NPV valuation problem?

COMPARING PROJECTS WITH UNEQUAL LIVES

Note that a replacement decision involves comparing two mutually exclusive projects: retaining the old asset versus buying a new one. To simplify matters, in our replacement example we assumed that the new machine had a life equal to the remaining life of the old machine. If, however, we were choosing between two mutually exclusive alternatives with significantly different lives, an adjustment would be necessary. We now discuss two procedures—(1) the replacement chain method and

FIGURE 12-1	Expected Net Cash Flows for Projects C and F

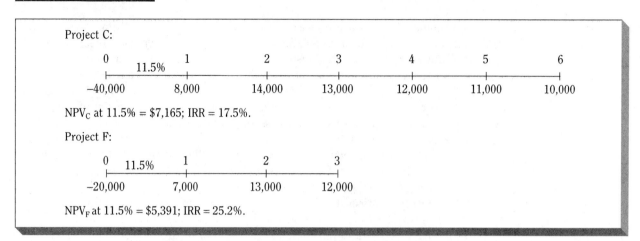

Project C:

NPV$_C$ at 11.5% = $7,165; IRR = 17.5%.

Project F:

NPV$_F$ at 11.5% = $5,391; IRR = 25.2%.

(2) the equivalent annual annuity method—to illustrate the problem and show how to deal with it.

Suppose RIC is planning to modernize its production facilities, and it is considering either a conveyor system (Project C) or some forklift trucks (Project F) for moving materials. Figure 12-1 shows both the expected net cash flows and the NPVs for these two mutually exclusive alternatives. We see that Project C, when discounted at an 11.5 percent cost of capital, has the higher NPV and thus appears to be the better project.

Replacement Chain (Common Life) Approach

Although the NPV shown in Figure 12-1 suggests that Project C should be selected, this analysis is incomplete, and the decision to choose Project C is actually incorrect. If we choose Project F, we will have an opportunity to make a similar investment in three years, and if cost and revenue conditions continue at the Figure 12-1 levels, this second investment will also be profitable. However, if we choose Project C, we give up the option to make this second investment. Therefore, to make a proper comparison of Projects C and F, we could apply the **replacement chain (common life) approach;** that is, we could find the NPV of Project F over a six-year period, and then compare this extended NPV with the NPV of Project C over the same six years.

The NPV for Project C as calculated in Figure 12-1 is already over the six-year common life. For Project F, however, we must add in a second project to extend the overall life of the combined projects to six years. Here we assume (1) that Project F's cost and annual cash inflows will not change if the project is repeated in three years and (2) that RIC's cost of capital will remain at 11.5 percent:

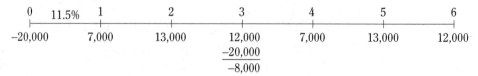

NPV at 11.5% = $9,281; IRR = 25.2%.

The NPV of this extended Project F is $9,281, and its IRR is 25.2 percent. (The IRR of two Project Fs is the same as the IRR for one Project F.) Since the $9,281 extended NPV of Project F over the common life of six years is greater than the $7,165 NPV of Project C, Project F should be selected.[9]

Equivalent Annual Annuity (EAA) Approach

Although the preceding example illustrates why an extended analysis is necessary if we are comparing mutually exclusive projects with different lives, the arithmetic is generally more complex in practice. For example, one project might have a six-year life versus a ten-year life for the other. This would require a replacement chain analysis over 30 years, the lowest common denominator of the two lives. In such a situation, it is often simpler to use a second procedure, the **equivalent annual annuity (EAA) method,** which involves three steps:

1. Find each project's NPV over its initial life. In Figure 12-1, we found $NPV_C = \$7,165$ and $NPV_F = \$5,391$.

2. There is some constant annuity cash flow (the equivalent annual annuity [EAA]) that has the same present value as a project's calculated NPV. For Project F, here is the time line:

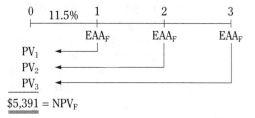

To find the value of EAA_F with a financial calculator, enter $N = 3$, $k = I = 11.5$, $PV = -5391$, and $FV = 0$, and solve for PMT. The answer is $2,225. This level annuity cash flow stream, when discounted back three years at 11.5 percent, has a present value equal to Project F's original NPV, $5,391. The $2,225 is called the project's "equivalent annual annuity (EAA)." The EAA for Project C can be found similarly, and it is $1,718. Thus, Project C has an NPV which is equivalent to an annuity of $1,718 per year, while Project F's NPV is equivalent to an annuity of $2,225.[10]

3. The project with the higher EAA will always have the higher NPV when extended out to any common life. Therefore, since F's EAA is larger than C's, we would choose Project F.

The EAA method is often easier to apply than the replacement chain method, but the replacement chain method is easier to explain to decision makers. Still, the two methods lead to the same decision if consistent assumptions are used.

---

[9]Alternatively, we could recognize that the value of the cash flow stream of two consecutive Project Fs can be summarized by two NPVs: one at Year 0 representing the value of the initial project, and one at Year 3 representing the value of the replication project:

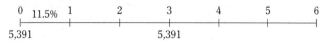

NPV = $9,281.

Ignoring rounding differences, the present value of these two cash flows, when discounted at 11.5 percent, is $9,281, so we again come to the conclusion that Project F should be selected.

[10]Some financial calculators have the EAA feature programmed in. For example, the HP-17B has the function in its cash flow register. One simply keys in the cash flows, enters the interest rate, and then presses the "NUS" key to get the EAA. Hewlett-Packard uses the term NUS (for "net uniform series") in lieu of the term EAA.

When should we worry about unequal life analysis? The unequal life issue (1) does not arise for independent projects, but (2) it can arise if mutually exclusive projects with significantly different lives are being compared. However, even for mutually exclusive projects, it is not always appropriate to extend the analysis to a common life. This should only be done if there is a high probability that the projects will actually be repeated at the end of their initial lives.

We should note several potentially serious weaknesses inherent in this type of analysis: (1) If inflation is expected, then replacement equipment will have a higher price. Moreover, both sales prices and operating costs will probably change. Thus, the static conditions built into the analysis would be invalid. (2) Replacements that occur down the road would probably employ new technology, which in turn might change the cash flows. This factor is not built into either replacement chain analysis or the EAA approach. (3) It is difficult enough to estimate the lives of most projects, so estimating the lives of a series of projects is often just a speculation.

In view of these problems, no experienced financial analyst would be too concerned about comparing mutually exclusive projects with lives of, say, eight years and ten years. Given all the uncertainties in the estimation process, such projects would, for all practical purposes, be assumed to have the same life. Still, it is important to recognize that a problem exists if mutually exclusive projects have substantially different lives. When we encounter such problems in practice, we use a computer spreadsheet and build expected inflation and/or possible efficiency gains directly into the cash flow estimates, and then use the replacement chain approach (but not the equivalent annual annuity method). The cash flow estimation is more complicated, but the concepts involved are exactly the same as in our example.

<table>
<tr><td>S E L F - T E S T
Q U E S T I O N S</td><td>Briefly describe the replacement chain (common life) approach.

Briefly describe the equivalent annual annuity (EAA) approach.

Why is it not always necessary to adjust project cash flow analyses for unequal lives?</td></tr>
</table>

ABANDONMENT VALUE

Projects are normally analyzed under the assumption that the firm will operate the asset over its full physical life. However, this may not be the best course of action—it may be best to abandon a project before the end of its potential life, and this possibility can materially affect the project's estimated profitability.[11] The situation in Table 12-8 can be used to illustrate the abandonment value concept and its effects on capital budgeting. The abandonment values listed in the third column are equivalent to net salvage values, except that they have been estimated for each year of Project A's life.

Using a 10 percent cost of capital, the expected NPV based on three years of operating cash flows and the zero abandonment (salvage) value is −$14.12:

```
  0    10%     1         2         3
  |-----+------|---------|---------|
($4,800)    $2,000    $2,000    $1,750
                                    0
```

$$\text{NPV} = -\$4,800 + \$2,000/(1.10)^1 + \$2,000/(1.10)^2 + \$1,750/(1.10)^3$$

$$= -\$14.12.$$

---

[11]The classic work on this subject is Alexander A. Robichek and James C. Van Horne, "Abandonment Value and Capital Budgeting," *Journal of Finance,* December 1967, 577–589.

TABLE 12-8	Project A: Investment, Operating, and Abandonment Cash Flows

YEAR (t)	INITIAL (YEAR 0) INVESTMENT AND OPERATING CASH FLOWS	NET ABANDONMENT VALUE AT END OF YEAR t
0	($4,800)	$4,800
1	2,000	3,000
2	2,000	1,650
3	1,750	0

Thus, Project A would not be accepted if we assume that it will be operated over its full three-year life. However, what would its NPV be if the project were abandoned after two years? In this case, we would receive operating cash flows in Years 1 and 2, plus the abandonment value at the end of Year 2, and the project's NPV would be $34.71:

$$
\begin{array}{cccc}
0 & 10\% & 1 & 2 \\
\vdash & & \dashv & \dashv \\
(\$4,800) & \$2,000 & & \$2,000 \\
& & & 1,650
\end{array}
$$

$$
\text{NPV} = -\$4,800 + \$2,000/(1.10)^1 + \$2,000/(1.10)^2 + \$1,650/(1.10)^2
$$

$$
= \$34.71.
$$

Thus, Project A would be profitable if we operate it for two years and then dispose of it. To complete the analysis, note that if the project were abandoned after one year, its NPV would be −$254.55. Thus, the optimal life for this project is two years. As a general rule, any project should be abandoned if its abandonment value is greater than the present value of all cash flows beyond the abandonment year, discounted to the abandonment decision point.

The abandonment option should be considered in the capital budgeting process because, as our example illustrates, there are cases where recognizing this option can change a project from unacceptable to acceptable. In addition, this type of analysis can be used to determine a project's **economic life,** which is the life that maximizes the project's NPV and thus maximizes shareholder wealth. For Project A, the economic life is two years versus the three-year **physical,** or **engineering, life.** Note that this analysis was based on the expected cash flows and the expected abandonment value, and it should always be conducted as a part of the capital budgeting evaluation of a proposed project.

Abandonment value also should be considered during routine post-audits of ongoing projects. As time goes by, additional information becomes available concerning both a project's current abandonment value and its expected future operating cash flows. If abandonment creates more value than continued operation, a project should be terminated. For example, a project might be right on track, with its actual cash flows equaling the cash flows that were initially expected. However, the actual current abandonment value might be significantly different than what was originally expected. This was the case with Eastman Kodak's Sterling Winthrop pharmaceutical business, which it sold in 1994 to Sanofi, a French health care and beauty products company. The business had more synergistic value to Sanofi than to Kodak because it provided Sanofi with U.S. distribution channels for its current and future drug products. In addition, the sale gave Kodak funds which it could use to build up its core film and digital imaging businesses.

Sometimes a project's operating cash flows turn out to be much lower than originally expected. Coca-Cola's "New Coke" is an example—shortly after its launch, it became apparent that the product would never be the money-maker the firm had anticipated. Note that both Kodak and Coca-Cola faced risks when they embarked on their projects: Future operating cash flows and abandonment values might be higher or lower than expected. Kodak realized "upside" potential due to a higher-than-expected abandonment value. Coca-Cola benefited by avoiding the "downside" losses which would have occurred due to the lower-than-anticipated operating cash flows by terminating the New Coke project. In general, the opportunity to abandon projects allows companies to limit downside losses but reap upside gains.

The actions of Kodak and Coca-Cola illustrate the **abandonment option,** which is the ability to abandon a project if the future operating cash flows and/or abandonment value are different than expected. The abandonment option reduces the riskiness of projects and thus increases their value, and it should be considered both when projects are originally evaluated and also during ongoing post-audits.

S E L F - T E S T
Q U E S T I O N S

Define the economic life of a project (as opposed to its physical life).

Should projects be viewed as having only one life, or should alternative lives be considered in the capital budgeting process?

What are the two main situations in which abandonment may be desirable?

ADJUSTING FOR INFLATION

Inflation is a fact of life in the United States and most other nations, so it must be considered in any sound capital budgeting analysis.[12]

Inflation-Induced Bias

Note that *in the absence of inflation,* the real rate, k_r, is equal to the nominal rate, k_n. Moreover, the real and nominal expected net cash flows—RCF_t and NCF_t—are also equal. Remember that *real* interest rates and cash flows do not include inflation effects, while *nominal* rates and flows do reflect the effects of inflation. In particular, an inflation premium, IP, is built into all nominal market interest rates. In the absence of inflation, NPV can thus be calculated in either of two ways:

$$NPV \text{ (no inflation)} = \sum_{t=0}^{n} \frac{RCF_t}{(1 + k_r)^t} = \sum_{t=0}^{n} \frac{NCF_t}{(1 + k_n)^t}. \tag{12-1}$$

Now suppose the expected rate of inflation is positive, and we expect *all* of the project's cash flows—including those related to depreciation—to rise at the rate i. Further, assume that this same inflation rate, i, is built into the market cost of capital as an inflation premium, IP = i. In this situation, the nominal net cash flow, NCF_t, will increase annually at the rate of i percent, producing this result:

$$NCF_t = RCF_t(1 + i)^t.$$

---

[12]For a formal discussion of this subject, see James C. Van Horne, "A Note on Biases in Capital Budgeting Introduced by Inflation," *Journal of Financial and Quantitative Analysis,* January 1971, 653–658; Philip L. Cooley, Rodney L. Roenfeldt, and It-Keong Chew, "Capital Budgeting Procedures under Inflation," *Financial Management,* Winter 1975, 18–27; and "Cooley, Roenfeldt, and Chew vs. Findlay and Frankle," *Financial Management,* Autumn 1976, 83–90.

For example, if we expected a net cash flow of $100 in Year 5 in the absence of inflation, then with a 5 percent annual rate of inflation, $NCF_5 = \$100(1.05)^5 = \$127.63$.

In general, the cost of capital used as the discount rate in capital budgeting analysis is based on the market-determined costs of debt and equity, so it is a nominal rate. To convert a real interest rate to a nominal rate when the inflation rate is i, we use this formula:

$$(1 + k_n) = (1 + k_r)(1 + i).$$

For example, if the real cost of capital is 7 percent and the inflation rate is 5 percent, then $1 + k_n = (1.07)(1.05) = 1.1235$, so $k_n = 12.35\%$.

Now if net cash flows increase at the rate of i percent per year, and if this same inflation premium is built into the firm's cost of capital, then the NPV would be calculated as follows:

$$\text{NPV (with inflation)} = \sum_{t=0}^{n} \frac{NCF_t}{(1+k_n)^t} = \sum_{t=0}^{n} \frac{RCF_t(1+i)^t}{(1+k_r)^t(1+i)^t}. \qquad \textbf{(12-2)}$$

Since the $(1 + i)^t$ terms in the numerator and denominator cancel, we are left with Equation 12-1:

$$\text{NPV} = \sum_{t=0}^{n} \frac{RCF_t}{(1+k_r)^t}.$$

Thus, if all costs and also the sales price, hence annual cash flows, are expected to rise at the same inflation rate that investors have built into the cost of capital, then the inflation-adjusted NPV as determined using Equation 12-2 is identical to the real NPV found using Equation 12-1.[13]

However, firms occasionally use base year, or constant (unadjusted), dollars throughout the analysis — say, 1999 dollars if the analysis is done in 1999 — along with a cost of capital as determined in the marketplace as we described in Chapter 10. This is wrong: *If the cost of capital includes an inflation premium, as it typically does, but the cash flows are all stated in constant (unadjusted) dollars, then the calculated NPV will be downward biased.* The denominator will reflect inflation, but the numerator will not, and this will produce a downward-biased NPV.

Making the Inflation Adjustment

There are two ways to adjust for inflation. First, all project cash flows can be expressed as real (unadjusted) flows, with no consideration of inflation, and then the cost of capital can be adjusted to a real rate by removing the inflation premiums from the component costs. This approach is relatively simple, but to produce an unbiased NPV it requires (1) that all project cash flows, including depreciation, be affected identically by inflation, and (2) that this rate of increase equals the inflation rate built into investors' required returns. Since these assumptions do not necessarily hold in practice, this method is not commonly used.

The second method involves leaving the cost of capital in its nominal form, and then adjusting the individual cash flows to reflect expected inflation. This is what we did

---

[13]To focus on inflation effects, we have simplified the situation somewhat. The actual project cost of capital is made up of debt and equity components, both of which are affected by inflation, but only the debt component is adjusted for tax effects. Thus, the relationship between nominal and real costs of capital is more complex than indicated in our discussion here.

earlier in our RIC example as summarized in Table 12-4. There we assumed that sales prices, variable costs, and fixed overhead costs would all increase at a rate of 6 percent per year but that depreciation charges would not be affected by inflation. Of course, we could have assumed different rates of inflation for sales prices, for variable costs, and for fixed overheads. For example, RIC might have long-term labor contracts which cause wage rates to rise with the Consumer Price Index (CPI), but its raw materials might be purchased under a fixed price contract, with the net result that variable costs are expected to rise by a smaller percentage than sales prices. In any event, one should build inflation into the cash flow analysis, with the specific adjustment reflecting as accurately as possible the most likely set of circumstances. With a spreadsheet, it is easy to make the adjustments.

Our conclusions about inflation may be summarized as follows. First, inflation is critically important, for it can and does have major effects on businesses. Therefore, it must be recognized and dealt with. Second, the most effective way of dealing with inflation in capital budgeting analyses is to build inflation estimates into each cash flow element, using the best available information on how each element will be affected. Third, since we cannot estimate future inflation rates with precision, errors are bound to be made. Thus, inflation adds to the uncertainty, or riskiness, of capital budgeting as well as to its complexity.

SELF-TEST QUESTIONS

Under what seemingly straightforward method of analysis would inflation cause a bias in a project's estimated NPV? Would the bias be upward or downward?

What is the best way of handling inflation, and how does this procedure eliminate the potential bias?

SUMMARY

This chapter discussed several issues in capital budgeting. The key concepts covered are listed below.

- The most important (and most difficult) step in analyzing a capital budgeting project is **estimating the incremental after-tax cash flows** the project will produce.

- **Project cash flow** is different from accounting income. Project cash flow includes: (1) **cash outlays for fixed assets,** (2) the **tax shield provided by depreciation,** and (3) cash flows due to **changes in net operating working capital.** Project cash flow does not include: (1) the **actual depreciation charge** or (2) **interest payments.**

- In determining incremental cash flows, **opportunity costs** (the cash flows foregone by using an asset) must be included, but **sunk costs** (cash outlays that have been made but which cannot be recouped) are not included. Any **externalities** (effects of a project on other parts of the firm) should also be reflected in the analysis.

- **Cannibalization** occurs when a new project leads to a reduction in sales of an existing product.

- **Tax laws** affect cash flow analysis in two ways: (1) They reduce operating cash flows, and (2) they determine the depreciation expense that can be taken in each year.

- The incremental cash flows from a typical project can be classified into three categories: (1) **initial investment outlay,** (2) **operating cash flows over the project's life,** and (3) **terminal year cash flows.**

- **Replacement analysis** is slightly different from that for **expansion projects** because the cash flows from the old asset must be considered in replacement decisions.

- Cash flow **estimation bias** will occur if managers are overly optimistic in their forecasts.

- A project may have an **option value** that is not accounted for in a conventional discounted cash flow analysis.

- If mutually exclusive projects have **unequal lives,** it may be necessary to adjust the analysis to put the projects on an equal life basis. This can be done using either the **replacement chain (common life) approach** or the **equivalent annual annuity (EAA) approach.**

- A project's true value may be greater than the NPV based on its **physical life** if it can be **abandoned** at the end of its **economic life,** which is earlier than its physical life.

- **Inflation effects** must be considered in project analysis. The best procedure is to build inflation directly into the cash flow estimates.

We continue our discussion of capital budgeting analysis in Chapter 13, where we discuss risk analysis.

Questions

12-1 Define each of the following terms:
   a. Cash flow; accounting income
   b. Incremental cash flow; sunk cost; opportunity cost
   c. Net working capital changes
   d. Salvage value
   e. Replacement decision
   f. Replacement chain
   g. Equivalent annual annuity
   h. Abandonment value
   i. Real rate of return, k_r, versus nominal rate of return, k_n
   j. Cash flow estimation bias
   k. Option value

12-2 Operating cash flows, rather than accounting profits, are listed in Table 12-4. What is the basis for this emphasis on cash flows as opposed to net income?

12-3 Why is it true, in general, that a failure to adjust expected cash flows for expected inflation biases the calculated NPV downward?

12-4 Suppose a firm is considering two mutually exclusive projects. One has a life of 6 years and the other a life of 10 years. Would the failure to employ some type of replacement chain analysis bias an NPV analysis against one of the projects? Explain.

12-5 Look at Table 12-7 and answer these questions:
   a. Why is the salvage value shown on Line 12 reduced for taxes on Line 13?
   b. Why is depreciation on the old machine deducted on Line 8 to get Line 9?
   c. What would happen if the new machine permitted a *reduction* in net working capital?
   d. Why are the cost savings on Line 6 reduced by multiplying the before-tax figure by $(1 - T)$, whereas the change in depreciation figure on Line 9 is multiplied by T?

12-6 Explain why sunk costs should not be included in a capital budgeting analysis, but opportunity costs and externalities should be included.

12-7 Explain how net working capital is recovered at the end of a project's life, and why it is included in a capital budgeting analysis.

12-8 In general, is an explicit recognition of incremental cash flows more important in new project or replacement analysis? Why?

Self-Test Problems (Solutions Appear in Appendix B)

ST-1
New Project Analysis

You have been asked by the president of the Farr Construction Company to evaluate the proposed acquisition of a new earth mover. The mover's basic price is $50,000, and it would cost another $10,000 to modify it for special use. Assume that the mover falls into the MACRS 3-year class, it would be sold after 3 years for $20,000, and it would require an increase in net working capital (spare parts inventory) of $2,000. The earth mover would have no effect on revenues, but it is expected to save the firm $20,000 per year in before-tax operating costs, mainly labor. The firm's marginal federal-plus-state tax rate is 40 percent.

a. What is the net cost of the earth mover? (That is, what are the Year 0 cash flows?)
b. What are the operating cash flows in Years 1, 2, and 3?
c. What are the additional (nonoperating) cash flows in Year 3?
d. If the project's cost of capital is 10 percent, should the earth mover be purchased?

ST-2
Replacement Project Analysis

The Erickson Toy Corporation currently uses an injection molding machine that was purchased 2 years ago. This machine is being depreciated on a straight line basis toward a $500 salvage value, and it has 6 years of remaining life. Its current book value is $2,600, and it can be sold for $3,000 at this time. Assume, for ease of calculation, that the annual depreciation expense is $350 per year.

The firm is offered a replacement machine which has a cost of $8,000, an estimated useful life of 6 years, and an estimated salvage value of $800. This machine falls into the MACRS 5-year class. The replacement machine would permit an output expansion, so sales would rise by $1,000 per year; even so, the new machine's much greater efficiency would still cause operating expenses to decline by $1,500 per year. The new machine would require that inventories be increased by $2,000, but accounts payable would simultaneously increase by $500.

The firm's marginal federal-plus-state tax rate is 40 percent, and its cost of capital is 15 percent. Should it replace the old machine?

Problems

12-1
Investment Outlay

Johnson Industries is considering an expansion project. The necessary equipment could be purchased for $9 million, and the project would also require an initial $3 million investment in net working capital. The company's tax rate is 40 percent. What is the project's initial investment outlay?

12-2
Operating Cash Flow

Nixon Communications is trying to estimate the first-year operating cash flow (at t = 1) for a proposed project. The financial staff has collected the following information:

Projected sales	$10 million
Operating costs (not including depreciation)	$7 million
Depreciation	$2 million
Interest expense	$2 million

The company faces a 40 percent tax rate. What is the project's operating cash flow for the first year (t = 1)?

12-3
Net Salvage Value

Carter Air Lines is now in the terminal year of a project. The equipment originally cost $20 million, of which 80 percent has been depreciated. Carter can sell the used equipment today to another airline for $5 million, and its tax rate is 40 percent. What is the equipment's after-tax net salvage value?

12-4
Replacement Analysis

The Sampras Company is considering the purchase of a new machine to replace an obsolete one. The machine being used for the operation has both a book value and a market value of zero; it is in good working order, however, and will last physically for at least another 10 years. The proposed replacement machine will perform the operation so much more efficiently that Sampras engineers estimate it will produce after-tax cash flows (labor savings and depreciation) of $9,000 per year. The new machine will cost $40,000 delivered and installed, and its economic life is estimated to be 10 years. It has zero salvage value. The firm's cost of capital is 10 percent, and its marginal tax rate is 35 percent. Should Sampras buy the new machine?

12-5
Replacement Analysis

Tennessee River Shipyards is considering the replacement of an 8-year-old riveting machine with a new one that will increase earnings before depreciation from $27,000 to $54,000 per year. The new machine will cost $82,500, and it will have an estimated life of 8 years and no salvage value. The new machine will be depreciated over its 5-year MACRS recovery period. The applicable corporate tax rate is 40 percent, and the firm's cost of capital is 12 percent. The old machine has been fully depreciated and has no salvage value. Should the old riveting machine be replaced by the new one?

12-6
Unequal Lives

Shao Airlines is considering two alternative planes. Plane A has an expected life of 5 years, will cost $100 million, and will produce net cash flows of $30 million per year. Plane B has a life of

10 years, will cost $132 million, and will produce net cash flows of $25 million per year. Shao plans to serve the route for 10 years. Inflation in operating costs, airplane costs, and fares is expected to be zero, and the company's cost of capital is 12 percent. By how much would the value of the company increase if it accepted the better project (plane)?

12-7
Unequal Lives

The Perez Company has the opportunity to invest in one of two mutually exclusive machines which will produce a product it will need for the foreseeable future. Machine A costs $10 million but realizes after-tax inflows of $4 million per year for 4 years. After 4 years, the machine must be replaced. Machine B costs $15 million and realizes after-tax inflows of $3.5 million per year for 8 years, after which it must be replaced. Assume that machine prices are not expected to rise because inflation will be offset by cheaper components used in the machines. If the cost of capital is 10 percent, which machine should the company use? Use both the replacement chain and equivalent annual annuity approaches.

12-8
New Project Analysis

The Campbell Company is evaluating the proposed acquisition of a new milling machine. The machine's base price is $108,000, and it would cost another $12,500 to modify it for special use by your firm. The machine falls into the MACRS 3-year class, and it would be sold after 3 years for $65,000. The machine would require an increase in net working capital (inventory) of $5,500. The milling machine would have no effect on revenues, but it is expected to save the firm $44,000 per year in before-tax operating costs, mainly labor. Campbell's marginal tax rate is 35 percent.
a. What is the net cost of the machine for capital budgeting purposes? (That is, what is the Year 0 net cash flow?)
b. What are the net operating cash flows in Years 1, 2, and 3?
c. What is the terminal year cash flow?
d. If the project's cost of capital is 12 percent, should the machine be purchased?

12-9
Depreciation Effects

Susan Fischer, great-granddaughter of the founder of Taussig Tile Products and current president of the company, believes in simple, conservative accounting. In keeping with her philosophy, she has decreed that the company shall use alternative straight line depreciation, based on the MACRS class lives, for all newly acquired assets. Your boss, the financial vice-president and the only nonfamily officer, has asked you to develop an exhibit which shows how much this policy costs the company in terms of market value. Ms. Fischer is interested in increasing the value of the firm's stock because she fears a family stockholder revolt which might remove her from office. For your exhibit, assume that the company spends $50 million each year on new capital projects, that the projects have on average a 10-year class life, that the company has a 10 percent cost of capital, and that its tax rate is 34 percent. (Hint: Show how much the NPV of projects in an average year would increase if Taussig used the standard MACRS recovery allowances. Also, ignore the half-year convention on the straight line calculation.)

12-10
New Project Analysis

You have been asked by the president of your company to evaluate the proposed acquisition of a new spectrometer for the firm's R&D department. The equipment's basic price is $70,000, and it would cost another $15,000 to modify it for special use by your firm. The spectrometer, which falls into the MACRS 3-year class, would be sold after 3 years for $30,000. Use of the equipment would require an increase in net working capital (spare parts inventory) of $4,000. The spectrometer would have no effect on revenues, but it is expected to save the firm $25,000 per year in before-tax operating costs, mainly labor. The firm's marginal federal-plus-state tax rate is 40 percent.
a. What is the net cost of the spectrometer? (That is, what is the Year 0 net cash flow?)
b. What are the net operating cash flows in Years 1, 2, and 3?
c. What is the additional (nonoperating) cash flow in Year 3?
d. If the project's cost of capital is 10 percent, should the spectrometer be purchased?

12-11
Replacement Analysis

The Wingler Equipment Company purchased a machine 5 years ago at a cost of $100,000. It had an expected life of 10 years at the time of purchase and an expected salvage value of $10,000 at the end of the 10 years. It is being depreciated by the straight line method toward a salvage value of $10,000, or by $9,000 per year.

A new machine can be purchased for $150,000, including installation costs. Over its 5-year life, it will reduce cash operating expenses by $50,000 per year. Sales are not expected to change. At the end of its useful life, the machine is estimated to be worthless. MACRS depreciation will be used, and it will be depreciated over its 3-year class life rather than its 5-year economic life.

The old machine can be sold today for $65,000. The firm's tax rate is 34 percent. The appropriate discount rate is 15 percent.
a. If the new machine is purchased, what is the amount of the initial cash flow at Year 0?
b. What incremental operating cash flows will occur at the end of Years 1 through 5 as a result of replacing the old machine?

c. What incremental nonoperating cash flow will occur at the end of Year 5 if the new machine is purchased?

d. What is the NPV of this project? Should the firm replace the old machine?

12-12
Unequal Lives

Filkins Fabric Company is considering the replacement of its old, fully depreciated knitting machine. Two new models are available: Machine 190-3, which has a cost of $190,000, a 3-year expected life, and after-tax cash flows (labor savings and depreciation) of $87,000 per year; and Machine 360-6, which has a cost of $360,000, a 6-year life, and after-tax cash flows of $98,300 per year. Knitting machine prices are not expected to rise, because inflation will be offset by cheaper components (microprocessors) used in the machines. Assume that Filkins' cost of capital is 14 percent.

a. Should the firm replace its old knitting machine, and, if so, which new machine should it use?

b. Suppose the firm's basic patents will expire in 9 years, and the company expects to go out of business at that time. Assume further that the firm depreciates its assets using the straight line method, that its marginal federal-plus-state tax rate is 40 percent, and that the used machines can be sold at their book values. Under these circumstances, should the company replace the old machine and, if so, which new model should the company purchase?

12-13
Abandonment Value

The Scampini Supplies Company recently purchased a new delivery truck. The new truck cost $22,500, and it is expected to generate net after-tax operating cash flows, including depreciation, of $6,250 per year. The truck has a 5-year expected life. The expected abandonment values (salvage values after tax adjustments) for the truck are given below. The company's cost of capital is 10 percent.

YEAR	ANNUAL OPERATING CASH FLOW	ABANDONMENT VALUE
0	($22,500)	$22,500
1	6,250	17,500
2	6,250	14,000
3	6,250	11,000
4	6,250	5,000
5	6,250	0

a. Should the firm operate the truck until the end of its 5-year physical life, or, if not, what is its optimal economic life?

b. Would the introduction of abandonment values, in addition to operating cash flows, ever *reduce* the expected NPV and/or IRR of a project?

12-14
Inflation Adjustments

The Rodriguez Company is considering an average-risk investment in a mineral water spring project that has a cost of $150,000. The project will produce 1,000 cases of mineral water per year indefinitely. The current sales price is $138 per case, and the current cost per case (all variable) is $105. The firm is taxed at a rate of 34 percent. Both prices and costs are expected to rise at a rate of 6 percent per year. The firm uses only equity, and it has a cost of capital of 15 percent. Assume that cash flows consist only of after-tax profits, since the spring has an indefinite life and will not be depreciated.

a. Should the firm accept the project? (Hint: The project is a perpetuity, so you must use the formula for a perpetuity to find its NPV.)

b. If total costs consisted of a fixed cost of $10,000 per year and variable costs of $95 per unit, and if only the variable costs were expected to increase with inflation, would this make the project better or worse? Continue with the assumption that the sales price will rise with inflation.

Spreadsheet Problems

Work the problems in this section only if you are using the computer problem diskette.

12-15
New Project Analysis

Use the model in File C12 to solve this problem. McLaughlin Mills is evaluating the proposed acquisition of a new milling machine. The machine's base price is $180,000, and it would cost another $25,000 to modify it for special use by your firm. The machine falls into the MACRS 3-year class, and it would be sold after 3 years for $80,000. The machine would require an increase in net working capital (inventory) of $7,500. The machine would have no effect on revenues, but it is expected to save the firm $75,000 per year in before-tax operating costs, mainly labor. McLaughlin's marginal tax rate is 34 percent.

a. What is the net cost of the machine for capital budgeting purposes? (That is, what is the Year 0 net cash flow?)
b. What are the operating cash flows in Years 1, 2, and 3?
c. What is the additional (nonoperating) cash flow in Year 3?
d. If the project's cost of capital is 10 percent, should the machine be purchased?
e. Determine the NPV if the cost of capital were (1) to rise to 12 percent or (2) to fall to 8 percent.
f. There is some uncertainty about the salvage value. It could be as low as $50,000 or as high as $90,000. What would the NPV be at those two salvage value levels? (Assume k = 10 percent.) Should this uncertainty affect the decision to invest? What salvage value (to the nearest thousand) would make you indifferent to the project?
g. Return to the original salvage value of $80,000. What would be the project's NPV if the corporate tax rate were increased to 46 percent?
h. Return the tax rate to 34 percent. Now assume that the manufacturer of the machine calls you with bad news: The base price of the machine has increased to $200,000. What does this do to the project's NPV? At what cost (to the nearest hundred) would McLaughlin be indifferent to the project?

12-16
Replacement Analysis

Use the second model in File C12 to solve this problem. The Orange Fizz Company is contemplating the replacement of one of its bottling machines with a newer and more efficient one. The old machine has a book value of $500,000 and a remaining useful life of 5 years. The firm does not expect to realize any return from scrapping the old machine in 5 years, but it can sell it now to another firm in the industry for $200,000. The old machine is being depreciated toward a zero salvage value, or by $100,000 per year, using the straight line method.

The new machine has a purchase price of $1.2 million, an estimated useful life and MACRS class life of 5 years, and an estimated salvage value of $175,000. It is expected to economize on electric power usage, labor, and repair costs, and also to reduce the number of defective bottles. In total, an annual savings of $275,000 will be realized if it is installed. The company is in the 40 percent federal-plus-state tax bracket, and it has a 10 percent cost of capital.
a. What is the initial cash outlay required for the new machine?
b. Calculate the annual depreciation allowances for both machines, and compute the change in the annual depreciation expense if the replacement is made.
c. What are the operating cash flows in Years 1 to 5?
d. What is the cash flow from the salvage value in Year 5?
e. Should the firm purchase the new machine? Support your answer.
f. In general, how would each of the following factors affect the investment decision, and how should each be treated?
(1) The expected life of the existing machine decreases.
(2) The cost of capital is not constant but is increasing.
g. The firm may be able to purchase an alternative new bottling machine from another supplier. Its purchase price would be $1,050,000, and its salvage value would be $250,000. This machine has a lower annual operating savings of $210,000. Should the firm purchase this machine?
h. If the salvage value on the alternative new machine were $200,000 rather than $250,000, how would this affect the decision?
i. With everything as in Part h, assume that the cost of capital declined from 10 percent to 8 percent. How would this affect the decision?

12-17
Inflation Adjustments

Use the third model in File C12 to solve this problem. The Dalrymple Company is evaluating an average-risk capital project having both a 3-year economic and MACRS class life. The net investment outlay at Time 0 is $18,800. The expected end-of-year cash flows, expressed in Time 0 dollars, are listed below: (Ignore salvage value and Year 4 depreciation.)

	YEAR 1	YEAR 2	YEAR 3
Revenues	$30,000	$30,000	$30,000
Variable costs	15,000	15,000	15,000
Fixed costs	6,500	6,500	6,500
Depreciation	6,204	8,460	2,820

The firm has a marginal federal-plus-state tax rate of 40 percent. Dalrymple's current cost of debt is 12 percent, and its cost of equity is 16 percent. These costs include an estimated inflation premium of 6 percent. The firm's target capital structure is 50 percent debt and 50 percent equity.
a. What is the firm's nominal WACC? Its real WACC?

b. What are the project's relevant real cash flows? What discount rate should be utilized when calculating a project's NPV based upon real cash flows? Why?

c. What is the NPV for this project? Should this project be accepted? What might have occurred if you had used the *nominal* WACC with *real* cash flows?

d. Now assume that all revenues and costs, except depreciation, are expected to increase at the inflation rate of 6 percent. What are the project's nominal cash flows and NPV based on these flows? Why is this NPV different from the NPV calculated in Part c?

e. Assume that the firm's management anticipates a rate of inflation resulting in a 6 percent inflation premium for Year 1 through Year 3. Based upon this assumption, the firm accepts the project. However, suppose the firm actually experiences nonneutral inflation such that revenues increase by only 6 percent, while variable and fixed costs increase by 7.5 percent. What are the actual after-tax cash flows in this case? What effect would the acceptance of the project, coupled with unanticipated nonneutral inflation, have had upon the value of the firm?

f. If a company, in its capital budgeting process, bases its cash flows on sales prices and unit costs at the time it analyzes the project, (1) would this tend to produce systematic errors in its capital budgeting evaluations, (2) would any such error be more serious for long-term or short-term projects, and (3) if you do think that systematic errors are likely to occur, how could they be corrected?

MINI CASE

John Crockett Furniture Company is considering adding a new line to its product mix, and the capital budgeting analysis is being conducted by Joan Samuels, a recently graduated finance MBA. The production line would be set up in unused space in Crockett's main plant. The machinery's invoice price would be approximately $200,000; another $10,000 in shipping charges would be required; and it would cost an additional $30,000 to install the equipment. Further, the firm's inventories would have to be increased by $25,000 to handle the new line, but its accounts payable would rise by $5,000. The machinery has an economic life of 4 years, and Crockett has obtained a special tax ruling which places the equipment in the MACRS 3-year class. The machinery is expected to have a salvage value of $25,000 after 4 years of use.

The new line would generate $125,000 in incremental net revenues (before taxes and excluding depreciation) in each of the next 4 years. The firm's tax rate is 40 percent, and its overall weighted average cost of capital is 10 percent.

a. Set up, without numbers, a time line for the project's cash flows.

b. (1) Construct incremental operating cash flow statements for the project's 4 years of operations.

   (2) Does your cash flow statement include any financial flows such as interest expense or dividends? Why or why not?

c. (1) Suppose the firm had spent $100,000 last year to rehabilitate the production line site. Should this cost be included in the analysis? Explain.

   (2) Now assume that the plant space could be leased out to another firm at $25,000 a year. Should this be included in the analysis? If so, how?

   (3) Finally, assume that the new product line is expected to decrease sales of the firm's other lines by $50,000 per year. Should this be considered in the analysis? If so, how?

d. Disregard the assumptions in Part c. What is Crockett's net investment outlay on this project? What is the net nonoperating cash flow at the time the project is terminated? Based on these cash flows, what are the project's NPV, IRR, MIRR, and payback? Do these indicators suggest that the project should be undertaken?

e. Assume now that the project is a replacement project rather than a new, or expansion, project. Describe how the analysis would differ for a replacement project.

f. Explain what is meant by cash flow estimation bias. What are some steps that Crockett's management could take to eliminate the incentives for bias in the decision process?

g. Do you think it likely that the project being considered here might have option value over and above the indicated NPV? If so, how might this be handled?

h. Assume that inflation is expected to average 5 percent over the next 4 years. Does it appear that Crockett's cash flow estimates are real or nominal? That is, are all the cash flows stated in the Time 0 dollars or have the cash flows been increased to account for expected inflation? Further, would it appear that the 10 percent cost of capital is a nominal or real interest rate?

Does it appear that the current NPV is biased because of inflation effects? If so, in what direction, and how could any bias be removed?

i. In an unrelated analysis, Joan was asked to choose between the following two mutually exclusive projects:

EXPECTED NET CASH FLOW

YEAR	PROJECT S	PROJECT L
0	($100,000)	($100,000)
1	60,000	33,500
2	60,000	33,500
3	—	33,500
4	—	33,500

The projects provide a necessary service, so whichever one is selected is expected to be repeated into the foreseeable future. Both projects have a 10 percent cost of capital.

(1) What is each project's initial NPV without replication?

(2) Now apply the replacement chain approach to determine the projects' extended NPVs. Which project should be chosen?

(3) Repeat the analysis using the equivalent annual annuity approach.

(4) Now assume that the cost to replicate Project S in 2 years will increase to $105,000 because of inflationary pressures. How should the analysis be handled now, and which project should be chosen?

j. Crockett is also considering another project which has a physical life of 3 years; that is, the machinery will be totally worn out after 3 years. However, if the project were abandoned prior to the end of 3 years, the machinery would have a positive salvage (or abandonment) value. Here are the project's estimated cash flows:

YEAR	INITIAL INVESTMENT AND OPERATING CASH FLOWS	END-OF-YEAR NET ABANDONMENT VALUE
0	($5,000)	$5,000
1	2,100	3,100
2	2,000	2,000
3	1,750	0

Using the 10 percent cost of capital, what is the project's NPV if it is operated for the full 3 years? Would the NPV change if the company planned to abandon the project at the end of Year 2? At the end of Year 1? What is the project's optimal (economic) life?

Selected Additional References and Cases

Several articles have been written regarding the implications of the Accelerated Cost Recovery System (ACRS). Among them are the following:

Angell, Robert J., and Tony R. Wingler, "A Note on Expensing versus Depreciating Under the Accelerated Cost Recovery System," *Financial Management,* Winter 1982, 34–35.

McCarty, Daniel E., and William R. McDaniel, "A Note on Expensing versus Depreciating Under the Accelerated Cost Recovery System: Comment," *Financial Management,* Summer 1983, 37–39.

For further information on replacement analysis, as well as other aspects of capital budgeting, see the texts by Bierman and Smidt; by Grant, Ireson, and Leavenworth; by Levy and Sarnat; and by Seitz and Ellison referenced in Chapter 11.

Three additional papers on the impact of inflation on capital budgeting are the following:

Bailey, Andrew D., and Daniel L. Jensen, "General Price Level Adjustments in the Capital Budgeting Decision," *Financial Management,* Spring 1977, 26–32.

Mehta, Dileep R., Michael D. Curley, and Hung-Gay Fung, "Inflation, Cost of Capital, and Capital Budgeting Procedures," *Financial Management,* Winter 1984, 48–54.

Rappaport, Alfred, and Robert A. Taggart, Jr., "Evaluation of Capital Expenditure Proposals Under Inflation," *Financial Management,* Spring 1982, 5–13.

For additional insights into unequal life analysis, see

Emery, Gary W., "Some Guidelines for Evaluating Capital Investment Alternatives with Unequal Lives," *Financial Management,* Spring 1982, 15–19.

For an interesting discussion on cash flow estimation and abandonment biases, see

Statman, Meir, and David Caldwell, "Applying Behavioral Finance to Capital Budgeting: Project Terminations," *Financial Management,* Winter 1987, 7–13.

Statman, Meir, and Tyzoon T. Tyebjee, "Optimistic Capital Budgeting Forecasts: An Experiment," *Financial Management,* Autumn 1985, 27–33.

The following articles pertain to other topics in this chapter:

Bjerksund, Petter, and Steinar Ekern, "Managing Investment Opportunities Under Price Uncertainty: From 'Last Chance' to 'Wait and See' Strategies," *Financial Management,* Autumn 1990, 65–83.

Chen, Son-Nan, "Optimal Asset Abandonment and Replacement: Tax and Replacement Considerations," *Financial Review,* May 1991, 157–177.

Kroll, Yoram, "On the Differences between Accrual Accounting Figures and Cash Flows: The Case of Working Capital," *Financial Management,* Spring 1985, 75–82.

Kulatilaka, Nalin, and Alan J. Marcus, "Project Valuation under Uncertainty: When Does DCF Fail?" *Journal of Applied Corporate Finance,* Fall 1992, 92–100.

Mukherjee, Tarun K., "Reducing the Uncertainty-Induced Bias in Capital Budgeting Decisions— A Hurdle Rate Approach," *Journal of Business Finance & Accounting,* September 1991, 747–753.

Triantis, Alexander J., and James E. Hodder, "Valuing Flexibility as a Complex Option," *Journal of Finance,* June 1990, 549–565.

The Cases in Financial Management: Dryden Request *series contains the following cases which focus on Chapter 11 and 12 material:*

Case 12, "Indian River Citrus Company (A), Case 12A, "Cranfield, Inc. (A)," and Case 14, "Robert Montoya, Inc. (A)," which focus on cash flow estimation but also include capital budgeting decision methods.

RISK ANALYSIS
AND REAL OPTIONS

S*implesse, a fat substitute developed by NutraSweet Corporation, was supposed to ensure the company's success and usher in an era of guilt-free gluttony for America's calorie counters and cholesterol watchers. It promised all the taste virtues of real fat but with none of the associated vices. To some, it seemed too good to be true.*

Simplesse is a highly processed mixture of whipped egg whites and skim milk intended to simulate not only the taste of fat but also its rich texture, its so-called "mouth-feel." Fat is what makes mayonnaise slippery and potato chips crunchy; it provides the creaminess in Häagen-Dazs ice cream and the gratifying greasiness in a Big Mac. However, consumers recognize the dark side of fat: It tastes great, but it can cause "spare tires" and heart disease.

Unfortunately, Simplesse is temperamental. It curdles when heated too high, which makes it hard to use in cooking. It also requires refrigeration, and its shelf life is short. Still, about $100 million went into the development of Simplesse. To justify the expenditure, NutraSweet's managers estimated that Simplesse would provide $444 million in revenues and $20 million in annual profits. Although most of the profits were expected to come from sales to other food companies for use in various food products, to get the ball rolling NutraSweet decided to develop a Simplesse product itself—Simple Pleasures, an imitation ice cream.

The research team's goal was to have Simple Pleasures rival Häagen-Dazs's vanilla flavor. During in-house testing, senior managers would give samples to junior managers and ask, "Doesn't it taste like Häagen-Dazs?" Needless to say, everyone replied, "Yes, it tastes just like Häagen-Dazs." In reality, it tasted more like chalk, and early versions of Simple Pleasures melted too slowly and left a scummy ring around the bowl. To add to the problems, NutraSweet badly underestimated how much it would cost to make and market the product, and how difficult it would be to move from making small batches in the lab to large-scale production runs.

In the end, Simple Pleasures captured about 8 percent of the nonfat ice cream market. The consensus among consumers seems to be that although Simple Pleasures isn't dreadful, it isn't real ice cream. And while it compares favorably in taste and texture with other nonfat ice creams, it is considerably more expensive.

What do NutraSweet's problems have to do with capital budgeting? It is clear that the cash flows associated with new projects are not known with certainty. Indeed, for most projects there is much uncertainty, which means much risk. In this chapter, we discuss procedures that are used to assess risk and incorporate it into the decision process. As you read the chapter, consider how NutraSweet might have used these procedures in its analysis of the Simplesse/Simple Pleasures project.

Up to now we have assumed that each project will produce a given stream of cash flows, and we then analyzed those cash flows to decide whether to accept or reject the project. Obviously, though, cash flows are not known with certainty, and we don't even know for sure that a project's forecasted "inflows" will be positive. We now turn to risk in capital budgeting, examining the techniques firms use to determine a project's risk and then to decide whether its profit potential is worth the risk. As a part of this analysis, we examine the impact of real options on projects' risks and returns.

INTRODUCTION TO PROJECT RISK ANALYSIS

As we noted in Chapter 10, three separate and distinct types of risk can be identified:

1. **Stand-alone risk,** which is the project's risk disregarding the fact that it is but one asset within the firm's portfolio of assets and that the firm is but one stock in a typical investor's portfolio of stocks. Stand-alone risk is measured by the variability of the project's expected returns.

2. **Corporate, or within-firm, risk,** which is the project's risk to the corporation, giving consideration to the fact that the project represents only one of the firm's portfolio of assets, hence that some of its risk to the firm's profits will be diversified away. Corporate risk is measured by the project's impact on uncertainty about the firm's future earnings.

3. **Market, or beta, risk,** which is the riskiness of the project as seen by a well-diversified stockholder who recognizes that the project is only one of the firm's assets and that the firm's stock is but one small part of the investor's total portfolio. Market risk is measured by the project's effect on the firm's beta.

As we shall see, a particular project may have high stand-alone risk, yet because of portfolio effects, taking it on may not have much effect on either the firm's risk or that of its owners.

Taking on a project with a high degree of either stand-alone or corporate risk will not necessarily affect the firm's beta. However, if the project has highly uncertain returns, and if those returns are highly correlated with returns on the firm's other assets and with most other assets in the economy, the project will have a high degree of all types of risk. Market risk is important because of its effect on a firm's stock price: Beta affects the cost of equity, k_s, which affects the stock price. Corporate risk is also important, for these three reasons:

1. Undiversified stockholders, including the owners of small businesses, are more concerned about corporate risk than about market risk.

2. Empirical studies generally find that both market and corporate risk affect stock prices. This suggests that investors, even those who are well diversified, consider factors other than market risk when they establish required returns.

3. The firm's stability is important to its managers, workers, customers, suppliers, and creditors, as well as to the community in which it operates. Firms that are in serious danger of bankruptcy, or even of suffering low profits and reduced output, have difficulty attracting and retaining good managers and workers. Also, both suppliers and customers are reluctant to depend on weak firms, and such firms have difficulty borrowing money at reasonable interest rates. These factors tend to reduce risky firms' profitability and hence their stock prices, and this makes corporate risk significant.

For these three reasons, corporate risk is important even if a firm's stockholders are well diversified.

What are the three types of project risk?

Why are (1) market and (2) corporate risk both important?

TECHNIQUES FOR MEASURING STAND-ALONE RISK

Why should a project's stand-alone risk be important to anyone? In theory, this type of risk should be of little or no concern. However, it is actually of great importance for two reasons:

1. It is easier to estimate a project's stand-alone risk than either its corporate risk or its market risk.
2. In the vast majority of cases, all three types of risk are highly correlated—if the general economy does well, so will the firm, and if the firm does well, so will most of its projects. Because of this high correlation, stand-alone risk is generally a good proxy for hard-to-measure corporate and market risk.

The starting point for analyzing a project's stand-alone risk involves determining the uncertainty inherent in its cash flows. This analysis can be handled in a number of ways, ranging from informal judgments to complex economic and statistical analyses involving large-scale computer models. To illustrate what is involved, we shall refer to the Regency Integrated Chips (RIC) watering system project that we discussed in Chapter 12. Many of the individual cash flows that were shown in Table 12-4 are subject to uncertainty. For example, sales for each year were projected at 25,000 units to be sold at a net price of $2,200 per unit, or $55 million in total. However, actual unit sales will almost certainly be somewhat higher or lower than 25,000, and the actual sales price will probably differ from the projected $2,200 per unit. *In effect, the sales quantity and the sales price estimates are really expected values based on probability distributions, as are many of the other values that were shown in Table 12-4.* The distributions could be relatively "tight," reflecting small standard deviations and low risk, or they could be "flat," denoting a great deal of uncertainty about the final value of the variable in question, hence a high degree of stand-alone risk.

The nature of the individual cash flow distributions, and their correlations with one another, determine the nature of the NPV probability distribution and, thus, the project's stand-alone risk. In the following sections, we discuss three techniques for assessing stand-alone risk: (1) sensitivity analysis, (2) scenario analysis, and (3) Monte Carlo simulation.

Sensitivity Analysis

Intuitively, we know that many of the variables that determine a project's cash flows are based on a probability distribution rather than being known with certainty. We also know that a change in a key input variable, such as units sold, will cause the NPV to change. **Sensitivity analysis** is a technique which indicates how much NPV will change in response to a given change in an input variable, other things held constant.

Sensitivity analysis begins with a *base-case* situation, which is developed using the *expected* values for each input. To illustrate, consider the data given back in Table

12-4, in which projected cash flow statements for RIC's watering system project were shown. The values used to develop the table, including unit sales, sales price, fixed costs, and variable costs, are the most likely, or base-case, values, and the resulting $12,075,384 NPV shown in Table 12-6 is called the **base-case NPV.** Now we ask a series of "what if" questions: "What if unit sales fall 20 percent below the most likely level?" "What if the sales price per unit falls?" "What if variable costs are 65 percent of dollar sales rather than the expected 60 percent?" Sensitivity analysis is designed to provide the decision maker with answers to questions such as these.

In a sensitivity analysis, each variable is changed by several percentage points above and below the expected value, holding other things constant. Then a new NPV is calculated using each of these values. Finally, the set of NPVs is plotted against the variable that was changed. Figure 13-1 shows the project's sensitivity graphs for three key input variables. The table below the graphs gives the NPVs that were used to construct the graphs. The slopes of the lines in the graphs show how sensitive NPV is to changes in each of the inputs: *The steeper the slope, the more sensitive the NPV is to a change in the variable.* In the figure, we see that the project's NPV is very sensitive to changes in variable costs, fairly sensitive to changes in unit sales, and not very sensitive to changes in the cost of capital.

If we were comparing two projects, the one with the steeper sensitivity lines would be riskier, because for that project a relatively small error in estimating a variable such as unit sales would produce a large error in the project's expected NPV. Thus, sensitivity analysis can provide useful insights into the riskiness of a project.

FIGURE 13-1   Sensitivity Analysis (Thousands of Dollars)

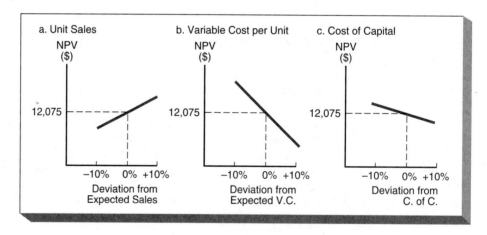

DEVIATION FROM BASE LEVEL (%)	NET PRESENT VALUE		
	UNITS SOLD	VARIABLE COST/UNIT	COST OF CAPITAL
−10	$ 7,944	$20,287	$13,772
0 (base case)	12,075	12,075	12,075
+10	16,207	3,864	10,521

NOTE: This analysis was performed using a spreadsheet, so the values are slightly different than those that would be obtained using interest factor tables because of rounding differences.

Before we move on, two additional points about sensitivity analysis warrant attention. First, spreadsheet computer models such as *Lotus 1-2-3* or *Microsoft Excel* are ideally suited for performing sensitivity analysis. We used a spreadsheet model to conduct the analyses represented in Figure 13-1; it generated the NPVs and then drew the graphs. Second, we could have plotted all of the sensitivity lines on one graph; this would have facilitated direct comparisons of the sensitivities among different input variables.

Scenario Analysis

Although sensitivity analysis is probably the most widely used risk analysis technique, it does have limitations. Consider, for example, a proposed coal mine project whose NPV is highly sensitive to changes in output, in variable costs, and in sales price. However, if a utility company has contracted to buy a fixed amount of coal at an inflation-adjusted price per ton, the mining venture could be quite safe in spite of its steep sensitivity lines. *In general, a project's stand-alone risk depends on (1) the sensitivity of NPV to changes in key variables and (2) the range of likely values of these variables as reflected in their probability distributions.* Because sensitivity analysis considers only the first factor, it is incomplete.

Scenario analysis is a risk analysis technique that considers both the sensitivity of NPV to changes in key variables and the likely range of variable values. In a scenario analysis, the financial analyst asks operating managers to specify the worst "reasonable" set of circumstances (low unit sales, low sales price, high variable cost per unit, high construction cost, and so on) and the best "reasonable" set. The NPVs under the bad and good conditions are then calculated and compared to the expected, or base-case, NPV.

As an example, let us return to the watering system project. RIC's managers are fairly confident of their estimates of all the project's cash flow variables except price and unit sales. Further, they regard a drop in sales below 15,000 units or a rise above 35,000 units as being extremely unlikely. Similarly, they expect the sales price as set in the marketplace to lie within the range of $1,700 to $2,700. Thus, 15,000 units at a price of $1,700 defines the lower bound, or the **worst-case scenario,** whereas 35,000 units at a price of $2,700 defines the upper bound, or the **best-case scenario.** Remember that the **base-case** values are 25,000 units at a price of $2,200.

To carry out the scenario analysis, we use the worst-case variable values to obtain the worst-case NPV and the best-case variable values to obtain the best-case NPV.[1] We actually performed the analysis using a spreadsheet model, and Table 13-1 summarizes the results of this analysis. We see that under the base-case forecast, a positive NPV results; the worst case produces a negative NPV; and the best case results in a very large positive NPV.

We can use the results of the scenario analysis to determine the expected NPV, the standard deviation of NPV, and the coefficient of variation. To begin, we need an estimate of the probabilities of occurrence of the three scenarios, the P_i values. Suppose management estimates that there is a 25 percent probability of the worst-case scenario,

---

[1]We could have included worst- and best-case values for fixed and variable costs, income tax rates, salvage values, and so on. For illustrative purposes, we limited the changes to only two variables. Also, note that we are treating sales price and quantity as independent of one another. That is, a low sales price could occur when unit sales were low, and a high sales price could be coupled with high unit sales, or vice versa. As we discuss in the next section, it is relatively easy to vary these assumptions if the facts of the situation suggest a different set of conditions.

| | TABLE 13-1 | | Scenario Analysis |

SCENARIO	PROBABILITY OF OUTCOME (P_i)	SALES VOLUME (UNITS)	SALES PRICE	NPV (THOUSANDS OF DOLLARS)
Worst case	0.25	15,000	$1,700	($10,079)
Base case	0.50	25,000	2,200	12,075
Best case	0.25	35,000	2,700	41,752
			Expected NPV =	$13,956
			σ_{NPV} =	$18,421
			CV_{NPV} =	1.3

a 50 percent probability of the base case, and a 25 percent probability of the best case. Of course, it is *very difficult* to estimate scenario probabilities precisely, but even ballpark estimates provide useful insights into a project's risk.

The scenario probabilities and NPVs constitute a probability distribution of returns like those we dealt with in Chapter 5, except that the returns are measured in dollars instead of percentages (rates of return). The expected NPV (in thousands of dollars) is $13,956:[2]

$$\text{Expected NPV} = \sum_{i=1}^{n} P_i(\text{NPV}_i)$$

$$= 0.25(-\$10,079) + 0.50(\$12,075) + 0.25(\$41,752)$$

$$= \$13,956.$$

The standard deviation of the NPV is $18,421 (in thousands of dollars):

$$\sigma_{NPV} = \sqrt{\sum_{i=1}^{n} P_i(\text{NPV}_i - \text{Expected NPV})^2}$$

$$= \sqrt{\begin{array}{l} 0.25(-\$10,079 - \$13,956)^2 + 0.50(\$12,075 - \$13,956)^2 \\ + 0.25(\$41,752 - \$13,956)^2 \end{array}}$$

$$= \$18,421.$$

Finally, the project's coefficient of variation is 1.3:

$$CV_{NPV} = \frac{\sigma_{NPV}}{E(\text{NPV})} = \frac{\$18,421}{\$13,956} = 1.3.$$

Now the project's coefficient of variation can be compared with the coefficient of variation of RIC's "average" project to get an idea of the relative riskiness of the watering system project. RIC's existing projects, on average, have a coefficient of variation of about 1.0, so, on the basis of this stand-alone risk measure, RIC's managers would conclude that the watering system project is 30 percent riskier than an "average" project.

---

[2]Note that the expected NPV, $13,956, is *not* the same as the base-case NPV, $12,075 (in thousands). This is because the two uncertain variables, sales volume and sales price, are multiplied together to obtain dollar sales, and this process causes the NPV distribution to be skewed to the right. A big number times another big number produces a very big number, which, in turn, causes the average, or expected value, to increase.

COCA-COLA TAKES ON THE HIGH-RISK, HIGH-RETURN MARKETS OF ASIA

Roughly half the world's population lives in China, India, and Indonesia. Since this region offers tremendous market potential, many U.S. companies are investing heavily in the area. For example, Coca-Cola, facing a relatively flat domestic market (soft-drink sales in the United States have grown by about 4 percent annually over the past decade) has aggressively looked overseas for growth. Over the next five to six years Coke expects to invest $2 billion in the three Asian giants—China, India, and Indonesia. These countries all have young, rapidly growing populations, and many people have yet to try their first Coke. So, while Coke sales in China have grown at a 49 percent annual rate during the past decade, the average Chinese citizen drinks only five Cokes a year. By contrast, per-capita consumption in the United States, at 343 servings a year, is pretty well saturated. Coke expects to capture 40 percent of a rapidly growing soft-drink market in China, and the consulting firm McKinsey & Company thinks Coke sales in China will hit $1 billion by the year 2000.

To be sure, such investments are risky. First, Coke faces political risk in each of the three countries. (See Chapter 4 for a discussion of country risk.) Many Chinese and Indians have a strong aversion to U.S. goods, partly because they fear losing control of their economies to foreigners. China, for example, has indicated that it is considering steps to restrict Coke's expansion. Clearly, Coke is at the mercy of local authorities, and its ability to operate in these markets could always be curtailed by a change in the political leadership or a backlash against American products.

In addition to political risk, the company also faces a host of logistical problems in its Far Eastern operations. Coke likes to distribute its product directly to retailers in order to manage inventory and to control quality, but that's tough, if not impossible, in many underdeveloped markets. In many cases, it must rely on local citizens riding bicycles to deliver its product in the more distant rural areas.

Despite the risks, Coca-Cola thinks the expected returns are worth the risks. At the same time, in a rather interesting way, investing in Coca-Cola has become an indirect way for investors to bet on the rapidly growing Asian markets. Jennifer Salomon, a beverage stock analyst for Salomon Brothers, says Coke tells potential investors, "Why bother investing in all of these different Asian companies when you can have 'one-stop shopping' with us?"

SOURCE: "Coke Pours into Asia: It's Promising Huge Growth in China, India, and Indonesia," *Business Week*, October 28, 1996, 72–77.

Scenario analysis provides useful information about a project's stand-alone risk. However, it is limited in that it only considers a few discrete outcomes (NPVs), even though there are an infinite number of possibilities. We briefly describe a more complete method of assessing a project's stand-alone risk in the next section.

Monte Carlo Simulation

Monte Carlo simulation, so named because this type of analysis grew out of work on the mathematics of casino gambling, ties together sensitivities and input probability distributions.[3] The first step in a Monte Carlo simulation is to create a computer model that develops the project's cash flows and NPV. Next, the analyst must specify the probability distribution of each uncertain input such as sales price and sales quantity. Continuous distributions, which allow analysts to specify uncertainty with only a mean and standard deviation, or distributions defined by a lower limit, most likely value, and upper limit, are usually used for this purpose. Once this has been done, the simulation proceeds as follows:

1. The Monte Carlo software chooses at random a value for each uncertain variable, based on its specified probability distribution. For example, a value for unit sales and a value for sales price would be chosen.

---

[3]The use of simulation analysis in capital budgeting was first reported by David B. Hertz, "Risk Analysis in Capital Investments," *Harvard Business Review,* January–February 1964, 95–106.

2. The value selected for each uncertain variable, along with values for the fixed inputs such as the tax rate and depreciation charges, are then used by the model to determine the net cash flow for each year, and these cash flows are then used to determine the project's NPV for this particular computer run.

3. Steps 1 and 2 are repeated many times, say, 1,000, resulting in 1,000 NPVs, which are then used to form a probability distribution of the NPV, with its own expected value and standard deviation.

Using this procedure, we performed a simulation analysis on RIC's watering system project. As in our scenario analysis, we simplified the illustration by specifying the distributions for only two key variables, unit sales and sales price. For all the other inputs, we merely specified their expected values.

In our simulation analysis, we assumed that sales price can be represented by a continuous normal distribution. Suppose the expected value is $2,200, and the actual sales price is not likely to vary by more than $500 from the expected value, that is, to fall below $1,700 or rise above $2,700. We know that in a normal distribution, the expected value plus or minus three standard deviations will encompass virtually the entire distribution. This implies that $500 represents about three standard deviations of potential sales price changes. Therefore, we assumed that $\sigma_{\text{Sales price}} = \$500/3 = \$166.67 \approx \$167$, so we instructed the computer to assume that the sales price distribution is normal, with an expected value of $2,200 and a standard deviation of $167.

Next, we assumed that the estimated distribution of unit sales has an expected value of 25,000 units, that sales could be as high as 40,000 units, given our production capacity, if demand is strong, but as low as 10,000 units if customers do not like the product. We could have again specified a normal distribution, but in the case of unit sales, we believed that a triangular distribution, with a most likely value of 25,000, a lower limit of 10,000, and an upper limit of 40,000, is most appropriate.

| TABLE 13-2 | Summary of Simulation Results (Thousands of Dollars) |

| | PROBABILITY OF NPV BEING EQUAL TO OR GREATER THAN THE INDICATED NPV | | | | | | | | | |
	0.90	0.857	0.80	0.70	0.60	0.50	0.40	0.30	0.20	0.10
NPV	($2,114)	$0.0	$2,577	$6,153	$8,993	$11,637	$14,740	$17,797	$21,417	$26,424

NPV DISTRIBUTION STATISTICS

Expected NPV	$12,096
Maximum NPV	$46,755
Minimum NPV	($13,888)
NPV range	$60,643
Probability of NPV > 0	85.7%
Probability of NPV < 0	14.3%
Standard deviation	$10,724
Coefficient of variation	$10,724/$12,096 = 0.89
Skewness	0.15[a]

[a]Positive skewness indicates that the NPV distribution is skewed to the right.

We used these data, plus a spreadsheet add-in program, to conduct the simulation. The output is summarized in Table 13-2, and the resulting NPV probability distribution is plotted in Figure 13-2. From the top part of Table 13-2 we see that there is a 90 percent probability that NPV will be no worse than –$2,114,000. Thus, there is a 10 percent probability of NPV being less than –$2,114,000. There is an 85.7 percent probability that the project would have NPV of at least zero, hence a 14.3 percent probability that the project would be unprofitable. Also, note that the simulation output includes the expected value (mean) and the standard deviation of the NPV.[4] Thus, the project's coefficient of variation of NPV can be calculated and stand-alone risk can be appraised in the same way as in scenario analysis.

In spite of its obvious appeal, Monte Carlo simulation has not been as widely used in industry as one might expect. The major problem is specifying each uncertain variable's probability distribution and the correlations among the distributions. Mechanically, it is easy to incorporate any type of correlation among variables into a simulation analysis; simulation software permits us to specify both intervariable and intertemporal correlations. However, it is *not* easy to determine correlations and probability distributions.

---

[4]Note that the standard deviation of NPV in the simulation is much smaller than the standard deviation we obtained in the scenario analysis. In the scenario analysis, we assumed that the low unit sales figure would be coupled with the low sales price for the worst case, and high values of each for the best case. That is, we assumed that these variables were *dependent* on one another, so high unit sales would mean high price, and vice versa. Thus, we ended up with only 3 NPVs, and a 25 percent probability of the worst (or best) case occurring.

In the simulation, we assumed that unit sales and price are *independent* of one another. Thus, in the simulation a high unit sales could be picked, and in the same run the computer could choose a low sales price. When the two variables are independent, the probability of a very low unit sales coupled with a very low sales price is remote. Further, in a simulation there are many possible values for each uncertain variable, while in a scenario analysis there is a discrete number (3 in our example). These two differences led to a lower standard deviation in the simulation analysis.

FIGURE 13-2   NPV Probability Distribution (Thousands of Dollars)

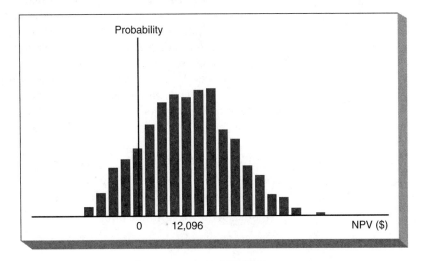

Expected NPV = $12,096.

$\sigma_{NPV} = \$10,724.$

$CV_{NPV} = \$10,724/\$12,096 = 0.89.$

Indeed, people who have tried to obtain such relationships from the operating managers who must estimate them have eloquently emphasized the difficulties involved. Clearly, the problem is not insurmountable, and simulation is being used in business with increasing frequency. Still, it is important not to underestimate the difficulty of obtaining valid estimates of variables' probability distributions, and correlations among the distributions.[5]

Evaluating Stand-Alone Risk

A problem with both scenario and simulation analysis is that even when the analysis has been completed, no clear-cut decision rule emerges. We end up with an expected NPV and a distribution about this expected value which we can use to judge the project's stand-alone risk. However, the analysis provides no criterion to indicate whether a project's profitability as measured by its expected NPV is sufficient to compensate for its risk as measured by σ_{NPV} or CV_{NPV}.

Finally, scenario and simulation analysis both focus on a project's stand-alone risk— they ignore the effects of diversification, both among projects within the firm and by investors in their personal investment portfolios. Thus, an individual project may have highly uncertain returns when evaluated on a "stand-alone" basis, but if those returns are not correlated with the returns on the firm's other assets or with stocks in general, then the project may not be very risky in terms of either corporate or market risk. Indeed, if the project's returns are negatively correlated with the firm's other assets, then it may decrease the firm's corporate risk, and in this case, the larger its σ_{NPV}, the more it will reduce the firm's overall risk. Similarly, if a project's returns are not positively correlated with the stock market, then even a project with highly variable returns might not be risky to well-diversified stockholders.

Despite these difficulties, it is important to measure projects' stand-alone risk. For example, consider a project with a large expected NPV but a 20 percent probability of having such large losses (and a negative NPV) that the company would go bankrupt. Moreover, if the company goes bankrupt, it may lose the going concern value embedded in all its other projects, and incur so many legal expenses that its value may be destroyed. Should such a project be accepted? Under the conditions described, it is doubtful that managers or owner-managers would accept the project. Moreover, managers, not computers, make the final decision on whether to accept or reject projects. Unlike computers, managers bring qualitative judgment into the decision process, and the stand-alone risk profile of a project can provide some extremely valuable insights.

SELF-TEST
QUESTIONS

List two reasons why, in practice, a project's stand-alone risk is important.

Differentiate between sensitivity and scenario analyses. What advantage does scenario analysis have over sensitivity analysis?

What is Monte Carlo simulation?

---

[5]For an interesting discussion of the pros and cons of simulation analysis, see Wilbur G. Lewellen and Michael S. Long, "Simulation versus Single-Value Estimates in Capital Expenditure Analysis," *Decision Sciences,* October 1972, 19–33. For more insight into the difficulties involved in estimating probability distributions and correlations in practice, see K. Larry Hastie, "One Businessman's View of Capital Budgeting," *Financial Management,* Winter 1974, 36–43. Hastie was treasurer of Bendix Corporation and later president of the Financial Management Association.

SHOULD FIRMS DIVERSIFY TO REDUCE CORPORATE RISK?

A project's *corporate risk* is the project's contribution to the firm's overall corporate risk, or, put another way, project corporate risk reflects the impact of the project on uncertainty about the firm's total cash flows. Corporate risk is a function of (1) the project's standard deviation and (2) its correlation with returns on the firm's other assets. As we learned in Chapter 5, a security may be risky if held in isolation but not very risky if held as part of a well-diversified portfolio. The same is true of capital budgeting; returns on an individual project may be highly uncertain, but if the project is small relative to the total firm, and if its returns are not highly correlated with the firm's other assets, the project may not be very risky in either the corporate or the beta sense.

Many firms make a serious effort to diversify; often this is a specific objective of the long-run strategic plan. For example, KeyCorp, a bank holding company with banks in New England, has weathered that region's economic storms because it also owns banks in the Pacific Northwest that have been profitable. Similarly, NCNB, a North Carolina–based banking concern that acquired Atlanta-based C&S/Sovran and Florida's Barnett Bank to become NationsBank, the third largest U.S. bank, stated: "We like having textiles and tobacco in North Carolina, citrus growing and tourism in Florida, cattle ranching and oil in Texas." One objective of moves such as those of KeyCorp and Nations-Bank is to stabilize earnings, reduce corporate risk, and raise the value of the firm's stock.

The wisdom of corporate diversification to reduce risk has been questioned — why should a firm diversify when stockholders can easily diversify themselves? In other words, although it may be true that if the returns on NCNB's, Barnett's, and C&S/Sovran's stocks are not perfectly positively correlated, hence merging the companies will reduce their risks somewhat, would it not be just as easy for investors to diversify directly, without the trouble and expense of a merger?

The answer is not simple. Although stockholders could directly obtain some of the risk-reducing benefits through personal diversification, other benefits can be gained only by diversification at the corporate level. For example, a more stable bank might be able to attract a better work force and also obtain funds cheaper than could two less stable banks. More important, there are often spillover effects from mergers. For example, NCNB became an expert at cleaning up bad real estate loans after it acquired banks in Texas, and that expertise helped it clean up bad loans at C&S/Sovran. Further, combining the administrative offices of the three banks resulted in economies of scale, lower costs, and, thus, higher profits.

S E L F - T E S T
Q U E S T I O N S

Define corporate risk.

Can a project's corporate risk be different from its stand-alone risk?

Does a merger that lowers a company's corporate risk by stabilizing earnings necessarily benefit stockholders?

Are there any good reasons why a firm might want to diversify through mergers even though its stockholders could diversify on their own?

MARKET RISK AND DIVISIONAL BETAS

The types of risk analysis discussed thus far provide insights into a project's risk and thus help managers make better accept/reject decisions. However, we have not yet taken account of portfolio risk. In this section, we show how the CAPM can be used to

HIGH-TECH CFOs

Recent improvements in technology have made it easier for corporations to utilize complex risk analysis techniques. New software and higher-powered computers enable financial managers to process large amounts of information, so technically astute finance people can consider a broad range of scenarios using computers to estimate the effects of changes in sales, operating costs, interest rates, the overall economy, and even the weather. Given such analysis, financial managers can make better decisions as to which course of action is most likely to generate the optimal trade-off between risk and return.

Done properly, risk analysis can also account for the correlation between various types of risk. For example, if interest rates and currencies tend to move together in a particular way, this tendency can be incorporated into the model. This can enable financial managers to better determine the likelihood and effect of "worst-case" outcomes.

While this type of risk analysis is undeniably useful, it is only as good as the information and assumptions that go into constructing the various models. Also, risk models frequently involve complex calculations, and they generate output which requires financial managers to have a fair amount of mathematical sophistication. However, technology is helping to solve these problems. New programs have been developed recently to present risk analysis output in an intuitive way. For example, Andrew Lo, an MIT finance professor, has developed a program which conveniently summarizes the risk, return, and liquidity profiles of various strategies using a new data visualization process that enables complicated relationships to be plotted along three-dimensional graphs that are easy to interpret. While some old-guard CFOs may bristle at these new approaches, younger and more computer-savvy CFOs are likely to embrace this technology. As Lo puts it: "The video-game generation just loves these 3-D tools."

SOURCE: Adapted from "The CFO Goes 3-D: Higher Math and Savvy Software Are Crucial," *Business Week*, October 28, 1996, 144, 150.

help overcome this shortcoming. Of course, the CAPM has shortcomings of its own, but it nevertheless offers useful insights into risk analysis in capital budgeting.

Recall from Chapter 5 that the Security Market Line equation expresses the risk/return relationship as follows:

$$k_s = k_{RF} + (k_M - k_{RF})b_i.$$

If b_i is the beta for an entire company, then k_s is the rate of return that stockholders require on their investment in the company. However, if b_i is the beta for a division, then k_s is the rate of return that stockholders require on their investment in the division. In fact, in theory each project has its own beta, which defines the rate of return that shareholders require on their investment in that particular project.

In Chapter 5 we discussed the estimation of betas for stocks, and we indicated the difficulties in estimating beta. The estimation of project betas is even more difficult, and more fraught with uncertainty. However, as we noted in Chapter 10, two approaches are used to estimate individual assets' betas — the pure play method and the accounting beta method. Because it is more frequently used, we will focus our discussion here on the pure play method.

This approach assumes initially that all projects within a single division have the same type of risk, and, therefore, the same beta. This is called the **divisional beta,** and it is the beta a company would have if the company consisted of only this single division. Just as the beta of a portfolio is the weighted average of the betas of the individual stocks within the portfolio, the beta of a company is the weighted average of its divisional betas.

If each division has a different beta, then each division will have a different **divisional cost of equity** and **divisional WACC.** The company's overall cost of equity is a weighted average of its divisional costs of equity, and its overall WACC is a weighted average of its divisional WACCs.

Before we discuss techniques for estimating divisional betas, it is important to understand how capital structures affect the betas of firms and divisions. The following section discusses the most commonly used procedure for adjusting betas to account for different capital structures.

Equity Betas, Asset Betas, and Capital Structure

If a firm were financed only with common equity, and if it had only one asset, then the beta of the firm and that of the asset (or project) would be identical. In this sense, we can think of an **asset beta** as being equal to the beta of an unleveraged, single-asset minifirm.

The beta of a firm with an all-equity capital structure (which means that the firm has zero financial leverage) is defined as an "unlevered beta." If the firm then begins to use debt, the riskiness inherent in its equity, and also its "levered beta," will begin to rise. In Chapter 16, we discuss in detail Robert Hamada's formula for the relationship between levered and unlevered betas:

$$\text{Hamada's formula: } b_L = b_U[1 + (1 - T)(D/S)]. \tag{13-1}$$

Here b_L is the beta given that the firm uses debt, b_U is the beta it would have if it used no debt, T is its tax rate, D is its dollars of debt, and S is the market value of its stock. If we were dealing with an unlevered, single-project firm, then its beta, b_U, would also be the beta of the firm's single asset. Thus, b_U can be thought of as an unlevered asset's beta.

The **equity beta** of a single-asset firm is a function of both the asset's business risk as measured by b_U and how the asset is financed, and it can be approximated by the Hamada equation. The beta on RIC's stock before it takes on the watering system project (its levered beta) is 1.8. This value was determined by regressing historical returns on the stock against those on the market. RIC's capital structure was already reflected in its 1.8 market-determined stock beta. However, what is the average underlying beta of RIC's existing assets, that is, the beta its stock would have if RIC used no debt? To find this average asset beta, we must remove the financing effect; this can be approximated by solving Equation 13-1, the Hamada formula, for b_U:

$$b_U = \frac{b_L}{1 + (1 - T)(D/S)}. \tag{13-1a}$$

For RIC, with a tax rate of 40 percent and a debt/equity ratio of 0.50/0.50, we obtain an asset beta of 1.125:

$$b_U = \frac{1.8}{1 + (0.60)(0.50/0.50)} = \frac{1.8}{1.6} = 1.125.$$

Thus, the beta of RIC's existing assets if the company used no debt is 1.125. Financial leverage has pushed the stock's beta up from 1.125 to 1.8.

Equations 13-1 and 13-1a enable us to convert asset betas to leveraged stock betas, and vice versa. However, in our discussion in Chapter 16, we will note that Equations 13-1 and 13-1a were derived under some very restrictive assumptions, so results based on those equations must be viewed as rough approximations. Nevertheless, we will use these equations in the next section, when we discuss the "pure play" method for estimating project betas.

The Pure Play Method

In the **pure play method,** the company tries to find one or more nonintegrated, single-product companies in the same line of business as the project being evaluated.[6] For example, suppose RIC could find several publicly traded firms that produced only watering systems. Further, suppose RIC believes that its new project would be subject

---

[6]One important article on this subject is Russell J. Fuller and Halbert S. Kerr, "Estimating the Divisional Cost of Capital: An Analysis of the Pure-Play Technique," *Journal of Finance,* December 1981, 997–1009. Fuller and Kerr used the method to estimate divisional betas and then tested the results empirically. They concluded that the pure play method is a valid technique for estimating the betas of major subparts of a firm.

to the same risks as those other firms. It could then determine the betas of these firms by the regular regression process, average them, and use this average as a proxy for the project's beta.

To illustrate, assume that RIC's analysts have identified three publicly owned companies engaged only in the production and distribution of watering control systems. Further, assume that the average stock beta of these firms is 2.23; that their average debt-to-equity ratio, D/S, is 0.4/0.6 = 0.67; and that their average federal-plus-state tax rate is 36 percent. We cannot conclude that the project's appropriate leverage-adjusted beta is 2.23, because RIC has a capital structure and tax rate different from those of the proxy firms.

To adjust for differences in financial leverage and tax rates, we can employ Equations 13-1 and 13-1a, using the following four steps:

Step 1. Note that the proxy firms' average stock beta of 2.23 reflects their average D/S ratio of 0.67 and their average tax rate of 36 percent.

Step 2. We can insert these values into Equation 13-1a to determine the three proxy firms' underlying asset beta:

$$b_U = \frac{2.23}{1 + (0.64)(0.67)} = 1.56.$$

Step 3. Now we can use Equation 13-1 to find what the proxy firms' stock betas would be if they had the same capital structure and tax rate as RIC:

$$b_L = 1.56[1 + (0.60)(0.50/0.50)]$$
$$= 2.50.$$

Step 4. Determine the project's cost of equity and its weighted average cost of capital, using 2.5 as the estimate for its beta:

$$k_{si} = 8\% + (13\% - 8\%)2.50 = 20.5\%.$$
$$\text{Project } k_i = 0.5(10\%)(0.60) + 0.5(20.5\%) = 13.25\%.$$

Note that the project's cost of capital, 13.25 percent, is greater than RIC's WACC of 11.5 percent. RIC's managers should either recalculate the project's NPV using a 13.25 percent cost of capital or justify their use of the lower 11.5 percent. In this case, RIC's managers concluded that the new watering system project would allow it to be one of the first-movers in a new and potentially large market. If the concept catches on with consumers, then RIC's early name recognition would provide them the opportunity to capitalize on the new market. Therefore, RIC's managers made a qualitative judgment to use the lower 11.5 percent cost of capital. We will have more to say in later sections about qualitative risk adjustments and options to expand.

The pure play approach is often difficult to implement because it is difficult to find pure play proxy firms. For our illustration, we assumed the existence of three pure play proxies. In reality, there is no pure play manufacturer of watering control systems. In fact, most systems are made by GE, Honeywell, and other large, multidivisional firms, and their watering system operations are combined with their other operations in a manner that makes it impossible to ascertain market betas for watering system projects. However, there are times when the method is feasible. For example, when the founders of Gateway Computer were considering going into the personal computer business, they were able to get data on Apple, Compaq, Dell, and several other essentially pure play personal computer companies. Similarly, Pillsbury was able to employ this technique when it considered capital budgeting decisions in its Godfather's Pizza, Steak and Ale, and Bennigan's divisions.[7]

What is the difference between corporate risk and market risk?

What is meant by the term "unleveraged asset beta," and how does its value differ from a project beta? From the firm's stock beta?

Briefly describe the pure play method for estimating a project's market risk.

OUR VIEW OF PROJECT RISK ANALYSIS

We have discussed the three types of risk normally considered in capital budgeting analysis—stand-alone risk, within-firm (or corporate) risk, and market risk—and we have discussed ways of assessing each. However, two important questions remain: (1) Should firms be concerned with stand-alone and corporate risk in their capital budgeting decisions, and (2) what do we do when the stand-alone, within-firm, and market risk assessments lead to different conclusions?

These questions do not have easy answers. From a theoretical standpoint, well-diversified investors should be concerned only with market risk, managers should be concerned only with stock price maximization, and these two factors should lead to the conclusion that market (beta) risk ought to be given virtually all the weight in capital budgeting decisions. However, if investors are not well diversified, if the CAPM does not operate exactly as theory says it should, or if measurement problems keep managers from having confidence in the CAPM approach in capital budgeting, it may be appropriate to give stand-alone and corporate risk more weight than financial theorists suggest. Note also that the CAPM ignores bankruptcy costs, even though such costs can be substantial, and the probability of bankruptcy depends on a firm's corporate risk, not on its beta risk. Therefore, one can easily conclude that even well-diversified investors should want a firm's management to give at least some consideration to a project's stand-alone risk and corporate risk instead of concentrating entirely on market risk.

Two methods are used to incorporate project risk into capital budgeting. One is called the **certainty equivalent** approach. Here all cash flows that are not known with certainty are scaled down, and the riskier the flows, the lower their certainty equivalent values. The Extension to this chapter provides a more detailed discussion of the certainty equivalent approach. The other method, and the one we focus on, is the **risk-adjusted discount rate** approach, under which differential project risk is dealt with by changing the discount rate. Average-risk projects are discounted at the firm's average cost of capital, higher-risk projects are discounted at a higher cost of capital, and lower-risk projects are discounted at a rate below the firm's average cost of capital. Unfortunately, unless one is willing to rely completely on the CAPM, there is no good way of specifying exactly *how much* higher or lower these discount rates should be; given the present state of the art, risk adjustments are necessarily judgmental and somewhat arbitrary.

In many cases, it is impossible to accurately assess a project's market risk, or even its corporate risk. Therefore, managers are often left with only an estimate of the project's

---

[7]For a technique that can be used when pure play companies are not available, see Yatin Bhagwat and Michael Ehrhardt, "A Full Information Approach for Estimating Divisional Betas," *Financial Management,* Summer 1991, 60–69.

Also, one can use the accounting beta method to estimate divisional betas. This topic was discussed in Chapter 10.

stand-alone risk. However, in most situations the project being evaluated is in the same line of business as the firm's other projects, and most firms' profitability is highly correlated with the national economy. Therefore, stand-alone, corporate, and market risk are usually highly correlated. In this case, a project with high stand-alone risk will typically have high corporate and market risk. This suggests that managers can get a feel for the relative risk of most projects on the basis of sensitivity, scenario, simulation, and/or decision tree analyses, even though these procedures measure only stand-alone risk.

Capital structure must also be taken into account if a firm finances different assets in different ways. For example, one division might have a lot of real estate which is well suited as collateral for loans, whereas some other division might have most of its capital tied up in research and development, which is not good collateral. As a result, the division with the real estate might have a higher **debt capacity** than the division with the R&D, hence an optimal capital structure which contains a higher percentage of debt. In this case, the financial staff might calculate the cost of capital differently for the two divisions.[8]

The corporate cost of capital provides the starting point for estimating a project's risk-adjusted discount rate. If all projects had equal risk and debt capacity, then all projects would be evaluated at the corporate cost of capital. However, larger firms typically have several divisions that vary in risk, and projects within divisions can also have risk differences. The first step in developing a project's cost of capital calls for adjusting the corporate cost of capital to reflect divisional risk and debt capacity. A division with above-average risk or below-average debt capacity would have a divisional cost of capital above the firm's corporate cost of capital. A division with below-average risk or above-average debt capacity would have a lower-than-average corporate cost of capital. (Of course, the average of the divisional costs of capital must equal the corporate cost of capital.) Most firms base these divisional costs of capital on divisional betas, using Hamada's formula in Equation 13-1 to account for any differences in divisional debt capacity.

Each project is then assigned to a risk category on the basis of its own risk relative to its division's average risk. If it is riskier than average for the division, then its risk-adjusted discount rate is set above the divisional cost of capital, and the opposite holds true if the project has below-average risk. Also, adjustments should be made when projects have debt capacities which differ widely from the divisional average. The most difficult part of this process is judging how large the divisional and project adjustments should be. If data are available, then the project's beta and the CAPM can be used to estimate the size of the adjustment. However, in most situations that adjustment is judgmental, and often a range of two to five percentage points is used.

This subjective risk-adjustment process is illustrated in Figure 13-3, which shows a firm with three divisions in separate lines of business. The overall (aggregate) risk and debt capacity of the company is such that the corporate WACC is 10 percent. Division HR is riskier than the corporation as a whole, it has a higher beta and lower debt capacity, so it has a divisional cost of capital of 13 percent. Division AR has average risk, so it is assigned a 10 percent divisional cost of capital. Division LR's relatively low risk gives it a cost of capital of 8 percent. Within each division, individual project riskiness is assessed *relative to an average project within the division,* and high-risk projects are assigned a project cost of capital three percentage points above the divisional cost of capital, while low-risk projects have a project cost of capital two percentage points below the divisional cost of capital. Thus, high-risk projects in Division HR would have a 16 percent project cost of capital, while that division's low-risk projects would have an 11 percent project

---

[8]We will say more about the optimal capital structure and debt capacity in Chapters 15 and 16.

FIGURE 13-3   The Risk-Adjustment Process for a Firm with Three Divisions

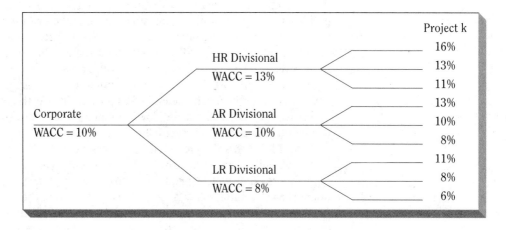

cost of capital. Overall, project costs of capital range from a low of 6 percent for a low-risk project in Division LR to 16 percent for a high-risk project in Division HR.

The end result of the process is a project cost of capital and an NPV which incorporates, to the extent possible, the project's debt capacity and relative riskiness. Managers may also have to consider other risk factors. For example, if the project could lead to litigation against the firm, then it has additional riskiness that should be taken into account—a number of drug, chemical, and asbestos companies have learned this, to their regret. Conversely, if the project can easily be abandoned, or if the assets can easily be converted to other uses within the firm, then it might be less risky than appears in a standard analysis. Such additional factors must be considered subjectively in making the final accept/reject decision. Typically, if the project involves new products and is large relative to the firm's average project, then these additional risk factors will be very important to the final decision—one large mistake can bankrupt a firm, and such "bet the company" decisions are not made lightly. On the other hand, if the project is a small replacement project, then the decision would probably be made on the basis of a straight numerical analysis.

Ultimately, capital budgeting decisions require a mix of objective and subjective analyses. Risk analysis is not very precise, so there is a temptation to ignore risk considerations because they are so nebulous. However, despite the imprecision and subjectiveness, risk should be assessed and incorporated into the capital budgeting process. Anything less would be tantamount to ignoring one of the basic principles of finance—projects with higher risk require higher returns.

SELF-TEST
QUESTIONS

In theory, should a firm be concerned with both stand-alone and corporate risk? In practice?

If a project's stand-alone, corporate, and market risk are highly correlated, would this make the task of measuring risk easier or harder? Explain.

Describe the process by which a project's risk and debt capacity are considered in capital budgeting decisions.

Describe some qualitative risk factors that managers should consider in the capital budgeting decision process that may not be included in a quantitative risk analysis.

RISKY CASH OUTFLOWS

Projects often have negative cash flows during their lives, and when this occurs, special problems may arise. To illustrate, suppose Duke Power Company has concluded that it needs a new generating plant, and it is choosing between a nuclear plant and a coal-fired plant. Both plants will produce the same amount of electricity, hence have the same revenues. However, the coal plant will have a smaller investment requirement but higher operating costs, hence smaller annual cash flows. Also, the nuclear plant will have to be closed down at the end of its 30-year life. At the present time, the company knows that the costs of tearing down the plant and removing the radioactive material will be high, but the exact cost is highly uncertain.

Table 13-3 shows the projected cash flows from the two plants. The coal plant has a cost of $2 billion, and it is expected to produce net cash flows of $250 million per year for 30 years. The nuclear plant has a cost of $4 billion, it is expected to produce cash flows of $474 million per year for 30 years, and then the company expects to have to spend $2 billion to decommission the radioactive plant. All of the cash flows except the decommissioning costs have the same risk as Duke Power's other cash flows, hence they are to be discounted at the company's WACC, 10 percent. However, the decommissioning costs are much more uncertain, hence should be discounted at a rate which reflects their higher risks.

At the bottom of Table 13-3 we show the projects' NPVs. That of the coal plant, discounting at the 10 percent WACC, is $357 million. At the 10 percent WACC, the nuclear plant has a slightly higher NPV, $364 million, but this value does not reflect nuclear's greater risk which results from uncertainty about decommissioning costs. Our first inclination is to discount the operating cash flows at WACC = 10% because those cash flows are assumed to be of average risk, but to discount the decommissioning costs at a higher rate to reflect their greater risk. Using a discount rate of 15 percent for the

---

TABLE 13-3   Expected Cash Flows, Coal versus Nuclear Power Plants (Millions of Dollars)

		CASH FLOWS FROM:	
	YEAR	COAL PLANT	NUCLEAR PLANT
	0	($2,000)	($4,000)
	1	250	474
	2	250	474
	.	.	.
	.	.	.
	.	.	.
	28	250	474
	29	250	474
	30	250	474
	31	0	(2,000)
NPV @ 10%		$ 357	$ 364
NPV nuclear plant @ 10% for operating CF but 15% for risky shutdown costs:			$ 442
NPV nuclear plant @ 10% for operating CF but 8% for risky shutdown costs:			$ 284

decommissioning costs, we get an NPV of $442. But note—something is amiss. We applied a higher risk-adjusted discount rate and this *improved* the relative position of the nuclear plant! Something is wrong!

What we conclude is that, whereas it is appropriate to increase the discount rate applied to risky cash *inflows* to adjust for their risk, *we must use a lower discount rate to reflect higher risks for cash outflows.* Therefore, we must discount the decommissioning cost at some lower rate to properly reflect its greater risk. When we discount this cost at an 8 percent rate, the nuclear plant's NPV is lowered, as it should be. When the discount rate problem is properly resolved, we see that the coal plant is the better choice. Quite a few U.S. utilities did not understand this situation, and that contributed to several bankruptcies, changes in management, and stockholder losses.

Many projects have especially risky cash outflows some time during their lives, and when this occurs it is important to remember the lessons of this section and discount these risky outflows at a relatively low rate. It is easy, in a complex set of cash flows, to forget about this and therefore produce a flawed NPV. This situation also comes up in other types of DCF analyses. For example, in certain leasing problems the salvage value at the end of a lease is more uncertain than the payment stream during the life of the lease. At times, the salvage value must be treated as an outflow—for example, if the lessee plans to continue using the asset, hence must buy it from the lessor. Here too the adjustment for the risky outflow is critical.[9]

S E L F - T E S T Q U E S T I O N	Describe some "real-world" situations in which risk adjustments must be applied to cash outflows. How are risky outflows handled?

INTRODUCTION TO REAL OPTIONS

According to traditional capital budgeting theory, a project's NPV is the present value of its expected future cash flows, discounted at a rate that reflects the riskiness of the expected future cash flows. If the NPV is positive, then the project should be accepted. Note, however, that traditional capital budgeting theory says nothing about actions that can be taken after the project has been accepted and placed in operation that might cause the cash flows to change. In other words, traditional capital budgeting theory assumes that a project is like a roulette wheel. A gambler can choose whether or not to spin the wheel, but once the wheel has been spun, there is nothing he or she can do to influence the outcome. Once the game begins, the outcome depends purely on chance, with no skill involved.

Contrast the roulette wheel with other games, such as draw poker. Chance plays a role in poker, and it continues to play a role after the initial deal because players receive additional cards throughout the game. Most important though, poker players are able to respond to their opponents' actions, so skillful players usually win.

Capital budgeting decisions have more in common with poker than roulette because (1) chance plays a continuing role throughout the life of the project and (2) managers

---

[9]The approach taken in this section, and our conclusions, have been criticized by some academicians. See Robert Ariel, "Risk Adjusted Discount Rates and the Present Value of Risky Costs," *The Financial Review*, Vol. 33, 1998, 17–30, for a review of the literature. Ariel argues that the same discount rate should be used for all cash flows, positive and negative, in projects such as the one in our example. Ariel and others base their argument on a CAPM analysis which accepts the CAPM as being completely valid, that risk premiums should be based strictly on betas, that project betas can be measured as accurately as security betas, and, implicitly, that corporate and stand-alone risk are irrelevant. If a firm faces many small projects with risky outflows, then Ariel's argument might well be valid, but we would question it in situations such as our power plant example.

can respond to changing market conditions and to competitors' actions. Opportunities to respond to changing circumstances are called **managerial options** because they give managers the option to influence the outcome of a project. They are also called **strategic options** because they are often associated with large, strategic projects rather than routine maintenance projects. Finally, they are also called **real options** and are differentiated from financial options because they involve real, rather than financial, assets.

Three key issues are associated with real options: (1) identifying the optimal response to changing conditions, (2) determining the value of a real option, and (3) structuring projects so as to create real options. The following sections discuss these issues in detail.

S E L F - T E S T Q U E S T I O N S	Explain the similarities and differences between capital budgeting projects and such games of chance as roulette and poker. What are real options, and how do they differ from financial options?

IDENTIFYING OPTIMAL RESPONSES TO CHANGING CONDITIONS: DECISION TREES

Up to this point we have focused primarily on techniques for estimating a project's stand-alone risk. Although this is an integral part of capital budgeting, managers are generally more interested in *reducing* risk than in *measuring* it. For example, sometimes projects can be structured so that expenditures do not have to be made all at one time, but, rather, can be made in stages over a period of years. This reduces risk by giving managers the opportunity to reevaluate decisions using new information and then either investing additional funds or canceling (abandoning) the project. Such projects can be evaluated using *decision trees*.

The Basic Decision Tree

For example, suppose United Robotics is considering the production of an industrial robot for the television manufacturing industry. The net investment for this project can be broken down into three stages, as set forth in Figure 13-4:

FIGURE 13-4	United Robotics: Decision Tree Analysis (Thousands of Dollars)

TIME							JOINT PROBABILITY	NPV	PRODUCT: PROB. × NPV
t = 0	t = 1	t = 2	t = 3	t = 4	t = 5	t = 6			
			$10,000	$10,000	$10,000	$10,000	0.144	$15,250	$2,196
		($10,000)	$4,000	$4,000	$4,000	$4,000	0.192	436	84
	($1,000)		($2,000)	($2,000)	($2,000)	($2,000)	0.144	(14,379)	(2,071)
($500)		Stop					0.320	(1,397)	(447)
	Stop						0.200	(500)	(100)
							1.000	Expected NPV =	($338)
								σ = $7,991	

Stage 1. At t = 0, which in this case is sometime in the near future, conduct a $500,000 study of the market potential for robots in television assembly lines.

Stage 2. If it appears that a sizable market does exist, then at t = 1 spend $1,000,000 to design and build a prototype robot. This robot would then be evaluated by television engineers, and their reactions would determine whether the firm should proceed with the project.

Stage 3. If reaction to the prototype robot is good, then at t = 2 build a production plant at a net cost of $10,000,000. If this stage were reached, the project would generate either high, medium, or low net cash flows over the following four years.

A **decision tree** such as the one in Figure 13-4 can be used to analyze such multi-stage, or sequential, decisions. Here we assume that one year goes by between decisions. Each circle represents a decision point, and it is called a **decision node.** The dollar value to the left of each decision node represents the net investment required at that decision point, and the cash flows shown under t = 3 to t = 6 represent the cash inflows if the project is pushed on to completion. Each diagonal line represents a **branch** of the decision tree, and each branch has an estimated probability. For example, if the firm decides to "go" with the project at Decision Point 1, it will spend $500,000 on a marketing study. Management estimates that there is a 0.8 probability that the study will produce favorable results, leading to the decision to move on to Stage 2, and a 0.2 probability that the marketing study will produce negative results, indicating that the project should be canceled after Stage 1. If the project is canceled, the cost to the company will be the $500,000 for the initial marketing study, and it will be a loss.

If the marketing study yields positive results, then United Robotics will spend $1,000,000 on the prototype robot at Decision Point 2. Management estimates (before even making the initial $500,000 investment) that there is a 60 percent probability that the television engineers will find the robot useful and a 40 percent probability that they will not like it.

If the engineers like the robot, the firm will spend the final $10,000,000 to build the plant and go into production. If the engineers do not like the prototype, the project will be dropped. If the firm does go into production, the operating cash flows over the project's four-year life will depend on how well the market accepts the final product. There is a 30 percent chance that acceptance will be quite good and net cash flows will be $10,000,000 per year, a 40 percent probability of $4,000,000 each year, and a 30 percent chance of losing $2,000,000 per year. These cash flows are shown under Years 3 through 6. Also, for now we assume that United Robotics would be contractually bound to continue production for four years, even if losses occur.

In summary, the decision tree in Figure 13-4 defines the decision nodes and the branches that leave the nodes. There are two types of nodes, decision nodes and outcome nodes. Decision nodes are the points at which management can respond to new information. The first decision node is at t = 1, after the company has completed the marketing study (Decision Point 1 in Figure 13-4). The second decision node is at t = 2, after the company has completed the prototype study (Decision Point 2 in Figure 13-4). The outcome nodes show the possible results if a particular decision is taken. In Figure 13-4, there is one relevant outcome node, the one occurring at t = 3, and its branches show the possible cash flows if the company goes ahead with the industrial robot project. Note that the decision tree also shows the probabilities of moving into each branch that leaves a node.

FIGURE 13-5 Continuous Probability Distribution of Returns for Industrial Television Robot Project

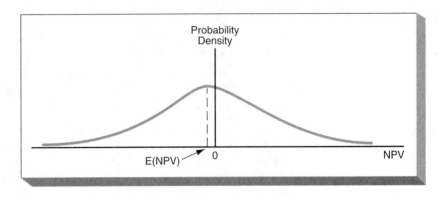

Extending the Decision Tree Concept

In Figure 13-4 we assumed that all uncertainty would be resolved by period t = 3. At that point, cash flows would be $10,000, $4,000, or −$2,000 per year for the remaining years of the project's life. It would, of course, be possible—and more realistic—to assume that cash flows after each year would themselves be subject to some uncertainty. This would lead to three (or more) additional branches from each node at t = 3. With three possibilities, there would be nine possible cash flows at t = 4. Then there could be another three branches from each of these nine cash flows, so there would be 27 possible cash flows at t = 5, and 27 × 3 = 81 at the end point, t = 6. Each of these end points would have a conditional probability, with the sum of the probabilities being 1.0. Each would also have a stream of cash flows, and we could calculate an NPV for each end point. Then, we could find the expected NPV and its standard deviation. If we specified more and more possible cash flows at each node, our final distribution would approach a continuous distribution, with an expected NPV and a standard deviation for that NPV. This continuous distribution might look like Figure 13-5.

If we attempted to construct and use the decision tree leading to Figure 13-5, we would encounter two significant problems:

- We would have to answer the question of whether the cash flows in one year were correlated with cash flows in the previous year. In other words, if the cash flows in Year 3 were high, would that mean that the cash flows in Year 4 were also likely to be high? If high cash flows in Year 3 signified market acceptance of the product, then sales would probably be high. However, if high cash flows in Year 3 merely indicated that the economy was strong, the Year 4 cash flows could be high, medium, or low. In the first situation, there would be high positive correlation among the yearly cash flows, while in the second the correlation would be close to zero.

- The riskiness of the cash flows would be changing over time, as the uncertainty about the size of the market was being resolved. This means that it might not be appropriate to discount all the cash flows at the same rate.

In practice, complex decision trees are used to analyze projects. Perhaps even more important, they are used to help structure projects and to help identify any real options that might be embedded in the projects. We take this up in the next section.

What are decision trees?

What are nodes and branches?

How could a decision tree be set up so that its final output was close to a continuous probability distribution for cash flows?

DETERMINING THE VALUE OF REAL OPTIONS

The valuation of real options is a complex subject, and we can only present the basics. Still, it is important for managers to know something about real options, so we will continue with the United Robotics example. We begin by finding the value of the project assuming that it has no real options. Then we introduce a real option, and we perform a preliminary valuation of that option.

United Robotics: Project Value without Real Options

The column of joint probabilities in Figure 13-4 above gives the probability of occurrence of each branch, hence of each NPV. Each joint probability is obtained by multiplying together all probabilities on a particular branch. For example, the probability that the company will, if Stage 1 is undertaken, move through Stages 2 and 3, and that a strong demand will produce $10,000,000 of inflows, is $(0.8)(0.6)(0.3) = 0.144 = 14.4\%$.

The company has a cost of capital of 11.5 percent, and management assumes initially that the project is of average risk. The NPV of the top (most favorable) branch as shown in the next to last column is $15,250 (in thousands of dollars):

$$\text{NPV} = -\$500 - \frac{\$1,000}{(1.115)^1} - \frac{\$10,000}{(1.115)^2} + \frac{\$10,000}{(1.115)^3} + \frac{\$10,000}{(1.115)^4} + \frac{\$10,000}{(1.115)^5} + \frac{\$10,000}{(1.115)^6}$$

$$= \$15,250.$$

The NPVs for other branches were calculated similarly.

The last column in Figure 13-4 gives the product of the NPV for each branch times the joint probability of that branch, and the sum of these products is the project's expected NPV. Based on the expectations set forth in Figure 13-4 and a cost of capital of 11.5 percent, the project's expected NPV is –$338,000.

Since the expected NPV is negative, it would appear that the project should be rejected, but that conclusion is not necessarily correct. First, recall that management assumed that the project is of average risk, hence we used the corporate cost of capital to evaluate it. However, we should now consider whether this project is more, less, or about as risky as an average project. The expected NPV is a negative $338,000, and the standard deviation of that NPV is $7,991,000. Therefore, the coefficient of variation is huge. This suggests that the project is extremely risky in terms of stand-alone risk. Note also that there is a $0.144 + 0.320 + 0.200 = 0.664$ probability of incurring a loss. Based on all this, the project appears to be totally unacceptable. However, it is possible that the project could be abandoned if sales are poor, and the option to abandon could have a considerable impact on the analysis. We discuss this point in the next section.

The Impact of a Real Option on NPV and Risk

Suppose United Robotics is not contractually bound to continue the industrial robot project. Thus, if sales are poor and cash flows are –$2,000 during the first year of operations (Year 3), and a similar cash flow situation is expected for the remainder of the project's life, the firm can abandon the project at the beginning of Year 4. (Here we are assuming that low first-year cash flow signifies that the product is not well received in the market, hence that future sales will be poor. In other situations, the cash flows could vary from year to year depending on economic conditions, in which case low first-year sales and cash flows might be followed by high cash flows in subsequent years.)

The ability to abandon the project changes the third branch of the decision tree. It now looks like this:

		JOINT PROBABILITY	NPV	PRODUCT: PROB. × NPV
③				
0.3	($2,000) ④ Stop			
		0.144	(10,883)	(1,567)

Changing this branch to reflect the abandonment option eliminates the $2 million cash losses in Years 4, 5, and 6, and this causes the NPV for the branch to be less negative. This increases the project's expected NPV from −$338,000 to a positive $166,000. Moreover, the abandonment option lowers the standard deviation from $7,991,000 to $7,157,000. Thus, abandonment possibilities change the project's NPV from negative to positive, and also lower its stand-alone risk as measured by either the standard deviation or the coefficient of variation.

We can find the value of the abandonment option for United Robotics. First, note that we found the value of the project assuming there was no abandonment. To do this, we applied traditional DCF analysis, discounting the expected future cash flows at a rate of 11.5 percent. This resulted in an NPV of *negative* $338,000. However, when we then added a real option—the option to abandon the project if the market turned out to be smaller than expected—this increased the expected cash flows because it eliminated some negative cash flows associated with a small market. When we applied DCF analysis to the new cash flows, we found a positive NPV of $166,000. So, the value of the option to abandon is

$$\text{Value of option} = \text{New NPV} − \text{Old NPV}$$

$$= \$166,000 − (−\$388,000) = \$504,000.$$

However, our analysis is not exactly correct: The true new NPV is probably greater than $166,000, hence the option value is probably greater than $504,000. Recall that we calculated the standard deviation of the expected NPV for the project with and without the abandonment option. Without abandonment, the standard deviation was $7,991,000, but it falls to $7,157,000 when the abandonment option is taken into account. Therefore, if 11.5 percent is appropriate for the project without the abandonment option, a lower rate probably should be used for the project with the option.

Unfortunately, we have no precise method to tell us the exact cost of capital to use when we have the abandonment option. The DCF analysis shows that the with-option project is worth at least $166,000, and that the option is worth at least $504,000, but we do not know exactly what the option is really worth because we do not know the correct cost of capital. In general, DCF techniques will not give perfectly accurate estimates of the value of a real option, because real options change a project's risk and resulting cost of capital.

Here are some additional points concerning decision tree analysis and real options:

1. Managers can reduce project risk if they can structure the decision process to include several decision points rather than just one. To illustrate, if United Robotics were to make a total commitment at t = 0, signing contracts that would in effect require completion of the project, it might save some money and accelerate the project, but in doing so it would substantially increase the project's riskiness.

2. Once production begins, if the firm can shut down or spin off the operation, this could dramatically reduce its risk. Indeed, firms do this frequently.

3. The cost of abandonment is generally reduced if the firm has alternative uses for the project's assets. If United Robotics could use its TV robot production equipment for an expansion of its auto robot production facilities, then the costs involved in abandoning the TV robot project might be lowered, hence its riskiness would be reduced.

4. Finally, note that capital budgeting is a dynamic process. Virtually all input values change over time, so firms must periodically review both their capital expenditure plans and their operating assets. In the United Robotics example, conditions might change between Decision Points 1 and 2, and if so, this new information should be used to revise probability and cash flow estimates.

The key concept to remember is that decisions can often be structured with multiple decision points. If so, and if the company has the willpower to admit it when a project is not working out as initially planned and then to abandon it, risks can be reduced and profitability increased.

SELF-TEST
QUESTIONS

How can the possibility of abandonment affect a project's profitability and stand-alone risk?

What are the costs and benefits of structuring large capital budgeting decisions in stages rather than as a single go/no-go decision?

DCF techniques do not give a completely accurate estimate of a real option's value. Why?

REAL OPTIONS AND FINANCIAL MANAGEMENT

The United Robotics example shows that the abandonment option can add value to a project. Managers should be able to identify all real options embedded in projects, they should know which types of options can be valued using quantitative techniques, and they should have some intuition about the qualitative aspects of options.

Identifying Embedded Real Options

There are many types of real options. The **flexibility option** allows managers to switch inputs in a manufacturing process. An example would be modifying power generating systems to permit switching between fuels, say, between coal, oil, and gas, depending on their costs. It generally costs more to build a flexible plant, but input flexibility can pay for itself rapidly if input prices are volatile. Another type of flexibility option allows a firm to respond to shifts in demand by switching outputs in a manufacturing facility.

The **capacity option** allows firms to manage their productive capacity in response to changing market conditions. In addition to the *abandonment option* we discussed earlier, many projects can be structured so that they contain *options to reduce or temporarily suspend operations* rather than completely close them down. Such options are common in natural resource projects, including mining, oil, and timber. Other projects can be structured so that they contain an *option to expand*. For example, at the cost of some additional up-front investment, the United Robotics facility might be configured in such a way that it would be relatively inexpensive to double production if demand for industrial robots turned out to be much higher than anticipated.

Projects can also contain an *option to expand into a new geographical market*. For example, many companies currently are investing in Eastern Europe, Russia, and China in projects that appear to have negative NPVs. However, if customers in those developing markets like the new products or services, then the option to open more facilities could be quite valuable.

New product options can also be valuable. For example, a company might accept a negative NPV project if it has embedded in it the *option to add complementary projects, or successive "generations"* of the original product. For example, Toshiba probably lost money on its first laptop computers, but the manufacturing skills and consumer recognition it gained helped turn its subsequent generations of laptops into money makers. In addition, Toshiba used its experience and name recognition in laptops as a springboard into the field of desktop computers.

Another important type of option is the **timing option.** For example, suppose Sony planned to introduce an interactive CD-TV system, and your software company has been invited to participate in the venture. You have a choice between two alternatives: (1) immediately begin full-scale production of game software on CDs for the new interactive TV or (2) receive an exclusive license to manufacture and distribute the software at a future time of your choosing. The license would in all likelihood be preferable, since it would give you the option to defer investment until you had a better idea of the size of the market for interactive CDs. This kind of *option to delay* is also valuable during periods of volatile interest rates, since the ability to wait can allow firms to raise capital for projects when interest rates are lower. Keep in mind, though, that the option to delay is valuable only if it more than offsets any harm that might come from delaying. For example, if you delayed implementing the interactive CD-TV project, some other company might establish a loyal customer base, or determine a standard, that would make it difficult for your company to later enter the market. Of course, your license might head off this possibility. Usually, the option to delay is most valuable to firms with proprietary technology, patents, licenses, or other barriers to entry.

Quantitative Analysis of Real Options

The addition of a real option to a project alters the risk of the project's cash flows, which makes it impossible to estimate perfectly the project's cost of capital. As we noted earlier, this makes it difficult to use DCF methods to estimate the value of a real option with precision. However, alternative techniques that do not suffer from this problem can sometimes be used. The basic idea behind these alternative approaches is to create a portfolio of financial securities in such a way that the cash flows of the financial portfolio are identical to the cash flows of the project. The financial portfolio is called a **replicating portfolio** because its cash flows replicate those of the project. Since the securites in the replicating portfolio all have observable prices, it is straightforward to calculate the total value of the portfolio. And since the project and the replicating portfolio have identical cash flows, the project must have the same value as the portfolio. One advantage of this approach is that it does not require the financial analyst to estimate the project's cost of capital.

There are three steps to applying the replicating portfolio approach:

1. Identify each source of risk that affects the real option and that risk's impact on the project's cash flows. Generally, there are multiple sources of risk, and it is often difficult to specify the effect each has on the project's cash flows.

2. Second, there must be assets that trade in efficient public markets (as do commodities, stocks, and several types of derivatives) whose cash flows and values depend on the same risks as those that affect the project. Obviously, we might not be able to find securities that isolate every source of risk. However, if the primary

risk is due to variations in input prices (or output prices for a commodity producer), there is a good chance an appropriate financial security exists. For example, there are futures contracts for most metals, foods, and fuels. There are also many securities whose prices are sensitive to interest rates, and those assets can be used in the valuation of financing timing options. Indeed, in recent years there has been a virtual explosion in the variety of financial securities, so every year more risks can be covered. The increase in the creation of derivative products by investment bankers is going hand in glove with the increased use of real options in financial management.

3. The third step in valuing real options is to "crunch the numbers." This is more difficult than traditional DCF analysis, but the availability of powerful microcomputers makes it feasible to calculate the value of many types of real options. A detailed description of quantitative techniques would go beyond the scope of this text, but the references at the end of the chapter contain several excellent sources that describe valuation techniques.

Qualitative Characteristics of Real Options

Conceptually, as we noted earlier, the true NPV of a project can be thought of as the value of the project without any embedded real options plus the value of the options:

$$\text{True NPV} = \text{NPV without options} + \text{NPV of the options}. \qquad (13\text{-}2)$$

We can usually calculate the value of the project without real options, since this is typically a traditional discounted cash flow analysis with a constant cost of capital. But sometimes it is not possible to quantify the value of a project with real options. However, managers should still think about real options within the framework of Equation 13-2. Here are some general rules-of-thumb:

1. Real options often add considerable value to projects, so ignoring them could lead to downward-biased NPVs and thus to systematic underinvestment.

2. In general, the longer before a real option must be "exercised," the more valuable it is.

3. The more volatile the underlying source of risk, the more valuable the option.

4. If interest rates rise, the values of real options will increase.

Smart managers never ignore real options. Smarter managers actually try to structure projects so as to build real options into those projects. Often it is not very expensive to configure a project so that it has real options, and those options can make the difference between a home run and a strikeout.

SELF-TEST QUESTION | List some different types of real options.

THE OPTIMAL CAPITAL BUDGET

The **optimal capital budget** is the set of projects that maximizes the value of the firm. Finance theory states that all projects with positive NPVs should be accepted, and that these positive NPV projects comprise the optimal capital budget. However, there are two complications to this in practice: (1) an increasing marginal cost of capital and (2) capital rationing. The following sections discuss these complications.

An Increasing Marginal Cost of Capital

The cost of capital itself can depend on the size of the capital budget. As we discussed in Chapter 10, the flotation costs associated with issuing new equity or public debt can be quite high. This means that the cost of capital jumps upward as soon as a company invests all of its internally generated cash and has to sell new common stock. In addition, investors often perceive extremely large capital investments to be riskier, which also serves to drive up the cost of capital as the size of the capital budget increases. As a result, a project might have a positive NPV if it is part of a "normal size" capital budget, but the same project might have a negative NPV if it is part of an unusually large capital budget. Fortunately, this problem occurs very rarely for most firms since it is unusual for an established firm to require new outside equity. The Extension at the end of the chapter contains a more detailed discussion of this problem and shows how to accommodate the problem of an increasing marginal cost of capital.

Capital Rationing

Armbrister Pyrotechnics, a manufacturer of fireworks and lasers for light shows, identified 40 potential independent projects, with 15 having a positive NPV based on the firm's 12 percent cost of capital. The total cost of implementing these 15 projects is $75 million. Based on finance theory, this optimal capital budget is $75 million, and Armbrister should accept the 15 projects with positive NPVs. However, Armbrister's management has imposed a limit of $50 million for capital expenditures during the upcoming year. Due to this restriction, Armbrister must forego a number of value-adding projects. This is an example of **capital rationing,** defined as a situation in which a firm limits its capital expenditures to less than the amount required to fund the optimal capital budget. Despite being at odds with finance theory, this practice is quite common.

Why would any company forego value-adding projects? Here are some potential explanations, along with some suggestions for better ways to handle these situations:

1. **Reluctance to issue new equity.** Many firms are extremely reluctant to issue new equity, so all their capital expenditures must be funded out of debt and internally generated cash. Also, most firms try to stay near their target capital structure, and, combined with the limit on equity, this limits the amount of debt that can be added during any one year. The result can be a serious constraint on the amount of funds available for investment in new projects.

    This reluctance to issue new equity could be based on some sound reasons: (a) flotation costs can be very expensive; (b) investors might perceive new stock offerings as a signal that the company's equity is overvalued; and (c) the company might have to reveal sensitive strategic information to investors, thereby reducing some of its competitive advantages. To avoid these costs, many companies simply limit their capital expenditures.

    However, rather than placing a somewhat artificial limit on capital expenditures, a company might be better off explicitly incorporating the costs of raising external capital into its cost of capital. If there still are positive NPV projects even using this higher cost of capital, then the company should go ahead and raise external equity and accept the projects. See the Extension section for more details concerning an increasing marginal cost of capital.

2. **Constraints on nonmonetary resources.** Sometimes a firm simply does not have the necessary managerial, marketing, or engineering talent to immediately accept all positive NPV projects. In other words, the potential projects are not really independent, because the firm cannot accept them all. To avoid potential problems due to

spreading existing talent too thinly, many firms simply limit the capital budget to a size that can be accommodated by their current personnel.

A better solution might be to employ a technique called **linear programming.** Each potential project has an expected NPV, and each potential project requires a certain level of support by different types of employees. A linear program can identify the set of projects that maximizes NPV, subject to the constraint that the total amount of support required for these projects does not exceed the available resources.[10]

3. **Controlling estimation bias.** As we discussed in Chapter 12, many managers become overly optimistic when estimating the cash flows for a project. Some firms try to control this estimation bias by requiring managers to use an unrealistically high cost of capital. Others try to control the bias by limiting the size of the capital budget. Neither solution is generally effective since managers quickly learn the rules of the game and then increase their own estimates of project cash flows, which might have been biased upward to begin with.

A better solution is to implement a post-audit program and to link the accuracy of forecasts to the compensation of the managers who initiated the projects.

S E L F - T E S T
Q U E S T I O N S

What factors can lead to an increasing marginal cost of capital? How might this affect capital budgeting?

What is capital rationing?

What are three explanations for capital rationing? How might firms handle these situations?

ESTABLISHING THE OPTIMAL CAPITAL BUDGET IN PRACTICE

To illustrate how companies generally apply capital budgeting in practice, we describe the procedures used by Swift Foods, a Midwestern grocery wholesaler. As indicated below, Swift's decision process combines quantitative measures and qualitative judgment:

Step 1. Swift's financial vice-president obtains an estimate of the firm's investment opportunities from the director of capital budgeting and an estimate of the WACC from the treasurer. If there were enough profitable investment opportunities, Swift would be willing to issue new stock, in which case the WACC would include equity flotation costs. However, reinvested earnings generally provide enough equity to support the capital budget. See the Extension for an explanation of the case in which a firm must issue new securities.

Step 2. The corporate WACC is scaled up or down for each division to reflect the division's capital structure and risk characteristics. Swift Foods, for example, assigns a factor of 0.9 to its stable, low-risk canned vegetables division, but a

---

[10]For further information on mathematical programming solutions to capital rationing, and for a review and analysis of the literature on this issue, see H. Martin Weingarten, "Capital Rationing: n Authors in Search of a Plot," *Journal of Finance*, December 1977, 1403–1431; and Stephen P. Bradley and Sherwood C. Frey, Jr., "Equivalent Mathematical Programming Models of Pure Capital Rationing," *Journal of Financial and Quantitative Analysis*, June 1978, 345–361.

factor of 1.1 to its more risky gourmet frozen foods group. Therefore, if the corporate WACC is determined to be 12.5 percent, the cost for the canned vegetables division is 0.9(12.5%) = 11.25%, while that for the gourmet frozen foods division is 1.1(12.5%) = 13.75%.

Step 3.   Each project within each division is classified into one of three groups—high risk, average risk, and low risk—and the same 0.9 and 1.1 factors are used to adjust the divisional WACCs. For example, a low-risk project in the canned vegetables division would have a cost of capital of 0.9(11.25%) = 10.13%, rounded to 10 percent, while a high-risk project in the gourmet frozen foods division would have a cost of 1.1(13.75%) = 15.13%, rounded to 15 percent.

Step 4.   Each project's NPV is then determined, using its risk-adjusted project cost of capital. The optimal capital budget consists of all independent projects with positive risk-adjusted NPVs plus those mutually exclusive projects with the highest positive risk-adjusted NPVs.

These steps implicitly assume that the projects taken on have, on average, about the same debt capacity and risk characteristics, and, consequently, the same weighted average cost of capital as the firm's existing assets. If this is not true, then the corporate WACC determined in Step 1 will not be correct, and it will have to be adjusted. However, given all the measurement errors and uncertainties inherent in the entire cost of capital/capital budgeting process, it would be unrealistic to push the adjustment process very far.

This type of analysis may seem more precise than the data warrant. Nevertheless, the procedure does force the firm to think carefully about each division's relative risk, about the risk of each project within the divisions, and about the relationship between the total amount of capital raised and the cost of that capital. Further, the procedure forces the firm to adjust its capital budget to reflect capital market conditions—if the costs of debt and equity rise, this fact will be reflected in the cost of capital used to evaluate projects, and projects that would be marginally acceptable when capital costs were low would (correctly) be ruled unacceptable when capital costs were high.

S E L F - T E S T
Q U E S T I O N

Describe the general procedures that firms follow when establishing their capital budgets.

SUMMARY

This chapter discussed four issues in capital budgeting: (1) assessing risk, (2) incorporating risk into capital budgeting decisions, (3) real options, and (4) determining the optimal capital budget. The key concepts covered are summarized below.

- A project's **stand-alone risk** is the risk the project would have if it were the firm's only asset and if the firm's stockholders held only that one stock. Stand-alone risk is measured by the variability of the asset's expected returns, and it is often used as a proxy for both market and corporate risk because (1) market and corporate risk are difficult to measure and (2) the three types of risk are usually highly correlated.

- **Within-firm,** or **corporate, risk** reflects the effects of a project on the firm's risk, and it is measured by the project's effect on the firm's earnings variability. Stockholder diversification is not taken into account.

- **Market risk** reflects the effects of a project on the riskiness of stockholders, assuming they hold diversified portfolios. In theory, market risk should be the most relevant type of risk.

- Corporate risk is important because it influences the firm's ability to use low-cost debt, to maintain smooth operations over time, and to avoid crises that might consume management's energy and disrupt employees, customers, suppliers, and the community.

- **Sensitivity analysis** is a technique which shows how much a project's NPV or IRR will change in response to a given change in an input variable such as sales, other things held constant.

- **Scenario analysis** is a risk analysis technique in which the best- and worst-case NPVs are compared with the project's expected NPV.

- **Monte Carlo simulation** is a risk analysis technique in which a computer is used to simulate probable future events and thus to estimate the profitability and riskiness of a project.

- The **risk-adjusted discount rate,** or **project cost of capital,** is the rate used to evaluate a particular project. It is based on the corporate WACC, which is increased for projects which are riskier than the firm's average project but decreased for less risky projects.

- The **pure play method** can be used to estimate betas for large projects or for divisions.

- When evaluating **risky outflows,** the risk-adjustment process is reversed; that is, **lower** rates are used to discount more risky outflows because the lower the discount rate, the greater the "penalty" imposed by a risky future cost.

- **Real options** exist when managers can influence the size and riskiness of a project's cash flows by taking different actions during or at the end of a project's life.

- Projects whose capital outlays are made in stages over several years are often evaluated using **decision trees.** Decision trees are also useful for identifying real options, which, in turn, may materially affect a project's true NPV.

- The **abandonment option** can increase a project's rate of return and decrease its riskiness.

- Other types of real options include: (1) flexibility options, (2) options to contract or temporarily suspend operations, (3) options to expand output, (4) options to enter a new geographical market, (5) options to introduce complementary products or successive generations of products, and (6) options to delay projects until more is known about future conditions.

- A **replicating portfolio** is a portfolio of publicly traded securities that mimics the cash flows of a project. The value of a project must equal the value of its replicating portfolio.

- Flotation costs and increased riskiness associated with unusually large expansion programs can cause the **marginal cost of capital** to rise as the size of the capital budget increases.

- **Capital rationing** occurs when management places a constraint on the size of the firm's capital budget during a particular period.

Questions

13-1   Define each of the following terms:
    a. Stand-alone risk; corporate (within-firm) risk; market (beta) risk
    b. Worst-case scenario; best-case scenario; base case
    c. Sensitivity analysis
    d. Scenario analysis

   e. Monte Carlo simulation analysis
   f. Coefficient of variation versus standard deviation
   g. Project beta versus corporate beta
   h. Pure play method of estimating divisional betas
   i. Corporate diversification versus stockholder diversification
   j. Risk-adjusted discount rate; project cost of capital
   k   Capital rationing
   l. Real option

13-2   Define (a) simulation analysis, (b) scenario analysis, and (c) sensitivity analysis. If AT&T were considering two investments, one calling for the expenditure of $200 million to develop a satellite communications system and the other involving the expenditure of $12,000 for a new truck, on which one would the company be more likely to use simulation analysis?

13-3   Distinguish between beta (or market) risk, within-firm (or corporate) risk, and stand-alone risk for a project being considered for inclusion in the capital budget. Which type of risk do you believe should be given the greatest weight in capital budgeting decisions? Explain.

13-4   Suppose Lima Locomotive Company, which has a high beta as well as a great deal of corporate risk, merged with Homestake Patterns Inc. Homestake's sales rise during recessions, when people are more likely to make their own clothes, and, consequently, its beta is negative but its corporate risk is relatively high. What would the merger do to the costs of capital in the consolidated company's locomotive engine division and in its patterns division?

13-5   Suppose a firm estimates its cost of capital for the coming year to be 10 percent. What are reasonable costs of capital for evaluating average-risk projects, high-risk projects, and low-risk projects?

Self-Test Problem (Solution Appears in Appendix B)

ST-1
Corporate Risk Analysis

The staff of Porter Manufacturing has estimated the following net cash flows and probabilities for a new manufacturing process:

	NET CASH FLOWS		
YEAR	P = 0.2	P = 0.6	P = 0.2
0	($100,000)	($100,000)	($100,000)
1	20,000	30,000	40,000
2	20,000	30,000	40,000
3	20,000	30,000	40,000
4	20,000	30,000	40,000
5	20,000	30,000	40,000
5*	0	20,000	30,000

Line 0 gives the cost of the process, Lines 1 through 5 give operating cash flows, and Line 5* contains the estimated salvage values. Porter's cost of capital for an average-risk project is 10 percent.

a. Assume that the project has average risk. Find the project's expected NPV. (Hint: Use expected values for the net cash flow in each year.)

b. Find the best-case and worst-case NPVs. What is the probability of occurrence of the worst case if the cash flows are perfectly dependent (perfectly positively correlated) over time? If they are independent over time?

c. Assume that all the cash flows are perfectly positively correlated, that is, there are only three possible cash flow streams over time: (1) the worst case, (2) the most likely, or base, case, and (3) the best case, with probabilities of 0.2, 0.6, and 0.2, respectively. These cases are represented by each of the columns in the table. Find the expected NPV, its standard deviation, and its coefficient of variation.

d. The coefficient of variation of Porter's average project is in the range 0.8 to 1.0. If the coefficient of variation of a project being evaluated is greater than 1.0, 2 percentage points are added to the firm's cost of capital. Similarly, if the coefficient of variation is less than 0.8, 1 percentage point is deducted from the cost of capital. What is the project's cost of capital? Should Porter accept or reject the project?

Problems

13-1
Corporate Risk Analysis

Shao Industries is considering a proposed project for its capital budget. The company estimates that the project's NPV is $12 million. This estimate assumes that the economy and market conditions will be average over the next few years. The company's CFO, however, forecasts that there is only a 50 percent chance that the economy will be average. Recognizing this uncertainty, she has also performed the following scenario analysis:

ECONOMIC SCENARIO	PROBABILITY OF OUTCOME	NPV
Recession	0.05	($70 million)
Below average	0.20	(25 million)
Average	0.50	12 million
Above average	0.20	20 million
Boom	0.05	30 million

What is the project's expected NPV, its standard deviation, and its coefficient of variation?

13-2
CAPM and Beta

Calgary Foods uses the SML to determine the cost of equity capital. Currently, the risk-free rate is 5 percent, the expected return on the market is 10 percent, and Calgary's beta is 1.4. The company is considering a proposed project which has an estimated beta of 0.7. What is the project's cost of equity? If selected, the proposed project would represent 20 percent of the firm's total assets. What would the firm's new beta and cost of equity be if it were to accept the project?

13-3
Risk Adjustment

The risk-free rate of return is 9 percent, and the market risk premium is 5 percent. The beta of the project under analysis is 1.4, with expected net cash flows estimated to be $1,500 per year for 5 years. The required investment outlay on the project is $4,500.
a. What is the required risk-adjusted return on the project?
b. Should the project be accepted?

13-4
Divisional Required Rates of Return

Dunlap Computer Corporation, a producer of office computer equipment, currently has assets of $15 million and a beta of 1.4. The risk-free rate is 8 percent and the market risk premium is 5 percent. Dunlap would like to expand into the risky home computer market. If the expansion is undertaken, Dunlap would create a new division with $3.75 million in assets. The new division would have a beta of 1.8.
a. What is Dunlap's current required rate of return?
b. If the expansion is undertaken, what would be the firm's new beta? What is the new overall required rate of return, and what rate of return must the home computer division produce to leave the new overall required rate of return unchanged?

13-5
Risky Cash Flows

The Bartram-Pulley Company (BPC) must decide between two mutually exclusive investment projects. Each project costs $6,750 and has an expected life of 3 years. Annual net cash flows from each project begin 1 year after the initial investment is made and have the following probability distributions:

PROJECT A		PROJECT B	
PROBABILITY	NET CASH FLOWS	PROBABILITY	NET CASH FLOWS
0.2	$6,000	0.2	$ 0
0.6	6,750	0.6	6,750
0.2	7,500	0.2	18,000

BPC has decided to evaluate the riskier project at a 12 percent rate and the less risky project at a 10 percent rate.

a. What is the expected value of the annual net cash flows from each project? What is the coefficient of variation (CV)? (Hint: $\sigma_B = \$5,798$ and $CV_B = 0.76$.)

b. What is the risk-adjusted NPV of each project?

c. If it were known that Project B was negatively correlated with other cash flows of the firm whereas Project A was positively correlated, how would this knowledge affect the decision? If Project B's cash flows were negatively correlated with gross domestic product (GDP), would that influence your assessment of its risk?

13-6
Risky Cash Outflows
Suwannee Electric and Gas Company is deciding if it should build an oil or a coal generating plant. Its cost of capital is 8 percent for low-risk projects, 10 percent for projects of average risk, and 12 percent for high-risk projects. Management believes that an oil plant is of average risk, but that a coal plant is of high risk due to the problem of acid rain. The cash *outflows* required to construct each plant are listed here. The revenues, fuel costs, and other operating costs are expected to be the same under both plans:

	CONSTRUCTION COSTS (THOUSANDS OF DOLLARS)	
YEAR	COAL PLANT	OIL PLANT
0	($100)	($400)
1	(500)	(1,000)
2	(1,500)	(1,000)
3	(1,500)	(1,000)
4	(1,500)	(1,500)
5	(1,000)	(1,000)
6	(500)	(200)

Which type of plant should be constructed?

13-7
Sequential Decisions
The Yoran Yacht Company (YYC), a prominent sailboat builder in Newport, may design a new 30-foot sailboat based on the "winged" keels first introduced on the 12-meter yachts that raced for the America's Cup.

First, YYC would have to invest $10,000 at t = 0 for the design and model tank testing of the new boat. YYC's managers believe that there is a 60 percent probability that this phase will be successful and the project will continue. If Stage 1 is not successful, the project will be abandoned with zero salvage value.

The next stage, if undertaken, would consist of making the molds and producing two proto-type boats. This would cost $500,000 at t = 1. If the boats test well, YYC would go into production. If they do not, the molds and prototypes could be sold for $100,000. The managers estimate that the probability is 80 percent that the boats will pass testing, and that Stage 3 will be undertaken.

Stage 3 consists of converting an unused production line to produce the new design. This would cost $1,000,000 at t = 2. If the economy is strong at this point, the net value of sales would be $3,000,000, while if the economy is weak, the net value would be $1,500,000. Both net values occur at t = 3, and each state of the economy has a probability of 0.5. YYC's corporate cost of capital is 12 percent.

a. Assume that this project has average risk. Construct a decision tree and determine the project's expected NPV.

b. Find the project's standard deviation of NPV and coefficient of variation (CV) of NPV. If YYC's average project had a CV of between 1.0 and 2.0, would this project be of high, low, or average stand-alone risk?

13-8
Divisional Market Risk Adjustments
SureGrip Rubber Company has two divisions: (1) the tire division, which manufactures tires for new autos, and (2) the recap division, which manufactures recapping materials that are sold to independent tire recapping shops throughout the United States. Since auto manufacturing fluctuates with the general economy, the tire division's earnings contribution to SureGrip's stock price is highly correlated with returns on most other stocks. If the tire division were operated as

a separate company, its beta coefficient would be about 1.60. The sales and profits of the recap division, on the other hand, tend to be countercyclical, since recap sales boom when people cannot afford to buy new tires. The recap division's beta is estimated to be 0.40. Approximately 75 percent of SureGrip's corporate assets are invested in the tire division and 25 percent are in the recap division.

Currently, the rate of interest on Treasury bonds is 10 percent, and the expected rate of return on an average share of stock is 15 percent. SureGrip uses only common equity capital, hence it has no debt outstanding.

a. What is the required rate of return on SureGrip's stock?

b. What discount rate should be used to evaluate capital budgeting projects? Explain your answer fully, and in the process, illustrate your answer with a project which costs $100,000, has a 10-year life, and provides expected after-tax net cash flows of $20,000 per year.

13-9
Simulation
Singleton Supplies Corporation (SSC) manufactures medical products for hospitals, clinics, and nursing homes. SSC may introduce a new type of X-ray scanner designed to identify certain types of cancers in their early stages. There are a number of uncertainties about the proposed project, but the following data are believed to be reasonably accurate.

	PROBABILITY	VALUE	RANDOM NUMBERS
Developmental costs	0.3	$2,000,000	00–29
	0.4	4,000,000	30–69
	0.3	6,000,000	70–99
Project life	0.2	3 years	00–19
	0.6	8 years	20–79
	0.2	13 years	80–99
Sales in units	0.2	100	00–19
	0.6	200	20–79
	0.2	300	80–99
Sales price	0.1	$13,000	00–09
	0.8	13,500	10–89
	0.1	14,000	90–99
Cost per unit (excluding developmental costs)	0.3	$5,000	00–29
	0.4	6,000	30–69
	0.3	7,000	70–99

SSC uses a cost of capital of 15 percent to analyze average-risk projects, 12 percent for low-risk projects, and 18 percent for high-risk projects. These risk adjustments reflect primarily the uncertainty about each project's NPV and IRR as measured by the coefficients of variation of NPV and IRR. SSC is in the 40 percent federal-plus-state income tax bracket.

a. What is the expected IRR for the X-ray scanner project? Base your answer on the expected values of the variables. Also, assume the after-tax "profits" figure you develop is equal to annual cash flows. All facilities are leased, so depreciation may be disregarded. Can you determine the value of σ_{IRR} short of actual simulation or a fairly complex statistical analysis?

b. Assume that SSC uses a 15 percent cost of capital for this project. What is the project's NPV? Could you estimate σ_{NPV} without either simulation or a complex statistical analysis?

c. Show the process by which a computer would perform a simulation analysis for this project. Use the random numbers 44, 17, 16, 58, 1; 79, 83, 86; and 19, 62, 6 to illustrate the process with the first computer run. Actually calculate the first-run NPV and IRR. Assume that the cash flows for each year are independent of cash flows for other years. Also, assume that the computer operates as follows: (1) A developmental cost and a project life are estimated for the first run. (2) Next, sales volume, sales price, and cost per unit are estimated and used to derive a cash flow for the first year. (3) Then, the next three random numbers are used to estimate sales volume, sales price, and cost per unit for the second year, hence the cash flow for the second year. (4) Cash flows for other years are developed similarly, on out to the first run's estimated life. (5) With the developmental cost and the cash flow stream established, NPV and IRR for the first run are derived and stored in the computer's memory. (6) The process is repeated to generate perhaps 500 other NPVs and IRRs. (7) Frequency distributions for NPV and IRR are plotted by the computer, and the distributions' means and standard deviations are calculated.

d. Does it seem a little strange to conduct a risk analysis such as the one here *after* having already established a cost of capital for use in the analysis? What might be done to improve this situation?

e. In this problem, we assumed that the probability distributions were all independent of one another. It would have been possible to use conditional probabilities where, for example, the probability distribution for cost per unit would vary from trial to trial, depending on the unit sales for the trial. Also, it would be possible to construct a simulation model such that the sales distribution in Year t would depend on the sales level attained in Year t − 1. Had these modifications been made in this problem, do you think the standard deviation of the NPV distribution would have been larger (riskier) or smaller (less risky) than where complete independence is assumed?

f. Name two *major* difficulties not mentioned earlier that occur in the kind of analysis discussed in this problem.

Spreadsheet Problem

Work the problem in this section only if you are using the computer problem diskette.

13-10
Scenario and Sensitivity Analysis

Use the model in File C13 to solve this problem. Your firm, Agrico, is considering the purchase of a tractor which will have a net cost of $30,000, will increase pre-tax operating cash flows exclusive of depreciation effects by $10,000 per year, and will be depreciated on a straight line basis to zero over 5 years at the rate of $6,000 per year, beginning the first year. (Annual cash flows will be $10,000, reduced by taxes, plus the tax savings that result from $6,000 of depreciation.) The board of directors, however, is having a heated debate as to whether the tractor will actually last 5 years. Specifically, Hugo Phillips insists that he knows of some that have lasted only 4 years. Joe Copeland agrees with Phillips, but he argues that most tractors do give 5 years of service. Kate Brown, on the other hand, says she has seen some last as long as 8 years.

a. Given this discussion, the board asks you to prepare a scenario analysis to ascertain the importance of the uncertainty about the tractor's life. Assume a 40 percent marginal federal-plus-state tax rate, a zero salvage value, and a marginal cost of capital of 10 percent. (Hint: The MACRS alternate straight line depreciation is based on the class life of the tractor and is not affected by the actual life. Also, ignore the half-year convention for this problem.)

b. The board would also like to know how changes in the cost of capital affect the analysis. Assume that the machine's life is 5 years, and analyze the effects of a change in the cost of capital to 8 percent or to 12 percent. Is the project very sensitive to changes in the cost of capital?

c. The board would like to determine the sensitivity of the project's NPV to changes in certain variables. First, they would like to examine the effect of changes in pre-tax operating revenues upon NPV. Calculate the project's NPV at plus 10, 20, and 30 percent of the estimated $10,000 pre-tax revenues, as well as minus 10, 20, and 30 percent of this figure. (Hold all other variables constant.) Second, calculate the effect upon NPV of various project lives. (Hint: Hold all other variables constant, and try lives ranging from 1 to 10 years.) Finally, examine NPV while changing the cost of capital. (Once again, hold all other variables constant at their original levels.) Plot a separate sensitivity diagram for each variable examined.

MINI CASE

The Chapter 12 Mini Case contains the details of a new-project capital budgeting evaluation being conducted by Joan Samuels at the John Crockett Furniture Company. However, in the initial analysis the riskiness of the project was not considered. The base case, or expected, cash flow estimates as they were estimated in Chapter 12 (in thousands of dollars) are given next. Crockett's corporate cost of capital (WACC) is 10 percent.

		YEAR			
	0	**1**	**2**	**3**	**4**
Investment in:					
Fixed assets	($240)				
Net working capital	(20)				
Unit sales		1,250	1,250	1,250	1,250
Sales price (dollars)		$200	$200	$200	$200
Gross revenue		$250	$250	$250	$250
Cash operating costs (50%)		125	125	125	125
Operating profit		$125	$125	$125	$125
Depreciation		79	108	36	17
EBIT		$ 46	$ 17	$ 89	$108
Taxes (40%)		18	7	36	43
Net operating income		$ 28	$ 10	$ 53	$ 65
Add back depreciation		79	108	36	17
Net operating cash flow		$107	$118	$ 89	$ 82
Salvage value					25
Tax on SV (40%)					(10)
Recovery of NWC					20
Net cash flow	($260)	$107	$118	$89	$117

NPV at 10% cost of capital = $82.

IRR = 23.8%.

MIRR = 17.8%.

As Joan's assistant, you have been directed to answer the following questions:
a. What does the term "risk" mean in the context of capital budgeting, to what extent can risk be quantified, and when risk is quantified, is the quantification based primarily on statistical analysis of historical data or on subjective, judgmental estimates?
b. (1) What are the three types of risk that are relevant in capital budgeting?
   (2) How is each of these risk types measured, and how do they relate to one another?
   (3) How is each type of risk used in the capital budgeting process?
c. (1) What is sensitivity analysis?
   (2) Perform a sensitivity analysis on the unit sales, salvage value, and cost of capital for the project. Assume that each of these variables can vary from its base case, or expected, value by plus and minus 10, 20, and 30 percent. Include a sensitivity diagram, and discuss the results.
   (3) What is the primary weakness of sensitivity analysis? What is its primary usefulness?
d. Assume that Joan Samuels is confident of her estimates of all the variables that affect the project's cash flows except unit sales: If product acceptance is poor, unit sales would be only 900 units a year, while a strong consumer response would produce sales of 1,600 units. In either case, cash costs would still amount to 50 percent of revenues. Joan believes that there is a 25 percent chance of poor acceptance, a 25 percent chance of excellent acceptance, and a 50 percent chance of average acceptance (the base case).
   (1) What is the worst-case NPV? The best-case NPV?
   (2) Use the worst-, base-, and best-case NPVs and probabilities of occurrence to find the project's expected NPV, standard deviation, and coefficient of variation.
e. (1) Assume that Crockett's average project has a coefficient of variation in the range of 0.2–0.4. Would the new furniture line be classified as high risk, average risk, or low risk? What type of risk is being measured here?

(2) Based on common sense, how highly correlated do you think that the project would be to the firm's other assets? (Give a correlation coefficient, or range of coefficients, based on your judgment.)

(3) How would this correlation coefficient and the previously calculated σ combine to affect the project's contribution to corporate, or within-firm, risk? Explain.

f. (1) Based on your judgment, what do you think the project's correlation coefficient would be with the general economy and thus with returns on "the market"?

(2) How would this correlation affect the project's market risk?

g. (1) Crockett typically adds or subtracts 3 percentage points to the overall cost of capital to adjust for risk. Should the new furniture line be accepted?

(2) Are there any subjective risk factors that should be considered before the final decision is made?

h. Define scenario analysis and simulation analysis, and discuss their principal advantages and disadvantages.

i. (1) Crockett's target capital structure is 50 percent debt and 50 percent common equity; its cost of debt is 12 percent; the risk-free rate is 10 percent; the market risk premium is 6 percent; and the firm's tax rate is 40 percent. If Joan's estimate of the new project's beta is 1.2, what is the project's market risk, and what is its cost of capital based on the CAPM?

(2) How does the project's market risk compare with the firm's overall market risk?

(3) How does the project's market risk compare with its stand-alone risk?

(4) Briefly describe a method that Joan could conceivably have used to estimate the project's market beta. How feasible do you think it would actually be in this case?

(5) What are the advantages and disadvantages of focusing on a project's market risk?

j. Crockett Furniture actually considers hundreds of potential projects each year, and it is not feasible for Joan to specify quantitatively a specific risk adjustment for each individual project. However, Joan has estimated divisional betas and divisional capital structures for each of Crockett's three divisions. The Heirloom Division produces handcrafted, luxury furniture, and its high beta and low debt capacity lead to a 14 percent divisional cost of capital. The Maple Division produces furniture targeted at middle-class consumers, and it has a 10 percent divisional cost of capital. The School Division produces cafeteria and office furniture for schools, and its stable demand gives it a low beta, a high debt capacity, and an 8 percent cost of capital. Joan classifies projects within each division as high, average, or low risk. She adds 2 percent to the divisional cost of capital for high-risk projects, she makes no adjustment for average-risk projects, and she subtracts 1 percent for low-risk projects.

(1) Specify the different costs of capital that could be used for different projects.

(2) If the original project is a high-risk one in the Heirloom Division, should Joan approve it?

k. As a completely different project, Crockett is also evaluating two different production line systems for its overstuffed furniture line. Plan W requires more workers but less capital, while Plan C requires more capital but fewer workers. Both systems have estimated 3-year lives. Since the production line choice has no impact on revenues, Joan will base her decision on the relative costs of the two systems as set forth next:

	EXPECTED NET COSTS	
YEAR	PLAN W	PLAN C
0	($500)	($1,000)
1	(500)	(300)
2	(500)	(300)
3	(500)	(300)

(1) Assume initially that the two systems are both of average risk. Which one should be chosen?

(2) Now assume that the worker-intensive plan (W) is judged to be riskier than average, because future wage rates are very difficult to forecast. Under this condition, which system should be chosen?

(3) What is Plan W's IRR?

l. In a discussion with some of Crockett's engineers, Joan learns that the manufacturing facilities that are being added for the new Heirloom project could be converted to manufacture products for the School Division if demand is low for the new Heirloom product.

    (1) How might this affect the value of the project?
    (2) How might this affect the use of DCF methodology?
    (3) Briefly describe some other types of real options.
    (4) What factors increase the value of real options?
m. After examining all the potential projects, Joan discovers that there are many more projects this year with positive NPVs than in a normal year. What two problems might this extra large capital budget cause?

Selected Additional References and Cases

The literature on risk analysis in capital budgeting is vast; here is a small but useful selection of additional references that bear directly on the topics covered in this chapter:

Ang, James S., and Wilbur G. Lewellen, "Risk Adjustment in Capital Investment Project Evaluations," *Financial Management,* Summer 1982, 5–14.

Bower, Richard S., and Jeffrey M. Jenks, "Divisional Screening Rates," *Financial Management,* Autumn 1975, 42–49.

Butler, J. S., and Barry Schachter, "The Investment Decision: Estimation Risk and Risk Adjusted Discount Rates," *Financial Management,* Winter 1989, 13–22.

Fama, Eugene F., "Risk-Adjusted Discount Rates and Capital Budgeting under Uncertainty," *Journal of Financial Economics,* August 1977, 3–24.

Findlay, M. Chapman III, Arthur E. Gooding, and Wallace Q. Weaver, Jr., "On the Relevant Risk for Determining Capital Expenditure Hurdle Rates," *Financial Management,* Winter 1976, 9–16.

Gehr, Adam K., Jr., "Risk-Adjusted Capital Budgeting Using Arbitrage," *Financial Management,* Winter 1981, 14–19.

Gup, Benton E., and S. W. Norwood III, "Divisional Cost of Capital: A Practical Approach," *Financial Management,* Spring 1982, 20–24.

Robichek, Alexander A., "Interpreting the Results of Risk Analysis," *Journal of Finance,* December 1975, 1384–1386.

Sick, Gordon A., "A Certainty-Equivalent Approach to Capital Budgeting," *Financial Management,* Winter 1986, 23–32.

Weaver, Samuel C., Peter J. Clemmens III, Jack A. Gunn, and Bruce D. Danneburg, "Divisional Hurdle Rates and the Cost of Capital," *Financial Management,* Spring 1989, 18–25.

Yagil, Joseph, "Divisional Beta Estimation under the Old and New Tax Laws," *Financial Management,* Winter 1987, 16–21.

Here is a reference on real options:

Trigeorgis, Lenos, *Real Options in Capital Investment: Models, Strategies, and Applications* (Westport, Conn.: Praeger, 1995).

Several journals have had special issues with sections devoted to the topic of real options:

Midland Corporate Finance Journal, Spring 1987.

Managerial Finance, Spring 1991.

Financial Management, Autumn 1993.

The Cases in Financial Management: Dryden Request *series contains the following cases which focus on capital budgeting under uncertainty:*

Case 13, "Indian River Citrus (B)," Case 13A, "Cranfield, Inc. (B)," Case 13B, "Tasty Foods (B)," Case 13C, "Heavenly Foods," and Case 15, "Robert Montoya, Inc. (B)," which illustrate project risk analysis. Case 58, "Universal Corporation," is a comprehensive case which illustrates Chapters 11, 12, and 13, as do Cases 47 and 48, "The Western Company (A and B)."

Case 16, "New England Seafood Company," Case 16A, "Gulf Coast Fisheries," and Case 59, "Sea King Corporation," which focus on sequential investments and decision trees.

EXTENSIONS

Incorporating Risk into Capital Budgeting Decisions: Certainty Equivalents and Risk-Adjusted Discount Rates

Two alternative methods have been developed for incorporating project risk into the capital budgeting decision process. One is the **certainty equivalent** method, in which the expected cash flows are adjusted to reflect project risk—risky cash flows are scaled down, and the riskier the flows, the lower their certainty equivalent values. The second is the **risk-adjusted discount rate** method, where differential project risk is dealt with by changing the discount rate—average-risk projects are discounted at the firm's corporate cost of capital, above-average-risk projects are discounted at a higher cost of capital, and below-average-risk projects are discounted at a rate below the corporate cost of capital. The risk-adjusted discount rate method is used by most companies, so we focused on it in the chapter. However, the certainty equivalent approach does have some advantages, so financial managers should be familiar with it.

The Certainty Equivalent Method.   The certainty equivalent (CE) method follows directly from the concept of utility theory. Under the CE approach, the decision maker must first evaluate a cash flow's risk and then specify how much money, with certainty, would make him or her indifferent between the riskless and the risky cash flows. To illustrate, suppose a rich eccentric offered you the following two choices:

1. Flip a fair coin. If a head comes up, you receive $1,000,000, but if a tail comes up, you get nothing. The expected value of the gamble is $(0.5)(\$1,000,000) + (0.5)(\$0) = \$500,000$, but the actual outcome will be either $0 or $1,000,000, so it is risky.

2. Do not flip the coin and simply pocket $300,000 cash.

If you find yourself indifferent between the two alternatives, then $300,000 is your certainty equivalent for this particular

risky $500,000 expected cash flow. The certain (or riskless) $300,000 thus provides you with the same utility as the risky $500,000 expected return.

Now ask yourself this question: In the preceding example, exactly how much cash-in-hand would it actually take to make *you* indifferent between a certain sum and the risky $500,000 expected return? If you are like most people, your certainty equivalent would be significantly less than $500,000, indicating that you are risk averse. In general, risk aversion exists, and the lower the certainty equivalent, the greater the decision maker's risk aversion.

The certainty equivalent concept can be applied to capital budgeting decisions, at least in theory, in the following way:

1. Estimate the certainty equivalent cash flow in each Year t, CE_t, based on the expected cash flow and its riskiness.

2. Given these certainty equivalents, discount by the risk-free rate to obtain the project's NPV.[1]

To illustrate, suppose Project A, whose expected net cash flows are shown in Table 13E-1, is to be evaluated using the certainty equivalent method. Assume that the initial net cost, $2,000, is fixed by contract and hence known with certainty. Further, assume that the capital budgeting analyst estimates that the cash inflows in Years 1 through 4 all have average risk, and that the appropriate certainty equivalent is $700. The project's NPV, found using a risk-free discount rate of 5 percent, is $482.17:

$$NPV_A = -\$2,000 + \frac{\$700}{(1.05)^1} + \frac{\$700}{(1.05)^2} + \frac{\$700}{(1.05)^3} + \frac{\$700}{(1.05)^4}$$

$$= \$482.17.$$

Since the risk-adjusted NPV is positive, the project should be accepted.

The certainty equivalent method is simple and neat. Further, it can easily accommodate differential risk among cash flows. For example, if the Year 4 expected net cash flow of $1,000 included a very risky estimated salvage value, we could

---

[1]Note that the risk-free rate normally does not reflect the tax advantage of debt as does the WACC. Thus, either the certainty equivalent estimates or the risk-free rate should be constructed so that they capture this benefit.

| **TABLE 13E-1** | Project A: Certainty Equivalent Analysis |

Year	Expected Net Cash Flow	Degree of Risk	Certainty Equivalent Cash Flow
0	($2,000)	Zero	($2,000)
1	1,000	Average	700
2	1,000	Average	700
3	1,000	Average	700
4	1,000	Average	700

simply reduce the certainty equivalent, say, from $700 to $500, and recalculate the project's NPV. Unfortunately, there is no practical way to estimate certainty equivalents. Each individual would have his or her own estimate, and these could vary significantly. To further complicate matters, certainty equivalents should reflect shareholders' risk preferences rather than those of management. For these reasons, the certainty equivalent method is not used to any extent in corporate decision making. However, it is conceptually a powerful tool, and in a later section we will use certainty equivalents to help see some assumptions embodied in constant risk-adjusted discount rates.

The Risk-Adjusted Discount Rate Method. With the risk-adjusted discount rate method, we use the expected cash flow values, CF_t, and the risk adjustment is made to the denominator of the NPV equation (the discount rate) rather than to the numerator. To illustrate, again consider Project A, whose expected cash flows were given in Table 13E-1. Suppose the firm evaluating Project A had a corporate cost of capital of 15 percent. Thus, all average-risk projects would be evaluated using a discount rate of 15 percent. Now assume that a risk analysis of Project A indicated that the project had above-average risk, and a project cost of capital of 22 percent was subjectively assigned to the project. In this situation, the risk-adjusted discount rate method produces an NPV of $493.64:

$$NPV_A = -\$2,000 + \frac{\$1,000}{(1.22)^1} + \frac{\$1,000}{(1.22)^2} + \frac{\$1,000}{(1.22)^3} + \frac{\$1,000}{(1.22)^4}$$

$$= \$493.64.$$

In theory, if managers were able to estimate precisely both a project's certainty equivalent cash flows and its risk-adjusted discount rate (or rates), the two methods would produce the identical NPV. However, the risk-adjusted discount rate method is easier to use in practice because the discount rate for average-risk projects (the firm's corporate cost of capital) can be estimated from observable market data, but no market data are available to help managers estimate certainty equivalent cash flows.

Certainty Equivalents versus Risk-Adjusted Discount Rates. As noted above, investment risk can be handled by making adjustments either to the numerator of the present value equation (the certainty equivalent, or CE, method) or to the denominator (the risk-adjusted discount rate, or RADR, method). The RADR method dominates in practice because people find it far easier to estimate suitable discount rates based on current market data than to derive certainty equivalent cash flows. Some financial theorists have suggested that the certainty equivalent approach is theoretically superior,[2] but other theorists have shown that if risk increases with time, then using a risk-adjusted discount rate is a valid procedure.[3]

Risk-adjusted rates lump together the pure time value of money as represented by the risk-free rate and a risk premium: $k = k_{RF} + RP$. On the other hand, the CE approach keeps risk and the time value of money separate. This separation gives a theoretical advantage to certainty equivalents, because lumping together the time value of money and the risk premium compounds the risk premium over time. By compounding the risk premium over time, the RADR method automatically assigns more risk to cash flows that occur in the distant future, and the farther into the future, the greater the implied risk. Since the CE method assigns risk to each cash flow individually, it does not impose any assumptions regarding the relationship between risk and time.

Implications. A firm using the RADR approach for its capital budgeting decisions will have a corporate cost of capital that reflects its overall market-determined riskiness. This rate should be used for "average" projects, that is, for projects which have the same risk as the firm's existing assets. Lower rates should be used for less risky projects, and higher rates should be used for riskier projects. To facilitate the decision process, corporate headquarters generally prescribes rates for different classes of investments (for example, replacement, expansion of existing lines, and expansion into new lines). Then, investments of a given class within a given division are analyzed in terms of the prescribed rate. For example, replacement decisions in the retailing division of an oil company might all be evaluated with a 10 percent discount rate, while exploratory drilling projects might be evaluated at a 20 percent rate.

However, a constant k implies that risk increases with time, and it therefore imposes a relatively severe burden on long-term projects. This means that short-payoff projects will tend to be selected over those with longer payoffs when, for example, there are alternative ways of performing a given task. This is often appropriate, but there are projects for which distant returns are *not* more risky than near-term returns. For example, the estimated returns on a water pipeline serving a developing community may be highly uncertain in the short run, because the rate of growth of the community is uncertain. However, the water company may be quite sure that, in time, the community will be fully developed and will utilize the full capacity of the pipeline. Similar situations could exist in many public projects — water projects, highway programs, schools, and so forth, and when industrial firms are building plants or retailers are building stores to serve growing geographic markets.

To the extent that the implicit assumption of rising risk over time reflects the facts, then a constant discount rate may be appropriate. Indeed, in the vast majority of business situations, risk undoubtedly is an increasing function of time, so a constant risk-adjusted discount rate is generally reasonable. However, one should be aware of the relationships described in this section and avoid the pitfall of unwittingly penalizing long-term projects when they are not, in fact, more risky than short-term projects.

---

[2]See Alexander A. Robichek and Stewart C. Myers, "Conceptual Problems in the Use of Risk-Adjusted Discount Rates," *Journal of Finance,* December 1966, 727–730.

[3]See Houng-Yhi Chen, "Valuation under Uncertainty," *Journal of Financial and Quantitative Analysis,* September 1967, 313–326.

The Optimal Capital Budget

In Chapter 10, we developed the concept of the weighted average cost of capital (WACC). Then, in Chapters 11, 12, and up to this point in Chapter 13, we have discussed how the cost of capital is used in capital budgeting. However, capital budgeting and the cost of capital are actually interrelated—we cannot determine the cost of capital until we determine the size of the capital budget, and we cannot determine the size of the capital budget until we determine the cost of capital. Therefore, as we show in this section, *the cost of capital and the capital budget must be determined simultaneously.* Citrus Grove Corporation, a producer of fruit juices, is used to illustrate the process.

The Investment Opportunity Schedule (IOS). Consider first Figure 13E-1, which provides information on Citrus Grove's potential projects for next year. The tabular data below the graphs show the six projects' cash flows and IRRs. The graph is defined as the firm's **investment opportunity schedule (IOS),** which is a plot of each project's IRR, in descending order, versus the dollars of new capital required

---

FIGURE 13E-1   Citrus Grove Corporation: IOS Schedules

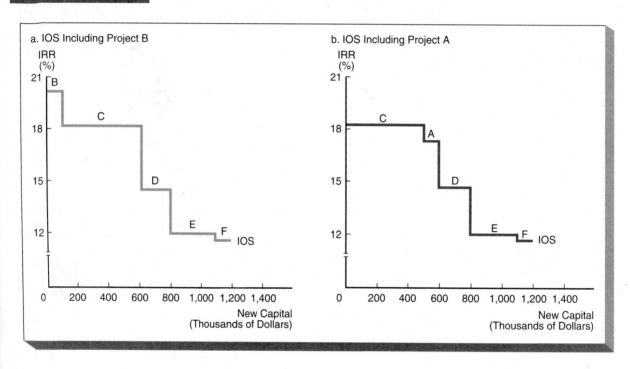

POTENTIAL CAPITAL PROJECTS' CASH FLOWS

YEAR	A[a]	B[a]	C	D	E	F
0	($100,000)	($100,000)	($500,000)	($200,000)	($300,000)	($100,000)
1	23,150	75,000	143,689	52,138	98,800	58,781
2	50,000	45,000	143,689	52,138	98,880	58,781
3	70,000	10,750	143,689	52,138	98,800	—
4	—	—	143,689	52,138	98,800	—
5	—	—	143,689	52,138	—	—
6	—	—	143,689	52,138	—	—
IRR	17.0%	20.0%	18.2%	14.5%	12.0%	11.5%

[a]Projects A and B are mutually exclusive, so only one can be in the final capital budget.

to finance it. For example, Project B has an IRR of 20 percent, shown on the vertical axis, and a cost of $100,000, shown on the horizontal axis.[4] Notice that Projects A and B are mutually exclusive. Thus, Citrus Grove has two possible IOS schedules: the one shown in panel a consists of Project B plus C, D, E, and F, and the one shown in panel b consists of Project A plus C, D, E, and F. Beyond $600,000, the two IOS schedules are identical. Thus, the two alternative schedules differ only in that one contains B, and thus ranks C second, while the other contains A, in which case C ranks first because IRR_C is greater than IRR_A. For now, we assume that all six projects have the same risk as Citrus Grove's average project.

The Marginal Cost of Capital (MCC) Schedule.

In Chapter 10, we discussed the concept of the weighted average cost of capital (WACC). We saw that the value of the WACC depends on the amount of new capital raised—the WACC will, after some point, rise if more and more capital is raised during a given year. This increase occurs because (1) flotation costs cause the cost of new equity to be higher than the cost of reinvested cash flow and (2) higher rates of return on debt, preferred stock, and common stock may be required to induce investors to supply additional capital to the firm.

Suppose Citrus Grove's cost of reinvested cash flow, or internal equity, is 15 percent, while its cost of new common stock is 16.8 percent. The company's target capital structure calls for 40 percent debt and 60 percent common equity; its marginal federal-plus-state tax rate is 40 percent; and its before-tax cost of debt is 10 percent. Thus, Citrus Grove's WACC using retained earnings as the common equity component is 11.4 percent:

$$WACC_1 = w_d(k_d)(1 - T) + w_{ce}k_s$$
$$= 0.4(10\%)(0.6) + 0.6(15\%) = 11.4\%.$$

Citrus Grove is forecasting $420,000 of reinvested cash flow during the planning period, hence the firm's break point is $700,000:

$$Break\ point = Reinvested\ cash\ flow/Equity\ fraction$$
$$= \$420,000/0.6 = \$700,000.$$

After $700,000 of new capital has been raised, Citrus Grove's WACC increases to 12.5 percent:

$$WACC_2 = 0.4(10\%)(0.6) + 0.6(16.8\%) \approx 12.5\%.$$

Thus, each dollar has a weighted average cost of 11.4 percent until the company has raised a total of $700,000. This $700,000 will consist of $280,000 of new debt with an after-tax cost of 6 percent and $420,000 of internal equity with a cost

of 15 percent. If the company raises $700,001 or more, each additional dollar will contain 60 cents of equity obtained by selling new common stock, so WACC rises from 11.4 to 12.5 percent.

Combining the MCC and IOS Schedules.

Now that we have estimated the MCC schedule, we can use it to determine the basic discount rate for the capital budgeting process; that is, we can use the MCC schedule to find the cost of capital for use in determining an average-risk project's net present value. To do this, we combine the IOS and MCC schedules on the same graph, as in Figure 13E-2, and then analyze this consolidated figure.

Finding the Marginal Cost of Capital.

Just how far down its IOS curve should Citrus Grove go? That is, which of the firm's available projects should it accept? First, Citrus Grove should accept all independent projects that have rates of return in excess of the cost of the capital that will be used to finance them, and it should reject all others. Projects E and F should be rejected, because they would have to be financed with capital that has a cost of 12.5 percent, and at that cost of capital, we know that these projects must have negative NPVs because their IRRs are below the cost of capital. Therefore, Citrus Grove's capital budget should consist of either A or B, plus C and D, and the firm should raise and invest a total of $800,000.[5]

The preceding analysis, as summarized in Figure 13E-2, reveals a very important point: The corporate cost of capital used in the capital budgeting process is determined at the intersection of the IOS and MCC schedules. This cost is called the firm's marginal cost of capital (MCC), and if it is used in capital budgeting, then the firm will make correct accept/reject decisions, and its level of investment will be optimal. If the firm uses any other rate for average-risk projects, its capital budget will not be optimal.

If Citrus Grove had fewer good investment opportunities, then its IOS schedule would be shifted to the left, possibly causing the intersection to occur on the $WACC_1 = 11.4\%$ portion of the MCC curve. Then, Citrus Grove's MCC would be 11.4 percent, and average-risk projects would be evaluated at that rate. Conversely, if the firm had more and better investment opportunities, its IOS would be shifted to the right, and if the shift were very far to the right, then the MCC might rise above 12.5 percent. Thus, we see that the discount rate used for evaluating average-risk projects is influenced by the set of potential projects. We have, of course, abstracted from differential project riskiness in this section, because we assumed that all of Citrus Grove's projects are equally risky.

Choosing between Mutually Exclusive Projects.

We have not yet completely determined Citrus Grove's optimal capital budget. We know that it should total $800,000, and that Projects C and D should be included, but we do not

[4]Do not be concerned by our use of IRR rather than MIRR or NPV. The fact is, we cannot calculate either MIRR or NPV until we know k, and we are using this analysis to develop a first-approximation estimate of k. Later on, we could switch to MIRR or NPV.

[5]Note that if the MCC schedule cuts through a project, and if that project must be accepted in total or else rejected, then we can calculate the average cost of the capital that will be used to finance the project (some at the higher WACC and some at the lower WACC) and compare that average WACC to the project's IRR.

FIGURE 13E-2   Citrus Grove Corporation: Combined IOS and MCC Schedules

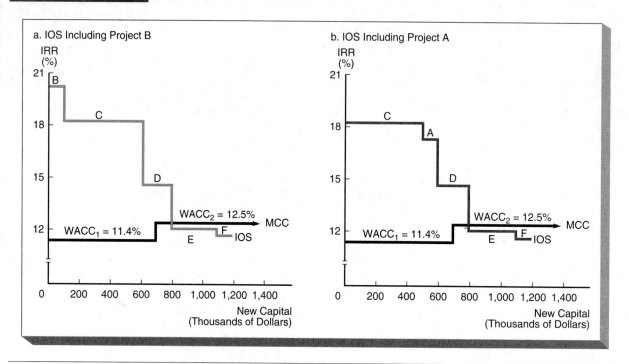

know which of the mutually exclusive projects, A or B, should be made part of the final budget. How should we choose between A and B? *The project with the higher NPV should be chosen.*

Notice that Figure 13E-1 contained the projects' IRRs, but no NPVs or MIRRs. We were not able to determine NPVs or MIRRs at that point because we did not know Citrus Grove's marginal cost of capital. Now, in Figure 13E-2, we see that the last dollar raised will cost 12.5 percent, so Citrus Grove's marginal cost of capital is 12.5 percent. Therefore, assuming the projects both have average risk, we can use a 12.5 percent discount rate to find $NPV_A = \$9,247$ and $NPV_B = \$9,772$. Citrus Grove should select Project B because its NPV is higher.

STRATEGIC FINANCING DECISIONS

V

CHAPTER 14
LONG-TERM
FINANCIAL PLANNING

CHAPTER 15
CAPITAL STRUCTURE
DECISIONS: THE BASICS

CHAPTER 16
CAPITAL STRUCTURE
DECISIONS: EXTENSIONS

CHAPTER 17
DISTRIBUTIONS TO
SHAREHOLDERS:
DIVIDENDS AND
REPURCHASES

Sir Norman Foster, architect of the Hong Kong Shanghai Bank, attempted to marry the solidity of oriental finance with the openness of the public space it occupies. The Shanghai Bank has a fully open public concourse at its base, from which elevators run to the indoor atrium and banking hall. The staggered profile with the varying elevations allows for garden terraces as well as more natural light inside.

© Doug Armand/Tony Stone Images

LONG-TERM
FINANCIAL PLANNING

Mitch Leibovitz, CEO of Pep Boys, the auto parts and service chain, wants to annihilate the competition. When intense competition from Pep Boys forces chains such as Auto Zone, Western Auto, or Genuine Parts to abandon a location, Leibovitz adds a snapshot of the closed store to his collection. "I don't believe in friendly competition. I want to put them out of business," he says. Consolidation is under way in the $125-billion-a-year after-market for automotive parts and servicing, so survival demands that Pep Boys be "a killer."

Alone among its competitors, Pep Boys can install what it sells. If customers don't want to do the work themselves, Pep Boys will do everything except body work or replacing engines and transmissions. Nearly all of its 682 stores have ten or more service bays that keep long hours. They stay open 13 hours a day Monday through Saturday, 9 hours on Sunday. No appointment is needed. The company can perform repairs more cheaply than dealers, largely because it charges no markup on parts. Mechanics get paid 32 to 38 percent of the service charge instead of an hourly wage, but, contrary to common practice, no share of the parts they install. If work has to be redone, mechanics must do it at their own expense.

Pep Boys was founded in 1921. The company grew to more than 100 stores by the early 1960s, after which conservative family management slowed expansion. Pep Boys went public in 1946, but the founding families kept control until the mid-1980s.

When Leibovitz took the helm in 1986, the company embarked on a major expansion program. Since 1986, Leibovitz has more than tripled the number of stores and more than tripled sales to more than $1.8 billion. Pep Boys's success demonstrates that unswerving dedication to a single concept, no matter how mundane, can create a dynamic, growing business.

Pep Boys now has more than 680 stores in 33 states. Analysts expect the store count to grow by 10 percent a year into the foreseeable future as the company enters new states and fills holes in existing markets. At this rate, the number of stores will double again in about seven years. Each new unit requires about $2.5 million for fixed assets and inventory, which Pep Boys funds primarily with internally generated equity plus debt supported by that equity.

According to Leibovitz, "If you want to have ho-hum results, have ho-hum goals." Pep Boys will have to do a lot of work to complete its expansion program. It will have to locate unserved markets, select sites, and line up the funds necessary to build the new outlets on schedule. In this chapter, we discuss financial forecasting, with an emphasis on how firms estimate the amount of capital needed to meet their growth targets. As you read the chapter, think about how Mitch Leibovitz might use the concepts presented here as he plans Pep Boys's expansion program. When you consider the potential impact of incorrect forecasting, you will quickly realize how important financial planning is to the success of any business.

For more information on Pep Boys, see http://www.pepboys.com.

Our primary objective in this book is to explain how managers can make their companies more valuable. If managers understand how investors determine the values of stocks and bonds, then they can better identify, evaluate, and implement projects that meet or exceed investor expectations. The book up to now has provided information on this process. However, value creation is impossible unless the company has a well-articulated plan. As Yogi Berra is reputed to have said, "You've got to be careful if you don't know where you're going, because you might not get there."

Pro forma, or **projected, financial statements** have three very important uses in the value creation process. Their first use is for estimating future free cash flows. These are necessary to implement the corporate valuation model, which enables management to measure the firm's current value, and, more importantly, to investigate the impact of proposed changes in strategy and operations. Second, the pro forma statements can be used to plan for the financing that will be required to execute the operating plans. And third, pro forma statements provide a basis for setting the targets used in the firm's compensation plan.

In this chapter, we explain how to create and use pro forma financial statements. We begin with the strategic plan, which forms the foundation for pro forma statements.

STRATEGIC PLANS

Most companies have a **mission statement,** which is in many ways a condensed version of their strategic plan. Figure 14-1 shows the mission statement of Coca-Cola, which we use to illustrate some of the key elements of strategic plans.

Corporate Purpose

Strategic plans, and mission statements, usually begin with a statement of the overall **corporate purpose.** Coca-Cola is very clear about its corporate purpose, stating that "We exist to create value for our shareowners."

FIGURE 14-1   The Mission Statement of the Coca-Cola Company
(http://www.cocacola.com/co/mission.html)

OUR MISSION

We exist to create value for our shareowners on a long-term basis by building a business that enhances The Coca-Cola Company's trademarks. This also is our ultimate commitment.

As the world's largest beverage company, we refresh the world. We do this by developing superior soft drinks, both carbonated and noncarbonated, and profitable nonalcoholic beverage systems that create value for our Company, our bottling partners, and our customers.

In creating value, we succeed or fail based on our ability to perform as stewards of several key assets:

1. Coca-Cola, the world's most powerful trademark, and other highly valuable trademarks.
2. The world's most effective and pervasive distribution system.
3. Satisfied customers, who make a good profit selling our products.
4. Our people, who are ultimately responsible for building this enterprise.
5. Our abundant resources, which must be intelligently allocated.
6. Our strong global leadership in the beverage industry in particular and in the business world in general.

This same corporate purpose is increasingly common for U.S. companies, but that has not always been the case. For example, Varian Associates, Inc., an NYSE company with sales of almost $2 billion, was, in 1990, regarded as one of the most technologically advanced electronics companies. However, Varian's management was more concerned with developing new technology than with marketing it, and its stock price was lower than it had been ten years earlier. Some of the larger stockholders were intensely unhappy with the state of affairs, and management was faced with the threat of a proxy fight or forced merger. In 1991, management announced a change in policy and stated that it would, in the future, emphasize both technological excellence *and* profitability, rather than focusing primarily on technology. Earnings improved dramatically, and the stock price rose from $6.75 to more than $60 within four years of the change in corporate purpose.

Stating that the corporate purpose is to create wealth for the company's owners is not yet as common abroad as it is in the United States. For example, Veba AG, one of Germany's largest companies, created a stir in 1996 when it stated in its annual report that "Our commitment is to create value for you, our shareholders." This was quite different from the usual German model, in which many companies have representatives from labor on their boards of directors and which explicitly state their commitments to a variety of stakeholders. However, Veba's stock has consistently outperformed the German stock market. As the trend in international investing continues, a higher percentage of many companies' owners will come from abroad, and it is likely that more non-U.S. companies will adopt a corporate purpose similar to that of Coke and Veba.

Corporate Scope

The **corporate scope** defines a firm's lines of business and geographic area of operations. As Coca-Cola's mission statement in Figure 14-1 states, the company limits its product scope to soft drinks, but it has a global geographic scope. Pepsi-Cola recently followed Coke's lead in restricting its scope by spinning off its food service businesses, including Taco Bell.

The steel industry provides a study in contrasts. For example, USX Corporation has diversified widely, from oil to financial services, while other companies such as Nucor Corporation have stuck closely to the basic steel business. Here is Nucor's position:

> We are a manufacturing company producing primarily steel products. Nucor's major strength is constructing plants economically and operating them efficiently.

During the last two decades, an investment in Nucor's stock has increased by more than 16 percent per year versus 4 percent for USX. Many factors caused these results, but scope and focus certainly were important determinants.

Corporate Objectives

The corporate purpose and scope state the general philosophy of the business, but they do not provide managers with operational objectives. The **corporate objectives** set forth specific goals for management to attain. Most organizations have both qualitative and quantitative objectives. For example, Coca-Cola's mission statement lists six corporate objectives, including "the world's most effective and pervasive distribution system" and "satisfied customers, who make a good profit selling our product." These are qualitative, but the objectives can be specified in quantitative terms, such as attaining a 50 percent market share, a 20 percent ROE, a 10 percent earnings growth rate, or a $100 million economic value added (EVA). Coca-Cola doesn't list any quantitative objectives in its mission statement, but it has them in its detailed strategic plan. Moreover, executive bonuses are based on achieving the stated objectives. Finally, most companies have multiple objectives, and those objectives are not static—companies revise their objectives as business conditions change.

Corporate Strategies

Once a firm has defined its purpose, scope, and objectives, it should develop a strategy for achieving its goals. **Corporate strategies** are broad approaches rather than detailed plans. For example, one airline may have a strategy of offering no-frills service between a limited number of cities, while another may plan to offer "staterooms in the sky." Strategies should be both attainable and compatible with the firm's purpose, scope, and objectives.

Some of the most interesting strategies that have been developed in recent years are those of the Bell operating companies in the wake of the forced breakup of AT&T in 1984. The seven regional telephone holding companies which emerged from the breakup all provide basic local telephone service, but beyond that, they have developed different strategies which are taking them in different directions. Some now sell a broad array of telecommunications equipment, while others have more limited offerings. Some are rapidly diversifying into nonregulated lines of business—Bell Atlantic has spent more than $2 billion for this purpose—while others are diversifying at a much slower pace. Others are moving abroad; for example, BellSouth recently won a $220 million contract to build a mobile phone system in Argentina. Even more surprising, two separate mergers between the operating companies—Bell Atlantic with NYNEX and SBC with Pacific Telesis—have recently been announced, so to some extent the breakup is being reversed.

<table>
<tr><td>S E L F - T E S T
Q U E S T I O N S</td><td>What are pro forma financial statements?

What are the three ways that pro forma financial statements are used in a company's plan for creating value?

Briefly describe the nature and use of the following corporate planning terms: (1) corporate purpose, (2) corporate scope, (3) corporate objectives, and (4) corporate strategies.</td></tr>
</table>

OPERATING PLANS

Operating plans can be developed for any time horizon, but most companies use a five-year horizon. A five-year plan is most detailed for the first year, with each succeeding year's plan becoming less specific. The plan is intended to provide detailed implementation guidance, based on the corporate strategy, in order to meet the corporate objectives. The plan explains in considerable detail who is responsible for what particular function, when specific tasks are to be accomplished, and the like.

Table 14-1 summarizes the annual planning schedule of MicroDrive Inc., a manufacturer of disk drives for microcomputers. This schedule illustrates the fact that for larger companies, the planning process is essentially continuous. Next, Table 14-2 outlines the key elements of MicroDrive's five-year plan. A full outline would require several pages, but Table 14-2 does at least provide insights into the format and content of a five-year plan. It should be noted that large, multidivisional companies such as General Electric break down their operating plans by divisions. Thus, each division has its own goals, mission, and plan for meeting its objectives, and these plans are then consolidated to form the corporate plan.[1]

---

[1]For more on the corporate planning process, see Benton E. Gup, *Guide to Strategic Planning* (New York: McGraw-Hill, 1980).

TABLE 14-1	MicroDrive Inc.: Annual Planning Schedule

MONTHS	ACTION
April–May	Planning department analyzes general economic and industry factors. Marketing department prepares sales forecast for each product group.
June–July	Engineering department prepares cost estimates for new manufacturing facilities and plant modernization programs.
August–September	Financial analysts evaluate proposed capital expenditures, divisional operating plans, and proposed sources and uses of funds.
October–November	Five-year plan is finalized by planning department, reviewed by divisional officers, and put into "semifinal" form.
December	Five-year plan is approved by the executive committee and then submitted to the board of directors for final approval.

TABLE 14-2	MicroDrive Inc.: Five-Year Operating Plan Outline

Part 1. Corporate purpose

Part 2. Corporate scope

Part 3. Corporate objectives

Part 4. Projected business environment

Part 5. Corporate strategies

Part 6. Summary of projected business results

Part 7. Product line plans and policies

    a. Marketing

    b. Manufacturing

    c. Finance

        1. Working capital

            (a) Overall working capital policy

            (b) Cash and marketable securities

            (c) Inventory management

            (d) Credit policy and receivables management

        2. Dividend policy

        3. Capital structure policy

        4. Financial forecast

            (a) Capital budget

            (b) Cash budget

            (c) Pro forma financial statements

            (d) External financing requirements

            (e) Financial condition analysis

        5. Accounting plan

        6. Control plan

    d. Administrative and personnel

    e. Research and development

    f. New products

What is the purpose of a firm's operating plan?

What is the most common time horizon for operating plans?

Briefly describe the contents of a typical operating plan.

THE FINANCIAL PLAN

The financial planning process can be broken down into six steps:

1. Set up a system of projected financial statements which can be used to analyze the effects of the operating plan on projected profits and various financial ratios. This system can also be used to monitor operations after the plan has been finalized and put into effect. Rapid awareness of deviations from plans is essential to a good control system, which, in turn, is essential to corporate success in a changing world.

2. Determine the funds needed to support the five-year plan. This includes funds for plant and equipment as well as for inventory and receivables, for R&D programs, and for major advertising campaigns.

3. Forecast funds availability over the next five years. This involves estimating the funds to be generated internally as well as those to be obtained from external sources. Any constraints on operating plans imposed by financial restrictions should be incorporated into the plan; examples include restrictions on the debt ratio, the current ratio, and the coverage ratios.

4. Establish and maintain a system of controls governing the allocation and use of funds within the firm. In essence, this involves making sure that the basic plan is carried out properly.

5. Develop procedures for adjusting the basic plan if the economic forecasts upon which the plan was based do not materialize. For example, if the economy turns out to be stronger than was forecasted, then these new conditions must be recognized and reflected in higher production schedules, larger marketing quotas, and the like, and as rapidly as possible. Thus, Step 5 is really a "feedback loop" which triggers modifications to the financial plan.

6. Establish a performance-based management compensation system. It is critically important that such a system rewards managers for doing what stockholders want them to do—maximize share prices. The EVA system is generally regarded as an especially effective procedure for this critical task.

In the remainder of this chapter, we focus on three key elements of the strategic plan: (1) the sales forecast, (2) pro forma financial statements, and (3) the external financing plan.

What are the six steps of the financial planning process?

SALES FORECASTS

The **sales forecast** generally starts with a review of sales during the past five to ten years, expressed in a graph such as that in Figure 14-2. The first part of the graph shows five years of historical sales for MicroDrive. The graph could have contained ten years of sales data, but MicroDrive typically focuses on sales figures for the latest five years because the firm's studies have shown that its future growth is more closely related to recent events than to the distant past.

| FIGURE 14-2 | MicroDrive Inc.: 1999 Sales Projection (Millions of Dollars) |

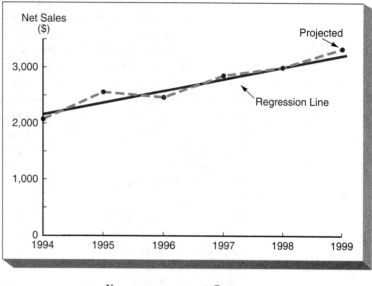

YEAR	SALES
1994	$2,058
1995	2,534
1996	2,472
1997	2,850
1998	3,000
1999	3,300 (Projected)

MicroDrive had its ups and downs during the period from 1994 to 1998. In 1996, poor performance of one of its drives led to bad publicity, which caused sales to fall below the 1995 level. Then, a banner year of microcomputer sales in 1997 pushed MicroDrive's sales up by 15 percent, an unusually high growth rate for the company. Based on a regression analysis, MicroDrive's forecasters determined that the average annual growth rate in sales over the past five years was 9.1 percent. On the basis of this historical sales trend, on planned new-product introductions, and on MicroDrive's forecast for the economy, the firm's planning committee projects 10 percent sales growth during 1999, to $3,300 million. Here are some of the factors that MicroDrive considered in its sales forecast:

1. MicroDrive has two divisions: standard drives and custom drives. The standard drive division produces large quantities of standardized disk drives, generally having capacities of less than 10,000 megabytes (10 gigabytes) and selling for less than $1,000. The custom division manufactures high-capacity, super-fast drives with capacities greater than 10 gigabytes; they sell for as much as $3,000 and are produced in relatively small quantities. Sales growth is seldom the same for each division, so to begin the forecasting process, independent divisional forecasts are made on the basis of historical growth, and then the divisional forecasts are combined to produce a "first approximation" corporate sales forecast.

2. Next, the level of economic activity and the overall demand for microcomputers are forecasted. Here, MicroDrive's planners must recognize that the firm's products are sold in two vastly different markets. Most drives are sold directly to personal computer manufacturers such as Packard-Bell, Gateway 2000, and Compaq. Such sales are high volume, and their prices are negotiated. In addition, a significant percentage of sales is made through wholesalers to individuals or small firms who are either making their own microcomputers or replacing disk drives that have failed.

3. Then, the forecasters must estimate MicroDrive's market share for each product line in each market, considering both the overall demand for disk drives and the competition among the major manufacturers. Consideration must be given to the firm's production capacity, to its competitors' capacities, and to new-product introductions both by microcomputer manufacturers and disk drive producers. Pricing strategies must also be considered—for example, should the company raise prices to boost margins, or should it lower prices to build market share and gain economies of scale in production?

4. MicroDrive sells all over the world. Its European sales represent about 20 percent of total sales, and Asian sales, which are currently only 4 percent of the total, were growing rapidly but have recently slumped. MicroDrive's foreign sales present unique forecasting problems. In particular, its planners must consider how exchange rate fluctuations would impact sales. MicroDrive must also consider the effects of trade agreements, governmental policies, and the like.

5. Inflation will also affect the firm's prices. Over the next five years, the inflation rate is expected to average 3 to 4 percent, and MicroDrive would like to increase prices, on average, by a like amount. In addition, the firm expects to expand its market share in certain products, resulting in a 4 percent growth rate in unit sales. The combination of unit sales growth and increases in sales prices has resulted in historical revenue growth rates in the 8 to 10 percent range, and this same situation is expected in the future.

6. Advertising campaigns, promotional discounts, credit terms, and the like, also affect sales, so developments in these areas must be factored in.

7. Forecasts are made for each division both in total and on an individual product basis. The individual product sales forecasts are summed, and this sum is compared with the overall divisional forecasts. Differences are reconciled, and the end result is a sales forecast for the company as a whole but with breakdowns by the two divisions and by individual products.

If the sales forecast is off, the consequences can be serious. First, if the market expands *more* than MicroDrive has geared up for, the company will not be able to meet demand. Its customers will end up buying competitors' products, and MicroDrive will lose market share. On the other hand, if its projections are overly optimistic, Micro-Drive could end up with too much plant, equipment, and inventory. This would mean low turnover ratios, high costs for depreciation and storage, and, possibly, write-offs of obsolete inventory. All of this would result in a low rate of return on equity, which in turn would depress the company's stock price. If MicroDrive had financed an unnecessary expansion with debt, its problems would be compounded. Thus, an accurate sales forecast is critical to the well-being of the firm.[2]

---

[2]A sales forecast is actually the *expected value of a probability distribution* with many possible levels of sales. Because any sales forecast is subject to uncertainty, financial planners are just as interested in the degree of uncertainty inherent in the sales forecast, as measured by the standard deviation, as in the expected level of sales.

SELF-TEST
QUESTIONS

How do past trends affect a sales forecast?

List some factors that should be considered when developing a sales forecast.

Explain why an accurate sales forecast is critical to profitability.

FINANCIAL STATEMENT FORECASTING: THE PERCENT OF SALES METHOD

Once sales have been forecasted, we must forecast future balance sheets and income statements. The most commonly used technique is the **percent of sales** method, which begins with the sales forecast, expressed as an annual growth rate in dollar sales revenues. Although we showed only one year in our earlier example, MicroDrive's managers actually forecasted sales for eight years, with these results:

YEAR	1999	2000	2001	2002	2003	2004	2005	2006
Growth rate in sales	10%	10%	10%	10%	9%	8%	7%	7%

This eight-year period is called the **explicit forecast period,** with the eighth year being the **forecast horizon.**

The initial forecasted growth rate is 10 percent, but high growth attracts competitors, and eventually the market becomes saturated. Therefore, population growth and inflation determine the **long-term sustainable growth rate** for most companies. Reasonable values for the sustainable growth rate are from 5 to 7 percent for most companies. MicroDrive's managers believe that a sustainable growth rate of 7 percent is reasonable because their company is in a high-tech industry. Its managers also believe that competition will drive their growth rate down to this sustainable level within seven or eight years, so they have chosen an eight-year forecast period.

Companies often have what is called a **competitive advantage period,** during which they can grow at rates higher than the long-term sustainable growth rate. For some companies with proprietary technology or strong brand identities, such as Microsoft or Coca-Cola, the competitive advantage period might be as long as 20 years. For companies that produce commodities or that are in highly competitive industries, the competitive advantage period might be as short as two or three years, or even be nonexistent.

To summarize, most financial plans have a forecast period of at least 5 years, while most corporate valuation models use a forecast period of 5 to 15 years, depending on the expected length of the competitive advantage period.

With the percent of sales forecasting method, many items on the income statement and balance sheets are assumed to increase proportionally with sales. For example, the inventories-to-sales ratio might be 20 percent, receivables/sales might be 15 percent, and so forth, for certain assets, liabilities, and costs. Then, as sales increase, those items that are tied to sales also increase, and the values of those items for a particular year are estimated as percentages of the forecasted sales for that year. The remaining items on the forecasted statements—items that are not tied directly to sales—depend on the company's policies and its managers' decisions.

Note that if the forecasted percentage of sales for each item is the same as the percentage for the year preceding the forecast period, then each item will grow at the same rate as sales. This approach is called the **constant ratio method of forecasting.** The advantage of this method is that it is easy to implement. The disadvantage is that it is not especially useful to managers, since one of the goals of operating managers is to limit the growth of certain items, such as costs and inventory, in order to improve profitability. In other words, *managers should strive to have improving, not constant, ratios!*

In the following sections we explain the percent of sales method and use it to forecast MicroDrive's financial statements.

Step 1. Forecasted Income Statement

First, we forecast the income statement for the coming year. This statement is needed to estimate income and the addition to retained earnings. Table 14-3 shows the forecast for 1999. Sales are forecasted to grow by 10 percent. Forecasted sales for 1999, shown on Row 1 of Column 3, are calculated by multiplying the 1998 sales, shown in Column 1, by (1 + growth rate) = 1.1. The result is a 1999 forecast of $3,300 million.

The percent of sales method assumes initially that all costs except depreciation are a specified percentage of sales. For 1998, MicroDrive's ratio of costs to sales is 87.2 percent ($2,616/$3,000 = 0.872). Thus, for each dollar of sales in 1998, MicroDrive incurred 87.2 cents of costs. Initially, the company's managers assume that the cost structure will remain unchanged in 1999. Later in the chapter we explore the impact of an improvement in the cost structure, but for now we assume that costs will equal 87.2 percent of sales. See Column 3, Row 2.

MicroDrive's managers assume that depreciation will be a fixed percentage of net plant and equipment. For 1998, the ratio of depreciation to net plant and equipment was 10 percent ($100/$1,000 = 0.10), and MicroDrive's managers believe that this is a

			1999 FORECAST			
TABLE 14-3 MicroDrive Inc.: Actual 1998 and Projected 1999 Income Statements (Millions of Dollars)	ACTUAL 1998 (1)	FORECAST BASIS (2)	FIRST PASS (3)	FEEDBACK (4)	SECOND PASS (5)	FINAL[c] (6)
1. Sales	$3,000	1.1 × 1998 Sales =	$3,300		$3,300	$3,300
2. Costs except depreciation	$2,616	0.872 × 1999 Sales =	$2,878		$2,878	$2,878
3. Depreciation	100	0.1 × 1999 Net plant =	110		110	110
4. Total operating costs	$2,716		$2,988		$2,988	$2,988
5. EBIT	$ 284		$ 312		$ 312	$ 312
6. Less interest	88		88[a]	+5	93	93
7. Earnings before taxes (EBT)	$ 196		$ 224		$ 219	$ 219
8. Taxes (40%)	78		89	−1	88	88
9. NI before preferred dividends	$ 118		$ 135		$ 131	$ 131
10. Dividends to preferred	4		4[a]		4	4
11. NI available to common	$ 114		$ 131		$ 127	$ 127
12. Dividends to common	$ 58		$ 63[b]	+3	$ 66	$ 66
13. Addition to retained earnings	$ 56		$ 68	−7	$ 61	$ 61

[a]Indicates a 1998 amount carried over for first-pass forecast.

[b]Indicates a projected amount. See text for explanation.

[c]If the dollars were taken out to several more digits, we would see differences between the "Second Pass" and "Final" columns due to successive feedbacks. But, as the data show, by the second pass most feedback effects have been accounted for.

good estimate of future depreciation. As we discuss in the next section, Table 14-4 shows that the forecasted net plant and equipment for 1999 is $1,100. Therefore, the forecasted depreciation for 1999 is 0.10($1,100) = $110.

Total operating costs, shown in Row 4 of Table 14-3, are the sum of costs and depreciation. EBIT is found by subtraction. For the first-pass forecast, shown on Row 4 of Column 3, we assume that debt for 1999 remains unchanged from 1998. Later, we modify this assumption to reflect the actual forecasted debt for 1999. For now, though, the interest expense shown on Row 6 is the same in 1999 as in 1998, because we initially assume that the amount of debt remains unchanged.

Earnings before taxes (EBT) are then calculated, as is net income before preferred dividends. Preferred dividends are carried over from the 1998 column, and they will remain constant unless MicroDrive decides to issue additional preferred stock. Net income available to common is then calculated, after which the 1999 first-pass dividends

| **TABLE 14-4** | MicroDrive Inc.: Actual 1998 and Projected 1999 Balance Sheets (Millions of Dollars) | | | | | |

| | ACTUAL 1998 (1) | FORECAST BASIS (2) | 1999 FORECAST | | | |
			FIRST PASS (3)	AFN[a] (4)	SECOND PASS (5)	FINAL (6)
Cash	$ 10	0.33% × 1999 Sales =	$ 11			
Accounts receivable	375	12.5% × 1999 Sales =	412			
Inventories	615	20.5% × 1999 Sales =	677			
Total current assets	$1,000		$1,100			
Net plant and equipment	1,000	33.33% × 1999 Sales =	1,100			
Total assets	$2,000		$2,200		$2,200	$2,200
Accounts payable	$ 60	2% × 1999 Sales =	$ 66		$ 66	$ 66
Notes payable	110		110[b]	+28	138	140
Accruals	140	4.67% × 1999 Sales =	154		154	154
Total current liabilities	$ 310		$ 330		$ 358	$ 360
Long-term bonds	754		754[b]	+28	782	784
Total debt	$1,064		$1,084		$1,140	$1,144
Preferred stock	$ 40		$ 40[b]		$ 40	$ 40
Common stock	$ 130		$ 130[b]	+56	$ 186	$ 189
Retained earnings	766	+68[c]	834		827	827
Total common equity	$ 896		$ 964		$1,013	$1,016
Total liabilities and equity	$2,000		$2,088	+112	$2,193	$2,200
Additional funds needed (AFN) this pass			$ 112		$ 7	$ 0
Cumulative AFN			$ 112		$ 119	$ 119

[a]AFN stands for "Additional Funds Needed." This figure is determined at the bottom of Column 3. Then, Column 4 shows how the required $112 of AFN will be raised.
[b]Indicates a 1998 amount carried over as the first-pass forecast.
[c]From Line 13 in Column 3 of Table 14-3.

are calculated as follows. The 1998 dividend per share is $1.15, and this dividend is expected to increase by about 8 percent, to $1.25. Since there are 50 million shares outstanding, the first-pass projected dividends are $1.25(50) = $62.5 million, rounded to $63 million. Like interest, this figure will be increased later in the analysis to reflect any additional shares issued.

To complete the first-pass forecasted income statement, the $63 million of projected dividends are subtracted from the $131 million projected net income, and the result is the first-pass projection of addition to retained earnings, $131 − $63 = $68 million. *Note, though, that this $68 million forecast for addition to retained earnings will turn out to be too high because it understates the actual 1999 interest and dividends. MicroDrive will have to borrow as well as issue new common stock to finance its asset additions, and this will change the forecasted income statement.* Those modifications will be made after we know how much additional financing will be required.

Step 2. Forecast the Balance Sheet

The assets shown on MicroDrive's balance sheet will have to increase if sales are to increase. For example, companies such as MicroDrive write checks and deposit checks every day. Because they don't know exactly when all of these checks will clear, they can't predict exactly what the balance in their checking accounts will be on any given day. Therefore, they must maintain a balance of cash and cash equivalents (such as short-term marketable securities) to avoid overdrawing their accounts. We discuss cash management in more detail in Chapter 21, but for now we simply assume that the amount of cash required to support the company's operations is proportional to its level of activity as measured by sales. MicroDrive's 1998 ratio of cash to sales was approximately 0.33 percent ($10/$3,000 = 0.0033), and its managers believe this ratio will remain constant in 1999. Therefore, the forecasted cash balance for 1999, shown in Column 3 of Table 14-4, is 0.0033($3,300) = $10.89 million, rounded to $11 million.

Unless a company changes its credit policy or has a change in its types of customers, accounts receivable will increase proportionately with sales. MicroDrive's 1998 ratio of accounts receivable to sales was $375/$3,000 = 0.125 = 12.5%. Later, we examine the effect of a change in credit policy, but for now we assume a constant credit policy and customer base. Therefore, the forecasted accounts receivable for 1999 is 0.125($3,300) = $412.5 million, rounded to $412 million as shown in Column 3 of Table 14-4.

As sales increase, companies generally need more inventory. For MicroDrive, the 1998 ratio of inventory to sales is $615/$3,000 = 20.5%. Assuming no change in Micro-Drive's inventory management, the forecasted inventory for 1999 is 0.205($3,300) = $676.5 million, rounded to $677 million as shown in Column 3 of Table 14-4.

It might be reasonable to assume that cash, accounts receivable, and inventory are proportional to sales, but will the amount of net plant and equipment go up and down as sales go up and down? The correct answer could be no or yes. When companies acquire plant and equipment, they often install greater capacity than they currently need, due to economies of scale. For example, it was more economically feasible for GM to build the Saturn automobile plant with a capacity of about 320,000 cars per year than to build the plant with a capacity of only 50,000 cars per year and then add capacity each year. Saturn's sales were far below 320,000 units for the first few years of production, so it was possible to increase sales during these years without also increasing plant and equipment. Even if a factory is at its maximum rated capacity, most companies can always squeeze out additional units by reducing the amount of downtime due to scheduled maintenance, running machinery at a higher than optimal speed, or running a second (or third) shift. Therefore, companies do not necessarily have a close relationship between sales and net plant and equipment in the short term.

However, some companies do have a fixed relationship between sales and plant and equipment, even in the short term. For example, new stores in many retail chains achieve the same sales during their first year as the chain's existing stores. Then, the only way these retailers can grow is by adding new stores, which results in a strong proportional relationship between fixed assets and sales.

In the long term, there is a relatively close relationship between sales and fixed assets for all companies: No company can continue to increase sales unless it eventually adds capacity. Therefore, as a first approximation it is reasonable to assume that the long-term ratio of net plant and equipment to sales will be constant.

For the first years of a forecast, managers generally use the actual planned investments in plant and equipment. If those estimates are not available, it is reasonable to assume an approximately constant ratio of net plant and equipment to sales. For Micro-Drive, the ratio of net plant and equipment to sales for 1998 is $1,000/$3,000 = 33.33%. MicroDrive's net plant and equipment have grown fairly steadily in the past, and its managers expect steady future growth. Therefore, they forecast net plant and equipment for 1999 to be 0.3333($3,300) = $1,100 million.

Once the individual asset accounts have been forecasted, they can be summed to complete the asset section of the balance sheet. For example, the total current assets forecasted for 1999 are $11 + $412 + $677 = $1,100 million, and fixed assets add another $1,100 million. Therefore, as Table 14-4 shows, MicroDrive will need a total of $2,200 million to support $3,300 million of sales in 1999.

Of course, if MicroDrive's assets are to increase, its liabilities and equity must also increase — the additional assets must be financed. Some items on the liability side can be expected to increase spontaneously with sales, producing what are called **spontaneously generated funds.** For example, as sales increase, so will MicroDrive's purchases of raw materials, and these larger purchases will spontaneously lead to a higher level of accounts payable. For MicroDrive, the 1998 ratio of accounts payable to sales is $60/$3,000 = 0.02 = 2%. MicroDrive's managers assume that their payables' policy will not change, so the forecasted accounts payable for 1999 is 0.02($3,300) = $66 million.

More sales will require more labor, and higher sales should also result in higher taxable income and thus taxes. Therefore, accrued wages and taxes will both increase. For MicroDrive, the 1998 ratio of accruals to sales is $140/$3,000 = 0.0467 = 4.67%. If this ratio does not change, then the forecasted level of accruals for 1999 will be 0.0467($3,300) = $154 million.

Retained earnings will also increase, but not at the same rate as sales: the new balance for retained earnings will be the old level plus the addition to retained earnings, which we calculated in Step 1. Also, notes payable, long-term bonds, preferred stock, and common stock will not rise spontaneously with sales — rather, the projected levels of these accounts will depend on financing decisions that we will discuss later.

In summary, (1) higher sales must be supported by additional assets, (2) some of the asset increases can be financed by spontaneous increases in accounts payable and accruals, and by retained earnings, and (3) any shortfall must be financed from external sources, using some combination of debt, preferred stock, and common stock.

The spontaneously increasing liabilities (accounts payable and accruals) are forecasted and shown in Column 3, the first-pass forecast. Then, those liability and equity accounts whose values reflect conscious management decisions — notes payable, long-term bonds, preferred stock, and common stock — are initially set at their 1998 levels. Thus, 1999 notes payable are initially set at $110 million, the long-term bond account is forecasted at $754 million, and so on. The 1999 value for the retained earnings (RE) account is obtained by adding the projected addition to retained earnings as developed in the 1999 income statement (see Table 14-3) to the 1998 ending balance:

$$1999 \text{ RE} = 1998 \text{ RE} + 1999 \text{ forecasted addition to RE}$$

$$= \$766 + \$68 = \$834 \text{ million.}$$

The forecast of total assets as shown in Column 3 (first-pass forecast) of Table 14-4 is $2,200 million, which indicates that MicroDrive must add $200 million of new assets in 1999 to support the higher sales level. However, the forecasted liability and equity accounts as shown in the lower portion of Column 3 rise by only $88 million, to $2,088 million. Since the balance sheet must balance, MicroDrive must raise an additional $2,200 − $2,088 = $112 million, which we designate as **Additional Funds Needed (AFN).** The AFN will be raised by borrowing from the bank as notes payable, by issuing long-term bonds, and by selling new common stock.

Step 3. Raising the Additional Funds Needed

MicroDrive's financial staff will base the financial mix on several factors, including the firm's target capital structure, the effect of short-term borrowing on its current ratio, conditions in the debt and equity markets, and restrictions imposed by existing debt agreements. The financial staff, after considering all of the relevant factors, decided on the following financing mix to raise the additional $112 million:

	AMOUNT OF NEW CAPITAL		
	PERCENT	DOLLARS (MILLIONS)	INTEREST RATE
Notes payable	25%	$ 28	8%
Long-term bonds	25	28	10
Common stock	50	56	—
	100%	$112	

These amounts, which are shown in Column 4 of Table 14-4, are added to the initially forecasted account totals as shown in Column 3 to generate the second-pass balance sheet. Thus, in Column 5 the notes payable account increases to $110 + $28 = $138 million, long-term bonds rise to $754 + $28 = $782 million, and common stock increases to $130 + $56 = $186 million.

If there were no changes in any other income statement or balance sheet account, the forecast would be complete — the initial shortfall was $112 million, and MicroDrive would raise that amount as shown above. However, when MicroDrive takes on new debt, its interest expenses will rise, and the additional shares of common stock will cause dividend payments to increase. These changes will affect the amount of retained earnings, as we discuss in the next section.

Step 4. Financing Feedbacks

One complexity that arises in financial forecasting relates to **financing feedbacks:** The external funds raised to pay for new assets create additional expenses which must be reflected in the income statement, and that lowers the initially forecasted addition to retained earnings. To handle financing feedbacks, we first forecast the additional interest expense and dividends that result from external financings. New short-term debt costs 8 percent, so the $28 million of new notes payable will increase MicroDrive's projected 1999 interest expense by 0.08($28) = $2.24 million. Similarly, new long-term bonds will add 0.10($28) = $2.80 million in interest expense, so the total increase in interest expense will be $5.04 million. When these feedbacks are considered, interest expense as shown in the projected 1999 second-pass income statement in Column 5 of Table 14-3 increases to $88 + $5 = $93 million. These higher interest charges will, of course, also affect the remainder of the income statement.

The financing plan also calls for issuing $56 million of new common stock. Micro-Drive's stock price was $23 at the end of 1998, and if we assume that new shares would be sold at this price, then $56/$23 = 2.4 million shares of new stock will have to be sold. Further, MicroDrive's 1999 dividend payment is projected to be $1.25 per share, so the 2.4 million shares of new stock will require 2.4($1.25) = $3 million of additional dividend payments. Thus, dividends to common stockholders as shown in the second-pass income statement increase to $63 + $3 = $66 million.

The net effect of the financing feedbacks is to reduce the addition to retained earnings by $7 million, from $68 million to $61 million. This reduces the balance sheet forecast of retained earnings by a like amount, so in Table 14-4 the second-pass 1999 balance sheet projection for retained earnings becomes $766 + $61 = $827 million, or $7 million less than in the initial forecast. Thus, a shortfall of $7 million will still exist as a result of financing feedback effects. This amount is shown toward the bottom of Column 5 in Table 14-4.

How would the second-pass shortfall be financed? In MicroDrive's case, 25 percent of the $7 million would be obtained as short-term debt, 25 percent as long-term bonds, and 50 percent as new common stock.

We could create a third-pass balance sheet by using this financing mix to add another $7 million to the liabilities and equity side. Would the third pass balance? No, because the additional $7 million in capital would require another increase in interest and dividend payments, and this would affect the third-pass income statement. There would still be a shortfall, although it would be much smaller than the $7 million shortfall on the second pass. We could then construct a fourth-pass forecasted income statement and balance sheet, fifth-pass statements, and so on. In each iteration, the additional financing would become smaller and smaller, and after about five iterations, the AFN would be essentially zero. We do not show the additional iterations, but the final results are shown in Column 6 of Tables 14-3 and 14-4.[3]

Analysis of the Forecast: Value-Based Management

The 1999 forecast as developed above is only the first part of MicroDrive's total planning process. We must go on to analyze the projected statements to determine how much value the plan creates for shareholders, and also whether it meets the firm's targets as set forth in its five-year financial plan. If the statements do not meet targets, then elements of the operating plan must be analyzed to see if changes should be made.

Table 14-5 shows selected information and key ratios for MicroDrive in 1998, projections for 1999, and the latest industry average ratios. (The table also shows some "Revised" data, which we discuss later. Disregard the "Revised" data for now.) The "Inputs" section shows that MicroDrive is planning no change in operations between 1998 and 1999 for three of the model's key drivers: (1) costs (excluding depreciation) as a percentage of sales, (2) accounts receivable as a percentage of sales, and (3) inventory as a percentage of sales. While MicroDrive's costs to sales ratio is only slightly worse than the industry average, its ratios of accounts receivable to sales and inventory to

---

[3]Given the fact that the forecast reflects estimates, there is not much point in going beyond two passes. However, with spreadsheets it is easy enough to iterate to a fully balanced solution.

TABLE 14-5	Value-Based Management: Projected Value, AFN, and Key Ratios			
	ACTUAL 1998	PRELIMINARY FORECAST FOR 1999[a]	REVISED FORECAST FOR 1999[a]	INDUSTRY AVERAGE 1998
Model Inputs				
Costs (excluding depreciation) as percentage of sales	87.2%	87.2%	86.0%	87.1%
Accounts receivable as percentage of sales	12.5	12.5	11.8	10.0
Inventory as percentage of sales	20.5	20.5	16.7	11.1
Model Outputs				
NOPAT (net operating profit after taxes)	$170	$187	$211	
Net operating working capital	$800	$880	$731	
Total operating capital	$1,800	$1,980	$1,831	
Free cash flow	($175)	$7	$180	
Value of operations (12/31/99)		$2,091	$3,442	
Estimated stock price per share (12/31/99)		$21.43	$52.02	
AFN		$119	($63)	
Current ratio	3.2×	3.1×	3.6×	4.2×
Inventory turnover	4.9×	4.9×	6.0×	9.0×
Days sales outstanding	45.0×	44.9×	42.5×	36.0×
Total assets turnover	1.5×	1.5×	1.6×	1.8×
Debt ratio[b]	55.2%	53.8%	51.7%	40.0%
Profit margin	3.8%	3.8%	4.8%	5.0%
Return on assets	5.7%	5.8%	7.7%	9.0%
Return on equity	12.7%	12.5%	15.9%	15.0%
NOPAT as percentage of sales	5.7%	5.7%	6.4%	5.7%
Total operating capital as percentage of sales	60.0%	60.0%	55.5%	50.3%
Return on invested capital	9.5%	9.5%	11.5%	11.4%

[a]The 1999 data reflect all financing feedbacks.
[b]Includes preferred stock.

sales are much worse than its competitors. Therefore, its investment is too high, and its return on assets, equity, and invested capital are too low.

The detailed model itself is not provided, but its key outputs as shown in the "Model Outputs" section indicate that MicroDrive initially forecasts a slight increase in NOPAT (net operating profit after taxes), but a very large increase in net operating working capital and in total operating capital. The result is a very small level of free cash flow. Although we do not show projections of the full financial statements for all eight years in the explicit forecast horizon, here are the initially projected free cash flows (FCFs):

YEAR	2000	2001	2002	2003	2004	2005	2006
FCF	8.4	8.9	9.8	34.6	63.7	96.9	103.7

Recall from Chapter 9 that the horizon, or terminal, value is the present value of all free cash flows beyond the horizon, discounted back to the horizon at the weighted average cost of capital. The horizon for MicroDrive is 2006, and its WACC is 10 percent. Because sales are expected to grow at a constant rate of 7 percent after the horizon, we can apply the constant growth formula from Chapter 9 to calculate the horizon value:

$$HV_{2006} = \frac{FCF_{2007}}{WACC - g} = \frac{FCF_{2006}(1 + g)}{WACC - g} = \frac{\$103.7(1 + 0.07)}{0.10 - 0.07} = \$3,698.6.$$

In other words, if all the assumptions used in the forecast hold true, then MicroDrive could sell its operations on December 31, 2006, for $3,698.6 million.

To find the expected value of operations at the end of the plan's first year (December 31, 1999), we need to find the present value of the horizon value plus the present values of the free cash flows occurring from December 31, 2000, through December 31, 2006. Here is a time line of the flows:

1999	2000	2001	2002	2003	2004	2005	2006
	$8.4	$8.9	$9.8	$34.6	$63.7	$96.9	$103.7
							$3,698.6
							$3,802.3

Remember that the $3,698.6 million horizon value is based on all the free cash flows *after* December 31, 2006, so we are not double counting by including the cash flow *at* 2006. Also, we do not include the free cash flow *at* 1999, because the value of any asset is based on future cash flows, not cash flows that have just occurred.

The present value of the free cash flows in the time line, discounted at MicroDrive's 10 percent WACC, is $2,091 million. Because the company has no nonoperating assets, such as short-term financial investments or minority interests in other companies, its total value, as of December 31, 1999, is $2,091 million. This is an estimate of the company's value if it executes its preliminary operating plan.

Is this value acceptable? To answer this question, we need to estimate the price of MicroDrive's stock as of December 31, 1999. According to the projected balance sheets in Table 14-4, on December 31, 1999, MicroDrive will owe $140 million on notes payable, $784 million on long-term bonds, and $40 million on preferred stock. The remaining value belongs to common stockholders, and it is $2,091 − $140 − $784 − $40 = $1,127 million. After all financing feedbacks, MicroDrive will have 52.6 million shares of stock outstanding as of December 31, 1999. Therefore, the expected price per share is $1,127/52.6 = $21.43. Since the current price is $23, this preliminary plan is judged to be unacceptable: *If MicroDrive's managers actually carry out the plan, the stock price will go down.*

A quick look at the "Ratios" section of Table 14-5 also shows weaknesses in the plan. MicroDrive's asset management ratios are much worse than the industry averages. For example, its total asset turnover ratio is 1.5 versus an industry average of 1.8. Even though its profits from operations (NOPAT/sales) are comparable to industry norms, the poor asset management ratios drag down the return on invested capital (9.5 percent for MicroDrive versus 11.4 percent for the industry average). Furthermore, MicroDrive finances more than the average amount of debt, and the extra interest expense reduces its profit margin (3.8 percent versus 5.0 percent for the industry). Much of the debt is short term, and this results in a current ratio of 3.2 versus the 4.2 industry average.

After reviewing its preliminary forecast, management decided to make several changes. Through the use of activity-based costing, MicroDrive identified some low-profit products and also a number of customers who require much more support — and cost — than the average customer. If it focuses its marketing efforts on high-profit products and low-cost customers, MicroDrive's managers believe they can lower operating costs from the current 87.2 percent of sales to 86 percent. Also, by screening credit customers more closely and by being more aggressive in collecting past-due accounts, the company believes it can reduce the ratio of accounts receivable to sales from 12.5 percent to 11.8 percent. In the manufacturing area, the company decided to change some of its assembly operations from traditional batch processing to a system that incorporates just-in-time production techniques. Finally, MicroDrive decided to work with its customers and suppliers to share information and thus streamline the entire logistics pipeline. Through these efforts, management believes it can reduce the inventory to sales ratio from 20.5 to 16.7 percent.

Based on these operating changes, MicroDrive created a revised set of forecasted statements. We do not show the actual statements, but their impact can be seen in the third column in Table 14-5. Here are the highlights of the revised forecast:

1. The reduction in operating costs improved NOPAT in 1999 by $211 − $187 = $24 million. Even more impressive, the improvements in the receivables policy and in inventory management freed up $149 million in working capital ($880 − $731 = $149). The net result is a very large increase in free cash flow for 1999, from a previously estimated $7 million to $180 million. Although we do not show it, the improvements in operations also led to significantly higher free cash flow for each year in the whole forecast period.

2. The improved free cash flows have an enormous impact on the company's value. As Table 14-5 shows, the revised value of operations is $3,442 million. Moreover, fewer shares of stock would be outstanding, so the forecasted stock price is $52.02. Thus, if MicroDrive can actually carry out these improvements in operations, the value of its stock will more than double.

3. The profit margin improves to 4.8 percent. Although MicroDrive's revised *operating* profit margin, NOPAT/sales, is greater than the industry average (6.4 percent versus 5.7 percent), its *net* profit margin still lags the industry average because of its higher than average interest payments.

4. The increase in the profit margin results in an increase in projected retained earnings. Further, by tightening inventory controls and reducing the days sales outstanding, MicroDrive projects a reduction in inventories and receivables. Taken together, these actions resulted in a *negative* 1999 AFN of $63 million, which means that MicroDrive would actually generate $63 million more from internal operations during 1999 than it needs for new assets. This $63 million of surplus funds could be used to reduce short-term debt, which would lead to a decrease in the forecasted debt ratio from 53.8 to 51.7 percent. The debt ratio would still be well above the industry average, but this is a step in the right direction.

5. The indicated changes would affect MicroDrive's current ratio, which would improve from 3.1 to 3.6.

6. These actions would raise the rate of return on assets from 5.8 to 7.7 percent, and they would boost the return on equity from 12.5 to 15.9 percent, which would even exceed the industry average. ·

Although MicroDrive's managers believe that the revised forecast is achievable, they cannot be sure of this. Accordingly, they want to know how variations in sales would affect the forecast. Therefore, a spreadsheet model was run using several different sales growth rates, and the results were analyzed to see how the ratios would change under different growth scenarios. To illustrate, if the sales growth rate increased from 10 to

20 percent, the additional funding requirement would change dramatically, from a $63 million *surplus* to an $83 million *shortfall*.

The spreadsheet model was also used to evaluate dividend policy. If MicroDrive decided to reduce its dividend growth rate, then additional funds would be generated, and these funds could be invested in plant, equipment, and inventories, used to reduce debt, or used to repurchase stock.

The model was also used to evaluate financing alternatives. For example, MicroDrive could use the forecasted $63 million of surplus funds to retire long-term bonds rather than to reduce short-term debt. Under this financing alternative, the current ratio would drop from 3.6 to 2.9, but the total debt ratio would still decline, and the interest coverage ratio would rise.

We see, then, that forecasting is an iterative process, both in the way the financial statements are generated and the way the financial plan is developed. For planning purposes, the financial staff develops a preliminary forecast based on a continuation of past policies and trends. This provides a starting point, or "baseline" forecast. Next, the model is modified to see what effects alternative operating plans would have on the firm's earnings and financial condition. This results in a revised forecast. Then alternative operating plans are examined under different sales growth scenarios, and the model is used to evaluate both dividend policy and capital structure decisions. The model can also be used to analyze alternative working capital policies—that is, to see the effects of changes in cash management, credit policy, inventory policy, and the use of different types of short-term credit. We examine MicroDrive's working capital policy within the framework of the company's financial model in Chapters 21, 22, and 23.

In summary, managers use financial planning models for three important purposes: (1) The models allow managers to measure the expected change in value, or stock price, under different strategic and operating alternatives. Thus, this process often is called **value-based management.** (2) The models help managers determine the amount of financing that will be required to support various operating plans. This is extremely important—since raising capital can be a lengthy process, managers need a lead time to finance in an optimal manner. (3) The models help identify appropriate targets for compensation plans. For example, it would be pointless to reward MicroDrive's managers for achieving the preliminary plan, since that plan would lead to a decrease in the stock's value. On the other hand, if MicroDrive's managers can hit the targets identified in the revised plan, they will deserve large bonuses.

SELF-TEST
QUESTIONS

Briefly describe the percent of sales method for financial forecasting.

What are "spontaneously generated funds"? List two common sources of spontaneous financing.

What is the AFN, and how is it estimated?

What is financing feedback, and how do feedbacks affect the estimated AFN?

What is value-based management?

THE AFN FORMULA

Most firms forecast their capital requirements by constructing pro forma income statements and balance sheets as described above. However, when the ratios are expected to remain constant, then the following formula is sometimes used to forecast financial requirements:

$$
\begin{array}{cccc}
\text{Additional} & \text{Required} & \text{Spontaneous} & \text{Increase in} \\
\text{funds} = & \text{increase} - & \text{increase in} - & \text{retained} \\
\text{needed} & \text{in assets} & \text{liabilities} & \text{earnings}
\end{array}
$$

$$
\text{AFN} = (A^*/S_0)\Delta S - (L^*/S_0)\Delta S - MS_1(1 - d). \tag{14-1}
$$

Here

AFN = additional funds needed.

A* = assets that are tied directly to sales, hence which must increase if sales are to increase. Note that A designates total assets and A* designates those assets that must increase if sales are to increase. When the firm is operating at full capacity, as is the case here, A* = A. Often, though, A* and A are not equal, and the equation must be modified or else the projected financial statement method must be used.

S_0 = sales during the last year, 1998 in our example.

A^*/S_0 = percentage of required assets to sales, which also shows the required dollar increase in assets per \$1 increase in sales. A^*/S_0 = \$2,000/\$3,000 = 0.6667 for MicroDrive. Thus, for every \$1 increase in sales, assets must increase by about 67 cents, based on 1998 data.

L* = liabilities that increase spontaneously. L* is normally much less than total liabilities (L).

L^*/S_0 = liabilities that increase spontaneously as a percentage of sales, or spontaneously generated financing per \$1 increase in sales. L^*/S_0 = (\$60 + \$140)/\$3,000 = 0.0667 = 6.67% for MicroDrive. Thus, every \$1 increase in sales generates about 7 cents of spontaneous financing.

S_1 = total sales projected for next year. Note that S_0 = \$3,000 designates last year's sales, and S_1 = \$3,300 million.

ΔS = change in sales = $S_1 - S_0$ = \$3,300 million − \$3,000 million = \$300 million for MicroDrive.

M = profit margin, or profit per \$1 of sales. M = \$114/\$3,000 = 0.0380 for MicroDrive. So, MicroDrive earns 3.8 cents on each dollar of sales.

d = percentage of earnings paid out in common dividends, or the dividend payout ratio; d = \$58/\$114 = 0.5088 = 50.88% for MicroDrive.

Inserting values for MicroDrive into Equation 14-1, we find the additional funds needed to be \$118 million:

$$
\begin{array}{cccc}
& \text{Required} & \text{Spontaneous} & \text{Increase} \\
\text{AFN} = & \text{asset} - & \text{liability} - & \text{in retained} \\
& \text{increase} & \text{increase} & \text{earnings}
\end{array}
$$

$$
= 0.667(\Delta S) - 0.067(\Delta S) - 0.038(S_1)(1 - 0.509)
$$

$$
= 0.667(\$300) - 0.067(\$300) - 0.038(\$3,300)(0.491)
$$

$$
= \$200 - \$20 - \$62
$$

$$
= \$118 \text{ million.}
$$

To increase sales by \$300 million, the formula suggests that MicroDrive must increase assets by \$200 million. The \$200 million of new assets must be financed in some manner. Of the total, \$20 million will come from a spontaneous increase in liabilities, while another \$62 million will be obtained from retained earnings. The remaining \$118 million must be raised from external sources. This value is an approximation, but it is only slightly different from the AFN figure ($119 million) we developed in Table 14-4.

Inherent in the formula are the assumptions (1) that each asset item must increase in direct proportion to sales increases, (2) that accounts payable and accruals also grow at the same rate as sales, (3) and that the profit margin is constant. Obviously, these assumptions do not always hold, so the formula does not always produce reliable results. Therefore, the formula is used primarily to get a rough-and-ready forecast of financial requirements under "business as usual" conditions.

Relationship between Sales Growth and Financial Requirements

The faster MicroDrive's growth rate in sales, the greater its need for additional financing. We can use Equation 14-1, which is plotted in Figure 14-3, to demonstrate this relationship. The tabular data show MicroDrive's additional financial requirements at various growth rates, and these data are plotted in the graph. The figure illustrates four important points:

1. **Financial feasibility.** At low growth rates, MicroDrive needs no external financing, and it even generates surplus cash. However, if the company grows faster than 3.21 percent, it must raise capital from outside sources.[4] Further, the faster the growth rate, the greater the capital requirements. If management foresees difficulties in raising the required capital, it should reconsider the feasibility of the expansion plans.

2. **Effect of dividend policy on financing needs.** Dividend policy as reflected in the payout ratio (d in Equation 14-1) also affects external capital requirements—the higher the payout ratio, the smaller the addition to retained earnings, hence the greater the need for external capital. Therefore, if MicroDrive foresees difficulties in raising capital, it should consider reducing the dividend payout ratio. This would lower (or shift to the right) the line in Figure 14-3, indicating smaller external capital requirements at all growth rates. However, before changing its dividend policy, management should consider the effects of such a decision on the stock price, as discussed in Chapter 17.

   Notice that the line in Figure 14-3 does *not* pass through the origin. Thus, at low growth rates (below 3.21 percent), surplus funds will be produced, because new retained earnings plus spontaneous funds will exceed the required asset increases. Only if the dividend payout ratio were 100 percent, meaning that the firm did not retain any of its earnings, would the "funds needed" line pass through the origin.

3. **Capital intensity.** The amount of assets required per dollar of sales, A^*/S_0 in Equation 14-1, is often called the **capital intensity ratio.** This ratio has a major effect on capital requirements. If the capital intensity ratio is low, sales can grow rapidly without much outside capital. However, if the firm is capital intensive, even a small growth in output will require a great deal of new outside capital.

4. **Profit margin.** The profit margin, M, is also an important determinant of the funds-required equation—the higher the margin, the lower the funds requirements. In terms of the graph, an increase in the profit margin would cause the line to shift down, and its slope would also become less steep. Because of the relationship between profit margins and additional capital requirements, some very rapidly growing firms do not need much external capital. For example, for many years, Xerox grew at a rapid rate with very little borrowing or stock sales. However, as the company lost patent

---

[4]We found the 3.21 percent growth rate by setting AFN equal to zero, substituting gS_0 for ΔS and $S_0 + g(S_0)$ for S_1 in the AFN equation, and then solving the equation $0 = 0.667(g)(S_0) - 0.067(g)(S_0) - 0.038(S_0 + gS_0)$ $(1 - 0.509)$ for g. The g that solved this equation was about 0.0321, or 3.21 percent.

FIGURE 14-3   Relationship between Growth in Sales and Financial Requirements, Assuming $S_0 = \$3,000$ (Millions of Dollars)

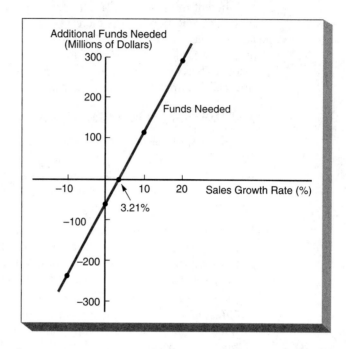

GROWTH RATE IN SALES (1)	INCREASE (DECREASE) IN SALES, ΔS (2)	FORECASTED SALES, S_1 (3)	ADDITIONAL FUNDS NEEDED (4)
20%	$600	$3,600	$293
10	300	3,300	118
3.21	96	3,096	0
0	0	3,000	−56
−10	−300	2,700	−230

Explanation of Columns:

Column 1: Assumed growth rate in sales, g.
Column 2: Increase (decrease) in sales, $\Delta S = g(S_0) = g(\$3,000)$.
Column 3: Forecasted sales, $S_1 = S_0 + g(S_0) = S_0(1 + g) = \$3,000(1 + g)$.
Column 4: Additional funds needed = $0.667(\Delta S) - 0.067(\Delta S) - 0.019(S_1)$.

---

protection and as competition intensified in the copier industry, Xerox's profit margin declined, its needs for external capital rose, and it began to borrow from banks and other sources.

S E L F - T E S T
Q U E S T I O N S

Under certain conditions a formula can be used to forecast AFN. Give the formula and briefly explain it.

How do the following factors affect external capital requirements?
(1) Dividend payout ratio.
(2) Capital intensity.
(3) Profit margin.

FORECASTING FINANCIAL REQUIREMENTS WHEN THE BALANCE SHEET RATIOS ARE SUBJECT TO CHANGE

Both the AFN formula and the projected financial statement method as we used it assume that the ratios of assets and liabilities to sales (A^*/S_0 and L^*/S_0) remain constant over time. This, in turn, requires the assumption that each "spontaneous" asset and liability item increases at the same rate as sales. In graph form, this implies the type of relationship shown in Panel a of Figure 14-4, a relationship that is (1) linear and (2) passes through the origin. Under those conditions, if the company's sales increase from $200 million to $400 million, or by 100 percent, inventory will also increase by 100 percent, from $100 million to $200 million.

The assumption of constant ratios and identical growth rates is appropriate at times, but there are times when it is incorrect. Three such conditions are described in the following sections.

Economies of Scale

There are economies of scale in the use of many kinds of assets, and when economies occur, the ratios are likely to change over time as the size of the firm increases. For example, retailers often need to maintain base stocks of different inventory items, even if current sales are quite low. As sales expand, inventories grow less rapidly than sales, so the ratio of inventory to sales (I/S) declines. This situation is depicted in Panel b of Figure 14-4. Here we see that the inventory/sales ratio is 1.5, or 150 percent, when sales are $200 million, but the ratio declines to 1.0 when sales climb to $400 million.

The relationship we use to illustrate economies of scale is linear, but nonlinear relationships often exist. Indeed, if the firm uses one popular model for establishing inventory levels (the EOQ model), its inventories will rise with the square root of sales. This situation is shown in Panel c of Figure 14-4, which shows a curved line whose slope decreases at higher sales levels. In this situation, very large sales increases would require very few additional inventories.

Lumpy Assets

In many industries, technological considerations dictate that if a firm is to be competitive, it must add fixed assets in large, discrete units; such assets are often referred to as **lumpy assets.** In the paper industry, for example, there are strong economies of scale in basic paper mill equipment, so when a paper company expands capacity, it must do so in large, lumpy increments. This type of situation is depicted in Panel d of Figure 14-4. Here we assume that the minimum economically efficient plant has a cost of $75 million, and that such a plant can produce enough output to reach a sales level of $100 million. If the firm is to be competitive, it simply must have at least $75 million of fixed assets.

Lumpy assets have a major effect on the fixed assets/sales (FA/S) ratio at different sales levels and, consequently, on financial requirements. At Point A in Panel d, which represents a sales level of $50 million, the fixed assets are $75 million, so the ratio FA/S = $75/$50 = 1.5. Sales can expand by $50 million, out to $100 million, with no additions to fixed assets. At that point, represented by Point B, the ratio FA/S = $75/$100 = 0.75. However, since the firm is operating at capacity (sales of $100 million), even a small increase in sales would require a doubling of plant

FIGURE 14-4   Four Possible Ratio Relationships (Millions of Dollars)

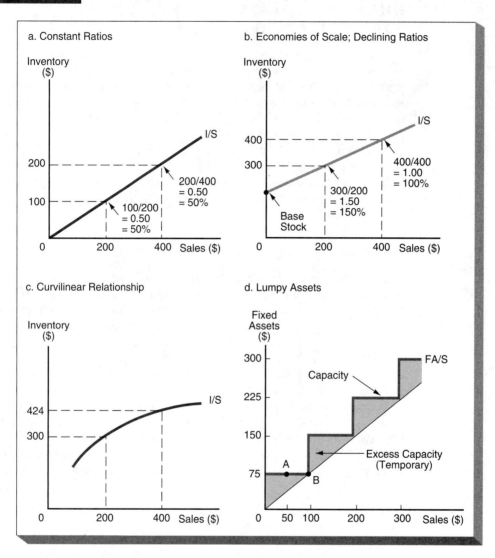

capacity, so a small projected sales increase would bring with it a very large financial requirement.[5]

---

[5]Several other points should be noted about Panel d of Figure 14-4. First, if the firm is operating at a sales level of $100 million or less, any expansion that calls for a sales increase above $100 million would require a *doubling* of the firm's fixed assets. A much smaller percentage increase would be involved if the firm were large enough to be operating a number of plants. Second, firms generally go to multiple shifts and take other actions to minimize the need for new fixed asset capacity as they approach Point B. However, these efforts can only go so far, and eventually a fixed asset expansion will be required. Third, firms often make arrangements to share excess capacity with other firms in their industry. For example, the situation in the electric utility industry is very much like that depicted in Panel d. However, electric companies often build jointly owned plants, or else they "take turns" building plants, and then they buy power from or sell power to other utilities to avoid building new plants that may be underutilized.

Excess Assets Due to Forecasting Errors

Panels a, b, c, and d of Figure 14-4 all focus on target, or projected, relationships between sales and assets. Actual sales, however, are often different from projected sales, and the actual asset/sales ratio at a given time may be quite different from the planned ratio. To illustrate, the firm depicted in Panel b of Figure 14-4 might, when its sales are at $200 million and its inventories at $300 million, project a sales expansion to $400 million and then increase its inventories to $400 million in anticipation of the sales expansion. However, suppose an unforeseen economic downturn were to hold sales to only $300 million. Actual inventories would then be $400 million, but inventories of only $350 million would be needed to support actual sales of $300 million. Thus, inventories would be $50 million larger than needed. In that situation, if the firm were making its forecast for the following year, it should recognize that sales could expand by $100 million with no increase whatever in inventories, but that any sales expansion beyond $100 million would require additional financing to increase inventories.

SELF-TEST
QUESTION

Describe three conditions under which the assumption that each "spontaneous" asset and liability item increases at the same rate as sales is *not* correct.

OTHER TECHNIQUES FOR FORECASTING FINANCIAL STATEMENTS

If any of the conditions noted above apply (economies of scale, excess capacity, or lumpy assets), the A^*/S_0 ratio will not be a constant, and the constant growth forecasting methods as discussed thus far should not be used. Rather, other techniques must be used to forecast asset levels and additional financing requirements. Two of these methods — linear regression and excess capacity adjustments — are discussed in the following sections.

Simple Linear Regression

If we assume that the relationship between a certain type of asset and sales is linear, then we can use simple linear regression techniques to estimate the requirements for that type of asset for any given sales increase. For example, MicroDrive's sales, inventories, and receivables during the last five years are shown in the lower section of Figure 14-5, and each current asset item is plotted in the upper section as a scatter diagram versus sales. Estimated regression equations determined using a financial calculator are also shown with each graph. For example, the estimated relationship between inventories and sales (in millions of dollars) is

$$\text{Inventories} = -\$35.7 + 0.186(\text{Sales}).$$

The plotted points are not very close to the regression line, which indicates a low degree of correlation. In fact, the correlation coefficient between inventories and sales is 0.71, indicating that there is only a moderate linear relationship between these two variables. Still, management may regard the regression relationship as providing a reasonable basis for forecasting target inventory levels.

We can use the estimated relationship between inventories and sales to forecast 1999 inventory levels. Since 1999 sales are projected at $3,300 million, 1999 inventories should be $578 million:

$$\text{Inventories} = -\$35.7 + 0.186(\$3,300) = \$578 \text{ million}.$$

FIGURE 14-5 MicroDrive Inc.: Linear Regression Models
(Millions of Dollars)

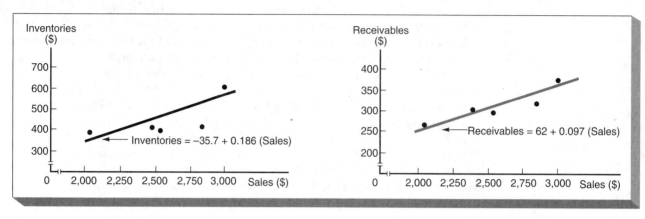

YEAR	SALES	INVENTORIES	ACCOUNTS RECEIVABLE
1994	$2,058	$387	$268
1995	2,534	398	297
1996	2,472	409	304
1997	2,850	415	315
1998	3,000	615	375

This is $99 million less than the preliminary forecast based on the projected financial statement method. The difference occurs because the projected financial statement method assumed that the ratio of inventories to sales would remain constant, when in fact it will probably decline. Note also that although our graphs show linear relationships, we could have easily used a nonlinear regression model had such a relationship been indicated.

After analyzing the regression results, MicroDrive's managers decided that a new forecast of AFN should be developed in which a lower days sales outstanding and a higher inventory turnover ratio are assumed. Management recognized that the 1998 levels of these accounts were above the industry averages, hence that the preliminary results projected for 1999 are unnecessarily high. When simple linear regression was used to forecast the receivables and inventories accounts, this caused the 1999 levels to reflect both the average relationships of these accounts to sales over the five-year period and also the trend in the variables' values. In contrast, the projected financial statement method we developed earlier assumed that the nonoptimal 1998 relationships would continue in 1999 and beyond.

Excess Capacity Adjustments

Consider again the MicroDrive example set forth in Tables 14-3 and 14-4, but now assume that excess capacity exists in fixed assets. Specifically, assume that fixed assets in 1998 were being utilized to only 96 percent of capacity. If fixed assets had been used to full capacity, 1998 sales could have been as high as $3,125 million, versus the $3,000 million in actual sales:

$$\begin{aligned}\text{Full}\\\text{capacity} &= \frac{\text{Actual sales}}{\substack{\text{Percentage of capacity}\\\text{at which fixed assets}\\\text{were operated}}} = \frac{\$3,000 \text{ million}}{0.96} = \$3,125 \text{ million.} \quad \textbf{(14-2)}\\\text{sales}\end{aligned}$$

This suggests that MicroDrive's Fixed assets/Sales ratio should be 32 percent:

$$\text{Target fixed assets/Sales ratio} = \frac{\text{Actual fixed assets}}{\text{Full capacity sales}} \quad \textbf{(14-3)}$$

$$= \frac{\$1,000}{\$3,125} = 0.32 = 32\%.$$

Therefore, if sales are to increase to $3,300 million, then fixed assets would have to increase to $1,056 million:

$$\substack{\text{Required level}\\\text{of fixed assets}} = (\text{Target fixed assets/Sales ratio})(\text{Projected sales}) \quad \textbf{(14-4)}$$

$$= 0.32(\$3,300) = \$1,056 \text{ million.}$$

We previously forecasted that MicroDrive would need to increase fixed assets at the same rate as sales, or by 10 percent. That meant an increase from $1,000 million to $1,100 million, or by $100 million. Now we see that the actual required increase is only from $1,000 million to $1,056 million, or by $56 million. Thus, the capacity-adjusted forecast is $100 million − $56 million = $44 million less than the earlier forecast. With a smaller fixed asset requirement, the projected AFN would decline from an estimated $112 million to $112 million − $44 million = $68 million.

Note also that when excess capacity exists, sales can grow to the capacity sales as determined above with no increase whatever in fixed assets, but sales beyond that level will require fixed asset additions as calculated in our example. The same situation could occur with respect to inventories, and the required additions would be determined in exactly the same manner as for fixed assets. Theoretically, the same situation could occur with other types of assets, but as a practical matter, excess capacity normally exists only with respect to fixed assets and inventories.

SELF-TEST
QUESTIONS

Would it be more important to use the regression method of forecasting asset requirements if the true situation were like that in Panel a or that in Panel b of Figure 14-4?

If excess capacity exists, how will that affect the AFN?

COMPUTERIZED FINANCIAL PLANNING MODELS

Although financial forecasting as described in this chapter can be done with a calculator, virtually all corporate forecasts are made using computerized forecasting models. Many computerized financial forecasting models are based on a spreadsheet program such as *Lotus 1-2-3* or *Microsoft Excel*. Spreadsheet models have two major advantages over pencil-and-paper calculations. First, it is much faster to construct a spreadsheet model than to make a "by hand" forecast if the forecast period extends beyond two or three years. Second, and more important, a spreadsheet model can recompute the projected financial statements and ratios almost instantaneously when the input variables are changed, thus making it easy for managers to determine the effects of changes in variables such as sales.[6]

Why are computerized planning models playing an increasingly important role in corporate management?

---

[6]It is becoming increasingly easy for companies to develop planning models as a result of the dramatic recent improvements in computer hardware and software. *Lotus 1-2-3* and *Excel* are the most widely used systems, although many companies also employ more complex and elaborate modeling systems. Increasingly, a knowledge of *Lotus 1-2-3*, *Excel,* or some similar spreadsheet program is becoming a requirement for getting even an entry-level job in many corporations. Indeed, surveys indicate that the probability of a business student getting an attractive job offer increases dramatically if he or she has a working knowledge of spreadsheets. In addition, starting salaries are materially higher for those students who have such a knowledge.

Note also that we have concentrated on long-run, or strategic, financial planning. Within the framework of the long-run strategic plan, firms also develop short-run financial plans. For example, in Table 14-4, we saw that MicroDrive Incorporated expects to need $119 million by the end of 1999, and that it plans to raise this capital by using short-term debt, long-term debt, and common stock. However, we do not know when during the year the funds will be needed, or when MicroDrive will obtain each of its different types of capital. To address these issues, the firm must develop a short-run financial plan, the centerpiece of which is the *cash budget,* which is a projection of cash inflows and outflows on a daily, weekly, or monthly basis during the coming year (or other budget period). We will discuss cash budgeting in Chapter 21, where we consider cash and marketable securities.

SUMMARY

This chapter described in broad outline how firms project their financial statements and determine their capital requirements. The key concepts covered are listed below.

- The primary planning documents are the **strategic plan,** the **operating plan,** and the **financial plan.**

- **Financial forecasting** generally begins with a forecast of the firm's sales, in terms of both units and dollars, for some future period.

- The **projected,** or **pro forma, financial statement method** and the **AFN formula method** are used to forecast financial requirements.

- A firm can determine its **additional funds needed (AFN)** by estimating the amount of new assets necessary to support the forecasted level of sales and then subtracting from that amount the spontaneous funds that will be generated from operations. The firm can then plan to raise the AFN through bank borrowing, by issuing securities, or both.

- The **higher a firm's sales growth rate,** the **greater** will be its need for additional financing. Similarly, the **larger a firm's dividend payout ratio,** the **greater** its need for additional funds.

- Adjustments must be made if **economies of scale** exist in the use of assets, if **excess capacity** exists, or if assets must be added in **lumpy increments.**

- **Linear regression** and **excess capacity adjustments** can be used to forecast asset requirements in situations in which assets cannot be expected to grow at the same rate as sales.

The type of forecasting described in this chapter is important for several reasons. First, if the projected operating results are unsatisfactory, management can "go back to the drawing board," reformulate its plans, and develop more reasonable targets for the coming year. Second, it is possible that the funds required to meet the sales forecast simply cannot be obtained. If so, it is obviously better to know this in advance and to scale back the projected level of operations than to suddenly run out of cash and have operations grind to a halt. And third, even if the required funds can be raised, it is desirable to plan for their acquisition well in advance.

Questions

14-1 Define each of the following terms:
  a. Operating plan; five-year plan
  b. Financial plan
  c. Sales forecast
  d. Percent of sales method
  e. Spontaneously generated funds
  f. Dividend payout ratio
  g. Pro forma financial statement
  h. Additional funds needed (AFN); AFN formula
  i. Capital intensity ratio
  j. Lumpy assets
  k. Financing feedback
  l. Simple linear regression
  m. Computerized financial planning model

14-2 Certain liability and net worth items generally increase spontaneously with increases in sales. Put a check ($\sqrt{}$) by those items that typically increase spontaneously:

Accounts payable	_____
Notes payable to banks	_____
Accrued wages	_____
Accrued taxes	_____
Mortgage bonds	_____
Common stock	_____
Retained earnings	_____

14-3 The following equation can, under certain assumptions, be used to forecast financial requirements:

$$AFN = (A^*/S_0)(\Delta S) - (L^*/S_0)(\Delta S) - MS_1(1 - d).$$

Under what conditions does the equation give satisfactory predictions, and when should it *not* be used?

14-4 Assume that an average firm in the office supply business has a 6 percent after-tax profit margin, a 40 percent debt/assets ratio, a total assets turnover of 2 times, and a dividend payout ratio of 40 percent. Is it true that if such a firm is to have *any* sales growth (g > 0), it will be forced either to borrow or to sell common stock (that is, it will need some nonspontaneous, external capital even if g is very small)?

14-5 Suppose a firm makes the following policy changes. If the change means that external, nonspontaneous financial requirements (AFN) will increase, indicate this by a (+); indicate a decrease by a (−); and indicate indeterminate or no effect by a (0). Think in terms of the immediate, short-run effect on funds requirements.
  a. The dividend payout ratio is increased.   _____
  b. The firm contracts to buy, rather than make, certain components used in its products.   _____
  c. The firm decides to pay all suppliers on delivery, rather than after a 30-day delay, to take advantage of discounts for rapid payment.   _____
  d. The firm begins to sell on credit (previously all sales had been on a cash basis).   _____
  e. The firm's profit margin is eroded by increased competition; sales are steady.   _____
  f. Advertising expenditures are stepped up.   _____
  g. A decision is made to substitute long-term mortgage bonds for short-term bank loans.   _____
  h. The firm begins to pay employees on a weekly basis (previously it had paid at the end of each month).   _____

Self-Test Problems   (Solutions Appear in Appendix B)

ST-1
Growth Rate

Weatherford Industries Inc. has the following ratios: $A^*/S_0 = 1.6$; $L^*/S_0 = 0.4$; profit margin = 0.10; and dividend payout ratio = 0.45, or 45 percent. Sales last year were $100 million. Assuming that these ratios will remain constant, use the AFN formula to determine the maximum growth rate Weatherford can achieve without having to employ nonspontaneous external funds.

ST-2
Additional Funds Needed

Suppose Weatherford's financial consultants report (1) that the inventory turnover ratio is sales/inventory = 3 times versus an industry average of 4 times and (2) that Weatherford could reduce inventories and thus raise its turnover to 4 without affecting sales, the profit margin, or the other asset turnover ratios. Under these conditions, use the AFN formula to determine the amount of additional funds Weatherford would require during each of the next 2 years if sales grew at a rate of 20 percent per year.

ST-3
Excess Capacity

Van Auken Lumber's 1998 financial statements are shown below.

VAN AUKEN LUMBER:
BALANCE SHEET AS OF DECEMBER 31, 1998
(THOUSANDS OF DOLLARS)

Cash	$ 1,800	Accounts payable	$ 7,200
Receivables	10,800	Notes payable	3,472
Inventories	12,600	Accruals	2,520
Total current assets	$25,200	Total current liabilities	$13,192
Net fixed assets	21,600	Mortgage bonds	5,000
		Common stock	2,000
		Retained earnings	26,608
Total assets	$46,800	Total liabilities and equity	$46,800

VAN AUKEN LUMBER:
INCOME STATEMENT FOR DECEMBER 31, 1998
(THOUSANDS OF DOLLARS)

Sales	$36,000
Operating costs	30,783
Earnings before interest and taxes	$ 5,217
Interest	1,017
Earnings before taxes	$ 4,200
Taxes (40%)	1,680
Net income	$ 2,520
Dividends (60%)	$ 1,512
Addition to retained earnings	$ 1,008

a. Assume that the company was operating at full capacity in 1998 with regard to all items *except* fixed assets; fixed assets in 1998 were being utilized to only 75 percent of capacity. By what percentage could 1999 sales increase over 1998 sales without the need for an increase in fixed assets?

b. Now suppose 1999 sales increase by 25 percent over 1998 sales. How much additional external capital will be required? Assume that Van Auken cannot sell any fixed assets. (Hint: Use the percent of sales method to develop a pro forma balance sheet and income statement as in Tables 14-3 and 14-4.) Assume that any required financing is borrowed as notes payable. Do not include any financing feedbacks, and use a pro forma income statement to determine the addition to retained earnings. (Another hint: Notes payable = $6,021.)

c. Use the financial statements developed in Part b to incorporate the financing feedback which results from the addition to notes payable. (That is, do the next financial statement iteration.) For purposes of this part, assume that the notes payable interest rate is 12 percent. What is the AFN for this iteration?

d. Suppose the industry average DSO and inventory turnover ratio are 90 days and 3.33, respectively, and that Van Auken Lumber matches these figures in 1999 and then uses the funds released to reduce equity. (It pays a special dividend out of retained earnings.) What would this do to the rate of return on year-end 1999 equity? Use the second-pass balance sheet and income statement as developed in Part c, and assume that the additional AFN amount calculated in that iteration is added to notes payable. (Hint: Notes payable is now $6,094.)

Problems

Carter Corporation's sales are expected to increase from $5 million in 1998 to $6 million in 1999, or by 20 percent. Its assets totaled $3 million at the end of 1998. Carter is at full capacity, so its assets must grow at the same rate as projected sales. At the end of 1998, current liabilities were $1 million, consisting of $250,000 of accounts payable, $500,000 of notes payable, and $250,000 of accruals. The after-tax profit margin is forecasted to be 5 percent, and the forecasted payout ratio is 70 percent. Use this information to answer Problems 14-1, 14-2, and 14-3.

14-1
AFN Formula

Use the AFN formula to forecast Carter's additional funds needed for the coming year.

14-2
AFN Formula

What would the additional funds needed be if the company's year-end 1998 assets had been $4 million? Assume that all other numbers are the same. Why is this AFN different from the one you found in Problem 14-1? Is the company's "capital intensity" the same or different?

14-3
AFN Formula

Return to the assumption that the company had $3 million in assets at the end of 1998, but now assume that the company pays no dividends. Under these assumptions, what would be the additional funds needed for the coming year? Why is this AFN different from the one you found in Problem 14-1?

14-4
Sales Increase

Pierce Furnishings generated $2.0 million in sales during 1998, and its year-end total assets were $1.5 million. Also, at year-end 1998, current liabilities were $500,000, consisting of $200,000 of notes payable, $200,000 of accounts payable, and $100,000 of accruals. Looking ahead to 1999, the company estimates that its assets must increase by 75 cents for every $1 increase in sales. Pierce's profit margin is 5 percent, and its payout ratio is 60 percent. How large a sales increase can the company achieve without having to raise funds externally?

14-5
Pro Forma
Statements and Ratios

Upton Computers makes bulk purchases of small computers, stocks them in conveniently located warehouses, and ships them to its chain of retail stores. Upton's balance sheet as of December 31, 1998, is shown here (millions of dollars):

Cash	$ 3.5	Accounts payable		$ 9.0
Receivables	26.0	Notes payable		18.0
Inventories	58.0	Accruals		8.5
Total current assets	$ 87.5	Total current liabilities		$ 35.5
Net fixed assets	35.0	Mortgage loan		6.0
		Common stock		15.0
		Retained earnings		66.0
Total assets	$122.5	Total liabilities and equity		$122.5

Sales for 1998 were $350 million, while net income for the year was $10.5 million. Upton paid dividends of $4.2 million to common stockholders. The firm is operating at full capacity. Assume that all ratios remain constant.

a. If sales are projected to increase by $70 million, or 20 percent, during 1999, use the AFN equation to determine Upton's projected external capital requirements.

b. Construct Upton's pro forma balance sheet for December 31, 1999. Assume that all external capital requirements are met by bank loans and are reflected in notes payable. Do not consider any financing feedback effects.

c. Now calculate the following ratios, based on your projected December 31, 1999, balance sheet. Upton's 1998 ratios and industry average ratios are shown here for comparison:

| | UPTON COMPUTERS | | INDUSTRY AVERAGE |
	12/31/99	12/31/98	12/31/98
Current ratio	_____	2.5×	3×
Debt/total assets	_____	33.9%	30%
Rate of return on equity	_____	13%	12%

d. Now assume that Upton grows by the same $70 million but that the growth is spread over 5 years—that is, that sales grow by $14 million each year. Do not consider any financing feedback effects.

   (1) Calculate total additional financial requirements over the 5-year period. (Hint: Use 1998 ratios, $\Delta S = \$70$, but total sales for the 5-year period.)

   (2) Construct a pro forma balance sheet as of December 31, 2003, using notes payable as the balancing item.

   (3) Calculate the current ratio, total debt/total assets ratio, and rate of return on equity as of December 31, 2003. [Hint: Be sure to use *total sales,* which amount to $1,960 million, to calculate retained earnings but 2003 profits to calculate the rate of return on equity— that is, return on equity = (2003 profits)/(12/31/03 equity).]

e. Do the plans outlined in Parts b and/or d seem feasible to you? That is, do you think Upton could borrow the required capital, and would the company be raising the odds on its bankruptcy to an excessive level in the event of some temporary misfortune?

14-6
Additional Funds Needed

Stevens Textile's 1998 financial statements are shown below.

STEVENS TEXTILE:
BALANCE SHEET AS OF DECEMBER 31, 1998
(THOUSANDS OF DOLLARS)

Cash	$ 1,080	Accounts payable	$ 4,320
Receivables	6,480	Accruals	2,880
Inventories	9,000	Notes payable	2,100
Total current assets	$16,560	Total current liabilities	$ 9,300
Net fixed assets	12,600	Mortgage bonds	3,500
		Common stock	3,500
		Retained earnings	12,860
Total assets	$29,160	Total liabilities and equity	$29,160

STEVENS TEXTILE:
INCOME STATEMENT FOR DECEMBER 31, 1998
(THOUSANDS OF DOLLARS)

Sales	$36,000
Operating costs	32,440
Earnings before interest and taxes	$ 3,560
Interest	560
Earnings before taxes	$ 3,000
Taxes (40%)	1,200
Net income	$ 1,800
Dividends (45%)	$ 810
Addition to retained earnings	$ 990

a. Suppose 1999 sales are projected to increase by 15 percent over 1998 sales. Determine the additional funds needed. Assume that the company was operating at full capacity in 1998, that it cannot sell off any of its fixed assets, and that any required financing will be borrowed as notes payable. Also, assume that assets, spontaneous liabilities, and operating costs are expected to increase by the same percentage as sales. Use the percent of sales method to develop a pro forma balance sheet and income statement for December 31, 1999. (Do not incorporate any financing feedback effects. Use the pro forma income statement to determine the addition to retained earnings.)

b. Use the financial statements developed in Part a to incorporate the financing feedback as a result of the addition to notes payable. (That is, do the next financial statement iteration.) For the purpose of this part, assume that the notes payable interest rate is 10 percent. What is the AFN for this iteration?

14-7
Additional Funds Needed

Garlington Technologies Inc.'s 1998 financial statements are shown below.

GARLINGTON TECHNOLOGIES INC.:
BALANCE SHEET AS OF DECEMBER 31, 1998

Cash	$ 180,000	Accounts payable	$ 360,000
Receivables	360,000	Notes payable	156,000
Inventories	720,000	Accruals	180,000
Total current assets	$1,260,000	Total current liabilities	$ 696,000
Fixed assets	1,440,000	Common stock	1,800,000
		Retained earnings	204,000
Total assets	$2,700,000	Total liabilities and equity	$2,700,000

GARLINGTON TECHNOLOGIES INC.:
INCOME STATEMENT FOR
DECEMBER 31, 1998

Sales	$3,600,000
Operating costs	3,279,720
EBIT	$ 320,280
Interest	20,280
EBT	$ 300,000
Taxes (40%)	120,000
Net income	$ 180,000
Per Share Data	
Common stock price	$24.00
Earnings per share (EPS)	$1.80
Dividends per share (DPS)	$1.08

a. Suppose that in 1999 sales increase by 10 percent over 1998 sales and that 1999 DPS will increase to $1.12. Construct the pro forma financial statements using the percent of sales method. How much additional capital will be required? Assume the firm operated at full capacity in 1998. Do not include any financing feedbacks.

b. Now assume that 50 percent of the additional capital required will be financed by selling common stock and the remainder by borrowing as notes payable. Assume that the interest rate on notes payable is 13 percent. Do the next iteration of financial statements incorporating financing feedbacks. What is the AFN for this iteration?

c. If the profit margin were to remain at 5 percent and the dividend payout rate were to remain at 60 percent, at what growth rate in sales would the additional financing requirements be exactly zero? (Hint: Set AFN equal to zero and solve for g.)

14-8

External Financing
Requirements

The 1998 balance sheet and income statement for the Damon Company are shown below.

DAMON COMPANY:
BALANCE SHEET AS OF DECEMBER 31, 1998
(THOUSANDS OF DOLLARS)

Cash	$ 80	Accounts payable		$ 160
Accounts receivable	240	Accruals		40
Inventories	720	Notes payable		252
Total current assets	$1,040	Total current liabilities		$ 452
Fixed assets	3,200	Long-term debt		1,244
		Total debt		$1,696
		Common stock		1,605
		Retained earnings		939
Total assets	$4,240	Total liabilities and equity		$4,240

DAMON COMPANY:
INCOME STATEMENT FOR DECEMBER 31, 1998
(THOUSANDS OF DOLLARS)

Sales	$8,000
Operating costs	7,450
EBIT	$ 550
Interest	150
EBT	$ 400
Taxes (40%)	160
Net income	$ 240

Per Share Data

Common stock price	$16.96
Earnings per share (EPS)	$1.60
Dividends per share (DPS)	$1.04

a. The firm operated at full capacity in 1998. It expects sales to increase by 20 percent during 1999 and expects 1999 dividends per share to increase to $1.10. Use the percent of sales method to determine how much outside financing is required, developing the firm's pro forma balance sheet and income statement, and use AFN as the balancing item.
b. If the firm must maintain a current ratio of 2.3 and a debt ratio of 40 percent, how much financing, after the first pass, will be obtained using notes payable, long-term debt, and common stock?
c. Make the second-pass financial statements incorporating financing feedbacks, using the ratios in Part b. Assume that the interest rate on debt averages 10 percent.

14-9

Long-Term Financing Needed

At year-end 1998, total assets for Bertin Inc. were $1.2 million and accounts payable were $375,000. Sales, which in 1998 were $2.5 million, are expected to increase by 25 percent in 1999. Total assets and accounts payable are proportional to sales and that relationship will be maintained. Bertin typically uses no current liabilities other than accounts payable. Common stock amounted to $425,000 in 1998, and retained earnings were $295,000. Bertin plans to sell new common stock in the amount of $75,000. The firm's profit margin on sales is 6 percent; 40 percent of earnings will be paid out as dividends.

a. What was Bertin's total debt in 1998?
b. How much new, long-term debt financing will be needed in 1999? (Hint: AFN – New stock = New long-term debt.) Do not consider any financing feedback effects.

14-10

Additional Funds Needed

The Booth Company's sales are forecasted to increase from $1,000 in 1998 to $2,000 in 1999. Here is the December 31, 1998, balance sheet:

Cash	$ 100	Accounts payable	$ 50
Accounts receivable	200	Notes payable	150
Inventories	200	Accruals	50
Net fixed assets	500	Long-term debt	400
		Common stock	100
		Retained earnings	250
Total assets	$1,000	Total liabilities and equity	$1,000

Booth's fixed assets were used to only 50 percent of capacity during 1998, but its current assets were at their proper levels. All assets except fixed assets increase at the same rate as sales, and fixed assets would also increase at the same rate if the current excess capacity did not exist. Booth's after-tax profit margin is forecasted to be 5 percent, and its payout ratio will be 60 percent. What is Booth's additional funds needed (AFN) for the coming year? Ignore financing feedback effects.

Spreadsheet Problem

Work the problem in this section only if you are using the computer problem diskette.

14-11
Additional Funds Needed

Use the model in File C14 to solve this problem. Roussakis Industries' 1998 financial statements are shown below.

ROUSSAKIS INDUSTRIES:
BALANCE SHEET AS OF DECEMBER 31, 1998
(MILLIONS OF DOLLARS)

Cash	$ 4.0	Accounts payable	$ 8.0
Receivables	12.0	Notes payable	5.0
Inventories	16.0	Total current liabilities	$13.0
Total current assets	$32.0	Long-term debt	12.0
Net fixed assets	40.0	Common stock	20.0
		Retained earnings	27.0
Total assets	$72.0	Total liabilities and equity	$72.0

ROUSSAKIS INDUSTRIES:
INCOME STATEMENT FOR DECEMBER 31, 1998
(MILLIONS OF DOLLARS)

Sales	$80.0
Operating costs	71.3
EBIT	$ 8.7
Interest	2.0
EBT	$ 6.7
Taxes (40%)	2.7
Net income	$ 4.0
Dividends (40%)	$1.60
Addition to retained earnings	$2.40

Assume that the firm has no excess capacity in fixed assets, that the average interest rate for debt is 12 percent, and that the projected annual sales growth rate for the next 5 years is 15 percent.
a. Roussakis plans to finance its additional funds needed with 50 percent short-term debt and 50 percent long-term debt. Using the percent of sales method, prepare the pro forma financial statements for 1999 through 2003, and then determine (1) additional funds needed, (2) the current ratio, (3) the debt ratio, and (4) the return on equity.

b. Sales growth could be 5 percentage points above or below the projected 15 percent. Determine the effect of such variances on AFN and the key ratios.

c. Perform an analysis to determine the sensitivity of AFN and the key ratios for 2003 to changes in the dividend payout ratio as specified in the following, assuming sales grow at a constant 15 percent. What happens to AFN if the dividend payout ratio (1) is raised from 40 to 70 percent or (2) is lowered from 40 to 20 percent?

MINI CASE

Sue Wilson, the new financial manager of Northwest Chemicals (NWC), an Oregon producer of specialized chemicals for use in fruit orchards, must prepare a financial forecast for 1999. NWC's 1998 sales were $2 billion, and the marketing department is forecasting a 25 percent increase for 1999. Sue thinks the company was operating at full capacity in 1998, but she is not sure about this. The 1998 financial statements, plus some other data, are shown below.

A. 1998 Balance Sheet (millions of dollars)

		PERCENT OF SALES			PERCENT OF SALES
Cash and securities	$ 20	1%	Accounts payable and accruals	$ 100	5%
Accounts receivable	240	12%	Notes payable	100	
Inventories	240	12%	Total current liabilities	$ 200	
Total current assets	$ 500		Long-term debt	100	
Net fixed assets	500	25%	Common stock	500	
			Retained earnings	200	
Total assets	$1,000		Total liabilities and equity	$1,000	

B. 1998 Income Statement (millions of dollars)

		PERCENT OF SALES
Sales	$2,000.00	
Variable costs	1,200.00	60%
Fixed costs	700.00	35%
Earnings before interest and taxes	$ 100.00	
Interest	16.00	
Earnings before taxes	$ 84.00	
Taxes (40%)	33.60	
Net income	$ 50.40	
Dividends (30%)	15.12	
Addition to retained earnings	$ 35.28	

C. Key Ratios

	NWC	INDUSTRY
Basic earning power	10.00%	20.00%
Profit margin	2.52	4.00
Return on equity	7.20	15.60
Days sales outstanding (360 days)	43.20 days	32.00 days
Inventory turnover	8.33×	11.00×

Fixed assets turnover	4.00	5.00
Total assets turnover	2.00	2.50
Debt/assets	30.00%	36.00%
Times interest earned	6.25×	9.40×
Current ratio	2.50	3.00
Payout ratio	30.00%	30.00%
Operating profit margin after taxes (NOPAT/Sales)	3.00%	5.00%
Operating capital requirement (Operating capital/Sales)	45.00%	35.00%
Return on invested capital (NOPAT/Operating capital)	6.67%	14.00%

Assume that you were recently hired as Wilson's assistant, and your first major task is to help her develop the forecast. She asked you to begin by answering the following set of questions.

a. Assume (1) that NWC was operating at full capacity in 1998 with respect to all assets, (2) that all assets must grow proportionally with sales, (3) that accounts payable and accruals will also grow in proportion to sales, and (4) that the 1998 profit margin and dividend payout will be maintained. Under these conditions, what will the company's financial requirements be for the coming year? Use the AFN equation to answer this question.

b. Now estimate the 1999 financial requirements using the percent of sales approach, making an initial forecast plus one additional "pass" to determine the effects of "financing feedbacks." Assume (1) that each type of asset, as well as payables, accruals, and fixed and variable costs, will be the same percent of sales in 1999 as in 1998; (2) that the payout ratio is held constant at 30 percent; (3) that external funds needed are financed 50 percent by notes payable and 50 percent by long-term debt (no new common stock will be issued); and (4) that all debt carries an interest rate of 8 percent.

c. Why do the two methods produce somewhat different AFN forecasts? Which method provides the more accurate forecast?

d. Calculate NWC's forecasted ratios, and compare them with the company's 1998 ratios and with the industry averages. How does NWC compare with the average firm in its industry, and is the company expected to improve during the coming year?

e. Calculate NWC's free cash flow for 1999.

f. Suppose NWC expects sales to grow 15 percent in 2000. In 2001 and all subsequent years, competition will cause NWC's sales to grow at a constant rate of 5 percent. If NWC's operations remain the same (i.e., the items that are a percent of sale will be the same percent of sales in years after 1998 and in 1998), the projected free cash flows for 2000 and 2001 are −$82.50 million and $25.88 million, respectively. After 2001, free cash flows are expected to grow at 5 percent per year. NWC's weighted average cost of capital is 9 percent. What is the value of NWC as of December 31, 1998? (Hint: Find the horizon value at 2001, and then find the present values of the horizon value and the free cash flows.)

g. Suppose you now learn that NWC's 1998 receivables and inventories were in line with required levels, given the firm's credit and inventory policies, but that excess capacity existed with regard to fixed assets. Specifically, fixed assets were operated at only 75 percent of capacity.

  (1) What level of sales could have existed in 1998 with the available fixed assets? What would the fixed assets/sales ratio have been if NWC had been operating at full capacity?

  (2) How would the existence of excess capacity in fixed assets affect the additional funds needed during 1999?

h. Without actually working out the numbers, how would you expect the ratios to change in the situation where excess capacity in fixed assets exists? Explain your reasoning.

i. Based on comparisons between NWC's days sales outstanding (DSO) and inventory turnover ratios with the industry average figures, does it appear that NWC is operating efficiently with respect to its inventories and accounts receivable? If the company were able to bring these ratios into line with the industry averages, what effect would this have on its AFN and its financial ratios? What effect would this have on free cash flow and the value of the company? (Note: Inventories and receivables will be discussed in detail in Chapter 21.)

j. The relationship between sales and the various types of assets is important in financial forecasting. The percent of sales approach, under the assumption that each asset item grows at the same rate as sales, leads to an AFN forecast that is reasonably close to the forecast using the AFN equation. Explain how each of the following factors would affect the accuracy of financial forecasts based on the AFN equation: (1) excess capacity, (2) base stocks of assets, such as shoes in a shoe store, (3) economies of scale in the use of assets, and (4) lumpy assets.

k. (1) How could regression analysis be used to detect the presence of the situations described above and then to improve the financial forecasts? Plot a graph of the following data, which is for a typical well-managed company in NWC's industry, to illustrate your answer.

YEAR	SALES	INVENTORIES
1996	$1,280	$118
1997	1,600	138
1998	2,000	162
1999 (est.)	2,500	192

(2) On the same graph that plots the above data, draw a line which shows how the regression line must appear to justify the use of the AFN formula and the percent of sales forecasting procedure. As a part of your answer, show the growth rate in inventories that results from a 10 percent increase in sales from a sales level of (a) $200 and (b) $2,000 based on both the actual regression line and a *hypothetical* regression line which is linear and which goes through the origin.

l. How would changes in these items affect the AFN? (1) The dividend payout ratio, (2) the profit margin, (3) the capital intensity ratio, and (4) NWC begins buying from its suppliers on terms which permit it to pay after 60 days rather than after 30 days. (Consider each item separately and hold all other things constant.)

Selected Additional References and Cases

The heart of successful financial planning is the sales forecast. On this key subject, see

Pan, Judy, Donald R. Nichols, and O. Maurice Joy, "Sales Forecasting Practices of Large U.S. Industrial Firms," *Financial Management,* Fall 1977, 72–77.

Hirschey, Mark, and James L. Pappas, *Managerial Economics* (Fort Worth, Tex.: Dryden Press, 1996).

Computer modeling is becoming increasingly important. For general references, see

Carleton, Willard T., Charles L. Dick, Jr., and David H. Downes, "Financial Policy Models: Theory and Practice," *Journal of Finance,* December 1973, 691–709.

Francis, Jack Clark, and Dexter R. Rowell, "A Simultaneous Equation Model of the Firm for Financial Analysis and Planning," *Financial Management,* Spring 1978, 29–44.

Grinyer, P. H., and J. Wooller, *Corporate Models Today — A New Tool for Financial Management* (London: Institute of Chartered Accountants, 1978).

Pappas, James L., and George P. Huber, "Probabilistic Short-Term Financial Planning," *Financial Management,* Autumn 1973, 36–44.

Traenkle, J. W., E. B. Cox, and J. A. Bullard, *The Use of Financial Models in Business* (New York: Financial Executives' Research Foundation, 1975).

Considerable effort has been expended to develop integrated financial planning models that identify optimal policies. For one example, see

Myers, Stewart C., and Gerald A. Pogue, "A Programming Approach to Corporate Financial Management," *Journal of Finance,* May 1974, 579–599.

For an article on control, see

Bierman, Harold, "Beyond Cash Flow ROI," *Midland Corporate Finance Journal,* Winter 1988, 36–39.

The Dryden Press Cases in Financial Management: Dryden Request series contains the following applicable cases:

Case 37, "Space-Age Materials, Inc.," Case 38, "Automated Banking Management, Inc.," Case 38A, "Expert Systems," Case 38B, "Medical Management Systems, Inc.," and Case 63, "Dental Records, Inc.," which all focus on using the percent of sales forecasting method to forecast future financing requirements.

CAPITAL STRUCTURE
DECISIONS: THE BASICS

To open its doors, a new business requires capital, and still more capital is needed if the firm is to expand. The required funds can come from many different sources and take many different forms. However, all capital can be classified into two basic types — debt and equity.

Raising capital as debt has several advantages. First, interest is tax deductible, which lowers the effective cost of debt. Second, debtholders are limited to a fixed return, so stockholders do not have to share profits if the business does exceptionally well. Finally, debtholders do not have voting rights, so stockholders can control a business with less money than would otherwise be required.

However, financing with debt also has disadvantages. First, the higher the debt ratio, the greater the risk and thus the higher the interest rate. At some point, rising interest rates overwhelm the tax advantages of debt. Second, if a company falls on hard times, and if its operating income is insufficient to cover interest charges, then stockholders will have to make up the shortfall, and if they cannot, the company may be forced into bankruptcy. Good times may be just around the corner, but too much debt can keep the company from getting there and can wipe out stockholders in the process.

Crown Cork & Seal Company, an $8.0 billion NYSE company, is a good example of a firm that used debt to good advantage. Over a ten-year period, from 1988 to 1998, Crown increased its long-term debt from a minuscule $9 million to a mighty $4 billion. This pushed its debt ratio up to a still-reasonable 42 percent. Crown used the borrowed funds to acquire other companies, and, since it earned more on the acquired assets than its cost of debt, that pushed up its ROE and, consequently, its stock price. Indeed, the stock price rose from $10 to more than $50 over the period.

On the other hand, debt financing is causing severe problems for some airlines, including U.S. Airways. In 1998, U.S. Airways had a long-term debt to capitalization ratio of almost 100 percent; that is, it was financed almost entirely by debt. Further, its annual interest expense was more than $200 million, considerably more than the company's operating income during most of the 1990s. U.S. Airways cannot pay dividends on its common stock, and its very survival is at stake. The airline industry is extremely cyclical, and large amounts of debt put tremendous pressures on a company when earnings turn south.

Companies can use either debt or equity capital to finance their assets. Is one form better than the other? If so, should firms be financed either with all debt or all equity? Or, if the best choice is some mix of debt and equity, what is the optimal mix? In this chapter, we discuss the key facets of the debt-versus-equity, or capital structure, decision. As you read the chapter, think about Crown Cork & Seal and U.S. Airways, and the ways the concepts discussed might aid the managers of these and other companies as they make capital structure decisions.[1]

---

[1]We have divided the material on capital structure into two chapters. Chapter 15 covers the basics, while Chapter 16 provides some extensions related primarily to the theory of capital structure. Both chapters are useful, but Chapter 15 does cover all of the concepts (including theory) needed to understand the material presented in succeeding chapters. Therefore, if time pressures preclude coverage of both chapters, Chapter 16 can be omitted.

One of the most perplexing issues facing financial managers is the relationship between **capital structure,** which is the mix of debt and equity financing, and stock prices. How does capital structure affect stock prices and the cost of capital? Should different industries, and different firms within industries, have different capital structures, and, if so, what factors lead to these differences? Although the optimal capital structure decision is complex and not well understood, the material in this chapter will help you deal with the issues involved.

BUSINESS AND FINANCIAL RISK

In Chapter 5, when we examined risk from the viewpoint of a stock investor, we distinguished between **market risk,** which is measured by the firm's beta coefficient, and **stand-alone risk,** which includes both market risk and an element of risk which can be eliminated by diversification. Now we introduce two new dimensions of risk: (1) **business risk,** or the riskiness of the firm's stock if it uses no debt, and (2) **financial risk,** which is the additional risk placed on the common stockholders as a result of the firm's decision to use debt.[2]

Conceptually, the firm has a certain amount of risk inherent in its operations: this is its business risk. If it uses debt, then, in effect, it partitions its investors into two groups and concentrates most of its business risk on one class of investors—the common stockholders. However, the common stockholders generally demand compensation for assuming more risk and thus require a higher rate of return. In this section, we examine business and financial risk within a stand-alone risk framework, which ignores the benefits of stockholder diversification.

Business Risk

Business risk in a stand-alone sense is a function of the uncertainty inherent in projections of a firm's future return on invested capital (ROIC), defined as follows:

$$ROIC = \frac{NOPAT}{Capital} = \frac{\text{Net income to common stockholders + After-tax interest payments}}{Capital}.$$

Here NOPAT is net operating profit after taxes. If a firm uses no debt, then its interest payments will be zero, its capital will be all equity, and its ROIC will equal its return on equity, ROE:

$$ROIC \text{ (zero debt)} = ROE = \frac{\text{Net income to common stockholders}}{\text{Common equity}}.$$

Therefore, the business risk of a *leverage-free* firm can be measured by the standard deviation of its ROE, σ_{ROE}.

To illustrate, consider Strasburg Electronics Company, a *debt-free (unlevered)* firm. Figure 15-1 gives some clues about the company's business risk. The top graph shows the trend in ROE from 1988 through 1998; this graph gives both security analysts and Strasburg's management an idea of the degree to which ROE has varied in the past and might vary in the future.

---

[2]Preferred stock also adds to financial risk. To simplify matters, we concentrate on debt and common equity in this chapter.

FIGURE 15-1 Strasburg Electronics: Trend in ROE, 1988–1998, and Subjective Probability Distribution of ROE, 1998

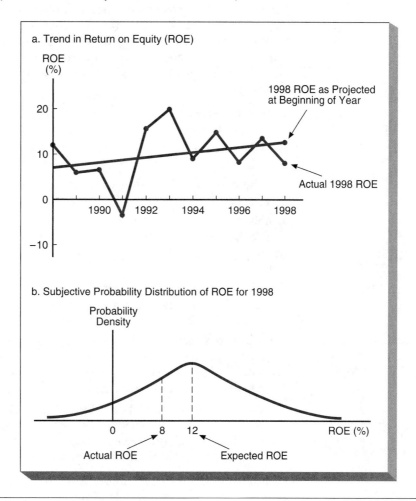

The lower graph shows the beginning-of-year subjectively estimated probability distribution of Strasburg's ROE for 1998, based on the trend line in the top section of Figure 15-1. As both graphs indicate, Strasburg's actual ROE in 1998 was only 8 percent, well below the expected value of 12 percent — 1998 was a bad year.

Strasburg's past fluctuations in ROE were caused by many factors — booms and recessions in the national economy, successful new products introduced both by Strasburg and by its competitors, labor strikes, a fire in Strasburg's main plant, and so on. Similar events will doubtless occur in the future, and when they do, the realized ROE will be higher or lower than the projected level. Further, there is always the possibility that a long-term disaster might strike, permanently depressing the company's earning power; for example, a competitor might introduce a new product that would permanently lower Strasburg's earnings. This uncertainty regarding Strasburg's future ROE, *assuming the firm uses no debt financing,* is defined as the company's *business risk.* Since Strasburg uses no debt, stockholders bear all of the company's business risk.

Business risk varies not only from industry to industry but also among firms in a given industry. Further, business risk can change over time. For example, the electric utilities were regarded for years as having little business risk, but a combination of events in recent years altered the utilities' situation, producing sharp declines in their ROEs and greatly increasing the industry's business risk. Now, food processors and grocery retailers frequently are given as examples of industries with low business risk, while cyclical manufacturing industries such as autos and steel, as well as many small startup companies, are regarded as having especially high business risk.[3]

Business risk depends on a number of factors, the more important of which are listed below:

1. **Demand variability.** The more stable the demand for a firm's products, other things held constant, the lower its business risk.

2. **Sales price variability.** Firms whose products are sold in highly volatile markets are exposed to more business risk than similar firms whose output prices are more stable.

3. **Input cost variability.** Firms whose input costs are highly uncertain are exposed to a high degree of business risk.

4. **Ability to adjust output prices for changes in input costs.** Some firms are better able than others to raise their own output prices when input costs rise. The greater the ability to adjust output prices to reflect cost conditions, the lower the degree of business risk.

5. **Ability to develop new products in a timely, cost-effective manner.** Firms in such high-tech industries as drugs and computers depend on a constant stream of new products. The faster its products become obsolete, the greater a firm's business risk.

6. **Foreign risk exposure.** Firms that generate a high percentage of their earnings overseas are subject to earnings declines due to exchange rate fluctuations. Also, if a firm operates in a politically unstable area, it may be subject to political risks. See Chapter 27 for a further discussion.

7. **The extent to which costs are fixed: operating leverage.** If a high percentage of costs are fixed, hence do not decline when demand falls off, then the firm is exposed to a relatively high degree of business risk. This factor is called *operating leverage,* and it is discussed at length in the next section.

Each of these factors is determined partly by the firm's industry characteristics, but each of them is also controllable to some extent by management. For example, most firms can, through their marketing policies, take actions to stabilize both unit sales and sales prices. However, this stabilization may require spending a great deal on advertising and/or price concessions to get commitments from customers to purchase fixed quantities at fixed prices in the future. Similarly, firms such as Strasburg Electronics can reduce the volatility of future input costs by negotiating long-term labor and materials supply contracts, but they may have to pay prices above the current spot price to obtain these contracts. Many firms also are using hedging techniques to reduce business risk, as we discuss in Chapter 24.

Operating Leverage

As noted above, business risk depends in part on the extent to which a firm builds fixed costs into its operations — if fixed costs are high, even a small decline in sales can lead to a large decline in ROE. So, other things held constant, the higher a firm's fixed costs,

---

[3]We have avoided any discussion of market versus company-specific risk in this section. We note now (1) that any action which increases business risk in the stand-alone risk sense will generally also increase a firm's beta coefficient, and (2) that a part of business risk as we define it will generally be company-specific, hence subject to elimination by diversification by the firm's stockholders. This point is discussed at some length in Chapter 16.

the greater its business risk. Higher fixed costs are generally associated with more highly automated, capital intensive firms and industries. However, businesses that employ highly skilled workers who must be retained and paid even during recessions also have relatively high fixed costs, as do firms with high product development costs, because the amortization of development costs is an element of fixed costs.

If a high percentage of total costs are fixed, then the firm is said to have a high degree of **operating leverage.** In physics, leverage implies the use of a lever to raise a heavy object with a small force. In politics, if people have leverage, their smallest word or action can accomplish a lot. *In business terminology, a high degree of operating leverage, other factors held constant, implies that a relatively small change in sales results in a large change in ROE.*

Figure 15-2 illustrates the concept of operating leverage by comparing the results that Strasburg could expect if it used different degrees of operating leverage. Plan A calls for a relatively small amount of fixed costs, $20,000. Here the firm would not have much automated equipment, so its depreciation, maintenance, property taxes, and so on would be low, but the total operating costs line has a relatively steep slope, indicating that variable costs per unit are higher than they would be if the firm used more operating leverage. Plan B calls for a higher level of fixed costs, $60,000. Here the firm uses automated equipment (with which one operator can turn out a few or many units at the same labor cost) to a much larger extent. The breakeven point is higher under Plan B—breakeven occurs at 60,000 units under Plan B versus only 40,000 units under Plan A.

We can calculate the breakeven quantity by recognizing that *operating breakeven* occurs when ROE = 0, hence when earnings before interest and taxes (EBIT) = 0:[4]

$$EBIT = 0 = PQ - VQ - F.$$

Here P is average sales price per unit of output, Q is units of output, V is variable cost per unit, and F is fixed operating costs. If we solve for the breakeven quantity, Q_{BE}, we get this expression:

$$Q_{BE} = \frac{F}{P - V}.$$

Thus for Plan A,

$$Q_{BE} = \frac{\$20,000}{\$2.00 - \$1.50} = 40,000 \text{ units,}$$

and for Plan B,

$$Q_{BE} = \frac{\$60,000}{\$2.00 - \$1.00} = 60,000 \text{ units.}$$

How does operating leverage affect business risk? *Other things held constant, the higher a firm's operating leverage, the higher its business risk.* This point is demonstrated in Figure 15-3, where we develop probability distributions for ROE under Plans A and B.

The left-hand section of Figure 15-3 graphs the probability distribution of sales that was presented in tabular form in Figure 15-2. The sales probability distribution depends on how demand for the product varies, not on whether the product is manufactured by Plan A or by Plan B. Therefore, the same sales probability distribution applies to both production plans; this distribution has expected sales of $220,000, and it ranges from zero to about $450,000, with a standard deviation of $\sigma_{Sales} = \$92,995$.

---

[4]This definition of breakeven does not include any fixed financial costs because Strasburg is an unlevered firm. If there were fixed financial costs, the firm would suffer an accounting loss at the operating breakeven point. We will introduce financial costs shortly.

| FIGURE 15-2 | Strasburg Electronics: Illustration of Operating Leverage |

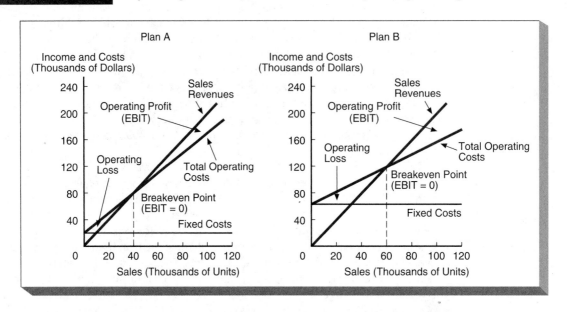

Selling price = $2.00   Selling price = $2.00
Fixed costs = $20,000   Fixed costs = $60,000
Variable costs = $1.50 per unit   Variable costs = $1.00 per unit

| | | | PLAN A | | | | | PLAN B | | | |
PROB-ABILITY	UNITS SOLD, Q	SALES	OPERATING COSTS	OPERATING EBIT	NI	ROE	OPERATING COSTS	OPERATING EBIT	NI	ROE
0.03	0	$ 0	$ 20,000	($20,000)	($12,000)	(6.9%)	$ 60,000	($ 60,000)	($36,000)	(20.6%)
0.07	40,000	80,000	80,000	0	0	0.0	100,000	(20,000)	(12,000)	(6.9)
0.15	60,000	120,000	110,000	10,000	6,000	3.4	120,000	0	0	0.0
0.50	110,000	220,000	185,000	35,000	21,000	12.0	170,000	50,000	30,000	17.1
0.15	160,000	320,000	260,000	60,000	36,000	20.6	220,000	100,000	60,000	34.3
0.07	180,000	360,000	290,000	70,000	42,000	24.0	240,000	120,000	72,000	41.1
0.03	220,000	440,000	350,000	90,000	54,000	30.9	280,000	160,000	96,000	54.9
Expected value		$220,000		$35,000	$21,000	12.0%		$ 50,000	$30,000	17.1%
Standard deviation		$ 92,995		$23,249	$13,949	8.0%		$ 46,497	$27,898	15.9%

NOTES:
a. Strasburg Electronics has a 40 percent federal-plus-state tax rate.
b. The firm uses no debt financing.
c. For simplicity, we assume assets = equity = $175,000 under both plans.

We use the sales probability distribution, together with the operating costs at each sales level, to develop graphs of the ROE probability distributions under Plans A and B. These are shown in the right-hand section of Figure 15-3. Plan B has a higher expected ROE, but this plan also entails a much higher probability of losses. Clearly, Plan B, the one with more fixed costs and a higher degree of operating leverage, is riskier. *In gen-*

FIGURE 15-3   Strasburg Electronics: Analysis of Business Risk

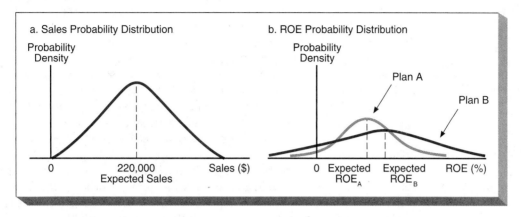

NOTE:
We are using continuous distributions to approximate the discrete distributions contained in Figure 15-2.

eral, holding other factors constant, the higher the degree of operating leverage, the greater the firm's business risk.

To what extent can firms control their operating leverage? To a large extent, operating leverage is determined by technology. Electric utilities, telephone companies, airlines, steel mills, and chemical companies simply *must* have large investments in fixed assets; this results in high fixed costs and operating leverage. Similarly, drug, auto, computer, and similar companies must spend heavily to develop new products, and product-development costs increase operating leverage. Grocery stores, on the other hand, generally have significantly lower fixed costs, hence lower operating leverage. Still, although industry factors do exert a major influence, all firms have some control over their operating leverage. For example, an electric utility can expand its generating capacity by building either a gas-fired or a coal-fired plant. The coal plant would require a larger investment and would have higher fixed costs, but its variable operating costs would be relatively low. The gas-fired plant, on the other hand, would require a smaller investment and would have lower fixed costs, but the variable costs (for gas) would be high. Thus, by its capital budgeting decisions, a utility (or any other company) can influence its operating leverage, hence its business risk.

The concept of operating leverage was originally developed for use in capital budgeting. Mutually exclusive projects which involve alternative methods for producing a given product often have different degrees of operating leverage, hence different breakeven points and different degrees of risk. Strasburg Electronics and many other companies regularly undertake a type of breakeven analysis (the sensitivity analysis discussed in Chapter 13) for each proposed project as a part of their regular capital budgeting process. Still, once a corporation's operating leverage has been established, this factor exerts a major influence on its capital structure decision.

Financial Risk

Financial risk is the additional risk placed on the common stockholders as a result of the decision to finance with debt. Conceptually, stockholders face a certain amount of risk which is inherent in a firm's operations—this is its business risk, which is defined as the uncertainty inherent in projections of future operating income. If a firm uses debt (financial leverage), this concentrates the business risk on common stockholders. To illustrate, suppose ten people decide to form a corporation to manufacture disk drives. There is a certain amount of business risk in the operation. If the firm is capitalized only with common equity, and if each person buys 10 percent of the stock, then each investor shares equally in the business risk. However, suppose the firm is capitalized with 50 percent debt and 50 percent equity, with five of the investors putting up their capital as debt and the other five putting up their money as equity. In this case, the five investors who put up the equity will have to bear all of the business risk, so the common stock will be twice as risky as it would have been had the firm been financed only with equity. Thus, the use of debt, or **financial leverage,** concentrates the firm's business risk on its stockholders. This concentration of business risk occurs because debtholders, who receive fixed interest payments, bear none of the business risk.

To illustrate the concentration of business risk, again consider Strasburg Electronics. Strasburg has $175,000 in assets and is all-equity financed.[5] If the firm were using Plan A from Figure 15-2, then its expected ROE would be 12.0 percent with a standard deviation of 8.0 percent. Now suppose the firm decides to change its capital structure by issuing $87,500 of debt at $k_d = 10\%$ and using these funds to replace $87,500 of equity. Its expected return on equity (which would now be only $87,500) would rise from 12 to 18 percent:

	OLD (UNLEVERAGED) SITUATION (SEE FIGURE 15-2)	NEW (LEVERAGED) SITUATION
Expected EBIT (unchanged)	$35,000	$35,000
Interest (10% on $87,500 of debt)	0	8,750
Earnings before taxes	$35,000	$26,250
Taxes (40%)	14,000	10,500
Net income	$21,000	$15,750
Expected ROE	$21,000/$175,000 = 12%	$15,750/$87,500 = 18%

Thus, the use of debt would "leverage up" the expected ROE from 12 percent to 18 percent. Note, however, that the expected return on invested capital (ROIC) is [$35,000(0.6)]/$175,000 = 0.12 = 12% in both the unleveraged and leveraged cases.

The total dollar return to all investors (both bondholders and stockholders) is Net income = $21,000 when no debt is used, but Net income + Interest = $15,750 + $8,750 = $24,500 when $87,500 of debt is used. Thus, the use of debt allows more of the $35,000 of EBIT to flow through to investors: $24,500 − $21,000 = $3,500. The leverage improvement results from interest tax savings—the interest expense of $8,750 reduced taxes by T(Interest) = 0.40($8,750) = $3,500. Thus, the use of debt shields a portion of a company's earnings from the tax collector.

Since raising half of its capital as debt would increase the expected dollar return to investors and leverage up the expected ROE to stockholders, should the firm use this amount of, or even more, debt financing? The answer would definitely be "yes" except

[5]A firm in business for at least ten years would likely have far more than $175,000 in assets. We are purposely keeping Strasburg Electronics small so that we may focus on the concepts without being overwhelmed by the numbers. Also note that, to be consistent with capital structure theory, we should be working with market values of securities rather than book values of assets. We are using book values at this point to simplify the illustration, but we will discuss market value relationships later in the chapter. In this regard, see Haim Levy and Robert Brooks, "Financial Break-Even Analysis and the Value of the Firm," *Financial Management,* Autumn 1986, 22–26.

for one problem: The use of financial leverage also increases the risk faced by the equity investors, and this higher risk will tend to offset the benefits of debt. To illustrate, suppose EBIT actually turned out to be $5,000 rather than the expected $35,000. If the firm used no debt, then ROE would decline from 12.0 percent to 1.7 percent. However, with debt financing, ROE would fall from 18.0 to –2.6 percent:

	ZERO DEBT	$87,500 OF DEBT
Actual EBIT	$5,000	$5,000
Interest (10%)	0	8,750
Earnings before taxes	$5,000	–$3,750
Taxes (40%)	2,000	– 1,500
Net income	$3,000	–$2,250
Actual ROE	1.7%	–2.6%
Expected ROE	12.0%	18.0%

A more complete analysis of the effects of leverage on Strasburg's ROE is illustrated in Figure 15-4. The two lines in the top graph show the ROE that would exist at different levels of EBIT under the two different capital structures. The greater the use of financial leverage, the more sensitive ROE is to changes in EBIT.

The lower panel of Figure 15-4 shows the effects of leverage on the firm's ROE probability distribution. With zero debt, expected ROE is 12 percent, and it has a relatively tight distribution. With 50 percent debt, the expected ROE rises to 18 percent, but the ROE distribution is flatter, indicating a more risky situation. In fact, the standard deviation of ROE is 8.0 percent at zero debt, but exactly twice as high, 16.0 percent, at 50 percent debt.

Our conclusions from this analysis are as follows:

1. The use of debt increases a firm's expected ROE, provided the expected return on invested capital exceeds the after-tax interest rate.

2. The standard deviation of ROE if the firm uses zero financial leverage, $\sigma_{ROE(U)}$, is a measure of the firm's business risk, and σ_{ROE} at any debt level is a measure of the stand-alone risk borne by stockholders. $\sigma_{ROE} = \sigma_{ROE(U)}$ if the firm does not use any financial leverage, but if the firm does use debt, then $\sigma_{ROE} > \sigma_{ROE(U)}$, because business risk is being concentrated on the stockholders.

3. The difference between σ_{ROE} and $\sigma_{ROE(U)}$ is a measure of the risk-increasing effects of financial leverage:

$$\text{Stand-alone risk} = \sigma_{ROE}.$$

$$\text{Business risk} = \sigma_{ROE(U)}.$$

$$\text{Financial risk} = \sigma_{ROE} - \sigma_{ROE(U)}.$$

In our example,

$$\text{Financial risk} = 16.0\% - 8.0\% = 8.0\%.$$

4. Operating leverage and financial leverage normally work in the same way; they both increase expected ROE, but they also increase the risk borne by stockholders.[6]

---

[6]Note that for operating leverage to benefit shareholders, the firm must be operating at a sales level above the breakeven point, and for financial leverage to be of benefit, the after-tax cost of debt must be less than the return on invested capital. Normally, when managers accept capital budgeting projects and make related financing decisions, they expect the firm to be operating above the breakeven point, and they also expect ROIC to exceed the after-tax cost of debt.

| FIGURE 15-4 | Strasburg Electronics: Effects of Financial Leverage on ROE |

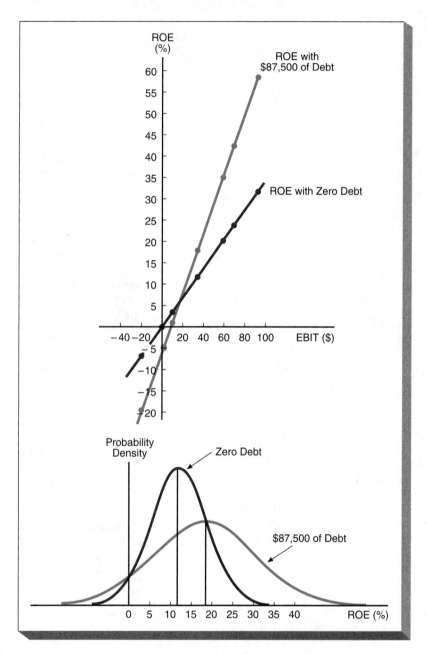

Operating leverage affects the firm's business risk, financial leverage affects the firm's financial risk, and they both affect the firm's stand-alone risk.

SELF-TEST
QUESTIONS

What is business risk, and how can it be measured?

What are some determinants of business risk?

What is financial risk, and how can it be measured?

What is operating leverage? What are the similarities between operating leverage and financial leverage?

CAPITAL STRUCTURE THEORY

In the previous section, we demonstrated that the use of financial leverage typically increases stockholders' expected returns, but, at the same time, it increases their risk. The question managers face, then, is this: Is the increase in expected return sufficient to compensate stockholders for the increase in risk? To help answer this question, it is useful to examine capital structure theory. Although theory does not provide all of the answers, it does provide insights into the effects of debt versus equity financing. Thus, an understanding of capital structure theory will aid managers in establishing their firms' optimal capital structures. This section provides the basics of capital structure theory, while Chapter 16 contains a more detailed discussion.

Modern capital structure theory began in 1958, when Professors Franco Modigliani and Merton Miller (hereafter MM) published what has been called the most influential finance article ever written.[7] MM proved, but under a very restrictive set of assumptions, that a firm's value is unaffected by its capital structure. Thus, MM's results suggest that it does not matter how a firm finances its operations, because at least under their assumptions, capital structure is irrelevant. One of the assumptions needed by MM to derive their results was the absence of taxes, both corporate and personal. With zero taxes, the increase in return to stockholders resulting from the use of leverage is exactly offset by the increase in risk. Thus, at any level of debt, the return to stockholders is just commensurate with the risk assumed, hence there is no net benefit to using financial leverage.

Despite the unrealistic assumptions, MM's irrelevance result is extremely important. By indicating the conditions under which capital structure is irrelevant, MM also provided us with some clues about what is required for capital structure to be relevant and hence to affect a firm's value.

The Effect of Taxes

MM published a follow-up paper in which they relaxed the assumption that there are no corporate taxes.[8] The tax code allows corporations to deduct interest payments as an expense. However, dividend payments to stockholders are not deductible. This differential treatment results in a net benefit to financial leverage and thus encourages corporations to use debt. Indeed, MM demonstrated that if all their other assumptions hold, this differential treatment leads to a situation which calls for 100 percent debt financing.

Several years later, Merton Miller (this time without Modigliani) extended the analysis to include personal taxes.[9] He noted that all of the income from bonds generally comes as interest, which is taxed as personal income at rates going up to 39.6 percent, while income from stocks generally comes partly from dividends and partly from capital gains. Further, capital gains are taxed at a maximum rate of 20 percent, and this tax is deferred until the stock is sold and the gain realized. If stock is held until the owner dies, no capital gains tax whatever must be paid. So, on balance, common stock returns are taxed at significantly lower effective rates than debt returns.

Because of the tax situation, investors are willing to accept relatively low before-tax returns on stock vis-à-vis the before-tax returns on bonds. For example, an investor

---

[7]Franco Modigliani and Merton H. Miller, "The Cost of Capital, Corporation Finance, and the Theory of Investment," *American Economic Review,* June 1958. Modigliani and Miller both won Nobel prizes for their work.

[8]Franco Modigliani and Merton H. Miller, "Corporate Income Taxes and the Cost of Capital: A Correction," *American Economic Review* 53, June 1963, 433–443.

[9]Merton H. Miller, "Debt and Taxes," *Journal of Finance* 32, May 1977, 261–275.

might require a return of 10 percent on Firm B's bonds, and if stock income were taxed at the same rate as bond income, the required rate of return on Firm B's stock might be 16 percent because of the stock's greater risk. However, in view of the favorable tax treatment of returns on the stock, investors might be willing to accept a before-tax return of only 14 percent on the stock.

Thus, as Miller pointed out, (1) the *deductibility of interest* favors the use of debt financing, but (2) the *favorable tax treatment of income from stocks* lowers the required rate of return on stock and thus favors the use of equity financing. It is difficult to say what the net effect of these two factors is. Most observers believe that interest deductibility has the stronger effect, hence that our tax system still favors the corporate use of debt. However, that effect is reduced by the lower capital gains tax rate.

One can observe changes in corporate financing patterns following major changes in tax rates. For example, in 1993 the top personal tax rate on interest and dividends was raised sharply, but the capital gains tax rate was not increased, and it was lowered in 1997. This resulted in an increased use of equity financing.

The Effect of Bankruptcy Costs

MM's results also depend on the assumption that there are no bankruptcy costs. However, bankruptcy can be quite costly. Firms in bankruptcy have very high legal and accounting expenses, and they also have a hard time retaining customers, suppliers, and employees. Moreover, bankruptcy often forces a firm to liquidate and to sell assets for less than they would be worth if the firm were to continue operating. Assets such as plant and equipment are often illiquid because they are configured to a company's individual needs, and also because they are difficult to disassemble and move.

Note too that the *threat of bankruptcy*, not just bankruptcy per se, brings about problems. Key employees jump ship, suppliers refuse to grant credit, customers seek more stable suppliers, and lenders demand higher interest rates or even refuse to extend credit.

Bankruptcy-related problems are most likely to arise when a firm has a lot of debt in its capital structure. Therefore, potential bankruptcy costs discourage firms from pushing their use of debt to excessive levels.

Bankruptcy-related costs depend on three things: (1) the probability of bankruptcy, (2) the costs the firm will incur if financial distress arises, and (3) the adverse effects that the potential for bankruptcy has on current operations. Firms whose earnings are more volatile, all else equal, face a greater chance of bankruptcy and, therefore, should use less debt than more stable firms. This is consistent with our earlier point that firms with a high degree of operating leverage, and thus greater business risk, should limit their use of financial leverage. Likewise, firms which would face high costs in the event of financial distress should rely less heavily on debt. For example, firms whose assets are illiquid and thus would have to be sold at "fire sale" prices should limit their use of debt financing. Finally, firms such as airlines, whose current sales are affected by anything that worries potential customers, should limit their use of debt.

A firm whose value primarily is due to growth opportunities and not to assets in place suffers from both a high cost of financial distress and from adverse effects on current operations. Consider a software developer versus a hotel chain. In the event of distress or liquidation, the hotel chain can raise funds by selling property. In contrast, the software developer cannot sell its assets, which consist primarily of its employees' intellectual capital. To avoid defaulting on loans, the software developer must reduce expenses, either by laying off employees or by cutting R&D. But, both these actions have significant negative impacts on the value of the company, making bankruptcy even more likely. As this example shows, potential financial distress is an especially serious situation for high-tech companies.

Trade-Off Theory

Research following the MM papers has led to a "trade-off theory of leverage," in which firms trade off the benefits of debt financing (favorable corporate tax treatment) against higher interest rates and bankruptcy costs. A summary of the trade-off theory is expressed graphically in Figure 15-5. Here are some observations about the figure:

1. The fact that interest is deductible makes debt less expensive than common or preferred stock. In effect, the government pays part of the cost of debt capital, or, to put it another way, debt provides *tax shelter benefits*. As a result, using debt causes more of the firm's operating income (EBIT) to flow through to investors, so the more debt a company uses, the higher its value and stock price. Under the MM assumptions, when corporate taxes are considered, a firm's stock price will be maximized if it uses 100 percent debt. The line labeled "MM Result Incorporating the Effects of Corporate Taxation" in Figure 15-5 expresses this relationship.

2. In the real world, firms rarely use 100 percent debt. One reason is because of the favorable personal tax treatment of income from stocks. However, the primary reason is that firms limit their use of debt to reduce the probability of financial distress (bankruptcy). Also, the interest rate on debt becomes prohibitively high at high debt levels.

3. There is some threshold level of debt, labeled D_1 in Figure 15-5, below which the probability of bankruptcy is so low as to be immaterial. Beyond D_1, however,

---

FIGURE 15-5   Effect of Leverage on Value of Stock: The Trade-Off Theory

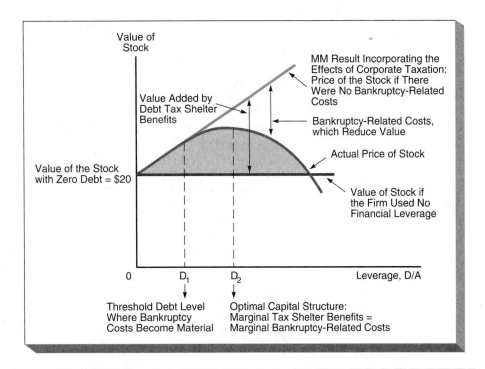

bankruptcy-related costs and rising interest rates become increasingly important, and they reduce the tax benefits of debt at an increasing rate. In the range from D_1 to D_2, bankruptcy-related costs reduce but do not completely offset the tax benefits of debt, so the firm's stock price rises (but at a decreasing rate) as its debt ratio increases. However, beyond D_2, bankruptcy-related costs exceed the tax benefits, so from this point on increasing the debt ratio lowers the value of the stock. Therefore, D_2 is the optimal capital structure.

4. Although it is not shown in Figure 15-5, there is a relationship between the firm's stock price and its weighted average cost of capital. As a firm uses more and more debt, its weighted average cost of capital first decreases, then reaches a minimum, and eventually begins to rise. Moreover, the minimum weighted average cost of capital occurs where the stock price is maximized—at Point D_2 in Figure 15-5. Thus, the same capital structure that maximizes the stock price also minimizes the overall cost of capital.

5. Both theoretical and empirical evidence support the preceding discussion. However, statistical problems prevent us from precisely identifying Points D_1 and D_2. So, while theoretical and empirical work supports the general shape of the curves in Figure 15-5, these curves must be taken as approximations, not as precisely defined functions. It is worth noting, however, that many theoretical models show that the maximum value of an optimally levered firm is from 10 to 20 percent greater than an unlevered firm. These models also indicate that the optimal amount of leverage is from 30 to 60 percent. These results contrast sharply with the case in which bankruptcy costs are ignored, in which the optimal leverage is 100 percent and the value of the levered firm can be more than 70 percent greater than an unlevered firm (depending on corporate tax rates and the firm's ROIC).

6. A disturbing empirical contradiction to capital structure theory as expressed in Figure 15-5 is the fact that many large, successful firms such as Intel and Microsoft use far less debt than the theory suggests. This point led to the development of the signaling theory, which is discussed next.

Signaling Theory

One of MM's assumptions is that investors and managers have exactly the same information about a firm's prospects—this is called **symmetric information.** However, managers often have better information than outside investors. This is called **asymmetric information,** and it has an important effect on capital structure. To see why, consider two situations, one in which a company's managers know that its prospects are extremely good (Firm G) and one in which the managers know that the future looks bad (Firm B).

Now suppose Firm G's R&D labs have just discovered a nonpatentable cure for the common cold. They want to keep the new product a secret as long as possible to delay competitors' entry into the market. Firm G must build plants to make the new product, so capital must be raised. How should Firm G's management raise the needed capital? If the firm sells stock, then, when profits from the new product start flowing in, the price of the stock would rise sharply, and the purchasers of the new stock would make a bonanza. The current stockholders (including the managers) would also do well, but not as well as they would have done if the company had not sold stock before the price increased, because then they would not have had to share the benefits of the new product with the new stockholders. *Therefore, one would expect a firm with very favorable prospects to try to avoid selling stock and, rather, to raise any required new capital by other means, including using debt beyond the normal optimal capital structure.*[10]

Now let's consider the bad firm, Firm B. Suppose its managers have information that new orders are off sharply because a competitor has installed new technology which has improved its products' quality. Firm B must upgrade its own facilities, at a high cost, just to maintain its current sales. As a result, its return on investment will fall (but not by as much as if it took no action, which would lead to a 100 percent loss through bankruptcy). How should Firm B raise the needed capital? Here the situation is just the reverse of that facing Firm G. *Firm B, because of its unfavorable prospects, would want to sell stock, which would mean bringing in new investors to share the losses!*[11]

The conclusions here are (1) that firms with extremely good prospects prefer to finance with debt, whereas (2) firms with poor prospects like to finance with stock. How should you, as an investor, react to this conclusion? You ought to say,

> If I see that a company plans to issue stock, this should worry me because I know that management would not want to issue stock if future prospects looked good, but it would want to issue stock if things looked bad. Therefore, I should lower my estimate of the firm's value, other things held constant.

The negative reaction should be stronger if the stock sale were by a large, established company such as GM or IBM, which has many financing options, than if it were by a small, unlisted company such as GeneSplicer. For GeneSplicer, a stock sale might signify truly extraordinary investment opportunities that cannot be exploited without raising new equity.

If you agree with the above answer, your views are consistent with those of sophisticated portfolio managers of institutions such as Morgan Guaranty Trust, Fidelity Investments, Prudential Insurance, and so forth. *So, in a nutshell, the announcement of a stock offering by a mature firm that has financing alternatives is taken as a signal that the firm's prospects as seen by its management are not bright.* This, in turn, suggests that when a mature firm announces a new stock offering, the price of its stock should decline. Empirical studies have shown that this situation does indeed exist.[12]

What is the implication of signaling theory for capital structure decisions? The answer is that firms should, in normal times, maintain a **reserve borrowing capacity** which can be used in the event that some especially good investment opportunity comes along. *This means that firms should, in normal times, use less debt than is suggested by the tax benefit/bankruptcy cost trade-off model expressed in Figure 15-5.*

Using Debt to Constrain Managers

In Chapter 1 we stated that agency problems may arise if managers and shareholders have different objectives. Such conflicts are particularly likely when the firm's managers have too much cash at their disposal. Then managers can use this cash to finance

---

[10]It would be illegal for Firm G's managers to personally purchase more shares on the basis of their inside knowledge of the new product. They could be sent to jail if they did.

[11]Of course, Firm B would have to make certain disclosures when it offered new shares to the public, but it might be able to meet the legal requirements without fully disclosing management's worst fears.

[12]Paul Asquith and David W. Mullins, Jr., "The Impact of Initiating Dividend Payments on Shareholders' Wealth," *Journal of Business*, January 1983, 77–96.

pet projects or for perquisites such as nicer offices, corporate jets, and tickets to sporting events, all of which may do little to raise stock prices.[13] By contrast, managers with constraints on free cash flow, such as commitments to make interest and principal payments, are less able to make wasteful expenditures. This is called "bonding" the free cash flow.

Firms can reduce, or bond, free cash flow in a variety of ways. One way is to funnel it back to shareholders through higher dividends or stock repurchases. Another alternative is to shift the capital structure toward more debt in the hope that higher debt service requirements will force managers to become more disciplined. If debt is not serviced as required, the firm will be forced into bankruptcy, in which case its managers would likely lose their jobs. Therefore, a manager is less likely to buy that expensive new corporate jet if the firm has large debt service requirements.

Leveraged buyouts (LBOs) bond free cash flow. In an LBO debt is used to finance the purchase of a company's shares, after which the firm "goes private." Many leveraged buyouts, which were especially common during the late 1980s, were designed specifically to reduce corporate waste.

Of course, increasing debt to bond free cash flow has a downside: It increases the risk of bankruptcy, which can be costly. One observer has argued that adding debt to a firm's capital structure is like putting a dagger pointing at the driver into the steering wheel of a car.[14] The dagger motivates you to drive more carefully, but you may get stabbed if someone runs into you, even if you are being careful. The analogy applies to corporations in the following sense: Higher debt forces managers to be more careful with shareholders' money, but even well-run firms could face bankruptcy (get stabbed) if some event beyond their control occurs. To continue the analogy, the capital structure decision comes down to deciding how big a dagger stockholders should employ to keep managers in line.

If you find our discussion of capital structure theory imprecise and somewhat unsatisfying, you are not alone. In truth, no one knows how to identify precisely a firm's optimal capital structure, or how to measure exactly the effects of capital structure on stock prices and the cost of capital. In practice, capital structure decisions must be made by combining judgment and numerical analysis. Still, an understanding of the theoretical issues presented here can help you make better judgments on capital structure issues.[15]

| SELF-TEST QUESTIONS | In what sense did MM's original theory produce an "irrelevance result"? |

In what sense did MM's original theory produce an "irrelevance result"?

How do corporate and personal taxes affect firms' capital structure decisions?

Explain how "asymmetric information" and "signals" affect capital structure decisions.

What is meant by *reserve borrowing capacity,* and why is it important to firms?

How can the use of debt serve to discipline firms' managers?

---

[13]If you don't believe corporate managers can waste money, read Bryan Burrough, *Barbarians at the Gate* (New York: Harper & Row, 1990), the story of the takeover of RJR-Nabisco.

[14]Ben Bernake, "Is There Too Much Corporate Debt?" Federal Reserve Bank of Philadelphia *Business Review,* September/October 1989, 3–13.

[15]One of the authors can report firsthand the usefulness of financial theory in the actual establishment of corporate capital structures. In recent years, he has served as a consultant to several of the regional telephone companies established after the breakup of AT&T, as well as to several large electric utilities. On the basis of finance theory and computer models which simulated results under a range of conditions, the companies were able to specify "optimal capital structure ranges" with at least a reasonable degree of confidence. Without finance theory, setting a target capital structure would have amounted to little more than throwing darts.

SETTING THE TARGET CAPITAL STRUCTURE WHEN CASH FLOWS ARE PERPETUITIES

Capital structure theory suggests that each firm has an optimal capital structure, one that maximizes its value and minimizes its overall cost of capital. However, research on capital structure theory also points out that there are many contradictory issues regarding capital structure decisions, and that theory cannot be used to specify a precisely optimal structure for a firm. In this section, we illustrate how a firm with perpetual cash flows might actually set its target capital structure. The example will reinforce many of the concepts discussed in previous sections, as well as help you understand how managers deal with real-world capital structure decisions. As you will see, actual capital structure decisions are based on *judgment,* but judgment supported by quantitative analysis plus an awareness of the theoretical issues we have discussed.

Hill Software Systems

Hill Software Systems (HSS) was founded in 1980 to develop and market a new type of graphics software for personal computers. The basic program was written and patented by Mark Hill, HSS's founder. Hill owns a majority of the stock, although a significant portion is held by institutional investors. The company has no debt, and HSS's key financial data are shown in Table 15-1. Assets are carried at a book value of $1 million, so the common equity also has a balance sheet value of $1 million. However, these balance sheet figures are not very meaningful because (1) the asset figures do not reflect the value of patents and (2) the fixed assets were purchased some years ago at prices lower than today's.

Mark Hill plans to retire shortly, and he wants to sell a major part of his stock to the public, using the proceeds to diversify his personal portfolio. As a part of the planning process, the question of capital structure has arisen. Should the firm continue its policy of using no debt, or should it recapitalize? And if it does decide to substitute some debt for equity, how far should it go? As in all such decisions, the correct answer is that *it should choose that capital structure which maximizes the value of the stock.* If the stock price is maximized, then the cost of capital will simultaneously be minimized.[16]

To simplify the analysis, we assume that the long-run demand for HSS's products is not expected to grow, so *its EBIT is expected to continue at $4 million indefinitely.* (However, future sales may turn out to be different from the expected level, so realized EBIT may be more or less than the expected $4 million.) Also, since the company has no need for new capital, *all of its income will be paid out as dividends.*

Now assume that HSS's treasurer consults with the firm's investment bankers and learns that debt can be sold, but the more debt used, the riskier the debt and, of course, the higher its interest rate, k_d. Also, the bankers state that the more debt HSS uses, the greater the riskiness of its stock, hence the higher its required rate of return on equity, k_s. Estimates of k_d, beta, and k_s at different debt levels are given in Figure 15-6, along with a graph of the relationship between k_s and debt level.

Given the data in Table 15-1, along with those in Figure 15-6, we can determine HSS's total market value, V, at different capital structures, and we can then use this

---

[16]In general, a firm's stock price is maximized when its total market value is maximized. However, in some relatively rare situations, a firm's stock price is greatest when its total value is less than maximum. To reach such a situation, the firm's bondholders must lose some value, and a portion of this loss is transferred to the firm's stockholders.

TABLE 15-1	Data on Hill Software Systems

Balance Sheet as of December 31, 1998

Current assets	$ 500,000	Debt	$ 0
Net fixed assets	500,000	Common equity (1.0 million shares outstanding)	1,000,000
Total assets	$1,000,000	Total claims	$1,000,000

Income Statement for 1998

Sales		$20,000,000
Fixed operating costs	$ 4,000,000	
Variable operating costs	12,000,000	16,000,000
Earnings before interest and taxes (EBIT)		$ 4,000,000
Interest		0
Taxable income		$ 4,000,000
Taxes (40% federal-plus-state)		1,600,000
Net income		$ 2,400,000

Other Data

1. Earnings per share = EPS = $2,400,000/1,000,000 shares = $2.40.
2. Dividends per share = DPS = $2,400,000/1,000,000 shares = $2.40. Thus, the company has a 100 percent payout ratio.
3. Book value per share = $1,000,000/1,000,000 shares = $1.
4. Market price per share = P_0 = $20. Thus, the stock sells at 20 times its book value.
5. Price/earnings ratio = P/E = $20/2.40 = 8.33 times.
6. Dividend yield = DPS/P_0 = $2.40/$20 = 12%.

information to establish the company's stock price as a function of its capital structure. These equations are used in the analysis:[17]

$$\text{Firm value: } V = D + S. \tag{15-1}$$

$$\text{Equity value: } S = \frac{\text{Dividend}}{k_s} = \frac{\text{Net income}}{k_s} = \frac{(\text{EBIT} - k_d D)(1 - T)}{k_s}. \tag{15-2}$$

$$\text{Stock price: } P_0 = \frac{\text{DPS}}{k_s} = \frac{\text{EPS}}{k_s}. \tag{15-3}$$

$$\text{Cost of capital: WACC} = (D/V)(k_d)(1 - T) + (S/V)(k_s). \tag{15-4}$$

We first substitute values for k_d, D, and k_s into Equation 15-2 to obtain values for S, the market value of common equity, at each level of debt, D, and we then sum S and D to find the total value of the firm. Table 15-2 and Figure 15-7, which plots selected data from the table, were developed by this process. The values shown in Columns 1, 2, and 3 of Table 15-2 were taken from Figure 15-6, while those in Column 4 were obtained by solving Equation 15-2 at different debt levels. The values given in Column 5 were obtained by summing Columns 1 and 4, D + S = V.

---

[17]Note that Equations 15-1 through 15-4 do not stem from a particular capital structure theory—they do not require acceptance of MM or any other theory. Rather, they are definitions and basic DCF valuation equations for perpetual cash flows.

FIGURE 15-6   HSS's Costs of Debt and Equity and Beta

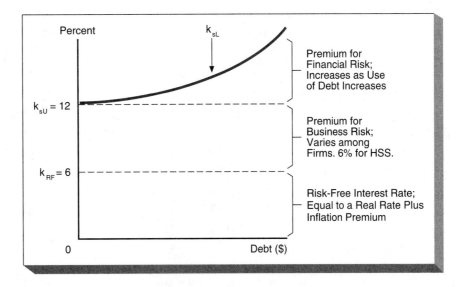

AMOUNT BORROWED[a] (1)	INTEREST RATE ON ALL DEBT, k_d (2)	ESTIMATED BETA COEFFICIENT OF STOCK, b^b (3)	REQUIRED RATE OF RETURN ON STOCK, k_s^c (4)
$ 0	—	1.50	12.0%
2,000,000	8.0%	1.55	12.2
4,000,000	8.3	1.65	12.6
6,000,000	9.0	1.80	13.2
8,000,000	10.0	2.00	14.0
10,000,000	12.0	2.30	15.2
12,000,000	15.0	2.70	16.8
14,000,000	18.0	3.25	19.0

[a]HSS is unable to borrow more than $14 million because of limitations on borrowing in its corporate charter.
[b]Note that the beta coefficient estimates do not correspond to Hamada's equation. The betas given here are subjective estimates furnished by investment bankers. See Chapters 13 and 16 for more discussion of Hamada's equation.
[c]We assume here that k_{RF} = 6% and k_M = 10%. Therefore, at zero debt, k_s = 6% + (10% − 6%)1.5 = 12%. Other values of k_s are calculated similarly.

To see how the stock prices shown in Column 6 of Table 15-2 were developed, visualize this series of events:

1. Initially, HSS has no debt. The firm's value is $20 million, or $20 for each of its 1 million shares. (See the top line of Table 15-2.)

2. Management announces a decision to change the capital structure; legally, the firm *must* make an explicit announcement or run the risk of having stockholders sue the directors. Any debt issued will be used to buy back stock. Because HSS is not growing, it does not require additional capital.

TABLE 15-2	HSS's Value, Stock Price, and Cost of Capital at Different Debt Levels

VALUE OF DEBT, D (IN MILLIONS) (1)	k_d (2)	k_s (3)	VALUE OF STOCK, S (IN MILLIONS) (4)	VALUE OF FIRM, V (IN MILLIONS) (1) + (4) = (5)	STOCK PRICE, P_0 (6)	D/V (7)	WACC (8)
$ 0.0	—	12.0%	$20.000	$20.000	$20.00	0.0%	12.0%
2.0	8.0%	12.2	18.885	20.885	20.89	9.6	11.5
4.0	8.3	12.6	17.467	21.467	21.47	18.6	11.2
6.0	**9.0**	**13.2**	**15.727**	**21.727**	**21.73**	**27.6**	**11.0**
8.0	10.0	14.0	13.714	21.714	21.71	36.8	11.1
10.0	12.0	15.2	11.053	21.053	21.05	47.5	11.4
12.0	15.0	16.8	7.857	19.857	19.86	60.4	12.1
14.0	18.0	19.0	3.158	17.158	17.16	81.6	12.3

NOTES:

a. The data in Columns 1 through 3 were taken from Figure 15-6.

b. The values for S in Column 4 were found by use of Equation 15-2.

$$S = \frac{\text{Net income}}{k_s} = \frac{(\text{EBIT} - k_d D)(1 - T)}{k_s}.$$

For example, at D = $0,

$$S = \frac{(\$4.0 - 0)(0.6)}{0.12} = \frac{\$2.4}{0.12} = \$20.0 \text{ million,}$$

and at D = $6.0,

$$S = \frac{[\$4.0 - 0.09(\$6.0)](0.6)}{0.132} = \frac{\$2.076}{0.132} = \$15.727 \text{ million.}$$

c. The values for V in Column 5 were obtained as the sum of D + S. For example, at D = $6.0, V = $6.0 + $15.727 = $21.727 million.

d. The stock prices shown in Column 6 are equal to the value of the firm as shown in Column 5 divided by the original number of shares outstanding, which, in this case, is 1 million. The logic behind this procedure is explained in the text.

e. Column 7 is found by dividing Column 1 by Column 5. For example, at D = $6.0, D/V = $6.0/$21.727 = 27.6%.

f. Column 8 is found by use of Equation 15-4. For example, at D = $6.0,
WACC = (D/V)(k_d)(1 − T) + (S/V)(k_s)
= (0.276)(9%)(0.6) + (0.724)(13.2%) = 11.0%.

g. At $14.0 million of debt, EBIT declines from $4 million to $3.52 million.

h. The row in boldface indicates the optimal amount of debt.

3. The values shown in Columns 1 through 5 of Table 15-2 are estimated as described previously. The major institutional investors, and the large brokerage companies which advise individual investors, have analysts just as capable of making these estimates as the firm's management. These analysts would start making their own estimates as soon as HSS announced the planned change in leverage, and they would presumably reach conclusions similar to those of the HSS analysts.

4. HSS's stockholders initially own the entire company. (There are not yet any bondholders.) They see, or are told by their advisor-analysts, that very shortly the value of the enterprise will rise from $20 million to some higher amount, presumably the maximum attainable, which is $21,727,000. Thus, they anticipate that the value of the firm will increase by $1,727,000.

FIGURE 15-7   Relationship between HSS's Capital Structure,
Cost of Capital, and Stock Price

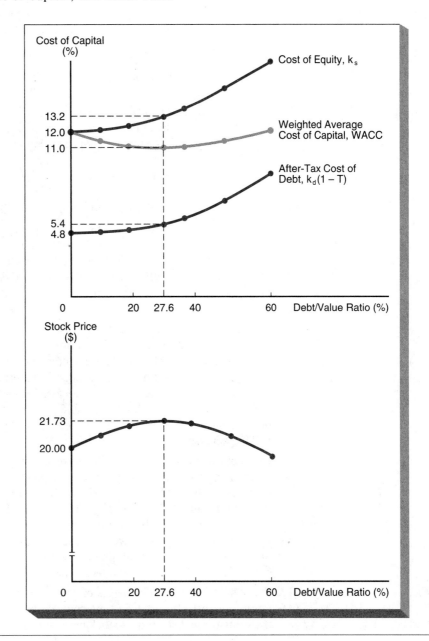

5. This additional $1,727,000 will accrue to the firm's current stockholders. Since there are 1 million shares of stock, each share will rise in value by $1.73, or from $20 to $21.73.

6. This price increase will occur *before* the transaction is completed. To see why, suppose the stock price remained at $20 after the announcement of the recapitalization plan. Shrewd investors would immediately recognize that the stock's price will soon go up to $21.73, and they would place orders to buy at any price below $21.73. This buying pressure would quickly run the price up to $21.73, at which point it

would remain constant. Thus, $21.73 is the *equilibrium stock price* for HSS once the decision to recapitalize is announced.

7. The firm sells $6 million of bonds at an interest rate of 9 percent. This money is used to buy stock at the market price, which is now $21.73, so 276,116 shares are repurchased:

$$\text{Shares repurchased} = \frac{\$6,000,000}{\$21.73} = 276,116.$$

8. The value of the equity after the 276,116 shares have been repurchased is $15,727,000, as shown in Column 4 of Table 15-2. There are 1,000,000 − 276,116 = 723,884 shares still outstanding, so the value per share of the remaining stock is

$$\text{Value per share} = \frac{\$15,727,000}{723,884} = \$21.73.$$

This confirms our earlier calculation of the equilibrium stock price.

9. The same process was used to find stock prices at other capital structures; these prices are given in Column 6 of Table 15-2 and plotted in the lower graph of Figure 15-7. *Since the maximum price occurs when HSS uses $6 million of debt, its optimal capital structure calls for $6 million of debt.* Note also that $6 million of debt corresponds to a firm value of $21.727 million. Thus, the optimal market value debt ratio, D/V*, is $6/$21.727 = 27.6%.

10. In this example, we assumed that EBIT would decline from $4 million to $3.52 million if the firm's debt rose to $14 million. The reason for the decline is that, at this very high level of debt, managers and employees would be worried about the firm's failing and about losing their jobs; suppliers would not sell to the firm on normal credit terms; orders would be lost because of customers' fears that the company might go bankrupt and thus be unable to deliver; and so on. EBIT is independent of financial leverage at "reasonable" debt levels, but at extreme degrees of leverage, EBIT is adversely affected.

11. Quite obviously, the situation in the real world is much more complex, and less exact, than this example suggests. Most important, different investors will have different estimates for EBIT and k_s, hence they will form different expectations about the equilibrium stock price. This means that HSS might have to pay more than $21.73 to repurchase its shares, or perhaps that the shares could be bought at a lower price. These changes would cause the optimal amount of debt to be somewhat higher or lower than $6 million. Still, $6 million represents our best estimate of the optimal debt level, so it is the level we should use as our target capital structure.

12. The WACC for the various levels of debt is shown in Column 8 of Table 15-2. The minimum cost of capital, 11.0 percent, corresponds to the level of debt at which the value of the firm and its stock price are maximized, $6.0 million.

The stock price and cost of capital relationships developed in Table 15-2 are graphed in Figure 15-7. Here we see that HSS's stock price is maximized, and its weighted average cost of capital is minimized, at the optimal D/V ratio, 27.6 percent.

The Effect of Financial Leverage on EPS

Thus far we have focused on the impact of leverage on a firm's total value and stock price. Before leaving the HSS illustration, we should also take a look at how leverage affects earnings per share (EPS); this is done in Table 15-3. Part I of the table gives

TABLE 15-3	HSS's EPS at Different Amounts of Debt (Millions of Dollars Except Per-Share Figures)

I. Operating Income (EBIT)

Probability of indicated sales	0.2	0.6	0.2
Sales	$10.00	$20.00	$30.00
Fixed operating costs	4.00	4.00	4.00
Variable costs (60% of sales)	6.00	12.00	18.00
Total costs (except interest)	$10.00	$16.00	$22.00
Earnings before interest and taxes (EBIT)	$0.00	$ 4.00	$ 8.00

II. Zero Debt

Less interest	0.00	0.00	0.00
Earnings before taxes	$ 0.00	$ 4.00	$ 8.00
Less taxes (40%)	0.00	1.60	3.20
Net income	$ 0.00	$ 2.40	$ 4.80
Earnings per share on 1 million shares (EPS)	$ 0.00	$ 2.40	$ 4.80
Expected EPS		$ 2.40	
Standard deviation of EPS[a]		$ 1.52	
Coefficient of variation of EPS[a]		0.63	

III. $10 Million of Debt

Less interest ($0.12 \times \$10,000,000$)	1.20	1.20	1.20
Earnings before taxes	($1.20)	$ 2.80	$ 6.80
Less taxes (40%)[b]	(0.48)	1.12	2.72
Net income	($0.72)	$ 1.68	$ 4.08
Earnings per share on 524,940 shares (EPS)[c]	($1.37)	$ 3.20	$ 7.77
Expected EPS		$ 3.20	
Standard deviation of EPS[a]		$ 2.90	
Coefficient of variation of EPS[a]		0.91	

[a]Procedures for calculating the standard deviation and the coefficient of variation were discussed in Chapter 5.
[b]Assume tax credit on losses. If credits were not available, expected EPS would be lower, and risk higher, at high debt levels.
[c]Shares outstanding is determined as follows:

$$\text{Shares} = \text{Original shares} - \frac{\text{Debt}}{\text{Stock price}} = 1,000,000 - \frac{\text{Debt}}{\text{Stock price}},$$

where the stock price is taken from Table 15-2, Column 6. With $10 million of debt, P = $21.05. After the recapitalization, 524,940 shares will remain outstanding:

$$\text{Shares} = 1,000,000 - \frac{\$10,000,000}{\$21.05} = 524,940.$$

EPS figures can also be calculated using this formula:

$$\text{EPS} = \frac{(\text{EBIT} - k_d D)(1 - T)}{\text{Original shares} - \text{Debt/Price}}.$$

For example, at D = $10 million,

$$\text{EPS} = \frac{[\$4,000,000 - (0.12)(\$10,000,000)](0.6)}{1,000,000 - \$10,000,000/\$21.05} = \frac{\$1,680,000}{524,940} = \$3.20.$$

| FIGURE 15-8 | Probability Distribution of EPS for HSS with Different Amounts of Financial Leverage |

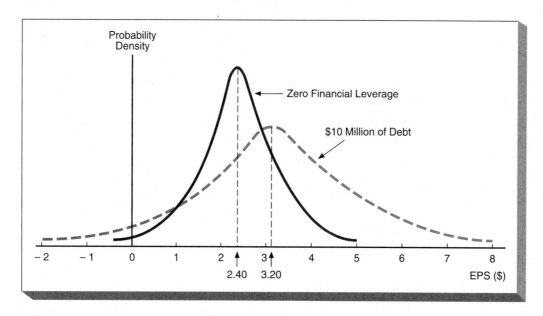

operating income data. It begins by recognizing that HSS's future EBIT is not known with certainty. Expected EBIT is $4 million, but the realized EBIT could be less than or greater than $4 million. To simplify matters, we have assumed a discrete distribution of sales, so EBIT has only three possible outcomes. Notice also that EBIT is assumed not to depend on financial leverage.[18]

Part II of Table 15-3 shows the situation that would exist if HSS continues to use no debt. Net income after taxes is divided by the 1 million shares outstanding to calculate EPS. If sales were as low as $10 million, EPS would be zero, but EPS would rise to $4.80 at sales of $30 million. Next, the EPS at each sales level is multiplied by the probability of that sales level to obtain the expected EPS, which is $2.40 if HSS uses no debt. We also calculate the standard deviation of EPS and its coefficient of variation to get an idea of the firm's stand-alone risk at a zero debt ratio: $\sigma_{EPS} = \$1.52$, and $CV_{EPS} = 0.63$.

Part III of Table 15-3 shows the financial results that would occur if the company decided to use $10 million of debt. The interest rate on the debt, 12 percent, is taken from Figure 15-6. With $10 million of 12 percent debt outstanding, the company's interest expense is $1.2 million per year. This is a fixed cost, and it is deducted from EBIT as calculated in Part I. Next, taxes are taken out, and we work on down to the EPS figures that would result at each sales level. With $10 million of debt, EPS would be −$1.37 if sales were as low as $10 million; it would rise to $3.20 if sales were $20 million; and it would soar to $7.77 if sales were as high as $30 million. The expected EPS is $3.20, $\sigma_{EPS} = \$2.90$, and $CV_{EPS} = 0.91$.

Continuous approximations of the EPS distributions under the two financial structures are graphed in Figure 15-8. Although expected EPS is much higher if the firm

---

[18]As we discussed earlier, capital structure does affect EBIT at very high debt levels. For example, we assumed that HSS's EBIT would fall from $4 million to $3.52 million if the level of debt rose to $14 million. However, debt in Table 15-3 is limited to $10 million, so the "excessive leverage effect on EBIT" is not present in this particular example.

uses financial leverage, the graph makes it clear that the risk of low, or even negative, EPS is also higher if debt is used. Figure 15-8 thus shows that using leverage involves a risk/return trade-off—higher leverage increases expected earnings per share, but it also increases the firm's risk. It is this increasing risk that causes k_s and k_d to increase at higher amounts of financial leverage.[19]

The relationship between expected EPS and financial leverage is plotted in the top section of Figure 15-9. Here we see that expected EPS first rises as the use of debt increases—interest charges rise, but the decreasing number of shares outstanding as debt is substituted for equity still causes EPS to increase. However, EPS peaks when $12 million of debt is used. Beyond this amount, interest rates rise rapidly, and EBIT begins to fall, so EPS is depressed in spite of the falling number of shares outstanding. Risk as measured by the coefficient of variation of EPS shown in the fourth column of the data in Figure 15-9 rises continuously, and at an increasing rate, as debt is substituted for equity.

Does the same amount of debt maximize both price and EPS? The answer is *no*. As we can see from the lower graph in Figure 15-9, HSS's stock price is maximized with $6 million of debt, while the upper graph shows that expected EPS is maximized by using $12 million of debt. *Since management is primarily interested in maximizing the value of the stock, the optimal capital structure calls for the use of $6 million of debt.*

Problems with the HSS Analysis

The Hill Software Systems example illustrated the effects of leverage on firm value, stock prices, earnings per share, and debt values. However, the example was obviously simplified to facilitate the discussion, and we cannot overemphasize the difficulties encountered when one attempts to use this type of analysis in practice. First, the capitalization rates (k_d and especially k_s) are very difficult to estimate. The cost of debt at different debt levels can be estimated with some confidence, but cost of equity estimates must be viewed as very rough approximations.[20]

Second, the mathematics of the valuation process make the outcomes very sensitive to the input estimates. Thus, fairly small errors in the estimates of k_d, k_s, and EBIT can lead to large errors in estimated EPS and stock price.

Third, our example was restricted to the case of a no-growth firm. In view of the input requirements to model even a simple no-growth situation, and the still greater requirements for the growth model, it is unrealistic to think that a precise optimal capital structure can ever be identified.

Finally, many firms are not publicly owned, and that causes still more difficulties. If a privately held firm's owner does not plan to have his or her firm go public, then potential market value data are really irrelevant. However, an analysis based on market values for a privately owned firm is useful if the owner is interested in knowing how the firm's market value would be affected by leverage should the decision be made to go public.

---

[19]Note that financial leverage has a similar effect on the risk of EPS as it does on that of ROE. Thus, Figure 15-8 is similar in appearance to the lower part of Figure 15-4.

[20]The statistical relationship between k_s and the debt ratio has been studied extensively using both cross-sectional and time series data. In the cross-sectional studies, a sample of firms is analyzed, with multiple regression techniques used in an attempt to "hold constant" all factors other than financial leverage that might influence k_s. The general conclusion of these studies is that k_s rises as leverage increases, but statistical problems preclude us from specifying the functional relationship with much confidence.

In the time series studies, a single firm's k_s is analyzed over time in an attempt to see how k_s changes in response to changes in its debt ratio. Here again, "other factors" do not remain constant, so it is impossible to specify exactly how k_s is affected by financial leverage.

| FIGURE 15-9 | Relationship between HSS's Expected EPS and Stock Price |

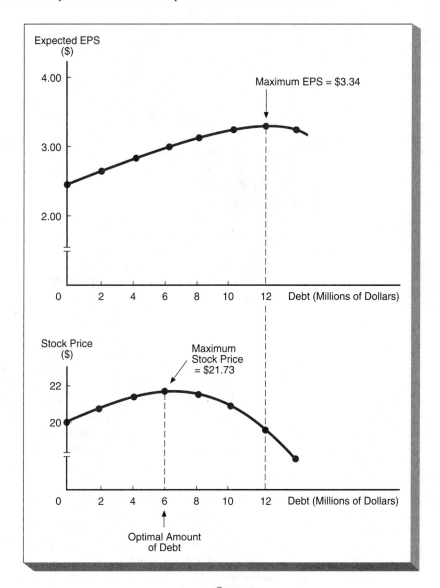

DEBT	EXPECTED EPS	STANDARD DEVIATION OF EPS	COEFFICIENT OF VARIATION	STOCK PRICE[b]
$ 0	$2.40[a]	$1.52[a]	0.63[a]	$20.00
2,000,000	2.55	1.68	0.66	20.89
4,000,000	2.70	1.87	0.69	21.47
6,000,000	2.87	2.09	0.73	21.73
8,000,000	3.04	2.40	0.80	21.71
10,000,000	3.20[a]	2.90[a]	0.91[a]	21.05
12,000,000	3.34	3.83	1.15	19.86
14,000,000	3.26	5.20	1.60	17.16

[a]These values are taken from Table 15-3. Values at other debt levels were calculated similarly.
[b]Stock prices are from Table 15-2.

S E L F - T E S T
Q U E S T I O N S

What are the key assumptions used in the Hill Software example?

Briefly describe the steps involved in finding Hill's optimal capital structure.

What problems occur when the procedures used in the Hill example are used to estimate real-world optimal capital structures?

SOME CONSIDERATIONS IN THE CAPITAL STRUCTURE DECISION

Since firms cannot determine their precise optimal capital structures, managers must apply judgment to their quantitative analyses. The judgmental analysis involves several different factors. In one situation a particular factor might have great importance. In another, that factor might be relatively unimportant. This section discusses some of the more important judgmental issues that should be taken into account.

Managerial Conservatism

Well-diversified investors have eliminated most, if not all, diversifiable risk from their portfolios. Therefore, the typical investor can tolerate some chance of financial distress, because a loss on one stock would probably be offset by gains on another. However, managers generally view financial stability as being quite important—they are typically not well diversified, and their careers, and thus the present value of their expected future earnings, can be seriously affected by financial distress. Thus, it is not difficult to imagine that managers might be more "conservative" in their use of leverage than the average stockholder would desire. If this is true, then managers would set somewhat lower target debt ratios than the ones which maximize stock prices. The managers of a publicly owned firm would never admit this, for unless they owned voting control, they would quickly be removed from office. However, in view of the uncertainties about what constitutes the value-maximizing structure, management could always say that the target capital structure employed is, in its judgment, the value-maximizing structure, and it would be difficult to prove otherwise.[21]

Lender and Rating Agency Attitudes

Regardless of a manager's own analysis of the proper leverage for his or her firm, there is no question but that lenders' and rating agencies' attitudes are frequently important determinants of financial structures. Generally, management will discuss the firm's financial structure with lenders and rating agencies and give much weight to their advice. However, if a particular firm's management is so confident of the future that it seeks to use leverage beyond the norms for its industry, its lenders may be unwilling to accept such debt increases, or may do so only at a high price.

Coverage ratios, which were discussed in detail in Chapter 3, often are used by lenders and rating agencies to measure the risk of financial distress. Accordingly, man-

---

[21]It is, of course, possible for a particular manager to be less conservative than his or her firm's average stockholder. However, this condition is less likely to occur than is excessive managerial conservatism, which is just another manifestation of the agency problem. If excessive conservatism exists, then managers, as agents of the stockholders, are not acting in the best interests of their principals. However, when managers become the primary owners of a company, such as in managerial buyouts (MBOs), they often become very aggressive in their use of financial leverage. By using extreme amounts of debt, they take on a great deal of risk, but, in the process, they open the door for big payoffs. Note too that the threat of takeovers motivates underleveraged firms' managers to use more debt than they otherwise would.

| TABLE 15-4 | HSS's Expected Times-Interest-Earned Ratio at Different Amounts of Debt |

AMOUNT OF DEBT (IN MILLIONS)	EXPECTED TIE[a]
$ 0	Undefined
2	25.0
4	12.1
6	7.4
8	5.0
10	3.3
12	2.2

[a]TIE = EBIT/Interest. Example: TIE = $4,000,000/$1,200,000 = 3.3 at $10 million of debt. Data are from Table 15-1 and Figure 15-6.

agements give considerable weight to such ratios as the **times-interest-earned (TIE) ratio,** which is defined as EBIT divided by total interest charges. The lower this ratio, the higher the probability that a firm will encounter financial distress.

Table 15-4 shows how HSS's expected TIE ratio declines as its use of debt increases. At zero debt, the TIE ratio is undefined, but it is almost infinitely high at very low debt levels. When $2 million of debt is used, the expected TIE is a high 25 times, but the interest coverage ratio declines rapidly as debt rises. Note, however, that these coverages are expected values—the actual TIE will be higher if sales exceed the expected $20 million level, but lower if sales fall below $20 million.

The variability of the TIE ratio is highlighted in Figure 15-10, which shows the probability distributions of the ratio at $8 million and $12 million of debt. The expected TIE is much higher if only $8 million of debt is used. Even more important, with less debt there is a much lower probability of a TIE of less than 1.0, the level at which the firm is not earning enough to meet its required interest payments.

Another coverage ratio that is often used by lenders and rating agencies is the **fixed charge coverage (FCC) ratio.** This ratio recognizes that there are fixed financial charges other than interest payments which could lead to financial distress. The FCC ratio is defined as follows:

$$FCC = \frac{EBIT + \text{Lease payments}}{\text{Interest} + \left(\begin{array}{c} \text{Lease} \\ \text{payments} \end{array}\right) + \left(\dfrac{\text{Sinking fund payments}}{1-T}\right)}.$$

Note that sinking fund payments reduce the debt—they are not deductible interest payments. Therefore, sinking fund payments must be "grossed up" in recognition of the fact that they must be made with after-tax dollars (net income). Interest and lease payments are fully deductible, hence they do not need to be grossed up.

If HSS had $1 million of lease payments and $1 million of sinking fund payments, its FCC ratio at a debt level of $10 million would be 1.3:

$$FCC = \frac{\$4,000,000 + \$1,000,000}{\$1,200,000 + \$1,000,000 + \dfrac{\$1,000,000}{0.6}}$$

$$= \frac{\$5,000,000}{\$3,866,667} = 1.3.$$

| FIGURE 15-10 | Probability Distributions of Times-Interest-Earned Ratio for HSS with Different Capital Structures |

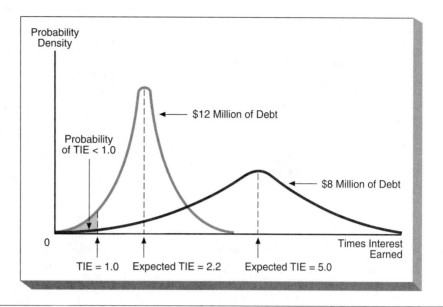

Thus, the coverage of total fixed charges is considerably less than the 3.3 times-interest-earned coverage at the same debt level.

Reserve Borrowing Capacity and Financing Flexibility

When we discussed asymmetric information and signaling, we noted that firms should maintain some reserve borrowing capacity, which preserves their ability to issue debt on favorable terms. For example, suppose Biotechnics Inc. had just successfully completed an R&D program, and its internal projections are for much higher earnings in the immediate future. However, the new earnings are not yet anticipated by investors, hence are not reflected in the price of its stock. Biotechnics would not want to issue stock—it would prefer to finance with debt until the higher earnings materialized and were reflected in the stock price, at which time it could sell an issue of common stock, retire the debt, and return to its target capital structure. Similarly, if the financial manager felt that interest rates were temporarily low, but were likely to rise fairly soon, he or she might want to issue long-term bonds and thus "lock in" the low rates for many years. To obtain this *financing flexibility*, firms generally use less debt under "normal" conditions, thus presenting a stronger financial picture than they would otherwise have. This is not suboptimal from a long-run standpoint, although it might appear so if viewed strictly on a short-run basis.

Note too that firms' debt contracts often specify that no new debt can be issued unless certain ratios exceed minimum levels. Very frequently, the TIE ratio is required to exceed 2 or 2.5 times as a condition for the issuance of additional debt. With this in mind, look back at Figure 15-10 and note that, if it used $12 million of debt, HSS's TIE would be less than 2.0 almost half the time, whereas the probability of a coverage less than 2.0 would be quite small if it used only $8 million of debt. Thus, if HSS sets a relatively high target debt ratio, its financing flexibility would be reduced in the sense that it could not count on using whatever type of capital it wanted to use at all times.

The emphasis that managers place on flexibility can be summed up by this statement made to the authors by a corporate treasurer:

> Our company can earn a lot more by making good capital budgeting decisions than by making good financing decisions. Indeed, we are not sure exactly how financing decisions affect our stock price, but we know for sure that foregoing a promising capital investment because funds are not available will hurt our stockholders. For this reason, my primary goal as treasurer is to always be in a position to raise the capital needed to support operations without having to sell new common stock and sending out a negative signal.

Control

The effect of debt on a management's control position may also influence the capital structure decision. If management just barely has majority control (just over 50 percent of the stock), but is not in a position to buy any more stock, debt may be the choice for new financings. On the other hand, a management group that is not concerned about voting control may decide to use equity rather than debt if the financial situation is so weak that the use of debt might subject the company to a serious risk of default. If the firm gets into trouble, creditors (through covenants in the debt agreements) may assume control and perhaps force a management change. This has happened to Chrysler, Navistar International (formerly International Harvester), Braniff, Continental Illinois Bank, and a number of other companies in recent years. However, if too little debt is used, management runs the risk of a takeover, where some other company or management group persuades stockholders to turn over control to the new group, which plans to boost earnings and stock prices by using financial leverage. This happened to Lenox, the china company, and to many other firms in recent years. Control considerations do not necessarily suggest the use of debt or of equity, but the effects of financing decisions on control must certainly be taken into account.

Business Risk

A firm that has relatively low business risk—small sales variability, low operating leverage, and so on—can take on more debt than can firms with high business risk. In essence, firms must limit their total risk, and the higher the business risk, the less "room" there is to take on financial risk.

Asset Structure

Firms whose assets are suitable as security for loans tend to use debt rather heavily. Thus, real estate companies, which have marketable assets, tend to be highly leveraged. However, companies involved in technological research employ relatively little debt.

Growth Rate

Other factors the same, faster-growing firms must rely more heavily on external capital—slow growth can be financed with retained earnings, but rapid growth generally requires the use of external funds. For reasons set forth in our discussion of signaling theory, and also because the flotation costs involved in selling common stock exceed those incurred when selling debt, firms prefer debt to new stock for meeting external funding needs. Thus, rapidly growing firms tend to use somewhat more debt than slower-growth companies.

Profitability

One often observes that firms with very high ROEs use relatively little debt. The reason seems to be that highly profitable firms such as Merck, 3M, and Microsoft simply do not need to do much debt financing—their high profits enable them to do most of their financing with retained earnings.

Taxes

Interest is a deductible expense, while dividends are not deductible. Therefore, the higher a firm's corporate tax rate, the greater the advantage of using debt.

Market Conditions

Conditions in the stock and bond markets undergo both long- and short-run changes that can affect a firm's optimal capital structure. For example, during a recent credit crunch, the junk bond market dried up, and it was essentially impossible for firms to issue lower-quality debt at "reasonable" interest rates. Therefore, low-rated companies in need of capital were forced to either issue stock or use short-term debt, regardless of their target capital structures. As conditions eased, however, such companies were able to sell bonds and move their capital structures back in line with their targets.

SELF-TEST QUESTIONS

Is the capital structure decision partly objective (made on the basis of numerical analysis) and partly subjective (judgmental, with many factors considered)?

List and discuss some factors that managers consider when setting the firm's target capital structure.

AN APPROACH TO SETTING THE TARGET CAPITAL STRUCTURE

Thus far in the chapter, we have discussed (1) the basics of business and financial risk, (2) several theories of capital structure, (3) a method of analysis based on perpetual cash flows, and (4) a number of factors that influence the capital structure decision. In this section, we describe a pragmatic approach to setting the target capital structure. Our approach requires judgmental assumptions, but it also requires managers to consider how alternative capital structures would affect future profitability, coverage, and external financing requirements under a variety of assumptions.

The starting point for the analysis is a forecasting model set up to test the effects of capital structure changes. Here is a brief description of the spreadsheet model we use in consulting assignments. Basically, the model generates forecasted data based on inputs supplied by the firm's financial staff. Each data item can be fixed, or it can be allowed to vary from year to year. The required data include the most recent balance sheet and income statement, plus the following items, all of which represent either expectations or management-determined policy variables:

1. Annual growth rates in an index of unit sales
2. Annual inflation rates for sales prices and input prices
3. Corporate tax rate
4. Variable costs as a percentage of sales

5. Fixed costs

6. Interest rates on already outstanding (or embedded) debt

7. Marginal component costs of capital

8. Capital structure percentages

9. Dividend growth rate

10. Long-term dividend payout ratio

The model uses the input data to forecast balance sheets and income statements for future years. Then it calculates and displays such data as external financing requirements, ROE, EPS, DPS, times-interest-earned, stock price, and WACC, along with a set of key ratios.

We begin by entering base-year balance sheet and income statement values plus data on the expected growth rate, expected inflation rates, and so on. These inputs are used by the model to forecast operating income and asset requirements. Next, the model brings in the financing mix. It uses as inputs both the debt/equity mix and the debt maturity structure. By debt maturity structure, we mean the proportion of short-term versus long-term debt. Further, we must estimate as best we can the effects of the firm's capital structure on its component costs—a higher debt ratio will lead to increases in the costs of all components, and vice versa if less debt is used. With all inputs entered, the model then forecasts financial statements and generates projected stock prices.

The model is then used to analyze alternative scenarios. This analysis takes two forms: (1) changing the financing inputs to get an idea about how the financing mix affects the key outputs and (2) changing the operating inputs to see how economic conditions affect the key outputs under various financing strategies. Finally, the model's output must be reviewed and analyzed, and a decision must be made as to the best capital structure. We pay particular attention to the forecasted EPS, interest coverage, external funding requirements, and projected stock price.

The model can generate output "answers" quite easily, but it is up to the financial analyst to assign input values, to interpret the output, and, finally, to recommend a target capital structure. The final decision will be made by the financial manager and/or top management, considering all the factors we have discussed. Reaching a decision is not easy, but a capital structure forecasting model such as the one we use does help managers analyze the effects of alternative courses of action, which is essential in good decision making.

It should be noted that *while capital structure decisions do affect stock prices, those effects are generally small in comparison to the effects of operating decisions.* A company's ability to identify (or create) market opportunities, and to produce and sell products or services efficiently, is the primary determinant of success. Financial arrangements can facilitate or hamper operations, but the best of financial plans cannot overcome deficiencies in the operations area. This statement is supported by empirical studies, which generally find a weak statistical relationship between capital structure and stock prices. It is also supported by runs of our computer model, which show stock prices to be affected significantly by changes in unit sales, sales prices, fixed costs, and variable costs, but only slightly by changes in capital structure. This last point can also be seen from the HSS example discussed earlier. Refer again to Table 15-2. Hill Software Systems' stock price is maximized at a D/V ratio of 27.6 percent. However, at a D/V of 18.6 percent, which is one-third lower, the firm's stock price drops only from $21.73 to $21.47, or by 1.2 percent, while if D/V rises to 36.8 percent, HSS's stock price hardly drops at all. Thus, HSS could set its target D/V ratio anywhere in the range from 18 to 40 percent and still come very close to maximizing its stock price.

Briefly describe the elements of a financial forecasting model designed to help set the target capital structure.

How critical is the optimal capital structure decision to the financial performance of the firm; that is, how important are small deviations from the optimal structure?

Should the target capital structure be thought of as a single point or as a range?

SOME ADDITIONAL INSIGHTS INTO CAPITAL STRUCTURE DECISIONS

At this point, one might have an uneasy feeling regarding both how to establish the target capital structure and its effect on risk, profitability, and stock prices. We can construct models which generate projected earnings, stock prices, coverage ratios, and so on, under different capital structures. However, our confidence in these results is limited, because we do not know for sure how k_d and k_s, hence stock prices, will really change with changes in the capital structure. We also know that in practice many subjective factors also influence the decision. Therefore, to gain more insights into capital structure decisions, it is useful to look at how managers say they actually establish target capital structures.

Professors David Scott and Dana Johnson surveyed a group of firms to find out how managers attempt to estimate the optimal capital structure, and whether managers really believe that one can be determined.[22] Scott and Johnson sent questionnaires to the chief financial officer (CFO) of each Fortune 1000 firm. Some 212 financial managers replied, and their answers provide useful insights into the decision process.

First, the respondents agreed that capital structure decisions do matter — in general, financial managers believe that the prudent use of debt can lower the firm's overall cost of capital, but that an excessive use of debt will increase the required rate of return on equity. Second, the most popular measures of financial leverage are (1) the long-term debt to total capitalization ratio,[23] (2) the times-interest-earned (TIE) ratio, and (3) the long-term debt to common equity ratio. However, when computing these ratios, accounting (or book) values rather than market values were virtually always used. Third, 64 percent of the responding managers indicated that their target long-term debt to total capitalization ratios were in the range of 26 to 40 percent, and the most popular reported target range was 26 to 30 percent. Because stock market values generally exceed book values, the debt ratio measured in market value terms would be quite a bit lower than these reported book value figures.

The survey also provided data on how various parties influence the capital structure decision. The data indicate that managers give the greatest weight to their own internal analyses, but that investment bankers and bond rating agencies also have a significant influence. Additionally, firms consider industry averages when setting their target

---

[22]See David F. Scott and Dana J. Johnson, "Financing Policies and Practices in Large Corporations," *Financial Management*, Summer 1982, 51–59.

[23]Total capitalization is defined as long-term debt plus preferred stock plus common equity. Therefore, current liabilities and deferred taxes are excluded.

capital structures, but they are willing to depart from the averages if their own conditions suggest that a departure is warranted.

Note that the Scott-Johnson survey was taken in 1982. Since then, many MBAs have graduated, gone into the work force, and now make important financial decisions. Our guess—supported by our own observations—is that if the survey were repeated today, more companies would report that they give weight to market value as well as book value capital structures.

Do practicing financial managers believe that capital structures matter?

Do investment bankers and rating agencies influence the capital structure decision?

SUMMARY

This chapter discussed capital structure decisions. The key concepts covered are listed below:

- **Business risk** is the inherent riskiness in a firm's operations if it uses no debt. **Financial risk** is the additional risk that is concentrated on the shareholders when debt financing is used.

- Within a **stand-alone risk framework,** business risk can be measured by $\sigma_{ROE(U)}$, stand-alone risk to stockholders can be measured by σ_{ROE}, and financial risk can be measured by Stand-alone risk – Business risk = $\sigma_{ROE} - \sigma_{ROE(U)}$.

- In 1958, **Franco Modigliani and Merton Miller (MM)** proved, under a restrictive set of assumptions including zero taxes, that capital structure is irrelevant; that is, according to the original MM article, a firm's value and cost of capital are not affected by its financing mix.

- When **corporate taxes** are added to the MM model, the results indicate that firms should use 100 percent debt financing. However, later work by Miller demonstrated that **personal taxes** reduce, but do not eliminate, the value of debt financing.

- The addition of financial distress and agency costs to either the MM corporate tax model or the Miller model results in a **trade-off model.** Here the marginal costs and benefits of debt are balanced against one another, and the result is an optimal capital structure that falls somewhere between zero and 100 percent debt.

- Unfortunately, capital structure theory does not provide neat, clean answers to the question of the optimal capital structure. Thus, many factors must be considered when actually choosing a target capital structure, and the final decision will be based on both quantitative analysis and judgment.

- If a firm has **perpetual cash flows,** then a relatively simple model can be used to estimate its value under different capital structures. In theory, this model can be used to find the capital structure that maximizes the stock price. However, the inputs to the model are very difficult, if not impossible, to estimate with any degree of precision. Further, most firms are growing, so they do not have constant cash flows.

- Since one cannot determine the optimal capital structure with quantitative models, managers must base decisions on analysis plus **qualitative factors,** including long-run viability, managerial conservatism, lender and rating agency attitudes, reserve borrowing capacity, control, asset structure, profitability, and taxes.

- Firms generally have **computerized planning models** which are used in the financial planning process. These models can be used to get a feel for the impact of capital structure changes on a firm's financial condition.

At this point, you should have a reasonably good idea about how capital structure affects stock prices and capital costs. In the next chapter, we will examine some additional issues which provide further insights into the capital structure decision.

Questions

15-1   Define each of the following terms:
   a. Capital structure
   b. Business risk
   c. Financial risk
   d. Operating leverage
   e. Financial leverage
   f. Breakeven point
   g. Capital structure theory
   h. Perpetual cash flow analysis
   i. Reserve borrowing capacity

15-2   What term refers to the uncertainty inherent in projections of future ROE(U)?

15-3   Firms with relatively high nonfinancial fixed costs are said to have a high degree of what?

15-4   "One type of leverage affects both EBIT and EPS. The other type affects only EPS." Explain this statement.

15-5   Why is the following statement true? "Other things being the same, firms with relatively stable sales are able to carry relatively high debt ratios."

15-6   Why do public utility companies usually have capital structures that are different from those of retail firms?

15-7   Some economists believe that swings in business cycles will not be as wide in the future as they have been in the past. Assuming that they are correct, what effect might this added stability have on the types of financing used by firms in the United States? Would your answer be true for all firms?

15-8   Why is EBIT generally considered to be independent of financial leverage? Why might EBIT actually be influenced by financial leverage at high debt levels?

15-9   If a firm with no debt could buy back and retire its stock at the pre-announcement price, would its final stock price be higher than that resulting from the procedure outlined in the chapter? Would it be fair for a firm to buy back its stock without telling stockholders that stock was being repurchased?

15-10   How might increasingly volatile inflation rates, interest rates, and bond prices affect the optimal capital structure for corporations?

15-11   If a firm went from zero debt to successively higher levels of debt, why would you expect its stock price to first rise, then hit a peak, and then begin to decline?

15-12   The stock of Gentech Company is currently selling at its low for the year, but management feels that the stock price is only temporarily depressed because of investor pessimism. The firm's capital budget this year is so large that the use of new outside equity is contemplated. However, management does not want to sell new stock at the current low price and is therefore considering a temporary departure from the firm's "optimal" capital structure by borrowing the funds it would otherwise have raised in the equity markets. Does this seem to be a wise move? Does this action conform to any of the theories presented in the chapter?

15-13   Why is the debt level that maximizes a firm's expected EPS generally higher than the debt level that maximizes its stock price?

Self-Test Problem   (Solution Appears in Appendix B)

ST-1
Optimal Capital Structure

The Rogers Company is currently in this situation: (1) EBIT = $4 million; (2) tax rate, T = 35%; (3) value of debt, D = $2 million; (4) k_d = 10%; (5) k_s = 15%; and (6) shares of stock outstanding, n = 600,000. The firm's market is stable, and it expects no growth, so all earnings are paid out as dividends. The debt consists of perpetual bonds.
   a. What is the total market value of the firm's stock, S, its price per share, P_0, and the firm's total market value, V?

b. What is the firm's weighted average cost of capital?
c. The firm can increase its debt by $8 million, to a total of $10 million, using the new debt to buy back and retire some of its shares. Its interest rate on all debt will be 12 percent (it will have to call and refund the old debt), and its cost of equity will rise from 15 to 17 percent. EBIT will remain constant. Should the firm change its capital structure?

Problems

15-1
Operating Leverage and Breakeven

Schweser Satellites Inc. produces satellite earth stations which sell for $100,000 each. The firm's fixed costs, F, are $2 million; 50 earth stations are produced and sold each year; profits total $500,000; and the firm's assets (all equity financed) are $5 million. The firm estimates that it can change its production process, adding $4 million to investment and $500,000 to fixed operating costs. This change will (1) reduce variable costs per unit by $10,000 and (2) increase output by 20 units, but (3) the sales price on all units will have to be lowered to $95,000 to permit sales of the additional output. The firm has tax loss carry-forwards that cause its tax rate to be zero, its cost of equity is 15 percent, and it uses no debt.
a. Should the firm make the change?
b. Would the firm's operating leverage increase or decrease if it made the change? What about its breakeven point?
c. Would the new situation expose the firm to more or less business risk than the old one?

15-2
Business and Financial Risk

Here are the estimated ROE distributions for Firms A, B, and C:

	PROBABILITY				
	0.1	0.2	0.4	0.2	0.1
Firm A: ROE_A	0.0%	5.0%	10.0%	15.0%	20.0%
Firm B: ROE_B	(2.0)	5.0	12.0	19.0	26.0
Firm C: ROE_C	(5.0)	5.0	15.0	25.0	35.0

a. Calculate the expected value and standard deviation for Firm C's ROE. $ROE_A = 10.0\%$, $\sigma_A = 5.5\%$; $ROE_B = 12.0\%$, $\sigma_B = 7.7\%$.
b. Discuss the relative riskiness of the three firms' returns. (Assume that these distributions are expected to remain constant over time.)
c. Now suppose all three firms have the same standard deviation of basic earning power (EBIT/Total assets), $\sigma_A = \sigma_B = \sigma_C = 5.5\%$. What can we tell about the financial risk of each firm?

15-3
Capital Structure Analysis

The following data reflect the current financial conditions of the Levine Corporation:

Value of debt (book = market)	$1,000,000
Market value of equity	$5,257,143
Sales, last 12 months	$12,000,000
Variable operating costs (50% of sales)	$6,000,000
Fixed operating costs	$5,000,000
Tax rate, T (federal-plus-state)	40%

At the current level of debt, the cost of debt, k_d, is 8 percent and the cost of equity, k_s, is 10.5 percent. Management questions whether or not the capital structure is optimal, so the financial vice-president has been asked to consider the possibility of issuing $1 million of additional debt and using the proceeds to repurchase stock. It is estimated that if the leverage were increased by raising the level of debt to $2 million, the interest rate on new debt would rise to 9 percent and k_s would rise to 11.5 percent. The old 8 percent debt is senior to the new debt, and it would remain outstanding, continue to yield 8 percent, and have a market value of $1 million. The firm is a zero-growth firm, with all of its earnings paid out as dividends.
a. Should the firm increase its debt to $2 million?
b. If the firm decided to increase its level of debt to $3 million, its cost of the additional $2 million of debt would be 12 percent and k_s would rise to 15 percent. The original 8 percent of

debt would again remain outstanding, and its market value would remain at $1 million. What level of debt should the firm choose: $1 million, $2 million, or $3 million?

c. The market price of the firm's stock was originally $20 per share. Calculate the new equilibrium stock prices at debt levels of $2 million and $3 million.

d. Calculate the firm's earnings per share if it uses debt of $1 million, $2 million, and $3 million. Assume that the firm pays out all of its earnings as dividends. If you find that EPS increases with more debt, does this mean that the firm should choose to increase its debt to $3 million, or possibly higher?

e. What would happen to the value of the old bonds if the firm uses more leverage and the old bonds are not senior to the new bonds?

15-4
Capital Structure Analysis   The Rivoli Company has no debt outstanding, and its financial position is given by the following data:

Assets (book = market)	$3,000,000
EBIT	$500,000
Cost of equity, k_s	10%
Stock price, P_0	$15
Shares outstanding, n	200,000
Tax rate, T (federal-plus-state)	40%

The firm is considering selling bonds and simultaneously repurchasing some of its stock. If it uses $900,000 of debt, its cost of equity, k_s, will increase to 11 percent to reflect the increased risk. Bonds can be sold at a cost, k_d, of 7 percent. Rivoli is a no-growth firm. Hence, all its earnings are paid out as dividends, and earnings are expectationally constant over time.

a. What effect would this use of leverage have on the value of the firm?

b. What would be the price of Rivoli's stock?

c. What happens to the firm's earnings per share after the recapitalization?

d. The $500,000 EBIT given previously is actually the expected value from the following probability distribution:

PROBABILITY	EBIT
0.10	($ 100,000)
0.20	200,000
0.40	500,000
0.20	800,000
0.10	1,100,000

What is the probability distribution of EPS with zero debt and with $900,000 of debt? Which EPS distribution is riskier?

e. Determine the probability distributions of the times-interest-earned ratio for each debt level. What is the probability of not covering the interest payment at the $900,000 debt level?

15-5
Capital Structure Analysis   Pettit Printing Company has a total market value of $100 million, consisting of 1 million shares selling for $50 per share and $50 million of 10 percent perpetual bonds now selling at par. The company's EBIT is $13.24 million, and its tax rate is 15 percent. Pettit can change its capital structure by either increasing its debt to $70 million or decreasing it to $30 million. If it decides to *increase* its use of leverage, it must call its old bonds and issue new ones with a 12 percent coupon. If it decides to *decrease* its leverage, it will call in its old bonds and replace them with new 8 percent coupon bonds. The company will sell or repurchase stock at the new equilibrium price to complete the capital structure change.

The firm pays out all earnings as dividends; hence, its stock is a zero growth stock. If it increases leverage, k_s will be 16 percent. If it decreases leverage, k_s will be 13 percent.

a. What is the firm's cost of equity at present?

b. Should the firm change its capital structure?

c. Suppose the tax rate is changed to 34 percent. This would lower after-tax income and also cause a decline in the price of the stock and the total value of the equity, other things held constant. Calculate the new stock price (at $50 million of debt).

d. Continue the scenario of Part c, but now re-examine the question of the optimal amount of debt. Does the tax rate change affect your decision about the optimal use of financial leverage?

e. Go back to Part b; that is, assume T = 15%. How would your analysis of the capital structure change be modified if the firm's presently outstanding debt could not be called, and it did not have to be replaced; that is, if the $50 million of 10 percent debt continued even if the company issued new 12 percent bonds?

f. Suppose these probabilities for EBIT exist: P[EBIT = $5 million] = 0.2; P[EBIT = $15 million] = 0.6; and P[EBIT = $25 million] = 0.2. Under the assumptions of Part e, what are (1) expected EPS and σ_{EPS} and (2) expected TIE and σ_{TIE}, assuming an increase in book value of debt to $70 million?

15-6

Subjective Analysis

You have been hired as a financial consultant by two firms, Alpha Industries (Firm A) and Zed Corporation (Firm Z). Firm A is in the fast-growing microcomputer retail sales industry, while Firm Z manufactures office equipment such as pencil sharpeners, staplers, and tape dispensers. Your task is to recommend the optimal capital structure for the two firms. Discuss the factors that would influence your decision, and specifically how each of these factors apply to each firm. Here are some additional points about the two firms:

(1) Firm A generally leases its stores, while Firm Z purchases its plants.

(2) Firm A's stock is widely held, while the family of Firm Z's founder holds 40 percent of its stock.

(3) Firm Z has a significant amount of accelerated depreciation expense each year, while Firm A has almost none.

(4) Firm A has demonstrated high growth and profitability over the last few years. On the other hand, Firm Z's growth has averaged a modest 5 percent per year, and its profit margins and ROEs have been unspectacular.

Spreadsheet Problem

Work this problem only if you are using the computerized problem diskette.

15-7

Capital Structure Analysis

Use the model in File C15 to solve this problem. The Norman Corporation is currently all-equity financed, but the firm is considering a change to 50 percent debt financing. The debt would cost 12 percent, and would be used to repurchase shares currently selling at $25 per share. Norman now has 40,000 shares outstanding and $1,000,000 in total assets. Its pro forma income statement for 1999, assuming zero debt usage, is as follows:

Sales	$900,000
Operating costs	750,000
EBIT	$150,000
Taxes (40%)	60,000
Net income	$ 90,000

a. What is the firm's expected EPS for 1999 using zero debt? At a debt level of $500,000?

b. Assume that operating costs remain at 83.33 percent of sales over a wide range of sales levels. Further, the 1999 pro forma income statement is based on expected sales of $900,000, but the actual sales distribution is as follows:

PROBABILITY	SALES
0.10	$500,000
0.15	700,000
0.50	900,000
0.15	1,100,000
0.10	1,300,000

Find the EPS at each sales level for both zero debt and 50 percent debt financing.

c. Make a plot of EPS versus sales level for both financing alternatives. Place the plots on the same set of axes. Interpret this graph.

d. At a zero debt level, Norman's expected ROE = $90,000/$1,000,000 = 9.0%, while at $500,000 of debt, expected ROE = $54,000/$500,000 = 10.8%. Determine the firm's ROE at each debt level for every possible sales level. Plot the two ROE distributions.

e. Now, assume that the $500,000 debt financing would cost 15 percent. Repeat the Part d analysis. Is there a significant difference? Why?

MINI CASE

Assume you have just been hired as business manager of PizzaPalace, a pizza restaurant located adjacent to campus. The company's EBIT was $500,000 last year, and since the university's enrollment is capped, EBIT is expected to remain constant (in real terms) over time. Since no expansion capital will be required, PizzaPalace plans to pay out all earnings as dividends. The management group owns about 50 percent of the stock, and the stock is traded in the over-the-counter market.

The firm is currently financed with all equity; it has 100,000 shares outstanding; and $P_0 = 20 per share. When you took your MBA corporate finance course, your instructor stated that most firms' owners would be financially better off if the firms used some debt. When you suggested this to your new boss, he encouraged you to pursue the idea. As a first step, assume that you obtained from the firm's investment banker the following estimated costs of debt and equity for the firm at different debt levels (in thousands of dollars):

AMOUNT BORROWED	k_d	k_s
$ 0	—	15.0%
250	10.0%	15.5
500	11.0	16.5
750	13.0	18.0
1,000	16.0	20.0

If the company were to recapitalize, debt would be issued, and the funds received would be used to repurchase stock. PizzaPalace is in the 40 percent state-plus-federal corporate tax bracket.

a. Now, to develop an example that can be presented to PizzaPalace's management to illustrate the effects of financial leverage, consider two hypothetical firms: Firm U, which uses no debt financing, and Firm L, which uses $10,000 of 12 percent debt. Both firms have $20,000 in assets, a 40 percent tax rate, and an expected EBIT of $3,000.
   (1) Construct partial income statements, which start with EBIT, for the two firms.
   (2) Now calculate ROE for both firms.
   (3) What does this example illustrate about the impact of financial leverage on ROE?

b. (1) What is business risk? What factors influence a firm's business risk?
   (2) What is operating leverage, and how does it affect a firm's business risk?

c. (1) What is meant by financial leverage and financial risk?
   (2) How does financial risk differ from business risk?

d. Now consider the fact that EBIT is not known with certainty, but rather has the following probability distribution:

ECONOMIC STATE	PROBABILITY	EBIT
Bad	0.25	$2,000
Average	0.50	3,000
Good	0.25	4,000

Redo the Part a analysis for Firms U and L, but add basic earning power (BEP), return on investment (ROI) [defined as (Net income + Interest)/(Debt + Equity)], and the times-interest-earned (TIE) ratio to the outcome measures. Find the values for each firm in each state of the economy, and then calculate the expected values. Finally, calculate the standard deviation and coefficient of variation of ROE. What does this example illustrate about the impact of debt financing on risk and return?

e. How are financial and business risk measured in a stand-alone risk framework?

f. What does capital structure theory attempt to do? What lessons can be learned from capital structure theory?

g. With the above points in mind, now consider the optimal capital structure for PizzaPalace.

   (1) What valuation equations can you use in the analysis?

   (2) Could either the MM or the Miller capital structure theories be applied directly in this analysis, and if you presented an analysis based on these theories, how do you think the owners would respond?

h. (1) Describe briefly, without using any numbers, the sequence of events that would take place if PizzaPalace does recapitalize.

   (2) What would be the new stock price if PizzaPalace recapitalized and used these amounts of debt: $250,000; $500,000; $750,000?

   (3) How many shares would remain outstanding after recapitalization under each debt scenario?

   (4) Considering only the levels of debt discussed, what is PizzaPalace's optimal capital structure?

i. It is also useful to determine the effect of any proposed recapitalization on EPS. Calculate the EPS at debt levels of $0, $250,000, $500,000, and $750,000, assuming that the firm begins at zero debt and recapitalizes to each level in a single step. Is EPS maximized at the same level that maximizes stock price?

j. Calculate the firm's WACC at each debt level. What is the relationship between the WACC and the stock price?

k. Suppose you discovered that PizzaPalace had more business risk than you originally estimated. Describe how this would affect the analysis. What if the firm had less business risk than originally estimated?

l. Is it possible to do an analysis similar to the PizzaPalace analysis for most firms? Why or why not? What type of analysis do you think a firm should actually use to help set its optimal, or target, capital structure? What other factors should managers consider when setting the target capital structure?

Selected Additional References and Cases

Chapter 16 provides references that focus on the theory of capital structure; the references listed here are oriented more toward applications than theory.

Donaldson's work on the setting of debt targets is old but still relevant:

Donaldson, Gordon, "New Framework for Corporate Debt Capacity," *Harvard Business Review,* March–April 1962, 117–131.

———, "Strategy for Financial Emergencies," *Harvard Business Review,* November–December 1969, 67–79.

For an article on signaling, see

Baskin, Jonathon, "An Empirical Investigation of the Pecking Order Hypothesis," *Financial Management,* Spring 1989, 26–35.

Definitive references on the empirical relationships between capital structure and (1) the cost of debt, (2) the cost of equity, (3) earnings, and (4) the price of a firm's stock are virtually nonexistent—statistical problems make the precise estimation of these relationships extraordinarily difficult, if not impossible. One good way to get a feel for the issues involved is to obtain a set of the cost of capital testimonies filed in a major utility rate case—such testimony is available from state public utility commissions, the Federal Communications Commission, the Federal Energy Regulatory Commission, and utility companies themselves. For an academic discussion of the issues, see

Caks, John, "Corporate Debt Decisions: A New Analytical Framework," *Journal of Finance,* December 1978, 1297–1315.

Gordon, Myron J., *The Cost of Capital to a Public Utility* (East Lansing, Mich.: Division of Research, Graduate School of Business Administration, Michigan State University, 1974).

Hamada, Robert S., "The Effect of the Firm's Capital Structure on the Systematic Risk of Common Stocks," *Journal of Finance,* May 1972, 435–452.

Masulis, Ronald W., "The Impact of Capital Structure Change on Firm Value: Some Estimates," *Journal of Finance,* March 1983, 107–126.

Piper, Thomas R., and Wolf A. Weinhold, "How Much Debt Is Right for Your Company?" *Harvard Business Review,* July–August 1982, 106–114.

Shalit, Sol S., "On the Mathematics of Financial Leverage," *Financial Management,* Spring 1975, 57–66.

Shiller, Robert J., and Franco Modigliani, "Coupon and Tax Effects on New and Seasoned Bond Yields and the Measurement of the Cost of Debt Capital," *Journal of Financial Economics,* September 1979, 297–318.

For some insights into how practicing financial managers view the capital structure decision, see

Kamath, Ravindra R., "Long-Term Financing Decisions: Views and Practices of Financial Managers of NYSE Firms," *Financial Review,* May 1997, 331–356.

Norton, Edgar, "Factors Affecting Capital Structure Decisions," *Financial Review,* August 1991, 431–446.

Pinegar, J. Michael, and Lisa Wilbricht, "What Managers Think of Capital Structure Theory: A Survey," *Financial Management,* Winter 1989, 82–91.

Scott, David F., and Dana J. Johnson, "Financing Policies and Practices in Large Corporations," *Financial Management,* Summer 1982, 51–59.

To learn more about the link between market risk and operating and financial leverage, see

Callahan, Carolyn M., and Rosanne M. Mohr, "The Determinants of Systematic Risk: A Synthesis," *The Financial Review,* May 1989, 157–181.

Gahlon, James M., and James A. Gentry, "On the Relationship between Systematic Risk and the Degrees of Operating and Financial Leverage," *Financial Management,* Summer 1982, 15–23.

Prezas, Alexandros P., "Effects of Debt on the Degrees of Operating and Financial Leverage," *Financial Management,* Summer 1987, 39–44.

Here are some additional articles which relate to this chapter:

Easterwood, John C., and Palani-Rajan Kadapakkam, "The Role of Private and Public Debt in Corporate Capital Structures," *Financial Management,* Autumn 1991, 49–57.

Garvey, Gerald T., "Leveraging the Underinvestment Problem: How High Debt and Management Shareholdings Solve the Agency Costs of Free Cash Flow," *Journal of Financial Research,* Summer 1992, 149–166.

Harris, Milton, and Artur Raviv, "Capital Structure and the Informational Role of Debt," *Journal of Finance,* June 1990, 321–349.

Israel, Ronen, "Capital Structure and the Market for Corporate Control: The Defensive Role of Debt Financing," *Journal of Finance,* September 1991, 1391–1409.

See the following three articles for additional insights into the relationship between industry characteristics and financial leverage:

Bowen, Robert M., Lane A. Daley, and Charles C. Huber, Jr., "Evidence on the Existence and Determinants of Inter-Industry Differences in Leverage," *Financial Management,* Winter 1982, 10–20.

Long, Michael, and Ileen Malitz, "The Investment-Financing Nexus: Some Empirical Evidence," *Midland Corporate Finance Journal,* Fall 1985, 53–59.

Scott, David F., Jr., and John D. Martin, "Industry Influence on Financial Structure," *Financial Management,* Spring 1975, 67–73.

For a discussion of the international implications of capital structure, see

Rutterford, Janette, "An International Perspective on the Capital Structure Puzzle," *Midland Corporate Finance Journal,* Fall 1985, 60–72.

The Winter 1995, Winter 1996, and Spring 1997 issues of the Journal of Applied Corporate Finance *all contain featured articles pertaining to the capital structure decision.*

The Dryden Press Cases in Financial Management: Dryden Request *series contains many of the concepts we present in Chapters 15 and 16.*

Case 9, "Home Security Systems, Inc.," Case 10, "Kleen Kar, Inc.," Case 10A, "Mountain Springs, Inc.," and Case 10B, "Greta Cosmetics, Inc.," which present a situation similar to the Hill Software Systems example in the text.

CAPITAL STRUCTURE
DECISIONS: EXTENSIONS*

*A*t a recent meeting of the Financial Management Association, a panel session focused on how firms actually set their target capital structures. The participants included financial managers from Hershey Foods, Bell Atlantic, EG&G (a high-tech firm), and a number of other firms in various industries. Although there were minor differences in philosophy and procedures among the companies, several themes emerged.

First, in practice it is impossible to specify an optimal capital structure—indeed, managers even feel uncomfortable about specifying an optimal capital structure range. Thus, financial managers worry primarily about whether their firms are using too little or too much debt, not about the precise optimal amount of debt. Second, even if a firm's actual capital structure varies widely from the theoretical optimum, this might not have much impact on its stock price. Thus, financial managers believe that capital structure decisions are secondary in importance to operating decisions, especially those relating to capital budgeting and the strategic direction of the firm.

In general, financial managers focus more on identifying a "prudent" level of debt than on setting a precise optimal level. A prudent level is defined as one that captures most of the benefits of debt yet (1) keeps financial risk at a manageable level, (2) ensures future financing flexibility, and (3) allows the firm to maintain a desirable credit rating. Thus, a prudent level of debt will protect the company against financial distress under all but the worst economic scenarios, and it will assure access to money and capital markets under most conditions.

As you read this chapter, think about how you would make capital structure decisions if you had that responsibility. At the same time, don't forget the very important message from the FMA panel session: Establishing the right capital structure is an imprecise process at best, and it should be based on both informed judgment and quantitative analyses.

Chapter 15 presented some basic material on capital structure, including a brief introduction to capital structure theory. We saw that debt concentrates a firm's business risk on its stockholders, but debt also increases the expected return on equity. We also saw that there is some optimal level of debt that maximizes a company's stock price, but that it is next to impossible to identify that optimal capital structure. Now we go into more detail on capital structure theory. This will give you a deeper understanding of the benefits and costs associated with debt financing.

---

*This chapter may be omitted without loss of continuity.

CAPITAL STRUCTURE THEORY: THE MODIGLIANI-MILLER MODELS

Until 1958, capital structure theory consisted of loose assertions about investor behavior rather than carefully constructed models which could be tested by formal statistical analysis. In what has been called the most influential set of financial papers ever published, Franco Modigliani and Merton Miller (MM) addressed capital structure in a rigorous, scientific fashion, and they set off a chain of research that continues to this day.[1]

Assumptions

To begin, MM made the following assumptions, some of which were later relaxed:

1. There are no personal or corporate taxes.

2. Business risk can be measured by σ_{EBIT}, and firms with the same degree of business risk are said to be in a *homogeneous risk class*.

3. All present and prospective investors have identical estimates of each firm's future EBIT; that is, investors have *homogeneous expectations* about expected future corporate earnings and the riskiness of those earnings.

4. Stocks and bonds are traded in *perfect capital markets*. This assumption implies, among other things, (a) that there are no brokerage costs and (b) that investors (both individuals and institutions) can borrow at the same rate as corporations.

5. The debt of firms and individuals is riskless, so the interest rate on all debt is the risk-free rate. Further, this situation holds regardless of how much debt a firm (or individual) uses.

6. All cash flows are perpetuities; that is, all firms expect zero growth, hence have an "expectationally constant" EBIT, and all bonds are perpetuities. "Expectationally constant" means that the best guess is that EBIT will be constant, but after the fact the realized level could be different from the expected level.

MM without Taxes

MM first analyzed leverage under the assumption that there are no corporate or personal income taxes. On the basis of their assumptions, they stated and algebraically proved two propositions:[2]

Proposition I. The value of any firm is established by capitalizing its expected net operating income (EBIT) at a constant rate (k_{sU}) which is based on the firm's risk class:

---

[1]See Franco Modigliani and Merton H. Miller, "The Cost of Capital, Corporation Finance and the Theory of Investment," *American Economic Review*, June 1958, 261–297; "The Cost of Capital, Corporation Finance and the Theory of Investment: Reply," *American Economic Review*, September 1958, 655–669; "Taxes and the Cost of Capital: A Correction," *American Economic Review*, June 1963, 433–443; and "Reply," *American Economic Review*, June 1965, 524–527. In a 1979 survey of Financial Management Association members, the original MM article was judged to have had the greatest impact on the field of finance of any work ever published. See Philip L. Cooley and J. Louis Heck, "Significant Contributions to Finance Literature," *Financial Management*, Tenth Anniversary Issue 1981, 23–33. Note that both Modigliani and Miller won Nobel prizes—Modigliani in 1985 and Miller in 1990.

[2]MM actually stated and proved three propositions, but the third one is not material to our discussion here.

$$V_L = V_U = \frac{EBIT}{WACC} = \frac{EBIT}{k_{sU}}. \qquad (16\text{-}1)$$

Here the subscript L designates a levered firm and U designates an unlevered firm. Both firms are assumed to be in the same business risk class, and k_{sU} is the required rate of return for an unlevered, or all-equity, firm. (For our purposes, it is easiest to think in terms of a single firm that has the option of either financing with all equity or using some combination of debt and equity.)

Since V as established by Equation 16-1 is a constant, *then under the MM model, when there are no taxes, the value of the firm is independent of its leverage.* As we shall see, this also implies that

1. The weighted average cost of capital to the firm is completely independent of its capital structure.

2. The WACC for the firm, regardless of the amount of debt it uses, is equal to the cost of equity it would have if it used no debt.

Proposition II.   The cost of equity to a levered firm, k_{sL}, is equal to (1) the cost of equity to an unlevered firm in the same risk class, k_{sU}, plus (2) a risk premium whose size depends on both the differential between an unlevered firm's costs of debt and equity and the amount of debt used:

$$k_{sL} = k_{sU} + \text{Risk premium} = k_{sU} + (k_{sU} - k_d)(D/S). \qquad (16\text{-}2)$$

Here D = market value of the firm's debt, S = market value of the firm's equity, and k_d = constant cost of debt. *Equation 16-2 states that as the firm's use of debt increases, its cost of equity also rises, and in a mathematically precise manner.*

Taken together, the two MM propositions imply that the inclusion of more debt in the capital structure will not increase the value of the firm, because the benefits of cheaper debt will be exactly offset by an increase in the riskiness, hence in the cost, of its equity. *Thus, MM argue that in a world without taxes, both the value of a firm and its WACC would be unaffected by its capital structure.*

MM's Arbitrage Proof

MM used an *arbitrage proof* to support their propositions.[3] They showed that, under their assumptions, if two companies differed only (1) in the way they are financed and (2) in their total market values, then investors would sell shares of the higher-valued firm, buy those of the lower-valued firm, and continue this process until the companies had exactly the same market value. To illustrate, assume that two firms, L and U, are identical in all important respects except financial structure. Firm L has $4,000,000 of 7.5 percent debt, while Firm U uses only equity. Both firms have EBIT = $900,000, and σ_{EBIT} is the same for both firms, so they are in the same business risk class.

MM assumed that all firms are in a zero-growth situation; that is, EBIT is expected to remain constant, and all earnings are paid out as dividends. Under this assumption, the total market value of a firm's common stock, S, is the present value of a perpetuity, which is found as follows:

---

[3]By *arbitrage* we mean the simultaneous buying and selling of essentially identical assets which sell at different prices. The buying increases the price of the undervalued asset, and the selling decreases the price of the overvalued asset. Arbitrage operations will continue until prices have been adjusted to the point where the arbitrageur can no longer earn a profit, at which point the markets are in equilibrium. In the absence of transaction costs, equilibrium requires that the prices of the two assets be equal.

$$S = \frac{\text{Dividends}}{k_s} = \frac{\text{Net income}}{k_s} = \frac{(\text{EBIT} - k_d D)(1 - T)}{k_s}. \qquad \textbf{(16-3)}$$

Equation 16-3 is merely the value of a perpetuity whose numerator is the net income available to common stockholders, which is all paid out as dividends, and whose denominator is the cost of common equity. In MM's zero-tax world, the tax rate, T, is zero, so Equation 16-3 becomes simply $(\text{EBIT} - k_d D)/k_s$.

Assume that initially, *before any arbitrage occurs*, both firms have the same equity capitalization rate: $k_{sU} = k_{sL} = 10\%$. Under this condition, according to Equation 16-3, the following situation would exist:

Firm U:

$$\text{Value of Firm U's stock} = S_U = \frac{\text{EBIT} - k_d D}{k_{sU}} = \frac{\$900{,}000 - \$0}{0.10} = \$9{,}000{,}000.$$

Total market value of Firm $U = V_U = D_U + S_U = \$0 + \$9{,}000{,}000 = \$9{,}000{,}000.$

Firm L:

$$\text{Value of Firm L's stock} = S_L = \frac{\text{EBIT} - k_d D}{k_{sL}}$$

$$= \frac{\$900{,}000 - 0.075(\$4{,}000{,}000)}{0.10} = \frac{\$600{,}000}{0.10} = \$6{,}000{,}000.$$

Total market value of Firm $L = V_L = D_L + S_L = \$4{,}000{,}000 + \$6{,}000{,}000 = \$10{,}000{,}000.$

Thus, before arbitrage, and assuming that $k_{sU} = k_{sL}$ (which implies that capital structure has no effect on the cost of equity), the value of the levered Firm L exceeds that of unlevered Firm U.

MM argued that this is a disequilibrium situation which cannot persist. To see why, suppose you owned 10 percent of L's stock, so the market value of your investment was $0.10(\$6{,}000{,}000) = \$600{,}000$. According to MM, you could increase your income without increasing your exposure to risk. For example, suppose you (1) sold your stock in L for $600,000, (2) borrowed an amount equal to 10 percent of L's debt ($400,000), and then (3) bought 10 percent of U's stock for $900,000. Notice that you would receive $1,000,000 from the sale of your 10 percent of L's stock plus your borrowing, and you would be spending only $900,000 on U's stock, so you would have an extra $100,000, which MM assumed you would invest in riskless debt to yield 7.5 percent, or $7,500 annually.

Now consider your income positions:

Old Income:	10% of L's $600,000 equity income		$60,000
New Income:	10% of U's $900,000 equity income	$90,000	
	Less 7.5% interest on $400,000 loan	(30,000)	$60,000
	Plus 7.5% interest on extra $100,000		7,500
	Total new income		$67,500

Thus, your net income from common stock would be exactly the same as before, $60,000, but you would have $100,000 left over for investment in riskless debt, which would increase your income by $7,500. Therefore, the total return on your $600,000 net worth would rise to $67,500. Further, your risk, according to MM, would be the same as before, because you would have simply substituted $400,000 of "homemade" leverage for your 10 percent share of Firm L's $4 million of corporate leverage. Thus, neither your "effective" debt nor your risk would have changed. Therefore, you would have increased your income without raising your risk, which is obviously a desirable thing to do.

MM argued that this arbitrage process would actually occur, with sales of L's stock driving its price down, and purchases of U's stock driving its price up, until the market values of the two firms were equal. Until this equality was established, gains could be obtained by switching from one stock to the other, hence the profit motive would force the equality to be reached. When equilibrium is established, the values of Firms L and U, and their weighted average costs of capital, would be equal. Thus, according to Modigliani and Miller, both a firm's value and its WACC must be independent of capital structure.

Note that each of the assumptions listed at the beginning of this section is necessary for the arbitrage proof to work. For example, if the companies do not have identical business risk, or if transactions costs are significant, then the arbitrage process cannot be invoked. We will discuss further implications of the assumptions later in the chapter.

Arbitrage with Short Sales

Even if you did not own any stock in L, you still could reap benefits if U and L do not have the same total market value. Now, your first step would be to sell short $600,000 of stock in L. To do this, your broker would let you borrow stock in L from one of the broker's other clients. Your broker would then sell the stock for you and give you the proceeds, or $600,000 in cash. You would supplement this $600,000 by borrowing $400,000. With the $1 million total, you would buy 10 percent of the stock in U for $900,000, and have $100,000 remaining.

Your position consists of $100,000 in cash and two portfolios. The first portfolio contains $900,000 of stock in U, and it generates $90,000 in income. Since you own the stock, we'll call it the "long" portfolio. The other portfolio consists of $600,000 of stock in L and $400,000 in debt. The value of this portfolio is $1 million, and it generates $60,000 in dividends and $30,000 in interest. However, you do not own this second portfolio—you "owe" it. Since you borrowed the $400,000, you owe the $30,000 in interest. And since you borrowed the stock in L, you "owe the stock" to the broker from whom it was borrowed. Therefore, you must pay your broker the $60,000 of dividends paid by L, which the broker would then pass on to the client from whom the stock was borrowed. So, your net cash flow from the second portfolio is a negative $90,000. Since you "owe" this portfolio, we'll call it the "short" portfolio.

Where are you going to get the $90,000 that you must pay on the short portfolio? The good news is that this is exactly the amount of cash flow generated by the long portfolio that you own. The cash flows generated by each portfolio are the same; in other words, the short portfolio "replicates" the long portfolio.

Here is the bottom line. You started out with no money of your own. By selling L short, borrowing $400,000, and purchasing stock in U, you ended up with $100,000 in cash plus the two portfolios. The portfolios replicate one another, so their net cash flow is zero. This is perfect arbitrage: You invest none of your own money, you have no risk, you have no future negative cash flows, but you end up with cash in your pocket.

Not surprising, many traders would want to do this. The selling pressure on L would cause its price to fall, and the buying pressure on U would cause its price to increase, until the two companies' values were equal. To put it another way, *if the long and short replicating portfolios have the same cash flows, then they must have the same value.*

This is one of the most important ideas in modern finance. Not only does the application of this idea give us insights into capital structure, but it is the fundamental building block underlying the Arbitrage Pricing Theory (APT) of stock returns in Chapter 6, the valuation of real options in Chapter 13, and the valuation of financial options and derivatives as discussed in Chapter 24. In fact, without this idea, the options and derivatives markets we have today would not exist.

MM with Corporate Taxes

MM's original work, published in 1958, assumed zero taxes. In 1963, they published a second article which incorporated corporate taxes. With corporate income taxes, they concluded that leverage will increase a firm's value. This occurs because interest is a tax-deductible expense, hence more of a leveraged firm's operating income flows through to investors. Here are the MM propositions when corporations are subject to income taxes:

Proposition I. The value of a levered firm is equal to the value of an unlevered firm in the same risk class (V_U) *plus* the gain from leverage. The gain from leverage is the value of the tax savings, found as the product of the corporate tax rate (T) times the amount of debt the firm uses (D):

$$V_L = V_U + TD. \tag{16-1a}$$

The important point here is that when corporate taxes are introduced, the value of the levered firm exceeds that of the unlevered firm by the amount TD. Since the gain from leverage increases as debt increases, in theory a firm's value is maximized at 100 percent debt financing.

Because all cash flows are assumed to be perpetuities, the value of the unlevered firm can be found by using Equation 16-4. With zero debt (D = $0), the value of the firm is its equity value:

$$S = V_U = \frac{EBIT(1 - T)}{k_{sU}}. \tag{16-4}$$

Proposition II. The cost of equity to a levered firm is equal to (1) the cost of equity to an unlevered firm in the same risk class plus (2) a risk premium whose size depends on the differential between the costs of equity and debt to an unlevered firm, the amount of financial leverage used, and the corporate tax rate:

$$k_{sL} = k_{sU} + (k_{sU} - k_d)(1 - T)(D/S). \tag{16-2a}$$

Note that Equation 16-2a is identical to the corresponding without-tax equation, 16-2, except for the term $(1 - T)$ in 16-2a. Since $(1 - T)$ is less than 1, corporate taxes cause the cost of equity to rise less rapidly with leverage than was true in the absence of taxes. Proposition II, coupled with the fact that taxes reduce the effective cost of debt, is what produces the Proposition I result, namely, that the firm's value increases as its leverage increases.

Illustration of the MM Models

To illustrate the MM models, assume that the following data and conditions hold for Fredrickson Water Company, an old, established firm that supplies water to residential customers in several no-growth upstate New York communities.

1. Fredrickson currently has no debt; it is an all-equity company.

2. Expected EBIT = $2,400,000. EBIT is not expected to increase over time, so Fredrickson is in a no-growth situation.

3. Needing no new capital, Fredrickson pays out all of its income as dividends.

4. If Fredrickson begins to use debt, it can borrow at a rate k_d = 8%. This borrowing rate is constant—it does not increase regardless of the amount of debt used. Any money raised by selling debt would be used to retire common stock, so *Fredrickson's assets would remain constant*.

5. The business risk inherent in Fredrickson's assets, and thus in its EBIT, is such that its required rate of return, k_{sU}, is 12 percent if no debt is used.

With Zero Taxes. To begin, assume that there are no taxes, so T = 0%. At any level of debt, Proposition I (Equation 16-1) can be used to find Fredrickson's value in an MM world, $20 million:

$$V_L = V_U = \frac{EBIT}{k_{sU}} = \frac{\$2.4 \text{ million}}{0.12} = \$20.0 \text{ million}.$$

If Fredrickson uses $10 million of debt, its stock value must be $10 million:

$$S = V - D = \$20 \text{ million} - \$10 \text{ million} = \$10 \text{ million}.$$

We can also find Fredrickson's cost of equity, k_{sL}, and its WACC at a debt level of $10 million. First, we use Proposition II (Equation 16-2) to find k_{sL}, Fredrickson's leveraged cost of equity:

$$k_{sL} = k_{sU} + (k_{sU} - k_d)(D/S)$$

$$= 12\% + (12\% - 8\%)(\$10 \text{ million}/\$10 \text{ million})$$

$$= 12\% + 4.0\% = 16.0\%.$$

Now we can find the company's weighted average cost of capital:

$$WACC = (D/V)(k_d)(1 - T) + (S/V)k_s$$

$$= (\$10/\$20)(8\%)(1.0) + (\$10/\$20)(16.0\%) = 12.0\%.$$

Fredrickson's value and cost of capital based on the MM model without taxes at various debt levels are shown in Panel a on the left side of Figure 16-1. Here we see that in an MM world without taxes, financial leverage simply does not matter: The value of the firm, and its overall cost of capital, are independent of the amount of debt.

With Corporate Taxes. To illustrate the MM model with corporate taxes, assume that all of the previous conditions hold except these two:

1. Expected EBIT = $4,000,000.[4]

2. Fredrickson has a 40 percent federal-plus-state tax rate, so T = 40%.

---

[4]If we had left Fredrickson's EBIT at $2.4 million, the introduction of corporate taxes would have reduced the firm's value from $20 million to $12 million:

$$V_U = \frac{EBIT (1 - T)}{k_{sU}} = \frac{\$2.4 \text{ million} (0.6)}{0.12} = \$12.0 \text{ million}.$$

Corporate taxes reduce the amount of operating income available to investors in an unlevered firm by the factor (1 − T), so the value of the firm would be reduced by a like amount.

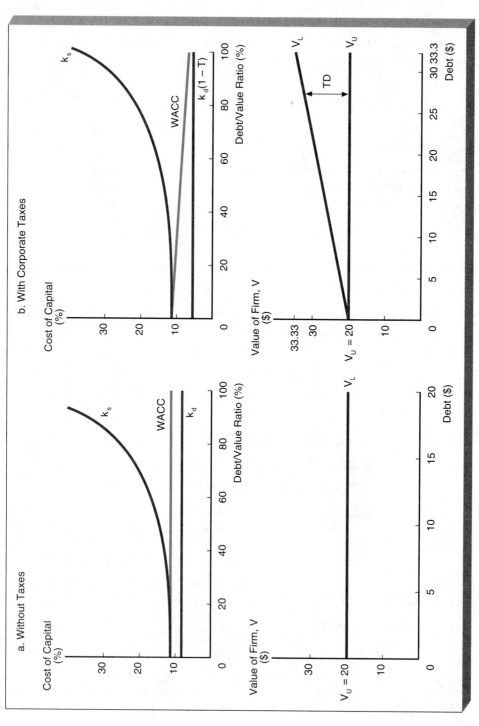

FIGURE 16-1 Effects of Leverage: MM Models (Millions of Dollars)

a. Without Taxes

Cost of Capital (%)

k_s

WACC

k_d

Debt/Value Ratio (%)

Value of Firm, V ($)

V_L

$V_U = 20$

Debt ($)

b. With Corporate Taxes

Cost of Capital (%)

k_s

WACC

$k_d(1 - T)$

Debt/Value Ratio (%)

Value of Firm, V ($)

V_L

$V_U = 20$

TD

Debt ($)

MM WITHOUT TAXES

D	V	S	D/V	k_d	k_s	WACC
$ 0	$20.00	$20.00	0.00%	8.0%	12.00%	12.00%
5	20.00	15.00	25.00	8.0	13.33	12.00
10	20.00	10.00	50.00	8.0	16.00	12.00
15	20.00	5.00	75.00	8.0	24.00	12.00
20	20.00	0.00	100.00	12.0	—	12.00

MM WITH CORPORATE TAXES

D	V	S	D/V	k_d	k_s	WACC
$ 0	$20.00	$20.00	0.00%	8.0%	12.00%	12.00%
5	22.00	17.00	22.73	8.0	12.71	10.91
10	24.00	14.00	41.67	8.0	13.71	10.00
15	26.00	11.00	57.69	8.0	15.27	9.23
20	28.00	8.00	71.43	8.0	18.00	8.57
25	30.00	5.00	83.33	8.0	24.00	8.00
30	32.00	2.00	93.75	8.0	48.00	7.50
33.33	33.33	0.00	100.00	12.0	—	12.00

Other things held constant, the introduction of corporate taxes would lower Fredrickson's net income, hence its value, so we increased EBIT from $2.4 million to $4 million to make the comparison between the two models easier.

When Fredrickson has zero debt but pays taxes, Equation 16-4 can be used to find its value, $20 million:

$$V_U = \frac{\text{EBIT} (1 - T)}{k_{sU}} = \frac{\$4 \text{ million } (0.6)}{0.12} = \$20.0 \text{ million.}$$

Now if Fredrickson uses $10 million of debt in a world with taxes, we see by Proposition I (Equation 16-1a) that its total market value rises to $24 million:

$$V_L = V_U + TD = \$20 \text{ million} + 0.4(\$10 \text{ million}) = \$24 \text{ million.}$$

Therefore, the value of Fredrickson's stock must be $14 million:

$$S = V - D = \$24 \text{ million} - \$10 \text{ million} = \$14 \text{ million.}$$

We can also find Fredrickson's cost of equity, k_{sL}, and its WACC at a debt level of $10 million. First, we use Proposition II (Equation 16-2a) to find k_{sL}, the leveraged cost of equity:

$$k_{sL} = k_{sU} + (k_{sU} - k_d)(1 - T)(D/S)$$

$$= 12\% + (12\% - 8\%)(0.6)(\$10 \text{ million}/\$14 \text{ million})$$

$$= 12\% + 1.71\% = 13.71\%.$$

The company's weighted average cost of capital is 10 percent:

$$\text{WACC} = (D/V)(k_d)(1 - T) + (S/V)k_s$$

$$= (\$10/\$24)(8\%)(0.6) + (\$14/\$24)(13.71\%) = 10.0\%.$$

Fredrickson's value and cost of capital at various debt levels with corporate taxes are shown in Panel b on the right side of Figure 16-1. In an MM world with corporate taxes, financial leverage does matter: The value of the firm is maximized, and its overall cost of capital is minimized, if it uses almost 100 percent debt financing. The increase in value is due solely to the tax deductibility of interest payments, which lowers both the cost of debt and the equity risk premium by $(1 - T)$.[5]

---

[5]In the limiting case, where the firm used 100 percent debt financing, the bondholders would own the entire company; thus, they would have to bear all the business risk. (Up until this point, MM assume that the stockholders bear all the risk.) If the bondholders bear all the risk, then the capitalization rate on the debt should be equal to the equity capitalization rate at zero debt, $k_d = k_{sU} = 12\%$.

The income stream to the stockholders in the all-equity case was $4,000,000(1 - T) = $2,400,000$, and the value of the firm was

$$V_U = \frac{\$2,400,000}{0.12} = \$20,000,000.$$

With all debt, the entire $4,000,000 of EBIT would be used to pay interest charges — k_d would be 12 percent, so $I = 0.12(\text{Debt}) = \$4,000,000$. Taxes would be zero, and investors (bondholders) would get the entire $4,000,000 of operating income; they would not have to share it with the government. Thus, at 100 percent debt, the value of the firm would be

$$V_L = \frac{\$4,000,000}{0.12} = \$33,333,333 = D.$$

There is, of course, a transition problem in all this — MM assume that $k_d = 8\%$ regardless of how much debt the firm has until debt reaches 100 percent, at which point k_d jumps to 12 percent, the cost of equity. As we shall see later in the chapter, k_d realistically rises as the use of financial leverage increases.

To conclude this section, compare the "Without Taxes" and "With Corporate Taxes" sections of Figure 16-1. Without taxes, both WACC and the firm's value (V) are constant. With corporate taxes, WACC declines and V rises as more and more debt is used, so the optimal capital structure, under MM with corporate taxes, is 100 percent debt.

What is the optimal capital structure under the MM zero-tax model?

What is the optimal capital structure under the MM model with corporate taxes?

How does the Proposition I equation differ in the two models?

How does the Proposition II equation differ in the two models?

Why do taxes result in a "gain from leverage" in the MM model with corporate taxes?

THE HAMADA MODEL: INTRODUCING MARKET RISK

In our discussion of business and financial risk in Chapter 15, we focused on stand-alone risk, using $\sigma_{ROE(U)}$ as the measure of business risk and $\sigma_{ROE(L)}$ as the measure of the stand-alone risk borne by stockholders if debt is used. Thus, in the stand-alone risk sense, $\sigma_{ROE(L)} - \sigma_{ROE(U)}$ is a measure of financial risk. Recall, though, that part of stand-alone risk can be eliminated if stockholders diversify their own portfolios. In this section, we consider business and financial risk from a **market risk** standpoint.

Robert Hamada combined the Capital Asset Pricing Model (CAPM) presented in Chapters 5 and 6 with the MM after-tax model to obtain this expression for k_{sL}, the cost of equity to a leveraged firm:[6]

$$k_{sL} = \begin{array}{c} \text{Risk-free} \\ \text{rate} \end{array} + \begin{array}{c} \text{Business risk} \\ \text{premium} \end{array} + \begin{array}{c} \text{Financial risk} \\ \text{premium} \end{array} \qquad \textbf{(16-5)}$$

$$= \quad k_{RF} \quad + \quad (k_M - k_{RF})b_U \quad + \quad (k_M - k_{RF})b_U(1 - T)(D/S).$$

Here b_U is the beta coefficient the firm would have if it used no financial leverage, and the other terms are as defined previously. In effect, Equation 16-5 partitions the required rate of return on a stock into three components: k_{RF}, the risk-free rate, which compensates shareholders for the time value of money; a premium for business risk as reflected by the term $(k_M - k_{RF})b_U$; and a premium for financial risk as reflected by the third term, $(k_M - k_{RF})b_U(1 - T)(D/S)$. If a firm has no financial leverage (D = $0), then the financial risk premium term would be zero (the third term would drop out) and equity investors would be compensated only for business risk.

As we will see, the MM model with corporate taxes does not hold exactly, and we also know that the CAPM does not fully describe investor behavior. Therefore, the Hamada model as expressed in Equation 16-5 must be regarded as an approximation. Nevertheless, the Hamada model can provide financial managers with some useful insights. As an illustration, assume that Firm U, an unlevered company with $b_U = 1.5$ and $100,000 of equity (S = $100,000), is considering replacing $20,000 of equity with debt. Assuming also that $k_{RF} = 10\%$, $k_M = 15\%$, and T = 34%, then Firm U's current unlevered required rate of return on equity would be 17.5 percent:

[6]See Robert S. Hamada, "Portfolio Analysis, Market Equilibrium, and Corporation Finance," *Journal of Finance,* March 1969, 13–31. Note that Thomas Conine and Maurry Tamarkin have extended Hamada's work to include risky debt. See "Divisional Cost of Capital Estimation: Adjusting for Leverage," *Financial Management,* Spring 1985, 54–58.

$$k_{sU} = 10\% + (15\% - 10\%)1.5$$
$$= 10\% + 7.5\% = 17.5\%.$$

This shows that the business risk premium is 7.5 percentage points. If the firm were to add \$20,000 of debt to its capital structure, then its new value, according to MM, would be $V_L = V_U + TD = \$100,000 + 0.34(\$20,000) = \$106,800$, and its k_s, using Equation 16-5, would rise to 18.64 percent:

$$k_{sL} = 10\% + (15\% - 10\%)1.5 + (15\% - 10\%)1.5(1 - 0.34)(\$20,000/\$86,800)$$
$$= 10\% + 7.5\% + 1.14\% = 18.64\%.$$

Thus, adding \$20,000 of debt to the capital structure would result in a financial risk premium on the stock of 1.14 percentage points, which would be added to the business risk premium of 7.5 percentage points.

Hamada also showed that Equation 16-5 can be used to derive another equation that analyzes the effect of financial leverage on beta. We know that the SML can be used to estimate a firm's required rate of return on equity:

$$\text{SML: } k_s = k_{RF} + (k_M - k_{RF})b.$$

Now, by equating the SML equation with Equation 16-5, we obtain:

$$k_{RF} + (k_M - k_{RF})b = k_{RF} + (k_M - k_{RF})b_U + (k_M - k_{RF})b_U(1 - T)(D/S)$$
$$(k_M - k_{RF})b = (k_M - k_{RF})b_U + (k_M - k_{RF})b_U(1 - T)(D/S) \qquad \textbf{(16-6)}$$
$$b = b_U + b_U(1 - T)(D/S),$$

or

$$b = b_U[1 + (1 - T)(D/S)]. \qquad \textbf{(16-6a)}$$

Thus, under the MM and CAPM assumptions, the equity beta of any firm is equal to the equity beta the firm would have if it used zero debt, adjusted upward by a factor that depends on (1) the corporate tax rate and (2) the amount of financial leverage employed.[7] Therefore, the stock's market risk, which is measured by b, depends on both the firm's business risk as measured by b_U and its financial risk as measured by $b - b_U = b_U(1 - T)(D/S)$.

To continue our illustration, if Firm U were to replace \$20,000 of equity with debt, its equity beta would increase from 1.5 to 1.728, according to Equation 16-6a:

$$b = b_U[1 + (1 - T)(D/S)]$$
$$= 1.5[1 + (1 - 0.34)(20,000/\$86,800)]$$
$$= 1.5(1.152) = 1.728.$$

We can confirm the Equation 16-5 value of $k_{sL} = 18.64\%$ by using $b = 1.728$ in the SML:

$$k_s = k_{RF} + (k_M - k_{RF})b$$
$$= 10\% + (15\% - 10\%)1.728 = 18.64\%.$$

---

[7]If a firm uses preferred stock, then Equation 16-6 becomes

$$b = b_U + b_U(P/S) + b_U(1 - T)(D/S),$$

where P = market value of preferred stock. Here the unlevered beta is adjusted upward by the preferred stock as well as the debt.

These relationships can be used to help estimate a company's or a division's cost of equity. In both instances, we proceed by obtaining betas for similar publicly traded firms and then "lever them up or down" to make them consistent with our own firm's (or division's) capital structure and tax rate. The result is an estimate of our firm's (or division's) equity beta, given (1) its business risk as measured by the equity betas of other firms in the same line of business and (2) its financial risk as measured by its own capital structure and tax rate.

According to Hamada, the required rate of return on a stock consists of three elements. What are they?

How is business risk measured within a market risk framework?

How is financial risk measured within a market risk framework?

What is the relationship between levered and unlevered betas according to Hamada?

CAPITAL STRUCTURE THEORY: THE MILLER MODEL

Although MM included **corporate** taxes in the second version of their model, they did not extend the model to include **personal** taxes. However, in his presidential address to the American Finance Association, Merton Miller introduced a model designed to show how leverage affects firms' values when both personal and corporate taxes are taken into account.[8] To explain Miller's model, let us begin by defining T_c as the corporate tax rate, T_s as the personal tax rate on income from stocks, and T_d as the personal tax rate on income from debt. Note that stocks' returns come partly as dividends and partly as capital gains, so T_s is a weighted average of the effective tax rates on dividends and capital gains, while essentially all debt income comes from interest, which is effectively taxed at investors' top rates.

With personal taxes included, *and under the same set of assumptions used in the earlier MM models,* the value of an unlevered firm is found as follows:

$$V_U = \frac{EBIT(1 - T_c)(1 - T_s)}{k_{sU}}. \tag{16-7}$$

The $(1 - T_s)$ term takes account of personal taxes. Therefore, the numerator shows how much of the firm's operating income is left after the unlevered firm pays corporate income taxes and its stockholders subsequently pay personal taxes on their equity income. Since the introduction of personal taxes lowers the income available to investors, personal taxes reduce the value of the unlevered firm, other things held constant.

Miller's results can be supported by an arbitrage proof similar to the one we presented earlier. However, the alternative proof shown below is easier to follow. To begin, we partition the levered firm's annual cash flows, CF_L, into those going to the stockholders and those going to the bondholders, after both corporate and personal taxes:

$$
\begin{aligned}
CF_L &= \text{Net CF to stockholders} \quad + \text{Net CF to bondholders} \\
&= (EBIT - I)(1 - T_c)(1 - T_s) + \quad\quad I(1 - T_d).
\end{aligned}
\tag{16-8}
$$

Here I is the annual interest payment. Equation 16-8 can be rearranged as follows:

$$CF_L = [EBIT(1 - T_c)(1 - T_s)] - [I(1 - T_c)(1 - T_s)] + [I(1 - T_d)]. \tag{16-8a}$$

---

[8]See Merton H. Miller, "Debt and Taxes," *Journal of Finance,* May 1977, 261–275.

The first term in Equation 16-8a is identical to the after-tax cash flow of an unlevered firm as shown in Equation 16-7, and its present value is found by discounting the perpetual cash flow by k_{sU}. The second and third terms, which reflect leverage, result from the cash flows associated with debt financing, which under the MM assumptions is assumed to be riskless. Their present values are obtained by discounting at the cost of debt, k_d. (Remember, these are all perpetual cash flows, so the basic perpetuity valuation model, $V = CF/k$, applies.) Combining the present values of the three terms, we obtain this value for the levered firm:

$$V_L = \frac{EBIT(1 - T_c)(1 - T_s)}{k_{sU}} - \frac{I(1 - T_c)(1 - T_s)}{k_d} + \frac{I(1 - T_d)}{k_d}. \tag{16-9}$$

The first term in Equation 16-9 is identical to V_U as set forth in Equation 16-7. Recognizing this, and when we consolidate the second two terms, we obtain this equation:

$$V_L = V_U + \frac{I(1 - T_d)}{k_d}\left[1 - \frac{(1 - T_c)(1 - T_s)}{(1 - T_d)}\right]. \tag{16-9a}$$

Now recognize that the after-tax perpetual interest payment divided by the required rate of return on debt, $I(1 - T_d)/k_d$, equals the market value of the debt, D. Substituting D into the preceding equation and rearranging, we obtain this expression, called the **Miller model:**

$$\text{Miller model: } V_L = V_U + \left[1 - \frac{(1 - T_c)(1 - T_s)}{(1 - T_d)}\right]D. \tag{16-10}$$

The Miller model provides an estimate of the value of a levered firm in a world with both corporate and personal taxes.

The Miller model has several important implications:

1. The term in brackets,

$$\left[1 - \frac{(1 - T_c)(1 - T_s)}{(1 - T_d)}\right],$$

when multiplied by D, represents the gain from leverage. The bracketed term thus replaces the corporate tax rate, T in the earlier MM model with corporate taxes, $V_L = V_U + TD$.

2. If we ignore all taxes, that is, if $T_c = T_s = T_d = 0$, then the bracketed term is zero, so in that case Equation 16-10 is the same as the original MM model without taxes.

3. If we ignore personal taxes, that is, if $T_s = T_d = 0$, then the bracketed term reduces to $[1 - (1 - T_c)] = T_c$, so Equation 16-10 is the same as the MM model with corporate taxes.

4. If the effective personal tax rates on stock and bond incomes were equal, that is, if $T_s = T_d$, then $(1 - T_s)$ and $(1 - T_d)$ would cancel, and the bracketed term would again reduce to T_c.

5. If $(1 - T_c)(1 - T_s) = (1 - T_d)$, then the bracketed term would go to zero, and the value of using leverage would also be zero. This implies that the tax advantage of debt to the firm would be exactly offset by the personal tax advantage of equity. Under this condition, capital structure would have no effect on a firm's value or its cost of capital, so we would be back to MM's original zero-tax theory.

6. Because taxes on capital gains are both lower than on ordinary income and can be deferred, the effective tax rate on stock income is normally less than that on bond income. This being the case, what would the Miller model predict as the gain from

leverage? To answer this question, assume that the tax rate on corporate income is $T_c = 34\%$, the effective rate on bond income is $T_d = 28\%$, and the effective rate on stock income is $T_s = 15\%$.[9] Using these values in the Miller model, we find that a levered firm's value increases over that of an unlevered firm by 22 percent of the market value of corporate debt:

$$\text{Gain from leverage} = \left[1 - \frac{(1 - T_c)(1 - T_s)}{(1 - T_d)}\right]D$$

$$= \left[1 - \frac{(1 - 0.34)(1 - 0.15)}{(1 - 0.28)}\right]D$$

$$= [1 - 0.78]D = 0.22D.$$

Note that the MM model with corporate taxes would indicate a gain from leverage of $T_c(D) = 0.34D$, or 34 percent of the amount of corporate debt. Thus, with these assumed tax rates, adding personal taxes to the model lowers but does not eliminate the benefit from corporate debt. In general, whenever the effective tax rate on income from stock is less than the effective rate on income from bonds, the Miller model produces a lower gain from leverage than is produced by the MM with-tax model.

In his paper, Miller argued that firms in the aggregate would issue a mix of debt and equity securities such that the before-tax yields on corporate securities and the personal tax rates of the investors who bought these securities would adjust until an equilibrium was reached. At equilibrium, $(1 - T_d)$ would equal $(1 - T_c)(1 - T_s)$, so, as we noted earlier in Point 5, the tax advantage of debt to the firm would be exactly offset by personal taxation, and capital structure would have no effect on a firm's value or its cost of capital. Thus, according to Miller, the conclusions derived from the original Modigliani-Miller zero-tax model are correct!

Others have extended and tested Miller's analysis. Generally, these extensions question Miller's conclusion that there is no advantage to the use of corporate debt. In the United States, the effective tax rate on income from stock is less than on income from bonds. Thus, it appears that $(1 - T_c)(1 - T_s)$ is less than $(1 - T_d)$, hence there is an advantage to the use of corporate debt. Still, Miller's work does show that personal taxes offset some of the benefits of corporate debt, so the tax advantages of corporate debt are less than were implied by the earlier MM model, where only corporate taxes were considered.

As we note in the next section, there are a number of problems with both the MM and the Miller models, so one should regard our examples as indicating the general effects of leverage on firms' value, not a precise relationship.

SELF-TEST
QUESTIONS

How does the Miller model differ from the MM model with corporate taxes?

What are the implications of the Miller model if $T_c = T_s = T_d = 0$?

What are the implications if $T_s = T_d = 0$?

Considering the current tax structure in the United States, what is the primary implication of the Miller model?

---

[9]In a 1978 article, Miller and Scholes described how investors could, theoretically, shelter or delay income from stock to the point where the effective personal tax rate on such income is essentially zero. See Merton H. Miller and Myron S. Scholes, "Dividends and Taxes," *Journal of Financial Economics,* December 1978, 333–364. However, the 1986 changes in the tax law eliminated most of the shelters Miller and Scholes discussed.

CRITICISMS OF THE MM AND MILLER MODELS

The conclusions of the MM and Miller models follow logically from their initial assumptions. However, both academicians and financial executives have voiced concerns over the validity of the MM and Miller models, and virtually no one believes they hold precisely. The MM zero-tax model leads to the conclusion that capital structure doesn't matter, yet we observe systematic capital structure patterns within industries. Further, when used with "reasonable" tax rates, both the MM model with corporate taxes and the Miller model lead to the conclusion that firms should use 100 percent debt financing, but virtually no firms deliberately go to that extreme.

People who disagree with the MM and Miller theories generally attack them on the grounds that their assumptions are not correct. Here are the main objections:

1. Both MM and Miller assume that personal and corporate leverage are perfect substitutes. However, an individual investing in a levered firm has less loss exposure as a result of corporate *limited liability* than if he or she used "homemade" leverage. For example, in our earlier illustration of the MM arbitrage argument, it should be noted that only the $600,000 our investor had in Firm L would be lost if that firm went bankrupt. However, if the investor engaged in arbitrage transactions and employed "homemade" leverage to invest in Firm U, then he or she could lose $900,000—the original $600,000 investment plus the $400,000 loan less the $100,000 investment in riskless bonds. This increased personal risk exposure would tend to restrain investors from engaging in arbitrage, and that could cause the equilibrium values of V_L, V_U, k_{sL}, and k_{sU} to be different from those specified by MM. Restrictions on institutional investors, who dominate capital markets today, may also retard the arbitrage process, because many institutional investors cannot legally borrow to buy stocks, hence are prohibited from engaging in homemade leverage.

2. If a leveraged firm's operating income declined, it would sell assets and take other measures to raise the cash necessary to meet its interest obligations and thus avoid bankruptcy. If the unleveraged firm experienced the same decline in operating income, it would probably take the less drastic measure of cutting dividends rather than selling assets. If dividends were cut, the investor who employed homemade leverage would not receive cash to pay the interest on his or her debt. Thus, homemade leverage puts stockholders in greater danger of bankruptcy than does corporate leverage.

3. Brokerage costs were assumed away by MM and Miller, making the switch from L to U costless. However, brokerage and other transaction costs (including "market pressure") do exist, and they too impede the arbitrage process.

4. MM initially assumed that corporations and investors can borrow at the risk-free rate. Although risky debt has been introduced into the analysis by others, to reach the MM and Miller conclusions it is still necessary to assume that both corporations and investors can borrow at the same rate. While major institutional investors probably can borrow at the corporate rate, many institutions are not allowed to borrow to buy securities. Further, most individual investors must borrow at higher rates than those paid by large corporations.

5. In his article, Miller concluded that an equilibrium would be reached, but to reach his equilibrium the tax benefit from corporate debt must be the same for all firms, and it must be constant for an individual firm regardless of the amount of leverage used. However, we know that tax benefits vary from firm to firm: Highly profitable companies gain the maximum tax benefit from leverage, while the benefits to firms that are struggling are much smaller. Further, some firms have other tax shields such as high depreciation, pension plan contributions, and operating loss

carry-forwards, and these shields reduce the tax savings from interest payments.[10] It also appears simplistic to assume that the expected tax shield is unaffected by the amount of debt used. Higher leverage increases the probability that the firm will not be able to use the full tax shield in the future, because higher leverage increases the probability of future unprofitability and consequently lower tax rates. All things considered, it appears likely that the interest tax shield from corporate debt is more valuable to some firms than to others.

6. MM and Miller assume that there are no costs associated with financial distress, and they ignore agency costs. Further, they assume that all market participants have identical information about firms' prospects, which is also incorrect. These topics are discussed in the next section.

SELF-TEST QUESTIONS

Should we accept that one of the models presented thus far (MM with zero taxes, MM with corporate taxes, or Miller) is correct? Why or why not?

Are any of the assumptions used in the models worrisome to you, and what does "worrisome" mean in this context?

CAPITAL STRUCTURE THEORY: THE TRADE-OFF MODELS

Some of the assumptions inherent in the MM and Miller models can be relaxed without changing the basic MM/Miller conclusions.[11] However, as we discuss next, when financial distress and agency costs are considered, the MM and Miller results are altered significantly.

Costs of Financial Distress

Financial distress includes, but is not restricted to, bankruptcy, and when financial distress occurs, several things can happen:

1. Arguments between claimants often delay the liquidation of assets. Bankruptcy cases can take many years to settle, and during this time machinery rusts, buildings are vandalized, inventories become obsolete, and the like.

2. Lawyers' fees, court costs, and administrative expenses can absorb a large part of the firm's value. Together, the costs of physical deterioration plus legal fees and administrative expenses are called the *direct costs* of financial distress.

3. Managers and other employees generally lose their jobs when a firm fails. Knowing this, the management of a firm that is in financial distress may take actions which keep it alive in the short run but which also dilute long-run value. For example, the firm may defer maintenance of machinery, sell off valuable assets at bargain prices to raise cash, or cut costs so much that the quality of its products or services is impaired and the firm's long-run market position is eroded.

---

[10]For a discussion of the impact of tax shields other than debt financing, see Harry DeAngelo and Ronald W. Masulis, "Optimal Capital Structure under Corporate and Personal Taxation," *Journal of Financial Economics,* March 1980, 3–30.

[11]For example, see Robert A. Haugen and James L. Pappas, "Equilibrium in the Pricing of Capital Assets, Risk-Bearing Debt Instruments, and the Question of Optimal Capital Structure," *Journal of Financial and Quantitative Analysis,* June 1971, 943–954; Joseph Stiglitz, "A Re-Examination of the Modigliani-Miller Theorem," *American Economic Review,* December 1969, 784–793; and Mark E. Rubenstein, "A Mean-Variance Synthesis of Corporate Financial Theory," *Journal of Finance,* March 1973, 167–181.

4. Both customers and suppliers are aware of the problems that can arise, and they often take "evasive action" that further damages the troubled firm. For example, Eastern Airlines, as it struggled to deal with its unions and to avoid liquidation, had trouble selling tickets because potential customers were worried about buying a seat for a future flight and then having the company shut down before they could take the trip. Some potential customers were also worried that the company might cut back on maintenance, and Eastern's suppliers were reluctant to grant normal credit terms or to gear up to supply parts and other materials on a long-term basis. Finally, Eastern had trouble attracting and retaining the highest-quality workers, as most workers with a choice preferred employment with a more stable airline to one that might go out of business at any time.

5. Nonoptimal managerial actions associated with financial distress, as well as the costs imposed by customers, suppliers, and capital providers, are called the *indirect costs* of financial distress. Of course, these costs may be incurred by a firm in financial distress even if it does not go into bankruptcy: Bankruptcy is just one point on the continuum of financial distress.

All things considered, the direct and indirect costs associated with financial distress are high.[12] Further, financial distress typically occurs only if a firm has debts — debt-free firms usually do not experience financial distress. *Therefore, the greater the use of debt financing, and the larger the fixed interest charges, the greater the probability that a decline in earnings will lead to financial distress, hence the higher the probability that costs associated with financial distress will be incurred.*

An increase in the probability of future financial distress lowers the current value of a firm and raises its cost of capital. To see why, suppose we estimate that Fredrickson Water will incur costs of $7 million if it fails at some future date, and that the *present value* of this possible future cost is $5 million. Further, the probability of financial distress increases with leverage, causing the expected present value of the cost of financial distress to rise from zero at zero debt to $4.75 million at $30 million of debt as shown in Table 16-1.

These expected costs must be subtracted from the values we previously calculated in Panel b of Figure 16-1 to find the firm's value at various amounts of leverage: They would reduce the values of V and S and, as a result, would raise k_s and the WACC. For example, at $20 million of debt, we would obtain the values in Table 16-2.[13] These changes would, of course, then have carry-through effects on the graphs in Panel b of Figure 16-1. Most important, they would (1) reduce the decline of the WACC line and (2) reduce the slope of the V_L line.

The effects of financial distress are also felt by a firm's bondholders. Firms experiencing financial distress have a higher probability of defaulting on debt payments, so the higher the probability of financial distress, the higher the required return on debt. Thus,

---

[12]See Edward I. Altman, "A Further Empirical Investigation of the Bankruptcy Cost Question," *Journal of Finance,* September 1984, 1067–1089. On the basis of a sample of 26 bankrupt companies, Altman found that bankruptcy costs exceed 20 percent of firm value.

[13]To find k_s and the WACC in Table 16-2, simply transpose Equation 16-3 and then apply the definition for the WACC:

$$k_s = \frac{(EBIT - k_dD)(1 - T)}{S} = \frac{[\$4 - 0.08(\$20)](1 - 0.4)}{\$5.5} = 26.18\%.$$

$$WACC = (D/V)(k_d)(1 - T) + (S/V)(k_s)$$

$$= (\$20/\$25.5)(8\%)(0.6) + (\$5.5/\$25.5)(26.18\%)$$

$$= 3.76\% + 5.65\% = 9.41\%.$$

| TABLE 16-1 | Fredrickson Water Company: Expected Costs of Financial Distress |

	AMOUNT OF DEBT				
	$0	$5 MILLION	$10 MILLION	$20 MILLION	$30 MILLION
Probability of financial distress	0.0	0.05	0.15	0.50	0.95
PV of expected costs of financial distress[a]	$0	$250,000	$750,000	$2,500,000	$4,750,000

[a]$5 million times the indicated probability.

| TABLE 16-2 | Fredrickson Water Company: Effects of Financial Distress (Millions of Dollars) |

	VALUES AT D = $20 MILLION WITH FINANCIAL DISTRESS EFFECTS IGNORED: PURE MM	VALUES AT D = $20 MILLION WITH FINANCIAL DISTRESS EFFECTS CONSIDERED: MODIFIED MM
V	$28.00	$28.00 – $2.5 = $25.5
S	$8.00	$8.00 – $2.5 = $5.5
k_s	18.00%	26.18%
WACC	8.57%	9.41%

as a firm uses more and more debt, hence increasing the probability of distress, the value of k_d also increases, causing several elements in Panel b of Figure 16-1 to change.

Agency Costs

We introduced the concept of agency costs in Chapter 1. One agency relationship is between a firm's stockholders and its bondholders. In the absence of any restrictions, management would be tempted to take actions that would benefit stockholders at the expense of bondholders. For example, if Fredrickson Water were to issue only a small amount of debt, then this debt would have relatively little risk, a high bond rating, and a low interest rate. After it issued the low-risk debt, Fredrickson might issue more debt secured by the same assets as the original debt. This would raise the risks faced by *all* bondholders, cause k_d to rise, and consequently cause the original bondholders to suffer capital losses. Similarly, after issuing debt Fredrickson might decide to restructure its assets, selling off those with low business risk and acquiring assets that were more risky but that also had higher expected rates of return. If things worked out well, the stockholders would get all of the benefit, but if things went sour, much of the loss would fall on the bondholders. So, stockholders would be playing a game of "heads, I win; tails, you lose" with bondholders.

Because stockholders might try to exploit bondholders in these and other ways, bonds are protected by restrictive covenants. These covenants hamper the corporation's legitimate operations to some extent. Further, the company must be monitored to ensure that the covenants are being obeyed, and the costs of monitoring are passed on to the stockholders in the form of higher debt costs. The lost efficiency plus monitoring costs are *agency costs* that increase the cost of debt and thus reduce its advantage.[14]

Value and Cost of Capital Considering Financial Distress and Agency Costs

If the MM model with corporate taxes were correct, a firm's value would rise continuously as it moved from zero debt toward 100 percent debt: The equation $V_L = V_U + TD$ shows that TD, hence V_L, is maximized if D is at a maximum. Recall that the increasing component of value, TD, is a direct result of the tax shelter provided by interest on the debt. However, as noted above, financial distress and agency costs could cause V_L to decline as the level of debt rises. Therefore, the relationship between a firm's value and its use of leverage has two negative components, so the true equation should look like this:

$$V_L = V_U + TD - \begin{pmatrix} \text{PV of} \\ \text{expected} \\ \text{costs of} \\ \text{financial} \\ \text{distress} \end{pmatrix} - \begin{pmatrix} \text{PV of} \\ \text{agency} \\ \text{costs} \end{pmatrix}. \qquad \textbf{(16-11)}$$

The relationship expressed in Equation 16-11 is graphed in Figure 16-2. The tax shelter effects totally dominate until the amount of debt reaches Point A. After Point A, financial distress and agency costs become increasingly important, offsetting some of the tax advantages. At Point B, the marginal tax shelter benefit of additional debt is exactly offset by the disadvantages of debt, and beyond Point B, the disadvantages outweigh the tax benefit.

Equation 16-10, the Miller model, can also be modified to reflect financial distress and agency costs. The equation would be identical to Equation 16-11, except that the gain from leverage term, TD, would reflect the addition of personal taxes. In either the MM or Miller models, the gain from leverage can at least be roughly estimated, but the value reduction resulting from potential financial distress and agency costs is almost entirely subjective. We know that these costs must increase as leverage rises, but we do not know the specific functional relationships.

The addition of financial distress and agency costs to either the MM tax model or the Miller model results in a **trade-off model** of capital structure. In such a model, the optimal capital structure can be visualized as a trade-off between the benefit of debt (the interest tax shelter) and the costs of debt (financial distress and agency costs).

Implications of the Trade-Off Models

The trade-off models cannot be used to specify a precise optimal capital structure, but they do enable us to make three statements about leverage:

1. Firms with more business risk ought to use less debt than lower-risk firms, other things being equal, because the greater the business risk, the greater the probabil-

---

[14]Michael C. Jensen and William H. Meckling point out that there are also agency costs between outside equityholders and management. See "Theory of the Firm: Managerial Behavior, Agency Costs, and Ownership Structure," *Journal of Financial Economics,* October 1976, 305–360. Their study further suggests that (1) bondholder agency costs increase as the debt ratio increases, but (2) outside stockholder agency costs move in reverse fashion, falling with increased use of debt.

FIGURE 16-2   Net Effects of Leverage on the Value of the Firm

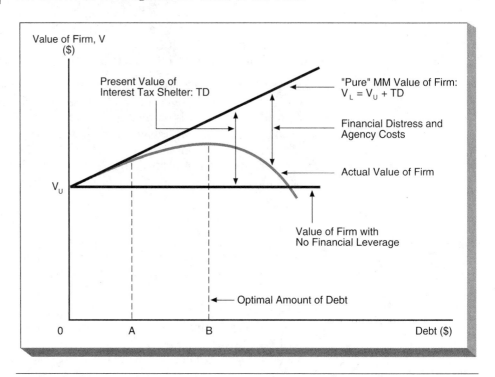

ity of financial distress at any level of debt, hence the greater the expected costs of distress. Thus, firms with lower business risk can borrow more before the expected costs of distress offset the tax advantages of borrowing (Point B in Figure 16-2).

2. Firms that have tangible, readily marketable assets such as real estate can use more debt than firms whose value is derived primarily from intangible assets such as patents and goodwill. The costs of financial distress depend not only on the probability of incurring distress but also on what happens if distress occurs. Specialized assets and intangible assets are more likely to lose value if financial distress occurs than are standardized, tangible assets.

3. Firms that are currently paying taxes at the highest rate, and that are likely to do so in the future, should use more debt than firms with lower tax rates. High corporate taxes lead to greater benefits from debt, other factors held constant, so more debt can be used before the tax shield is offset by financial distress and agency costs.

According to the trade-off models, each firm should set its target capital structure such that the costs and benefits of leverage are balanced at the margin, because such a structure will maximize its value. If the trade-off models are correct, we should find actual target structures that are consistent with the three points just noted. Further, we should find that firms within a given industry have similar capital structures, because such firms should have roughly the same types of assets, business risk, and profitability.

The Empirical Evidence

The trade-off models have intuitive appeal because they lead to the conclusion that both no-debt and all-debt are bad, while a "moderate" debt level is good. However, we must ask ourselves whether these models explain actual behavior. If they do not, then we must search for other explanations.

In fact, the trade-off models have very limited empirical support.[15] It does turn out that firms which invest primarily in tangible assets do tend to borrow more heavily than firms whose value stems from intangibles. However, empirical evidence refutes other aspects of the trade-off models. First, several studies have examined models of financing behavior to see if firms' financing decisions are consistent with a target capital structure. There is some evidence that this occurs, but the explanatory power of the models is very low, suggesting that trade-off models capture only a part of actual behavior. Second, studies have not consistently demonstrated that a firm's tax rate has a predictable, material effect on its capital structure. Indeed, firms used about as much debt before corporate income taxes even existed as they do today. Finally, actual debt ratios tend to vary widely across apparently similar firms within given industries, whereas the trade-off models suggest that similar firms should have similar debt ratios.

All in all, the empirical support for the trade-off models is weak, which suggests that factors not incorporated into these models are also at work. In other words, the trade-off models do not tell the full story.

SELF-TEST QUESTIONS	Describe some types of financial distress and agency costs.
	How are these costs related to the use of financial leverage?
	How are the basic MM with corporate taxes and Miller models affected by the inclusion of financial distress and agency costs?
	What is a trade-off model of capital structure?
	What implications do the trade-off models have regarding capital structure?
	Does the empirical evidence support the trade-off models?

CAPITAL STRUCTURE THEORY: THE SIGNALING MODEL

Some time ago, Professor Gordon Donaldson of Harvard conducted an extensive study of how corporations actually establish their capital structures.[16] Here is a summary of his findings:

1. Firms prefer to finance with internally generated funds, that is, with retained earnings and depreciation cash flow.

2. Firms set target dividend payout ratios based on expected future investment opportunities and expected future cash flows. The target payout ratio is set at a level such that retained earnings plus depreciation will cover capital expenditures under normal conditions.

3. Dividends are "sticky" in the short run—firms are reluctant to raise dividends unless they are confident that the higher dividend can be maintained, and they are

---

[15]For examples of the empirical research in this area, see Robert A. Taggart, Jr., "A Model of Corporate Financing Decisions," *Journal of Finance,* December 1977, 1467–1484; and Paul Marsh, "The Choice between Equity and Debt: An Empirical Study," *Journal of Finance,* March 1982, 121–144.

[16]Gordon Donaldson, *Corporate Debt Capacity: A Study of Corporate Debt Policy and the Determination of Corporate Debt Capacity* (Boston: Harvard Graduate School of Business Administration, 1961).

especially reluctant to cut the dividend. Indeed, they generally do not reduce the dividend unless things are so bad that they simply have to.

4. If a firm has more internal cash flow than is needed to cover its capital expenditures, then it will invest in marketable securities, use the funds to retire debt, increase dividends, repurchase stock, or acquire other firms. On the other hand, if it has insufficient internal cash flow to finance nonpostponable new projects, it will first draw down its marketable securities portfolio, then go to the external capital markets. If it has to go to the external markets, it will first issue debt, then convertible bonds, and then common stock only as a last resort. *Thus, Donaldson observed that there is a "pecking order" of financing, not a balanced approach as would result if the trade-off models accurately described real-world behavior.*

Professor Stewart Myers noted the inconsistency between Donaldson's findings and the trade-off models, and that inconsistency led Myers to propose a new theory.[17] First, Myers noted that Donaldson's pecking-order findings led away from, rather than toward, a well-defined capital structure. Equity is raised in two forms—retained earnings and new stock. Retained earnings are at the top of the pecking order, while new common stock is at the bottom. Therefore, if retained earnings are high relative to investment requirements, the equity ratio will increase, while if retained earnings are insufficient, the firm will borrow rather than issue stock, causing the debt ratio to increase. The trade-off models, on the other hand, assume that equity from the sale of stock is equivalent to that from retained earnings, and they suggest that the debt/equity ratio should remain constant over time.

Next, Myers noted that a critical assumption in the trade-off models is that all market participants have homogeneous expectations, which implies (1) that all participants have the same information and (2) that any changes in operating income are purely random as opposed to being anticipated by some but not all parties. Myers had the insight to see that if expectations are not homogeneous, meaning that different groups of market participants have asymmetric (or different) information, then Donaldson's results can be explained in a logical manner. Myers's work resulted in what is now called the **signaling,** or **asymmetric information, theory** of capital structure.

To illustrate, assume that a firm has 10,000 common shares outstanding. They sell at a price of $19 per share, so the market value of its equity is $190,000. However, its managers have better information regarding the firm's future than stockholders, and the managers believe that the actual value per share based on existing assets is $21, giving the equity a total "intrinsic" value of $210,000. Such an information asymmetry (or difference) could easily exist, for managers often know more about their firms' prospects than do current and potential investors.[18]

Suppose further that management now identifies a new project which would require $100,000 of external financing and which has an estimated NPV of $5,000. [Remember that a project's NPV represents economic value added (EVA), and that it accrues to the shareholders.] This project is unanticipated by the firm's investors, so the $5,000 NPV has not been incorporated into the $190,000 equity market value. Should the firm

---

[17]Stewart C. Myers, "The Capital Structure Puzzle," *Journal of Finance,* July 1984, 575–592. It is interesting to note that, like the Miller model, Myers's paper was first presented as a presidential address to the American Finance Association.

[18]This assumption is contrary to the strong-form efficient markets hypothesis (EMH) presented in Chapter 9, but as we noted there, few observers—including people who strongly support weak-form and semistrong-form efficiency—are willing to accept strong-form efficiency.

accept the project? To begin, suppose the firm issues new stock to raise the $100,000 to finance the project. Several possibilities exist:

1. **Symmetric information.** First, as a point of departure, consider the situation in which management can convey all the information to the public, hence all investors have the same information as management regarding existing asset values. Under these conditions, the stock would immediately rise to its $21 intrinsic value. Then, when the new project comes along and is financed, the firm would have to sell $100,000/$21 = 4,762 new shares. Acceptance of the project would then increase the stock price from $21 to $21.34:

$$\text{New stock price} = \frac{\text{Original market value} + \text{New money raised} + \text{NPV}}{\text{Original shares} + \text{New shares}}$$

$$= \frac{\$210,000 + \$100,000 + \$5,000}{10,000 + 4,762} = \frac{\$315,000}{14,762} = \$21.34.$$

Both old and new shareholders would benefit if the project were accepted; each group would gain $21.34 − $21.00 = $0.34 per share as a result of the new project.

2. **Asymmetric information prior to stock issue.** Now suppose management is unable to inform investors about the stock's intrinsic value. Perhaps it is necessary to hold back such information to maintain a competitive edge, or perhaps SEC regulations cause management to refrain from "touting" the stock prior to the new issue (if things did not work out as expected, new shareholders might sue the managers who had provided the rosy forecast). In this situation, new stock would fetch the current price, $19 per share, so the company would have to sell $100,000/$19 = 5,263 shares in order to raise the required $100,000. If this were done, this new price would result after the project was accepted and the information asymmetry was removed:

$$\text{New stock price} = \frac{\text{New market value} + \text{New money raised} + \text{NPV}}{\text{Original shares} + \text{New shares}}$$

$$= \frac{\$210,000 + \$100,000 + \$5,000}{10,000 + 5,263} = \frac{\$315,000}{15,263} = \$20.64.$$

Under this condition, the project should not be undertaken. If the project were not accepted, so no new shares were sold, then the price of the stock would rise to its $21 intrinsic value when the information asymmetry was eventually removed. The sale of new stock at $19 per share would lead to a $0.36 per share loss to the firm's existing shareholders. There would be a $1.64 gain to the new shareholders, but management wants to maximize the value of *current* stockholders, not new ones.

3. **A more profitable project.** Now suppose the project had an NPV of $20,000 rather than $5,000, the stock sold for $19, and other conditions in Scenario 2 were unchanged. Now the firm's stock price would rise to $21.62 if it undertook the project:

$$\text{New stock price} = \frac{\$210,000 + \$100,000 + \$20,000}{10,000 + 5,263} = \frac{\$330,000}{15,263} = \$21.62.$$

Under these conditions, the firm should take on the project. Note, though, that most of the positive NPV would go to the new stockholders, who would pay $19 per share and thus enjoy a capital gain of $2.62 versus a gain of only $0.62 for the original stockholders.

4. **Dark clouds on the horizon.** Now suppose an entirely different—and bad—situation faced the firm. Stockholders think the firm is worth $19 per share, but managers know (a) that outside investors are entirely too optimistic about growth opportunities, (b) that investors have not factored in proposed legislation which will require large, nonearning investments in pollution control equipment, and (c) that the current stock price does not reflect the need for new R&D expenditures which will be required to keep the firm's products competitive. If all of these bad events materialize, profit margins will be under pressure, cash flows will fall, and the company will have difficulty servicing its debt.

Faced with these conditions, management might well conclude that the stock's intrinsic value is only $17 per share, and then decide to sell a new issue of 10,000 shares at the current price of $19, raising $190,000 and using the funds to retire debt or to support this year's capital budget. This action would increase the intrinsic value of the stock from $17 to $18:

$$\text{New intrinsic value} = \frac{\text{Old intrinsic market value} + \text{New money}}{\text{Original shares} + \text{New shares}}$$

$$= \frac{\$170,000 + \$190,000}{10,000 + 10,000} = \frac{\$360,000}{20,000} = \$18.00.$$

Current stockholders will, if management's expectations come true, suffer a loss when the bad news becomes known, but the sale of new stock would reduce that loss. (Note: Management would have to carefully word the prospectus for the new issue, pointing out the potential problems. However, virtually all prospectuses are filled with cautionary language, so investors have difficulty telling from them what management really expects.)

5. **Finance the original $5,000 NPV project with debt.** If the firm used debt to finance the original $100,000 project (Scenario 2), *and then the information asymmetry were removed,* the new stock price would be $21.50 versus the $20.64 we found under Scenario 2:

$$\text{New stock price} = \frac{\text{New market value} + \text{NPV}}{\text{Original shares}}$$

$$= \frac{\$210,000 + \$5,000}{10,000} = \frac{\$215,000}{10,000} = \$21.50.$$

Thus, if debt were used, all of the intrinsic value of the firm's existing assets, plus the NPV of the new project, would accrue to the original shareholders. If stock were used, we saw earlier that the value of the original stock would end up at $20.64 rather than $21, the intrinsic value without the new investment.[19]

What does all this suggest about corporate financial policy? First, in a world where asymmetric information exists, corporations should issue new shares only in the unlikely event that they have extraordinarily profitable investments that cannot be either postponed, signaled to investors, or financed by debt, or in situations where

---

[19]If the additional debt were not proportionally matched with retained earnings, issuing new debt would increase the firm's risk and consequently its required rate of return on equity. Similarly, the issuance of new equity in the previous scenarios might reduce risk and thus lower the cost of equity. We abstract from these effects because (1) they are of second order importance and (2) incorporating them into the analysis would unnecessarily complicate the examples.

management thinks the shares are overvalued. Second, investors recognize all this, so selling pressure drives down a company's share price when it announces plans to issue new shares. Third, the pecking order that Donaldson observed is rational when asymmetric information exists—it pays to retain a large fraction of earnings, and also to keep the equity ratio up and the debt ratio down, so as to maintain a "reserve borrowing capacity" which can be used to support the capital budget if and when an unusually large number of positive NPV projects come along, or if problems arise which require outside capital.[20]

Note that signaling effects, and their impact on investors' perceptions, differ substantially across firms. To illustrate, asymmetry is typically much greater in the drug and semiconductor industries than in the retailing and trucking industries, because success in the drug and semiconductor industries depends on secretive proprietary research and development. Thus, managers in these industries have significantly more information about their firms' prospects than do outside investors. Also, emerging firms with limited capital but good growth opportunities are recognized as having to use external financing, so the announcement of new stock offerings by a new company is not viewed with as much concern by investors as are offerings by mature firms with limited growth opportunities. Thus, although signaling affects all firms, its impact varies from firm to firm.

SELF-TEST QUESTIONS

Briefly explain the asymmetric information (signaling) theory.

What does this theory suggest about capital structure decisions?

Is the signaling theory equally applicable to all firms?

CAPITAL STRUCTURE THEORY: OUR VIEW

The great contribution of the trade-off models developed by MM, Miller, and their followers is that these models identified the specific benefits and costs of using debt—the tax benefits, financial distress costs, and so on. Prior to MM, no capital structure theory existed, so we had no systematic way of analyzing the effects of debt financing.

The trade-off models are summarized graphically in Figure 16-3. The top graph shows the relationships between the debt ratio and the cost of debt, the cost of equity, and the WACC. Both k_s and $k_d(1 - T_c)$ rise steadily with increases in leverage, but the rate of increase accelerates at higher debt levels, reflecting agency costs and the increased probability of financial distress. The WACC first declines, then hits a minimum at D/V*, and then begins to rise. Note that the value of D in D/V* in the upper graph is D*, the level of debt in the lower graph that maximizes the firm's value. Thus, a firm's WACC is minimized and its value is maximized at the same capital structure. Note also that the general shapes of the curves apply regardless of whether we are using the modified MM with corporate taxes model, the Miller model, or a variant of these models.

Unfortunately, it is impossible to quantify accurately the costs and benefits of debt financing, so it is impossible to pinpoint D/V*, the capital structure that maximizes a firm's value. Most experts believe such a structure exists for every firm, but that it

---

[20]Flotation costs also play a role in capital structure theory. In general, flotation costs are smaller on debt than on equity issues, and this provides an additional rationale for using debt rather than outside equity. We will discuss this issue in more detail in Chapter 18.

FIGURE 16-3   Effects of Leverage: The Trade-Off Models

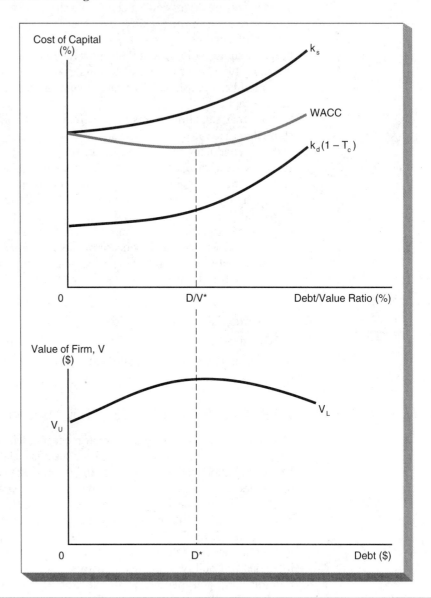

changes over time as firms' operations and investors' preferences change. Most experts also believe that, as shown in Figure 16-3, the relationship between value and leverage is relatively flat over a fairly broad range, so large deviations from the optimal capital structure can occur without materially affecting the stock price.

Now consider the signaling theory. Because of asymmetric information, investors know less about a firm's prospects than its managers know. Further, managers try to maximize value for *current* stockholders, not new ones. Therefore, if the firm has excellent prospects, management will not want to issue new shares, but if things look bleak, then a new stock offering would benefit current stockholders. Consequently, investors take a stock offering to be a signal of bad news, so stock prices tend to decline when new issues are announced. As a result, new equity financings are relatively expensive. The net effect of signaling effects is to motivate firms to maintain a reserve borrowing capacity designed to permit future investment opportunities to be financed by debt if internal funds are not available.

By combining the trade-off and asymmetric information theories, we obtain this explanation for firms' behavior: (1) Debt financing provides benefits because of the tax deductibility of interest, so firms should have some debt in their capital structures. (2) However, financial distress and agency costs place limits on debt usage—beyond some point, these costs offset the tax advantage of debt. The costs of financial distress are especially harmful to firms whose values consist primarily of intangible growth options, such as R&D. Such firms should have lower levels of debt than firms whose asset bases consist mostly of tangible assets. (3) Because of problems due to asymmetric information and flotation costs, low-growth firms should follow a pecking order, with capital raised first from internal sources, then by borrowing, and finally by issuing new stock. In fact, such low-growth firms rarely need to issue external equity. High-growth firms whose growth is occurring primarily through increases in tangible assets should follow the same pecking order, but usually will need to issue new stock as well as debt. High-growth firms whose values consist primarily of intangible growth options may run out of internally generated cash, but they should emphasize stock rather than debt due to the severe problems that financial distress imposes on such firms. (4) Finally, because of asymmetric information, firms should maintain a reserve of borrowing capacity in order to be able to take advantage of good investment opportunities without having to issue stock at low prices, and this reserve will cause the actual debt ratio to be lower than that suggested by the trade-off models.

SELF-TEST
QUESTIONS

Summarize the trade-off and signaling theories of capital structure.

Are the trade-off and signaling theories mutually exclusive; that is, might both be correct?

Does capital structure theory provide managers with a model that can be used to set a precise optimal capital structure?

VARIATIONS IN CAPITAL STRUCTURES

As might be expected, wide variations in the use of financial leverage occur both across industries and among individual firms in each industry. Table 16-3 illustrates differences for selected industries; the ranking is in descending order of common equity ratios, as shown in Column 1.[21]

Drug and electronics companies use relatively little debt—the uncertainties inherent in industries that are cyclical, oriented toward research, or subject to huge product liability suits render the heavy use of debt unwise. Also, these companies are generally quite profitable, hence are able to finance largely with retained earnings. Utility and retailing companies, on the other hand, use debt relatively heavily. The utilities have traditionally used large amounts of debt, particularly long-term debt—their fixed

---

[21]Information on capital structures and financial strength is available from a multitude of sources. We used the *Compustat* data tapes to develop Table 16-3, but published sources include *The Value Line Investment Survey, Robert Morris Associates Annual Studies,* and *Dun & Bradstreet Key Business Ratios.*

TABLE 16-3	Capital Structure Percentages, 1995: Four Industries Ranked by Common Equity Ratios						
INDUSTRY	COMMON EQUITY (1)	PREFERRED STOCK (2)	TOTAL DEBT (3)	LONG-TERM DEBT (4)	SHORT-TERM DEBT (5)	TIMES-INTEREST-EARNED RATIO (6)	RETURN ON EQUITY (7)
Drugs	74.4%	0.0%	25.6%	18.7%	6.9%	17.1×	26.4%
Electronics	68.4	0.0	31.6	24.5	7.1	6.4	11.7
Retailing	53.6	1.0	45.4	39.4	6.0	5.1	16.2
Utilities	46.9	5.3	47.8	43.8	4.0	2.5	5.6
Composite (average of all industries, not just those listed above)	37.7%	1.5%	60.8%	38.7%	22.1%	3.2×	11.7%

NOTE: These ratios are based on accounting (or book) values. Stated on a market-value basis, the equity percentages would rise, because most stocks sell at prices that are two to three times higher than their book values.

SOURCE: *Compustat* Industrial Data Tape, 1995.

assets make good security for mortgage bonds, and their relatively stable sales has made it safe for them to carry more debt than would be true for firms with more business risk. Note, though, that the utilities are rapidly being deregulated, hence they face rapidly increasing competition. As a result, virtually every utility has revised its target capital structure to include less debt. This demonstrates that firms change their target capital structures as their business risks change.

Particular attention should be given to the times-interest-earned (TIE) ratio because it gives an indication of how safe the debt is and how vulnerable the company is to financial distress. TIE ratios depend on three factors: (1) the percentage of debt, (2) the interest rate on the debt, and (3) the company's profitability. Generally, the least leveraged industries, such as the drug industry, have the highest coverage ratios, whereas the utility industry, which finances heavily with debt, has a low average coverage ratio. Again, it should be noted that both Moody's and Standard & Poor recently changed their "guidelines" for the utility industry, raising the coverage ratios (and lowering the debt ratios) that are necessary to receive bond ratings such as AA, A, and so forth.

Wide variations also exist among firms within given industries. For example, although the average debt ratio in 1995 for the drug industry was 25.6 percent, Merck's ratio was only 7 percent, while that of American Home Products was 62 percent. Two particularly important factors in explaining such variation in leverage ratios are the stability of earnings and the presence of growth opportunities. Empirical studies show that firms with more stability in their earnings typically have higher than average leverage ratios when compared with the industry average. Also, firms with greater than average investment growth opportunities typically have lower than average leverage ratios. Thus, factors unique to individual firms, including managerial attitudes, play an important role in setting target capital structures.

Professor Ravindra R. Kamath recently surveyed a large number of CFOs.[22] About one-third of the CFOs said they try to maintain a target capital structure when raising

[22]See Ravindra R. Kamath, "Long-Term Financing Decisions: Views and Practices of Financial Managers of NYSE Firms," *The Financial Review,* May 1997, 350–356.

new capital, and about two-thirds said that they follow a "hierarchy in which the most advantageous sources of funds are exhausted before other sources are used." The hierarchy usually followed the pecking order of internally generated cash flow, external debt, and external equity. But there were occasions in which common equity was the first source of financing. This probably is because the firm had so much leverage that additional debt would be a more costly source of financing than equity. In other words, the firm was far above the optimal degree of leverage, so it issued equity to get closer to the optimal, or target, level of debt. Therefore, many firms do not explicitly state that they have a target capital structure, but their actions imply that a target capital structure does exist for the firm.

S E L F - T E S T
Q U E S T I O N
| Why do wide variations in the use of financial leverage occur both across industries and among the individual firms in each industry?

BOOK WEIGHTS VERSUS MARKET WEIGHTS

In Chapter 10, we calculated the weighted average cost of capital with market value rather than book value weights. Further, in our discussions of capital structure thus far in Chapters 15 and 16, we have focused primarily on market values, not book values. However, survey data indicate that financial managers generally focus on book value structures. Thus, there seems to be a conflict between academic theory and business practice. Here are some thoughts on this issue:

1. If stocks and bonds do not sell exactly at book value—and they almost never do—then it would be impossible for a growing firm to establish and maintain at constant levels both a target book value and a target market value capital structure. The firm could stay on its book value target or on its market value target, but not on both. To illustrate, assume that a company has, at book value, $50 million of debt and $50 million of equity, for a total book value of $100 million. However, its stock sells at 2.0 times book, so the market value of its equity is $100. Here is the capital structure situation, with dollars in millions:

	BOOK VALUE		MARKET VALUE	
Debt	$ 50	50%	$ 50	33%
Equity	50	50	100	67
Total	$100	100%	$150	100%

Now suppose the company needs to raise an additional $100 million. If it sells $50 million of debt and $50 million of common stock, it will add these amounts to its balance sheet, so its book value capital structure will remain constant. However, adding $50 million to both debt and equity will cause its market value capital structure to change. On the other hand, if it raises $33 million as debt and $67 million as equity, its market value capital structure will remain constant, but its book value structure will change. Thus, it can maintain either its book value or its market value capital structure, but not both.

2. Book values as reported on balance sheets reflect the historical costs of assets. However, historical costs have little to do with the actual value of assets or with their ability to produce cash flows. Market values would almost always better reflect cash generation and debt service ability.

3. As we have repeatedly noted throughout this chapter and the last one, the point of capital structure analysis is to find that capital structure which maximizes the firm's market value, hence its stock price. Since this optimum is defined in terms of stock prices, it can only be determined by an analysis of market values.

4. Now suppose a firm found its optimal market value structure, but then financed so as to maintain a constant book value structure. This would lead to a departure from value maximization. Therefore, if a firm is growing, it must finance so as to hold constant its market value structure. That will, as we saw above, normally lead to changes in the book value structure.

5. Since the firm should, to keep its value at a maximum, finance so as to hold its market value structure constant, the weighted average cost of capital, WACC, should be found using market value weights.

6. Business executives prefer stability and predictability to volatility and uncertainty. Book values are far more predictable than market values. Further, a financial manager can set a target book value capital structure and then attain it, right on the money. It would be virtually impossible to stay at a target market value structure because of bond and stock price fluctuations. This is one reason executives focus on book value structures rather than on the more logical market value structures. Also, many financial executives have accounting backgrounds, and accountants focus on accounting numbers. However, as financial executives gain a knowledge of financial (as opposed to accounting) theory, the focus is shifting more toward market values.

7. For purposes of developing the weighted average cost of capital, we strongly recommend the use of market value weights. However, if a company focuses on a book value capital structure, seeks to maintain that structure, and finances in accordance with book value weights, then its weighted average cost of capital should be based on book weights.

8. Some executives have argued against the use of market value weights on the grounds that as stock prices change, so would capital structure weights, with the result being a volatile cost of capital. This argument is incorrect. The cost of capital should be based on *target* weights, not on the actual capital structure, and there is no reason to think that a target market value structure would be any less stable than a target book value structure. In fact, as we discuss in Point 9 below, target market value weights are probably more stable than target book weights.

9. Now consider a fairly typical situation. Firm X currently has a 50/50 debt/equity ratio at book, and a 33/67 ratio at market. It targets on the book value ratio. Several years go by. The company takes on projects with positive NPVs, and that raises its market value above its book value. Also, inflation occurs, so new assets cost more. Output prices are based on marginal costs, which have risen because of inflation. With the new, higher prices, the rate of return on old assets increases, as does the value of the old assets, and the firm's stock price rises. Book values per share are relatively stable, so the increasing stock price leads to an increase in the market/book ratio. Debt values, on the other hand, remain close to book. Rising stock prices, when combined with stable bond prices, could cause the market value debt/equity ratio to remain constant at the 33/67 level, or even to increase, even though the firm finances on a 50/50 book basis.

10. Note also that, under our scenario, the rising ROE will lead to improved coverage ratios. This fact, together with analysts' knowledge that the firm's book values are understated, will support an increase in the debt ratio measured at book.

What can we conclude from all this? We are absolutely convinced that firms should focus on market value capital structures and base their cost of capital calculations on target market value weights. Because market values do change, it would be impossible to keep the actual capital structure on target at all times, but this fact in no way detracts from the validity of market value targets.

SELF-TEST QUESTIONS | Should the target capital structure be expressed in book value or market value weights? Why do practicing financial managers prefer to work with book weights?

SUMMARY

In this chapter, we discussed a variety of topics related to capital structure decisions. The key concepts covered are listed below:

- In 1958, **Franco Modigliani and Merton Miller (MM)** proved, under a restrictive set of assumptions including zero taxes, that capital structure is irrelevant; that is, according to the original MM article, a firm's value is not affected by its financing mix.

- MM later added **corporate taxes** to their model and reached the conclusion that capital structure does matter. Indeed, their model led to the conclusion that firms should use 100 percent debt financing.

- MM's model with corporate taxes demonstrated that the primary benefits of debt stem from the **tax deductibility of interest payments.**

- Much later, Miller extended the theory to include **personal taxes.** The introduction of personal taxes reduces, but does not eliminate, the benefits of debt financing. Thus, the **Miller model** also leads to 100 percent debt financing.

- The addition of financial distress and agency costs to either the MM corporate tax model or the Miller model results in a **trade-off model.** Here the marginal costs and benefits of debt are balanced against one another, and the result is an optimal capital structure that falls somewhere between zero and 100 percent debt.

- The **Hamada equation** combines the CAPM with MM (with corporate taxes):

$$k_{sL} = k_{RF} + (k_M - k_{RF})b_U + (k_M - k_{RF})b_U(1 - T)(D/S).$$

This equation shows that the required rate of return on a levered company's stock is equal to the risk-free rate, which compensates investors for the time value of money, plus premiums for business risk and financial risk.

- Within a **market risk framework,** business risk can be measured by b_U, market risk can be measured by b, and financial risk can be measured by $b - b_U = b_U(1 - T)(D/S)$.

- The **asymmetric information,** or **signaling, theory,** which recognizes that managers have better information than most investors, postulates that there is a preferred "pecking order" of financing: first retained earnings (and depreciation), then debt, and then, as a last resort only, new common stock.

- The signaling theory leads to the conclusion that firms should maintain a **borrowing capacity reserve** so that they can always issue debt on reasonable terms rather than have to issue new equity at the wrong time.

- There are clearly benefits to debt financing, but firms should use different amounts of debt depending on their tax rates, asset structures, and business risks.

- Wide variations in capital structure exist, both across industries and among individual firms within industries. The variations across industries can be explained to a large extent by the economic fundamentals of the industry. Variations within industries also reflect fundamental differences, but they additionally reflect differences in managers' attitudes toward debt.

- The optimal capital structure should be thought of in market value rather than book value terms, even though managers often seem to focus on book values.

Questions

16-1 Define each of the following terms.
a. MM Proposition I without taxes; with corporate taxes
b. MM Proposition II without taxes; with corporate taxes
c. Miller model
d. Financial distress costs
e. Agency costs
f. Trade-off model
g. Asymmetric information, or signaling, theory
h. Hamada equation
i. Reserve borrowing capacity

16-2 Explain why agency costs would probably be more of a problem for a large, publicly owned firm that uses both debt and equity capital than for a small, unleveraged, owner-managed firm.

16-3 Explain, verbally, how MM use the arbitrage process to prove the validity of Proposition I. Also, list the major MM assumptions and explain why each of these assumptions is necessary in the arbitrage proof.

16-4 A utility company is supposed to be allowed to charge prices high enough to cover all costs, including its cost of capital. Public service commissions are supposed to take actions to stimulate companies to operate as efficiently as possible in order to keep costs, hence prices, as low as possible. Some time ago, AT&T's debt ratio was about 33 percent. Some people (Myron J. Gordon in particular) argued that a higher debt ratio would lower AT&T's cost of capital and permit it to charge lower rates for telephone service. Gordon thought an optimal debt ratio for AT&T was about 50 percent. Do the theories presented in the chapter support or refute Gordon's position?

Self-Test Problem (Solution Appears in Appendix B)

ST-1
MM with Financial
Distress Costs

B. Gibbs Inc. is an unleveraged firm, and it has constant expected operating earnings (EBIT) of $2 million per year. The firm's tax rate is 40 percent, and its market value is $V = S = \$12$ million. Management is considering the use of some debt financing. (Debt would be issued and used to buy back stock, so the size of the firm would remain constant.) Since interest expense is tax deductible, the value of the firm would tend to increase as debt is added to the capital structure, but there would be an offset in the form of a rising risk of financial distress. The firm's analysts have estimated, as an approximation, that the present value of any future financial distress costs is $8 million, and that the probability of distress would increase with leverage according to the following schedule:

VALUE OF DEBT	PROBABILITY OF FINANCIAL DISTRESS
$ 2,500,000	0.00%
5,000,000	1.25
7,500,000	2.50
10,000,000	6.25
12,500,000	12.50
15,000,000	31.25
20,000,000	75.00

a. What is the firm's cost of equity and weighted average cost of capital at this time?
b. According to the "pure" MM with-tax model, what is the optimal level of debt?
c. What is the optimal capital structure when financial distress costs are included?
d. Plot the value of the firm, with and without distress costs, as a function of the level of debt.

Problems

16-1
Business and Financial Risk

Air Tampa has just been incorporated, and its board of directors is currently grappling with the question of optimal capital structure. The company plans to offer commuter air services between Tampa and smaller surrounding cities. Jaxair has been around for a few years, and it has about the same basic business risk as Air Tampa would have. Jaxair's market-determined beta is 1.8, and it has a current market value debt ratio (total debt/total assets) of 50 percent and a federal-plus-state tax rate of 40 percent. Air Tampa expects only to be marginally profitable at startup, hence its tax rate would only be 25 percent. Air Tampa's owners expect that the total book and market value of the firm's stock, if it uses zero debt, would be $10 million.

a. Estimate the beta of an unleveraged firm in the commuter airline business based on Jaxair's market-determined beta. (Hint: Jaxair's market-determined beta is a leveraged beta. Use Equation 16-6a and solve for b_U.)
b. Now assume that $k_{RF} = 10\%$ and $k_M = 15\%$. Find the required rate of return on equity for an unleveraged commuter airline. What is the business risk premium for this industry?
c. Air Tampa is considering three capital structures: (1) $2 million debt, (2) $4 million debt, and (3) $6 million debt. Estimate Air Tampa's k_s for these debt levels. What is the financial risk premium at each level?
d. Calculate Air Tampa's k_s and financial risk premium at $6 million debt assuming its federal-plus-state tax rate is now 40 percent. Compare this with your corresponding answer to Part c. (Hint: The increase in the tax rate causes V_U to drop to $8 million.)

16-2
MM without Taxes

Companies U and L are identical in every respect except that U is unleveraged while L has $10 million of 5 percent bonds outstanding. Assume (1) that all of the MM assumptions are met, (2) that there are no corporate or personal taxes, (3) that EBIT is $2 million, and (4) that the cost of equity to Company U is 10 percent.

a. What value would MM estimate for each firm?
b. What is k_s for Firm U? For Firm L?
c. Find S_L, and then show that $S_L + D = V_L = \$20$ million.
d. What is the WACC for Firm U? For Firm L?
e. Suppose $V_U = \$20$ million and $V_L = \$22$ million. According to MM, do these values represent an equilibrium? If not, explain the process by which equilibrium would be restored.

16-3
MM with Corporate Taxes

Refer to Problem 16-2. Assume that all the facts hold, except that both firms are subject to a 40 percent federal-plus-state corporate tax rate.

a. What value would MM now estimate for each firm? (Use Proposition I.)
b. What is k_s for Firm U? Firm L?
c. Find S_L, and then show that $S_L + D = V_L$ results in the same value as obtained in Part a.
d. What is the WACC for Firm U? For Firm L?

16-4
Miller Model

Refer to Problems 16-2 and 16-3. Assume that all facts hold, except that both corporate and personal taxes apply. Assume that both firms must pay a federal-plus-state corporate tax rate of $T_c = 40\%$, and that investors in both firms face a tax rate of $T_d = 28\%$ on debt income and $T_s = 20\%$, on average, on stock income.

a. What is the value of the unleveraged firm, V_U? (Note that V_U is now reduced by the personal tax on stock income, hence $V_U \neq \$12$ million as in Problem 16-3.)
b. What is the value of V_L?
c. What is the gain from leverage in this situation? Compare this with the gain from leverage in Problem 16-3.
d. Set $T_c = T_s = T_d = 0$. What is the value of the leveraged firm? The gain from leverage?
e. Now suppose $T_s = T_d = 0$. What are the value of the leveraged firm and the gain from leverage?
f. Assume that $T_d = 28\%$, $T_s = 28\%$, and $T_c = 40\%$. Now what are the value of the leveraged firm and the gain from leverage?

16-5
MM with and without Taxes

International Associates (IA) is just about to commence operations as an international trading company. The firm will have book assets of $10 million, and it expects to earn a 16 percent return on these assets before taxes. However, because of certain tax arrangements with foreign governments, IA will not pay any taxes; that is, its tax rate will be zero. Management is trying to decide how to raise the required $10 million. It is known that the capitalization rate for an all-equity firm in this business is 11 percent, that is, $k_{sU} = 11\%$. Further, IA can borrow at a rate $k_d = 6\%$. Assume that the MM assumptions apply.

a. According to MM, what will be the value of IA if it uses no debt? If it uses $6 million of 6 percent debt?

b. What are the values of the WACC and k_s at debt levels of D = $0, D = $6 million, and D = $10 million? What effect does leverage have on firm value? Why?

c. Assume the initial facts of the problem ($k_d = 6\%$, EBIT = $1.6 million, $k_{sU} = 11\%$), but now assume that a 40 percent federal-plus-state corporate tax rate exists. Find the new market values for IA with zero debt and with $6 million of debt, using the MM formulas.

d. What are the values of the WACC and k_s at debt levels of D = $0, D = $6 million, and D = $10 million, assuming a 40 percent corporate tax rate? Plot the relationships between the value of the firm and the debt ratio, and between capital costs and the debt ratio.

e. What is the maximum dollar amount of debt financing that can be used? What is the value of the firm at this debt level? What is the cost of this debt?

f. How would each of the following factors tend to change the values you plotted in your graph?
   (1) The interest rate on debt increases as the debt ratio rises.
   (2) At higher levels of debt, the probability of financial distress rises.

16-6
Agency Costs

Until recently, the Prestopino Company carried a triple-A bond rating and was strong in every respect. However, a series of problems has afflicted the firm: It is currently in severe financial distress, and its ability to make future payments on outstanding debt is questionable. If the firm were forced into bankruptcy at this time, the common stockholders would almost certainly be wiped out. Although the firm has limited financial resources, its cash flows (primarily from depreciation) are sufficient to support one of two mutually exclusive investments, each costing $150 million and having a 10-year expected life. These projects have the same market risk, but different total risk as measured by the variance of returns. Each project has the following after-tax cash inflows for 10 years:

	ANNUAL CASH INFLOWS	
PROBABILITY	PROJECT A	PROJECT B
0.5	$30,000,000	$10,000,000
0.5	35,000,000	50,000,000

Assume that both projects have the same market risk as the firm's "average" project. The firm's weighted average cost of capital is 15 percent.

a. What is the expected annual cash inflow from each project?
b. Which project has the greater total risk?
c. Which project would you choose if you were a stockholder? Why?
d. Which project would the bondholders prefer to see management select? Why?
e. If the choices conflict, what "protection" do the bondholders have against the firm's making a decision that is contrary to their interests?
f. Who bears the cost of this "protection"? How is this cost related to leverage and the optimal capital structure?

16-7
MM with Financial Distress Costs

The Boisjoly Company currently has no debt. An in-house research group has just been assigned the job of determining whether the firm should change its capital structure. Because of the importance of the decision, management has also hired the investment banking firm of Stanley Morgan & Company to conduct a parallel analysis of the situation. Mr. Harris, the in-house analyst, who is well versed in modern finance theory, has decided to carry out the analysis using the MM framework. Ms. Broske, the Stanley Morgan consultant, who has a good knowledge of capital market conditions and is confident of her ability to predict the firm's debt and equity costs at various levels of debt, has decided to estimate the optimal capital structure as that structure which minimizes the firm's weighted average cost of capital. The following data are relevant to both analyses:

EBIT = $4 million per year, in perpetuity.

Federal-plus-state tax rate = 40%.

Dividend payout ratio = 100%.

Current required rate of return on equity = 12%.

The cost of capital schedule predicted by Mr. Harris follows:

	AT A DEBT LEVEL OF (MILLIONS OF DOLLARS)							
	$0	$2	$4	$6	$8	$10	$12	$14
Interest rate (%)	—	8.0	8.3	9.0	10.0	11.0	13.0	16.0
Cost of equity (%)	12.0	12.25	12.75	13.0	13.15	13.4	14.65	17.0

Ms. Broske estimated the present value of financial distress costs at $8 million. Additionally, she estimated the following probabilities of financial distress:

	AT A DEBT LEVEL OF (MILLIONS OF DOLLARS)							
	$0	$2	$4	$6	$8	$10	$12	$14
Probability of financial distress	0	0	0.05	0.07	0.10	0.17	0.47	0.90

a. What level of debt would Mr. Harris and Ms. Broske recommend as optimal?
b. Comment on the similarities and differences in their recommendations.

Spreadsheet Problem

Work this problem only if you are using the computerized problem diskette.

16-8
MM with Financial
Distress Costs

Use the model in File C16 to solve this problem. The Brandt Corporation is an unleveraged firm, and it has constant expected operating earnings (EBIT) of $2 million per year. Brandt's federal-plus-state tax rate is 40 percent, its cost of equity is 10 percent, and its market value is $V = S = \$12$ million. Management is considering the use of debt which would cost the firm 8 percent regardless of the amount used. (Debt would be issued and used to buy back stock, so the size of the firm would remain constant.) Since interest expense is tax deductible, the value of the firm would tend to increase as debt is added to the capital structure, but there would be an offset in the form of rising risk of financial distress. The firm's analysts have estimated, as an approximation, that the present value of any future financial distress costs is $8 million, and that the probability of distress would increase with leverage according to the following schedule:

VALUE OF DEBT	PROBABILITY OF DISTRESS
$ 0	0.0%
2,500,000	2.5
5,000,000	5.0
7,500,000	10.0
10,000,000	25.0
12,500,000	50.0
15,000,000	75.0

a. According to the "pure" MM with corporate taxes model, what is the optimal level of debt? (Consider only those debt values listed in the table.)
b. What is the optimal capital structure when financial distress costs are included?
c. Plot the value of the firm, with and without financial distress costs, as a function of the level of debt.
d. Assume that the firm's unleveraged cost of equity is 8 percent. What is the firm's optimal capital structure now? (From this point on, include financial distress costs in all your analyses.)
e. Return to the base-case k_{sU} of 10 percent. Now assume that the firm's tax rate increases to 60 percent. What effect does this change have on the firm's optimal capital structure?
f. Return to the base-case tax rate of 40 percent. Assume that the estimated present value of financial distress costs is only $5 million. Now what is the firm's optimal capital structure?

MINI CASE

Donald Cheney, the CEO of Cheney Electronics, is concerned about his firm's level of debt financing. The company uses short-term debt to finance its temporary working capital needs, but it does not use any permanent (long-term) debt. Other electronics companies average about 30 percent debt, and Mr. Cheney wonders why the difference occurs, and what its effects are on stock prices. To gain some insights into the matter, he poses the following questions to you, his recently hired assistant:

a. *Business Week* recently ran an article on companies' debt policies, and the names Modigliani and Miller (MM) were mentioned several times as leading researchers on the theory of capital structure. Briefly, who are MM, and what assumptions are embedded in the MM and Miller models?

b. Assume that Firms U and L are in the same risk class, and that both have EBIT = $500,000. Firm U uses no debt financing, and its cost of equity is $k_{sU} = 14\%$. Firm L has $1 million of debt outstanding at a cost of $k_d = 8\%$. There are no taxes. Assume that the MM assumptions hold, and then:
   (1) Find V, S, k_s, and WACC for Firms U and L.
   (2) Graph (a) the relationships between capital costs and leverage as measured by D/V, and (b) the relationship between value and D.

c. Using the data given in Part b, but now assuming that firms L and U are both subject to a 40 percent corporate tax rate, repeat the analysis called for in b(1) and b(2) under the MM with-tax model.

d. Now suppose investors are subject to the following tax rates: $T_d = 30\%$ and $T_s = 12\%$.
   (1) What is the gain from leverage according to the Miller model?
   (2) How does this gain compare to the gain in the MM model with corporate taxes?
   (3) What does the Miller model imply about the effect of corporate debt on the value of the firm, that is, how do personal taxes affect the situation?

e. What capital structure policy recommendations do the three theories (MM without taxes, MM with corporate taxes, and Miller) suggest to financial managers? Empirically, do firms appear to follow any one of these guidelines?

f. What are financial distress and agency costs? How does the addition of these costs change the MM and Miller models? (Express your answer in words, in equation form, and in graphical form.)

g. How are financial and business risk measured in a market risk framework?

h. What is the asymmetric information, or signaling, theory of capital structure?

i. What is the "pecking order" theory of capital structure?

Selected Additional References and Cases

The body of literature on capital structure—and the number of potential references—is huge. Therefore, only a sampling can be given here. For an extensive review of the recent literature, as well as a detailed bibliography, see

Beranek, William, "Research Directions in Finance," *Quarterly Review of Business and Economics,* Spring 1981, 6–24.

The major theoretical works on capital structure theory are discussed in an integrated framework in

Copeland, Thomas E., and J. Fred Weston, *Financial Theory and Corporate Policy* (Reading, Mass.: Addison-Wesley, 1988).

Harris, Milton, and Artur Raviv, "The Theory of Capital Structure," *Journal of Finance,* March 1991, 297–355.

The Fall 1988 issue of The Journal of Economic Perspectives *and the Summer 1989 issue of* Financial Management *each contain several interesting and very readable articles which review the MM propositions after 30 years of debate and testing.*

In addition to Miller's work, the effect of personal taxes on capital structure decisions has been addressed by

Gordon, Myron J., and Lawrence I. Gould, "The Cost of Equity Capital with Personal Income Taxes and Flotation Costs," *Journal of Finance,* September 1978, 1201–1212.

Some other references of relevance include the following:

Ben-Horim, Moshe, Shalom Hochman, and Oded Palmon, "The Impact of the 1986 Tax Reform Act on Corporate Financial Policy," *Financial Management,* Autumn 1987, 29–35.

Bradley, Michael, Gregg A. Jarrell, and E. Han Kim, "On the Existence of an Optimal Capital Structure: Theory and Evidence," *Journal of Finance,* July 1984, 857–878.

Conine, Thomas E., Jr., "Debt Capacity and the Capital Budgeting Decision: Comment," *Financial Management,* Spring 1980, 20–22.

Crutchley, Claire E., and Robert S. Hansen, "A Test of the Agency Theory of Managerial Ownership, Corporate Leverage, and Corporate Dividends," *Financial Management,* Winter 1989, 36–46.

Dugan, Michael T., and Keith A. Shriver, "An Empirical Comparison of Alternative Methods for Estimating the Degree of Operating Leverage," *Financial Review,* May 1992, 309–321.

Ferri, Michael, and Wesley H. Jones, "Determinants of Financial Structure: A New Methodological Approach," *Journal of Finance,* June 1979, 631–644.

Flath, David, and Charles R. Knoeber, "Taxes, Failure Costs, and Optimal Industry Capital Structure," *Journal of Finance,* March 1980, 89–117.

Ghosh, Dilip K., "Optimum Capital Structure Redefined," *Financial Review,* August 1992, 411–429.

Kelly, William A., Jr., and James A. Miles, "Capital Structure Theory and the Fisher Effect," *The Financial Review,* February 1989, 53–73.

Lee, Wayne Y., and Henry H. Barker, "Bankruptcy Costs and the Firm's Optimal Debt Capacity: A Positive Theory of Capital Structure," *Southern Economic Journal,* April 1977, 1453–1465.

Mackie-Mason, Jeffrey K., "Do Taxes Affect Corporate Financing Decisions," *Journal of Finance,* December 1990, 1471–1493.

Martin, John D., and David F. Scott, "Debt Capacity and the Capital Budgeting Decision: A Revisitation," *Financial Management,* Spring 1980, 23–26.

Miller, Merton H., "The Modigliani-Miller Propositions after Thirty Years," *Journal of Applied Corporate Finance,* Spring 1989, 6–18.

———, "Leverage," *Journal of Finance,* June 1991, 479–488.

Pinegar, J. Michael, and Lisa Wilbricht, "What Managers Think of Capital Structure Theory: A Survey," *Financial Management,* Winter 1989, 82–91.

Scherr, Frederick C., "A Multiperiod Mean-Variance Model of Optimal Capital Structure," *The Financial Review,* February 1987, 1–31.

Schneller, Meir I., "Taxes and the Optimal Capital Structure of the Firm," *Journal of Finance,* March 1980, 119–127.

Taggart, Robert A., Jr., "Taxes and Corporate Capital Structure in an Incomplete Market," *Journal of Finance,* June 1980, 645–659.

Thakor, Anjan V., "Strategic Issues in Financial Contracting: An Overview," *Financial Management,* Summer 1989, 39–58.

There has been considerable discussion in the literature concerning a financial leverage clientele effect. Many theorists postulate that firms with low leverage are favored by high-tax-bracket investors and vice versa. Two articles on this subject are

Harris, John M., Jr., Rodney L. Roenfeldt, and Philip L. Cooley, "Evidence of Financial Leverage Clienteles," *Journal of Finance,* September 1983, 1125–1132.

Kim, E. Han, "Miller's Equilibrium, Shareholder Leverage Clienteles, and Optimal Capital Leverage," *Journal of Finance,* May 1982, 301–319.

For a very readable discussion of the many issues involved in capital structure theory, see

"A Discussion of Corporate Capital Structure," *Midland Corporate Finance Journal*, Fall 1985, 19–48.

The Dryden Press Cases in Financial Management: Dryden Request *series has the following cases that apply to this chapter:*

Case 7, "Seattle Steel Products," Case 9, "Kleen Kar, Inc.," Case 10, "Aspeon Sparkling Water," Case 10A, "Mountain Springs," Case 10B, "Greta Cosmetics," and Case 45, "The Western Company," focus on capital structure theory.

Case 8, "Johnson Window Company," and Case 8A, "Isle Marine Boat Company," cover operating and financial leverage.

DISTRIBUTIONS TO SHAREHOLDERS: DIVIDENDS AND REPURCHASES

At 9:02 on the morning of January 26, 1993, the financial news wire carried a short announcement indicating that IBM had slashed its dividend. Shortly thereafter, IBM provided this additional information.

The Board of Directors took this action only after serious deliberation and careful consideration of both IBM's earnings and the investment required for the long-term development of the Company's businesses, as well as IBM's intention to pay an appropriate return to shareholders. After weighing all factors, and taking into account the need to maintain IBM's strong financial position, the Board decided to act now in the best long-term interests of the Company and its shareholders.

IBM's dividend cut—the first ever for the company—reduced the annual dividend from $4.84 to $1.58. The $4.84 amount had been established in 1989, and the dividend growth rate prior to 1989 had averaged 7 percent per year.

Many analysts and investors had been expecting a dividend cut because IBM had been hammered by the shift from mainframe to personal computers. So, IBM was trapped with most of its resources devoted to poor-selling products. Meanwhile, nimbler companies such as Microsoft and Intel were earning record profits from the software and microchip businesses that IBM, in effect, gave them in the 1980s. The end result was that IBM set a record for corporate losses in 1992, saw a 60 percent drop in its stock price, and was forced to cut its dividend.

IBM's problems mounted in 1993, forcing it to cut the dividend again. However, in 1994 a new management team began to turn things around, and earnings per share began a steady climb. With profitability restored, IBM now faces two related questions: (1) How much of its free cash flow should it pass on to stockholders, and (2) should it provide this cash to stockholders by raising the dividend or by repurchasing stock? Thus far, IBM's board has spent more than $10 billion repurchasing common stock, and it has also raised the dividend. Further, most analysts expect to see the dividend continue to increase in the years ahead. For example, Value Line *forecasts that IBM's dividend will grow at an average rate of 14.5 percent over the next five years. These prospects lifted the stock price from a 1993 low of $20.40 to a 1998 high of $129 after adjusting for a two-for-one stock split in 1997.* Value Line *forecasts continued stock price increases, but what really happens remains to be seen.*

This chapter discusses the many facets of dividend policy. As you read the chapter, put yourself in the shoes of an IBM board member. If the board had seen the company's problems on the horizon a few years earlier, why didn't it cut the dividend then? Also, if things looked so bleak, why didn't the board eliminate the dividend instead of just cutting it? Finally, if IBM continues to improve, should the dividend be raised, should more shares be repurchased, or should the company do some of each? By the end of the chapter, you should have a good idea of both how dividend decisions are made and the dilemma faced by IBM's board.

Successful companies earn income. That income can then be reinvested in operating assets, used to acquire securities, used to retire debt, or distributed to stockholders. If the decision is made to distribute income to stockholders, three key issues arise: (1) What percentage should be distributed? (2) Should the distribution be as cash dividends, or should the cash be passed on to shareholders by buying back some stock? (3) How stable should the distribution be; that is, should the funds paid out from year to year be stable and dependable, which stockholders would probably prefer, or be allowed to vary with the firm's cash flows and investment requirements, which would probably be better from the firm's standpoint? These three issues are the primary focus of this chapter, but we also consider two related issues, stock dividends and stock splits.

DIVIDENDS VERSUS CAPITAL GAINS: WHAT DO INVESTORS PREFER?

When deciding how much cash to distribute to stockholders, financial managers must keep in mind that the firm's objective is to maximize shareholder value. Consequently, the **target payout ratio**—defined as the percentage of net income to be paid out as cash dividends—should be based in large part on investors' preferences for dividends versus capital gains: do investors prefer (1) to have the firm distribute income as cash dividends or (2) to have it either repurchase stock or else plow the earnings back into the business, both of which should result in capital gains? This preference can be considered in terms of the constant growth stock valuation model:

$$\hat{P}_0 = \frac{D_1}{k_s - g}.$$

If the company increases the payout ratio, it raises D_1. This increase in the numerator, taken alone, would cause the stock price to rise. However, if D_1 is raised, then less money will be available for reinvestment, that will cause the expected growth rate to decline, and that would tend to lower the stock's price. Thus, any change in payout policy will have two opposing effects. Therefore, the firm's **optimal dividend policy** must strike a balance between current dividends and future growth so as to maximize the stock price.

In this section we examine three theories of investor preference: (1) the dividend irrelevance theory, (2) the "bird-in-the-hand" theory, and (3) the tax preference theory.

Dividend Irrelevance Theory

It has been argued that dividend policy has no effect on either the price of a firm's stock or its cost of capital. If dividend policy has no significant effects, then it would be *irrelevant*. The principal proponents of the **dividend irrelevance theory** are Merton Miller and Franco Modigliani (MM).[1] They argued that the firm's value is determined only by its basic earning power and its business risk. In other words, MM argued that the value of the firm depends only on the income produced by its assets, not on how this income is split between dividends and retained earnings.

To understand MM's argument that dividend policy is irrelevant, recognize that any shareholder can construct his or her own dividend policy. For example, if a firm does not pay dividends, a shareholder who wants a 5 percent dividend can "create" it by sell-

---

[1]Merton H. Miller and Franco Modigliani, "Dividend Policy, Growth, and the Valuation of Shares," *Journal of Business,* October 1961, 411–433.

ing 5 percent of his or her stock. Conversely, if a company pays a higher dividend than an investor desires, the investor can use the unwanted dividends to buy additional shares of the company's stock. If investors could buy and sell shares and thus create their own dividend policy without incurring costs, then the firm's dividend policy would truly be irrelevant. Note, though, that investors who want additional dividends must incur brokerage costs to sell shares and perhaps pay capital gains taxes, and investors who do not want dividends must first pay taxes on the unwanted dividends and then incur brokerage costs to purchase shares with the after-tax dividends. Since taxes and brokerage costs certainly exist, dividend policy may well be relevant.

In developing their dividend theory, MM made a number of assumptions, especially the absence of taxes and brokerage costs. Therefore, the MM irrelevance theory may not be true. However, MM argued (correctly) that all economic theories are based on simplifying assumptions, and that the validity of a theory must be judged by empirical tests, not by the realism of its assumptions. We will discuss empirical tests of MM's dividend irrelevance theory shortly.

Bird-in-the-Hand Theory

The principal conclusion of MM's dividend irrelevance theory is that dividend policy does not affect the required rate of return on equity, k_s. This conclusion has been hotly debated in academic circles. In particular, Myron Gordon and John Lintner argued that k_s decreases as the dividend payout is increased because investors are less certain of receiving the capital gains which are supposed to result from retaining earnings than they are of receiving dividend payments.[2] Gordon and Lintner said, in effect, that investors value a dollar of expected dividends more highly than a dollar of expected capital gains because the dividend yield component, D_1/P_0, is less risky than the g component in the total expected return equation, $k_s = D_1/P_0 + g$.

MM disagreed. They argued that k_s is independent of dividend policy, which implies that investors are indifferent between D_1/P_0 and g and, hence, between dividends and capital gains. MM called the Gordon-Lintner argument the **bird-in-the-hand** fallacy because, in MM's view, most investors plan to reinvest their dividends in the stock of the same or similar firms, and, in any event, the riskiness of the firm's cash flows to investors in the long run is determined by the riskiness of operating cash flows, not by dividend payout policy.

Tax Preference Theory

There are three tax-related reasons for thinking that investors might prefer a low dividend payout to a high payout: (1) Recall from Chapter 2 that long-term capital gains are taxed at a maximum rate of 20 percent, whereas dividend income is taxed at effective rates which go up to 39.6 percent. Therefore, wealthy investors (who own most of the stock and receive most of the dividends) might prefer to have companies retain and plow earnings back into the business. Earnings growth would presumably lead to higher stock prices, and thus lower-taxed capital gains would be substituted for higher-taxed dividends. (2) Taxes are not paid on the gain until a stock is sold. Due to time value effects, a dollar of taxes paid in the future has a lower effective cost than a dollar paid today. (3) If a stock is held by someone until he or she dies, no capital gains tax is

[2]Myron J. Gordon, "Optimal Investment and Financing Policy," *Journal of Finance,* May 1963, 264–272, and John Lintner, "Dividends, Earnings, Leverage, Stock Prices, and the Supply of Capital to Corporations," *Review of Economics and Statistics,* August 1962, 243–269.

due at all—the beneficiaries who receive the stock can use the stock's value on the death day as their cost basis and thus completely escape the capital gains tax.

Because of these tax advantages, investors may prefer to have companies retain most of their earnings. If so, investors would be willing to pay more for low-payout companies than for otherwise similar high-payout companies.

Illustration of the Three Dividend Policy Theories

Figure 17-1 illustrates the three alternative dividend policy theories: (1) Miller and Modigliani's dividend irrelevance theory, (2) Gordon and Lintner's bird-in-the-hand theory, and (3) the tax preference theory. To understand the three theories, consider the case of Hardin Electronics, which has from its inception plowed all earnings back into the business and thus has never paid a dividend. Hardin's management is now reconsidering its dividend policy, and it wants to adopt the policy that will maximize its stock price.

Consider first the data presented below the graph. The three rows show three alternative payout policies: (1) Pay zero and retain all earnings, which is the present policy, (2) pay out 50 percent of earnings, and (3) pay out 100 percent of earnings. In the example, we assume that the company will have a 15 percent ROE regardless of which payout policy it follows, so with a book value per share of $30, EPS will be 0.15($30) = $4.50 under all payout policies.[3] Given an EPS of $4.50, dividends per share are shown in Column 3 under each payout policy.

Under the assumption of a constant ROE, the growth rate shown in Column 4 will be g = (% Retained)(ROE), and it will vary from 15 percent at a zero payout to zero at a 100 percent payout. For example, if Hardin pays out 50 percent of its earnings, then its dividend growth rate will be g = 0.5(15%) = 7.5%.

Columns 5, 6, and 7 show the situation if MM's irrelevance theory were correct. Under this theory, neither the stock price nor the cost of equity would be affected by the payout policy—the stock price would remain constant at $30, and k_s would be stable at 15 percent. Note that k_s is found as the sum of the growth rate in Column 4 plus the dividend yield in Column 6.

Columns 8, 9, and 10 show the situation if the bird-in-the-hand theory were true. Under this theory, investors prefer dividends, and the more of its earnings the company pays out, the higher its stock price and the lower its cost of equity. In our example, the bird-in-the-hand theory indicates that adopting a 100 percent payout policy would cause the stock price to rise from $30 to $40, and the cost of equity would decline from 15 percent to 11.25 percent.

Finally, Columns 11, 12, and 13 show the situation if the tax preference theory were correct. Under this theory, investors prefer companies which retain earnings and thus provide returns in the form of lower-taxed capital gains rather than higher-taxed dividends. If the tax preference theory were correct, then an increase in the dividend payout ratio from its current zero level would cause the stock price to decline and the cost of equity to rise.

The data in the table are plotted to produce the two graphs shown in Figure 17-1. The upper graph shows how the stock price would react to dividend policy under each of the theories, and the lower graph shows how the cost of equity would be affected. Note that

---

[3]When the three theories were developed, it was assumed that a company's investment opportunities would be held constant and that if the company increased its dividends, its capital budget could be funded by selling common stock. Conversely, if a high-payout company lowered its payout to the point where earnings exceeded good investment opportunities, it was assumed that the company would repurchase shares. Transactions costs were assumed to be immaterial. We maintain those assumptions in our example.

| FIGURE 17-1 | Dividend Irrelevance, Bird-in-the-Hand, and Tax Preference Dividend Theories |

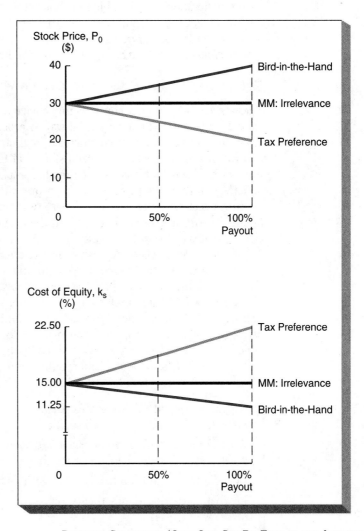

ALTERNATIVE PAYOUT POLICIES				POSSIBLE SITUATIONS (ONLY ONE CAN BE TRUE IN THE AGGREGATE)								
				MM: IRRELEVANCE			BIRD-IN-THE-HAND			TAX PREFERENCE		
PERCENT PAYOUT (1)	PERCENT RETAINED (2)	DPS (3)	g (4)	P_0 (5)	D/P_0 (6)	k_s (7)	P_0 (8)	D/P_0 (9)	k_s (10)	P_0 (11)	D/P_0 (12)	k_s (13)
0%	100%	$0.00	15.0%	$30	0.0%	15.0%	$30	0.00%	15.00%	$30	0.0%	15.0%
50	50	2.25	7.5	30	7.5	15.0	35	6.43	13.93	25	9.0	16.5
100	0	4.50	0.0	30	15.0	15.0	40	11.25	11.25	20	22.5	22.5

NOTES:

1. Book value = Initial market value = $30 per share.
2. ROE = 15%.
3. EPS = $30(0.15) = $4.50.
4. g = (% retained)(ROE) = (% retained)(15%). Example: At payout = 50%, g = 0.5(15%) = 7.5%.
5. k_s = Dividend yield + Growth rate.

different individual stockholders might prefer different policies. Someone in a low tax bracket who needed cash dividends to meet living expenses might prefer the 100 percent payout policy. Someone in a high tax bracket who did not need cash income might prefer a 0 percent payout. And some stockholders might be truly indifferent. *However, the net effect on the stock price and the cost of equity would depend on how many of each type of stockholder there were, that is, on the aggregate view of investors.*

Using Empirical Evidence to Decide Which Theory Is Best

These three theories offer contradictory advice to corporate managers, so which, if any, should we believe? The most logical way to proceed is to test the theories empirically. Many such tests have been conducted, but their results have been unclear. There are two reasons for this: (1) For a valid statistical test, things other than dividend policy must be held constant; that is, the sample companies must differ only in their dividend policies, and (2) we must be able to measure with a high degree of accuracy each sample firm's cost of equity. Neither of these two conditions holds: We cannot find a set of publicly owned firms that differ only in their dividend policies, nor can we obtain precise estimates of the cost of equity.

Therefore, no one can establish a clear relationship between dividend policy and the cost of equity. Investors cannot be seen to uniformly prefer either higher or lower dividends. Nevertheless, *individual* investors do have strong preferences. Some prefer high dividends, while others prefer all capital gains. These differences among individuals help explain why it is difficult to reach any definitive conclusions regarding the optimal dividend payout. Even so, both evidence and logic suggest that investors prefer firms which follow a *stable, predictable* dividend policy (regardless of the payout level). We will consider the issue of dividend stability later in the chapter.

SELF-TEST
QUESTIONS

Explain the dividend irrelevance theory, the bird-in-the-hand theory, and the tax preference theory. Use a graph such as Figure 17-1 to illustrate your answer.

What did Modigliani and Miller assume about taxes and brokerage costs when they developed their dividend irrelevance theory?

How did the bird-in-the-hand theory get its name?

In what sense does MM's theory represent a middle-ground position between the other two theories?

What have been the results of empirical tests of the dividend theories?

OTHER DIVIDEND POLICY ISSUES

Before we discuss how dividend policy is set in practice, we must examine two other theoretical issues that could affect our views toward dividend policy: (1) the *information content,* or *signaling, hypothesis* and (2) the *clientele effect.*

Information Content, or Signaling, Hypothesis

When MM set forth their dividend irrelevance theory, they assumed that everyone—investors and managers alike—has identical information regarding the firm's future earnings and dividends. In reality, however, different investors have different views on both the level of future dividend payments and the uncertainty inherent in those payments, and managers have better information about future prospects than public stockholders.

It has been observed that an increase in the dividend is often accompanied by an increase in the price of a stock, while a dividend cut generally leads to a stock price decline. This could indicate that investors, in the aggregate, prefer dividends to capital gains. However, MM argued differently. They noted the well-established fact that corporations are reluctant to cut dividends, hence do not raise dividends unless they anticipate good earnings in the future. Thus, MM argued that a higher-than-expected dividend increase is a "signal" to investors that the firm's management forecasts good future earnings.[4] Conversely, a dividend reduction, or a smaller-than-expected increase, is a signal that management is forecasting poor earnings in the future. Thus, MM argued that investors' reactions to changes in dividend policy do not necessarily show that investors prefer dividends to retained earnings. Rather, they argue that price changes following dividend actions simply indicate that there is an important **information, or signaling, content** in dividend announcements.

Like most other aspects of dividend policy, empirical studies of signaling have had mixed results. There is clearly some information content in dividend announcements. However, it is difficult to tell whether the stock price changes that follow increases or decreases in dividends reflect only signaling effects or both signaling and dividend preference. Still, signaling effects should definitely be considered when a firm is contemplating a change in dividend policy.

Clientele Effect

As we indicated earlier, different groups, or *clienteles,* of stockholders prefer different dividend payout policies. For example, retired individuals and university endowment funds generally prefer cash income, so they may want the firm to pay out a high percentage of its earnings. Such investors (and pension funds) are often in low or even zero tax brackets, so taxes are of no concern. On the other hand, stockholders in their peak earning years might prefer reinvestment, because they have less need for current investment income and would simply reinvest dividends received, after first paying income taxes on those dividends.

If a firm retains and reinvests income rather than paying dividends, those stockholders who need current income would be disadvantaged. The value of their stock might increase, but they would be forced to go to the trouble and expense of selling off some of their shares to obtain cash. Also, some institutional investors (or trustees for individuals) would be legally precluded from selling stock and then "spending capital." On the other hand, stockholders who are saving rather than spending dividends might favor the low dividend policy, for the less the firm pays out in dividends, the less these stockholders will have to pay in current taxes, and the less trouble and expense they will have to go through to reinvest their after-tax dividends. Therefore, investors who want current investment income should own shares in high-dividend-payout firms, while investors with no need for current investment income should own shares in low-dividend-payout firms. For example, investors seeking high cash income might invest in electric utilities, which averaged a 78 percent payout from 1993 through 1997, while

---

[4]Stephen Ross has suggested that managers can use capital structure as well as dividends to give signals concerning firms' future prospects. For example, a firm with good earnings prospects can carry more debt than a similar firm with poor earnings prospects. This theory, called *incentive signaling,* rests on the premise that signals with cash-based variables (either debt interest or dividends) cannot be mimicked by unsuccessful firms because such firms do not have the future cash-generating power to maintain the announced interest or dividend payment. Thus, investors are more likely to believe a glowing verbal report when it is accompanied by a dividend increase or a debt-financed expansion program. See Stephen A. Ross, "The Determination of Financial Structure: The Incentive-Signaling Approach," *The Bell Journal of Economics,* Spring 1977, 23–40.

those favoring growth could invest in the semiconductor industry, which paid out only 7 percent.

To the extent that stockholders can switch firms, a firm can change from one dividend payout policy to another and then let stockholders who do not like the new policy sell to other investors who do. However, frequent switching would be inefficient because of (1) brokerage costs, (2) the likelihood that stockholders who are selling will have to pay capital gains taxes, and (3) a possible shortage of investors who like the firm's newly adopted dividend policy. Thus, management should be hesitant to change its dividend policy, because a change might cause current shareholders to sell their stock, forcing the stock price down. Such a price decline might be temporary, but it might also be permanent—if few new investors are attracted by the new dividend policy, then the stock price would remain depressed. Of course, the new policy might attract an even larger clientele than the firm had before, in which case the stock price would rise.

Evidence from several studies suggests that there is in fact a **clientele effect.**[5] MM and others have argued that one clientele is as good as another, so the existence of a clientele effect does not necessarily imply that one dividend policy is better than any other. MM may be wrong, though, and neither they nor anyone else can prove that the aggregate makeup of investors permits firms to disregard clientele effects. This issue, like most others in the dividend arena, is still up in the air.

<table>
<tr><td>S E L F - T E S T
Q U E S T I O N</td><td>Define (1) information content and (2) the clientele effect, and explain how they affect dividend policy.</td></tr>
</table>

DIVIDEND STABILITY

The stability of dividends is also important. Profits and cash flows vary over time, as do investment opportunities. Taken alone, this suggests that corporations should vary their dividends over time, increasing them when cash flows are large and the need for funds is low and lowering them when cash is in short supply relative to investment opportunities. However, many stockholders rely on dividends to meet expenses, and they would be seriously inconvenienced if the dividend stream were unstable. Further, reducing dividends to make funds available for capital investment could send incorrect signals to investors who might then push down the stock price because they interpreted the dividend cut to mean that the company's future earnings prospects had been diminished. Thus, maximizing its stock price requires a firm to balance its internal needs for funds against the needs and desires of its stockholders.

How should this balance be struck; that is, how stable and dependable should a firm attempt to make its dividends? It is impossible to give a definitive answer to this question, but the following points are relevant:

1. Virtually every publicly owned company makes a five- to ten-year financial forecast of earnings and dividends. Such forecasts are never made public—they are used for internal planning purposes only. However, security analysts construct similar forecasts and do make them available to investors; see *Value Line* for an example. Further, virtually every internal five- to ten-year corporate forecast we have seen for a "normal" company projects a trend of higher earnings and dividends. Both man-

---

[5]For example, see R. Richardson Pettit, "Taxes, Transactions Costs and the Clientele Effect of Dividends," *The Journal of Financial Economics,* December 1977, 419–436.

agers and investors know that economic conditions may cause actual results to differ from forecasted results, but "normal" companies expect to grow.

2. Years ago, when inflation was not persistent, the term "stable dividend policy" meant a policy of paying the same dollar dividend year after year. AT&T was a prime example of a company with a stable dividend policy—it paid $9 per year ($2.25 per quarter) for 25 straight years. Today, though, most companies and stockholders expect earnings to grow over time as a result of retained earnings and inflation. Further, dividends are normally expected to grow more or less in line with earnings. Thus, today a "stable dividend policy" generally means increasing the dividend at a reasonably steady rate. For example, Rubbermaid made this statement in a recent annual report:

> Dividends per share were increased . . . for the 34th consecutive year. . . . Our goal is to increase sales, earnings, and earnings per share by 15% per year, while achieving a 21% return on shareholders' equity. It is also the Company's objective to pay approximately 30% of current year's earnings as dividends, which will permit us to retain sufficient capital to provide for future growth.

Rubbermaid used the word "approximately" in discussing its payout ratio, because even if earnings vary a bit from the target level, the company still planned to increase the dividend by the target growth rate. Even though Rubbermaid did not mention the dividend growth rate in the statement, analysts can calculate the growth rate and see that it is the same 15 percent as indicated for sales and earnings:

$$g = b(ROE)$$
$$= (1 - Payout)(ROE)$$
$$= 0.7(21\%) \approx 15\%.$$

Here b is the fraction of earnings that are retained, or 1.0 minus the payout ratio.

Companies with volatile earnings and cash flows would be reluctant to make a commitment to increase the dividend each year, so they would not make such a detailed statement. Even so, most companies would like to be able to exhibit the kind of stability Rubbermaid has shown, and they try to come as close to it as they can.

Dividend stability has two components: (a) How dependable is the growth rate, and (b) can we count on at least receiving the current dividend in the future? The most stable policy, from an investor's standpoint, is that of a firm whose dividend growth rate is predictable—such a company's total return (dividend yield plus capital gains yield) would be relatively stable over the long run, and its stock would be a good hedge against inflation. The second most stable policy is where stockholders can be reasonably sure that the current dividend will not be reduced—it may not grow at a steady rate, but management will probably be able to avoid cutting the dividend. The least stable situation is where earnings and cash flows are so volatile that investors cannot count on the company to maintain the current dividend over a typical business cycle.

3. Most observers believe that dividend stability is desirable. Assuming this position is correct, investors prefer stocks that pay more predictable dividends to stocks which pay the same average amount of dividends but in a more erratic manner. This means that the cost of equity will be minimized, and the stock price maximized, if a firm stabilizes its dividends as much as possible.

SELF-TEST QUESTIONS

What does the term "stable dividend policy" mean?

What are the two components of dividend stability?

ESTABLISHING THE DIVIDEND POLICY IN PRACTICE

In the preceding sections we saw that investors may or may not prefer dividends to capital gains, but that they do prefer predictable to unpredictable dividends. Given this situation, how should firms set their basic dividend policies? For example, how should a company like Rubbermaid establish the specific percentage of earnings it will pay out? Rubbermaid's target is 30 percent, but why not 40 percent, 50 percent, or some other percentage? In this section, we describe how firms actually set their dividend policies.

Setting the Target Payout Ratio: The Residual Dividend Model[6]

When deciding how much cash to distribute to stockholders, two points should be kept in mind: (1) The overriding objective is to maximize shareholder value, and (2) the firm's cash flows really belong to its shareholders, so management should refrain from retaining income unless it can be reinvested to produce returns higher than shareholders could themselves earn by investing the cash in investments of equal risk. On the other hand, recall from Chapter 10 that internal equity (retained earnings) is cheaper than external equity (new common stock). This encourages firms to retain earnings because they add to the equity base and thus reduce the likelihood that the firm will have to raise external equity at a later date to fund future investment projects.

When establishing a dividend policy, one size does not fit all. Some firms produce a lot of cash but have limited investment opportunities—this is true for firms in profitable but mature industries where few opportunities for growth exist. Such firms typically distribute a large percentage of their cash to shareholders, thereby attracting investment clienteles which prefer high dividends. Other firms generate little or no excess cash but have many good investment opportunities—this is often true of new firms in rapidly growing industries. Such firms generally distribute little or no cash but enjoy rising earnings and stock prices, thereby attracting investors who prefer capital gains.

As Table 17-1 suggests, dividend payouts and dividend yields for large corporations vary considerably. Generally, firms in stable, cash-producing industries such as utilities, financial services, and tobacco pay relatively high dividends, whereas companies in rapidly growing industries such as computer and cable TV tend to pay lower dividends.

For a given firm, the optimal payout ratio is a function of four factors: (1) investors' preferences for dividends versus capital gains, (2) the firm's investment opportunities, (3) its target capital structure, and (4) the availability and cost of external capital. The last three elements are combined in what we call the **residual dividend model.** Under this model a firm follows these four steps when deciding its target payout ratio: (1) It determines the optimal capital budget; (2) it determines the amount of equity needed to finance that budget, given its target capital structure; (3) it uses retained earnings to meet equity requirements to the extent possible; and (4) it pays dividends only if more earnings are available than are needed to support the optimal capital budget. The word *residual* implies "leftover," and the residual policy implies that dividends are paid out of "leftover" earnings.

If a firm rigidly follows the residual dividend policy, then dividends paid in any given year can be expressed as follows:

---

[6]The term "payout ratio" can be interpreted in two ways: (1) the conventional way, where the payout ratio means the percentage of net income to common paid out as cash dividends, or (2) the percentage of net income distributed to stockholders as dividends and through share repurchases. In this section, we assume that no repurchases occur. Increasingly, though, firms are using the residual model to determine "distributions to shareholders" and then making a separate decision as to the form of that distribution. Further, an increasing percentage of the distribution is in the form of repurchases.

| TABLE 17-1 | Dividend Payouts | | |

COMPANY	INDUSTRY	DIVIDEND PAYOUT	DIVIDEND YIELD
I. Companies That Pay High Dividends			
Orange & Rockland	Utility	81.0%	7.3%
RJR Nabisco Holdings	Tobacco/food	80.0	5.7
H.J. Heinz	Food processor	63.0	3.1
Bankers Trust NY	Banking	62.0	5.3
Philip Morris	Consumer products/tobacco	55.0	4.5
Mellon Bank	Banking	48.0	4.0
II. Companies That Pay Low or No Dividends			
McDonald's	Fast-food restaurants	15.0%	0.6%
Intel	Semiconductors	3.0	0.2
Compaq Computer	Computers	0.0	0.0
Apple Computer	Computers	0.0	0.0
Microsoft	Computer software	0.0	0.0
Health Management Association	Health care services	0.0	0.0

SOURCE: *Value Line Investment Survey,* various 1997 issues.

Dividends = Net income − Retained earnings required to help finance new investments

= Net income − [(Target equity ratio)(Total capital budget)].

For example, if net income is $100, the target equity ratio is 60 percent, and the firm plans to spend $50 on capital projects, then its dividends would be $100 − [(0.6)($50)] = $100 − $30 = $70. So, if the company had $100 of earnings and a capital budget of $50, it could use $30 of the retained earnings plus $50 − $30 = $20 of new debt to finance the capital budget, and this would keep its capital structure on target. Note that the amount of equity needed to finance new investments might exceed the net income; in our example, this would happen if the capital budget were $200. In such instances, no dividends would be paid, and the company would have to raise external equity if it wanted to maintain its target capital structure.

Most firms have a target capital structure that calls for at least some debt, so new financing is done partly with debt and partly with equity. As long as the firm finances with the optimal mix of debt and equity, and provided it uses only internally generated equity (retained earnings), then the marginal cost of each new dollar of capital will be minimized. Internally generated equity is available for financing a certain amount of new investment, but beyond that amount, the firm must turn to more expensive new common stock. At the point where new stock must be sold, the cost of equity, and consequently the marginal cost of capital, rises.

To illustrate these points in more detail, consider the case of Texas and Western (T&W) Transport Company. T&W's overall composite cost of capital is 10 percent. However, this cost assumes that all new equity comes from retained earnings. If the company must issue new stock, its cost of capital will be higher. T&W has $60 million in net income and a target capital structure of 60 percent equity and 40 percent debt. Provided that it does not pay any cash dividends, T&W could make net investments (investments in addition to asset replacements from depreciation) of $100 million, consisting of $60 million from retained earnings plus $40 million of new debt supported by the retained earnings, at a 10 percent marginal cost of capital. If the capital budget exceeded $100 million, the required equity component would exceed net income, which is of course the maximum amount of retained earnings. In this case, T&W would have to issue new common stock, thereby pushing its cost of capital above 10 percent.[7]

At the beginning of its planning period, T&W's financial staff considers all proposed projects for the upcoming period. Independent projects are accepted if their estimated returns exceed the risk-adjusted cost of capital. In choosing among mutually exclusive projects, T&W chooses the project with the highest positive NPV. The capital budget represents the amount of capital that is required to finance all accepted projects. Since T&W follows a strict residual dividend policy, we can see from Table 17-2 that the estimated capital budget has a profound effect on its dividend payout ratio.

If T&W forecasts poor investment opportunities, its estimated capital budget will be only $40 million. To maintain the target capital structure, 40 percent of this capital ($16 million) must be raised as debt, and 60 percent ($24 million) must be equity. If it followed a strict residual policy, T&W would retain $24 million to help finance new investments, then pay out the remaining $36 million as dividends. Under this scenario, the company's dividend payout ratio would be $36 million/$60 million = 0.6 = 60%.

By contrast, if the company's investment opportunities were average, its optimal capital budget would rise to $70 million. Here it would require $42 million of retained earnings, so dividends would be $60 − $42 = $18 million, for a payout of $18/$60 = 30%. Finally, if investment opportunities are good, the capital budget would be $150 million, which would require 0.6($150) = $90 million of equity. T&W would retain all of its net income ($60 million), and thus pay no dividends. Moreover, since the required equity exceeds the retained earnings, the company would have to issue new common stock in order to maintain the target capital structure.

Since investment opportunities and earnings will surely vary from year to year, strict adherence to the residual dividend policy would result in unstable dividends. One year the firm might pay zero dividends because it needed the money to finance good investment opportunities, but the next year it might pay a large dividend because investment

---

[7]If T&W does not retain all of its earnings, its cost of capital will rise above 10 percent before its capital budget reaches $100 million. For example, if T&W chose to retain $36 million, its cost of capital would increase once the capital budget exceeded $36/0.6 = $60 million. To see this point, note that a capital budget of $60 million would require $36 million of equity—if the capital budget rose above $60 million, the company's required equity capital would exceed its retained earnings, thereby requiring it to issue new common stock.

TABLE 17-2   T&W's Dividend Payout Ratio with $60 Million of Net Income When Faced with Different Investment Opportunities (Dollars in Millions)

| | INVESTMENT OPPORTUNITIES | | |
	POOR	AVERAGE	GOOD
Capital budget	$40	$70	$150
Net income	$60	$60	$ 60
Required equity (0.6 × Capital budget)	24	42	90
Dividends paid (Net income − Required equity)	$36	$18	−$30[a]
Dividends payout ratio (Dividend/NI)	60%	30%	0%

[a]With a $150 capital budget, T&W would retain all of its earnings and also issue $30 million of new stock.

opportunities were poor and it therefore did not need to retain much. Similarly, fluctuating earnings could also lead to variable dividends, even if investment opportunities were stable. Therefore, following the residual dividend policy would almost certainly lead to fluctuating, unstable dividends. Thus, the residual policy would be optimal only if investors were not bothered by fluctuating dividends. However, since investors prefer stable, dependable dividends, k_s would be higher, and the stock price lower, if the firm followed the residual model in a strict sense rather than attempting to stabilize its dividends over time. Therefore, a firm should

1. Estimate what its earnings and investment opportunities are likely to look like, on average, over the next five or so years.
2. Use this forecasted information to find the residual model payout ratio and dollars of dividends during the planning period.
3. Then set a *target payout ratio* based on the projected data.

Thus, the firm should use the residual policy to help set its long-run target payout ratios, but not as a guide to the payout in any one year.

Companies use the residual dividend model as discussed above to help understand the determinants of an optimal dividend policy, but they typically use a computerized financial forecasting model when setting the target payout ratio. Most larger corporations forecast their financial statements over the next five to ten years. Information on projected capital expenditures and working capital requirements is entered into the model, along with sales forecasts, profit margins, depreciation, and the other elements required to forecast cash flows. The target capital structure is also specified, and the model shows the amount of debt and equity that will be required to meet the capital budgeting requirements while maintaining the target capital structure.

Then, dividend payments are introduced. Naturally, the higher the payout ratio, the greater the required external equity. Most companies then use the model to find a dividend pattern over the forecast period (generally five years) that will provide sufficient equity to support the capital budget without having to sell new common stock or move the capital structure ratios outside the optimal range. The end result might include a statement, in a memo from the financial vice-president to the chairman of the board, such as the following:

> We forecasted the total market demand for our products, what our share of the market is likely to be, and our required investments in capital assets and working capital. Using this information, we developed projected balance sheets and income statements for the period 1999–2003.
>
> Our 1998 dividends totaled $50 million, or $2 per share. On the basis of projected earnings, cash flows, and capital requirements, we can increase the dividend by 8 percent per year. This is consistent with a payout ratio of 42 percent, on average, over the forecast period. Any faster dividend growth rate (or higher payout) would require us to sell common stock, cut the capital budget, or raise the debt ratio. Any slower growth rate would lead to a buildup of the common equity ratio. Therefore, I recommend that the Board increase the dividend for 1999 by 8 percent, to $2.16, and that it plan for similar increases in the future.
>
> Events over the next five years will undoubtedly lead to differences between our forecasts and actual results. If and when changes occur, we will want to reexamine our position. However, I am confident that we can meet any random cash shortfalls by increasing our borrowings—we have unused debt capacity which gives us flexibility in this regard.
>
> We ran the corporate model under several recession scenarios. If the economy really crashes, our earnings will not cover the dividend. However, in all "reasonable" scenarios cash flows do cover the dividend. I know the Board does not want to push the dividend up to a level where we would have to cut it under bad economic conditions. Our model runs indicate, though, that the $2.16 dividend can be maintained under any reasonable set of forecasts. Only if we increased the dividend to over $3 would we be seriously exposed to the danger of having to cut the dividend.

I might also note that *Value Line* and most other analysts' reports are forecasting that our dividends will grow in the 6 percent to 8 percent range. Thus, if we go to $2.16, we will be at the high end of the range, which should give our stock a boost. With takeover rumors so widespread, getting the stock up a bit would make us all breathe a little easier.

Finally, we considered distributing cash to shareholders through a stock repurchase program. Here we would reduce the dividend payout ratio and use the funds so generated to buy our stock on the open market. Such a program has several advantages, but it would also have drawbacks. I do not recommend that we institute a stock repurchase program at this time. However, if our free cash flows exceed our forecasts, I would recommend that we use these surpluses to buy back stock. Also, I plan to continue looking into a regular repurchase program, and I may recommend such a program in the future.

This company, like Rubbermaid, has very stable operations, so it can plan its dividends with a fairly high degree of confidence. Other companies, especially those in cyclical industries, have difficulty maintaining in bad times a dividend that is really too low in good times. Such companies set a very low "regular" dividend and then supplement it with an "extra" dividend when times are good. General Motors, Ford, and other auto companies have followed the **low-regular-dividend-plus-extras** policy in the past. Each company announced a low regular dividend that it was sure could be maintained "through hell or high water," and stockholders could count on receiving this dividend under all conditions. Then when times were good and profits and cash flows were high, the companies paid a clearly designated extra dividend. Investors recognized that the extras might not be maintained in the future, so they did not interpret them as a signal that the companies' earnings were going up permanently, nor did they take the elimination of the extra as a negative signal. In recent years, however, the auto companies and other companies have replaced the "extras" in their low-regular-dividend-plus-extras policy with stock repurchases.

Earnings, Cash Flows, and Dividends

We normally think of earnings as being the primary determinant of dividends, but in reality cash flows are even more important. This situation is revealed in Figure 17-2, which gives data for Chevron Corporation from 1972 through 1997. Chevron's dividends increased steadily from 1972 to 1981; during that period both earnings and cash flows were rising, as was the price of oil. After 1981, oil prices declined sharply, pulling earnings down. Cash flows, though, remained well above the dividend requirement.

Chevron acquired Gulf Oil in 1984, and it issued over $10 billion of debt to finance the acquisition. Interest on the debt hurt earnings immediately after the merger, as did certain write-offs connected with the merger. Further, Chevron's management wanted to pay off the new debt as fast as possible. All of this influenced the company's decision to hold the dividend constant from 1982 through 1987. Earnings improved dramatically in 1988, and the dividend has increased more or less steadily since then. Note that the dividend was increased in 1991 in spite of the weak earnings and cash flow resulting from the Persian Gulf War.

Now look at Columns 4 and 6, which show payout ratios based on earnings and on cash flows. The earnings payout is quite volatile—dividends ranged from 26 percent to 113 percent of earnings. The cash flow payout, on the other hand, is much more stable—it ranged from 19 percent to 33 percent of cash flows. Further, the correlation between dividends and cash flows was 0.95 versus only 0.72 between dividends and earnings. Thus, dividends clearly depend more on cash flows, which reflect the company's *ability* to pay dividends, than on current earnings, which are heavily influenced by accounting practices and which do not necessarily reflect the ability to pay dividends.

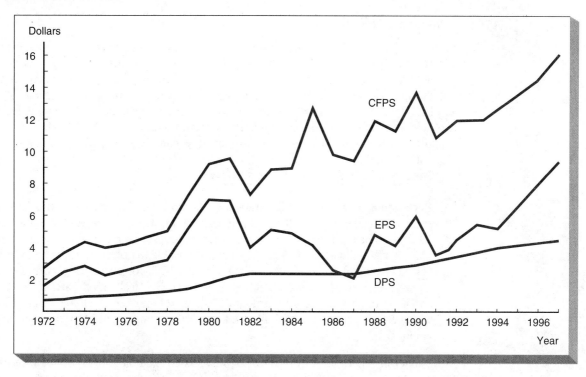

FIGURE 17-2 Chevron: Earnings, Cash Flows, and Dividends, 1972–1997

YEAR (1)	DIVIDENDS PER SHARE (2)	EARNINGS PER SHARE (3)	EARNINGS PAYOUT (4)	CASH FLOW PER SHARE (5)	CASH FLOW PAYOUT (6)
1972	$0.73	$1.61	45%	$2.72	27%
1973	0.78	2.49	31	3.68	21
1974	0.96	2.86	34	4.36	22
1975	1.00	2.28	44	4.00	25
1976	1.08	2.59	42	4.22	26
1977	1.18	2.98	40	4.68	25
1978	1.28	3.24	40	5.06	25
1979	1.45	5.22	28	7.29	20
1980	1.80	7.02	26	9.26	19
1981	2.20	6.96	32	9.61	23
1982	2.40	4.03	60	7.35	33
1983	2.40	5.15	47	8.93	27
1984	2.40	4.94	49	9.00	27
1985	2.40	4.19	57	12.76	19
1986	2.40	2.63	91	9.86	24
1987	2.40	2.13	113	9.47	25
1988	2.55	4.86	52	11.97	21
1989	2.80	4.16	67	11.33	25
1990	2.95	6.02	49	13.75	21
1991	3.25	3.69	88	11.14	29
1992	3.30	4.70	70	12.88	26
1993	3.50	5.60	62	13.12	27
1994	3.70	5.20	71	12.66	29
1995	3.85	6.02	64	13.36	29
1996	4.16	8.12	51	14.90	28
1997	4.56	9.40	49	16.10	28

NOTE: For consistency, data after 1993 have been adjusted to remove the effect of a two-for-one split in 1994.

SOURCE: *Value Line Investment Survey*, various issues.

Payment Procedures

Dividends are normally paid quarterly, and if conditions permit, the dividend is increased once each year. For example, Katz Corporation paid $0.50 per quarter in 1998, or at an annual rate of $2.00. In common financial parlance, we say that in 1998 Katz's *regular quarterly dividend* was $0.50, and its *annual dividend* was $2.00. In late 1998, Katz's board of directors met, reviewed projections for 1999, and decided to keep the 1999 dividend at $2.00. The directors announced the $2 rate, so stockholders could count on receiving it unless the company experiences unanticipated operating problems.

The actual payment procedure is as follows:

1. **Declaration date.** On the declaration date—say, on November 9—the directors meet and declare the regular dividend, issuing a statement similar to the following: "On November 9, 1998, the directors of Katz Corporation met and declared the regular quarterly dividend of 50 cents per share, payable to holders of record on December 11, payment to be made on January 4, 1999." For accounting purposes, the declared dividend becomes an actual liability on the declaration date. If a balance sheet were constructed, the amount ($0.50) × (Number of shares outstanding) would appear as a current liability, and retained earnings would be reduced by a like amount.

2. **Holder-of-record date.** At the close of business on the holder-of-record date, December 11, the company closes its stock transfer books and makes up a list of shareholders as of that date. If Katz Corporation is notified of the sale before 5 P.M. on December 11, then the new owner receives the dividend. However, if notification is received on or after December 12, the previous owner gets the dividend check.

3. **Ex-dividend date.** Suppose Jean Buyer buys 100 shares of stock from John Seller on December 7. Will the company be notified of the transfer in time to list Buyer as the new owner and thus pay the dividend to her? To avoid conflict, the securities industry has set up a convention under which the right to the dividend remains with the stock until four business days prior to the holder-of-record date; on the fourth day before that date, the right to the dividend no longer goes with the shares. The date when the right to the dividend leaves the stock is called the ex-dividend date. In this case, the ex-dividend date is four days prior to December 11, or December 7:

Dividend goes with stock:	December 6	Buyer would receive the dividend.
Ex-dividend date:	December 7	Seller would receive the dividend.
	December 8	
	December 9	
	December 10	
Holder-of-record date:	December 11	

Therefore, if Buyer is to receive the dividend, she must buy the stock on or before December 6. If she buys it on December 7 or later, Seller will receive the dividend because he will be the official holder of record.

Katz's dividend amounts to $0.50, so the ex-dividend date is important. Barring fluctuations in the stock market, one would normally expect the price of a stock to drop by approximately the amount of the dividend on the ex-dividend date. Thus, if

Katz closed at \$30½ on December 6, it would probably open at about \$30 on December 7.[8]

4. **Payment date.** The company actually mails the checks to the holders of record on January 4, the payment date.

S E L F - T E S T
Q U E S T I O N S

Explain the logic of the residual dividend model, the steps a firm would take to implement it, and why it is more likely to be used to establish a long-run payout target than to set the actual year-by-year payout ratio.

How do firms use planning models to help set dividend policy?

Which are more critical to the dividend decision, earnings or cash flow? Explain.

Explain the procedures used to actually pay the dividend.

Why is the ex-dividend date important to investors?

CHANGING DIVIDEND POLICIES

From our previous discussion, it is obvious that firms should try to establish a rational dividend policy and then stick with it. Dividend policy can be changed, but this can cause problems because such changes can inconvenience the firm's existing stockholders, send unintended signals, and convey the impression of dividend instability, all of which can have negative implications for stock prices. Still, economic circumstances do change, and occasionally such changes dictate that a firm should alter its dividend policy.

One of the most striking examples of a dividend policy change occurred in May 1994, when FPL Group, a utility holding company whose primary subsidiary is Florida Power & Light, announced a cut in its quarterly dividend from \$0.62 per share to \$0.42. At the same time, FPL stated it would buy back 10 million of its common shares over the next three years to bolster its stock price.[9] Here is the text of the letter to its stockholders in which FPL announced these changes:

---

[8]December 6, 1998, is a Sunday. Therefore, the buyer would actually have to purchase the stock on Friday, December 4, to receive the dividend. Also, tax effects cause the price decline on average to be less than the full amount of the dividend. Suppose you were an investor in the 40 percent federal-plus-state tax bracket. If you bought Katz's stock on December 4, you would receive the dividend, but you would almost immediately pay 40 percent of it out in taxes. Thus, you would want to wait until December 7 to buy the stock if you thought you could get it for \$0.50 less per share. Your reaction, and those of others, would influence stock prices around dividend payment dates. Here is what would happen:

1. Other things held constant, a stock's price should rise during the quarter, with the daily price increase (for Katz) equal to \$0.50/90 = \$0.005556. Therefore, if the price started at \$30 just after its last ex-dividend date, it would rise to \$30.50 on December 6.

2. In the absence of taxes, the stock's price would fall to \$30 on December 7 and then start up as the next dividend accrual period began. Thus, over time, if everything else were held constant, the stock's price would follow a sawtooth pattern if it were plotted on a graph.

3. Because of taxes, the stock's price would neither rise by the full amount of the dividend nor fall by the full dividend amount when it goes ex-dividend.

4. The amount of the rise and subsequent fall would depend on the average investor's marginal tax rate.

See Edwin J. Elton and Martin J. Gruber, "Marginal Stockholder Tax Rates and the Clientele Effect," *Review of Economics and Statistics,* February 1970, 68–74, for an interesting discussion of all this.

[9]For a complete discussion of the FPL decision, see Dennis Soter, Eugene Brigham, and Paul Evanson, "The Dividend Cut Heard 'Round the World: The Case of FPL," *Journal of Applied Corporate Finance,* Spring 1996, 4–15. Also, note that stock repurchases are discussed in a later section.

Dear Shareholder,

Over the past several years, we have been working hard to enhance shareholder value by aligning our strategy with a rapidly changing business environment. . . . The Energy Policy Act of 1992 has brought permanent changes to the electric industry. Although we have taken effective and sometimes painful steps to prepare for these changes, one critical problem remains. Our dividend payout ratio of 90 percent—the percentage of our earnings paid to shareholders as dividends—is far too high for a growth company. It is well above the industry average, and it has limited the growth in the price of our stock.

To meet the challenges of this competitive marketplace and to ensure the financial strength and flexibility necessary for success, the Board of Directors has announced a change in our financial strategy that includes the following milestones:

- A new dividend policy that provides for paying out 60 to 65 percent of prior years' earnings. This means a reduction in the quarterly dividend from 62 to 42 cents per share beginning with the next payment.

- The authorization to repurchase 10 million shares of common stock over the next three years, including at least 4 million shares in the next year.

- An earlier dividend evaluation beginning in February 1995 to more closely link dividend rates to annual earnings.

We believe this financial strategy will enhance long-term share value and will facilitate both earnings per share and dividend growth to about 5 percent per year over the next several years.

Adding to shareholder wealth in this manner should be increasingly significant given recent changes in the tax law, which have made capital gains more attractive than dividend income. . . . We take this action from a position of strength. We are not being forced into a defensive position by expectations of poor financial performance. Rather, it is a strategic decision to align our dividend policy and your total return as a shareholder with the growth characteristics of our company.

We appreciate your understanding and support, and we will continue to provide updates on our progress in forthcoming shareholder reports.

Several analysts called the FPL decision a watershed event for the electric utility industry. Furthermore, other utilities have followed FPL's lead. FPL saw its circumstances changing—its core electric business was moving from a regulated monopoly environment to one of increasing competition, and the new environment required a stronger balance sheet and more financial flexibility than was consistent with a 90 percent payout policy.

What did the market think about FPL's dividend policy change? The company's stock price fell by 14 percent the day the announcement was made. In the past, hundreds of dividend cuts followed by sharply lower earnings had conditioned investors to expect the worst when a company reduces its dividend—this is the signaling effect discussed earlier. However, over the next few months, as they understood FPL's actions better, analysts began to praise the decision and to recommend the stock. As a result, FPL's stock outperformed the average utility and soon exceeded the pre-announcement price. The policy change was painful to FPL's stockholders in the short run, but it was clearly the proper move, and it proved to be beneficial to stockholders in the longer run.

S E L F - T E S T   Why do companies change their dividend policies?
Q U E S T I O N S   What is the best strategy for announcing dividend policy changes?

DIVIDEND REINVESTMENT PLANS

During the 1970s, most large companies instituted **dividend reinvestment plans (DRPs or DRIPs),** whereby stockholders can automatically reinvest their dividends in the stock of the paying corporation.[10] Today most larger companies offer DRIPs, and although participation rates vary considerably, about 25 percent of the average firm's shareholders are enrolled. There are two types of DRIPs: (1) plans which involve only "old stock" that is already outstanding and (2) plans which involve newly issued stock. In either case, the stockholder must pay taxes on the dividends, even though stock rather than cash is received.

Under both types of DRIPs, stockholders choose between continuing to receive dividend checks or having the company use the dividends to buy more stock in the corporation. Under the "old stock" type of plan, if a stockholder elects reinvestment, a bank, acting as trustee, takes the total funds available for reinvestment, purchases the corporation's stock on the open market, and allocates the shares purchased to the participating stockholders' accounts on a pro rata basis. The transactions costs of buying shares (brokerage costs) are low because of volume purchases, so these plans benefit small stockholders who do not need cash dividends for current consumption.

The "new stock" type of DRIP invests the dividends in newly issued stock, hence these plans raise new capital for the firm. AT&T, Xerox, Union Carbide, and many other companies have had new stock plans in effect in recent years, using them to raise substantial amounts of new equity capital. No fees are charged to stockholders, and many companies offer stock at a discount of 3 percent to 5 percent below the actual market price. The companies offer discounts as a trade-off against flotation costs that would be incurred if new stock had been issued through investment bankers rather than through the dividend reinvestment plans.

One interesting aspect of DRIPs is that they are forcing corporations to reexamine their basic dividend policies. A high participation rate in a DRIP suggests that stockholders might be better off if the firm simply reduced cash dividends, which would save stockholders some personal income taxes. Quite a few firms are surveying their stockholders to learn more about their preferences and to find out how they would react to a change in dividend policy. A more rational approach to basic dividend policy decisions may emerge from this research.

Note that companies start or stop using new stock DRIPs depending on their need for equity capital. Thus, both Union Carbide and AT&T recently stopped offering a new stock DRIP with a 5 percent discount because their needs for equity capital declined, but about the same time Xerox began such a plan.

Some companies have expanded their DRIPs by moving to "open enrollment," whereby anyone can purchase the firm's stock directly and thus bypass brokers' commissions. Exxon not only allows investors to buy their initial shares at no fee but also lets them pick up additional shares through automatic bank account withdrawals. Several plans, including Mobil's, offer dividend reinvestment for individual retirement accounts, and some, such as U.S. West, allow participants to invest weekly or monthly rather than on the quarterly dividend schedule. In all of these plans, and many others, stockholders can invest more than the dividends they are foregoing—they simply send a check to the company and buy shares without a brokerage commission. According to First Chicago Trust, which handles the paperwork for 13 million shareholder DRIP accounts, at least half of all DRIPs will offer open enrollment, extra purchases, and other expanded services within the next few years.

---

[10]See Richard H. Pettway and R. Phil Malone, "Automatic Dividend Reinvestment Plans," *Financial Management,* Winter 1973, 11–18, for an excellent discussion of the subject.

What are dividend reinvestment plans?

What are their advantages and disadvantages from both the stockholders' and the firm's perspectives?

SUMMARY OF FACTORS INFLUENCING DIVIDEND POLICY

In earlier sections, we described both the major theories of investor preference and some issues concerning the effects of dividend policy on the value of a firm. We also discussed the residual dividend model for setting a firm's long-run target payout ratio. In this section, we discuss several other factors that affect the dividend decision. These factors may be grouped into four broad categories: (1) constraints on dividend payments, (2) investment opportunities, (3) availability and cost of alternative sources of capital, and (4) effects of dividend policy on k_s. Each of these categories has several subparts, which we discuss in the following paragraphs.

Constraints

1. **Bond indentures.** Debt contracts often limit dividend payments to earnings generated after the loan was granted. Also, debt contracts often stipulate that no dividends can be paid unless the current ratio, times-interest-earned ratio, and other safety ratios exceed stated minimums.

2. **Preferred stock restrictions.** Typically, common dividends cannot be paid if the company has omitted its preferred dividend. The preferred arrearages must be satisfied before common dividends can be resumed.

3. **Impairment of capital rule.** Dividend payments cannot exceed the balance sheet item "retained earnings." This legal restriction, known as the *impairment of capital rule,* is designed to protect creditors. Without the rule, a company that is in trouble might distribute most of its assets to stockholders and leave its debtholders out in the cold. (*Liquidating dividends* can be paid out of capital, but they must be indicated as such, and they must not reduce capital below the limits stated in debt contracts.)

4. **Availability of cash.** Cash dividends can be paid only with cash. Thus, a shortage of cash in the bank can restrict dividend payments. However, the ability to borrow can offset this factor.

5. **Penalty tax on improperly accumulated earnings.** To prevent wealthy individuals from using corporations to avoid personal taxes, the tax code provides for a special surtax on improperly accumulated income. Thus, if the IRS can demonstrate that a firm's dividend payout ratio is being deliberately held down to help its stockholders avoid personal taxes, the firm is subject to heavy penalties. This factor is relevant only to privately owned firms—we have never heard of a publicly owned firm being accused of improperly accumulating earnings.

Investment Opportunities

1. **Number of profitable investment opportunities.** If a firm typically has a large number of profitable investment opportunities, this will tend to produce a low target payout ratio, and vice versa if the firm's profitable investment opportunities are few in number.

2. **Possibility of accelerating or delaying projects.** The ability to accelerate or to postpone projects will permit a firm to adhere more closely to a stable dividend policy.

Alternative Sources of Capital

1. **Cost of selling new stock.** If a firm needs to finance a given level of investment, it can obtain equity by retaining earnings or by issuing new common stock. If flotation costs (including any negative signaling effects of a stock offering) are high, the cost of new equity will be well above k_s, making it better to set a low payout ratio and to finance through retention rather than through sale of new common stock. On the other hand, a high dividend payout ratio is more feasible for a firm whose flotation costs are low. Flotation costs differ among firms — for example, the flotation percentage is generally higher for small firms, so they tend to set low payout ratios.

2. **Ability to substitute debt for equity.** A firm can finance a given level of investment with either debt or equity. As noted above, low stock flotation costs permit a more flexible dividend policy because equity can be raised either by retaining earnings or by selling new stock. A similar situation holds for debt policy: if the firm can adjust its debt ratio without raising costs sharply, it can pay the expected dividend, even if earnings fluctuate, by using a variable debt ratio.

3. **Control.** If management is concerned about maintaining control, it may be reluctant to sell new stock, hence the company may retain more earnings than it otherwise would. However, if stockholders want higher dividends and a proxy fight looms, then the dividend will be increased. This factor motivated Chrysler to raise its dividend in 1996.

Effects of Dividend Policy on k_s

The effects of dividend policy on k_s may be considered in terms of four factors: (1) stockholders' desire for current versus future income, (2) perceived riskiness of dividends versus capital gains, (3) the tax advantage of capital gains over dividends, and (4) the information content of dividends (signaling). Since we discussed each of these factors in detail earlier, we need only note here that the importance of each factor in terms of its effect on k_s varies from firm to firm depending on the makeup of its current and possible future stockholders.

It should be apparent from our discussion that dividend policy decisions are truly exercises in informed judgment, not decisions based on quantified rules. Even so, to make rational dividend decisions, financial managers must take account of all the points discussed in the preceding sections.

SELF-TEST
QUESTIONS

Identify the four broad sets of factors which affect dividend policy.

What constraints affect dividend policy?

How do investment opportunities affect dividend policy?

How does the availability and cost of outside capital affect dividend policy?

OVERVIEW OF THE DIVIDEND POLICY DECISION

In many ways, our discussion of dividend policy parallels our discussion of capital structure: We have presented the relevant theories and issues, and we have listed some additional factors that influence dividend policy, but we have not come up with any hard-and-fast guidelines that managers can follow. Dividend policy decisions are exercises in informed judgment, not decisions that can be based on a precise mathematical model.

In practice, dividend policy is not an independent decision—the dividend decision is made jointly with capital structure and capital budgeting decisions. The underlying reason for this joint decision process is asymmetric information, which influences managerial actions in two ways:

1. In general, managers do not want to issue new common stock. First, new common stock involves issuance costs—commissions, fees, and so on—and those costs can be avoided by using retained earnings to finance the firm's equity needs. Also, as we discussed in Chapter 15, asymmetric information causes investors to view new common stock issues as negative signals and thus lowers expectations regarding the firm's future prospects. The end result is that the announcement of a new stock issue usually leads to a decrease in the stock price. Considering the total costs involved, including both issuance and asymmetric information costs, managers strongly prefer to use retained earnings as their primary source of new equity.

2. Dividend changes provide signals about managers' beliefs as to their firms' future prospects. Thus, dividend reductions, or worse yet, omissions, generally have a significant negative effect on a firm's stock price. Since managers recognize this, they try to set dollar dividends low enough so that there is only a remote chance that the dividend will have to be reduced in the future. Of course, unexpectedly large dividend increases can be used to provide positive signals.

The effects of asymmetric information suggest that, to the extent possible, managers should avoid both new common stock sales and dividend cuts, because both actions tend to lower stock prices. Thus, in setting dividend policy, managers should begin by considering the firm's future investment opportunities relative to its projected internal sources of funds. The firm's target capital structure also plays a part, but because the optimal capital structure is a *range,* firms can vary their actual capital structures somewhat from year to year. Since it is best to avoid issuing new common stock, the target long-term payout ratio should be designed to permit the firm to meet all of its equity capital requirements with retained earnings. In effect, managers should use the residual dividend model to set dividends, but in a long-term framework. Finally, the current dollar dividend should be set so that there is an extremely low probability that the dividend, once set, will ever have to be lowered or omitted.

Of course, the dividend decision is made during the planning process, so there is uncertainty about future investment opportunities and operating cash flows. Thus, the actual payout ratio in any year will probably be above or below the firm's long-range target. However, the dollar dividend should be maintained, or increased as planned, unless the firm's financial condition deteriorates to the point where the planned policy simply cannot be maintained. A steady or increasing stream of dividends over the long run signals that the firm's financial condition is under control. Further, investor uncertainty is decreased by stable dividends, so a steady dividend stream reduces the negative effect of a new stock issue, should one become absolutely necessary.

In general, firms with superior investment opportunities should set lower payouts, hence retain more earnings, than firms with poor investment opportunities. The degree of uncertainty also influences the decision. If there is a great deal of uncertainty in the forecasts of free cash flows, then it is best to be conservative and to set a lower current dollar dividend. Also, firms with postponable investment opportunities can afford to set a higher dollar dividend, because, in times of stress, investments can be postponed for a year or two, thus increasing the cash available for dividends. Finally, firms whose cost of capital is largely unaffected by changes in the debt ratio can also afford to set a higher payout ratio, because they can, in times of stress, more easily issue additional debt to maintain the capital budgeting program without having to cut dividends or issue stock.

Firms have only one opportunity to set the dividend payment from scratch. There-fore, today's dividend decisions are constrained by policies that were set in the past, hence setting a policy for the next five years necessarily begins with a review of the current situation.

Although we have outlined a rational process for managers to use when setting their firms' dividend policies, dividend policy still remains one of the most judgmental decisions that firms must make. For this reason, dividend policy is always set by the board of directors—the financial staff analyzes the situation and makes a recommendation, but the board makes the final decision.

SELF-TEST QUESTION | Describe the dividend policy decision process. Be sure to discuss all the factors that influence the decision.

STOCK DIVIDENDS AND STOCK SPLITS

Stock dividends and stock splits are related to the firm's cash dividend policy. The rationale for stock dividends and splits can best be explained through an example. We will use Porter Electronic Controls Inc., a $700 million electronic components manufacturer, for this purpose. Since its inception, Porter's markets have been expanding, and the company has enjoyed growth in sales and earnings. Some of its earnings have been paid out in dividends, but some are also retained each year, causing its earnings per share and stock price to grow. The company began its life with only a few thousand shares outstanding, and, after some years of growth, each of Porter's shares had a very high EPS and DPS. When a "normal" P/E ratio was applied, the derived market price was so high that few people could afford to buy a "round lot" of 100 shares. This limited the demand for the stock and thus kept the total market value of the firm below what it would have been if more shares, at a lower price, had been outstanding. To correct this situation, Porter "split its stock," as described in the next section.

Stock Splits

Although there is little empirical evidence to support the contention, there is never-theless a widespread belief in financial circles that an *optimal price range* exists for stocks. "Optimal" means that if the price is within this range, the price/earnings ratio, hence the firm's value, will be maximized. Many observers, including Porter's manage-ment, believe that the best range for most stocks is from $20 to $80 per share. Accord-ingly, if the price of Porter's stock rose to $80, management would probably declare a two-for-one **stock split,** thus doubling the number of shares outstanding, halving the earnings and dividends per share, and thereby lowering the stock price. Each stock-holder would have more shares, but each share would be worth less. If the post-split price were $40, Porter's stockholders would be exactly as well off as they were before the split. However, if the stock price were to stabilize above $40, stockholders would be better off. Stock splits can be of any size—for example, the stock could be split two-for-one, three-for-one, one-and-a-half-for-one, or in any other way.[11]

Stock Dividends

Stock dividends are similar to stock splits in that they "divide the pie into smaller slices" without affecting the fundamental position of the current stockholders. On a 5

---

[11]*Reverse splits,* which reduce the shares outstanding, can even be used. For example, a company whose stock sells for $5 might employ a one-for-five reverse split, exchanging one new share for five old ones and raising the value of the shares to about $25, which is within the optimal price range. LTV Corporation did this after several years of losses had driven its stock price down below the optimal range.

percent stock dividend, the holder of 100 shares would receive an additional 5 shares (without cost); on a 20 percent stock dividend, the same holder would receive 20 new shares; and so on. Again, the total number of shares is increased, so earnings, dividends, and price per share all decline.

If a firm wants to reduce the price of its stock, should it use a stock split or a stock dividend? Stock splits are generally used after a sharp price run-up to produce a large price reduction. Stock dividends used on a regular annual basis will keep the stock price more or less constrained. For example, if a firm's earnings and dividends were growing at about 10 percent per year, its stock price would tend to go up at about that same rate, and it would soon be outside the desired trading range. A 10 percent annual stock dividend would maintain the stock price within the optimal trading range. Note, though, that small stock dividends create bookkeeping problems and unnecessary expenses, so firms today use stock splits far more often than stock dividends.[12]

Price Effects

If a company splits its stock or declares a stock dividend, will this increase the market value of its stock? Several empirical studies have sought to answer this question, and here is a summary of their findings.[13]

1. On average, the price of a company's stock rises shortly after it announces a stock split or dividend.

2. However, these price increases are more the result of the fact that investors take stock splits/dividends as signals of higher future earnings and dividends than of a desire for stock dividends/splits per se. Since only companies whose managements think things look good tend to split their stocks, the announcement of a stock split is taken as a signal that earnings and cash dividends are likely to rise. Thus, the price increases associated with stock splits/dividends are probably the result of signals of favorable prospects for earnings and dividends, not a desire for stock splits/dividends per se.

3. If a company announces a stock split or dividend, its price will tend to rise. However, if during the next few months it does not announce an increase in earnings and dividends, then its stock price will drop back to the earlier level.

4. As we noted earlier, brokerage commissions are generally higher in percentage terms on lower-priced stocks. This means that it is more expensive to trade low-priced than high-priced stocks, and this, in turn, means that stock splits may reduce the liquidity of a company's shares. This particular piece of evidence suggests that stock splits/dividends might actually be harmful, although a lower price does mean that more investors can afford to trade in round lots (100 shares), which carry lower commissions than do odd lots (less than 100 shares).

---

[12]Accountants treat stock splits and stock dividends somewhat differently. For example, in a two-for-one stock split, the number of shares outstanding is doubled and the par value is halved, and that is about all there is to it. With a stock dividend, a bookkeeping entry is made transferring "retained earnings" to "common stock." For example, if a firm had 1,000,000 shares outstanding, if the stock price was $10, and if it wanted to pay a 10 percent stock dividend, then (1) each stockholder would be given one new share of stock for each ten shares held, and (2) the accounting entries would involve showing 100,000 more shares outstanding and transferring 100,000($10) = $1,000,000 from "retained earnings" to "common stock." The retained earnings transfer limits the size of stock dividends, but that is not important because companies can always split their stock in any way they choose.

[13]See Eugene F. Fama, Lawrence Fisher, Michael C. Jensen, and Richard Roll, "The Adjustment of Stock Prices to New Information," *International Economic Review,* February 1969, 1–21; Mark S. Grinblatt, Ronald M. Masulis, and Sheridan Titman, "The Valuation Effects of Stock Splits and Stock Dividends," *Journal of Financial Economics,* December 1984, 461–490; and C. Austin Barker, "Evaluation of Stock Dividends," *Harvard Business Review,* July–August 1958, 99–114.

What do we conclude from all this? From a pure economic standpoint, stock dividends and splits are just additional pieces of paper. However, they provide management with a relatively low-cost way of signaling that the firm's prospects look good. Further, we should note that since few large, publicly owned stocks sell at prices above several hundred dollars, we simply do not know what the effect would be if Microsoft, Xerox, Hewlett-Packard, and other highly successful firms had never split their stocks, and consequently had sold at prices in the thousands or even tens of thousands of dollars. All in all, it probably makes sense to employ stock dividends/splits when a firm's prospects are favorable especially if the price of its stock has gone beyond the normal trading range.[14]

SELF-TEST
QUESTIONS

What are stock dividends and stock splits?

What impact do stock dividends and splits have on stock prices? Why?

In what situations should managers consider the use of stock dividends?

In what situations should they consider the use of stock splits?

STOCK REPURCHASES

Several years ago, a *Fortune* article entitled "Beating the Market by Buying Back Stock" discussed the fact that during a one-year period, more than 600 major corporations repurchased significant amounts of their own stock. It also gave illustrations of some specific companies' repurchase programs and their effects on stock prices. The article's conclusion was that "buy-backs have made a mint for shareholders who stay with the companies carrying them out."

In addition, we noted earlier that both IBM and FPL recently cut their dividends but simultaneously instituted programs to repurchase shares of their stocks. Thus they substituted share repurchases for cash dividends as a way to distribute funds to stockholders. IBM and FPL are not alone—during 1997 Philip Morris, GE, Disney, Citicorp, Merck, and more than 800 other companies took similar actions, and the dollars used to repurchase shares approximately matched the amount paid out as dividends.

Why are stock repurchase programs becoming so popular? The short answer is that they enhance shareholder value: A more complete answer is given in the remainder of this section, where we explain what a **stock repurchase** is, how it is carried out, and how the financial manager should analyze a possible repurchase program.

There are two principal types of repurchases: (1) situations where the firm has cash available for distribution to its stockholders, and it distributes this cash by repurchasing shares rather than by paying cash dividends, and (2) situations where the firm concludes that its capital structure is too heavily weighted with equity, and then it sells debt and uses the proceeds to buy back its stock.

Stock that has been repurchased by a firm is called *treasury stock*. If some of the outstanding stock is repurchased, fewer shares will remain outstanding. Assuming that the repurchase does not adversely affect the firm's future earnings, the earnings per share on the remaining shares will increase, resulting in a higher market price per share. As a result, capital gains will have been substituted for dividends.

---

[14]It is interesting to note that Berkshire Hathaway, which is controlled by billionaire Warren Buffett, one of the most successful financiers of the twentieth century, has never had a stock split, and its stock sold on the NYSE for $71,000 per share in late 1998. But, in response to investment trusts that were being formed to sell fractional units of the stock, Buffett created a new class of Berkshire Hathaway stock (Class B) worth about $\frac{1}{30}$ of a Class A (regular) share.

The Effects of Stock Repurchases

Many companies have been repurchasing their stock in recent years. Until the 1980s, most repurchases amounted to a few million dollars, but in 1985, Phillips Petroleum announced plans for the largest repurchase on record up to that time—81 million of its shares with a market value of $4.1 billion. Other large repurchases have been made by Texaco, IBM, CBS, Coca-Cola, Teledyne, Atlantic Richfield, Goodyear, and Xerox. Indeed, since 1985, more shares have been repurchased than issued.

The effects of a repurchase can be illustrated with data on American Development Corporation (ADC). The company expects to earn $4.4 million in 1999, and 50 percent of this amount, or $2.2 million, has been allocated for distribution to common shareholders. There are 1.1 million shares outstanding, and the market price is $20 a share. ADC believes that it can either use the $2.2 million to repurchase 100,000 of its shares through a tender offer at $22 a share or else pay a cash dividend of $2 a share.[15]

The effect of the repurchase on the EPS and market price per share of the remaining stock can be analyzed in the following way:

1. Current EPS $= \dfrac{\text{Total earnings}}{\text{Number of shares}} = \dfrac{\$4.4 \text{ million}}{1.1 \text{ million}} = \$4$ per share.

2. P/E ratio $= \dfrac{\$20}{\$4} = 5\times.$

3. EPS after repurchasing 100,000 shares $= \dfrac{\$4.4 \text{ million}}{1 \text{ million}} = \$4.40$ per share.

4. Expected market price after repurchase $= (\text{P/E})(\text{EPS}) = (5)(\$4.40) = \$22$ per share.

It should be noted from this example that investors would receive before-tax benefits of $2 per share in any case, either in the form of a $2 cash dividend or a $2 increase in the stock price. This result would occur because we assumed, first, that shares could be repurchased at exactly $22 a share and, second, that the P/E ratio would remain constant. If shares could be bought for less than $22, the operation would be even better for *remaining* stockholders, but the reverse would hold if ADC had to pay more than $22 a share. Furthermore, the P/E ratio might change as a result of the repurchase operation, rising if investors viewed it favorably and falling if they viewed it unfavorably. Some factors that might affect P/E ratios are considered next.

Advantages of Repurchases

The advantages of repurchases are as follows:

1. Repurchase announcements are viewed as positive signals by investors because the repurchase is often motivated by management's belief that the firm's shares are undervalued.

---

[15]Stock repurchases are generally made in one of three ways: (1) A publicly owned firm can simply buy its own stock through a broker on the open market. (2) It can make a *tender offer,* under which it permits stockholders to send in (that is, "tender") their shares to the firm in exchange for a specified price per share. In this case, it generally indicates that it will buy up to a specified number of shares within a particular time period (usually about two weeks); if more shares are tendered than the company wishes to purchase, purchases are made on a pro rata basis. (3) The firm can purchase a block of shares from one large holder on a negotiated basis. If a negotiated purchase is employed, care must be taken to ensure that this one stockholder does not receive preferential treatment over other stockholders or that any preference given can be justified by "sound business reasons." Texaco's management was sued by stockholders who were unhappy over the company's repurchase of about $600 million of stock from the Bass Brothers' interests at a substantial premium over the market price. The suit charged that Texaco's management, afraid the Bass Brothers would attempt a takeover, used the buyback to get them off its back. Such payments have been dubbed "greenmail."

STOCK REPURCHASES: AN EASY WAY TO BOOST STOCK PRICES?

Looking for a way to boost your company's stock price? Why not buy back some of your company's shares? That reflects the thinking of an increasing number of financial managers. By mid-1996, a record 850 companies had indicated that they would repurchase shares, up from 655 announcements over the same time period in 1995 and 535 in 1994. Moreover, repurchase programs are increasing in size — during 1995 and the first half of 1996, 37 companies have announced buybacks that exceed $1 billion.

The buyback rage is in some ways surprising. Given the recent performance of the stock market, it has become quite expensive to buy back shares. Nevertheless, the market's response to a buyback announcement is usually positive. For example, in mid-1996 Reebok announced that it would buy back one-third of its outstanding shares, and on the announcement day, the stock price rose 10 percent. Reebok's experience is not unique. A recent study found (1) that the average company's stock rose 3.5 percent the day a buyback was announced and (2) that companies which repurchase shares outperform the market over a four-year period following the announcement.[a]

Why are buybacks so popular with investors? The general view is that financial managers are signaling to the investment community a belief that the stock is undervalued, hence that the company thinks its own stock is an attractive investment. In this respect, stock repurchases have the opposite effect of stock issuances, which are thought to signal that the firm's stock is overvalued. Buybacks also help assure investors that the company is not wasting its shareholders' money by investing in subpar investments. Michael O'Neill, the CFO of BankAmerica, puts it this way: "We look very hard internally, but if we don't have a profitable use for capital, we think we should return it to shareholders."

Despite all the recent hoopla surrounding buybacks, many analysts stress that in some instances they have a downside: If a firm's stock is actually overvalued, buying back shares at the inflated price will harm the remaining stockholders. In this regard, buybacks should not be viewed as a gimmick to boost stock prices in the short run, but should be used only if they are part of a well-thought-out strategy for investment and for distributing cash to stockholders. Indeed, buybacks do not always succeed — Disney, for example, announced a buyback in April 1996, and its stock price fell more than 10 percent in the next six months.

[a]David Ikenberry, Josef Lakonishok, and Theo Vermaelen, "Market Under-Reaction to Open Market Share Repurchases," *Rice University Working Paper,* June 1994.

SOURCE: Adapted from "Buybacks Make News, But Do They Make Sense?" *BusinessWeek,* August 12, 1996, 76.

2. The stockholders have a choice when the firm distributes cash by repurchasing stock — they can sell or not sell. With a cash dividend, on the other hand, stockholders must accept a dividend payment and pay the tax. Thus, those stockholders who need cash can sell back some of their shares, while those who do not want additional cash can simply retain their stock. From a tax standpoint, a repurchase permits both types of stockholders to get what they want.

3. A third advantage is that a repurchase can remove a large block of stock that is "overhanging" the market and keeping the price per share down.

4. Dividends are "sticky" in the short run because managements are reluctant to raise the dividend if the increase cannot be maintained in the future — managements dislike cutting cash dividends because of the negative signal a cut gives. Hence, if the excess cash flow is thought to be only temporary, management may prefer to make the distribution in the form of a share repurchase rather than to declare an increased cash dividend that cannot be maintained.

5. Companies can use the residual model to set a *target cash distribution* level, then divide the distribution into a *dividend component* and a *repurchase component.* The dividend payout ratio will be relatively low, but the dividend itself will be relatively secure, and it will grow as a result of the declining number of shares outstanding. The company has more flexibility in adjusting the total distribution than it would if the entire distribution were in the form of cash dividends, because repurchases can be varied from year to year without giving off adverse signals. This procedure, which is

what FPL did, has much to recommend it, and it is a primary reason for the dramatic increase in the volume of share repurchases.

6. Repurchases can be used to produce large-scale changes in capital structures. For example, several years ago Consolidated Edison decided to repurchase $400 million of its common stock in order to increase its debt ratio. The repurchase was necessary because even if the company financed its capital budget only with debt, it would still have taken several years to get the debt ratio up to the target level. Con Ed used the repurchase to produce an instantaneous change in its capital structure.

7. Companies such as Microsoft and Intel that grant large numbers of stock options to employees can repurchase stock and then reissue those shares when options are exercised. This avoids the dilution that would occur if new shares were sold to cover exercised options.

Disadvantages of Repurchases

Disadvantages of repurchases include the following:

1. Stockholders may not be indifferent between dividends and capital gains, and the price of the stock might benefit more from cash dividends than from repurchases. Cash dividends are generally dependable, but repurchases are not.

2. The *selling* stockholders may not be fully aware of all the implications of a repurchase, or they may not have all pertinent information about the corporation's present and future activities. However, firms generally announce repurchase programs before embarking on them to avoid potential stockholder suits.

3. The corporation may pay too high a price for the repurchased stock, to the disadvantage of remaining stockholders. If its shares are not actively traded, and if the firm seeks to acquire a relatively large amount of its stock, then the price may be bid above its equilibrium level and then fall after the firm ceases its repurchase operations.

Conclusions on Stock Repurchases

When all the pros and cons on stock repurchases have been totaled, where do we stand? Our conclusions may be summarized as follows:

1. Because of the lower capital gains tax rate and the deferred tax on capital gains, repurchases have a significant tax advantage over dividends as a way to distribute income to stockholders. This advantage is reinforced by the fact that repurchases provide cash to stockholders who want cash but allow those who do not need current cash to delay its receipt. On the other hand, dividends are more dependable and are thus better suited for those who need a steady source of income.

2. Because of signaling effects, companies should not vary their dividends—this would lower investors' confidence in a company and adversely affect its cost of equity and its stock price. However, cash flows vary over time, as do investment opportunities, so the "proper" dividend in the residual model sense varies. To get around this problem, a company can set its dividend at a level low enough to keep dividend payments from constraining operations and then use repurchases on a more or less regular basis to distribute excess cash. Such a procedure would provide regular, dependable dividends plus additional cash flow to those stockholders who want it.

3. Repurchases are also useful when a firm wants to make a large shift in its capital structure within a short period of time, or when it wants to distribute cash from a one-time event such as the sale of a division.

In an earlier edition of this book, we argued that companies ought to be doing more repurchasing and paying out less cash as dividends than they were. Increases in the size

SHARE REPURCHASES ARE LESS COMMON OVERSEAS

While stock repurchases have become quite common in the United States, they are considerably less common, and often illegal, overseas. During the 1990s, 50 European companies have announced stock buyback programs—in contrast to more than 800 U.S. companies announcing buyback plans during just the first eight months of 1996. Moreover, most of the European buybacks have occurred in one country—Great Britain. Even in England, where buybacks are allowed and are fairly common, regulators still view them with some skepticism. For example, England recently closed a tax loophole which had encouraged buybacks—this change led Reuters to cancel a proposed buyback.

Nevertheless, there are some indications that buybacks may become more common overseas. Germany and France are taking steps to eliminate laws which prohibit buybacks. Likewise, regulators in other European and Asian countries are slowly beginning to reconsider their long-held opposition to buybacks.

SOURCE: "Business This Week: Taking Credits," *The Economist,* October 12, 1996, 5; "Share Repurchases," *The Economist,* July 2, 1994, 70.

and frequency of repurchases in recent years suggest that companies have reached this same conclusion.

SELF-TEST QUESTIONS

Explain how repurchases can (1) help stockholders hold down taxes and (2) help firms change their capital structures.

What is treasury stock?

What are three ways a firm can repurchase its stock?

What are some advantages and disadvantages of stock repurchases?

How can stock repurchases help a company operate in accordance with the residual dividend model?

SUMMARY

Dividend policy involves the decision to pay out earnings versus retaining them for reinvestment in the firm. The key concepts covered in the chapter are listed below.

- **Dividend policy** involves three issues: (1) What fraction of earnings should be distributed, on average, over time? (2) Should the distribution be in the form of cash dividends or stock repurchases? (3) Should the firm maintain a steady, stable dividend growth rate?

- The **optimal dividend policy** strikes a balance between current dividends and future growth so as to maximize the firm's stock price.

- Miller and Modigliani developed the **dividend irrelevance theory,** which holds that a firm's dividend policy has no effect on either the value of its stock or its cost of capital.

- The **bird-in-the-hand theory** holds that the firm's value will be maximized by a high dividend payout ratio, because cash dividends are less risky than potential capital gains.

- The **tax preference theory** states that because long-term capital gains are subject to less onerous taxes than dividends, investors prefer to have companies retain earnings rather than pay them out as dividends.

- **Empirical tests** of the three theories **have been inconclusive.** Therefore, academicians cannot tell corporate managers how a given change in dividend policy will affect stock prices and capital costs.

- Dividend policy should take account of the **information content of dividends (signaling)** and the **clientele effect.** The information content, or signaling, effect relates to the fact that investors regard an unexpected dividend change as a signal of management's forecast of future earnings. The clientele effect suggests that a firm will attract investors who like the firm's dividend payout policy. Both factors should be considered by firms that are considering a change in dividend policy.

- In practice, most firms try to follow a policy of paying a **steadily increasing dividend.** This policy provides investors with stable, dependable income, and departures from it give investors signals about management's expectations for future earnings.

- Most firms use the **residual dividend model** to set the long-run target payout ratio at a level which will permit the firm to satisfy its equity requirements with retained earnings.

- A **dividend reinvestment plan (DRP, or DRIP)** allows stockholders to have the company automatically use dividends to purchase additional shares of stock. DRIPs are popular because they allow stockholders to acquire additional shares without incurring brokerage fees.

- **Legal constraints, investment opportunities, availability and cost of funds from other sources,** and **taxes** are also considered when firms establish dividend policies.

- A **stock split** increases the number of shares outstanding. In theory, splits should reduce the price per share in proportion to the increase in shares because splits merely "divide the pie into smaller slices." However, firms generally split their stocks only if (1) the price is quite high and (2) management thinks the future is bright. Therefore, stock splits are often taken as positive signals and thus boost stock prices.

- A **stock dividend** is a dividend paid in additional shares of stock rather than in cash. Both stock dividends and splits are used to keep stock prices within an "optimal" trading range.

- Under a **stock repurchase plan,** a firm buys back some of its outstanding stock, thereby decreasing the number of shares, which should increase both EPS and the stock price. Repurchases are useful for making major changes in capital structure, as well as for distributing temporary excess cash.

Questions

17-1 Define each of the following terms:
   a. Optimal dividend policy
   b. Dividend irrelevance theory; bird-in-the-hand theory; tax preference theory
   c. Information content, or signaling, hypothesis; clientele effect
   d. Residual dividend model
   e. Extra dividend
   f. Declaration date; holder-of-record date; ex-dividend date; payment date
   g. Dividend reinvestment plan (DRIP)
   h. Stock split; stock dividend
   i. Stock repurchase

17-2 How would each of the following changes tend to affect aggregate (that is, the average for all corporations) payout ratios, other things held constant? Explain your answers.
   a. An increase in the personal income tax rate.
   b. A liberalization of depreciation for federal income tax purposes—that is, faster tax write-offs.
   c. A rise in interest rates.
   d. An increase in corporate profits.
   e. A decline in investment opportunities.
   f. Permission for corporations to deduct dividends for tax purposes as they now do interest charges.
   g. A change in the tax code so that both realized and unrealized capital gains in any year were taxed at the same rate as dividends.

17-3 Discuss the pros and cons of having the directors formally announce what a firm's dividend policy will be in the future.

17-4 Most firms would like to have their stock selling at a high P/E ratio, and they would also like to have extensive public ownership (many different shareholders). Explain how stock dividends or stock splits may help achieve these goals.

17-5 What is the difference between a stock dividend and a stock split? As a stockholder, would you prefer to see your company declare a 100 percent stock dividend or a two-for-one split? Assume that either action is feasible.

17-6 "The cost of retained earnings is less than the cost of new outside equity capital. Consequently, it is totally irrational for a firm to sell a new issue of stock and to pay dividends during the same year." Discuss this statement.

17-7 Would it ever be rational for a firm to borrow money in order to pay dividends? Explain.

17-8 "Executive salaries have been shown to be more closely correlated to the size of the firm than to its profitability. If a firm's board of directors is controlled by management instead of by outside directors, this might result in the firm's retaining more earnings than can be justified from the stockholders' point of view." Discuss the statement, being sure (a) to discuss the interrelationships among cost of capital, investment opportunities, and new investment and (b) to explain the implied relationship between dividend policy and stock prices.

17-9 Modigliani and Miller (MM) on the one hand and Gordon and Lintner (GL) on the other have expressed strong views regarding the effect of dividend policy on a firm's cost of capital and value.
a. In essence, what are the MM and GL views regarding the effect of dividend policy on the cost of capital and stock prices?
b. How does the tax preference theory differ from the views of MM and GL?
c. According to the text, which of the theories, if any, has received statistical confirmation from empirical tests?
d. How could MM use the *information content, or signaling, hypothesis* to counter their opponents' arguments? If you were debating MM, how would you counter them?
e. How could MM use the *clientele effect* concept to counter their opponents' arguments? If you were debating MM, how would you counter them?

17-10 More NYSE companies had stock dividends and stock splits during 1983 and 1984 than ever before. What events in these years could have made stock splits and stock dividends so popular? Explain the rationale that a financial vice-president might give his or her board of directors to support a stock split/dividend recommendation.

17-11 One position expressed in the financial literature is that firms set their dividends as a residual after using income to support new investment.
a. Explain what a residual dividend policy implies, illustrating your answer with a table showing how different investment opportunities could lead to different dividend payout ratios.
b. Think back to Chapter 15, where we considered the relationship between capital structure and the cost of capital. If the WACC-versus-debt-ratio plot was shaped like a sharp V, would this have a different implication for the importance of setting dividends according to the residual policy than if the plot was shaped like a shallow bowl (or a flattened U)?

17-12 Indicate whether the following statements are true or false. If the statement is false, explain why.
a. If a firm repurchases its stock in the open market, the shareholders who tender the stock are subject to capital gains taxes.
b. If you own 100 shares in a company's stock and the company's stock splits two for one, you will own 200 shares in the company following the split.
c. Some dividend reinvestment plans increase the amount of equity capital available to the firm.
d. The tax code encourages companies to pay a large percentage of their net income in the form of dividends.
e. If your company has established a clientele of investors who prefer large dividends, the company is unlikely to adopt a residual dividend policy.
f. If a firm follows a residual dividend policy, holding all else constant, its dividend payout will tend to rise whenever the firm's investment opportunities improve.

Self-Test Problem (Solution Appears in Appendix B)

ST-1
Alternative Dividend Policies

Components Manufacturing Corporation (CMC) has an all-common-equity capital structure. It has 200,000 shares of $2 par value common stock outstanding. When CMC's founder, who was also its research director and most successful inventor, retired unexpectedly to the South Pacific in late 1998, CMC was left suddenly and permanently with materially lower growth expectations and relatively few attractive new investment opportunities. Unfortunately, there was no way to replace the founder's contributions to the firm. Previously, CMC found it necessary to plow back most of its earnings to finance growth, which averaged 12 percent per year. Future growth at a 5 percent rate is considered realistic, but that level would call for an increase in the dividend payout. Further, it now appears that new investment projects with at least the 14 percent rate of return required by CMC's stockholders ($k_s = 14\%$) would amount to only $800,000 for 1999 in comparison to a projected $2,000,000 of net income. If the existing 20 percent dividend payout were continued, retained earnings would be $1.6 million in 1999, but, as noted, investments which yield the 14 percent cost of capital would amount to only $800,000.

The one encouraging thing is that the high earnings from existing assets are expected to continue, and net income of $2 million is still expected for 1999. Given the dramatically changed circumstances, CMC's management is reviewing the firm's dividend policy.

a. Assuming that the acceptable 1999 investment projects would be financed entirely by earnings retained during the year, calculate DPS in 1999, assuming that CMC uses the residual dividend model.

b. What payout ratio does your answer to Part a imply for 1999?

c. If a 60 percent payout ratio is maintained for the foreseeable future, what is your estimate of the present market price of the common stock? How does this compare with the market price that should have prevailed under the assumptions existing just before the news about the founder's retirement? If the two values of P_0 are different, comment on why.

d. What would happen to the price of the stock if the old 20 percent payout were continued? Assume that if this payout is maintained, the average rate of return on the retained earnings will fall to 7.5 percent and the new growth rate will be

$$g = (1.0 - \text{Payout ratio})(\text{ROE})$$

$$= (1.0 - 0.2)(7.5\%)$$

$$= (0.8)(7.5\%) = 6.0\%.$$

Problems

17-1
Residual Dividend Model

Axel Telecommunications has a target capital structure which consists of 70 percent debt and 30 percent equity. The company anticipates that its capital budget for the upcoming year will be $3,000,000. If Axel reports net income of $2,000,000 and it follows a residual dividend payout policy, what will be its dividend payout ratio?

17-2
Stock Split

Gamma Medical's stock trades at $90 a share. The company is contemplating a 3-for-2 stock split. Assuming that the stock split will have no effect on the total market value of its equity, what will be the company's stock price following the stock split?

17-3
Stock Repurchases

Beta Industries has net income of $2,000,000 and it has 1,000,000 shares of common stock outstanding. The company's stock currently trades at $32 a share. Beta is considering a plan where it will use available cash to repurchase 20 percent of its shares in the open market. The repurchase is expected to have no effect on either net income or the company's P/E ratio. What will be its stock price following the stock repurchase?

17-4
External Equity Financing

Northern Pacific Heating and Cooling Inc. has a 6-month backlog of orders for its patented solar heating system. To meet this demand, management plans to expand production capacity by 40 percent with a $10 million investment in plant and machinery. The firm wants to maintain a 40 percent debt-to-total-assets ratio in its capital structure; it also wants to maintain its past dividend policy of distributing 45 percent of last year's net income. In 1998, net income was $5 million. How much external equity must Northern Pacific seek at the beginning of 1999 to expand capacity as desired?

17-5
Residual Dividend Policy

Petersen Company has a capital budget of $1.2 million. The company wants to maintain a target capital structure which is 60 percent debt and 40 percent equity. The company forecasts that its net income this year will be $600,000. If the company follows a residual dividend policy, what will be its payout ratio?

17-6
Dividend Payout

The Wei Corporation expects next year's net income to be $15 million. The firm's debt ratio is currently 40 percent. Wei has $12 million of profitable investment opportunities, and it wishes to maintain its existing debt ratio. According to the residual dividend model, how large should Wei's dividend payout ratio be next year?

17-7
Stock Split

After a 5-for-1 stock split, the Strasburg Company paid a dividend of $0.75 per new share, which represents a 9 percent increase over last year's pre-split dividend. What was last year's dividend per share?

17-8
Dividend Residual Policy

The Welch Company is considering three independent projects, each of which requires a $5 million investment. The estimated internal rate of return (IRR) and cost of capital for these projects are presented below:

Project H (High Risk):	Cost of Capital = 16%; IRR = 20%
Project M (Medium Risk):	Cost of Capital = 12%; IRR = 10%
Project L (Low Risk):	Cost of Capital = 8%; IRR = 9%

Note that the projects' cost of capital varies because the projects have different levels of risk. The company's optimal capital structure calls for 50 percent debt and 50 percent common equity. Welch expects to have net income of $7,287,500. If Welch bases its dividends on the residual model, what will its payout ratio be?

17-9
Alternative Dividend Policies

In 1998 the Keenan Company paid dividends totaling $3,600,000 on net income of $10.8 million. 1998 was a normal year, and for the past 10 years, earnings have grown at a constant rate of 10 percent. However, in 1999, earnings are expected to jump to $14.4 million, and the firm expects to have profitable investment opportunities of $8.4 million. It is predicted that Keenan will not be able to maintain the 1999 level of earnings growth — the high 1999 earnings level is attributable to an exceptionally profitable new product line introduced that year — and the company will return to its previous 10 percent growth rate. Keenan's target debt ratio is 40 percent.

a. Calculate Keenan's total dividends for 1999 if it follows each of the following policies:
  (1) Its 1999 dividend payment is set to force dividends to grow at the long-run growth rate in earnings.
  (2) It continues the 1998 dividend payout ratio.
  (3) It uses a pure residual dividend policy (40 percent of the $8.4 million investment is financed with debt).
  (4) It employs a regular-dividend-plus-extras policy, with the regular dividend being based on the long-run growth rate and the extra dividend being set according to the residual policy.

b. Which of the preceding policies would you recommend? Restrict your choices to the ones listed, but justify your answer.

c. Assume that investors expect Keenan to pay total dividends of $9,000,000 in 1999 and to have the dividend grow at 10 percent after 1999. The stock's total market value is $180 million. What is the company's cost of equity?

d. What is Keenan's long-run average return on equity? [Hint: g = (Retention rate)(ROE) = (1.0 − Payout rate)(ROE).]

e. Does a 1999 dividend of $9,000,000 seem reasonable in view of your answers to Parts c and d? If not, should the dividend be higher or lower?

17-10
Alternative Dividend Policies

Buena Terra Corporation is reviewing its capital budget for the upcoming year. It has paid a $3.00 dividend per share (DPS) for the past several years, and its shareholders expect the dividend to remain constant for the next several years. The company's target capital structure is 60 percent equity and 40 percent debt; it has 1,000,000 shares of common equity outstanding; and its net income is $8 million. The company forecasts that it would require $10 million to fund all of its profitable (that is, positive NPV) projects for the upcoming year.

a. If Buena Terra follows the residual dividend model, how much retained earnings will it need to fund its capital budget?

b. If Buena Terra follows the residual dividend model, what will be the company's dividend per share and payout ratio for the upcoming year?

c. If Buena Terra maintains its current $3.00 DPS for next year, how much retained earnings will be available for the firm's capital budget?

d. Can the company maintain its current capital structure, maintain the $3.00 DPS, and maintain a $10 million capital budget without having to raise new common stock?

e. Suppose that Buena Terra's management is firmly opposed to cutting the dividend; that is, it wishes to maintain the $3.00 dividend for the next year. Also assume that the company was committed to funding all profitable projects, and was willing to issue more debt (along with the available retained earnings) to help finance the company's capital budget. Assume that the resulting change in capital structure has a minimal impact on the company's composite cost of capital, so that the capital budget remains at $10 million. What portion of this year's capital budget would have to be financed with debt?

f. Suppose once again that Buena Terra's management wants to maintain the $3.00 DPS. In addition, the company wants to maintain its target capital structure (60 percent equity, 40 percent debt), and maintain its $10 million capital budget. What is the minimum dollar amount of new common stock that the company would have to issue in order to meet each of its objectives?

g. Now consider the case where Buena Terra's management wants to maintain the $3.00 DPS and its target capital structure, but it wants to avoid issuing new common stock. The company is willing to cut its capital budget in order to meet its other objectives. Assuming that the company's projects are divisible, what will be the company's capital budget for the next year?

h. What actions can a firm that follows the residual dividend policy take when its forecasted retained earnings are less than the retained earnings required to fund its capital budget?

MINI CASE

Southeastern Steel Company (SSC) was formed 5 years ago to exploit a new continuous-casting process. SSC's founders, Donald Brown and Margo Valencia, had been employed in the research department of a major integrated-steel company, but when that company decided against using the new process (which Brown and Valencia had developed), they decided to strike out on their own. One advantage of the new process was that it required relatively little capital in comparison with the typical steel company, so Brown and Valencia have been able to avoid issuing new stock, and thus they own all of the shares. However, SSC has now reached the stage where outside equity capital is necessary if the firm is to achieve its growth targets yet still maintain its target capital structure of 60 percent equity and 40 percent debt. Therefore, Brown and Valencia have decided to take the company public. Until now, Brown and Valencia have paid themselves reasonable salaries but routinely reinvested all after-tax earnings in the firm, so dividend policy has not been an issue. However, before talking with potential outside investors, they must decide on a dividend policy.

Assume that you were recently hired by Arthur Adamson & Company (AA), a national consulting firm, which has been asked to help SSC prepare for its public offering. Martha Millon, the senior AA consultant in your group, has asked you to make a presentation to Brown and Valencia in which you review the theory of dividend policy and discuss the following questions.

a. (1) What is meant by the term "dividend policy"?
   (2) The terms "irrelevance," "bird-in-the-hand," and "tax preference" have been used to describe three major theories regarding the way dividend policy affects a firm's value. Explain what these terms mean, and briefly describe each theory.
   (3) What do the three theories indicate regarding the actions management should take with respect to dividend policy?
   (4) Explain the relationships between dividend policy, stock price, and the cost of equity under each dividend policy theory by constructing two graphs such as those shown in Figure 17-1. Dividend payout should be placed on the X axis.
   (5) What results have empirical studies of the dividend theories produced? How does all this affect what we can tell managers about dividend policy?

b. Discuss (1) the information content, or signaling, hypothesis, (2) the clientele effect, and (3) their effects on dividend policy.

c. (1) Assume that SSC has an $800,000 capital budget planned for the coming year. You have determined that its present capital structure (60 percent equity and 40 percent debt) is optimal, and its net income is forecasted at $600,000. Use the residual dividend model approach to determine SSC's total dollar dividend and payout ratio. In the process, explain what the residual dividend model is. Then, explain what would happen if net income were forecasted at $400,000, or at $800,000.
   (2) In general terms, how would a change in investment opportunities affect the payout ratio under the residual payment policy?
   (3) What are the advantages and disadvantages of the residual policy? (Hint: Don't neglect signaling and clientele effects.)

d. What is a dividend reinvestment plan (DRIP), and how does it work?

e. Describe the series of steps that most firms take in setting dividend policy in practice.

f. What are stock repurchases? Discuss the advantages and disadvantages of a firm's repurchasing its own shares.

g. What are stock dividends and stock splits? What are the advantages and disadvantages of stock dividends and stock splits?

Selected Additional References and Cases

Dividend policy has been studied extensively by academicians. The first major academic work, and still a classic that we recommend highly, is Lintner's analysis of the way corporations actually set their dividend payment policies.

Lintner, John, "Distribution of Incomes of Corporations among Dividends, Retained Earnings, and Taxes," *American Economic Review*, May 1956, 97–113.

The effects of dividend policy on stock prices and capital costs have been examined by many researchers. The classic theoretical argument that dividend policy is important, and that stockholders like dividends, was set forth by Gordon, while Miller and Modigliani (MM) developed the notion that dividend policy is not important. Many researchers have extended both Gordon's and MM's theoretical arguments, and have attempted to test the effects of dividend policy in a variety of ways. Although statistical problems have precluded definitive conclusions, the following articles, among others, have helped to clarify the issues:

Brennan, Michael, "Taxes, Market Valuation, and Corporate Financial Policy," *National Tax Journal*, Spring 1975, 417–427.

Hayes, Linda S., "Fresh Evidence That Dividends Don't Matter," *Fortune*, May 4, 1981, 351–354.

Lewellen, Wilbur G., Kenneth L. Stanley, Ronald C. Lease, and Gary G. Schlarbaum, "Some Direct Evidence on the Dividend Clientele Phenomenon," *Journal of Finance*, December 1978, 1385–1399.

Mukherjee, Tarun, and Larry M. Austin, "An Empirical Investigation of Small Bank Stock Valuation and Dividend Policy," *Financial Management*, Spring 1980, 27–31.

On stock dividends and stock splits, see

Baker, H. Kent, and Patricia L. Gallagher, "Management's View of Stock Splits," *Financial Management*, Summer 1980, 73–77.

Baker, H. Kent, Aaron L. Phillips, and Gary E. Powell, "The Stock Distribution Puzzle: A Synthesis of the Literature on Stock Splits and Stock Dividends," *Financial Practice and Education*, Spring/Summer 1995, 24–37.

Copeland, Thomas E., "Liquidity Changes Following Stock Splits," *Journal of Finance*, March 1979, 115–141.

McNichols, Maureen, and Ajay Dravid, "Stock Dividends, Stock Splits, and Signaling," *Journal of Finance*, July 1990, 857–879.

On repurchases, see

Denis, David J., "Defensive Changes in Corporate Payout Policy: Share Repurchases and Special Dividends," *Journal of Finance*, December 1990, 1433–1456.

Finnerty, Joseph E., "Corporate Stock Issue and Repurchase, *Financial Management*, Autumn 1975, 62–71.

Gay, Gerald D., Jayant R. Kale, and Thomas H. Noe, "Share Repurchase Mechanisms: A Comparative Analysis of Efficacy, Shareholder Wealth and Corporate Control Effects," *Financial Management*, Spring 1991, 44–59.

Klein, April, and James Rosenfeld, "The Impact of Targeted Share Repurchases on the Wealth of Non-Participating Shareholders," *Journal of Financial Research*, Summer 1988, 89–97.

Netter, Jeffry M., and Mark L. Mitchell, "Stock-Repurchase Announcements and Insider Transactions after the October 1987 Stock Market Crash," *Financial Management*, Autumn 1989, 84–96.

Pugh, William, and John S. Jahera, Jr., "Stock Repurchases and Excess Returns: An Empirical Examination," *The Financial Review*, February 1990, 127–142.

Stewart, Samuel S., Jr., "Should a Corporation Repurchase Its Own Stock?" *Journal of Finance*, June 1976, 911–921.

Wansley, James W., William R. Lane, and Salil Sarkar, "Managements' View on Share Repurchase and Tender Offer Premiums," *Financial Management*, Autumn 1989, 97–110.

Woolridge, J. Randall, and Donald R. Chambers, "Reverse Splits and Shareholder Wealth," *Financial Management*, Autumn 1983, 5–15.

For surveys of managers' views on dividend policy, see

Baker, H. Kent, Gail E. Farrelly, and Richard B. Edelman, "A Survey of Management Views on Dividend Policy," *Financial Management*, Autumn 1985, 78–84.

Pruitt, Stephen W., and Lawrence J. Gitman, "The Interactions between the Investment, Financing, and Dividend Decisions of Major U.S. Firms," *Financial Review,* August 1991, 409–430.

Other pertinent articles include

Asquith, Paul, and David W. Mullins, Jr., "Signalling with Dividends, Stock Repurchases, and Equity Issues," *Financial Management,* Autumn 1986, 27–44.

Born, Jeffrey A., "Insider Ownership and Signals—Evidence from Dividend Initiation Announcement Effects," *Financial Management,* Spring 1988, 38–45.

Brealey, Richard A., "Does Dividend Policy Matter?" *Midland Corporate Finance Journal,* Spring 1983, 17–25.

Brennan, Michael J., and Anjan V. Thakor, "Shareholder Preferences and Dividend Policy," *Journal of Finance,* September 1990, 993–1018.

Chang, Rosita P., and S. Ghon Rhee, "The Impact of Personal Taxes on Corporate Dividend Policy and Capital Structure Decisions," *Financial Management,* Summer 1990, 21–31.

DeAngelo, Harry, and Linda DeAngelo, "Dividend Policy and Financial Distress: An Empirical Investigation of Troubled NYSE Firms," *Journal of Finance,* December 1990, 1415–1432.

DeAngelo, Harry, Linda DeAngelo, and Douglas J. Skinner, "Dividends and Losses," *Journal of Finance,* December 1992, 1837–1863.

Dempsey, Stephen J., and Gene Laber, "Effects of Agency and Transactions Costs on Dividend Payout Ratios: Further Evidence of the Agency-Transaction Cost Hypothesis," *Journal of Financial Research,* Winter 1992, 317–321.

Fehrs, Donald H., Gary A. Benesh, and David R. Peterson, "Evidence of a Relation between Stock Price Reactions Around Cash Dividend Changes and Yields," *Journal of Financial Research,* Summer 1988, 111–123.

Ghosh, Chinmoy, and J. Randall Woolridge, "An Analysis of Shareholder Reaction to Dividend Cuts and Omissions," *Journal of Financial Research,* Winter 1988, 281–294.

Healy, Paul M., and Krishna G. Palepu, "How Investors Interpret Changes in Corporate Financial Policy," *Journal of Applied Corporate Finance,* Fall 1989, 59–64.

Impson, C. Michael, and Imre Karafiath, "A Note on the Stock Market Reaction to Dividend Announcements," *The Financial Review,* May 1992, 259–271.

Kale, Jayant R., and Thomas H. Noe, "Dividends, Uncertainty, and Underwriting Costs Under Asymmetric Information," *Journal of Financial Research,* Winter 1990, 265–277.

Manakyan, Herman, and Carolyn Carroll, "An Empirical Examination of the Existence of a Signaling Value Function for Dividends," *Journal of Financial Research,* Fall 1990, 201–210.

Miller, Merton H., "Behavioral Rationality in Finance: The Case of Dividends," *Midland Corporate Finance Journal,* Winter 1987, 6–15.

Peterson, David R., and Pamela P. Peterson, "A Further Understanding of Stock Distributions: The Case of Reverse Stock Splits," *Journal of Financial Research,* Fall 1992, 189–205.

Peterson, Pamela P., David R. Peterson, and Norman H. Moore, "The Adoption of New-Issue Dividend Reinvestment Plans and Shareholder Wealth," *Financial Review,* May 1987, 221–232.

Talmor, Eli, and Sheridan Titman, "Taxes and Dividend Policy," *Financial Management,* Summer 1990, 32–35.

Wansley, James W., C. F. Sirmans, James D. Shilling, and Young-jin Lee, "Dividend Change Announcement Effects and Earnings Volatility and Timing," *Journal of Financial Research,* Spring 1991, 37–49.

Woolridge, J. Randall, and Chinmoy Ghosh, "Dividend Cuts: Do They Always Signal Bad News?" *Midland Corporate Finance Journal,* Summer 1985, 20–32.

The following cases in the Cases in Financial Management: Dryden Request *series focus on the issues contained in this chapter:*

Case 19, "Georgia Atlantic Company," Case 19A, "Floral Fragrance, Inc.," Case 19B, "Cook Transportation, Inc.," and Case 20, "Bessemer Steel Products, Inc.," which illustrate the dividend policy decision. Case 60, "Consolidated Electric," is a longer and more comprehensive case on dividend policy.

CHAPTER 18
ISSUING SECURITIES, REFUNDING OPERATIONS, AND OTHER TOPICS

CHAPTER 19
LEASE FINANCING

CHAPTER 20
HYBRID FINANCING: PREFERRED STOCK, WARRANTS, AND CONVERTIBLES

John Hancock Mutual Life Insurance Company began more than 130 years ago with four people in a small office. In May 1998, Chairman Stephen Brown made a statement promising conversion from a mutual company to a stockholder-owned organization. Today the company retains its corporate headquarters in the John Hancock Tower, Boston, Massachusetts, and is New England's tallest building at 740 feet.

© Walter Bibikow/FPG International

ISSUING SECURITIES, REFUNDING OPERATIONS, AND OTHER TOPICS

*O*n any given day, thousands of businesses go to the markets to raise vast amounts of new capital. One good way to become familiar with the types of securities businesses issue is to read the announcements in The Wall Street Journal. The following actions were among the thousands that occurred during just one week in October 1997:

1. *Bell Canada International issued 20.7 million shares of common stock at a price of $16.30 per share. Although equity investors put up some $337 million, Bell Canada netted only $310 million—the remaining $27 million went to brokers, lawyers, accountants, and others who helped create the issue and bring it to market.*

2. *AmeriPath sold 5.6 million common shares at $16 each in an initial public offering. This company, which had been privately held, went public for two reasons: (a) to raise capital and (b) to create a liquid market for the stock held by the company's founders and key employees. Several brokerage firms, including Donaldson, Lufkin, & Jenrette, handled the issue.*

3. *Associates Corporation issued $600 million of new debt in two "tranches." (Tranche is the term used to designate different classes, generally maturities, when a single security issue is broken into two or more parts.) The first tranche consisted of $325 million of four-year notes carrying a coupon rate of 6.467 percent. The second tranche consisted of $275 million of five-year notes having a coupon rate of 6.5 percent. Both tranches were rated AA3 by Moody's and AA- by Standard & Poor's.*

4. *CellStar Corporation issued $150 million of 5 percent convertible subordinated notes due in 2002. After 90 days, and at any time before maturity, each note can be converted into 18 shares of common stock. Since investors paid $1,000 for each note, the conversion price, or cost of shares received upon conversion, is $1,000/18 = $55.56. At the time of issue, CellStar's stock was selling for $42 a share.*

5. *Southern Pacific, the railroad company, filed a "shelf registration" with the Securities and Exchange Commission to sell up to $1 billion in secured notes. In effect, the securities "sit on the shelf," and Southern Pacific can actually issue them as needed over the next year without going through a complicated and lengthy filing process.*

6. *Pharmacia & Upjohn, Inc., announced that it had established a new $500 million bank facility (line of credit) with a group of banks led by Citibank. The unsecured credit line, which will be available at any time during the next seven years, will be used for general corporate purposes, including use as a backup for the company's commercial paper. Pharmacia & Upjohn paid a fee of six basis points, or 0.006 ($500 million) = $3 million, for the commitment. Any borrowings on the line will have an interest rate tied to short-term Treasury securities.*

7. *Transit Group, Inc., announced that it extended the expiration date for 690,000 common stock warrants until November 16, 2000. These warrants, which were issued in November 1989, were set to expire on November 16, 1997. For every two warrants, holders may purchase one share of the company's common stock for $7.50. The warrants may be redeemed for $0.05 per warrant with 30 days' notice, provided the stock price has been above $8.50 for ten consecutive trading days. At the time of the announcement, Transit Group's common stock was selling for $7.00 per share.*

8. *The Bank of New York announced that it issued 4,743,800 American Depository Shares (ADSs) of Portugal Telecom in conjunction with that firm's global offering of 37.5 million shares. The Bank of New York is the largest depository for American and Global Depository Receipts, which permit non-U.S. companies to offer dollar-denominated securities to investors in the United States and Europe. Each ADS represents ownership of one Telecom share.*

Although these issues represent only a small sample of the week's financing activity, they give you an idea of the wide range of financing alternatives available to businesses. After reading this chapter, you should have a better understanding of the procedures used by firms when they issue securities, and of how the security markets are regulated.

In Chapters 8 and 9 we introduced the basics of bond and stock financing, including how they are valued. Now, in Chapter 18, we discuss some additional topics related to long-term financing, including why firms sell equity to the public, how stocks and bonds are issued, the regulation of securities markets, and how bonds and preferred stocks are refunded.

THE DECISION TO GO PUBLIC

"Going public" means selling some of a company's stock to outside investors and then letting the stock trade in public markets. Most businesses begin life as proprietorships or partnerships, and then, as the more successful ones grow, at some point they find it desirable to convert into corporations. Initially, most corporations' stocks are owned by the firm's officers, key employees, and/or a very few investors who are not actively involved in management. However, if growth continues, at some point the company may decide to go public. For example, Hertz, MGM, Polo Ralph Lauren, and hundreds of other companies took this step in 1997. The advantages and disadvantages of public stock ownership are discussed next.

Advantages of Going Public

1. **Permits founder diversification.** As a company grows and becomes more valuable, its founders often have most of their wealth tied up in the company. By selling some of their stock in a public offering, they can diversify their holdings, thereby reducing the riskiness of their personal portfolios.

2. **Increases liquidity.** The stock of a closely held firm is illiquid: it has no ready market. If one of the owners wants to sell some shares to raise cash, it is hard to find a ready buyer, and even if a buyer is located, there is no established price on which to base the transaction. These problems do not exist with publicly owned firms.

3. **Facilitates raising new corporate cash.** If a privately held company wants to raise cash by a sale of new stock, it must either go to its existing owners, who may not have any money or may not want to put more eggs in this particular basket, or else shop around for wealthy investors. However, it is usually quite difficult to get outsiders to put money into a closely held company, because if the outsiders do not have voting control (over 50 percent of the stock), the inside stockholders/managers can run roughshod over them. The insiders can pay or not pay dividends, pay themselves exorbitant salaries, have private deals with the company, and so on. For example, the president might buy a warehouse and lease it to the company at a high rental, get the use of a Rolls Royce, and enjoy frequent "all-the-frills" travel to conventions. The insiders can even keep the outsiders from knowing the company's actual earnings, or its real worth. There are few positions more vulnerable than that of an outside stockholder in a closely held company, and for this reason, it is hard for closely held companies to raise new equity capital. Going public, which brings with it both public disclosure of information and regulation by the Securities and Exchange Commission (SEC), greatly reduces these problems, makes people more willing to invest in the company, and thus makes it easier for the firm to raise capital.

4. **Establishes a value for the firm.** For a number of reasons, it is often useful to establish a firm's value in the marketplace. For one thing, when the owner of a privately owned business dies, state and federal tax appraisers must set a value on the company for estate tax purposes. Often, these appraisers set too high a value, which creates an obvious problem. However, a company that is publicly owned has an established value. Similarly, if a company wants to give incentive stock options to key employees, it is useful to know the exact value of those options, and employees much prefer to own stock, or options on stock, that is publicly traded and therefore liquid.

Disadvantages of Going Public

1. **Cost of reporting.** A publicly owned company must file quarterly and annual reports with the SEC and/or various state agencies. These reports can be a costly pain, especially for small firms.

2. **Disclosure.** Management may not like the idea of reporting operating data, because such data will then be available to competitors. Similarly, the owners of the company may not want people to know their net worth, and since a publicly owned company must disclose the number of shares owned by its officers, directors, and major stockholders, it is easy enough for anyone to multiply shares held by price per share to estimate the net worth of the insiders.

3. **Self-dealings.** The owners/managers of closely held companies have many opportunities for various types of questionable but legal self-dealings, including the payment of high salaries, nepotism, personal transactions with the business (such as a leasing arrangement), and not-truly-necessary fringe benefits. Such self-dealings, which are often designed to minimize their personal tax liabilities, are much harder to arrange if a company is publicly owned.

4. **Inactive market/low price.** If the firm is very small, and if its shares are not traded frequently, its stock will not really be liquid, and the market price may not represent the stock's true value. Security analysts and stockbrokers simply will not follow the stock, because there will not be sufficient trading activity to generate enough brokerage commissions to cover the costs of following the stock.

5. **Control.** Because of the recent dramatic increase in tender offers and proxy fights, the managers of publicly owned firms who do not have voting control must be con-

cerned about maintaining control. Further, there is pressure on such managers to produce annual earnings gains, even when it might be in the shareholders' best long-term interests to adopt a strategy that reduces short-term earnings but raises them in future years. These factors have led a number of public companies to "go private" in "leveraged buyout" deals where the managers borrow the money to buy out the nonmanagement stockholders. We discuss the decision to go private in a later section.

Conclusions on Going Public

There are no hard-and-fast rules regarding if or when a company should go public. This is an individual decision that should be made on the basis of the company's and stockholders' own unique circumstances. If a company does decide to go public, either by selling newly issued stock to raise new capital or by the sale of stock by the current owners, the key issue is setting the price at which shares will be offered to the public. The company and its current owners want to set the price as high as possible — the higher the offering price, the smaller the fraction of the company the current owners will have to give up to obtain any specified amount of money. On the other hand, potential buyers want the price set as low as possible. We will return to the establishment of the offering price later in the chapter, after we have described some other aspects of common stock financing.

S E L F - T E S T Q U E S T I O N S	What are the major advantages of going public?
	What are the major disadvantages?

THE DECISION TO LIST

The decision to go public is truly a milestone in a company's life — it marks a major change in the relationship between the firm and its owners. The decision to **list the stock** and have it trade on an exchange rather than in the over-the-counter market, on the other hand, is not a major event. The company will have to file a few new reports and abide by the rules of the exchange; stockholders will generally purchase or sell shares through a stockbroker who acts as an **agent** rather than a **dealer;** and the stock's price will be quoted in the newspaper under a stock exchange rather than in the over-the-counter section. These are not significant differences.

In order to have its stock listed, a company must apply to an exchange, pay a relatively small fee, and meet the exchange's minimum requirements. These requirements relate to the size of the company's net income and the number of shares outstanding and in the hands of outsiders (as opposed to the number held by insiders, who generally do not trade their stock very actively). Also, the company must agree to disclose certain information to the exchange; this information is designed to help the exchange track trading patterns and thus try to ensure that no one is attempting to manipulate the price of the stock.[1] The size qualifications increase as one moves from the regional exchanges to the AMEX and on to the NYSE.

---

[1] It is illegal for anyone to attempt to manipulate the price of a stock. During the 1920s, and earlier, syndicates would buy and sell stocks back and forth at rigged prices so the public would believe that a particular stock was worth more or less than its true value. The exchanges, with the encouragement and support of the SEC, utilize sophisticated computer programs to help spot any irregularities that suggest manipulation, and they require disclosures to help identify manipulators. This same system helps to identify illegal insider trading.

Assuming a company qualifies, many people believe that listing is beneficial both to it and to its stockholders. Listed companies receive a certain amount of free advertising and publicity, and their status as a listed company may enhance their prestige and reputation. This may have a beneficial effect on the sales of the firm's products. Investors respond favorably to increased information, increased liquidity, and confidence that the quoted price is not being manipulated. By providing investors with these benefits in the form of listing their companies' stocks, financial managers may be able to lower their firms' cost of equity and increase the value of their stock.

However, due to improvements in telecommunications and computer technologies, the differences between the OTC market and the exchanges have become less distinct. As a result, some very large companies such as MCI, Microsoft, Intel, and Apple, which almost certainly would have been listed on the NYSE in earlier days, have elected to remain in the OTC market. Today, corporate CFOs are more conscious than ever that alternative markets have benefits that may exceed the prestige of a NYSE listing.

SELF-TEST QUESTION | What are the major advantages and disadvantages to a company listing its stock on an exchange?

PROCEDURES FOR SELLING NEW COMMON STOCK

If a company plans to sell stock to raise new capital, the new shares may be sold in one of five ways: (1) on a pro rata basis to existing stockholders through a rights offering, (2) through investment bankers to the general public in a public offering, (3) to a single buyer (or a very small number of buyers) in a private placement, (4) to employees through employee stock purchase plans, or (5) through a dividend reinvestment plan. We discussed dividend reinvestment plans in Chapter 17, but the other procedures are considered in the following sections.

Rights Offerings

As discussed in Chapter 9, common stockholders often have the **preemptive right** to purchase any additional shares sold by the firm. If the preemptive right is contained in a particular firm's charter, the company must offer any newly issued common stock to existing stockholders. If the charter does not prescribe a preemptive right, the firm has the option of selling to its existing stockholders or to the public at large. If it sells to the existing stockholders, the issue is called a **rights offering.** Each stockholder is issued an option to buy a certain number of new shares, and the terms of the option are listed on a certificate called a **stock purchase right**, or simply a **right.** If a stockholder does not wish to purchase any additional shares, then he or she can sell the rights to some other person who does want to buy the stock.[2]

Public Offerings

If the preemptive right exists in a company's charter, it must sell new stock through a rights offering. If the preemptive right does not apply, the company can choose between a rights offering and a **public offering.** We discuss procedures for public offerings later in the chapter.

---

[2]For more details on the mechanics of a rights offering, see Eugene F. Brigham and Louis C. Gapenski, *Intermediate Financial Management,* 5th Ed. (Forth Worth, Tex.: Dryden Press, 1996), Chapter 14.

Private Placements

In a **private placement,** securities are sold to one or a few investors, generally institutional investors. Private placements are most common with bonds, but they also occur with stocks. The primary advantages of private placements are (1) lower flotation costs and (2) greater speed, since the shares do not have to go through the SEC registration process.

The most common type of private placement occurs when a company places securities directly with a financial institution, often an insurance company or a pension fund. In fact, Prudential Insurance Company has begun sending salespeople to call on businesses—not to sell them policies, but to sell them on raising funds privately from Prudential. To illustrate a private placement, AT&T recently sold 6.3 million shares of common stock worth about $650 million to Capital Group Inc., a Los Angeles institutional investor that manages both mutual and pension funds. The transaction was a blow to three Wall Street firms, Morgan Stanley, Dillon Reed, and Goldman Sachs, which wanted to sell the stock in a conventional public offering. AT&T's treasurer said selling the stock in a private placement saved about 2.5 percent, or $16.3 million, in underwriting expenses.

One type of private placement that is occurring with increasing frequency is where a large company makes an equity investment in a smaller supplier. For example, Compaq Computer and AMP Corporation each recently invested several million in Intellon Corporation, a telecommunications equipment manufacturer. Intellon needed capital for expansion, and Compaq and AMP were both engaged in joint development ventures with Intellon and wanted it to be financially strong. Similar arrangements are quite common, and some of them go back many years. For example, Sears, Roebuck has for many years supplied equity capital to some of its major suppliers, including Johnson Controls, which furnishes Sears with "Die-Hard" batteries, and with DeSoto Chemical, which supplies most of the paints that Sears sells.

The primary disadvantage of a private placement is that the securities generally do not go through the SEC registration process, so under SEC rules they cannot be sold except to another large, "sophisticated" purchaser in the event the original buyer wants to sell them. However, SEC rules permit any institution with $100 million or more to buy and sell private placement securities. Since many institutions exceed that limit, private placements are becoming increasingly popular, and today they constitute almost 40 percent of all nonbank debt financing.

Employee Purchase Plans and ESOPs

Many companies have plans that allow employees to purchase stock on favorable terms. Under executive stock option plans, key managers are given options to purchase stock. These managers generally have a direct, material influence on the company's fortunes, so if they perform well, the stock will go up and the options will become valuable. There are also plans for lower-level employees. For example, IBM permits employees who are not participants in its stock option plan to allocate up to 10 percent of their salaries to its stock purchase plan, and the funds are then used to buy newly issued shares at 85 percent of the market value on the purchase date. Often, the company's contribution (in IBM's case, the 15 percent discount) is not vested in an employee until five years after the purchase date. This type of plan is designed both to improve employee performance and to reduce turnover.

Another type of plan calls for the stock bought for employees to be purchased out of a share of the company's profits. Congress has sought to encourage employee ownership through tax policy—under an **Employee Stock Ownership Plan (ESOP)**, companies can claim a tax credit equal to a percentage of wages, provided that the funds are used to buy newly issued stock for the benefit of employees. The amount of the credit varies from year to year, depending on the whims of Congress: currently it is ½ of 1 percent of total wages.

To start a typical ESOP, a company borrows money to buy its own stock, either newly issued stock or on the open market, and places the stock in the hands of the ESOP trustee, who then allocates the stock ownership to the firm's employees on the basis of relative salaries. Then, after the ESOP is initially funded, additional stock is bought and paid for out of annual earnings and the tax saving. Often, ESOPs are set up to supplement or to replace entirely employee retirement programs. ESOPs generally have one thing in common with leveraged buyouts (LBOs) — they increase debt, hence result in higher financial leverage. However, the similarity ends there. While an LBO usually makes owners out of a small group of managers, an ESOP makes owners out of practically everyone on the payroll.

The advantages of ESOPs are as follows:

1. **Tax breaks.** Companies get a huge tax advantage from ESOPs—they get a tax credit, plus they can deduct (a) the interest on the debt used to buy stock for the ESOP, (b) some of the principal payments on the ESOP-funding debt, and (c) the dividends they pay on the ESOP-held shares.

2. **Anti-takeover defense.** The more of a company's stock the ESOP holds, the better able a company is to fend off a raider, because the ESOP's trustee will generally support current management over a raider who may be planning to lay off many of the current employees.

3. **Pension cost control.** When a company uses an ESOP to reduce or even replace its conventional pension plan, it can save heavily. Some companies drop their retirement medical benefits, telling employees that they can dip into their ESOP accounts to buy medical coverage.

4. **Productivity enhancement.** Once the employees are owners as well as workers, they are presumably motivated to become more productive and more concerned about product quality.

Although their advantages are very real, ESOPs have some disadvantages:

1. **Balance of power.** ESOPs transform workers into a large bloc of shareholders with intimate knowledge about the company who may favor higher wages over higher profits. Also, if a firm's managers alienate the employee-owners, workers could vote their shares in favor of a raider.

2. **Legal considerations.** The Labor Department and the courts are on the lookout for ESOP abuses. If they perceive an ESOP to be a hastily constructed takeover defense, designed primarily to protect current management, they could reject the ESOP plan. Also, ESOP tax laws could be changed by Congress at any time to make them less favorable to the firm.

3. **Retiree benefits.** The more retirees' benefits are tied to an ESOP, the more dependent retirees become on the price of the company's stock. That leaves retirees vulnerable to both the whims of Wall Street and management mistakes, and it puts a lot of employees' retirement eggs into one basket.

4. **Obligation to repurchase stock.** Private companies with ESOPs must repurchase stock at the current appraised value when employees leave the company or retire. If a large number of employees quit or retire in a given year, the repurchases can put a significant strain on the company's cash position.

Although employee purchase plans are designed more to provide incentives to improve employee performance than to raise capital, these plans do produce a surprisingly large amount of new equity. Note, though, that a company may choose to purchase shares for its ESOP on the open market rather than issue new shares. The decision to use newly issued shares or repurchased shares depends upon the company's need for funds in a given year. Still, employee purchase plans have the potential for raising a great deal of equity capital.

S E L F - T E S T
Q U E S T I O N S

What is a rights offering?

What is a private placement? What are its primary advantages over a public offering?

Briefly describe employee purchase plans.

What is an Employee Stock Ownership Plan (ESOP)? What are its major advantages and disadvantages?

ADVANTAGES AND DISADVANTAGES OF FINANCING WITH COMMON STOCK

In this section we briefly discuss the advantages and disadvantages of financing with common stock.

Advantages of Common Stock

1. Common stock does not entail fixed charges. If the company does not generate enough earnings, it does not have to pay common stock dividends. If the firm uses debt, it must make interest and principal payments regardless of the level of earnings.

2. Common stock has no maturity date—it is permanent capital which does not have to be "paid back."

3. Since common stock strengthens the position of creditors, its use improves access to debt markets and lowers the cost of debt.

4. Common stock can, at times, be sold more easily than debt. It appeals to certain investor groups because (a) it typically carries a higher expected return than does preferred stock or debt, (b) it provides investors with a better hedge against inflation than does preferred stock or bonds, and (c) most of the returns are taxed as capital gains, and taxes can be deferred until the gains are realized.

Disadvantages of Common Stock

1. The sale of common stock normally gives voting rights to the new investors. For this reason, equity financing is often avoided by small firms, whose owner-managers may be unwilling to share control with outsiders. Note, though, that firms can use special classes of common stock that do not carry voting rights.

2. Debt enables the firm to acquire funds at a fixed cost, whereas common stock "dilutes the equity," which means that more stockholders will share in the firm's future profits.

3. The costs of underwriting and distributing common stock are higher than those for preferred stock or debt.

4. The sale of new common stock may be perceived by investors as a negative signal, hence may cause the stock to fall.

What are the advantages of financing with common stock?

What are some disadvantages of financing with common stock?

SECURITIES REGULATION AND THE INVESTMENT BANKING PROCESS

In this section, we describe the regulation of securities markets, the way securities are issued, and the role of investment bankers in the process.

Regulation of Securities Markets

Sales of new securities, and also sales in the secondary markets, are regulated by the **Securities and Exchange Commission (SEC)** and, to a lesser extent, by each of the 50 states. Here are the primary elements of SEC regulation:

1. The SEC has jurisdiction over all **interstate public offerings** in amounts of $1.5 million or more.

2. Newly issued securities (stocks and bonds) must be registered with the SEC at least 20 days before they are publicly offered. The **registration statement** provides financial, legal, and technical information about the company to the SEC, and the **prospectus** summarizes this information for investors. The SEC's lawyers and accountants analyze both the registration statement and the prospectus; if the information is inadequate or misleading, the SEC will delay or stop the public offering.

3. After the registration has become effective, new securities may be offered, but all sales solicitations must be accompanied by the prospectus. Preliminary, or **"red herring," prospectuses** may be distributed to potential buyers during the 20-day waiting period, but no sales may be finalized during this time. The "red herring" prospectus contains all the key information that will appear in the final prospectus except the price, which is generally set after the market closes the day before the new securities are actually offered to the public.

4. If the registration statement or prospectus contains **misrepresentations or omissions** of material facts, any purchaser who suffers a loss may sue for damages. Severe penalties may be imposed on the issuer or its officers, directors, accountants, engineers, appraisers, underwriters, and all others who participated in the preparation of the registration statement or prospectus.

5. The SEC also **regulates all national stock exchanges,** and companies whose securities are listed on an exchange must file annual reports similar to the registration statement with both the SEC and the exchange.

6. The SEC has control over trading by corporate **insiders.** Officers, directors, and major stockholders must file monthly reports of changes in their holdings of the stock of the corporation. Any short-term profits from such transactions must be turned over to the corporation.

7. The SEC has the power to **prohibit manipulation** by such devices as pools (large amounts of money used to buy or sell stocks to artificially affect prices) or wash sales (sales between members of the same group to record artificial transaction prices).

8. The SEC has **control over the proxy statement** and the way the company uses it to solicit votes.

Control over credit used to buy securities is exercised by the Federal Reserve Board through **margin requirements,** which specify the maximum percentage of the purchase price someone can borrow. If a great deal of margin borrowing has been going on, then a decline in stock prices can result in inadequate coverages. This could force stockbrokers to issue **margin calls,** which require investors either to put up more money or have their margined stock sold to pay off their loans. Such forced sales further depress the stock market and thus can set off a downward spiral. The initial margin requirement has been 50 percent since 1974 (subsequent "maintenance margins" are lower and are generally set by individual lenders).

States also have some control over the issuance of new securities within their boundaries. This control is usually exercised by a "corporation commissioner" or someone with a similar title. State laws relating to security sales are called **blue sky laws,** because they were put into effect to keep unscrupulous promoters from selling securities that offered the "blue sky" but which actually had little or no asset backing.

The securities industry itself realizes the importance of stable markets, sound brokerage firms, and the absence of stock manipulation. Therefore, the various exchanges work closely with the SEC to police transactions and to maintain the integrity and credibility of the system. Similarly, the **National Association of Securities Dealers (NASD)** cooperates with the SEC to police trading in the OTC market. These industry groups also cooperate with regulatory authorities to set net worth and other standards for securities firms, to develop insurance programs to protect the customers of brokerage houses, and the like.

In general, government regulation of securities trading, as well as industry self-regulation, is designed to ensure (1) that investors receive information that is as accurate as possible, (2) that no one artificially manipulates the market price of a given stock, and (3) that corporate insiders do not take advantage of their position to profit in their companies' stocks at the expense of other stockholders. Neither the SEC, the state regulators, nor the industry itself can prevent investors from making foolish decisions or from having "bad luck," but they can and do help investors obtain the best data possible for making sound investment decisions.

The Investment Banking Process

The investment banking process takes place in two stages.

Stage I Decisions.   At Stage I, the firm itself makes some initial, preliminary decisions, including the following:

1. **Dollars to be raised.** How much new capital is needed?
2. **Type of securities used.** Should common, preferred, bonds, hybrid securities, or a combination, be used? Further, if common stock is to be issued, should it be done as a rights offering or by a direct sale to the general public?
3. **Competitive bid versus a negotiated deal.** Should the company simply offer a block of its securities for sale to the highest bidder, or should it negotiate a deal with an investment banker? These two procedures are called **competitive bids** and **negotiated deals,** respectively. Only about 100 of the largest firms listed on the NYSE, whose securities are already well known to the investment banking community, are in a position to use the competitive bidding process. The investment banks must do a great deal of investigative work ("due diligence") to bid on an issue unless they are

already quite familiar with the firm, and such costs would be too high to make it worthwhile unless the bank was sure of getting the deal. Therefore, except for the largest firms, offerings of stock and bonds are generally on a negotiated basis.

4. **Selection of an investment banker.** Most deals are negotiated, so the firm must select an investment banker. This can be an important decision for a firm that is going public. On the other hand, an older firm that has already "been to market" will have an established relationship with an investment banker. However, it is easy to change bankers if the firm is dissatisfied. Different investment banking houses are better suited for different companies. The older, larger "establishment houses" such as Morgan Stanley deal mainly with companies such as AT&T, IBM, and Exxon. Other bankers handle more speculative issues. Some houses specialize in new issues, while others are not well suited to handle such issues because their brokerage clients are relatively conservative. (Investment banking houses sell new issues largely to their own regular brokerage customers, so the nature of these customers has a major effect on the ability of the house to do a good job for corporate issuers.) Table 18-1 lists the top ten U.S. underwriters for 1997 as measured by the dollar amount of securities underwritten.

Stage II Decisions. Stage II decisions, which are made jointly by the firm and its selected investment banker, include the following:

1. **Reevaluating the initial decisions.** The firm and its banker will reevaluate the initial decisions regarding the size of the issue and the type of securities to use. For example, the firm may have decided initially to raise $50 million by selling common stock, but the investment banker may convince management that it would be better off, in view of current market conditions, to limit the stock issue to $25 million and to raise the other $25 million as debt.

TABLE 18-1	Top Ten Underwriters of U.S. Debt and Equity	
		TOTAL AMOUNT MANAGED (IN BILLIONS OF DOLLARS)
	1. Merrill Lynch	$208.1
	2. Salomon Smith Barney	167.0
	3. Morgan Stanley Dean Witter	139.5
	4. Goldman, Sachs	137.3
	5. Lehman Brothers	121.0
	6. JP Morgan	104.0
	7. Credit Suisse First Boston	67.7
	8. Bear, Stearns	57.5
	9. Donaldson, Lufkin & Jenrette	46.0
	10. Chase Manhattan	33.1

SOURCE: *The Wall Street Journal,* January 2, 1998, p. R38. Reprinted by permission of *The Wall Street Journal,* © 1998. Dow Jones & Company, Inc. All Rights Reserved Worldwide.

2. **Best efforts or underwritten issues.** The firm and its investment banker must decide whether the banker will work on a **best efforts** basis or will **underwrite** the issue. In a best efforts sale, the banker does not guarantee that the securities will be sold or that the company will get the cash it needs, only that it will put forth its best efforts to sell the issue. On an underwritten issue, the company does get a guarantee, because the banker agrees to buy the entire issue and then resell the stock to its customers. Therefore, the banker bears significant risks in underwritten offerings. For example, on one IBM bond issue, interest rates rose sharply, and bond prices fell, after the deal had been set but before the investment bankers could sell the bonds to ultimate purchasers. The bankers lost somewhere between $10 million and $20 million. Had the offering been on a best efforts basis, IBM would have been the loser.

3. **Banker's compensation and other expenses.** The investment banker's compensation must be negotiated. Also, the firm must estimate the other underwriting expenses it will incur in connection with the issue — lawyers' fees, accountants' costs, printing and engraving, and so on. In an underwritten issue, the banker will buy the issue from the company at a discount below the price at which the securities are to be offered to the public, with this "spread" being set to cover the banker's costs and to provide a profit.

   In the Extension to Chapter 10, we presented data on the issuance costs associated with public issues of bonds and common stock. As the data show, costs as a percentage of the proceeds are higher for stocks than for bonds, and costs are higher for small than for large issues. The relationship between size of issue and flotation cost is due primarily to the existence of fixed costs — certain costs must be incurred regardless of the size of the issue, so the percentage flotation cost is quite high for small issues.

   Also, it should be noted that when companies go public to raise new capital, the new shares are typically underpriced, so the stock often closes on the first day of trading at a price well above the issue price. For example, Boston Chicken's stock soared from its $20 offering price to close the first day at $51. Underpricing represents a potentially large cost to existing shareholders. Further, the investment bankers frequently take part of their compensation in the form of options to buy stock in the firm. For example, Glasgo Technologies recently went public with a $10 million issue by selling 1 million shares at a price of $10 per share. Its investment bankers bought the stock from the company at a price of $9.75 per share, so the direct underwriting fee was only $1,000,000($10.00 − $9.75) = $250,000$, or 2.5 percent, but they also received a five-year option to buy 200,000 shares at a price of $10 per share. If the stock should go up to $15 per share, which the bankers expected it to do, then the investment banking firm would make a $1 million profit, which would in effect be an additional underwriting fee.

4. **Setting the offering price.** If the company is already publicly owned, the offering price will be based upon the existing market price of the stock. Typically, the investment banker buys the securities at a prescribed number of points below the closing price on the last day of registration. For example, suppose that in October 1998, the stock of Microwave Telecommunications Inc. (MTI) had a current price of $28.60 per share, and the stock had traded between $25 and $30 per share during the previous three months. Suppose further that MTI and its underwriter agreed that the investment banker would buy 10 million new shares at $1 per share below the closing price on the last day of registration. If the stock closed at $25 on the day the SEC released the issue, MTI would receive $24 per share. Typically, such agreements have an escape clause that provides for the contract to be voided if the price of the securities drops below some predetermined figure. In the illustrative case, this "upset" price might be set at $24 per share. Thus, if the closing price of the shares on the

last day of registration had been $23.50, MTI would have had the option of withdrawing from the agreement.

The investment banker will have an easier job if the issue is priced relatively low. However, the issuer naturally wants as high a price as possible. A conflict of interest on price therefore arises between the investment banker and the issuer. If the issuer is financially sophisticated and makes comparisons with similar security issues, the investment banker will be forced to price close to the market.

As we discussed in Chapters 15 and 16, the announcement of a new stock offering by a mature firm is often taken as a negative signal—if the firm's prospects were good, management would not want to issue new stock and thus share the rosy future with new stockholders. Therefore, the announcement of a new offering is taken as bad news. Consequently, the price will probably fall when the announcement is made, so the offering price will probably have to be set at a price substantially below the pre-announcement market price. Consider Figure 18-1, in which d_0 is the estimated market demand curve for MTI's stock and S_0 is the number of shares currently outstanding. Initially, there are 50 million shares outstanding, and the equilibrium price is $28.60 per share, determined as follows:

$$\hat{P}_0 = \frac{D_1}{k_s - g} = \frac{\$2.00}{0.12 - 0.05} \approx \$28.60.$$

The values shown for D_1, k_s, and g are the *estimates of a marginal investor.* Investors who do not now own MTI's stock probably, on average, regard the stock as being riskier

---

FIGURE 18-1   Microwave Telecommunications Inc.:
Estimated Common Stock Demand Curves

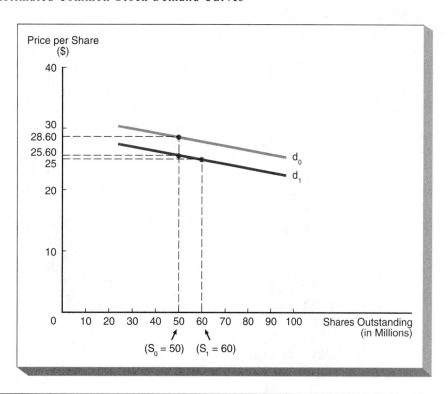

and thus assign it a higher k_s, or perhaps they estimate the company's growth rate as being lower than do people who now own the stock. In any event, people who do not now own the stock think it is worth less than $28.60.

When MTI announces that it plans to sell another 10 million shares, this is taken as a negative signal. Consequently, the demand curve for the stock drops from d_0 to d_1, and the price falls. The new equilibrium price, if 50 million shares were outstanding and if the marginal investor now expects MTI's growth rate to be 4.2 percent, would be about $25.60:

$$\hat{P}_0 = \frac{\$2.00}{0.12 - 0.042} \approx \$25.60.$$

However, if MTI is to sell another 10 million shares of stock, it will either have to attract investors who would not be willing to own the stock at the $25.60 per share price or else induce present stockholders to buy additional shares. There are two ways this can be accomplished: (1) by reducing the offering price of the stock or (2) by "promoting" or "advertising" the company and thus shifting the demand curve for its stock back to the right.[3] If the demand curve does not shift at all from d_1, we see from Figure 18-1 that the only way the 10 million additional shares could be sold would be by setting the offering price at about $25 per share. However, if the investment banker could promote the stock sufficiently to shift the demand curve back up to d_0, then the offering price could be set much closer to the pre-announcement equilibrium price of $28.60 per share.[4]

The extent to which the demand curve can be shifted depends primarily on two factors: (1) what investors think the company can do with the money brought in by the stock sale and (2) how effectively the brokers promote the issue. If investors can be convinced that the new money will be invested in highly profitable projects that will raise earnings and the earnings growth rate, then the demand curve shift will occur, and the stock price might actually go above $28.60. Even if investors do not radically change their expectations about the company's fundamental factors, the fact that MTI's stock is brought to the attention of new investors may shift the demand curve. The extent to which this promotion campaign is successful in shifting the demand curve depends, of course, upon the effectiveness of the investment banking firm. Therefore, the effectiveness of different investment bankers, as perceived by MTI's financial manager, will be an important factor in the choice of an underwriter.

One final point is that *if pressure from the new shares and/or negative signaling effects drives down the price of the stock, all shares outstanding, not just the new shares, are affected.* Thus, if MTI's stock should fall from $28.60 to $25 per share as a result of the financing, and if the price should remain at that new level, then the company would incur a loss of $3.60 on each of the 50 million shares previously outstanding, or a total market value loss of $180 million. This loss, like underwriting expenses, is a flotation cost, and it should be considered as a cost associated with the stock issue.

---

[3]It should be noted that investors can buy newly issued stock without paying normal brokerage commissions, and brokers are quick to point this out to potential purchasers. Thus, if an investor were to buy MTI's stock at $28 per share in the regular market, the commission would be about 1 percent, or 28 cents per share. If the stock were purchased in an underwriting, this commission would be avoided.

It should also be noted that for years many academicians argued that the demand curve for a firm's stock is either horizontal or has an extremely slight downward slope, and that signaling effects are minimal. Most corporate treasurers, on the other hand, have long felt that both effects exist for mature companies, and empirical studies confirm the treasurers' position. For example, see Andrei Shleifer, "Do Demand Curves for Stocks Slope Down?" *Journal of Finance,* July 1986, 579–590.

[4]Note that the supply curve is a vertical line, first at 50 million and then, after the new issue, at 60 million.

However, if the company's prospects really were poorer than investors thought, then the price decline would have occurred sooner or later anyway. On the other hand, if the company's prospects are really not all that bad (the signal was incorrect), then over time MTI's demand curve will move back to d_0, or even above d_0, so the company would not suffer a permanent loss anywhere close to $180 million.

If the company is "going public," there will be no established price or demand curve, so the bankers will have to estimate the **equilibrium price** at which the stock will sell after issue. Note that if the offering price is set below the true equilibrium price, as with Boston Chicken and most other IPOs, the stock will rise sharply after the issue, and the company and its selling stockholders will have given away too many shares to raise the required capital. If the offering price is set above the true equilibrium price, either the issue will fail or, if the bankers succeed in selling the stock to their retail clients, these clients will be unhappy when the stock subsequently falls to its equilibrium level. Therefore, it is important that the equilibrium price be closely approximated, although it is hard to estimate this price.[5]

Selling Procedures.   Once the company and its investment bankers have decided how much money to raise, the types of securities to issue, and the basis for pricing the issue, they will prepare and file an SEC registration statement and a prospectus. It generally takes about 20 days for the issue to be approved by the SEC. The final price of the stock (or the interest rate on a bond issue) is set at the close of business the day the issue clears the SEC, and the securities are offered to the public the following day.

Investors are required to pay for securities within ten days, and the investment banker must pay the issuing firm within four days of the official commencement of the offering. Typically, the banker sells the stock within a day or two after the offering begins, but on occasion, the banker miscalculates, sets the offering price too high, and thus is unable to move the issue. At other times, the market declines during the offering period, forcing the banker to reduce the price of the stock or bonds. In either instance, on an underwritten offering the firm receives the price that was agreed upon, so the banker must absorb any losses that are incurred.

Because they are exposed to large potential losses, investment bankers typically do not handle the purchase and distribution of issues single-handedly unless the issue is a very small one. If the sum of money involved is large, investment bankers form **underwriting syndicates** in an effort to minimize the risk each banker faces. The banking house which sets up the deal is called the **lead,** or **managing, underwriter.**

In addition to the underwriting syndicate, on larger offerings still more investment bankers are included in a **selling group,** which handles the distribution of securities to individual investors. The selling group includes all members of the underwriting syndicate plus additional dealers who take relatively small percentages of the total issue from the members of the underwriting syndicate. Thus, the underwriters act as wholesalers, while members of the selling group act as retailers. The number of houses in a selling group depends partly upon the size of the issue. For example, the one set up when Communications Satellite Corporation (Comsat) went public consisted of 385 members.

---

[5]IPOs are almost always underpriced; in the period 1990–1994, underpricing averaged more than 12 percent; see the Extension to Chapter 10 for more details. Various theories have been put forth to explain this phenomenon. The best explanation seems to be that (1) both the company and the investment bankers want to create excitement, and a price run-up does that; (2) a small percentage of the company's stock is generally offered to the public, so current stockholders give away less due to underpricing than appears at first glance; and (3) IPO companies generally plan to have further offerings in the future, and the best way to ensure future success is to have a successful IPO, which underpricing guarantees.

A new selling procedure has recently emerged which does not require an underwriting syndicate. In this type of sale, called an **unsyndicated stock offering,** the managing underwriter, acting alone, sells the issue entirely to institutional investors, thus bypassing both retail stockbrokers and individual investors. In recent years, about 50 percent of all stock sold has been by unsyndicated offerings. Behind this phenomenon is a simple motivating force: money. The fees that issuers pay on a syndicated offering, which includes commissions paid to retail brokers, can run at least a full percentage point higher than those on unsyndicated offerings. Further, although total fees are lower if there is no syndicate, managing underwriters usually come out ahead because they do not have to share the fees with an underwriting syndicate. Recent issuers of unsyndicated stock include Transamerica Corporation and Public Service Company of New Mexico. However, some types of stock do not appeal to institutional investors, so not all firms can use unsyndicated offers.

Shelf Registrations.   The selling procedures described previously, including the 20-day waiting period after registration with the SEC, apply to most security sales. However, under the SEC's Rule 415, large, well-known public companies which issue securities frequently may file a master registration statement with the SEC and then update it with a short-form statement just prior to each individual offering. Under this procedure, the company can decide at 10 A.M. to sell securities and have the sale completed before noon. This procedure is known as **shelf registration** because, in effect, the company puts its new securities "on the shelf" and then sells them to investors when it feels the market is "right." Firms with less than $150 million in stock held by outside investors cannot use shelf registrations. The rationale for this distinction is to protect investors who may not be able to get adequate financial data about a little-known company in the short time between announcement of a shelf issue and its sale. Shelf registrations have two advantages over standard registrations: (1) lower flotation costs and (2) more control over the timing of the issue.

Maintenance of the Secondary Market.   In the case of a large, established firm such as IBM or GM, the investment banking firm's job is finished after it has disposed of the stock and turned the net proceeds over to the issuing firm. However, in the case of a small company going public for the first time, the investment banker is under some obligation to maintain a market in the shares after the issue has been completed. Such stocks are typically traded in the over-the-counter market, and the lead underwriter generally agrees to "make a market" in the stock so as to keep it reasonably liquid. The company wants a good market to exist for its stock, as do the stockholders. Therefore, if the banking house wants to do business with the company in the future, to keep its own brokerage customers happy, and to have future referral business, it will hold an inventory and help to maintain an active secondary market in the stock.

SELF-TEST QUESTIONS

What are the key features of security market regulations?

What is the difference between Stage I and Stage II decisions?

What is the difference between a best efforts and an underwritten issue?

What are some potential problems encountered when setting the offering price on a stock issue?

Briefly explain the selling procedures used on a new securities issue.

What is a shelf registration? What are the advantages of shelf registrations over standard registrations?

RECENT INNOVATIONS IN TYPES OF BONDS

In Chapter 8 we introduced basic debt securities, but the last 15 years have witnessed many innovations in long-term debt financing. We will discuss three in this section. The first—zero coupon bonds—is a result of the extreme volatility in interest rates which has characterized the period. The second and third, project financing and securitization, permit a firm to tie a debt issue to a specific asset.

Zero (or Very Low) Coupon Bonds

Some bonds pay no interest but are offered at a substantial discount below their par values and hence provide capital appreciation rather than interest income. These securities are called **zero coupon bonds ("zeros")**, or **original issue discount bonds (OIDs).** Corporations first used zeros in a major way in 1981. In recent years IBM, Alcoa, JCPenney, ITT, Cities Service, GMAC, Martin-Marietta, and many other companies have used them to raise billions of dollars. Municipal governments also sell "zero munis."

Shortly after corporations began to issue zeros, investment bankers figured out a way to create zeros from U.S. Treasury bonds, which are issued only in coupon form. In 1983 Salomon Brothers bought $1 billion of 7 percent, 30-year Treasuries. Each bond had 60 coupons worth $35 each, which represented the interest payments due every six months. Salomon then in effect clipped the coupons and placed them in 60 piles; the last pile also contained the now "stripped" bond itself, which represented a promise of $1,000 in the year 2013. These 60 piles of U.S. Treasury promises were then placed with the trust department of a bank and used as collateral for "zero coupon U.S. Treasury Trust Certificates," which are, in essence, zero coupon Treasury bonds. A pension fund that expected to need money in 2004 could have bought 21-year certificates backed by the interest the Treasury will pay in 2004.

In 1985 the Treasury Department began allowing investors to strip long-term U.S. Treasury bonds and directly register the newly created zero coupon bonds, called STRIPs, with the Treasury Department. This bypasses the role fomerly played by investment banks. Now virtually all U.S. Treasury zeros are held in the form of STRIPs. These STRIPs are, of course, safer than corporate zeros, so they are very popular with pension fund managers.

To understand how zeros are used and analyzed, consider the zeros of Vandenberg Corporation, a shopping center developer. Vandenberg is developing a new shopping center in Orange County, California, and it needs $50 million. The company does not anticipate major cash flows from the project for about five years. However, Pieter Vandenberg, the president, plans to sell the center once it is fully developed and rented, which should take about five years. Therefore, Vandenberg wants to use a financing vehicle that will not require cash outflows for five years. He has decided on a five-year zero coupon bond, with a maturity value of $1,000.

Vandenberg Corporation is an A-rated company, and A-rated zeros with five-year maturities yield 9 percent at this time (five-year coupon bonds also yield 9 percent). The company is in the 40 percent federal-plus-state tax bracket. Pieter Vandenberg wants to know the firm's after-tax cost of capital if it uses 9 percent, five-year maturity zeros, and he also wants to know what the bond's cash flows will be. Table 18-2 provides an analysis of the situation, and the following numbered paragraphs explain the table itself.

1. The information in the "Basic Data" section, except the issue price, was given in the preceding paragraph, and the information in the "Analysis" section was calculated using the known data. The maturity value of the bond is always set at $1,000 or some multiple thereof.

TABLE 18-2	Analysis of a Zero Coupon Bond

Basic Data:

Maturity value	$1,000
k_d	9.00%
Maturity	5 years
Corporate tax rate	40.00%
Issue price	$649.93

Analysis:

				Years		
	0	1	2	3	4	5
(1) Year-end accrued value	649.93	708.42	772.18	841.68	917.43	1000.00
(2) Interest deduction		58.49	63.76	69.50	75.75	82.57
(3) Tax savings (40%)		23.40	25.50	27.80	30.30	33.03
(4) Cash flow	+649.93	+23.40	+25.50	+27.80	+30.30	−966.97

After-tax cost of debt = 5.40%.
Number of $1,000 zeros the company must issue to raise $50 million = Amount needed/Price per bond

$$= \$50,000,000/\$649.93$$
$$= 76,931 \text{ bonds.}$$

Face amount of bonds: (76,931)($1,000) = $76,931,000.

---

2. The issue price is the PV of $1,000, discounted back five years at the rate $k_d = 9\%$. Using a financial calculator, we input N = 5, I = 9, and FV = 1000, then press the PV key to find PV = $649.93. Note that $649.93, compounded annually for five years at 9 percent, will grow to $1,000 as shown on the time line in Table 18-2.

3. The accrued values as shown on Line 1 in the analysis section represent the compounded value of the bond at the end of each year. The accrued value for Year 0 is the issue price; the accrued value for Year 1 is found as $649.93(1.09)^1 = \$708.42$; the accrued value at the end of Year 2 is $649.93(1.09)^2 = \$772.18$; and, in general, the value at the end of any Year n is

$$\text{Accrued value at the end of Year n} = \text{Issue price} \times (1 + k_d)^n.$$

4. The interest deduction as shown on Line 2 represents the increase in accrued value during the year. Thus, interest in Year 1 = $708.42 − $649.93 = $58.49. In general,

$$\text{Interest in Year n} = \text{Accrued value}_n - \text{Accrued value}_{n-1}.$$

This method of calculating taxable interest is specified in the Tax Code.

5. The company can take a tax deduction for interest each year, even though the payment is not made in cash. This deduction lowers the taxes that would otherwise be paid, producing the following savings:

$$\text{Tax savings} = (\text{Interest deduction})(T)$$
$$= \$58.49(0.4)$$
$$= \$23.40 \text{ in Year 1.}$$

6. Line 4 represents a cash flow time line; it shows the cash flow at the end of Years 0 through 5. At Year 0, the company receives the $649.93 issue price. The company then has positive cash inflows equal to the tax savings during Years 1 through 4. Finally, in Year 5, it must pay the $1,000 maturity value, but it gets one more interest tax saving for that year. Therefore, the net cash flow in Year 5 is −$1,000 + $33.03 = −$966.97.

7. We can find the IRR of the cash flows shown on Line 4 using the IRR function of a financial calculator by simply inputting the annual cash flows in the cash flow register. The IRR is 5.4 percent, and it is the after-tax cost of zero coupon debt to the company. Conceptually, here is the situation:

$$\sum_{t=0}^{n} \frac{CF_n}{(1 + k_{d(AT)})^n} = 0$$

$$\frac{\$649.93}{(1 + k_{d(AT)})^0} + \frac{\$23.40}{(1 + k_{d(AT)})^1} + \frac{\$25.50}{(1 + k_{d(AT)})^2} + \frac{\$27.80}{(1 + k_{d(AT)})^3} + \frac{\$30.30}{(1 + k_{d(AT)})^4} + \frac{-\$966.97}{(1 + k_{d(AT)})^5} = 0.$$

The value $k_{d(AT)} = 0.054 = 5.4\%$, found with a financial calculator, produces the equality, and it is the after-tax cost of the zero coupon bond.

8. Note that $k_d(1 - T) = 9\%(0.6) = 5.4\%$. As we saw in Chapter 10, the cost of capital for regular coupon debt is found using the formula $k_d(1 - T)$. Thus, there is symmetrical treatment for tax purposes for zero coupon and regular coupon debt, so both have the same tax implications. This was Congress's intent, and it is why the Tax Code specifies the treatment set forth in Table 18-2.[6]

Not all original issue discount bonds (OIDs) have zero coupons. For example, Vandenberg might have sold an issue of five-year bonds with a 5 percent coupon at a time when other bonds with similar ratings and maturities were yielding 9 percent. Such a bond would have had a value of $844.41:

$$\text{Bond value} = \sum_{t=1}^{5} \frac{\$50}{(1.09)^t} + \frac{\$1,000}{(1.09)^5} = \$844.41.$$

If an investor had purchased these bonds at a price of $844.41, the yield to maturity would have been 9 percent. The discount of $1,000 − $844.41 = $155.59 would have been amortized over the bond's five-year life, and it would have been handled by both Vandenberg and the bondholders exactly as the discount on the zeros was handled.

Thus, zero coupon bonds are just one type of original issue discount bond. Any non-convertible bond whose coupon rate is set below the going market rate at the time of its issue will sell at a discount, and it will be classified (for tax and other purposes) as an OID bond.

---

[6]The purchaser of a zero coupon bond must calculate interest income on the bond in the same manner as the issuer calculates the interest deduction. Thus, in Year 1, a buyer of a bond would report interest income of $58.49 and would pay taxes in the amount of T(Interest income), even though no cash was received. T, of course, would be the bondholder's personal tax rate. Because of the tax situation, most zero coupon bonds are bought by pension funds and other tax-exempt entities. Individuals do, however, buy taxable zeros for their Individual Retirement Accounts (IRAs). Also, state and local governments issue "tax-exempt muni zeros," which are purchased by individuals in high tax brackets.

Note too that we have analyzed the bond as if the cash flows accrued annually. Generally, to facilitate comparisons with semiannual payment coupon bonds, the analysis is conducted on a semiannual basis.

Corporate (and municipal) zeros are generally callable at the option of the issuer, just like coupon bonds, after some stated call protection period. The call price is set at a premium over the accrued value at the time of the call. Stripped U.S. Treasury bonds (Treasury zeros) are not callable. Thus, Treasury zeros are completely protected against reinvestment risk (the risk of having to invest cash flows from a bond at a lower rate because of a decline in interest rates).

Project Financing

In recent years, many large projects such as the Alaska pipeline have been financed by what is called **project financing.**[7] We can only present an overview of the concept, for in practice it involves very complicated provisions and can take many forms.

Project financing has been used to finance energy explorations, oil tankers, refineries, and electric generating plants. Generally, one or more firms will sponsor the project, putting up the required equity capital, while the remainder of the financing is furnished by lenders or lessors.[8] Most often, a separate legal entity is formed to operate the project. Normally, the project's creditors do not have full recourse against the sponsors. In other words, the lenders and lessors must be paid from the project's cash flows, plus the sponsors' equity in the project, because the creditors have no claims against the sponsors' other assets or cash flows. Often the sponsors write "comfort" letters, giving general assurances that they will strive diligently to make the project successful, but these letters are not legally binding. Therefore, in project financing the lenders and lessors must focus their analysis on the inherent merits of the project plus the equity cushion provided by the sponsors.[9]

Project financing is not a new development. Indeed, back in 1299, the English Crown negotiated a loan with Florentine merchant bankers that was to be repaid with one year's output from the Devon silver mines. Essentially, the Italians were allowed to operate the mines for one year, paying all the operating costs and mining as much ore as they could. The Crown made no guarantees as to how much ore could be mined, or the value of the refined silver. A more current example involved GE Capital, the credit arm of General Electric, which recently financed a $72 million project to build an aluminum can plant. The plant is owned by several beverage makers, but it is operated independently, and GE Capital must depend on the cash flows from the plant to repay the loan. About half of all project financings in recent years have been for electric generating plants, including both plants owned by electric utilities and cogeneration plants operated by industrial companies. Project financings are generally characterized by large size and a high degree of complexity. However, since project financing is tied to a specific project, it can be tailored to meet the specific needs of both the creditors and the sponsors. In particular, the financing can be structured so that both the funds provided during

---

[7]For an excellent discussion of project financing, see John W. Kensinger and John D. Martin, "Project Finance: Raising Money the Old-Fashioned Way," *Journal of Applied Corporate Finance,* Fall 1988, 69–81.

[8]A lessor is an individual or firm that owns buildings and equipment and then leases them to another firm. Leasing is discussed in Chapter 19.

[9]In another type of project financing, each sponsor guarantees its share of the project's debt obligations. Here the creditors would also consider the creditworthiness of the sponsors in addition to the project's own prospects. It should be noted that project financing with multiple sponsors in the electric utility industry has led to problems when one or more of the sponsors has gotten into financial trouble. For example, Long Island Lighting, one of the sponsors in the Nine Mile Point nuclear project, became unable to meet its commitments to the project, which forced other sponsors to shoulder an additional burden or else see the project cancelled and lose all their investment up to that point. Utility executives have stated that this default, and others, will make companies reluctant to enter into similar projects in the future.

the construction phase and the subsequent repayments match the timing of the project's projected cash outflows and inflows.

Project financing offers several potential benefits over conventional debt financing. For one, project financing usually restricts the usage of the project's cash flows, which means that the lenders, rather than the managers, can decide whether to reinvest excess cash flows or to use them to reduce the loan balance by more than the minimum required. Conferring this power on the lenders reduces their risks. Project financings also have advantages for borrowers. First, because risks to the lenders are reduced, the interest rate built into a project financing deal may be relatively low. Second, since suppliers of project financing capital have no recourse against the sponsoring firms' other assets and cash flows, project financings insulate the firms' other assets from risks associated with the project being financed. Managers may be more willing to take on a very large, risky project if they know that the company's existence would not be threatened if it fails.

Project financings increase the number and type of investment opportunities, hence they make capital markets "more complete." At the same time, project financings reduce the costs to investors of obtaining information and monitoring the borrower's operations. To illustrate, consider an oil and gas exploration project that is funded using project financing. If the project were financed as an integral part of the firm's normal operations, investors in all the firm's outstanding securities would need information on the project. By isolating the project, the need for information is confined to the investors in the project financing, and they need to monitor only the project's operations, and not those of the entire firm.

Project financings also permit firms whose earnings are below the minimum requirements specified in their existing bond indentures to obtain additional debt financing. In such situations, lenders look only at the merits of the new project, and its cash flows may support additional debt even though the firm's existing assets would not. Project financings also permit managers to reveal proprietary information to a smaller group of investors, hence project financings increase the ability of a firm to maintain confidentiality. Finally, project financings can improve incentives for key managers by enabling them to take direct ownership stakes in the operations under their control. By establishing separate projects, companies can provide incentives that are much more directly based upon individual performance than is typically possible within a large corporation.

Securitization

As the term is generally used, a **security** refers to a publicly traded financial instrument, as opposed to a privately placed instrument. Thus, securities have greater liquidity than otherwise similar instruments that are not traded in an open market. In recent years, procedures have been developed to **securitize** various types of debt instruments, thus increasing their liquidity, lowering the cost of capital to borrowers, and generally increasing the efficiency of the financial markets.[10]

Securitization has occurred in two major ways. First, some debt instruments that were formerly rarely traded are now actively traded, with the change being due to decisions by certain financial institutions to "make a market," which means to stand willing to buy or sell the security, and to hold an inventory of the security in order to balance buy and sell orders. This occurred many years ago in the case of common stocks and investment-grade bonds. More recently, it occurred in the commercial

[10]The Fall 1988 issue of the *Journal of Applied Corporate Finance* is devoted to securitization.

paper market, in which large, financially strong firms issue short-term, unsecured debt in lieu of obtaining bank loans. The commercial paper market has grown from about $50 billion outstanding in the mid-1970s to over $350 billion today, and this market permits large firms to finance their working capital needs at lower cost than with bank loans.

Another example of securitization is the junk bond market. Before this market developed, firms with poor credit were forced to obtain debt financing on a private placement basis, typically from the firm's bank. It was difficult for firms to shop around for the best rate, because lenders who were not familiar with them were unwilling to spend the time and money necessary to determine the feasibility of the loan, and lenders were also concerned about (and hence charged a higher rate for) the illiquidity of privately placed debt. Then, Michael Milken developed procedures for analyzing the repayment feasibility of junk bonds, and Drexel Burnham Lambert put its reputation and credibility behind these issues and made a market for them in case a purchaser needed to cash out. Subsequently, Morgan Stanley, Merrill Lynch, Salomon Brothers, and the other major investment bankers entered the junk bond market, and today it has "securitized" much of the old private placement market for below-investment-grade debt.

The second major development in securitization involves the pledging of specific assets, **asset securitization,** or the creation of **asset-backed securities.** The oldest type of asset securitization is the mortgage-backed bond. Here, individual home mortgages are combined into pools, and then bonds are created which use the pool of mortgages as collateral. The financial institution that originated the mortgage generally continues to act as the servicing agent, but the mortgage itself is sold to other investors. The securitization of mortgages has created a national mortgage market with many players, hence it has benefited borrowers. The development has also benefited lenders, for the original lending institution, often a savings and loan, no longer owns the relatively long-term mortgage, hence it is better able to match the maturity of its assets (loans) with its liabilities (savings accounts and certificates of deposit). Today, many different types of assets are being used as collateral, including auto loans, credit card balances, and even the royalties from David Bowie's music!

The asset securitization process involves the pooling and repackaging of loans secured by relatively homogeneous, small-dollar assets into liquid securities. In the past, such financing was provided by a single lending institution, which would write the loan, structure the terms, absorb the credit and interest rate risk, provide the capital, and service the collections. Under securitization, several different institutions are involved, with each playing a different functional role. A savings and loan might originate the loan, an investment banker might pool the loans and structure the security, a federal agency might insure against credit risk, a second investment banker might sell the securities, and a pension fund might supply the final capital.

The process of securitization has, in general, lowered costs and increased the availability of funds to borrowers, decreased risks to lenders, and created new investment opportunities for many investors. With these potential benefits, we predict that securitization will continue to expand in the future.

| S E L F - T E S T QUESTIONS | What are zero coupon bonds? What are their advantages and disadvantages for issuers and purchasers? |

What is project financing? What are its advantages and disadvantages?

What is securitization? What are its advantages to borrowers? What are its advantages to lenders?

ADVANTAGES AND DISADVANTAGES OF LONG-TERM DEBT

From the issuer's viewpoint, there are several advantages and disadvantages to long-term debt. The major advantages are as follows:

1. The cost of debt is independent of earnings, so debtholders do not participate if profits soar. There is, however, a flip side to this argument—if profits fall, the company must still pay the interest on its debt.
2. Because of the tax deductibility of interest payments, the risk-adjusted component cost of debt is lower than that of common stock.
3. The owners of the corporation do not have to share control when debt financing is used.

The major disadvantages are as follows:

1. Since debt service (interest plus scheduled principal repayments) is a fixed charge, a decline in operating income may result in insufficient cash flow to meet debt service requirements. This can lead to bankruptcy.
2. As discussed in Chapters 15 and 16, financial leverage increases the firm's riskiness, hence raises its cost of both debt and equity.
3. Debt normally has a fixed maturity date at which time the firm must repay the principal.
4. In a long-term contractual relationship, it is necessary for the indenture provisions to be much more stringent than in a short-term credit agreement. Thus, the firm will be subject to more restrictions than if it had borrowed on a short-term basis or had issued common stock.
5. There is a limit to the amount of funds which can be raised at a "reasonable" rate. Widely accepted lending standards dictate that the debt ratio should not exceed certain limits (which vary from industry to industry), and when debt goes beyond these limits, its cost becomes prohibitive.

SELF-TEST QUESTIONS | What are the major advantages to long-term debt financing?

What are the major disadvantages?

FACTORS THAT INFLUENCE LONG-TERM FINANCING DECISIONS

As we show in this section, many factors influence a firm's long-term financing decisions. Their relative importance varies among firms at any point in time and also for any given firm over time, but all should be considered when a firm raises capital.

Capital Structure Considerations

One of the most important factors in any financing decision is the relationship between the firm's actual capital structure and its target capital structure. Remember that firms establish an optimal, or target, capital structure (or at least a range) and, over time, finance in accordance with this target. Of course, in any one year few firms finance exactly in accordance with their target capital structures, primarily because of flotation costs: Smaller issues of new securities have proportionally larger flotation costs, so firms tend to issue common stock and long-term debt sporadically, while retained earnings are generated continuously.

Note that having fewer, but larger, security offerings causes a firm's capital structure to fluctuate about its optimal level rather than stay right on target. However, (1) small fluctuations about the optimal capital structure have little effect on the weighted average cost of capital, (2) investors recognize that this procedure is prudent, and (3) the firm saves substantial amounts of flotation costs by financing in this manner. So, while over the long haul firms finance in accordance with their target capital structures, flotation costs plus the factors discussed in the following sections influence the specific financing decisions in any given year.

We should also point out that firms can, and often do, arrange financings in advance. Thus, if a firm concluded that it would need $8 million of debt over a two-year period, it might arrange with an insurance company to lend it $4 million in each of the next two years, with the second $4 million being firmly committed at the time the first $4 million is borrowed. Such financings can reduce flotation costs, because the lender needs to make only one detailed credit analysis. Similarly, larger firms can use shelf registrations, which we discussed earlier in this chapter, to hold down financing costs even though they sell relatively small blocks of securities. Both commitment financings and shelf registrations make it possible for firms to adhere reasonably closely to their optimal capital structures without incurring unduly high flotation costs.

Maturity Matching

Assume that Consolidated Tools, a Cincinnati machine tool manufacturer, made the decision to float a $25 million nonconvertible bond issue to help finance its 1999 capital budget. It must choose a maturity for the issue, taking into consideration the shape of the yield curve, management's own expectations about future interest rates, and the maturity of the assets being financed. To illustrate how asset maturities affect the choice of debt maturities, suppose Consolidated's capital projects consist primarily of new milling machinery. This machinery has an expected economic life of ten years (even though it falls into the MACRS five-year class life). Should Consolidated use debt with a 5-year, 10-year, 20-year, or 30-year, or some other, maturity?

Note that some of the new capital will come from common equity, which is permanent capital. On the other hand, debt maturities can be specified at the time of issue. If Consolidated financed its capital budget with ten-year sinking fund bonds, it would be matching asset and liability maturities. The cash flows resulting from the new machinery could be used to make the interest and sinking fund payments on the issue, so the bonds would be retired as the machinery wore out. If Consolidated used one-year debt, it would have to pay off this debt with cash flows derived from assets other than the machinery in question. Conversely, if it used 20-year or 30-year debt, it would have to service the debt long after the assets that were purchased with the funds had been scrapped and had ceased providing cash flows. This would worry lenders.

Of course, the one-year debt could probably be rolled over year after year, out to the ten-year asset maturity. However, if interest rates rose, Consolidated would have to pay a higher rate when it rolled over its debt, and if the company experienced difficulties, it might not be able to refund the debt at any reasonable rate.

For all these reasons, the best all-around financing strategy is to match debt maturities with asset maturities. In recognition of this fact, firms generally do place great emphasis on maturity matching, and this factor often dominates the debt portion of the financing decision.

Effects of Interest Rate Levels and Forecasts

Financial managers also consider interest rate levels and forecasts, both absolute and relative, when making financing decisions. For example, if long-term interest rates are high by historical standards and are expected to fall, managers will be reluctant to issue long-term debt and thus lock in those costs for long periods. We already know that one solution to this problem is for firms to use a call provision—callability permits refunding should interest rates drop. However, there is a cost, because the firm must set a higher coupon on callable debt. Also, floating rate debt could be used. Another alternative would be to finance with short-term debt whenever long-term rates were historically high, and then, assuming that interest rates subsequently fall, sell a long-term issue to replace the short-term debt. Of course, this strategy has its risks: If interest rates move even higher, the firm will be forced to renew its short-term debt at higher and higher rates, or to replace the short-term debt with a long-term bond which costs even more than it would have when the original decision was made.

One could argue that capital markets are efficient, hence that it is impossible to predict what future interest rates will be because these rates will be determined by information which is not now known. Thus, under the efficient markets hypothesis, it would be unproductive for firms to try to "beat the market" by forecasting future capital costs and then acting on these forecasts. According to this view, financial managers ought to arrange their capital structures in such a manner that they can ride out almost any economic storm, and this generally calls for (1) using some "reasonable" mix of debt and equity and (2) using debt with maturities which more or less match the maturities of the assets being financed.

Although the efficient markets hypothesis has merit, there is no question that many managers disagree. They are influenced by current cost levels and forecasts, and they act accordingly. One manifestation of this behavior is the heavy use of shelf registrations. Some firms use shelf registrations because managers believe that financing "windows" exist. In the volatile interest rate environment that has characterized recent years, a company might decide to issue bonds when the rate is 8 percent but then find, six weeks later when it has SEC approval to go ahead with the issue, that rates are up to 9 percent. If it had "bonds on the shelf," it could have gone ahead and sold the issue while the low-cost window was open. (Another way to protect against rising rates is to hedge against this possibility with interest rate futures. We discuss futures markets and the use of futures for hedging in Chapter 24.)

A few years ago, the interest rate on AAA corporate bonds was about 12.5 percent. Exxon's investment bankers advised the company to tap the Eurobond market for relatively cheap fixed-rate financing.[11] At the time, Exxon could issue its bonds in London at 0.4 percentage points *below* comparable maturity U.S. Treasury bonds. However, one of Exxon's officers was quoted as saying, "I say so what. The absolute level of rates is too high. Our people would rather wait." The managers of Exxon, as well as many other companies, were betting that the next move in interest rates would be down. Since interest rates are now much lower, it turned out that Exxon was right.

These attitudes confirm that many firms base their financing decisions on expectations about future interest rates. It is easy to be right on one interest rate call—if you predict a decline in interest rates, you have a 50-50 chance of being correct. However, the success of a strategy based on forecasting rates requires that those forecasts be right more often than they are wrong, and it is very difficult to find someone with a long-term track record which is better than 50-50. Finance would be easy if we could

---

[11]See Chapter 27 for a discussion of Eurobonds.

accurately predict future interest rates. Unfortunately, predicting future interest rates with consistent accuracy is somewhere between difficult and impossible — people who make a living selling interest rate forecasts say it is difficult; many others say it is impossible.

Information Asymmetries

In Chapter 8, we discussed bond ratings and the effects of changes in ratings on the cost and availability of capital. If a firm's current financial condition is poor, its managers may be reluctant to issue new long-term debt because (1) a new debt issue would probably trigger a review by the rating agencies, and (2) debt issued when a firm is in poor financial shape would probably cost more and be subject to more severe restrictive covenants than debt issued from strength. Further, in Chapters 15 and 16 we pointed out that firms are reluctant to use new common stock financing, especially when this might be taken as a negative signal. Thus, a firm that is in a weakened condition, but which is forecasting a better time in the future, would be inclined to delay permanent financing of any type until things improved. Such a firm would be motivated to use short-term debt even to finance long-term assets, with the expectation of replacing the short-term debt in the future with cheaper, higher-rated long-term debt.

Conversely, a firm that is strong now, but which forecasts a potentially bad time in the period just ahead, would be motivated to finance long term now rather than to wait. Each of these scenarios implies either that the capital markets are inefficient or that investors do not have the same information regarding the firm's future as does its financial manager. The second situation is undoubtedly true at times, and the first one possibly is too at times.

The firm's earnings outlook, and the extent to which forecasted higher earnings per share are reflected in stock prices, also has an effect on the choice of securities. If a successful R&D program has just been concluded, and as a result management forecasts higher earnings than do most investors, then the firm would not want to issue common stock. It would use debt and then, once earnings rise and push up the stock price, sell common to restore the capital structure to its target level.

Amount of Financing Required

Obviously, the amount of financing required will influence the financing decision. This is mainly due to flotation costs. A $5 million debt financing would most likely be done with a term loan or a privately placed bond issue, while a firm seeking $100 million of new debt would most likely use a public offering.

Availability of Collateral

Generally, secured debt will be less costly than unsecured debt. Thus, firms with large amounts of marketable fixed assets are likely to use a relatively large amount of debt, especially mortgage bonds. Additionally, each year's financing decision would be influenced by the amount of qualified assets available as security for new bonds.

SELF-TEST QUESTIONS	What are some factors that financial managers consider when making long-term financing decisions?
	How do information asymmetries affect financing decisions?

REFUNDING OPERATIONS

A great deal of long-term corporate debt was sold during the late 1980s at interest rates in the 9 to 12 percent range. Because the period of call protection on much of this debt has ended or is about to end, and because interest rates have fallen since the debt was issued, many companies are analyzing the pros and cons of bond refundings. Refunding decisions actually involve two separate questions: (1) Is it profitable to call an outstanding issue in the current period and replace it with a new issue; and (2) even if refunding is currently profitable, would the value of the firm be increased even more if the refunding were postponed to a later date? We consider both questions in this section.

Note that the decision to refund a security is analyzed in much the same way as a capital budgeting expenditure. The costs of refunding (the investment outlays) are (1) the call premium paid for the privilege of calling the old issue, (2) the tax savings from writing off the unexpensed flotation costs on the old issue, and (3) the net interest that must be paid while both issues are outstanding (the new issue is often sold one month before the refunding to ensure that the funds will be available). The annual cash flows, in a capital budgeting sense, are the interest payments that are saved each year plus the net tax savings which the firm receives for amortizing the flotation expenses. For example, if the interest expense on the old issue is $1,000,000 whereas that on the new issue is $700,000, the $300,000 reduction in interest savings constitutes an annual benefit.[12]

The net present value method is used to analyze the advantages of refunding: the future cash flows are discounted back to the present, and then this discounted value is compared with the cash outlays associated with the refunding. The firm should refund the bond if the present value of the savings exceeds the cost — that is, if the NPV of the refunding operation is positive.

In the discounting process, the after-tax cost of the new debt should be used as the discount rate. The reasons for this are (1) there is relatively little risk to the savings — cash flows in a refunding are known with relative certainty, which is quite unlike the situation with cash flows in most capital budgeting decisions, and (2) the cash outlay required to refund the old issue is generally obtained by increasing the amount of the new issue (see Footnote 15).

The easiest way to examine the refunding decision is through an example. Microchip Computer Company has outstanding a $60 million bond issue which has a 15 percent annual coupon and 20 years remaining to maturity. This issue, which was sold five years ago, had flotation costs of $3 million, which the firm has been amortizing on a straight line basis over the 25-year original life of the issue. The bond has a call provision which makes it possible for the company to retire the bonds at this time by calling them in at a 10 percent call premium. Investment bankers have assured the company that it could sell an additional $60 million to $70 million worth of new annual coupon 20-year bonds at an interest rate of 12 percent. To ensure that the funds required to pay off the old debt will be available, the new bonds would be sold one month before the old issue is called, so for one month, interest would have to be paid on both issues. Current short-term interest rates are 11 percent; for the one-month overlap period, proceeds from the new

---

[12]During the early 1980s, there was a flurry of work on the pros and cons of refunding bond issues that had fallen to deep discounts as a result of rising interest rates. At such times, the company could go into the market, buy its debt at a low price, and retire it. The difference between the bonds' par value and the price the company paid would be reported as income, and taxes would have to be paid on it. The results of the research on the refunding of discount issues suggest that bonds should not, in general, be refunded after a rise in rates. See Andrew J. Kalotay, "On the Structure and Valuation of Debt Refundings," *Financial Management*, Spring 1982, 41–42; and Robert S. Harris, "The Refunding of Discounted Debt: An Adjusted Present Value Analysis," *Financial Management*, Winter 1980, 7–12.

TABLE 18-3 Bond Refunding Decision Worksheet

	AMOUNT BEFORE TAX	AMOUNT AFTER TAX	PRESENT VALUE AT 7.92%
Investment Outlay: t = 0			
1. Call premium on old issue	($6,000,000)	($3,960,000)	($ 3,960,000)
2. Flotation costs on new issue	(2,650,000)	(2,650,000)	(2,650,000)
3. Tax savings on old issue flotation costs	2,400,000	816,000	816,000
4. Extra interest cost on old issue	(750,000)	(495,000)	(495,000)
5. Interest earned on short-term investment	550,000	363,000	363,000
6. Net investment outlay at t = 0			($ 5,926,000)
Annual Flotation Cost Tax Effects: t = 1 – 20			
7. Annual benefit from new issue flotation costs	$ 132,500	$ 45,050	$ 444,953
8. Annual lost benefit from old issue flotation costs	(120,000)	(40,800)	(402,976)
9. PV of amortization tax effects			$ 41,977
Savings Due to Refunding: t = 1 – 20			
10. Interest payment on old issue	$9,000,000	$5,940,000	
11. Interest payment on new issue	7,200,000	4,752,000	
12. Net interest savings		$1,188,000	$11,733,727
NPV of Refunding Decision			$ 5,849,704

issue will be invested in short-term securities. Predictions are that long-term interest rates are unlikely to fall below 12 percent.[13] Flotation costs on a new refunding issue would amount to $2,650,000. Microchip's marginal tax rate is 34 percent. Should the company refund the $60 million of 15 percent bonds?

The following steps outline the decision process; the steps are summarized in worksheet form in Table 18-3.

Step 1. **Determine the investment outlay required to refund the issue.**
    a. **Call premium**

$$Before tax: 0.10(\$60,000,000) = \$6,000,000.$$

$$After tax: \$6,000,000(1 - T) = \$6,000,000(0.66)$$

$$= \$3,960,000.$$

Although Microchip must expend $6 million on the call premium, this is a tax-deductible expense in the year the call is made. Since the company is in the 34 percent tax bracket, it saves 0.34($6,000,000) = $2,040,000 in taxes. Therefore, the after-tax cost of the call is only $3.96 million. This amount is shown as a cost, or outflow, on Line 1 of Table 18-3.

    b. **Flotation costs on new issue**
Flotation costs on the new issue are $2,650,000, as shown on Line 2 of the worksheet. For tax purposes, flotation costs cannot be expensed. Therefore, the before-tax and after-tax figures are the same. However, these costs can

---

[13]The firm's management has estimated that there is a 75 percent probability that interest rates will remain at their present level of 12 percent or else rise; there is only a 25 percent probability that they will fall further.

be written off over the life of the new bond, or 20 years, producing an annual tax deduction of

$$\frac{\$2,650,000}{20} = \$132,500.$$

Since Microchip is in the 34 percent tax bracket, it has a tax savings of $132,500(0.34) = $45,050 a year for 20 years. This is an annuity of $45,050 for 20 years. In a refunding analysis, all cash flows should be discounted at the after-tax cost of new debt, in this case $12\%(1 - T) = 12\%(0.66) = 7.92\%$. The present value of the tax savings, discounted at 7.92 percent, is $444,953, which is shown on Line 7 as an inflow.

c. **Flotation costs on old issue**
The old issue has an unamortized flotation cost of $(20/25)(\$3,000,000) = \$2.4$ million at this time. If the issue is retired, the unamortized flotation cost may be recognized immediately as an expense, thus creating an after-tax savings of $2,400,000(0.34) = $816,000, which is shown on Line 3 of the worksheet. The firm will, however, no longer receive a tax deduction of $120,000 a year for 20 years, or an after-tax benefit of $40,800 a year. The present value of this tax savings, discounted at 7.92 percent, is $402,976, which is shown on Line 8 as an opportunity cost of the refunding. It is important to note that because of the refunding, the old flotation costs provide an immediate tax saving rather than annual savings over the next 20 years. Thus, the $816,000 − $402,976 = $413,024 net savings simply reflects the difference between the present value of benefits received in the future without the refunding versus an immediate benefit if the refunding occurs.

d. **Additional interest**
One month "extra" interest on the old issue, after taxes, costs $495,000:

$$(\text{Dollar amount})(1/12 \text{ of } 15\%)(1 - T) = \text{Interest cost}$$

$$(\$60,000,000)(0.0125)(0.66) = \$495,000.$$

However, the proceeds from the new issue can be invested in short-term securities for one month. Thus, $60 million invested at a rate of 11 percent will return $363,000 in after-tax interest:

$$(\$60,000,000)(1/12 \text{ of } 11\%)(1 - T) = \text{Interest earned}$$

$$(\$60,000,000)(0.009167)(0.66) = \$363,000.$$

These figures are reflected in Lines 4 and 5.

e. **Total after-tax investment outlay**
The total investment outlay required to refund the bond issue, which will be financed by debt, is thus $5,926,000.[14] This is shown on Line 6 of Table 18-3.

Step 2. Calculate the PV of the flotation cost tax effects.
The net effect of the amortization of the flotation costs on the old and new issues is $41,977 in savings on a present value basis. This amount is shown on Line 9.

---

[14]The net cash investment outlay (in this case, about $6 million) is usually obtained by increasing the amount of the new bond issue. Thus, the new issue would be about $66 million. However, the interest on the additional debt *should not* be deducted at Step 2 because the net investment outlay itself will be deducted at Step 3. If additional interest on the $6 million were deducted at Step 2, then interest would, in effect, be deducted twice. The situation here is exactly like that in regular capital budgeting decisions. Even though some debt may be used to finance a project, interest on that debt is not subtracted when developing the annual cash flows. Rather, the annual cash flows are discounted by the project's cost of capital.

Step 3. **Calculate the PV of the annual interest savings.**

a. **Interest on old bond, after tax**

The annual after-tax interest on the old issue is $5,940,000:

$$(\$60,000,000)(0.15)(0.66) = \$5,940,000.$$

This is shown on Line 10.

b. **Interest on new bond, after tax**

The new issue has an annual after-tax cost of $4,752,000.

$$(\$60,000,000)(0.12)(0.66) = \$4,752,000.$$

This is shown on Line 11.

c. **Annual savings**

Thus, the annual after-tax savings is $1,188,000:

Interest on old bond, after tax	$5,940,000
Interest on new bond, after tax	(4,752,000)
Annual net savings	$1,188,000

This is shown on Line 12.

d. **PV of annual savings**

The PV of $1,188,000 per year at 7.92 percent for 20 years is $11,733,727. This is also shown on Line 12.

Step 4. **Determine the NPV of the refunding.**

Net investment outlay	($5,926,000)
Amortization tax effects	41,977
Interest savings	11,733,727
NPV from refunding	$ 5,849,704

Since the net present value of the refunding is positive, it would benefit stockholders to refund the old bond.

Several other points should be noted. First, since the cash flows are based on differences between contractual obligations, their risk is the same as that of the bonds. Therefore, the present values of the cash flows should be found by discounting at the after-tax cost of the new bonds. Second, since the refunding operation is advantageous to the firm, it must be disadvantageous to bondholders; they must give up their 15 percent bonds and reinvest in new ones that yield 12 percent. This points out the danger of the call provision to bondholders, and it also explains why bonds without a call provision command higher prices than callable bonds. Third, although it is not emphasized in the example, we assumed that the firm raises the investment required to undertake the refunding operation (the $5,926,000 shown on Line 6 of Table 18-3) as debt. This should be feasible, since the refunding operation will improve the interest coverage ratio even though, if the investment outlay is raised as debt, a larger amount of debt will be outstanding.[15] Fourth, we set up our example in such a way that the new

---

[15]See Aharon R. Ofer and Robert A. Taggart, Jr., "Bond Refunding: A Clarifying Analysis," *Journal of Finance,* March 1977, 21–30, for a discussion of how the method of financing the refunding affects the analysis. Ofer and Taggart prove that (1) if the refunding investment outlay is to be raised as debt, the after-tax cost of debt is the proper discount rate, while (2) if these funds are to be raised as common equity, then the before-tax cost of debt is the proper rate. Since a profitable refunding will virtually always raise the firm's debt-carrying capacity (because total interest charges after the refunding will be lower than before the refunding), it is more logical to use debt than either equity or a combination of debt and equity to finance the operation. Therefore, firms generally do use additional debt to finance refunding operations, so we assume debt financing for the costs of refunding and discount at the after-tax cost of debt.

issue had the same maturity as the remaining life of the old issue. Often, the old bonds have only a relatively short time to maturity (say, 5 to 10 years), while the new bonds would have a longer maturity (say, 25 to 30 years). In this situation, a replacement chain analysis is required. Although the interest savings benefit occurs over a much shorter period, refunding now pushes future flotation costs out further into the future, and this value can most easily be captured by a replacement chain analysis. Fifth, refunding decisions are well suited for analysis with a spreadsheet program. A refunding spreadsheet is easy to set up, and once it is, it is easy to vary the assumptions, especially the assumption about the interest rate on the new issue, and to see the way such changes affect the NPV.

One final point should be addressed: Although our analysis shows that the refunding would increase the value of the firm, would refunding *at this time* truly maximize the firm's expected value? Note that if interest rates continue to fall, then the company might be better off waiting, for this could increase the NPV of the refunding operation even more. The mechanics of calculating the NPV of a refunding are simple, but the decision on *when* to refund is not a simple one at all, because it requires a forecast of future interest rates. Thus, refund now versus waiting for a possibly more favorable future refunding is a judgmental decision.

To illustrate the timing decision, assume that Microchip's managers forecast that long-term interest rates have a 50 percent probability of remaining at their present level of 12 percent over the next year. However, there is a 25 percent probability that rates could fall to 10 percent, and a 25 percent probability that they could rise to 14 percent. Further, assume that short-term rates are expected to remain one percentage point below long-term rates, and that the call premium would be reduced by one-twentieth if the call were delayed for one year.

The refunding analysis could then be repeated, as previously, but assuming it would take place one year from now. Thus, the old bonds would have only 19 years remaining to maturity. We performed the analysis and found the NPV distribution of refunding one year from now:

PROBABILITY	LONG-TERM INTEREST RATE	NPV OF REFUNDING ONE YEAR FROM NOW
25%	10%	$15,328,674
50	12	5,770,191
25	14	(2,158,208)

At first blush, it would seem reasonable to calculate the expected NPV of refunding next year in terms of the probability distribution. However, that would not be correct. If interest rates did rise to 14 percent, Microchip would not refund the issue; therefore, the actual NPV if rates rise to 14 percent would be zero. The expected NPV from refunding one year hence is, therefore, $0.25(\$15,328,674) + 0.50(\$5,770,191) + 0.25(\$0) = \$6,717,264$ versus $5,849,704 if refunding occurred today.

Even though the expected NPV of refunding in one year is higher, Microchip's managers would probably decide to refund today. The $5,849,704 represents a certain increase in firm value, whereas the $6,717,264 is only an expected increase. Also, proper comparison requires that the $6,717,264 be discounted back one year to today. Microchip's managers should opt to delay refunding only if the expected NPV from later refunding is sufficiently above today's certain NPV to compensate for the risk and time value involved.

Clearly, the decision to refund now versus refund later is complicated by the fact that there would be numerous opportunities to refund in the future rather than just a single opportunity one year from now. Furthermore, the decision must be based on a large set of interest rate forecasts, a daunting task in itself. Fortunately, financial managers making bond refunding decisions can now use the values of derivative securities to estimate the value of the bond issue's embedded call option. If the call option is worth more than the NPV of refunding today, the issue should not be immediately refunded. Rather, the issuer should either delay the refunding to take advantage of the information obtained from the derivative market or actually create a derivative transaction to lock in the value of the call option.[16]

---

[16]For more information on derivatives in general, see Chapter 24. For more information on the use of derivatives to help make call decisions, see Andrew J. Kalotay and George O. Williams, "How to Succeed in Derivatives without Really Buying," *Journal of Applied Corporate Finance,* Fall 1993, 100–103.

SUMMARY

- **Going public** facilitates stockholder diversification, increases liquidity of the firm's stock, makes it easier for the firm to raise capital, and establishes a value for the firm. However, reporting costs are high, operating data must be disclosed, management self-dealings are harder to arrange, the price may sink to a low level if the stock is not traded actively, and public ownership may make it harder for management to maintain control.

- The decision to **list** the stock on a major exchange is not as critical as the decision to go public.

- New common stock may be sold in five ways: (1) on a pro rata basis to existing stockholders through a **rights offering,** (2) through investment bankers to the general public in a **public offering,** (3) to a single buyer, or a small number of buyers, in a **private placement,** (4) to employees through an **employee purchase plan,** and (5) to shareholders through a **dividend reinvestment plan.**

- The major **advantages of common stock** are as follows: (1) there is no obligation to make fixed payments, (2) common stock never matures, (3) the use of common stock increases the creditworthiness of the firm, (4) stock can often be sold more easily than debt, and (5) using stock helps the firm maintain its reserve borrowing capacity.

- The major **disadvantages of common stock** are (1) it extends voting rights to new stockholders, (2) new stockholders share in the firm's profits, (3) the costs of issuing stock are high, (4) using stock can raise the firm's cost of capital, and (5) dividends paid on common stock are not tax deductible.

- Securities markets are regulated by the **Securities and Exchange Commission (SEC).**

- **Investment bankers** assist in the issuing of securities by helping the firm determine the size of the issue and the type of securities to be used, by establishing the selling price, by selling the issue, and, in some cases, by maintaining an after-market for the stock.

- Recent innovations in long-term financing include **zero coupon bonds,** which pay no interest but are issued at a discount, **project financing,** and **securitization.**

- A firm's long-term financing decisions are influenced by its **target capital structure,** the **maturity of its assets,** its current and forecasted **financial condition,** the suitability of its **assets for use as collateral,** and current and forecasted **interest rate levels.**

- If a bond has a call provision, the issuer may **refund (call)** the bond prior to maturity. Firms use a type of NPV analysis to make the call decision.

Questions

18-1 Define each of the following terms:

     a. Going public; new issue market; initial public offering (IPO)
     b. Rights offering
     c. Public offering; private placement
     d. Employee purchase plan; ESOP
     e. Securities and Exchange Commission (SEC); registration statement; shelf registration; "blue sky" laws; margin requirement; insiders
     f. Prospectus; "red herring" prospectus
     g. National Association of Securities Dealers (NASD)
     h. Best efforts arrangement; underwritten arrangement
     i. Zero coupon bond; original issue discount bond (OID)
     j. Refunding
     k. Project financing
     l. Securitization
     m. Maturity matching

18-2 Is it true that the "flatter," or more nearly horizontal, the demand curve for a particular firm's stock, and the less important investors regard the signaling effect of the offering, the more important the role of investment bankers when the company sells a new issue of stock?

18-3 The SEC attempts to protect investors who are purchasing newly issued securities by making sure that the information put out by a company and its investment bankers is correct and is not misleading. However, the SEC does not provide an opinion about the real value of the securities; hence, an investor might pay too much for some new stock and consequently lose heavily. Do you think the SEC should, as a part of every new stock or bond offering, render an opinion to investors on the proper value of the securities being offered? Explain.

18-4 How do you think each of the following items would affect a company's ability to attract new capital and the flotation costs involved in doing so?
     a. A decision to list a company's stock; the stock now trades in the over-the-counter market.
     b. A decision of a privately held company to go public.
     c. The increasing institutionalization of the "buy side" of the stock and bond markets.
     d. The trend toward "financial conglomerates" as opposed to stand-alone investment banking houses.
     e. Elimination of the preemptive right.
     f. The introduction of "shelf registrations" in 1981.

18-5 Before entering a formal agreement, investment bankers carefully investigate the companies whose securities they underwrite; this is especially true of the issues of firms going public for the first time. Since the bankers do not themselves plan to hold the securities but intend to sell them to others as soon as possible, why are they so concerned about making careful investigations?

18-6 It is frequently stated that the primary purpose of the preemptive right is to allow individuals to maintain their proportionate share of the ownership and control of a corporation.
     a. How important do you suppose this consideration is for the average stockholder of a firm whose shares are traded on the New York or American Stock Exchanges?
     b. Is the preemptive right likely to be of more importance to stockholders of publicly owned or closely held firms? Explain.
     c. Is a firm likely to get a wider distribution of shares if it sells new stock through a preemptive rights offering to existing stockholders or directly to underwriters?
     d. Why would management be interested in getting a wider distribution of its shares?

18-7 Draw an SML graph. Put dots on the graph to show (approximately) where you think a particular company's (a) common stock and (b) bonds would lie. Now put on dots to represent a riskier company's stock and bonds.

18-8 Suppose you work for the treasurer of a large, profitable corporation. Your company has some surplus funds to invest. You can buy these securities:
     (1) Aaa-rated Exxon 20-year bonds which sell at par and yield 9 percent.
     (2) Aa-rated Exxon preferred stock which yields 7 percent.
     (3) Ca-rated Continental Airlines bonds which yield 13 percent.
     (4) C-rated Continental Airlines preferred stock which yields 14 percent.
     (5) A-rated Alabama Power floating rate preferred stock which currently yields 5 percent.
     (6) Treasury bills which yield 4 percent.
     a. Does it appear that these securities are in equilibrium?
     b. If these were your only choices, which would you recommend? Why?

Problems

18-1
Profit or Loss on New Stock Issue

Security Brokers Inc. specializes in underwriting new issues by small firms. On a recent offering of Beedles Inc., the terms were as follows:

Price to public:	$5 per share
Number of shares:	3 million
Proceeds to Beedles:	$14,000,000

The out-of-pocket expenses incurred by Security Brokers in the design and distribution of the issue were $300,000. What profit or loss would Security Brokers incur if the issue were sold to the public at an average price of
a. $5 per share?
b. $6 per share?
c. $4 per share?

18-2
Underwriting and Flotation Expenses

The Beranek Company, whose stock price is now $25, needs to raise $20 million in common stock. Underwriters have informed the firm's management that they must price the new issue to the public at $22 per share because of a downward-sloping demand curve. The underwriters' compensation will be 5 percent of the issue price, so Beranek will net $20.90 per share. The firm will also incur expenses in the amount of $150,000.

How many shares must the firm sell to net $20 million after underwriting and flotation expenses?

18-3
New Stock Issue

The Edelman Gem Company, a small jewelry manufacturer, has been successful and has enjoyed a good growth trend. Now Edelman is planning to go public with an issue of common stock, and it faces the problem of setting an appropriate price on the stock. The company and its investment bankers believe that the proper procedure is to select several similar firms with publicly traded common stock and to make relevant comparisons.

Several jewelry manufacturers are reasonably similar to Edelman with respect to product mix, asset composition, and debt/equity proportions. Of these companies, Kennedy Jewelers and Strasburg Fashions are most similar. When analyzing the following data, assume that 1993 and 1998 were reasonably "normal" years for all three companies — that is, these years were neither especially good nor especially bad in terms of sales, earnings, and dividends. At the time of the analysis, k_{RF} was 8 percent and k_M was 12 percent. Kennedy is listed on the AMEX and Strasburg on the NYSE, while Edelman will be traded in the OTC market.

	KENNEDY	STRASBURG	EDELMAN (TOTALS)
Earnings per share			
1998	$ 4.50	$ 7.50	$ 1,200,000
1993	3.00	5.50	816,000
Price per share			
1998	$36.00	$65.00	—
Dividends per share			
1998	$ 2.25	$ 3.75	$ 600,000
1993	1.50	2.75	420,000
Book value per share, 1998	$30.00	$55.00	$ 9 million
Market/book ratio, 1998	120%	118%	—
Total assets, 1998	$28 million	$ 82 million	$20 million
Total debt, 1998	$12 million	$ 30 million	$11 million
Sales, 1998	$41 million	$140 million	$37 million

a. Assume that Edelman has 100 shares of stock outstanding. Use this information to calculate earnings per share (EPS), dividends per share (DPS), and book value per share for Edelman. (Hint: Edelman's 1998 EPS = $12,000.)
b. Calculate earnings and dividend growth rates for the three companies. (Hint: Edelman's EPS growth rate is 8 percent.)
c. On the basis of your answer to Part a, do you think Edelman's stock would sell at a price in the same "ballpark" as that of Kennedy and Strasburg, that is, in the range of $25 to $100 per share?

d. Assuming that Edelman's management can split the stock so that the 100 shares could be changed to 1,000 shares, 100,000 shares, or any other number, would such an action make sense in this case? Why?

e. Now assume that Edelman did split its stock and has 400,000 shares. Calculate new values for EPS, DPS, and book value per share. (Hint: Edelman's new 1998 EPS is $3.00.)

f. Return on equity (ROE) can be measured as EPS/book value per share or as total earnings/total equity. Calculate ROEs for the three companies for 1998. (Hint: Edelman's 1998 ROE = 13.3%.)

g. Calculate dividend payout ratios for the three companies for both years. (Hint: Edelman's 1998 payout ratio is 50%.)

h. Calculate debt/total assets ratios for the three companies for 1998. (Hint: Edelman's 1998 debt ratio is 55%.)

i. Calculate the P/E ratios for Kennedy and Strasburg for 1998. Are these P/Es reasonable in view of relative growth, payout, and ROE data? If not, what other factors might explain them? (Hint: Kennedy's P/E = 8×).

j. Now determine a range of values for Edelman's stock price, with 400,000 shares outstanding, by applying Kennedy's and Strasburg's P/E ratios, price/dividends ratios, and price/book value ratios to your data for Edelman. For example, one possible price for Edelman's stock is (P/E Kennedy)(EPS Edelman) = 8($3) = $24 per share. Similar calculations would produce a range of prices based on both Kennedy's and Strasburg's data. (Hint: Our range was $24 to $27.)

k. Using the equation $k_s = D_1/P_0 + g$, find approximate k_s values for Kennedy and Strasburg. Then use these values in the constant growth stock price model to find a price for Edelman's stock. (Hint: We averaged the EPS and DPS g's for Edelman.)

l. At what price do you think Edelman's shares should be offered to the public? You will want to select a price that will be low enough to induce investors to buy the stock but not so low that it will rise sharply immediately after it is issued. Think about relative growth rates, ROEs, dividend yields, and total returns ($k_s = D_1/P_0 + g$).

Spreadsheet Problem

Work this problem in this section only if you are using the computer problem diskette.

18-4
Zero Coupon Bonds

Use the model in File C18 to solve this problem. Suppose Southern States Insurance Company needs to raise $400 million, and its investment bankers have indicated that 10-year zero coupon bonds could be sold at a YTM of 12 percent while a 14 percent yield would be required on *annual* payment coupon bonds sold at par. Southern State's tax rate is 34 percent. (Assume that the discount can be amortized by the issuer using the straight line method. This cannot be done under current tax laws, but assume it anyway.)

a. How many $1,000 par value bonds would Southern States have to sell under each plan?

b. What would be the after-tax YTM on each type of bond (1) to a holder who is tax exempt and (2) to a taxpayer in the 50 percent federal-plus-state bracket?

c. What would be the after-tax cost of each type of bond to Southern States?

d. Why would investors be willing to buy the zero coupon bonds?

e. Why might Southern States turn down the offer to issue zero coupon bonds?

f. Redo Parts a, b, and c assuming that the YTM on zero coupon bonds falls to 10 percent and that on annual coupon bonds falls to 12 percent. As in the previous analysis, the after-tax yield to investors on the annual coupon bond exceeds that of the zero coupon bond. Has the differential between the annual and zero coupon bond yields changed? Would investors be more willing to purchase the zero coupon bond under the original assumptions or under the new assumptions? If the before-tax YTM were 10 percent on each type of bond, what would the after-tax YTMs be to zero and to 50 percent taxpayers, what would the after-tax cost be to the company, and what type of investors would be likely to hold the zeros and what type the regular coupon bonds?

MINI CASE

Randy's, a family-owned restaurant chain operating in Alabama, has grown to the point where expansion throughout the entire Southeast is feasible. The proposed expansion would require the firm to raise about $15 million in new capital. Because Randy's currently has a debt ratio of 50 percent, and also because the family members already have all their personal wealth invested in the company, the family would like to sell common stock to the public to raise the $15 million.

However, the family does want to retain voting control. You have been asked to brief the family members on the issues involved by answering the following questions:

a. What agencies regulate securities markets?

b. What are some of the decisions faced by firms needing external financing?

c. Would the stock sale be an initial public offering (IPO)? What would be the advantages to the family members of having the firm go public? Would there be any disadvantages? If you were a key employee, but not a family member, or a potential key employee being interviewed as a part of the expansion process, how would the decision affect you?

d. What does it mean for a stock to be listed? Do you think that Randy's stock would be listed shortly after the company goes public? If not, where would the stock trade?

e. What is a rights offering? Would it make sense for Randy's to use a rights offering to raise the $15 million? Even if you do not think a rights offering should be employed, could one be used?

f. What is the difference between a private placement and a public offering? What are the advantages and disadvantages of each type of placement? Which type would be most suitable for Randy's?

g. What is meant by going private? Assume for the sake of this question that Randy's previously went public. What are the advantages and disadvantages of the firm's going private?

h. (1) Would Randy's be likely to sell the $15 million of stock by itself or through an investment banker?

   (2) If an investment banker were used, would the sale most likely be on the basis of a competitive bid or a negotiated deal?

   (3) If it were a negotiated deal, would it most likely be done on a best efforts or an underwritten basis? In each case, explain your answer.

i. Without doing any calculations, describe the procedure by which the company and its investment banker would determine the price at which the stock would be offered to the public.

j. Suppose the decision were made to issue 1.5 million shares at $10 per share. What would be the net amount raised if the flotation cost on the issue were 18 percent? What if the firm were already publicly owned and the flotation costs were 9 percent? Would there be a difference in costs between a best efforts and an underwritten offering?

k. What are some of the factors a firm should consider when deciding whether to issue long-term debt or equity?

l. Describe the key features of the following securities:

   (1) Project financing

   (2) Securitization

m. Under what conditions would a firm exercise a bond's call provision?

Selected Additional References and Cases

For a wealth of facts and figures on a major segment of the stock market, see New York Stock Exchange, Fact Book (New York: published annually).

For a discussion of the current state of investment banking and trends in the industry, see

Auerbach, Joseph, and Samuel L. Hayes III, *Investment Banking and Diligence: What Price Deregulation* (Boston: HBS Press, 1986).

Eccles, Robert G., and Dwight B. Crane, *Doing Deals: Investment Bankers at Work* (Boston: HBS Press, 1988).

Hayes, S. L., "The Transformation of Investment Banking," *Harvard Business Review,* January–February 1979, 153–170.

Rogowski, Robert, and Eric Sorensen, "The New Competitive Environment of Investment Banking: Transactional Finance and Concession Pricing of New Issues," *Midland Corporate Finance Journal,* Spring 1986, 64–71.

For additional insights on the benefits of listing, see

Baker, H. Kent, and Richard B. Edelman, "AMEX-to-NYSE Transfers, Market Microstructure, and Shareholder Wealth," *Financial Management,* Winter 1992, 60–72.

Edelman, Richard B., and H. Kent Baker, "Liquidity and Stock Exchange Listing," *The Financial Review,* May 1990, 231–249.

Other good references on specific aspects of equity financing include the following:

Aggarwal, Reena, and Pietra Rivoli, "Fads in the Initial Public Offering Market?" *Financial Management,* Winter 1990, 45–57.

Block, Stanley, and Marjorie Stanley, "The Financial Characteristics and Price Movement Patterns of Companies Approaching the Unseasoned Securities Market in the Late 1970s," *Financial Management,* Winter 1980, 30–36.

Bowyer, John W., and Jess B. Yawitz, "Effect of New Equity Issues on Utility Stock Prices," *Public Utilities Fortnightly,* May 22, 1980, 25–28.

Brickley, James A., and Kathleen T. Hevert, "Direct Employee Stock Ownership: An Empirical Investigation," *Financial Management,* Summer 1991, 70–84.

Carter, Richard, and Steven Manaster, "Initial Public Offerings and Underwriter Reputation," *Journal of Finance,* September 1990, 1045–1067.

Denis, David J., "The Costs of Equity Issues Since Rule 415: A Closer Look," *Journal of Financial Research,* Spring 1993, 77–88.

Fabozzi, Frank J., "Does Listing on the AMEX Increase the Value of Equity?" *Financial Management,* Spring 1981, 43–50.

Hansen, Robert S., and John M. Pinkerton, "Direct Equity Financing: A Resolution to a Paradox," *Journal of Finance,* June 1982, 651–665.

Ibbotson, Roger G., Jody L. Sindelar, and Jay R. Ritter, "Initial Public Offerings," *Journal of Applied Corporate Finance,* Summer 1988, 37–45.

———, "The Market's Problems with the Pricing of Initial Public Offerings," *Journal of Applied Corporate Finance,* Spring 1994, 66–74.

Jurin, Bruce, "Raising Equity in an Efficient Market," *Midland Corporate Finance Journal,* Winter 1988, 53–60.

Loderer, Claudio, John W. Cooney, and Leonard D. Van Drunen, "The Price Elasticity of Demand for Common Stock," *Journal of Finance,* June 1991, 621–651.

Logue, Dennis, and Robert A. Jarrow, "Negotiation versus Competitive Bidding in the Sale of Securities by Public Utilities," *Financial Management,* Autumn 1978, 31–39.

Lucas, Deborah J., and Robert L. McDonald, "Equity Issues and Stock Price Dynamics," *Journal of Finance,* September 1990, 1019–1043.

Michaely, Roni, and Wayne H. Shaw, "The Choice of Going Public: Spin-offs vs. Carve-outs," *Financial Management,* Autumn 1995, 5–21.

Muscarella, Chris J., and Michael R. Vetsuypens, "The Underpricing of 'Second' Initial Public Offerings," *Journal of Financial Research,* Fall 1989, 183–192.

Ritter, Jay R., "The Long-Run Performance of Initial Public Offerings," *Journal of Finance,* March 1991, 3–27.

For more information on shelf registration, see

Bhagat, Sanjai, "The Evidence on Shelf Registration," *Midland Corporate Finance Journal,* Spring 1984, 6–12.

For an excellent discussion of the various procedures used to raise capital, see

Smith, Clifford W., Jr., "Raising Capital: Theory and Evidence," *Midland Corporate Finance Journal,* Spring 1986, 6–22. Also, pages 72–76 of the Spring 1986 issue of the *Midland Corporate Finance Journal* contain a bibliography of recent articles pertaining to investment banking and capital acquisition.

The Spring 1990 issue of Financial Management *is devoted to Employee Stock Ownership Plans (ESOPs).*

The Spring 1993 issue of Financial Management *contains several articles on IPOs and LBOs.*

The Winter 1993 issue of the Journal of Applied Corporate Finance *is devoted to the SEC and securities regulation.*

References on bond refunding include the following:

Ang, James S., "The Two Faces of Bond Refunding," *Journal of Finance,* June 1975, 869–874.

——, "The Two Faces of Bond Refunding: Reply," *Journal of Finance,* March 1978, 354–356.

Chiang, Raymond C., and M. P. Narayanan, "Bond Refunding in Efficient Markets: A Dynamic Analysis with Tax Effects," *Journal of Financial Research,* Winter 1991, 287–302.

Dyl, Edward A. and Michael D. Joehnk, "Refunding Tax Exempt Bonds," *Financial Management,* Summer 1976, 59–66.

Emery, Douglas R., "Overlapping Interest in Bond Refunding: A Reconsideration," *Financial Management,* Summer 1978, 19–20.

Finnerty, John D., "Refunding High-Coupon Debt," *Midland Corporate Finance Journal,* Winter 1986, 59–74.

Harris, Robert S., "The Refunding of Discounted Debt: An Adjusted Present Value Analysis," *Financial Management,* Winter 1980, 7–12.

Kalotay, Andrew J., "On the Advanced Refunding of Discounted Debt," *Financial Management,* Summer 1978, 14–18.

——, "On the Structure and Valuation of Debt Refundings," *Financial Management,* Spring 1982, 41–42.

Kraus, Alan, "An Analysis of Call Provisions and the Corporate Refunding Decision," *Midland Corporate Finance Journal,* Spring 1983, 46–60.

Laber, Gene, "The Effect of Bond Refunding of Discounted Debt," *Financial Management,* June 1979, 795–799.

——, "Implications of Discount Rates and Financing Assumptions for Bond Refunding Decisions," *Financial Management,* Spring 1979, 7–12.

——, "Repurchases of Bonds through Tender Offers: Implications for Shareholder Wealth," *Financial Management,* Summer 1978, 7–13.

Livingston, Miles, "The Effect of Bond Refunding on Shareholder Wealth: Comment," *Journal of Finance,* June 1979, 801–804.

——, "Bond Refunding Reconsidered: Comment," *Journal of Finance,* March 1980, 191–196.

Mauer, David C., "Optimal Bond Call Policies under Transactions Costs," *Journal of Financial Research,* Spring 1993, 23–37.

Mayor, Thomas H., and Kenneth G. McCoin, "Bond Refunding: One or Two Faces?" *Journal of Finance,* March 1978, 349–353.

Ofer, Aharon R., and Robert A. Taggart, Jr., "Bond Refunding: Reconsidered: Reply," *Journal of Finance,* March 1980, 197–200.

Riener, Kenneth D., "Financial Structure Effects of Bond Refunding," *Financial Management,* Summer 1980, 18–23.

Thatcher, Janet S., and John G. Thatcher, "An Empirical Test of the Timing of Bond-Refunding Decisions," *Journal of Financial Research,* Fall 1992, 219–230.

Yawitz, Jess B., and James A. Anderson, "The Effect of Bond Refunding on Shareholder Wealth," *Journal of Finance,* December 1977, 1738–1746.

——, "The Effect of Bond Refunding on Shareholder Wealth: Reply," *Journal of Finance,* June 1979, 805–809.

Zeise, Charles H., and Roger K. Taylor, "Advance Refunding: A Practitioner's Perspective," *Financial Management,* Summer 1977, 73–76.

The following cases from the Cases in Financial Management: Dryden Request *series focus on the issues contained in this chapter:*

Case 21, "Sun Coast Savings Bank," which illustrates the decision to go public.

Case 22, "Precision Tool Company," which emphasizes the investment banking process.

Case 23, "Art Deco Reproductions, Inc.," which focuses on the analysis of a rights offering.

Case 24, "Bay Area Telephone Company," Case 24A, "Shenandoah Power Company," and Case 24B, "Tucson Entertainment, Inc.," which illustrate the bond refunding decision.

LEASE FINANCING

Some of the biggest players in the airline business have never issued a ticket, lost a passenger's luggage, or landed a plane in bad weather. They are the aircraft leasing companies—the merchant bankers of aviation—and their role is to help finance aircraft and to help airlines respond more quickly and efficiently to market changes. Among the major players in aircraft leasing are GPA Group, a closely held company based in Shannon, Ireland, and International Lease Finance of Beverly Hills.

Aircraft leasing companies purchase airplanes from manufacturers such as Boeing and Airbus Industrie and then lease them, often on a relatively short-term basis, to carriers such as American, British Airways, Delta, Lufthansa, and United. Leasing separates the risks and rewards of owning aircraft from those of operating them. Currently, leasing companies buy about 50 percent of all new commercial aircraft sold.

The airline industry is undergoing major changes due to global deregulation. The highly competitive nature of the industry has forced both TWA and Continental to seek bankruptcy protection twice and has caused many airlines to fail, including Braniff, Eastern, Midway, and Pan Am. In the days of regulation, airlines knew precisely the routes they would serve, and their prices could be raised to cover any cost increases. Thus, airlines could buy planes confident that route structures would be relatively stable and that revenues would cover financing costs. Now, however, airlines are constantly dropping and adding routes in response to changing competitive conditions. Because different types of aircraft are better suited for some routes than others, for optimal operations airlines must frequently restructure their fleets. If an airline had purchased all of its aircraft, it could not respond quickly to changing conditions. The leasing companies, on the other hand, lease all types of aircraft to all types of airlines, and there is usually some airline somewhere interested in a given aircraft when its lease is dropped by another airline. Therefore, leasing provides badly needed flexibility.

Global deregulation also has spawned a host of startup airlines, both in the United States and in Europe. Such airlines find it difficult to raise the capital needed to purchase aircraft, but leasing helps them get started. Startup airlines typically are in a precarious financial condition, and leasing companies often are more willing than lenders to take the financing risk because lessors are in a more favorable legal position should the airline actually go bankrupt. Thus, it is easier for leasing companies to repossess and redeploy aircraft than it would be for lenders.

Interestingly, Airbus Industrie, the European aircraft consortium, has adopted short-term leases as a sales tool. In recent years, Delta and United "bought" aircraft from Airbus on "walkaway" leases, under which the aircraft could be returned to the manufacturer in less than a year. U.S. manufacturers complained that Airbus can offer such terms only because it is subsidized by the four European countries that back the consortium. The Clinton administration reportedly lobbied to force Airbus to discontinue its short-term lease program, which would help Boeing but potentially hurt U.S. airlines.

As you read this chapter, think about the airline industry and why leasing can be more attractive than buying. Also, think about why leasing companies and manufac-

turers are able to offer such attractive lease rates. When you finish the chapter, you should understand both how leases are analyzed, and also the conditions under which leasing is likely to be attractive.

Firms generally own fixed assets and report them on their balance sheets, but it is the *use* of assets that is important, not their ownership per se. One way to obtain the use of facilities and equipment is to buy them, but an alternative is to lease them. Prior to the 1950s, leasing was generally associated with real estate — land and buildings. Today, however, it is possible to lease virtually any kind of fixed asset, and currently over 30 percent of all new capital equipment is financed through lease arrangements.[1]

THE TWO PARTIES TO LEASING

Lease transactions involve two parties: the **lessor**, who owns the property, and the **lessee,** who obtains use of the property in exchange for one or more **lease,** or **rental, payments.** (Note that the term *lessee* is pronounced "less-ee," not "lease-ee," and *lessor* is pronounced "less-or.") Since both parties must agree before a lease transaction can be completed, this chapter discusses leasing from the perspectives of both the lessor and the lessee.

SELF-TEST QUESTIONS | Who are the two parties to a lease transaction?

TYPES OF LEASES

Leasing takes several different forms, the four most important being (1) operating leases, (2) financial, or capital, leases, (3) sale-and-leaseback arrangements, and (4) combination leases.

Operating Leases

Operating leases, sometimes called **service leases,** generally provide for both *financing* and *maintenance*. IBM was one of the pioneers of the operating lease contract, and computers and office copying machines, together with automobiles, trucks, and aircraft, are the primary types of equipment involved in operating leases. Ordinarily, operating leases require the lessor to maintain and service the leased equipment, and the cost of the maintenance is built into the lease payments.

Another important characteristic of operating leases is the fact that they are *not fully amortized*. In other words, the rental payments required under the lease contract are not sufficient for the lessor to recover the full cost of the asset. However, the lease contract is written for a period considerably less than the expected economic life of the asset, and the lessor expects to recover all costs either by subsequent renewal payments, by re-leasing the asset to other lessees, or by selling the asset.

---

[1]For a detailed treatment of leasing, see James S. Schallheim, *Lease or Buy? Principles for Sound Decision Making* (Boston: Harvard Business School Press, 1994).

A final feature of operating leases is that they often contain a *cancellation clause* which gives the lessee the right to cancel the lease and to return the asset before the expiration of the basic lease agreement. This is an important consideration to the lessee, for it means that the asset can be returned if it is rendered obsolete by technological developments or is no longer needed because of a change in the lessee's business.

Financial, or Capital, Leases

Financial leases, sometimes called **capital leases,** are differentiated from operating leases in that (1) they *do not* provide for maintenance service, (2) they *are not* cancellable, and (3) they *are* fully amortized (that is, the lessor receives rental payments equal to the full price of the leased equipment plus a return on invested capital). In a typical arrangement, the firm that will use the equipment (the lessee) selects the specific items it requires and negotiates the price with the manufacturer. The user firm then arranges to have a leasing company (the lessor) buy the equipment from the manufacturer and simultaneously executes a lease contract. The terms of the lease generally call for full amortization of the lessor's investment, plus a rate of return on the unamortized balance which is close to the percentage rate the lessee would have paid on a secured loan. For example, if the lessee would have to pay 10 percent for a loan, then a rate of about 10 percent would be built into the lease contract.

The lessee is generally given an option to renew the lease at a reduced rate upon expiration of the basic lease. However, the basic lease usually cannot be cancelled unless the lessor is paid in full. Also, the lessee generally pays the property taxes and insurance on the leased property. Since the lessor receives a return *after,* or *net of,* these payments, this type of lease is often called a "net, net" lease.

Sale-and-Leaseback Arrangements

Under a **sale-and-leaseback arrangement,** a firm that owns land, buildings, or equipment sells the property to another firm and simultaneously executes an agreement to lease the property back for a stated period under specific terms. The capital supplier could be an insurance company, a commercial bank, a specialized leasing company, the finance arm of an industrial firm, or an individual investor. The sale-and-leaseback plan is an alternative to a mortgage.

Note that the seller immediately receives the purchase price put up by the buyer. At the same time, the seller-lessee retains the use of the property. The parallel to borrowing is carried over to the lease payment schedule. Under a mortgage loan arrangement, the lender would normally receive a series of equal payments just sufficient to amortize the loan and to provide a specified rate of return on the outstanding loan balance. Under a sale-and-leaseback arrangement, the lease payments are set up exactly the same way—the payments are just sufficient to return the full purchase price to the investor, plus a stated return on the lessor's investment.

Sale-and-leaseback arrangements are almost the same as financial leases, the major difference being that the leased equipment is used and the lessor buys it from the user-lessee instead of from a manufacturer or a distributor. A sale and leaseback may, then, be thought of as a special type of financial lease.

Combination Leases

Many lessors now offer leases under a wide variety of terms. Therefore, in practice, leases often do not fit exactly into the operating lease or financial lease category, but, rather, combine some features of each. Such leases are called **combination leases.** To illustrate, cancellation clauses are normally associated with operating leases, but many of today's financial leases also contain cancellation clauses. However, in financial leases these clauses generally include prepayment provisions whereby the lessee must make penalty payments sufficient to enable the lessor to recover the unamortized cost of the leased property.

SELF-TEST
QUESTIONS

What is the difference between an operating lease and a financial, or capital, lease?

What is a sale-and-leaseback transaction?

What is a combination lease?

TAX EFFECTS

The full amount of the lease payments is a tax-deductible expense for the lessee *provided the Internal Revenue Service agrees that a particular contract is a genuine lease and not simply an installment loan called a lease.* This makes it important that a lease contract be written in a form acceptable to the IRS. A lease that complies with all IRS requirements is called a **guideline,** or **tax-oriented, lease,** and the tax benefits of ownership (depreciation and any investment tax credits) belong to the lessor. The main provisions of the tax guidelines are as follows:[2]

1. The lease term (including any extensions or renewals at a fixed rental rate) must not exceed 80 percent of the estimated useful life of the equipment at the commencement of the lease transaction. Thus, an asset with a ten-year life can be leased for no more than eight years. Further, the remaining useful life must not be less than one year. Note that an asset's useful life is normally much longer than its MACRS depreciation class life.

2. The equipment's estimated residual value (in constant dollars without adjustment for inflation) at the expiration of the lease must equal at least 20 percent of its value at the start of the lease. This requirement can have the effect of limiting the maximum lease term.

3. Neither the lessee nor any related party can have the right to purchase the property at a predetermined fixed price at the lease's inception. However, the lessee can be given an option to buy the asset at its fair market value.

4. Neither the lessee nor any related party can pay or guarantee payment of any part of the price of the leased equipment. Simply put, the lessee cannot make any investment in the equipment, other than through the lease payments.

5. The leased equipment must not be "limited use" property, defined as equipment that can only be used by the lessee or a related party at the end of the lease.

The reason for the IRS's concern about lease terms is that, without restrictions, a company could set up a "lease" transaction calling for very rapid payments, which would be tax deductions. The effect would be to depreciate the equipment over a much shorter period than its MACRS class life. For example, suppose a firm planned to acquire a $2,000,000 computer which had a three-year MACRS class life. The

---

[2]See Schallheim, *op. cit.,* Chapter 3, for more on taxes and leasing.

annual depreciation allowances would be $660,000 in Year 1, $900,000 in Year 2, $300,000 in Year 3, and $140,000 in Year 4. If the firm were in the 40 percent federal-plus-state tax bracket, the depreciation would provide a tax saving of $264,000 in Year 1, $360,000 in Year 2, $120,000 in Year 3, and $56,000 in Year 4, for a total savings of $800,000. At a 6 percent discount rate, the present value of these tax savings would be $714,567.

Now suppose the firm could acquire the computer through a one-year lease arrangement with a leasing company for a payment of $2 million, with a 1-dollar purchase option. If the $2,000,000 payment were treated as a lease payment, it would be fully deductible, so it would provide a tax savings of 0.4($2,000,000) = $800,000 versus a present value of only $714,567 for the depreciation shelters. Thus, the lease payment and the depreciation would both provide the same total amount of tax savings (40% of $2,000,000, or $800,000), but the savings would come in faster, hence have a higher present value, with the one-year lease. Therefore, if just any type of contract could be called a lease and given tax treatment as a lease, then the timing of the tax shelters could be speeded up as compared with ownership depreciation tax shelters. This speedup would benefit companies, but it would be costly to the government. For this reason, the IRS has established the rules described above for defining a lease for tax purposes.

Even though leasing can be used only within limits to speed up the effective depreciation schedule, there are still times when very substantial tax benefits can be derived from a leasing arrangement. For example, if a firm has incurred losses and hence has no current tax liabilities, then depreciation shelters are not very useful. In this case, a leasing company set up by profitable companies like GE or Philip Morris can buy the equipment, receive the depreciation shelters, and then share these benefits with the lessee by charging lower lease payments. This point will be discussed in detail later in the chapter, but the point to be made now is that if firms are to obtain tax benefits from leasing, the lease contract must be written in a manner that will qualify it as a true lease under IRS guidelines. If there is any question about the legal status of the contract, the financial manager must be sure to have the firm's lawyers and accountants check the latest IRS regulations.[3]

Note that a lease which does not meet the tax guidelines is called a **non-tax-oriented lease.** For this type of lease, the lessee (1) is the effective owner of the leased property, (2) can depreciate it for tax purposes, and (3) can deduct only the interest portion of each lease payment.

SELF-TEST QUESTIONS

What is the difference between a tax-oriented lease and a non-tax-oriented lease?

What are some lease provisions that would cause a lease to be classified as a non-tax-oriented lease?

Why does the IRS place limits on lease provisions?

---

[3]In 1981, Congress relaxed the normal IRS rules to permit *safe harbor leases,* which had virtually no IRS restrictions and which were explicitly designed to permit the transfer of tax benefits from unprofitable companies which could not use them to high-profit companies which could. The point of safe harbor leases was to provide incentives for capital investment to companies which had little or no tax liability—under safe harbor leasing, companies with no tax liability could sell the benefit to companies in a high marginal tax bracket. In 1981 and 1982, literally billions of dollars were paid by such profitable firms as IBM and Philip Morris for the tax shelters of such unprofitable ones as Ford and Eastern Airlines. However, in 1983, Congress sharply curtailed the use of safe harbor leases.

FINANCIAL STATEMENT EFFECTS[4]

Under certain conditions, neither the leased assets nor the liabilities under the lease contract appear directly on the firm's balance sheet. For this reason, leasing is often called *off-balance sheet* financing. This point is illustrated in Table 19-1 by the balance sheets of two hypothetical firms, B and L. Initially, the balance sheets of both firms are identical, and they both have debt ratios of 50 percent. Next, each firm decides to acquire a fixed asset costing $100. Firm B borrows $100 and buys the asset, so both an asset and a liability go on its balance sheet, and its debt ratio rises from 50 to 75 percent. Firm L leases the equipment. The lease may call for fixed charges as high or even higher than the loan, and the obligations assumed under the lease may be equally or more dangerous from the standpoint of potential bankruptcy, but the firm's debt ratio remains at only 50 percent.

To correct this problem, the Financial Accounting Standards Board issued FASB Statement 13, which requires that, for an unqualified audit report, firms that enter into financial (or capital) leases must restate their balance sheets to report the leased asset as a fixed asset and the present value of the future lease payments as a liability. This process is called **capitalizing the lease,** and its net effect is to cause Firms B and L to have similar balance sheets, both of which will, in essence, resemble the one shown for Firm B.

The logic behind Statement 13 is as follows. If a firm signs a financial lease contract, its obligation to make lease payments is just as binding as if it had signed a loan agreement—the failure to make lease payments can bankrupt a firm just as fast as the failure to make principal and interest payments on a loan. Therefore, for all intents and purposes, a financial lease is identical to a loan.[5] This being the case, if a firm signs a financial lease agreement, this has the effect of raising its true debt ratio, and thus its true capital structure is changed. Therefore, if the firm had previously established a target capital structure, and if there is no reason to think that the optimal capital structure has changed, then using lease financing requires additional equity support exactly like debt financing.

If disclosure of the lease in our Table 19-1 example were not made, then Firm L's investors could be deceived into thinking that its financial position is stronger than it really is. Thus, even before FASB Statement 13 was issued, firms were required to disclose the existence of long-term leases in footnotes to their financial statements. At that time, it was debated as to whether or not investors recognized fully the impact of leases and, in effect, would see that Firms B and L were in essentially the same financial position. Some people argued that leases were not fully recognized, even by sophisticated investors. If this were the case, then leasing could alter the capital structure decision in a significant manner—a firm could increase its true

---

[4]FASB Statement 13, "Accounting for Leases," spells out in detail both the conditions under which the lease must be capitalized and the procedures for capitalizing it. Also, see Schallheim, *op. cit.,* Chapter 4, for more on the accounting treatment of leases.

[5]There are, however, certain legal differences between loans and leases. In the event of liquidation in bankruptcy, a lessor is entitled to take possession of the leased asset, and if the value of the asset is less than the required payments under the lease, the lessor can enter a claim (as a general creditor) for one year's lease payments. Also, after bankruptcy has been declared but before the case has been resolved, lease payments may be continued, whereas all payments on debts are generally stopped. In a reorganization, the lessor receives the asset plus three years' lease payments if needed to cover the value of the lease. The lender under a secured loan arrangement has a security interest in the asset, meaning that if it is sold, the lender will be given the proceeds, and the full unsatisfied portion of the lender's claim will be treated as a general creditor obligation. It is not possible to state, as a general rule, whether a supplier of capital is in a stronger position as a secured creditor or as a lessor. However, in certain situations, lessors may bear less risk than secured lenders if financial distress occurs.

| TABLE 19-1 | Balance Sheet Effects of Leasing |

BEFORE ASSET INCREASE				AFTER ASSET INCREASE							
FIRMS B AND L				FIRM B, WHICH BORROWS AND BUYS				FIRM L, WHICH LEASES			
Current assets	$ 50	Debt	$ 50	Current assets	$ 50	Debt	$150	Current assets	$ 50	Debt	$ 50
Fixed assets	50	Equity	50	Fixed assets	150	Equity	50	Fixed assets	50	Equity	50
	$100		$100		$200		$200		$100		$100
Debt/assets ratio:			50%				75%				50%

leverage through a lease arrangement, and this procedure would have a smaller effect on its cost of conventional debt, k_d, and on its cost of equity, k_s, than if it had borrowed directly and reflected this fact on its balance sheet. These benefits of leasing would accrue to existing investors at the expense of new investors who would, in effect, be deceived by the fact that the firm's balance sheet did not reflect its true financial leverage.

The question of whether investors were truly deceived was debated but never resolved. Those who believed strongly in efficient markets thought that investors were not deceived and that footnotes were sufficient, while those who questioned market efficiency thought that all leases should be capitalized. Statement 13 represents a compromise between these two positions, though one that is tilted heavily toward those who favor capitalization.

A lease is classified as a capital lease, hence must be capitalized and shown directly on the balance sheet, if one or more of the following conditions exist:

1. Under the terms of the lease, ownership of the property is effectively transferred from the lessor to the lessee.

2. The lessee can purchase the property at less than its true market value when the lease expires.

3. The lease runs for a period equal to or greater than 75 percent of the asset's life. Thus, if an asset has a ten-year life and the lease is written for eight years, the lease must be capitalized.

4. The present value of the lease payments is equal to or greater than 90 percent of the initial value of the asset.[6]

These rules, together with strong footnote disclosure rules for operating leases, are sufficient to ensure that no one will be fooled by lease financing; thus, leases are regarded as debt for capital structure purposes, and they have the same effects as debt on k_d and k_s. Therefore, leasing is not likely to permit a firm to use more financial leverage than could be obtained with conventional debt.[7]

---

[6]The discount rate used to calculate the present value of the lease payments must be the lower of (1) the rate used by the lessor to establish the lease payments (this rate is discussed later in the chapter) or (2) the rate of interest which the lessee would have to pay for new debt with a maturity equal to that of the lease. Also, note that any maintenance payments embedded in the lease payment must be stripped out prior to checking this condition.

[7]Schallheim, op. cit., in Chapter 5, argues that leases and debt may not be strict substitutes. The evidence on this point is not conclusive. However, the lease analysis models are based on the assumption that leasing is a substitute for borrowing, and that assumption is probably valid in most situations.

Why is lease financing sometimes referred to as off-balance sheet financing?

What is the intent of FASB Statement 13?

What is the difference in the balance sheet treatment of a lease that is capitalized and one that is not?

EVALUATION BY THE LESSEE

Leases are evaluated by both the lessee and the lessor. The lessee must determine whether leasing an asset is less costly than buying it, and the lessor must decide whether the lease payments provide a satisfactory return on the capital invested in the leased asset. This section focuses on the lessee's analysis.

In the typical case, the events leading to a lease arrangement follow the sequence described below. We should note that a degree of uncertainty exists regarding the theoretically correct way to evaluate lease-versus-purchase decisions, and some very complex decision models have been developed to aid in the analysis. However, the simple analysis given here leads to the correct decision in all the cases we have ever encountered.

1. The firm decides to acquire a particular building or piece of equipment; this decision is based on regular capital budgeting procedures. Whether or not to acquire the asset is *not* part of the typical lease analysis—in a lease analysis, we are concerned simply with whether to obtain the use of the machine by lease or by purchase. Thus, for the lessee, the lease decision is typically just a financing decision. However, if the effective cost of capital obtained by leasing is substantially lower than the cost of debt, then the cost of capital used in the capital budgeting decision would have to be recalculated, and perhaps projects formerly deemed unacceptable might become acceptable. See the Extensions section at the end of this chapter for more information on feedback effects.

2. Once the firm has decided to acquire the asset, the next question is how to finance its acquisition. Well-run businesses do not have excess cash lying around, so capital to finance new assets must be obtained from some source.

3. Funds to purchase the asset could be obtained from internally generated cash flows, by borrowing, or by selling new equity. Alternatively, the asset could be leased. Because of the capitalization/disclosure provision for leases, leasing normally has the same capital structure effect as borrowing.

4. As indicated earlier, a lease is comparable to a loan in the sense that the firm is required to make a specified series of payments, and a failure to meet these payments could result in bankruptcy. If a company has a target capital structure, then $1 of lease financing displaces $1 of debt financing. Thus, the most appropriate comparison is lease financing versus debt financing. Note that the analysis should compare the cost of leasing with the cost of debt financing *regardless* of how the asset purchase is actually financed. The asset may be purchased with available cash if not leased, but since leasing is a substitute for debt financing, and has the same capital structure effect, the appropriate comparison would still be with debt financing.

To illustrate the basic elements of lease analysis, consider this simplified example. The Thompson-Grammatikos Company (TGC) requires the use of a two-year asset that costs $100, and the company must choose between leasing and buying the asset.

If the asset is purchased, the bank would lend TGC the $100 at a rate of 10 percent on a two-year, simple interest loan. Thus, the firm would have to pay the bank $10 in interest at the end of each year, plus return the $100 of principal at the end of Year 2. For simplicity, assume (1) that TGC could depreciate the asset over two years for tax purposes by the straight line method if it is purchased, resulting in tax depreciation of $50 in each year, and (2) that the asset's value at the end of two years is estimated to be $0.

Alternatively, TGC could lease the asset under a guideline lease for two years for a payment of $55 at the end of each year. TGC's tax rate is 40 percent. The analysis for the lease-versus-borrow decision consists of (1) estimating the cash flows associated with borrowing and buying the asset, that is, the flows associated with debt financing, (2) estimating the cash flows associated with leasing the asset, and (3) comparing the two financing methods to determine which has the lower cost. Here are the borrow-and-buy flows, set up to produce a cash flow time line:

CASH FLOWS IF TGC BUYS	YEAR 0	YEAR 1	YEAR 2
Equipment cost	($100)		
Loan amount	100		
Interest expense		($10)	($ 10)
Tax savings from interest		4	4
Principal repayment			(100)
Tax savings from depreciation		20	20
Net cash flow (time line)	$ 0	$14	($ 86)

The net cash flow is zero in Year 0, positive in Year 1, and negative in Year 2. The operating cash flows are not shown, but they must, of course, be positive or else TGC would not want to acquire the asset. Since the operating cash flows will be the same regardless of whether the asset is leased or purchased, they can be ignored.

Here are the cash flows associated with the lease:

CASH FLOWS IF TGC LEASES	YEAR 0	YEAR 1	YEAR 2
Lease payment		($55)	($55)
Tax savings from payment		22	22
Net cash flow (time line)	$0	($33)	($33)

Note that the two sets of cash flows reflect the tax deductibility of interest and depreciation if the asset is purchased, or the lease payments if it is leased. Thus, the net cash flows include the tax savings from these items.[8]

To compare the cost streams of buying versus leasing, we must put them on a present value basis. As we explain later, the correct discount rate is the after-tax cost of debt, which for TGC is $10\%(1 - 0.4) = 6.0\%$. Applying this rate, we find the present value cost of buying to be $63.33 versus a present value cost of leasing of $60.50. Since leasing has the lower present value of costs, the company should lease this particular asset.

---

[8]If the lease had not met IRS guidelines, then ownership would effectively reside with the lessee, and TGC would depreciate the asset for tax purposes whether it was leased or purchased. However, only the implied interest portion of the lease payment would be tax deductible. Thus, the analysis for a nonguideline lease would consist of simply comparing the after-tax financing flows on the loan with the after-tax lease payment stream.

Now we examine a more realistic example, one from the Anderson Equipment Company, which is conducting a lease analysis on some assembly line equipment that it will procure during the coming year. The following data have been developed:

1. Anderson plans to acquire automated assembly line equipment with a ten-year life at a cost of $10 million, delivered and installed. However, Anderson plans to use the equipment for only five years, and then discontinue the product line.

2. Anderson can borrow the required $10 million at a before-tax cost of 10 percent.

3. The equipment's estimated scrap value is $50,000 after ten years of use, but its estimated salvage value after only five years of use is $1,000,000. Thus, if Anderson buys the equipment, it would expect to receive $1,000,000 before taxes when the equipment is sold in five years. Note that in leasing, the asset's value at the end of the lease period is called its **residual value.**

4. Anderson can lease the equipment for five years at a rental charge of $2,750,000, payable at the beginning of each year, but the lessor will own the equipment upon the expiration of the lease. (The lease payment schedule is established by the potential lessor, as described in the next major section, and Anderson can accept it, reject it, or negotiate.)

5. The lease contract stipulates that the lessor will maintain the equipment at no additional charge to Anderson. However, if Anderson borrows and buys, it will have to bear the cost of maintenance, which will be done by the equipment manufacturer at a fixed contract rate of $500,000 per year, payable at the beginning of each year.

6. The equipment falls in the MACRS five-year class life, Anderson's marginal tax rate is 40 percent, and the lease qualifies as a guideline lease.

Table 19-2 shows the steps involved in the analysis. Part I of the table is devoted to the costs of borrowing and buying. The company borrows $10 million, uses it to pay for the equipment, and then makes the *after-tax* interest and principal payments shown on Line 1. Line 2 shows the maintenance cost. Line 3 gives the maintenance tax savings. Line 4 contains the depreciation tax savings, which is the depreciation expense times the tax rate. Lines 5 and 6 contain the residual (or salvage) value cash flows. The tax is on the excess of the residual value over the asset's book value, not on the full residual value. Line 7 contains the net cash flows, and Line 8 shows the net present value of these flows, discounted at 6 percent.

Part II of Table 19-2 analyzes the lease. The lease payments, shown on Line 9, are $2,750,000 per year; this rate, which includes maintenance, was established by the prospective lessor and offered to Anderson Equipment. If Anderson accepts the lease, the full amount will be a deductible expense, so the tax savings, shown on Line 10, is 0.40(Lease payment) = 0.40($2,750,000) = $1,100,000. Thus, the after-tax cost of the lease payment is Lease payment − Tax savings = $2,750,000 − $1,100,000 = $1,650,000. This amount is shown on Line 11, Years 0 through 4.

The next step is to compare the net cost of owning with the net cost of leasing. However, we must first put the annual cash flows of leasing and borrowing on a common basis. This requires converting them to present values, which brings up the question of the proper rate at which to discount the costs. We know that the discount rate must reflect the riskiness of the cash flows being discounted. This principle was observed in our discussions of security valuation and capital budgeting, and it also applies in lease analysis. Just how risky are the cash flows under consideration here? Most of them are relatively certain, at least when compared with the types of cash flow estimates that were developed in capital budgeting. For example, the loan payment schedule is set by

| **TABLE 19-2** | Anderson Equipment Company: Dollar Cost Analysis (Thousands of Dollars) |

	YEAR 0	YEAR 1	YEAR 2	YEAR 3	YEAR 4	YEAR 5
I. Cost of Owning (Borrowing and Buying)						
1. After-tax loan payments		($ 600)	($ 600)	($ 600)	($ 600)	($10,600)
2. Maintenance cost	($ 500)	(500)	(500)	(500)	(500)	
3. Maintenance tax savings	200	200	200	200	200	
4. Depreciation tax savings		800	1,280	760	480	$ 440
5. Residual value						1,000
6. Tax on residual value						(160)
7. Net cash flow (time line)	($ 300)	($ 100)	$ 380	($ 140)	($ 420)	($ 9,320)
8. PV cost of owning = $7,471						
II. Cost of Leasing						
9. Lease payment	($2,750)	($2,750)	($2,750)	($2,750)	($2,750)	
10. Payment tax savings	1,100	1,100	1,100	1,100	1,100	
11. Net cash flow (time line)	($1,650)	($1,650)	($1,650)	($1,650)	($1,650)	$0
12. PV cost of leasing = $7,367						
III. Cost Comparison						

13. Net advantage to leasing (NAL) = PV cost of owning − PV cost of leasing = $7,471 − $7,367 = $104.

NOTES:

a. The net cash flows shown in Lines 7 and 11 are discounted at the lessee's after-tax cost of debt, 6.0 percent.

b. The MACRS depreciation allowances are 0.20, 0.32, 0.19, 0.12, and 0.11 in Years 1 through 5, respectively. Thus, the depreciation expense is 0.20($10,000) = $2,000 in Year 1, and so on. The depreciation tax savings in each year is 0.4(Depreciation).

c. The residual value is $1,000 while the book value is $600. Thus, Anderson would have to pay 0.4($1,000 − $600) = $160 in taxes, producing a net after-tax residual value of $1,000 − $160 = $840. These amounts are shown in Lines 5 and 6 in the cost of owning analysis.

d. In practice, a lease analysis such as this would be done using a spreadsheet model.

e. In the NAL equation on Line 13, the PV costs are stated as positive values. If the PV costs are treated as negative values, or outflows, the NAL must be redefined as follows: NAL = PV cost of leasing − PV cost of owning = −$7,367 − (−$7,471) = $104.

contract, as is the lease payment schedule. The depreciation expenses are also established by law and not subject to change, and the $500,000 annual maintenance cost is fixed by contract as well. The tax savings are somewhat uncertain, but they will be as projected so long as Anderson's marginal tax rate remains at 40 percent. The residual value is the least certain of the cash flows, but even here, Anderson's management is fairly confident about the estimate.

Since the cash flows under the lease and under the borrow-and-purchase alternatives are both relatively certain, they should be discounted at a relatively low rate. Most analysts recommend that the company's cost of debt be used, and this rate seems reasonable in our example. Further, since the cash flows are after taxes, *the **after-tax cost of debt,** which is 10%(1 − T) = 10%(0.6) = 6%, should be used.* Accordingly, we discount the net cash flows on Lines 7 and 11 using a rate of 6.0 percent. The resulting present values are $7,471,000 for the cost of owning and $7,367,000 for the cost of leasing, as shown on Lines 8 and 12. The financing method that produces the smaller present value of costs is the one that should be selected. We define the **net advantage to leasing (NAL)** as follows (see Note e to Table 19-2):

$$NAL = PV \text{ cost of owning} - PV \text{ cost of leasing}$$

$$= \$7,471,00 \qquad - \$7,367,000$$

$$= \$104,000.$$

The PV cost of owning exceeds the PV cost of leasing, so the NAL is positive. Therefore, Anderson should lease the equipment.[9]

In this section, we have focused on the dollar cost of leasing versus borrowing and buying, which is analogous to the NPV method used in capital budgeting. A second method that lessees can use to evaluate leases focuses on the percentage cost of leasing and is analogous to the IRR method used in capital budgeting. The percentage approach is discussed in the Extension to this chapter.

<table>
<tr><td>S E L F - T E S T
Q U E S T I O N S</td><td>Explain how the cash flows are structured in order to estimate the net advantage to leasing.

What discount rate should be used to evaluate a lease? Why?

Define the term "net advantage to leasing, NAL."</td></tr>
</table>

EVALUATION BY THE LESSOR

Thus far we have considered leasing only from the lessee's viewpoint. It is also useful to analyze the transaction as the lessor sees it: Is the lease a good investment for the party who must put up the money? The lessor will generally be a specialized leasing company, a bank or bank affiliate, an individual or group of individuals, or a manufacturer such as IBM or GM that uses leasing as a sales tool. The specialized leasing companies are often owned by profitable companies such as General Electric, which owns General Electric Capital, the largest leasing company in the world. Investment banking houses such as Merrill Lynch also set up and/or work with specialized leasing companies, where brokerage clients' money is made available to leasing customers in deals which permit the investors to share in the tax shelters provided by the lease.

Any potential lessor needs to know the rate of return on the capital invested in the lease, and this information is also useful to the prospective lessee: Lease terms on large leases are generally negotiated, so the lessee should know what return the lessor is earning. The lessor's analysis involves (1) determining the net cash outlay,

---

[9]The more complicated methods which exist for analyzing leasing generally focus on the issue of the discount rate that should be used to discount the cash flows. Conceptually, we could assign a separate discount rate to each individual cash flow component, then find the present values of each of the cash flow components, and finally sum these present values to determine the net advantage or disadvantage to leasing. This approach has been taken by Stewart C. Myers, David A. Dill, and Alberto J. Bautista (MDB) in "Valuation of Financial Lease Contracts," *Journal of Finance,* June 1976, 799–819, among others. MDB correctly note that the use of a single discount rate is valid only if (1) leases and loans are viewed by investors as being equivalent and (2) all cash flows are equally risky, hence appropriately discounted at the same rate. The first assumption is probably valid for most financial leases, and even where it is not, no one knows how to adjust properly for any capital structure effects that leases might have. Regarding the second assumption, advocates of multiple discount rates often point out that the residual value is less certain than are the other cash flows and thus recommend discounting it at a higher rate. However, there is no way of knowing precisely how much to increase the after-tax cost of debt to account for the increased riskiness of the residual value cash flow. Further, in a market risk sense, all cash flows could be equally risky even though individual items such as the residual value might have more or less total variability than others. To complicate matters even more, the market risk of the residual value will usually be different than the firm's market risk. For more on residual value risk, see Schallheim, *op. cit.,* Chapter 8.

which is usually the invoice price of the leased equipment less any lease payments made in advance; (2) determining the periodic cash inflows, which consist of the lease payments minus both income taxes and any maintenance expense the lessor must bear; (3) estimating the after-tax residual value of the property when the lease expires; and (4) determining whether the rate of return on the lease exceeds the lessor's opportunity cost of capital or, equivalently, whether the NPV of the lease exceeds zero.

To illustrate the lessor's analysis, we assume the same facts as for the Anderson Equipment Company lease, plus the following: (1) The potential lessor is a wealthy individual whose current income is in the form of interest, and whose marginal federal-plus-state income tax rate, T, is 40 percent. (2) The investor can buy five-year bonds that have a 9 percent yield to maturity, providing an after-tax yield of $(9\%)(1 - T) = (9\%)(0.6) = 5.4\%$. This is the after-tax return that the investor can obtain on alternative investments of similar risk. (3) The before-tax residual value is $1,000,000. Since the asset will be depreciated to a book value of $600,000 at the end of the five-year lease, $400,000 of this $1 million will be taxable at the 40 percent rate because of the recapture of depreciation rule, so the lessor can expect to receive $1,000,000 $- 0.4(\$400,000) = \$840,000$ after taxes from the sale of the equipment after the lease expires.

The lessor's cash flows are developed in Table 19-3. Here we see that the lease as an investment has a net present value of $26,000. On a present value basis, the investor who invests in the lease rather than in the 9 percent bonds (5.4 percent after taxes) is better off by $26,000, indicating that he or she should be willing to write the lease. As

| TABLE 19-3 | Lease Analysis from the Lessor's Viewpoint (Thousands of Dollars) | | | | | |

	YEAR 0	YEAR 1	YEAR 2	YEAR 3	YEAR 4	YEAR 5
1. Net purchase price	($10,000)					
2. Maintenance cost	(500)	($ 500)	($ 500)	($ 500)	($ 500)	
3. Maintenance tax savings	200	200	200	200	200	
4. Depreciation tax savings[a]		800	1,280	760	480	$ 440
5. Lease payment	2,750	2,750	2,750	2,750	2,750	
6. Tax on lease payment	(1,100)	(1,100)	(1,100)	(1,100)	(1,100)	
7. Residual value						1,000
8. Tax on residual value[b]						(160)
9. Net cash flow	($ 8,650)	$2,150	$2,630	$2,110	$1,830	$1,280

$$NPV = \sum_{t=0}^{5} \frac{NCF_t}{(1 + k)^t} = \$26 \text{ when } k = 5.4\%.$$

$$IRR: NPV = 0 = \sum_{t=0}^{5} \frac{NCF_t}{(1 + IRR)^t}; IRR = 5.5\%.$$

NOTES:
[a]Depreciation times the lessor's tax rate.
[b](Residual value − Book value)T.

we saw earlier, the lease is also advantageous to Anderson Equipment Company, so the transaction should be completed.

The investor can also calculate the lease investment's IRR based on the net cash flows shown on Line 9 of Table 19-3. The IRR of the lease, which is that discount rate which forces the NPV of the lease to zero, is 5.5 percent. Thus, the lease provides a 5.5 percent after-tax return to this 40 percent tax rate investor. This exceeds the 5.4 percent after-tax return on 9 percent bonds. So, using either the IRR or the NPV method, the lease would appear to be a satisfactory investment.[10]

Setting the Lease Payment

In the preceding sections we evaluated the lease assuming that the lease payments had already been specified. However, in large leases the parties generally sit down and work out an agreement on the size of the lease payments, with these payments being set so as to provide the lessor with some specific required rate of return. In situations where the lease terms are not negotiated, which is often the case for small leases, the lessor must still go through the same type of analysis, setting terms which provide a target rate of return, and then offering these terms to the potential lessee on a take-it-or-leave-it basis.

To illustrate all this, suppose the potential lessor described earlier, after examining other alternative investment opportunities, decides that the 5.5 percent return on the Anderson Equipment Company lease is too low, and that the required return on the lease is 6.0 percent. What lease payment schedule would provide this return?

To answer this question, note again that Table 19-3 contains the lessor's cash flow analysis. If the basic analysis is computerized, it is easy to first change the discount rate to 6 percent, and then change the lease payment — either by trial-and-error or by using the goal-seeking function — until the lease's NPV = $0 or, equivalently, its IRR = 6.0 percent. When we did this with a spreadsheet lease evaluation model, we found that the lessor must set the lease payment at $2,788,591.50 to obtain an after-tax rate of return of 6.0 percent. If this lease payment is not acceptable to the lessee, Anderson Equipment Company, then it may not be possible to strike a deal. Naturally, competition among leasing companies forces lessors to build market-related returns into their lease payment schedules.

Note that a lease payment of $2,788,591.50 would drive Anderson's NAL down to exactly zero. Thus, both the lessee and the lessor would have NAL = NPV = $0. Leasing is not always a zero sum game, but if the inputs to the lessee and the lessor are identical, as in this case, then a positive NAL to the lessee implies an equal but negative NPV to the lessor. *However, conditions are often such that leasing can provide net benefits to both parties. This situation arises because of differentials, generally in taxes, in estimated residual values, or in the ability to bear the residual value risk.* We will explore this issue in detail in a later section.

Note that the lessor can, under certain conditions, increase the return on the lease by borrowing some of the funds used to purchase the leased asset. Such a lease is called a **leveraged lease.** Whether or not a lease is leveraged has no effect on the lessee's analysis, but it can have a significant effect on the cash flows to the lessor, hence on the lessor's expected rate of return. We discuss leveraged leases in more detail in the Extension to this chapter.

---

[10]Note that the lease investment is actually slightly more risky than the alternative bond investment because the residual value cash flow is less certain than a principal repayment. Thus, the lessor might require an expected return somewhat above the 5.4 percent promised on a bond investment.

| What discount rate is used in a lessor's NPV analysis?

What is the economic interpretation of the lessor's IRR?

OTHER ISSUES IN LEASE ANALYSIS

The basic methods of analysis used by lessees and lessors were presented in the previous sections. However, some other issues warrant discussion.

Estimated Residual Value

It is important to note that the lessor owns the property upon expiration of a lease, hence the lessor has claim to the asset's residual value. Superficially, it would appear that if residual values are expected to be large, owning would have an advantage over leasing. However, this apparent advantage does not hold up. If expected residual values are large — as they may be under inflation for certain types of equipment and also if real estate is involved — competition between leasing companies and other financing sources, as well as competition among leasing companies themselves, will force leasing rates down to the point where potential residual values are fully recognized in the lease contract. Thus, the existence of large residual values is not likely to result in materially higher costs for leasing.

Increased Credit Availability

As noted earlier, leasing is sometimes said to have an advantage for firms that are seeking the maximum degree of financial leverage. First, it is sometimes argued that firms can obtain more money, and for longer terms, under a lease arrangement than under a loan secured by a specific piece of equipment. Second, since some leases do not appear on the balance sheet, lease financing has been said to give the firm a stronger appearance in a *superficial* credit analysis and thus to permit the firm to use more leverage than would be possible if it did not lease.

There may be some truth to these claims for smaller firms, but since firms are required to capitalize financial leases and to report them on their balance sheets, this point is of questionable validity for any firm large enough to have audited financial statements. However, leasing can be a way to circumvent existing loan covenants. If restrictive covenants prohibit a firm from issuing more debt but fail to restrict lease payments, then the firm could effectively increase its leverage by leasing additional assets. Also, firms that are in very poor financial condition and facing possible bankruptcy may be able to obtain lease financing at a lower cost than comparable debt financing because (1) lessors often have a more favorable position than lenders should the lessee actually go bankrupt and (2) lessors that specialize in certain types of equipment may be in a better position to dispose of repossessed equipment than banks or other lenders.

Real Estate Leases

Most of our examples have focused on equipment leasing. However, leasing originated with real estate, and such leases still constitute a huge segment of total lease financing. (We distinguish between housing rentals and long-term business leases; our concern is with business leases.) Retailers lease many of their stores. In some situations, retailers have no choice but to lease — this is true of locations in malls and certain buildings. In other situations, they have a choice of building and owning versus leasing. The same situation exists for business firms' offices and other facilities. Law firms and accounting firms, for example, can choose between buying their own facilities or leasing on a long-term basis (up to 20 or more years).

The type of lease-versus-purchase analysis we discussed in this chapter is just as applicable for real estate as for equipment—conceptually, there is no difference. Of course, such things as maintenance, who the other tenants will be, what alterations can be made, who will pay for alterations, and the like, become especially important with real property, but the analytical procedures upon which the lease-versus-buy decision is based are no different from any other lease analysis.

Auto Leases

Auto leasing is very popular today, both for large corporations and for individuals, especially professionals such as MBAs, doctors, lawyers, and accountants. For corporations, the key factor is often maintenance and disposal of used vehicles—the leasing companies are specialists here, and many businesses prefer to "outsource" services related to autos. For individuals, leasing is often more convenient, and it may be easier to justify tax deductions on leased than owned vehicles. Also, most auto leasing to individuals is through dealers. These dealers (and manufacturers) use leasing as a sales tool, and they often make the terms quite attractive, especially when it comes to the down payment, which may be nonexistent in the case of a lease.

Auto leasing also permits many individuals to drive more expensive cars than would otherwise be possible. For example, the monthly payment on a new BMW might be $1,000 when financed with a three-year loan, but the same car, if leased for three years, might only cost $499 a month. At first glance, it appears that leasing is less expensive than owning because the monthly payment is so much lower. However, such a simplistic analysis ignores the fact that payments end after the loan is paid off but continue indefinitely under leasing. By using the techniques described in this chapter, individuals can assess the true costs associated with auto leases and then rationally judge the merits of each type of auto financing.

Spreadsheet Models

Lease analysis, like capital budgeting, is particularly well suited for spreadsheets. Setting the analysis up on a computer is especially useful when negotiations are under way, and when investment banking houses such as Merrill Lynch are working out a leasing deal between a group of investors and a company, the analysis is always computerized.

Leasing and Tax Laws[11]

The ability to structure leases that are advantageous to both lessor and lessee depends in large part on tax laws. The four major tax factors that influence leasing are (1) investment tax credits, (2) depreciation rules, (3) tax rates, and (4) the alternative minimum tax. In this section, we briefly discuss each of these factors and how they influence leasing decisions.

The investment tax credit (ITC), when it is allowed, is a direct reduction of taxes that occurs when a firm purchases new capital equipment. Prior to 1987 firms could imme-

---

[11]See Schallheim, *op. cit.*, Chapters 3 and 6, for an in-depth discussion of tax effects on leasing.

diately deduct up to 10 percent of the cost of new capital investments from their corporate tax bills. Thus, a company that bought a $1,000,000 mainframe computer system would get a $100,000 reduction in current-year taxes. Since the ITC goes to the owner of the capital asset, low-tax-bracket companies that could not otherwise use the ITC could use leasing as a vehicle to pass immediate tax savings to high-tax-bracket lessors. Congress eliminated the ITC in 1987, but it could be reinstated in the future. If the ITC is put back into law, leasing would become more attractive to low-tax-bracket firms.

Owners recover their investments in capital assets through depreciation, which is a tax-deductible expense. Because of the time value of money, the faster an asset can be depreciated, the greater the tax advantages of ownership. Recent tax laws have tended to slow depreciation write-offs, thus reducing the value of ownership. This has also reduced the advantage to leasing by low-tax-bracket lessees from high-tax-bracket lessors. Any move to liberalize depreciation rules would tend to make leasing more desirable in many situations. The value of depreciation also depends on the firm's tax rate, because the depreciation tax saving equals the amount of depreciation multiplied by the tax rate. Thus, higher corporate tax rates mean greater ownership tax savings, hence more incentive for tax-driven leases.

Finally, the alternative minimum tax (AMT) also impacts leasing activity. Corporations are permitted to use accelerated depreciation and other tax shelters on their tax books but then use straight line depreciation for reporting results to shareholders. Thus, some firms report to the IRS that they are doing poorly and hence pay little or no taxes, but report high earnings to shareholders. The corporate AMT, which is roughly computed by applying a 20 percent tax rate to the profits reported to shareholders, is designed to force highly profitable companies to pay at least some taxes even if they have tax shelters that push their taxable income to zero. In effect, all firms (and individuals) must compute the "regular" tax and the AMT tax, and then pay the higher of the two.

Companies that have large AMT liabilities look for ways to reduce their tax bills by lowering reported income. Leasing can be beneficial here—a relatively short-term lease with high annual payments will increase reported expenses, hence lower reported profits. Note that the lease does not have to qualify as a guideline lease and be deducted for regular tax purposes—all that is needed is to lower reported income as shown on the income statement.

We see that tax laws and differential tax rates between lessors and lessees can be a motivating force for leasing. However, as we discuss in the next section, there are sound economic reasons why firms lease plant and equipment.

S E L F - T E S T
Q U E S T I O N S

Does leasing lead to increased credit availability?

How do tax laws affect leasing?

OTHER REASONS FOR LEASING

Up to this point, we have noted that tax rate or other differentials are generally necessary to make leasing attractive to both the lessee and lessor. If the lessee and lessor are facing different tax situations, including the alternative minimum tax, then it is often possible to structure a lease that is beneficial to both parties. However, there are other reasons firms might want to lease an asset rather than buy it.

As discussed in the opening section, more than half of all commercial aircraft are leased, and smaller airlines, especially in developing nations, lease an even higher percentage of their planes. One of the reasons for this lease usage is that airlines can reduce their risks by leasing. If an airline purchases all its aircraft, it would be hampered in its ability to respond to changing market conditions. Because they have become specialists at matching airlines with available aircraft, the aircraft lessors are quite good at managing the changing demand for different types of aircraft. This permits them to offer attractive lease terms. In this situation, **leasing provides operating flexibility.** Leasing is not necessarily less expensive than buying, but the operating flexibility is quite valuable.

Leasing is also an attractive alternative for many high-technology items that are subject to rapid and unpredictable technological obsolescence. Say a small rural hospital wants to buy a magnetic resonance imaging (MRI) device. If it buys the MRI equipment, it is exposed to the risk of technological obsolescence. In a short time some new technology might lower the value of the current system and thus render the project unprofitable. Since it does not use much equipment of this nature, the hospital would bear a great deal of risk if it bought the MRI device. However, a lessor that specializes in state-of-the-art medical equipment would be exposed to significantly less risk. By purchasing and then leasing many different items, the lessor benefits from diversification. Of course, over time some items will probably lose more value than the lessor expected, but this will be offset by other items that retained more value than was expected. Also, since such a leasing company will be especially familiar with the market for used medical equipment, it can refurbish the equipment and then get a better price in the resale market than could a remote rural hospital. For these reasons, leasing can reduce the risk of technological obsolescence.

Leasing can also be attractive when a firm is uncertain about the demand for its products or services, and thus about how long the equipment will be needed. Again, consider the hospital industry. Hospitals often offer services that are dependent on a single staff member — for example, a physician who does liver transplants. To support the physician's practice, the hospital might have to invest millions in equipment that can be used only for this particular procedure. The hospital will charge for the use of the equipment, and if things go as expected, the investment will be profitable. However, if the physician leaves the hospital, and if no replacement can be recruited, then the project is dead, and the equipment becomes useless to the hospital. In this case, a lease with a cancellation clause would permit the hospital to simply return the equipment. The lessor would charge something for the cancellation clause, and this would lower the expected profitability of the project, but it would provide the hospital with an option to abandon the equipment, and the value of the option could easily exceed the incremental cost of the cancellation clause. The leasing company would be willing to write this option because it is in a better position to remarket the equipment, either by writing another lease or by selling it outright.

The leasing industry recently introduced a type of lease that even transfers some of a project's operating risk from the lessee to the lessor, and also motivates the lessor to maintain the leased equipment in good working order. Instead of making a fixed rental payment, the lessee pays a fee each time the leased equipment is used. This type of lease originated with copy machines, where the lessee pays so much per month plus an additional amount per copy made. If the machine breaks down, no copies are made, and the lessor's rental income declines. This motivates the lessor to repair the machine quickly.

This type of lease is also used in the health care industry, where it is called a "per-procedure lease." For example, a hospital might lease an X-ray machine for a fixed fee per X-ray, say, $5. If demand for the machine's X rays is less than expected by the hospital, revenues will be lower than expected, but so will the machine's capital costs. Conversely, high demand would lead to higher-than-expected lease costs, but these would be offset by higher-than-expected revenues. By using a per-procedure lease, the hospital is converting a fixed cost for the equipment into a variable cost, hence reducing the machine's operating leverage and breakeven point. The net effect is to reduce the project's risk. Of course, the expected cost of a per-procedure lease might be more than the cost of a conventional lease, but the risk reduction benefit could be worth the cost. Note too that if the lessor writes a large number of per-procedure leases, much of the riskiness inherent in such leases could be eliminated by diversification, so the risk premiums that lessors build into per-procedure lease payments could be low enough to attract potential lessees.

Some companies also find leasing attractive because the lessor is able to provide servicing on favorable terms. For example, Virco Manufacturing, a company that makes school desks and other furniture, recently leased 25 truck tractors and 140 trailers which it uses to ship furniture from its plant. The lease agreement, with a large leasing company which specializes in purchasing, maintaining, and then reselling trucks, permitted the replacement of an aging fleet that Virco had built up over the years. "We are pretty good at manufacturing furniture, but we aren't very good at maintaining a truck fleet," said Virco's CFO.

There are other reasons that might cause a firm to lease an asset rather than buy it. Often, these reasons are difficult to quantify, hence they cannot be easily incorporated into an NPV or IRR analysis. Nevertheless, a sound lease decision must begin with a quantitative analysis, and then qualitative factors can be considered before making the final lease-or-buy decision.

SELF-TEST QUESTION | Describe some economic factors which might provide an advantage to leasing.

SUMMARY

In the United States, more than 30 percent of all equipment is leased, as is a great deal of real estate. Consequently, leasing is an important financing vehicle. In this chapter, we discussed the leasing decision from the standpoints of both the lessee and lessor. The key concepts covered are listed below:

- The four most important types of lease agreement are (1) **operating lease,** (2) **financial,** or **capital, lease,** (3) **sale and leaseback,** and (4) **combination lease.**
- The IRS has specific guidelines that apply to lease arrangements. A lease that meets these guidelines is called a **guideline,** or **tax-oriented, lease,** because the IRS permits the lessor to deduct the asset's depreciation and allows the lessee to deduct the lease payments. A lease that does not meet the IRS guidelines is called a **non-tax-oriented lease.** In these leases, ownership for tax purposes resides with the lessee rather than the lessor.
- **FASB Statement 13** spells out the conditions under which a lease must be **capitalized** (shown directly on the balance sheet) as opposed to shown only in the notes to the financial statements. Generally, leases that run for a period equal to or greater than 75 percent of the asset's life must be capitalized.
- The lessee's analysis consists basically of a comparison of the PV of costs associated with leasing versus the PV of costs associated with owning. The difference in these costs is called the **net advantage to leasing (NAL).**

- One of the key issues in the lessee's analysis is the appropriate discount rate. Since the cash flows in a lease analysis are stated on an after-tax basis and are known with relative certainty, the appropriate discount rate is the **lessee's after-tax cost of debt.** A higher discount rate may be used on the **residual value** if it is substantially riskier than the other flows.

- The lessor evaluates the lease as an **investment.** If the lease's NPV is greater than zero, or if its IRR is greater than the lessor's opportunity cost, then the lease should be written.

- Leasing is motivated by various differences between lessees and lessors. Three of the most important reasons for leasing are (1) **tax rate differentials,** (2) leases in which the lessor is better able to bear the **residual value risk** than the lessee, and (3) situations where the lessor can maintain the leased equipment more efficiently than the lessee.

The Extension to this chapter provides some additional information on leasing.

Questions

19-1   Define each of the following terms:
a. Lessee; lessor
b. Operating lease; financial lease; sale and leaseback; combination lease; leveraged lease
c. "Off-balance sheet" financing; capitalizing
d. FASB Statement 13
e. Guideline lease
f. Residual value
g. Lessee's analysis; lessor's analysis
h. Net advantage to leasing (NAL)
i. Alternative minimum tax (AMT)

19-2   Distinguish between operating leases and financial leases. Would you be more likely to find an operating lease employed for a fleet of trucks or for a manufacturing plant?

19-3   Would you be more likely to find that lessees are in high or low income tax brackets as compared with lessors?

19-4   Commercial banks moved heavily into equipment leasing during the early 1970s, acting as lessors. One major reason for this invasion of the leasing industry was to gain the benefits of accelerated depreciation and the investment tax credit on leased equipment. During this same period, commercial banks were investing heavily in municipal securities, and they were also making loans to real estate investment trusts (REITs). In the mid-1970s, these REITs got into such serious difficulty that many banks suffered large losses on their REIT loans. Explain how its investments in municipal bonds and REITs could reduce a bank's willingness to act as a lessor.

19-5   One alleged advantage of leasing voiced in the past is that it kept liabilities off the balance sheet, thus making it possible for a firm to obtain more leverage than it otherwise could have. This raised the question of whether or not both the lease obligation and the asset involved should be capitalized and shown on the balance sheet. Discuss the pros and cons of capitalizing leases and related assets.

19-6   Suppose there were no IRS restrictions on what constituted a valid lease. Explain, in a manner that a legislator might understand, why some restrictions should be imposed. Illustrate your answer with numbers.

19-7   Suppose Congress enacted new tax law changes that would (1) permit equipment to be depreciated over a shorter period, (2) lower corporate tax rates, and (3) reinstate the investment tax credit. Discuss how each of these potential changes would affect the relative volume of leasing versus conventional debt in the U.S. economy.

19-8   In our Anderson Equipment Company example, we assumed that the lease could not be cancelled. What effect would a cancellation clause have on the lessee's analysis? On the lessor's analysis?

Self-Test Problem (Solution Appears in Appendix B)

ST-1
Lease versus Buy

The Randolph Teweles Company (RTC) has decided to acquire a new truck. One alternative is to lease the truck on a 4-year guideline contract for a lease payment of $10,000 per year, with payments to be made at the *beginning* of each year. The lease would include maintenance. Alternatively, RTC could purchase the truck outright for $40,000, financing the purchase by a bank loan for the net purchase price and amortizing the loan over a 4-year period at an interest rate of 10 percent per year. Under the borrow-to-purchase arrangement, RTC would have to maintain the truck at a cost of $1,000 per year, payable at year end. The truck falls into the MACRS 3-year class. It has a residual value of $10,000, which is the expected market value after 4 years, when RTC plans to replace the truck irrespective of whether it leases or buys. RTC has a marginal federal-plus-state tax rate of 40 percent.

a. What is RTC's PV cost of leasing?
b. What is RTC's PV cost of owning? Should the truck be leased or purchased?
c. The appropriate discount rate for use in the analysis is the firm's after-tax cost of debt. Why?
d. The residual value is the least certain cash flow in the analysis. How might RTC incorporate differential riskiness of this cash flow into the analysis?

Problems

19-1
Balance Sheet Effects

Reynolds Construction needs a piece of equipment that costs $200. Reynolds either can lease the equipment or borrow $200 from a local bank and buy the equipment. If the equipment is leased, the lease would *not* have to be capitalized. Reynolds' balance sheet prior to the acquisition of the equipment is as follows:

Current assets	$300	Debt	$400
Net fixed assets	500	Equity	400
Total assets	$800	Total claims	$800

a. (1) What is Reynolds' current debt ratio?
   (2) What would be the company's debt ratio if it purchased the equipment?
   (3) What would be the debt ratio if the equipment were leased?
b. Would the company's financial risk be different under the leasing and purchasing alternatives?

19-2
Lease versus Buy

Assume that Reynolds' tax rate is 40 percent and the equipment's depreciation would be $100 per year. If the company leased the asset on a 2-year lease, the payment would be $110 at the beginning of each year. If Reynolds borrowed and bought, the bank would charge 10 percent interest on the loan. Should Reynolds lease or buy the equipment?

19-3
Lease versus Buy

Big Sky Mining Company must install $1.5 million of new machinery in its Nevada mine. It can obtain a bank loan for 100 percent of the purchase price, or it can lease the machinery. Assume that the following facts apply:

(1) The machinery falls into the MACRS 3-year class.
(2) Estimated maintenance expenses are $75,000 per year, payable at the beginning of each year.
(3) The firm's tax rate is 40 percent.
(4) The loan would have an interest rate of 15 percent.
(5) The lease terms call for $400,000 payments at the end of each of the next 4 years.
(6) Under either the lease or the purchase, Big Sky must pay for insurance, property taxes, and maintenance.
(7) Assume that Big Sky Mining will continue to use the machine beyond the expiration of the lease and must purchase it at an estimated residual value of $250,000 at the end of the 4th year.

What is the NAL of the lease?

19-4
Balance Sheet Effects

Two companies, Energen and Hastings Corporation, began operations with identical balance sheets. A year later, both required additional manufacturing capacity at a cost of $50,000. Energen obtained a 5-year, $50,000 loan at an 8 percent interest rate from its bank. Hastings, on the other hand, decided to lease the required $50,000 capacity for 5 years, and an 8 percent return was built into the lease. The balance sheet for each company, before the asset increases, follows:

		Debt	$ 50,000
		Equity	100,000
Total assets	$150,000	Total claims	$150,000

a. Show the balance sheets for both firms after the asset increases and calculate each firm's new debt ratio. (Assume that the lease is not capitalized.)

b. Show how Hastings's balance sheet would look immediately after the financing if it capitalized the lease.

c. Would the rate of return (1) on assets and (2) on equity be affected by the choice of financing? How?

19-5
Lease versus Buy

A. Sadik Industries must install $1 million of new machinery in its Texas plant. It can obtain a bank loan for 100 percent of the required amount. Alternatively, a Texas investment banking firm which represents a group of investors believes that it can arrange for a lease financing plan. *Assume* that these facts apply:

(1) The equipment falls in the MACRS 3-year class.

(2) Estimated maintenance expenses are $50,000 per year.

(3) The firm's tax rate is 34 percent.

(4) If the money is borrowed, the bank loan will be at a rate of 14 percent, amortized in 3 equal installments at the end of each year.

(5) The tentative lease terms call for payments of $320,000 at the end of each year for 3 years. The lease is a guideline lease.

(6) Under the proposed lease terms, the lessee must pay for insurance, property taxes, and maintenance.

(7) Sadik must use the equipment if it is to continue in business, so it will almost certainly want to acquire the property at the end of the lease. If it does, then under the lease terms it can purchase the machinery at its fair market value at that time. The best estimate of this market value is $200,000, but it could be much higher or lower under certain circumstances.

To assist management in making the proper lease-versus-buy decision, you are asked to answer the following questions:

a. Assuming that the lease can be arranged, should the firm lease or borrow and buy the equipment? Explain. (Hint: In this situation, the firm plans to use the asset beyond the term of the lease. Thus, the residual value becomes a *cost* to leasing in Year 3. Also, there is no Year 3 residual value tax consequence, as the firm cannot immediately deduct the Year 3 purchase price from taxable income.)

b. Consider the $200,000 estimated residual value. Is it appropriate to discount it at the same rate as the other cash flows? What about the other cash flows — are they all equally risky? (Hint: Riskier cash flows are normally discounted at higher rates, but when the cash flows are *costs* rather than *inflows,* the normal procedure must be reversed.)

Spreadsheet Problems

Work these problems only if you are using the computer problem diskette.

19-6
Lessor's Analysis

Use the first model in File C19 to solve this problem. The Dorfman Company has decided to acquire some new R&D equipment. One alternative is to lease the equipment on a 4-year guideline contract for a lease payment of $11,500 per year, payments to be made at the *beginning* of each year. The lease, which would include maintenance, is being offered by Bankston Credit Corporation, a local leasing company. Bankston would purchase the equipment outright for $40,000, and would have to pay the local dealer $1,000 at the beginning of each year to provide maintenance service. The equipment falls into the MACRS 3-year class; and it has a residual value of $10,000, which is the expected market value after 4 years. The lessor's marginal state-plus-federal tax rate is 40 percent. The analysts at Bankston compare the returns on potential leases with returns available on comparable maturity commercial loans which the firm also writes. Currently, Bankston is charging 9 percent on 4-year commercial loans.

a. What is the NPV on the lease investment?

b. Should Bankston write the lease? Why or why not?

c. Assume that interest rates rise, and Bankston can now earn 16 percent (before taxes) on its commercial loans. How does this affect the lease analysis?

d. What lease payment must Bankston charge to be indifferent between writing the lease and loaning at 16 percent?

e. Return to the original situation. Suppose there is a 25 percent chance that the residual value will be only $5,000, and another 25 percent probability that the residual value will be $15,000. There is a 50 percent probability that the residual value will be $10,000. What is Bankston's best-case and worst-case NPV? Suppose that the Bankston analysts account for differential risk by increasing the residual value discount rate. What residual value discount rate forces NPV = $0 when the residual value is $10,000?

19-7

Lessee's Analysis

Use the second model in File C19 to solve this problem. As part of its overall plant modernization and cost reduction program, Western Fabrics' management has decided to install a new automated weaving loom. In the capital budgeting analysis of this equipment, the IRR of the project was found to be 29 percent versus a project required return of 14 percent.

The loom has an invoice price of $100,000, including delivery and installation charges. The funds needed could be borrowed from the bank through a 4-year amortized loan at a 15 percent interest rate, with payments to be made at the end of each year. In the event the loom is purchased, the manufacturer will contract to maintain and service it for a fee of $8,000 per year paid at the end of each year. The loom falls in the MACRS 5-year class, and Western's marginal federal-plus-state tax rate is 40 percent.

Aubey Automation Inc., maker of the loom, has offered to lease the loom to Western for $30,500 upon delivery and installation (at t = 0) plus 4 additional annual lease payments of $30,500 to be made at the end of Years 1 to 4. (Note that there are 5 lease payments in total.) The lease agreement includes maintenance and servicing. Actually, the loom has an expected life of 8 years, at which time its expected salvage value is zero; however, after 4 years, its market value is expected to equal its book value. Western plans to build an entirely new plant in 4 years, so it has no interest in either leasing or owning the proposed loom for more than that period.

a. Should the loom be leased or purchased?
b. Western's managers disagree on the appropriate discount rate to be used in the analysis. What effect would a discount rate change have on the lease-versus-purchase decision?
c. The salvage value is clearly the most uncertain cash flow in the analysis. What effect would a salvage value risk adjustment have on the analysis? (Assume that the appropriate salvage value pre-tax discount rate is 18 percent.)
d. The original analysis assumed that the firm would not need the loom after 4 years. Now assume that the firm will continue to use it after the lease expires. Thus, if it leased, Western would have to buy the asset after 4 years at the then existing market value, which is assumed to equal the book value. What effect would this requirement have on the basic analysis?
e. Under the original lease terms, it was to Western's advantage to purchase the loom. However, if you had analyzed the lease from the lessor's viewpoint, you would have found that it was more profitable for Aubey Automation to lease the machine than to sell it — in fact, the manager of Aubey has found that the company can lower the lease payment to $30,000 and still make more by leasing the machine than by selling it. With an annual lease payment of $30,000, should the loom be leased or bought?
f. Perform the lease analysis assuming that Western's marginal tax rate is (1) 0 percent and (2) 50 percent. Assume a lease payment of $30,500 and a 15 percent pre-tax discount rate. What effect, if any, would the lessee's tax rate have on the lease-buy decision?

MINI CASE

Lewis Securities Inc. has decided to acquire a new market data and quotation system for its Richmond home office. The system receives current market prices and other information from several on-line data services, then either displays the information on a screen or stores it for later retrieval by the firm's brokers. The system also permits customers to call up current quotes on terminals in the lobby.

The equipment costs $1,000,000, and, if it were purchased, Lewis could obtain a term loan for the full purchase price at a 10 percent interest rate. The equipment is classified as a special-purpose computer, so it falls into the MACRS 3-year class. If the system were purchased, a 4-year maintenance contract could be obtained at a cost of $20,000 per year, payable at the *beginning* of each year. The equipment would be sold after 4 years, and the best estimate of its residual value at that time is $100,000. However, since real-time display system technology is changing rapidly, the actual residual value is uncertain.

As an alternative to the borrow-and-buy plan, the equipment manufacturer informed Lewis that Consolidated Leasing would be willing to write a 4-year guideline lease on the equipment, including maintenance, for payments of $280,000 at the *beginning* of each year. Lewis's marginal federal-plus-state tax rate is 40 percent. You have been asked to analyze the lease-versus-purchase decision, and in the process to answer the following questions:

a. (1) Who are the two parties to a lease transaction?
   (2) What are the four primary types of leases, and what are their characteristics?
   (3) How are leases classified for tax purposes?
   (4) What effect does leasing have on a firm's balance sheet?
   (5) What effect does leasing have on a firm's capital structure?
b. (1) What is the present value cost of owning the equipment? (Hint: Set up a time line which shows the net cash flows over the period t = 0 to t = 4, and then find the PV of these net cash flows, or PV cost of owning.)
   (2) Explain the rationale for the discount rate you used to find the PV.
c. What is Lewis's present value cost of leasing the equipment? (Hint: Again, construct a time line.)
d. What is the net advantage to leasing (NAL)? Does your analysis indicate that Lewis should buy or lease the equipment? Explain.
e. Now assume that the equipment's residual value could be as low as $0 or as high as $200,000, but that $100,000 is the expected value. Since the residual value is riskier than the other cash flows in the analysis, this differential risk should be incorporated into the analysis. Describe how this could be accomplished. (No calculations are necessary, but explain how you would modify the analysis if calculations were required.) What effect would increased uncertainty about the residual value have on Lewis's lease-versus-purchase decision?
f. The lessee compares the cost of owning the equipment with the cost of leasing it. Now put yourself in the lessor's shoes. In a few sentences, how should you analyze the decision to write or not write the lease?
g. (1) Assume that the lease payments were actually $300,000 per year, that Consolidated Leasing is also in the 40 percent tax bracket, and that it also forecasts a $100,000 residual value. Also, to furnish the maintenance support, Consolidated would have to purchase a maintenance contract from the manufacturer at the same $20,000 annual cost, again paid in advance. Consolidated Leasing can obtain an expected 10 percent pre-tax return on investments of similar risk. What would Consolidated's NPV and IRR of leasing be under these conditions?
   (2) What do you think the lessor's NPV would be if the lease payment were set at $280,000 per year? (Hint: The lessor's cash flows would be a "mirror image" of the lessee's cash flows.)
h. Lewis's management has been considering moving to a new downtown location, and they are concerned that these plans may come to fruition prior to the expiration of the lease. If the move occurs, Lewis would buy or lease an entirely new set of equipment, and hence management would like to include a cancellation clause in the lease contract. What impact would such a clause have on the riskiness of the lease from Lewis's standpoint? From the lessor's standpoint? If you were the lessor, would you insist on changing any of the lease terms if a cancellation clause were added? Should the cancellation clause contain any restrictive covenants and/or penalties of the type contained in bond indentures or provisions similar to call premiums?

Selected Additional References and Cases

For a description of lease analysis in practice, as well as a comprehensive bibliography of the leasing literature, see

Mukherjee, Tarun K., "A Survey of Corporate Leasing Analysis," *Financial Management,* Autumn 1991, 96–107.

O'Brien, Thomas J., and Bennie H. Nunnally, Jr., "A 1982 Survey of Corporate Leasing Analysis," *Financial Management,* Summer 1983, 30–36.

Many of the theoretical issues surrounding lease analysis are discussed in the following articles:

Finucane, Thomas J., "Some Empirical Evidence on the Use of Financial Leases," *The Journal of Financial Research,* Fall 1988, 321–333.

Hochman, Shalom, and Ramon Rabinovitch, "Financial Leasing under Inflation," *Financial Management,* Spring 1984, 17–26.

Levy, Haim, and Marshall Sarnat, "Leasing, Borrowing, and Financial Risk," *Financial Management,* Winter 1979, 47–54.

Lewellen, Wilbur G., Michael S. Long, and John J. McConnell, "Asset Leasing in Competitive Capital Markets," *Journal of Finance,* June 1976, 787–798.

Miller, Merton H., and Charles W. Upton, "Leasing, Buying, and the Cost of Capital Services," *Journal of Finance,* June 1976, 761–786.

Schall, Lawrence D., "The Evaluation of Lease Financing Opportunities," *Midland Corporate Finance Journal,* Spring 1985, 48–65.

Leveraged lease analysis is discussed in these articles:

Athanasopoulos, Peter J., and Peter W. Bacon, "The Evaluation of Leveraged Leases," *Financial Management,* Spring 1980, 76–80.

Dyl, Edward A., and Stanley A. Martin, Jr., "Setting Terms for Leveraged Leases," *Financial Management,* Winter 1977, 20–27.

Grimlund, Richard A., and Robert Capettini, "A Note on the Evaluation of Leveraged Leases and Other Investments," *Financial Management,* Summer 1982, 68–72.

Perg, Wayne F., "Leveraged Leasing: The Problem of Changing Leverage," *Financial Management,* Autumn 1978, 47–51.

For a discussion of realized returns on lease contracts, see

Lease, Ronald C., John J. McConnell, and James S. Schallheim, "Realized Returns and the Default and Prepayment Experience of Financial Leasing Contracts," *Financial Management,* Summer 1990, 11–20.

The Summer 1987 issue of Financial Management *contains articles by H. Martin Weingartner, Roger L. Cason, and Lawrence D. Schall which focus on the impact of asset life uncertainty on lease analysis.*

The Option Pricing Model (OPM) has been used in lease analysis by

Copeland, Thomas E., and J. Fred Weston, "A Note on the Evaluation of Cancellable Operating Leases," *Financial Management,* Summer 1982, 60–67.

Lee, Wayne Y., John D. Martin, and Andrew J. Senchack, "The Case for Using Options to Evaluate Salvage Values in Financial Leases," *Financial Management,* Autumn 1982, 33–41.

For a discussion of the impact of the AMT on lease decisions, see

"The Effect of the Corporate Alternative Minimum Tax: Amount, Duration, and Effect on the Lease versus Buy Decision," *The Journal of Equipment Lease Financing,* Spring 1989, 7–26.

The Cases in Financial Management: Dryden Request *series contains the following cases which deal with lease analysis:*

Case 25, "Environmental Sciences, Inc.," Case 25A, "Agro Chemical Corporation," and Case 25B, "Friendly Food Stores, Inc.," Case 26, "Prudent Solutions, Inc.," and Case 61, "AgroGrow, Inc.," all of which examine the lease decision from the perspectives of both the lessee and the lessor.

EXTENSIONS

Percentage Cost Analysis

Anderson's lease-versus-purchase decision could also be analyzed using the percentage cost approach. Here we know the after-tax cost of debt, 6.0 percent, so we can find the *after-tax cost rate implied in the lease contract* and compare it with the cost of the loan. Signing a lease is similar to signing a loan contract—the firm has the use of equipment, but it must make a series of payments under either type of contract. We know the rate built into the loan; it is 6.0 percent after taxes

for Anderson. There is an equivalent cost rate built into the lease. If the equivalent after-tax cost rate in the lease is less than the after-tax interest rate on the debt, then there is an advantage to leasing.

Table 19E-1 sets forth the cash flows needed to determine the equivalent loan cost. Here is an explanation of the table:

1. The net cost to purchase the equipment, which is avoided if Anderson leases, is shown on Line 1 as a positive cash flow (an inflow) at Year 0. If Anderson leases, it avoids hav-

TABLE 19E-1	Anderson Equipment Company: IRR Analysis (Thousands of Dollars)					
	YEAR 0	YEAR 1	YEAR 2	YEAR 3	YEAR 4	YEAR 5
1. Avoided net purchase price	$10,000					
2. After-tax lease payment	(1,650)	($1,650)	($1,650)	($1,650)	($1,650)	
3. Lost depreciation tax savings		(800)	(1,280)	(760)	(480)	($ 440)
4. Avoided after-tax maintenance cost	300	300	300	300	300	
5. Lost after-tax residual value						(840)
6. Net cash flow	$ 8,650	($2,150)	($2,630)	($2,110)	($1,830)	($1,280)

$$NPV = \sum_{t=0}^{5} \frac{NCF_t}{(1 + k_L)^t} = 0 \text{ when } k_L = IRR = 5.5\%.$$

ing to pay the net purchase price for the equipment—the lessor pays that cost—so Anderson saves $10 million. That is a positive cash flow at Year 0.

2. Next, we must determine what Anderson must give up (or "pay back") if it leases. As we saw earlier, Anderson must make annual lease payments of $2,750,000, which amount to $1,650,000 on an after-tax basis. These amounts are reported as cash outflows on Line 2, Years 0 through 4.

3. If Anderson elects to lease, it will give up the right to depreciate the asset. The lost depreciation tax savings, which represent an opportunity cost of leasing, are shown as outflows on Line 3, Years 1 through 5.

4. If Anderson decides to lease rather than borrow and buy, it will avoid the maintenance cost of $500,000 per year, or $300,000 after taxes. This is shown on Line 4 as an inflow, or benefit of leasing.

5. Finally, if Anderson leases the equipment, it will give up the net after-tax residual value of $840,000. This is also an opportunity cost of leasing, and it is shown on Line 5 as an outflow in Year 5.

6. Line 6 is a time line of the annual net cash flows. If Anderson leases, there is an inflow at Year 0 followed by outflows in Years 1 to 5. Note that the Line 6 net cash flows are simply the net cash flows of leasing rather than buying, or Line 11 minus Line 7 in Table 19-2.

By entering the cash flows on Line 6 into the cash flow register of a calculator and then pressing the IRR button, we can find the IRR for the stream; it is 5.5 percent, and this is the equivalent after-tax cost rate implied in the lease contract. If Anderson leases, it is using up $10 million of its debt capacity, and the implied cost rate is 5.5 percent. Since this cost rate is less than the 6.0 percent after-tax cost of a regular loan, this IRR analysis confirms the NPV analysis: Anderson should lease rather than buy the equipment. The NPV and IRR approaches will always lead to the same deci-

sion. Thus, one method is as good as the other from a decision standpoint.[1]

Feedback Effect on Capital Budgeting

Up to now, we have assumed that the potential lessee has already made a firm decision to acquire the new equipment. Thus, the lease analysis was conducted only to determine whether the equipment should be leased or purchased. However, if the cost of leasing is less than the cost of debt, it is possible for projects formerly deemed unacceptable to become acceptable.

To illustrate this point, assume that Anderson's target capital structure calls for 50 percent debt and 50 percent common equity, that Anderson's cost of debt, k_d, is 10 percent, and that its cost of equity, k_s, is 15 percent. Thus, Anderson's weighted average cost of capital is

$$WACC = 0.5(10\%)(0.60) + 0.5(15\%)$$

$$= 0.5(6.0\%) + 0.5(15\%) = 10.5\%.$$

Further, assume that the firm's initial capital budgeting analysis on this equipment, using a 10.5 percent project cost of capital for average-risk projects, resulted in an NPV of −$50,000. As we saw in the preceding section, the after-tax cost of leasing for this project is 5.5 percent, compared with Anderson's after-tax cost of debt of 6.0 percent. Thus, this project can be financed at a lower cost than other projects which involve equipment that cannot be leased.

What should we do now? There are two possible polar positions, depending on Anderson's opportunity to substitute lease financing for regular debt financing:

1. **The debt component of all projects can be financed by leasing on similar terms.** In this case, Anderson should never borrow—all "debt" financing should come from leasing. If it had a capital budget of $100 million, and if its

---

[1]Note that the net cash flows shown on Line 6 are the incremental cash flows to Anderson if it leases rather than borrows and buys. Thus, the NPV of these flows is the net advantage to leasing. When discounted at a rate of 6.0 percent, the NPV of the Line 6 flows is $103,389, which, except for a rounding difference, is the same as we obtained in the Table 19-2 NPV analysis.

optimal capital structure called for 50 percent debt, then it should lease assets with a cost of $50 million and finance the remainder with equity. All projects should be evaluated at a WACC based on the debt cost implied in the lease contracts, 5.5 percent in our example. Thus for all average-risk projects,

$$\text{WACC for use in capital budgeting} = 0.5(5.5\%) + 0.5(15\%) = 10.25\%.$$

Anderson's capital budgeting director should now recalculate the project's NPV using a cost of capital of 10.25 percent versus the average project cost of capital, ignoring leasing, of 10.5 percent. Assume that the project's NPV is now +$20,000. The availability of lease financing has made the project acceptable.

2. **The project under consideration is unique—it is the only one for which favorable lease terms are available.** In this case, with the further assumption that the cost of the project does not exceed the company's incremental debt capacity, the NPV of the project for capital budgeting purposes should be determined as follows:

$$\text{Adjusted NPV} = \frac{\text{NPV based on}}{\text{"regular" WACC}} + \frac{\text{NAL from}}{\text{Table 19-2}}$$

$$= -\$50,000 + \$104,000 = \$54,000.$$

Here the firm has enough debt capacity to finance the project entirely by leasing, so the firm will get the entire NAL. (If all projects were suitable for leasing, they still could not all be leased because some equity would be required. Therefore, under the conditions of the preceding paragraph, this procedure would not be appropriate.) The entire NAL should be allocated to this project. All other projects should be evaluated on the basis of the WACC with "regular" debt.

If neither polar position holds, or if different projects can be leased on different lease terms with different equivalent loan rates, then no simple rule can be used. Note, though, that as a practical matter we rarely need to go into the feedback effects of leasing on capital budgeting in the first place, because few projects that are not acceptable under one financing method would be acceptable under another. Given all the uncertainties about capital budgeting cash flows, few managers would change their minds about the acceptability of a project as a result of a few basis points change in the WACC. Still, for certain types of businesses the availability of lease financing could make the difference in the go/no-go decision. Therefore, it is important for financial managers to know how leasing might affect capital budgeting analysis.

Leveraged Lease Analysis

When leasing began, only two parties were involved in a lease transaction—the lessor, who put up the money, and the lessee. In recent years, however, a new type of lease, the *leveraged lease,* has come into widespread use. Under a leveraged lease, the lessor arranges to borrow part of the required funds, generally giving the lender a first mortgage on the plant or equipment being leased. The lessor still receives the tax benefits associated with accelerated depreciation. However, the lessor now has a riskier position, because of the use of financial leverage.

Such leveraged leases, often with syndicates of wealthy individuals seeking tax shelters acting as owner-lessors, are an important part of the financial scene today. Incidentally, whether or not a lease is leveraged is not important to the lessee; from the lessee's standpoint, the method of analyzing a proposed lease is unaffected by whether or not the lessor borrows part of the required capital.

The example in Table 19E-1 is not set up as a leveraged lease. However, it would be easy enough to modify the analysis if the lessor borrows all or part of the required $10 million, making the transaction a leveraged lease. First, we would add a set of lines to Table 19E-1 to show the financing cash flows. The interest component would represent another tax deduction, while the loan repayments would constitute additional cash outlays. The initial cost of the asset would be reduced by the amount of the loan. With these changes made, a new NPV and IRR could be calculated and used to evaluate whether or not the lease represents a good investment.

To illustrate, assume that the lessor can borrow $5 million of the $10 million net purchase price at a rate of 9 percent on a five-year simple interest loan. Table 19E-2 contains the lessor's leveraged lease NPV analysis. The NPV of the leveraged lease investment based on the net cash flows shown on Line 3 is $26,000, which is the same as the $26,000 NPV for the

TABLE 19E-2	Leveraged Lease Analysis (Thousands of Dollars)					
	YEAR 0	**YEAR 1**	**YEAR 2**	**YEAR 3**	**YEAR 4**	**YEAR 5**
1. Net cash flow from Table 19E-1	($8,650)	$2,150	$2,630	$2,110	$1,830	$1,280
2. Leveraging cash flows[a]	5,000	(270)	(270)	(270)	(270)	(5,270)
3. Net cash flow	($3,650)	$1,880	$2,360	$1,840	$1,560	($3,990)

$$\text{NPV} = \sum_{t=0}^{5} \frac{\text{NCF}_t}{(1+k)^t} = \$26 \text{ when } k = 5.4\%.$$

[a]The lessor borrows $5 million at t = 0 and repays it at t = 5. Interest expense, payable at the end of each year, is 0.09($5,000) = $450, but it is tax deductible, so the after-tax interest cash flow is −$450(1 − T) = −$450(0.6) = −$270.

unleveraged lease. Note, though, that the lessor has spent only $3.65 million on this lease. Therefore, the lessor could invest in a total of 2.37 similar leveraged leases for the same $8.65 million investment required to finance a single unleveraged lease, producing a total net present value of 2.37($26,000) = $61,620.

The effect of leverage on the lessor's return is also reflected in the leveraged lease's IRR. The IRR is that discount rate which equates the sum of the present values of the Line 3 cash flows to zero. We find the IRR of the leveraged lease to be about 8.5 percent, which is substantially higher than the 5.5 percent after-tax return on the unleveraged lease.[2]

Typically, leveraged leases provide lessors with higher expected rates of return (IRRs) and higher NPVs per dollar of invested capital than unleveraged leases. However, such leases are also riskier for the same reason that any leveraged investment is riskier. Since leveraged leases are a relatively new development, no standard methodology has been developed for analyzing them in a risk/return framework. However, sophisticated lessors are now developing Monte Carlo simulations similar to those described in Chapter 13. Then, given the apparent riskiness of the lease investment, the lessor can decide whether the returns built into the contract are sufficient to compensate for the risk involved.

---

[2]Note two additional points concerning the leveraged lease analysis. First, in this situation, leveraging had no impact on the lessor's per-lease NPV. This is because the cost of the loan to the lessor (5.4 percent after taxes) equals the discount rate, and hence the leveraging cash flows are netted out on a present value basis. Second, the leveraged lease has multiple IRRs, one at 0.0 percent and another at approximately 8.5 percent. Leveraged leases frequently have two IRRs.

HYBRID FINANCING:
PREFERRED STOCK,
WARRANTS, AND CONVERTIBLES

*T*he use of convertible securities—generally bonds or preferred stocks that can be exchanged for common stock of the issuing corporation—has soared during the last decade. In 1995, U.S. firms issued $125 billion of convertibles, a fourfold increase from ten years earlier.

Why do companies use convertibles so heavily? To answer this question, recognize that convertibles virtually always have coupon rates that are lower than would be required on straight, nonconvertible bonds or preferred stocks. Therefore, if a company raises $100 million by issuing convertible bonds, its interest expense is lower than if it financed with nonconvertible debt. But why would investors be willing to buy convertibles, given their lower cash payments? The answer lies in the conversion feature—if the price of the issuer's stock rises, the holder of the convertible can exchange it for stock and realize a capital gain. So, convertibles hold down the cash costs of financing by giving investors an opportunity for capital gains.

Convertibles can work out well or badly for investors and companies alike. To illustrate, a few years ago MCI issued $1.3 billion of convertible bonds at a rate 4 percentage points lower than its cost would have been on nonconvertible debt. Investors who purchased the issue expected MCI's stock price to rise, at which point they would exchange the debt for stock and earn a capital gain. However, MCI's stock price didn't rise to the point where it was attractive to convert, and when the issue became callable, MCI called the bonds, thus eliminating the conversion option and any possibility of capital gains.

An example with a different result is Hercules Inc.'s $68 million issue in 1990. The coupon rate was set at 8 percent, 3.5 percentage points less than the 11.5 percent required on the company's nonconvertible debt. However, Hercules's stock has since soared, and a $1,000 original investment in the convertibles was worth $3,310 in 1998.

Investors also like convertibles because they are safer than stocks—if things don't go well for the company, the convertibles still have the stability associated with debt. However, even the best laid financial plans can go awry. For example, in 1994 Boston Chicken, whose stock price had recently gone from $20 to $51 in one day, issued $130 million of convertible bonds. Then, the issue was hit with a "double whammy"—the stock price fell, and interest rates rose. This lowered the value of both the underlying bond and the conversion option, and, as a result, the convertibles dropped by 30 percent.

Like all securities, convertibles offer pros and cons to both issuers and investors. When you finish this chapter, you should have a much better understanding of how convertibles are valued and why a firm might choose to issue a convertible bond rather than either straight debt or common stock.

In earlier chapters, we have examined common stock, various types of long-term debt, and leasing. In this chapter, we examine three other sources of long-term capital: preferred stock, which is a hybrid security that represents a cross between debt and common equity; warrants, which are derivative securities; and convertibles, which are hybrids between debt (or preferred stock) and warrants.

PREFERRED STOCK

Preferred stock is a **hybrid**—it is similar to bonds in some respects and to common stock in other ways. Accountants classify preferred stock as equity, hence show it on the balance sheet as an equity account. However, from a finance perspective preferred stock lies somewhere between debt and common equity—it imposes a fixed charge and thus increases the firm's financial leverage, yet omitting the preferred dividend does not force a company into bankruptcy. We first describe the basic features of preferred, after which we describe some recent innovations in preferred stock financing.

Basic Features

Preferred stock has a par (or liquidating) value, often either $25 or $100. The dividend is stated as either a percentage of par, as so many dollars per share, or both ways. For example, several years ago Klondike Paper Company sold 150,000 shares of $100 par value perpetual preferred stock for a total of $15 million. This preferred had a stated annual dividend of $12 per share, so the preferred dividend yield was $12/$100 = 0.12, or 12 percent, at the time of issue. The dividend was set when the stock was issued; it will not be changed in the future. Therefore, if the required rate of return on preferred, k_{ps}, changes from 12 percent after the issue date—as it did—then the market price of the preferred stock will go up or down. Currently, k_{ps} for Klondike Paper's preferred is 9 percent, and the price of the preferred has risen from $100 to $12/0.09 = $133.33.

If the preferred dividend is not earned, the company does not have to pay it. However, most preferred issues are **cumulative**, meaning that the cumulative total of all unpaid preferred dividends must be paid before dividends can be paid on the common stock. Unpaid preferred dividends are called **arrearages.** Dividends in arrears do not earn interest; thus, arrearages do not grow in a compound interest sense—they only grow from additional nonpayments of the preferred dividend. Also, many preferred stocks accrue arrearages for only a limited number of years, say, three years, meaning that the cumulative feature ceases after three years. However, the dividends in arrears continue in force until they are paid.

Preferred stock normally has no voting rights. However, most preferred issues stipulate that the preferred stockholders can elect a minority of the directors—say, three out of ten—if the preferred dividend is passed (omitted). Jersey Central Power & Light, one of the companies that owned a share of the Three Mile Island (TMI) nuclear plant, had preferred stock outstanding which could elect a *majority* of the directors if the preferred dividend was passed for four successive quarters. Jersey Central kept paying its preferred dividends even during the dark days following the TMI accident. Had the preferred not been entitled to elect a majority of the directors, the dividend would probably have been passed.

Although nonpayment of preferred dividends will not bankrupt a company, corporations issue preferred with every intention of paying the dividend. Even if passing the dividend does not give the preferred stockholders control of the company, failure to pay a preferred dividend precludes payment of common dividends. In addition, passing the dividend makes it difficult to raise capital by selling bonds, and virtually impossible to sell more preferred or common stock. However, having preferred stock outstanding does give a firm the chance to overcome its difficulties—if bonds had been used instead of preferred stock, Jersey Central would have been in danger of being forced into bankruptcy before it could straighten out its problems. *Thus, from the viewpoint of the issuing corporation, preferred stock is less risky than bonds.*

However, for investors preferred stock is riskier than bonds: (1) Preferred stockholders' claims are subordinated to those of bondholders in the event of liquidation, and (2) bondholders are more likely to continue receiving income during hard times than are preferred stockholders. Accordingly, investors require a higher after-tax rate of return on a given firm's preferred stock than on its bonds. However, since 70 percent of preferred dividends is exempt from corporate taxes, preferred stock is attractive to corporate investors. In recent years, high-grade preferred stock, on average, has sold on a lower pre-tax yield basis than have high-grade bonds. As an example, Du Pont's preferred stock recently had a market yield of about 7.0 percent, whereas its bonds provided a yield of 8.3 percent, or 1.3 percentage points *more* than its preferred. The tax treatment accounted for this differential; the *after-tax yield* to corporate investors was greater on the preferred stock than on the bonds.[1]

About half of all preferred stock issued in recent years has been convertible into common stock. For example, Enron Corporation issued preferred stock which stipulated that one share of preferred could be converted into three shares of common, at the option of the preferred stockholder. Convertibles are discussed at length in a later section.

Some preferred stocks are similar to perpetual bonds in that they have no maturity date, but most new issues now have specified maturities. For example, many preferred shares have a sinking fund provision which calls for the retirement of 2 percent of the issue each year, meaning that the issue will "mature" in a maximum of 50 years. Also, many preferred issues are callable by the issuing corporation, which can also limit the life of the preferred.[2]

Nonconvertible preferred stock is virtually all owned by corporations, which can take advantage of the 70 percent dividend exclusion to obtain a higher after-tax yield on preferred stock than on bonds. Individuals should not own preferred stocks (except convertible preferreds)—they can get higher yields on safer bonds, so it is not logical for them to hold preferreds. As a result of this ownership pattern, the volume of preferred stock financing is geared to the supply of money in the hands of corporate investors. When the supply of such money is plentiful, the prices of preferred stocks are

---

[1] The after-tax yield on an 8.3 percent bond to a corporate investor in the 34 percent marginal tax rate bracket is $8.3\%(1 - T) = 8.3\%(0.66) = 5.48\%$. The after-tax yield on a 7.0 percent preferred stock is $7.0\%(1 -$ Effective $T) = 7.0\%[1 - (0.30)(0.34)] = 7.0\%(0.898) = 6.29\%$. Also, note that tax law prohibits firms from issuing debt and then using the proceeds to purchase another firm's preferred or common stock. If debt is used for stock purchases, then the 70 percent dividend exclusion is voided. This provision is designed to prevent a firm from engaging in "tax arbitrage," using tax-deductible debt to purchase largely tax-exempt preferred stock.

[2] Prior to the late 1970s, virtually all preferred stock was perpetual, and almost no issues had sinking funds or call provisions. Then, insurance company regulators, worried about the unrealized losses the companies had been incurring on preferred holdings as a result of rising interest rates, put into effect some regulatory changes which essentially mandated that insurance companies buy only limited life preferreds. From that time on, virtually no new preferred has been perpetual. This example illustrates the way securities change as a result of changes in the economic environment.

bid up, their yields fall, and investment bankers suggest that companies which need financing consider issuing preferred stock.

For issuers, preferred stock has a tax *disadvantage* relative to debt—interest expense is deductible, but preferred dividends are not. Still, firms with low tax rates may have an incentive to issue preferred stock which can be bought by corporate investors with high tax rates, who can take advantage of the 70 percent dividend exclusion. If a firm has a lower tax rate than potential corporate buyers, the firm might be better off issuing preferred stock than debt. The key here is that the tax advantage to a high-tax-rate corporation is greater than the tax disadvantage to a low-tax-rate issuer. To illustrate, assume that risk differentials between debt and preferred would require an issuer to set the interest rate on new debt at 10 percent and the dividend yield on new preferred at 12 percent in a no-tax world. However, when taxes are considered, a corporate buyer with a high tax rate, say, 40 percent, might be willing to buy the preferred stock if it has an 8 percent before-tax yield. This would produce an $8\%(1 - \text{Effective T}) = 8\%[1 - 0.30(0.40)] = 7.04\%$ after-tax return on the preferred versus $10\%(1 - 0.40) = 6.0\%$ on the debt. If the issuer has a low tax rate, say, 10 percent, its after-tax costs would be $10\%(1 - T) = 10\%(0.90) = 9\%$ on the bonds and 8 percent on the preferred. Thus, the security with lower risk to the issuer, preferred stock, also has a lower cost. Such situations can make preferred stock a logical financing choice.[3]

Other Types of Preferred Stock

In addition to the "plain vanilla" variety of preferred stocks, several variations are also used. Two of these, floating rate and market auction preferred, are discussed in the Extension to this chapter.

Advantages and Disadvantages of Preferred Stock

There are both advantages and disadvantages to financing with preferred stock. Here are the major advantages from the issuers' standpoint:

1. In contrast to bonds, the obligation to pay preferred dividends is not contractual, and passing a preferred dividend cannot force a firm into bankruptcy.
2. By issuing preferred stock, the firm avoids the dilution of common equity that occurs when common stock is sold.
3. Since preferred stock sometimes has no maturity, and since preferred sinking fund payments, if present, are typically spread over a long period, preferred issues reduce the cash flow drain from repayment of principal that occurs with debt issues.

There are two major disadvantages:

1. Preferred stock dividends are not deductible to the issuer, hence the after-tax cost of preferred is typically higher than the after-tax cost of debt. However, the tax advantage of preferreds to corporate purchasers lowers its pre-tax cost and thus its effective cost.
2. Although preferred dividends can be passed, investors expect them to be paid, and firms intend to pay the dividends if conditions permit. Thus, preferred dividends are

---

[3]For a more rigorous treatment of the tax hypothesis of preferred stock, see Iraj Fooladi and Gordon S. Roberts, "On Preferred Stock," *Journal of Financial Research*, Winter 1986, 319–324. For an example of an empirical test of the hypothesis, see Arthur L. Houston, Jr., and Carol Olson Houston, "Financing with Preferred Stock," *Financial Management*, Autumn 1990, 42–54.

considered to be a fixed cost. Therefore, their use, like that of debt, increases financial risk and thus the cost of common equity.

S E L F - T E S T
Q U E S T I O N S

Should preferred stock be considered as equity or debt? Explain.

Who are the major purchasers of nonconvertible preferred stock? Why?

What are the advantages and disadvantages of preferred stock to the issuer?

WARRANTS

A **warrant** is a certificate issued by a company which gives the holder the right to buy a stated number of shares of the company's stock at a specified price for some specified length of time. Generally, warrants are distributed with debt, and they are used to induce investors to buy long-term debt with a lower coupon rate than would otherwise be required. For example, when Infomatics Corporation, a rapidly growing high-tech company, wanted to sell $50 million of 20-year bonds in 1998, the company's investment bankers informed the financial vice-president that the bonds would be difficult to sell, and that a coupon rate of 10 percent would be required. However, as an alternative the bankers suggested that investors might be willing to buy the bonds with a coupon rate of only 8 percent if the company would offer 20 warrants with each $1,000 bond, each warrant entitling the holder to buy one share of common stock at an **exercise price** of $22 per share. The stock was selling for $20 per share at the time, and the warrants would expire in the year 2008 if they had not been exercised previously.

Why would investors be willing to buy Infomatics' bonds at a yield of only 8 percent in a 10 percent market just because warrants were also offered as part of the package? It is because the warrants are long-term **call options** which have value because holders can buy the firm's common stock at the exercise price regardless of how high the market price climbs. This option offsets the low interest rate on the bonds and makes the package of low-yield bonds plus warrants attractive to investors. (See Chapter 24 for a more complete discussion of options.)

Initial Market Price of a Bond with Warrants

The Infomatics bonds, if they had been issued as straight debt, would have carried a 10 percent interest rate. However, with warrants attached, the bonds were sold to yield 8 percent. Someone buying the bonds at their $1,000 initial offering price would thus be receiving a package consisting of an 8 percent, 20-year bond plus 20 warrants. Since the going interest rate on bonds as risky as those of Infomatics was 10 percent, we can find the straight-debt value of the bonds, assuming an annual coupon for ease of illustration, as follows:

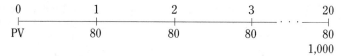

Using a financial calculator, input $N = 20$, $I = 10$, $PMT = 80$, and $FV = 1000$. Then, press the PV key to obtain the bond's value, $829.73, or approximately $830. Thus, a person buying the bonds in the initial underwriting would pay $1,000 and receive in exchange a straight bond worth about $830 plus 20 warrants presumably worth about $1,000 − $830 = $170:

$$\frac{\text{Price paid for}}{\text{bond with warrants}} = \frac{\text{Straight-debt}}{\text{value of bond}} + \frac{\text{Value of}}{\text{warrants}}$$

$$\$1,000 \quad = \quad \$830 \quad + \quad \$170.$$

Since investors receive 20 warrants with each bond, each warrant has an implied value of $170/20 = $8.50.

The key issue in setting the terms of a bond-with-warrants is valuing the warrants. The straight-debt value can be estimated quite accurately, as was done above. However, it is more difficult to estimate the value of the warrants. The Black-Scholes Option Pricing Model (OPM), which we discuss in Chapter 24, can be used to find the value of a call option. There is a temptation to use this model to find the value of a warrant, since call options are similar to warrants in many respects: Both give the investor the right to buy a share of stock at a fixed exercise price on or before the expiration date. However, there is a major difference between call options and warrants. When call options are exercised, the stock provided to the option-holder comes from the secondary market, but when warrants are exercised, the stock provided to the warrant holders are newly issued shares. This means that the exercise of warrants dilutes the value of the original equity, which could cause the value of the original warrant to differ from the value of a similar call option. Therefore, investment bankers cannot use the Black-Scholes model to determine the value of warrants.

It is extremely important to assign the correct value to the warrants. If, when the issue is originally priced, the value assigned to the warrants is greater than their true market value, then the coupon rate on the bonds will be set too low, and it will be impossible to sell the bond-with-warrants package at its par value. In this case, Infomatics will not be able to raise the full $50 million that it needs to fund its growth.

Conversely, if the value of the warrants is underestimated, then the coupon rate will be set too high. This means that the true value of the bonds with warrants will be greater than the issue price. Suppose this happens, and the true value of the bonds with warrants is $60 million. Investors will eagerly buy all of the bonds with warrants at the issue price, and Infomatics will receive the full $50 million that it needs. But this is not good news for the existing shareholders.

To see this, think of the total value of Infomatics as being analogous to a pie. The size of the pie is equal to the present value of all the future cash flows expected to be generated by Infomatics' operations and investments. Pieces of the pie belong to different groups of investors, such as debtholders and holders of bonds with warrants. Shareholders come last and get the remaining piece of the pie, after the other investors have received their fair share.

At the time of the bond offering, Infomatics had 10 million shares of common stock outstanding and no other debt or preferred stock. The stock price was $20 per share, so the total market value of Infomatics was 10($20) = $200 million. The offering itself will raise $50 million in cash, which will subsequently be invested in projects. Therefore, immediately after the offering the total value of Infomatics is $250 million ($200 million in stock plus $50 million in cash).[4] If investors in the bonds with warrants pay only

---

[4]We assume that the average expected net present value of these projects is zero. If the NPV of the projects is greater than zero, then the total value of Infomatics will be greater than $250 million. In this case, there will be little change in the price of the bonds, since bondholders receive the fixed coupon payment no matter how well the company does. However, the stock price and the value of the warrants will increase, since the total value of the company has increased without a commensurate increase in the value committed to the bondholders. The reverse would occur if the expected NPV of the projects is less than zero.

$50 million for a piece of pie that is worth $60 million, then the piece of pie remaining for the original shareholders is only worth $190 million ($250 million − $60 million). The result is a $10 million transfer of wealth from the original shareholders to the investors in the bonds with warrants. Therefore, it is extremely important for Infomatics to correctly estimate the value of the warrants at the time the bonds with warrants are issued.

Use of Warrants in Financing

Warrants generally are used by small, rapidly growing firms as "sweeteners" when they sell debt or preferred stock. Such firms frequently are regarded by investors as being highly risky, so their bonds can be sold only at extremely high coupon rates and with very restrictive indenture provisions. To avoid this, firms such as Infomatics often offer warrants along with the bonds. However, some years ago, AT&T raised $1.57 billion by selling bonds with warrants. This was the largest financing of any type ever undertaken by a business firm, and it marked the first use ever of warrants by a large, strong corporation.[5]

Getting warrants along with bonds enables investors to share in the company's growth, assuming it does in fact grow and prosper. Therefore, investors are willing to accept a lower interest rate and less restrictive indenture provisions. A bond with warrants has some characteristics of debt and some characteristics of equity. It is a hybrid security that provides the financial manager with an opportunity to expand the firm's mix of securities and thus to appeal to a broader group of investors.

Virtually all warrants today are **detachable.** Thus, after a bond with attached warrants is sold, the warrants can be detached and traded separately from the bond. Further, even after the warrants have been exercised, the bond (with its low coupon rate) remains outstanding.

The exercise price on warrants is generally set some 20 to 30 percent above the market price of the stock on the date the bond is issued. If the firm grows and prospers, and if its stock price rises above the exercise price at which shares may be purchased, warrant holders could exercise their warrants and buy stock at the stated price. However, without some incentive, warrants would never be exercised prior to maturity—their value in the open market would be greater than their value if exercised, so holders would sell warrants rather than exercise them. There are three conditions which encourage holders to exercise their warrants: (1) Warrant holders will surely exercise and buy stock if the warrants are about to expire and the market price of the stock is above the exercise price. (2) Warrant holders will exercise voluntarily if the company raises the dividend on the common stock by a sufficient amount. No dividend is earned on the warrant, so it provides no current income. However, if the common stock pays a high dividend, it provides an attractive dividend yield but limits price growth. This induces warrant holders to exercise their

---

[5]It is interesting to note that before the AT&T issue, the New York Stock Exchange's stated policy was that warrants could not be listed because they were "speculative" instruments rather than "investment" securities. When AT&T issued warrants, however, the Exchange changed its policy, agreeing to list warrants that met certain requirements. Many other warrants have since been listed.

It is also interesting to note that, prior to the sale, AT&T's treasury staff, working with Morgan Stanley analysts, estimated the value of the warrants as a part of the underwriting decision. The package was supposed to sell for a total price in the neighborhood of $1,000. The bond value could be determined accurately, so the trick was to estimate the equilibrium value of the warrant under different possible exercise prices and years to expiration, and then to use an exercise price and life which would cause Bond value + Warrant value ≈ $1,000. Using a warrant pricing model, the AT&T/Morgan Stanley analysts set terms which caused the warrant to sell on the open market at a price that was only 35¢ off from the estimated price.

option to buy the stock. (3) Warrants sometimes have **stepped-up exercise prices,** which prod owners into exercising them. For example, Williamson Scientific Company has warrants outstanding with an exercise price of $25 until December 31, 2002, at which time the exercise price rises to $30. If the price of the common stock is over $25 just before December 31, 2002, many warrant holders will exercise their options before the stepped-up price takes effect and the value of the warrants falls.

Another desirable feature of warrants is that they generally bring in funds only if funds are needed. If the company grows, it will probably need new equity capital. At the same time, growth will cause the price of the stock to rise and the warrants to be exercised, hence the firm will obtain additional cash. If the company is not successful, and it cannot profitably employ additional money, the price of its stock will probably not rise sufficiently to induce exercise of the warrants.

Wealth Effects and Dilution Due to Warrants

Assume that the value of Infomatics' operations and investments, which is $250 million immediately after issuing the bonds with warrants, is expected to grow, and does grow, at 9 percent per year. When the warrants are due to expire in ten years, the total value of Infomatics will be $250(1.09)^{10} = 591.841 million. How is this value allocated among the original stockholders, the bondholders, and the warrant holders?

The bonds will have ten years remaining until maturity, with a fixed coupon payment of $80. If the expected market interest rate is still 10 percent, then:

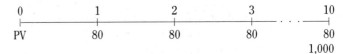

Using a financial calculator, input N = 10, I = 10, PMT = 80, and FV = 1000. Press the PV key to obtain the bond's value, $877.11. The total value of all of the bonds is 50,000($877.11) = $43.856 million.

The value remaining for the original stockholders and the warrant holders is equal to the remaining value of the firm, after deducting the value due to the bondholders. This remaining value is $591.841 − $43.856 = $547.985 million. If there had been no warrants, then the original stockholders would have been entitled to all of this remaining value. Recall that there are 10 million shares of stock, so the price per share would be $547.895/10 = $54.80. Suppose the company has a basic earning power of 13.5 percent (recall that BEP = EBIT/Total Assets) and total assets of $591.841 million.[6] This means that EBIT is 0.135($591.841) = $79.899 million; interest payments are $4 million ($80 coupon payment per bond × 50,000 bonds); and earnings before taxes are $79.899 − $4 = $75.899 million. With a tax rate of 40 percent, after-tax earnings are equal to $75.899(1 − 0.4) = $45.539 million, and earnings per share are $45.539/10 = $4.55. Therefore, if Infomatics had no warrants, the stock price would be $54.80 per share, and the earnings per share would be $4.55.

But Infomatics *does* have warrants, and with the stock price over $50 the warrant holders surely will choose to exercise their warrants. Infomatics will receive $22 mil-

---

[6]In this case, the total market value equals the book value of assets, but the same calculations would follow even if market and book values were not equal.

lion when the 1 million warrants are exercised at a price of $22 per warrant. This makes the total value $613.841 million (the $591.841 million value of operations plus the $22 million raised by the exercise of the warrants). The total value remaining for stockholders is now $569.985 million ($613.841 million less the $43.856 million allocated to bondholders). There are now 11 million shares of stock (the original 10 million plus the new 1 million due to the exercise of the warrants), so the stock price is $569.985/11 = $51.82 per share. Notice that this is lower than the $54.80 price per share that Infomatics would have had if there had been no warrants. In other words, the warrants have diluted the value of the stock.

A similar dilution occurs with earnings per share. After exercise, the asset base would increase from $591.841 million to $613.841 million, with the additional $22 million coming from the purchase of 1 million shares of stock at $22 per share. If the new funds have the same basic earning power as the existing funds, then the new EBIT would be 0.135($613.841) = $82.869 million. Interest payments would still be $4 million, so earnings before taxes would be $82.869 − $4 = $78.869 million, and after-tax earnings will be $78.869(1 − 0.4) = $47.321 million. With 10 + 1 = 11 million shares now outstanding, EPS would be $47.321/11 = $4.30, down from $4.55. Therefore, exercising the warrants would dilute EPS.

Has this wealth transfer harmed the original shareholders? The answer is yes and no. Yes, because the original shareholders clearly are worse off than they would have been if there had been no warrants. However, if there had been no warrants attached to the bonds, then the bonds would have had a 10 percent coupon rate instead of the 8 percent coupon rate. Also, if the value of the company had not increased as expected, then it might not have been profitable for the warrant holders to exercise their warrants. In other words, the original shareholders were willing to trade off the potential dilution for the lower coupon rate. In this example, the original stockholders and the investors in the bonds with warrants got what they expected. Therefore, the answer is no, the wealth transfer at the time of exercise did not harm the original shareholder, because they expected an eventual transfer and were fairly compensated by the lower coupon payments. As we show later, there are other instances when the wealth transfer is different than expected, leading to a real transfer of wealth from one class of investors to another.

Note too that investors would recognize the situation, so the actual wealth transfer would occur gradually over time, not in a fell swoop when the warrants were exercised. First, EPS would have been reported on a fully diluted basis over the years, and on that basis, there would be no decline whatever in EPS. Also, investors would know what was happening, so the stock price, over time, would reflect the likely future dilution, so it too would be stable when the warrants were exercised. So, whereas our calculations show the effects of the warrants, those effects would actually be reflected in EPS and the stock price on a gradual basis over time.

The Component Cost of Bonds with Warrants

When Infomatics issued its debt with warrants, the firm received $50 million, or $1,000 for each bond. Simultaneously, the company assumed an obligation to pay $80 interest for 20 years plus $1,000 at the end of 20 years. The pre-tax cost of the money would have been 10 percent if no warrants had been attached, but each Infomatics bond had 20 warrants, each of which entitles its holder to buy one share of Infomatics stock for $22. What is the percentage cost of the $50 million? As we shall see, the cost is well above the 8 percent coupon rate on the bonds.

As we demonstrated earlier, when the warrants expire ten years from now, the expected stock price is $51.82. The company would then have to issue one share of stock worth $51.82 for each warrant exercised and, in return, Infomatics would receive the exercise price, $22. Thus, a purchaser of the bonds, if he or she holds the complete package, would realize a profit in Year 10 of $51.82 − $22 = $29.82 for each common share issued. Since each bond has 20 warrants attached, investors would have a gain of 20($29.82) = $596.40 per bond at the end of Year 10. Here is a time line of the cash flow stream to an investor:

0	1		9	10	11		20
−$1,000	+$80	. . .	+$80	+$ 80.00	+$80	. . .	+ $ 80
				+ 596.40			+ 1,000
				+$676.40			+ $1,080

The IRR of this stream is 10.7 percent, which is the investor's overall pre-tax rate of return on the issue. This return is 70 basis points higher than the return on straight debt. This reflects the fact that the issue is riskier to investors than a straight-debt issue because some of the return is expected to come in the form of stock price appreciation, and that part of the return is relatively risky.

The expected rate of return to investors is the before-tax cost to the company—this was true of common stocks, straight bonds, and preferred stocks, and it is also true of bonds sold with warrants.

Problems with Warrant Issues

Although warrants are bought by investors with the expectation of receiving a total return commensurate with the overall riskiness of the package of securities being purchased, things do not always work out as expected. For example, in 1989 Sony paid $3.4 billion for Columbia Pictures, a U.S. movie studio. To help finance the deal, in 1990 Sony sold $470 million of four-year bonds with warrants at an incredibly low 0.3 percent coupon interest rate. The rate was so low because the warrants, which also had a maturity of four years, allowed investors to purchase Sony stock at 7,670 yen per share, only 2.5 percent above the share price at the time the bonds with warrants were issued.

Investors snapped up the issue, and many of the warrants were "peeled off" and sold separately on the open market. The warrant buyers obviously believed that Sony's stock would climb well above the exercise price. From Sony's point of view, the bond-with-warrants package provided a very low-cost "bridge loan" (the bonds) that would be replaced with equity financing when the warrants were exercised, presumably in four years when the bonds became due. This very low cost capital encouraged Japanese firms to acquire foreign companies and to invest huge amounts in new plant and equipment.

However, the willingness of investors to buy Japanese warrants suffered a severe blow when the Japanese stock market fell by 40 percent. By 1994, when the warrants expired, Sony's stock sold for only 5,950 yen versus the 7,670-yen exercise price, so the warrants were not exercised. Thus, Sony's planned infusion of equity capital never materialized, and it had to refinance the four-year bond issue at much higher rates.

Both Sony and its investors lost on the deal. The investors lost because they did not get the return they expected on the issue. Sony lost because it had to alter its financing plans due to the fact that the warrants were not exercised. In spite of presumably good planning by both the company and investors, this bond-with-warrants issue, and many like it, did not work out as anticipated.

What is a warrant?

Describe how a new bond issue with warrants is valued.

How are warrants used in corporate financing?

The use of warrants lowers the coupon rate on the corresponding debt issue. Does this mean that the component cost of a debt-plus-warrants package is less than the cost of straight debt? Explain.

CONVERTIBLES

Convertible securities are bonds or preferred stocks which, under specified terms and conditions, can be exchanged for (that is, converted into) common stock at the option of the holder. Unlike the exercise of warrants, which brings in additional funds to the firm, conversion does not provide capital: debt (or preferred stock) is simply replaced on the balance sheet by common stock. Of course, reducing the debt or preferred stock will improve the firm's financial strength and make it easier to raise additional capital, but that requires a separate action.

Conversion Ratio and Conversion Price

One of the most important provisions of a convertible security is the **conversion ratio, CR,** defined as the number of shares of stock a bondholder will receive upon conversion. Related to the conversion ratio is the **conversion price, P_c,** which is the effective price investors pay for the common stock when conversion occurs. The relationship between the conversion ratio and the conversion price can be illustrated by the Silicon Valley Software Company's convertible debentures, issued at their $1,000 par value in July of 1998. At any time prior to maturity on July 15, 2018, a debenture holder can exchange a bond for 20 shares of common stock; therefore, the conversion ratio, CR, is 20. The bond cost purchasers $1,000, the par value, when it was issued. Dividing the $1,000 par value by the 20 shares received gives a conversion price of $50 a share:

$$\text{Conversion price} = P_c = \frac{\text{Par value of bond}}{\text{Shares received}}$$

$$= \frac{\$1,000}{\text{CR}} = \frac{\$1,000}{20} = \$50.$$

Conversely, by solving for CR, we obtain the conversion ratio:

$$\text{Conversion ratio} = \text{CR} = \frac{\$1,000}{P_c} = \frac{\$1,000}{\$50} = 20 \text{ shares.}$$

Once CR is set, the value of P_c is established, and vice versa.

Like a warrant's exercise price, the conversion price is typically set at from 20 to 30 percent above the prevailing market price of the common stock at the time the convertible issue is sold. Exactly how the conversion price is established can best be understood after examining some of the reasons firms use convertibles.

Generally, the conversion price and conversion ratio are fixed for the life of the bond, although sometimes a stepped-up conversion price is used. For example, the 1998 convertible debentures for Breedon Industries are convertible into 12.5 shares until 2008; into 11.76 shares from 2008 until 2018; and into 11.11 shares from 2018 until maturity in 2028. The conversion price thus starts at $80, rises to $85, and then goes to $90. Breedon's convertibles, like most, have a ten-year call-protection period.

Another factor that may cause a change in the conversion price and ratio is a standard feature of almost all convertibles—the clause protecting the convertible against dilution from stock splits, stock dividends, and the sale of common stock at prices below the conversion price. The typical provision states that if common stock is sold at a price below the conversion price, then the conversion price must be lowered (and the conversion ratio raised) to the price at which the new stock was issued. Also, if the stock is split, or if a stock dividend is declared, the conversion price must be lowered by the percentage amount of the stock dividend or split. For example, if Breedon Industries were to have a two-for-one stock split during the first ten years of its convertible's life, the conversion ratio would automatically be adjusted from 12.5 to 25, and the conversion price lowered from $80 to $40. If this protection were not contained in the contract, a company could completely thwart conversion by the use of stock splits and stock dividends. Warrants are similarly protected against dilution.

The standard protection against dilution from selling new stock at prices below the conversion price can, however, get a company into trouble. For example, assume that Breedon's stock was selling for $65 per share at the time the convertible was issued. Further, suppose the market went sour, and Breedon's stock price dropped to $50 per share. If Breedon needed new equity to support operations, a new common stock sale would require the company to lower the conversion price on the convertible debentures from $80 to $50. That would raise the value of the convertibles and, in effect, transfer wealth from current shareholders to the convertible holders. This transfer would, de facto, amount to an additional flotation cost on the new common stock issue. Potential problems such as this must be kept in mind by firms considering the use of convertibles or bonds with warrants.

The Component Cost of Convertibles

In the spring of 1998, Silicon Valley Software was evaluating the use of the convertible bond issue described earlier. The issue would consist of 20-year convertible bonds which would sell at a price of $1,000 per bond; this $1,000 would also be the bond's par (and maturity) value. The bonds would pay a 10 percent annual coupon interest rate, or $100 per year. Each bond would be convertible into 20 shares of stock, so the conversion price would be $1,000/20 = $50. The stock was expected to pay a dividend of $2.80 during the coming year, and it sold at $35 per share. Further, the stock price was expected to grow at a constant rate of 8 percent per year. Therefore, $k_s = \hat{k}_s = D_1/P_0 + g = \$2.80/\$35 + 8\% = 8\% + 8\% = 16\%$. If the bonds were not made convertible, they would have to offer a yield of 13 percent, given their riskiness and the general level of interest rates. The convertible bonds would not be callable for ten years, after which they could be called at a price of $1,050, with this price declining by $5 per year thereafter. If, after ten years, the conversion value exceeds the call price by at least 20 percent, management would probably call the bonds.

Figure 20-1 shows the expectations of both an average investor and the company.[7]

1. The horizontal line at M = $1,000 represents the par (and maturity) value. Also, $1,000 is the price at which the bond is initially offered to the public.

---

[7]For a more complete discussion of how the terms of a convertible offering are determined, see M. Wayne Marr and G. Rodney Thompson, "The Pricing of New Convertible Bond Issues," *Financial Management*, Summer 1984, 31–37.

| FIGURE 20-1 | Silicon Valley Software: Convertible Bond Model |

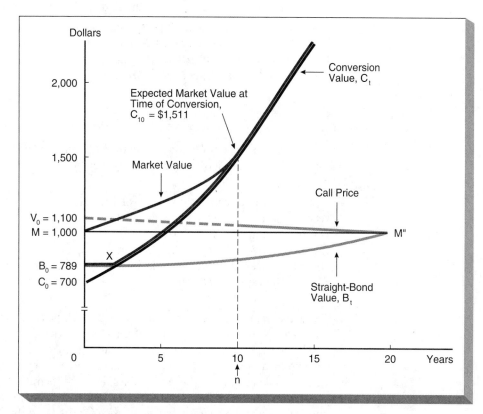

YEAR	PURE-BOND VALUE, B_t	CONVERSION VALUE, C_t	MATURITY VALUE, M	MARKET VALUE	FLOOR VALUE	PREMIUM
0	$ 789	$ 700	$1,000	$1,000	$ 789	$211
1	792	756	$1,000	1,023	792	231
2	795	816	$1,000	1,071	816	255
3	798	882	$1,000	1,147	882	265
4	802	952	$1,000	1,192	952	240
5	806	1,029	$1,000	1,241	1,029	212
6	811	1,111	$1,000	1,293	1,111	182
7	816	1,200	$1,000	1,344	1,200	144
8	822	1,296	$1,000	1,398	1,296	102
9	829	1,399	$1,000	1,453	1,399	54
10	837	1,511	$1,000	1,511	1,511	0
11	846	1,632	$1,000	1,632	1,632	0
.	.	.	.	.	.	.
.	.	.	.	.	.	.
.	.	.	.	.	.	.
20	1,000	3,263	$1,000	3,263	3,263	0

2. The bond is protected against call for ten years. It is initially callable at a price of $1,050, and the call price declines thereafter by $5 per year. Thus, the call price is represented by the solid section of the line V_0M''.

3. Since the convertible has a 10 percent coupon rate, and since the yield on a non-convertible bond of similar risk was stated to be 13 percent, the expected "straight-bond" value of the convertible, B_t, must be less than par. At the time of issue, assuming an annual coupon, B_0 is $789:

$$B_0 = \sum_{t=1}^{20} \frac{\$100}{(1.13)^t} + \frac{\$1,000}{(1.13)^{20}} = \$789.$$

Note, however, that the bond's straight-debt value must be $1,000 just prior to maturity, so the straight-debt value rises over time. B_t follows the line B_0M'' in the graph.

4. The bond's initial conversion value, or the value of the stock the investor would receive if the bonds were converted at $t = 0$, is $700: the bond's conversion value is $P_t(CR)$, so at $t = 0$, conversion value $= P_0(CR) = \$35(20$ shares$) = \$700$. Since the stock price is expected to grow at an 8 percent rate, the conversion value should rise over time. For example, in Year 5 it should be $P_5(CR) = \$35(1.08)^5(20) = \$1,029$. The expected conversion value over time is given by the line C_t in Figure 20-1.

5. The actual market price of the bond can never fall below the higher of its straight-debt value or its conversion value. If the market price dropped below the straight-bond value, those who wanted bonds would recognize the bargain and buy the convertible as a bond. Similarly, if the market price dropped below the conversion value, people would buy the convertibles, exercise them to get stock, and then sell the stock at a profit. Therefore, the higher of the bond value and conversion value curves in the graph represents a *floor price* for the bond. In Figure 20-1, the floor price is represented by the thicker shaded line B_0XC_t.

6. The bond's market value will typically exceed its floor value. It will exceed the straight-bond value because the option to convert is worth something—a 10 percent bond with conversion possibilities is worth more than a 10 percent bond without this option. The convertible's price will also exceed its conversion value because holding the convertible is equivalent to holding a call option, and, prior to expiration, the option's true value is higher than its expiration (or conversion) value. Without using a sophisticated pricing model, we cannot say exactly where the market value line will lie, but as a rule it will be at or above the floor set by the straight-bond and conversion value lines.

7. At some point, the market value line will touch the conversion value line. This convergence will occur for two reasons. First, the stock should pay higher and higher dividends as the years go by, but the interest payments on the convertible are fixed. For example, Silicon's convertibles would pay $100 in interest annually, while the dividends on the 20 shares received upon conversion would initially be $20(\$2.80) = \$56$. However, at an 8 percent growth rate, the dividends after ten years would be up to $120.90, while the interest would still be $100. Thus, at some point, rising dividends could be expected to push against the fixed interest payments, causing the premium to disappear and investors to convert voluntarily. Second, once the bond becomes callable, its market value cannot exceed the higher of the conversion value and the call price without exposing investors to

the danger of a call. For example, suppose that ten years after issue (when the bonds were callable), the market value of the bond was $1,600, the conversion value was $1,500, and the call price was $1,050. If the company called the bonds the day after you bought ten bonds for $16,000, you would be forced to convert into stock worth only $15,000, so you would suffer a loss of $100 per bond, or $1,000, in one day. Recognizing this danger, you and other investors would simply not pay a premium over the higher of the call price or the conversion value once the bond becomes callable. Therefore, in Figure 20-1, we assume that the market value line hits the conversion value line in Year 10, when the bond becomes callable.

8. Let n represent the year when investors expect conversion to occur, either voluntarily because of rising dividends or because the company calls the convertibles to strengthen its balance sheet by substituting equity for debt. In our example, we assume that n = 10, the first call date.

9. Since n = 10, the expected market value at Year 10 is $35(1.08)^{10}(20) = $1,511$. An investor can find the expected rate of return on the convertible bond, k_c, by finding the IRR of the following cash flow stream:

0	1	9	10
−$1,000	+$100	+$100	+$ 100
			+ 1,511
			+$1,611

The solution is k_c = IRR = 12.8 percent.

10. The return on a convertible is expected to come partly from interest income and partly from capital gains; in this case, the total expected return is 12.8 percent, with 10 percent representing interest income and 2.8 percent representing the expected capital gain. The interest component is relatively assured, while the capital gain component is more risky. Therefore, a convertible's expected return is more risky than that of a straight bond. This leads us to conclude that k_c should be larger than the cost of straight debt, k_d. Thus, it would seem that the expected rate of return on Silicon's convertibles, k_c, should lie between its cost of straight debt, k_d = 13%, and its cost of common stock, k_s = 16%.

11. Investment bankers use the type of model described here, plus a knowledge of the market, to set the terms on convertibles (the conversion ratio, coupon interest rate, and years of call protection) such that the security will just "clear the market" at its $1,000 offering price. In our example, the required conditions do not hold—the calculated rate of return on the convertible is only 12.8 percent, which is less than the 13 percent cost of straight debt. Therefore, the terms on the bond must be made more attractive to investors. Silicon Valley Software would have to increase the coupon interest rate on the convertible above 10 percent, raise the conversion ratio above 20 (and thereby lower the conversion price from $50 to a level closer to the current $35 market price of the stock), lengthen the call-protected period, or use a combination of these three such that the expected rate of return on the convertible ends up between 13 and 16 percent.[8]

_____

[8] In this discussion, we ignore the tax advantages to investors associated with capital gains. In some situations, tax effects could result in k_c being less than k_d.

Use of Convertibles in Financing

Convertibles have two important advantages from the issuer's standpoint: (1) Convertibles, like bonds with warrants, offer a company the chance to sell debt with a low interest rate in exchange for a chance to participate in the company's success if it does well. (2) In a sense, convertibles provide a way to sell common stock at prices higher than those currently prevailing. Some companies actually want to sell common stock, not debt, but feel that the price of their stock is temporarily depressed. Management may know, for example, that earnings are depressed because of startup costs associated with a new project, but they expect earnings to rise sharply during the next year or so, pulling the price of the stock up with them. Thus, if the company sold stock now, it would be giving up more shares than necessary to raise a given amount of capital. However, if it set the conversion price 20 to 30 percent above the present market price of the stock, then 20 to 30 percent fewer shares would be given up when the bonds were converted than if stock were sold directly at the current time. Notice, however, that management is counting on the stock's price to rise above the conversion price to make the bonds attractive in conversion. If earnings do not rise and pull the stock price up, hence conversion does not occur, then the company will be saddled with debt in the face of low earnings, which could be disastrous.

How can the company be sure that conversion will occur if the price of the stock rises above the conversion price? Typically, convertibles contain a call provision that enables the issuing firm to force holders to convert. Suppose the conversion price is $50, the conversion ratio is 20, the market price of the common stock has risen to $60, and the call price on a convertible bond is $1,050. If the company calls the bond, bondholders can either convert into common stock with a market value of 20($60) = $1,200 or allow the company to redeem the bond for $1,050. Naturally, bondholders prefer $1,200 to $1,050, so conversion would occur. The call provision gives the company a way to force conversion, provided the market price of the stock is greater than the conversion price. Note, however, that most convertibles have a fairly long period of call protection—ten years is typical. Therefore, if the company wants to be able to force conversion fairly early, then it will have to set a short call-protection period. This will, in turn, require that it set a higher coupon rate or a lower conversion price.

From the standpoint of the issuer, convertibles have three important disadvantages: (1) Although the use of a convertible bond may give the company the opportunity to sell stock at a price higher than the price at which it could be sold currently, if the stock greatly increases in price, the firm would probably find that it would have been better off if it had used straight debt in spite of its higher cost and then later sold common stock and refunded the debt. (2) Convertibles typically have a low coupon interest rate, and the advantage of this low-cost debt will be lost when conversion occurs. (3) If the company truly wants to raise equity capital, and if the price of the stock does not rise sufficiently after the bond is issued, then the company will be stuck with debt.

Convertibles and Agency Costs

One of the potential agency problems between bondholders and stockholders discussed in Chapter 1 is asset substitution. Stockholders have an "option-related" incentive to take on projects with high upside potential even though they increase the riskiness of the firm. When such an action is taken, there is potential for a wealth transfer between bondholders and stockholders. However, when convertible debt is issued, actions which increase the riskiness of the company may also increase the value of the convertible debt. Thus, some of the gains to shareholders from taking on high-risk projects have to be shared with convertible bondholders. This sharing of benefits lowers agency costs. The same general logic applies to convertible preferred and to warrants.

SELF-TEST QUESTIONS	What is a conversion ratio? A conversion price? A straight-bond value? What is meant by a convertible's floor value? What are the advantages and disadvantages of convertibles to issuers? To investors? How do convertibles reduce agency costs?

A FINAL COMPARISON OF WARRANTS AND CONVERTIBLES

Convertible debt can be thought of as straight debt with nondetachable warrants. Thus, at first blush, it might appear that debt with warrants and convertible debt are more or less interchangeable. However, a closer look reveals one major and several minor differences between these two securities.[9] First, as we discussed previously, the exercise of warrants brings in new equity capital, while the conversion of convertibles results only in an accounting transfer.

A second difference involves flexibility. Most convertible issues contain a call provision that allows the issuer either to refund the debt or to force conversion, depending on the relationship between the conversion value and call price. However, most warrants are not callable, so firms generally must wait until maturity for the warrants to generate new equity capital. Generally, maturities also differ between warrants and convertibles. Warrants typically have much shorter maturities than convertibles, and warrants typically expire before their accompanying debt matures. Further, warrants provide for fewer future common shares than do convertibles because with convertibles all of the debt is converted to common whereas debt remains outstanding when warrants are exercised. Together, these facts suggest that debt-plus-warrant issuers are actually more interested in selling debt than in selling equity.

In general, firms that issue debt with warrants are smaller and riskier than those that issue convertibles. One possible rationale for the use of option securities, especially the use of debt with warrants by small firms, is the difficulty investors have assessing the risk of small companies. If a startup with a new, untested product seeks debt financing, it is very difficult for potential lenders to judge the riskiness of the venture, hence it is difficult to set a fair interest rate. Under these circumstances, many potential investors will be reluctant to invest, making it necessary to set very high interest rates to attract debt capital. By issuing debt with warrants, investors obtain a package that offers upside potential to offset the risks of loss.

Finally, there is a significant difference in issuance costs between debt with warrants and convertible debt. Bonds with warrants typically require issuance costs that are about 1.2 percentage points more than the flotation costs for convertibles. In general, bond-with-warrant financings have underwriting fees that closely reflect the weighted

---

[9]For a more detailed comparison of warrants and convertibles, see Michael S. Long and Stephen E. Sefcik, "Participation Financing: A Comparison of the Characteristics of Convertible Debt and Straight Bonds Issued in Conjunction with Warrants," *Financial Management,* Autumn 1990, 23–34.

average of the fees associated with debt and equity issues, while underwriting costs for convertibles are substantially lower.

S E L F - T E S T
Q U E S T I O N S

What are some differences between debt-with-warrant financing and convertible debt?

Explain how bonds with warrants might help small, risky firms sell debt securities.

OTHER TOPICS IN HYBRID FINANCING

When warrants or convertibles are outstanding, the firm has several alternative formats for reporting earnings per share. The Extension section provides a brief discussion of these choices.

Although the exercise of warrants is typically triggered by expiration, conversion is generally forced by a call. Thus, firms that issue convertibles are faced with making a call decision. Such decisions also are discussed in the Extension section.

Finally, in recent years investment bankers have created some unusual types of hybrid securities which are tax deductible to the issuer. These securities are discussed in the Extension section.

SUMMARY

In this chapter, we discussed preferred stock, warrants, and convertibles. The key concepts are listed below:

- **Preferred** stock is a hybrid — it is similar to bonds in some respects and to common stock in other ways.

- A **warrant** is a long-term call option issued along with a bond. Warrants are generally detachable from the bond, and they trade separately in the market. When warrants are exercised, the firm receives additional equity capital, and the original bonds remain outstanding.

- A **convertible** security is a bond or preferred stock that can be exchanged for common stock at the option of the holder. When a security is converted, debt or preferred stock is replaced with common stock, and no money changes hands.

- Warrant and convertible issues are generally structured so that the exercise or conversion price is 20 to 30 percent above the stock's price at time of issue.

- Although both warrants and convertibles are option securities, there are several differences between the two, including separability, impact when exercised, callability, maturity, and flotation costs.

- Warrants and convertibles are **"sweeteners"** which are used to make the underlying debt or preferred stock issue more attractive to investors. Although the coupon rate or dividend yield is lower when options are part of the issue, the overall cost of the issue is higher than the cost of straight debt or preferred, because option-related securities are riskier.

The Extension to this chapter discusses several new types of hybrid securities. It also discusses how earnings per share are reported when convertibles or warrants are outstanding, as well as information regarding when convertible bonds should be called to force conversion.

Questions

20-1 Define each of the following terms:
  a. Preferred stock
  b. Cumulative dividends; arrearages
  c. Warrant; detachable warrant
  d. Stepped-up price
  e. Convertible security
  f. Conversion ratio; conversion price; conversion value
  g. "Sweetener"

20-2 Is preferred stock more like bonds or common stock? Explain.

20-3 What effect does the trend in stock prices (subsequent to issue) have on a firm's ability to raise funds through (a) convertibles and (b) warrants?

20-4 If a firm expects to have additional financial requirements in the future, would you recommend that it use convertibles or bonds with warrants? What factors would influence your decision?

20-5 How does a firm's dividend policy affect each of the following?
  a. The value of its long-term warrants.
  b. The likelihood that its convertible bonds will be converted.
  c. The likelihood that its warrants will be exercised.

20-6 Evaluate the following statement: "Issuing convertible securities represents a means by which a firm can sell common stock at a price above the existing market."

20-7 Why do corporations often sell convertibles on a rights basis?

20-8 Suppose a company simultaneously issues $50 million of convertible bonds with a coupon rate of 10 percent and $50 million of straight bonds with a coupon rate of 14 percent. Both bonds have the same maturity. Does the fact that the convertible issue has the lower coupon rate suggest that it is less risky than the straight bond? Is the cost of capital lower on the convertible than on the straight bond? Explain.

Problems

20-1
Warrants

Gregg Company recently issued two types of bonds. The first issue consisted of 20-year straight debt with an 8 percent annual coupon. The second issue consisted of 20-year bonds with a 6 percent annual coupon and attached warrants. Both issues sold at their $1,000 par values. What is the implied value of the warrants attached to each bond?

20-2
Convertibles

Peterson Securities recently issued convertible bonds with a $1,000 par value. The bonds have a conversion price of $40 a share. What is the convertible issue's conversion ratio?

20-3
Warrants

Maese Industries Inc. has warrants outstanding that permit the holders to purchase 1 share of stock per warrant at a price of $25.
  a. Calculate the exercise value of the firm's warrants if the common sells at each of the following prices: (1) $20, (2) $25, (3) $30, (4) $100. (Hint: A warrant's exercise value is the difference between the stock price and the purchase price specified by the warrant if the warrant were to be exercised.)
  b. At what approximate price do you think the warrants would actually sell under each condition indicated above? What premium above exercise value is implied in your price? Your answer is a guess, but your prices and premiums should bear reasonable relationships to one another.
  c. How would each of the following factors affect your estimates of the warrants' prices and premiums in Part b?
    (1) The life of the warrant.
    (2) Expected variability (σ_p) in the stock's price.
    (3) The expected growth rate in the stock's EPS.
    (4) The company announces a change in dividend policy: whereas it formerly paid no dividends, henceforth it will pay out *all* earnings as dividends.
  d. Assume the firm's stock now sells for $20 per share. The company wants to sell some 20-year, annual interest, $1,000 par value bonds. Each bond will have attached 50 warrants, each exercisable into 1 share of stock at an exercise price of $25. The firm's straight bonds yield 12 percent. Regardless of your answer to Part b, assume that each warrant will have a market value of $3 when the stock sells at $20. What coupon interest rate, and dollar coupon, must the company set on the bonds with warrants if they are to clear the market?

20-4
Convertible Premiums

The Tsetsekos Company was planning to finance an expansion in the summer of 1998. The principal executives of the company all agreed that an industrial company such as theirs should finance growth by means of common stock rather than by debt. However, they felt that the price of the company's common stock did not reflect its true worth, so they decided to sell a convertible security. They considered a convertible debenture but feared the burden of fixed interest charges if the common stock did not rise in price to make conversion attractive. They decided on an issue of convertible preferred stock, which would pay a dividend of $2.10 per share.

The common stock was selling for $42 a share at the time. Management projected earnings for 1998 at $3 a share and expected a future growth rate of 10 percent a year in 1999 and beyond. It was agreed by the investment bankers and the management that the common stock would sell at 14 times earnings, the current price/earnings ratio.

a. What conversion price should be set by the issuer? The conversion ratio will be 1.0; that is, each share of convertible preferred can be converted into 1 share of common. Therefore, the convertible's par value (and also the issue price) will be equal to the conversion price, which, in turn, will be determined as a percentage over the current market price of the common. Your answer will be a guess, but make it a reasonable one.

b. Should the preferred stock include a call provision? Why?

20-5
Convertible Bond Analysis

In June 1976, U.S. Steel (now USX Corporation) sold $400 million of convertible bonds. The bonds had a 25-year maturity, a 5¾ percent coupon rate, and were sold at their $1,000 par value. The conversion price was set at $62.75 against a current price of $55 per share of common. The bonds were subordinated debentures, and they were given an A rating; straight nonconvertible debentures of the same quality yielded about 8¾ percent at the time.

a. Calculate the premium on the bonds, that is, the percentage excess of the conversion price over the current stock price.

b. What is U.S. Steel's annual interest savings on the convertible issue versus a straight-debt issue?

c. Look up U.S. Steel's (USX's) current stock price in the paper. On the basis of this price, do you think it likely that the bonds would have been converted? (Calculate the value of the stock one would receive by converting a bond.)

d. The bonds originally sold for $1,000. If interest rates on A-rated bonds had remained constant at 8¾ percent, what do you think would have happened to the price of the convertible bonds?

e. Now suppose the price of U.S. Steel's common stock had fallen from $55 on the day the bonds were issued to $32.75 at present. (At the time this problem was written, that is exactly what had happened.) Suppose also that the rate of interest had fallen from 8¾ to 5¾ percent. (This had not happened when the problem was being written—the interest rate on A-rated bonds was about 10 percent.) Under these conditions, what do you think would have happened to the price of the bonds?

f. Set up a graphic model to illustrate how investors valued the U.S. Steel convertibles in 1976. How well were these expectations realized?

20-6
Warrant/Convertible Decisions

The Howland Carpet Company has grown rapidly during the past 5 years. Recently, its commercial bank urged the company to consider increasing its permanent financing. Its bank loan under a line of credit has risen to $250,000, carrying an 8 percent interest rate. Howland has been 30 to 60 days late in paying trade creditors.

Discussions with an investment banker have resulted in the decision to raise $500,000 at this time. Investment bankers have assured the firm that the following alternatives are feasible (flotation costs will be ignored):

- *Alternative 1:* Sell common stock at $8.

- *Alternative 2:* Sell convertible bonds at an 8 percent coupon, convertible into 100 shares of common stock for each $1,000 bond (that is, the conversion price is $10 per share).

- *Alternative 3:* Sell debentures at an 8 percent coupon, each $1,000 bond carrying 100 warrants to buy common stock at $10.

John L. Howland, the president, owns 80 percent of the common stock and wishes to maintain control of the company. One hundred thousand shares are outstanding. The following are extracts of Howland's latest financial statements:

BALANCE SHEET

		Current liabilities	$400,000
		Common stock, par $1	100,000
		Retained earnings	50,000
Total assets	$550,000	Total claims	$550,000

INCOME STATEMENT

Sales	$1,100,000
All costs except interest	990,000
EBIT	$ 110,000
Interest	20,000
EBT	$ 90,000
Taxes (40%)	36,000
Net income	$ 54,000
Shares outstanding	100,000
Earnings per share	$0.54
Price/earnings ratio	15.83×
Market price of stock	$8.55

a. Show the new balance sheet under each alternative. For Alternatives 2 and 3, show the balance sheet after conversion of the bonds or exercise of the warrants. Assume that half of the funds raised will be used to pay off the bank loan and half to increase total assets.

b. Show Mr. Howland's control position under each alternative, assuming that he does not purchase additional shares.

c. What is the effect on earnings per share of each alternative, if it is assumed that profits before interest and taxes will be 20 percent of total assets?

d. What will be the debt ratio under each alternative?

e. Which of the three alternatives would you recommend to Howland, and why?

20-7
Convertible Bond Analysis

Niendorf Incorporated needs to raise $25 million to construct production facilities for a new model diskette drive. The firm's straight nonconvertible debentures currently yield 14 percent. Its stock sells for $30 per share; the last dividend was $2; and the expected growth rate is a constant 9 percent. Investment bankers have tentatively proposed that the firm raise the $25 million by issuing convertible debentures. These convertibles would have a $1,000 par value, carry a coupon rate of 10 percent, have a 20-year maturity, and be convertible into 20 shares of stock. The bonds would be noncallable for 5 years, after which they would be callable at a price of $1,075; this call price would decline by $5 per year in Year 6 and each year thereafter. Management has called convertibles in the past (and presumably it will call them again in the future), once they were eligible for call, when the bonds' conversion value was about 20 percent above the bonds' par value (not their call price).

a. Draw an accurate graph similar to Figure 20-1 representing the expectations set forth above. (Assume an annual coupon.)

b. What is the expected rate of return on the proposed convertible issue?

c. Do you think that these bonds could be successfully offered to the public at par? That is, does $1,000 seem to be an equilibrium price in view of the stated terms? If not, suggest the type of change that would have to be made to cause the bonds to trade at $1,000 in the secondary market, assuming no change in capital market conditions.

d. Suppose the projects outlined here work out on schedule for 2 years, but then the firm begins to experience extremely strong competition from Japanese firms. As a result, Niendorf's expected growth rate drops from 9 percent to zero. Assume that the dividend at the time of the drop is $2.38. The company's credit strength is not impaired, and its value of k_s is also unchanged. What would happen (1) to the stock price, and (2) to the convertible bond's price? Be as precise as you can.

MINI CASE

Paul Duncan, financial manager of EduSoft Inc., is facing a dilemma. The firm was founded 5 years ago to provide educational software for the rapidly expanding primary and secondary school markets. Although EduSoft has done well, the firm's founder believes that an industry shakeout is imminent. To survive, EduSoft must grab market share now, and this will require a large infusion of new capital.

Because he expects earnings to continue rising sharply and looks for the stock price to follow suit, Mr. Duncan does not think it would be wise to issue new common stock at this time. On the other hand, interest rates are currently high by historical standards, and with the firm's B rating, the interest payments on a new debt issue would be prohibitive. Thus, he has narrowed his choice of financing alternatives to two securities: (1) bonds with warrants, or (2) convertible bonds. As Duncan's assistant, you have been asked to help in the decision process by answering the following questions:

a. How does preferred stock differ from both common equity and debt? Is preferred stock more risky than common stock?

b. What is a call option? How can a knowledge of call options help a financial manager to better understand warrants and convertibles?

c. One of the firm's alternatives is to issue a bond with warrants attached. EduSoft's current stock price is $20, and its investment banker estimates that the cost of a 20-year, annual coupon bond without warrants would be 12 percent. The bankers suggest attaching 50 warrants, each with an exercise price of $25, to each $1,000 bond. It is estimated that each warrant, when detached and traded separately, would have a value of $3.

   (1) What coupon rate should be set on the bond with warrants if the total package is to sell for $1,000?

   (2) Suppose the bonds were issued and the warrants immediately traded on the open market for $5 each. What would this imply about the terms of the issue? Did the company "win" or "lose"?

   (3) When would you expect the warrants to be exercised? Assume they have a 10-year life; that is, they expire 10 years after issue.

   (4) Will the warrants bring in additional capital when exercised? If so, how much, and what type of capital?

   (5) Since warrants lower the cost of the accompanying debt issue, shouldn't all debt be issued with warrants? What is the expected return to the holders of the bond with warrants (or the expected cost to the company) if the warrants are expected to be exercised in 5 years, when EduSoft's stock price is expected to be $36.75? How would you expect the cost of the bond with warrants to compare with the cost of straight debt? With the cost of common stock?

d. As an alternative to the bond with warrants, Mr. Duncan is considering convertible bonds. The firm's investment bankers estimate that EduSoft could sell a 20-year, 10.5 percent annual coupon, callable convertible bond for its $1,000 par value, whereas a straight-debt issue would require a 12 percent coupon. The convertibles would be call protected for 5 years, the call price would be $1,100, and the company would probably call the bonds as soon as possible after their conversion value exceeds $1,200. Note, though, that the call must occur on an issue date anniversary. EduSoft's current stock price is $20, its last dividend was $1.48, and the dividend is expected to grow at a constant 8 percent rate. The convertible could be converted into 40 shares of EduSoft stock at the owner's option.

   (1) What conversion price is built into the bond?

   (2) What is the convertible's straight-debt value? What is the implied value of the convertibility feature?

   (3) What is the formula for the bond's expected conversion value in any year? What is its conversion value at Year 0? At Year 10?

   (4) What is meant by the "floor value" of a convertible? What is the convertible's expected floor value at Year 0? At Year 10?

   (5) Assume that EduSoft intends to force conversion by calling the bond as soon as possible after its conversion value exceeds 20 percent above its par value, or 1.2($1,000) = $1,200. When is the issue expected to be called? (Hint: Recall that the call must be made on an anniversary date of the issue.)

   (6) What is the expected cost of capital for the convertible to EduSoft? Does this cost appear to be consistent with the riskiness of the issue?

e. EduSoft's market value capital structure is as follows (in millions of dollars):

Debt	$ 50
Equity	50
	$100

If the company raises $20 million in additional capital by selling (1) convertibles or (2) bonds with warrants, what would its WACC be, and how would those figures compare with its current WACC? EduSoft's tax rate is 40 percent.

f. Mr. Duncan believes that the costs of both the bond with warrants and the convertible bond are close enough to one another to call them even, and also consistent with the risks involved. Thus, he will make his decision based on other factors. What are some of the factors which he should consider?

Selected Additional References and Cases

For additional discussions on preferred stock, see

Alderson, Michael J., and Donald R. Fraser, "Financial Innovations and Excesses Revisited: The Case of Auction Rate Preferred Stock," *Financial Management,* Summer 1993, 61–75.

Alderson, Michael J., Keith C. Brown, and Scott L. Lummer, "Dutch Auction Rate Preferred Stock," *Financial Management,* Summer 1987, 68–73.

Fooladi, Iraj, and Gordon S. Roberts, "On Preferred Stock," *Journal of Financial Research,* Winter 1986, 319–324.

Wansley, James W., Fayez A. Elayan, and Brian A. Maris, "Preferred Stock Returns, CreditWatch, and Preferred Stock Rating Changes," *The Financial Review,* May 1990, 265–285.

Winger, Bernard J., et al., "Adjustable Rate Preferred Stock," *Financial Management,* Spring 1986, 48–57.

Quite a bit of work has been done on warrant pricing. Some of the articles include

Ehrhardt, Michael C., and Ronald E. Shrieves, "The Impact of Warrants and Convertible Securities on the Systematic Risk of Common Equity," *Financial Review,* November 1995, 843–856.

Galai, Dan, and Mier I. Schneller, "The Pricing of Warrants and the Value of the Firm," *Journal of Finance,* December 1978, 1333–1342.

Lauterbach, Beni, and Paul Schultz, "Pricing Warrants: An Empirical Study of the Black-Scholes Model and Its Alternatives," *Journal of Finance,* September 1990, 1181–1209.

Leonard, David C., and Michael E. Solt, "On Using the Black-Scholes Model to Value Warrants," *Journal of Financial Research,* Summer 1990, 81–92.

Phelps, Katherine L., William T. Moore, and Rodney L. Roenfeldt, "Equity Valuation Effects of Warrant-Debt Financing," *Journal of Financial Research,* Summer 1991, 93–103.

Schwartz, Eduardo S., "The Valuation of Warrants: Implementing a New Approach," *Journal of Financial Economics,* January 1977, 79–93.

For more insights into convertible pricing and use, see

Alexander, Gordon J., and Roger D. Stover, "Pricing in the New Issue Convertible Debt Market," *Financial Management,* Fall 1977, 35–39.

Alexander, Gordon J., Roger D. Stover, and D. B. Kuhnau, "Market Timing Strategies in Convertible Debt Financing," *Journal of Finance,* March 1979, 143–155.

Asquith, Paul, and David W. Mullins, Jr., "Convertible Debt: Corporate Call Policy and Voluntary Conversion," *Journal of Finance,* September 1991, 1273–1289.

Billingsley, Randall S., and David M. Smith, "Why Do Firms Issue Convertible Debt?" *Financial Management,* Summer 1996, 93–99.

Brennan, Michael, "The Case for Convertibles," *Issues in Corporate Finance* (New York: Stern Stewart Putnam & Macklis, 1983), 102–111.

Emery, Douglas R., Mai E. Iskandor-Datta, and Jong-Chul Rhim, "Capital Structure Management as a Motivation for Calling Convertible Debt," *Journal of Financial Research,* Spring 1994, 91–104.

Harikumar, T., P. Kadapakkam, and Ronald F. Singer, "Convertible Debt and Investment Incentives," *Journal of Financial Research,* Spring 1994, 15–29.

Ingersoll, Jonathan E., "A Contingent Claims Valuation of Convertible Securities," *Journal of Financial Economics,* May 1977, 289–322.

Janjigian, Vahan, "The Leverage Changing Consequences of Convertible Debt Financing," *Financial Management,* Autumn 1987, 15–21.

Krishnan, V. Sivarama, and Ramesh P. Rao, "Financial Distress Costs and Delayed Calls of Convertible Bonds," *Financial Review,* November 1996, 913–925.

The following case from the Cases in Financial Management: Dryden Request *series covers many of the issues presented in this chapter:*

Case 27, "Virginia May Chocolate Company," which illustrates convertible bond valuation.

EXTENSIONS

Adjustable Rate and Market Auction Preferred Stocks

Instead of paying fixed dividends, **adjustable rate preferred stocks (ARPs)** have their dividends tied to the rate on Treasury securities. The ARPs, which are issued mainly by utilities and large commercial banks, were touted as nearly perfect short-term corporate investments since (1) only 30 percent of the dividends are taxable to corporations, and (2) the floating rate feature was supposed to keep the issue trading at near par. The new security proved to be so popular as a short-term investment for firms with idle cash that mutual funds designed just to invest in them sprouted like weeds (shares of the funds, in turn, were purchased by corporations). However, the ARPs still had some price volatility due (1) to changes in the riskiness of the issues (some big banks which had issued ARPs, such as Continental Illinois, ran into serious loan default problems) and (2) to the fact that Treasury yields fluctuated between dividend rate adjustments dates. Thus, the ARPs had too much price instability to be held in the liquid asset portfolios of many corporate investors.

To solve this problem, investment bankers introduced **money market,** or **market auction, preferred.** Here the underwriter conducts an auction on the issue every seven weeks (to get the 70 percent exclusion from taxable income, buyers must hold the stock at least 46 days). Holders who want to sell their shares can put them up for auction at par value. Buyers then submit bids in the form of the yields they are willing to accept over the next seven-week period. The yield set on the issue for the coming period is the lowest yield sufficient to sell all the shares being offered at that auction. The buyers pay the sellers the par value, hence holders are virtually assured that their shares can be sold at par. The issuer then must pay a dividend rate over the next seven-week period as determined by the auction. From the holder's standpoint, market auction preferred is a low-risk, largely tax-exempt, seven-week maturity security which can be sold between auction dates at close to par. However, if there are not enough buyers to match the sellers (in spite of the high yield), then the auction can fail, which has occurred on occasion. For example, a few years ago, an auction of MCorp (a Texas bank holding company) failed to attract enough buyers. Analysts attributed the failure to the downgrading of MCorp's preferred stock from double A to single B, which caused potential buyers to think (correctly, as it turned out) that the company would go bankrupt and not pay the dividends expected.

Adjustable rate and market auction preferreds are also issued by industrial and service companies. For example, Texas Instruments recently issued $225 million of market auction preferred. About the only thing investors do not like about ARPs and auction market preferreds is that, as stock, they are more vulnerable to an issuer's financial problems than debt would be, as evidenced by the MCorp example.

Reporting Earnings When Warrants or Convertibles Are Outstanding

If warrants or convertibles are outstanding, a firm could theoretically report earnings per share in one of three ways:

1. *Basic EPS,* where earnings available to common stockholders are divided by the average number of shares actually outstanding during the period.

2. *Primary EPS,* where earnings available are divided by the average number of shares that would have been outstanding if warrants and convertibles "likely to be converted in the near future" had actually been exercised or converted. In calculating primary EPS, earnings are first adjusted by "backing out" the interest on the convertibles, after which the adjusted earnings are divided by the adjusted number of shares. Accountants have a formula which basically compares the conversion or exercise price with the actual market value of the stock to determine the likelihood of conversion when deciding on the need to use this adjustment procedure.

3. *Diluted EPS,* which is similar to primary EPS except that *all* warrants and convertibles are assumed to be exercised or converted, regardless of the likelihood of exercise or conversion.

Under SEC rules, firms are required to report both basic and diluted EPS. For firms with large amounts of option securities outstanding, there can be a substantial difference between the basic and diluted EPS figures. For financial statement purposes, firms reported diluted EPS until 1997, when the Financial Accounting Standards Board (FASB) changed to basic EPS. According to FASB, the change was made to give investors a simpler picture of a company's underlying performance. Also, the change makes it easier for investors to compare the performance of U.S. firms with their foreign counterparts, which tend to use basic EPS.

Calling Convertible Issues

Most convertible issues have provisions that allow the issuer to call the issue prior to maturity. In such cases, the issuing firm must make the decision when, if at all, to call the convertible. If a convertible is called when its conversion value is less than the stock price, convertible holders will accept the call and receive the call price. The firm will have to pay cash to redeem the issue, and no new equity will appear on the balance sheet. If the call is made when the conversion price exceeds the stock price, holders will convert their securities into common stock. In this case, the firm will not have a cash outlay, and a balance sheet transfer will be made from debt (or preferred) to common equity.

When should a convertible be called? To begin, consider the situation where the conversion value is less than the convertible's call price. In our Chapter 20 convertible bond example, assume that Silicon Valley's stock price does not rise, and that the conversion value at Year 10 is $35(20 \text{ shares}) = 700, much less than the $1,050 call price. Further, assume that interest rates have stayed the same, so that a new straight-debt issue would cost 13 percent, well above the convertible's 10 percent coupon rate. In this situation, the firm has no incentive to call the convertible, because the convertible coupon rate is less than that currently required on straight debt. However, if interest rates fall, and new straight debt costs less than the convertible coupon rate, the convertible should be called. The rationale here is the same as for calling a nonconvertible bond.

What about the situation when the issuer's stock price, hence conversion value, has risen? When a convertible is converted into common stock, the difference between the stock's current price and the convertible's conversion price constitutes a wealth transfer from current stockholders to convertible holders. Since managers are motivated to act in the best interest of current stockholders, and hence to minimize the amount of wealth transfer, theory dictates that the call should be made as soon as the conversion value reaches the call price,

assuming the deferral period has ended. (In reality, because of transactions costs, the call should be made when the conversion value is slightly above the call price.) To illustrate, if after ten years, Silicon Valley's stock price has risen to $60, then the conversion value is $60(20) = $1,200$, and a call at $1,050 would force holders to convert to get $1,200 worth of common stock, resulting in a wealth transfer of (Stock price − Conversion price)(Number of shares) = ($60 − $50)(20) = $200 per bond. If the call were not made, and the stock price subsequently rose to $75, the wealth transfer would increase to ($75 − $50)(20) = $500 per bond.

To view this from another perspective, a firm's value is split among its security holders. As a firm's fortunes rise, the values of its debt securities are fixed, but the value of its common stock rises, and so does the value of its convertibles, which have a call option on the stock. However, the existence of the convertible issue lowers the value of the common stock, and the greater the value of the call option (of the convertible), the lower the value of the common stock. By calling the convertible as soon as the conversion value equals the call price, the firm's managers "kill" the conversion option, and hence remove the opportunity for convertible holders to share in future stock price increases.

Interestingly, several studies have shown that firms do not call convertibles when conversion value reaches call price, but rather tend to wait until the conversion value is well above the call price.[1] One reason proposed to explain this observed behavior is that the firm may want to save near-term cash flow. For example, Silicon Valley's common dividend might be $6 per share when the convertible bonds become callable. Assuming a 40 percent tax rate, current after-tax interest on each bond is $100(0.60) = $60 per year, while conversion into 20 shares of common would require $120 of annual dividend payments. Another possible explanation involves signaling—if a firm calls its convertibles at the earliest possible time, then investors will be less interested in future convertible issues it might decide to use.

Some Innovative New Hybrids

Over the past three years, investment bankers have devised some new preferred stock hybrids having significant appeal to both issuers and investors. For example, RJR Nabisco recently issued trust-oriented preferred securities (TOPrS), which combine features of both preferred stock and bonds. TOPrS are sold at just $25 a share, which makes them more accessible to small investors than corporate bonds with $1,000 or $5,000 par values, although most buyers purchase round lots of 100 shares. Several versions of these securities have been issued by different companies under names such as monthly income preferred securities (MIPS) and quarterly income preferred securities (QUIPS). In fact, in recent years these new hybrids have accounted for more than half of the total preferred stock issued.

---

[1]For example, see Jonathon Ingersoll, "An Examination of Corporate Call Policies on Convertible Securities," *Journal of Finance,* May 1977, 463–478.

Unlike conventional preferred, these new hybrids offer yields higher than those set on the firm's debt securities, which makes them attractive to individual investors. For example, RJR Nabisco's TOPrS were set at 8 percent while its bonds yielded about 7.2 percent at the time. The key to the higher yield is the securities' tax deductibility for the issuer. The deal works in this way: The parent company creates a partnership or trust that actually issues the securities. Then the proceeds are loaned to the parent, which repays the loan with tax-deductible interest payments. These payments, in turn, are timed to coincide with the dividend payments made to the hybrid holders.

The new securities tend to have long maturities—typically 30 to 40 years—so holders are subject to considerable price risk, just as on any long-term fixed-rate investment. The hybrids have call provisions, but most offer five years of call protection. After that, a sharp drop in interest rates would likely trigger a call. Most of these hybrids are traded on the New York Stock Exchange, which makes it easy for investors to monitor values and ensures liquidity. Of course, if the company faces financial trouble, the preferred dividends may be stopped. But, as with more conventional preferred, issuers do not want to omit the dividends on these hybrids because this action creates constraints both on common dividends and on future capital acquisition.

The creation of these new hybrids is but one example of the avalanche of new types of securities that have been developed over the past two decades. Changes in the economic environment, coupled with increased volatility in interest and exchange rates, have fueled the surge. To be a success, new securities must enable issuers or investors to do something that they could not do previously, or to do the same thing in a more cost-efficient way. New securities must create value, perhaps by reallocating risk to a class of investor more able to bear it, or by reducing transactions costs, or by increasing liquidity. Taxes also create an opportunity for value creation—if taxes can be reduced to investors without increasing the corporate tax liability, or vice versa, then value can be created. The new hybrids capture tax benefits by creating a tax-deductible preferred stock that has the same tax consequences to investors as does conventional preferred.

CHAPTER 21
CURRENT ASSET MANAGEMENT

CHAPTER 22
SHORT-TERM FINANCING

CHAPTER 23
WORKING CAPITAL MANAGEMENT: EXTENSIONS

When the Deutsche Bank was first constructed in 1870, banking was in the throes of radical change. Why? It was beginning to accept deposits in cash. The bank built a solid base in deposit taking, and between 1871 and 1873 the Deutsche Bank opened five branches — in Bremen, Yokohama, Shanghai, Hamburg, and London.

© Chris Ladd/Masterfile

CURRENT ASSET MANAGEMENT

*C*ore *Industries Inc. is a $200 million electrical equipment manufacturer whose stock is listed on the NYSE. The stock traded in the range of $12 to $17 per share during most of the 1980s, but during the recession of 1990, earnings plunged and the stock dropped to $4. Then Core's directors made several key managerial changes, including the chief financial officer (CFO), and things improved dramatically.*

At an annual meeting of stockholders, the new CFO, Ray Steben, kicked off the presentations, informing stockholders that while sales had increased by 12 percent, profits jumped 29 percent and the stock price 79 percent.

What caused this dramatic improvement? According to Steben, the improvement resulted primarily from the company's renewed focus on stockholder value and better working capital management:

> *These strong sales and earnings figures are further evidence that shareholder value will continue to be focused upon, and your management will be stewards of the capital entrusted to it. Return on beginning equity jumped from 7.2 percent to 13.3 percent, a level not exceeded since 1981. As you know, our stated objective is to better 15 percent. Return on average capital employed improved almost 50 percent, from 4.5 percent to 6.8 percent. And the company was considerably more efficient in its use of working capital. As a direct result of a company-wide program, operating working capital was reduced from $0.50 to $0.40 per dollar of sales. Operating working capital is basically receivables and inventory less payables and accruals. The cash freed up by this program was used to reduce debt and to invest in operations and acquisitions that will return better than our cost of capital.*

Following Steben's address, Core's president, Dave Zimmer, elaborated on Core's improvement and the ways management planned to maintain the momentum in the coming years. Like Steben, Zimmer stressed the improvement in working capital management, especially the fact that capital previously locked up in excessive inventories and receivables had been freed and was now earning returns for stockholders. Zimmer also informed stockholders that "your top management has placed a significant portion of its compensation at risk both through the annual bonus plan and the new, long-term incentive plan." He then explained that EVA will be used to tie management's compensation directly to stock price performance, so managers will do well only if stockholders do well.

Since the focus on EVA and working capital began, Core has continued to perform well. It has continued to improve the ratio of working capital to sales, and this has led to continued increases in cash flow. So, the stock price has continued to move up nicely.

While generally pleased with its recent performance, Core's management has been resolute in its desire to continue improving operations. It plans to continue shrinking working capital, and as noted, it has also taken steps to implement the Economic Value Added (EVA) concept discussed in Chapter 2. An expert on EVA, Mark MacGuidwin, was brought in, and employees throughout the corporation are now compensated based on the EVA of their division.

While we were revising this book, Core was acquired by United Dominion Ltd, for $25 per share. So, the focus on improving working capital management led to a 525 percent gain in the stock's price.

About 60 percent of a typical financial manager's time is devoted to working capital management, and many students' first jobs will involve working capital. This is particularly true in smaller businesses, where most new jobs in the United States are being created.

Working capital policy involves two basic questions: (1) What is the appropriate amount of current assets for the firm to carry, both in total and for each specific account, and (2) how should current assets be financed? This chapter addresses current asset holdings, and Chapter 22 addresses their financing.

WORKING CAPITAL TERMINOLOGY

We begin our discussion of working capital policy by reviewing some basic definitions and concepts:

1. **Working capital,** sometimes called *gross working capital,* simply refers to current assets used in operations.
2. **Net working capital** is defined as current assets minus current liabilities.
3. **Net operating working capital** is defined as non-interest-bearing current assets minus non-interest-charging current liabilities. Generally, net operating working capital is equal to cash, accounts receivable, and inventories less accounts payable and accruals.
4. The **current ratio,** which was discussed in Chapter 3, is calculated by dividing current assets by current liabilities, and it is intended to measure liquidity. However, a high current ratio does not ensure that a firm will have the cash required to meet its needs. If inventories cannot be sold, or if receivables cannot be collected in a timely manner, then the apparent safety reflected in a high current ratio could be illusory.
5. The **quick ratio,** or **acid test,** also attempts to measure liquidity, and it is found by subtracting inventories from current assets and then dividing by current liabilities. The quick ratio removes inventories from current assets because they are the least liquid of current assets. Therefore, the quick ratio is an "acid test" of a company's ability to meet its current obligations.
6. The best and most comprehensive picture of a firm's liquidity position is shown by its **cash budget.** This statement, which forecasts cash inflows and outflows, focuses on what really counts, namely, the firm's ability to generate sufficient cash inflows to meet its required cash outflows. We will discuss cash budgets in detail later in the chapter.
7. **Working capital policy** refers to the firm's policies regarding (1) target levels for each category of current assets and (2) how current assets will be financed.
8. **Working capital management** involves both setting working capital policy and carrying out that policy in day-to-day operations.

The term *working capital* originated with the old Yankee peddler, who would load up his wagon with goods and then go off on his route to peddle his wares. The merchandise was called working capital because it was what he actually sold, or "turned over," to produce his profits. The wagon and horse were his fixed assets. He generally owned the horse and wagon, so they were financed with "equity" capital, but he borrowed the funds to buy the merchandise. These borrowings were called *working capital loans,* and they had to be repaid after each trip to demonstrate to the bank that the credit was sound. If the peddler was able to repay the loan, then the bank would make another loan, and banks that followed this procedure were said to be employing "sound banking practices."

SELF-TEST
QUESTIONS

Why is the quick ratio also called an acid test?

How did the term "working capital" originate?

ALTERNATIVE CURRENT ASSET INVESTMENT POLICIES

Figure 21-1 shows three alternative policies regarding the total amount of current assets carried. Essentially, these policies differ with regard to the amount of current assets carried to support any given level of sales, hence in the turnover of those assets. The line with the steepest slope represents a **relaxed current asset investment** (or "fat cat") **policy,** where relatively large amounts of cash, marketable securities, and inven-

---

FIGURE 21-1   Alternative Current Asset Investment Policies (Millions of Dollars)

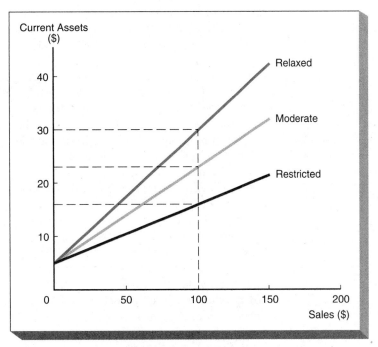

POLICY	CURRENT ASSETS TO SUPPORT SALES OF $100	TURNOVER OF CURRENT ASSETS
Relaxed	$30	3.3×
Moderate	23	4.3×
Restricted	16	6.3×

NOTE: The sales/current assets relationship is shown here as being linear, but the relationship is often curvilinear.

tories are carried, and where sales are stimulated by the use of a credit policy that provides liberal financing to customers and a corresponding high level of receivables. Conversely, with the **restricted current asset investment** (or "lean-and-mean") **policy,** the holdings of cash, securities, inventories, and receivables are minimized. Under the restricted policy, current assets are turned over more frequently, so each dollar of current assets is forced to "work harder." The **moderate current asset investment policy** lies between the two extremes. Core Industries, as discussed in the opening vignette, brought in a new management team which switched from a relaxed to a restricted policy, with good results.

The Impact of Uncertainty and Technology on Working Capital

Under conditions of certainty—where sales, costs, lead times, payment periods, and so on, are known for sure—all firms would hold only minimal levels of current assets. Any larger amounts would increase the need for external funding without a corresponding increase in profits, while any smaller holdings would involve late payments to suppliers along with lost sales due to inventory shortages and an overly restrictive credit policy.

However, the picture changes when uncertainty is introduced. Now the firm requires some minimum amount of cash and inventories based on expected payments, expected sales, expected order lead times, and so on, plus additional holdings, or *safety stocks,* which enable it to deal with variations from the expected values. Similarly, accounts receivable levels are determined by credit terms, and the tougher the credit terms, the lower the receivables for any given level of sales. With a restricted current asset investment policy, the firm would hold minimal safety stocks of cash and inventories, and it would have a tight credit policy even though this meant running the risk of losing sales. A restricted, lean-and-mean current asset investment policy generally provides the highest expected return on this investment, but it entails the greatest risk, while the reverse is true under a relaxed policy. The moderate policy falls in between the two extremes in terms of expected risk and return.

Changing technology can lead to dramatic changes in the optimal current asset investment policy. For example, if new technology makes it possible for a manufacturer such as Core Industries to speed up the production of a given product from ten days to five days, then its work-in-progress inventory can be cut in half. Similarly, retailers such as Wal-Mart or Home Depot have installed systems under which bar codes on all merchandise are read at the cash register. The information on the sale is electronically transmitted to a computer which maintains a record of the inventory of each item, and the computer automatically transmits orders to suppliers' computers when stocks fall to prescribed levels. With such a system, inventories will be held at optimal levels; orders will reflect exactly what styles, colors, and sizes consumers are buying; and the firm's profits will be maximized.

Managing the Components of Working Capital

Working capital consists of four main components: cash, marketable securities, inventory, and accounts receivable. The remainder of this chapter focuses on the issues involved with managing each of these components. As you will see, a common thread underlies all current asset management. For each type of asset, firms face a fundamental trade-off: current assets (that is, working capital) are necessary to conduct business, and the greater the holdings of current assets, the smaller the danger of running out, hence the lower the firm's operating risk. However, holding working capital is costly— if inventories are too large, then the firm will have assets which earn a zero or even

---

EVA AND WORKING CAPITAL

Economic Value Added (EVA), which we first discussed in Chapter 2, provides a useful way of thinking about working capital—this is the approach taken by Core Industries, the company discussed at the beginning of this chapter. The EVA formula is as follows:

$$EVA = NOPAT - (\text{Cost of capital} \times \text{Total capital}).$$

If a company such as Core can reduce inventories, cash holdings, or receivables without seriously affecting operating income, then cash will be freed up. This cash can then be used to pay off debt or to repurchase stock, both of which reduce capital. If capital is reduced, then financing costs will decline, and this will raise EVA. Many firms have reported that when division managers and other operating people think about working capital in these terms, they find ways to reduce it, because their compensation depends on their divisions' EVAs.

We can also think of working capital management in terms of ROE and the Du Pont equation:

$$ROE = \frac{\text{Profit}}{\text{margin}} \times \frac{\text{Total assets turnover}}{} \times \frac{\text{Leverage}}{\text{factor}}$$

$$= \frac{\text{Net income}}{\text{Sales}} \times \frac{\text{Sales}}{\text{Total assets}} \times \frac{\text{Assets}}{\text{Equity}}.$$

If working capital and hence total assets can be reduced without adversely affecting the profit margin, this will increase the total assets turnover and, consequently, ROE.

---

negative return if storage and spoilage costs are high. And, of course, firms must use capital to buy assets such as inventory, this capital has a cost, and this increases the downward drag from excessive holdings of inventories (or receivables or even cash). So, there is pressure to hold the amount of working capital to the minimum consistent with running the business without interruption.

Firms typically follow a cycle in which they purchase inventory, sell goods on credit, and then collect accounts receivable. This cycle is referred to as the cash conversion cycle, and it is discussed in detail in Chapter 23. Sound working capital policy is designed to minimize the time between cash expenditures on materials and the collection of cash on sales.

S E L F - T E S T
Q U E S T I O N S

Identify and explain three alternative current asset investment policies.

What are the principal components of working capital?

What are the reasons for not wanting to hold too little working capital? For not wanting to hold too much?

What is the fundamental trade-off that managers face when managing working capital?

THE CONCEPT OF ZERO WORKING CAPITAL

At first glance, it might seem that working capital management is not as important as capital budgeting, dividend policy, and other decisions that determine a firm's long-term direction. However, in today's world of intense global competition, working capital management is receiving increasing attention from managers striving for peak efficiency. In fact, the goal of many leading companies today—including American Standard, Campbell Soup, General Electric, Quaker Oats, and Whirlpool—is *zero working capital*. Proponents of the zero working capital concept claim that a movement toward this goal not only generates cash but also speeds up production and helps businesses make more timely deliveries and operate more efficiently. The concept has its own definition of working capital: Inventories + Receivables − Payables. The ratio-

An article entitled "Cutting Working Capital" can be found at http://www.sbc1.com/sbc/info/PreviousOAAB.html. The article is reprinted from *Small Business News,* and it provides an excellent discussion of the advantages and pitfalls of cutting working capital.

American Standard provides a detailed discussion of how they are applying demand flow production concepts to reengineered manufacturing and office processes in an attempt to achieve zero working capital. The site can be accessed at http://www.teamflow. Look for American Standard under User Profiles.

nale here is (1) that inventories and receivables are the keys to making sales, but (2) that inventories can be financed by suppliers through accounts payable.

On average, companies use 20 cents of working capital for each dollar of sales. So, on average, working capital is turned over five times per year. Reducing working capital and thus increasing turnover has two major financial benefits. First, every dollar freed up by reducing inventories or receivables, or by increasing payables, results in a one-time contribution to cash flow. Second, a movement toward zero working capital permanently raises a company's earnings. Like all capital, funds invested in working capital cost money, so reducing the amount of working capital yields permanent savings in capital costs. In addition to the financial benefits, reducing working capital forces a company to produce and deliver faster than its competitors, which helps it gain new business and charge premium prices for providing good service. As inventories disappear, warehouses can be sold off, both labor and handling equipment needs are reduced, and obsolete and/or out-of-style goods are minimized.

To illustrate the benefits of striving for zero working capital, in just one year Campbell Soup pared its working capital by $80 million. It used the cash to develop new products and to buy companies in Britain, Australia, and other countries. Equally important, the company expects to increase annual profits by $50 million over the next few years by lowering overtime labor and storage costs.

The most important factor in moving toward zero working capital is increased speed. If the production process is fast enough, companies can produce items as they are ordered rather than having to forecast demand and build up large inventories that are managed by bureaucracies. The best companies are able to start production after an order is received yet still meet customer delivery requirements. This system is known as *demand flow,* or *demand-based management,* and it builds on the just-in-time method of inventory control which we will discuss later in this chapter. (See the box entitled "American Standard Embraces Demand Flow Management.") However, demand flow management is broader than just-in-time, because it requires that all elements of a production system operate quickly and efficiently.

Achieving zero working capital requires that every order and part move at maximum speed, which generally means replacing paper with electronic data. Then, orders streak from the processing department to the plant, flexible production lines produce each product every day, and finished goods flow directly from the production line onto waiting trucks or rail cars. Instead of cluttering plants or warehouses with inventories, products move directly into the pipeline. As efficiency rises, working capital dwindles.

Clearly, it is not possible for most firms to achieve zero working capital and infinitely efficient production. Still, a focus on minimizing receivables and inventories while maximizing payables will help a firm lower its investment in working capital and achieve financial and production economies.

S E L F - T E S T
Q U E S T I O N

What is the basic idea of zero working capital, and how is working capital defined in this concept?

CASH MANAGEMENT

Approximately 1.5 percent of the average industrial firm's assets are held in the form of cash, which is defined as demand deposits plus currency. Cash is often called a "nonearning asset." It is needed to pay for labor and raw materials, to buy fixed assets, to pay taxes, to service debt, to pay dividends, and so on. However, cash itself (and also most commercial checking accounts) earns no interest. Thus, the goal of the cash manager

AMERICAN STANDARD EMBRACES DEMAND FLOW MANAGEMENT

The recent history of New Jersey based American Standard provides an interesting illustration of how demand flow management can dramatically improve corporate performance. Fighting off a hostile bid from Black and Decker, American Standard's management undertook a leveraged buyout in 1988. The resulting debt load and a weak economy devastated the company, so in 1989, the newly promoted CEO, Emmanuel Kampouris, began looking for ways to improve the company's profitability.

Kampouris decided that demand flow management would improve efficiency. So far, the strategy has paid off handsomely. The company has dramatically reduced the time it takes to produce a wide variety of products. For example, bathroom fixtures, which had taken three weeks to produce, are now ready for sale in less than four days. As a result, working capital as a percentage of sales has shrunk dramatically. Sales have risen, but inventories have fallen, and inventory turnover has increased sharply.

American Standard's achievements have drawn the attention of many companies, including General Electric. After implementing its own demand flow management, GE succeeded in reducing inventories in some of its plants by up to 30 percent.

SOURCE: "American Standard Wises Up," *Business Week,* November 18, 1996, 70–74.

is to minimize the amount of cash the firm must hold for use in conducting its normal business activities, yet, at the same time, to have sufficient cash (1) to take trade discounts, (2) to maintain its credit rating, and (3) to meet unexpected cash needs. We begin our analysis with a discussion of the reasons for holding cash.

Rationale for Holding Cash

Firms hold cash for two primary reasons:

1. **Transactions.** Cash balances are necessary in business operations. Payments must be made in cash, and receipts are deposited in the cash account. Cash balances associated with routine payments and collections are known as **transactions balances.**
2. **Compensation to banks for providing loans and services.** A bank makes money by lending out funds that have been deposited with it, so the larger its deposits, the better the bank's profit position. If a bank is providing services to a customer, it may require the customer to leave a minimum balance on deposit to help offset the costs of providing the services. Also, banks may require borrowers to hold deposits at the bank. Both types of deposits are defined as **compensating balances,** and they are discussed in detail later in this chapter.

Two other reasons for holding cash have been noted in the finance and economics literature: for *precaution* and for *speculation.* Cash inflows and outflows are unpredictable, with the degree of predictability varying among firms and industries. Therefore, firms need to hold some cash in reserve for random, unforeseen fluctuations in inflows and outflows. These "safety stocks" are called **precautionary balances,** and the less predictable the firm's cash flows, the larger such balances should be. However, if the firm has easy access to borrowed funds — that is, if it can borrow on short notice — its need for precautionary balances is reduced. Also, as we note later in this chapter, firms that would otherwise need large precautionary balances tend to hold highly liquid marketable securities rather than cash per se. Marketable securities serve many of the purposes of cash, but they provide greater interest income than bank deposits.

Some cash balances may be held to enable the firm to take advantage of bargain purchases that might arise; these funds are called **speculative balances.** However, firms today are more likely to rely on reserve borrowing capacity and/or marketable securities portfolios than on cash per se for speculative purposes.

The cash accounts of most firms can be thought of as consisting of transactions, compensating, precautionary, and speculative balances. However, we cannot calculate the amount needed for each purpose, sum them, and produce a total desired cash balance, because the same money often serves more than one purpose. For instance, precautionary and speculative balances can also be used to satisfy compensating balance requirements. Firms do, however, consider all four factors when establishing their target cash positions.

Advantages of Holding Adequate Cash and Near-Cash Assets

In addition to the four motives just discussed, sound working capital management requires that an ample supply of cash and near-cash assets be maintained for several specific reasons:

1. It is essential that the firm have sufficient cash and near-cash assets to take **trade discounts.** Suppliers frequently offer customers discounts for early payment of bills. As we will see in the next chapter, the cost of not taking discounts is very high, so firms should have enough cash to permit payment of bills in time to take discounts.

2. Adequate holdings of cash and near-cash assets can help the firm maintain its credit rating by keeping its current and acid test ratios in line with those of other firms in its industry. A strong credit rating enables the firm both to purchase goods from suppliers on favorable terms and to maintain an ample line of low-cost credit with its bank.

3. Cash and near-cash assets are useful for taking advantage of favorable business opportunities, such as special offers from suppliers or the chance to acquire another firm.

4. The firm should have sufficient cash and near-cash assets to meet such emergencies as strikes, fires, or competitors' marketing campaigns, and to weather seasonal and cyclical downturns.

SELF-TEST
QUESTIONS

Why is cash management important?

What are the two primary motives for holding cash?

What are the two secondary motives for holding cash as noted in the finance and economics literature?

THE CASH BUDGET

The firm estimates its needs for cash as a part of its general budgeting, or forecasting, process. First, it forecasts sales, its fixed asset and inventory requirements, and the times when payments must be made. This information is combined with projections about when accounts receivable will be collected, taxes paid, dividend and interest payment dates, and so on. All of this information is summarized in the **cash budget,** which shows the firm's projected cash inflows and outflows over some specified period. Generally, firms use a daily cash budget forecasted over the next month, plus less detailed monthly cash budgets for the coming year. The monthly cash budgets are used for planning purposes, and the daily or weekly budgets for actual cash control.

The cash budget provides more detailed information concerning future cash flows than do the forecasted financial statements. In Chapter 14, we developed MicroDrive

Incorporated's 1999 forecasted financial statements. MicroDrive's projected 1999 sales were $3,300 million, resulting in a net cash flow provided by operations of $162 million. When all expenditures and financing flows are considered, MicroDrive's cash account is projected to increase by $1 million in 1999. Does this mean that MicroDrive will not have to worry about cash shortages during 1999? To answer this question, we must construct MicroDrive's cash budget for 1999.

To simplify the example, we will only consider MicroDrive's cash budget for the last half of 1999. Further, we will not list every cash flow but rather focus on the operating cash flows. MicroDrive's sales peak is in September, when personal computer manufacturers are beginning their peak sales season. All sales are made on terms of 2/10, net 40, meaning that a 2 percent discount is allowed if payment is made within 10 days, and, if the discount is not taken, the full amount is due in 40 days. However, like most companies, MicroDrive finds that some of its customers delay payment up to 90 days. Experience has shown that payment on 20 percent of MicroDrive's dollar sales is made during the month in which the sale is made—these are the discount sales. On 70 percent of sales, payment is made during the month immediately following the month of sale, and on 10 percent of sales payment is made in the second month following the month of sale.

The costs of component parts and packaging materials average 70 percent of the sales prices of the finished products. These purchases are generally made one month before the firm expects to sell the finished products, but MicroDrive's purchase terms with its suppliers allow it to delay payments for 30 days. Accordingly, if July sales are forecasted at $300 million, then purchases during June will amount to $210 million, and this amount will actually be paid in July.

Such other cash expenditures as wages and rent are also built into the cash budget, and MicroDrive must make estimated tax payments of $30 million on September 15 and $20 million on December 15. Also, a $100 million payment for a new plant must be made in October. Assuming that MicroDrive's **target cash balance** is $10 million, and that it projects $15 million to be on hand on July 1, 1999, what will its monthly cash surpluses or shortfalls be for the period from July to December?

The monthly cash flows are shown in Table 21-1. Section I of the table provides a worksheet for calculating both collections on sales and payments on purchases. Line 1 gives the sales forecast for the period from May through December. (May and June sales are necessary to determine collections for July and August.) Next, Lines 2 through 5 show cash collections. Line 2 shows that 20 percent of the sales during any given month are collected during that month. Customers who pay in the first month, however, take the discount, so the cash collected in the month of sale is reduced by 2 percent; for example, collections during July for the $300 million of sales in that month will be 20 percent times sales times 1.0 minus the 2 percent discount = $(0.20)($300)(0.98) \approx 59 million. Line 3 shows the collections on the previous month's sales, or 70 percent of sales in the preceding month; for example, in July, 70 percent of the $250 million June sales, or $175 million, will be collected. Line 4 gives collections from sales two months earlier, or 10 percent of sales in that month; for example, the July collections for May sales are $(0.10)($200) = 20 million. The collections during each month are summed and shown on Line 5; thus, the July collections represent 20 percent of July sales (minus the discount) plus 70 percent of June sales plus 10 percent of May sales, or $254 million in total.

Next, payments for purchases of raw materials are shown. July sales are forecasted at $300 million, so MicroDrive will purchase $210 million of materials in June (Line 6) and pay for these purchases in July (Line 7). Similarly, MicroDrive will purchase $280 million of materials in July to meet August's forecasted sales of $400 million.

| TABLE 21-1 | | MicroDrive Inc.: Cash Budget (Millions of Dollars) | | | | | |

	MAY	JUN	JUL	AUG	SEP	OCT	NOV	DEC
I. COLLECTIONS AND PURCHASES WORKSHEET								
(1) Sales (gross)[a]	$200	$250	$300	$400	$500	$350	$250	$200
Collections								
(2) During month of sale: (0.2)(0.98)(month's sales)			59	78	98	69	49	39
(3) During first month after sale: 0.7(previous month's sales)			175	210	280	350	245	175
(4) During second month after sale: 0.1(sales 2 months ago)			20	25	30	40	50	35
(5) Total collections (2 + 3 + 4)			$254	$313	$408	$459	$344	$249
Purchases								
(6) 0.7(next month's sales)		$210	$280	$350	$245	$175	$140	
(7) Payments (prior month's purchases)			$210	$280	$350	$245	$175	$140
II. CASH GAIN OR LOSS FOR MONTH								
(8) Collections (from Section I)			$254	$313	$408	$459	$344	$249
(9) Payments for purchases (from Section I)			$210	$280	$350	$245	$175	$140
(10) Wages and salaries			30	40	50	40	30	30
(11) Rent			15	15	15	15	15	15
(12) Other expenses			10	15	20	15	10	10
(13) Taxes					30			20
(14) Payment for plant construction						100		
(15) Total payments			$265	$350	$465	$415	$230	$215
(16) Net cash gain (loss) during month (Line 8 − Line 15)			($ 11)	($ 37)	($ 57)	$44	$114	$ 34
III. LOAN REQUIREMENT OR CASH SURPLUS								
(17) Cash at start of month if no borrowing is done[b]			$ 15	$ 4	($ 33)	($ 90)	($ 46)	$ 68
(18) Cash (cash at start +gain or −loss = Line 16 + Line 17)			$ 4	($ 33)	($ 90)	($ 46)	$ 68	$102
(19) Target cash balance			10	10	10	10	10	10
(20) Cumulative surplus cash (or loans outstanding) to maintain $10 target cash balance: (Line 18 − Line 19)[c]			($ 6)	($ 43)	($100)	($ 56)	$ 58	$ 92

[a]Although the budget period is July through December, sales and purchases data for May and June are needed to determine collections and payments during July and August. Gross sales are before discounts have been deducted.

[b]The amount shown on Line 17 for July, the $15 balance (in millions), is on hand initially. The values shown for each of the following months on Line 17 are equal to the cumulative cash as shown on Line 18 for the preceding month; for example, the $4 shown on Line 17 for August is taken from Line 18 in the July column.

[c]When the target cash balance of $10 (Line 19) is deducted from the cash balance (Line 18), a resulting negative figure on Line 20 (shown in parentheses) represents a required loan, whereas a positive figure represents surplus cash. Loans are required from July through October, and surpluses are expected during November and December. Note also that firms can borrow or pay off loans on a daily basis, so the $6 million borrowed during July would be done on a daily basis, as needed, and during October the $100 million loan that existed at the beginning of the month would be reduced daily to the $56 million ending balance, which, in turn, would be completely paid off during November.

With Section I completed, Section II can be constructed. Cash from collections is shown on Line 8. Lines 9 through 14 list payments made during each month, and these payments are summed on Line 15. The difference between cash receipts and cash payments (Line 8 minus Line 15) is the net cash gain or loss during the month. For July there is a net cash loss of $11 million, as shown on Line 16.

In Section III, we first determine the cash balance MicroDrive would have at the start of each month, assuming no borrowing is done. This is shown on Line 17. Micro-Drive will have $15 million on hand on July 1. The beginning cash balance (Line 17) is then added to the net cash gain or loss during the month (Line 16) to obtain the cash that would be on hand if no financing were done (Line 18). At the end of July, Micro-Drive forecasts a cash balance of $4 million in the absence of borrowing.

The target cash balance, $10 million, is then subtracted from the Line 17 cash balance to determine the firm's borrowing requirements, shown in parentheses, or its surplus cash. Because MicroDrive expects to have cumulative cash, as shown on Line 18, of only $4 million in July, it will have to borrow $6 million to bring the cash account up to the target balance of $10 million. Assuming that this amount is indeed borrowed, loans outstanding will total $6 million at the end of July. (MicroDrive did not have any loans outstanding on July 1.) The cash surplus or required loan balance is given on Line 20; a positive value indicates a cash surplus, whereas a negative value indicates a loan requirement. Note that the surplus cash or loan requirement shown on Line 20 is a *cumulative amount*. MicroDrive must borrow $6 million in July. Then, it has an additional cash shortfall during August of $37 million as reported on Line 16, so its total loan requirement at the end of August is $6 + $37 = $43 million, as reported on Line 20. MicroDrive's arrangement with the bank permits it to increase its outstanding loans on a daily basis, up to a prearranged maximum, just as you could increase the amount you owe on a credit card. MicroDrive will use any surplus funds it generates to pay off its loans, and because the loan can be paid down at any time, on a daily basis, the firm will never have both a cash surplus and an outstanding loan balance.

This same procedure is used in the following months. Sales will peak in September, accompanied by increased payments for purchases, wages, and other items. Receipts from sales will also go up, but the firm will still be left with a $57 million net cash outflow during the month. The total loan requirement at the end of September will hit a peak of $100 million, the cumulative cash plus the target cash balance. The $100 million can also be found as the $43 million needed at the end of August plus the $57 million cash deficit for September.

Sales, purchases, and payments for past purchases will fall sharply in October, but collections will be the highest of any month because they will reflect the high September sales. As a result, MicroDrive will enjoy a healthy $44 million net cash gain during October. This net gain can be used to pay off borrowings, so loans outstanding will decline by $44 million, to $56 million.

MicroDrive will have an even larger cash surplus in November, which will permit it to pay off all of its loans. In fact, the company is expected to have $58 million in surplus cash by the month's end, and another cash surplus in December will swell the excess cash to $92 million. With such a large amount of unneeded funds, MicroDrive's treasurer will certainly want to invest in interest-bearing securities or to put the funds to use in some other way.

Here are some additional points about cash budgets:

1. For simplicity, our illustrative budget for MicroDrive omitted many important cash flows that are anticipated for 1999, such as dividends and proceeds from stock and

bond sales. Some of these are projected to occur in the first half of the year, but those that are projected for the July–December period could easily be added to the table. The final cash budget should contain all projected cash inflows and outflows, and it should be consistent with the forecasted financial statements.

2. Our cash budget does not reflect interest on loans or income from investing surplus cash. This refinement could easily be added.

3. If cash inflows and outflows are not uniform during the month, we could seriously understate the firm's peak financing requirements. The data in Table 21-1 show the situation expected on the last day of each month, but on any given day during the month, it could be quite different. For example, if all payments had to be made on the fifth of each month, but collections came in uniformly throughout the month, the firm would need to borrow much larger amounts than those shown in Table 21-1. In this case, we would need a daily cash budget.

4. Since depreciation is a noncash charge, it does not appear on the cash budget other than through its effect on taxable income, hence on taxes paid.

5. Since the cash budget represents a forecast, all the values in the table are *expected* values. If actual sales, purchases, and so on, are different from the forecasted levels, then the projected cash deficits and surpluses will also be incorrect. Thus, MicroDrive might end up needing to borrow larger amounts than are indicated on Line 20, so it should arrange a line of credit in excess of that amount. For example, if MicroDrive's monthly sales turn out to be only 80 percent of their forecasted levels, its maximum cumulative borrowing requirement will turn out to be $126 million rather than $100 million, a 26 percent increase from the expected figure.

6. Spreadsheet programs are particularly well suited for constructing and analyzing cash budgets, especially with respect to the sensitivity of cash flows to changes in sales levels, collection periods, and the like. We could change any assumption, say, the projected monthly sales or the lag before customers pay, and the cash budget would automatically and instantly be recalculated. This would show us how the firm's borrowing requirements would change if conditions changed. Also, with a spreadsheet model, it is easy to add features like interest paid on loans, interest earned on marketable securities, and so on. We have written such a model for the computer-related problem at the end of the chapter.

7. Finally, we should note that the target cash balance probably will be adjusted over time, rising and falling with seasonal patterns and with long-term changes in the scale of the firm's operations. Thus, MicroDrive will probably plan to maintain larger cash balances during August and September than at other times, and as the company grows, so will its required cash balance. Also, the firm might even set the target cash balance at zero—this could be done if it carried a portfolio of marketable securities which could be sold to replenish the cash account, or if it had an arrangement with its bank that permitted it to borrow any funds needed on a daily basis. In that event, the cash budget would simply stop with Line 18, and the amounts on that line would represent projected loans outstanding or surplus cash. Note, though, that most firms would find it difficult to operate with a zero-balance bank account, just as you would, and the costs of such an operation would in most instances offset the costs associated with maintaining a positive cash balance. Therefore, most firms do set a positive target cash balance. Statistics are not available on whether transactions balances or compensating balances actually control most firms' target cash balances, but compensat-

ing balance requirements do often dominate, especially during periods of high interest rates and tight money.[1]

S E L F - T E S T
Q U E S T I O N S

What is the purpose of a cash budget?

What are the three major sections of a cash budget?

Suppose a firm's cash flows do not occur uniformly throughout the month. What impact would this have on the accuracy of the forecasted borrowing requirements?

How could uncertainty be handled in a cash budget?

Does depreciation appear in a cash budget? Explain.

CASH MANAGEMENT TECHNIQUES

Cash management has changed significantly over the last 20 years for two reasons. First, from the early 1970s to the mid-1980s, there was an upward trend in interest rates that increased the opportunity cost of holding cash. This encouraged financial managers to search for more efficient ways of managing cash. Second, technological developments, particularly computerized electronic funds transfer mechanisms, changed the way cash is managed.

Most cash management activities are performed jointly by the firm and its banks. Effective cash management encompasses proper management of cash inflows and outflows, which entails (1) improving forecasts of cash flows, (2) synchronizing cash inflows and outflows, (3) using float, (4) accelerating collections, (5) getting available funds to where they are needed, and (6) controlling disbursements. Most business is conducted by large firms, many of which operate regionally, nationally, or even globally. They collect cash from many sources and make payments from a number of different cities or even countries. For example, companies such as IBM, General Motors, and Hewlett-Packard have manufacturing plants all around the world, even more sales offices, and bank accounts in virtually every city where they do business. Their collection points follow sales patterns. Some disbursements are made from local offices, but most are made in the cities where manufacturing occurs, or else from the home office. Thus, a major corporation might have hundreds or even thousands of bank accounts, and since there is no reason to think that inflows and outflows will balance in each account, a system must be in place to transfer funds from where they come in to where they are needed, to arrange loans to cover net corporate shortfalls, and to invest net corporate surpluses without delay. We discuss the most commonly used techniques for accomplishing these tasks in the following sections.

Cash Flow Synchronization

If you as an individual were to receive income once a year, you would probably put it in the bank, draw down your account periodically, and have an average balance during the year equal to about half your annual income. If you received income monthly instead

---

[1]This point was underscored by an incident that occurred at a professional finance meeting. A professor presented a scholarly paper that used operations research techniques to determine "optimal cash balances" for a sample of firms. He then reported that the firms' actual cash balances greatly exceeded their optimal balances, suggesting inefficiency and the need for more refined techniques. The discussant of the paper made her comments short and sweet. She reported that she had written each of the sample firms and asked them why they had so much cash; they had uniformly replied that their cash holdings were set by compensating balance requirements. Thus, the model might have been useful to determine the optimal cash balance in the absence of compensating balance requirements, but it was precisely those requirements that determined actual balances.

of once a year, you would operate similarly, but now your average balance would be much smaller. If you could arrange to receive income daily and to pay rent, tuition, and other charges on a daily basis, and if you were confident of your forecasted inflows and outflows, then you could hold a very small average cash balance.

Exactly the same situation holds for businesses—by improving their forecasts and by arranging things so that cash receipts coincide with cash requirements, firms can reduce their transactions balances to a minimum. Recognizing all this, utility companies, oil companies, credit card companies, and so on, arrange to bill customers, and to pay their own bills, on regular "billing cycles" throughout the month. This **synchronization of cash flows** provides cash when it is needed and thus enables firms to reduce cash balances, decrease bank loans, lower interest expenses, and boost profits.

Speed Up the Check-Clearing Process

When a customer writes and mails a check, this *does not* mean that the funds are immediately available to the receiving firm. Most of us have been told by someone that "the check is in the mail," and we have also deposited a check in our account and then been told that we cannot write our own checks against this deposit until the **check-clearing** process has been completed. Our bank must first make sure that the check we deposited is good and the funds are available before it will give us cash.

In practice, it may take some time for a firm to process incoming checks and obtain the use of the money. A check must first be delivered through the mail and then be cleared through the banking system before the money can be put to use. Checks received from customers in distant cities are especially subject to delays because of mail time and also because more parties are involved. For example, assume that we receive a check and deposit it in our bank. Our bank must send the check to the bank on which it was drawn. Only when this latter bank transfers funds to our bank are the funds available for us to use. Checks are generally cleared through the Federal Reserve System or through a clearinghouse set up by the banks in a particular city. Of course, if the check is deposited in the same bank on which it was drawn, that bank merely transfers funds by bookkeeping entries from one depositor to another. The length of time required for checks to clear is thus a function of the distance between the payer's and the payee's banks. In the case of private clearinghouses, it can range from one to three days. Checks are generally cleared through the Federal Reserve System in about two days, but mail delays can slow down things on each end of the Fed's involvement in the process.

Using Float

Float is defined as the difference between the balance shown in a firm's (or individual's) checkbook and the balance on the bank's records. Suppose a firm writes, on average, checks in the amount of $5,000 each day, and it takes six days for these checks to clear and to be deducted from the firm's bank account. This will cause the firm's own checkbook to show a balance $30,000 smaller than the balance on the bank's records; this difference is called **disbursement float.** Now suppose the firm also receives checks in the amount of $5,000 daily, but it loses four days while they are being deposited and cleared. This will result in $20,000 of **collections float.** In total, the firm's **net float**— the difference between the $30,000 positive disbursement float and the $20,000 negative collections float—will be $10,000.

If the firm's own collection and clearing process is more efficient than that of the recipients of its checks—which is generally true of larger, more efficient firms—then the firm could actually show a *negative* balance on its own books but have a *positive* balance on its bank records. Some firms indicate that they *never* have positive book cash balances. One large manufacturer of construction equipment stated that while its account, according to its bank's records, shows an average cash balance of about $20 million, its *book* cash balance is *minus* $20 million—it has $40 million of net float. Obviously, the firm must be able to forecast its disbursements and collections accurately in order to make such heavy use of float.

E. F. Hutton provides an example of pushing cash management too far. Hutton, a leading brokerage firm at the time, did business with banks across the country, and it had to keep compensating balances in these banks. The sizes of the required compensating balances were known, and any excess funds in these banks were sent electronically, on a daily basis, to New York and San Francisco banks, where they were immediately invested in interest-bearing securities. However, rather than waiting to see what the end-of-day balances actually were, Hutton began estimating inflows and outflows, and it transferred out for investment the *estimated* end-of-day excess. But then Hutton got greedy and began *kiting* checks. Hutton deliberately overestimated its deposits and underestimated clearings of its own checks, thereby deliberately overstating its estimated end-of-day balances. As a result, Hutton was chronically overdrawn at its local banks, and it was in effect earning interest on funds which really belonged to those local banks. It is entirely proper to forecast what your bank will have recorded as your balance and then to make decisions based on the estimate, even if that balance is different from the balance your own books show. However, it is illegal to forecast an overdrawn situation but then to tell the bank that you expect to have a positive balance.[2]

Delays that cause float arise because it takes time for checks (1) to travel through the mail (mail float), (2) to be processed by the receiving firm (processing float), and (3) to clear through the banking system (clearing, or availability, float). Basically, the size of a firm's net float is a function of its ability to speed up collections on checks received and to slow down collections on checks written. Efficient firms go to great lengths to speed up the processing of incoming checks, thus putting the funds to work faster, and they try to stretch their own payments out as long as possible.

Acceleration of Receipts

Financial managers have searched for ways to collect receivables faster since credit transactions began. Although cash collection is the financial manager's responsibility, the speed with which checks are cleared depends on the banking system. Several techniques are now used both to speed collections and to get funds where they are needed. Included are (1) lockbox plans established close to customers and (2) requiring large customers to pay by wire or automatic debit.

Lockboxes.   A **lockbox plan** is one of the oldest cash management tools. In a lockbox system, incoming checks are sent to post office boxes rather than to corporate headquarters. For example, a firm headquartered in New York City might have its West Coast customers send their payments to a box in San Francisco, its customers in the

---

[2] A question raised during the Hutton investigation was this: "Why didn't the banks recognize that Hutton was systematically overdrawing its account and call the company to task?" The answer is that some banks, with tight controls, did exactly that—they refused to let Hutton get away with the practice. Other banks were lax. Still other banks apparently let Hutton get away with being chronically overdrawn out of fear of losing its business: Hutton used its economic muscle to force the banks to let it get away with an illegal act. In many people's opinion, the banks were as much at fault as Hutton. Still, in business dealings, honesty is presumed, and Hutton was dishonest in its dealings with the banks. This dishonesty severely damaged Hutton's reputation, cost the company profits totaling hundreds of millions of dollars, cost its top managers their jobs, and contributed to the ultimate demise of the company.

Southwest send their checks to Dallas, and so on, rather than having all checks sent to New York City. Several times a day a local bank will collect the contents of the lockbox and deposit the checks into the company's local account. The bank then provides the firm with a daily record of the receipts collected, usually via an electronic data transmission system in a format that permits on-line updating of the firm's accounts receivable records.

A lockbox system reduces the time required for a firm to receive incoming checks, to deposit them, and to get them cleared through the banking system so the funds are available for use. Lockbox services can often increase the availability of funds by two to five days over the "regular" system.

Payment by Wire or Automatic Debit.   Firms are increasingly demanding payments of larger bills by wire, or even by automatic electronic debits, whereby funds are automatically deducted from one account and added to another. This is, of course, the ultimate in a speeded-up collection process, and computer technology is making such a process increasingly feasible and efficient.

SELF - TEST
QUESTIONS

What is float? How do firms use float to increase cash management efficiency?

What are some methods firms can use to accelerate receipts?

MARKETABLE SECURITIES

Realistically, the management of cash and marketable securities cannot be separated—management of one implies management of the other. In the first part of the chapter, we focused on cash management. Now, we turn to **marketable securities.**

Marketable securities typically provide much lower yields than operating assets. For example, at the end of 1997 Ford held a $19 billion portfolio of short-term marketable securities that yielded about 6 percent, but its operating assets provided a much higher return. Why would a company such as Ford have such large holdings of low-yielding assets?

In many cases, companies hold marketable securities for the same reasons they hold cash. Although these securities are not the same as cash, in most cases they can be converted to cash on very short notice (often just a few minutes) with a single telephone call. Moreover, while cash and most commercial checking accounts yield nothing, marketable securities provide at least a modest return. For this reason, many firms hold at least some marketable securities in lieu of larger cash balances, liquidating part of the portfolio to increase the cash account when cash outflows exceed inflows. In such situations, the marketable securities could be used as a substitute for transactions balances, for precautionary balances, for speculative balances, or for all three. In most cases, the securities are held primarily for precautionary purposes—most firms prefer to rely on bank credit to make temporary transactions or to meet speculative needs, but they may still hold some liquid assets to guard against a possible shortage of bank credit.

Although setting the target cash balance is, to a large extent, judgmental, analytical rules can be applied to help formulate better judgments. For example, years ago William Baumol recognized that the trade-off between cash and marketable securities is similar to the one firms face when setting the optimal level of inventory.[3] Baumol

---

[3]William J. Baumol, "The Transactions Demand for Cash: An Inventory Theoretic Approach," *Quarterly Journal of Economics,* November 1952, 545–556.

applied the EOQ inventory model to determine the optimal level of cash balances.[4] He suggested that cash holdings should be higher if costs are high and the time to liquidate marketable securities is long, but that those holdings should be lower if interest rates are low. His logic was that if it is expensive and time consuming to convert securities to cash, and if securities do not earn much because interest rates are low, then it does not pay to hold securities as opposed to cash. It does pay to hold securities if interest rates are high and the securities can be converted to cash quickly and cheaply.

SELF-TEST
QUESTIONS

Why might a company hold low-yielding marketable securities when it could earn a much higher return on operating assets?

Why would a low interest rate environment lead to larger cash balances?

How might improvements in telecommunications technology affect the level of corporations' cash balances?

INVENTORY

Inventories, which may be classified as (1) *supplies,* (2) *raw materials,* (3) *work-in-process,* and (4) *finished goods,* are an essential part of virtually all business operations. As is the case with accounts receivable, inventory levels depend heavily upon sales. However, whereas receivables build up *after* sales have been made, inventory must be acquired *ahead* of sales. This is a critical difference, and the necessity of forecasting sales before establishing target inventory levels makes inventory management a difficult task. Also, since errors in the establishment of inventory levels quickly lead either to lost sales or to excessive carrying costs, inventory management is as important as it is difficult.

Inventory management techniques are covered in depth in production management courses. Still, since financial managers have a responsibility both for raising the capital needed to carry inventory and for the firm's overall profitability, we need to cover the financial aspects of inventory management here. Two examples will make clear the types of issues involved in inventory management, and the financial problems poor inventory control can cause.

Retail Clothing Store

Chicago Discount Clothing (CDC) must order swimsuits for summer sales in January, and it must take delivery by April to be sure of having enough suits to meet the heavy May–June demand. Bathing suits come in many styles, colors, and sizes, and if CDC stocks incorrectly, either in total or in terms of the style-color-size distribution, then the store will have trouble. It will lose potential sales if it stocks too few suits, and it will be forced to lower prices and take losses if it stocks too many or the wrong types.

The effects of inventory changes on the balance sheet are important. For simplicity, assume that CDC has a $10,000 base stock of inventory which is financed by common stock. Its balance sheet is as follows:

Inventory (base stock)	$10,000	Common stock	$10,000
Total assets	$10,000	Total claims	$10,000

[4]A more complete description of the Economic Ordering Quantity (EOQ) model can be found in Chapter 23.

Now it anticipates that it will sell $5,000 of swimsuits (at cost) this summer. Dollar sales will actually be greater than $5,000, since CDC makes about $200 in profits for every $1,000 of inventory sold. CDC finances its seasonal inventory with bank loans, so its pre-summer balance sheet would look like this:

Inventory (seasonal)	$ 5,000	Notes payable to bank	$ 5,000
Inventory (base stock)	10,000	Common stock	10,000
Total assets	$15,000	Total claims	$15,000

If everything works out as planned, sales will be made, inventory will be converted to cash, the bank loan will be retired, and the company will earn a profit. The balance sheet, after a successful season, might look like this:

Cash	$ 1,000	Notes payable to bank	$ 0
Inventory (seasonal)	0	Common stock	10,000
Inventory (base stock)	10,000	Retained earnings	1,000
Total assets	$11,000	Total claims	$11,000

The company is now in a highly liquid position and is ready to begin a new season.

But suppose the season had not gone well, and CDC had only sold $1,000 of its inventory. As fall approached, the balance sheet would look like this:

Cash	$ 200	Notes payable to bank	$ 4,000
Inventory (seasonal)	4,000	Common stock	10,000
Inventory (base stock)	10,000	Retained earnings	200
Total assets	$14,200	Total claims	$14,200

Now suppose the bank insists on repayment of the $4,000 outstanding on the loan, and it wants cash, not swimsuits. But if the swimsuits did not sell well in the summer, how will out-of-style suits sell in the fall? Assume that CDC is forced to mark the seasonal suits down to half their cost (not half the selling price) in order to sell them to raise cash to repay the bank loan. Here is the result:

Cash	$ 2,200	Notes payable to bank	$ 4,000
Inventory (base stock)	10,000	Common stock	10,000
		Retained earnings	(1,800)
Total assets	$12,200	Total claims	$12,200

At this point, CDC is in serious trouble. It does not have the cash to pay off the loan, and the firm's shareholders have lost $1,800 of their equity. If the bank will not extend the loan, and if other sources of cash are not available, CDC will have to mark down its base stock prices in an effort to stimulate sales, and if this does not work, CDC could be forced into bankruptcy. Clearly, poor inventory decisions can spell trouble.

Appliance Manufacturer

Now consider a different situation, that of Housepro Corporation, an appliance manufacturer. Here is its inventory position, in millions of dollars:

Raw materials	$ 200
Work-in-process	200
Finished goods	600
Total inventory	$1,000

Suppose Housepro anticipates that the economy is about to get much stronger and that the demand for appliances will rise sharply. If it is to share in the expected boom, Housepro will have to increase production. This means it will have to increase inventory, and, since the inventory buildup must precede sales, additional financing will be required—some liability account, perhaps notes payable, will have to be increased in order to finance the inventory buildup.

Proper inventory management requires close coordination among the sales, purchasing, production, and finance departments. The sales/marketing department is generally the first to spot changes in demand. These changes must be worked into the company's purchasing and manufacturing schedules, and the financial manager must arrange any financing needed to support the inventory buildup. Lack of coordination among departments, poor sales forecasts, or both, can lead to disaster.

SELF-TEST
QUESTIONS

Why is good inventory management essential to a firm's success?

What departments should be involved in inventory decisions?

INVENTORY COSTS

The twin goals of inventory management are (1) to ensure that the inventories needed to sustain operations are available, but (2) to hold the costs of ordering and carrying inventories to the lowest possible level. Table 21-2 gives a listing of the typical costs associated with inventory, divided into three categories: carrying costs,

TABLE 21-2   Costs Associated with Inventory

	APPROXIMATE ANNUAL COST AS A PERCENTAGE OF INVENTORY VALUE
I. Carrying Costs	
Cost of capital tied up	12.0%
Storage and handling costs	0.5
Insurance	0.5
Property taxes	1.0
Depreciation and obsolescence	12.0
Total	26.0%
II. Ordering, Shipping, and Receiving Costs	
Cost of placing orders, including production and set-up costs	Varies
Shipping and handling costs	2.5%
III. Costs of Running Short	
Loss of sales	Varies
Loss of customer goodwill	Varies
Disruption of production schedules	Varies

NOTE: These costs vary from firm to firm, from item to item, and also over time. The figures shown are U.S. Department of Commerce estimates for an average manufacturing firm. Where costs vary so widely that no meaningful numbers can be assigned, the term "Varies" is reported.

ordering and receiving costs, and the costs that are incurred if the firm runs short of inventory.

Inventory is costly to store; therefore, there is always pressure to reduce inventory as part of firms' overall cost-containment strategies. A recent article in *Fortune* highlights the fact that an increasing number of corporations are taking drastic steps to control inventory costs.[5] For example, Trane Corporation, which makes air conditioners, recently adopted the just-in-time inventory procedures described in the next section.

In the past, Trane produced parts on a steady basis, stored them as inventory, and had them ready whenever the company received an order for a batch of air conditioners. However, the company reached the point where its inventory covered an area equal to three football fields, and it still sometimes took as long as 15 days to fill an order. To make matters worse, occasionally some of the necessary components simply could not be located, while in other instances the components were located but found to have been damaged from long storage.

Then Trane adopted a new inventory policy—it began producing components only after an order is received, and then sending the parts directly from the machines which make them to the final assembly line. The net effect: Inventories fell nearly 40 percent even as sales increased by 30 percent.

However, as Table 21-2 indicates, there are costs associated with holding too little inventory, and these costs can be severe. Generally, if a business carries small inventories, it must reorder frequently. This increases ordering costs. Even more important, firms can miss out on profitable sales, and also suffer a loss of goodwill which can lead to lower future sales. So, it is important to have enough inventory on hand to meet customer demands.

Suppose IBM has developed a new line of notebook computers. How much inventory should it produce and have on hand when the marketing campaign is launched? If it fails to produce enough inventory, retailers and customers are likely to be frustrated because they cannot immediately purchase the highly advertised product. Rather than wait, many customers will purchase a notebook computer elsewhere. On the other hand, if IBM has too much inventory, it will incur unnecessarily high carrying costs. In addition, computers become obsolete quickly, so if inventory levels are high but sales are mediocre, the company may have to discount the notebooks to sell them. Apart from reducing the profit margin on this year's line of computers, these discounts may push down computer prices in general, thereby reducing profit margins on the company's other products as well.

SELF-TEST QUESTIONS

What are the three categories of inventory costs?

What are some components of inventory carrying costs?

What are some components of inventory ordering costs?

INVENTORY CONTROL SYSTEMS

Inventory management requires the establishment of an *inventory control system.* Inventory control systems run the gamut from very simple to extremely complex, depending on the size of the firm and the nature of its inventory. For example, one simple control procedure is the **red-line method**—inventory items are stocked in a bin, a

---

[5]Shawn Tully, "Raiding a Company's Hidden Cash," *Fortune*, August 22, 1994, 82–87.

red line is drawn around the inside of the bin at the level of the reorder point, and the inventory clerk places an order when the red line shows. The **two-bin method** has inventory items stocked in two bins. When the working bin is empty, an order is placed and inventory is drawn from the second bin. These procedures work well for parts such as bolts in a manufacturing process, or for many items in retail businesses.

Computerized Systems

Most companies today employ **computerized inventory control systems.** The computer starts with an inventory count in memory. As withdrawals are made, they are recorded by the computer, and the inventory balance is revised. When the reorder point is reached, the computer automatically places an order, and when the order is received, the recorded balance is increased. As we noted earlier, retailers such as Wal-Mart have carried this system quite far — each item has a bar code, and, as an item is checked out, the code is read, a signal is sent to the computer, and the inventory balance is adjusted at the same time the price is fed into the cash register tape. When the balance drops to the reorder point, an order is placed. In Wal-Mart's case, the order goes directly from its computer to those of its suppliers.

A good inventory control system is dynamic, not static. A company such as Wal-Mart or General Motors stocks hundreds of thousands of different items. The sales (or use) of individual items can rise or fall separately from rising or falling overall corporate sales. As the usage rate for an item begins to rise or fall, the inventory manager must adjust its balance to avoid running short or ending up with obsolete items. If the change in the usage rate appears to be permanent, the safety stock should be reconsidered, and the computer model used in the control process should be reprogrammed.

Just-in-Time Systems

An approach to inventory control called the **just-in-time (JIT) system** was developed by Japanese firms but has gained popularity throughout the world. Toyota provides a good example of the just-in-time system. Eight of Toyota's ten factories, along with most of its suppliers, dot the countryside around Toyota City. Delivery of components is tied to the speed of the assembly line, and parts are generally delivered no more than a few hours before they are used. The just-in-time system reduces the need for Toyota and other manufacturers to carry large inventories, but it requires a great deal of coordination between the manufacturer and its suppliers, both in the timing of deliveries and the quality of the parts. Component parts must be perfect; otherwise, a few bad parts could stop the entire production line. Therefore, JIT inventory management has been developed in conjunction with total quality management (TQM).

Not surprisingly, U.S. automobile manufacturers were among the first domestic firms to move toward just-in-time systems. Ford has been restructuring its production system with a goal of increasing its inventory turnover from 20 times a year to 30 or 40 times. Of course, just-in-time systems place considerable pressure on suppliers. GM formerly kept a ten-day supply of seats and other parts made by Lear Siegler; now GM sends in orders at four- to eight-hour intervals and expects immediate shipment. A Lear Siegler spokesman stated, "We can't afford to keep things sitting around either," so Lear Siegler has had to be tougher on its own suppliers.

Just-in-time systems are also being adopted by smaller firms. In fact, some production experts say that small companies are better positioned than large ones to use just-in-time methods, because it is easier to redefine job functions and to educate people in small firms. One small-firm example is Fireplace Manufacturers Inc., a manufacturer of prefabricated fireplaces. The company was recently having cash flow problems, and it

KEEPING INVENTORY LEAN

What do just-in-time (JIT) inventory methods and supercomputers have in common? The answer is that both are being used, in a coordinated manner, to keep U.S. business inventories remarkably lean. Recent statistics show that retail, wholesale, and factory inventories—taken together and adjusted for inflation—amount to just 1.4 times monthly sales, the lowest reading on record. And leaner inventories mean lower inventory carrying costs for businesses, hence greater profits.

JIT became the watchword for many U.S. manufacturers in the mid-1980s, as they began to adopt this Japanese method of inventory delivery. JIT involves redesigning production so that parts and raw materials flow into the factory just as they are needed, thus allowing manufacturers to save the cost of carrying inventories. Large firms, including General Motors, Campbell Soup, Motorola, Hewlett-Packard, and Intel, as well as dozens of small firms such as Omark Industries, an Oregon manufacturer of power saw chains, have converted to JIT. A recent survey of 385 manufacturing plants in the United States found that more than 16 percent were "extremely skilled" in JIT procedures, and another 44 percent had plans under way to "excel" in JIT operations. Importantly, the inventory turnover ratios of plants using JIT procedures were twice as high as those for the survey groups as a whole.

Large corporations started the just-in-time trend in the United States, but Robert W. Hall of Indiana University, who has written several books on the subject, says smaller companies are actually better positioned to adopt the method. Hall points out that small firms usually have only one plant to convert, and they usually have simpler accounting and planning systems. Also, their management groups are smaller and can make faster decisions than can larger firms. Another advantage for many small firms is that smaller, nonunionized labor forces make it easier to redesign job functions.

Worker attitudes toward these changes have generally been the greatest stumbling block for companies—large or small—that convert to JIT methods. One company president says employee acceptance depends on management. "It's just a matter of managers getting their mind-sets correct." This can be difficult, though, since managers must give up the security of large inventories and trust their suppliers more than they ever have before. It is essential for managers to work closely with suppliers to ensure that parts or materials get to the plant at the right time and in the right sequence for the assembly line.

Cadbury Schweppes PLC, the London food and beverage producer, has inventory levels that are a fraction of what they were in the mid-1980s as a result of "closer cooperation with a smaller but better informed set of suppliers." The Schweppes unit gets 80 percent of its glass containers from a single supplier, as compared with 30 percent seven years ago. The firm's director of purchasing commented, "We used to play one off against the other and keep them guessing, but now we work very closely together, providing sales forecasts and other data we once kept to ourselves." By working in this way, the Schweppes unit has been able to reduce its inventory carrying costs, including financing and warehousing costs, dramatically.

When a company adopts the JIT method, it is essential that managers be concerned not only with their own problems but also with those faced by their suppliers. Xerox, for instance, went into the new system with the idea that "this was an inventory reduction program for our benefit," according to the materials manager for the copier division, "and we treated it that way, asking suppliers to hold inventories without compensation. Suppliers protested, and good relationships built over many years began to deteriorate." To improve the situation, Xerox reorganized its production and

was carrying $1.1 million in inventory to support annual sales of about $8 million. The company went to a just-in-time system, trimmed its raw material and work-in-process inventory to $750,000, and freed up $350,000 of cash, even as sales doubled.

The close coordination required between the parties using JIT procedures has led to an overall reduction of inventory throughout the production-distribution system, and to a general improvement in economic efficiency. This point is made by companies such as Wal-Mart and Toyota, and it is borne out by economic statistics, which show that inventory as a percentage of sales has been declining since the use of just-in-time procedures began.

Out-Sourcing

Another important development related to inventory is **out-sourcing,** which is the practice of purchasing components rather than making them in-house. Thus, if GM arranged to buy radiators, axles, and other parts from suppliers rather than making ordering schedules so suppliers could plan better. It also formed classes to teach JIT to its suppliers. One supplier, Rockford Dynatorq, reduced the time needed to make one brake part from three and a half weeks to just one day with the help of Xerox. Rockford's inventory dropped by 10 percent in just six months.

Improvement in quality control is a common by-product of JIT. First, with smaller inventories it is more critical than ever that there be few unusable units. In addition, many wasteful procedures are also discovered when manufacturers reevaluate their production processes for JIT conversion. Costs that add nothing to a product's value are incurred every time an item is moved, inspected, or stored in inventory, and JIT helps trim these costs.

Retailers such as Kmart, Wal-Mart, and Dayton Hudson are using a sophisticated approach to maintaining lean inventories and reducing carrying costs. These firms are using supercomputers, extraordinarily powerful parallel computers, to help managers decide what to buy, where to stock it, and when to cut prices. Wayne Hood, a retail analyst with Prudential Securities, states that "Technology like this is absolutely critical . . . It's going to separate the winners from the losers in retailing. Companies that don't invest in tech-nology—even in hard times—won't make it."

The parallel design of these supercomputers, where thousands of small processors work as one instead of having two to four large processors as in mainframe computers, permits retailing managers to quickly access data. For example, managers can obtain data on-line instantly from every register, in every store, during the last year: What was sold, when, and what were the colors, styles, sizes, and prices? These managers can then act on this information. Mainframe computers would choke on this terabyte (a trillion characters of information) of data. In addition to having the capability of accessing such information, the supercomputers are less costly than the mainframes.

Supercomputers have been especially effective in managing seasonal inventory items. Seasonal merchandise, such as Christmas and Valentine's Day items, have high profit margins, so it is bad to have them go out of stock. But they also have a "death date"—a time at which they must be completely sold out. Therefore, such items need to be tightly managed. By using supercomputers, Kmart was able to determine that it sold 50 percent of its Valentine inventory in a particular store in the last two days, hence that there was no need to panic and mark down prices to move the stock. Thus, the store managers were able to avoid unnecessary price cuts, and this increased the stores' profits.

It is apparent from firms' statements and from reported statistics that the trend to lower inventory levels represents a long-term, serious commitment. According to Geoffrey Moore, a Columbia University economist, the trend toward leaner inventories will reduce the volatility of U.S. business cycles because with smaller stockpiles of inventories, inventory draw-downs during recessions cannot last as long. Therefore, production must pick up sooner than would be the case if initial inventories were larger. Thus, it appears that JIT procedures, combined with supercomputers, will lower companies' costs and help stabilize the economy. But they will also make life increasingly difficult for smaller, less efficient firms.

SOURCES: "Small Manufacturers Shifting to 'Just-in-Time' Techniques," *The Wall Street Journal,* December 21, 1987; "Having a Hard Time," *Fortune,* June 9, 1986; "General Motors' Little Engine That Could," *Business Week,* August 3, 1987; "Firms' Inventories Are Remarkably Lean," *The Wall Street Journal,* November 3, 1992; "Supercomputers Manage Holiday Stock," *The Wall Street Journal,* December 23, 1992.

them itself, it would be increasing its use of out-sourcing. Out-sourcing is often combined with just-in-time systems to reduce inventory levels. However, perhaps the major reason for out-sourcing has nothing to do with inventory policy—a bureaucratic, unionized company like GM can often buy parts from a smaller, nonunionized supplier at a lower cost than if it made them itself.

The Relationship between Production Scheduling and Inventory Levels

A final point relating to inventory levels is *the relationship between production scheduling and inventory levels.* A firm such as a greeting card manufacturer has highly seasonal sales. Such a firm could produce on a steady, year-round basis, or it could let production rise and fall with sales. If it established a level production schedule, its production costs would be relatively low, but its inventory would rise sharply during periods when sales were low and then decline during peak sales periods, and the average inventory held would be substantially higher than if production rose and fell with sales.

Our discussions of just-in-time systems, out-sourcing, and production scheduling all point out the necessity of coordinating inventory policy with manufacturing/procurement policies. Companies try to minimize *total production and distribution costs,* and inventory costs are just one part of total costs. Still, they are an important cost, and financial managers should be aware of the determinants of inventory costs and how they can be minimized.

S E L F - T E S T
Q U E S T I O N S

Describe some inventory control systems that are used in practice.

What are just-in-time systems? What are their advantages? Why is quality especially important if a JIT system is used?

What is out-sourcing?

Describe the relationship between production scheduling and inventory levels.

RECEIVABLES MANAGEMENT

Firms would, in general, rather sell for cash than on credit, but competitive pressures force most firms to offer credit. Thus, goods are shipped, inventories are reduced, and an **account receivable** is created.[6] Eventually, the customer will pay the account, at which time (1) the firm will receive cash and (2) its receivables will decline. Carrying receivables has both direct and indirect costs, but it also has an important benefit— increased sales.

Receivables management begins with the decision of whether or not to grant credit. In this section, we discuss the manner in which receivables build up, and we also discuss several alternative ways to monitor receivables. A monitoring system is important, because without it receivables will build up to excessive levels, cash flows will decline, and bad debts will offset the profits on sales. Corrective action is often needed, and the only way to know whether the situation is getting out of hand is with a good receivables control system.

The Accumulation of Receivables

The total amount of accounts receivable outstanding at any given time is determined by two factors: (1) the volume of credit sales and (2) the average length of time between sales and collections. For example, suppose Boston Lumber Company (BLC), a wholesale distributor of lumber products, opens a warehouse on January 1 and, starting the first day, makes sales of $1,000 each day. For simplicity, we assume that all sales are on credit, and customers are given ten days to pay. At the end of the first day, accounts receivable will be $1,000; they will rise to $2,000 by the end of the second day; and by January 10, they will have risen to 10($1,000) = $10,000. On January 11, another $1,000 will be added to receivables, but payments for sales made on January 1 will

---

[6]Whenever goods are sold on credit, two accounts are created—an asset item entitled *accounts receivable* appears on the books of the selling firm, and a liability item called *accounts payable* appears on the books of the purchaser. At this point, we are analyzing the transaction from the viewpoint of the seller, so we are concentrating on the variables under its control, in this case, the receivables. We will examine the transaction from the viewpoint of the purchaser in Chapter 22, where we discuss accounts payable as a source of funds and consider their cost relative to the cost of funds obtained from other sources.

reduce receivables by $1,000, so total accounts receivable will remain constant at $10,000. In general, once the firm's operations have stabilized, this situation will exist:

$$\begin{matrix} \text{Accounts} \\ \text{receivable} \end{matrix} = \begin{matrix} \text{Credit sales} \\ \text{per day} \end{matrix} \times \begin{matrix} \text{Length of} \\ \text{collection period} \end{matrix} \qquad \textbf{(21-1)}$$

$$= \quad \$1,000 \quad \times \quad 10 \text{ days} \quad = \$10,000.$$

If either credit sales or the collection period changes, such changes will be reflected in accounts receivable.

Notice that the $10,000 investment in receivables must be financed. To illustrate, suppose that when the warehouse opened on January 1, BLC's shareholders had put up $800 as common stock and used this money to buy the goods sold the first day. The $800 of inventory will be sold for $1,000, so BLC's gross profit on the $800 investment is $200, or 25 percent. In this situation, the beginning balance sheet would be as follows:[7]

Inventories	$800	Common stock	$800
Total assets	$800	Total liabilities and equity	$800

At the end of the day, the balance sheet would look like this:

Accounts receivable	$1,000	Common stock	$ 800
Inventories	0	Retained earnings	200
Total assets	$1,000	Total liabilities and equity	$1,000

To remain in business, BLC must replenish inventories. To do so requires that $800 of goods be purchased, and this requires $800 in cash. Assuming that BLC borrows the $800 from the bank, the balance sheet at the start of the second day will be as follows:

Accounts receivable	$1,000	Notes payable to bank	$ 800
Inventories	800	Common stock	800
		Retained earnings	200
Total assets	$1,800	Total liabilities and equity	$1,800

At the end of the second day, the inventories will have been converted to receivables, and the firm will have to borrow another $800 to restock for the third day.

This process will continue, provided the bank is willing to lend the necessary funds, until the beginning of the 11th day, when the balance sheet reads as follows:

Accounts receivable	$10,000	Notes payable to bank	$ 8,000
Inventories	800	Common stock	800
		Retained earnings	2,000
Total assets	$10,800	Total liabilities and equity	$10,800

From this point on, $1,000 of receivables will be collected every day, and $800 of these funds can be used to purchase new inventories.

This example makes it clear (1) that accounts receivable depend jointly on the level of credit sales and the collection period, (2) that any increase in receivables must be

---

[7]Note that the firm would need other assets such as cash, fixed assets, and a permanent stock of inventory. Also, overhead costs and taxes would have to be deducted, so retained earnings would be less than the figures shown here. We abstract from these details here so that we may focus on receivables.

financed in some manner, but (3) that the entire amount of receivables does not have to be financed because the profit portion ($200 of each $1,000 of sales) does not represent a cash outflow. In our example, we assumed bank financing, but, as we demonstrate in Chapter 22, there are many alternative ways to finance current assets.

Monitoring the Receivables Position

Investors—both stockholders and bank loan officers—should pay close attention to accounts receivable management, for, as we shall see, one can be misled by reported financial statements and later suffer serious losses on an investment.

When a credit sale is made, the following events occur: (1) Inventories are reduced by the cost of goods sold, (2) accounts receivable are increased by the sales price, and (3) the difference is profit, which is added to retained earnings. If the sale is for cash, then the cash from the sale has actually been received by the firm, but if the sale is on credit, the firm will not receive the cash from the sale until the account is collected. Firms have been known to encourage "sales" to very weak customers in order to report high profits. This could boost the firm's stock price, at least until credit losses begin to lower earnings, at which time the stock price will fall. Analyses along the lines suggested in the following sections will detect any such questionable practice, as well as any unconscious deterioration in the quality of accounts receivable. Such early detection could help both investors and bankers avoid losses.[8]

Days Sales Outstanding (DSO).   Suppose Super Sets Inc., a television manufacturer, sells 200,000 television sets a year at a price of $198 each. Further, assume that all sales are on credit with the following terms: if payment is made within 10 days, customers will receive a 2 percent discount; otherwise the full amount is due within 30 days. Finally, assume that 70 percent of the customers take discounts and pay on Day 10, while the other 30 percent pay on Day 30.

Super Sets's **days sales outstanding (DSO),** sometimes called the **average collection period (ACP),** is 16 days:

$$DSO = ACP = 0.7(10 \text{ days}) + 0.3(30 \text{ days}) = 16 \text{ days.}$$

Super Sets's **average daily sales (ADS),** assuming a 360-day year, is $110,000:

$$ADS = \frac{\text{Annual sales}}{360} = \frac{(\text{Units sold})(\text{Sales price})}{360} \qquad \textbf{(21-2)}$$

$$= \frac{200,000(\$198)}{360} = \frac{\$39,600,000}{360} = \$110,000.$$

Super Sets's accounts receivable, assuming a constant, uniform rate of sales throughout the year, will at any point in time be $1,760,000:

$$\text{Receivables} = (ADS)(DSO) \qquad \textbf{(21-3)}$$

$$= (\$110,000)(16) = \$1,760,000.$$

Note also that its DSO, or average collection period, is a measure of the average length of time it takes Super Sets's customers to pay off their credit purchases, and the DSO is often compared with an industry average DSO. For example, if all television manufac-

---

[8]Accountants are increasingly interested in these matters. Investors have sued several of the major accounting firms for substantial damages when (1) profits were overstated and (2) it could be shown that the auditors should have conducted an analysis along the lines described here and then reported the results to stockholders in their audit opinion.

turers sell on the same credit terms, and if the industry average DSO is 25 days versus Super Sets's 16 days, then Super Sets either has a higher percentage of discount customers or else its credit department is exceptionally good at ensuring prompt payment.

Finally, if you know both the annual sales and the receivables balance, you can calculate DSO as follows:

$$\text{DSO} = \frac{\text{Receivables}}{\text{Sales per day}} = \frac{\$1,760,000}{\$110,000} = 16 \text{ days.}$$

The DSO can also be compared with the firm's own credit terms. For example, suppose Super Sets's DSO had been averaging 35 days. With a 35-day DSO, some customers would obviously be taking more than 30 days to pay their bills. In fact, if many customers were paying within 10 days to take advantage of the discount, the others must, on average, be taking much longer than 35 days. One way to check this possibility is to use an aging schedule as described in the next section.

Aging Schedules.   An **aging schedule** breaks down a firm's receivables by age of account. Table 21-3 contains the December 31, 1998, aging schedules of two television manufacturers, Super Sets and Wonder Vision. Both firms offer the same credit terms, and both show the same total receivables. However, Super Sets's aging schedule indicates that all of its customers pay on time—70 percent pay on Day 10 while 30 percent pay on Day 30. Wonder Vision's schedule, which is more typical, shows that many of its customers are not abiding by its credit terms—some 27 percent of its receivables are more than 30 days past due, even though Wonder Vision's credit terms call for full payment by Day 30.

Aging schedules cannot be constructed from the type of summary data reported in financial statements; they must be developed from the firm's accounts receivable ledger. However, well-run firms have computerized their accounts receivable records, so it is easy to determine the age of each invoice, to sort electronically by age categories, and thus to generate an aging schedule.

Management should constantly monitor both the DSO and the aging schedule to detect trends, to see how the firm's collection experience compares with its credit terms, and to see how effectively the credit department is operating in comparison with other firms in the industry. If the DSO starts to lengthen, or if the aging schedule begins to show an increasing percentage of past-due accounts, then the firm's credit policy may need to be tightened.

TABLE 21-3   Aging Schedules

AGE OF ACCOUNTS (DAYS)	SUPER SETS		WONDER VISION	
	VALUE OF ACCOUNTS	PERCENTAGE OF TOTAL VALUES	VALUE OF ACCOUNTS	PERCENTAGE OF TOTAL VALUE
0–10	$1,232,000	70%	$ 825,000	47%
11–30	528,000	30	460,000	26
31–45	0	0	265,000	15
46–60	0	0	179,000	10
Over 60	0	0	31,000	2
Total receivables	$1,760,000	100%	$1,760,000	100%

Although a change in the DSO or the aging schedule should signal the firm to investigate its credit policy, a deterioration in either of these measures does not necessarily indicate that the firm's credit policy has weakened. In fact, if a firm experiences sharp seasonal variations, or if it is growing rapidly, then both the aging schedule and the DSO may be distorted. To see this point, note that the DSO is calculated as follows:

$$DSO = \frac{\text{Accounts receivable}}{\text{Sales}/360}.$$

Since receivables at a given point in time reflect sales in the last month or so, but sales as shown in the denominator of the equation are for the last 12 months, a seasonal increase in sales will increase the numerator more than the denominator, hence will raise the DSO. This will occur even if customers are still paying exactly as before. Similar problems arise with the aging schedule if sales fluctuate widely. Therefore, a change in either the DSO or the aging schedule should be taken as a signal to investigate further, but not necessarily as a sign that the firm's credit policy has weakened. Still, days sales outstanding and the aging schedule are useful tools for reviewing the credit department's performance.[9]

SELF - TEST
QUESTIONS

Explain how a new firm's receivables balance is built up over time.

Define days sales outstanding (DSO). What can be learned from it? How is it affected by sales fluctuations?

What is an aging schedule? What can be learned from it? How is it affected by sales fluctuations?

CREDIT POLICY

The success or failure of a business depends primarily on the demand for its products—as a rule, the higher its sales, the larger its profits and the higher its stock price. Sales, in turn, depend on a number of factors, some exogenous but others under the firm's control. The major controllable determinants of demand are sales prices, product quality, advertising, and the firm's **credit policy.** Credit policy, in turn, consists of these four variables:

1. *Credit period,* which is the length of time buyers are given to pay for their purchases.

2. *Credit standards,* which refer to the required financial strength of acceptable credit customers.

3. *Collection policy,* which is measured by its toughness or laxity in attempting to collect on slow-paying accounts.

4. *Discounts* given for early payment, including the discount percentage and how rapidly payment must be made to qualify for the discount.

The credit manager is responsible for administering the firm's credit policy. However, because of the pervasive importance of credit, the credit policy itself is normally

---

[9]See Chapter 23 for a more complete discussion of the problems with the DSO and aging schedule and ways to correct for them.

established by the executive committee, which usually consists of the president plus the vice-presidents of finance, marketing, and production.

SELF-TEST
QUESTION | What are the four credit policy variables?

SETTING THE CREDIT PERIOD AND STANDARDS

A firm's regular **credit terms,** which include the **credit period** and **discount,** might call for sales on a 2/10, net 30 basis to all "acceptable" customers. Here customers who pay within 10 days would be given a 2 percent discount, and others would be required to pay within 30 days. Its **credit standards** would be applied to determine which customers qualify for the regular credit terms, and the amount of credit available to each customer.

Credit Standards

Credit standards refer to the financial strength and creditworthiness a customer must exhibit in order to qualify for credit. If a customer does not qualify for the regular credit terms, it can still purchase from the firm, but under more restrictive terms. For example, a firm's "regular" credit terms might call for payment after 30 days, and these terms might be extended to all qualified customers. The firm's credit standards would be applied to determine which customers qualified for the regular credit terms, and how much credit each should receive. The major factors considered when setting credit standards relate to the likelihood that a given customer will pay slowly or perhaps end up as a bad debt loss.

Setting credit standards requires a measurement of **credit quality,** which is defined in terms of the probability of a customer's default. The probability estimate for a given customer is, for the most part, a subjective judgment. Nevertheless, credit evaluation is a well-established practice, and a good credit manager can make reasonably accurate judgments of the probability of default by different classes of customers.

Managing a credit department requires fast, accurate, and up-to-date information. To help get such information, the National Association of Credit Management (a group with 43,000 member firms) persuaded TRW, a large credit-reporting agency, to develop a computer-based telecommunications network for the collection, storage, retrieval, and distribution of credit information. A typical business credit report would include the following pieces of information:

1. A summary balance sheet and income statement.

2. A number of key ratios, with trend information.

3. Information obtained from the firm's suppliers telling whether it pays promptly or slowly, and whether it has recently failed to make any payments.

4. A verbal description of the physical condition of the firm's operations.

5. A verbal description of the backgrounds of the firm's owners, including any previous bankruptcies, lawsuits, divorce settlement problems, and the like.

6. A summary rating, ranging from A for the best credit risks down to F for those that are deemed likely to default.

Although a great deal of credit information is available, it must still be processed in a judgmental manner. Computerized information systems can assist in making better credit decisions, but, in the final analysis, most credit decisions are really exercises in informed judgment.[10]

SELF-TEST
QUESTIONS

What are credit terms?

What is credit quality, and how is it assessed?

SETTING THE COLLECTION POLICY

Collection policy refers to the procedures the firm follows to collect past-due accounts. For example, a letter might be sent to customers when a bill is 10 days past due; a more severe letter, followed by a telephone call, would be sent if payment is not received within 30 days; and the account would be turned over to a collection agency after 90 days.

The collection process can be expensive in terms of both out-of-pocket expenditures and lost goodwill—customers dislike being turned over to a collection agency. However, at least some firmness is needed to prevent an undue lengthening of the collection period and to minimize outright losses. A balance must be struck between the costs and benefits of different collection policies.

Changes in collection policy influence sales, the collection period, and the bad debt loss percentage. All of this should be taken into account when setting the credit policy.

SELF-TEST
QUESTION

How does collection policy influence sales, the collection period, and the bad debt loss percentage?

CASH DISCOUNTS

The last element in the credit policy decision, the use of **cash discounts** for early payment, is analyzed by balancing the costs and benefits of different cash discounts. For example, a firm might decide to change its credit terms from "net 30," which means that customers must pay within 30 days, to "2/10, net 30," where a 2 percent discount is given if payment is made in ten days. This change should produce two benefits: (1) It should attract new customers who consider the discount to be a price reduction, and (2) the discount should cause a reduction in the days sales outstanding, because some existing customers will pay more promptly in order to get the discount. Offsetting these benefits is the dollar cost of the discounts. The optimal discount percentage is established at the point where the marginal costs and benefits are exactly offsetting.

If sales are seasonal, a firm may use **seasonal dating** on discounts. For example, Slimware Inc., a swimsuit manufacturer, sells on terms of 2/10, net 30, May 1 dating. This means that the effective invoice date is May 1, even if the sale was made back in January. The discount may be taken up to May 10; otherwise, the full amount must be

---

[10]Credit analysts use procedures ranging from highly sophisticated, computerized "credit-scoring" systems, which actually calculate the statistical probability that a given customer will default, to informal procedures, which involve going through a checklist of factors that should be considered when processing a credit application. The credit-scoring systems use various financial ratios such as the current ratio and the debt ratio (for businesses) and income, years with the same employer, and the like (for individuals) to determine the statistical probability of default. Credit is then granted to those with low default probabilities. The informal procedures often involve examining the "5 C's of Credit": character, capacity, capital, collateral, and conditions. Character is obvious; capacity is a subjective estimate of ability to repay; capital means how much net worth the borrower has; collateral means assets pledged to secure the loan; and conditions refers to business conditions, which affect ability to repay.

paid on May 30. Slimware produces throughout the year, but retail sales of bathing suits are concentrated in the spring and early summer. By offering seasonal dating, the company induces some of its customers to stock up early, saving Slimware some storage costs and also "nailing down sales."

How can cash discounts be used to influence sales volume and the DSO?

What is seasonal dating?

OTHER FACTORS INFLUENCING CREDIT POLICY

In addition to the factors discussed in previous sections, two other points should be made regarding credit policy.

Profit Potential

We have emphasized the costs of granting credit. *However, if it is possible to sell on credit and also to impose a carrying charge on the receivables that are outstanding, then credit sales can actually be more profitable than cash sales.* This is especially true for consumer durables (autos, appliances, and so on), but it is also true for certain types of industrial equipment. Thus, GM's General Motors Acceptance Corporation (GMAC) unit, which finances automobiles, is highly profitable, as is Sears' credit subsidiary.[11] Some encyclopedia companies even lose money on cash sales but more than make up these losses from the carrying charges on their credit sales. Obviously, such companies would rather sell on credit than for cash!

The carrying charges on outstanding credit are generally about 18 percent on a nominal basis: 1.5 percent per month, so $1.5\% \times 12 = 18\%$. This is equivalent to an effective annual rate of $(1.015)^{12} - 1.0 = 19.6\%$. Having receivables outstanding that earn more than 18 percent is highly profitable unless there are too many bad debt losses.

Legal Considerations

It is illegal, under the Robinson-Patman Act, for a firm to charge prices that discriminate between customers unless these differential prices are cost-justified. The same holds true for credit — it is illegal to offer more favorable credit terms to one customer or class of customers than to another, unless the differences are cost-justified.

How do profit potential and legal considerations affect a firm's credit policy?

---

[11]Companies that do a large volume of sales financing typically set up subsidiary companies called *captive finance companies* to do the actual financing. Thus, General Motors, Chrysler, and Ford all have captive finance companies, as do Sears, IBM, and General Electric.

SUMMARY

This chapter discussed the management of current assets, particularly cash, marketable securities, inventory, and receivables. The key concepts are listed below:

- **Working capital** refers to current assets, and **net working capital** is defined as current assets minus current liabilities. **Working capital policy** refers to decisions relating to current assets and their financing.

- Under a **relaxed current asset policy,** a firm would hold relatively large amounts of each type of current asset. Under a **restricted current asset policy,** the firm would hold minimal amounts of these items.

- A policy which strives for **zero working capital** not only generates cash but also speeds up production and helps businesses operate more efficiently. This concept has its own definition of working capital: Inventories + Receivables − Payables. The rationale is that inventories and receivables are the keys to making sales, and that inventories can be financed by suppliers through accounts payable.

- The **primary goal of cash management** is to reduce the amount of cash held to the minimum necessary to conduct business.

- The **transactions balance** is the cash necessary to conduct day-to-day business, whereas the **precautionary balance** is a cash reserve held to meet random, unforeseen needs. A **compensating balance** is a minimum checking account balance that a bank requires as compensation either for services provided or as part of a loan agreement. Firms also hold **speculative balances,** which allow them to take advantage of bargain purchases. Note, though, that borrowing capacity and marketable security holdings both reduce the need for precautionary and speculative balances.

- A **cash budget** is a schedule showing projected cash inflows and outflows over some period. The cash budget is used to predict cash surpluses and deficits, and it is the primary cash management planning tool.

- **Cash management techniques** generally fall into five categories: (1) synchronizing cash flows, (2) using float, (3) accelerating collections, (4) determining where and when funds will be needed, and (5) controlling disbursements.

- **Disbursement float** is the amount of funds associated with checks written by a firm that are still in process and hence have not yet been deducted from the firm's bank account.

- **Collections float** is the amount of funds associated with checks written to a firm that have not been cleared, hence are not yet available for the firm's use.

- **Net float** is the difference between disbursement float and collections float, and it also is equal to the difference between the balance in the firm's own checkbook and the balance on the bank's records. The larger the net float, the smaller the cash balance the firm must maintain, so net float is good.

- Two techniques that can be used to speed up collections are (1) **lockboxes** and (2) **wire transfers.**

- Firms can reduce their cash balances by holding **marketable securities,** which can be sold on short notice at close to their quoted prices. Marketable securities serve both as a substitute for cash and as a temporary investment for funds that will be needed in the near future. Safety is the primary consideration when selecting marketable securities.

- **Inventory management** involves determining how much inventory to hold, when to place orders, and how many units to order.

- **Inventory** can be grouped into four categories: (1) supplies, (2) raw materials, (3) work-in-process, and (4) finished goods.

- **Inventory costs** can be divided into three types: carrying costs, ordering costs, and stock-out costs. In general, carrying costs increase as the level of inventory rises, but ordering costs and stock-out costs decline with larger inventory holdings.

- Firms use inventory control systems such as the **red-line method** and the **two-bin method,** as well as **computerized inventory control systems,** to help them keep track of actual inventory levels and to ensure that inventory levels are adjusted as sales change. **Just-in-time (JIT) systems** are used to hold down inventory costs and, simultaneously, to improve the production process.

- When a firm sells goods to a customer on credit, an **account receivable** is created.

- A firm can use an **aging schedule** and the **days sales outstanding (DSO)** to help keep track of its receivables position and to help avoid an increase in bad debts.

- A firm's **credit policy** consists of four elements: (1) credit period, (2) discounts given for early payment, (3) credit standards, and (4) collection policy. The first two, when combined, are called the **credit terms.**

- Two major sources of external credit information are **credit associations,** which are local groups that meet frequently and correspond with one another to exchange information on credit customers, and **credit-reporting agencies,** which collect credit information and sell it for a fee.

- Additional factors that influence a firm's overall credit policy are (1) **profit potential** and (2) **legal considerations.**

- The basic objective of the credit manager is to increase profitable sales by extending credit to worthy customers and therefore adding value to the firm.

Working capital policy involves two basic issues. The first, determining the appropriate level for each type of current asset, was addressed in this chapter. The second, how current assets should be financed, will be addressed in Chapter 22.

Questions

21-1 Define each of the following terms:
a. Working capital; net working capital; working capital policy
b. Relaxed current asset investment policy; restricted current asset investment policy; moderate current asset investment policy
c. Transactions balance; compensating balance; precautionary balance; speculative balance
d. Cash budget; target cash balance
e. Trade discounts
f. Synchronized cash flows
g. Check clearing; net float; disbursement float; collections float
h. Lockbox plan
i. Marketable securities
j. Red-line method; two-bin method; computerized inventory control system
k. Just-in-time system; out-sourcing
l. Account receivable; days sales outstanding
m. Aging schedule
n. Credit policy; credit period; credit standards; collection policy; credit terms
o. Cash discounts
p. Seasonal dating

21-2 Assuming the firm's sales volume remained constant, would you expect it to have a higher cash balance during a tight-money period or during an easy-money period? Why?

21-3 What are the two principal reasons for holding cash? Can a firm estimate its target cash balance by summing the cash held to satisfy each of the two?

21-4 Explain how each of the following factors would probably affect a firm's target cash balance if all other factors were held constant.
a. The firm institutes a new billing procedure which better synchronizes its cash inflows and outflows.

b. The firm develops a new sales forecasting technique which improves its forecasts.

c. The firm reduces its portfolio of U.S. Treasury bills.

d. The firm arranges to use an overdraft system for its checking account.

e. The firm borrows a large amount of money from its bank and also begins to write far more checks than it did in the past.

f. Interest rates on Treasury bills rise from 5 percent to 10 percent.

21-5   Why would a lockbox plan make more sense for a firm that makes sales all over the United States than for a firm with the same volume of business but concentrated in its home city?

21-6   Is it true that when one firm sells to another on credit, the seller records the transaction as an account receivable while the buyer records it as an account payable and that, disregarding discounts, the receivable typically exceeds the payable by the amount of profit on the sale?

21-7   What are the four elements of a firm's credit policy? To what extent can firms set their own credit policies as opposed to having to accept policies that are dictated by "the competition"?

21-8   Suppose that a firm makes a purchase and receives the shipment on February 1. The terms of trade as stated on the invoice read "2/10, net 40, May 1 dating." What is the latest date on which payment can be made and the discount still be taken? What is the date on which payment must be made if the discount is not taken?

21-9   a. What is the days sales outstanding (DSO) for a firm whose sales are $2,880,000 per year and whose accounts receivable are $312,000? (Use 360 days per year.)

b. Is it true that if this firm sells on terms of 3/10, net 40, its customers probably all pay on time?

21-10   Is it true that if a firm calculates its days sales outstanding, it has no need for an aging schedule?

21-11   Firm A had no credit losses last year, but 1 percent of Firm B's accounts receivable proved to be uncollectible and resulted in losses. Should Firm B fire its credit manager and hire A's?

21-12   Indicate by a (+), (−), or (0) whether each of the following events would probably cause accounts receivable (A/R), sales, and profits to increase, decrease, or be affected in an indeterminant manner:

	A/R	**SALES**	**PROFITS**
The firm tightens its credit standards.	_____	_____	_____
The terms of trade are changed from 2/10, net 30, to 3/10, net 30.	_____	_____	_____
The terms are changed from 2/10, net 30, to 3/10, net 40.	_____	_____	_____
The credit manager gets tough with past-due accounts.	_____	_____	_____

21-13   A firm can reduce its investment in inventory by having its suppliers hold raw materials inventory and its customers hold finished goods inventory. Explain actions a firm can take which would result in larger inventory for its suppliers and customers and smaller inventory for itself. What are the limitations of such actions?

Self-Test Problems   (Solutions Appear in Appendix B)

ST-1
Working Capital Policy

The Calgary Company is attempting to establish a current assets policy. Fixed assets are $600,000, and the firm plans to maintain a 50 percent debt-to-assets ratio. The interest rate is 10 percent on all debt. Three alternative current asset policies are under consideration: 40, 50, and 60 percent of projected sales. The company expects to earn 15 percent before interest and taxes on sales of $3 million. Calgary's effective federal-plus-state tax rate is 40 percent. What is the expected return on equity under each alternative?

ST-2
Float

The Upton Company is setting up a new checking account with Howe National Bank. Upton plans to issue checks in the amount of $1 million each day and to deduct them from its own records at the close of business on the day they are written. On average, the bank will receive and clear the checks at 5 P.M. the third day after they are written; for example, a check written on Monday will be cleared on Thursday afternoon. The firm's agreement with the bank requires it to maintain a $500,000 average compensating balance; this is $250,000 greater than the cash balance the firm would otherwise have on deposit. It makes a $500,000 deposit at the time it opens the account.

a. Assuming that the firm makes deposits at 4 P.M. each day (and the bank includes them in that day's transactions), how much must it deposit daily in order to maintain a sufficient balance once it reaches a steady state? Indicate the required deposit on Day 1, Day 2, Day 3, if any, and each day thereafter, assuming that the company will write checks for $1 million on Day 1 and each day thereafter.

b. How many days of float does Upton have?

c. What ending daily balance should the firm try to maintain (1) on the bank's records and (2) on its own records?

Problems

21-1
Net Float

On a typical day, Troan Corporation writes $10,000 in checks. It generally takes 4 days for those checks to clear. Each day the firm typically receives $10,000 in checks that take 3 days to clear. What is the firm's average net float?

21-2
Cash Management

Williams & Sons last year reported sales of $10 million and an inventory turnover ratio of 2. The company is now adopting a just-in-time inventory system. If the new system is able to reduce the firm's inventory level and increase the firm's inventory turnover ratio to 5, while maintaining the same level of sales, how much cash will be freed up?

21-3
Receivables Investment

Medwig Corporation has a DSO of 17 days. The company averages $3,500 in credit sales each day. What is the company's average accounts receivable?

21-4
Lockbox System

I. Malitz and Associates Inc. operates a mail-order firm doing business on the West Coast. Malitz receives an average of $325,000 in payments per day. On average, it takes 4 days from the time customers mail checks until Malitz receives and processes them. Malitz is considering the use of a lockbox system to reduce collection and processing float. The system will cost $6,500 per month and will consist of 10 local depository banks and a concentration bank located in San Francisco. Under this system, customers' checks should be received at the lockbox locations 1 day after they are mailed, and daily totals will be transferred to San Francisco using wire transfers costing $9.75 each. Assume that Malitz has an opportunity cost of 10 percent and that there are $52 \times 5 = 260$ working days, hence 260 transfers from each lockbox location, in a year.

a. What is the total annual cost of operating the lockbox system?

b. What is the benefit of the lockbox system to Malitz?

c. Should Malitz initiate the system?

21-5
Receivables Investment

McDowell Industries sells on terms of 3/10, net 30. Total sales for the year are $900,000. Forty percent of the customers pay on the 10th day and take discounts; the other 60 percent pay, on average, 40 days after their purchases.

a. What is the days sales outstanding?

b. What is the average amount of receivables?

c. What would happen to average receivables if McDowell toughened up on its collection policy with the result that all nondiscount customers paid on the 30th day?

21-6
Working Capital Policy

The Rentz Corporation is attempting to determine the optimal level of current assets for the coming year. Management expects sales to increase to approximately $2 million as a result of an asset expansion presently being undertaken. Fixed assets total $1 million, and the firm wishes to maintain a 60 percent debt ratio. Rentz's interest cost is currently 8 percent on both short-term and longer-term debt (which the firm uses in its permanent structure). Three alternatives regarding the projected current asset level are available to the firm: (1) a tight policy requiring current assets of only 45 percent of projected sales, (2) a moderate policy of 50 percent of sales in current assets, and (3) a relaxed policy requiring current assets of 60 percent of sales. The firm expects to generate earnings before interest and taxes at a rate of 12 percent on total sales.

a. What is the expected return on equity under each current asset level? (Assume a 40 percent effective federal-plus-state tax rate.)

b. In this problem, we have assumed that the level of expected sales is independent of current asset policy. Is this a valid assumption?

c. How would the overall riskiness of the firm vary under each policy?

21-7
Net Float

The Stendardi-Stephens Company (SSC) is setting up a new checking account with National Bank. SSC plans to issue checks in the amount of $1.6 million each day and to deduct them from its own records at the close of business on the day they are written. On average, the bank will receive and clear (that is, deduct from the firm's bank balance) the checks at 5 P.M. the fourth day after they are written; for example, a check written on Monday will be cleared on Friday afternoon. The firm's agreement with the bank requires it to maintain a $1.2 million average compensating balance; this is $400,000 greater than the cash balance the firm would otherwise have on deposit. It makes a $1.2 million deposit at the time it opens the account.

a. Assuming that the firm makes deposits at 4 P.M. each day (and the bank includes them in that day's transactions), how much must it deposit daily in order to maintain a sufficient balance once it reaches a steady state? Indicate the required deposit on Day 1, Day 2, Day 3, Day 4, if any, and each day thereafter, assuming that the company will write checks for $1.6 million on Day 1 and each day thereafter.

b How many days of float does SSC carry?

c. What ending daily balance should the firm try to maintain (1) on the bank's records and (2) on its own records?

d. Explain how net float can help increase the value of the firm's common stock.

21-8
Lockbox System

The Hardin-Gehr Corporation (HGC) began operations 5 years ago as a small firm serving customers in the Detroit area. However, its reputation and market area grew quickly, so that today HGC has customers throughout the entire United States. Despite its broad customer base, HGC has maintained its headquarters in Detroit and keeps its central billing system there. HGC's management is considering an alternative collection procedure to reduce its mail time and processing float. On average, it takes 5 days from the time customers mail payments until HGC is able to receive, process, and deposit them. HGC would like to set up a lockbox collection system, which it estimates would reduce the time lag from customer mailing to deposit by 3 days—bringing it down to 2 days. HGC receives an average of $1,400,000 in payments per day.

a. How many days of collection float now exist (HGC's customers' disbursement float) and what would it be under the lockbox system? What reduction in cash balances could HGC achieve by initiating the lockbox system?

b. If HGC has an opportunity cost of 10 percent, how much is the lockbox system worth on an annual basis?

c. What is the maximum monthly charge HGC should pay for the lockbox system?

21-9
Cash Budgeting

Dorothy Koehl recently leased space in the Southside Mall and opened a new business, Koehl's Doll Shop. Business has been good, but Koehl has frequently run out of cash. This has necessitated late payment on certain orders, which, in turn, is beginning to cause a problem with suppliers. Koehl plans to borrow from the bank to have cash ready as needed, but first she needs a forecast of just how much she must borrow. Accordingly, she has asked you to prepare a cash budget for the critical period around Christmas, when needs will be especially high.

Sales are made on a cash basis only. Koehl's purchases must be paid for during the following month. Koehl pays herself a salary of $4,800 per month, and the rent is $2,000 per month. In addition, she must make a tax payment of $12,000 in December. The current cash on hand (on December 1) is $400, but Koehl has agreed to maintain an average bank balance of $6,000—this is her target cash balance. (Disregard till cash, which is insignificant because Koehl keeps only a small amount on hand in order to lessen the chances of robbery.)

The estimated sales and purchases for December, January, and February are shown below. Purchases during November amounted to $140,000.

	SALES	PURCHASES
December	$160,000	$40,000
January	40,000	40,000
February	60,000	40,000

a. Prepare a cash budget for December, January, and February.

b. Now, suppose Koehl were to start selling on a credit basis on December 1, giving customers 30 days to pay. All customers accept these terms, and all other facts in the problem are unchanged. What would the company's loan requirements be at the end of December in this case? (Hint: The calculations required to answer this question are minimal.)

21-10

Cash Budgeting

Helen Bowers, owner of Helen's Fashion Designs, is planning to request a line of credit from her bank. She has estimated the following sales forecasts for the firm for parts of 1999 and 2000:

May 1999	$180,000
June	180,000
July	360,000
August	540,000
September	720,000
October	360,000
November	360,000
December	90,000
January 2000	180,000

Collection estimates obtained from the credit and collection department are as follows: collections within the month of sale, 10 percent; collections the month following the sale, 75 percent; collections the second month following the sale, 15 percent. Payments for labor and raw materials are typically made during the month following the one in which these costs have been incurred. Total labor and raw materials costs are estimated for each month as follows:

May 1999	$ 90,000
June	90,000
July	126,000
August	882,000
September	306,000
October	234,000
November	162,000
December	90,000

General and administrative salaries will amount to approximately $27,000 a month; lease payments under long-term lease contracts will be $9,000 a month; depreciation charges will be $36,000 a month; miscellaneous expenses will be $2,700 a month; income tax payments of $63,000 will be due in both September and December; and a progress payment of $180,000 on a new design studio must be paid in October. Cash on hand on July 1 will amount to $132,000, and a minimum cash balance of $90,000 will be maintained throughout the cash budget period.

a. Prepare a monthly cash budget for the last 6 months of 1999.

b. Prepare an estimate of the required financing (or excess funds)—that is, the amount of money Bowers will need to borrow (or will have available to invest)—for each month during that period.

c. Assume that receipts from sales come in uniformly during the month (that is, cash receipts come in at the rate of ⅟₃₀ each day), but all outflows are paid on the 5th of the month. Will this have an effect on the cash budget—in other words, would the cash budget you have prepared be valid under these assumptions? If not, what can be done to make a valid estimate of peak financing requirements? No calculations are required, although calculations can be used to illustrate the effects.

d. Bowers produces on a seasonal basis, just ahead of sales. Without making any calculations, discuss how the company's current ratio and debt ratio would vary during the year assuming all financial requirements were met by short-term bank loans. Could changes in these ratios affect the firm's ability to obtain bank credit?

Spreadsheet Problem

Work the problem in this section only if you are using the computer problem diskette.

21-11

Cash Budgeting

Use the model in the File C21 to solve this problem.

a. Refer to Problem 21-10. Suppose that by offering a 2 percent cash discount for paying within the month of sale, the credit manager of Helen's Fashion Designs has revised the collection percentages to 50 percent, 35 percent, and 15 percent, respectively. How will this affect the loan requirements?

b. Return the payment percentages to their base-case values: 10 percent, 75 percent, and 15 percent, respectively, and the discount to zero percent. Now suppose sales fall to only 70 percent of the forecasted level. Production is maintained, so cash outflows are unchanged. How does this affect Bowers's financial requirements?

c. Return sales to the forecasted level (100%), and suppose collections slow down to 3 percent, 10 percent, and 87 percent for the 3 months, respectively. How does this affect financial requirements? If Bowers went to a cash-only sales policy, how would that affect requirements, other things held constant?

MINI CASE

Dan Barnes, financial manager of Ski Equipment Inc. (SKI), is excited, but apprehensive. The company's founder recently sold his 51 percent controlling block of stock to Kent Koren, who is a big fan of EVA (Economic Value Added). EVA is found by taking the after-tax operating profit and then subtracting the dollar cost of all the capital the firm uses:

$$EVA = NOPAT - \text{Capital costs}$$

$$= EBIT(1 - T) - WACC \text{ (Capital employed)}.$$

If EVA is positive, then the firm is creating value. On the other hand, if EVA is negative, the firm is not covering its cost of capital, and stockholders' value is being eroded. Koren rewards managers handsomely if they create value, but those whose operations produce negative EVAs are soon looking for work. Koren frequently points out that if a company can generate its current level of sales with less assets, it would need less capital. That would, other things held constant, lower capital costs and increase its EVA.

Shortly after he took control of SKI, Kent Koren met with SKI's senior executives to tell them of his plans for the company. First, he presented some EVA data which convinced everyone that SKI had not been creating value in recent years. He then stated, in no uncertain terms, that this situation must change. He noted that SKI's designs of skis, boots, and clothing are acclaimed throughout the industry, but something is seriously amiss elsewhere in the company. Costs are too high, prices are too low, or the company employs too much capital, and he wants SKI's managers to correct the problem or else.

Barnes has long felt that SKI's working capital situation should be studied—the company may have the optimal amounts of cash, securities, receivables, and inventories, but it may also have too much or too little of these items. In the past, the production manager resisted Dan's efforts to question his holdings of raw materials inventories, the marketing manager resisted questions about finished goods, the sales staff resisted questions about credit policy (which affects accounts receivable), and the treasurer did not want to talk about her cash and securities balances. Koren's speech made it clear that such resistance would no longer be tolerated.

Dan also knows that decisions about working capital cannot be made in a vacuum. For example, if inventories could be lowered without adversely affecting operations, then less capital would be required, the dollar cost of capital would decline, and EVA would increase. However, lower raw materials inventories might lead to production slowdowns and higher costs, while lower finished goods inventories might lead to the loss of profitable sales. So, before inventories are changed, it will be necessary to study operating as well as financial effects. The situation is the same with regard to cash and receivables. Following are some ratios for SKI:

	SKI	INDUSTRY
Current	1.75	2.25
Quick	0.83	1.20
Debt/assets	58.76%	50.00%
Turnover of cash and securities	16.67	22.22
Days sales outstanding	45.00	32.00
Inventory turnover	4.82	7.00
Fixed assets turnover	11.35	12.00
Total assets turnover	2.08	3.00
Profit margin on sales	2.07%	3.50%
Return on equity (ROE)	10.45%	21.00%

a. Dan plans to use the preceding ratios as the starting point for discussions with SKI's operating executives. He wants everyone to think about the pros and cons of changing each type of current asset and how changes would interact to affect profits and EVA. Based on the data in the table, does SKI seem to be following a relaxed, moderate, or restricted working capital policy?

b. How can one distinguish between a relaxed but rational working capital policy and a situation where a firm simply has a lot of current assets because it is inefficient? Does SKI's working capital policy seem appropriate?

c. What might SKI do to reduce its cash and securities without harming operations?

d. What is "float," and how is it affected by the firm's cash manager (treasurer)?

In an attempt to better understand SKI's cash position, Dan developed a cash budget. Data for the first 2 months of the year are shown at the end of this Mini Case. (Note that Dan's preliminary cash budget does not account for interest income or interest expense.) He has the figures for the other months, but they are not shown in this Mini Case.

e. Should depreciation expense be explicitly included in the cash budget? Why or why not?

f. In his preliminary cash budget, Dan has assumed that all sales are collected and, thus, that SKI has no bad debts. Is this realistic? If not, how would bad debts be dealt with in a cash budgeting sense? (Hint: Bad debts will affect collections but not purchases.)

g. Dan's cash budget for the entire year, although not given here, is based heavily on his forecast for monthly sales. Sales are expected to be extremely low between May and September but then increase dramatically in the fall and winter. November is typically the firm's best month, when SKI ships equipment to retailers for the holiday season. Interestingly, Dan's forecasted cash budget indicates that the company's cash holdings will exceed the targeted cash balance every month except for October and November, when shipments will be high but collections will not be coming in until later. Based on the ratios in the first table, does it appear that SKI's target cash balance is appropriate? In addition to possibly lowering the target cash balance, what actions might SKI take to better improve its cash management policies, and how might that affect its EVA?

h. What reasons might SKI have for maintaining a relatively high amount of cash?

i. What are the three categories of inventory costs? If the company takes steps to reduce its inventory, what effect would this have on the various costs of holding inventory?

j. Is there any reason to think that SKI may be holding too much inventory? If so, how would that affect EVA and ROE?

k. If the company reduces its inventory without adversely affecting sales, what effect should this have on the company's cash position (1) in the short run and (2) in the long run? Explain in terms of the cash budget and the balance sheet.

l. Dan knows that SKI sells on the same credit terms as other firms in its industry. Use the ratios presented in the first table to explain whether SKI's customers pay more or less promptly than those of its competitors. If there are differences, does that suggest that SKI should tighten or loosen its credit policy? What four variables make up a firm's credit policy, and in what direction should each be changed by SKI?

m. Does SKI face any risks if it tightens its credit policy?

n. If the company reduces its DSO without seriously affecting sales, what effect would this have on its cash position (1) in the short run and (2) in the long run? Answer in terms of the cash budget and the balance sheet. What effect should this have on EVA in the long run?

	NOV	DEC	JAN	FEB	MAR	APR
I. COLLECTIONS AND PURCHASES WORKSHEET						
(1) Sales (gross)	$71,218	$68,212	$65,213	$52,475	$42,909	$30,524
Collections						
(2) During month of sale (0.2)(0.98)(month's sales)			12,781.75	10,285.10		
(3) During first month after sale (0.7)(previous month's sales)			47,748.40	45,649.10		
(4) During second month after sale (0.1)(sales 2 months ago)			7,121.80	6,821.20		
(5) Total collections (Lines 2 + 3 + 4)			$67,651.95	$62,755.40		
Purchases						
(6) (0.85)(forecasted sales 2 months from now)		$44,603.75	$36,472.65	$25,945.40		
(7) Payments (1-month lag)			44,603.75	36,472.65		
II. CASH GAIN OR LOSS FOR MONTH						
(8) Collections (from Section I)			$67,651.95	$62,755.40		
(9) Payments for purchases (from Section I)			44,603.75	36,472.65		
(10) Wages and salaries			6,690.56	5,470.90		
(11) Rent			2,500.00	2,500.00		
(12) Taxes						
(13) Total payments			$53,794.31	$44,443.55		
(14) Net cash gain (loss) during month (Line 8 − Line 13)			$13,857.64	$18,311.85		
III. CASH SURPLUS OR LOAN REQUIREMENT						
(15) Cash at beginning of month if no borrowing is done			$ 3,000.00	$16,857.64		
(16) Cumulative cash (cash at start + gain or − loss = Line 14 + Line 15)			16,857.64	35,169.49		
(17) Target cash balance			1,500.00	1,500.00		
(18) Cumulative surplus cash or loans outstanding to maintain $1,500 target cash balance (Line 16 − Line 17)			$15,357.64	$33,669.49		

Selected Additional References and Cases

The following books focus on short-term financial management:

Gallinger, George W., and P. Basil Healy, *Liquidity Analysis and Management* (Reading, Mass.: Addison-Wesley, 1991).

Hill, Ned C., and William L. Sartoris, *Short-Term Financial Management* (New York: Prentice-Hall, 1995).

Maness, Terry S., and John T. Zietlow, *Short-Term Financial Management: Text, Cases, and Readings* (Minneapolis/St. Paul: West, 1993).

The following articles provide more information on short-term financial management:

Gentry, James A., "State of the Art of Short-Run Financial Management," *Financial Management,* Summer 1988, 41–57.

Gentry, James A., and Jesus M. De La Garza, "Monitoring Accounts Payables," *Financial Review,* November 1990, 559–576.

Gentry, James A., R. Vaidyanathan, and Hei Wai Lee, "A Weighted Cash Conversion Cycle," *Financial Management,* Spring 1990, 90–99.

Lambrix, R. J., and S. S. Singhvi, "Managing the Working Capital Cycle," *Financial Executive,* June 1979, 32–41.

Maier, Steven F., and James H. Vander Weide, "A Practical Approach to Short-Run Financial Planning," *Financial Management,* Winter 1978, 10–16.

Merville, Larry J., and Lee A. Tavis, "Optimal Working Capital Policies: A Chance-Constrained Programming Approach," *Journal of Financial and Quantitative Analysis,* January 1973, 47–60.

Mitchell, Karlyn, "The Debt Maturity Choice: An Empirical Investigation," *Journal of Financial Research,* Winter 1993, 309–320.

Yardini, Edward E., "A Portfolio-Balance Model of Corporate Working Capital," *Journal of Finance,* May 1979, 535–552.

Perhaps the best way to get a good feel for the current state of the art in cash management is to look through recent issues of The Journal of Cash Management, *a publication aimed at professionals in the field.*

For more information on transfer systems, see

Summers, Bruce J., "Clearing and Payment Systems: The Role of the Central Bank," *Federal Reserve Bulletin,* February 1991, 81–91.

Wood, John C., and Dolores D. Smith, "Electronic Transfer of Government Benefits," *Federal Reserve Bulletin,* April 1991, 204–207.

For more information on float management, see

Batlin, C. A., and Susan Hinko, "Lockbox Management and Value Maximization," *Financial Management,* Winter 1981, 39–44.

Gitman, Lawrence J., D. Keith Forrester, and John R. Forrester, Jr., "Maximizing Cash Disbursement Float," *Financial Management,* Summer 1976, 32–41.

Nauss, Robert M., and Robert E. Markland, "Solving Lockbox Location Problems," *Financial Management,* Spring 1979, 21–31.

The following articles provide more information on cash concentration systems:

Stone, Bernell K., and Ned C. Hill, "Cash Transfer Scheduling for Efficient Cash Concentration," *Financial Management,* Autumn 1980, 35–43.

_____, "The Design of a Cash Concentration System," *Journal of Financial and Quantitative Analysis,* September 1981, 301–322.

Stone, Bernell K., and Tom W. Miller, "Daily Cash Forecasting with Multiplicative Models of Cash Flow Patterns," *Financial Management,* Winter 1987, 45–54.

For greater insights into compensating balance requirements, see

Campbell, Tim S., and Leland Brendsel, "The Impact of Compensating Balance Requirements on the Cash Balances of Manufacturing Corporations," *Journal of Finance,* March 1977, 31–40.

Frost, Peter A., "Banking Services, Minimum Cash Balances, and the Firm's Demand for Money," *Journal of Finance,* December 1970, 1029–1039.

For more information on marketable securities, see

Brown, Keith C., and Scott L. Lummer, "A Reexamination of the Covered Call Option Strategy for Corporate Cash Management," *Financial Management,* Summer 1986, 13–17.

Kamath, Ravindra R., et al., "Management of Excess Cash: Practices and Developments," *Financial Management,* Autumn 1985, 70–77.

Stigum, M., *The Money Market: Myth, Reality, and Practice* (Homewood, Ill.: Dow Jones-Irwin, 1978).

Van Horne, J. C., *Financial Market Rates and Flows* (Englewood Cliffs, N.J.: Prentice-Hall, 1984).

Zivney, Terry L., and Michael J. Alderson, "Hedged Dividend Capture with Stock Index Options," *Financial Management,* Summer 1986, 5–12.

The following articles and books provide additional insights into the problems of inventory management:

Arvan, L., and L. N. Moses, "Inventory Management and the Theory of the Firm," *American Economic Review,* March 1982, 186–193.

Bierman, H., Jr., C. P. Bonini, and W. H. Hausman, *Quantitative Analysis for Business Decisions* (Homewood, Ill.: Irwin, 1977).

Brooks, L. D., "Risk-Return Criteria and Optimal Inventory Stocks," *Engineering Economist,* Summer 1980, 275–299.

Followill, Richard A., Michael Schellenger, and Patrick H. Marchand, "Economic Order Quantities, Volume Discounts, and Wealth Maximization," *The Financial Review,* February 1990, 143–152.

Kallberg, Jarl G., and Kenneth L. Parkinson, *Current Asset Management: Cash, Credit, and Inventory* (New York: Wiley, 1984).

Magee, John F., "Guides to Inventory Policy, I," *Harvard Business Review,* January–February 1956, 49–60.

_____, "Guides to Inventory Policy, II," *Harvard Business Review,* March–April 1956, 103–116.

_____, "Guides to Inventory Policy, III," *Harvard Business Review,* May–June 1956, 57–70.

Mehta, Dileep R., *Working Capital Management* (Englewood Cliffs, N.J.: Prentice-Hall, 1974).

Shapiro, A., "Optimal Inventory and Credit Granting Strategies under Inflation and Devaluation," *Journal of Financial and Quantitative Analysis,* January 1973, 37–46.

Smith, Keith V., *Guide to Working Capital Management* (New York: McGraw-Hill, 1979).

Articles which address credit policy and receivables management include the following:

Atkins, Joseph C., and Yong H. Kim, "Comment and Correction: Opportunity Cost in the Evaluation of Investment in Accounts Receivable," *Financial Management,* Winter 1977, 71–74.

Ben-Horim, Moshe, and Haim Levy, "Management of Accounts Receivable under Inflation," *Financial Management,* Spring 1983, 42–48.

Dyl, Edward A., "Another Look at the Evaluation of Interest in Accounts Receivable," *Financial Management,* Winter 1977, 67–70.

Gallinger, George W., and A. James Ifflander, "Monitoring Accounts Receivable Using Variance Analysis," *Financial Management,* Winter 1986, 69–76.

Gentry, James A., and Jesus M. De La Garza, "A Generalized Model for Monitoring Accounts Receivable," *Financial Management,* Winter 1985, 28–38.

Hill, Ned C., and Kenneth D. Riener, "Determining the Cash Discount in the Firm's Credit Policy," *Financial Management,* Spring 1979, 68–73.

Kim, Yong H., and Joseph C. Atkins, "Evaluating Investments in Accounts Receivable: A Wealth Maximizing Framework," *Journal of Finance,* May 1978, 403–412.

Mian, Shehzad L., and Clifford W. Smith, "Extending Trade Credit and Financing Receivables," *Journal of Applied Corporate Finance,* Spring 1994, 75–84.

Oh, John S., "Opportunity Cost in the Evaluation of Investment in Accounts Receivables," *Financial Management,* Summer 1976, 32–36.

Roberts, Gordon S., and Jeremy A. Viscione, "Captive Finance Subsidiaries: The Manager's View," *Financial Management,* Spring 1981, 36–42.

Sachdeva, Kanwal S., and Lawrence J. Gitman, "Accounts Receivable Decisions in a Capital Budgeting Framework," *Financial Management,* Winter 1981, 45–49.

Walia, Tinlochan S., "Explicit and Implicit Cost of Changes in the Level of Accounts Receivable and the Credit Policy Decision of the Firm," *Financial Management,* Winter 1977, 75–78.

Weston, J. Fred, and Pham D. Tuan, "Comment on Analysis of Credit Policy Changes," *Financial Management,* Winter 1980, 59–63.

The following cases from the Cases in Financial Management: Dryden Request *casebook focus on the credit policy decision:*

Case 29, "Office Mates, Inc.," which illustrates how changes in current asset policy affect expected profitability and risk.

Case 32, "Alpine Wear, Inc.," which illustrates the mechanics of the cash budget and the rationale behind its use.

Two new cash budgeting cases, Case 32A, "Toy World, Inc.," and Case 32B, "Sorenson Stove Company," have been added to the Dryden case set.

Case 33, "Upscale Toddlers, Inc.," which deals with credit policy changes.

Case 34, "Texas Rose Company," which focuses on receivables management.

Case 62, "Western Supply Company," which illustrates the effects of a change in credit policy on corporate profitability and cash flow.

SHORT-TERM FINANCING

At the beginning of the last chapter, we discussed steps Core Industries has taken to improve its working capital management. Core reduced its cash, receivables, and inventories, and the result was lower operating costs and higher profits. Even so, Core still has substantial holdings of current assets, and the funds invested in these assets must be obtained from some source. This involves "working capital financing policy," the focus of the current chapter.

Most firms use several types of short-term debt to finance their working capital requirements. Included are bank loans, trade credit, commercial paper, and accruals. However, companies structure their current liabilities in a manner that depends on the nature of their business. For example, the sales of Toys R Us are very seasonal—nearly half of all sales occur in the final three months of the year. To meet holiday demands, Toys R Us must dramatically increase its inventories during early fall. This inventory buildup must be financed until the Christmas season, when sales bring cash into the till and debts can be reduced. The company finances the buildup with trade credit, loans from U.S. and foreign banks, commercial paper, and the sale of marketable securities built up during the slack season.

Short-term credit is generally cheaper than long-term capital, but it is a riskier, less dependable source of financing. Interest rates can increase dramatically, and changes in a company's financial position can affect both the cost and availability of short-term credit.

Core Industries finances its working capital in several ways. First, trade credit and accruals are essentially free, so Core naturally uses them. In addition, it uses bank loans, including a five-year, $50 million revolving credit agreement. Currently, Core is highly liquid, and it is in a good position to finance its rapid growth.

After you have completed this chapter, you will have a better understanding of the various ways corporations finance their current assets, and the costs associated with each type of financing.

In the last chapter, we discussed the first step in working capital management—determining the optimal level for each type of current asset. Now we turn to the second step—financing current assets. We begin with a discussion of alternative financing policies.

ALTERNATIVE CURRENT ASSET FINANCING POLICIES

Most businesses experience seasonal and/or cyclical fluctuations. For example, construction firms have peaks in the spring and summer, retailers peak around Christmas, and the manufacturers who supply construction companies or retailers follow similar patterns. Similarly, virtually all businesses must build up current assets when the economy is strong, but they reduce inventories and receivables when the economy slacks off. Still, current assets rarely drop to zero—companies have some **permanent current assets,** which are the current assets on hand at the low point of the cycle. Then, as sales increase during the upswing, current assets must be increased, and these additional current assets are defined as **temporary current assets.** The manner in which the permanent and temporary current assets are financed is called the firm's *current asset financing policy.*

Maturity Matching, or "Self-Liquidating," Approach

The **maturity matching, or "self-liquidating," approach** calls for matching asset and liability maturities as shown in Panel a of Figure 22-1. This strategy recognizes that temporary current assets will be converted into cash in the near term, hence the company finances those assets with short-term capital.

At the limit, a firm could attempt to match exactly the maturity structure of its assets and liabilities. Inventory expected to be sold in 30 days could be financed with a 30-day bank loan; a machine expected to last for 5 years could be financed with a 5-year loan; a 20-year building could be financed with a 20-year mortgage bond; and so forth. Actually, of course, two factors prevent this exact maturity matching: (1) there is uncertainty about the lives of assets, and (2) some common equity must be used, and common equity has no maturity. To illustrate the uncertainty factor, a firm might finance inventories with a 30-day loan, expecting to sell the inventories and then use the cash to retire the loan. But if sales were slow, the cash would not be forthcoming, and the use of short-term credit could end up causing a problem. Still, if a firm makes an attempt to match asset and liability maturities, we would define this as a moderate current asset financing policy.

Aggressive Approach

Panel b of Figure 22-1 illustrates the situation for an aggressive firm which finances all of its fixed assets with long-term capital and part of its permanent current assets with short-term, nonspontaneous credit. Note that there can be different *degrees* of aggressiveness. For example, the dashed line in Panel b could have been drawn *below* the line designating fixed assets, indicating that all of the permanent current assets and part of the fixed assets were financed with short-term credit; this would be a highly aggressive, extremely nonconservative position, and the firm would be very much subject to dangers from rising interest rates as well as to loan renewal problems. However, short-term debt is often cheaper than long-term debt, and some firms are willing to sacrifice safety for the chance of higher profits.

Students can access various types of historical interest rates, including fixed and variable rates, at the St. Louis Federal Reserve's FRED site. The address is http://www.stls.frb.org/fred/.

Conservative Approach

Panel c of Figure 22-1 has the dashed line *above* the line designating permanent current assets, indicating that permanent capital is being used to finance all permanent asset requirements and also to meet some of the seasonal needs. In this situation, the firm uses a small amount of short-term, nonspontaneous credit to meet its peak requirements, but it also meets a part of its seasonal needs by "storing liquidity" in the form of marketable securities. The humps above the dashed line represent short-term financing, while the troughs below the dashed line represent short-term security holdings. Panel c represents a safe, conservative current asset financing policy. Like the aggressive approach, there are different degrees of conservatism. If the dashed line in Panel c were moved to the top of the temporary current asset "humps," no short-term, nonspontaneous debt would be used, and the company would be following a very conservative policy.

Chrysler, which in 1996 had $8.7 billion of cash and marketable securities, fits the Panel c pattern. Its chairman, Robert Eaton, stated that these liquid assets would be

FIGURE 22-1   Alternative Current Asset Financing Policies

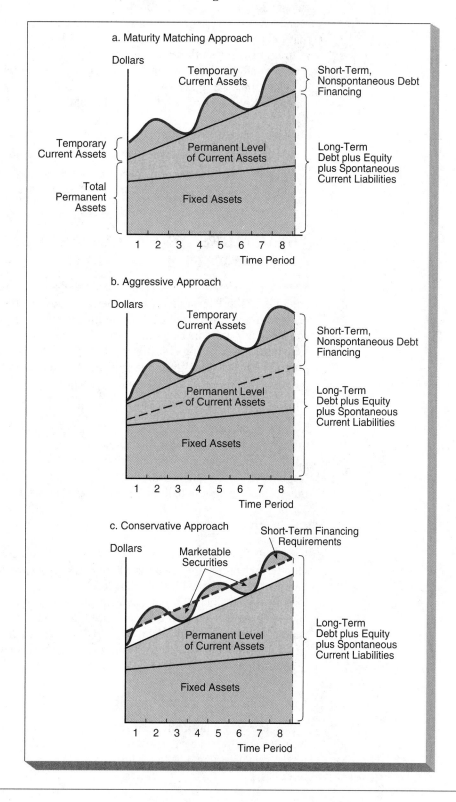

needed during the next recession, and he cited as evidence the fact that Chrysler had an operating cash deficit of more than $4 billion during the 1991–1992 recession. However, some of Chrysler's stockholders, notably Lee Iacocca and Kirk Kerkorian, argued that only $2 billion was necessary. They felt that Chrysler could borrow funds in the future if need be, so the extra $6.7 billion should be redeployed to earn more than the 3 percent after taxes it was getting. The Chrysler example illustrates the fact that reasonable people can disagree—there is no clear, precise answer to the question of how much cash and securities a firm should hold.

<table>
<tr><td>S E L F - T E S T
Q U E S T I O N S</td><td>What is meant by the term "permanent current assets"?

What is meant by the term "temporary current assets"?

What is meant by the term "current asset financing policy"?

What are three alternative current asset financing policies? Is one best?</td></tr>
</table>

ADVANTAGES AND DISADVANTAGES OF SHORT-TERM FINANCING

The three possible financing policies described above were distinguished by the relative amounts of short-term debt used under each policy. The aggressive policy calls for the greatest use of short-term debt, while the conservative policy calls for the least. Maturity matching falls in between. Although short-term credit is generally riskier than long-term credit, using short-term funds does have some significant advantages. The pros and cons of short-term financing are considered in this section.

Speed

A short-term loan can be obtained much faster than a long-term loan. Lenders will insist on a more thorough financial examination before extending long-term credit, and the loan agreement will have to be spelled out in considerable detail because a lot can happen during the life of a 10- to 20-year loan. Therefore, if funds are needed in a hurry, the firm should look to the short-term markets.

Flexibility

If it needs funds for seasonal or cyclical use, a firm may not want to commit itself to long-term debt for three reasons: (1) Flotation costs are higher for long-term debt than for short-term credit. (2) Although long-term debt can be repaid early, provided the loan agreement includes a prepayment provision, prepayment penalties can be expensive. Accordingly, if a firm thinks its need for funds will diminish in the near future, it should choose short-term debt. (3) Long-term loan agreements always contain provisions, or covenants, which constrain future actions. Short-term credit agreements are generally less restrictive.

Cost of Long-Term versus Short-Term Debt

The yield curve is normally upward sloping, indicating that interest rates are generally lower on short-term debt. Thus, under normal conditions, interest costs at the time the funds are obtained will be lower if the firm borrows on a short-term rather than a long-term basis.

Risks of Long-Term versus Short-Term Debt

Even though short-term rates are often lower than long-term rates, short-term credit is riskier for two reasons: (1) If a firm borrows on a long-term basis, its interest costs will be relatively stable over time, but if it uses short-term credit, its interest expense will fluctuate widely, at times going quite high. For example, the prime rate banks charge large corporations for short-term debt more than tripled over a two-year period in the 1980s, rising from 6.25 to 21 percent. Many firms that had borrowed heavily on a short-term basis simply could not meet their rising interest costs, and, as a result, bankruptcies hit record levels during that period. (2) If a firm borrows heavily on a short-term basis, a temporary recession may make it impossible to repay the debt on schedule. If the borrower is in a weak financial position, the lender may not extend the loan, which could force the firm into bankruptcy. Braniff Airlines, which failed during a credit crunch in the 1980s, is an example.

A good example of the riskiness of short-term debt is provided by Transamerica Corporation, a major financial services company. Transamerica's chairman, Mr. Beckett, described how during a period of rising rates his company was moving to reduce its dependency on short-term loans. According to Beckett, Transamerica had reduced its variable-rate (short-term) loans by about $450 million over a two-year period. "We aren't going to go through the enormous increase in debt expense again that had such a serious impact on earnings," he said. The company's earnings fell sharply because money rates rose to record highs. "We were almost entirely in variable-rate debt," he said, but currently "about 65 percent is fixed rate and 35 percent variable. We've come a long way, and we'll keep plugging away at it." Transamerica's earnings were badly depressed by the increase in short-term rates, but other companies were even less fortunate — they simply could not pay the rising interest charges, and this forced them into bankruptcy.

S E L F - T E S T
Q U E S T I O N

What are the advantages and disadvantages of short-term debt over long-term debt?

SOURCES OF SHORT-TERM FINANCING

Statements about the flexibility, cost, and riskiness of short-term versus long-term debt depend, to a large extent, on the type of short-term credit that is actually used. There are numerous sources of short-term funds, and in the following sections we describe four major types: (1) accruals, (2) accounts payable (trade credit), (3) bank loans, and (4) commercial paper.

ACCRUALS

Firms generally pay employees on a weekly, biweekly, or monthly basis, so the balance sheet will typically show some accrued wages. Similarly, the firm's own estimated income taxes, Social Security and income taxes withheld from employee payrolls, and sales taxes collected are generally paid on a weekly, monthly, or quarterly basis. Therefore, the balance sheet will typically show some accrued taxes along with accrued wages.

These **accruals** increase automatically, or spontaneously, as a firm's operations expand. Further, this type of debt is "free" in the sense that no explicit interest is paid on funds raised through accruals. However, a firm cannot ordinarily control its accruals:

The timing of wage payments is set by economic forces and industry custom, while tax payment dates are established by law. Thus, firms use all the accruals they can, but they have little control over the levels of these accounts.

What types of short-term credit are classified as accruals?

What is the cost of accruals?

How much control do financial managers have over the dollar amount of accruals?

ACCOUNTS PAYABLE (TRADE CREDIT)

Firms generally make purchases from other firms on credit, recording the debt as an *account payable*. Accounts payable, or **trade credit,** is the largest single category of short-term debt, representing about 40 percent of the current liabilities of the average nonfinancial corporation. The percentage is somewhat larger for smaller firms: Because small companies often do not qualify for financing from other sources, they rely especially heavily on trade credit.[1]

Trade credit is a "spontaneous" source of financing in the sense that it arises from ordinary business transactions. For example, suppose a firm makes average purchases of $2,000 a day on terms of net 30, meaning that it must pay for goods 30 days after the invoice date. On average, it will owe 30 times $2,000, or $60,000, to its suppliers. If its sales, and consequently its purchases, were to double, then its accounts payable would also double, to $120,000. So, simply by growing, the firm would spontaneously generate an additional $60,000 of financing. Similarly, if the terms under which it bought were extended from 30 to 40 days, its accounts payable would expand from $60,000 to $80,000. Thus, lengthening the credit period, as well as expanding sales and purchases, generates additional financing.

The Cost of Trade Credit

Firms that sell on credit have a *credit policy* that includes certain *terms of credit*. For example, Microchip Electronics sells on terms of 2/10, net 30, meaning that it gives its customers a 2 percent discount if they pay within 10 days of the invoice date, but the full invoice amount is due and payable within 30 days if the discount is not taken.

Note that the true price of Microchip's products is the net price, or 0.98 times the list price, because any customer can purchase an item at that price as long as the customer pays within 10 days. Now consider Personal Computer Company (PCC), which buys its memory chips from Microchip. One commonly used memory chip is listed at $100, so the "true" price to PCC is $98. Now if PCC wants an additional 20 days of credit beyond the 10-day discount period, it must incur a finance charge of $2 per chip for that credit. Thus, the $100 list price consists of two components:

List price = $98 true price + $2 finance charge.

The question PCC must ask before it turns down the discount to obtain the additional 20 days of credit from Microchip is this: Could we obtain credit under better terms

---

[1] In a credit sale, the seller records the transaction as a receivable, the buyer as a payable. We examined accounts receivable as an asset in Chapter 21. Our focus in this chapter is on accounts payable, a liability item. We might also note that if a firm's accounts payable exceed its receivables, it is said to be *receiving net trade credit*, whereas if its receivables exceed its payables, it is *extending net trade credit*. Smaller firms frequently receive net credit; larger firms generally extend it.

from some other source, say, a bank? In other words, could 20 days of credit be obtained for less than $2 per chip?

PCC buys an average of $11,760,000 of memory chips from Microchip each year at the net, or true, price. This amounts to $11,760,000/360 = $32,666.67 per day. For simplicity, assume that Microchip is PCC's only supplier. If PCC decides not to take the additional trade credit — that is, if it pays on the 10th day and takes the discount — its payables will average 10($32,666.67) = $326,667. Thus, PCC will be receiving $326,667 of free credit from Microchip.

Now suppose PCC decides to take the additional 20 days credit and thus must pay the finance charge. Since PCC will now pay on the 30th day, its accounts payable will increase to 30($32,666.67) = $980,000.[2] Microchip will now be supplying PCC with an additional $980,000 − $326,667 = $653,333 of credit, which PCC could use to build up its cash account, to pay off debt, to expand inventories, or even to extend credit to its own customers, hence increasing its own accounts receivable.

The additional trade credit offered by Microchip has a cost — PCC must pay a finance charge equal to the 2 percent discount it is foregoing. PCC buys $11,760,000 of chips at the true price, and the added finance charges increase the total cost to $11,760,000/0.98 = $12 million. Therefore, the annual financing cost is $12,000,000 − $11,760,000 = $240,000. Dividing the $240,000 financing cost by the $653,333 of additional credit, we find the nominal annual cost rate of the additional trade credit to be 36.7 percent:

$$\text{Nominal annual cost} = \frac{\$240,000}{\$653,333} = 36.7\%.$$

If PCC can borrow from its bank (or from other sources) at an interest rate less than 36.7 percent, it should take discounts and forgo the additional trade credit.

The following equation can be used to calculate the nominal cost, on an annual basis, of not taking discounts, illustrated with terms of 2/10, net 30:

$$\begin{matrix} \text{Nominal} \\ \text{annual} \\ \text{cost} \end{matrix} = \frac{\text{Discount percent}}{100 - \begin{matrix}\text{Discount}\\\text{percent}\end{matrix}} \times \frac{360\ \text{days}}{\begin{matrix}\text{Days credit is}\\\text{outstanding}\end{matrix} - \begin{matrix}\text{Discount}\\\text{period}\end{matrix}} \qquad \textbf{(22-1)}$$

$$= \frac{2}{98} \times \frac{360}{20} = 2.04\% \times 18 = 36.7\%.$$

The numerator of the first term, Discount percent, is the cost per dollar of credit, while the denominator in this term, 100 − Discount percent, represents the funds made available by not taking the discount. Thus, the first term, 2.04%, is the cost per period for the trade credit. The denominator of the second term is the number of days of extra credit obtained by not taking the discount, so the entire second term shows how many times each year the cost is incurred, 18 times in this example.

The nominal annual cost formula does not take account of compounding, and in effective annual interest terms, the cost of trade credit is even higher. The discount amounts to interest, and with terms of 2/10, net 30, the firm gains use of the funds for

---

[2]A question arises here: Should accounts payable reflect gross purchases or purchases net of discounts? Generally accepted accounting principles permit either treatment if the difference is not material, but if the discount is material, then the transaction must be recorded net of discounts, or at "true" prices. Then, the higher payment that results from not taking discounts is reported as an additional expense called "discounts lost." *Thus, we show accounts payable net of discounts even if the company does not expect to take discounts.*

30 − 10 = 20 days, so there are 360/20 = 18 "interest periods" per year. Remember that the first term in Equation 22-1, (Discount percent)/(100 − Discount percent) = 0.02/0.98 = 0.0204, is the periodic interest rate. This rate is paid 18 times each year, so the effective annual cost of trade credit is

$$\text{Effective annual rate} = (1.0204)^{18} - 1.0 = 1.439 - 1.0 = 43.9\%.$$

Thus, the 36.7 percent nominal cost calculated with Equation 22-1 understates the true cost.

Notice, however, that the cost of trade credit can be reduced by paying late. Thus, if PCC could get away with paying in 60 days rather than in the specified 30 days, then the effective credit period would become 60 − 10 = 50 days, the number of times the discount would be lost would fall to 360/50 = 7.2, and the nominal cost would drop from 36.7 percent to 2.04% × 7.2 = 14.7%. The effective annual rate would drop from 43.9 to 15.7 percent:

$$\text{Effective annual rate} = (1.0204)^{7.2} - 1.0 = 1.157 - 1.0 = 15.7\%.$$

In periods of excess capacity, firms may be able to get away with deliberately paying late, or **stretching accounts payable.** However, they will also suffer a variety of problems associated with being branded a "slow payer." These problems are discussed later in the chapter.

The costs of the additional trade credit from foregoing discounts under some other purchase terms are shown below:

	COST OF ADDITIONAL CREDIT IF THE CASH DISCOUNT IS NOT TAKEN	
CREDIT TERMS	NOMINAL COST	EFFECTIVE COST
1/10, net 20	36.4%	43.6%
1/10, net 30	18.2	19.8
2/10, net 20	73.5	106.9
3/15, net 45	37.1	44.1

As these figures show, the cost of not taking discounts can be substantial. Incidentally, throughout the chapter, we assume that payments are made either on the *last day* for taking discounts or on the *last day* of the credit period, unless otherwise noted. It would be foolish to pay, say, on the 5th day or on the 20th day if the credit terms were 2/10, net 30.[3]

Effects of Trade Credit on the Financial Statements

A firm's policy with regard to taking or not taking discounts can have a significant effect on its financial statements. To illustrate, assume that PCC is just beginning its operations. On the first day, it makes net purchases of $32,666.67. This amount is

[3]A financial calculator can also be used to determine the cost of trade credit. If the terms of credit are 2/10, net 30, this implies that for every $100 of goods purchased at the full list price, the customer has the choice of paying the full amount in 30 days or else paying $98 in 10 days. If a customer decides not to take the discount, then it is in effect borrowing $98, the amount it would otherwise have to pay, from Day 11 to Day 30, or for 20 days. It will then have to pay $100, which is the $98 loan plus a $2 financing charge, at the end of the 20-day loan period. To calculate the interest rate, enter N = 1, PV = 98, PMT = 0, FV = −100, and then press I to obtain 2.04 percent. This is the rate for 20 days. To calculate the effective annual interest rate on a 360-day basis, enter N = 20/360 = 0.05556, PV = 98, PMT = 0, FV = −100, and then press I to obtain 43.86 percent. The 20/360 = 0.05556 is the fraction of a year the "loan" is outstanding, and the 43.86 percent is the annualized cost of not taking discounts.

recorded on its balance sheet under accounts payable.[4] The second day it buys another $32,666.67. The first day's purchases are not yet paid for, so at the end of the second day, accounts payable total $65,333.34. Accounts payable increase by another $32,666.67 on the third day, for a total of $98,000, and after ten days, accounts payable are up to $326,667.

If PCC takes discounts, then on the 11th day it will have to pay for the $32,666.67 of purchases made on the first day, which will reduce accounts payable. However, it will buy another $32,666.67, which will increase payables. Thus, after the 10th day of operations, PCC's balance sheet will level off, showing a balance of $326,667 in accounts payable, assuming the company pays on the 10th day and takes discounts.

Now suppose PCC decides not to take discounts. In this case, on the 11th day it will add another $32,666.67 to payables, but it will not pay for the purchases made on the 1st day. Thus, the balance sheet figure for accounts payable will rise to 11($32,666.67) = $359,333.37. This buildup will continue through the 30th day, at which point payables will total 30($32,666.67) = $980,000. On the 31st day, PCC will buy another $32,666.67 of goods, which will increase accounts payable, but it will also pay for the purchases made the 1st day, which will reduce payables. Thus, its accounts payable will stabilize at $980,000 after 30 days if it does not take discounts.

The top section of Table 22-1 shows PCC's balance sheet, after it reaches a steady state, under the two trade credit policies. Total assets are unchanged by this policy decision, and we also assume that the accruals and common equity accounts are unchanged. The differences show up in accounts payable and notes payable; when PCC elects to take discounts and thus gives up some of the trade credit it otherwise could have obtained, it will have to raise $653,333 from some other source. It could have sold more common stock, or it could have used long-term bonds, but it chose to use bank credit, which has a 10 percent cost and is reflected in the notes payable account.

The bottom section of Table 22-1 shows PCC's income statement under the two policies. If the company does not take discounts, then its interest expense will be zero, but it will have a $240,000 expense for discounts lost. On the other hand, if it does take discounts, it will incur an interest expense of $65,333, but it will avoid the cost of discounts lost. Since discounts lost exceed the interest expense, the take-discounts policy results in a higher net income and, thus, in a higher stock price.

Components of Trade Credit: Free versus Costly

On the basis of the preceding discussion, trade credit can be divided into two components: (1) **free trade credit,** which involves credit received during the discount period and which for PCC amounts to 10 days' net purchases, or $326,667, and (2) **costly trade credit,** which involves credit in excess of the free trade credit and whose cost is an implicit one based on the foregone discounts.[5] PCC could obtain $653,333, or 20 days' net purchases, of nonfree trade credit at a nominal cost of 37 percent. *Firms should always use the free component, but they should use the costly component only after analyzing the cost of this capital to make sure that it is less than the cost of funds*

---

[4]Inventories also increase by $32,666.67, but we are not now concerned with inventories. Again, note that both inventories and receivables are recorded net of discounts regardless of whether discounts are taken.

[5]There is some question as to whether any credit is really "free," because the supplier will have a cost of carrying receivables which must be passed on to the customer in the form of higher prices. Still, if suppliers sell on standard terms such as 2/10, net 30, and if the base price cannot be negotiated downward for early payment, then for all intents and purposes, the ten days of trade credit is indeed "free."

TABLE 22-1	PCC's Financial Statements with Different Trade Credit Policies

	TAKE DISCOUNTS; BORROW FROM BANK (1)	DO NOT TAKE DISCOUNTS; USE MAXIMUM TRADE CREDIT (2)	DIFFERENCE (1) − (2)
I. Balance Sheets			
Cash	$ 500,000	$ 500,000	$ 0
Receivables	1,000,000	1,000,000	0
Inventories	2,000,000	2,000,000	0
Fixed assets	2,980,000	2,980,000	0
Total assets	$ 6,480,000	$ 6,480,000	$ 0
Accounts payable	$ 326,667	$ 980,000	$−653,333
Notes payable (10%)	653,333	0	+653,333
Accruals	500,000	500,000	0
Common equity	5,000,000	5,000,000	0
Total claims	$ 6,480,000	$ 6,480,000	$ 0
II. Income Statements			
Sales	$15,000,000	$15,000,000	$ 0
Less: Purchases	11,760,000	11,760,000	0
Labor	2,000,000	2,000,000	0
Interest	65,333	0	+65,333
Discounts lost	0	240,000	−240,000
Earnings before taxes (EBT)	$ 1,174,667	$ 1,000,000	$+174,667
Taxes (40%)	469,867	400,000	−69,867
Net income	$ 704,800	$ 600,000	$+104,800

which could be obtained from other sources. Under the terms of trade found in most industries, the costly component is relatively expensive, so stronger firms will avoid using it.

We noted earlier that firms sometimes can and do deviate from the stated credit terms, thus altering the percentage cost figures cited earlier. For example, a California manufacturing firm that buys on terms of 2/10, net 30, makes a practice of paying in 15 days (rather than 10), but it still takes discounts. Its treasurer simply waits until 15 days after receipt of the goods to pay, then writes a check for the invoiced amount less the 2 percent discount. The company's suppliers want its business, so they tolerate this practice. Similarly, a Wisconsin firm that also buys on terms of 2/10, net 30, does not take discounts, but it pays in 60 rather than in 30 days, thus "stretching" its trade credit. As we saw earlier, both practices reduce the calculated cost of trade credit. Neither of these firms is "loved" by its suppliers, and neither could continue these practices in times when suppliers were operating at full capacity and had order backlogs, but these practices can and do reduce the costs of trade credit during times when suppliers have excess capacity.

SELF-TEST
QUESTIONS

What is trade credit?

What is the difference between free trade credit and costly trade credit?

What is the formula for finding the nominal annual cost of trade credit? What is the formula for the effective annual cost rate of trade credit?

How does the cost of costly trade credit generally compare with the cost of short-term bank loans?

SHORT-TERM BANK LOANS

Commercial banks, whose loans generally appear on firms' balance sheets as notes payable, are second in importance to trade credit as a source of short-term financing for non-financial corporations.[6] The banks' influence is actually greater than it appears from the dollar amounts because banks provide *nonspontaneous* funds. As a firm's financing needs increase, it requests additional funds from its bank. If the request is denied, the firm may be forced to abandon attractive growth opportunities. Although banks do make longer-term loans, *the bulk of their lending is on a short-term basis*— about two-thirds of all bank loans mature in a year or less. Bank loans to businesses are frequently written as 90-day notes, in which case the loan must be repaid or renewed at the end of 90 days. Of course, if a borrower's financial position has deteriorated, the bank may refuse to renew the loan. This can mean serious trouble for the borrower. The key features of bank loans are discussed in the following paragraphs.

Promissory Note

When a bank loan is approved, the agreement is executed by signing a **promissory note.** When the note is signed, the bank credits the borrower's checking account with the funds, so on the borrower's balance sheet both cash and notes payable increase. Here are the key elements contained in most promissory notes:

1. **Amount borrowed.** The note must specify the amount of the loan.

2. **Interest only versus amortized.** Loans are either *interest-only,* where only interest is paid during the life of the loan, and the principal is repaid when the loan matures, or *amortized,* meaning that some of the principal is repaid on each payment date. Amortized loans are called *installment loans.*

3. **Collateral.** If a short-term loan is secured by some specific collateral, generally accounts receivable or inventories, this fact is indicated in the note. If the collateral is to be kept on the premises of the borrower, then a form called a *UCC-1* (Uniform Commercial Code-1) is filed with the secretary of the state in which the collateral resides, along with a *Security Agreement* (also part of the Uniform Commercial Code) which describes the nature of the agreement. These filings prevent the borrower from using the same collateral to secure loans from different lenders, and they spell out conditions under which the lender can seize the collateral.

4. **Loan guarantees.** If the borrower is a small corporation, its bank will probably insist that the larger stockholders *personally guarantee* the loan. Banks have often

---

[6]Although commercial banks remain the primary source of short-term loans, other sources are available. For example, GE Capital Corporation (GECC) had several billion dollars in commercial loans outstanding. Firms such as GECC, which was initially established to finance consumers' purchases of GE's durable goods, often find business loans to be more profitable than consumer loans.

seen a troubled company's owner divert assets from the company to some other entity he or she owned, so banks protect themselves by insisting on personal guarantees. However, stockholder guarantees are virtually impossible to get in the case of larger corporations with many stockholders. Also, guarantees are unnecessary for proprietorships or partnerships because here the owners are already personally liable for the business's debts.

5. **Nominal, or stated, interest rate.** The interest rate can be either *fixed* or *floating*. If it floats, it is generally indexed to the bank's prime rate, to the T-bill rate, or to the London Inter-Bank Offer Rate (LIBOR). Most loans of any size ($25,000 and up) have floating rates if their maturities are greater than 90 days. The note will also indicate whether the bank uses a *360-* or *365-day year* for purposes of calculating interest; most banks use a 360-day year.

6. **Frequency of interest payments.** If the note is on an interest-only basis, it will indicate *how frequently interest must be paid.* Interest is typically calculated on a daily basis but paid monthly.

7. **Maturity.** Long-term loans always have specific maturity dates. A short-term loan may or may not have a specified maturity. For example, a loan may mature in 30 days, 90 days, 6 months, or 1 year, or it may call for "payment on demand," in which case the loan can remain outstanding as long as the borrower wants to continue using the funds and the bank agrees. Banks virtually never call demand notes unless the borrower's creditworthiness deteriorates, so many "short-term loans" remain outstanding for years, with the interest rate floating with rates in the economy.

8. **Discount interest.** Most loans call for interest to be paid after it has been earned, but *discount loans* require that interest be paid in advance. If the loan is on a discount basis, the borrower actually receives less than the face amount of the loan, and this increases the loan's effective cost. We discuss discount loans in a later section.

9. **Add-on basis installment loans.** Auto loans and other types of consumer installment loans are generally set up on an "add-on basis," which means that interest charges over the life of the loan are calculated and then added to the face amount of the loan. Thus, the borrower signs a note for the funds received plus the interest. The add-on feature also raises the effective cost of a loan, as we demonstrate in a later section.

10. **Other cost elements.** Some loans require compensating balances, and revolving credit agreements often require commitment fees. Both of these conditions will be spelled out in the loan agreement, and both raise the effective cost of a loan above its stated nominal rate, as we illustrate in a later section.

Compensating Balances

Banks sometimes require borrowers to maintain an average demand deposit (checking account) balance equal to from 10 to 20 percent of the face amount of the loan. This is called a **compensating balance,** and such balances raise the effective interest rate on the loans. For example, if a firm needs $80,000 to pay off outstanding obligations, but if it must maintain a 20 percent compensating balance, then it must borrow $100,000 to obtain a usable $80,000. If the stated annual interest rate is 8 percent, the effective cost is actually 10 percent: $8,000 interest divided by $80,000 of usable funds equals 10 percent.[7]

---

[7]Note, however, that the compensating balance may be set as a minimum monthly *average,* and if the firm would maintain this average anyway, the compensating balance requirement would not raise the effective interest rate. Also, note that these *loan* compensating balances are added to any compensating balances that the firm's bank may require for *services performed,* such as clearing checks.

Informal Line of Credit

A **line of credit** is an informal agreement between a bank and a borrower indicating the maximum credit the bank will extend to the borrower. For example, on December 31, a bank loan officer might indicate to a financial manager that the bank regards the firm as being "good" for up to $80,000 during the forthcoming year, provided the borrower's financial condition does not deteriorate. If on January 10 the financial manager signs a promissory note for $15,000 for 90 days, this would be called "taking down" $15,000 of the total line of credit. This amount would be credited to the firm's checking account at the bank, and before repayment of the $15,000, the firm could borrow additional amounts up to a total of $80,000 outstanding at any one time.

Many lines of credit have a "cleanup" clause requiring the borrower to have a zero balance on the loan for some period during the year. For example, a toy retailer might draw on the line of credit during the fall inventory buildup, and then repay the loan during the winter after collecting on sales made during the holiday season. Banks are willing to fund this type of temporary financing need with a line of credit, and the cleanup clause prevents the line of credit from becoming a permanent source of financing.

Revolving Credit Agreement

A **revolving credit agreement** is a formal line of credit often used by large firms. To illustrate, in 1997 Texas Petroleum Company negotiated a revolving credit agreement for $100 million with a group of banks. The banks were formally committed for four years to lend the firm up to $100 million if the funds were needed. Texas Petroleum, in turn, paid an annual commitment fee of $\frac{1}{4}$ of 1 percent on the unused balance of the commitment to compensate the banks for making the commitment. Thus, if Texas Petroleum did not take down any of the $100 million commitment during a year, it would still be required to pay a $250,000 annual fee, normally in monthly installments of $20,833.33. If it borrowed $50 million on the first day of the agreement, the unused portion of the line of credit would fall to $50 million, and the annual fee would fall to $125,000. Of course, interest would also have to be paid on the money Texas Petroleum actually borrowed. As a general rule, the interest rate on "revolvers" is pegged to the prime rate, the T-bill rate, or some other market rate, so the cost of the loan varies over time as interest rates change.[8] Texas Petroleum's rate was set at prime plus 0.5 percentage point.

Note that a revolving credit agreement is similar to an informal line of credit, but with an important difference: The bank has a *legal obligation* to honor a revolving credit agreement, and it receives a commitment fee. Neither the legal obligation nor the fee exists under the informal line of credit.

SELF-TEST QUESTION | Explain how a firm that expects to need funds during the coming year might make sure the needed funds will be available.

---

[8]Each bank sets its own prime rate, but, because of competitive forces, most banks' prime rates are identical. Further, most banks follow the rate set by the large New York City banks.

In recent years many banks have been lending to the strongest companies at rates below the prime rate. As we discuss later in this chapter, larger firms have ready access to the commercial paper market, and if banks want to do business with these larger companies, they must match, or at least come close to, the commercial paper rate.

THE COST OF BANK LOANS

The cost of bank loans varies for different types of borrowers at any given point in time and for all borrowers over time. Interest rates are higher for riskier borrowers, and rates are also higher on smaller loans because of the fixed costs involved in making and servicing loans. If a firm can qualify as a "prime credit" because of its size and financial strength, it can borrow at the **prime rate,** which at one time was the lowest rate banks charged. Rates on other loans are generally scaled up from the prime rate, but loans to very large, strong customers are made at rates below prime. Thus, loans to smaller, riskier borrowers are generally stated to carry an interest rate of "prime *plus* some number of percentage points," but loans to larger, less risky borrowers may have a rate stated as "prime *minus* some percentage points."

Bank rates vary widely over time depending on economic conditions and Federal Reserve policy. When the economy is weak, then (1) loan demand is usually slack, (2) inflation is low, and (3) the Fed also makes plenty of money available to the system. As a result, rates on all types of loans are relatively low. Conversely, when the economy is booming, loan demand is typically strong, the Fed restricts the money supply, and the result is high interest rates. As an indication of the kinds of fluctuations that can occur, the prime rate during 1980 rose from 11 percent to 21 percent in just four months, and it rose from 6 to 9 percent during 1994. The prime rate is currently (March 1998) 8.50 percent. Interest rates on other bank loans also vary, generally moving with the prime rate.

Regular, or Simple, Interest

In this and the following sections, we explain how to calculate the effective cost of different bank loans. For illustrative purposes, we assume a loan of $10,000 at a nominal interest rate of 12 percent, with a 365-day year.

For business loans, the most common procedure is called **regular,** or **simple, interest,** based on an interest-only loan. We begin by dividing the nominal interest rate, 12 percent in this case, by 365 (or 360 in some cases) to get the rate per day:

$$\text{Interest rate per day} = \frac{\text{Nominal rate}}{\text{Days in year}} \tag{22-2}$$

$$= 0.12/365 = 0.00032876712.$$

This rate is then multiplied by the actual number of days during the specific payment period, and then times the amount of the loan. For example, if the loan is interest-only, with monthly payments, then the interest payment for January would be $101.92:

$$\text{Interest charge for period} = (\text{Days in period})(\text{Rate per day})(\text{Amount of loan}) \tag{22-3}$$

$$= (31 \text{ days})(0.00032876712)(\$10,000) = \$101.92.$$

If interest were payable quarterly, and if there were 91 days in the particular quarter, then the interest payment would be $299.18. The annual interest would be 365 × 0.00032876712 × $10,000 = $1,200.00. Note that if the bank had based the interest calculation on a 360-day year, as most banks do, the interest rate per day would have been slightly higher. Obviously, banks use a 360-day year to boost their earnings.

The effective interest rate on a loan depends on how frequently interest must be paid—the more frequently, the higher the effective rate. We demonstrate this point with two time lines, one for interest paid once a year and one for quarterly payments:

Interest paid annually:

0	0.25	0.5	0.75	1.0
10,000	0	0	0	−1,200.00
				−10,000.00
				−11,200.00

The borrower gets $10,000 at t = 0 and pays $11,200 at t = 1. With a financial calculator, enter N = 1, PV = 10000, PMT = 0, and FV = −11200, and then press I to get the effective cost of the loan, 12 percent.

Interest paid quarterly:

0	0.25	0.5	0.75	1.0
10,000	−299.18	−299.18	−302.47	−299.18
				−10,000.00
				−10,299.18

Note that the third quarter has 92 days. We enter the data in the cash flow register of a financial calculator (being sure to use the +/− key to enter −299.18), and we find the periodic rate to be 2.9999 percent. The effective annual rate is 12.55 percent:

$$\text{Effective annual rate, quarterly} = (1 + 0.029999)^4 - 1 = 12.55\%.$$

Had the loan called for interest to be paid monthly, the effective rate would have been 12.68 percent, and if interest had been paid daily, the rate would have been 12.75 percent. These rates would be higher if the bank used a 360-day year.

In these examples, we assumed that the loan matured in one year but that interest was paid at various times during the year. The rates we calculated would have been exactly the same as the ones above even if the loan had matured on each interest payment date. In other words, the effective rate on a monthly payment loan would be 12.68 percent regardless of whether it matured after one month, six months, one year, or ten years, providing the stated rate remains at 12 percent.

Discount Interest

In a **discount interest** loan, the bank deducts the interest in advance (*discounts* the loan). Thus, the borrower receives less than the face value of the loan. On a one-year, $10,000 loan with a 12 percent (nominal) rate, discount basis, the interest is $10,000(0.12) = $1,200. Therefore, the borrower obtains the use of only $10,000 − $1,200 = $8,800. If the loan were for less than a year, the interest charge (the discount) would be lower; in our example, it would be $600 if the loan were for six months, hence the amount received would be $9,400.

The effective rate on a discount loan is always higher than the rate on an otherwise similar simple interest loan. To illustrate, consider the situation for a discounted 12 percent loan for one year:

Discount interest, paid annually:

0	0.25	0.5	0.75	1.0
10,000	0	0	0	−10,000
−1,200				
8,800				

THE TRAVAILS OF JAMESWAY
The travails of Jamesway Corporation, a retailer which operates primarily in the northeastern United States, provides a vivid illustration of the difficulty of maintaining an inexpensive source of funds. After 28 profitable years, Jamesway's financial position deteriorated as a result of unforeseen problems when it implemented a new automated merchandise ordering system. Order errors led to excessive inventory buildup, which, in turn, required the firm to mark down its goods and to book large losses.

Jamesway's lead lender, which had been providing the company with short-term credit to finance its inventories, cut its line of credit in half. The problems were exacerbated because a considerable amount of long-term debt was coming due in the near future. This situation caused suppliers to restrict credit to Jamesway, squeezing it still further.

In the end, the company was unable to finance the purchase of inventory needed for the "Back-to-School" and Christmas holiday seasons, and it was forced to declare bankruptcy.

After working out a plan of reorganization, the company emerged from bankruptcy in early 1995. Needless to say, a key element of the reorganization plan was to obtain a firmly committed revolving credit agreement.

With a financial calculator, enter N = 1, PV = 8800, PMT = 0, and FV = −10000, and then press I to get the effective cost of the loan, 13.64 percent.[9]

If a discount loan matures in less than a year, say, after one quarter, we have this situation:

Discount interest, one quarter:

0	0.25	0.5	0.75	1.0
10,000	−10,000	0	0	0
−300				
9,700				

Enter N = 1, PV = 9700, PMT = 0, and FV = −10000, and then press I to find the periodic rate, 3.092784 percent per quarter, which corresponds to an effective annual rate of 12.96 percent. Thus, shortening the period of a discount loan lowers the effective rate of interest. This occurs because there is a delay in paying interest relative to a longer-term discount loan ($300 paid each quarter rather than $1,200 paid up front).

Effects of Compensating Balances on Discount Loans

If the bank requires a compensating balance, and if the amount of the required balance exceeds the amount the firm would normally hold on deposit, then the excess must be

---

[9]Note that the firm actually receives less than the face amount of the loan:

$$\text{Funds received} = \text{Face amount of loan} \, (1.0 - \text{Nominal interest rate}).$$

We can solve for the face amount as follows:

$$\text{Face amount of loan} = \frac{\text{Funds received}}{1.0 - \text{Nominal rate (decimal)}}.$$

Therefore, if the borrowing firm actually requires $10,000 of cash, it must borrow $11,363.64:

$$\text{Face value} = \frac{\$10,000}{1.0 - 0.12} = \frac{\$10,000}{0.88} = \$11,363.64.$$

Now, the borrower will receive $11,363.64 − 0.12($11,363.64) = $10,000. Increasing the face value of the loan does not change the effective rate of 13.64 percent on the $10,000 of usable funds.

deducted at t = 0 and then added back when the loan matures. This raises the effective rate on the loan. To illustrate, here is the setup for a one-year discount loan, with a 20 percent compensating balance which the firm would not otherwise hold on deposit:

Discount interest, paid annually, with 20 percent compensating balance:

0	0.25	0.5	0.75	1.0
10,000	0	0	0	−10,000
−1,200				2,000
−2,000				
6,800				−8,000

Note that the bank initially gives, and the borrower gets, $10,000 at time 0. However, the bank takes out the $1,200 of interest in advance, and the company must leave $2,000 in the bank as a compensating balance, hence the borrower's effective net cash flow at t = 0 is $6,800. At t = 1, the borrower must repay the $10,000, but $2,000 is already in the bank (the compensating balance), so the company must repay a net amount of $8,000.

With a financial calculator, enter N = 1, PV = 6800, PMT = 0, and FV = −8000, and then press I to get the effective cost of the discount loan with a compensating balance, 17.65 percent.

Installment Loans: Add-On Interest

Lenders typically charge **add-on interest** on automobile and other types of installment loans. The term "add-on" means that the interest is calculated and then added to the amount received to determine the loan's face value. To illustrate, suppose you borrow $10,000 on an add-on basis at a nominal rate of 12 percent to buy a car, with the loan to be repaid in 12 monthly installments. At a 12 percent add-on rate, you will pay a total interest charge of $10,000(0.12) = $1,200. To determine the effective rate of an add-on loan, we proceed as follows:

1. The amount to be repaid is $10,000 of principal plus $1,200 of interest, or a total of $11,200.

2. The monthly payment is $11,200/12 = $933.33.

3. You are, in effect, paying off a 12-period annuity of $933.33 in order to receive $10,000 today, so $10,000 is the present value of the annuity. Here is the time line:

0	i = ?	1	2	11	12 Months
10,000		−933.33	−933.33	−933.33	−933.33

4. With a financial calculator, enter N = 12, PV = 10000, PMT = −933.33, FV = 0, and then press I to obtain 1.7880 percent. However, this is a monthly rate.

5. The effective annual rate is found as follows:[10]

$$\text{Effective annual rate}_{\text{Add-on}} = (1 + k_d)^n - 1.0$$
$$= (1.01788)^{12} - 1.0$$
$$= 1.2370 - 1.0 = 23.7\%.$$

---

[10]Note that if an installment loan is paid off ahead of schedule, additional complications arise. For the classic discussion of this point, see Dick Bonker, "The Rule of 78," *Journal of Finance*, June 1976, 877–888.

The **annual percentage rate (APR),** which by law the bank is required to state in bold print on all "consumer loan" agreements, would be 21.46 percent:

$$\text{APR rate} = (\text{Periods per year})(\text{Rate per period})$$

$$= 12(1.7880\%) = 21.46\%.$$

Prior to the passage of the truth in lending laws in the 1970s, most banks would have called this a 12 percent loan, period. The truth in lending laws apply primarily to consumer as opposed to business loans.

S E L F - T E S T
Q U E S T I O N S

What are some different ways banks can calculate interest on loans?

What is a compensating balance? What effect does a compensating balance requirement have on the effective interest rate on a loan?

CHOOSING A BANK

Individuals whose only contact with their bank is through the use of its checking services generally choose a bank for the convenience of its location and the competitive cost of its services. However, a business that borrows from banks must look at other criteria, and a borrower seeking a banking relationship should recognize that important differences exist among banks. Some of these differences are considered next.

Willingness to Assume Risks

Banks have different basic policies toward risk. Some are inclined to follow relatively conservative lending practices, while others engage in what are properly termed "creative banking practices." These policies reflect partly the personalities of bank officers and partly the characteristics of the bank's deposit liabilities. Thus, a bank with fluctuating deposit liabilities in a static community will tend to be a conservative lender, while a bank whose deposits are growing with little interruption may follow more liberal credit policies. Similarly, a large bank with broad diversification over geographic regions and across industries can obtain the benefit of combining and averaging risks. Thus, marginal credit risks that might be unacceptable to a small or specialized bank can be pooled by a branch banking system to reduce the overall risk of a group of marginal accounts.[11]

Advice and Counsel

Some bank loan officers are active in providing counsel and in stimulating development loans to firms in their early and formative years. Certain banks have specialized departments which make loans to firms expected to grow and thus to become more important customers. The personnel of these departments can provide valuable counseling to customers: The bankers' experience with other firms in growth situations may enable them to spot, and then to warn their customers about, developing problems.

---

[11]Bank deposits are insured by a federal agency, and banks are required to pay premiums to cover the cost of this insurance. Logically, riskier banks should pay higher premiums, but to date political forces have limited the use of risk-based insurance premiums. As an alternative, banks with riskier loan portfolios are required to have more equity capital per dollar of deposits than less risky banks. The savings and loan industry, until the 1980s, had federal insurance, no differential capital requirements, and lax regulations. As a result, some S&L operators wrote very high interest rate, but very risky, loans using low-cost, insured deposits. If the loans paid off, the S&L owners would get rich. If they went into default, the taxpayers would have to pay off the deposits. Those government policies ended up costing taxpayers more than $100 billion.

Loyalty to Customers

Banks differ in their support of borrowers in bad times. This characteristic is referred to as the degree of *loyalty* of the bank. Some banks may put great pressure on a business to liquidate its loans when the firm's outlook becomes clouded, whereas others will stand by the firm and work diligently to help it get back on its feet. An especially dramatic illustration of this point was Bank of America's bailout of Memorex Corporation. The bank could have forced Memorex into bankruptcy, but instead it loaned the company additional capital and helped it survive a bad period. Memorex's stock price subsequently rose from $1.50 to $68, so Bank of America's help was indeed beneficial.

Specialization

Banks differ greatly in their degrees of loan specialization. Larger banks have separate departments that specialize in different kinds of loans—for example, real estate loans, farm loans, and commercial loans. Within these broad categories, there may be a specialization by line of business, such as steel, machinery, cattle, or textiles. The strengths of banks are also likely to reflect the nature of the business and the economic environment in which they operate. For example, some California banks have become specialists in lending to electronics companies, while many Midwestern banks are agricultural specialists. A sound firm can obtain more creative cooperation and more active support by going to a bank that has experience and familiarity with its particular type of business. Therefore, a bank that is excellent for one firm may be unsatisfactory for another.

Maximum Loan Size

The size of a bank can be an important factor. Since the maximum loan a bank can make to any one customer is limited to 15 percent of the bank's capital accounts (capital stock plus retained earnings), it is generally not appropriate for large firms to develop borrowing relationships with small banks.

Merchant Banking

The term "merchant bank" was originally applied to banks which not only made loans but also provided customers with equity capital and financial advice. Prior to 1933, U.S. commercial banks performed all types of merchant banking functions. However, about one-third of the U.S. banks failed during the Great Depression, in part because of these activities, so in 1933 the Glass-Steagall Act was passed in an effort to reduce banks' exposure to risk. In recent years, commercial banks have been attempting to get back into merchant banking, in part because their foreign competitors offer such services, and U.S. banks compete with foreign banks for multinational corporations' business. Currently, the larger banks, often through subsidiaries, are being permitted to get back into merchant banking, at least to a limited extent. This trend will probably continue, and if it does, corporations will need to consider a bank's ability to provide a full range of commercial and merchant banking services when choosing a bank.

Other Services

Banks can also provide cash management services, assist with electronic funds transfers, help firms obtain foreign exchange, and the like, and the availability of such services should be taken into account when selecting a bank. Also, if the firm is a small business whose manager owns most of its stock, the bank's willingness and ability to provide trust and estate services should also be considered.

What are some factors that should be considered when choosing a bank?

COMMERCIAL PAPER

Commercial paper is a type of unsecured promissory note issued by large, strong firms and sold primarily to other business firms, to insurance companies, to pension funds, to money market mutual funds, and to banks. In early 1998, there was approximately $970 billion of commercial paper outstanding, versus about $870 billion of bank loans. Much of this commercial paper outstanding was issued by financial institutions.

Maturity and Cost

Maturities of commercial paper generally vary from one day to nine months, with an average of about five months.[12] The interest rate on commercial paper fluctuates with supply and demand conditions — it is determined in the marketplace, varying daily as conditions change. Recently, commercial paper rates have ranged from 1½ to 3 percentage points below the stated prime rate, and about ⅛ to ½ of a percentage point above the T-bill rate. For example, in March 1998, the average rate on three-month commercial paper was 5.45 percent, the stated prime rate was 8.5 percent, and the three-month T-bill rate was 5.09 percent.

Use of Commercial Paper

The use of commercial paper is restricted to a comparatively small number of very large concerns that are exceptionally good credit risks. Dealers prefer to handle the paper of firms whose net worth is $100 million or more and whose annual borrowing exceeds $10 million. One potential problem with commercial paper is that a debtor who is in temporary financial difficulty may receive little help because commercial paper dealings are generally less personal than are bank relationships. Thus, banks are generally more able and willing to help a good customer weather a temporary storm than is a commercial paper dealer. On the other hand, using commercial paper permits a corporation to tap a wide range of credit sources, including financial institutions outside its own area and industrial corporations across the country, and this can reduce interest costs.

What is commercial paper?

What types of companies can use commercial paper to meet their short-term financing needs?

How does the cost of commercial paper compare with the cost of short-term bank loans? With the cost of Treasury bills?

USE OF SECURITY IN SHORT-TERM FINANCING

Thus far, we have not addressed the question of whether or not short-term loans should be secured. Commercial paper is never secured, but other types of loans can be secured

---

[12]The maximum maturity without SEC registration is 270 days. Also, commercial paper can only be sold to "sophisticated" investors; otherwise, SEC registration would be required even for maturities of 270 days or less.

if this is deemed necessary or desirable. Other things held constant, it is better to borrow on an unsecured basis, since the bookkeeping costs of secured loans are often high. However, firms often find that they can borrow only if they put up some type of collateral to protect the lender, or that by using security they can borrow at a much lower rate.

Several different kinds of collateral can be employed, including marketable stocks or bonds, land or buildings, equipment, inventory, and accounts receivable. Marketable securities make excellent collateral, but few firms that need loans also hold portfolios of stocks and bonds. Similarly, real property (land and buildings) and equipment are good forms of collateral, but they are generally used as security for long-term loans rather than for working capital loans. Therefore, most secured short-term business borrowing involves the use of accounts receivable and inventories as collateral.

To understand the use of security, consider the case of a Chicago hardware dealer who wanted to modernize and expand his store. He requested a $200,000 bank loan. After examining his business's financial statements, the bank indicated that it would lend him a maximum of $100,000 and that the interest rate would be 10 percent, discount interest, for an effective rate of 11.1 percent. The owner had a substantial personal portfolio of stocks, and he offered to put up $300,000 of high-quality stocks to support the $200,000 loan. The bank then granted the full $200,000 loan, and at the prime rate of 8.25 percent, simple interest. The store owner might also have used his inventories or receivables as security for the loan, but processing costs would have been high. Procedures for using accounts receivable and inventories as security for short-term credit are described in the Extension to this chapter.[13]

SELF-TEST
QUESTIONS

What is a secured loan?

What are some types of current assets that are pledged as security for short-term loans?

[13]The term "asset-based financing" is often used as a synonym for "secured financing." In recent years, accounts receivable have been used as security for long-term bonds, and this permits corporations to borrow from lenders such as pension funds rather than being restricted to banks and other traditional short-term lenders.

SUMMARY

This chapter examined the types of credit that can be used to finance current assets. The key concepts covered are listed below.

- **Permanent current assets** are those current assets that the firm holds even during slack times, whereas **temporary current assets** are the additional current assets that are needed during seasonal or cyclical peaks. The methods used to finance permanent and temporary current assets define the firm's **current asset financing policy.**

- A **moderate** approach to current asset financing involves matching, to the extent possible, the maturities of assets and liabilities, so that temporary current assets are financed with short-term nonspontaneous debt, and permanent current assets and fixed assets are financed with long-term debt or equity, plus spontaneous debt. Under an **aggressive** approach, some permanent current assets, and perhaps even some fixed assets, are financed with short-term debt. A **conservative** approach would be to use long-term capital to finance all permanent assets and some of the temporary current assets.

- The advantages of short-term credit are (1) the **speed** with which short-term loans can be arranged, (2) increased **flexibility,** and (3) the fact that short-term **interest rates** are generally **lower** than long-term rates. The principal disadvantage of short-term credit is the **extra risk** the borrower must bear because (1) the lender can demand payment on short notice and (2) the cost of the loan will increase if interest rates rise.

- **Short-term credit** is defined as any liability originally scheduled for payment within one year. The four major sources of short-term credit are (1) accruals, (2) accounts payable, (3) loans from commercial banks and finance companies, and (4) commercial paper.

- **Accruals,** which are continually recurring short-term liabilities, represent free, spontaneous credit.

- **Accounts payable,** or **trade credit,** is the largest category of short-term debt. Trade credit arises spontaneously as a result of credit purchases. Firms should use all the **free trade credit** they can obtain, but they should use **costly trade credit** only if it is less expensive than other forms of short-term debt. Suppliers often offer discounts to customers who pay within a stated discount period. The following equation may be used to calculate the nominal cost, on an annual basis, of not taking discounts:

$$\text{Nominal cost} = \frac{\text{Discount percent}}{100 - \text{Discount percent}} \times \frac{360}{\text{Days credit is outstanding} - \text{Discount period}}.$$

- **Bank loans** are an important source of short-term credit. Interest on bank loans may be quoted as **simple interest, discount interest,** or **add-on interest.** The effective rate on a bank loan always exceeds the quoted nominal rate except for a simple interest loan where the interest is paid once a year.

- When a bank loan is approved, a **promissory note** is signed. It specifies: (1) the amount borrowed, (2) the percentage interest rate, (3) the repayment schedule, (4) the collateral, and (5) any other conditions to which the parties have agreed.

- Banks sometimes require borrowers to maintain **compensating balances,** which are deposit requirements set at between 10 and 20 percent of the loan amount. Compensating balances raise the effective interest rate on bank loans.

- A **line of credit** is an informal agreement between the bank and the borrower indicating the maximum amount of credit the bank will extend to the borrower.

- A **revolving credit agreement** is a formal line of credit often used by large firms; it involves a **commitment fee.**

- **Commercial paper** is unsecured short-term debt issued by large, financially strong corporations. Although the cost of commercial paper is lower than the cost of bank loans, it can be used only by large firms with exceptionally strong credit ratings.

- Sometimes a borrower will find that it is necessary to borrow on a **secured basis,** in which case the borrower pledges assets such as real estate, securities, equipment, inventories, or accounts receivable as collateral for the loan.

Questions

22-1　Define each of the following terms:
a. Permanent current assets; temporary current assets
b. Moderate current asset financing policy; aggressive current asset financing policy; conservative current asset financing policy
c. Maturity matching, or "self-liquidating," approach
d. Accruals

e. Trade credit; stretching accounts payable; free trade credit; costly trade credit
f. Promissory note; line of credit; revolving credit agreement
g. Prime rate
h. Simple interest; discount interest; add-on interest
i. Compensating balance (CB)
j. Commercial paper
k. Secured loan

22-2 How does the seasonal nature of a firm's sales influence its decision regarding the amount of short-term credit to use in its financial structure?

22-3 What are the advantages of matching the maturities of assets and liabilities? What are the disadvantages?

22-4 From the standpoint of the borrower, is long-term or short-term credit riskier? Explain. Would it ever make sense to borrow on a short-term basis if short-term rates were above long-term rates?

22-5 If long-term credit exposes a borrower to less risk, why would people or firms ever borrow on a short-term basis?

22-6 "Firms can control their accruals within fairly wide limits; depending on the cost of accruals, financing from this source will be increased or decreased." Discuss.

22-7 Is it true that both trade credit and accruals represent a spontaneous source of capital for financing growth? Explain.

22-8 Is it true that most firms are able to obtain some free trade credit and that additional trade credit is often available, but at a cost? Explain.

22-9 The availability of bank credit is often more important to a small firm than to a large one. Why?

22-10 What kinds of firms use commercial paper? Could Mama and Papa Gus's Corner Grocery borrow using this form of credit?

22-11 Given that commercial paper interest rates are generally lower than bank loan rates to a given borrower, why might firms which are capable of selling commercial paper also use bank credit?

22-12 Suppose a firm can obtain funds by borrowing at the prime rate or by selling commercial paper.
a. If the prime rate is 8.25 percent, what is a reasonable estimate for the cost of commercial paper?
b. If a substantial cost differential exists, why might a firm like this one actually borrow some of its funds in each market?

Self-Test Problem   (Solution Appears in Appendix B)

ST-1
Current Asset Financing

Vanderheiden Press Inc. and the Herrenhouse Publishing Company had the following balance sheets as of December 31, 1998 (thousands of dollars):

	VANDERHEIDEN PRESS	**HERRENHOUSE PUBLISHING**
Current assets	$100,000	$ 80,000
Fixed assets (net)	100,000	120,000
Total assets	$200,000	$200,000
Current liabilities	$ 20,000	$ 80,000
Long-term debt	80,000	20,000
Common stock	50,000	50,000
Retained earnings	50,000	50,000
Total liabilities and equity	$200,000	$200,000

Earnings before interest and taxes for both firms are $30 million, and the effective federal-plus-state tax rate is 40 percent.
a. What is the return on equity for each firm if the interest rate on current liabilities is 10 percent and the rate on long-term debt is 13 percent?
b. Assume that the short-term rate rises to 20 percent. While the rate on new long-term debt rises to 16 percent, the rate on existing long-term debt remains unchanged. What would be the return on equity for Vanderheiden Press and Herrenhouse Publishing under these conditions?
c. Which company is in a riskier position? Why?

Problems

22-1
Cost of Trade Credit

What is the nominal and effective cost of trade credit (on a 360-day basis) under the credit terms of 3/15, net 30?

22-2
Cost of Trade Credit

A large retailer obtains merchandise under the credit terms of 1/15, net 45, but routinely takes 60 days to pay its bills. Given that the retailer is an important customer, suppliers allow the firm to stretch its credit terms. What is the retailer's effective cost of trade credit (on a 360-day basis)?

22-3
Accounts Payable

A chain of appliance stores, APP Corporation, purchases inventory with a net price of $500,000 each day. The company purchases the inventory under the credit terms of 2/15, net 40. APP always takes the discount, but takes the full 15 days to pay its bills. What is the average accounts payable for APP?

22-4
Cost of Bank Loan

On March 1, Minnerly Motors obtained a business loan from a local bank. The loan is a $25,000 interest-only loan with a nominal rate of 11 percent. Interest is calculated on a simple interest basis with a 365-day year. What is Minnerly's interest charge for the first month (assuming 31 days in the month)?

22-5
Cost of Bank Loan

Mary Jones recently obtained an automobile loan from a local bank. The loan is for $15,000 with a nominal interest rate of 11 percent. However, this is an installment loan, so the bank also charges add-on interest. Mary must make monthly payments on the loan, and the loan is to be repaid in 1 year. What is the effective annual rate on the loan (assuming a 365-day year)?

22-6
Cost of Trade Credit

Calculate the nominal annual cost of nonfree trade credit under each of the following terms. Assume payment is made either on the due date or on the discount date.
a. 1/15, net 20.
b. 2/10, net 60.
c. 3/10, net 45.
d. 2/10, net 45.
e. 2/15, net 40.

22-7
Cost of Trade Credit

a. If a firm buys under terms of 3/15, net 45, but actually pays on the 20th day and *still takes the discount,* what is the nominal cost of its nonfree trade credit?
b. Does it receive more or less credit than it would if it paid within 15 days?

22-8
Cost of Bank Loans

Del Hawley, owner of Hawley's Hardware, is negotiating with First City Bank for a $50,000, 1-year loan. First City has offered Hawley the following alternatives. Calculate the effective annual interest rate for each alternative. Which alternative has the lowest effective annual interest rate?
a. A 12 percent annual rate on a simple interest loan, with no compensating balance required and interest due at the end of the year.
b. A 9 percent annual rate on a simple interest loan, with a 20 percent compensating balance required and interest again due at the end of the year.
c. An 8.75 percent annual rate on a discounted loan, with a 15 percent compensating balance.
d. Interest is figured as 8 percent of the $50,000 amount, *payable at the end of the year,* but the $50,000 is repayable in monthly installments during the year.

22-9
Cost of Trade Credit

Grunewald Industries sells on terms of 2/10, net 40. Gross sales last year were $4.5 million, and accounts receivable averaged $437,500. Half of Grunewald's customers paid on the 10th day and took discounts. What are the nominal and effective costs of trade credit to Grunewald's nondiscount customers? (Hint: Calculate sales/day based on a 360-day year; then get average receivables of discount customers; then find the DSO for the nondiscount customers.)

22-10
Effective Cost of Short-Term Credit

The D. J. Masson Corporation needs to raise $500,000 for 1 year to supply working capital to a new store. Masson buys from its suppliers on terms of 3/10, net 90, and it currently pays on the 10th day and takes discounts, but it could forego discounts, pay on the 90th day, and get the needed $500,000 in the form of costly trade credit. Alternatively, Masson could borrow from its bank on a 12 percent discount interest rate basis. What is the effective annual interest rate of the lower-cost source?

22-11
Effective Cost of Short-Term Credit

Yonge Corporation must arrange financing for its working capital requirements for the coming year. Yonge can (a) borrow from its bank on a simple interest basis (interest payable at the end of the loan) for 1 year at a 12 percent nominal rate; (b) borrow on a 3-month, but renewable, loan at an 11.5 percent nominal rate; (c) borrow on an installment loan basis at a 6 percent add-on rate with 12 end-of-month payments; or (d) obtain the needed funds by no longer taking discounts and thus increasing its accounts payable. Yonge buys on terms of 1/15, net 60. What is the effective annual cost (*not* the nominal cost) of the *least expensive* type of credit, assuming 360 days per year?

22-12
Cash Discounts

Suppose a firm makes purchases of $3.6 million per year under terms of 2/10, net 30, and takes discounts.

a. What is the average amount of accounts payable net of discounts? (Assume that the $3.6 million of purchases is net of discounts—that is, gross purchases are $3,673,469, discounts are $73,469, and net purchases are $3.6 million. Also, use 360 days in a year.)

b. Is there a cost of the trade credit the firm uses?

c. If the firm did not take discounts but it did pay on the due date, what would be its average payables and the cost of this nonfree trade credit?

d. What would its cost of not taking discounts be if it could stretch its payments to 40 days?

22-13
Trade Credit versus Bank Credit

The Thompson Corporation projects an increase in sales from $1.5 million to $2 million, but it needs an additional $300,000 of current assets to support this expansion. The money can be obtained from the bank at an interest rate of 13 percent, discount interest; no compensating balance is required. Alternatively, Thompson can finance the expansion by no longer taking discounts, thus increasing accounts payable. Thompson purchases under terms of 2/10, net 30, but it can delay payment for an additional 35 days—paying in 65 days and thus becoming 35 days past due—without a penalty because of its suppliers' current excess capacity problems.

a. Based strictly on effective, or equivalent, annual interest rate comparisons, how should Thompson finance its expansion?

b. What additional qualitative factors should Thompson consider before reaching a decision?

22-14
Bank Financing

The Raattama Corporation had sales of $3.5 million last year, and it earned a 5 percent return, after taxes, on sales. Recently, the company has fallen behind in its accounts payable. Although its terms of purchase are net 30 days, its accounts payable represent 60 days' purchases. The company's treasurer is seeking to increase bank borrowings in order to become current in meeting its trade obligations (that is, to have 30 days' payables outstanding). The company's balance sheet is as follows (thousands of dollars):

Cash	$ 100	Accounts payable	$ 600
Accounts receivable	300	Bank loans	700
Inventory	1,400	Accruals	200
Current assets	$1,800	Current liabilities	$1,500
Land and buildings	600	Mortgage on real estate	700
Equipment	600	Common stock, $0.10 par	300
		Retained earnings	500
Total assets	$3,000	Total liabilities and equity	$3,000

a. How much bank financing is needed to eliminate the past-due accounts payable?

b. Would you as a bank loan officer make the loan? Why?

22-15
Cost of Bank Loans

Gifts Galore Inc. borrowed $1.5 million from National City Bank. The loan was made at a simple annual interest rate of 9 percent a year for 3 months. A 20 percent compensating balance requirement raised the effective interest rate.

a. The nominal annual rate on the loan was 11.25 percent. What is the true effective rate?

b. What would be the effective cost of the loan if the note required discount interest?

c. What would be the nominal annual interest rate on the loan if the bank did not require a compensating balance but required repayment in 3 equal monthly installments?

22-16
Short-Term Financing Analysis

Malone Feed and Supply Company buys on terms of 1/10, net 30, but it has not been taking discounts and has actually been paying in 60 rather than 30 days. Malone's balance sheet follows (thousands of dollars):

Cash	$ 50	Accounts payable[a]	$ 500
Accounts receivable	450	Notes payable	50
Inventory	750	Accruals	50
Current assets	$1,250	Current liabilities	$ 600
		Long-term debt	150
Fixed assets	750	Common equity	1,250
Total assets	$2,000	Total liabilities and equity	$2,000

[a]Stated net of discounts.

Now, Malone's suppliers are threatening to stop shipments unless the company begins making prompt payments (that is, paying in 30 days or less). The firm can borrow on a 1-year note (call this a current liability) from its bank at a rate of 15 percent, discount interest, with a 20 percent compensating balance required. (Malone's $50,000 of cash is needed for transactions; it cannot be used as part of the compensating balance.)

a. Determine what action Malone should take by calculating (1) the cost of nonfree trade credit and (2) the cost of the bank loan.

b. Assume that Malone foregoes discounts and then borrows the amount needed to become current on its payables from the bank. How large will the bank loan be?

c. Based on your conclusion in Part b, construct a pro forma balance sheet. (Hint: You will need to include an account entitled "prepaid interest" under current assets.)

22-17
Alternative Financing
Arrangements

Suncoast Boats Inc. estimates that because of the seasonal nature of its business, it will require an additional $2 million of cash for the month of July. Suncoast Boats has the following 4 options available for raising the needed funds:

(1) Establish a 1-year line of credit for $2 million with a commercial bank. The commitment fee will be 0.5 percent per year on the unused portion, and the interest charge on the used funds will be 11 percent per annum. Assume that the funds are needed only in July, and that there are 30 days in July and 360 days in the year.

(2) Forgo the trade discount of 2/10, net 40, on $2 million of purchases during July.

(3) Issue $2 million of 30-day commercial paper at a 9.5 percent per annum interest rate. The total transactions fee, including the cost of a backup credit line, on using commercial paper is 0.5 percent of the amount of the issue.

(4) Issue $2 million of 60-day commercial paper at a 9 percent per annum interest rate, plus a transactions fee of 0.5 percent. Since the funds are required for only 30 days, the excess funds ($2 million) can be invested in 9.4 percent per annum marketable securities for the month of August. The total transactions cost of purchasing and selling the marketable securities is 0.4 percent of the amount of the issue.

a. What is the dollar cost of each financing arrangement?

b. Is the source with the lowest expected cost necessarily the one to select? Why or why not?

Spreadsheet Problem

Work the problem in this section only if you are using the computer problem diskette.

22-18
Working Capital Financing

Use the model in File C22 to solve this problem. Three companies—Aggressive, Moderate, and Conservative—have different working capital management policies as implied by their names. For example, Aggressive employs only minimal current assets, and it finances almost entirely with current liabilities plus equity. This restricted approach has a dual effect. It keeps total assets low, which tends to increase return on assets; but because of stock-outs and credit rejections, total sales are reduced, and because inventory is ordered more frequently and in smaller quantities, variable costs are increased. Condensed balance sheets for the three companies follow:

	AGGRESSIVE	MODERATE	CONSERVATIVE
Current assets	$225,000	$300,000	$450,000
Fixed assets	300,000	300,000	300,000
Total assets	$525,000	$600,000	$750,000
Current liabilities (12%)	$300,000	$150,000	$ 75,000
Long-term debt (10%)	0	150,000	300,000
Total debt	$300,000	$300,000	$375,000
Equity	225,000	300,000	375,000
Total liabilities and equity	$525,000	$600,000	$750,000
Current ratio	0.75×	2×	6×

The cost of goods sold functions for the three firms are as follows:

$$\text{Cost of goods sold} = \text{Fixed costs} + \text{Variable costs}.$$

Aggressive: Cost of goods sold = $300,000 + 0.70(\text{Sales}).$

Moderate: Cost of goods sold = $405,000 + 0.65(Sales).

Conservative: Cost of goods sold = $577,500 + 0.60(Sales).

Because of the working capital differences, sales for the three firms under different economic conditions are expected to vary as follows:

	AGGRESSIVE	MODERATE	CONSERVATIVE
Strong economy	$1,800,000	$1,875,000	$1,950,000
Average economy	1,350,000	1,500,000	1,725,000
Weak economy	1,050,000	1,200,000	1,575,000

a. Construct income statements for each company for strong, average, and weak economies using the following format:

> Sales
>
> Less cost of goods sold
>
> Earnings before interest and taxes (EBIT)
>
> Less interest expense
>
> Earnings before taxes (EBT)
>
> Less taxes (40%)
>
> Net income

b. Compare the basic earning power (EBIT/Assets) and return on equity for the companies. Which company is best in a strong economy? In an average economy? In a weak economy?
c. Suppose that, with sales at the average-economy level, short-term interest rates rose to 20 percent. How would this affect the three firms?
d. Suppose that because of production slowdowns caused by inventory shortages, the aggressive company's variable cost ratio rose to 80 percent. What would happen to its ROE? Assume a short-term interest rate of 12 percent.
e. What considerations for management of working capital are indicated by this problem?

MINI CASE

Bats and Balls (B&B) Inc., a baseball equipment manufacturer, is a small company with seasonal sales. Each year before the baseball season, B&B purchases inventory which is financed through a combination of trade credit and short-term bank loans. At the end of the season, B&B uses sales revenues to repay its short-term obligations. The company is always looking for ways to become more profitable, and senior management has asked one of its employees, Ann Taylor, to review the company's current asset financing policies. Putting together her report, Ann is trying to answer each of the following questions:
a. B&B tries to match the maturity of its assets and liabilities. Describe how B&B could adopt either a more aggressive or more conservative financing policy.
b. What are the advantages and disadvantages of using short-term credit as a source of financing?
c. Is it likely that B&B could make significantly greater use of accruals?
d. Assume that B&B buys on terms of 1/10, net 30, but that it can get away with paying on the 40th day if it chooses not to take discounts. Also, assume that it purchases $3 million of components per year, net of discounts. How much free trade credit can the company get, how much costly trade credit can it get, and what is the percentage cost of the costly credit? Should B&B take discounts?
e. What is commercial paper, and would it be feasible for B&B to finance with commercial paper?
f. Suppose B&B decided to raise an additional $100,000 as a 1-year loan from its bank, for which it was quoted a rate of 8 percent. What is the effective annual cost rate assuming (1) simple interest, (2) discount interest, (3) discount interest with a 10 percent compensating

balance, and (4) add-on interest on a 12-month installment loan? For the first three of these assumptions, would it matter if the loan were for 90 days, but renewable, rather than for a year?

g. How large would the loan actually be in each of the cases in Part g?

h. What are the pros and cons of borrowing on a secured versus an unsecured basis?

Selected Additional References

For more on trade credit, see

Adams, Paul D., Steve R. Wyatt, and Yong H. Kim, "A Contingent Claims Analysis of Trade Credit," *Financial Management*, Autumn 1992, 104–112.

Brosky, John J., *The Implicit Cost of Trade Credit and Theory of Optimal Terms of Sale* (New York: Credit Research Foundation, 1969).

Schwartz, Robert A., "An Economic Analysis of Trade," *Journal of Financial and Quantitative Analysis*, September 1974, 643–658.

For more on bank lending and commercial credit in general, see

Campbell, Tim S., "A Model of the Market for Lines of Credit," *Journal of Finance*, March 1978, 231–243.

Stone, Bernell K., "Allocating Credit Lines, Planned Borrowing, and Tangible Services over a Company's Banking System," *Financial Management*, Summer 1975, 65–78.

For a discussion of effective yields, see

Finnerty, John D., "Bank Discount, Coupon Equivalent, and Compound Yields: Comment," *Financial Management*, Summer 1983, 40–44.

Glasgo, Philip W., William J. Landes, and A. Frank Thompson, "Bank Discount, Coupon Equivalent, and Compound Yields," *Financial Management*, Autumn 1982, 82–84.

EXTENSIONS

Secured Short-Term Financing

This extension discusses procedures for using accounts receivable and inventories as security for short-term loans. As noted earlier in the chapter, secured loans involve quite a bit of paperwork and other administrative costs, which make them relatively expensive. However, this is often the only type of financing available to weaker firms.

Accounts Receivable Financing. Accounts receivable financing involves either the pledging of receivables or the selling of receivables (called factoring). The *pledging of accounts receivable,* or putting accounts receivable up as security for a loan, is characterized by the fact that the lender not only has a claim against the receivables but also has *recourse* to the borrower: If the person or firm that bought the goods does not pay, the selling firm must take the loss. Therefore, the risk of default on the pledged accounts receivable remains with the borrower. The buyer of the goods is not ordinarily notified about the pledging of the receivables, and the financial institution that lends on the security of accounts receivable is generally either a commercial bank or one of the large industrial finance companies.

Factoring, or selling accounts receivable, involves the purchase of accounts receivable by the lender, generally without recourse to the borrower, which means that if the purchaser of the goods does not pay for them, the lender rather than the seller of the goods takes the loss. Under factoring, the buyer of the goods is typically notified of the transfer and is asked to make payment directly to the financial institution. Since the factoring firm assumes the risk of default on bad accounts, it must make the credit check. Accordingly, factors provide not only money, but also a credit department for the borrower. Incidentally, the same financial institutions that make loans against pledged receivables also serve as factors. Thus, depending on the circumstances and the wishes of the borrower, a financial institution will provide either form of receivables financing.

■ **Procedure for Pledging Accounts Receivable.** The financing of accounts receivable is initiated by a legally binding agreement between the seller of the goods and the financing institution. The agreement sets forth in detail the procedures to be followed and the legal obligations of both parties. Once the working relationship has been established, the seller periodically takes a batch of invoices to the financing institution. The lender reviews the invoices and makes credit appraisals of the buyers. Invoices of companies that do not meet the lender's credit standards are not accepted for pledging.

The financial institution seeks to protect itself at every phase of the operation. First, selection of sound invoices is one way the lender safeguards itself. Second, if the buyer of the goods does not pay the invoice, the lender still has recourse against the seller. Third, additional protection is afforded the lender because the loan will generally be less than 100 percent of the pledged receivables; for example, the lender may advance the selling firm only 75 percent of the amount of the pledged invoices.

- **Procedure for Factoring Accounts Receivable.** The procedures used in factoring are somewhat different from those for pledging. Again, an agreement between the seller and the factor specifies legal obligations and procedural arrangements. When the seller receives an order from a buyer, a credit approval slip is written and immediately sent to the factoring company for a credit check. If the factor approves the credit, shipment is made and the invoice is stamped to notify the buyer to make payment directly to the factoring company. If the factor does not approve the sale, the seller generally refuses to fill the order; if the sale is made anyway, the factor will not buy the account.

The factor normally performs three functions: (1) credit checking, (2) lending, and (3) risk bearing. However, the seller can select various combinations of these functions by changing provisions in the factoring agreement. For example, a small- or medium-sized firm may have the factor perform the risk-bearing function and thus avoid having to establish a credit department. The factor's service is often less costly than a credit department that would have excess capacity for the firm's credit volume. At the same time, if the selling firm uses someone who is not really qualified for the job to perform credit checking, then that person's lack of education, training, and experience could result in excessive losses.

The seller may have the factor perform the credit-checking and risk-taking functions without performing the lending function. The following procedure illustrates the handling of a $10,000 order under this arrangement. The factor checks and approves the invoices. The goods are shipped on terms of net 30. Payment is made to the factor, who remits to the seller. If the buyer defaults, however, the $10,000 must still be remitted to the seller, and if the $10,000 is never paid, the factor sustains a $10,000 loss. Note that in this situation, the factor does not remit funds to the seller until either they are received from the buyer of the goods or the credit period has expired. Thus, the factor does not supply any credit.

Now consider the more typical situation in which the factor performs the lending, risk-bearing, and credit-checking functions. The goods are shipped, and even though payment is not due for 30 days, the factor immediately makes funds available to the seller. Suppose $10,000 worth of goods are shipped. Further, assume that the factoring commission for credit checking and risk bearing is 2.5 percent

of the invoice price, or $250, and that the interest expense is computed at a 9 percent annual rate on the invoice balance, or $75.[1] The selling firm's accounting entry is as follows:

Cash	$9,175	
Interest expense	75	
Factoring commission	250	
Reserve due from factor on collection of account	500	
Accounts receivable		$10,000

The $500 due from the factor upon collection of the account is a reserve established by the factor to cover disputes between the seller and buyers over damaged goods, goods returned by the buyers to the seller, and the failure to make an outright sale of goods. The reserve is paid to the selling firm when the factor collects on the account.

Factoring is normally a continuous process instead of the single cycle just described. The firm that sells the goods receives an order; it transmits this order to the factor for approval; upon approval, the firm ships the goods; the factor advances the invoice amount minus withholdings to the seller; the buyer pays the factor when payment is due; and the factor periodically remits any excess in the reserve to the seller of the goods. Once a routine has been established, a continuous circular flow of goods and funds takes place between the seller, the buyers of the goods, and the factor. Thus, once the factoring agreement is in force, funds from this source are *spontaneous* in the sense that an increase in sales will automatically generate additional credit.

- **Cost of Receivables Financing.** Both accounts receivable pledging and factoring are convenient and advantageous, but they can be costly. The credit-checking and risk-bearing fee is 1 to 3 percent of the amount of invoices accepted by the factor, and it may be even more if the buyers are poor credit risks. The cost of money is reflected in the interest rate (usually 2 to 3 percentage points over the prime rate) charged on the unpaid balance of the funds advanced by the factor.

- **Evaluation of Receivables Financing.** It cannot be said categorically that accounts receivable financing is always either a good or a poor way to raise funds. Among the advantages is, first, the flexibility of this source of financing: As the firm's sales expand, more financing is needed, but a larger volume of invoices, and hence a larger amount of receivables financing, is generated automatically. Second, receivables can be used as security for loans that would not otherwise be granted. Third, factoring can provide the services of a credit department that might otherwise be available only at a higher cost.

---

[1]Since the interest is only for one month, we multiply 1/12 of the quoted rate (9 percent) by the $10,000 invoice price:

$$(1/12)(0.09)(\$10,000) = \$75.$$

The effective annual interest rate is above 9 percent because (1) the term is for less than one year and (2) a discounting procedure is used and the borrower does not get the full $10,000. In many instances, however, the factoring contract calls for interest to be calculated on the invoice price minus the factoring commission and the reserve account.

Accounts receivable financing also has disadvantages. First, when invoices are numerous and relatively small in dollar amount, the administrative costs involved may be excessive. Second, since receivables represent the firm's most liquid noncash assets, some trade creditors may refuse to sell on credit to a firm that factors or pledges its receivables on the grounds that this practice weakens the position of other creditors.

▪ **Future Use of Receivables Financing.** We may make a prediction at this point: In the future, accounts receivable financing will increase in relative importance. Computer technology is rapidly advancing toward the point where credit records of individuals and firms can be kept on disks and magnetic tapes. For example, one device used by retailers consists of a box which, when an individual's magnetic credit card is inserted, gives a signal that the credit is "good" and that a bank is willing to "buy" the receivable created as soon as the store completes the sale. The cost of handling invoices will be greatly reduced over present-day costs because the new systems will be so highly automated. This will make it possible to use accounts receivable financing for very small sales, and it will reduce the cost of all receivables financing. The net result will be a marked expansion of accounts receivable financing. In fact, when consumers use credit cards such as MasterCard or Visa, the seller is in effect factoring receivables. The seller receives the amount of the purchase, minus a percentage fee, the next working day. The buyer receives 30 days' (or so) credit, at which time he or she remits payment directly to the credit card company or sponsoring bank.

Inventory Financing.

A substantial amount of credit is secured by business inventories. If a firm is a relatively good credit risk, the mere existence of the inventory may be a sufficient basis for receiving an unsecured loan. However, if the firm is a relatively poor risk, the lending institution may insist upon security in the form of a *lien* against the inventory. Methods for using inventories as security are discussed in this section.

▪ **Blanket Liens.** The *inventory blanket lien* gives the lending institution a lien against all the borrower's inventories. However, the borrower is free to sell inventories, and thus the value of the collateral can be reduced below the level that existed when the loan was granted.

▪ **Trust Receipts.** Because of the inherent weakness of the blanket lien, another procedure for inventory financing has been developed — the *security instrument* (also called the *trust receipt*), which is an instrument acknowledging that the goods are held in trust for the lender. Under this method, the borrowing firm, as a condition for receiving funds from the lender, signs and delivers a trust receipt for the goods. The goods can be stored in a public warehouse or held on the premises of the borrower. The trust receipt

states that the goods are held in trust for the lender or are segregated on the borrower's premises on the lender's behalf, and that any proceeds from the sale of the goods must be transmitted to the lender at the end of each day. Automobile dealer financing is one of the best examples of trust receipt financing.

One defect of trust receipt financing is the requirement that a trust receipt be issued for specific goods. For example, if the security is autos in a dealer's inventory, the trust receipts must indicate the cars by registration number. In order to validate its trust receipts, the lending institution must send someone to the borrower's premises periodically to see that the auto numbers are correctly listed because auto dealers who are in financial difficulty have been known to sell cars backing trust receipts and then use the funds obtained for other operations rather than to repay the bank. Problems are compounded if the borrower has a number of different locations, especially if they are separated geographically from the lender. To offset these inconveniences, *warehousing* has come into wide use as a method of securing loans with inventory.

▪ **Warehouse Receipts.** *Warehouse receipt financing* is another way to use inventory as security. It is a method of financing which uses inventory as a security and which requires public notification, physical control of the inventory, and supervision by a custodian of the field warehousing concern. A *public warehouse* is an independent third-party operation engaged in the business of storing goods. Items which must age, such as tobacco and liquor, are often financed and stored in public warehouses. Sometimes a public warehouse is not practical because of the bulkiness of goods and the expense of transporting them to and from the borrower's premises. In such cases, a *field warehouse* may be established on the borrower's grounds. To provide inventory supervision, the lending institution employs a third party in the arrangement, the field warehousing company, which acts as its agent.

Field warehousing can be illustrated by a simple example. Suppose a firm which has iron stacked in an open yard on its premises needs a loan. A field warehousing concern can place a temporary fence around the iron, erect a sign stating "This is a field warehouse supervised by the Smith Field Warehousing Corporation," and then assign an employee to supervise and control the fenced-in inventory.

This example illustrates the three essential elements for the establishment of a field warehouse: (1) public notification, (2) physical control of the inventory, and (3) supervision by a custodian of the field warehousing concern. When the field warehousing operation is relatively small, the third condition is sometimes violated by hiring an employee of the borrower to supervise the inventory. This practice is viewed as undesirable by most lenders because there is no control over the collateral by a person independent of the borrowing firm.[2]

---

[2]This absence of independent control was the main cause of the breakdown that resulted in more than $200 million of losses on loans to the Allied Crude Vegetable Oil Company by Bank of America and other banks. American Express Field Warehousing Company was handling the operation, but it hired men from Allied's own staff as custodians. Their dishonesty was not discovered because of another breakdown — the fact that the American Express touring inspector did not actually take a physical inventory of the warehouses. As a consequence, the swindle was not discovered until losses running into the hundreds of millions of dollars had been suffered.

The field warehouse financing operation is best described by an actual case. A California tomato cannery was interested in financing its operations by bank borrowing. It had sufficient funds to finance 15 to 20 percent of its operations during the canning season. These funds were adequate to purchase and process an initial batch of tomatoes. As the cans were put into boxes and rolled into the storerooms, the cannery needed additional funds for both raw materials and labor. Because of the cannery's poor credit rating, the bank decided that a field warehousing operation was necessary to secure its loans.

The field warehouse was established, and the custodian notified the bank of the description, by number, of the boxes of canned tomatoes in storage and under warehouse control. With this inventory as collateral, the lending institution established for the cannery a deposit on which it could draw. From this point on, the bank financed the operations. The cannery needed only enough cash to initiate the cycle. The farmers brought in more tomatoes; the cannery processed them; the cans were boxed; the boxes were put into the field warehouse; field warehouse receipts were drawn up and sent to the bank; the bank established further deposits for the cannery on the basis of the additional collateral, and the cannery could draw on the deposits to continue the cycle.

Of course, the cannery's ultimate objective was to sell the canned tomatoes. As it received purchase orders, it transmitted them to the bank, and the bank directed the custodian to release the inventories. It was agreed that as remittances were received by the cannery, they would be turned over to the bank. These remittances thus paid off the loans.

Note that a seasonal pattern existed. At the beginning of the tomato harvesting and canning season, the cannery's cash needs and loan requirements began to rise, and they reached a peak just as the season ended. It was expected that well before the new canning season began, the cannery would have sold a sufficient volume to pay off the loan. If the cannery had experienced a bad year, the bank might have carried the loan over for another year to enable the company to work off its inventory.

- **Acceptable Products.** In addition to canned foods, which account for about 17 percent of all field warehouse loans, many other types of products provide a basis for field warehouse financing. Some of these are miscellaneous groceries, which represent about 13 percent; lumber products, about 10 percent; and coal and coke, about 6 percent. These products are relatively nonperishable and are sold in well-developed, organized markets. Nonperishability protects the lender if it should have to take over the security. For this reason, a bank would not make a field warehousing loan on perishables such as fresh fish, but frozen fish, which can be stored for a long time, can be field warehoused.

- **Cost of Financing.** The fixed costs of a field warehousing arrangement are relatively high; such financing is therefore not suitable for a very small firm. If a field warehousing company sets up a field warehouse, it will typically set a minimum charge of about $5,000 per year, plus about 1 to 2 percent of the amount of credit extended to the borrower. Furthermore, the financing institution will charge an interest rate of 2 to 3 percentage points over the prime rate. An efficient field warehousing operation requires a minimum inventory of at least $1 million.

- **Evaluation of Inventory Financing.** The use of inventory financing, especially field warehouse financing, as a source of funds has many advantages. First, the amount of funds available is flexible because the financing is tied to inventory growth, which, in turn, is related directly to financing needs. Second, the field warehousing arrangement increases the acceptability of inventories as loan collateral; some inventories simply would not be accepted by a bank as security without such an arrangement. Third, the necessity for inventory control and safe-keeping, as well as the use of specialists in warehousing, often results in improved warehouse practices, which, in turn, save handling costs, insurance charges, theft losses, and so on. Thus, field warehousing companies often save money for firms in spite of the costs of financing that we have discussed. The major disadvantages of field warehousing include the paperwork, physical separation requirements, and, for small firms, the fixed-cost element.

WORKING CAPITAL
MANAGEMENT: EXTENSIONS*

*F*or many Americans, the mention of baseball cards brings to mind the name of Topps Company, the founder of the sports card industry. For many years, Topps had the sports card market to itself, but competitors rushed into the market in the 1980s, when news of collectors' paying thousands of dollars for a single classic card helped create a new interest among both serious and casual collectors. Today, about 100 companies vie for a share of the $1.5 billion annual sales generated by sports and entertainment cards. With more than 30 percent of the market, Topps remains the biggest player. Its current line includes the traditional packs of cards covering baseball and three other sports, plus premium packs with fancier pictures, more statistics, and higher prices.

The sports card business is inherently risky because "sales" to wholesalers and retailers—which account for 75 percent of the business—can be returned to manufacturers. Thus, a sale can be "undone" by merely returning the merchandise. Topps records its sales, less a reserve for returns, when it ships its products. Customers have 21 days to pay for cards, but Topps must refund the full price of all cards returned. At the end of each year (but not at the end of each quarter), Topps compares the dollar amount of returned merchandise with the amount placed in reserve. If the actual dollar amount of returned merchandise exceeds the reserve, the difference is subtracted from earnings. On the other hand, if returns are less than the amount built into the reserve, earnings are boosted.

After covering Chapters 21 and 22, it should be apparent that Topps's sales and returns policy creates special problems for its inventory and receivables managers. For all practical purposes, the bulk of its finished goods inventory is held by wholesalers and retailers, not by the manufacturer. Accordingly, the quantity in stock is not known, so Topps is somewhat in the dark concerning production requirements. A production run on a particular set of cards would be wasted if a large number of returns were to materialize on that set. A similar problem occurs with receivables—their value is not known, because receivables may be paid off with returned cards rather than cash. Indeed, given its returns policy, a "sale" by Topps is not a sale at all until the cards are sold by the retailer. This keeps both Topps's managers and outside analysts in the dark until the company tabulates end-of-year results. Without interim information on returns, outside analysts cannot get a good grasp on true sales until the reserve account is reconciled and the ending balance reported.

In Chapters 21 and 22, we presented the basic elements of current asset management and short-term financing. Now, in Chapter 23, we present a more in-depth treatment of several working capital topics, including (1) the cash conversion cycle, (2) the target cash balance, (3) accounting for inventory, (4) the EOQ model, and (5) monitoring the receivables position.

---

*All or parts of this chapter may be omitted without loss of continuity.

THE CASH CONVERSION CYCLE

As we noted in Chapter 21, the concept of working capital management originated with the old Yankee peddler, who would borrow to buy inventory, sell the inventory to pay off the bank loan, and then repeat the cycle. That general concept has been applied to more complex businesses, and the cash flow cycle concept is used for analyzing the effectiveness of a firm's working capital management.

We can illustrate the concept with data from Real Time Computer Corporation (RTC), which in early 1998 received an order from a government agency for 40 of its new super-minicomputers at a price of $250,000 each. The effects of the order on RTC's working capital position are as follows:

1. RTC will order and then receive the materials it needs to produce the 40 computers. Because RTC and most other firms purchase materials on credit, this transaction will create an account payable, but there will be no immediate cash payment.

2. Labor will be used to convert the materials into finished computers. However, wages will not be fully paid at the time the work is done, so accrued wages will build up.

3. The finished computers will be shipped and billed, but billing will create receivables, not immediate cash inflows.

4. At some point during the cycle, RTC must pay off its accounts payable and accrued wages. Because these payments will be made before RTC has collected cash from its receivables, the payments must be financed.

5. The cycle will be completed when RTC's receivables have been collected. At that time, the company will be in a position to pay off the credit that was used to finance production.

The **cash conversion cycle** model diagrams the length of time between when the company makes payments and when it receives cash. The following terms are used in the model:[1]

1. The **inventory conversion period,** which is the average length of time required to convert materials into finished goods and then to sell those goods, is calculated by dividing inventory on hand by sales per day. For RTC's contract, average inventories are $2 million and sales are $10 million, so the inventory conversion period is 72 days:

$$\text{Inventory conversion period} = \frac{\text{Inventory}}{\text{Sales per day}} = \frac{\text{Inventory}}{\text{Sales}/360}$$

$$= \frac{\$2,000,000}{\$10,000,000/360} = 72 \text{ days.}$$

Thus, it takes an average of 72 days to convert raw materials into finished goods and then to sell those goods.

2. The **receivables collection period,** which is the average length of time required to convert receivables into cash, that is, to collect cash following a sale, is calculated by dividing accounts receivable by the average credit sales per day. If

---

[1]See Verlyn D. Richards and Eugene J. Laughlin, "A Cash Conversion Cycle Approach to Liquidity Analysis," *Financial Management,* Spring 1980, 32–38. A similar approach was set forth earlier by Lawrence J. Gitman, "Estimating Corporate Liquidity Requirements: A Simplified Approach," *The Financial Review,* 1974, 79–88.

receivables average $666,667 and sales are $10 million, the receivables collection period is:

$$\text{Receivables collection period} = \text{DSO} = \frac{\text{Receivables}}{\text{Sales/360}}$$

$$= \frac{\$666,667}{\$10 \text{ million/360}} = 24 \text{ days.}$$

Thus, it takes 24 days after a sale to convert the receivables into cash.

3. The **payables deferral period** is the average length of time between the purchase of materials and labor and the payment of cash for them. For example, if the firm on average has 30 days to pay for labor and materials, if its cost of goods sold is $8 million per year, and if its accounts payable average $666,667, then its payables deferral period can be calculated as follows:

$$\text{Payables deferral period} = \text{Payables/Credit purchases per day}$$

$$= \text{Payables/(Cost of goods sold/360)}$$

$$= \$666,667/(\$8,000,000/360) = 30 \text{ days.}$$

The calculated figure is consistent with the stated 30-day payment period.

4. The **cash conversion cycle** nets out the three periods just defined and thus equals the length of time between the firm's actual cash expenditures for productive resources and its own cash receipts from the sale of products. The cash conversion cycle equals the average length of time a dollar is tied up in current assets.

We can now use these definitions and calculated values to analyze RTC's cash conversion cycle:

(1)	+	(2)	−	(3)	=	(4)	
Inventory conversion period	+	Receivables collection period	−	Payables deferral period	=	Cash conversion cycle	**(23-1)**
72	+	24	−	30	=	66 days.	

The concept is diagrammed in Figure 23-1. It takes RTC an average of 72 days to convert raw materials to computers and then sell them, and another 24 days to collect on receivables. However, 30 days normally elapse between receipt of raw materials and payment for them. Thus, the cash conversion cycle is 66 days. To look at it another way,

$$\text{Receipts delay} \quad - \text{ Payment delay} = \text{Net delay}$$

$$(72 \text{ days} + 24 \text{ days}) - \quad 30 \text{ days} \quad = 66 \text{ days.}$$

Given these data, RTC knows when it starts producing a computer that it will have to finance its outlays for a 66-day period. The firm's goal should be to shorten its cash conversion cycle as much as possible without hurting operations. This would improve profits, because the longer the cash conversion cycle, the greater the need for external financing, and such financing has a cost.

The cash conversion cycle can be shortened (1) if the firm can reduce the inventory conversion period by processing and selling goods more quickly, (2) if it can reduce the receivables collection period by speeding up collections, or (3) if it can lengthen the payables deferral period by slowing down its own payments. To the extent that these

FIGURE 23-1   The Cash Conversion Cycle Model

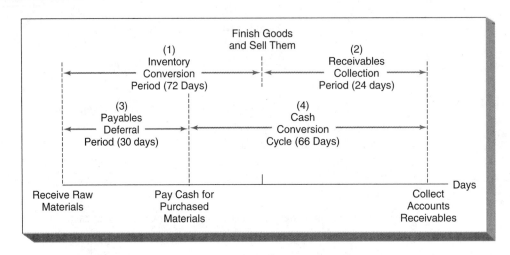

actions can be taken *without increasing costs or depressing sales,* they should be carried out.

To illustrate, suppose RTC must spend $200,000 on materials and labor to produce one computer, and it takes three days to produce a computer. Thus, it must invest $200,000/3 = $66,667 for each day's production. This investment must be financed for 66 days—the length of the cash conversion cycle. Therefore, the company's working capital financing needs will be 66 × $66,667 = $4.4 million. Since RTC does not have $4.4 million of idle cash, it will have to line up $4.4 million of financing before it accepts the order. However, if RTC could reduce the cash conversion cycle to 56 days by deferring payment of its accounts payable an additional ten days, or by speeding up either the production process or the collection of its receivables, it could reduce its working capital financing requirements by about $667,000. We see, then, that actions which affect the inventory conversion period, the receivables collection period, and the payables deferral period all affect the cash conversion cycle, hence they influence the firm's need for current assets and current asset financing.

Firms can use the cash conversion cycle analysis to consider their "regular, ongoing" business operations, or when they are analyzing special orders such as RTC's sale of the 40 computers. Both types of usages are important. Analysis of regular operations can lead to dramatic reductions in working capital and corresponding improvements in free cash flow, EVA, and MVA as discussed in Chapter 2. Analysis of new, incremental business can be used to determine the effects of this business on financial requirements, and it can also be used when negotiating price and payment terms, and in discussions with suppliers. You should keep the cash conversion cycle concept in mind as you go through the remainder of this chapter.

SELF-TEST
QUESTIONS

What steps are involved in estimating the cash conversion cycle?

What do the following terms mean?
   (1) Inventory conversion period
   (2) Receivables collection period
   (3) Payables deferral period

What is the cash conversion cycle model? How can it be used to improve current asset management? EVA?

SETTING THE TARGET CASH BALANCE

In Chapter 21, when we discussed MicroDrive Incorporated's cash budget, we took as a given the $10 million target cash balance. We also discussed how lockboxes, synchronizing inflows and outflows, and float can reduce the required cash balance. Now we consider how target cash balances are set in practice.

Note (1) that cash per se earns no return, (2) that it is an asset which appears on the left side of the balance sheet, (3) that cash holdings must be financed by raising either debt or equity, and (4) that both debt and equity capital have a cost. If cash holdings could be reduced without hurting sales or other aspects of a firm's operations, this reduction would permit a reduction in either debt or equity, or both, which would increase the return on capital and thus boost the value of the firm's stock. *Therefore, the general operating goal of the cash manager is to minimize the amount of cash held subject to the constraint that enough cash be held to enable the firm to operate efficiently.*

For most firms, cash as a percentage of assets and/or sales has declined sharply in recent years as a direct result of technological developments in computers and telecommunications. Years ago, it was difficult to move money from one location to another, and it was also difficult to forecast exactly how much cash would be needed in different locations at different points in time. As a result, firms had to hold relatively large "safety stocks" of cash to be sure they had enough when and where it was needed. Also, they held relatively large amounts of short-term securities as a backup, and they also had backup lines of credit which permitted them to borrow on short notice to build up the cash account if it became depleted.

Now think how computers and telecommunications affect the situation. With a good computer system, tied together with good telecommunications links, a company can get real-time information on its cash balances, whether it operates in a single location or all over the world. Further, it can use statistical procedures to forecast cash inflows and outflows, and good forecasts reduce the need for safety stocks. Finally, improvements in telecommunications systems make it possible for a treasurer to replenish his or her cash accounts within minutes by simply calling a lender and stating that the firm wants to borrow a given amount under its line of credit. The lender then wires the funds to the desired location. Similarly, marketable securities can be sold with close to the same speed and with the same minimal transactions costs.

General Telephone (Gen Tel) can be used to illustrate this. Gen Tel knows exactly how much it must pay and when, and it can forecast quite accurately when it will receive checks. For example, the treasurer of Gen Tel's Florida operation knows when the major employers in Tampa pay their workers and how long after that people generally pay their phone bills. Armed with this information, Gen Tel's Florida treasurer can forecast with great accuracy any cash surpluses or deficits on a daily basis. Of course, no forecast will be exact, so slight overages or underages will occur. But this presents no problem. The treasurer knows by 11 A.M. the checks that must be covered by 4 P.M. that day, how much cash has come in, and consequently how much of a cash surplus or deficit will exist. Then a simple phone call is made, and the company borrows to cover any deficit or buys securities (or pays off outstanding loans) with any surplus. Thus, Gen Tel can maintain cash balances that are very close to zero, a situation that would have been impossible a few years ago.

Today, cash management in reasonably sophisticated firms is largely a job for systems people, and, except for the very largest firms, it is generally most efficient to have a bank handle the actual operations of the cash management system. Banks do this for a living, and there are economies of scale in operating cash management systems. Also, many banks are willing and able to offer such services, so competition has driven the

FIGURE 23-2 Cash Balances under the Baumol Model's Assumptions

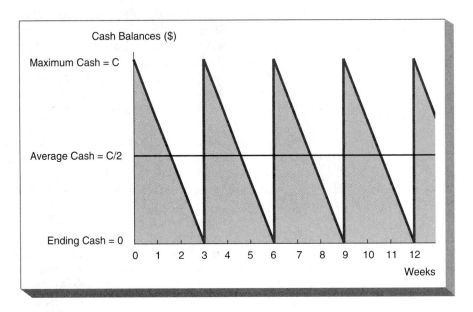

cost of cash management down to a reasonable level. Still, it is essential that corporate treasurers know enough about cash management procedures to be able to negotiate and then work with the banks to ensure that they get the best price (interest rate) on credit lines, the best yield on short-term investments, and a reasonable cost for other banking services. To provide perspective on these issues, we discuss next a theoretical model for cash balances plus a practical approach to setting the target cash balance.

The Baumol Model

William Baumol first noted that cash balances are, in many respects, similar to inventories, and that the EOQ inventory model, which will be developed in a later section, can be used to establish a target cash balance.[2] Baumol's model assumes that the firm uses cash at a steady, predictable rate — say $1 million per week — and that the firm's cash inflows from operations also occur at a steady, predictable rate — say, $900,000 per week. Therefore, the firm's net cash outflows, or net need for cash, also occur at a steady rate — in this case, $100,000 per week.[3] Under these steady-state assumptions, the firm's cash position will resemble the situation shown in Figure 23-2.

If our illustrative firm started at Time 0 with a cash balance of C = $300,000, and if its outflows exceeded its inflows by $100,000 per week, then its cash balance would drop to zero at the end of Week 3, and its average cash balance would be C/2 = $300,000/2 = $150,000. Therefore, at the end of Week 3 the firm would have to replenish its cash balance, either by selling marketable securities, if it had any, or by borrowing.

If C were set at a higher level, say, $600,000, then the cash supply would last longer (six weeks), and the firm would have to sell securities (or borrow) less frequently. How-

---

[2]William J. Baumol, "The Transactions Demand for Cash: An Inventory Theoretic Approach," *Quarterly Journal of Economics,* November 1952, 545–556.

[3]Our hypothetical firm is experiencing a $100,000 weekly cash shortfall, but this does not necessarily imply that it is headed for bankruptcy. The firm could, for example, be highly profitable and be enjoying high earnings, but be expanding so rapidly that it is experiencing chronic cash shortages that must be made up by borrowing or by selling common stock. Or, the firm could be in the construction business and therefore receive major cash inflows at wide intervals, but have net cash outflows of $100,000 per week between major inflows.

FIGURE 23-3   Determination of the Target Cash Balance

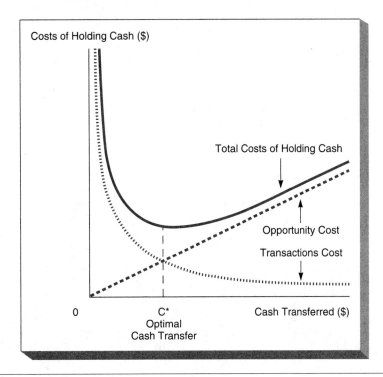

ever, its average cash balance would rise from $150,000 to $300,000. Brokerage or some other type of transactions cost must be incurred to sell securities (or to borrow), so holding larger cash balances will lower the transactions costs associated with obtaining cash. On the other hand, cash provides no income, so the larger the average cash balance, the higher the opportunity cost, which is the return that could have been earned on securities or other assets held in lieu of cash. Thus, we have the situation that is graphed in Figure 23-3. The optimal cash balance is found by using the following variables and equations:

C = amount of cash raised by selling marketable securities or by borrowing. $C/2$ = average cash balance.

C^* = optimal amount of cash to be raised by selling marketable securities or by borrowing. $C^*/2$ = optimal average cash balance.

F = fixed costs of selling securities or of obtaining a loan.

T = total amount of net new cash needed for transactions during the entire period (usually a year).

k = opportunity cost of holding cash, set equal to either the rate of return foregone on marketable securities or the cost of borrowing to hold cash.

The total costs of cash balances consist of holding (or opportunity) costs plus transactions costs:[4]

---

[4]Total costs can be expressed on either a before-tax or an after-tax basis. Both methods lead to the same conclusions regarding target cash balances and comparative costs. For simplicity, we present the model here on a before-tax basis.

$$\text{Total costs} = \text{Holding costs} + \text{Transactions costs}$$

$$= \left(\begin{array}{c}\text{Average cash}\\ \text{balance}\end{array}\right)\left(\begin{array}{c}\text{Opportunity}\\ \text{cost}\end{array}\right) + \left(\begin{array}{c}\text{Number of}\\ \text{transactions}\end{array}\right)\left(\begin{array}{c}\text{Cost per}\\ \text{transaction}\end{array}\right) \quad \textbf{(23-2)}$$

$$= \frac{C}{2}(k) + \frac{T}{C}(F).$$

The minimum total costs are achieved when C is set equal to C*, the optimal cash transfer. C* is found as follows:[5]

$$C^* = \sqrt{\frac{2(F)(T)}{k}}. \quad \textbf{(23-3)}$$

Equation 23-3 is the **Baumol model** for determining optimal cash balances. To illustrate its use, suppose F = $150; T = 52 weeks × $100,000/week = $5,200,000; and k = 15% = 0.15. Then

$$C^* = \sqrt{\frac{2(\$150)(\$5,200,000)}{0.15}} = \$101,980.$$

Therefore, the firm should sell securities (or borrow if it does not hold securities) in the amount of $101,980 when its cash balance approaches zero, thus building its cash balance back up to $101,980. If we divide T by C*, we have the number of transactions per year: $5,200,000/$101,980 = 50.99 ≈ 51, or about once a week. The firm's average cash balance is $101,980/2 = $50,990 ≈ $51,000.

Notice that the optimal cash balance increases less than proportionately with increases in the amount of cash needed for transactions. For example, if the firm's size, and consequently its net new cash needs, doubled from $5,200,000 to $10,400,000 per year, average cash balances would increase by only 41 percent, from $51,000 to $72,000. This suggests that there are economies of scale in holding cash balances, and this, in turn, gives larger firms an edge over smaller ones.[6]

Of course, the firm would probably want to hold a safety stock of cash designed to reduce the probability of a cash shortage. However, if the firm is able to sell securities or to borrow on short notice—and most larger firms can do so in a matter of minutes simply by making a telephone call—the safety stock can be quite low.

The Baumol model is obviously simplistic. Most important, it assumes relatively stable, predictable cash inflows and outflows, and it does not take into account seasonal or cyclical trends. Other models have been developed to deal both with uncertainty and with trends, but all of them have limitations and are more useful as conceptual models than for actually setting target cash balances.

Monte Carlo Simulation

Although the Baumol model and other theoretical models provide insights into the optimal cash balance, they are generally not practical for actual use. Rather, firms generally set their target cash balances based on some "safety stock" of cash that holds the

---

[5]Equation 23-2 is differentiated with respect to C. The derivative is set equal to zero, and we then solve for C = C* to derive Equation 23-3. This model, applied to inventories and called the EOQ model, is discussed further in a later section.

[6]This edge may, of course, be more than offset by other factors—after all, cash management is only one aspect of running a business.

risk of running out of money to some acceptably low level. One commonly used procedure is Monte Carlo simulation.[7] To illustrate, consider the cash budget for MicroDrive Incorporated presented in Table 21-1 in Chapter 21. Sales and collections are the driving forces in the cash budget and, of course, are subject to uncertainty. In the cash budget, we used expected values for sales and collections, as well as for all other cash flows. However, it would be relatively easy to use Monte Carlo simulation, first discussed in Chapter 13, to introduce uncertainty. If the cash budget were constructed using a spreadsheet program with Monte Carlo add-in software, then the key uncertain variables could be specified as continuous probability distributions rather than point values.

The end result of the simulation would be a distribution for each month's net cash gain or loss instead of the single values shown on Line 16 of Table 21-1. Suppose September's net cash loss distribution looked like this (in millions):

SEPTEMBER CASH LOSS	PROBABILITY OF THIS LOSS OR MORE
($83)	10%
(75)	20
(68)	30
(62)	40
(57)	50
(52)	60
(46)	70
(39)	80
(31)	90

Now suppose MicroDrive's managers want to be 90 percent confident that the firm will not run out of cash during September. They would set the beginning-of-month balance at $83 million, well above the current $10 million, because there is only a 10 percent probability that September's cash flow will be worse than an $83 million outflow. With a balance of $83 million at the beginning of the month, there would be only a 10 percent chance that MicroDrive would run out of cash during September. Of course, Monte Carlo simulation could be applied to the remaining months in the Table 21-1 cash budget, and the amounts obtained to meet some confidence level could be used to set each month's target cash balance instead of using a fixed target across all months.

The same type of analysis could be used to determine the amount of short-term securities to hold, or the size of a requested line of credit. Of course, as in all simulations, the hard part is estimating the probability distributions for sales, collections, and the other highly uncertain variables. If these inputs are not good representations of the actual uncertainty facing the firm, then the resulting target balances will not offer the protection against cash shortages implied by the simulation. There is no substitute for experience, and cash managers will adjust the target balances obtained by Monte Carlo simulation to reflect actual results.

SELF-TEST
QUESTIONS

How has technology changed the way target cash balances are set?

What is the Baumol model, and how is it used?

Explain how Monte Carlo simulation can be used to set a firm's target cash balance.

---

[7]See Eugene M. Lerner, "Simulating a Cash Budget," in *Readings on the Management of Working Capital*, 2d ed., Keith V. Smith, ed. (St. Paul, Minn.: West, 1980).

ACCOUNTING FOR INVENTORY

When finished goods are sold, the firm must assign a cost of goods sold. The cost of goods sold appears on the income statement as an expense for the period, and the balance sheet inventory account is reduced by a like amount. Four methods can be used to value the cost of goods sold, and hence to value the remaining inventory: (1) specific identification, (2) first-in, first-out (FIFO), (3) last-in, first-out (LIFO), and (4) weighted average.

Specific Identification

Under **specific identification,** a unique cost is attached to each item in inventory. Then, when an item is sold the inventory value is reduced by that specific amount. This method is used only when the items are high cost and move relatively slowly, such as cars for an automobile dealer.

First-In, First-Out (FIFO)

In the **FIFO** method, the units sold during a given period are assumed to be the first units that were placed in inventory. As a result, the cost of goods sold is based on the cost of the oldest inventory items, and the remaining inventory consists of the newest goods.

Last-In, First-Out (LIFO)

LIFO is the opposite of FIFO. The cost of goods sold is based on the last units placed in inventory, while the remaining inventory consists of the first goods placed in inventory. Note that this is purely an accounting convention—the actual physical units sold could be either the earlier or the later units placed in inventory, or some combination. For example, Del Monte has in its LIFO inventory accounts catsup bottled in the 1920s, but all the catsup in its warehouses was bottled in 1998 or 1999.

Weighted Average

The **weighted average** method involves calculating the weighted average unit cost of goods available for sale from inventory, and this average is then used to determine the cost of goods sold. This method results in a cost of goods sold and an ending inventory that fall somewhere between the FIFO and LIFO methods.

Comparison of Inventory Accounting Methods

To illustrate these methods and their effects on financial statements, assume that Custom Furniture Inc. manufactured five identical antique reproduction dining tables during a one-year accounting period. During the year, a new labor contract plus dramatically increasing mahogany prices caused manufacturing costs to almost double, resulting in the following inventory costs:

Table Number:	1	2	3	4	5	Total
Cost:	$10,000	$12,000	$14,000	$16,000	$18,000	$70,000

There were no tables in stock at the beginning of the year, and Tables 1, 3, and 5 were sold during the year.

If Custom used the specific identification method, the cost of goods sold would be reported as $10,000 + $14,000 + $18,000 = $42,000, while the end-of-period inventory value would be $70,000 − $42,000 = $28,000. If Custom used the FIFO method, its cost of goods sold would be $10,000 + $12,000 + $14,000 = $36,000, and ending inventory would be $70,000 − $36,000 = $34,000. If Custom used the LIFO method, its cost of goods sold would be $48,000, and its ending inventory would be $22,000. Finally, if Custom used the weighted average method, its average cost per unit of inventory would be $70,000/5 = $14,000, its cost of goods sold would be 3($14,000) = $42,000, and its ending inventory would be $70,000 − $42,000 = $28,000.

If Custom's actual sales revenues from the tables were $80,000, or an average of $26,667 per unit sold, and if its other costs were minimal, the following is a summary of the effects of the four methods:

METHOD	SALES	COST OF GOODS SOLD	REPORTED PROFIT	ENDING INVENTORY VALUE
Specific identification	$80,000	$42,000	$38,000	$28,000
FIFO	80,000	36,000	44,000	34,000
LIFO	80,000	48,000	32,000	22,000
Weighted average	80,000	42,000	38,000	28,000

Ignoring taxes, Custom's cash flows would not be affected by its choice of inventory methods, yet its balance sheet and reported profits would vary with each method. In an inflationary period such as in our example, FIFO gives the lowest cost of goods sold and thus the highest net income. FIFO also shows the highest inventory value, so it produces the strongest apparent liquidity position as measured by net working capital or the current ratio. On the other hand, LIFO produces the highest cost of goods sold, the lowest reported profits, and the weakest apparent liquidity position. However, when taxes are considered, LIFO provides the greatest tax deductibility, and thus it results in the lowest tax burden. Consequently, after-tax cash flows are highest if LIFO is used.

Of course, these results apply only to periods when costs are increasing. If costs were constant, all four methods would produce the same cost of goods sold, ending inventory, taxes, and cash flows. However, inflation has been a fact of life in recent years, so most firms use LIFO to take advantage of its greater tax and cash flow benefits.

SELF-TEST QUESTIONS

What are the four methods used to account for inventory?

What impact does the method used have on the firm's reported profits? On ending inventory levels?

Which method should be used if management anticipates a period of inflation? Why?

THE ECONOMIC ORDERING QUANTITY (EOQ) MODEL

As discussed in Chapter 21, inventories are obviously necessary, but it is equally obvious that a firm's profitability will suffer if it has too much or too little inventory. Most firms use a pragmatic approach to setting inventory levels, in which past experience plays a major role. However, as a starting point in the process, it is useful for managers to consider the insights provided by the **economic ordering quantity (EOQ)** model.

The EOQ model first specifies the costs of ordering and carrying inventories and then combines these costs to obtain the total costs associated with inventory holdings. Finally, optimization techniques are used to find that order quantity, hence inventory level, that minimizes total costs. Note that a third category of inventory costs, the costs of running short (stock-out costs), are not considered in our initial discussion. These costs are dealt with by adding safety stocks, as we will discuss later. Similarly, we shall discuss quantity discounts in a later section. The costs that remain for consideration at this stage are carrying costs and ordering, shipping, and receiving costs.

Carrying Costs

Carrying costs generally rise in direct proportion to the average amount of inventory carried. Inventories carried, in turn, depend on the frequency with which orders are placed. To illustrate, if a firm sells S units per year, and if it places equal-sized orders N times per year, then S/N units will be purchased with each order. If the inventory is used evenly over the year, and if no safety stocks are carried, then the average inventory, A, will be

$$A = \frac{\text{Units per order}}{2} = \frac{S/N}{2}. \qquad (23\text{-}4)$$

For example, if S = 120,000 units in a year, and N = 4, then the firm will order 30,000 units at a time, and its average inventory will be 15,000 units:

$$A = \frac{S/N}{2} = \frac{120,000/4}{2} = \frac{30,000}{2} = 15,000 \text{ units.}$$

Just after a shipment arrives, the inventory will be 30,000 units; just before the next shipment arrives, it will be zero; and on average, 15,000 units will be carried.

Now assume the firm purchases its inventory at a price P = \$2 per unit. The average inventory value is thus (P)(A) = \$2(15,000) = \$30,000. If the firm has a cost of capital of 10 percent, it will incur \$3,000 in financing charges to carry the inventory for one year. Further, assume that each year the firm incurs \$2,000 of storage costs (space, utilities, security, taxes, and so forth), that its inventory insurance costs are \$500, and that it must mark down inventories by \$1,000 because of depreciation and obsolescence. The firm's total cost of carrying the \$30,000 average inventory is thus \$3,000 + \$2,000 + \$500 + \$1,000 = \$6,500, and the annual percentage cost of carrying the inventory is \$6,500/\$30,000 = 0.217 = 21.7%.

Defining the annual percentage carrying cost as C, we can, in general, find the annual total carrying cost, TCC, as the percentage carrying cost, C, times the price per unit, P, times the average number of units, A:

$$\text{TCC} = \text{Total carrying cost} = (C)(P)(A). \qquad (23\text{-}5)$$

In our example,

$$\text{TCC} = (0.217)(\$2)(15,000) \approx \$6,500.$$

Ordering Costs

Although we assume that carrying costs are entirely variable and rise in direct proportion to the average size of inventories, ordering costs are often fixed. For example, the costs of placing and receiving an order—interoffice memos, long-distance telephone calls, setting up a production run, and taking delivery—are essentially fixed regardless of the size of an order, so this part of inventory cost is simply the fixed cost of placing and receiving orders times the number of orders placed per year.[8] We define the fixed costs associated with ordering inventories as F, and if we place N orders per year, the total ordering cost is given by Equation 23-6:

$$\text{Total ordering cost} = \text{TOC} = (F)(N). \tag{23-6}$$

Here TOC = total ordering cost, F = fixed costs per order, and N = number of orders placed per year.

Equation 23-4 may be rewritten as N = S/2A, and then substituted into Equation 23-6:

$$\text{Total ordering cost} = \text{TOC} = F\left(\frac{S}{2A}\right). \tag{23-7}$$

To illustrate the use of Equation 23-7, if F = \$100, S = 120,000 units, and A = 15,000 units, then TOC, the total annual ordering cost, is \$400:

$$\text{TOC} = \$100\left(\frac{120,000}{30,000}\right) = \$100(4) = \$400.$$

Total Inventory Costs

Total carrying cost, TCC, as defined in Equation 23-5, and total ordering cost, TOC, as defined in Equation 23-7, may be combined to find total inventory costs, TIC, as follows:

$$\text{Total inventory costs} = \text{TIC} = \quad \text{TCC} \quad + \quad \text{TOC}$$
$$= (C)(P)(A) + F\left(\frac{S}{2A}\right). \tag{23-8}$$

Recognizing that the average inventory carried is A = Q/2, or one-half the size of each order quantity, Q, we may rewrite Equation 23-8 as follows:

$$\text{TIC} = \quad \text{TCC} \quad + \quad \text{TOC}$$
$$= (C)(P)\left(\frac{Q}{2}\right) + (F)\left(\frac{S}{Q}\right). \tag{23-9}$$

Here we see that total carrying cost equals average inventory in units, Q/2, multiplied by unit price, P, times the percentage annual carrying cost, C. Total ordering cost equals the number of orders placed per year, S/Q, multiplied by the fixed cost of placing and receiving an order, F. Finally, total inventory costs equal the sum of total carrying cost plus total ordering cost. We will use this equation in the next section to develop the optimal inventory ordering quantity.

Derivation of the EOQ Model

Figure 23-4 illustrates the basic premise on which the EOQ model is built, namely, that some costs rise with larger inventories while other costs decline, and there is an optimal

---

[8]Note that in reality both carrying and ordering costs can have variable and fixed-cost elements, at least over certain ranges of average inventory. For example, security and utilities charges are probably fixed in the short run over a wide range of inventory levels. Similarly, labor costs in receiving inventory could be tied to the quantity received, and hence could be variable. To simplify matters, we treat all carrying costs as variable and all ordering costs as fixed. However, if these assumptions do not fit the situation at hand, the cost definitions can be changed. For example, one could add another term for shipping costs if there are economies of scale in shipping, such that the cost of shipping a unit is smaller if shipments are larger. However, in most situations shipping costs are not sensitive to order size, so total shipping costs are simply the shipping cost per unit times the units ordered (and sold) during the year. Under this condition, shipping costs are not influenced by inventory policy, hence they may be disregarded for purposes of determining the optimal inventory level and the optimal order size.

order size (and associated average inventory) which minimizes the total costs of inventories. First, as noted earlier, the average investment in inventories depends on how frequently orders are placed and the size of each order — if we order every day, average inventories will be much smaller than if we order once a year. Further, as Figure 23-4 shows, the firm's carrying costs rise with larger orders: larger orders mean larger average inventories, so warehousing costs, interest on funds tied up in inventory, insurance, and obsolescence costs will all increase. However, ordering costs decline with larger orders and inventories: the cost of placing orders, suppliers' production set-up costs, and order handling costs will all decline if we order infrequently and consequently hold larger quantities.

If the carrying and ordering cost curves in Figure 23-4 are added, the sum represents total inventory costs, TIC. The point where the TIC is minimized represents the **economic ordering quantity (EOQ),** and this, in turn, determines the optimal average inventory level.

The EOQ is found by differentiating Equation 23-9 with respect to ordering quantity, Q, and setting the derivative equal to zero:

$$\frac{d(TIC)}{dQ} = \frac{(C)(P)}{2} - \frac{(F)(S)}{Q^2} = 0.$$

Now, solving for Q we obtain:

$$\frac{(C)(P)}{2} = \frac{(F)(S)}{Q^2}$$

$$Q^2 = \frac{2(F)(S)}{(C)(P)}$$

$$Q = EOQ = \sqrt{\frac{2(F)(S)}{(C)(P)}}. \qquad \textbf{(23-10)}$$

FIGURE 23-4   Determination of the Optimal Order Quantity

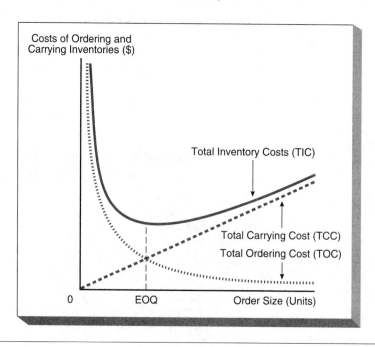

Here

EOQ = economic ordering quantity, or the optimal quantity to be ordered each time an order is placed.

  F = fixed costs of placing and receiving an order.

  S = annual sales in units.

  C = annual carrying costs expressed as a percentage of average inventory value.

  P = purchase price the firm must pay per unit of inventory.

Equation 23-10 is the EOQ model.[9] The assumptions of the model, which will be relaxed shortly, include the following: (1) sales can be forecasted perfectly, (2) sales are evenly distributed throughout the year, and (3) orders are received when expected.

EOQ Model Illustration

To illustrate the EOQ model, consider the following data supplied by Cotton Tops Inc., a distributor of budget-priced, custom-designed T-shirts which it sells to concessionaires at various theme parks in the United States:

S = annual sales = 26,000 shirts per year.

C = percentage carrying cost = 25 percent of inventory value.

P = purchase price per shirt = $4.92 per shirt. (The sales price is $9, but this is irrelevant for our purposes here.)

F = fixed cost per order = $1,000. Cotton Tops designs and distributes the shirts, but the actual production is done by another company. The bulk of this $1,000 cost is the labor cost for setting up the equipment for the production run, which the manufacturer bills separately from the $4.92 cost per shirt.

Substituting these data into Equation 23-10, we obtain an EOQ of 6,500 units:

$$EOQ = \sqrt{\frac{2(F)(S)}{(C)(P)}} = \sqrt{\frac{(2)(\$1,000)(26,000)}{(0.25)(\$4.92)}}$$

$$= \sqrt{42,276,423} \approx 6,500 \text{ units.}$$

With an EOQ of 6,500 shirts and annual usage of 26,000 shirts, Cotton Tops will place 26,000/6,500 = 4 orders per year. Notice that average inventory holdings depend directly on the EOQ. This relationship is illustrated graphically in Figure 23-5, where we see that average inventory = EOQ/2. Immediately after an order is received, 6,500 shirts are in stock. The usage rate, or sales rate, is 500 shirts per week (26,000/52 weeks), so inventories are drawn down by this amount each week. Thus, the actual number of units held in inventory will vary from 6,500 shirts just after an order is received to zero just before a new order arrives. With a 6,500 beginning balance, a zero ending balance, and a uniform sales rate, inventories will average one-half the EOQ, or 3,250 shirts, during the year. At a cost of $4.92 per shirt, the average investment in inventories will be (3,250)($4.92) ≈ $16,000. If inventories are financed by bank loans,

---

[9]The EOQ model can also be written as

$$EOQ = \sqrt{\frac{2(F)(S)}{C^*}},$$

where C* is the annual carrying cost per unit expressed in *dollars*.

FIGURE 23-5   Inventory Position without Safety Stock

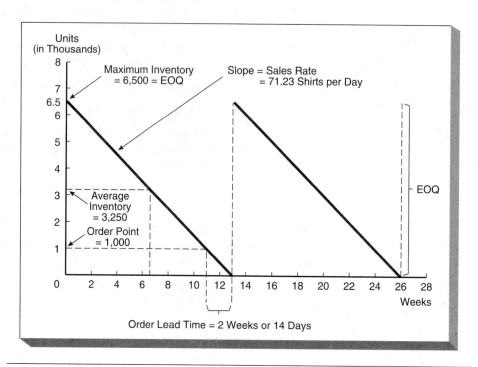

the loan will vary from a high of $32,000 to a low of $0, but the average amount out-standing over the course of a year will be $16,000.

Notice that the EOQ, hence average inventory holdings, rises with the square root of sales. Therefore, a given increase in sales will result in a less-than-proportionate increase in inventories, so the inventory/sales ratio will tend to decline as a firm grows. For example, Cotton Tops's EOQ is 6,500 shirts at an annual sales level of 26,000, and the average inventory is 3,250 shirts, or $16,000. However, if sales were to increase by 100 percent, to 52,000 shirts per year, the EOQ would rise only to 9,195 units, or by 41 percent, and the average inventory would rise by this same percentage. This suggests that there are economies of scale in holding inventories.[10]

Finally, look at Cotton Tops's total inventory costs for the year, assuming that the EOQ is ordered each time. Using Equation 23-9, we find total inventory costs are $8,000:

$$
\begin{aligned}
\text{TIC} &= \quad \text{TCC} \quad + \quad \text{TOC} \\
&= \quad (C)(P)\left(\frac{Q}{2}\right) \quad + \quad (F)\left(\frac{S}{Q}\right) \\
&= 0.25(\$4.92)\left(\frac{6,500}{2}\right) + (\$1,000)\left(\frac{26,000}{6,500}\right) \\
&\approx \quad\quad \$4,000 \quad\quad + \quad\quad \$4,000 \quad = \$8,000.
\end{aligned}
$$

---

[10]Note, however, that these scale economies relate to each particular item, not to the entire firm. Thus, a large distributor with $500 million of sales might have a higher inventory/sales ratio than a much smaller distributor if the small firm has only a few high-sales-volume items while the large firm distributes a great many low-volume items.

Note these two points: (1) The $8,000 total inventory cost represents the total of carrying costs and ordering costs, but this amount does *not* include the 26,000($4.92) = $127,920 annual purchasing cost of the inventory itself. (2) As we see both in Figure 23-4 and in the calculation above, at the EOQ, total carrying cost (TCC) equals total ordering cost (TOC). This property is not unique to our Cotton Tops illustration; it always holds.

Setting the Order Point

If a two-week lead time is required for production and shipping, what is Cotton Tops's order point level? Cotton Tops sells 26,000/52 = 500 shirts per week. Thus, if a two-week lag occurs between placing an order and receiving goods, Cotton Tops must place the order when there are 2(500) = 1,000 shirts on hand. During the two-week production and shipping period, the inventory balance will continue to decline at the rate of 500 shirts per week, and the inventory balance will hit zero just as the order of new shirts arrives.

If Cotton Tops knew for certain that both the sales rate and the order lead time would never vary, it could operate exactly as shown in Figure 23-5. However, sales do change, and production and/or shipping delays are sometimes encountered. To guard against these events, the firm must carry additional inventories, or safety stocks, as discussed in the next section.

S E L F - T E S T
Q U E S T I O N S

What are some specific inventory carrying costs? As defined here, are these costs fixed or variable?

What are some inventory ordering costs? As defined here, are these costs fixed or variable?

What are the components of total inventory costs?

What is the concept behind the EOQ model?

What is the relationship between total carrying cost and total ordering cost at the EOQ?

What assumptions are inherent in the EOQ model as presented here?

EOQ MODEL EXTENSIONS

The basic EOQ model was derived under several restrictive assumptions. In this section, we relax some of these assumptions and, in the process, extend the model to make it more useful.

The Concept of Safety Stocks

The concept of a **safety stock** is illustrated in Figure 23-6. First, note that the slope of the sales line measures the expected rate of sales. The company *expects* to sell 500 shirts per week, but let us assume that the maximum likely sales rate is twice this amount, or 1,000 units each week. Further, assume that Cotton Tops sets the safety stock at 1,000 shirts, so it initially orders 7,500 shirts, the EOQ of 6,500 plus the 1,000-unit safety stock. Subsequently, it reorders the EOQ whenever the inventory level falls to 2,000 shirts, the safety stock of 1,000 shirts plus the 1,000 shirts expected to be used while awaiting delivery of the order.

Notice that the company could, over the two-week delivery period, sell 1,000 units a week, or double its normal expected sales. This maximum rate of sales is shown by the

FIGURE 23-6   Inventory Position with Safety Stock Included

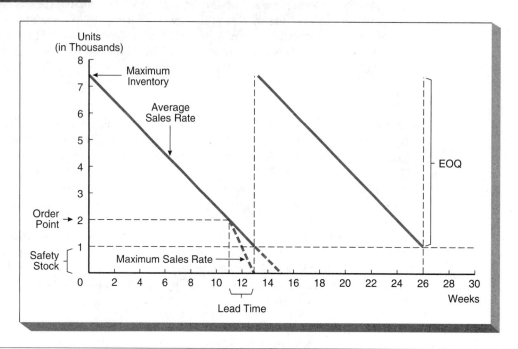

steeper dashed line in Figure 23-6. The condition that makes this higher sales rate possible is the safety stock of 1,000 shirts.

The safety stock is also useful to guard against delays in receiving orders. The expected delivery time is two weeks, but with a 1,000-unit safety stock, the company could maintain sales at the expected rate of 500 units per week for an additional two weeks if something should delay an order.

However, carrying a safety stock has a cost. The average inventory is now EOQ/2 plus the safety stock, or 6,500/2 + 1,000 = 3,250 + 1,000 = 4,250 shirts, and the average inventory value is now (4,250)($4.92) = $20,910. This increase in average inventory causes an increase in annual inventory carrying costs equal to (Safety stock)(P)(C) = 1,000($4.92)(0.25) = $1,230.

The optimal safety stock varies from situation to situation, but, in general, it *increases* (1) with the uncertainty of demand forecasts, (2) with the costs (in terms of lost sales and lost goodwill) that result from inventory shortages, and (3) with the probability that delays will occur in receiving shipments. The optimal safety stock *decreases* as the cost of carrying this additional inventory increases.

Setting the Safety Stock Level

The critical question with regard to safety stocks is this: How large should the safety stock be? To answer this question, first examine Table 23-1, which contains the probability distribution of Cotton Tops's unit sales for an average two-week period, the time it takes to receive an order of 6,500 T-shirts. Note that the expected sales over an average two-week period is 1,000 units. Why do we focus on a two-week period? Because shortages can occur only during the two weeks it takes an order to arrive.

Cotton Tops's managers have estimated that the annual carrying cost is 25 percent of inventory value. Since each shirt has an inventory value of $4.92, the annual carrying cost per unit is 0.25($4.92) = $1.23, and the carrying cost for each 13-week

TABLE 23-1	Two-Week Sales Probability Distribution

PROBABILITY	UNIT SALES
0.1	0
0.2	500
0.4	1,000
0.2	1,500
0.1	2,000
1.0	Expected sales = 1,000

inventory period is $1.23(13/52) = $0.308 per unit. Even though shortages can occur only during the 2-week order period, safety stocks must be carried over the full 13-week inventory cycle. Next, Cotton Tops's managers must estimate the cost of shortages. Assume that when shortages occur, 50 percent of Cotton Tops's buyers are willing to accept back orders, while 50 percent of its potential customers simply cancel their orders. Remember that each shirt sells for $9.00, so each one-unit shortage produces expected lost profits of 0.5($9.00 − $4.92) = $2.04. With this information, the firm can calculate the costs of different safety stock levels. This is done in Table 23-2.

For each safety stock level, we determine the expected cost of a shortage based on the sales probability distribution in Table 23-1. There is an expected shortage cost of $408 if no safety stock is carried; $102 if the safety stock is set at 500 units; and no expected shortage, hence no shortage cost, with a safety stock of 1,000 units. The cost of carrying each safety level is merely the cost of carrying a unit of inventory over the 13-week inventory period, $0.308, times the safety stock; for example, the cost of carrying a safety stock of 500 units is $0.308(500) = $154. Finally, we sum the expected shortage cost in Column 6 and the safety stock carrying cost in Column 7 to obtain the total cost figures given in Column 8. Since the 500-unit safety stock has the lowest expected total cost, Cotton Tops should carry this safety level.

Of course, the optimal safety level is highly sensitive to the estimates of the sales probability distribution and shortage costs. Errors here could result in incorrect safety stock levels. Note also that in calculating the $2.04 per unit shortage cost, we implicitly assumed that a lost sale in one period would not result in lost sales in future periods. If shortages cause customer ill will, this could lead to permanent sales reductions. Then the situation would be much more serious, stock-out costs would be far higher, and the firm should consequently carry a larger safety stock.

The stock-out example is just one example of the many judgments required in inventory management—the mechanics are relatively simple, but the inputs are judgmental and difficult to obtain.

Quantity Discounts

Now suppose the T-shirt manufacturer offered Cotton Tops a **quantity discount** of 2 percent on large orders. If the quantity discount applied to orders of 5,000 or more, then Cotton Tops would continue to place the EOQ order of 6,500 shirts and take the quantity discount. However, if the quantity discount required orders of 10,000 or more, then Cotton Tops would have to compare the savings in purchase price that would result if its ordering quantity were increased to 10,000 units with the increase in total inventory costs caused by the departure from the 6,500-unit EOQ.

| TABLE 23-2 | | Safety Stock Analysis | | | | | |

SAFETY STOCK (1)	SALES DURING TWO-WEEK DELIVERY PERIOD (2)	PROBABILITY (3)	SHORTAGE[a] (4)	SHORTAGE COST (LOST PROFITS): $2.04 \times (4)$ = (5)	EXPECTED SHORTAGE COST: $(3) \times (5)$ = (6)	SAFETY STOCK CARRYING COST: $0.308 \times (1)$ = (7)	EXPECTED TOTAL COST: (6) + (7) = (8)
0	0	0.1	0	$ 0	$ 0		
	500	0.2	0	0	0		
	1,000	0.4	0	0	0		
	1,500	0.2	500	1,020	204		
	2,000	0.1	1,000	2,040	204		
		1.0		Expected shortage cost = $408		$ 0	$408
500	0	0.1	0	$ 0	$ 0		
	500	0.2	0	0	0		
	1,000	0.4	0	0	0		
	1,500	0.2	0	0	0		
	2,000	0.1	500	1,020	102		
		1.0		Expected shortage cost = $102		$154	$256
1,000	0	0.1	0	$ 0	$ 0		
	500	0.2	0	0	0		
	1,000	0.4	0	0	0		
	1,500	0.2	0	0	0		
	2,000	0.1	0	0	0		
		1.0		Expected shortage cost = $ 0		$308	$308

[a]Shortage = Actual sales − (1,000 Stock at order point + Safety stock); positive values only.

First, consider the total costs associated with Cotton Tops's EOQ of 6,500 units. We found earlier that total inventory costs are $8,000:

$$TIC = \qquad TCC \qquad + \qquad TOC$$

$$= \qquad (C)(P)\left(\frac{Q}{2}\right) \qquad + \qquad (F)\left(\frac{S}{Q}\right)$$

$$= 0.25(\$4.92)\left(\frac{6,500}{2}\right) + (\$1,000)\left(\frac{26,000}{6,500}\right)$$

$$\approx \qquad \$4,000 \qquad + \qquad \$4,000 \qquad = \$8,000.$$

Now, what would total inventory costs be if Cotton Tops ordered 10,000 units instead of 6,500? The answer is $8,625:

$$TIC = 0.25(\$4.82)\left(\frac{10,000}{2}\right) + (\$1,000)\left(\frac{26,000}{10,000}\right)$$

$$= \qquad \$6,025 \qquad + \qquad \$2,600 \qquad = \$8,625.$$

Notice that when the discount is taken, the price, P, is reduced by the amount of the discount; the new price per unit would be 0.98($4.92) = $4.82. Also note that when the ordering quantity is increased, carrying costs increase because the firm is carrying a larger average inventory, but ordering costs decrease since the number of orders per year decreases. If we were to calculate total inventory costs at an ordering quantity of 5,000, we would find that carrying costs would be less than $4,000, and ordering costs would be more than $4,000, but the total inventory costs would be more than $8,000, since they are at a minimum when 6,500 units are ordered.[11]

Thus, inventory costs would increase by $8,625 − $8,000 = $625 if Cotton Tops were to increase its order size to 10,000 shirts. *However, this cost increase must be compared with Cotton Tops's savings if it takes the discount.* Taking the discount would save 0.02($4.92) = $0.0984 per unit. Over the year, Cotton Tops orders 26,000 shirts, so the annual savings is $0.0984(26,000) ≈ $2,558. Here is a summary:

Reduction in purchase price = 0.02($4.92)(26,000) =	$2,558
Increase in total inventory cost =	625
Net savings from taking discounts	$1,933

Obviously, the company should order 10,000 units at a time and take advantage of the quantity discount.

Inflation

Moderate inflation — say, 3 percent per year — can largely be ignored for purposes of inventory management, but higher rates of inflation must be explicitly considered. If the rate of inflation in the types of goods the firm stocks tends to be relatively constant, it can be dealt with quite easily — simply deduct the expected annual rate of inflation from the carrying cost percentage, C, in Equation 23-10, and use this modified version of the EOQ model to establish the ordering quantity. The reason for making this deduction is that inflation causes the value of the inventory to rise, thus offsetting somewhat the effects of depreciation and other carrying costs. Since C will now be smaller, the calculated EOQ, and the average inventory, will increase. However, the higher the rate of inflation, the higher are interest rates, and this factor will cause C to increase, thus lowering the EOQ and average inventories.

On balance, there is no evidence that inflation either raises or lowers the optimal inventories of firms in the aggregate. Inflation should still be explicitly considered, however, for it will raise the individual firm's optimal holdings if the rate of inflation for its own inventories is above average (and is greater than the effects of inflation on interest rates), and vice versa.

Seasonal Demand

For most firms, it is unrealistic to assume that the demand for an inventory item is uniform throughout the year. What happens when there is seasonal demand, as would hold true for an ice cream company? Here the standard annual EOQ model is obviously not appropriate. However, it does provide a point of departure for setting inventory

---

[11]At an ordering quantity of 5,000 units, total inventory costs are $8,275:

$$TIC = (0.25)(\$4.92)\left(\frac{5,000}{2}\right) + (\$1,000)\left(\frac{26,000}{5,000}\right)$$

$$= \$3,075 + \$5,200 = \$8,275.$$

| TABLE 23-3 | EOQ Sensitivity Analysis |

ORDERING QUANTITY	TOTAL INVENTORY COSTS	PERCENTAGE DEVIATION FROM OPTIMAL
3,000	$10,512	+31.4%
4,000	8,960	+12.0
5,000	8,275	+3.4
6,000	8,023	+0.3
6,500	8,000	0.0
7,000	8,019	+0.2
8,000	8,170	+2.1
9,000	8,423	+5.3
10,000	8,750	+9.4

parameters, which are then modified to fit the particular seasonal pattern. We divide the year into the seasons in which annualized sales are relatively constant, say, summer, spring and fall, and winter. Then, the EOQ model is applied separately to each period. During the transitions between seasons, inventories would be either run down or else built up with special seasonal orders.

EOQ Range

Thus far, we have interpreted the EOQ and the resulting inventory values as single point estimates. It can be easily demonstrated that small deviations from the EOQ do not appreciably affect total inventory costs, and, consequently, that the optimal ordering quantity should be viewed more as a range than as a single value.[12]

To illustrate this point, we examine the sensitivity of total inventory costs to ordering quantity for Cotton Tops. Table 23-3 contains the results. We conclude that the ordering quantity could range from 5,000 to 8,000 units without affecting total inventory costs by more than 3.4 percent. Thus, managers can adjust the ordering quantity within a fairly wide range without significantly increasing total inventory costs.

SELF-TEST QUESTIONS

Why are safety stocks required?

Conceptually, how would you evaluate a quantity discount offer from a supplier?

What impact does inflation typically have on the EOQ?

Can the EOQ model be used when a company faces seasonal demand fluctuations?

What is the effect of minor deviations from the EOQ on total inventory costs?

THE PAYMENTS PATTERN APPROACH TO MONITORING RECEIVABLES

In Chapter 21, we discussed two methods for monitoring a firm's receivables position: days sales outstanding and aging schedules. These procedures are useful, especially for

---

[12]This is somewhat analogous to the optimal capital structure in that small changes in capital structure around the optimum do not have much effect on the firm's weighted average cost of capital.

TABLE 23-4	Hanover Company: Receivables Data for 1998 (Thousands of Dollars)

MONTH (1)	CREDIT SALES FOR MONTH (2)	RECEIVABLES AT END OF MONTH (3)	BASED ON QUARTERLY SALES DATA		BASED ON YEAR-TO-DATE SALES DATA	
			ADS[a] (4)	DSO[b] (5)	ADS (6)	DSO (7)
January	$ 60	$ 54				
February	60	90				
March	60	102	$2.00	51 days	$2.00	51 days
April	60	102				
May	90	129				
June	120	174	3.00	58	2.50	70
July	120	198				
August	90	177				
September	60	132	3.00	44	2.67	49
October	60	108				
November	60	102				
December	60	102	2.00	51	2.50	41

[a]ADS = Average daily sales.
[b]DSO = Days sales outstanding.

monitoring an individual customer's account, but neither is totally suitable for monitoring the aggregate payment performance of all credit customers, especially for a firm that experiences fluctuating credit sales. In this section, we present another way to monitor receivables, the **payments pattern approach.**

The primary point in analyzing the aggregate accounts receivable situation is to see if customers, on average, are paying more slowly. If so, accounts receivable will build up, as will the cost of carrying receivables. Further, the payment slowdown may signal a decrease in the quality of the receivables, hence an increase in bad debt losses down the road. The DSO and aging schedules are useful in monitoring credit operations, but both are affected by increases and decreases in the level of sales. Thus, changes in sales levels, including normal seasonal or cyclical changes, can change a firm's DSO and aging schedule even though its customers' payment behavior has not changed at all. For this reason, a procedure called the *payments pattern approach* has been developed to measure any changes that might be occurring in customers' payment behavior.[13] To illustrate the payments pattern approach, consider the Hanover Company, a small manufacturer of hand tools which commenced operations in January 1998. Table 23-4 contains Hanover's credit sales and receivables data for 1998. Column 2 shows that Hanover's credit sales are seasonal, with the lowest sales in the fall and winter months and the highest during the summer.

[13]See Wilbur G. Lewellen and Robert W. Johnson, "A Better Way to Monitor Accounts Receivable," *Harvard Business Review,* May–June 1972, 101–109; and Bernell Stone, "The Payments-Pattern Approach to the Forecasting and Control of Accounts Receivable," *Financial Management,* Autumn 1976, 65–82.

Now assume that 10 percent of Hanover's customers pay in the month the sale is made, that 30 percent pay in the first month following the sale, that 40 percent pay in the second month, and that the remaining 20 percent pay in the third month. Further, assume that Hanover's customers have the same payment behavior throughout the year; that is, they always take the same length of time to pay. Column 3 of Table 23-4 contains Hanover's receivables balance at the end of each month. For example, during January Hanover has $60,000 in sales. Ten percent of the customers paid during the month of sale, so the receivables balance at the end of January was $60,000 − 0.1($60,000) = (1.0 − 0.1)($60,000) = 0.9($60,000) = $54,000. By the end of February, 10% + 30% = 40% of the customers had paid for January's sales, and 10 percent had paid for February's sales. Thus, the receivables balance at the end of February was 0.6($60,000) + 0.9($60,000) = $90,000. By the end of March, 80 percent of January's sales had been collected, 40 percent of February's had been collected, and 10 percent of March's sales had been collected, so the receivables balance was 0.2($60,000) + 0.6($60,000) + 0.9($60,000) = $102,000; and so on.

Columns 4 and 5 give Hanover's average daily sales (ADS) and days sales outstanding (DSO), respectively, as these measures would be calculated from quarterly financial statements. For example, in the April–June quarter, ADS = ($60,000 + $90,000 + $120,000)/90 = $3,000, and the end-of-quarter (June 30) DSO = $174,000/$3,000 = 58 days. Columns 6 and 7 also show ADS and DSO, but here they are calculated on the basis of accumulated sales throughout the year. For example, at the end of June ADS = $450,000/180 = $2,500 and DSO = $174,000/$2,500 = 70 days. (For the entire year, sales are $900,000; ADS = $2,500, and DSO at year-end = 41 days. These last two figures are shown at the bottom of the last two columns.)

The data in Table 23-4 illustrate two major points. First, fluctuating sales lead to changes in the DSO, which suggests that customers are paying faster or slower, even though we know that customers' payment patterns are not changing at all. The rising monthly sales trend causes the calculated DSO to rise, whereas falling sales (as in the third quarter) cause the calculated DSO to fall, even though nothing is changing with regard to when customers actually pay. Second, we see that the DSO depends on an averaging procedure, but regardless of whether quarterly, semiannual, or annual data are used, the DSO is still unstable even though payment patterns are *not* changing. Therefore, it is difficult to use the DSO as a monitoring device if the firm's sales exhibit seasonal or cyclical patterns.

Seasonal or cyclical variations also make it difficult to interpret aging schedules. Table 23-5 contains Hanover's aging schedules at the end of each quarter of 1998. At the end of June, Table 23-4 showed that Hanover's receivables balance was $174,000.

TABLE 23-5 Hanover Company: Quarterly Aging Schedules for 1998
(Thousands of Dollars)

AGE OF ACCOUNTS (DAYS)	VALUE AND PERCENTAGE OF TOTAL ACCOUNTS RECEIVABLE AT THE END OF EACH QUARTER:							
	MARCH 31		JUNE 30		SEPTEMBER 30		DECEMBER 31	
0–30	$ 54	53%	$108	62%	$ 54	41%	$ 54	53%
31–60	36	35	54	31	54	41	36	35
61–90	12	12	12	7	24	18	12	12
	$102	100%	$174	100%	$132	100%	$102	100%

THE PAYMENTS PATTERN APPROACH TO MONITORING RECEIVABLES   891

Eighty percent of April's $60,000 of sales had been collected, 40 percent of May's $90,000 of sales had been collected, and 10 percent of June's $120,000 of sales had been collected. Thus, the end-of-June receivables balance consisted of 0.2($60,000) = $12,000 of April sales, 0.6($90,000) = $54,000 of May sales, and 0.9($120,000) = $108,000 of June sales. Note again that Hanover's customers had not changed their payment patterns. However, rising sales during the second quarter created the impression of faster payments when judged by the percentage aging schedule, and falling sales after July created the opposite appearance. Thus, neither the DSO nor the aging schedule provides an accurate picture of customers' payment patterns if sales fluctuate during the year or are trending up or down.

With this background, we can now examine another basic tool, the *uncollected balances schedule,* as shown in Table 23-6. At the end of each quarter, the dollar amount of receivables remaining from each of the three month's sales is divided by that month's sales to obtain three receivables-to-sales ratios. For example, at the end of the first quarter $12,000 of the $60,000 January sales, or 20 percent, are still outstanding; 60 percent of February sales are still out; and 90 percent of March sales are uncollected. Exactly the same situation is revealed at the end of each of the next three quarters. Thus, Table 23-6 shows that Hanover's customers' payment behavior has remained constant.

TABLE 23-6	Hanover Company: Quarterly Uncollected Balances Schedules for 1998 (Thousands of Dollars)		

QUARTER	MONTHLY SALES	REMAINING RECEIVABLES AT END OF QUARTER	REMAINING RECEIVABLES AS PERCENT OF MONTH'S SALES AT END OF QUARTER
Quarter 1:			
January	$ 60	$ 12	20%
February	60	36	60
March	60	54	90
		$102	170%
Quarter 2:			
April	$ 60	$ 12	20%
May	90	54	60
June	120	108	90
		$174	170%
Quarter 3:			
July	$120	$ 24	20%
August	90	54	60
September	60	54	90
		$132	170%
Quarter 4:			
October	$ 60	$ 12	20%
November	60	36	60
December	60	54	90
		$102	170%

Recall that at the beginning of the example we assumed the existence of a constant payments pattern. In a normal situation, the firm's customers' payments pattern would probably vary somewhat over time. Such variations would be shown in the last column of the uncollected balances schedule. For example, suppose customers began to pay their accounts slower in the second quarter. That might cause the second quarter uncollected balances schedule to look like this (in thousands of dollars):

QUARTER 2, 1998	SALES	NEW REMAINING RECEIVABLES	NEW RECEIVABLES/SALES
April	$ 60	$ 16	27%
May	90	70	78
June	120	110	92
		$196	197%

We see that the receivables-to-sales ratios are now higher than in the corresponding months of the first quarter. This causes the total uncollected balances percentage to rise from 170 to 197 percent, which, in turn, should alert Hanover's managers that customers are paying slower than they did earlier in the year.

The uncollected balances schedule permits a firm to monitor its receivables better, and it can also be used to forecast future receivables balances. When Hanover's pro forma 1999 quarterly balance sheets are constructed, management can use the historical receivables-to-sales ratios, coupled with 1999 sales estimates, to project each quarter's receivables balance. For example, with projected sales as given below, and using the same payments pattern as in 1998, Hanover's projected end-of-June 1999 receivables balance would be as follows:

QUARTER 2, 1999	PROJECTED SALES	RECEIVABLES/SALES	PROJECTED RECEIVABLES
April	$ 70,000	20%	$ 14,000
May	100,000	60	60,000
June	140,000	90	126,000
		Total projected receivables =	$200,000

The payments pattern approach permits us to remove the effects of seasonal and/or cyclical sales variation and to construct a more accurate measure of customers' payments patterns. Thus, it provides financial managers with better aggregate information than the days sales outstanding or the aging schedule. Managers should use the payments pattern approach to monitor collection performance as well as to project future receivables requirements.

Except possibly in the inventory and cash management areas, nowhere in the typical firm have computers had more of an impact than in accounts receivable management. A well-run business will use a computer system to record sales, to send out bills, to keep track of when payments are made, to alert the credit manager when an account becomes past due, and to take action automatically to collect past-due accounts (for example, to prepare form letters requesting payment). Additionally, the payment history of each customer can be summarized and used to help establish credit limits for customers and classes of customers, and the data on each account can be aggregated and used for the firm's accounts receivable monitoring system. Finally, historical data can be stored in the firm's database and used to develop inputs for studies related to credit policy changes, as we discuss in the next section.

S E L F - T E S T
Q U E S T I O N S

Define days sales outstanding (DSO). What can be learned from it? Does it have any deficiencies when used to monitor collections over time?

What is an aging schedule? What can be learned from it? Does it have any deficiencies when used to monitor collections over time?

What is the uncollected balances schedule? What advantages does it have over the DSO and the aging schedule for monitoring receivables? How can it be used to forecast a firm's receivables balance?

ANALYZING PROPOSED CHANGES IN CREDIT POLICY

In Chapter 21, we discussed credit policy, including setting the credit period, credit standards, collection policy, and discount percentage, as well as the factors that influence credit policy. A firm's credit policy is reviewed periodically, and policy changes may be proposed. However, before a new policy is adopted, it should be analyzed to determine if it is indeed preferable to the existing policy. In this section, we discuss procedures for analyzing proposed changes in credit policy.

If a firm's credit policy is *eased* by such actions as lengthening the credit period, relaxing credit standards, following a less tough collection policy, or offering cash discounts, then sales should increase: *Easing the credit policy stimulates sales.* Of course, if credit policy is eased and sales rise, then costs will also rise because more labor, materials, and so on, will be required to produce the additional goods. Additionally, receivables outstanding will also increase, which will increase carrying costs. Moreover, bad debts and/or discount expenses may also rise. Thus, the key question when deciding on a proposed credit policy change is this: Will sales revenues increase more than costs, including credit-related costs, causing cash flow to increase, or will the increase in sales revenues be more than offset by higher costs?

Table 23-7 illustrates the general idea behind the analysis of credit policy changes. Column 1 shows the projected 1999 income statement for Monroe Manufacturing under the assumption that the firm's current credit policy is maintained throughout the year. Column 2 shows the expected effects of easing the credit policy by extending the credit period, offering larger discounts, relaxing credit standards, and easing collection efforts. Specifically, Monroe is analyzing the effects of changing its credit terms from 1/10, net 30, to 2/10, net 40, relaxing its credit standards, and putting less pressure on slow-paying customers. Column 3 shows the projected 1999 income statement incorporating the expected effects of an easing in credit policy. The generally looser policy is expected to increase sales and lower collection costs, but discounts and several other types of costs would rise. The overall, bottom-line effect is a $7 million increase in projected net income. In the following paragraphs, we explain how the numbers in the table were calculated.

Monroe's annual sales are $400 million. Under its current credit policy, 50 percent of those customers who pay do so on Day 10 and take the discount, 40 percent pay on Day 30, and 10 percent pay late, on Day 40. Thus, Monroe's days sales outstanding is $(0.5)(10) + (0.4)(30) + (0.1)(40) = 21$ days, and discounts total $(0.01)(\$400,000,000)(0.5) = \$2,000,000$.

The cost of carrying receivables is equal to the average receivables balance times the variable cost percentage times the cost of money used to carry receivables. The firm's

TABLE 23-7	Monroe Manufacturing Company: Analysis of Changing Credit Policy (Millions of Dollars)		
	PROJECTED 1999 NET INCOME UNDER CURRENT CREDIT POLICY (1)	**EFFECT OF CREDIT POLICY CHANGE (2)**	**PROJECTED 1999 NET INCOME UNDER NEW CREDIT POLICY (3)**
Gross sales	$400	+$130	$530
Less discounts	2	+ 4	6
Net sales	$398	+$126	$524
Production costs, including overhead	280	+ 91	371
Profit before credit costs and taxes	$118	+$ 35	$153
Credit-related costs:			
Cost of carrying receivables	3	+ 2	5
Credit analysis and collection expenses	5	− 3	2
Bad debt losses	10	+ 22	32
Profit before taxes	$100	+$ 14	$114
State-plus-federal taxes (50%)	50	+ 7	57
Net income	$ 50	+$ 7	$ 57

NOTE: The above statements include only those cash flows incremental to the credit policy decision.

variable cost ratio is 70 percent, and its pre-tax cost of capital invested in receivables is 20 percent. Thus, its cost of carrying receivables is $3 million:

$$(DSO)\left(\begin{array}{c}\text{Sales} \\ \text{per} \\ \text{day}\end{array}\right)\left(\begin{array}{c}\text{Variable} \\ \text{cost} \\ \text{ratio}\end{array}\right)\left(\begin{array}{c}\text{Cost} \\ \text{of} \\ \text{funds}\end{array}\right) = \text{Cost of carrying receivables}$$

$$(21)(\$400,000,000/360)(0.70)(0.20) = \$3,266,667 \approx \$3 \text{ million.}$$

Only variable costs enter this calculation because this is the only cost element in receivables that must be financed. We are seeking the cost of carrying receivables, and variable costs represent the firm's investment in the cost of goods sold.

Even though Monroe spends $5 million annually to analyze accounts and to collect bad debts, 2.5 percent of sales will never be collected. Bad debt losses therefore amount to $(0.025)(\$400,000,000) = \$10,000,000$.

Monroe's new credit policy would be 2/10, net 40 versus the old policy of 1/10, net 30, so it would call for a larger discount and a longer payment period, as well as a relaxed collection effort and lower credit standards. The company believes that these changes will lead to a $130 million increase in sales, to $530 million per year. Under the new terms, management believes that 60 percent of the customers who pay will take the 2 percent discount, so discounts will increase to $(0.02)(\$530,000,000)(0.60) = \$6,360,000 \approx \$6$ million. Half of the nondiscount customers will pay on Day 40, and the remainder on Day 50. The new DSO is thus estimated to be 24 days:

$$(0.6)(10) + (0.2)(40) + (0.2)(50) = 24 \text{ days.}$$

Also, the cost of carrying receivables will increase to $5 million:

$$(24)(\$530,000,000/360)(0.70)(0.20) = \$4,946,667 \approx \$5 \text{ million.}[14]$$

The company plans to reduce its annual credit analysis and collection expenditures to $2 million. The reduced credit standards and the relaxed collection effort are expected to raise bad debt losses to about 6 percent of sales, or to $(0.06)(\$530,000,000) = \$31,800,000 \approx \$32,000,000$, which is an increase of $22 million from the previous level.

The combined effect of all the changes in credit policy is a projected $7 million annual increase in net income. There would, of course, be corresponding changes on the projected balance sheet—the higher sales would necessitate somewhat larger cash balances, inventories, and, depending on the capacity situation, perhaps more fixed assets. Accounts receivable would, of course, also increase. Since these asset increases would have to be financed, certain liabilities and/or equity would have to be increased.

The $7 million expected increase in net income is, of course, an estimate, and the actual effects of the change could be quite different. In the first place, there is uncertainty—perhaps quite a lot—about the projected $130 million increase in sales. Indeed, if the firm's competitors matched its changes, sales might not rise at all. Similar uncertainties must be attached to the number of customers who would take discounts, to production costs at higher or lower sales levels, to the costs of carrying additional receivables, and to bad debt losses. In the final analysis, the decision will be based on judgment, especially concerning the risks involved, but the type of quantitative analysis set forth above is essential to the process.

SELF-TEST
QUESTIONS

Describe the procedure for evaluating a change in credit policy using the income statement approach.

Do you think that credit policy decisions are made more on the basis of numerical analyses or on judgmental factors?

---

[14]Since the credit policy change will result in a longer DSO, the firm will have to wait longer to receive its profit on the goods it sells. Therefore, the firm will incur an opportunity cost due to not having the cash from these profits available for investment. The dollar amount of this opportunity cost is equal to the old sales per day times the change in DSO times the contribution margin (1 − Variable cost ratio) times the firm's cost of carrying receivables, or

$$\text{Opportunity cost} = (\text{Old sales}/360)(\Delta\text{DSO})(1 - v)(k)$$
$$= (\$400/360)(3)(0.3)(0.20)$$
$$= \$0.2 = \$200,000.$$

For simplicity, we have ignored this opportunity cost in our analysis. For a more complete discussion of credit policy change analysis, see Eugene F. Brigham and Louis C. Gapenski, *Intermediate Financial Management*, 5th ed. (Fort Worth, Tex.: Dryden Press, 1996), Chapter 23.

SUMMARY

- The **cash conversion cycle** is the length of time between paying for raw materials and receiving cash from the sale of finished goods:

$$\begin{matrix} \text{Cash} & & \text{Inventory} & & \text{Receivables} & & \text{Payables} \\ \text{conversion} & = & \text{conversion} & + & \text{collection} & - & \text{deferral}. \\ \text{cycle} & & \text{period} & & \text{period} & & \text{period} \end{matrix}$$

- The **Baumol model** provides insights into the optimal cash balance. The model balances the opportunity cost of holding cash against the transactions costs associated with obtaining cash either by selling marketable securities or by borrowing.

$$\text{Optimal cash infusion} = \sqrt{\frac{2(F)(T)}{k}}.$$

- Firms generally set their target cash balances at the level which holds the risk of running out of cash to some acceptable level. **Monte Carlo simulation** can be helpful in setting the target cash balance.

- Inventory can be grouped into four categories: (1) **raw materials,** (2) **work-in-process,** (3) **finished goods,** and (4) **supplies.**

- **Inventory costs** also can be divided into three parts: carrying costs, ordering costs, and stock-out costs. In general, **carrying costs** increase as the level of inventory rises, but **ordering costs** and **stock-out costs** decline with larger inventory holdings.

- **Total carrying cost (TCC)** is equal to the percentage cost of carrying inventory (C) times the purchase price per unit of inventory (P) times the average number of units held (A): TCC = (C)(P)(A).

- **Total ordering cost (TOC)** is equal to the fixed cost of placing an order (F) times the number of orders placed per year (N): TOC = (F)(N).

- **Total inventory costs (TIC)** equal total carrying cost (TCC) plus total ordering cost (TOC): TIC = TCC + TOC.

- The **economic ordering quantity (EOQ)** model is a formula for determining the order quantity that will minimize total inventory costs:

$$\text{EOQ} = \sqrt{\frac{2(F)(S)}{(C)(P)}}.$$

Here F is the fixed cost per order, S is annual sales in units, C is the percentage cost of carrying inventory, and P is the purchase price per unit.

- The **reorder point** is the inventory level at which new items must be ordered.

- **Safety stocks** are held to avoid shortages (1) if sales increase more than was expected or (2) if shipping delays are encountered on inventory ordered. The cost of carrying a safety stock, which is separate from that based on the EOQ model, is equal to the percentage cost of carrying inventory times the purchase price per unit times the number of units held as the safety stock.

- Firms can use **days sales outstanding (DSO)** and **aging schedules** to help monitor their receivables position, but the best way to monitor aggregate receivables is the **payments pattern approach.** The primary tool in this approach is the **uncollected balances schedule.**

- If a firm **eases its credit policy** by lengthening the credit period, relaxing its credit standards and collection policy, and offering (or raising) its cash discount, its sales should increase. However, its costs will also increase. A firm should ease its credit policy only if the costs of doing so will be offset by higher expected revenues. In general, credit policy changes should be evaluated on the basis of incremental profits.

This chapter concludes our discussion of working capital management and financing. In Part VIII, we discuss several special topics, beginning with derivatives and risk management in Chapter 24.

Questions

23-1   Define each of the following terms:
   a. Cash conversion cycle; inventory conversion period; receivables collection period; payables deferral period
   b. Baumol model
   c. Total carrying cost; total ordering cost; total inventory costs
   d. Economic ordering quantity (EOQ); EOQ model; EOQ range
   e. Reorder point; safety stock
   f. Aging schedule; days sales outstanding (DSO)
   g. Payments pattern approach; uncollected balances schedule

23-2   Indicate by a +, −, or 0 whether each of the following events would probably cause average annual inventory holdings to rise, fall, or be affected in an indeterminate manner:
   a. Our suppliers change from delivering by train to air freight.   _____
   b. We change from producing just-in-time to meet seasonal demand to steady, year-round production.   _____
   c. Competition in the markets in which we sell increases.   _____
   d. The general rate of inflation rises.   _____
   e. Interest rates rise; other things are constant.   _____

Self-Test Problems   (Solutions Appear in Appendix B)

ST-1
Credit Policy Changes

The McCue Company expects to have sales of $10 million this year under its current operating policies. Its variable costs as a percentage of sales are 80 percent, and its cost of capital is 16 percent. Currently the firm's credit policy is net 25 (no discount for early payment). However, its DSO is 30 days, and its bad debt loss percentage is 2 percent. McCue spends $50,000 per year to collect bad debts, and its federal-plus-state-plus-local tax rate is 50 percent.

The credit manager is considering two alternative proposals, given below, for changing the firm's credit policy. Find the expected change in net income, taking into consideration anticipated changes in carrying costs for accounts receivable, the probable bad debt losses, and the discounts likely to be taken, for each proposal. Should a change in credit policy be made?

Proposal 1: Lengthen the credit period by going from net 25 to net 30. The bad debt collection expenditures will remain constant. Under this proposal, sales are expected to increase by $1 million annually, and the bad debt loss percentage on *new* sales is expected to rise to 4 percent (the loss percentage on old sales should not change). In addition, the DSO is expected to increase from 30 to 45 days on all sales.

Proposal 2: Shorten the credit period by going from net 25 to net 20. Again, collection expenses will remain constant. The anticipated effects of this change are (1) a decrease in sales of $1 million per year, (2) a decline in the DSO from 30 to 22 days, and (3) a decline in the bad debt loss percentage to 1 percent on all sales.

ST-2
EOQ Model

The Bertin Breads Company buys and then sells (as bread) 2.6 million bushels of wheat annually. The wheat must be purchased in multiples of 2,000 bushels. Ordering costs, which include grain elevator removal charges of $3,500, are $5,000 per order. Annual carrying costs are 2 percent of the purchase price per bushel of $5. The company maintains a safety stock of 200,000 bushels. The delivery time is 6 weeks.
   a. What is the EOQ?
   b. At what inventory level should a reorder be placed to prevent having to draw on the safety stock?
   c. What are the total inventory costs?
   d. The wheat processor agrees to pay the elevator removal charges if Bertin Breads will purchase wheat in quantities of 650,000 bushels. Would it be to the firm's advantage to order under this alternative?

Problems

23-1
Cash Conversion Cycle

The Boudreaux Corporation has an inventory conversion period of 75 days, a receivables collection period of 38 days, and a payables deferral period of 30 days.
   a. What is the length of the firm's cash conversion cycle?

b. If Boudreaux's annual sales are $3,375,000 and all sales are on credit, what is the firm's investment in accounts receivable?

c. How many times per year does Boudreaux turn over its inventory?

23-2
Relaxing Collection Efforts

The Boyd Corporation has annual credit sales of $1.6 million. Current expenses for the collection department are $35,000, bad debt losses are 1.5 percent, and the days sales outstanding is 30 days. The firm is considering easing its collection efforts such that collection expenses will be reduced to $22,000 per year. The change is expected to increase bad debt losses to 2.5 percent and to increase the days sales outstanding to 45 days. In addition, sales are expected to increase to $1,625,000 per year.

Should the firm relax collection efforts if the opportunity cost of funds is 16 percent, the variable cost ratio is 75 percent, and taxes are 40 percent?

23-3
Economic Ordering Quantity

The Gentry Garden Center sells 90,000 bags of lawn fertilizer annually. The optimal safety stock (which is on hand initially) is 1,000 bags. Each bag costs the firm $1.50, inventory carrying costs are 20 percent, and the cost of placing an order with its supplier is $15.

a. What is the economic ordering quantity?

b. What is the maximum inventory of fertilizer?

c. What will be the firm's average inventory?

d. How often must the company order?

23-4
Tightening Credit Terms

Kim Mitchell, the new credit manager of the Vinson Corporation, was alarmed to find that Vinson sells on credit terms of net 90 days while industrywide credit terms have recently been lowered to net 30 days. On annual credit sales of $2.5 million, Vinson currently averages 95 days of sales in accounts receivable. Mitchell estimates that tightening the credit terms to 30 days would reduce annual sales to $2,375,000, but accounts receivable would drop to 35 days of sales and the savings on investment in them should more than overcome any loss in profit.

Vinson's variable cost ratio is 85 percent, and taxes are 40 percent. If the interest rate on funds invested in receivables is 18 percent, should the change in credit terms be made?

23-5
Monitoring of Receivables

The Russ Fogler Company, a small manufacturer of cordless telephones, began operations on January 1, 1998. Its credit sales for the first 6 months of operations were as follows:

MONTH	CREDIT SALES
January	$ 50,000
February	100,000
March	120,000
April	105,000
May	140,000
June	160,000

Throughout this entire period, the firm's credit customers maintained a constant payments pattern: 20 percent paid in the month of sale, 30 percent paid in the month following the sale, and 50 percent paid in the second month following the sale.

a. What was Fogler's receivables balance at the end of March and at the end of June?

b. Assume 90 days per calendar quarter. What were the average daily sales (ADS) and days sales outstanding (DSO) for the first quarter and for the second quarter? What were the cumulative ADS and DSO for the first half-year?

c. Construct an aging schedule as of June 30. Use 0–30, 31–60, and 61–90 day account ages.

d. Construct the uncollected balances schedule for the second quarter as of June 30.

23-6
Optimal Cash Transfer

Barenbaum Industries projects that cash outlays of $4.5 million will occur uniformly throughout the year. Barenbaum plans to meet its cash requirements by periodically selling marketable securities from its portfolio. The firm's marketable securities are invested to earn 12 percent, and the cost per transaction of converting securities to cash is $27.

a. Use the Baumol model to determine the optimal transaction size for transfers from marketable securities to cash.

b. What will be Barenbaum's average cash balance?

c. How many transfers per year will be required?

d. What will be Barenbaum's total annual cost of maintaining cash balances? What would the total cost be if the company maintained an average cash balance of $50,000 or of $0 (it deposits funds daily to meet cash requirements)?

Spreadsheet Problems

Work the problems in this section only if you are using the computer problem diskette.

23-7
Accounts Receivable
Management

Use the first model in File C23 to solve this problem. Altman Auto Parts is considering changing its credit terms from 2/15, net 30, to 3/10, net 30, inorder to speed collections. At present, 60 percent of the firm's customers take the 2 percent discount. Under the new terms, discount customers are expected to rise to 70 percent. Regardless of the credit terms, half of the customers who do not take the discount are expected to pay on time, while the remainder will pay 10 days late. The change does not involve a relaxation of credit standards; therefore, bad debt losses are not expected to rise above their present 2 percent level. However, the more generous cash discount terms are expected to increase sales from $1 million to $1.2 million per year. The firm's variable cost ratio is 75 percent, the interest rate on funds invested in accounts receivable is 12 percent, and its tax rate is 40 percent.

a. What is the days sales outstanding before and after the change?
b. Calculate the discount costs before and after the change.
c. Calculate the dollar cost of carrying receivables before and after the change.
d. Calculate the bad debt losses before and after the change.
e. What is the incremental profit from the change in credit terms? Should the firm change its credit terms?
f. (1) Suppose the sales forecast is lowered to $1,100,000. Should the firm change its credit policy? What if the sales forecast dropped to $1,036,310?
   (2) Suppose the payment pattern of customers remains unchanged with the new credit plan; that is, 60 percent still take the discount, 20 percent pay on time, and 20 percent pay late. Also, the variable cost ratio rises to 78 percent. How does all this affect the decision, assuming the sales forecast remains at $1,200,000?

23-8
Inventory Management

Use the second model in File C23 to solve this problem. The following inventory data have been established for the Adler Corporation:

(1) Orders must be placed in multiples of 100 units.
(2) Annual sales are 338,000 units.
(3) The purchase price per unit is $3.
(4) Carrying cost is 20 percent of the purchase price of goods.
(5) Cost per order placed is $24.
(6) Desired safety stock is 14,000 units; this amount is on hand initially.
(7) Two weeks are required for delivery.

a. What is the EOQ?
b. How many orders should the firm place each year?
c. At what inventory level should a reorder be made? [Hint: Reorder point = Safety stock + (Weeks to deliver × Weekly usage) − Goods in transit.]
d. Calculate the total costs of ordering and carrying inventories if the order quantity is (1) 4,000 units, (2) 4,800 units, or (3) 6,000 units. What are the total costs if the order quantity is the EOQ?
e. What are the EOQ and total inventory costs if
   (1) Sales increase to 500,000 units?
   (2) Fixed order costs increase to $30? Sales remain at 338,000 units.
   (3) Purchase price increases to $4? Leave sales and fixed costs at original values.

MINI CASE

SECTION I: Receivables Management Rich Jackson, a recent finance graduate, is planning to go into the wholesale building supply business with his brother, Jim, who majored in building construction. The firm would sell primarily to general contractors, and it would start operating next January. Sales would be slow during the cold months, rise during the spring, and then fall off again in the summer, when new construction in the area slows. Sales estimates for the first 6 months are as follows (in thousands of dollars):

| January | $100 | March | $300 | May | $200 |
| February | 200 | April | 300 | June | 100 |

The terms of sale are net 30, but because of special incentives, the brothers expect 30 percent of the customers (by dollar value) to pay on the 10th day following the sale, 50 percent to pay on the 40th day, and the remaining 20 percent to pay on the 70th day. No bad debt losses are expected, because Jim, the building construction expert, knows which contractors are having financial problems.

a. Assume that, on average, the brothers expect annual sales of 18,000 items at an average price of $100 per item. (Use a 360-day year.)
   (1) What is the firm's expected days sales outstanding (DSO)?
   (2) What is its expected average daily sales (ADS)?
   (3) What is its expected average accounts receivable level?
   (4) Assume that the firm's profit margin is 25 percent. How much of the receivables balance must be financed? What would the firm's balance sheet figures for accounts receivable, notes payable, and retained earnings be at the end of 1 year if notes payable are used to finance the investment in receivables? Assume that the cost of carrying receivables had been deducted when the 25 percent profit margin was calculated.
   (5) If bank loans have a cost of 12 percent, what is the annual dollar cost of carrying the receivables?

b. What are some factors which influence (1) a firm's receivables level and (2) the dollar cost of carrying receivables?

c. Assuming that the monthly sales forecasts given previously are accurate, and that customers pay exactly as was predicted, what would the receivables level be at the end of each month? *To reduce calculations, assume that 30 percent of the firm's customers pay in the month of sale, 50 percent pay in the month following the sale, and the remaining 20 percent pay in the second month following the sale. Note that this is a different assumption than was made earlier.* Use the following format to answer Parts c and d:

MONTH	SALES	END-OF-MONTH RECEIVABLES	QUARTERLY SALES	ADS	DSO = (A/R)(ADS)
Jan	$100	$ 70			
Feb	200	160			
Mar	300	250	$600	$6.67	37.5
Apr	$300				
May	200				
Jun	100				

d. What is the firm's forecasted average daily sales for the first 3 months? For the entire half-year? The days sales outstanding is commonly used to measure receivables performance. What DSO is expected at the end of March? At the end of June? What does the DSO indicate about customers' payments? Is DSO a good management tool in this situation? If not, why not?

e. Construct aging schedules for the end of March and the end of June (use the format given below). Do these schedules properly measure customers' payment patterns? If not, why not?

AGE OF ACCOUNT (DAYS)	MARCH A/R	MARCH %	JUNE A/R	JUNE %
0–30	$210	84%		
31–60	40	16		
61–90	0	0	——	——
	$250	100%		

f. Construct the uncollected balances schedules for the end of March and the end of June. Use the format given below. Do these schedules properly measure customers' payment patterns?

	MARCH			JUNE		
MONTH	SALES	CONTRIBUTION TO A/R	A/R-TO-SALES RATIO	MONTH	SALES	CONTRIBUTION TO A/R	A/R-TO-SALES RATIO
Jan	$100	$ 0	0%	Apr			
Feb	200	40	20	May			
Mar	300	210	70	Jun		____	____

g. Assume that it is now July of Year 1, and the brothers are developing pro forma financial statements for the following year. Further, assume that sales and collections in the first half-year matched the predicted levels. Using the Year 2 sales forecasts as shown next, what are next year's pro forma receivables levels for the end of March and for the end of June?

MONTH	PREDICTED SALES	PREDICTED A/R-TO-SALES RATIO	PREDICTED CONTRIBUTION TO RECEIVABLES
Jan	$150	0%	$ 0
Feb	300	20	60
Mar	500	70	350
	Projected March 31 A/R balance =		$410
Apr	$400		
May	300		
Jun	200		
	Projected June 30 A/R balance =		

h. Assume now that it is several years later. The brothers are concerned about the firm's current credit terms, which are now net 30, which means that contractors buying building products from the firm are not offered a discount, and they are supposed to pay the full amount in 30 days. Gross sales are now running $1,000,000 a year, and 80 percent (by dollar volume) of the firm's *paying* customers generally pay the full amount on Day 30, while the other 20 percent pay, on average, on Day 40. Two percent of the firm's gross sales end up as bad debt losses.

　　The brothers are now considering a change in the firm's credit policy. The change would entail (1) changing the credit terms to 2/10, net 20, (2) employing stricter credit standards before granting credit, and (3) enforcing collections with greater vigor than in the past. Thus, cash customers and those paying within 10 days would receive a 2 percent discount, but all others would have to pay the full amount after only 20 days. The brothers believe that the discount would both attract additional customers and encourage some existing customers to purchase more from the firm—after all, the discount amounts to a price reduction. Of course, these customers would take the discount and, hence, would pay in only 10 days. The net expected result is for sales to increase to $1,100,000; for 60 percent of the paying customers to take the discount and pay on the 10th day; for 30 percent to pay the full amount on Day 20; for 10 percent to pay late on Day 30; and for bad debt losses to fall from 2 percent to 1 percent of gross sales. The firm's operating cost ratio will remain unchanged at 75 percent, and its cost of carrying receivables will remain unchanged at 12 percent.

To begin the analysis, describe the four variables which make up a firm's credit policy, and explain how each of them affects sales and collections. Then use the information given in Part h to answer Parts i through n.

i. Under the current credit policy, what is the firm's days sales outstanding (DSO)? What would the expected DSO be if the credit policy change were made?

j. What is the dollar amount of the firm's current bad debt losses? What losses would be expected under the new policy?

k. What would be the firm's expected dollar cost of granting discounts under the new policy?

l. What is the firm's current dollar cost of carrying receivables? What would it be after the proposed change?

m. What is the incremental after-tax profit associated with the change in credit terms? Should the company make the change? (Assume a tax rate of 40 percent.)

	NEW	OLD	DIFFERENCE
Gross sales		$1,000,000	
Less discounts	_____	0	_____
Net sales		$1,000,000	
Production costs	_____	750,000	_____
Profit before credit costs and taxes		$ 250,000	
Credit-related costs:			
Carrying costs		8,000	
Bad debt losses	_____	20,000	_____
Profit before taxes		$ 222,000	
Taxes (40%)	_____	88,800	_____
Net income		$ 133,200	

n. Suppose the firm makes the change, but its competitors react by making similar changes to their own credit terms, with the net result being that gross sales remain at the current $1,000,000 level. What would the impact be on the firm's post-tax profitability?

SECTION II: **Inventory Management**   Andria Mullins, financial manager of Webster Electronics, has been asked by the firm's CEO, Fred Weygandt, to evaluate the company's inventory control techniques and to lead a discussion of the subject with the senior executives. Andria plans to use as an example one of Webster's "big ticket" items, a customized computer microchip which the firm uses in its laptop computer. Each chip costs Webster $200, and in addition it must pay its supplier a $1,000 setup fee on each order. Further, the minimum order size is 250 units; Webster's annual usage forecast is 5,000 units; and the annual carrying cost of this item is estimated to be 20 percent of the average inventory value.

Andria plans to begin her session with the senior executives by reviewing some basic inventory concepts, after which she will apply the EOQ model to Webster's microchip inventory. As her assistant, you have been asked to help her by answering the following questions:
a. Why is inventory management vital to the financial health of most firms?
b. What assumptions underlie the EOQ model?
c. Write out the formula for the total costs of carrying and ordering inventory, and then use the formula to derive the EOQ model.
d. What is the EOQ for custom microchips? What are total inventory costs if the EOQ is ordered?
e. What is Webster's added cost if it orders 400 units at a time rather than the EOQ quantity? What if it orders 600 per order?
f. Suppose it takes 2 weeks for Webster's supplier to set up production, make and test the chips, and deliver them to Webster's plant. Assuming certainty in delivery times and usage, at what inventory level should Webster reorder? (Assume a 52-week year, and assume that Webster orders the EOQ amount.)
g. Of course, there is uncertainty in Webster's usage rate as well as in delivery times, so the company must carry a safety stock to avoid running out of chips and having to halt production. If a 200-unit safety stock is carried, what effect would this have on total inventory costs? What is the new reorder point? What protection does the safety stock provide if usage increases, or if delivery is delayed?
h. Now suppose Webster's supplier offers a discount of 1 percent on orders of 1,000 or more. Should Webster take the discount? Why or why not?
i. For many firms, inventory usage is not uniform throughout the year, but, rather, follows some seasonal pattern. Can the EOQ model be used in this situation? If so, how?
j. How would these factors affect an EOQ analysis?
   (1) The use of just-in-time procedures.
   (2) The use of air freight for deliveries.
   (3) The use of a computerized inventory control system, wherein as units were removed from stock, an electronic system automatically reduced the inventory account and, when the

order point was hit, automatically sent an electronic message to the supplier placing an order. The electronic system ensures that inventory records are accurate, and that orders are placed promptly.

(4) The manufacturing plant is redesigned and automated. Computerized process equipment and state-of-the-art robotics are installed, making the plant highly flexible in the sense that the company can switch from the production of one item to another at a minimum cost and quite quickly. This makes short production runs more feasible than under the old plant setup.

Selected Additional References and Cases

Key references on cash balance models include the following:

Daellenbach, Hans G., "Are Cash Management Optimization Models Worthwhile?" *Journal of Financial and Quantitative Analysis,* September 1974, 607–626.

Miller, Merton H., and Daniel Orr, "The Demand for Money by Firms: Extension of Analytic Results," *Journal of Finance,* December 1968, 735–759.

Mullins, David Wiley, Jr., and Richard B. Homonoff, "Applications of Inventory Cash Management Models," in *Modern Developments in Financial Management,* Stewart C. Myers, ed. (New York: Praeger, 1976).

Stone, Bernell K., "The Use of Forecasts for Smoothing in Control-Limit Models for Cash Management," *Financial Management,* Spring 1972, 72–84.

The following cases from the Cases in Financial Management: Dryden Request *series focus on the credit policy decision:*

Case 33, "Upscale Toddlers, Inc.," Case 50, "Mitchell Lumber Co.," and Case 62, "Western Supply," which deal with credit policy changes.

Case 34, "Texas Rose Company," and Case 34A, "Bridgewater Pool Company," which focus on receivables management.

CHAPTER 24
DERIVATIVES AND
RISK MANAGEMENT

CHAPTER 25
BANKRUPTCY,
REORGANIZATION, AND
LIQUIDATION

CHAPTER 26
MERGERS, LBOS,
DIVESTITURES, AND
HOLDING COMPANIES

CHAPTER 27
MULTINATIONAL FINANCIAL
MANAGEMENT

CHAPTER 28
PENSION PLAN
MANAGEMENT

Located in Kuala Lumpur's
business district, the Petrona
Towers were designed and
built to meet office space
requirements. Currently, the
Towers' offices have a less
than 5 percent vacancy rate,
but when the interior's 2.57
million square feet of office
space is completed, property
consultant Henry Butcher
estimates vacancy will jump
to 30 percent due to an
overbuilt market.

© David Lawrence/Prime
Images, 1997

DERIVATIVES AND RISK MANAGEMENT

*C*orporate financial managers are generally thought of as models of caution, paid to manage a company's finances prudently and conservatively. But recent events at Procter & Gamble, Gibson Greetings, and Metallgesellschaft, a major German company, have shaken that image. Each of these companies incurred huge losses on derivatives transactions which were supposedly undertaken to reduce risk.

A look at how P&G got into trouble with risky derivatives shows how tempting it can be for a company to try to magnify its returns, but how difficult it is to predict the risks involved. P&G profited handsomely with derivatives in the early 1990s. Sensing more opportunity for gain, the P&G treasury staff asked Bankers Trust to create a derivative whose returns would depend on both U.S. and German interest rates. Bankers Trust, perhaps the most aggressive dealer in exotic securities, gave P&G three choices. P&G chose the most aggressive, the derivative that promised the greatest reward but entailed the greatest risk.

The transaction involved two complex swaps. P&G was allowed to issue floating rate debt at below-market rates, but, in return, the company had to give Bankers Trust a series of "put options" that gave the bank the right to sell to P&G U.S. Treasury bonds and German government bonds at a fixed price. If interest rates in both countries were constant or fell, there would be no problem for P&G—the bonds would be worth more on the open market than the fixed price, so Bankers Trust would not require P&G to buy them. But if rates rose, P&G would have to buy bonds at above-market prices.

Rates climbed rapidly after the deal was struck, causing bond prices to plunge, so P&G was saddled with a rising liability to buy bonds at above-market prices. Bankers Trust said that it advised P&G to cut its losses by closing out the transactions, but P&G wouldn't budge. When the first losses hit, the P&G folks who set the transaction up probably said, "Oh-oh, we have a problem. But let's wait and see what interest rates do before we tell the boss." By the time P&G bit the bullet and closed out the position, it had a pre-tax loss of $157 million.

P&G contended that it was victimized by Bankers Trust, and it sued, contending that the bank did not disclose all the risks involved in the transactions. Said a P&G spokesperson, "These transactions were intended to be hedges. We use swaps to manage and reduce our borrowing costs, not to make money. The swaps turned out to be speculative transactions that were highly leveraged and clearly did not fit our policy." On the other hand, Bankers Trust claimed that P&G is a sophisticated company and that it knew the rules of the game. The lawsuit was finally settled after more than two years of haggling, with Bankers Trust agreeing to cover about 80 percent of P&G's losses. However, derivatives' use and abuse has continued to be one of the hottest topics in the financial press.

As you read this chapter, think about P&G, and try to answer these questions: Why should companies try to manage risk? What financial techniques can be used to manage risk? And what safeguards should companies put in place to prevent programs designed to limit risks from actually increasing them?

In this chapter, we discuss risk management, a topic of increasing importance to financial managers. The term *risk management* can mean many things, but in business it involves identifying events that could have adverse financial consequences and then taking actions to prevent and/or minimize the damage caused by these events. Years ago, corporate risk managers dealt primarily with insurance — they made sure the firm was adequately insured against fire, theft, and other casualties, and that it had adequate liability coverage. More recently, the scope of risk management has been broadened to include such things as controlling the costs of key inputs like petroleum by purchasing oil futures, or protecting against changes in interest rates or exchange rates through dealings in the interest rate or foreign exchange markets. In addition, risk managers try to ensure that actions designed to hedge against risk — as P&G claimed its derivatives transactions were supposed to be — are not actually increasing risks.

REASONS TO MANAGE RISK

We know that investors dislike risk. We also know that most investors hold well-diversified portfolios, so at least in theory the only "relevant risk" is systematic risk. Therefore, if you asked corporate executives what type of risk they were concerned about, you might expect the answer to be, "beta." However, this is almost certainly not the answer you would get. The most likely answer, if you asked a CEO to define risk, is something like this: "Risk is the possibility that our future earnings and free cash flows will be significantly lower than we expect." For example, consider Plastics Inc., which manufactures dashboards, interior door panels, and other plastic components used by auto companies. Petroleum is the key feedstock for plastic and thus makes up a large percentage of its costs. Plastics has a three-year contract with an auto company to deliver 500,000 door panels each year, at a price of $20 each. When the company signed this contract, oil sold for $19 per barrel, and oil was expected to stay at that level for the next three years. If oil prices fall, Plastics will have higher than expected profits and free cash flows, but if oil rises, profits will fall. Since Plastics' value depends on its profits and free cash flow, a change in the price of oil will cause stockholders to earn either more or less than they anticipated.

Now suppose Plastics announces that it plans to lock in a three-year supply of oil at a guaranteed price of $19 per barrel, and the cost of getting the guarantee is zero. Would that cause its stock price to rise? At first glance, it seems that the answer should be yes, but maybe that's not correct. Recall that the long-run value of a stock depends on the present value of its expected future free cash flows, discounted at the weighted average cost of capital (WACC). Locking in the cost of oil will cause an increase in Plastics' stock price if and only if (1) it causes the expected future free cash flows to increase or (2) it causes the WACC to decline.

Consider first the free cash flows. Before the announcement of guaranteed oil costs, investors had formed an estimate of the expected future free cash flows, based on an expected oil price of $19 per barrel. Therefore, while locking in the cost of oil at $19 per barrel will lower the riskiness of the expected future free cash flows, it will not change the *size* of these cash flows, because investors already expected a price of $19 per barrel.

Now what about the WACC? It will change only if locking in the cost of oil causes a change in the cost of debt or equity, or the target capital structure. Assuming the foreseeable increases in the price of oil were not enough to cause bankruptcy, Plastics' cost of debt should not change, and neither should its target capital structure. Regarding the cost of equity, recall from Chapter 5 that most investors hold well-diversified portfolios, which means that the cost of equity should depend only on systematic risk. Moreover, even though an increase in oil prices would have a negative impact on Plastics' stock price, it would not have a negative impact on all stocks. Indeed, oil producers should have higher than expected returns and stock prices. Assuming that Plastics' investors hold well-diversified portfolios, including stocks of oil-producing companies, there would not appear to be much reason to expect its cost of equity to decrease. The bottom line is this: If Plastics' expected future cash flows and WACC will not change significantly due to an elimination of the risk of oil price increases, then neither should the value of its stock.

We discuss futures contracts and hedging in detail in the next section, but for now let's assume that Plastics has *not* locked in oil prices. Therefore, if oil prices increase, its stock price will fall. However, its stockholders know this, so they can build portfolios that contain oil futures whose values will rise or fall with oil prices and thus offset changes in the price of Plastics' stock. By choosing the correct amount of the futures contracts, investors can thus "hedge" their portfolios and completely eliminate the risk due to changes in oil prices. There will be a cost to hedging, but that cost to large, sophisticated investors should be about the same as the cost to Plastics. Since stockholders can hedge away oil price risk themselves, why should they pay a higher price for Plastics' stock just because the company itself hedged away the risk? In other words, if investors can use "homemade" hedging, then the stock of a company that hedges its own operations should be the same as it would be if the company did not hedge its operations. This should remind you of the Modigliani-Miller results in Chapter 15: If investors can use homemade leverage, then the price of levered and unlevered firms should be equal.

Still, a 1995 survey reported that 59 percent of firms with market values greater than $250 million engage in risk management, and that percentage is surely much higher today.[1] Although there is no proof that risk management adds value, here are several good reasons for companies to manage risks:

1. **Debt capacity.** Risk management can reduce the volatility of cash flows, and this decreases the probability of bankruptcy. As we discussed in Chapters 15 and 16, firms with lower operating risks can use more debt, and this can lead to higher stock prices due to the interest tax shield.

2. **Maintaining the optimal capital budget over time.** Recall from Chapters 15 and 16 that firms are reluctant to raise external equity due to high flotation costs and market pressure. This means that the capital budget must generally be financed with debt plus internally generated funds, mainly retained earnings and depreciation. In years when internal cash flows are low, they may be too small to support the optimal capital budget, causing firms to either slow investment below the optimal rate or else incur the high costs associated with external equity. By smoothing out the cash flows, risk management can alleviate this problem.

3. **Financial distress.** Financial distress—which can range from worrying stockholders to higher interest rates on debt to customer defections to bankruptcy—is associated with having cash flows fall below expected levels. Risk management can reduce the likelihood of low cash flows, hence of financial distress.

4. **Comparative advantages in hedging.** Many investors cannot implement a homemade hedging program as efficiently as can a company. First, firms generally have

---

[1]See Gordon M. Bodnar, Gregory S. Hayt, and Richard C. Marston, "1995 Wharton Survey of Derivative Usage by U.S. Non-Financial Firms," *Financial Management,* Winter 1996, 113–133.

lower transactions costs due to a larger volume of hedging activities. Second, there is the problem of asymmetric information—managers know more about the firm's risk exposure than outside investors, hence managers can create more effective hedges. And third, effective risk management requires specialized skills and knowledge that firms are more likely to have.

5. **Borrowing costs.** As discussed later in the chapter, firms can sometimes reduce input costs, especially the interest rate on debt, through the use of derivative instruments called "swaps." Any such cost reduction adds value to the firm.

6. **Tax effects.** Companies with volatile earnings pay more taxes than more stable companies due to the treatment of tax credits and the rules governing corporate loss carry-forwards and carry-backs. Moreover, if volatile earnings lead to bankruptcy, then tax loss carry-forwards are generally lost. Therefore, our tax system encourages risk management to stabilize earnings.[2]

7. **Compensation systems.** Many compensation systems establish "floors" and "ceilings" on bonuses or else reward managers for meeting targets. To illustrate, suppose a firm's compensation system calls for a manager to receive no bonus if net income is below $1 million, a bonus of $10,000 if income is between $1 million and $2 million, and one of $20,000 if income is $2 million or more. Moreover, the manager will receive an additional $10,000 if actual income is at least 90 percent of the forecasted level, which is $1 million. Now consider the following two situations. First, if income is stable at $2 million each year, the manager gets a $30,000 bonus each year, for a two-year total of $60,000. However, if income is zero the first year and $4 million the second, the manager gets no bonus the first year and $30,000 the second, for a two-year total of $30,000. So, even though the company has the same total income ($4 million) over the two years, the manager's bonus is higher if earnings are stable. So, even if hedging does not add much value for stockholders, it may still be beneficial to managers.

Since perhaps the most important aspect of risk management involves derivative securities, the next section explains **derivatives,** which are securities whose values are determined by the market price of some other asset. Derivatives include *options,* whose values depend on the price of some underlying asset; *interest rate and exchange rate futures and swaps,* whose values depend on interest rate and exchange rate levels; and *commodity futures,* whose values depend on commodity prices.

SELF-TEST
QUESTIONS

Explain why finance theory, combined with well-diversified investors and "home-made hedging," might suggest that risk management should not add much value to a company.

List and explain some reasons why companies might actually employ risk management techniques.

BACKGROUND ON DERIVATIVES

An historical perspective is useful when studying derivatives. One of the first formal markets for derivatives was the futures market for wheat. Farmers were concerned about the price they would receive for their wheat when they sold it in the fall, and

---

[2]See Clifford W. Smith, and René Stulz, "The Determinants of Firms' Hedging Policies," *The Journal of Financial and Quantitative Analysis,* December 1985, 395–406.

The Chicago Board of Trade has an excellent web site at http://www.cbot.com/menu.htm. Make sure to check out the Visitor's Center for a wealth of information on the history and operation of the exchange.

millers were concerned about the price they would have to pay. The risks faced by both parties could be reduced if they could establish a price earlier in the year. Accordingly, mill agents would go out to the wheat belt and make contracts with farmers which called for the farmers to deliver grain at a predetermined price. Both parties benefited from the transaction in the sense that their risks were reduced. The farmers could concentrate on growing their crop without worrying about the price of grain, and the millers could concentrate on their milling operations. Thus, *hedging with futures* lowered aggregate risk in the economy.

These early futures dealings were between two parties who arranged transactions between themselves. Soon, though, middlemen came into the picture, and *trading* in futures was established. The Chicago Board of Trade was an early marketplace for this dealing, and *futures dealers* helped make a market in futures contracts. Thus, farmers could sell futures on the exchange, and millers could buy them there. This improved the efficiency and lowered the cost of hedging operations.

Quickly, a third group—*speculators*—entered the scene. As we will see in the next section, most derivatives, including futures, are highly leveraged, meaning that a small change in the value of the underlying asset will produce a large change in the price of the derivative. This leverage appealed to speculators. At first blush, one might think that the appearance of speculators would increase risk, but this is not true. Speculators add capital and players to the market, and this tends to stabilize the market. Of course, derivatives markets are inherently volatile due to the leverage involved, hence risk to the speculators themselves is high. Still, their bearing that risk makes the derivatives markets more stable for the hedgers.

Natural hedges, defined as situations in which aggregate risk can be reduced by derivatives transactions between two parties (called *counterparties*), exist for many commodities, for foreign currencies, for interest rates on securities with different maturities, and even for common stocks where portfolio managers want to "hedge their bets." Natural hedges occur when futures are traded between cotton farmers and cotton mills, copper mines and copper fabricators, importers and foreign manufacturers for currency exchange rates, electric utilities and coal miners, and oil producers and oil users. In all such situations, hedging reduces aggregate risk and thus benefits the economy.

Hedging can also be done in situations where no natural hedge exists. Here one party wants to reduce some type of risk, and another party agrees to sell a contract which protects the first party from that specific event or situation. Insurance is an obvious example of this type of hedge. Note, though, that with nonsymmetric hedges, risks are generally *transferred* rather than *eliminated*. Even here, though, insurance companies can reduce certain types of risk through diversification.

The derivatives markets have grown more rapidly than any other major market in recent years, for a number of reasons. First, analytical techniques such as the Black-Scholes Option Pricing Model, which is discussed in the next section, have been developed to help establish "fair" prices, and having a better basis for pricing hedges makes the counterparties more comfortable with deals. Second, computers and electronic communications make it much easier for counterparties to deal with one another. Third, globalization has greatly increased the importance of currency markets and the need for reducing the exchange rate risks brought on by global trade. Recent trends and developments are sure to continue if not accelerate, so the use of derivatives for risk management is bound to grow.

Note, though, that derivatives do have a potential downside. These instruments are highly leveraged, so small miscalculations can lead to huge losses. Also, they are complicated, hence not well understood by most people. This makes mistakes more likely

An excellent article about the fiasco in Orange County, entitled "Orange County: Don't Blame Derivatives," can be found on NYU's Stern Business School website at http://equity.stern.nyu.edu/Webzine/Sternbusiness/Spring95/orange.html. The article, written by Stephen Figlewski and Lawrence J. White, professors at NYU, provides an excellent discussion of what derivatives are, how they work, and why Orange County got into trouble in the first place.

ORANGE COUNTY BLUES

It was too good to be true. For more than 20 years, the investment fund managed by California's Orange County produced impressive returns. However, this all came to an end in December 1994, when the county announced that the fund had generated more than $2 billion in losses. The county's treasurer, Robert Citron, was forced to resign, and both the county and its fund were declared bankrupt.

What happened? During the 1980s, fund manager Citron had followed a strategy of investing in long-term securities. The trend in interest rates was downward. When rates decline, long-term bond prices rise, so Citron's fund had earned both interest and capital gains. Furthermore, Citron started borrowing at low short-term rates and investing in higher-yielding long-term bonds, which further increased the fund's interest income and capital gains.

Such a strategy works wonderfully during a period of declining rates: The fund's record was outstanding, and Citron was a hero in Orange County. However, Citron's confidence in his ability to beat the market turned to overconfidence, and he failed to display a reasonable degree of prudence. In November 1993, he became convinced that interest rates were poised for another dramatic decline, so he began borrowing heavily and using the money to purchase "high octane" — exceptionally risky — derivative products whose values were extremely sensi-

tive to changes in interest rates. One of Citron's favorites was a derivative called an "inverse floater," whose interest payments rise when interest rates fall, and vice versa. Another favorite was a complicated derivative product that was designed to go up in value if the yield curve steepened, that is, if long-term rates increased relative to short-term rates.

Citron was betting (1) that interest rates in general were going to decline and (2) that short-term rates were going to decline more than long-term rates. However, his predictions were completely wrong. The economy strengthened in 1994, causing the Fed to raise interest rates dramatically. Further, short-term rates went up almost 4 percentage points versus less than 2 percentage points for long-term rates, so the yield curve flattened instead of growing steeper.

These changes caused the value of inverse floaters and yield curve derivatives to plunge, and the general increase in rates also reduced the value of the "plain vanilla" securities the fund held. Further, the problem was exacerbated because the fund had borrowed on a short-term basis to finance its investments, and its own interest costs rose steadily as interest rates increased.

The fund used its assets (securities) as collateral for its loans. It took in some $7.5 billion in tax receipts, fees, and the like from school districts, cities in the county such as Anaheim (home of Disneyland), and water districts. This money was

"invested" in derivatives and other securities until such time as it was needed for payrolls and the like. In the meantime, its "investments" were used as collateral for loans to buy still more derivatives.

Interestingly, most of the derivatives in which Orange County invested were based on securities issued by the federal government. Those securities could decline in value even though there will be no default on their cash payments. Of course, if the amount of cash received declines, as it would on an inverse floater if interest rates rise, the value of the security will decline, and such a security is certainly not riskless.

Orange County is the fifth largest county in the country — and one of the wealthiest — and it is slowly recovering from Citron's folly. But the losses have had some profound effects on Orange County's citizens. The county's bonds were downgraded from AA to junk, causing its interest rates to soar. Highway projects were canceled, and some employees had to be laid off.

More recently, Orange County has issued new debt. In early 1997, more than a year after the county declared bankruptcy, it sold $880 million in bonds, but at a high cost. Moreover, many problems are still unresolved. For example, the county has filed lawsuits against both its investment banker, Merrill Lynch, and its auditor, KPMG Peat Marwick. The outcome of these lawsuits may not be resolved for several years.

---

than with less complex instruments, and it makes it harder for a firm's top management to exercise proper control over derivatives transactions. One 28-year-old, relatively low-level employee, operating in the Far East, entered into transactions that led to the bankruptcy of Britain's oldest bank (Barings Bank), the institution that held the accounts of the Queen of England. P&G's problems were discussed earlier, and Orange County, California, went bankrupt due to its treasurer's speculation in derivatives. Hundreds of other horror stories could be told.

The P&G, Orange Country, and Barings Bank affairs make the headlines, causing some people to argue that derivatives should be regulated out of existence to "protect the public." However, derivatives are used far more often to hedge risks than in harmful speculations, but these beneficial transactions never make the headlines. So, while the horror stories point out the need for top managers to exercise control over the personnel who deal with derivatives, they certainly do not justify the elimination of derivatives.

In the balance of this chapter, we discuss how firms can manage risks, and how derivatives are used in risk management.

<table>
<tr><td>S E L F - T E S T
Q U E S T I O N S</td><td>What is a "natural hedge"? Give some examples of natural hedges.

List three reasons the derivatives markets have grown more rapidly than any other major market in recent years.</td></tr>
</table>

OPTIONS

An **option** is a contract which gives its holder the right to buy (or sell) an asset at some predetermined price within a specified period of time. Financial managers should understand option theory both for risk management and also because such an understanding will help them structure warrant and convertible financings.

Option Types and Markets

There are many types of options and option markets.[3] To illustrate how options work, suppose you owned 100 shares of General Computer Corporation (GCC), which on Friday, March 20, 1998, sold for $53.50 per share. You could sell to someone the right to buy your 100 shares at any time during the next four months at a price of, say, $55 per share. The $55 is called the **strike, or exercise, price.** Such options exist, and they are traded on a number of exchanges, with the Chicago Board Options Exchange (CBOE) being the oldest and the largest. This type of option is defined as a **call option,** because the purchaser has a "call" on 100 shares of stock. The seller of an option is called the option *writer.* An investor who "writes" call options against stock held in his or her portfolio is said to be selling *covered options.* Options sold without the stock to back them up are called *naked options.* When the exercise price exceeds the current stock price, a call option is said to be *out-of-the-money.* When the exercise price is below the current price of the stock, the option is *in-the-money.*

You can also buy an option which gives you the right to *sell* a stock at a specified price within some future period — this is called a **put option.** For example, suppose you think GCC's stock price is likely to decline from its current level of $53.50 sometime during the next four months. Table 24-1 provides data on GCC's options. You could buy a four-month put option (the July put option) for $218.75 ($2³/₁₆ × 100) which would give you the right to sell 100 shares (which you would not necessarily own) at a price of $50 per share ($50 is the strike price). Suppose you bought this 100-share contract for $218.75 and then GCC's stock fell to $45. You could buy a share of stock for $45 and exercise your put option by selling the stock for $50. Your profit from exercising the option would be ($50 − $45)(100) = $500. After subtracting the $218.75 you paid for the option, your profit (before taxes and commissions) would be $281.25.

Table 24-1 contains an extract from the Listed Options Quotations Table for Friday, March 20, 1998, as it would appear the next day in a daily newspaper. Sport World's April $55 call option sold for $0.50. Thus, for $0.50(100) = $50 you could buy options

---

[3]For an in-depth treatment of options, see Don M. Chance, *An Introduction to Derivatives* (Fort Worth, TX: Dryden, 1995).

TABLE 24-1   March 20, 1998, Listed Options Quotations

		CALLS — LAST QUOTE			PUTS — LAST QUOTE		
CLOSING PRICE	STRIKE PRICE	APRIL	MAY	JULY	APRIL	MAY	JULY
General Computer Corporation (GCC)							
53½	50	4¼	4¾	5½	⅝	1⅜	2³⁄₁₆
53½	55	1⁵⁄₁₆	2¹⁄₁₆	3⅛	2⅝	r	4½
53½	60	⁵⁄₁₆	¹¹⁄₁₆	1½	6⅝	r	8
U.S. Medical							
56⅝	55	4¼	5⅛	7	2¼	3¾	r
Sport World							
53⅛	55	½	1⅛	r	2⅛	r	r

NOTE: r means not traded on March 20.

that would give you the right to purchase 100 shares of Sport World stock at a price of $55 per share from March until April, or during the next month.[4] If the stock price stayed below $55 during that period, you would lose your $50, but if it rose to $65, your $50 investment would increase in value to ($65 − $55)(100) = $1,000 in less than 30 days. That translates into a very healthy annualized rate of return. Incidentally, if the stock price did go up, you would not actually exercise your options and buy the stock — rather, you would sell the options, which would then have a value of $1,000 versus the $50 you paid, to another option buyer or back to the original seller.

In addition to options on individual stocks, options are also available on several stock indexes such as the NYSE Index and the S&P 100 Index. Index options permit one to hedge (or bet) on a rise or fall in the general market as well as on individual stocks.

Option trading is one of the hottest financial activities in the United States. The leverage involved makes it possible for speculators with just a few dollars to make a fortune almost overnight. Also, investors with sizable portfolios can sell options against their stocks and earn the value of the option (less brokerage commissions), even if the stock's price remains constant. Most importantly, though, options can be used to create *hedges* which protect the value of an individual stock or portfolio. We will discuss hedging strategies in more detail later in the chapter.[5]

Conventional options are generally written for six months or less, but a new type of option called a **Long-term Equity AnticiPation Security (LEAPS)** has been trading in recent years. Like conventional options, LEAPS are listed on exchanges and are tied both to individual stocks and to stock indexes. The major difference is that LEAPS are long-term options, having maturities of up to 2½ years. One-year LEAPS cost about

---

[4]Actually, the *expiration date*, which is the last date that the option can be exercised, is the Friday before the third Saturday of the exercise month. Also, note that option contracts are generally written in 100-share multiples.

[5]It should be noted that insiders who trade illegally generally buy options rather than stock because the leverage inherent in options increases the profit potential. Note, though, that it is illegal to use insider information for personal gain, and an insider using such information would be taking advantage of the option seller. Insider trading, in addition to being unfair and essentially equivalent to stealing, hurts the economy: Investors lose confidence in the capital markets and raise their required returns because of an increased element of risk, and this raises the cost of capital and thus reduces the level of real investment.

twice as much as the matching three-month option, but because of their much longer time to expiration, LEAPS provide buyers with more potential for gains and offer better long-term protection for a portfolio.

Corporations on whose stocks options are written have nothing to do with the option market. Corporations do not raise money in the option market, nor do they have any direct transactions in it. Moreover, option holders do not vote for corporate directors or receive dividends. There have been studies by the SEC and others as to whether option trading stabilizes or destabilizes the stock market, and whether this activity helps or hinders corporations seeking to raise new capital. The studies have not been conclusive, but option trading is here to stay, and many regard it as the most exciting game in town.

Factors That Affect the Value of a Call Option

A study of Table 24-1 provides some insights into call option valuation. First, we see that there are at least three factors which affect a call option's value: (1) The higher the stock's market price in relation to the strike price, the higher will be the call option price. Thus, Sport World's $55 April call option sells for $0.50, whereas U.S. Medical's $55 April option sells for $4.25. This difference arises because U.S. Medical's current stock price is $56⅝ versus only $53⅛ for Sport World. (2) The higher the strike price, the lower the call option price. Thus, all of GCC's call options, regardless of exercise month, decline as the strike price increases. (3) The longer the option period, the higher the option price. This occurs because the longer the time before expiration, the greater the chance that the stock price will climb substantially above the exercise price. Thus, option prices increase as the expiration date is lengthened. Other factors that affect option values, especially the volatility of the underlying stock, are discussed in later sections.

Exercise Value versus Option Price

How is the actual price of a call option determined in the market? In the next section, we present a widely used model (the Black-Scholes model) for pricing call options, but first it is useful to establish some basic concepts. To begin, we define a call option's **exercise value** as follows:

$$\text{Exercise value} = \text{Current price of the stock} - \text{Strike price.}$$

The exercise value is what the option would be worth if you had to exercise it immediately. For example, if a stock sells for $50 and its option has a strike price of $20, then you could buy the stock for $20 by exercising the option. You would own a stock worth $50, but you would only have to pay $20. Therefore, the option would be worth $30 if you had to exercise it immediately. Note that the calculated exercise value of a call option could be negative, but realistically the minimum "true" value of an option is zero, because no one would exercise an out-of-the-money option. Note also that an option's exercise value is only a first approximation value—it merely provides a starting point for finding the actual value of the option.

Now consider Figure 24-1, which presents some data on Space Technology Inc. (STI), a company which recently went public and whose stock price has fluctuated widely during its short history. The third column in the tabular data shows the exercise values for STI's call option when the stock was selling at different prices; the fourth column gives the actual market prices for the option; and the fifth column shows the premium of the actual option price over its exercise value. At any stock price below $20, the exercise value is set at zero, but above $20, each $1 increase in the price of the

FIGURE 24-1   Space Technology Inc.: Option Price and Exercise Value

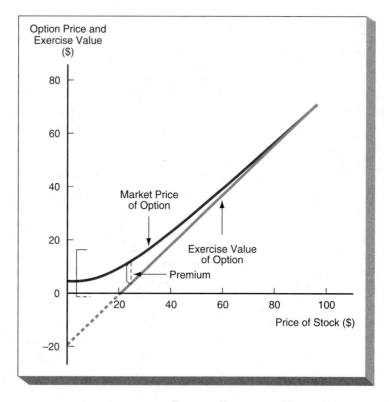

PRICE OF STOCK (1)	STRIKE PRICE (2)	EXERCISE VALUE OF OPTION (1) − (2) = (3)	MARKET PRICE OF OPTION (4)	PREMIUM (4) − (3) = (5)
$20.00	$20.00	$ 0.00	$ 9.00	$9.00
21.00	20.00	1.00	9.75	8.75
22.00	20.00	2.00	10.50	8.50
35.00	20.00	15.00	21.00	6.00
42.00	20.00	22.00	26.00	4.00
50.00	20.00	30.00	32.00	2.00
73.00	20.00	53.00	54.00	1.00
98.00	20.00	78.00	78.50	0.50

stock brings with it a $1 increase in the option's exercise value. Note, however, that the actual market price of the option lies above the exercise value at each price of the common stock, although the premium declines as the price of the stock increases. For example, when the stock sold for $20 and the option had a zero exercise value, its actual price, and the premium, was $9. Then, as the price of the stock rose, the *exercise value's increase* matched the stock's increase dollar for dollar, but the *market price* of the option climbed less rapidly, causing the premium to decline. The premium was $9 when the stock sold for $20 a share, but it had declined to $1 by the time the stock price had risen to $73 a share. Beyond that point, the premium virtually disappeared.

Why does this pattern exist? Why should a call option ever sell for more than its exercise value, and why does the premium decline as the price of the stock increases? The answer lies in part in the speculative appeal of options—they enable someone to gain a high degree of personal leverage when buying securities. To illustrate, suppose STI's option sold for exactly its exercise value. Now suppose you were thinking of investing in the company's common stock at a time when it was selling for $21 a share. If you bought a share and the price rose to $42, you would have made a 100 percent capital gain. However, had you bought the option at its exercise value ($1 when the stock was selling for $21), your capital gain would have been $22 − $1 = $21 on a $1 investment, or 2,100 percent! At the same time, your total loss potential with the option would be only $1 versus a potential loss of $21 if you purchased the stock. The huge capital gains potential, combined with the loss limitation, is clearly worth something—the exact amount it is worth to investors is the amount of the premium. Note, however, that buying the option is riskier than buying STI's stock, because there is a higher probability of losing money on the option. If STI's stock price fell to $20, you would have a 4.76 percent loss if you bought the stock (ignoring transaction costs), but you would have a 100 percent loss on the option investment.

Why does the premium decline as the price of the stock rises? Part of the answer is that both the leverage effect and the loss protection feature decline at high stock prices. For example, if you were thinking of buying STI stock when its price was $73 a share, the exercise value of the option would be $53. If the stock price doubled to $146, you would have a 100 percent gain on the stock. Now note that the exercise value of the option would go from $53 to $126, for a percentage gain of 138 percent versus 2,100 percent in the earlier case. Notice also that the potential loss per dollar of potential gain on the option is much greater when the option is selling at high prices. These two factors, the declining leverage impact and the increasing danger of larger losses, help explain why the premium diminishes as the price of the common stock rises.

In addition to the stock price and the exercise price, the price of an option depends on three other factors: (1) the option's term to maturity, (2) the variability of the stock price, and (3) the risk-free rate. We will explain precisely how these factors affect call option prices later, but for now, note these points:

1. The longer a call option has to run, the greater its value and the larger its premium. If an option expires at 4 P.M. today, there is not much chance that the stock price will go up very much, so the option must sell at close to its exercise value, and its premium must be small. On the other hand, if the expiration date is a year away, the stock price could rise sharply, pulling the option's value up with it.

2. An option on an extremely volatile stock is worth more than one on a very stable stock. If the stock price rarely moves, then there is only a small chance of a large gain. However, if the stock price is highly volatile, the option could easily become very valuable. At the same time, losses on options are limited—you can make an unlimited amount, but you can only lose what you paid for the option. Therefore, a large decline in a stock's price does not have a corresponding bad effect on option holders. As a result of the unlimited upside but limited downside, the more volatile a stock, the higher the value of its options.

3. The payoff on an option will occur in the future, so the value of the option is, in a sense, the present value of an expected future payoff. The higher the discount rate used to find the PV, the lower the value of the call option.

Because of Points 1 and 2, in a graph such as Figure 24-1 the longer an option's life, the higher its market price line would be above the exercise value line. Similarly, the more volatile the price of the underlying stock, the higher is the market price line. We will see precisely how these factors, and also the discount rate, affect option values when we discuss the Black-Scholes option pricing model.

What is an option? A call option? A put option?

Define a call option's exercise value. Why is the actual market price of a call option usually above its exercise value?

What are some factors which affect a call option's value?

INTRODUCTION TO OPTION PRICING MODELS

In the next section, we discuss a widely used but complex option pricing model, the Black-Scholes model. First, though, we go through a simple example to illustrate basic principles. To begin, note that all option pricing models are based on the concept of a **riskless hedge.** Here an investor buys a stock and simultaneously sells a call option on that stock. If the stock's price goes up, the investor will earn a profit on the stock, but the holder of the option will exercise it, and that will cost the investor money. Conversely, if the stock goes down, the investor will lose on his or her investment in the stock, but gain from the option (which will expire worthless if the stock price declines). As we demonstrate, it is possible to set things up such that the investor will end up with a riskless position—regardless of what the stock does, the value of the investor's portfolio will remain constant. Thus, a riskless investment will have been created.

If an investment is riskless, it must, in equilibrium, yield the riskless rate. If it offered a higher rate of return, arbitrageurs would buy it and in the process push the rate of return down, and vice versa if it offered less than the riskless rate.

Given the price of the stock, its potential volatility, the option's exercise price, the life of the option, and the risk-free rate, there is but one price for the option if it is to meet the equilibrium condition, namely, that a portfolio which consists of the stock and the call option will earn the riskless rate. We value an illustrative option below, and then we use the Black-Scholes model to value options under more realistic conditions.

1. **Assumptions of the example.** The stock of Western Cellular, a manufacturer of cell phones, sells for $40 per share. Options exist which permit the holder to buy one share of Western at an exercise price of $35. These options will expire at the end of one year, at which time Western's stock will be selling at one of two prices, either $30 or $50. Also, the risk-free rate is 8.0 percent. Based on these assumptions, we must find the value of the options.

2. **Find the range of values at expiration.** When the option expires at the end of the year, Western's stock will sell for either $30 or $50, and here is the situation with regard to the value of the options:

	ENDING STOCK PRICE	−	STRIKE PRICE VALUE	=	ENDING OPTION VALUE	
	$30.00	−	$35.00	=	$ 0.00	(The option will be worthless. It cannot have a negative value.)
	50.00	−	35.00	=	15.00	
Range	$20.00				$15.00	

3. **Equalize the range of payoffs for the stock and the option.** As shown above, the ranges of payoffs for the stock and the option are $20 and $15. To construct the risk-

less portfolio, we need to equalize these ranges. We do so by buying 0.75 share and selling one option (or 75 shares and 100 options) to produce the following situation, where the range for both the stock and the option is $15:

ENDING STOCK PRICE	×	0.75	=	ENDING VALUE OF STOCK	ENDING VALUE OF OPTION
$30.00	×	0.75	=	$22.50	$ 0.00
50.00	×	0.75	=	37.50	15.00
Range $20.00				$15.00	$15.00

4. **Create a riskless hedged investment.** We can now create a riskless investment portfolio by buying 0.75 share of Western's stock and selling one call option. Here is the situation:

ENDING STOCK PRICE	×	0.75	=	ENDING VALUE OF STOCK IN THE PORTFOLIO	+	ENDING VALUE OF OPTION IN THE PORTFOLIO	=	ENDING TOTAL VALUE OF THE PORTFOLIO
$30.00	×	0.75	=	$22.50	+	$ 0.00	=	$22.50
50.00	×	0.75	=	37.50	+	−15.00	=	22.50

The stock in the portfolio will have a value of either $22.50 or $37.50, depending on what happens to the price of the stock. The call option that was sold will have no effect on the value of the portfolio if Western's price falls to $30, because it will then not be exercised—it will expire worthless. However, if the stock price ends at $50, the holder of the option will exercise it, paying the $35 exercise price for stock that would cost $50 on the open market, so in that case, the option would have a cost of $15 to the holder of the portfolio.

Now notice that the value of the portfolio is $22.50 regardless of whether Western's stock goes up or down. So, the portfolio is riskless. A hedge has been created that protects against both increases or decreases in the price of the stock.

5. **Pricing the call option.** To this point, we have not mentioned the price of the call option which was sold to create the riskless hedge. How much should it sell for? Obviously, the seller would like to get a high price, but the buyer would want a low price. What is the *fair*, or *equilibrium*, price? To find this price, we proceed as follows:

  a. The value of the portfolio will be $22.50 at the end of the year, regardless of what happens to the price of the stock. This $22.50 is riskless.

  b. The risk-free rate is 8 percent, so the present value of the riskless $22.50 year-end value is

$$PV = \$22.50/(1.08) = \$20.83.$$

  c. Since Western's stock is currently selling for $40, and since the portfolio contains 0.75 share, the cost of the stock in the portfolio is

$$0.75(\$40) = \$30.00.$$

  d. If one paid $30 for the stock, and if the present value of the portfolio is $20.83, the option would have to sell for at least $9.17:

$$\text{Price of option} = \text{Cost of stock} - \text{PV of portfolio}$$

$$= \$30 - \$20.83 = \$9.17.$$

If this option sold at a price higher than $9.17, other investors could create riskless portfolios as described above and earn more than the riskless rate. Investors would create such portfolios—and options—until their price fell to $9.17, at which point the market would be in equilibrium. Conversely, if the options sold for less than $9.17, investors would refuse to create them, and the resulting supply shortage would drive the price up to $9.17. Thus, investors (or arbitrageurs) would buy and sell in the market until the options were priced at their equilibrium level.

Clearly, this example is unrealistic—Western's stock price could be almost anything after one year, and you could not purchase 0.75 share of stock (but you could do so in effect by buying 75 shares and selling 100 options). Still, the example does illustrate that investors can, in principle, create riskless portfolios by buying stocks and selling call options against those stocks, and the return on such portfolios should be the risk-free rate. If call options are not priced to reflect this condition, arbitrageurs will actively trade stocks and options until option prices reflect equilibrium conditions. In the next section, we discuss the Black-Scholes Option Pricing Model, which is based on the general premise we developed here—the creation of a riskless portfolio—but which is applicable to "real-world" option pricing because it allows for a complete range of ending stock prices.

SELF-TEST QUESTIONS

Describe how a risk-free portfolio can be created using stocks and options.

How can such a portfolio be used to help estimate a call option's value?

THE BLACK-SCHOLES OPTION PRICING MODEL (OPM)

The *Black-Scholes Option Pricing Model (OPM),* developed in 1973, helped give rise to the rapid growth in options trading.[6] This model, which has even been programmed into the permanent memories of some hand-held calculators, is widely used by option traders.

In deriving their option pricing model, Fischer Black and Myron Scholes made the following assumptions:

1. The stock underlying the call option provides no dividends or other distributions during the life of the option.

2. There are no transaction costs for buying or selling either the stock or the option.

3. The short-term, risk-free interest rate is known and is constant during the life of the option.

4. Any purchaser of a security may borrow any fraction of the purchase price at the short-term, risk-free interest rate.

5. Short selling is permitted, and the short seller will receive immediately the full cash proceeds of today's price for a security sold short.[7]

---

[6]See Fischer Black and Myron Scholes, "The Pricing of Options and Corporate Liabilities," *Journal of Political Economy,* May/June 1973, 637–659.

[7]Suppose an investor (or speculator) does not now own any IBM stock. If the investor anticipates a rise in the stock price and consequently buys IBM stock, he or she is said to have *gone long* in IBM. On the other hand, if the investor thinks IBM's stock is likely to fall, he or she could *go short,* or *sell IBM short.* Since the short seller has no IBM stock, he or she would have to borrow the shares sold short from a broker. If the stock price falls, the short seller could, later on, buy shares on the open market and pay back the ones borrowed from the broker. The short seller's profit, before commissions and taxes, would be the difference between the price received from the short sale and the price paid later to purchase the replacement stock.

6. The call option can be exercised only on its expiration date.

7. Trading in all securities takes place continuously, and the stock price moves randomly.

The derivation of the Black-Scholes model rests on the concept of a riskless hedge such as the one we set up in the last section. By buying shares of a stock and simultaneously selling call options on that stock, an investor can create a risk-free investment position, where gains on the stock will exactly offset losses on the option. This riskless hedged position must earn a rate of return equal to the risk-free rate. Otherwise, an arbitrage opportunity would exist, and people trying to take advantage of this opportunity would drive the price of the option to the equilibrium level as specified by the Black-Scholes model.

The Black-Scholes model consists of the following three equations:

$$V = P[N(d_1)] - Xe^{-k_{RF}t}[N(d_2)]. \tag{24-1}$$

$$d_1 = \frac{\ln(P/X) + [k_{RF} + (\sigma^2/2)]t}{\sigma\sqrt{t}}. \tag{24-2}$$

$$d_2 = d_1 - \sigma\sqrt{t}. \tag{24-3}$$

Here

V = current value of the call option.

P = current price of the underlying stock.

$N(d_1)$ = probability that a deviation less than d_1 will occur in a standard normal distribution. Thus, $N(d_1)$ and $N(d_2)$ represent areas under a standard normal distribution function.

X = exercise, or strike, price of the option.

$e \approx 2.7183$.

k_{RF} = risk-free interest rate.

t = time until the option expires (the option period).

$\ln(P/X)$ = natural logarithm of P/X.

σ^2 = variance of the rate of return on the stock.

Note that the value of the option is a function of the variables we discussed earlier: (1) P, the stock's price; (2) t, the option's time to expiration; (3) X, the strike price; (4) σ^2, the variance of the underlying stock; and (5) k_{RF}, the risk-free rate. We do not derive the Black-Scholes model—the derivation involves some extremely complicated mathematics that go far beyond the scope of this text. However, it is not difficult to use the model. Under the assumptions set forth previously, if the option price is different from the one found by Equation 24-1, this would provide the opportunity for arbitrage profits, which would force the option price back to the value indicated by the model.[8] As we noted earlier, the Black-Scholes model is widely used by traders, so actual option prices conform reasonably well to values derived from the model.

In essence, the first term of Equation 24-1, $P[N(d_1)]$, can be thought of as the expected present value of the terminal stock price, while the second term, $Xe^{-k_{RF}t}[N(d_2)]$, can be thought of as the present value of the exercise price. However, rather than try to figure out exactly what the equations mean, it is more productive to plug in some numbers to see how changes in the inputs affect the value of an option.

Robert's Online Option Pricer can be accessed at http://www.intrepid.com/~robertl/option-pricer.html. The site is designed to provide a financial service over the Internet to small investors for option pricing, giving anyone a means to price option trades without having to buy expensive software and hardware.

---

[8]*Programmed trading,* in which stocks are bought and options are sold, or vice versa, is an example of arbitrage between stocks and options.

OPM Illustration

The current stock price, P, the exercise price, X, and the time to maturity, t, can all be obtained from a newspaper such as *The Wall Street Journal*. The risk-free rate, k_{RF}, is the yield on a Treasury bill with a maturity equal to the option expiration date. The annualized variance of stock returns, σ^2, can be estimated by multiplying the variance of the percentage change in daily stock prices for the past year [that is, the variance of $(P_t - P_{t-1})/P_t$] by 365 days.

Assume that the following information has been obtained:

P = $20.

X = $20.

t = 3 months or 0.25 year.

k_{RF} = 12% = 0.12.

σ^2 = 0.16. Note that if σ^2 = 0.16, then $\sigma = \sqrt{0.16} = 0.4$.

Given this information, we can now use the OPM by solving Equations 24-1, 24-2, and 24-3. Since d_1 and d_2 are required inputs for Equation 24-1, we solve Equations 24-2 and 24-3 first:

$$d_1 = \frac{\ln(\$20/\$20) + [0.12 + (0.16/2)](0.25)}{0.40(0.50)}$$

$$= \frac{0 + 0.05}{0.20} = 0.25.$$

$$d_2 = d_1 - 0.4\sqrt{0.25} = 0.25 - 0.20 = 0.05.$$

Note that $N(d_1) = N(0.25)$ and $N(d_2) = N(0.05)$ represent areas under a standard normal distribution function. From Table A-5 in Appendix A at the end of the book, we see that the value $d_1 = 0.25$ implies a probability of $0.0987 + 0.5000 = 0.5987$, so $N(d_1) = 0.5987$. Similarly, $N(d_2) = 0.5199$. We can use those values to solve Equation 24-1:

$$V = \$20\,[N(d_1)] - \$20e^{-(0.12)(0.25)}[N(d_2)]$$

$$= \$20[N(0.25)] - \$20(0.9704)[N(0.05)]$$

$$= \$20(0.5987) - \$19.41(0.5199)$$

$$= \$11.97 - \$10.09 = \$1.88.$$

Thus the value of the option, under the assumed conditions, is $1.88. Suppose the actual option price were $2.25. Arbitrageurs could simultaneously sell the option, buy the underlying stock, and earn a riskless profit. Such trading would occur until the price of the option was driven down to $1.88. The reverse would occur if the option sold for less than $1.88. Thus, investors would be unwilling to pay more than $1.88 for the option, and they could not buy it for less, so $1.88 is the *equilibrium value* of the option.

To see how the five OPM factors affect the value of the option, consider Table 24-2. Here the top row shows the base-case input values which were used above to illustrate the OPM and the resulting option value, V = $1.88. In each of the subsequent rows, the boldfaced factor is increased, while the other four are held constant at their base-case levels. The resulting value of the call option is given in the last column. Now let's consider the effects of the changes:

1. **Current stock price.** If the current stock price, P, increases from $20 to $25, the option value increases from $1.88 to $5.81. Thus, the value of the option increases

| TABLE 24-2 | Effects of OPM Factors on the Value of a Call Option |

	INPUT FACTORS					OUTPUT
CASE	P	X	t	k_{RF}	σ^2	V
Base case	$20	$20	0.25	12%	0.16	$1.88
Increase P by $5	**25**	20	0.25	12	0.16	5.81
Increase X by $5	20	**25**	0.25	12	0.16	0.39
Increase t to 6 months	20	20	**0.50**	12	0.16	2.81
Increase k_{RF} to 16%	20	20	0.25	**16**	0.16	1.99
Increase σ^2 to 0.25	20	20	0.25	12	**0.25**	2.27

as the stock price increases, but by less than the stock price increase, $3.93 versus $5.00. Note, though, that the percentage increase in the option value, ($5.81 − $1.88)/$1.88 = 209%, far exceeds the percentage increase in the stock price, ($25 − $20)/$20 = 25%.

2. **Exercise price.** If the exercise price, X, increases from $20 to $25, the value of the option declines. Again, the decrease in the option value is less than the exercise price increase, but the percentage change in the option value, ($0.39 − $1.88)/$1.88 = −79%, exceeds the percentage change in the exercise price, ($25 − $20)/$20 = 25%.

3. **Option period.** As the time to expiration increases from t = 3 months (or 0.25 year) to t = 6 months (or 0.50 year), the value of the option increases from $1.88 to $2.81. This occurs because the value of the option depends on the chances for an increase in the price of the underlying stock, and the longer the option has to go, the higher the stock price may climb. Thus, a six-month option is worth more than a three-month option.

4. **Risk-free rate.** As the risk-free rate increases from 12 to 16 percent, the value of the option increases slightly, from $1.88 to $1.99. Equations 24-1, 24-2, and 24-3 suggest that the principal effect of an increase in k_{RF} is to reduce the present value of the exercise price, $Xe^{-k_{RF}t}$, hence to increase the current value of the option.[9] The risk-free rate also plays a role in determining the values of the normal distribution functions $N(d_1)$ and $N(d_2)$, but this effect is of secondary importance. Indeed, option prices in general are not very sensitive to interest rate changes, at least not to changes within the ranges normally encountered.

5. **Variance.** As the variance increases from the base case 0.16 to 0.25, the value of the option increases from $1.88 to $2.27. Therefore, the riskier the underlying security, the more valuable the option. This result is logical. First, if you bought an option to buy a stock that sells at its exercise price, and if $\sigma^2 = 0$, then there would be a zero probability of the stock going up, hence a zero probability of making money on the option. On the other hand, if you bought an option on a high-variance stock, there would be a fairly high probability that the stock would go way up, hence that you

The Chicago Board Options Exchange provides 20-minute delayed quotes for equity, index, and LEAP options at http://www.cboe.com.

---

[9]At this point, you may be wondering why the first term in Equation 24-1, $P[N(d_1)]$, is not discounted. In fact, it has been, because the current stock price, P, already represents the present value of the expected stock price at expiration. In other words, P is a discounted value, and the discount rate used in the market to determine today's stock price includes the risk-free rate. Thus, Equation 24-1 can be thought of as the present value of the end-of-option-period spread between the stock price and the strike price, adjusted for the probability that the stock price will be higher than the strike price.

would make a large profit on the option. Of course, a high-variance stock could go way down, but as an option holder, your losses would be limited to the price paid for the option—only the right-hand side of the stock's probability distribution counts. Put another way, an increase in the price of the stock helps options holders more than a decrease hurts them, so the greater the variance, the greater is the value of the option. This makes options on risky stocks more valuable than those on safer, low-variance stocks.

Myron Scholes and Robert Merton were awarded the 1997 Nobel Prize in Economics, and Fischer Black would have been a co-recipient had he still been living.[10] Their work provided analytical tools and methodologies that are widely used to solve many types of financial problems, not just option pricing. Indeed, the entire field of modern risk management is based primarily on their contributions. This concludes our discussion of options and option pricing theory. The next section discusses some other types of derivative securities.

SELF-TEST QUESTIONS	What is the purpose of the Black-Scholes Option Pricing Model?

Explain what a "riskless hedge" is and how the riskless hedge concept is used in the Black-Scholes OPM.

Describe the effect of a change in each of the following factors on the value of a call option:
(1) Stock price.
(2) Exercise price.
(3) Option life.
(4) Risk-free rate.
(5) Stock price variance, that is, riskiness of stock.

OTHER TYPES OF DERIVATIVES

Put and call options represent an important class of derivative securities, but there are other types of derivatives, including forward contracts, futures, swaps, structured notes, inverse floaters, and a host of other "exotic" contracts.

Forward Contracts versus Futures Contracts

Forward contracts are agreements where one party agrees to buy a commodity at a specific price on a specific future date and the other party agrees to make the sale. *Goods are actually delivered under forward contracts.* Unless both parties are financially strong, there is a danger that one party will default on the contract, especially if the price of the commodity changes markedly after the agreement is reached.

A **futures contract** is similar to a forward contract, but with three key differences: (1) Futures contracts are "marked to market" on a daily basis, meaning that gains and losses are noted and money must be put up to cover losses. This greatly reduces the risk of default that exists with forward contracts. (2) With futures, physical delivery of the underlying asset is virtually never taken—the two parties simply settle up with cash for the difference between the contracted price and the actual price on the expiration date. (3) Futures contracts are generally standardized instruments that are

---

[10]See Robert C. Merton, "Theory of Rational Option Pricing," *Bell Journal of Economics and Management Science,* Vol. 4, 1973, 141–183.

traded on exchanges, whereas forward contracts are generally tailor-made, are negotiated between two parties, and are not traded after they have been signed.

Futures and forward contracts were originally used for commodities such as wheat, where farmers would sell forward contracts to millers, enabling both parties to lock in prices and thus reduce their risk exposure. Commodities contracts are still important, but today more trading is done in foreign exchange and interest rate futures. To illustrate how foreign exchange contracts are used, suppose GE arranges to buy electric motors from a German manufacturer on terms that call for GE to pay 1 million marks in 180 days. GE would not want to give up the free trade credit, but if the mark appreciated against the dollar during the next six months, the dollar cost of the million marks would rise. GE could hedge the transaction by buying a forward contract under which it agreed to buy the million marks in 180 days at a fixed dollar price. This would lock in the dollar cost of the motors. This transaction would probably be conducted through a money center bank, which would try to find a German company (a "counterparty") that needed dollars in six months. Alternatively, GE could buy a futures contract on an exchange.

Interest rate futures represent another huge and growing market. For example, suppose Simonset Corporation decides to build a new plant at a cost of $20 million. It plans to finance the project with 20-year bonds which would carry a 10 percent interest rate if they were issued today. However, the company will not need the money for about six months. Simonset could go ahead and sell 20-year bonds now, locking in the 10 percent rate, but it would have the money before it was needed, so it would have to invest in short-term securities which would yield less than 10 percent. However, if Simonset waits six months to sell the bond issue, interest rates might be higher than they are today, in which case the value of the plant would be reduced, perhaps to the point of making it unprofitable.

One solution to Simonset's dilemma involves *interest rate futures,* which are based on a hypothetical 20-year Treasury bond with an 8 percent semiannual coupon. If interest rates in the economy go up, the value of the hypothetical T-bond will go down, and vice versa. In our example, Simonset is worried about an increase in interest rates. Should rates rise, the hypothetical Treasury bond's value would decline. Therefore, Simonset could sell T-bond futures for delivery in six months to hedge its position. If interest rates rise, Simonset will have to pay more when it issues its own bonds. However, it will make a profit on its futures position because it will have pre-sold the bonds at a higher price than it will have to pay to cover (repurchase) them. Of course, if interest rates decline, Simonset will lose on its futures position, but this will be offset by the fact that it will get to pay a lower interest rate when it issues its bonds.

Our examples show that forward contracts and futures can be used to hedge, or reduce, risks. It has been estimated that more than 95 percent of all transactions are indeed designed as hedges, with banks and futures dealers serving as middlemen between hedging counterparties. Interest rate and exchange rate futures can, of course, be used for speculative as well as hedging purposes. One can buy a T-bond contract on $100,000 of bonds with only $5,000 down, in which case a small change in interest rates will result in a very large gain or loss. Still, the primary motivation behind the vast majority of these transactions is to hedge risks, not to create them.

Swaps

A **swap** is just what the name implies—two parties agree to swap something, generally obligations to make specified payment streams. Most swaps today involve either interest payments or currencies. To illustrate an interest rate swap, suppose Company S has a 20-year, $100 million floating rate bond outstanding, while Company F has a $100 million, 20-year, fixed rate issue outstanding. Thus, each company has an obligation to make a stream of interest payments, but one payment stream is fixed while the other will vary as interest rates change in the future.

Now suppose Company S has stable cash flows, and it wants to lock in its cost of debt. Company F has cash flows that fluctuate with the economy, rising when the economy is strong and falling when it is weak. Recognizing that interest rates also move up and down with the economy, Company F has concluded that it would be better off with variable rate debt. If the companies swapped their payment obligations, an *interest rate swap* would occur. Company S would now have to make fixed payments, which is consistent with its stable cash inflows, and Company F would have a floating stream, which for it is less risky.

Our example illustrates how swaps can reduce risk by allowing each company to match the variability of its interest payments with that of its cash flows. However, there also are situations where swaps can reduce both the riskiness and the amount of interest payments. For example, Antron Corporation, which has a high credit rating, can issue either floating rate debt at LIBOR + 1 percent or fixed rate debt at 10 percent.[11] Bosworth Industries is less creditworthy, and its cost for floating rate debt would be LIBOR + 1.5 percent, and its fixed rate cost would be 10.4 percent. Due to the nature of its operations, Antron's CFO has decided that it would be better off with fixed rate debt, while Bosworth's CFO would prefer floating rate debt. Paradoxically, both firms can benefit by issuing the type of debt they do not want, but then swapping their payment obligations.

First, each company would issue an identical amount of debt, which is called the **notional principal.** Even though Antron wants fixed rate debt, it issues floating rate debt at LIBOR + 1 percent, and Bosworth issues fixed rate debt at 10.4 percent. Next, the two companies swap their interest payments: Antron will make 10.4 percent fixed rate payments to Bosworth, and Bosworth will make LIBOR + 1 percent payments to Antron.[12] In addition, Bosworth must make a fixed **side payment** of 0.45 percent to Antron.

Table 24-3 shows the net payments made by each company. Note that Antron ends up making fixed payments, which it desires, but because of the swap, the rate paid is 9.95 percent versus the 10 percent rate it would have paid had it issued fixed rate debt directly. At the same time, the swap leaves Bosworth with floating rate debt, which it wanted, but at a rate of LIBOR + 0.45 percent versus the LIBOR + 0.50 percent it would have paid on directly issued floating rate debt. As the example illustrates, swaps can sometimes lower the interest rate paid by each party.

Other swap arrangements can also involve side payments. For example, if interest rates had fallen sharply since Company F issued its bonds, then its old payment obligations would be relatively high, and it would have to make a side payment to get S to agree to the swap. Similarly, if the credit risk of one company was higher than that of the other, the stronger company would be concerned about the ability of its weaker "counterparty" to make the required payments. This too would lead to the need for a side payment.

---

[11]LIBOR stands for the London Interbank Offer Rate, the rate charged on interbank dollar loans in the Eurodollar market.

[12]Actually, such transactions are generally arranged by large money center banks, and payments are made to the bank, which in turn pays the interest on the original loans. The bank would assume the credit risk and guarantee the payments should one of the parties default. For it services, the bank would receive a percentage of the payments as its fee.

TABLE 24-3	Anatomy of an Interest Rate Swap			
ANTRON'S PAYMENTS: BORROWS FIXED, SWAPS FOR FLOATING			**BOSWORTH'S PAYMENTS: BORROWS FLOATING, SWAPS FOR FIXED**	
Payment to lender	−(LIBOR + 1%)		Payment to lender	−10.40% fixed
Payment from Bosworth	+(LIBOR + 1%)		Payment from Antron	+10.40% fixed
Payment to Bosworth	− 10.40% fixed		Payment to Antron	−(LIBOR + 1%)
Side payment received from Bosworth	+0.45% fixed		Side payment made to Antron	−0.45% fixed
Net payment by Antron	−9.95% fixed		Net payment by Bosworth	−(LIBOR + 1.45%)

Currency swaps are similar to interest rate swaps. To illustrate, suppose Company A, an American firm, had issued $100 million of dollar-denominated bonds in the United States to fund an investment in Germany. Meanwhile, Company G, a German firm, had issued $100 million of mark-denominated bonds in Germany to make an investment in the United States. Company A would earn marks but be required to make payments in dollars, and Company G would be in a reverse situation. Thus, both companies would be exposed to exchange rate risk. However, both companies' risks would be eliminated if they swapped payment obligations. As with interest rate swaps, differences in interest rates or credit risks would require side payments.

Originally, swaps were arranged between companies by money center banks, which would match up counterparties. Such matching still occurs, but today most swaps are between companies and banks, with the banks then taking steps to ensure that their own risks are hedged. For example, Citibank might arrange a swap with Company A, which would agree to make specified payments in marks to the bank, and the bank would make the dollar payments Company A would otherwise owe. Citibank would charge a fee for setting up the swap, and these charges would reflect the creditworthiness of Company A. To protect itself against exchange rate movements, the bank would hedge its position, either by lining up a German company which needed to make dollar payments or else by using currency futures.

Structured Notes

The term **structured note** often means a debt obligation which is derived from some other debt obligation. For example, in the early 1980s, investment bankers began buying large blocks of 30-year, noncallable Treasury bonds and then **stripping** them to create a series of zero coupon bonds. The zero with the shortest maturity was backed by the first interest payment on the T-bond issue, the second shortest zero was backed by the next interest payment, and so forth, on out to a 30-year zero backed by the last interest payment plus the maturity value of the T-bond. Zeros formed by stripping T-bonds were one of the first types of structured notes.

Another important type of structured note is backed by the interest and principal payments on mortgages. In the 1970s, Wall Street firms began to buy large packages of mortgages backed by federal agencies and then place these packages, or "pools," with a trustee. Then bonds called **Collateralized Mortgage Obligations (CMOs),** backed by the mortgage pool held in trust, were sold to pension funds, individuals for their IRA accounts, and other investors who were willing to invest in CMOs but who would not have purchased individual mortgages. This *securitization* of mortgages made billions of dollars of new capital available to home buyers.

CMOs are more difficult to evaluate than straight bonds for several reasons. First, the underlying mortgages can be prepaid at any time, and when this occurs the prepayment proceeds are used to retire part of the CMO debt itself. Therefore, the holder of a CMO is never sure when his or her bond will be called. This situation is further complicated by the fact that when interest rates decline, this causes bond prices to rise. However, declining rates also lead to mortgage prepayments, which cause the CMOs to be called especially rapidly.

It should also be noted that a variety of structured notes can be created, ranging from notes whose cash flows can be predicted with virtual certainty to other notes whose payment streams are highly uncertain. For example, investment bankers can (and do) create notes called **IOs** (for **Interest Only**), which provide cash flows from the interest component of the mortgage amortization payments, and **POs** (for **Principal Only**), which are paid from the principal repayment stream. In each case, the value of the note is found as the PV of an expected payment stream, but the length and size of the stream are uncertain. Suppose, for example, that you are offered an IO which you expect to provide payments of $100 for ten years (you expect the mortgages to be refinanced after ten years, at which time your payments will cease). Suppose further that you discount the expected payment stream at a rate of 10 percent and determine that the value is $614.46. You have $614.46 to invest, so you buy the IO, expecting to earn 10 percent on your money.

Now suppose interest rates decline. If rates fall, the discount rate would drop, and that would normally imply an increase in the IO's value. However, if rates decline sharply, this would lead to a rash of mortgage refinancings, in which case your payments, which come from interest only, would cease (or be greatly reduced), and the value of your IO would fall sharply. On the other hand, a sharp increase in interest rates would reduce refinancing, lengthen your expected payment stream, and probably increase the value of your IO.

Investment bankers can slice and dice a pool of mortgages into a bewildering array of structured notes, ranging from "plain vanilla" ones with highly predictable cash flows to "exotic" ones (sometimes called "toxic waste") whose risks are almost incalculable but are surely large.

Securitizing mortgages through CMOs serves a useful economic function—it provides an investment outlet for pension funds and others with money to invest, and it makes more money available to homeowners at a reasonable cost. Also, some investors want relatively safe investments, while others are willing to buy more speculative securities for the higher expected returns they provide. Structured notes permit a partitioning of risks to give investors what they want. There are dangers, though. The "toxic waste" is often bought by naive officials managing money for local governments like Orange County, California, when they really ought to be holding only safe securities.

Inverse Floaters

A floating rate note has an interest rate that rises and falls with some interest rate index. For example, the interest rate on a $100,000 note at prime plus 1 percent would be 9 percent when the prime rate is 8 percent, and the note's rate would move up and down with the prime rate. Since both the cash flows associated with the note and the discount rate used to value it rise and fall together, the market value of the note would be relatively stable.

With an **inverse floater,** the rate paid on the note moves counter to market rates. Thus, if interest rates in the economy rose, the interest rate paid on an inverse floater would fall, lowering its cash interest payments. At the same time, the discount rate used to value the inverse floater's cash flows would rise along with other rates. The combined effect of lower cash flows and a higher discount rate would lead to a very large decline in the value of the inverse floater. Thus, inverse floaters are exceptionally vulnerable to increases in interest rates. Of course, if interest rates fall, the value of an inverse floater will soar.

We have discussed the most important types of derivative securities, but certainly not all types. This discussion should, though, give you a good idea of how and why derivatives are created, and how they can be used and misused.

<table>
<tr><td>S E L F - T E S T
Q U E S T I O N S</td><td>Briefly describe the following types of derivative securities:
(1) Futures and forward contracts.
(2) Swaps.
(3) Structured notes.
(4) Inverse floaters.</td></tr>
</table>

RISK MANAGEMENT

As businesses become increasingly complex, it is becoming more and more difficult for CEOs and directors to know what problems might lie in wait. Therefore, companies need to have someone systematically look for potential problems and design safeguards to minimize potential damage. With this in mind, most larger firms have designated "risk managers" who report to the chief financial officer, while the CFOs of smaller firms personally assume risk management responsibilities. In any event, **risk management** is becoming increasingly important, and it is something finance students should understand. Therefore, in the remainder of this chapter we discuss the basics of risk management, with particular emphasis on how derivatives can be used to hedge financial risks.

FUNDAMENTALS OF RISK MANAGEMENT

It is useful to begin our discussion of risk management by defining some commonly used terms that describe different risks. Some of these risks can be mitigated, or managed, and that is what risk management is all about.

1. **Pure risks** are risks that offer only the prospect of a loss. Examples include the risk that a plant will be destroyed by fire or that a product liability suit will result in a large judgment against the firm.

2. **Speculative risks** are situations that offer the chance of a gain but might result in a loss. Thus, investments in new projects and marketable securities involve speculative risks.

3. **Demand risks** are associated with the demand for a firm's products or services. Because sales are essential to all businesses, demand risk is one of the most significant risks that firms face.

4. **Input risks** are risks associated with input costs, including both labor and materials. Thus, a company that uses copper as a raw material in its manufacturing process faces the risk that the cost of copper will increase and that it will not be able to pass this increase on to its customers.

**MICROSOFT'S GOAL:
MANAGE EVERY RISK!**

Twenty years ago, risk management meant buying insurance against fire, theft, and liability losses. Today, though, due to globalization, volatile markets, and a host of lawyers looking for someone to sue, a multitude of risks can adversely affect companies. Microsoft addressed these risks by creating a virtual consulting practice, called Microsoft Risk Co., to help manage the risks faced by its sales, operations, and product groups.

In a recent article in *CFO*, Scott Lange, head of Microsoft Risk, identified these 12 major sources of risk:

1. *Business partners* (interdependency, confidentiality, cultural conflict, contractual risks).
2. *Competition* (market share, price wars, industrial espionage, antitrust allegations, etc.).
3. *Customers* (product liability, credit risk, poor market timing, inadequate customer support).
4. *Distribution systems* (transportation, service availability, cost, dependence on distributors).
5. *Financial* (foreign exchange, portfolio, cash, interest rate, stock market).
6. *Operations* (facilities, contractual risks, natural hazards, internal processes and control).
7. *People* (employees, independent contractors, training, staffing inadequacy).
8. *Political* (civil unrest, war, terrorism, enforcement of intellectual property rights, change in leadership, revised economic policies).
9. *Regulatory and legislative* (antitrust, export licensing, jurisdiction, reporting and compliance, environmental).
10. *Reputations* (corporate image, brands, reputations of key employees).
11. *Strategic* (mergers and acquisitions, joint ventures and alliances, resource allocation and planning, organizational agility).
12. *Technological* (complexity, obsolescence, the year 2000 problem, workforce skill-sets).

According to Lange, it is important to resist the idea that risk should be categorized by how the insurance industry views it. Insurance coverage lines are a tiny subset of the risks a modern enterprise faces in the pursuit of its business objectives. He also defined the role of finance in risk management: The role of finance is to put on paper all the risks that can be identified and to try to quantify them. When possible, use a number—one number, perhaps, or a probability distribution. For example, what is the probability of losing $1 million on a product, or $10 million? At Microsoft, the finance department works with the product groups to determine the exposure. "We try to use common sense," Lange says.

In many ways risk management mirrors the quality movement of the 1980s and 1990s. The goal of the quality movement was to take the responsibility for quality out of a separate Quality Control Department and to make all managers and employees responsible for quality. Lange has a similar goal for Microsoft—to have risk management permeate the thinking of all Microsoft managers and employees.

SOURCE: Edward Teach, "Microsoft's Universe of Risk," *CFO*, March 1997, 69–72.

5. **Financial risks** are risks that result from financial transactions. As we have seen, if a firm plans to issue new bonds, it faces the risk that interest rates will rise before the bonds can be brought to market. Similarly, if the firm enters into contracts with foreign customers or suppliers, it faces the risk that fluctuations in exchange rates will result in unanticipated losses.

6. **Property risks** are associated with destruction of productive assets. Thus, the threat of fire, floods, and riots imposes property risks on a firm.

7. **Personnel risks** are risks that result from employees' actions. Examples include the risks associated with employee fraud or embezzlement, or suits based on charges of age or sex discrimination.

8. **Environmental risks** include risks associated with polluting the environment. Public awareness in recent years, coupled with the huge costs of environmental cleanup, has increased the importance of this risk.

9. **Liability risks** are associated with product, service, or employee actions. Examples include the very large judgments assessed against asbestos manufacturers and

some health care providers, as well as costs incurred as a result of improper actions of employees, such as driving corporate vehicles in a reckless manner.

10. **Insurable risks** are risks that can be covered by insurance. In general, property, personnel, environmental, and liability risks can be transferred to insurance companies. Note, though, that the *ability* to insure a risk does not necessarily mean that the risk *should be* insured. Indeed, a major function of risk management involves evaluating all alternatives for managing a particular risk, including self-insurance, and then choosing the optimal alternative.

Note that the risk classifications we used are somewhat arbitrary, and different classifications are commonly used in different industries. However, the list does give an idea of the wide variety of risks to which a firm can be exposed.

An Approach to Risk Management

Firms often use the following process for managing risks.

1. **Identify the risks faced by the firm.** Here the risk manager identifies the potential risks faced by his or her firm. (See the Microsoft box on page 930.)

2. **Measure the potential impact of each risk.** Some risks are so small as to be immaterial, whereas others have the potential for dooming the company. It is useful to segregate risks by potential impact and then to focus on the most serious threats.

3. **Decide how each relevant risk should be handled.** In most situations, risk exposure can be reduced through one of the following techniques:

    a. **Transfer the risk to an insurance company.** Often, it is advantageous to insure against, hence transfer, a risk. However, insurability does not necessarily mean that a risk should be covered by insurance. In many instances, it might be better for the company to *self-insure,* which means bearing the risk directly rather than paying another party to bear it.

    b. **Transfer the function that produces the risk to a third party.** For example, suppose a furniture manufacturer is concerned about potential liabilities arising from its ownership of a fleet of trucks used to transfer products from its manufacturing plant to various points across the country. One way to eliminate this risk would be to contract with a trucking company to do the shipping, thus passing the risks to a third party.

    c. **Purchase derivative contracts to reduce risk.** As we indicated earlier, firms use derivatives to hedge risks. Commodity derivatives can be used to reduce input risks. For example, a cereal company may use corn or wheat futures to hedge against increases in grain prices. Similarly, financial derivatives can be used to reduce risks that arise from changes in interest rates and exchange rates.

    d. **Reduce the probability of occurrence of an adverse event.** The expected loss arising from any risk is a function of both the probability of occurrence and the dollar loss if the adverse event occurs. In some instances, it is possible to reduce the probability that an adverse event will occur. For example, the probability that a fire will occur can be reduced by instituting a fire prevention program, by replacing old electrical wiring, and by using fire-resistant materials in areas with the greatest fire potential.

    e. **Reduce the magnitude of the loss associated with an adverse event.** Continuing with the fire risk example, the dollar cost associated with a fire can be reduced

BARINGS AND SUMITOMO SUFFER LARGE LOSSES IN THE DERIVATIVE MARKETS

Barings, a conservative English Bank with a long, impressive history dating back to its financing of the Louisiana Purchase in the 19th century, collapsed in 1995 when one of its traders lost $1.4 billion in derivatives trades. Nicholas Leeson, a 28-year-old trader in Barings' Singapore office, had speculated in Japanese stock index and interest rate futures without his superiors' knowledge. A lack of internal controls at the bank allowed him to accumulate large losses without being detected. Leeson's losses caught many by surprise, and they provided ammunition to those who argue that trading in derivatives should be more highly regulated if not sharply curtailed.

Most argue that the blame goes beyond Leeson—that both the bank and the exchanges were at fault for failing to provide sufficient oversight. For misreporting his trades, Leeson is currently serving a 6½-year sentence in a Singapore prison. What remained of Barings was ultimately sold to a Dutch banking concern.

Many analysts, including those who argued that the Barings episode was just an unsettling but isolated incident, were startled by a similar case a year and a half after the Barings debacle. In June 1996, Japan's Sumitomo Corporation disclosed that its well-respected chief copper trader, Yasuo Hamanaka, had been conducting unauthorized speculative trades for more than a decade. The cumulative loss on these trades was $2.6 billion. Hamanaka has been indicted on charges of fraud and forgery.

These two events illustrate both the dangers of derivatives and the importance of internal controls. While it is unsettling to learn that the actions of a single, relatively low-level employee can suddenly cripple a giant corporation, these losses should be placed in perspective. The overwhelming majority of firms that use derivatives have been successful in enhancing performance and/or reducing risk. For this reason, most analysts argue that it would be a huge mistake to use the rare instances where fraud occurred to limit a market which has, for the most part, been a resounding success. However, given the volume of business in this market, we can in the future expect to see other problems similar to those encountered by Barings and Sumitomo.

by such actions as installing sprinkler systems, designing facilities with self-contained fire zones, and locating facilities close to a fire station.

f. **Totally avoid the activity that gives rise to the risk.** For example, a company might discontinue a product or service line because the risks outweigh the rewards, as with the recent decision by Dow-Corning to discontinue its manufacture of silicon breast implants.

Note that risk management decisions, like all corporate decisions, should be based on a cost/benefit analysis for each feasible alternative. For example, suppose it would cost $50,000 per year to conduct a comprehensive fire safety training program for all personnel in a high-risk plant. Presumably, this program would reduce the expected value of future fire losses. An alternative to the training program would be to place $50,000 annually in a reserve fund set aside to cover future fire losses. Both alternatives involve expected cash flows, and from an economic standpoint the choice should be made on the basis of the lowest present value of future costs. Thus, the same financial management techniques applied to other corporate decisions can also be applied to risk management decisions. Note, though, that if a fire occurs and a life is lost, the trade-off between fire prevention and expected losses may not sit well with a jury. The same thing holds true for product liability, as Ford, GM, and others have learned.

The Extension to this chapter describes ways in which companies can use insurance to manage certain types of risks, such as property and liability loss exposure. Also, some types of interest rate risk can be managed through the use of immunization, a financial technique that does not require the use of derivatives, and the Extension also describes immunization techniques. The remainder of this chapter focuses on the use of derivatives to manage risk.

Define the following terms:
  (1) Pure risks.
  (2) Speculative risks.
  (3) Demand risks.
  (4) Input risks.
  (5) Financial risks.
  (6) Property risks.
  (7) Personnel risks.
  (8) Environmental risks.
  (9) Liability risks.
  (10) Insurable risks.
  (11) Self-insurance.

Should a firm insure itself against all of the insurable risks it faces? Explain.

USING DERIVATIVES TO REDUCE RISKS

Firms are subject to numerous risks related to interest rate, stock price, and exchange rate fluctuations in the financial markets. For an investor, one of the most obvious ways to reduce financial risks is to hold a broadly diversified portfolio of stocks and debt securities, including international securities and debt of varying maturities. However, derivatives can also be used to reduce the risks associated with financial and commodity markets.[13]

Hedging with Futures

Information from the CBOT on the financial market futures they trade is available at http://www.cbot.com. The site provides some general information on the various types of financial market instruments which are available and provides information on how to order specific literature or the CBOT's publication catalog.

One of the most useful tools for reducing interest rate, exchange rate, and commodity risk is to hedge in the futures markets. Most financial and real asset transactions occur in what is known as the *spot,* or *cash, market,* where the asset is delivered immediately (or within a few days). *Futures,* or *futures contracts,* on the other hand, call for the purchase or sale of an asset at some future date, but at a price which is fixed today.

In 1997, futures contracts were available on more than 30 real and financial assets traded on 14 U.S. exchanges, the largest of which are the Chicago Board of Trade (CBOT) and the Chicago Mercantile Exchange (CME). Futures contracts are divided into two classes, **commodity futures** and **financial futures.** Commodity futures, which cover oil, various grains, oilseeds, livestock, meats, fibers, metals, and wood, were first traded in the United States in the mid-1800s. Financial futures, which were first traded in 1975, include Treasury bills, notes, bonds, certificates of deposit, Eurodollar deposits, foreign currencies, and stock indexes.

You can obtain daily closing prices on Treasury bond futures and other types of futures contracts from the web site of Ira Epstein & Company at http://www.iepstein.com/quotes.html.

To illustrate how futures contracts work, consider the CBOT's contract on Treasury bonds. The basic contract is for $100,000 of a hypothetical 8 percent coupon, semiannual payment Treasury bond with 20 years to maturity. Table 24-4 shows an extract from the Treasury bond futures table which appeared in the November 13, 1997, issue of *The Wall Street Journal.*

The first column gives the delivery month; the next three columns give the opening, high, and low prices for that contract on that day. The opening price for the December future, 117-28, means 117 plus 28/32, or 117.875 percent of par. Column 5 gives the settlement price, which is typically the price at the close of trading. Column 6 reports

---

[13]In Chapter 27, we discuss both the risks involved with holding foreign currencies and procedures for reducing such risks.

TABLE 24-4	Futures Prices

Treasury Bonds (CBT) — $100,000; pts. 32nds of 100%

Delivery Month (1)	Open (2)	High (3)	Low (4)	Settle (5)	Change (6)	Lifetime High (7)	Lifetime Low (8)	Open Interest (9)
Dec	117-28	118-13	117-22	118-05	+7	119-02	100-08	591,944
Mar	108-03	118-03	117-13	117-25	+8	118-24	104-21	120,353
June	117-03	117-17	117-03	117-17	+8	118-02	104-03	13,597

SOURCE: *The Wall Street Journal*, November 13, 1997, C18.

the change in the settlement price from the preceding day — the December contract rose by 7/32. Columns 7 and 8 give the life-of-contract highs and lows. Finally, Column 9 shows the "open interest," which is the number of contracts outstanding.

To illustrate, we focus on the Treasury bonds for June delivery. The settlement price was 117-17, or 117 plus 17/32 percent of the $100,000 contract value. Thus, the price at which one could buy $100,000 face value of 8 percent, 20-year Treasury bonds to be delivered in June was 117.53125 percent of par, or 1.1753125($100,000) = $117,531.25. The contract price increased by 8/32 of 1 percent of $100,000, or by $250, from the previous day, so if you had bought the contract yesterday, you would have made $250. Over its life, the contract's price has ranged from 104.09375 to 118.0625, and there were 13,597 contracts outstanding, representing a total value of about $1.6 billion.

Note that the contract increased by 8/32 of a percent on this particular day. Why would the value of the bond futures contract increase? Since bond prices increase when interest rates fall, we know that interest rates fell on that day. Moreover, we can calculate the implied rates inherent in the futures contracts. (*The Wall Street Journal* formerly provided the implied yields, but now one must calculate them.) Recall that the contract relates to a hypothetical 20-year, semiannual payment, 8 percent coupon bond. The closing price (settlement price) was 117 and 17/32, or 117.53125 percent of par. Using a financial calculator, we can solve for k_d in the following equation:

$$\$1,175.3125 = \sum_{t=1}^{40} \frac{\$40}{(1 + k_d/2)^t} + \frac{\$1,000}{(1 + k_d/2)^{40}}.$$

The solution value for the six-month rate is 3.215, which is equivalent to a nominal annual rate of 6.430 percent. Since the price of the bond rose by 8/32 that day, we could find the previous day's closing (settlement) price and its implied interest rate, which would turn out to be 6.450 percent. Therefore, interest rates fell by 2 basis points, which was enough to increase the value of the contract by $250.00.

Thus, the futures contract for June delivery of this hypothetical bond sold for $117,531.25 for 100 bonds with a par value of $100,000, which translates to a yield to maturity of about 6.4 percent. This yield reflects investors' beliefs about what the interest rate level will be in June. The spot yield on T-bonds was about 6.2 percent at the time, so the marginal trader in the futures market was predicting a 20-basis-point increase in yields over the next seven months. That prediction could, of course, turn out to be incorrect.

Now suppose that three months later interest rates in the futures market had fallen from the earlier levels, say, from 6.4 to 5.9 percent. Falling interest rates mean rising bond prices, and we could calculate that the June contract would then be worth about $124,468. Thus, the contract's value would have increased by $124,468 − $117.531 = $6,937.

When futures contracts are purchased, the purchaser does not have to put up the full amount of the purchase price; rather, the purchaser is required to post an initial *margin,* which for CBT Treasury bond contracts is $3,000 per $100,000 contract. However, investors are required to maintain a certain value in the margin account, called a *maintenance margin.* If the value of the contract declines, then the owner may be required to add additional funds to the margin account, and the more the contract value falls, the more money must be added. The value of the contract is checked at the end of every working day, and margin account adjustments are made at that time. This is called "marking to market." If an investor purchased our illustrative contract and then sold it later for $124,468, he or she would have made a profit of $6,937 on a $3,000 investment, or a return of over 200 percent in only three months. It is clear, therefore, that futures contracts offer a considerable amount of leverage. Of course, if interest rates had risen, then the value of the contract would have declined, and the investor could easily have lost his or her $3,000, or more. Futures contracts are never settled by delivery of the securities involved. Rather, the transaction is completed by reversing the trade, which amounts to selling the contract back to the original seller.[14] The actual gains and losses on the contract are realized when the futures contract is closed.

Futures contracts and options are similar to one another—so similar that people often confuse the two. Therefore, it is useful to compare the two instruments. A *futures contract* is a definite agreement on the part of one party to buy something on a specific date and at a specific price, and the other party agrees to sell on the same terms. No matter how low or how high the price goes, the two parties must settle the contract at the agreed-upon price. An *option,* on the other hand, gives someone the right to buy (call) or sell (put) an asset, but the holder of the option does not have to complete the transaction. Note also that options exist both for individual stocks and for "bundles" of stocks such as those in the S&P and *Value Line* indexes, but generally not for commodities. Futures, on the other hand, are used for commodities, debt securities, and stock indexes. The two types of instruments can be used for the same purposes. One is not necessarily better or worse than another—they are simply different.

Security Price Exposure

Firms are obviously exposed to losses due to changes in security prices when securities are held in investment portfolios, and they are also exposed during times when securities are being issued. In addition, firms are exposed to risk if they use floating rate debt to finance an investment that produces a fixed income stream. Risks such as these can often be mitigated by using derivatives. As we discussed earlier, derivatives are securities whose value stems, or is derived, from the values of other assets. Thus, options and futures contracts are derivatives, because their values depend on the prices of some underlying asset. Now we will explore further the use of two types of derivatives, futures and swaps, to help manage certain types of risk.

---

[14]The buyers and sellers of most financial futures contracts do not actually trade with one another—each trader's contractual obligation is with a futures exchange. This feature helps to guarantee the fiscal integrity of the trade. Incidentally, commodities futures traded on the exchanges are settled in the same way as financial futures, but in the case of commodities much of the contracting is done off the exchange, between farmers and processors, as *forward contracts,* in which case actual deliveries occur.

Futures.   Futures are used for both speculation and hedging. **Speculation** involves betting on future price movements, and futures are used because of the leverage inherent in the contract. **Hedging,** on the other hand, is done by a firm or individual to protect against a price change that would otherwise negatively affect profits. For example, rising interest rates and commodity (raw material) prices can hurt profits, as can adverse currency fluctuations. If two parties have mirror-image risks, then they can enter into a transaction that eliminates, as opposed to transfers, risks. This is a "natural hedge." Of course, one party to a futures contract could be a speculator, the other a hedger. Thus, to the extent that speculators broaden the market and make hedging possible, they help decrease risk to those who seek to avoid it.

There are two basic types of hedges: (1) **long hedges,** in which futures contracts are *bought* in anticipation of (or to guard against) price increases, and (2) **short hedges,** where a firm or individual *sells* futures contracts to guard against price declines. Recall that rising interest rates lower bond prices and thus decrease the value of bond futures contracts. Therefore, if a firm or individual needs to guard against an *increase* in interest rates, a futures contract that makes money if rates rise should be used. That means selling, or going short, on a futures contract. To illustrate, assume that in January Carson Foods is considering a plan to issue $10,000,000 of 20-year bonds in June to finance a capital expenditure program. The interest rate would be 10 percent if the bonds were issued today, and at that rate the project would have a positive NPV. However, interest rates may rise over the next five months, and when the issue is actually sold, the interest rate might be substantially above 10 percent, which would make the project a bad investment. Carson can protect itself against a rise in rates by hedging in the futures market.

In this situation, Carson would be hurt by an increase in interest rates, so it would use a short hedge. It would choose a futures contract on that security most similar to the one it plans to issue, long-term bonds. In this case, Carson would probably hedge with Treasury bond futures. Since it plans to issue $10,000,000 of bonds, it would sell $10,000,000/$100,000 = 100 Treasury bond contracts for delivery in June. Carson would have to put up 100($3,000) = $300,000 in margin money and also pay brokerage commissions. For illustrative purposes we use the numbers in Table 24-4. We can see from Table 24-4 that each June contract has a value of 117 plus 17/32 percent, so the total value of the 100 contracts is 1.1753125($100,000)(100) = $11,753,125. Now suppose renewed fears of inflation push the interest rate on Carson's debt up by 100 basis points, to 11 percent, over the next five months. If Carson issued 10 percent coupon bonds, they would bring only $920 per bond, because investors now require an 11 percent return. Thus, Carson would lose $80 per bond times 10,000 bonds, or $800,000, as a result of delaying the financing. However, the increase in interest rates would also bring about a change in the value of Carson's short position in the futures market. Since interest rates have increased, the value of the futures contract would fall, and if the interest rate on the futures contract also increased by the same full percentage point, from 6.43 to 7.43 percent, the contract value would fall to $10,588,831. Carson would then close its position in the futures market by repurchasing for $10,588,831 the contracts which it earlier sold short for $11,753,125, giving it a profit of $1,164,294, less commissions.

Thus, Carson would, if we ignore commissions and the opportunity cost of the margin money, offset the loss on the bond issue. In fact, in our example Carson more than offsets the loss, pocketing an additional $364,294. Of course, if interest rates had fallen, Carson would have lost on its futures position, but this loss would have been offset by the fact that Carson could now sell its bonds with a lower coupon.

If futures contracts existed on Carson's own debt, and interest rates moved identically in the spot and futures markets, then the firm could construct a **perfect hedge,** in which gains on the futures contract would exactly offset losses on the bonds. In reality, it is virtually impossible to construct perfect hedges, because in most cases the underlying asset is not identical to the futures asset, and even when they are, prices (and interest rates) may not move exactly together in the spot and futures markets.

Note too that if Carson had been planning an equity offering, and if its stock tended to move fairly closely with one of the stock indexes, the company could have hedged against falling stock prices by selling short the index future. Even better, if options on Carson's stock were traded in the option market, then it could use options rather than futures to hedge against falling stock prices.

The futures and options markets permit flexibility in the timing of financial transactions, because the firm can be protected, at least partially, against changes that occur between the time a decision is reached and the time when the transaction will be completed. However, this protection has a cost — the firm must pay commissions. Whether or not the protection is worth the cost is a matter of judgment. The decision to hedge also depends on management's risk aversion as well as the company's strength and ability to assume the risk in question. In theory, the reduction in risk resulting from a hedge transaction should have a value exactly equal to the cost of the hedge. Thus, a firm should be indifferent to hedging. However, many firms believe that hedging is worthwhile. Trammell Crow, a large Texas real estate developer, recently used T-bill futures to lock in interest costs on floating rate construction loans, while Dart & Kraft used Eurodollar futures to protect its marketable securities portfolio. Merrill Lynch, Salomon Brothers, and the other investment banking houses hedge in the futures and options markets to protect themselves when they are engaged in major underwritings.

Swaps.   A *swap* is another method for reducing financial risks. As we noted earlier, a swap is an exchange.[15] In finance, it is an exchange of cash payment obligations, in which each party to the swap prefers the payment type or pattern of the other party. In other words, swaps occur because the counterparties prefer the terms of the other's debt contract, and the swap enables each party to obtain a preferred payment obligation. Generally, one party has a fixed rate obligation and the other a floating rate obligation, or one has an obligation denominated in one currency and the other in another currency.

Major changes have occurred over time in the swaps market. First, standardized contracts have been developed for the most common types of swaps, and this has had two effects: (1) Standardized contracts lower the time and effort involved in arranging swaps, and thus lower transactions costs. (2) The development of standardized contracts has led to a secondary market for swaps, which has increased the liquidity and efficiency of the swaps market. A number of international banks now make markets in swaps and offer quotes on several standard types. Also, as noted above, the banks now take counterparty positions in swaps, so it is not necessary to find another firm with mirror-image needs before a swap transaction can be completed. The bank would generally find a final counterparty for the swap at a later date, so its positioning helps make the swap market more operationally efficient.[16]

---

[15]For more information on swaps, see Clifford W. Smith, Jr., Charles W. Smithson, and Lee Macdonald Wakeman, "The Evolving Market for Swaps," *Midland Corporate Finance Journal,* Winter 1986, 20–32; and Mary E. Ruth and Steve R. Vinson, "Managing Interest Rate Uncertainty amidst Change," *Public Utilities Fortnightly,* December 22, 1988, 28–31.

[16]The role of banks in the global swap market is worrisome to the Federal Reserve and other central banks. When banks take positions in swaps, they are themselves exposed to various risks, and if the counterparties cannot meet their obligations, a bank could suddenly become liable for making two sets of payments. Further, swaps are "off balance sheet" transactions, so it is currently impossible to tell just how large the swap market is or who has what obligation. The fear is that if one large multinational bank gets into trouble, the entire worldwide swap market could collapse like a house of cards. See "Swap Fever: Big Money, Big Risks," *Fortune,* June 1, 1992.

To further illustrate a swap transaction, consider the following situation. An electric utility currently has outstanding a five-year floating rate note tied to the prime rate. The prime rate could rise significantly over the period, so the note carries a high degree of interest rate risk. The utility could, however, enter into a swap with a counterparty, say, Citibank, wherein the utility would pay Citibank a fixed series of interest payments over the five-year period, and Citibank would make the company's required floating rate payments. As a result, the utility would have converted a floating rate loan to a fixed rate loan, and the risk of rising interest rates would have been passed from the utility to Citibank. Such a transaction can lower both parties' risks — because banks' revenues rise as interest rates rise, Citibank's risk would actually be lower if it had floating rate obligations.

Longer-term swaps can also be made. Recently, Citibank entered into a 17-year swap in an electricity cogeneration project financing deal. The project's sponsors were unable to obtain fixed rate financing on reasonable terms, and they were afraid that interest rates would increase and make the project unprofitable. The project's sponsors were, however, able to borrow from local banks on a floating rate basis and then arrange a simultaneous swap with Citibank for a fixed rate obligation.

Commodity Price Exposure

As we noted earlier, futures markets were established for many commodities long before they began to be used for financial instruments. We can use Porter Electronics, which uses large quantities of copper as well as several precious metals, to illustrate inventory hedging. Suppose that in May 1998, Porter foresaw a need for 100,000 pounds of copper in March 1999 for use in fulfilling a fixed price contract to supply solar power cells to the U.S. government. Porter's managers are concerned that a strike by Chilean copper miners will occur, which could raise the price of copper in world markets and possibly turn the expected profit on the solar cells into a loss.

Porter could, of course, go ahead and buy the copper that it will need to fulfill the contract, but if it does it will incur substantial carrying costs. As an alternative, the company could hedge against increasing copper prices in the futures market. The New York Commodity Exchange trades standard copper futures contracts of 25,000 pounds each. Thus, Porter could buy four contracts (go long) for delivery in March 1999. Assume that these contracts were trading in May for about $1.00 per pound, and that the spot price at that date was about $1.02 per pound. If copper prices do rise appreciably over the next ten months, the value of Porter's long position in copper futures would increase, thus offsetting some of the price increase in the commodity itself. Of course, if copper prices fall, Porter would lose money on its futures contract, but the company would be buying the copper on the spot market at a cheaper price, so it would make a higher-than-anticipated profit on its sale of solar cells. Thus, hedging in the copper futures market locks in the cost of raw materials and removes some risk to which the firm would otherwise be exposed.

Eastman Kodak uses silver futures to hedge against short-term increases in the price of silver, which is the primary ingredient in black-and-white film. Many other manufacturers, such as Alcoa with aluminum and Archer Daniels Midland with grains, routinely use the futures markets to reduce the risks associated with input price volatility.

The Use and Misuse of Derivatives

Most of the news stories about derivatives are related to financial disasters. Much less is heard about the benefits of derivatives. However, because of these benefits, more than 90 percent of large U.S. companies use derivatives on a regular basis. Moreover, according to McKinsey & Company, by the year 2000 it will be necessary for all CFOs to understand derivatives to do their job well. Even now, sophisticated investors and analysts are demanding that firms use derivatives to hedge certain risks. For example, Compaq Computer was recently sued by a shareholder group for failing to properly hedge its foreign exchange exposure. The shareholders lost the suit, but Compaq got the message and now uses currency futures to hedge its international operations. In another example, Prudential Securities reduced its earnings estimate for Cone Mills, a North Carolina textile company, because Cone did not sufficiently hedge its exposure to changing cotton prices. These examples lead to one conclusion: if a company can safely and inexpensively hedge its risks, it should do so.

There can, however, be a downside to the use of derivatives. Hedging is invariably cited by authorities as a "good" use of derivatives, whereas speculating with derivatives is often cited as a "bad" use. Some people and organizations can afford to bear the risks involved in speculating with derivatives, but others are either not sufficiently knowledgeable about the risks they are taking or else should not be taking those risks in the first place. Most would agree that the typical corporation should use derivatives only to hedge risks, not to speculate in an effort to increase profits. Hedging allows managers to concentrate on running their core businesses without having to worry about interest rate, currency, and commodity price variability. However, problems can arise quickly when hedges are improperly constructed or when a corporate treasurer, eager to report relatively high returns, uses derivatives for speculative purposes.

One interesting example of a derivatives debacle involved Kashima Oil, a Japanese firm that imports oil. It pays with U.S. dollars but then sells oil in the Japanese market for yen. Kashima began by using currency futures to hedge, but then it started to speculate on dollar-yen price movements, hoping to increase profits. When the currency markets moved against Kashima's speculative position, lax accounting rules permitted it to avoid reporting the losses by simply rolling over the contract. By the time Kashima bit the bullet and closed its position, it had lost $1.5 billion. Other companies have experienced similar problems.

Our position is that derivatives can and should be used to hedge against certain risks, but that the leverage inherent in derivatives contracts makes them potentially dangerous instruments. Also, CFOs, CEOs, and board members should be reasonably knowledgeable about the derivatives their firms use, should establish policies regarding when they can and cannot be used, and should establish audit procedures to ensure that the policies are actually carried out. Moreover, a firm's derivatives position should be reported to stockholders, because stockholders have a right to know when situations such as that involving P&G or Kashima might arise.

SELF-TEST QUESTIONS

What is a futures contract?

Explain how a company can use the futures market to hedge against rising interest rates.

What is a swap? Describe the mechanics of a fixed rate to floating rate swap.

Explain how a company can use the futures market to hedge against rising raw materials prices.

How should derivatives be used in risk management? What problems can occur?

SUMMARY

This chapter provided an introduction to derivative securities and corporate risk management. The key concepts covered are listed below:

- There are six reasons **risk management** might increase the value of a firm. Risk management allows corporations (1) to increase their **use of debt,** (2) to maintain their **capital budget** over time, (3) to avoid costs associated with **financial distress,** (4) to utilize their **comparative advantages in hedging** relative to the hedging ability of individual investors, (5) to reduce both the risks and costs of borrowing by using **swaps,** and (6) to reduce the **higher taxes** that result from fluctuating earnings.

- **Derivatives** are securities whose values are determined by the market price or interest rate of some other security.

- A **hedge** is a transaction which lowers risk. A **natural hedge** is a transaction between two **counterparties** where both parties' risks are reduced.

- **Options** are financial instruments that (1) are created by exchanges rather than firms, (2) are bought and sold primarily by investors, and (3) are of importance to both investors and financial managers.

- The two primary types of options are (1) **call options,** which give the holder the right to purchase a specified asset at a given price (the **exercise,** or **strike, price**) for a given period of time, and (2) **put options,** which give the holder the right to sell an asset at a given price for a given period of time.

- A call option's **exercise value** is defined as the current price of the stock less the strike price.

- The **Black-Scholes Option Pricing Model (OPM)** can be used to estimate the value of a call option.

- A **futures contract** is a standardized contract that is traded on an exchange and is "marked to market" daily, but where physical delivery of the underlying asset usually does not occur.

- Under a **forward contract,** one party agrees to buy a commodity at a specific price and a specific future date and the other party agrees to make the sale. Delivery does occur.

- A **structured note** is a debt obligation derived from another debt obligation.

- A **swap** is an exchange of cash payment obligations. Swaps occur because the parties involved prefer someone else's payment stream.

- In general, **risk management** involves the management of unpredictable events that have adverse consequences for the firm.

- The three steps in risk management are as follows: (1) **identify** the risks faced by the company, (2) **measure** the potential impacts of these risks, and (3) **decide** how each relevant risk should be dealt with.

- In most situations, risk exposure can be dealt with by one or more of the following techniques: (1) **transfer the risk** to an insurance company, (2) **transfer the function** that produces the risk to a third party, (3) **purchase derivative contracts,** (4) **reduce the probability** of occurrence of an adverse event, (5) **reduce the magnitude** of the loss associated with an adverse event, and (6) totally **avoid** the activity that gives rise to the risk.

- **Financial futures** markets permit firms to create **hedge** positions to protect themselves against fluctuating interest rates, stock prices, and exchange rates.

- **Commodity futures** can be used to hedge against input price increases.

- **Long hedges** involve buying futures contracts to guard against price increases.

- **Short hedges** involve selling futures contracts to guard against price declines.

- A **perfect hedge** occurs when the gain or loss on the hedged transaction exactly offsets the loss or gain on the unhedged position.

Questions

24-1   Define each of the following terms:
a.   Derivative
b.   Option; call option; put option
c.   Exercise value; strike price
d.   Black-Scholes Option Pricing Model
e.   Corporate risk management
f.   Financial futures; forward contract
g.   Hedging; natural hedge; long hedges; short hedges; perfect hedge
h.   Swap; structured note
i.   Commodity futures

24-2   Give two reasons stockholders might be indifferent between owning the stock of a firm with volatile cash flows and that of a firm with stable cash flows.

24-3   List six reasons risk management might increase the value of a firm.

24-4   Why do options typically sell at prices higher than their exercise values?

24-5   Discuss some of the techniques available to reduce risk exposures.

24-6   Explain how the futures markets can be used to reduce interest rate and input price risk.

24-7   How can swaps be used to reduce the risks associated with debt contracts?

Self-Test Problems   (Solutions Appear in Appendix B)

ST-1   A call option on the stock of Bedrock Boulders has a market price of $7. The stock sells for $30
Options   a share, and the option has an exercise price of $25 a share.
a.   What is the exercise value of the call option?
b.   What is the premium on the option?

ST-2   Which of the following events are likely to increase the market value of a call option on a com-
Options   mon stock? Explain.
a.   An increase in the stock's price.
b.   An increase in the volatility of the stock price.
c.   An increase in the risk-free rate.
d.   A decrease in the time until the option expires.

Problems

24-1   Assume you have been given the following information on Purcell Industries:
Black-Scholes Model

Current stock price = $15	Exercise price of option = $15
Time to maturity of option = 6 months	Risk-free rate = 10%
Variance of stock price = 0.12	$d_1 = 0.32660$
$d_2 = 0.08165$	$N(d_1) = 0.62795$
$N(d_2) = 0.53252$	

Using the Black-Scholes Option Pricing Model, what would be the value of the option?

24-2   The exercise price on one of Flanagan Company's options is $15, its exercise value is $22, and its
Options   premium is $5. What are the option's market value and the price of the stock?

24-3   What is the implied interest rate on a Treasury bond ($100,000) futures contract that settled at
Futures   100-16? If interest rates increased by 1 percent, what would be the contract's new value?

24-4   The Zinn Company plans to issue $10,000,000 of 10-year bonds in June to help finance a new
Hedging   research and development laboratory. It is now November, and the current cost of debt to the high-risk biotech company is 11 percent. However, the firm's financial manager is concerned that interest rates will climb even higher in coming months.
a.   Use data in Table 24-4 to create a hedge against rising interest rates.
b.   Assume that interest rates in general increase by 200 basis points. How well did your hedge perform?
c.   What is a perfect hedge? Are most real-world hedges perfect? Explain.

Spreadsheet Problem

Work the problem in this section only if you are using the computer problem diskette.

24-5
Options
Use the model in File C24 to solve this problem. Considine Software Corporation (CSC) options are actively traded on one of the regional exchanges. CSC's current stock price is $10, with a 0.16 instantaneous variance of returns. The current 6-month risk-free rate is 12 percent.

   a. What is the value of CSC's 6-month option with an exercise price of $10 according to the Black-Scholes model?

   b. What would be the effect on the option price if CSC redeployed its assets and thereby reduced its variance of returns to 0.09?

   c. Assume that CSC returns to its initial asset structure; that is, its stock return variance is 0.16. Now assume that CSC's current stock price is $15. What effect does the stock price increase have on the option value?

   d. Return to base-case (Part a) values. Now assume that the strike price is $15. What is the new option value?

MINI CASE

Assume that you have just been hired as a financial analyst by Tropical Sweets Inc., a mid-sized California company that specializes in creating exotic candies from tropical fruits such as mangoes, papayas, and dates. The firm's CEO, George Yamaguchi, recently returned from an industry corporate executive conference in San Francisco, and one of the sessions he attended was on the pressing need for smaller companies to institute corporate risk management programs. Since no one at Tropical Sweets is familiar with the basics of derivatives and corporate risk management, Yamaguchi has asked you to prepare a brief report that the firm's executives could use to gain at least a cursory understanding of the topics.

To begin, you gathered some outside materials on derivatives and corporate risk management and used these materials to draft a list of pertinent questions that need to be answered. In fact, one possible approach to the paper is to use a question-and-answer format. Now that the questions have been drafted, you have to develop the answers.

   a. Why might stockholders be indifferent whether or not a firm reduces the volatility of its cash flows?

   b. What are six reasons risk management might increase the value of a corporation?

   c. What is an option? What is the single most important characteristic of an option?

   d. Options have a unique set of terminology. Define the following terms:
      (1) Call option
      (2) Put option
      (3) Exercise price
      (4) Striking, or strike, price
      (5) Option price
      (6) Expiration date
      (7) Exercise value
      (8) Covered option
      (9) Naked option
      (10) In-the-money call
      (11) Out-of-the-money call
      (12) LEAP

   e. Consider Tropical Sweets' call option with a $25 strike price. The following table contains historical values for this option at different stock prices:

STOCK PRICE	CALL OPTION PRICE
$25	$ 3.00
30	7.50
35	12.00
40	16.50
45	21.00
50	25.50

     (1) Create a table which shows (a) stock price, (b) strike price, (c) exercise value, (d) option price, and (e) the premium of option price over exercise value.
     (2) What happens to the premium of option price over exercise value as the stock price rises? Why?
f. In 1973, Fischer Black and Myron Scholes developed the Black-Scholes Option Pricing Model (OPM).
     (1) What assumptions underlie the OPM?
     (2) Write out the three equations that constitute the model.
     (3) What is the value of the following call option according to the OPM?

$$\text{Stock price} = \$27.00$$

$$\text{Exercise price} = \$25.00$$

$$\text{Time to expiration} = 6 \text{ months}$$

$$\text{Risk-free rate} = 6.0\%$$

$$\text{Stock return variance} = 0.11$$

g. What impact does each of the following call option parameters have on the value of a call option?
     (1) Current stock price
     (2) Exercise price
     (3) Option's term to maturity
     (4) Risk-free rate
     (5) Variability of the stock price
h. What is corporate risk management? Why is it important to all firms?
i. Risks that firms face can be categorized in many ways. Define the following types of risk:
     (1) Speculative risks
     (2) Pure risks
     (3) Demand risks
     (4) Input risks
     (5) Financial risks
     (6) Property risks
     (7) Personnel risks
     (8) Environmental risks
     (9) Liability risks
     (10) Insurable risks
j. What are the three steps of corporate risk management?
k. What are some actions that companies can take to minimize or reduce risk exposures?
l. What is financial risk exposure? Describe the following concepts and techniques that can be used to reduce financial risks:
     (1) Derivatives
     (2) Futures markets
     (3) Hedging
     (4) Swaps
m. Describe how commodity futures markets can be used to reduce input price risk.

Selected Additional References

For additional insights into the use of financial futures for hedging, see the following publications:

Bacon, Peter W., and Richard Williams, "Interest Rate Futures Trading: A New Tool for the Financial Manager," *Financial Management,* Spring 1976, 32–38.

Blake, Marshall, and Nelda Mahady, "How Mid-Sized Companies Manage Risk," *Journal of Applied Corporate Finance,* Spring 1991, 59–65.

Block, Stanley B., and Timothy J. Gallagher, "The Use of Interest Rate Futures and Options by Corporate Managers," *Financial Management,* Autumn 1986, 73–78.

Castelino, Mark G., Jack C. Francis, and Avner Wolf, "Cross-Hedging: Basis Risk and Choice of the Optimal Hedging Vehicle," *Financial Review,* May 1991, 179–210.

Kolb, Robert W., *Understanding Futures Markets* (Glenview, Ill.: Scott, Foresman, 1985).

McCabe, George M., and Charles T. Franckle, "The Effectiveness of Rolling the Hedge Forward in the Treasury Bill Futures Market," *Financial Management,* Summer 1983, 21–29.

Siegel, Daniel R., and Diane F. Siegel, *Futures Markets* (Hinsdale, Ill.: Dryden Press, 1990).

For information on hedging, see

Dolde, Walter, "The Trajectory of Corporate Financial Risk Management," *Journal of Applied Corporate Finance,* Fall 1993, 33–41.

——, "Hedging, Leverage, and Primitive Risk," *Journal of Financial Engineering,* Vol. 4, No. 2.

Marshall, John F., Vipul K. Bansal, Anthony F. Herbst, and Alan L. Tucker, "Hedging Business Cycle Risk with Macro Swaps and Options," *Journal of Applied Corporate Finance,* Winter 1992, 103–108.

For more information on swaps, see

Brown, Keith C., and Donald J. Smith, "Default Risk and Innovations in the Design of Interest Rate Swaps," *Financial Management,* Summer 1993, 94–105.

Einzig, Robert, and Bruce Lange, "Swaps at Transamerica: Applications and Analysis," *Journal of Applied Corporate Finance,* Winter 1990, 48–58.

Goodman, Laurie S., "The Uses of Interest Rate Swaps in Managing Corporate Liabilities," *Journal of Applied Corporate Finance,* Winter 1990, 35–47.

The original Black-Scholes article tested the OPM to see how well predicted prices conformed to market values. For additional empirical tests, see

Galai, Dan, "Tests of Market Efficiency of the Chicago Board Options Exchange," *Journal of Business,* April 1977, 167–197.

Gultekin, N. Bulent, Richard J. Rogalski, and Seha M. Tinic, "Option Pricing Model Estimates: Some Empirical Results," *Financial Management,* Spring 1982, 58–69.

MacBeth, James D., and Larry J. Merville, "An Empirical Examination of the Black-Scholes Call Option Pricing Model," *Journal of Finance,* December 1979, 1173–1186.

Much of the Fall 1993 issue of the Journal of Applied Corporate Finance *is devoted to risk management issues.*

For more information on the derivatives markets, see

Chance, Don M., *An Introduction to Derivatives* (Fort Worth, Tex.: Dryden Press, 1995).

Chapman, Alger B. "Duke," "Future of the Derivatives Markets: Products, Technology, and Participants," *Financial Practice and Education,* Fall/Winter 1994, 124–128.

EXTENSIONS

Risk Management with Insurance and Bond Portfolio Immunization

In the main body of the chapter, we explained risk management techniques that employed derivative securities. We discuss two alternative techniques for managing risk in this Extension — insurance and bond portfolio immunization.

Corporate Insurance Programs. The first step in a corporate insurance program is to identify all potential losses, and the second step is to assess their likelihoods of occurrence and loss potentials. In this section, we discuss risk identification and measurement.

Risk Identification and Measurement. Risk identification is the process by which a business systematically and continuously identifies those current and potential risks that might adversely affect it. Most corporate risk managers use a checklist to identify risks, and smaller firms without risk managers usually rely on the risk management services of insurance companies or else hire risk management consultants to identify and measure the risks that they face. The checklists, which are published by insurance companies, the American Management Association, and the Risk and Insurance Management Society, are many pages long, so we will not present one here.[1] For small firms, it may be possible for a single individual to apply the checklist to his or her firm to

---

[1]For one example, see C. Arthur Williams, Jr., Michael L. Smith, and Peter C. Young, *Risk Management and Insurance* (New York: McGraw-Hill, 1995), Chapter 3.

identify the risks, but larger, multidivisional firms must involve a number of people in the risk identification process.

After risks have been identified, it is necessary to measure the firm's degree of exposure to each risk. This involves estimating (1) **loss frequency** (or loss probability) and (2) **loss severity** (dollar value of each loss). In general, loss exposure is more a function of the severity of losses than of their frequency. A potential catastrophic loss, even though its frequency is rare, is far more serious than frequent small losses. For example, suppose a company uses trucks to deliver its products. In any year, the probability of an accident that damages one of its trucks is relatively high, whereas the probability of a death or injury liability claim is relatively low. However, the potential severity of the liability loss is so much greater than potential damage losses that virtually all firms consider their liability risk exposure to be greater than their collision risk exposure.

There are several approaches to measuring loss severity. Two of the most common are (1) the maximum loss approach, and (2) the average loss approach. The **maximum loss** is the dollar loss associated with the worst-case scenario, while the **average loss** is the average dollar loss associated with a particular peril, such as a plant fire, considering that a wide range of possible losses can occur.

To illustrate, Table 24E-1 contains a risk manager's estimates for the probabilities and dollar losses associated with a fire at a given plant. There is a 99 percent probability that no fire will occur and a 1 percent probability that there will be a fire. The expected loss is only $5,650, but if a fire does occur, the damage could range from $100,000 to $2,000,000. The company could easily afford the $5,650 annual expected loss, but a large fire loss would put it out of business, and it would lose all of its value as a going concern.

A fire insurance policy which fully protects against fire would cost $5,650 plus administrative costs and insurance company profit. In this case, all risk of fire would be transferred to the insurance company. However, the risk manager might decide that the company could withstand losses of up to $1 million, hence that only the risk of losses of $1 million or more should be transferred to an insurer. The probability of a loss of $1 million or more during a given year is 0.10% + 0.05% = 0.15%, and the expected loss to an insurance company which assumed that risk would be $2,000. Therefore, the firm could buy a policy with a $1 million deductible at a relatively low premium cost.[2]

Property Loss Exposures. One of the first risks that comes to mind when discussing corporate risk management is the risk of property losses. In general, property is divided into two classes: (1) **real property,** which consists of land and buildings, and (2) **personal property,** which is all property other than real property. In a business setting, real property is the company's land and buildings such as corporate headquarters, plants, stores, and warehouses, while personal property includes the company's manufacturing equipment, vehicles, furniture and fixtures, and inventories.

The perils most commonly associated with property losses are (1) **physical perils,** which include such natural events as fires, floods, explosions, and windstorms; (2) **social perils,** which are associated with the behavior of people and include theft, strikes, vandalism, and embezzlement; and (3) **economic perils,** which stem from external economic events, such as a competitor's introduction of a new product that significantly reduces the value of inventory.

Property losses are classified as direct or indirect. **Direct losses** occur when the property itself is destroyed, damaged, or lost. Thus, the loss of a manufacturing plant and its contents by fire is a direct loss. **Indirect losses** stem from direct loss; the loss of profits during the time when fire damage is being repaired is an example.

To measure a firm's potential exposure to property losses, the risk manager must attach a value to the firm's property. Property appraisers have developed several standards of measurement for assigning property values. Here are the six most common appraisal measurements:

---

[2]Although we have been dealing with discrete distributions here, loss probabilities could be specified by continuous distributions, hence Monte Carlo simulation could be a useful tool in the risk measurement process.

TABLE 24E-1   Probabilities and Dollar Losses from a Fire

PROBABILITY OF OCCURRENCE	DOLLAR LOSS
99.00%	$ 0
0.15	100,000
0.20	250,000
0.30	500,000
0.20	750,000
0.10	1,000,000
0.05	2,000,000
100.00%	Expected loss = $ 5,650

1. **Original cost.** The original cost of property is merely the dollar cost at the time of acquisition. In general, original cost is not a very good measure of an asset's true value, primarily because it does not consider the impact of factors that affect value over time.

2. **Book value.** Book value is the original cost of the property less the accumulated amount of accounting depreciation. Book value does consider the wear and tear on an asset, at least as measured by accountants, but it does not consider the impact of inflation, competition, or technological change.

3. **Market value.** The market value of an asset is the current value of the asset as set by supply and demand conditions in the marketplace. Some assets, such as vehicles, have an easily determined market value, but for assets such as a manufacturing plant it may be virtually impossible to determine a market value.

4. **Tax appraisal value.** Many types of property are appraised for tax purposes, so this value is known for many corporate assets. However, tax appraisals may not be current, and they are often set at less than true market value to reduce valuation appeals.

5. **Economic value.** The economic value of an asset is the present value of the cash flows it is expected to produce. For some assets, such as securities, the economic value should be the same as the market value. For other assets, such as a manufacturing plant, the economic and market values may differ depending on who operates the plant, because different owners may be able to create different cash flow streams due to varying management skills and synergies. Also, some assets, such as office equipment, do not directly produce cash flow streams, and for them the economic value method is obviously inappropriate.

6. **Replacement value.** Replacement value is the cost to replace the property. Because of inflation, the replacement values for many assets are considerably higher than their book values, but in some cases technological or other developments make it possible to replace an asset at less than its book value.

In general, property loss exposures are managed either by retaining the risk or by passing it to an insurer. Basic insurance can usually be purchased to cover losses associated with fire, smoke, lightning, windstorm and hail, explosion, riot, and aircraft and vehicle accidents. Because of the adverse selection problem associated with flood insurance, this type of coverage can generally be obtained only through subsidized government programs.[3]

In addition to basic coverage, additional coverage can usually be obtained to protect against losses due to burglary and vandalism. Finally, coverage can be purchased that offers protection against income loss and employee dishonesty. Needless to say, the more risk that is passed on to the insurer, the higher the cost of the policy. One of the biggest issues in risk management is to determine what risks should be retained by the firm rather than passed on to insurers.

Liability Loss Exposures.   In addition to property loss exposure, businesses also face exposure to liability losses. For our purposes, the term **liability** involves the concept of a cost that can be imposed when a responsibility is not met. Companies risk liability losses through five categories of exposure: (1) bailee exposure, (2) ownership exposure, (3) business operation exposure, (4) employee action exposure, and (5) professional exposure.

In many business activities, a business takes possession of personal property owned by a person or another business and performs some service pertaining to the property, such as repair or storage, and then returns the property to the owner. In legal language, such transactions are called **bailments,** and the business having temporary possession of the property is called the **bailee.** Although the legal complexities associated with bailment are too extensive to discuss here, it is obviously important for companies that act as bailees to fully understand the liability exposure that such arrangements create.

Ownership of real and personal property brings with it significant liability exposures. In essence, injuries that occur on a business's real property and/or as a result of its personal property can give rise to liability losses. Again, the legal specifics go beyond the scope of this chapter, but risk managers must be familiar with the nature of the potential liability that results from property ownership.

The liability exposure that arises from business operations is often the most critical exposure that firms face. First, businesses may be sued for creating a **nuisance,** which is an activity that harms third parties. Much of what is now controlled by environmental regulation was formerly considered as a nuisance. Thus, water and air pollution, as well as noise pollution, may subject a firm to civil suits as well as to the penalties specified in our environmental protection laws.

Another potential liability exposure is **patent and copyright infringement.** Here, firms violate invention or creative work protection laws, hence wrongfully use the works of others. Suits of this nature, if won, tend to have very large settlements, so they can constitute large risks for some firms. For example, Apple Computer sued Microsoft Corporation for $5.5 billion for copyright infringement. Apple argued that Microsoft's Windows software illegally duplicated the "look and feel" inherent in the screen images (icons) that helped make Apple's Macintosh computer successful. "I'll move to Canada if Apple wins," said Steve Ballmer, one of Microsoft's vice-presidents. However, the move was not necessary, because the court dismissed Apple's claim, ruling that the general appearance of a program is not protected by copyright law. On the day following the ruling, Microsoft's shares surged $11\frac{7}{8}$ to $128\frac{7}{8}$, a sign that the potential liability was clearly worrying investors.

A firm that uses **unfair trade practices** also creates the potential for large liability exposures. In fact, treble damages can be assessed in such suits, which can present a serious financial threat to just about any firm.

Firms also face potential liability problems from defects in the goods and services they provide. Such risk exposure is called **product liability.** Auto manufacturers have lost millions of dollars in suits related to faulty design and construction. For example, Audi faced hundreds of lawsuits related to "sudden acceleration" problems, and other automakers lost millions of dollars on lawsuits connected with faulty gas tanks. Similarly, four

---

[3]Only those businesses that face high risk of floods would buy flood insurance. Further, because floods typically cause widespread damage, the premiums charged by commercial insurers for flood insurance would be exorbitantly high.

firms associated with producing breast implants were forced to establish a $4.5 billion fund to settle class action lawsuits related to implant injuries. Of course, the exposure to such liability varies a great deal depending on the type of product or service sold. Because of inflation and the generous temperament of many juries, product liability exposures have become increasingly important in recent years. Thus, every risk manager has to constantly monitor his or her firm's product liability exposure, for it can have negative effects both through damage judgments and through sales lost due to bad publicity.

To illustrate the difficulties encountered in identifying potential risks, consider the situation faced by Keene Corporation, once a NYSE company and a leading manufacturer of heat-absorbing composite materials used in a variety of aerospace, defense, and commercial applications. In 1968, Keene acquired for $8 million a small manufacturer of insulation products which, to conform to customers' specifications at the time, contained asbestos. Keene stopped production of these products in 1972 and closed the company down in 1976—losing its entire investment. Unfortunately for Keene, this did not mark the end of the saga. Laws passed *after the insulation business was closed, and enforced retroactively,* forced Keene and its insurers to spend over $500 million on asbestos litigation, and these charges eventually forced the company into bankruptcy. In total, Keene lost more than a half-billion dollars and ended up bankrupt because it made the mistake of acquiring a company—which it bought 20 years earlier for $8 million—with a product liability exposure.

Another type of liability involves **improper actions by employees,** such as sexual harassment. For example, in 1994 the world's largest law firm, Baker & McKenzie, was hit with $6.9 million in punitive damages in a sexual harassment suit brought by a former secretary in the firm. Punitive damages, which generally are not covered by insurance, are meant to deter and punish wrongdoing. In this instance, the firm was punished for not doing enough to prevent sexual harassment by a senior partner who brought in a lot of revenue and also for not taking appropriate action after the sexual harassment had been reported. The jury's award was nearly twice the $3.7 million in punitive damages sought by the secretary's lawyers. If the decision is not reversed, it will amount to about 10 percent of the law firm's net worth.

The final type of liability exposure applies to professionals such as doctors, lawyers, accountants, and architects. In general, businesses that provide services requiring advance training and licensing are exposed to **professional liability.** There has been a dramatic increase in the number of malpractice lawsuits in recent years and in the dollar amounts of the judgments. Professional liability losses can be especially damaging because they affect both the firm's cash and its reputation. As with property loss exposures, the usual approach for handling liability exposures is either to self-insure or to pass the risk to an insurer. Liability insurance, including professional liability, can be purchased, but it is often difficult for insurers to adequately pool the risks involved. For example, liability losses among some physicians in southern Florida became so great in the late 1980s that malpractice premiums, which are based on location, rose above $100,000 a year. Many physicians were unable to afford such premiums, so they either retired or left

to practice elsewhere. Hospitals face a similar problem, and to deal with it, many states require hospitals to join insurance pools for malpractice protection.

For all types of liability coverage, deductibles are common, whereby the business has to pay some part of the award, say, $100,000, with the insurer covering the remainder.

Bond Portfolio Immunization. In our discussion of bond valuation in Chapter 8, we discussed interest rate and reinvestment rate risk. **Interest rate (price) risk** is the risk that the price of a debt security will fall as a result of increases in interest rates, and **reinvestment rate risk** is the risk of earning a return less than expected when debt principal or interest payments are reinvested at rates less than the original yield to maturity.

To illustrate how to reduce interest rate and reinvestment rate risks, we will consider a firm which is obligated to pay a worker a lump sum retirement benefit of $10,000 at the end of ten years.[4] Assume that the yield curve is horizontal, the current interest rate on all Treasury securities is 9 percent, and the type of security used to fund the retirement benefit is Treasury bonds. The present value of $10,000, discounted back ten years at 9 percent, is $10,000(0.4224) = $4,224. Therefore, the firm could invest $4,224 in Treasury bonds and expect to be able to meet its obligation ten years hence.

Suppose, however, interest rates change from the current 9 percent rate immediately after the firm has bought the Treasury bonds. How would this affect the situation? The answer is, "It all depends." If rates fall, then the value of the bonds in the portfolio will rise, but this benefit will be offset to a greater or lesser degree by a decline in the rate at which the coupon payment of 0.09($4,224) = $380.16 can be reinvested. The reverse would hold if interest rates rise above 9 percent. Here are some examples (for simplicity, we assume annual coupons):

1. **The firm buys $4,224 of 9 percent, ten-year maturity bonds; rates fall to 7 percent immediately after the purchase and remain at that level:**

$$\text{Portfolio value at the end of 10 years} = \begin{array}{c}\text{Future value of}\\ \text{10 interest payments}\\ \text{of \$380.16 each}\\ \text{compounded at 7\%}\end{array} + \begin{array}{c}\text{Maturity}\\ \text{value}\end{array}$$
$$= \$5,252 + \$4,224 = \$9,476.$$

Therefore, the firm cannot meet its $10,000 obligation, and it must contribute additional funds.

2. **The firm buys $4,224 of 9 percent, 40-year bonds; rates fall to 7 percent immediately after the purchase and remain at that level:**

$$\text{Portfolio value at the end of 10 years} = \$5,252 + \begin{array}{c}\text{Value of 30-year, 9\% bonds}\\ \text{when } k_d = 7\%\end{array}$$
$$= \$5,252 + \$5,272 = \$10,524.$$

In this situation, the firm has excess capital at the end of the ten-year period.

3. **The firm buys \$4,224 of 9 percent, ten-year bonds; rates rise to 12 percent immediately after the purchase and remain at that level:**

$$\begin{array}{l}\text{Portfolio value at} \\ \text{the end of 10 years}\end{array} = \begin{array}{c}\text{Future value of} \\ \text{10 interest payments} \\ \text{of \$380.16 each} \\ \text{compounded at 12\%}\end{array} + \begin{array}{c}\text{Maturity} \\ \text{value}\end{array}$$

$$= \$6,671 + \$4,224 = \$10,895.$$

This situation also produces a funding surplus.

4. **The firm buys \$4,224 of 9 percent, 40-year bonds; rates rise to 12 percent immediately after the purchase and remain at that level:**

$$\begin{array}{l}\text{Portfolio value at} \\ \text{the end of 10 years}\end{array} = \$6,671 + \begin{array}{c}\text{Value of 30-year, 9\% bonds} \\ \text{when } k_d = 12\%\end{array}$$

$$= \$6,671 + \$3,203 = \$9,874.$$

This time, a shortfall occurs.

Here are some generalizations drawn from the examples:

1. If interest rates *fall*, and the portfolio is invested in relatively short-term bonds, then the reinvestment rate penalty exceeds the capital gains, so a net shortfall occurs. However, if the portfolio had been invested in relatively long-term bonds, a drop in rates would produce capital gains which would more than offset the shortfall caused by low reinvestment rates.

2. If interest rates *rise,* and the portfolio is invested in relatively short-term bonds, then gains from high reinvestment rates will more than offset capital losses, and the final portfolio value will exceed the required amount. However, if the portfolio had been invested in long-term bonds, then capital losses would more than offset reinvestment gains, and a net shortfall would result.

If a company has many cash obligations expected in the future, the complexity of estimating the effects of interest rate changes is obviously expanded. Still, methods have been devised to help deal with the risks associated with changing interest rates. Several methods are discussed in the following sections.

Zero Coupon Bonds and Stripped Treasuries. We discussed zero coupon bonds in Chapter 18, where we indicated that they were devised to eliminate reinvestment rate risk. In our example of a firm needing \$10,000 in ten years, the purchase of a ten-year zero coupon bond would eliminate all risks associated with changes in interest rates. The firm would, in our example, simply purchase a zero coupon bond which promised to pay \$10,000 in ten years.

Immunization. Bond portfolios can be **immunized** against interest rate and reinvestment rate risk, much as people can be immunized against flu. In brief, immunization involves selecting bonds with coupons and maturities such that the benefits or losses from changes in reinvestment rates are exactly offset by losses or gains in the prices of the bonds. In other words, if a bond's reinvestment rate risk exactly matches its interest rate price risk, then the bond is immunized against the adverse effects of changes in interest rates.

To see what's involved, refer back to our example of a firm which buys \$4,224 of 9 percent Treasury bonds to meet a \$10,000 obligation ten years hence. In the example, we see that if the firm buys bonds with a ten-year maturity and interest rates remain constant, then the obligation can be met exactly. However, if interest rates fall from 9 percent to 7 percent, a shortfall will occur because the coupons received will be reinvested at a rate of 7 percent rather than the 9 percent reinvestment rate required to reach the \$10,000 target. But, suppose the firm had bought 40-year rather than ten-year bonds. A decline in interest rates would still have the same effect on the compounded coupon payments, but now the firm would hold 9 percent coupon, 30-year bonds in a 7 percent market 10 years hence, so the bonds would have a value greater than par. In this case, the bonds would have risen by more than enough to offset the shortfall in compounded interest. Bonds with a maturity somewhere between 10 and 40 years would result in a breakeven situation in which the reinvestment shortfall was exactly offset by capital gains.

Duration. The key to immunizing a portfolio is to buy bonds which have a **duration** equal to the years until the funds will be needed. Duration cannot be defined in simple terms like maturity, but it can be thought of as the weighted average maturity of all the cash flows (coupon payments plus maturity value) provided by a bond, and it is exceptionally useful to help manage the risk inherent in a bond portfolio. The duration formula and an example of the calculation are provided below, but first we present some additional points about duration:

1. Duration is to a bond what payback is to a capital budgeting project, because the longer the duration, the longer funds are tied up in the bond.

2. To immunize a bond portfolio, buy bonds which have a duration equal to the number of years until the funds will be needed. In our example, the firm should buy bonds with a duration of ten years.

3. A corporate treasurer (or any other investor) who is terribly concerned about declines in the market value of his or her portfolio should buy bonds with low durations. (This is important even if the investor buys a bond mutual fund.) The percentage change in the value of a bond (or bond portfolio) will be approximately equal to the bond's duration times the percentage point change in interest rates. Therefore, a 2 percentage point increase in interest rates will lower the value of a bond with a ten-year duration by about 20 percent, but the value of a five-year duration bond will fall by only 10 percent. So, twice the duration, twice the volatility.

4. The duration of a zero coupon bond is equal to its maturity, but the duration of any coupon bond is less than its maturity. (Remember, the duration is a weighted average maturity of the cash flows, the only cash flow from a zero occurs at maturity, and coupon bonds have cash flows prior to maturity.) Further, the higher the coupon rate, the shorter the duration, other things held constant, because a high-coupon bond provides significant early cash flows even if it has a long maturity.

Duration is calculated using this formula:

$$\text{Duration} = \sum_{t=1}^{n} \frac{t(\text{PVCF}_t)}{\sum_{t=1}^{n} \text{PVCF}_t} = \sum_{t=1}^{n} \frac{t(\text{PVCF}_t)}{\text{Value}}.$$

Here n is the bond's years to maturity, t is the year each cash flow occurs, and $PVCF_t$ is the present value of the cash flow at Year t discounted at the current rate of interest. Note that the denominator of the equation is the PV of the cash flows, which is the current market value of the bond.

To illustrate the duration calculation, consider a 20-year, 9 percent annual coupon bond bought at its par value of $1,000. It provides cash flows of $90 per year for 19 years, and $1,090 in the 20th year. To calculate duration, we used a spreadsheet set up as follows:

t (1)	CF (2)	PVCF (9%) (3)	PVCF/VALUE = PVCF/$1,000 (4)	t(PVCF/VALUE) (5)
1	$ 90	$ 82.57	0.08257	0.08257
2	90	75.75	0.07575	0.15150
.	.	.	.	.
.	.	.	.	.
.	.	.	.	.
19	90	17.50	0.01750	0.33258
20	1,090	194.49	0.19449	3.88979
		Value = $1,000.00		Duration = 9.95011

Column 1 gives the year each cash flow occurs, Column 2 gives the cash flows, Column 3 shows the PV of each cash flow, Column 4 shows the percentage of each PV cash flow to the total PV of cash flows, and Column 5 multiplies each year by its percentage of the PV of total cash flows. The sum of the weighted percentages is the bond's duration.

Since a 20-year bond's 9.95 duration is close to that of our illustrative firm's 10-year liability, if the firm bought a portfolio of 20-year bonds and then reinvested the coupons as they came in, the accumulated interest payments, plus the value of the bond after ten years, would be close to $10,000 irrespective of whether interest rates rose, fell, or remained constant at 9 percent.

Unfortunately, other complications arise. Our simple example looked at a single interest rate change which occurred immediately after funding. In reality, interest rates change every day, which causes bonds' durations to change, and this, in turn, requires that bond portfolios be **rebalanced** periodically to remain immunized. Still, this can be done, and computer programs are available to assist in the rebalancing process.

BANKRUPTCY, REORGANIZATION, AND LIQUIDATION

In June 1993, Continental Airlines performed, for the second time, a feat few companies accomplish even once—emerge from bankruptcy. (TWA managed to duplicate Continental's feat, while Braniff Airlines went into bankruptcy twice but only came out once.) When Continental Airlines Holdings Inc., along with 53 subsidiaries, filed for bankruptcy court protection in December 1990, it owed $3.96 billion. When it emerged from bankruptcy in 1993, the firm had only four subsidiaries, it had shaved its debt to $1.8 billion, and it had $635 million in cash. However, with equity of only $600 million, the company still had an equity ratio of only 25 percent.

While under court protection—which means that the Bankruptcy Court prevented Continental's creditors from seizing the assets securing their debt, or even collecting interest due them—the company was able to take actions unavailable to its non-bankrupt competitors. In particular, it was able to abrogate its labor contracts and lower wages substantially. This action, along with not having to pay interest on its debt, permitted it to offer very low fares and still generate good cash flows.

However, the operating and financing advantages provided by the bankruptcy were costly to some parties. The company's reorganization plan, which provided the road map out of bankruptcy, called for paying creditors only a fraction of what they were owed. For example, unsecured creditors received from 5 cents to 40 cents per dollar of claims, depending on the exact type of debt. Creditors also were required to take some stock in the "new" Continental. In addition, 55 percent of the equity went to Air Canada and to Air Partners, a Fort Worth investor group, which, between them, poured $450 million of new cash into the airline. In fact, all of the equity went to creditors and new investors—the firm's original stockholders were wiped out.

After emerging from bankruptcy, Continental instituted a new strategy that focused on transoceanic services to Europe and Asia while cutting back on short-haul flights. Continental, along with the rest of the industry, also enjoyed a period of stable fuel and labor costs and rapid passenger growth. Combined, these factors resulted in Continental reporting positive earnings in both 1995 and 1996, the first time in many years. As a further sign of its recovery from bankruptcy, Continental announced in 1997 that it will purchase 30 new aircraft from Boeing, and it has been winning rave reviews for both on-time performance and customer satisfaction.

Continental is one of the success stories of bankruptcy—the corporation itself has survived, its customers are receiving good service, its employees have jobs, its creditors got more than they would have in a liquidation, and its new equity investors have made money. As we discuss in the chapter, though, other bankrupt firms have not fared so well. The decisions that firms' managers, creditors, and other stakeholders make before and during bankruptcy proceedings determine the final results.

As you go through the chapter, think about the decisions that Continental's managers and creditors had to make regarding bankruptcy and reorganization, and the effects the firm's bankruptcy has had on all of its stakeholders as well as on competing airlines.

Thus far, we have dealt with issues faced by growing, successful enterprises. However, many firms encounter financial difficulties, and some, including such big names as Pan American Airlines and Texaco, are forced into bankruptcy. When a firm encounters financial distress, its managers must try to ward off the firm's total collapse and thereby reduce its losses. The ability of a firm to hang on during rough times often means the difference between forced liquidation versus rehabilitation and eventual success. An understanding of bankruptcy is also critical to the executives of healthy firms, because they must know the best way to handle things when their customers or suppliers face the threat of bankruptcy.

FINANCIAL DISTRESS AND ITS CONSEQUENCES

We begin with some background on financial distress and its consequences.[1]

Causes of Business Failure

A recent Dun & Bradstreet compilation assigned percentage values to business failure causes, as shown in Table 25-1. Economic factors include industry weakness and poor location. Financial factors include too much debt and insufficient capital. The importance of the different factors varies over time, depending on such things as the state of the economy and the level of interest rates. Also, most business failures occur because a number of factors combine to make the business unsustainable. Further, case studies show that financial difficulties are usually the result of a series of errors, misjudgments, and interrelated weaknesses that can be attributed directly or indirectly to management. As you might guess, signs of potential financial distress are generally evident in a ratio analysis long before the firm actually fails, and researchers use ratio analysis to predict the probability that a given firm will go bankrupt.

The Business Failure Record

How widespread is business failure in the United States? In Table 25-2, we see that a fairly large number of businesses fail each year, although the failures in any one year are not a large percentage of the total business population. It is interesting to note that

---

[1] Much of the current academic work in the area of financial distress and bankruptcy is based on writings by Edward I. Altman. For a summary of his work and that of others, see Edward I. Altman, *Bankruptcy and Distressed Restructuring* (Homewood, Ill.: Irwin, 1992).

TABLE 25-1   Causes of Business Failure

CAUSE OF FAILURE	PERCENTAGE OF TOTAL
Economic factors	37.1%
Financial factors	47.3
Neglect, disaster, and fraud	14.0
Other factors	1.6
	100.0%

SOURCE: Dun & Bradstreet Inc., *Business Failure Record* (New York, updated annually).

| TABLE 25-2 | Historical Failure Rate of U.S. Businesses |

Years	Average Number of Failures per Year	Average Failure Rate per 10,000 Businesses	Average Liability per Failure
1950–1959	11,119	42	$ 41,082
1960–1969	13,110	52	92,271
1970–1979	9,311	36	296,497
1980	11,742	42	394,744
1981	17,041	61	414,147
1982	24,908	89	626,738
1983	31,334	110	512,953
1984	52,078	107	562,016
1985	57,253	115	645,160
1986	61,616	120	725,850
1987	61,111	102	568,209
1988	57,097	98	693,084
1989	50,361	65	840,507
1990	60,747	74	923,996
1991	88,140	107	1,098,539
1992	97,069	110	971,653
1993	86,133	109	554,438
1994	71,558	86	404,955
1995	71,194	90	525,833
1996	71,800	83	470,354

NOTE: Due to statistical revision, data prior to 1984 are not directly comparable to data in 1984 and thereafter.
SOURCE: Dun & Bradstreet, Inc., *Business Failure Record* (New York, updated annually).

whereas the failure rate per 10,000 businesses fluctuates with the state of the economy, the average liability per failure has tended to increase over time, at least into the early 1990s. This is due primarily to inflation, but it also reflects the fact that some very large firms have failed in recent years.

Although bankruptcy is more frequent among smaller firms, it is clear from Table 25-3 that large firms are not immune. However, some firms might be too big or too important to be allowed to fail, and mergers or governmental intervention are often used as an alternative to outright failure and liquidation. The decision to give federal aid to Chrysler in the 1980s is an excellent illustration. Also, in recent years federal regulators have arranged the absorption of many "problem" financial institutions by financially sound institutions. In addition, several U.S. government agencies, principally the Defense Department, were able to bail out Lockheed when it otherwise would have failed, and the "shotgun marriage" of Douglas Aircraft and McDonnell was designed to prevent Douglas's failure. Another example of intervention is that of Merrill Lynch taking over the brokerage firm Goodbody & Company, which would otherwise have gone bankrupt and would have frozen the accounts of its 225,000 customers while a bankruptcy settlement was being worked out. Goodbody's failure would have panicked investors across the country, so New York Stock Exchange member firms put up $30

TABLE 25-3	Twelve Largest Nonbank Bankruptcies (Billions of Dollars)

COMPANY	LIABILITIES	DATE
Texaco	$21.6	April 1987
Olympia & York	19.8	May 1992
Executive Life Insurance	14.6	April 1991
Mutual Benefit Life	13.5	July 1991
Campeau (Allied and Federated)	9.9	January 1990
First Capital Holdings	9.3	May 1991
Baldwin United	9.0	September 1983
Continental Airlines	6.2	December 1990
Lomas Financial	6.1	September 1989
Macy's	5.3	January 1992
Columbia Gas	5.0	July 1991
LTV	4.7	July 1986

NOTE: There are motivations for filing for bankruptcy other than immediate financial distress. For example, Texaco's bankruptcy was the result of a lawsuit, and Continental Airline's first filing in 1983 was motivated by a desire to abrogate union contracts.

SOURCE: Data supplied by Edward I. Altman.

million as an inducement to get Merrill Lynch to keep Goodbody from folding. Similar instances in other industries could also be cited.

Why do government and industry seek to avoid failure among larger firms? There are many reasons. In the case of banks, the main reason is to prevent an erosion of confidence and a consequent run on the banks. With Lockheed and Douglas, the Defense Department wanted not only to maintain viable suppliers but also to avoid disrupting local communities. With Chrysler, the government wanted to preserve jobs as well as a competitor in the U.S. auto industry. Even when the public interest is not at stake, the fact that bankruptcy is a very expensive process gives private industry strong incentives to avoid outright bankruptcy. The costs and complexities of a formal bankruptcy are discussed in subsequent sections of this chapter, after we examine some less formal and less expensive procedures.

SELF-TEST
QUESTIONS

What are the major causes of business failure?

Do business failures occur evenly over time?

Which size of firm, large or small, is most prone to business failure? Why?

ISSUES FACING A FIRM IN FINANCIAL DISTRESS

Financial distress begins when a firm is unable to meet scheduled payments or when cash flow projections indicate that it will soon be unable to do so. As the situation develops, these central issues arise:

1. Is the firm's inability to meet scheduled debt payments a temporary cash flow problem, or is it a permanent problem caused by asset values having fallen below debt obligations?

2. If the problem is a temporary one, then an agreement with creditors that gives the firm time to recover and to satisfy everyone may be worked out. However, if basic long-run asset values have truly declined, then economic losses have occurred. In this event, who should bear the losses, and who should get whatever value remains?

3. Is the company "worth more dead than alive"? That is, would the business be more valuable if it were maintained and continued in operation or if it were liquidated and sold off in pieces?

4. Should the firm file for protection under Chapter 11 of the Bankruptcy Act, or should it try to use informal procedures? (Both reorganization and liquidation can be accomplished either informally or under the direction of a bankruptcy court.)

5. Who should control the firm while it is being liquidated or rehabilitated? Should the existing management be left in charge, or should a trustee be placed in charge of operations?

In the remainder of the chapter, we discuss these questions.

SELF-TEST QUESTION What five major issues must be addressed when a firm is in financial distress?

SETTLEMENTS WITHOUT GOING THROUGH FORMAL BANKRUPTCY

When a firm experiences financial distress, its managers and creditors must decide whether the problem is temporary, and the firm is really financially viable, or whether a permanent problem exists that endangers the firm's life. Then, the parties must decide whether to try to solve the problem informally or under the direction of a bankruptcy court. Because of costs associated with formal bankruptcy, including the disruptions that occur when a firm's customers, suppliers, and employees learn that it has filed under the Bankruptcy Act, it is desirable if possible to reorganize (or liquidate) a firm outside of formal bankruptcy. We first discuss informal settlement procedures, then procedures under a formal bankruptcy.

Informal Reorganization

In the case of an economically sound company whose financial difficulties appear to be temporary, creditors are generally willing to work with the company to help it to recover and reestablish itself on a sound financial basis. Such voluntary plans, commonly called **workouts,** usually require a **restructuring** of the firm's debt, because current cash flows are insufficient to service the existing debt. Restructuring typically involves extension and/or composition. In an **extension,** creditors postpone the dates of required interest or principal payments, or both. In a **composition,** creditors voluntarily reduce their fixed claims on the debtor by accepting a lower principal amount, by reducing the interest rate on the debt, by taking equity for debt, or by some combination of these changes.

A debt restructuring begins with a meeting between the failing firm's managers and creditors. The creditors appoint a committee consisting of four or five of the largest creditors, plus one or two of the smaller ones. This meeting is often arranged and conducted by an **adjustment bureau** associated with and run by a local credit managers' association.[2] The first step is for management to draw up a list of creditors, with amounts of debt owed. There are typically different classes of debt, ranging from first-mortgage holders to unsecured creditors. Next, the company develops information showing the value of the firm under different scenarios. Typically, one scenario is going out of business, selling off the assets, and then distributing the proceeds to the various creditors in accordance with the priority of their claims, with any surplus going to the common stockholders. The company may hire an appraiser to get an appraisal of the value of the firm's property to use as a basis for this scenario. Other scenarios include continued operations, frequently with some improvements in capital equipment, marketing, and perhaps some management changes.

This information is then shared with the firm's bankers and other creditors. Frequently, it can be demonstrated that the firm's debts exceed its liquidating value, and it can also be shown that legal fees and other costs associated with a formal liquidation under federal bankruptcy procedures would materially lower the net proceeds available to creditors. Further, it generally takes at least a year, and often several years, to resolve matters in a formal proceeding, so the present value of the eventual proceeds will be lower still. This information, when presented in a credible manner, often convinces creditors that they would be better off accepting something less than the full amount of their claims rather than holding out for the full face amount. If management and the major creditors agree that the problems can probably be resolved, then a more formal plan is drafted and presented to all the creditors, along with the reasons creditors should be willing to compromise on their claims.

In developing the reorganization plan, creditors prefer an extension because it promises eventual payment in full. In some cases, creditors may agree not only to postpone the date of payment but also to subordinate existing claims to vendors who are willing to extend new credit during the workout period. Similarly, creditors may agree to accept a lower interest rate on loans during the extension, perhaps in exchange for a pledge of collateral. Because of the sacrifices involved, the creditors must have faith that the debtor firm will be able to solve its problems.

In a composition, creditors agree to reduce their claims. Typically, creditors receive cash and/or new securities that have a combined market value that is less than the amounts owed them. The cash and securities, which might have a value of only 10 percent of the original claim, are taken as full settlement of the original debt. Bargaining will take place between the debtor and the creditors over the savings that result from avoiding the costs of legal bankruptcy: administrative costs, legal fees, investigative costs, and so on. In addition to escaping such costs, the debtor gains in that the stigma of bankruptcy may be avoided. As a result, the debtor may be induced to part with most of the savings from avoiding formal bankruptcy.

Often, the bargaining process will result in a restructuring which involves both extension and composition. For example, the settlement may provide for a cash payment of 25 percent of the debt immediately, plus a new note promising six future installments of 10 percent each, for a total payment of 85 percent.

Voluntary settlements are both informal and simple, and also relatively inexpensive because legal and administrative expenses are held to a minimum. Thus, voluntary procedures generally result in the largest return to creditors. Although creditors do not obtain immediate payment and may even have to accept less than is owed them,

---

[2]There is a nationwide group called the National Association of Credit Management, which consists of bankers and industrial companies' credit managers. This group sponsors research on credit policy and problems, conducts seminars on credit management, and operates local chapters in cities throughout the nation. These local chapters frequently operate adjustment bureaus.

they generally recover more money, and sooner, than if the firm were to file for bankruptcy.

In recent years, one factor that has motivated some creditors, especially banks and insurance companies, to agree to voluntary restructurings is the fact that restructurings can sometimes help creditors avoid showing a loss. Thus, a bank that is "in trouble" with its regulators over weak capital ratios may agree to extend further loans which are used to pay the interest on earlier loans in order to keep the bank from having to write down the value of its earlier loans. This particular type of restructuring depends on (1) the willingness of the regulators to go along with the process, and (2) whether the bank is likely to recover more in the end by restructuring the debt than by forcing the borrower into bankruptcy immediately.

We should point out that informal voluntary settlements are not reserved for small firms. International Harvester (now Navistar International) avoided formal bankruptcy proceedings by getting its creditors to agree to restructure more than $3.5 billion of debt. Likewise, Chrysler's creditors accepted both an extension and a composition to help it through its bad years. The biggest problem with informal reorganizations is getting all the parties to agree to the voluntary plan. This problem, called the **holdout problem,** is discussed in a later section.

Informal Liquidation

When it is obvious that a firm is more valuable dead than alive, informal procedures can also be used to **liquidate** the firm. **Assignment** is an informal procedure for liquidating a firm, and it usually yields creditors a larger amount than they would get in a formal bankruptcy liquidation. However, assignments are feasible only if the firm is small and its affairs are not too complex. An assignment calls for title to the debtor's assets to be transferred to a third party, known as an **assignee** or **trustee.** The assignee is instructed to liquidate the assets through a private sale or public auction and then to distribute the proceeds among the creditors on a pro rata basis. The assignment does not automatically discharge the debtor's obligations. However, the debtor may have the assignee write on the check to each creditor the requisite legal language to make endorsement of the check acknowledgment of full settlement of the claim.

Assignment has some advantages over liquidation in federal bankruptcy courts in terms of time, legal formality, and expense. The assignee has more flexibility in disposing of property than does a federal bankruptcy trustee, so action can be taken sooner, before inventory becomes obsolete or machinery rusts. Also, since the assignee is often familiar with the debtor's business, better results may be achieved. However, an assignment does not automatically result in a full and legal discharge of all the debtor's liabilities, nor does it protect the creditors against fraud. Both of these problems can be reduced by formal liquidation in bankruptcy, which we discuss in a later section.

SELF-TEST QUESTIONS

Define the following terms:
- (1) Restructuring
- (2) Extension
- (3) Composition
- (4) Assignment
- (5) Assignee (trustee)

What are the advantages of liquidation by assignment versus a formal bankruptcy liquidation?

FEDERAL BANKRUPTCY LAW

U.S. bankruptcy laws were first enacted in 1898. They were modified substantially in 1938, then they were changed substantially again in 1978, and some fine-tuning was done in 1986. The primary purpose of the bankruptcy law is to avoid having firms that are worth more as ongoing concerns be put out of business by individual creditors who could force liquidation without regard to the effects on other parties.

Currently, our bankruptcy law consists of eight odd-numbered chapters, plus one even-numbered chapter. (The old even-numbered chapters were deleted when the act was revised in 1978.) Chapters 1, 3, and 5 contain general provisions applicable to the other chapters. Chapter 11, which deals with business reorganization, is the most important section from a financial management viewpoint. Chapter 7 details the procedures to be followed when liquidating a firm; generally, Chapter 7 does not come into play unless it has been determined that reorganization under Chapter 11 is not feasible. Chapter 9 deals with financially distressed municipalities; Chapter 12 covers special procedures for family-owned farms; Chapter 13 covers the adjustment of debts for "individuals with regular income"; and Chapter 15 sets up a system of trustees who help administer proceedings under the act.

A firm is officially bankrupt when it files for bankruptcy with a federal court. When you read that a company such as Southland (the owner of the 7-Eleven convenience store chain) has "filed for court protection under Chapter 11," this means that the company is attempting to reorganize under the supervision of a bankruptcy court. Formal bankruptcy proceedings are designed to protect both the firm and its creditors. On the one hand, if the problem is temporary insolvency, then the firm may use bankruptcy proceedings to gain time to solve its cash flow problems without asset seizure by its creditors. On the other hand, if the firm is truly bankrupt in the sense that liabilities exceed assets, the creditors can use bankruptcy procedures to stop the firm's managers from continuing to operate, lose more money, and thus deplete assets which should go to creditors.

Bankruptcy law is flexible in that it provides scope for negotiations between a company, its creditors, and its stockholders. A case is opened by filing a petition with one of the 291 bankruptcy courts serving 90 judicial districts. The petition may be either **voluntary** or **involuntary;** that is, it may be filed either by the firm's management or by its creditors. After a filing, a committee of unsecured creditors is then appointed by the court to negotiate with management for a reorganization, which may include the restructuring of debt. A **trustee** will be appointed if the court deems current management incompetent or if fraud is suspected. Otherwise, the existing management will retain control. If no fair and feasible reorganization can be worked out, the bankruptcy judge will order that the firm be liquidated under procedures spelled out in Chapter 7 of the Bankruptcy Act.

SELF-TEST
QUESTIONS

Define the following terms:
  (1) Bankruptcy law
  (2) Chapter 11
  (3) Chapter 7
  (4) Trustee
  (5) Voluntary bankruptcy
  (6) Involuntary bankruptcy

How does a firm formally declare bankruptcy?

REORGANIZATION IN BANKRUPTCY

It might appear that most reorganizations should be handled informally because informal reorganizations are faster and less costly than formal bankruptcy. However, two problems often arise to stymie informal reorganizations and thus force debtors into Chapter 11 bankruptcy—the common pool problem and the holdout problem.[3]

To illustrate these problems, consider a firm that is having financial difficulties. It is worth $9 million as a going concern (this is the present value of its expected future operating cash flows) but only $7 million if it is liquidated. The firm's debt totals $10 million at face value—ten creditors with equal priority each have a $1 million claim. Now suppose the firm's liquidity deteriorates to the point where it defaults on one of its loans. The holder of that loan has the contractual right to *accelerate* the claim, which means the creditor can *foreclose* on the loan and demand payment of the entire balance. Further, since most debt agreements have *cross-default provisions,* defaulting on one loan effectively places all loans in default.

The firm's market value is less than the $10 million face value of debt, regardless of whether it remains in business or liquidates. Therefore, it would be impossible to pay off all of the creditors in full. However, the creditors in total would be better off if the firm is not shut down, because they can recover $9 million if the firm remains in business but only $7 million if it is liquidated. The problem here, which is called the **common pool problem,** is that, in the absence of protection under the Bankruptcy Act, individual creditors would have an incentive to foreclose on the firm even though it is worth more as an ongoing concern.

An individual creditor would have the incentive to foreclose because it could then force the firm to liquidate a portion of its assets to pay off that particular creditor's $1 million claim in full. The payment to that creditor would reduce the value of the assets, hence operating cash flow, so the value of the remaining creditors' claims would decline. Of course, all the creditors would recognize the gains to be had from this strategy, so they would storm the debtor with foreclosure notices. Even those creditors who understand the merits of keeping the firm alive would be forced to foreclose, because the foreclosures of the other creditors would reduce the payoff to those who do not. In our hypothetical example, if seven creditors foreclosed and forced liquidation, they would be paid in full, and the remaining three creditors would receive nothing.

With many creditors, as soon as a firm defaults on one loan, there is the potential for a disruptive flood of foreclosures that would make the creditors collectively worse off. In our example, the creditors would lose $2 million in value if a flood of foreclosures were to force the firm to liquidate. If the firm had only one creditor, say, a single bank loan, the common pool problem would not exist. If a bank had loaned the company $10 million, it would not force liquidation to get $7 million when it could keep the firm alive and eventually realize $9 million.

Chapter 11 of the Bankruptcy Act provides a solution to the common pool problem through its **automatic stay** provision. *An automatic stay, which is forced on all creditors in a bankruptcy, limits the ability of creditors to foreclose to collect their individual claims.* However, the creditors can collectively foreclose on the debtor and force liquidation.

While bankruptcy gives the firm a chance to work out its problems without the threat of creditor foreclosure, management does not have a completely free reign

---

[3]The issues discussed in this section are covered in more detail in Thomas H. Jackson, *The Logic and Limits of Bankruptcy Law* (Cambridge, Mass.: Harvard University Press, 1986).

over the firm's assets. First, bankruptcy law requires the debtor firm to request permission from the court to take many actions, and the law also gives creditors the right to petition the bankruptcy court to block almost any action the firm might take while in bankruptcy. Second, **fraudulent conveyance** statutes, which are part of debtor-creditor law, protect creditors from unjustified transfers of property by a firm in financial distress.

To illustrate fraudulent conveyance, suppose a holding company is contemplating bankruptcy protection for one of its subsidiaries. The holding company might be tempted to sell some or all of the subsidiary's assets to itself (the parent company) for less than the true market value. This transaction would reduce the value of the subsidiary by the difference between the true market value of its assets and the amount paid, and the loss would be borne primarily by the subsidiary's creditors. Such a transaction would be voided by the courts as a fraudulent conveyance. Note also that transactions that favor one creditor at the expense of another can be voided under the same law. For example, a transaction in which an asset is sold and the proceeds are used to pay one creditor in full at the expense of other creditors could be voided. Thus, fraudulent conveyance laws also protect creditors from each other.[4]

The second problem that the bankruptcy law mitigates is the **holdout problem.** To illustrate this problem, consider again our example with ten creditors owed $1 million each but with only $9 million worth of assets. The goal of the firm is to avoid liquidation by remedying the default. In an informal workout, this would require a reorganization plan that is agreed to by each of the ten creditors. Suppose the firm offers each creditor new debt with a face value of $850,000 in exchange for the old $1,000,000 face value debt. If each of the creditors accepted the offer, the firm could be successfully reorganized. The reorganization would leave the equity holders with some value—the market value of the equity would be $9,000,000 − 10($850,000) = $500,000. Further, the creditors would have claims worth $8.5 million, much more than the $7 million value of their claims in liquidation.

Although such an exchange offer seems to benefit all parties, it is unlikely to be accepted by the creditors. Here's why: Suppose seven of the ten creditors tender their bonds; thus, seven creditors each now have claims with a face value of $850,000 each, or $5,950,000 in total, while the three creditors that did not tender their bonds each have a claim with a face value of $1 million. The total face value of the debt at this point is $8,950,000, which is less than the $9 million value of the firm. In this situation, the three holdout creditors would receive the full face value of their debt. However, this would not happen, because (1) all of the creditors would be sophisticated enough to realize this could happen, and (2) each creditor would want to be one of the three holdouts that gets paid in full. Thus, it is likely that none of the creditors would accept the offer. Thus, the holdout problem makes it difficult to restructure the firm's debts. Again, if the firm had a single creditor, there would be no holdout problem.

The holdout problem is mitigated in bankruptcy proceedings by the bankruptcy court's ability to lump creditors into classes. Each class is considered to have accepted a reorganization plan if two-thirds of the amount of debt and one-half the number of claimants vote for the plan, and the plan will be approved by the court if it is deemed to be "fair and equitable" to the dissenting parties. This procedure, in which the court mandates a reorganization plan in spite of dissent, is called a **cramdown,** because the court crams the plan down the throats of the dissenters. The ability of the court to force acceptance of a reorganization plan greatly reduces the incentive for creditors to

---

[4]The bankruptcy code requires that all transactions undertaken by the firm in the six months prior to a bankruptcy filing be reviewed by the court for fraudulent conveyance.

hold out. Thus, in our example, if the reorganization plan offered each creditor a new claim worth $850,000 in face value, along with information that each creditor would probably receive only $700,000 under the liquidation alternative, it would have a good chance of success.

It is easier for a firm with few creditors to informally reorganize than it is for a firm with many creditors. A recent study examined 169 publicly traded firms that experienced severe financial distress from 1978 to 1987.[5] About half of the firms reorganized without filing for bankruptcy, while the other half were forced to reorganize in bankruptcy. The firms that reorganized without filing for bankruptcy owed most of their debt to a few banks, and they had fewer creditors. Generally, bank debt can be reorganized outside of bankruptcy, but a publicly traded bond issue held by thousands of individual bondholders makes reorganization difficult.

Filing for bankruptcy under Chapter 11 has several features in addition to the automatic stay and cramdown provisions:

1. Interest and principal payments, including interest on delayed payments, may be delayed without penalty until a reorganization plan is approved, and the plan itself may call for even further delays. This permits cash generated from operations to be used to sustain operations rather than be paid to creditors.

2. The firm is permitted to issue **debtor-in-possession (DIP) financing.** DIP financing enhances the ability of the firm to borrow funds for short-term liquidity purposes, because such loans are, under the law, senior to all previous unsecured debt.

3. The debtor firm's managers are given the exclusive right for 120 days after filing for bankruptcy protection to submit a reorganization plan, plus another 60 days to obtain agreement on the plan from the affected parties. The court may also extend these dates. After management's first right to submit a plan has expired, any party to the proceedings may propose its own reorganization plan.

Under the early bankruptcy laws, most formal reorganization plans were guided by the **absolute priority doctrine.** This doctrine holds that creditors should be compensated for their claims in a rigid hierarchical order, and that senior claims must be paid in full before junior claims can receive even a dime. If there was any chance that a delay would lead to losses by senior creditors, then the firm would be shut down and liquidated. However, an alternative position, the **relative priority doctrine,** holds that more flexibility should be allowed in a reorganization, and that a balanced consideration should be given to all claimants. The current law represents a movement away from absolute priority toward relative priority.

The primary role of the bankruptcy court in a reorganization is to determine the **fairness** and the **feasibility** of the proposed plan of reorganization. The basic doctrine of fairness states that claims must be recognized in the order of their legal and contractual priority. Feasibility means that there is a reasonable chance that the reorganized company will be viable. Carrying out the concepts of fairness and feasibility in a reorganization involves the following steps:

1. Future sales must be estimated.

2. Operating conditions must be analyzed so that future earnings and cash flows can be predicted.

3. The appropriate capitalization rate must be determined.

---

[5]See Stuart Gilson, Kose John, and Larry Lang, "Troubled Debt Restructurings: An Empirical Study of Private Reorganization of Firms in Default," *Journal of Financial Economics,* October 1990, 315–354.

4. This capitalization rate must then be applied to the estimated cash flows to obtain an estimate of the company's value.[6]

5. An appropriate capital structure for the company after it emerges from Chapter 11 must be determined.

6. The reorganized firm's securities must be allocated to the various claimants in a fair and equitable manner.

The primary test of feasibility in a reorganization is whether the fixed charges after reorganization will be adequately covered by earnings. Adequate coverage generally requires an improvement in earnings, a reduction of fixed charges, or both. Among the actions that must generally be taken are the following:

1. Debt maturities are usually lengthened, interest rates may be lowered, and some debt is usually converted into equity.

2. When the quality of management has been substandard, a new team must be given control of the company.

3. If inventories have become obsolete or depleted, they must be replaced.

4. Sometimes the plant and equipment must be modernized before the firm can operate and compete successfully.

5. Reorganization may also require an improvement in production, marketing, advertising, and other functions.

6. It is sometimes necessary to develop new products or markets to enable the firm to move from areas where economic trends are poor into areas with more potential for growth.

These actions usually require at least some new money, so most reorganization plans include new investors who are willing to put up new capital.

Illustration of a Reorganization

Reorganization procedures may be illustrated with an example involving the Columbia Software Company, a regional firm that specializes in selling, installing, and servicing accounting software for small businesses.[7] Table 25-4 gives Columbia's balance sheet as of March 31, 1998. The company had been suffering losses running to $2.5 million a year, and, as will be made clear in the following discussion, the asset values in the balance sheet are overstated relative to their market values. The firm was **insolvent,** which means that the book values of its liabilities were greater than the market values of its assets, so it filed a petition with a federal court for reorganization under Chapter 11. Management filed a plan of reorganization with the court on June 13, 1998. The plan was subsequently submitted for review by the SEC.[8]

---

[6]Several different approaches can be used to estimate a company's value. Market-determined multiples such as the price/earnings ratio, which are obtained from an analysis of comparable firms, can be applied to some measure of the company's earnings or cash flow. Alternatively, discounted cash flow techniques may be used. The key point here is that fairness requires that the value of a company facing reorganization be estimated so that potential offers can be rationally evaluated by the bankruptcy court.

[7]This example is based on an actual reorganization, although the company name has been changed and the numbers have been changed slightly to simplify the analysis.

[8]Reorganization plans must be submitted to the Securities and Exchange Commission (SEC) if (1) the securities of the debtor are publicly held, and (2) total indebtedness exceeds $3 million. However, in recent years the only bankruptcy cases that the SEC has become involved in are those that are either precedent setting or that involve issues of national interest.

TABLE 25-4   Columbia Software Company: Balance Sheet as of March 31, 1998 (Millions of Dollars)

Assets	
Current assets	$ 3.50
Net fixed assets	12.50
Other assets	0.70
Total assets	$16.70
Liabilities and Equity	
Accounts payable	$ 1.00
Accrued taxes	0.25
Notes payable	0.25
Other current liabilities	1.75
7½% first mortgage bonds, due 2006	6.00
9% subordinated debentures, due 2001[a]	7.00
Common stock ($1 par)	1.00
Paid-in capital	3.45
Retained earnings	(4.00)
Total liabilities and equity	$16.70

[a]The debentures are subordinated to the notes payable.

The plan concluded that the company could not be internally reorganized and that the only feasible solution would be to combine Columbia with a larger, nationwide software company. Accordingly, management solicited the interest of a number of software companies. Late in July 1998, Moreland Software showed an interest in Columbia. On August 3, 1998, Moreland made a formal proposal to take over Columbia's $6 million of 7½ percent first-mortgage bonds, to pay the $250,000 in taxes owed by Columbia, and to provide 40,000 shares of Moreland common stock to satisfy the remaining creditor claims. Since the Moreland stock had a market price of $75 per share, the value of the stock was $3 million. Thus, Moreland was offering $3 million of stock plus assuming $6 million of loans and $250,000 of taxes—a total of $9.25 million for assets that had a book value of $16.7 million.

Moreland's plan is shown in Table 25-5. As in most Chapter 11 plans, the secured creditors' claims are paid in full (in this case, the mortgage bonds are taken over by Moreland Software). However, the total remaining unsecured claims equal $10 million against only $3 million of Moreland stock. Thus, each unsecured creditor would be entitled to receive 30 percent before the adjustment for subordination. Before this adjustment, holders of the notes payable would receive 30 percent of their $250,000 claim, or $75,000 in stock. However, the debentures are subordinated to the notes payable, so an additional $175,000 must be allocated to notes payable from the $2.1 million initially allocated to the subordinated debentures. In Column 5, the dollar claims of each class of debt are restated in terms of the number of shares of Moreland common stock received by each class of unsecured creditors. Finally, Column 6 shows the percentage of the original claim each group received. Of course,

TABLE 25-5	Columbia Software Company: Reorganization Plan (Millions of Dollars)

SENIOR CLAIMS

Taxes	$ 250,000	Paid off by Moreland
Mortgage bonds	$6,000,000	Assumed by Moreland

The reorganization plan for the remaining $10 million of liabilities, based on 40,000 shares at a price of $75 for a total market value of $3 million, or 30 percent of the remaining liabilities, is as follows:

JUNIOR CLAIMS (1)	ORIGINAL AMOUNT (2)	30% OF CLAIM AMOUNT (3)	CLAIM AFTER SUBORDINATION (4)	NUMBER OF SHARES OF COMMON STOCK (5)	PERCENTAGE OF ORIGINAL CLAIM RECEIVED (6)
Notes payable	$ 250,000	$ 75,000	$ 250,000[a]	3,333	100%
Unsecured creditors	2,750,000	825,000	825,000	11,000	30
Subordinated debentures	7,000,000	2,100,000	1,925,000[a]	25,667	28
	$10,000,000	$3,000,000	$3,000,000	40,000	30%

[a]Because the debentures are subordinated to the notes payable, $250,000 − $75,000 = $175,000 must be redistributed from the debentures to the notes payable.

both the taxes and the secured creditors were paid off in full, while the stockholders received nothing.[9]

The bankruptcy court first evaluated the proposal from the standpoint of fairness. The court began by considering the value of Columbia Software as estimated by the unsecured creditors' committee and by a subgroup of debenture holders. After discussions with various experts, one group had arrived at estimated post-reorganization sales of $25 million per year. It further estimated that the profit margin on sales would equal 6 percent, thus producing estimated future annual earnings of $1.5 million.

This subgroup analyzed price/earnings ratios for comparable companies and arrived at 8 times future earnings for a capitalization factor. Multiplying 8 by $1.5 million gave an indicated equity value of the company of $12 million. This value was four times that of the 40,000 shares of Moreland stock offered for the remainder of the company. Thus, the subgroup concluded that the plan for reorganization did not meet the test of fairness. Note that under both Moreland's plan and the subgroup's plan, the holders of common stock were to receive nothing, which is one of the risks of ownership, while the holders of the first-mortgage bonds were to be assumed by Moreland, which amounts to being paid in full.

The bankruptcy judge examined management's plan for feasibility, observing that in the reorganization Moreland Software would take over Columbia's properties. The committee judged that the direction and aid of Moreland would remedy the deficiencies that had troubled Columbia. Whereas the debt/assets ratio of Columbia Software had become unbalanced, Moreland has only a moderate amount of debt. After consolidation, Moreland would still have a relatively low 27 percent debt ratio.

---

[9]We do not show it, but $365,000 of fees for Columbia's attorneys and $123,000 of fees for the creditors' committee lawyers were also deducted. The current assets shown in Table 25-4 were net of these fees. Creditors joke (often bitterly) about the "lawyers first" rule in payouts in bankruptcy cases. It is often said, with much truth, that the only winners in bankruptcy cases are the attorneys.

Moreland's net income before interest and taxes had been running at a level of approximately $15 million. The interest on its long-term debt after the merger would be $1.5 million and, taking short-term borrowings into account, would total a maximum of $2 million per year. The $15 million in earnings before interest and taxes would therefore provide an interest charge coverage of 7.5 times, exceeding the norm of 5 times for the industry.

Notice that the question of feasibility would have been irrelevant had Moreland offered $3 million in cash rather than in stock, and had it offered to pay off the bonds rather than take them over. It is the court's responsibility to protect the interests of Columbia's creditors. Since the creditors are being forced to take common stock or bonds guaranteed by another firm, the law requires the court to look into the feasibility of the transaction. If Moreland had made a cash offer, however, the feasibility of its own operation after the transaction was completed would not have been a concern.

Moreland Software was told of the subgroup's analysis and concern over the fairness of the plan. Further, Moreland was asked to increase the number of shares it offered. Moreland refused, and no other company offered to acquire Columbia. Because no better offer could be obtained, and since the only alternative to the plan was liquidation (with an even lower realized value), Moreland's proposal was ultimately accepted by the creditors despite some disagreement with the valuation.

Prepackaged Bankruptcies

In recent years, a new type of reorganization that combines the advantages of both the informal workout and formal Chapter 11 reorganization has become popular. This new hybrid is called a **prepackaged bankruptcy,** or **pre-pack.**[10]

In an informal workout, a debtor negotiates a restructuring with its creditors. Even though complex workouts typically involve corporate officers, lenders, lawyers, and investment bankers, workouts are still less expensive and less damaging to reputations than are Chapter 11 reorganizations. In a prepackaged bankruptcy, the debtor firm gets all, or most of, the creditors to agree to the reorganization plan *prior* to filing for bankruptcy. Then, a reorganization plan is filed along with, or shortly after, the bankruptcy petition. If enough creditors have signed on before the filing, a cramdown can be used to bring reluctant creditors along.

A logical question arises: Why would a firm that can arrange an informal reorganization want to file for bankruptcy? The three primary advantages of a prepackaged bankruptcy are (1) reduction of the holdout problem, (2) preserving creditors' claims, and (3) taxes. Perhaps the biggest benefit of a prepackaged bankruptcy is the reduction of the holdout problem—a bankruptcy filing permits a cramdown that would otherwise be impossible. By eliminating holdouts, bankruptcy forces all creditors in each class to participate on a pro rata basis, which preserves the relative value of all claimants. Also, filing for formal bankruptcy can at times have positive tax implications. First, in an informal reorganization in which the debtholders trade debt for equity, if the original equity holders end up with less than 50 percent ownership, the company loses its accumulated tax losses. In formal bankruptcy, the firm may get to keep its loss carryforwards. Second, in a workout, when debt worth, say, $1,000, is exchanged for debt worth, say, $500, the reduction in debt of $500 is considered to be taxable income to the corporation. However, if this same situation

---

[10]For more information on prepackaged bankruptcies, see John J. McConnell and Henri Servaes, "The Economics of Pre-Packaged Bankruptcy," *Journal of Applied Corporate Finance,* Summer 1991, 93–97.

occurs in a Chapter 11 reorganization, the difference is not treated as taxable income.[11]

All in all, prepackaged bankruptcies make sense in many situations. If sufficient agreement can be reached among creditors through informal negotiations, a subsequent filing can solve the holdout problem and result in favorable tax treatment. For these reasons, the number of prepackaged bankruptcies has grown dramatically in recent years.

Reorganization Time and Expense

The time, expense, and headaches involved in a reorganization are almost beyond comprehension. Even in $2 to $3 million bankruptcies, many people and groups are involved: lawyers representing the company, the U.S. Bankruptcy Trustee, each class of secured creditor, the general creditors as a group, tax authorities, and the stockholders if they are upset with management. There are time limits within which things are supposed to be done, but the process generally takes at least a year and probably much longer. The company must be given time to file its plan, and creditor groups must be given time to study and seek clarifications to it and then file counterplans to which the company must respond. Also, different creditor classes often disagree among themselves as to how much each class should receive, and hearings must be held to resolve such conflicts.

Management will want to remain in business, while some well-secured creditors may want the company liquidated as quickly as possible. Often, some party's plan will involve selling the business to another concern, as was the case with Columbia Software in our earlier example. Obviously, it can take months to seek out and negotiate with potential merger candidates.

The typical bankruptcy case takes about two years from the time the company files for protection under Chapter 11 until the final reorganization plan is approved or rejected. While all of this is going on, the company's business suffers. Sales certainly won't be helped, key employees may leave, and the remaining employees will be worrying about their jobs rather than concentrating on their work. Further, management will be spending much of its time on the bankruptcy rather than running the business, and it won't be able to take any significant action without court approval, which requires filing a formal petition with the court and giving all parties involved a chance to respond.

Even if its operations do not suffer, the company's assets will surely be reduced by its own legal fees and the required court and trustee costs. Good bankruptcy lawyers charge from $150 to $250 per hour, depending on the location, so those costs are not trivial. The creditors will also be incurring legal costs. Indeed, the sound of all of those meters ticking at $200 an hour in a slow-moving hearing can be deafening.

Note that creditors also lose the time value of their money. A creditor with a $100,000 claim and a 10 percent opportunity cost who ends up getting $50,000 after two years would have been better off settling for $41,500 initially. When the creditor's legal fees, executive time, and general aggravation are taken into account, it might even make sense to settle for $20,000 or $25,000.

Both the troubled company and its creditors know the drawbacks of formal bankruptcy, or their lawyers will inform them. Armed with a knowledge of how bankruptcy

---

[11]Note that in both tax situations—loss carryforwards and debt value reductions—favorable tax treatment can be available in workouts if the firm is deemed to be legally insolvent, that is, if the market value of its assets is demonstrated to be less than the face value of its liabilities.

works, management may be in a strong position to persuade creditors to accept a work-out which on the surface appears to be unfair and unreasonable. Or, if a Chapter 11 case has already begun, creditors may at some point agree to settle just to stop the bleeding.

One final point should be made before closing this section. In most reorganization plans, creditors with claims of less than $1,000 are paid off in full. Paying off these "nuisance claims" does not cost much money, and it saves time and gets votes to support the plan.

SELF-TEST QUESTIONS

Define the following terms:
 (1) Common pool problem
 (2) Holdout problem
 (3) Automatic stay
 (4) Cramdown
 (5) Fraudulent conveyance
 (6) Absolute priority doctrine
 (7) Relative priority doctrine
 (8) Fairness
 (9) Feasibility
 (10) Debtor-in-possession financing
 (11) Prepackaged bankruptcy

What are the advantages of a formal reorganization under Chapter 11?

What has been the recent trend regarding absolute versus relative priority doctrines?

How do courts assess the fairness of proposed reorganization plans?

How do courts assess the feasibility of proposed reorganization plans?

Why have prepackaged bankruptcies become so popular in recent years?

LIQUIDATION IN BANKRUPTCY

If a company is "too far gone" to be reorganized, then it must be liquidated. Liquidation should occur when the business is worth more dead than alive, or when the possibility of restoring it to financial health is remote and the creditors are exposed to a high risk of greater loss if operations are continued. Earlier we discussed assignment, which is an informal liquidation procedure. Now we consider **liquidation in bankruptcy,** which is carried out under the jurisdiction of a federal bankruptcy court.

Chapter 7 of the Federal Bankruptcy Reform Act deals with liquidation. It (1) provides safeguards against fraud by the debtor, (2) provides for an equitable distribution of the debtor's assets among the creditors, and (3) allows insolvent debtors to discharge all their obligations and thus be able to start new businesses unhampered by the burdens of prior debt. However, formal liquidation is time consuming and costly, and it extinguishes the business.

The distribution of assets in a liquidation under Chapter 7 is governed by the following priority of claims:

1. **Past-due property taxes.**

2. **Secured creditors, who are entitled to the proceeds of the sale of specific property pledged for a lien or a mortgage.** If the proceeds from the sale of the pledged

property do not fully satisfy a secured creditor's claim, the remaining balance is treated as a general creditor claim (see Item 10 below).[12]

3. **Legal fees and other expenses to administer and operate the bankrupt firm.** These costs include legal fees incurred in trying to reorganize.

4. **Expenses incurred after an involuntary case has begun but before a trustee is appointed.**

5. **Wages due workers if earned within three months prior to the filing of the petition in bankruptcy.** The amount of wages is limited to $2,000 per employee.

6. **Claims for unpaid contributions to employee pension plans that should have been paid within six months prior to filing.** These claims, plus wages in Item 5, may not exceed the $2,000-per-wage-earner limit.

7. **Unsecured claims for customer deposits.** These claims are limited to a maximum of $900 per individual.

8. **Taxes due to federal, state, county, and other government agencies.**

9. **Unfunded pension plan liabilities.** These liabilities have a claim above that of the general creditors for an amount up to 30 percent of the common and preferred equity, and any remaining unfunded pension claims rank with the general creditors.[13]

10. **General, or unsecured, creditors.** Holders of trade credit, unsecured loans, the unsatisfied portion of secured loans, and debenture bonds are classified as general creditors. Holders of subordinated debt also fall into this category, but they must turn over required amounts to the senior debt.

11. **Preferred stockholders.** These stockholders can receive an amount up to the par value of their stock.

12. **Common stockholders.** These stockholders receive any remaining funds.[14]

To illustrate how this priority system works, consider the balance sheet of Whitman Inc., shown in Table 25-6. Assets have a book value of $90 million. The claims are shown on the right-hand side of the balance sheet. Note that the debentures are sub-

---

[12]When a firm or individual who goes bankrupt has a bank loan, the bank will attach any deposit balances. The loan agreement may stipulate that the bank has a first-priority claim on any deposits. If this is the case, the deposits are used to offset all or part of the bank loan; this is called, in legal terms, "the right of offset." In this case, the bank will not have to share the deposits with other creditors. Loan contracts often designate compensating balances as security against a loan. Even if the bank has no explicit claim against deposits, the bank will attach the deposits and hold them for the general body of creditors, including the bank itself. Without an explicit statement in the loan agreement, the bank does not receive preferential treatment with regard to attached deposits.

[13]Pension plan liabilities have a significant bearing on bankruptcy settlements. As we discuss in Chapter 28, pension plans may be funded or unfunded. Under a funded plan, the firm makes cash payments to an insurance company or to a trustee (generally a bank), which then uses these funds (and interest earned on them) to pay retirees' pensions. Under an unfunded plan, the firm is obligated to make payments to retirees, but it does not provide cash in advance. Many plans are actually partially funded—some money has been paid in advance, but not enough to provide full pension benefits to all employees.

If a firm goes bankrupt, the funded part of the pension plan remains intact and is available for retirees. Prior to 1974, employees had no explicit claims for unfunded pension liabilities, but under the Employees' Retirement Income Security Act of 1974 (ERISA), an amount up to 30 percent of the equity (common and preferred) is earmarked for employees' pension plans and has a priority over the general creditors, with any remaining pension claims having status equal to that of the general creditors. This means, in effect, that the funded portion of a bankrupt firm's pension plan is completely secured, but that the unfunded portion ranks somewhat above the general creditors. Obviously, unfunded pension fund liabilities should be of great concern to a firm's unsecured creditors.

[14]Note that if different classes of common stock have been issued, differential priorities may exist in stockholder claims.

| TABLE 25-6 | Whitman Inc.: Balance Sheet at Liquidation (Millions of Dollars) |

Current assets	$80.0	Accounts payable	$20.0
Net fixed assets	10.0	Notes payable (to banks)	10.0
		Accrued wages (1,400 @ $500)	0.7
		Federal taxes	1.0
		State and local taxes	0.3
		Current liabilities	$32.0
		First mortgage	$ 6.0
		Second mortgage	1.0
		Subordinated debentures[a]	8.0
		Total long-term debt	$15.0
		Preferred stock	$ 2.0
		Common stock	26.0
		Paid-in capital	4.0
		Retained earnings	11.0
		Total equity	$43.0
Total assets	$90.0	Total liabilities and equity	$90.0

[a]The debentures are subordinated to the notes payable.

ordinated to the notes payable to banks. Whitman filed for bankruptcy under Chapter 11, but since no fair and feasible reorganization could be arranged, the trustee is liquidating the firm under Chapter 7.

The assets as reported in the balance sheet are greatly overstated; they are, in fact, worth less than half the $90 million at which they are carried. The following amounts are realized on liquidation:

From sale of current assets	$28,000,000
From sale of fixed assets	5,000,000
Total receipts	$33,000,000

The distribution of proceeds from the liquidation is shown in Table 25-7. The first-mortgage holders receive the $5 million in net proceeds from the sale of fixed property, leaving $28 million available to the remaining creditors, including a $1 million unsatisfied claim of the first-mortgage holders. Next are the fees and expenses of administering the bankruptcy, which are typically about 20 percent of gross proceeds (including the bankrupt firm's own legal fees); in this example, they are assumed to be $6 million. Next in priority are wages due workers, which total $700,000, and taxes due, which amount to $1.3 million. Thus far, the total amount of claims paid from the $33 million received from the asset sale is $13 million, leaving $20 million for the general creditors. In this example, we assume that there are no claims for unpaid benefit plans or unfunded pension liabilities.

The claims of the general creditors total $40 million. Since $20 million is available, claimants will initially be allocated 50 percent of their claims, as shown in Column 3. However, the subordination adjustment requires that the subordinated debentures turn over to the notes payable all amounts received until the notes are satisfied. In

TABLE 25-7	Whitman Inc.: Distribution of Liquidation Proceeds (Millions of Dollars)

Distribution to Priority Claimants

Proceeds from the sale of assets	$33.0
Less:	
1. First mortgage (paid from the sale of fixed assets)	5.0
2. Fees and expenses of bankruptcy	6.0
3. Wages due to workers within three months of bankruptcy	0.7
4. Taxes due to federal, state, and local governments	1.3
Funds available for distribution to general creditors	$20.0

Distribution to General Creditors

GENERAL CREDITORS' CLAIMS (1)	AMOUNT OF CLAIM[a] (2)	PRO RATA DISTRIBUTION[b] (3)	DISTRIBUTION AFTER SUBORDINATION ADJUSTMENT[c] (4)	PERCENTAGE OF ORIGINAL CLAIM RECEIVED[d] (5)
Unsatisfied portion of first mortgage	$ 1.0	$ 0.5	$ 0.5	92%
Second mortgage	1.0	0.5	0.5	50
Notes payable (to banks)	10.0	5.0	9.0	90
Accounts payable	20.0	10.0	10.0	50
Subordinated debentures	8.0	4.0	0.0	0
Total	$40.0	$20.0	$20.0	

[a]Column 2 is the claim of each class of general creditor. Total claims equal $40.0 million.

[b]From the top section of the table, we see that $20 million is available for distribution to general creditors. Since there are $40 million of general creditor claims, the pro rata distribution will be $20/$40 = 0.50, or 50 cents on the dollar.

[c]The debentures are subordinate to the notes payable, so up to $5 million could be reallocated from debentures to notes payable. However, only $4 million is available to the debentures, so this entire amount is reallocated.

[d]Column 5 shows the results of dividing the Column 4 final allocation by the original claim shown in Column 2, except for the first mortgage, where the $5 million received from the sale of fixed assets is included in the calculation.

this situation, the claim of the notes payable is $10 million, but only $5 million is available; the deficiency is therefore $5 million. After transfer of $4 million from the subordinated debentures, there remains a deficiency of $1 million on the notes; this amount will remain unsatisfied.

Note that 90 percent of the bank claim is satisfied, whereas a maximum of 50 percent of other unsecured claims will be satisfied. These figures illustrate the usefulness of the subordination provision to the security to which the subordination is made.

Since no other funds remain, the claims of the holders of preferred and common stocks, as well as the subordinated debentures, are completely wiped out. Studies of the proceeds in bankruptcy liquidations reveal that unsecured creditors receive, on the average, about 15 cents on the dollar, while common stockholders generally receive nothing.

SELF-TEST QUESTIONS

Describe briefly the priority of claims in a formal liquidation.

What is the impact of subordination on the final allocation of proceeds from liquidation?

In general, how much do unsecured creditors receive from a liquidation? How much do stockholders receive?

OTHER MOTIVATIONS FOR BANKRUPTCY

Normally, bankruptcy proceedings do not commence until a company has become so financially weak that it cannot meet its current obligations. However, bankruptcy law also permits a company to file for bankruptcy if its financial forecasts indicate that a continuation of current conditions would lead to insolvency. This provision was used by Continental Airlines in 1983 to break its union contract and hence lower its labor costs. Continental demonstrated to a bankruptcy court that operations under the then-current union contract would lead to insolvency in a matter of months. The company then filed a reorganization plan that included major changes in all its contracts, including its union contract. The court sided with Continental and allowed the company to abrogate its contract. Continental then reorganized as a nonunion carrier, and that reorganization turned the company from a money loser into a money maker.[15] Congress changed the law after the Continental affair to make it more difficult for companies to use bankruptcy to break union contracts, but this case did set the precedent for using bankruptcy to help head off financial problems as well as to help solve existing ones.

Bankruptcy law has also been used to hasten settlements in major product liability suits. The Manville asbestos and A. H. Robins dalkon shield cases are examples. In both situations, the companies were being bombarded by thousands of lawsuits, and the very existence of such huge contingent liabilities made normal operations impossible. Further, in both cases it was relatively easy to prove (1) that if the plaintiffs won, the companies would be unable to pay the full amount of the claims, (2) that a larger amount of funds would be available to the claimants if the companies continued to operate rather than liquidate, (3) that continued operations were possible only if the suits were brought to a conclusion, and (4) that a timely resolution of all the suits was impossible because of their vast number and variety. The bankruptcy statutes were used to consolidate all the suits and to reach settlements under which the plaintiffs obtained more money than they otherwise would have received, and the companies were able to stay in business. The stockholders did poorly under these plans, because most of the companies' future cash flows were assigned to the plaintiffs, but even so, the stockholders probably fared better than they would have if the suits had been concluded through the jury system.

SELF-TEST
QUESTION

What are some situations other than immediate financial distress that lead firms to file for bankruptcy?

SOME CRITICISMS OF BANKRUPTCY LAWS

Although bankruptcy laws, for the most part, exist to protect creditors, many critics claim that current laws are not doing what they were intended to do. Before 1978, most bankruptcies ended quickly in liquidation. Then Congress rewrote the laws, giving companies more opportunity to stay alive, on the grounds that this was best for managers, employees, creditors, and stockholders. Before the reform, 90 percent of Chapter 11 filers were liquidated, but now that percentage is less than 80 percent, and the average time between filing and liquidation has almost doubled. Indeed, large public corporations with the ability to hire high-priced legal help can avoid, or at least delay, liquidation, often at the expense of creditors and shareholders.

---

[15]As we discussed in the opening section, Continental's fortunes declined again in 1990 when it was unable to successfully integrate several acquisitions, including Eastern, and the company filed for bankruptcy a second time. It emerged successfully, and in 1998 it was doing well.

Critics believe that bankruptcy is great for businesses these days—especially for consultants, lawyers, and investment bankers, who reap hefty fees during bankruptcy proceedings, and for managers, who continue to collect their salaries and bonuses as long as the business is kept alive. The problem, according to critics, is that bankruptcy courts allow cases to drag on too long, depleting assets that could be sold to pay off creditors and shareholders. Too often, quick resolution is impossible because bankruptcy judges are required to deal with issues such as labor disputes, pension plan funding, and environmental liability—social questions that could be solved by legislative action rather than by bankruptcy courts.

For example, LTV Corporation was in bankruptcy from 1986 to 1993, mainly because of pension disputes between the company, its workers, retirees, and the federal government. During this time, the Dallas-based conglomerate spent $162 million in legal and consulting fees, but, under the final reorganization plan, creditors got only 4 to 53 cents on the dollar, and stockholders got nothing.

Critics contend that bankruptcy judges ought to realize that some sick companies should be allowed to die—and die quickly. Maintaining companies on life support does not serve the interests of the parties the bankruptcy laws were meant to protect. One proposal for overhauling the system calls for limiting the time that companies have to file a reorganization plan. A debtor is supposed to have only 120 days, but the deadline is almost never enforced. It might make more sense to set a deadline of six months or a year and then stick to it. "Bankruptcy is like open-heart surgery—the longer you stay under the knife, the lower the chance of success," says James E. Spiotto, a creditor's lawyer with Chapman & Cutler in Chicago. "We should be seeking a quick, efficient way to give companies a fresh start."

Other critics think the entire bankruptcy system of judicial protection and supervision needs to be scrapped. Some even have proposed a kind of auction procedure, where shareholders and creditors would have the opportunity to gain control of a bankrupt company by raising the cash needed to pay the bills. The rationale here is that the market is a better judge than a bankruptcy court as to whether a company is worth more dead or alive.

Finally, note that companies operating under the protection of Chapter 11 can damage and perhaps even bankrupt their otherwise healthy competitors. To illustrate, Eastern Airlines' cash costs were low during its bankruptcy because it did not have to service its debt, and it was also generating cash by selling off assets. Eastern used its cash to advertise heavily and to cut fares, both of which siphoned off traffic from other airlines. Obviously, this hurt the other airlines and indeed led to other airline bankruptcies. Had Eastern been put down in a timely fashion, the airline industry would be a lot healthier today.

SELF-TEST QUESTION | According to critics, what are some problems with the bankruptcy system?

OTHER TOPICS IN BANKRUPTCY

Some additional insights into the reorganization and liquidation process can be gained by reviewing recent bankruptcies. Therefore, in the Extensions section of this chapter, we discuss the Eastern Airlines and Revco bankruptcies. Also, financial analysts are constantly seeking ways to assess a firm's likelihood of going bankrupt. We discuss one method, Multiple Discriminant Analysis (MDA), in the Extensions section.

SUMMARY

This chapter discussed the main issues involved in bankruptcy and financial distress in general. The key concepts are listed below:

- The proportion of businesses that fail fluctuates with the economy, but the average liability per failure has tended to increase over time due to inflation and to an increase in the number of billion-dollar bankruptcies in recent years.

- The fundamental issue that must be addressed when a company encounters financial distress is whether it is "worth more dead than alive"; that is, would the business be more valuable if it continued in operation or if it were liquidated and sold off in pieces?

- In the case of a fundamentally sound company whose financial difficulties appear to be temporary, creditors will frequently work directly with the company, helping it to recover and reestablish itself on a sound financial basis. Such voluntary reorganization plans are called **workouts.**

- Reorganization plans usually require some type of **restructuring** of the firm's debts, involving either an **extension,** which postpones the date of required payment of past-due obligations, or a **composition,** by which the creditors voluntarily reduce their claims on the debtor or the interest rate on their claims.

- When it is obvious that a firm is worth more dead than alive, informal procedures can sometimes be used to **liquidate** the firm. **Assignment** is an informal procedure for liquidating a firm, and it usually yields creditors a larger amount than they would receive in a formal bankruptcy liquidation. However, assignments are feasible only if the firm is small and its affairs are not too complex.

- Current **bankruptcy law** consists of nine chapters, designated by Arabic numbers. For businesses, the most important chapters are **Chapter 7,** which details the procedures to be followed when liquidating a firm, and **Chapter 11,** which contains procedures for formal reorganizations.

- Since the first bankruptcy laws, most formal reorganization plans have been guided by the **absolute priority doctrine.** This doctrine holds that creditors should be compensated for their claims in a rigid hierarchical order, and that senior claims must be paid in full before junior claims can receive even a dime.

- Another position, the **relative priority doctrine,** holds that more flexibility should be allowed in a reorganization, and that a balanced consideration should be given to all claimants. In recent years, there has been a shift away from absolute priority toward relative priority. The primary effect of this shift has been to delay liquidations so as to give managements more time to rehabilitate companies in an effort to provide value to junior claimants.

- The primary role of the bankruptcy court in a reorganization is to determine the **fairness** and the **feasibility** of proposed plans of reorganization.

- Even if some creditors or stockholders dissent and do not accept a reorganization plan, the plan may still be approved by the court if the plan is deemed to be "fair and equitable" to all parties. This procedure, in which the court mandates a reorganization plan in spite of dissent, is called a **cramdown.**

- In the last few years, a new type of reorganization that combines the advantages of both the informal workout and formal Chapter 11 reorganization has become popular. This new hybrid is called a **prepackaged bankruptcy.**

- The distribution of assets in a **liquidation** under Chapter 7 of the Bankruptcy Act is governed by a specific priority of claims.

Questions

25-1 Define each of the following terms:
a. Informal restructuring; reorganization in bankruptcy
b. Assignment; liquidation in bankruptcy

    c. Fairness; feasibility
    d. Absolute priority doctrine; relative priority doctrine
    e. Bankruptcy Reform Act of 1978; Chapter 11; Chapter 7
    f. Priority of claims in liquidation
    g. Extension; composition
    h. Workout; cramdown
    i. Prepackaged bankruptcy
    j. Holdout

25-2 "A certain number of business failures is a healthy sign. If there are no failures, this is an indication (a) that entrepreneurs are overly cautious, and hence not as inventive and as willing to take risks as a healthy, growing economy requires; (b) that competition is not functioning to weed out inefficient producers; or (c) that both situations exist." Discuss this statement.

25-3 Why do creditors usually accept a plan for financial rehabilitation rather than demand liquidation of the business?

25-4 Would it be possible to form a profitable company by merging two companies, both of which are business failures? Explain.

25-5 Would it be a sound rule to liquidate whenever the liquidation value is above the value of the corporation as a going concern? Discuss.

25-6 Why do liquidations usually result in losses for the creditors or the owners, or both? Would partial liquidation or liquidation over a period limit their losses? Explain.

25-7 Are liquidations likely to be more common for public utility, railroad, or industrial corporations? Why?

Problems

25-1
Reorganization

The Verbrugge Publishing Company's 1998 balance sheet and income statement are as follows (in millions of dollars). Verbrugge and its creditors have agreed upon a voluntary reorganization plan. In this plan, each share of the $6 preferred will be exchanged for one share of $2.40 preferred with a par value of $37.50 plus one 8 percent subordinated income debenture with a par value of $75. The $10.50 preferred issue will be retired with cash.

Balance Sheet

Current assets	$168	Current liabilities	$ 42
Net fixed assets	153	Advance payments	78
Goodwill	15	Reserves	6
		$6 preferred stock, $112.50 par value (1,200,000 shares)	135
		$10.50 preferred stock, no par, callable at $150 (60,000 shares)	9
		Common stock, $1.50 par value (6,000,000 shares)	9
		Retained earnings	57
Total assets	$336	Total claims	$336

Income Statement

Net sales	$540.0
Operating expense	516.0
Net operating income	$ 24.0
Other income	3.0
EBT	$ 27.0
Taxes (50%)	13.5
Net income	$ 13.5
Dividends on $6 preferred	7.2
Dividends on $10.50 preferred	0.6
Income available to common stockholders	$ 5.7

a. Construct the pro forma balance sheet assuming that reorganization takes place. Show the new preferred at its par value.

b. Construct the pro forma income statement. How much does the proposed recapitalization increase income available to common shareholders?

c. *Required earnings* is defined as the amount that is just enough to meet fixed charges (debenture interest and/or preferred dividends). What are the required pre-tax earnings before and after the recapitalization?

d. How is the debt ratio affected by the reorganization? If you were a holder of Verbrugge's common stock, would you vote in favor of the reorganization?

25-2
Liquidation

At the time it defaulted on its interest payments and filed for bankruptcy, the McDaniel Mining Company had the following balance sheet (in thousands of dollars). The court, after trying unsuccessfully to reorganize the firm, decided that the only recourse was liquidation under Chapter 7. Sale of the fixed assets, which were pledged as collateral to the mortgage bondholders, brought in $400,000, while the current assets were sold for another $200,000. Thus, the total proceeds from the liquidation sale were $600,000. Trustee's costs amounted to $50,000; no single worker was due more than $2,000 in wages; and there were no unfunded pension plan liabilities.

Current assets	$ 400	Accounts payable	$ 50
Net fixed assets	600	Accrued taxes	40
		Accrued wages	30
		Notes payable	180
		Total current liabilities	$ 300
		First-mortgage bonds[a]	300
		Second-mortgage bonds[a]	200
		Debentures	200
		Subordinated debentures[b]	100
		Common stock	50
		Retained earnings	(150)
Total assets	$1,000	Total claims	$1,000

[a]All fixed assets are pledged as collateral to the mortgage bonds.
[b]Subordinated to notes payable only.

a. How much will McDaniel's shareholders receive from the liquidation?

b. How much will the mortgage bondholders receive?

c. Who are the other priority claimants in addition to the mortgage bondholders? How much will they receive from the liquidation?

d. Who are the remaining general creditors? How much will each receive from the distribution before subordination adjustment? What is the effect of adjusting for subordination?

25-3
Liquidation

The following balance sheet represents Boles Electronics Corporation's position at the time it filed for bankruptcy (in thousands of dollars):

Cash	$ 10	Accounts payable	$ 1,600
Receivables	100	Notes payable	500
Inventories	890	Wages payable	150
		Taxes payable	50
Total current assets	$ 1,000	Total current liabilities	$ 2,300
Net plant	4,000	Mortgage bonds	2,000
Net equipment	5,000	Subordinated debentures	2,500
		Preferred stock	1,500
		Common stock	1,700
Total assets	$10,000	Total claims	$10,000

The mortgage bonds are secured by the plant, but not by the equipment. The subordinated debentures are subordinated to notes payable. The firm was unable to reorganize under Chapter 11; therefore, it was liquidated under Chapter 7. The trustee, whose legal and administrative fees amounted to $200,000, sold off the assets and received the following proceeds (in thousands of dollars):

Asset	Proceeds
Plant	$1,600
Equipment	1,300
Receivables	50
Inventories	240
Total	$3,190

In addition, the firm had $10,000 in cash available for distribution. No single wage earner had over $2,000 in claims, and there were no unfunded pension plan liabilities.

a. What is the total amount available for distribution to all claimants? What is the total of creditor and trustee claims? Will the preferred and common stockholders receive any distributions?

b. Determine the dollar distribution to each creditor and to the trustee. What percentage of each claim is satisfied?

MINI CASE

Kimberly MacKenzie, president of Kim's Clothes Inc., a medium-sized manufacturer of women's casual clothing, is worried. Her firm has been selling clothes to Russ Brothers Department Store for more than 10 years, and she has never experienced any problems in collecting payment for the merchandise sold. Currently, Russ Brothers owes Kim's Clothes $65,000 for spring sportswear that was delivered to the store just 2 weeks ago. Kim's concern was brought about by an article that appeared in yesterday's *Wall Street Journal* that indicated that Russ Brothers was having serious financial problems. Further, the article stated that Russ Brothers' management was considering filing for reorganization, or even liquidation, with a federal bankruptcy court.

Kim's immediate concern was whether or not her firm would collect its receivables if Russ Brothers went bankrupt. In pondering the situation, Kim also realized that she knew nothing about the process that firms go through when they encounter severe financial distress. To learn more about bankruptcy, reorganization, and liquidation, Kim asked Ron Mitchell, the firm's chief financial officer, to prepare a briefing on the subject for the entire board of directors. In turn, Ron asked you, a newly hired financial analyst, to do the groundwork for the briefing by answering the following questions.

a. (1) What are the major causes of business failure?
   (2) Do business failures occur evenly over time?
   (3) Which size of firm, large or small, is more prone to business failure? Why?
b. What key issues must managers face in the financial distress process?
c. What informal remedies are available to firms in financial distress? In answering this question, define the following terms:
   (1) Workout
   (2) Restructuring
   (3) Extension
   (4) Composition
   (5) Assignment
   (6) Assignee (trustee)
d. Briefly describe U.S. bankruptcy law, including the following terms:
   (1) Chapter 11
   (2) Chapter 7
   (3) Trustee
   (4) Voluntary bankruptcy
   (5) Involuntary bankruptcy
e. What are the major differences between an informal reorganization and reorganization in bankruptcy? In answering this question, be sure to discuss the following items:
   (1) Common pool problem
   (2) Holdout problem

(3) Automatic stay
(4) Cramdown
(5) Fraudulent conveyance

f. What is a prepackaged bankruptcy? Why have prepackaged bankruptcies become more popular in recent years?

g. Briefly describe the priority of claims in a Chapter 7 liquidation.

h. Assume that Russ Brothers did indeed fail, and that it had the following balance sheet when it was liquidated (in millions of dollars):

Current assets	$40.0	Accounts payable	$10.0
Net fixed assets	5.0	Notes payable (to banks)	5.0
		Accrued wages	0.3
		Federal taxes	0.5
		State and local taxes	0.2
		Current liabilities	$16.0
		First mortgage	$ 3.0
		Second mortgage	0.5
		Subordinated debentures[a]	4.0
		Total long-term debt	$ 7.5
		Preferred stock	$ 1.0
		Common stock	13.0
		Paid-in capital	2.0
		Retained earnings	5.5
		Total equity	$21.5
Total assets	$45.0	Total claims	$45.0

[a]The debentures are subordinated to the notes payable.

The liquidation sale resulted in the following proceeds:

From sale of current assets	$14,000,000
From sale of fixed assets	2,500,000
Total receipts	$16,500,000

For simplicity, assume that there were no trustee's fees or any other claims against the liquidation proceeds. Also, assume that the mortgage bonds are secured by the entire amount of fixed assets. What would each claimant receive from the liquidation distribution?

Selected Additional References and Cases

For a better understanding of multiple discriminant analysis and its use to predict corporate bankruptcy, see

Collins, Robert A., "An Empirical Comparison of Bankruptcy Prediction Models," *Financial Management,* Summer 1980, 52–57.

Eisenbeis, Robert A., "Pitfalls in the Application of Discriminant Analysis," *Journal of Finance,* June 1977, 875–900.

Joy, O. Maurice, and John O. Tollefson, "On the Financial Application of Discriminant Analysis," *Journal of Financial and Quantitative Analysis,* December 1975, 723–739.

For more information on bankruptcy costs, see

Altman, Edward I., "A Further Empirical Investigation of the Bankruptcy Cost Question," *Journal of Finance,* September 1984, 1067–1089.

Guffey, Daryl M., and William T. Moore, "Direct Bankruptcy Costs: Evidence from the Trucking Industry," *Financial Review,* May 1991, 223–235.

Warner, Jerold B., "Bankruptcy Costs: Some Evidence," *Journal of Finance,* May 1977, 337–347.

In addition to those articles cited in the chapter, the Summer 1991 issue of the Journal of Applied Corporate Finance *contains the following relevant works:*

Fitts, Peter, et al., "Bankruptcies, Workouts, and Turnarounds: A Roundtable Discussion," 34–61.

Gilson, Stuart C., "Managing Default: Some Evidence on How Firms Choose between Workouts and Chapter 11," 62–70.

Weiss, Lawrence A., "The Bankruptcy Code and Violations of Absolute Priority," 71–78.

The following articles and publications provide insights into various aspects of bankruptcy:

Betker, Brian L., "An Empirical Examination of Prepackaged Bankruptcy," *Financial Management,* Spring 1995, 3–18.

Beranek, William, Robert Boehmer, and Brooke Smith, "Much Ado about Nothing: Absolute Priority Deviations in Chapter 11," *Financial Management,* Autumn 1996, 102–109.

Brown, David T., "Claimholder Incentive Conflicts in Reorganization: The Role of Bankruptcy Law," *Review of Financial Studies,* 1989, 109–123.

Business Failure Record (New York: Dun & Bradstreet, Inc., updated annually).

Chatterjee, Sris, Upinder S. Dhillon, and Gabriel G. Ramirez, "Resolution of Financial Distress: Debt Restructurings via Chapter 11, Prepackaged Bankruptcies, and Workouts," *Financial Management,* Spring 1996, 5–18.

Chen, Yehning, J. Fred Weston, and Edward I. Altman, "Financial Distress and Restructuring Models," *Financial Management,* Summer 1995, 57–75.

Eberhart, Allan C., William T. Moore, and Rodney Roenfeldt, "Security Pricing and Deviations from the Absolute Priority Rule in Bankruptcy Proceedings," *Journal of Finance,* December 1990, 1457–1469.

Franks, Julian R., and Walter N. Torous, "An Empirical Investigation of U.S. Firms in Reorganization," *Journal of Finance,* July 1989, 747–769.

Harris, Richard, "The Consequences of Costly Default," *Economic Inquiry,* October 1978, 477–496.

Kaiser, Kevin M. J., "European Bankruptcy Laws: Implications for Corporations Facing Financial Distress," *Financial Management,* Autumn 1996, 67–85.

McConnell, John J., Ronald C. Lease, and Elizabeth Tashjian, "Prepacks as a Mechanism for Resolving Financial Distress," *Journal of Applied Corporate Finance,* Winter 1996, 99–106.

The following bankruptcy case can be found in the Cases in Financial Management: Dryden Request *series:*

Case 65, "Bubbling Springs Water Company," which examines both liquidation and restructuring alternatives for a firm in financial distress.

EXTENSIONS

Recent Business Failures

This section sketches two of the more prominent recent business failures. They provide additional insights into the bankruptcy process.

Eastern Airlines. During the 1980s, Eastern Airlines was plagued by seemingly unending woes, from incessant labor strife to occasionally poor service, which caused the airline to lose hundreds of millions of dollars.[1] Finally, under its chairman, Frank Lorenzo, the company filed for Chapter 11 bankruptcy in March 1989 after a showdown with its unions. Lorenzo, who was determined to break the unions' strike, insisted that he could restore Eastern to profitability if given enough time. Every few months, the company would submit projections to the bankruptcy court showing that the airline

---

[1]For more information on the Eastern bankruptcy, see "Eastern: The Wings of Greed," which was published in the November 11, 1991, issue of *Business Week.*

was about to turn the corner, while creditors complained that the forecasts were wildly optimistic.

The bankruptcy judge stated early on that keeping Eastern flying was in the "public interest" and that this goal outweighed the "parochial" concerns of the creditors. Thus, the court allowed Lorenzo to sell off assets and use the proceeds to cover operating losses. In early 1990, the unsecured creditors demanded that a trustee be appointed to run Eastern, and Martin Shugrue was appointed by the court in April. By then, however, $1.2 billion in assets that could have gone to creditors had been sold, and the funds had evaporated. Although analysts gave Eastern almost no chance of surviving, Shugrue launched an expensive program to restore the carrier to health. About $35 million was spent on national TV ads featuring the trustee as the leader of a new Eastern, and millions more were poured into new leather seats and increased flight attendants for first-class passengers to try to steal full-fare passengers from rival carriers which had better reputations for service, such as Delta.

When the Persian Gulf war slowed air travel and sent fuel prices upward, it became obvious to all, even the court, that Eastern would never make it, so the court finally agreed to shut it down for good on January 18, 1991. By that time, however, Eastern had wasted another $530 million in its attempt to stay afloat.

It took from January 1991 to December 1994 for the bankruptcy court to approve the liquidation plan. By that time, more than $95 million had been paid out to lawyers and other bankruptcy officials, and hundreds of millions had been vaporized in operating losses. All priority claims—including those to employees, the pension plan, and secured creditors—were paid in full, which required more than $1 billion of the liquidation proceeds. The 70,000 general creditors fared less well: They received roughly 11 cents on the dollar. Clearly, a more timely liquidation would have greatly increased the payout to the unsecured creditors.

What about Martin Shugrue, the trustee? He moved on to greener pastures; he is now president of a resurrected Pan American, which is trying to muscle its way back into the very competitive skies of commercial aviation.

Revco. On December 29, 1986, Revco Drug Stores went private in a leveraged buyout.[2] At the time, Revco was one of the nation's largest retail drug chains, operating over 2,000 stores in 30 states. The buyout increased management's ownership in the company from 3 percent to 31 percent, but it also raised the company's indebtedness from $309 million to $1.3 billion, including $700 million in subordinated notes (junk bonds). Immediately after the buyout, the company only had $35 million in common equity out of $1.7 billion in capital, for an equity ratio of only 2 percent. Given the heavy debt burden, several analysts stated that a hiccup would throw the company into bankruptcy.

Indeed, on April 15, 1988, Revco announced that it could not make a $46 million interest payment on its subordinated notes. In a press release issued that day, the company said: "Revco believes that its business is strong and its operations solid; however, our current capitalization is not the appropriate one for the company. After evaluation, Revco's board has determined that a financial restructuring is appropriate." The company and its creditors wanted to avoid the costs of a Chapter 11 bankruptcy, so they made several attempts at a workout. For example, in mid-May Revco's management proposed that bondholders exchange their subordinated notes for a new class of common stock that would leave then-current stockholders with only 5 percent ownership. Such a restructuring was consistent with the argument that the LBO team paid too much for the company and that any equity value remaining after the overpayment was destroyed by poor operating performance. However, this proposal failed because the company's stockholders would not agree to go along with it.

As Revco's fortunes fell, Magten Asset Management, a firm that specializes in investing in distressed companies, began buying Revco's senior subordinated notes at about 50 cents on the dollar. By late June, Magten had accumulated more than 25 percent of that particular security, which gave it veto power over any reorganization plan, whether private or under court supervision. Such power gave Magten the right to hold out for higher returns before consenting to any reorganization plan. On July 7, 1988, bondholders agreed to a one-month "standstill," whereby creditors agreed not to take action against Revco for missing its June interest payments. However, the company's cash flow was not improving, and on July 22 Magten demanded full and immediate payment of all principal and interest due. This action triggered cross-default provisions, which put Revco in default on all its borrowings. On July 28, 1988, Revco filed for protection under Chapter 11 of the Bankruptcy Act.

Following the formal bankruptcy filing, numerous reorganization plans were proposed, but most failed because of disagreements among the various claimants. In September 1991, creditors filed a plan in which they would get 100 percent ownership of the company in return for agreeing to lighten Revco's current debt load of $1.5 billion. In addition, the plan called for Salomon Brothers, an investment bank which had collected almost $40 million in fees on the original over-leveraged LBO deal, to pay $9.5 million to the creditors in return for an agreement to drop several proposed suits against Salomon. In the plan, banks that had lent Revco $306 million would receive $205 million of new 12 percent notes due December 31, 1998, a small amount of cash, and some new convertible preferred stock. The value of this package of securities was estimated at about 60 cents on the dollar. Holders of Revco's subordinated notes did not fare even that well. They would get common stock in the post-bankruptcy Revco, but no cash or notes. These notes had been trading at about 18 cents on the dollar, reflecting investors' beliefs that the final reorganization plan would leave little for bondholders. Revco's stockholders would receive nothing—stockholders are almost always wiped out when creditors are forced to accept less than their original claims.

Finally, in June 1992 the plan was accepted, and Revco emerged from bankruptcy with fewer than 1,200 stores. With several former creditors now on the board, the first order of

---

[2]For more detail on the Revco buyout and subsequent failure, see Karen H. Wruck, "What Really Went Wrong at Revco," *Journal of Applied Corporate Finance,* Summer 1991, 79–92.

business was to fire the chairman, Boake Sells. Then, the board created a committee of five executives to lead the company. In spite of its years of problems, many analysts predicted a bright future for Revco once it shed its onerous debt burden. In fact, the company did well, becoming an industry leader in the use of technology to fill and track prescriptions. Today, Revco is the second largest drug store chain, with more than 2,200 stores. It has fully recovered from its reorganization, and it is poised for rapid growth as the population ages.

Using Multiple Discriminant Analysis to Predict Bankruptcy

As we have seen, bankruptcy, or even the possibility of bankruptcy, can cause significant trauma for a firm's managers, investors, suppliers, customers, and community. Thus, it would be beneficial to be able to predict the likelihood of bankruptcy so that steps could be taken to avoid it or at least to reduce its impact. One approach to bankruptcy prediction is *Multiple Discriminant Analysis (MDA)*, a statistical technique similar to regression analysis. In this section, we discuss MDA in detail, and we illustrate its application to bankruptcy prediction.[3]

The Basics of Multiple Discriminant Analysis.   Suppose a bank loan officer wants to segregate corporate loan applications into those likely to default and those not likely to default. Assume that data for some past period are available on a group of firms which includes both companies that went bankrupt and companies that did not. For simplicity, we assume that only the current ratio and the debt/assets ratio are analyzed. These ratios for our sample of firms are given in Columns 2 and 3 at the bottom of Figure 25E-1. The Xs in the graph represent firms that went bankrupt, while the dots represent firms that remained solvent. For example, Point A in the upper left section is the point for Firm 2, which had a current ratio of 3.0 and a debt ratio of 20 percent, and a dot indicates that the firm did not go bankrupt. Point B, in the lower right section, represents Firm 19, which had a current ratio of 1.0 and a debt ratio of 60 percent, and the X indicates that it did go bankrupt.

The objective of discriminant analysis is to construct a boundary line through the graph such that if the firm is to the left of the line, it is not likely to become insolvent, whereas it is likely to go bankrupt if it falls to the right. This boundary line is called the *discriminant function,* and in our example it takes this form:

$$Z = a + b_1(\text{Current ratio}) + b_2(\text{Debt ratio}).$$

Here Z is called the *Z score,* a is a constant term, and b_1 and b_2 indicate the effects of the current ratio and the debt ratio on the probability of a firm going bankrupt.

Although a full discussion of discriminant analysis would go well beyond the scope of this book, some useful insights may be gained by observing these points:

1. The discriminant function is fitted (that is, the values of a, b_1, and b_2 are obtained) using historical data for a sample of firms that either went bankrupt or did not during some past period. When the data in the lower part of Figure 25E-1 were fed into a "canned" discriminant analysis program (the computing centers of most universities and large corporations have such programs), the following discriminant function was obtained:

   $$Z = -0.3877 - 1.0736(\text{Current ratio}) + 0.0579(\text{Debt ratio}).$$

2. This equation was plotted on Figure 25E-1 as the locus of points for which Z = 0. All combinations of current ratios and debt ratios shown on the line result in Z = 0.[4] Companies that lie to the left of the line (and also have Z values less than zero) are not likely to go bankrupt, while those to the right (and have Z greater than zero) are likely to go bankrupt. It can be seen from the graph that one X, indicating a failing company, lies to the left of the line, while two dots, indicating nonbankrupt companies, lie to the right of the line. Thus, the discriminant analysis failed to properly classify three companies.

3. Once we have determined the parameters of the discriminant function, we can calculate the Z scores for other companies, say, loan applicants at a bank. The Z scores for our hypothetical companies, along with their probabilities for going bankrupt, are given in Columns 5 and 6 of Figure 25E-1. The higher the Z score, the worse the company looks from the standpoint of bankruptcy. Here is an interpretation:

   Z = 0: 50-50 probability of future bankruptcy (say, within two years). The company lies exactly on the boundary line.

   Z < 0: If Z is negative, there is a less than 50 percent probability of bankruptcy. The smaller (more negative) the Z score, the lower the probability of bankruptcy. The computer output from MDA programs gives this probability, and it is shown in Column 6 of Figure 25E-1.

---

[3]This section is based largely on the work of Edward I. Altman, especially these three papers: (1) "Financial Ratios, Discriminant Analysis, and the Prediction of Corporate Bankruptcy," *Journal of Finance,* September 1968, 589–609; (2) with Robert G. Haldeman and P. Narayanan, "Zeta Analysis: A New Model to Identify Bankruptcy Risk of Corporations," *Journal of Banking and Finance,* June 1977, 29–54; and (3) Salomon Brothers, with John Hartzell and Matthew Peck, "Emerging Market Corporate Bonds, A Scoring System," May 15, 1995. The last article reviews and updates Altman's earlier work and applies it internationally.

[4]To plot the boundary line, let D/A = 0% and 80%, and then find the current ratio that forces Z = 0 at those two values. For example, at D/A = 0,

$$Z = -0.3877 - 1.0736(\text{Current ratio}) + 0.0579(0) = 0$$
$$0.3877 = -1.0736(\text{Current ratio})$$
$$\text{Current ratio} = 0.3877/(-1.0736) = -0.3611.$$

Thus, −0.3611 is the vertical axis intercept. Similarly, the current ratio at D/A = 80% is found to be 3.9533. Plotting these two points on Figure 25E-1, and then connecting them, provides the discriminant boundary line, which is the line that best partitions the companies into bankrupt and nonbankrupt. It should be noted that nonlinear discriminant functions may be used, and we could also use more dependent variables.

FIGURE 25E-1   Discriminant Boundary between Bankrupt and Solvent Firms

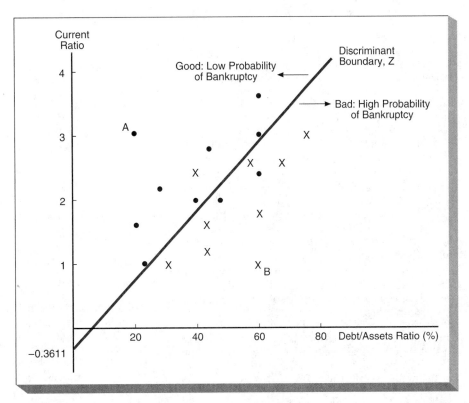

FIRM NUMBER (1)	CURRENT RATIO (2)	DEBT/ASSETS RATIO (3)	DID FIRM GO BANKRUPT? (4)	Z SCORE (5)	PROBABILITY OF BANKRUPTCY (6)
1	3.6×	60%	No	−0.780	17.2%
2(A)	3.0	20	No	−2.451	0.8
3	3.0	60	No	−0.135	42.0
4	3.0	76	Yes	0.791	81.2
5	2.8	44	No	−0.847	15.5
6	2.6	56	Yes	0.062	51.5
7	2.6	68	Yes	0.757	80.2
8	2.4	40	Yes[a]	−0.649	21.1
9	2.4	60	No[a]	0.509	71.5
10	2.2	28	No	−1.129	9.6
11	2.0	40	No	−0.220	38.1
12	2.0	48	No[a]	0.244	60.1
13	1.8	60	Yes	1.153	89.7
14	1.6	20	No	−0.948	13.1
15	1.6	44	Yes	0.441	68.8
16	1.2	44	Yes	0.871	83.5
17	1.0	24	No	−0.072	45.0
18	1.0	32	Yes	0.391	66.7
19(B)	1.0	60	Yes	2.012	97.9

continued

Z > 0: If Z is positive, the probability of bankruptcy is greater than 50 percent, and the larger Z, the greater the probability of bankruptcy.

4. The mean Z score of the companies that did not go bankrupt is −0.583, while that for the bankrupt firms is +0.648. These means, along with approximations of the Z score probability distributions of the two groups, are shown in Figure 25E-2. We may interpret this graph as indicating that if Z is less than about −0.3, there is a very small probability that the firm will go bankrupt, whereas if Z is greater than +0.3, there is only a small probability that it will remain solvent. If Z is in the range ±0.3, called the *zone of ignorance,* we are uncertain about how the firm should be classified.

5. The signs of the coefficients of the discriminant function are logical. A high current ratio is good, and since its coefficient is negative, the higher the current ratio, the lower the probability of failure. Similarly, high debt ratios produce high Z scores, and this is consistent with a higher probability of bankruptcy.

6. Our illustrative discriminant function has only two variables, but other characteristics could be introduced. For example, we could add such variables as the rate of return on assets, the times-interest-earned ratio, the days sales outstanding, the quick ratio, and so forth.[5] Had the rate of return on assets been introduced, it might have turned out that Firm 8 (which failed) had a low ROA, while Firm 9 (which did not fail) had a high ROA. A new discriminant function would be calculated:

$$Z = a + b_1(\text{Current ratio}) + b_2(\text{D/A}) + b_3(\text{ROA}).$$

Firm 8 might now have a positive Z, while Firm 9's Z might become negative. Thus, it is likely that by adding more characteristics we would improve the accuracy of our bankruptcy forecasts. In terms of Figure 25E-2, this would cause each probability distribution to become tighter, narrow the zone of ignorance, and lead to fewer misclassifications.

Altman's Model. In a classic paper, Edward Altman applied MDA to a sample of corporations, and he developed a discriminant function that has had wide use in actual practice. Altman's function was fitted as follows:

$$Z = 0.012X_1 + 0.014X_2 + 0.033X_3$$
$$+ 0.006X_4 + 0.999X_5. \qquad \textbf{(25E-1)}$$

Here

X_1 = net working capital/total assets.

X_2 = retained earnings/total assets.[6]

X_3 = EBIT/total assets.

X_4 = market value of common and preferred stock/book value of debt.[7]

X_5 = sales/total assets.

The first four variables in Equation 25E-1 are expressed as percentages rather than as decimals. (For example, if X_3 = 13.3%, then 13.3, *not* 0.133, is used as its value.) Also, Altman's 50-50 point was 2.675, and not 0.0 as in our hypothetical example; his zone of ignorance was from Z = 1.81 to Z = 2.99; and in his model the *larger* the Z score, the less the probability of bankruptcy.[8]

Altman's function can be used to calculate a Z score for MicroDrive Inc. based on the data presented previously in Chapter 2, Tables 2-1 and 2-2. Here is the calculation, ignoring the small amount of preferred stock, for 1998:

Figure 25E-1 footnote

[a]If the "Z score" in Column 5 is negative, the firm should not go bankrupt, but a positive Z score predicts bankruptcy. There were three misclassifications. Firm 8 had Z = −0.649, so MDA predicted no bankruptcy, but it did go bankrupt. Similarly, MDA predicted bankruptcy for Firms 9 and 12, but they did not go bankrupt. The following tabulation shows bankruptcy and solvency predictions versus actual results:

	Z POSITIVE: MDA PREDICTS BANKRUPTCY	Z NEGATIVE: MDA PREDICTS SOLVENCY
Did subsequently go bankrupt	8	1
Remained solvent	2	8

The model did not perform perfectly, as two predicted bankruptcies remained solvent and one firm that was expected to remain solvent went bankrupt. Thus, the model misclassified 3 out of 19 firms, or 16 percent of the sample. Its success rate was 84 percent.

---

[5]With more than two variables, it is difficult to graph the function, but this presents no problem in actual usage because graphs are only used to explain MDA.

[6]Retained earnings is the balance sheet figure, not the addition to retained earnings for the year.

[7][(Shares of common outstanding)(Price per share) + (Shares of preferred)(Price per share of preferred)]/Balance sheet value of total debt, including all short-term liabilities.

[8]These differences reflect the software package Altman used to generate the discriminant function. Altman's program did not specify a constant term, and his program simply reversed the sign of Z from ours.

FIGURE 25E-2   Probability Distributions of Z Scores

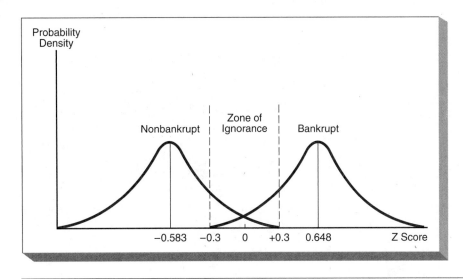

$X_1 = \$400/\$2,000 = 0.200 = 20.0\%$ $20.0 \times 0.012 = 0.240$

$X_2 = \$660/\$2,000 = 0.330 = 33.0\%$ $33.0 \times 0.014 = 0.462$

$X_3 = \$266/\$2,000 = 0.133 = 13.3\%$ $13.3 \times 0.033 = 0.439$

$X_4 = [50(\$28.50) + 1(\$102)]/$

     $(\$300 + \$800) = 1.388 = 138.8\%$ $138.8 \times 0.006 = 0.833$

$X_5 = \$3,000/\$2,000 = 1.5$ $1.5 \times 0.999 = \underline{1.499}$

$$Z = \underline{\underline{3.473}}$$

Since MicroDrive's Z score of 3.473 is above the 2.99 upper limit of Altman's zone of ignorance, the data indicate that there is virtually no chance that MicroDrive will go bankrupt within the next two years. (Altman's model predicts bankruptcy reasonably well for about two years into the future.)

Altman and his colleagues' later work updated and improved his original study. In their more recent work, they explicitly considered such factors as capitalized lease obligations, and they applied smoothing techniques to level out random fluctuations in the data. The new model was able to predict bankruptcy with a high degree of accuracy for two years into the future, and with a slightly lower but still reasonable degree of accuracy (70 percent) for about five years.

MDA has been used with success by credit analysts to establish default probabilities for both consumer and corporate loan applicants, and by portfolio managers considering both stock and bond investments. It can also be used to evaluate a set of pro forma ratios as developed in Chapter 14, or to gain insights into the feasibility of a reorganization plan filed under the Bankruptcy Act. Altman's model has also been used by Salomon Brothers, Morgan Stanley, and other investment banking houses to appraise the quality of junk bonds used to finance takeovers and leveraged buyouts. The technique is described in detail in many statistics texts, while several articles cited at the end of this chapter discuss financial applications of MDA. The interested reader is urged to study this literature, for MDA has many potentially valuable applications in finance.

When using MDA in practice it is best to create your own discriminant data using a recent sample from the industry in question. It is not reasonable to assume that the financial ratios of a steel company facing imminent bankruptcy are the same as for a retail grocery chain in equally dire straits. If both firms were analyzed using Z scores calculated with the same equation, it might turn out that the grocery chain had a relatively high score, signifying (incorrectly) a low probability of bankruptcy, while the steel company had a relatively low score, indicating (correctly) a high probability of bankruptcy. The misclassification of the grocery company could result from the fact that it has very high sales for the amount of its book assets, hence its X_5, which has the largest coefficient, is much higher than for an average firm in an average industry facing potential bankruptcy. To remove any such industry bias, the MDA analysis should be based on a sample with characteristics similar to those of the firm being analyzed. Unfortunately, though, it is often not possible to find enough firms that have recently gone bankrupt to conduct an industry MDA.

MERGERS, LBOs, DIVESTITURES, AND HOLDING COMPANIES

*O*n October 1, 1997, WorldCom Inc. chairman Bernie Ebbers called MCI chairman Bert Roberts and announced that he planned to offer $30 billion for MCI. This was the largest merger offer in history, and one that would reshape the entire telecommunications industry, from local phone service to control of the Internet.

Until the late 1960s, AT&T had a monopoly on U.S. telephone service. A copper wire network tied phone users together, and it would have been terribly inefficient to have more than one national company. In exchange for its government-granted monopoly, AT&T agreed to price local residential service rates below cost and to offset losses in this sector by charging high rates to businesses, to long-distance users, and for telephone equipment. Moreover, all residential users were charged essentially the same rates, regardless of the cost of providing service. As a result, rates of return on some of AT&T's assets were much higher than on other assets.

By the 1980s, the natural monopoly no longer existed. Microwave, satellite, fiberoptic, and wireless (cellular) technologies made it possible for many companies to operate and bring competition to the industry. Moreover, it is well known that competitive firms are more efficient than monopolistic ones, so there was pressure to knock down the regulatory barriers and let competition in.

If a company could enter the high-profit sectors and avoid the low-profit residential sector, it could make a killing. MCI's founders recognized this, so they sought and received permission to set up microwave systems between such major cities as New York and Chicago, thereby undercutting AT&T's artifically high rates, and they made a fortune "skimming cream." AT&T protested, but without avail, and its monopoly was broken. Other companies entered other profitable sectors. Finally, in 1983, Congress broke AT&T up, creating seven regional Bell companies that were to provide local service (deemed to still be a natural monopoly) and a new AT&T which was to retain the "competitive" services, primarily long distance and equipment manufacturing.

MCI was highly profitable from the start, and by 1997 its revenues had grown to $28 billion. It had a state-of-the-art fiber-optic network, and it was one of the major players in the rapidly growing Internet market. Moreover, MCI had agreed with British Telecom (BT) to merge and create the first global telecom powerhouse.

Now enter WorldCom. In September 1983, shortly after the AT&T breakup, Bernie Ebbers, a high school basketball coach who had gotten into the hotel business, met for coffee with three friends to discuss the telephone situation. As hotel operators, they had seen how profitable long-distance service was, so they decided to set up a long-distance company themselves. They would lease transmission lines from existing companies at relatively low bulk rates, resell use of the lines to AT&T's overcharged business customers, and make a profit on the transaction. By 1997, WorldCom had become the largest player in the Internet market, had one of the largest and most modern fiberoptic long-distance networks, and had a foothold in most of the larger urban markets.

WorldCom had been eyeing MCI for some time, because Ebbers could see tremendous cost-cutting and revenue-increasing synergies if WorldCom and MCI merged. However, MCI was a much larger company (revenues of $28 billion versus $8 billion for WorldCom), and it is hard for a minnow to swallow a whale. However, Ebbers still decided to strike, offering $30 billion for MCI's stock versus BT's $20 billion.

Assuming the MCI acquisition is completed, WorldCom will suddenly be in a position to oust AT&T as the world's most powerful telecommunications company. Indeed, it will have almost recreated the old AT&T, with local and long-distance service plus almost 60 percent of the new Internet market.

The MCI/WorldCom merger was, when it was announced, the largest business combination in history. More recently, the Citicorp/Travelers, NationsBank/BankAmerica, and Chrysler/Daimler-Benz proposed mergers exceeded it. Technology and markets are changing rapidly and producing potential economies of scale and scope in many industries, both in the United States and around the world, and that is leading to ever-increasing numbers of larger and larger mergers. So, the MCI/WorldCom situation is just one example of the kind of activity that is happening every day to change the face of companies and industries around the world.

SOURCES: "The New World Order," *Business Week*, October 13, 1997, 26–34; "WorldCom's MCI Bid Alters Playing Field for Telecom Industry," *The Wall Street Journal*, October 2, 1997, 1.

Most corporate growth occurs by *internal expansion*, which takes place when a firm's existing divisions grow through normal capital budgeting activities. However, the most dramatic examples of growth, and often the largest increases in firms' stock prices, result from *mergers*, the first topic covered in this chapter. *Leveraged buyouts*, or *LBOs*, occur when a firm's stock is acquired by a small group of investors rather than by another operating company. Since LBOs are similar to mergers in many respects, they are also covered in this chapter. Conditions change over time, causing firms to sell off, or *divest*, major divisions to other firms that can better utilize the divested assets. Divestitures are also discussed in the chapter. Finally, we discuss the *holding company* form of organization, wherein one corporation owns the stock of one or more other companies.

RATIONALE FOR MERGERS

Many reasons have been proposed by financial managers and theorists to account for the high level of U.S. merger activity. The primary motives behind corporate **mergers** are presented in this section.[1]

Synergy

The primary motivation for most mergers is to increase the value of the combined enterprise. If Companies A and B merge to form Company C, and if C's value exceeds that of A and B taken separately, then **synergy** is said to exist. Such a merger should be beneficial to both A's and B's stockholders.[2] Synergistic effects can arise from four

---

[1] As we use the term, *merger* means any combination that forms one economic unit from two or more previous ones. For legal purposes, there are distinctions among the various ways these combinations can occur, but our focus is on the fundamental economic and financial aspects of mergers.

[2] If synergy exists, then the whole is greater than the sum of the parts. Synergy is also called the "2 plus 2 equals 5 effect." The distribution of the synergistic gain between A's and B's stockholders is determined by negotiation. This point is discussed later in the chapter.

sources: (1) *operating economies,* which result from economies of scale in management, marketing, production, or distribution; (2) *financial economies,* including lower transactions costs and better coverage by security analysts; (3) *differential efficiency,* which implies that the management of one firm is more efficient and that the weaker firm's assets will be more productive after the merger; and (4) *increased market power* due to reduced competition. Operating and financial economies are socially desirable, as are mergers that increase managerial efficiency, but mergers that reduce competition are socially undesirable and illegal.[3]

Lotus Development Corporation was acquired recently by IBM. Lotus had an outstanding group of software developers, and it owned the Notes system for communicating between PC users. However, its marketing was relatively weak, and it had a shortage of capital. IBM, on the other hand, had an outstanding marketing organization and a huge pool of capital, so it was able to increase the market value of Lotus's assets. The recently announced merger between Morgan Stanley and Dean Witter is another synergistic merger. This deal "unites Wall Street with Main Street." Morgan Stanley, an elite investment bank which specializes in underwriting securities for the world's leading corporations, is joining forces with Dean Witter, which has thousands of sales representatives and 40 million retail customers. After the merger, Dean Witter's brokers can distribute securities brought in by Morgan Stanley's investment bankers, and this should help both organizations in the increasingly competitive securities markets. The NationsBank/BankAmerica merger will provide almost nationwide banking, and the Citicorp/Travelers merger will provide one-stop shopping for financial services.

Tax Considerations

Tax considerations have stimulated a number of mergers. For example, a profitable firm in the highest tax bracket could acquire a firm with large accumulated tax losses. These losses could then be turned into immediate tax savings rather than carried forward and used in the future.[4] Also, mergers can serve as a way of minimizing taxes when disposing of excess cash. For example, if a firm has a shortage of internal investment opportunities compared with its free cash flow, it could (1) pay an extra dividend, (2) invest in marketable securities, (3) repurchase its own stock, or (4) purchase another firm. If it pays an extra dividend, its stockholders would have to pay immediate taxes on the distribution. Marketable securities often provide a good temporary parking place for money, but they generally earn a rate of return less than that required by stockholders. A stock repurchase might result in a capital gain for the remaining stockholders. However, using surplus cash to acquire another firm would avoid all these problems, and this has motivated a number of mergers.

Purchase of Assets below Their Replacement Cost

Sometimes a firm will be touted as an acquisition candidate because the cost of replacing its assets is considerably higher than its market value. For example, in the early

---

[3]In the 1880s and 1890s, many mergers occurred in the United States, and some of them were obviously directed toward gaining market power rather than increasing efficiency. As a result, Congress passed a series of acts designed to ensure that mergers are not used as a method of reducing competition. The principal acts include the Sherman Act (1890), the Clayton Act (1914), and the Celler Act (1950). These acts make it illegal for firms to combine if the combination tends to lessen competition. The acts are enforced by the antitrust division of the Justice Department and by the Federal Trade Commission.

[4]Mergers undertaken only to use accumulated tax losses would probably be challenged by the IRS. In recent years Congress has made it increasingly difficult for firms to pass along tax savings after mergers.

1980s oil companies could acquire reserves cheaper by buying other oil companies than by doing exploratory drilling. Thus, Chevron acquired Gulf Oil to augment its reserves. Similarly, in the 1980s several steel company executives stated that it was cheaper to buy an existing steel company than to construct a new mill. For example, LTV (the fourth largest steel company) acquired Republic Steel (the sixth largest) to create the second largest firm in the industry.

Diversification

Managers often cite diversification as a reason for mergers. They contend that diversification helps stabilize a firm's earnings and thus benefits its owners. Stabilization of earnings is certainly beneficial to employees, suppliers, and customers, but its value is less certain from the standpoint of stockholders. Why should Firm A acquire Firm B to stabilize earnings when stockholders can simply buy the stock of both firms?

Of course, if you were the owner-manager of a closely held firm, it might be nearly impossible to sell part of your stock to diversify. Also, selling your stock would probably lead to a large capital gains tax. So, a diversification merger might be the best way to achieve personal diversification.

Managers' Personal Incentives

Financial economists like to think that business decisions are based only on economic considerations, especially maximization of firms' values. However, many business decisions are based more on managers' personal motivations than on economic analyses. Business leaders like power, and more power is attached to running a larger corporation than a smaller one. Obviously, no executive would admit that his or her ego was the primary reason behind a merger, but egos do play a prominent role in many mergers.

It has also been observed that executive salaries are highly correlated with company size—the bigger the company, the higher the salaries of its top officers. This too could play a role in corporate acquisition programs.

Personal considerations deter as well as motivate mergers. After most takeovers, some managers of the acquired companies lose their jobs, or at least their autonomy. Therefore, managers who own less than 51 percent of their firms' stock look to devices that will lessen the chances of a takeover. Mergers can serve as such a device. For example, when Enron was under attack, it arranged to buy Houston Natural Gas, paying for Houston primarily with debt. That merger made Enron much larger, hence harder for any potential acquirer to "digest," and the much higher debt level made it harder for an acquiring company to use debt to buy Enron. Such **defensive mergers** are hard to defend on economic grounds. The managers involved invariably argue that synergy, not a desire to protect their own jobs, motivated the acquisition, but observers suspect that many mergers were designed more to benefit managers than stockholders.

Breakup Value

Firms can be valued by book value, economic value, or replacement value. Recently, takeover specialists have begun to recognize **breakup value** as another basis for valuation. Analysts estimate a company's breakup value, which is the value of the individual parts of the firm if they were sold off separately. If this value is higher than the firm's current market value, then a takeover specialist could acquire the firm at or even above its current market value, sell it off in pieces, and earn a substantial profit.

Define synergy. Is synergy a valid rationale for mergers? Describe several situations that might produce synergistic gains.

Give two examples of how tax considerations can motivate mergers.

Suppose your firm could purchase another firm for only half of its replacement value. Would that be a sufficient justification for the acquisition?

Discuss the pros and cons of diversification as a rationale for mergers.

What is breakup value?

TYPES OF MERGERS

Economists classify mergers into four types: (1) horizontal, (2) vertical, (3) congeneric, and (4) conglomerate. A **horizontal merger** occurs when one firm combines with another in its same line of business—the NationsBank/BankAmerica merger is an example. An example of a **vertical merger** would be a steel producer's acquisition of one of its own suppliers, such as an iron or coal mining firm, or an oil producer's acquisition of a petrochemical firm which uses oil as a raw material. *Congeneric* means "allied in nature or action," hence a **congeneric merger** involves related enterprises but not producers of the same product (horizontal) or firms in a producer-supplier relationship (vertical). The Citicorp/Travelers merger is an example. A **conglomerate merger** occurs when unrelated enterprises combine, as illustrated by Mobil Oil's acquisition of Montgomery Ward.

Operating economies (and also anticompetitive effects) are at least partially dependent on the type of merger involved. Vertical and horizontal mergers generally provide the greatest synergistic operating benefits, but they are also the ones most likely to be attacked by the Department of Justice as anticompetitive. In any event, it is useful to think of these economic classifications when analyzing prospective mergers.

What are the four economic types of mergers?

LEVEL OF MERGER ACTIVITY

Five major "merger waves" have occurred in the United States. The first was in the late 1800s, when consolidations occurred in the oil, steel, tobacco, and other basic industries. The second was in the 1920s, when the stock market boom helped financial promoters consolidate firms in a number of industries, including utilities, communications, and autos. The third was in the 1960s, when conglomerate mergers were the rage. The fourth occurred in the 1980s, when LBO firms and others began using junk bonds to finance all manner of acquisitions. The fifth, which involves strategic alliances designed to enable firms to compete better in the global economy, is in progress today.

As can be seen from Table 26-1, some huge mergers have occurred in recent years, and, as indicated in the opening vignette, much bigger ones are in the works.[5] The table lists only mergers involving U.S. firms, but large mergers are not unique to the

---

[5]For detailed reviews of the 1980s merger wave, see Andrei Shleifer and Robert W. Vishny, "The Takeover Wave of the 1980s," *Journal of Applied Corporate Finance,* Fall 1991, 49–56; Edmund Faltermayer, "The Deal Decade: Verdict on the '80s," *Fortune,* August 26, 1991, 58–70; and "The Best and Worst Deals of the '80s: What We Learned from All Those Mergers, Acquisitions, and Takeovers," *Business Week,* January 15, 1990, 52–57.

TABLE 26-1	The Five Biggest Mergers through 1996 Involving U.S. Corporations (Billions of Dollars)		

COMPANY	YEAR	VALUE	PAID THE ACQUIRED FIRM'S STOCKHOLDERS WITH:
AT&T-McCaw Cellular	1994	$18.9	Stock
Disney-Capital Cities/ABC	1996	18.8	Cash and stock
Wells Fargo-First Interstate	1996	14.2	Stock
Time-Warner Communications	1990	14.1	Cash
Boeing-McDonnell Douglas	1996	14.0	Stock
Chevron-Gulf	1984	13.3	Cash

United States. For example, in 1996, global drug companies Ciba-Geigy and Sandoz Ltd. announced a merger which was valued at more than $30 billion. In general, the mergers in the 1990s have been significantly different from those of the 1980s. Most 1980s mergers were financial transactions in which buyers sought companies that were selling at less than their true values as a result of incompetent or sluggish management. If a target company could be managed better, if redundant assets could be sold, and if operating and administrative costs could be cut, profits and stock prices would rise. In the 1990s, on the other hand, most of the mergers have been strategic in nature—companies are merging to gain economies of scale or scope and thus be better able to compete in the world economy. Indeed, many recent mergers have involved companies in the financial, defense, media, computer, telecommunications, and health care industries, all of which are experiencing structural changes and intense competition.

Other differences between the 1980s and the 1990s are the way the mergers were financed and how the target firms' stockholders were compensated. In the 1980s, cash was the preferred method of payment, because large cash payments could convince even the most reluctant shareholder to approve the deal. Moreover, the cash was generally obtained by borrowing, which left the consolidated company with a heavy debt burden, which often led to difficulties. In the 1990s, stock has replaced borrowed cash as the merger currency for two reasons: (1) Many of the 1980s mergers were financed with junk bonds which later went into default. These defaults, along with the demise of Drexel Burnham, the leading junk bond dealer, have made it difficult to arrange debt-financed mergers. (2) During the 1990s, most mergers have been strategic—as between NationsBank and BankAmerica, IBM and Lotus, and Disney and Cap Cities/ABC—where both companies' managers realized that they needed one another. Most of these mergers have been friendly, and stock swaps are easier to arrange in friendly mergers than in hostile ones. Also, both sets of managers have been concerned about the postmerger financial strength of the consolidated company, and the surviving company will obviously be stronger if the deal is financed with stock rather than debt.

Although the larger 1990s mergers have generally been stock-for-stock, many of the smaller mergers have been for cash. Even here, though, things have been different. In the 1980s, companies typically borrowed to get the money to finance cash acquisitions. In the 1990s, corporate cash flows have been very high, so companies have been able to pay for their smaller acquisitions out of cash flow.

Yet another factor in the 1990s has been the increase in cross-border mergers. Many of these mergers have been motivated by large shifts in the value of the world's leading currencies. For example, in the early 1990s, the dollar was weak relative to the yen and the mark. The decline in the dollar made it easier for Japanese and German acquirers to buy U.S. corporations.

SELF-TEST
QUESTIONS

What five major "merger waves" have occurred in the United States?

What are some reasons for the current wave?

HOSTILE VERSUS FRIENDLY TAKEOVERS

In the vast majority of merger situations, one firm (generally the larger of the two) simply decides to buy another company, negotiates a price with the management of the target firm, and then acquires the target company. Occasionally, the acquired firm will initiate the action, but it is much more common for a firm to seek acquisitions than to seek to be acquired.[6] Following convention, we call a company that seeks to acquire another firm the **acquiring company** and the one which it seeks to acquire the **target company.**

Once an acquiring company has identified a possible target, it must (1) establish a suitable price, or range of prices, and (2) tentatively set the terms of payment—will it offer cash, its own common stock, bonds, or some combination? Next, the acquiring firm's managers must decide how to approach the target company's managers. If the acquiring firm has reason to believe that the target's management will approve the merger, then it will simply propose a merger and try to work out some suitable terms. If an agreement is reached, then the two management groups will issue statements to their stockholders indicating that they approve the merger, and the target firm's management will recommend to its stockholders that they agree to the merger. Generally, the stockholders are asked to *tender* (or send in) their shares to a designated financial institution, along with a signed power of attorney which transfers ownership of the shares to the acquiring firm. The target firm's stockholders then receive the specified payment, either common stock of the acquiring company (in which case the target company's stockholders become stockholders of the acquiring company), cash, bonds, or some mix of cash and securities. This is a **friendly merger.**

The 1997 acquisition of Celebrity Cruise Lines by Royal Caribbean International typifies a friendly merger. After secret negotiations between the two boards, an agreement was announced at a joint press conference. The acquisition was fought briefly by Carnival Corporation, which made its own offer for Celebrity, but Royal Caribbean increased its offer by $15 million, and the deal was sealed. The merger was approved by the shareholders of both companies, and no antitrust issues were raised. Therefore, the merger was completed just a few months after the initial announcement. Royal Caribbean paid $515 million in cash and common stock for Celebrity, and it also assumed $800 million of Celebrity's debt.

The acquisition gives Royal Caribbean, which will operate Celebrity as a separate brand, instant access to the upscale cruise market. Furthermore, Celebrity now has economies of scale that it could never achieve operating independently. Mergers in the highly competitive cruise industry have been commonplace in recent years, and many observers predict that only a handful of companies will survive into the next century.

---

[6]However, if a firm is in financial difficulty, if its managers are elderly and do not think that suitable replacements are on hand, or if it needs the support (often the capital) of a larger company, then it may seek to be acquired. Thus, when a number of Texas, Ohio, and Maryland financial institutions were in trouble in the 1980s, they lobbied to get their state legislatures to pass laws that would make it easier for them to be acquired. Out-of-state banks then moved in to help salvage the situation and minimize depositor losses.

By 2000, Royal Caribbean is expected to have about 30,000 berths, but Carnival, the world's largest cruise line, will still dominate the industry with about 50,000.

Often, however, the target company's management resists the merger. Perhaps they feel that the price offered is too low, or perhaps they simply want to keep their jobs. In either case, the acquiring firm's offer is said to be *hostile* rather than friendly, and the acquiring firm must make a direct appeal to the target firm's stockholders. In a **hostile merger,** the acquiring company will again make a **tender offer,** and again it will ask the stockholders of the target firm to tender their shares in exchange for the offered price. This time, though, the target firm's managers will urge stockholders not to tender their shares, generally stating that the price offered (cash, bonds, or stocks in the acquiring firm) is too low.

The battle between Shamrock Holdings and Polaroid illustrates a failed hostile merger attempt. It began when Polaroid's stock was trading in the low $30s. At the time, many analysts had declared that Polaroid was a likely takeover candidate because of its sluggish performance but strong brand name. Also, Polaroid was expected to receive a substantial settlement from its successful suit against Eastman Kodak, which had been found guilty of violating Polaroid's instant camera patents.

Shamrock Holdings, the investment vehicle of the Roy E. Disney family, proposed a friendly takeover, was rebuffed, and then made a $45-per-share hostile tender offer. Polaroid responded to the unwanted offer (1) by selling a block of its stock to a newly established employee stock ownership plan (ESOP), (2) by selling another block to a friendly investor (a *white squire*), and (3) by buying back 22 percent of its outstanding shares at $50 a share. To finance all of this, Polaroid added $536 million in bank debt. Additionally, Polaroid announced that it was restructuring its operations by cutting its work force by 15 percent, and that was expected to boost profits. Shamrock responded to these actions (1) by initiating a **proxy fight** to elect a new slate of officers at Polaroid, and (2) by filing a court suit challenging the legitimacy of Polaroid's defensive maneuvers.

After nine months of heated exchange, an accord was reached. Polaroid agreed to pay Shamrock $20 million in compensation for expenses incurred in the battle, and Shamrock signed an agreement promising not to seek control of Polaroid for ten years. Also, Polaroid agreed to spend $5 million in advertising on Shamrock's radio and television stations and to distribute to shareholders much of its pending award from Kodak. Although defeated, Shamrock ended up making about $35 million before taxes, considering both the cash settlement and the price increase on the Polaroid shares it owned. Polaroid ended up with more debt and less cash. Polaroid's president and CEO said, "The fundamental changes and initiatives put in place during this period made us stronger, despite the pressure." (Note: In the spring of 1998, Polaroid's stock was selling for $40, or $5 below the $45 offered several years earlier. Meanwhile, the market as measured by the Dow Jones industrials had more than doubled. Were Polaroid's shareholders well served by its managers' resistance to the Shamrock takeover?)

The battle of Ingersoll-Rand for Clark Equipment illustrates a hostile takeover that succeeded. The battle began when Ingersoll-Rand, an industrial machinery maker, approached Clark, a construction equipment manufacturer, with a proposal to negotiate a friendly acquisition. After Clark's management rebuffed the proposal, Ingersoll-Rand announced a hostile, all-cash tender offer of $77 per share for Clark's stock. The shares, which were selling for just over $50 prior to the offer, immediately jumped to $83 in anticipation of a competing bidder at a higher price. Clark's board rejected the offer, but in view of the high price set on the bid, the board came under intense pressure to negotiate a deal. Adding to the pressure was the fact that Clark, unlike most companies, elected all of its directors each year, so the entire seven-member board ran the risk of being ousted at the next shareholder meeting—only a month away. With the pressure mounting, Clark's board agreed to a sweetened $86-per-share deal only one week after the hostile tender offer was launched.

The Clark acquisition illustrates three points. First, an all-cash offer that is high enough will generally overcome any resistance by the target firm's management. Second, and this appears to be a trend in the 1990s wave, strategic buyers often begin the hostile bidding process with a "preemptive" or "blowout" bid. The idea here is to offer such a high premium over the preannouncement price that no other bidders will be willing to jump into the fray and the target company's board cannot simply reject the bid. Third, if a hostile bid is eventually accepted by the target's board, the deal ends up as "friendly," regardless of the acrimony during the hostile phase.

IBM is reported to have negotiated with Lotus for almost two years before launching its hostile tender offer. The week before the offer was announced, Lotus's stock sold for $30 per share. IBM offered $60 per share, a 100 percent premium. IBM decided to make a preemptive bid, one so high that Lotus's stockholders would tender their stock and that no "white knight" could match or exceed. IBM had a cash hoard in excess of $10 billion, so it was unlikely that its bid could be stopped. Lotus's board agreed to the takeover at a price of $64 per share, so again, a hostile offer ended up as a friendly merger.

S E L F - T E S T
Q U E S T I O N | What's the difference between a hostile and a friendly merger?

MERGER REGULATION

Prior to the mid-1960s, friendly acquisitions generally took place as simple exchange-of-stock mergers, and a proxy fight was the primary weapon used in hostile control battles. However, in the mid-1960s corporate raiders began to operate differently. First, it took a long time to mount a proxy fight—raiders had to first request a list of the target company's stockholders, be refused, and then get a court order forcing management to turn over the list. During that time, the target's management could think through and then implement a strategy to fend off the raider. As a result, management won most proxy fights.

Then raiders began saying to themselves, "If we could bring the decision to a head quickly, before management can take countermeasures, that would greatly increase our probability of success." That led the raiders to turn from proxy fights to tender offers, which had a much shorter response time. For example, the stockholders of a company whose stock was selling for $20 might be offered $27 per share and be given two weeks to accept. The raider, meanwhile, would have accumulated a substantial block of the shares in open market purchases, and additional shares might have been purchased by institutional friends of the raider who promised to tender their shares in exchange for the tip that a raid was to occur.

Faced with a well-planned raid, managements were generally overwhelmed. The stock might actually be worth more than the offered price, but management simply did not have time to get this message across to stockholders or to find a competing bidder. This situation seemed unfair, so Congress passed the Williams Act in 1968. This law had two main objectives: (1) to regulate the way acquiring firms can structure takeover offers and (2) to force acquiring firms to disclose more information about their offers. Basically, Congress wanted to put target managements in a better position to defend against hostile offers. Additionally, Congress believed that shareholders needed easier access to information about tender offers—including information on any securities that might be offered in lieu of cash—in order to make rational tender-versus-don't-tender decisions.

The Williams Act placed the following four restrictions on acquiring firms: (1) Acquirers must disclose their current holdings and future intentions within ten days of amassing at least 5 percent of a company's stock. (2) Acquirers must disclose the source of the funds to be used in the acquisition. (3) The target firm's shareholders must be allowed at least 20 days to tender their shares; that is, the offer must be "open" for at least 20 days. (4) If the acquiring firm increases the offer price during the 20-day open period, all shareholders who tendered prior to the new offer must receive the higher price. In total, these restrictions were intended to reduce the acquiring firm's ability to surprise management and to stampede target shareholders into accepting an inadequate offer. Prior to the Williams Act, offers were generally made on a first-come, first-served basis, and they were often accompanied by an implicit threat to lower the bid price after 50 percent of the shares were in hand. The legislation also gave the target more time to mount a defense, and it gave rival bidders and white knights a chance to enter the fray and thus help a target's stockholders obtain a better price.

Many states have also passed laws designed to protect firms in their states from hostile takeovers. At first, these laws focused on disclosure requirements, but by the late 1970s several states had enacted takeover statutes so restrictive that they virtually precluded hostile takeovers. In 1979, MITE Corporation, a Delaware firm, made a hostile tender offer for Chicago Rivet and Machine Co., a publicly held Illinois corporation. Chicago Rivet sought protection under the Illinois Business Takeover Act. The constitutionality of the Illinois act was contested, and the U.S. Supreme Court found the law unconstitutional. The court ruled that the market for securities is a national market, and even though the issuing firm was incorporated in Illinois, the state of Illinois could not regulate interstate securities transactions.

The Illinois decision effectively eliminated the first generation of state merger regulations. However, the states kept trying to protect their state-headquartered companies, and in 1987 the U.S. Supreme Court upheld an Indiana law which radically changed the rules of the takeover game. Specifically, the Indiana law first defined "control shares" as enough shares to give an investor 20 percent of the vote. It went on to state that when an investor buys control shares, those shares can be voted only after approval by a majority of "disinterested shareholders," defined as those who are neither officers nor inside directors of the company, nor associates of the raider. The law also gives the buyer of control shares the right to insist that a shareholders' meeting be called within 50 days to decide whether the shares may be voted. The Indiana law dealt a major blow to raiders, mainly because it slows down the action. Delaware (the state in which most large companies are incorporated) later passed a similar bill, as did New York and a number of other important states.

The new state laws also have some features which protect target stockholders from their own managers. Included are limits on the use of golden parachutes, onerous debt-financing plans, and some types of takeover defenses. Since these laws do not regulate tender offers per se, but rather govern the practices of firms in the state, they have withstood all legal challenges to date. But when companies such as IBM offer 100 percent premiums for companies such as Lotus, it is hard for any defense to hold them off.

SELF-TEST QUESTIONS

Is there a need to regulate mergers? Explain.

Do the states play a role in merger regulation, or is it all done at the national level?

MERGER ANALYSIS

In theory, merger analysis is quite simple. The acquiring firm simply performs an analysis to value the target company and then determines whether the target can be bought at that value or, preferably, for less than the estimated value. The target company, on the other hand, should accept the offer if the price exceeds either its value if it continued to operate independently or the price it can get from some other bidder. Theory aside, however, some difficult issues are involved. In this section, we first discuss valuing the target firm, which is the initial step in a merger analysis. Then we discuss setting the bid price and postmerger control. In the next section, we discuss structuring the takeover bid.

Valuing the Target Firm

Several methodologies are used to value target firms, but we will confine our discussion to the two most common: (1) the discounted cash flow approach and (2) the market multiple method. However, regardless of the valuation methodology, it is crucial to recognize two facts. First, the target company typically will not continue to operate as a separate entity, but will become part of the acquiring firm's portfolio of assets. Therefore, changes in operations will affect the value of the business and must be considered in the analysis. Second, the goal of merger valuation is to value the target firm's equity, because a firm is acquired from its owners, not from its creditors. Thus, although we use the phrase "valuing the firm," our focus is on the value of the equity rather than on total value.

Discounted Cash Flow Analysis. The **discounted cash flow (DCF)** approach to valuing a business involves the application of capital budgeting procedures to an entire firm rather than to a single project. To apply this method, two key items are needed: (1) pro forma statements that forecast the incremental free cash flows expected to result from the merger and (2) a discount rate, or cost of capital, to apply to these projected cash flows.

Pro Forma Cash Flow Statements. Obtaining accurate postmerger cash flow forecasts is by far the most important task in the DCF approach. In a pure **financial merger,** in which no synergies are expected, the incremental postmerger cash flows are simply the expected cash flows of the target firm. In an **operating merger,** where the two firms' operations are to be integrated, forecasting future cash flows is more difficult.

Table 26-2 shows the projected cash flow statements for Apex Corporation, which is being considered as a target by Hightech, a large conglomerate. The projected data are for the postmerger period, and all synergistic effects have been included. Apex currently uses 50 percent debt, and if it were acquired, Hightech would keep the debt ratio at 50 percent. Both Hightech and Apex have a 40 percent marginal federal-plus-state tax rate.

Lines 1 through 4 of the table show the operating information that Hightech expects for the Apex subsidiary if the merger takes place, and Line 5 contains the earnings before interest and taxes (EBIT) for each year. Unlike a typical capital budgeting analysis, a merger analysis usually *does* incorporate interest expense into the cash flow forecast, as shown on Line 6. This is done for three reasons: (1) acquiring firms often assume the debt of the target firm, so old debt at different coupon rates is often part of the deal; (2) the acquisition is often financed partially by debt; and (3) if the subsidiary is to grow in the future, new debt will have to be issued over time to support the expansion. Thus, debt associated with a merger is typically more complex than the single issue of new debt associated with a normal capital project, and the easiest way to properly account for the complexities of merger debt is to specifically include each year's

TABLE 26-2	Projected Postmerger Cash Flow Statements for the Apex Subsidiary as of December 31 (Millions of Dollars)				
	1999	2000	2001	2002	2003
1. Net sales	$105.0	$126.0	$151.0	$174.0	$191.0
2. Cost of goods sold	75.0	89.0	106.0	122.0	132.0
3. Selling and administrative expenses	10.0	12.0	13.0	15.0	16.0
4. Depreciation	8.0	8.0	9.0	9.0	10.0
5. EBIT	$ 12.0	$ 17.0	$ 23.0	$ 28.0	$ 33.0
6. Interest[a]	8.0	9.0	10.0	11.0	11.0
7. EBT	$ 4.0	$ 8.0	$ 13.0	$ 17.0	$ 22.0
8. Taxes (40%)[b]	1.6	3.2	5.2	6.8	8.8
9. Net income	$ 2.4	$ 4.8	$ 7.8	$ 10.2	$ 13.2
10. Plus depreciation	8.0	8.0	9.0	9.0	10.0
11. Cash flow	$ 10.4	$ 12.8	$ 16.8	$ 19.2	$ 23.2
12. Less retentions needed for growth[c]	4.0	4.0	7.0	9.0	12.0
13. Plus terminal value[d]					150.2
14. Net cash flow to Hightech[e]	$ 6.4	$ 8.8	$ 9.8	$ 10.2	$161.4

[a]Interest payments are estimates based on Apex's existing debt, plus additional debt required to finance growth.

[b]Hightech will file a consolidated tax return after the merger. Thus, the taxes shown here are the full corporate taxes attributable to Apex's operations: there will be no additional taxes on any cash flows passed from Apex to Hightech.

[c]Some of the cash flows generated by the Apex subsidiary after the merger must be retained to finance asset replacements and growth, while some will be transferred to Hightech to pay dividends on its stock or for redeployment within the corporation. These retentions are net of any additional debt used to help finance growth.

[d]Apex's available cash flows are expected to grow at a constant 10 percent rate after 2003. The value of all post-2003 cash flows as of December 31, 2003, is estimated by use of the constant growth model to be $150.2 million:

$$V_{2003} = \frac{CF_{2004}}{k_s - g} = \frac{(\$23.2 - \$12.0)(1.10)}{0.182 - 0.10} = \$150.2 \text{ million.}$$

In the next section, we discuss the estimated 18.2 percent cost of equity. The $150.2 million is the PV at the end of 2003 of the stream of cash flows for year 2004 and thereafter.

[e]These are the net cash flows projected to be available to Hightech by virtue of the acquisition. The cash flows could be used for dividend payments to Hightech's stockholders, to finance asset expansion in Hightech's other divisions and subsidiaries, and so on.

expected interest expense in the cash flow forecast. Therefore, we are using what is called the *equity residual method* to value the target firm. Here the estimated net cash flows are a residual which belongs solely to the acquiring firm's shareholders. Therefore, they should be discounted at the cost of equity. This is in contrast to the corporate value model of Chapter 9, where the free cash flows (which belong to all investors, not just shareholders) are discounted at the WACC. Both methods lead to the same estimate of equity value.

Line 7 contains the earnings before taxes (EBT), and Line 8 gives taxes based on Hightech's 40 percent marginal rate. Line 9 lists each year's net income, and depreciation is added back on Line 10 to obtain each year's cash flow as shown on Line 11. Since some of Apex's assets will wear out or become obsolete, and since Hightech plans to expand the Apex subsidiary should the acquisition occur, some equity funds must be retained and reinvested in the business. These retentions, which are not available for transfer to the parent, are shown on Line 12. Finally, we have projected only five years of cash flows, but Hightech would likely operate the Apex subsidiary for many years—in theory, forever.

Therefore, we applied the constant growth model to the 2003 cash flow to estimate the value of all cash flows beyond 2003. (See Note d to Table 26-2.) This "terminal value" represents Apex's projected value at the end of 2003, and it is shown on Line 13.

The net cash flows shown on Line 14 would be available to Hightech's stockholders, and they are the basis of the valuation.[7] Of course, the postmerger cash flows are extremely difficult to estimate, and in a complete merger valuation, just as in a complete capital budgeting analysis, sensitivity, scenario, and simulation analyses should be conducted. Indeed, in a friendly merger the acquiring firm would send a team consisting of literally dozens of accountants, engineers, and so forth, to the target firm's headquarters. They would go over its books, estimate required maintenance expenditures, set values on assets such as real estate and petroleum reserves, and the like. Such an investigation, which is called **due diligence,** is an essential part of any merger analysis.

Estimating the Discount Rate.   The bottom-line net cash flows shown on Line 14 are after interest and taxes, hence they represent equity. Therefore, they should be discounted at the cost of equity rather than at the overall cost of capital. Further, the discount rate used should reflect the riskiness of the cash flows in the table. The most appropriate discount rate is Apex's cost of equity, not that of either Hightech or the consolidated postmerger firm.

Although we will not illustrate it here, Hightech could perform a risk analysis on the Table 26-2 cash flows just as it does on any set of capital budgeting flows. Sensitivity analysis, scenario analysis, and/or Monte Carlo simulation could be used to give Hightech's management a feel for the risks involved with the acquisition. Apex is a publicly traded company, so we can assess directly its market risk. Apex's market-determined premerger beta was 1.63. Because the merger would not change Apex's capital structure or tax rate, its postmerger beta would remain at 1.63.

We use the Security Market Line to estimate Apex's postmerger cost of equity. If the risk-free rate is 10 percent and the market risk premium is 5 percent, then Apex's cost of equity, k_s, after the merger with Hightech, would be about 18.2 percent.[8]

$$k_s = k_{RF} + (RP_M)b = 10\% + (5\%)1.63 = 18.15\% \approx 18.2\%.$$

Valuing the Cash Flows.   The current value of Apex's stock to Hightech is the present value of the cash flows expected to Hightech, discounted at 18.2 percent (in millions of dollars):

$$V_{1998} = \frac{\$6.4}{(1.182)^1} + \frac{\$8.8}{(1.182)^2} + \frac{\$9.8}{(1.182)^3} + \frac{\$10.2}{(1.182)^4} + \frac{\$161.4}{(1.182)^5} \approx \$92.8.$$

Thus, the value of Apex's stock to Hightech is $92.8 million.

---

[7]We purposely kept the cash flows relatively simple to help focus on key issues. In an actual merger valuation, the cash flows would be much more complex, normally including such items as additional capital furnished by the acquiring firm, tax loss carry-forwards, tax effects of plant and equipment valuation adjustments, and cash flows from the sale of some of the subsidiary's assets.

[8]In this example, we used the Capital Asset Pricing Model to estimate Apex's cost of equity, and thus we assumed that investors require a premium for market risk only. We could have also conducted a corporate risk analysis, in which the relevant risk would be the contribution of Apex's cash flows to the total risk of the postmerger firm.

In actual merger situations among large firms, companies almost always hire an investment banker to help develop valuation estimates. For example, when General Electric acquired Utah International, GE hired Morgan Stanley to determine Utah's value. We discussed the valuation process with the Morgan Stanley analyst in charge of the appraisal, and he confirmed that they applied all of the standard procedures discussed in this chapter. Note, though, that merger analysis, like the analysis of any other complex issue, requires judgment, and people's judgments differ as to how much weight to give to different methods in any given situation.

Note that in a merger analysis, the value of the target consists of the target's pre-merger value plus any value created by operating or financial synergies. In this example, we held the target's capital structure and tax rate constant. Therefore, the only synergies were operating synergies, and these effects were incorporated into the forecasted cash flows. If there had been financial synergies, the analysis would have to be modified to reflect this added value. For example, if Apex had been operating with only 30 percent debt, and if Hightech could lower Apex's overall cost of capital by increasing the debt ratio to 50 percent, then Apex's merger value would have exceeded the $92.8 million calculated above.

Market Multiple Analysis. The second method of valuing a target company is **market multiple analysis,** which applies a market-determined multiple to net income, earnings per share, sales, book value, or, for businesses such as cable TV or cellular telephone systems, the number of subscribers. While the DCF method applies valuation concepts in a precise manner, focusing on expected cash flows, market multiple analysis is more judgmental. To illustrate the concept, note that Apex's forecasted net income is $2.4 million in 1999, and it rises to $13.2 million in 2003, for an average of $7.7 million over the five-year forecast period. The average P/E ratio for publicly traded companies similar to Apex is 12.

To estimate Apex's value using the market P/E multiple approach, simply multiply its $7.7 million average net income by the market multiple of 12 to obtain the value of $7.7(12) = $92.4 million. This is the equity, or ownership, value of the firm. Note that we used the average net income over the coming five years to value Apex. The market P/E multiple of 12 is based on the current year's income of comparable companies, but Apex's current income does not reflect synergistic effects or managerial changes that will be made. By averaging future net income, we are attempting to capture the value added by Hightech to Apex's operations.

Note that measures other than net income can be used in the market multiple approach. For example, another commonly used measure is *earnings before interest, taxes, depreciation, and amortization (EBITDA).* The procedure would be identical to that just described, except that the market multiple would be price divided by EBITDA rather than earnings per share, and this multiple would be multiplied by Apex's EBITDA.

As noted above, in some businesses such as cable TV and cellular telephone, an important element in the valuation process is the number of customers a company has. The acquirer has an idea of the cost required to obtain a new customer and the average cash flow per customer. For example, telephone companies have been paying about $2,000 per customer for cellular operators. Managed care companies such as HMOs have applied similar logic in acquisitions, basing their valuations on the number of people insured.

Setting the Bid Price

Using the DCF valuation results, $92.8 million is the most Hightech could pay for Apex—if it pays more, then Hightech's own value will be diluted. On the other hand, if Hightech can get Apex for less than $92.8 million, Hightech's stockholders will gain value. Therefore, Hightech will bid something less than $92.8 million when it makes an offer for Apex.

Figure 26-1 graphs the merger situation. The $92.8 million is shown as a point on the horizontal axis, and it is the maximum price that Hightech can afford to pay. If Hightech pays less, say, $82.8 million, then its stockholders will gain $10 million from the merger, while if it pays more, its stockholders will lose. What we have, then, is a 45-

A video clip entitled "T. Boone Pickens on White Knights," which discusses mergers and takeovers, is available at Ohio State University's web site at http://www.cob.ohio-state.edu/~fin/clips.htm. The clip requires a QuickTime video player for either Windows or Macintosh machines (which you download for free over the Internet at http://www.quicktime.apple.com/sw/). One caveat is that the video clip is in excess of 5 MB in size and should therefore only be accessed with a rapid Internet connection.

FIGURE 26-1   A View of Merger Analysis (Millions of Dollars)

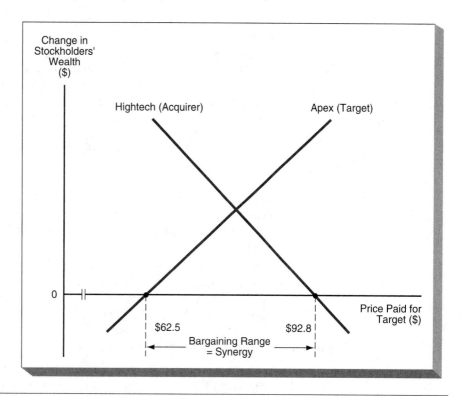

degree line which cuts the X axis at $92.8 million, and that line shows how much High-tech's stockholders can expect to gain or lose at different acquisition prices.

Now consider the target company, Apex. It has 10 million shares of stock which sell for $6.25, so its value as an independent operating company is presumably $62.5 million. [In making this statement, we assume (1) that the company is being operated as well as possible by its present management, and (2) that the $6.25 market price per share does not include a "speculative merger premium" in addition to the PV of its operating cash flows.] If Apex is acquired at a price greater than $62.5 million, its stockholders will gain value, while they will lose value at any lower price. Thus, we can draw another 45-degree line, this one with an upward slope, to show how the merger price affects Apex's stockholders.

The difference between $62.5 and $92.8 million, or $30.3 million, represents synergistic benefits expected from the merger. Here are some points to note:

1. If there were no synergistic benefits, the maximum bid would be equal to the current value of the target company. The greater the synergistic gains, the greater the gap between the target's current price and the maximum the acquiring company could pay.

2. The greater the synergistic gains, the more likely a merger is to be consummated.

3. The issue of how to divide the synergistic benefits is critically important. Obviously, both parties will want to get as much as possible. In our example, if Apex's management knew the maximum price that Hightech could pay, it would argue for a price close to $92.8 million. Hightech, on the other hand, would try to get Apex at a price as close to $62.5 million as possible.

4. Where, within the $62.5 to $92.8 million range, will the actual price be set? The answer depends on a number of factors, including whether Hightech offers to pay with cash or securities, the negotiating skills of the two management teams, and, most importantly, the bargaining positions of the two parties as determined by fundamental economic conditions. To illustrate the latter point, suppose there are many companies similar to Apex that Hightech could acquire, but no company other than Hightech that could gain synergies by acquiring Apex. In this case, Hightech would probably make a relatively low, take-it-or-leave-it offer, and Apex would probably take it because some gain is better than none. On the other hand, if Apex has some unique technology or other asset that many companies want, then once Hightech announces its offer, others will probably make competing bids, and the final price will probably be close to or even above $92.8 million. A price above $92.8 million would presumably be paid by some other company which had a better synergistic fit or, perhaps, whose management was more optimistic about Apex's cash flow potential. In Figure 26-1, this situation would be represented by a line parallel to that for Hightech but shifted to the right of the Hightech line.

5. Hightech would, of course, want to keep its maximum bid secret, and it would plan its bidding strategy carefully and consistently with the situation. If it thought that other bidders would emerge, or that Apex's management might resist in order to preserve their jobs, it might make a high "preemptive" bid in hopes of scaring off competing bids and/or management resistance. On the other hand, it might make a low-ball bid in hopes of "stealing" the company.

We will have more to say about these points in the sections that follow, and you should keep Figure 26-1 in mind as you go through the rest of the chapter.

Postmerger Control

The employment/control situation is often of vital interest in a merger analysis. First, consider the situation in which a small, owner-managed firm sells out to a larger concern. The owner-manager may be anxious to retain a high-status position, and he or she may also have developed a camaraderie with the employees and thus be concerned about their retention after the merger. If so, these points would be stressed during the merger negotiations.[9] When a publicly owned firm that is not owned by its managers is merged into another company, the acquired firm's managers will be worried about their postmerger positions. If the acquiring firm agrees to retain the old management, then management may be willing to support the merger and to recommend its accep-

---

[9]The acquiring firm may also be concerned about this point, especially if the target firm's management is quite good. Indeed, a condition of the merger may be that the management team agree to stay on for a period such as five years after the merger. In this case, the price paid may be contingent on the acquired firm's performance subsequent to the merger. For example, when International Holdings acquired Walker Products, the price paid was an immediate 100,000 shares of International Holdings stock worth $63 per share plus an additional 30,000 shares each year for the next three years, provided Walker Products earned at least $1 million during each of these years. Since Walker's managers owned the stock and would receive the bonus, they had a strong incentive to stay on and help the firm meet its targets.

Finally, if the managers of the target company are highly competent but do not wish to remain on after the merger, the acquiring firm may build into the merger contract a noncompete agreement with the old management. Typically, the acquired firm's principal officers must agree not to affiliate with a new business which is competitive with the one they sold for a specified period, say, five years. Such agreements are especially important with service-oriented businesses.

WHEN YOU MERGE YOU COMBINE MORE THAN JUST FINANCIAL STATEMENTS

When corporations merge, they combine more than just their financial statements. Mergers bring together two organizations with different histories and corporate cultures. Deals that look good on paper can fail if the individuals involved are unwilling or unable to work together to generate the potential synergies. Consequently, when analyzing a potential merger, it is important to determine whether the two companies are compatible.

Many deals fall apart because, during the "due diligence" phase, synergistic benefits are revealed to be less than was originally anticipated, so there is little economic rationale for the merger. Other negotiations break off because the two parties cannot agree on the price to be paid for the acquired firm's stock. In addition, merger talks often collapse because of "social issues." These social issues include both the "chemistry" of the companies and their personnel and such basic issues as these: What will be the name of the combined company? Where will headquarters be located? And, most important: Who will run the combined company? Robert Kindler, a partner at Cravath, Swaine & Moore, a prominent New York law firm that specializes in mergers, summarizes the importance of these issues as follows: "Even transactions that make absolute economic sense don't happen unless the social issues work."

Investment bankers, lawyers, and other professionals state that mergers tend to be most successful if there is a clear and well-arranged plan spelling out who will run the company. This issue is straightforward if one firm is clearly dominant and is acquiring the other. However, in cases where there is "a merger of equals," senior personnel issues often become sticky. This situation is made considerably easier if one of the chief executives is at or near the retirement age.

Some analysts believe that social issues often play too large a role, derailing mergers that should take place. In other cases where a merger occurs, concerns about social issues preclude managers from undertaking the necessary changes—like laying off redundant staff—for the deal to benefit shareholders.

SOURCE: "In Many Merger Deals, Ego and Pride Play Big Roles in Which Way Talks Go," *The Wall Street Journal,* August 22, 1996, C1. ©1996 Dow Jones & Company, Inc. All Rights Reserved Worldwide.

---

tance to the stockholders. If the old management is to be removed, then it will probably resist the merger.[10]

SELF-TEST QUESTIONS

What is the difference between an operating merger and a financial merger?

Describe the way postmerger cash flows are estimated in a DCF analysis.

What is the basis for the discount rate in a DCF analysis? Describe how this rate might be estimated.

Describe the market multiple approach.

What are some factors that acquiring firms consider when they set a bid price?

How do control issues affect mergers?

STRUCTURING THE TAKEOVER BID

The acquiring firm's offer to the target's shareholders can be in the form of cash, stock of the acquiring firm, debt of the acquiring firm, or some combination. The structure of the bid affects (1) the capital structure of the postmerger firm, (2) the tax treatment

---

[10]Managements of firms that are thought to be attractive merger candidates often arrange *golden parachutes* for themselves. Golden parachutes are extremely lucrative retirement plans which take effect if a merger is consummated. Thus, when Bendix was acquired by Allied, Bill Agee, Bendix's chairman, "pulled the ripcord of his golden parachute" and walked away with $4 million. If a golden parachute is large enough, it can also function as a poison pill—for example, where the president of a firm worth $10 million would have to be paid $8 million if the firm is acquired, this will prevent a takeover. Stockholders are increasingly resisting such arrangements, but some still exist.

of both the acquiring firm and the target's stockholders, (3) the ability of the target firm's stockholders to benefit from future merger-related gains, and (4) the types of federal and state regulations to which the acquiring firm will be subjected. In this section, we discuss how acquiring firms structure their offers.

The form of payment offered to the target's shareholders determines the personal tax treatment of these stockholders. Target shareholders do not have to pay taxes on stock they receive in the transaction provided at least 50 percent of the payment to target shareholders, in total, is in the form of shares (either common or preferred) of the acquiring firm. In such *nontaxable offers,* target shareholders do not realize any capital gains or losses until they sell the equity securities they received. However, capital gains are taxed in the transaction year if an offer consists of more than 50 percent cash and/or debt securities. Also, even in "nontaxable deals," capital gains taxes must be paid by any stockholders who receive cash.

All other things equal, stockholders prefer nontaxable offers, since they may then postpone capital gains taxes. Furthermore, if the target firm's stockholders receive stock, they will benefit from synergistic gains resulting from the merger. Most target shareholders are thus willing to give up their stock for a lower price in a nontaxable than in a taxable offer. As a result, one might expect nontaxable bids to dominate. However, this is not the case—roughly half of all mergers have been taxable, and, as noted in Table 26-1, two of the top five mergers were all-cash deals.

Prior to 1986, if a firm paid more than book value for a target firm's assets in a taxable merger, it could write up those assets, depreciate the marked-up value for tax purposes, and thus lower the postmerger firm's taxes vis-à-vis the taxes of the two firms operating separately. At the same time, the target firm did not have to pay any taxes on the write-up at the time of the merger. Under current law, if the acquiring company writes up the target company's assets for tax purposes, then the target company must pay capital gains taxes in the year the merger occurs. (These taxes can be avoided if the acquiring company elects not to write up acquired assets and depreciates them on their old basis.) However, the marked-up assets, plus goodwill (discussed in the next section), can be depreciated for tax purposes.

Securities laws also have an effect on the construction of the offer. The SEC has oversight over the issuance of new securities, including stock or debt issued in connection with a merger. Therefore, whenever a corporation bids for control of another firm through the exchange of equity or debt, the entire process must take place under the scrutiny of the Securities and Exchange Commission. The time required for such reviews allows target managements to implement defensive tactics and other firms to make competing offers, and as a result, nearly all hostile tender offers are for cash rather than securities.

SELF-TEST
QUESTIONS

What are some alternative ways of structuring takeover bids?

How do taxes influence the payment structure?

How do securities laws affect the payment structure?

ACCOUNTING TREATMENT FOR MERGERS

Although a detailed discussion of accounting is best left to accounting courses, the accounting implications of mergers cannot be ignored. Mergers are handled in either of two basic ways: (1) as a pooling of interests or (2) as a purchase. The method used can have a significant effect on postmerger reported profits, and this, in turn, can influence the desirability of the merger.

TABLE 26-3	Accounting for Mergers: A Acquires B

POOLING OF INTERESTS

	FIRM A	FIRM B	POSTMERGER: FIRM A
Current assets	$ 50	$25	$ 75
Fixed assets	50	25	75
Total assets	$100	$50	$150
Debt	$ 40	$20	$ 60
Common equity	60	30	90
Total claims	$100	$50	$150

PURCHASE ACCOUNTING

			POSTMERGER: FIRM A		
	FIRM A (1)	FIRM B (2)	$20 PAID[a] (3)	$30 PAID[a] (4)	$50 PAID[a] (5)
Current assets	$ 50	$25	$ 75	$ 75	$ 80[c]
Fixed assets	50	25	65[b]	75	80[c]
Goodwill[d]	0	0	0	0	10[d]
Total assets	$100	$50	$140	$150	$170
Debt	$ 40	$20	$ 60	$ 60	$ 60
Equity	60	30	80[e]	90	110[f]
Total claims	$100	$50	$140	$150	$170

[a]The price paid is the *net asset value,* that is, total assets minus debt.

[b]Here we assume that Firm B's fixed assets are written down from $25 to $15 before constructing the consolidated balance sheet.

[c]Here we assume that Firm B's current and fixed assets are both increased to $30.

[d]*Goodwill* refers to the excess paid for a firm above the appraised value of the physical assets purchased. Goodwill represents payment both for intangibles such as patents and for "organization value" such as that associated with having an effective sales force.

[e]Firm B's common equity is reduced by $10 prior to consolidation to reflect the fixed asset write-off.

[f]Firm B's equity is increased to $50 to reflect the above-book purchase price.

Pooling of Interests Accounting

A **pooling of interests** is, in theory, a merger among equals, and hence the consolidated balance sheet is constructed by simply adding together the balance sheets of the merged companies. The top section of Table 26-3 shows the essential elements of the consolidated balance sheet after Firms A and B have merged under a pooling of interests. This final balance sheet holds regardless of how many shares Firm A (the survivor) gave up to acquire Firm B. (In a pooling, shares, not cash, must be exchanged.)

Purchase Accounting

The lower section of Table 26-3, which uses the same data as for the pooled companies, illustrates purchase accounting. Here Firm A is assumed to have "bought" Firm B in much the same way it would buy any capital asset, paying for it with cash, debt, or stock of the acquiring company. If the price paid is exactly equal to the acquired firm's **net asset value,** which is defined as its total assets minus its liabilities, then the consolidated balance sheet will be identical to that under pooling. Otherwise, there is an important difference. If the price paid exceeds the net asset value, then asset values will be increased to reflect the price actually paid, whereas if the price paid is less than the net asset value, then assets must be written down when preparing the consolidated balance sheet.

Note that Firm B's net asset value is $30, which is also its reported common equity value. This $30 book value could be equal to the market value (which is determined by the firm's earning power), but book value could also be more or less than the market value. Three situations are considered in the lower section of Table 26-3. First, in Column 3 we assume that Firm A gives cash or stock worth $20 for Firm B. Thus, B's assets as reported on its balance sheet were overvalued, and A pays less than B's net asset value. The overvaluation could be in either fixed or current assets; an appraisal would be made but we assume that it is fixed assets which are overvalued. Accordingly, we reduce B's fixed assets and also its common equity by $10 before constructing the consolidated balance sheet shown in Column 3. Next, in Column 4, we assume that A pays exactly the net asset value for B. In this case, pooling and purchase accounting would produce identical balance sheets.

Finally, in Column 5 we assume that A pays more than the net asset value for B: $50 is paid for $30 of net assets. This excess is assumed to be partly attributable to undervalued assets (land, buildings, machinery, and inventories), so to reflect this undervaluation, current and fixed assets are each increased by $5. In addition, we assume that $10 of the $20 excess of market value over book value is due to a superior sales organization, or some other intangible factor, and we post this excess as **goodwill.** B's common equity is increased by $20, the sum of the increases in current and fixed assets plus goodwill, and this markup is also reflected in A's postmerger equity account.[11]

Income Statement Effects

Significant differences can also arise in reported profits under the two accounting methods. If asset values are increased, as they often are under a purchase, this must be reflected in higher depreciation charges (and also in a higher cost of goods sold if inventories are written up). This, in turn, will further reduce reported profits. Also, goodwill represents the excess paid for a firm over its adjusted net asset value. This excess is presumably paid because of the acquired firm's superior earning power, which will probably be eroded over time as patents expire, as new firms enter the industry, and so forth. Thus, goodwill is written off, or "amortized," over a period corresponding to the expected life of the superior earning power, but in no case more than 40 years. Goodwill is certainly not a trivial issue. For example, when Philip Morris acquired Seven-Up for a price of $520 million, approximately $390 million of the purchase price represented goodwill.

Table 26-4 illustrates the income statement effects of the higher current and fixed assets, and also the write-off of goodwill, under pooling versus purchase. For the purchase, we assume that A purchased B for $50, creating $10 of goodwill and $10 of

---

[11]This example assumes that additional debt was not issued to help finance the acquisition. If the acquisition were totally debt financed, the postmerger balance sheet would show increases in the debt account rather than increases in the equity account. If it were financed by a mix of debt and equity, both accounts would be changed.

TABLE 26-4   Income Effects of Pooling versus Purchase Accounting

	PREMERGER		POSTMERGER: FIRM A	
	FIRM A (1)	FIRM B (2)	POOLING (3)	PURCHASE (4)
Sales	$100.0	$50.0	$150.0	$150.0
Operating costs	72.0	36.0	108.0	109.0[a]
Operating income	$ 28.0	$14.0	$ 42.0	$ 41.0[a]
Interest (10%)	4.0	2.0	6.0	6.0
Taxable income	$ 24.0	$12.0	$ 36.0	$ 35.0
Taxes (40%)	9.6	4.8	14.4	14.0
Earnings after tax	$ 14.4	$ 7.2	$ 21.6	$ 21.0
Goodwill write-off	0	0	0	1.0[b]
Net income	$ 14.4	$ 7.2	$ 21.6	$ 20.0
EPS[c]	$ 2.40	$2.40	$ 2.40	$ 2.22

[a]Operating costs are $1 higher than they otherwise would be to reflect the higher reported costs (depreciation and cost of goods sold) caused by the physical asset markup at the time of purchase.

[b]($10 of increased goodwill)/10 years = $1 write-off per year.

[c]Firm A had six shares and Firm B had three shares before the merger. A gives one of its shares for each of B's, so A has nine shares outstanding after the merger.

higher physical asset value. Further, we assume that this $20 will be written off over ten years.[12] As Column 4 indicates, the writing off of goodwill and asset markups under purchase accounting causes reported profits to be lower than they would be under pooling.

The write-off of goodwill is also reflected in earnings per share. In our hypothetical merger, we assume that nine shares exist in the consolidated firm. (Six of these shares went to A's stockholders, and three to B's.) Under pooling, EPS = $2.40, while under purchase, EPS = $2.22. Further, the greater the amount of goodwill, the larger is the write-off and the more significant is the dilution in reported earnings per share. This fact causes managers to prefer pooling to purchase accounting.

Several conditions must be met to use the pooling method, the most important of which is that the acquisition must be paid for with common stock of the acquiring firm.[13] This, coupled with other conditions, restricts the use of pooling in practice. Nevertheless, about 90 percent of all recent acquisitions over $100 million have used pooling, which does not lower the combined firm's reported earnings.

SELF-TEST QUESTIONS

What is the difference between pooling of interests and purchase accounting for mergers?

What is goodwill? What impact does goodwill have on the firm's balance sheet? On its income statement?

---

[12]The write-off of goodwill is not a deduction for income tax purposes, but the other excess write-offs (fixed assets and inventories) were deductible prior to 1986.

[13]See Accounting Principles Board Opinions #16 and #17. Also, note that the Financial Accounting Standards Board is currently considering changes that would further restrict or even end pooling.

ANALYSIS FOR A "TRUE CONSOLIDATION"

Most of our analysis in the preceding sections assumed that one firm plans to acquire another. However, in many situations it is hard to identify an "acquirer" and a "target"—the merger appears to be a true "merger of equals," as was the case with the Citicorp/Travelers and NationsBank/BankAmerica mergers. In such cases, how is the analysis handled? Here are the steps one would go through:

1. Develop pro forma financial statements for the consolidated corporation. What are the projected sales, costs, interest charges, taxes, net income, and free cash flows, assuming the two firms merge? How will the consolidated balance sheets look? Such mergers are virtually always handled on a pooling of interests basis, so the balance sheets are combined, with no write-up or write-down. Synergies are generally expected to be important, so they must be worked into the pro forma income statements. If antitrust considerations require the disposal of certain assets (say, some branches if two banks with overlapping service areas merge), that must be reflected in the projected statements. The key set of figures is the projected consolidated free cash flows available to stockholders.

2. Estimate the new company's cost of equity, and use that rate to discount the equity flows of the consolidated company. This is the value of the equity of the consolidated company.

3. Decide how to allocate the new company's stock between the two sets of old stockholders. Normally, one would expect the consolidated value to exceed the sum of the pre-announcement values of the two companies because of synergy. For example, Company A might have had a premerger equity value of $10 billion, found as (Number of shares)(Price per share), and Company B might have had a premerger value of $15 billion. If the postmerger value of new Company AB is estimated to be $30 billion, then that value must be allocated. Company A's stockholders will have to receive enough shares to cause its stockholders to have a projected value of at least $10 billion, and Company B's stockholders will have to receive at least $15 billion. But how will the remaining $5 billion of synergistic-induced value be divided?

This is a key issue, and one that the two management groups will negotiate long and hard over. There is no rule, or formula, that can be applied, but one basis for the allocation is the relative pre-announcement values of the two companies. For example, in our hypothetical merger of A and B to form AB, the companies might agree to give $10/$25 = 40% of the new stock to A's stockholders and 60% to B's stockholders. Unless a case could be made for giving a higher percentage of the shares to one of the companies because it was responsible for more of the synergistic value, then the premerger value proportions would seem to be a "fair" solution. In any event, the premerger proportions will probably be given the greatest weight in reaching the final decision.

It should also be noted that control of the consolidated company is always an issue in mergers such as the Citicorp/Travelers and NationsBank/BankAmerica deals. Generally, the companies hold a press conference and announce that the CEO of one firm will be chairman of the new company, that the other CEO will be president, that the new board will consist of directors from both old boards, and that power will be shared. With huge mergers such as those we have been seeing lately, there is plenty of power to be shared.

How does merger analysis differ in the case of a large company acquiring a smaller one versus a "true merger of equals"?

Do you think the same guidelines for allocating synergistic gains would be used in both types of mergers?

THE ROLE OF INVESTMENT BANKERS

Investment bankers are involved with mergers in a number of ways: (1) they help arrange mergers, (2) they help target companies develop and implement defensive tactics, (3) they help value target companies, (4) they help finance mergers, and (5) they invest in the stocks of potential merger candidates. These merger-related activities have been quite profitable. For example, the investment bankers and lawyers who arranged the Campeau-Federated merger earned fees of about $83 million — First Boston and Wasserstein Perella split $29 million from Campeau, and Goldman Sachs, Hellman & Friedman, and Shearson Lehman Hutton divided up $54 million for representing Federated. No wonder investment banking houses are able to make top offers to finance graduates!

Arranging Mergers

The major investment banking firms have merger and acquisition groups which operate within their corporate finance departments. (Corporate finance departments offer advice, as opposed to underwriting or brokerage services, to business firms.) Members of these groups identify firms with excess cash that might want to buy other firms, companies that might be willing to be bought, and firms that might, for a number of reasons, be attractive to others. Also, if an oil company, for instance, decided to expand into coal mining, then it might enlist the aid of an investment banker to help it acquire a coal company. Similarly, dissident stockholders of firms with poor track records might work with investment bankers to oust management by helping to arrange a merger. Investment bankers are reported to have offered packages of financing to corporate raiders, where the package includes both designing the securities to be used in the tender offer, plus lining up people and firms who will buy the target firm's stock now and then tender it once the final offer is made.

Investment bankers have occasionally taken illegal actions in the merger arena. For one thing, they are reported to have *parked stock* — purchasing it for a raider under a guaranteed buy-back agreement — to help the raider de facto accumulate more than 5 percent of the target's stock without disclosing the position. People have gone to jail for this.

Developing Defensive Tactics

Target firms that do not want to be acquired generally enlist the help of an investment banking firm, along with a law firm that specializes in mergers. Defenses include such tactics as (1) changing the bylaws so that only one-third of the directors are elected each year and/or so that a 75 percent approval (a *super-majority*) versus a simple majority is required to approve a merger; (2) trying to convince the target firm's stockholders that the price being offered is too low; (3) raising antitrust issues in the hope that the Justice Department will intervene; (4) repurchasing stock in the open market in an effort to push the price above that being offered by the potential acquirer; (5) getting a **white knight** who is acceptable to the target firm's management to compete with the potential acquirer; (6) getting a "white squire" who is friendly to current management to buy enough of the target firm's shares to block the merger; and (7) taking a poison pill, as described next.

Poison pills — which occasionally really do amount to committing economic suicide to avoid a takeover — are such tactics as borrowing on terms that require immediate repayment of all loans if the firm is acquired, selling off at bargain prices the assets that originally made the firm a desirable target, granting such lucrative **golden parachutes** to their executives that the cash drain from these payments would render the merger infeasible, and planning defensive mergers which would leave the firm with new assets of questionable value and a huge debt load. Currently, the most popular poison pill is for a company to give its stockholders *stock purchase rights* which allow them to buy at half-price the stock of an acquiring firm, should the firm be acquired. The blatant use of poison pills is constrained by directors' awareness that excessive use could trigger personal suits by stockholders against directors who voted for them, and, perhaps in the near future, by laws that would further limit management's use of pills. Still, investment bankers and antitakeover lawyers are busy thinking up new poison pill formulas, and others are just as busy trying to come up with antidotes.[14]

To illustrate a typical poison pill, consider Chrysler's poison pill share rights purchase plan. Chrysler's stockholders received one full right in the poison pill plan for each share of common stock held. Each right entitles the holder to buy one-hundredth of a share of Chrysler junior participating cumulative preferred stock for $120. However, the primary purpose of the rights is to act as a poison pill. Certain events, as described next, will cause the rights either to "kick in" and hence entitle holders to buy Chrysler common stock at half its market value, or to "flip over" and hence entitle holders to buy common stock in an acquiring entity at half its market value.

A "kick in" will occur if a shareholder acquires 20 percent or more of the firm's common stock. Further, Chrysler's board could trigger the "kick in" if an owner of 10 percent or more of the firm's stock has "adverse" intentions, where "adverse" intentions are defined as any intentions to take actions that are detrimental to the long-term interests of Chrysler and its shareholders. A "kick over" will occur if a hostile takeover occurs, which is any takeover that is not supported by Chrysler's board of directors.

Another takeover defense that is being used is the employee stock ownership plan (ESOP). ESOPs are designed to give lower-level employees an ownership stake in the firm, and current tax laws provide generous incentives for companies to establish such plans and fund them with the firm's common stock. As we discussed earlier, Polaroid used an ESOP to help fend off Shamrock Holdings's hostile takeover attempt. Also, Procter & Gamble recently set up an ESOP that, along with an existing profit-sharing plan, eventually will give employees a 20 percent ownership stake in the company. Since the trustees of ESOPs generally support current management in any takeover attempt, and since up to 85 percent of the votes is often required to complete a merger, an ESOP can provide an effective defense against a hostile tender offer. Procter & Gamble stated that its ESOP was designed primarily to lower its costs by utilizing the plan's tax advantages and to improve employees' retirement security. However, the company also noted that the ESOP would strengthen its defenses against a takeover.

---

[14]It has become extremely difficult and expensive for companies to buy "directors' insurance" which protects the board from such contingencies as stockholders' suits, and even when insurance is available it often does not pay for losses if the directors have not exercised due caution and judgment. This exposure is making directors extremely leery of actions that might trigger stockholder suits.

Establishing a Fair Value

If a friendly merger is being worked out between two firms' managements, it is important to document that the agreed-upon price is a fair one; otherwise, the stockholders of either company may sue to block the merger. Therefore, in most large mergers each side will hire an investment banking firm to evaluate the target company and to help establish the fair price. For example, General Electric employed Morgan Stanley to determine a fair price for Utah International, as did Royal Dutch to help establish the price it paid for Shell Oil. Even if the merger is not friendly, investment bankers may still be asked to help establish a price. If a surprise tender offer is to be made, the acquiring firm will want to know the lowest price at which it might be able to acquire the stock, while the target firm may seek help in "proving" that the price being offered is too low.[15]

Financing Mergers

Many mergers are financed with the acquiring company's excess cash. However, if the acquiring company has no excess cash, it will require a source of funds. Perhaps the single most important factor behind the 1980s merger wave was the development of junk bonds for use in financing acquisitions.

Drexel Burnham Lambert was the primary developer of junk bonds, defined as bonds rated below investment grade (BBB/Baa). Prior to Drexel's actions, it was almost impossible to sell low-grade bonds to raise new capital. Drexel then pioneered a procedure under which a target firm's situation would be appraised very closely, and a cash flow projection similar to that in Table 26-2 (but much more detailed) would be developed.

With the cash flows having been forecasted, Drexel's analysts would figure out a debt structure — amount of debt, maturity structure, and interest rate — that could be serviced by the cash flows. With this information, Drexel's junk bond people, operating out of Beverly Hills, would approach financial institutions (savings and loans, insurance companies, pension funds, and mutual funds) with a financing plan, and they would offer a rate of return several percentage points above the rate on more conservative investments. Drexel's early deals worked out well, and the institutions that bought the bonds were quite pleased. These results enabled Drexel to expand its network of investors, which increased its ability to finance larger and larger mergers. T. Boone Pickens, who went after Phillips, Texaco, and several other oil giants, was an early Drexel customer, as was Ted Turner.

To be successful in the mergers and acquisitions (M&A) business, an investment banker must be able to offer a financing package to clients, whether they are acquirers who need capital to take over companies or target companies trying to finance stock repurchase plans or other defenses against takeovers. Drexel was the leading player in the merger financing game during the 1980s, but since Drexel's bankruptcy Merrill Lynch, Morgan Stanley, Salomon Brothers, and others are all vying for the title.

Arbitrage Operations

Arbitrage generally means simultaneously buying and selling the same commodity or security in two different markets at different prices, and pocketing a risk-free return.

---

[15]Such investigations must obviously be done in secret, for if someone knew that Company A was thinking of offering, say, $50 per share for Company T, which was currently selling at $35 per share, then huge profits could be made. One of the biggest scandals to hit Wall Street was the disclosure that Ivan Boesky was buying information from Dennis Levine, a senior member of the investment banking house of Drexel Burnham Lambert, about target companies that Drexel was analyzing for others. Purchases based on such insider information would, of course, raise the prices of the stocks and thus force Drexel's clients to pay more than they otherwise would have had to pay. Levine and Boesky, among others, went to jail for their improper use of insider information.

However, the major brokerage houses, as well as some wealthy private investors, are engaged in a different type of arbitrage called *risk arbitrage.* The *arbitrageurs,* or "arbs," speculate in the stocks of companies that are likely takeover targets. Vast amounts of capital are required to speculate in a large number of securities and thus reduce risk, and also to make money on narrow spreads. However, the large investment bankers have the wherewithal to play the game. To be successful, arbs need to be able to sniff out likely targets, assess the probability of offers reaching fruition, and move in and out of the market quickly and with low transactions costs.

The risk arbitrage business has been rocked by insider trading scandals. Indeed, the most famous arb of all, Ivan Boesky, was caught buying inside information from executives of some leading investment banking houses and law firms. The Boesky affair slowed down risk arbitrage activity, but with deals such as IBM's offer of $60 per share for Lotus's $30 stock, risk arbitrage is not about to go away.

S E L F - T E S T
Q U E S T I O N S

What are some defensive tactics that firms can use to resist hostile takeovers?

What is the difference between pure arbitrage and risk arbitrage?

What role did junk bonds play in the merger wave of the 1980s?

WHO WINS: THE EMPIRICAL EVIDENCE

All the recent merger activity has raised two questions: (1) Do corporate acquisitions create value, and, (2) if so, how is the value shared between the parties?

Most researchers agree that takeovers increase the wealth of the shareholders of target firms, for otherwise they would not agree to the offer. However, there is a debate as to whether mergers benefit the acquiring firm's shareholders. In particular, managements of acquiring firms may be motivated by factors other than shareholder wealth maximization. For example, they may want to merge merely to increase the size of the corporations they manage, because increased size usually brings larger salaries plus job security, perquisites, power, and prestige.

The validity of the competing views on who gains from corporate acquisitions can be tested by examining the stock price changes that occur around the time of a merger or takeover announcement. Changes in the stock prices of the acquiring and target firms represent market participants' beliefs about the value created by the merger, and about how that value will be divided between the target and acquiring firms' shareholders. So, examining a large sample of stock price movements can shed light on the issue of who gains from mergers.

One cannot simply examine stock prices around merger announcement dates, because other factors influence stock prices. For example, if a merger was announced on a day when the entire market advanced, the fact that the target firm's price rose would not necessarily signify that the merger was expected to create value. Hence, studies examine *abnormal returns* associated with merger announcements, where abnormal returns are defined as that part of a stock price change caused by factors other than changes in the general stock market.

Many studies have examined both acquiring and target firms' stock price responses to mergers and tender offers.[16] Jointly, these studies have covered nearly every acquisi-

---

[16]For an excellent summary of the effects of mergers on value, see Michael C. Jensen and Richard S. Ruback, "The Market for Corporate Control: The Scientific Evidence," *Journal of Financial Economics,* April 1983, 5–50.

tion involving publicly traded firms from the early 1960s to the present, and they are remarkably consistent in their results: on average, the stock prices of target firms increase by about 30 percent in hostile tender offers, while in friendly mergers the average increase is about 20 percent. However, for both hostile and friendly deals, the stock prices of acquiring firms, on average, remain constant. Thus, the evidence strongly indicates (1) that acquisitions do create value, but (2) that shareholders of target firms reap virtually all the benefits.

In hindsight, these results are not too surprising. First, target firms' shareholders can always say no, so they are in the driver's seat. Second, takeovers are a competitive game, so if one potential acquiring firm does not offer full value for a potential target, then another firm will generally jump in with a higher bid. Finally, managements of acquiring firms might well be willing to give up all the value created by the merger, because the merger would enhance the acquiring managers' personal positions without harming their shareholders.

It has also been argued that acquisitions may increase shareholder wealth at the expense of bondholders—in particular, concern has been expressed that leveraged buyouts dilute the claims of bondholders. Specific instances can be cited where bonds were downgraded and bondholders did suffer losses, sometimes quite large ones, as a direct result of an acquisition. However, most studies find no evidence to support the contention that bondholders on average lose in corporate acquisitions.

SELF-TEST QUESTIONS	Explain how researchers can study the effects of mergers on shareholder wealth.
	Do mergers create value? If so, who profits from this value?
	Do the research results discussed in this section seem logical? Explain.

CORPORATE ALLIANCES

Mergers are one way for two companies to join forces, but many companies are striking cooperative deals, called **corporate,** or **strategic, alliances,** which stop far short of merging. Whereas mergers combine all of the assets of the firms involved, as well as their ownership and managerial expertise, alliances allow firms to create combinations that focus on specific business lines that offer the most potential synergies. These alliances take many forms, from simple marketing agreements to joint ownership of worldwide operations.

One form of corporate alliance is the **joint venture,** in which parts of companies are joined to achieve specific, limited objectives.[17] A joint venture is controlled by a management team consisting of representatives of the two (or more) parent companies. Joint ventures have been used often by U.S., Japanese, and European firms to share technology and/or marketing expertise. For example, Whirlpool recently announced a joint venture with the Dutch electronics giant Philips to produce appliances under Philips's brand names in five European countries. By joining with their foreign counterparts, U.S. firms are attempting to gain a stronger foothold in Europe. Although alliances are new to some firms, they are established practices to others. For example, Corning Glass now obtains over half of its profits from 23 joint ventures, two-thirds of

---

[17]Cross-licensing, consortia, joint bidding, and franchising are still other ways for firms to combine resources. For more information on joint ventures, see Sanford V. Berg, Jerome Duncan, and Phillip Friedman, *Joint Venture Strategies and Corporate Innovation* (Cambridge, Mass.: Oelgeschlager, Gunn and Hain, 1982).

them with foreign companies representing almost all of Europe, as well as Japan, China, South Korea, and Australia.

SELF-TEST
QUESTIONS

What is the difference between a merger and a corporate alliance?

What is a joint venture? Give some reasons why joint ventures may be advantageous to the parties involved.

LEVERAGED BUYOUTS

In a **leveraged buyout (LBO)** a small group of investors, usually including current management, acquires a firm in a transaction financed largely by debt. The debt is serviced with funds generated by the acquired company's operations and, often, by the sale of some of its assets. Sometimes, the acquiring group plans to run the acquired company for a number of years, boost its sales and profits, and then take it public again as a stronger company. In other instances, the LBO firm plans to sell off divisions to other firms that can gain synergies. In either case, the acquiring group expects to make a substantial profit from the LBO, but the inherent risks are great due to the heavy use of financial leverage. To illustrate the profit potential, Kohlberg Kravis Roberts & Company (KKR), a leading LBO specialist firm, averaged a spectacular 50 percent annual return on its LBO investments during the 1980s. However, strong stock prices for target firms have dampened the returns on LBO investments, so recent activity has been slower than in its heyday of the 1980s.

A good example of an LBO was KKR's buyout of RJR Nabisco. RJR, a leading producer of tobacco and food products with brands such as Winston, Camel, Planters, Ritz, Oreo, and Del Monte, was trading at about $55 a share in October 1988. Then, F. Ross Johnson, the company's chairman and CEO, announced a $75-a-share, or $17.6 billion, offer to outside stockholders in a plan to take the firm private. This deal, if completed, would have been the largest business transaction up to that time. After the announcement, RJR's stock price soared to $77.25, which indicated that investors thought the final price would be even higher than Johnson's opening bid. A few days later KKR offered $90 per share, or $20.6 billion, for RJR. The battle between the two bidders raged until late November, when RJR's board accepted KKR's revised bid of cash and securities worth about $106 a share, for a total value of about $25 billion. Of course, the investment bankers' fees reflected the record size of the deal—the bankers received almost $400 million, with Drexel Burnham Lambert alone getting over $200 million. Johnson lost his job, but he walked away with a multimillion-dollar golden parachute.

KKR wasted no time in restructuring the newly private RJR. In June 1989, RJR sold its five European businesses to France's BSN for $2.5 million. Then, in September RJR sold the tropical fruit portion of its Del Monte foods unit to Polly Peck, a London-based food company, for $875 million. In the same month, RJR sold the Del Monte canned foods business to an LBO group led by Citicorp Venture Capital for $1.48 billion. Next, in October 1990 RJR sold its Baby Ruth, Butterfinger, and Pearson candy businesses to Nestlé, a Swiss company, for $370 million. In total, RJR sold off more than $5 billion worth of businesses in 1990 to help pay down the tremendous debt taken on in the LBO. In addition to asset sales, in 1991 RJR went public again by issuing more than $1 billion in new common stock, which placed about 25 percent of the firm's common stock in public hands. Also, as the firm's credit rating improved due to the retirement of some of its debt, RJR issued about $1 billion of new debt at significantly lower rates and used the proceeds to retire even more of its high-cost debt.

The RJR Nabisco story is the classic LBO tale—a company is taken private in a highly leveraged deal, the private firm's high-cost junk debt is reduced through asset sales, and finally the company again goes public, which gives the original LBO deal-makers the opportunity to "cash out." This story, however, did not have a fairytale ending. When KKR finally sold the last of its RJR shares in early 1995, it made a profit of about $60 million on a $3.1 billion investment, hardly a stellar return. The best a KKR spokesman could say about the deal was that "it preserved investors' equity." The transaction was largely financed by outside investors, with KKR putting up only $126 million of the original investment. Even though the return on their investment was the same as that received by outside investors, KKR earned an additional $500 million in transactions, advisor, management, and directors' fees.

Regardless of the outcome of the RJR Nabisco deal, there have been some spectacularly successful LBOs. For example, in an early deal that helped fuel the LBO wave, William Simon and Raymond Chambers bought Gibson Greeting Cards in 1982 for $1 million in equity and $79 million in debt. Less than 18 months later, Simon's personal investment of $330,000 was worth $66 million in cash and stock. However, there have also been some spectacular failures. For example, in 1988 Revco became the first large LBO to file for Chapter 11 bankruptcy. It turned out that sales were nearly $1 billion short of the $3.4 billion forecasted at the time of the drugstore chain's buyout.[18]

<table>
<tr><td>SELF-TEST
QUESTIONS</td><td>What is an LBO?

Have LBOs been profitable in recent years?

What actions do companies typically take to meet the large debt burdens resulting from LBOs?

How do LBOs typically affect bondholders?</td></tr>
</table>

DIVESTITURES

Although corporations do more buying than selling of productive facilities, a good bit of selling does occur. In this section, we briefly discuss the major types of divestitures, after which we present some recent examples and rationales for divestitures.

Types of Divestitures

There are four types of **divestitures:** (1) sale of an operating unit to another firm, (2) setting up the business to be divested as a separate corporation and then "spinning it off" to the divesting firm's stockholders, (3) following the steps for a spin-off but selling only some of the shares, and (4) outright liquidation of assets.

Sale to another firm generally involves the sale of an entire division or unit, usually for cash but sometimes for stock of the acquiring firm. In a **spin-off,** the firm's existing stockholders are given new stock representing separate ownership rights in the division which was divested. The division establishes its own board of directors and officers, and it becomes a separate company. The stockholders end up owning shares of

---

[18]For a more detailed discussion of the impact of the RJR LBO on the firm's different classes of investors, see Nancy Mohan and Carl R. Chen, "A Review of the RJR-Nabisco Buyout," *Journal of Applied Corporate Finance,* Summer 1990, 102–108. For interesting discussions of highly leveraged takeovers, see Martin S. Fridson, "What Went Wrong with the Highly Leveraged Deals? (Or, All Variety of Agency Costs)," *Journal of Applied Corporate Finance,* Fall 1991, 57–67; and "The Economic Consequences of High Leverage and Stock Market Pressures on Corporate Management: A Round Table Discussion," *Journal of Applied Corporate Finance,* Summer 1990, 6–57.

GOVERNMENTS ARE DIVESTING STATE-OWNED BUSINESSES TO SPUR ECONOMIC EFFICIENCY

In many countries governments have traditionally owned or controlled a number of key businesses. When Margaret Thatcher became prime minister of Britain in 1979, she set out to reverse this trend, and soon her officials were devising methods for the government to divest state-owned enterprises. Thatcher coined the term "privatization" to describe the process of transferring productive operations and assets from the public sector to the private sector.

The privatization momentum picked up in the early and mid-1980s, expanding to other countries including France, Germany, Japan, and Singapore. Privatization accelerated further as the communist countries and authoritarian regimes across Eastern Europe, Asia, and Latin America shifted toward market-based economies.

Telecommunications, electric power, and airlines are examples of industries that have undergone extensive privatization throughout the world. These industries are vitally important to the economic infrastructure of every nation, and for this reason governments have historically been heavily involved in owning and regulating them within their national borders. Generally, the government-owned enterprise was granted monopoly power to supply the service in question and was subsidized in an effort to hold down costs to consumers. However, economists have long argued that government operations are inherently less efficient than are enterprises which are subject to competitive pressures and whose managers are guided by the profit motive. Thus, in recent years there have been numerous privatizations in these important industries, and as governments have sold their interests, competition has led to lower costs and improved service.

In Western Europe, privatizations in the telecommunications industry have been given an extra push by a European Union plan which opened markets to competition. Because most European telecoms were government owned, the resulting privatizations brought to market tens of billions of dollars of telecom stock. Globally, governments have raised hundreds of billions of dollars through privatizations.

The results are not all in, but it is clear that the removal of bureaucrats and politicians from the control of key enterprises often results in increased economic efficiency and a higher standard of living.

---

two firms instead of one, but no cash has been transferred. In a **carve-out,** a minority interest in a corporate subsidiary is sold to new shareholders, so the parent gains new equity financing yet retains control. Finally, in a **liquidation** the assets of a division are sold off piecemeal, rather than as an operating entity. To illustrate the different types of divestitures, we present some recent examples in the next section.

Divestiture Illustrations

1. Pepsi recently announced plans to spin off its fast-food business, which includes Pizza Hut, Taco Bell, and Kentucky Fried Chicken. Pepsi originally acquired the chains because it wanted to increase the distribution channels for its soft drinks. Over time, however, Pepsi began to realize that the soft-drink and restaurant businesses were quite different, and synergies between them were less than anticipated. The proposed spin-off is part of Pepsi's attempt to once again focus on its core business. However, Pepsi will try to maintain these distribution channels by signing long-term contracts which ensure that Pepsi products will be sold exclusively in each of the three spun-off chains. While the terms of the divestiture have not been finalized, the initial response from investors has been positive.

2. United Airlines sold its Hilton International Hotels subsidiary to Ladbroke Group PLC of Britain for $1.1 billion, and also sold its Hertz rental car unit and its Westin hotel group. The sales culminated a disastrous strategic move by United to build a full-service travel empire. The failed strategy resulted in the firing of Richard J. Ferris, the company's chairman. The move into nonairline travel-related businesses had been viewed by many analysts as a mistake, because there were few synergies to be gained. Further, analysts feared that United's managers, preoccupied by running

hotels and rental car companies, would not maintain the company's focus in the highly competitive airline industry. The funds raised by the divestitures were paid out to United's shareholders as a special dividend.

3. General Motors (GM) spun off its Electronic Data Systems (EDS) subsidiary. EDS, a computer services company founded in 1962 by Ross Perot, prospered as an independent company until it was acquired by GM in 1984. The rationale for the acquisition was that EDS's expertise would help GM both operate better in the information age and build cars that encompassed leading-edge computer technology. However, the spread of desktop computers and the movement of companies to downsize their internal computer staffs caused EDS's non-GM business to soar. Ownership by GM hampered EDS's ability to strike alliances and, in some cases, to enter into business agreements. The best way for EDS to compete in its industry was as an independent, hence it was spun off.

4. As noted in the opening vignette, AT&T was broken up in 1983 to settle a Justice Department antitrust suit filed in the 1970s.[19] For almost 100 years AT&T had operated as a holding company which owned Western Electric (its manufacturing subsidiary), Bell Labs (its research arm), a huge long-distance network which was operated as a division of the parent company, and 22 Bell operating companies, such as Pacific Telephone, New York Telephone, Southern Bell, and Southwestern Bell. In 1984, AT&T was reorganized into eight separate companies—a slimmed-down AT&T which kept Western Electric, Bell Labs, and the long-distance operations, plus seven new regional telephone holding companies that were created from the 22 old operating telephone companies. The stock of the seven new telephone companies was then spun off to the old AT&T's stockholders. A person who held 100 shares of old AT&T stock owned, after the divestiture, 100 shares of the "new" AT&T plus 10 shares of each of the seven new operating companies. These 170 shares were backed by the same assets that had previously backed 100 shares of old AT&T common.

The AT&T divestiture resulted from a suit by the Justice Department, which wanted to divide the Bell System into a regulated monopoly segment (the seven regional telephone companies) and a manufacturing/long-distance segment which would be exposed to competition. The breakup was designed to strengthen competition and thus speed up technological change in those parts of the telecommunications industry that are not natural monopolies.

5. After its forced breakup, AT&T lost little time in building itself up. In 1991 it acquired computer maker NCR, and in 1994 it bought McCaw Cellular Communications, a cellular phone operator. Then, in 1995, AT&T made a surprise announcement. Its massive combination of technology assets was not paying off, and AT&T's stock was in the doldrums. Then the company split itself into three parts. The surviving AT&T includes the core $53 billion long-distance and cellular phone businesses. The division which makes the switching equipment used by local and long-distance companies was spun off under the name Lucent Technologies. AT&T also spun off its loss-plagued computer business (the former NCR). AT&T shares took off on the announcement, adding more than $6 to the share price and $11 billion to AT&T's total value—more than enough to make up for the purchase of NCR and the ensuing losses. One reason for the breakup was the fact that AT&T and the local

---

[19]Another forced divestiture involved Du Pont and General Motors. In 1921, GM was in serious financial trouble, and Du Pont supplied capital in exchange for 23 percent of the stock. In the 1950s, the Justice Department won an antitrust suit which required Du Pont to spin off (to Du Pont's stockholders) its GM stock.

telephone companies were entering one another's markets, and the locals were reluctant to buy equipment from a competitor (AT&T). Therefore, Lucent was losing business to other manufacturers. Also, the breakup permitted the managers of each entity to focus exclusively on the problems and opportunities of their own businesses. Now they can concentrate on those areas where they have the greatest expertise without distraction from events in other business lines.

6. Some years ago, Woolworth liquidated all of its 336 Woolco discount stores. This made the company, which had had sales of $7.2 billion before the liquidation, 30 percent smaller. Woolco had posted operating losses of $19 million the year before the liquidation, and its losses in the latest six months had climbed to an alarming $21 million. Woolworth's CEO, Edward F. Gibbons, was quoted as saying, "How many losses can you take?" Woolco's problems necessitated a write-off of $325 million, but management believed it was better to go ahead and "bite the bullet" rather than let the losing stores bleed the company to death.

7. As a result of some imprudent loans to oil companies and to developing nations, Continental Illinois, one of the largest U.S. bank holding companies at the time, was threatened with bankruptcy. Continental then sold off several profitable divisions, such as its leasing and credit card operations, to raise funds to cover bad-loan losses. In effect, Continental sold assets in order to stay alive. Ultimately, Continental was bailed out by the Federal Deposit Insurance Corporation and the Federal Reserve, which arranged a $7.5 billion rescue package and provided a blanket guarantee for all of Continental's $40 billion of deposits, which kept deposits in excess of $100,000 from fleeing the bank because of their uninsured status.

As the preceding examples illustrate, the reasons for divestitures vary widely. Sometimes the market feels more comfortable when firms "stick to their knitting"; the Pepsi and United Airlines divestitures are examples. Other companies need cash either to finance expansion in their primary business lines or to reduce a large debt burden, and divestitures can be used to raise this cash; Continental Bank illustrates this point. The divestitures also show that running a business is a dynamic process—conditions change, corporate strategies change in response, and as a result firms alter their asset portfolios by acquisitions and/or divestitures. Some divestitures, such as Woolworth's liquidation of its Woolco stores, are to unload losing assets that would otherwise drag the company down. The first AT&T example is one of the many instances in which a divestiture is the result of an antitrust settlement. The AT&T and GM spin-offs illustrate situations where parts of the business can operate more efficiently alone than together.

SELF-TEST QUESTIONS

What are some reasons companies divest assets?

What are three major motives for divestitures?

HOLDING COMPANIES

Holding companies date from 1889, when New Jersey became the first state to pass a law permitting corporations to be formed for the sole purpose of owning the stocks of other companies. Many of the advantages and disadvantages of holding companies are identical to those of any large-scale organization. Whether a company is organized on a divisional basis or with subsidiaries kept as separate companies does not affect the basic reasons for conducting a large-scale, multiproduct, multiplant operation. However, as we show next, the use of holding companies to control large-scale operations has some distinct advantages and disadvantages.

Advantages of Holding Companies

1. **Control with fractional ownership.** Through a holding company operation, a firm may buy 5, 10, or 50 percent of the stock of another corporation. Such fractional ownership may be sufficient to give the holding company effective working control over the operations of the company in which it has acquired stock ownership. Working control is often considered to entail more than 25 percent of the common stock, but it can be as low as 10 percent if the stock is widely distributed. One financier says that the attitude of management is more important than the number of shares owned: "If management thinks you can control the company, then you do." In addition, control on a very slim margin can be held through relationships with large stockholders outside the holding company group.

2. **Isolation of risks.** Because the various **operating companies** in a holding company system are separate legal entities, the obligations of any one unit are separate from those of the other units. Therefore, catastrophic losses incurred by one unit of the holding company system may not be translatable into claims on the assets of the other units. However, we should note that while this is a customary generalization, it is not always valid. First, the **parent company** may feel obligated to make good on the subsidiary's debts, even though it is not legally bound to do so, in order to keep its good name and to retain customers. An example of this was American Express's payment of more than $100 million in connection with a swindle that was the responsibility of one of its subsidiaries. Second, a parent company may feel obligated to supply capital to an affiliate in order to protect its initial investment; General Public Utilities' continued support of its subsidiaries' Three Mile Island nuclear plant after the accident at that plant is an example. And, third, when lending to one of the units of a holding company system, an astute loan officer may require a guarantee by the parent holding company. To some degree, therefore, the assets in the various elements of a holding company are not really separate. Still, a catastrophic loss, as could occur if a drug company's subsidiary distributed a batch of toxic medicine, may be avoided.[20]

Disadvantages of Holding Companies

1. **Partial multiple taxation.** Provided the holding company owns at least 80 percent of a subsidiary's voting stock, the IRS permits the filing of consolidated returns, in which case dividends received by the parent are not taxed. However, if less than 80 percent of the stock is owned, then tax returns cannot be consolidated. Firms that own more than 20 percent but less than 80 percent of another corporation can deduct 80 percent of the dividends received, while firms that own less than 20 percent may deduct only 70 percent of the dividends received. This partial double taxation somewhat offsets the benefits of holding company control with limited ownership, but whether the tax penalty is sufficient to offset other possible advantages is a matter that must be decided in individual situations.

2. **Ease of enforced dissolution.** It is relatively easy to require dissolution by disposal of stock ownership of a holding company operation found guilty of antitrust violations. For instance, in the 1950s Du Pont was required to dispose of its 23 percent

---

[20]Note, though, that the parent company would still be held accountable for such losses if it were deemed to exercise operating control over the subsidiary. Thus, Union Carbide was held responsible for its subsidiary's Bhopal, India, disaster, and Dow Chemical may be held liable for Dow-Corning's multibillion-dollar silicone breast implant product liability judgment.

MERGING AS A MEANS OF EXITING A CLOSELY HELD BUSINESS

Imagine a small family-run business that has achieved success. The entire family fortune may be tied up in the firm, as might be the case if a successful entrepreneur—say, Grandpa—started a business, brought his sons and daughters in as they reached adulthood, and continued to run the enterprise as it grew.

In such a situation, particularly if the firm is valued in the millions, the family's entire financial well-being may depend on the success of this business. As long as Grandpa is healthy and continues to run things, everything is fine. Grandpa may, in fact, be reluctant to sell the business; it gives him something to pass on to his family, and it provides a place for his children and grandchildren to work.

Closely held family businesses are fairly common in the United States, yet for several reasons, maintaining the business in its closely held form may not be in the family's best interests. First, there is the problem of succession. Because at some point Grandpa will retire or die, the issue of who will succeed him is important. Sometimes there is a clear choice for the successor, and everyone agrees with the choice. More often, however, even in families that are very close, the problem of succession can split the family apart. This problem is especially acute if Grandpa dies unexpectedly. At a highly emotional time, a key business decision—the choice of a new president—needs to be made, and the choice is not a simple one. It is, therefore, essential that Grandpa and the other principals set up a plan of succession. If the issue is not resolvable, plans should be made for the outright sale of the business in the event of Grandpa's death.

A second problem is that the business represents the family's primary asset, but family members have no easy way to realize that value when they need cash because the business is not liquid. Sometimes a plan will be made for someone to buy a family member's stock at a predetermined price, such as at its book value per share. This enables the family member to obtain cash, but the price paid probably bears little relation to the market value of the shares. Thus, a family member gives up a valuable asset for the sake of liquidity, taking a potential loss in the process. An alternative is to register the shares and take the company public so that family members can use their equity as they choose. A disadvantage to this approach is the potential loss of control as the number of shares held by the public increases.

A third problem is that as the firm grows, the family may be unable to provide the financial resources necessary to support that growth. If external funds are needed, they will generally be more difficult to obtain in a private, closely held business.

Perhaps an even more serious problem is that, since the family's entire wealth is tied up in a single business, the family holds an *undiversified portfolio*. As was explained in Chapter 5, diversification reduces a portfolio's risk. Thus, the goals of maintaining control and reducing risk through diversification are in conflict. Again, a public offering would allow family members to sell some of their stock and to diversify their own personal portfolios.

Both the diversification motive and family members' liquidity needs often indicate that a business's ownership structure should be changed. There is, however, another alternative besides going public—that of selling the business outright to another company or of merging it into a larger firm. This alternative is often overlooked by owners of closely held businesses, because it frequently means an immediate and complete loss of control. Selling out deserves special consideration, however, because it can often produce far greater value than can be achieved in a public offering.

With the sale of the business, the family gives up control, yet that control is what makes the firm more valuable in a merger than in a public offering. Merger premiums for public companies often range from 50 to 70 percent over the market price. Therefore, a company worth $10 million in the public market might be acquired for a price of $15 to $17 million in a merger. In contrast, initial public offerings (IPOs) are normally made at below-market prices. Furthermore, if the owners sell a significant amount of their stock in the IPO, the market will take that as a signal that the company's future is dim, and the price will be depressed even more.

What are the disadvantages to a merger? An obvious disadvantage is the loss of control. Also, family members risk losing employment in the firm. In such a case, however, they will have additional wealth to sustain them while they seek other opportunities.

The owners of a closely held family business must consider the costs and benefits of continuing to be closely held versus either going public or being acquired in a merger. Of the three alternatives, the merger alternative is likely to provide the greatest benefits to the family members.

stock interest in General Motors Corporation, acquired in the early 1920s. Because there was no fusion between the corporations, there were no difficulties from an operating standpoint in requiring the separation of the two companies. However, if complete amalgamation had taken place, it would have been much more difficult to break up the company after so many years, and the likelihood of forced divestiture would have been reduced.

Holding Companies as a Leveraging Device

The holding company vehicle has been used to obtain huge degrees of financial leverage. In the 1920s, several tiers of holding companies were established in the electric utility, railroad, and other industries. In those days, an operating company at the bottom of the pyramid might have $100 million of assets, financed by $50 million of debt and $50 million of equity. Then, a first-tier holding company might own the stock of the operating firm as its only asset and be financed with $25 million of debt and $25 million of equity. A second-tier holding company, which owned the stock of the first-tier company, might be financed with $12.5 million of debt and $12.5 million of equity. Such systems were extended to five or six levels. With six holding companies, $100 million of operating assets could be controlled at the top by only $0.78 million of equity, and the operating assets would have to provide enough cash income to support $99.22 million of debt. *Such a holding company system is highly leveraged—its consolidated debt ratio is 99.22 percent, even though each of the individual components shows only a 50 percent debt/assets ratio.* Because of this consolidated leverage, even a small decline in profits at the operating company level could bring the whole system down like a house of cards. This situation existed in the electric utility industry in the 1920s, and the Depression of the 1930s wreaked havoc with the holding companies and led to federal legislation which constrained holding companies in that industry.

S E L F - T E S T
Q U E S T I O N S

What is a holding company?

What are some of the advantages of holding companies? What are some of the disadvantages?

SUMMARY

This chapter included discussions of mergers, divestitures, holding companies, and LBOs. The key concepts covered are summarized below:

- A **merger** occurs when two firms combine to form a single company. The primary motives for mergers are (1) synergy, (2) tax considerations, (3) purchase of assets below their replacement costs, (4) diversification, and (5) gaining control over a larger enterprise.

- Mergers can provide economic benefits through **economies of scale** and through putting assets in the hands of **more efficient managers.** However, mergers also have the potential for reducing competition, and for this reason they are carefully regulated by government agencies.

- In most mergers, one company (the **acquiring firm**) initiates action to take over another (the **target firm**).

- A **horizontal merger** occurs when two firms in the same line of business combine.

- A **vertical merger** combines a firm with one of its customers or suppliers.

- A **congeneric merger** involves firms in related industries, but where no customer-supplier relationship exists.

- A **conglomerate merger** occurs when firms in totally different industries combine.

- In a **friendly merger,** the managements of both firms approve the merger, whereas in a **hostile merger,** the target firm's management opposes it.

- An **operating merger** is one where the operations of the two firms are combined. A **financial merger** is one where the firms continue to operate separately, hence no operating economies are expected.

- In a typical **merger analysis,** the key issues to be resolved are (1) the price to be paid for the target firm and (2) the employment/control situation. If the merger is a consolidation of two relatively equal firms, an issue is, "What percentage of the ownership do each merger partner's shareholders receive?"

- Two methods are commonly used to determine the **value of the target firm:** (1) the **discounted cash flow (DCF)** method and (2) the **market multiple** method.

- For accounting purposes, mergers are handled in one of two ways: (1) as a **pooling of interests** or (2) as a **purchase.**

- A **joint venture** is a **corporate alliance** in which two or more companies combine some of their resources to achieve a specific, limited objective.

- A **divestiture** is the sale of some of a company's operating assets. A divestiture may involve (1) selling an operating unit to another firm, (2) **spinning off** a unit as a separate company, or (3) the outright **liquidation** of a unit's assets.

- The **reasons for divestiture** include to settle antitrust suits, to clarify what a company actually does, to enable management to concentrate on a particular type of activity, and to raise capital needed to strengthen the corporation's core business.

- A **holding company** is a corporation which owns sufficient stock in another firm to control it. The holding company is also known as the **parent company,** and the companies which it controls are called **subsidiaries,** or **operating companies.**

- Advantages to holding company operations include (1) control can often be obtained for a smaller cash outlay, (2) risks may be segregated, and (3) regulated companies can operate separate subsidiaries for their regulated and unregulated businesses.

- Disadvantages to holding company operations include (1) tax penalties and (2) the fact that incomplete ownership, if it exists, can lead to control problems.

- A **leveraged buyout (LBO)** is a transaction in which a firm's publicly owned stock is acquired in a mostly debt-financed tender offer, and a privately owned, highly leveraged firm results. Often, the firm's own management initiates the LBO.

Questions

26-1   Define each of the following terms:
   a. Synergy; merger
   b. Horizontal merger; vertical merger; congeneric merger; conglomerate merger
   c. Friendly merger; hostile merger; defensive merger; tender offer; target company; breakup value; acquiring company
   d. Operating merger; financial merger
   e. Discounted cash flow method; market multiple method
   f. Pooling of interests; purchase accounting
   g. White knight; poison pill; golden parachute; proxy fight
   h. Joint venture; corporate alliance
   i. Divestiture; spin-off; leveraged buyout (LBO)
   j. Holding company; operating company; parent company
   k. Arbitrage; risk arbitrage

26-2   Four economic classifications of mergers are (1) horizontal, (2) vertical, (3) conglomerate, and (4) congeneric. Explain the significance of these terms in merger analysis with regard to (a) the likelihood of governmental intervention and (b) possibilities for operating synergy.

26-3   Firm A wants to acquire Firm B. Firm B's management agrees that the merger is a good idea. Might a tender offer be used?

26-4   Distinguish between operating mergers and financial mergers.

26-5   In the spring of 1984, Disney Productions' stock was selling for about $3.125 per share (all prices have been adjusted for 4-for-1 splits in 1986 and 1992). Then Saul Steinberg, a New York financier, began acquiring it, and after he had 12 percent, he announced a tender offer for another 37 percent of the stock—which would bring his holdings up to 49 percent—at a price of $4.22 per share. Disney's management then announced plans to buy Gibson Greeting Cards and Arvida Corporation, paying for them with stock. It also lined up bank credit and (according to Steinberg) was prepared to borrow up to $2 billion and use the funds to repurchase shares at a higher price than Steinberg was offering. All of these efforts were designed to keep Steinberg from taking control. In June, Disney's management agreed to pay Steinberg $4.84 per share, which gave him a gain of about $60 million on a 2-month investment of about $26.5 million.

When Disney's buy-back of Steinberg's shares was announced, the stock price fell almost instantly from $4.25 to $2.875. Many Disney stockholders were irate, and they sued to block the buyout. Also, the Disney affair added fuel to the fire in a Congressional committee that was holding hearings on proposed legislation that would (1) prohibit someone from acquiring more than 10 percent of a firm's stock without making a tender offer for all the remaining shares, (2) prohibit poison pill tactics such as those Disney's management had used to fight off Steinberg, (3) prohibit buy-backs such as the deal eventually offered to Steinberg (greenmail) unless there was an approving vote by stockholders, and (4) prohibit (or substantially curtail) the use of golden parachutes (the one thing Disney's management did not try).

Set forth the arguments for and against this type of legislation. What provisions, if any, should it contain? Also, look up Disney's current stock price to see how its stockholders have actually fared.

26-6 Two large, publicly owned firms are contemplating a merger. No operating synergy is expected. However, since returns on the 2 firms are not perfectly positively correlated, the standard deviation of earnings would be reduced for the combined corporation. One group of consultants argues that this risk reduction is sufficient grounds for the merger. Another group thinks this type of risk reduction is irrelevant because stockholders can themselves hold the stock of both companies and thus gain the risk-reduction benefits without all the hassles and expenses of the merger. Whose position is correct?

Problems

The following information is required to work Problems 26-1, 26-2, and 26-3.

Harrison Corporation is interested in acquiring Van Buren Corporation. Assume that the risk-free rate of interest is 5 percent and the market risk premium is 6 percent.

26-1
Valuation
Van Buren currently expects to pay a year-end dividend of $2.00 a share ($D_1 = 2.00). Van Buren's dividend is expected to grow at a constant rate of 5 percent a year, and its beta is 0.9. What is the current price of Van Buren's stock?

26-2
Merger Valuation
Harrison estimates that if it acquires Van Buren, the year-end dividend will remain at $2.00 a share, but synergies will enable the dividend to grow at a constant rate of 7 percent a year (instead of the current 5 percent). Harrison also plans to increase the debt ratio of what would be its Van Buren subsidiary—the effect of this would be to raise Van Buren's beta to 1.1. What is the per-share value of Van Buren to Harrison Corporation?

26-3
Merger Bid
On the basis of your answers to Problems 26-1 and 26-2, if Harrison were to acquire Van Buren, what would be the range of possible prices that it could bid for each share of Van Buren common stock?

26-4
Merger Analysis
Apilado Appliance Corporation is considering a merger with the Vaccaro Vacuum Company. Vaccaro is a publicly traded company, and its current beta is 1.30. Vaccaro has been barely profitable, so it has paid an average of only 20 percent in taxes during the last several years. In addition, it uses little debt, having a debt ratio of just 25 percent.

If the acquisition were made, Apilado would operate Vaccaro as a separate, wholly owned subsidiary. Apilado would pay taxes on a consolidated basis, and the tax rate would therefore increase to 35 percent. Apilado also would increase the debt capitalization in the Vaccaro subsidiary to 40 percent of assets, which would increase its beta to 1.50. Apilado's acquisition department estimates that Vaccaro, if acquired, would produce the following net cash flows to Apilado's shareholders (in millions of dollars):

YEAR	NET CASH FLOWS
1	$1.30
2	1.50
3	1.75
4	2.00
5 and beyond	Constant growth at 6%

These cash flows include all acquisition effects. Apilado's cost of equity is 14 percent, its beta is 1.0, and its cost of debt is 10 percent. The risk-free rate is 8 percent.

a. What discount rate should be used to discount the estimated cash flow? (Hint: Use Apilado's k_s to determine the market risk premium.)

b. What is the dollar value of Vaccaro to Apilado?

c. Vaccaro has 1.2 million common shares outstanding. What is the maximum price per share that Apilado should offer for Vaccaro? If the tender offer is accepted at this price, what will happen to Apilado's stock price?

26-5
Capital Budgeting Analysis

The Stanley Stationery Shoppe wishes to acquire The Carlson Card Gallery for $400,000. Stanley expects the merger to provide incremental earnings of about $64,000 a year for 10 years. Ken Stanley has calculated the marginal cost of capital for this investment to be 10 percent. Conduct a capital budgeting analysis for Stanley to determine whether or not he should purchase The Carlson Card Gallery.

26-6
Merger Analysis

TransWorld Communications Inc., a large telecommunications company, is evaluating the possible acquisition of Georgia Cable Company (GCC), a regional cable company. TransWorld's analysts project the following postmerger data for GCC (in thousands of dollars):

		1999	2000	2001	2002
Net sales		$450	$518	$555	$600
Selling and administrative expense		45	53	60	68
Interest		18	21	24	27
Tax rate after merger	35%				
Cost of goods sold as a percent of sales	65%				
Beta after merger	1.50				
Risk-free rate	8%				
Market risk premium	4%				
Terminal growth rate of cash flow available to TransWorld	7%				

If the acquisition is made, it will occur on January 1, 1999. All cash flows shown in the income statements are assumed to occur at the end of the year. GCC currently has a capital structure of 40 percent debt, but TransWorld would increase that to 50 percent if the acquisition were made. GCC, if independent, would pay taxes at 20 percent, but its income would be taxed at 35 percent if it were consolidated. GCC's current market-determined beta is 1.40, and its investment bankers think that its beta would rise to 1.50 if the debt ratio were increased to 50 percent. The cost of goods sold is expected to be 65 percent of sales, but it could vary somewhat. Depreciation-generated funds would be used to replace worn-out equipment, so they would not be available to TransWorld's shareholders. The risk-free rate is 8 percent, and the market risk premium is 4 percent.

a. What is the appropriate discount rate for valuing the acquisition?

b. What is the terminal value? What is the value of GCC to TransWorld?

Spreadsheet Problem

Work the problem in this section only if you are using the computer problem diskette.

26-7
Merger Analysis

Use the model in File C26 to work this problem.

a. Refer back to Problem 26-6. Rework the problem assuming that sales in each year were $100,000 higher than the base-case amounts and that the cost of goods sold/sales ratio was 60 percent rather than 65 percent. What would be the value of GCC to TransWorld under these assumptions?

b. With sales and the cost of goods sold ratio at the levels specified in Part a, what would be GCC's value if its beta were 1.60, if k_{RF} rose to 9 percent, and if RP_M rose to 5 percent?

c. Leaving all values at their Part b levels, what would be the value of the acquisition if the terminal growth rate rose to 12 percent or dropped to 3 percent?

MINI CASE

Smitty's Home Repair Company, a regional hardware chain which specializes in "do-it-yourself" materials and equipment rentals, is cash rich because of several consecutive good years. One of the alternative uses for the excess funds is an acquisition. Linda Wade, Smitty's treasurer and your boss, has been asked to place a value on a potential target, Hill's Hardware, a small chain which operates in an adjacent state, and she has enlisted your help.

The table below indicates Wade's estimates of Hill's earnings potential if it came under Smitty's management (in millions of dollars). The interest expense listed here includes the interest (1) on Hill's existing debt, (2) on new debt that Smitty's would issue to help finance the acquisition, and (3) on new debt expected to be issued over time to help finance expansion within the new "H division," the code name given to the target firm. The retentions represent earnings that will be reinvested within the H division to help finance its growth.

Security analysts estimate Hill's beta to be 1.3. The acquisition would not change Hill's capital structure or tax rate. Wade realizes that Hill's Hardware also generates depreciation cash flows, but she believes that these funds would have to be reinvested within the division to replace worn-out equipment.

Wade estimates the risk-free rate to be 9 percent and the market risk premium to be 4 percent. She also estimates that net cash flows after 2002 will grow at a constant rate of 6 percent. Following are projections for sales and other items.

	1999	2000	2001	2002
Net sales	$60.0	$90.0	$112.5	$127.5
Cost of goods sold (60%)	36.0	54.0	67.5	76.5
Selling/administrative expense	4.5	6.0	7.5	9.0
Interest expense	3.0	4.5	4.5	6.0
Necessary retained earnings	0.0	7.5	6.0	4.5

Smitty's management is new to the merger game, so Wade has been asked to answer some basic questions about mergers as well as to perform the merger analysis. To structure the task, Wade has developed the following questions, which you must answer and then defend to Smitty's board.

a. Several reasons have been proposed to justify mergers. Among the more prominent are (1) tax considerations, (2) risk reduction, (3) control, (4) purchase of assets at below-replacement cost, (5) synergy, and (6) globalization. In general, which of the reasons are economically justifiable? Which are not? Which fit the situation at hand? Explain.

b. Briefly describe the differences between a hostile merger and a friendly merger.

c. Use the data developed in the table to construct the H division's cash flow statements for 1999 through 2002. Why is interest expense deducted in merger cash flow statements, whereas it is not normally deducted in a capital budgeting cash flow analysis? Why are earnings retentions deducted in the cash flow statement?

d. Conceptually, what is the appropriate discount rate to apply to the cash flows developed in Part c? What is your actual estimate of this discount rate?

e. What is the estimated terminal value of the acquisition; that is, what is the estimated value of the H division's cash flows beyond 2002? What is Hill's value to Smitty's? Suppose another firm were evaluating Hill's as an acquisition candidate. Would they obtain the same value? Explain.

f. Assume that Hill's has 10 million shares outstanding. These shares are traded relatively infrequently, but the last trade, made several weeks ago, was at a price of $9 per share. Should Smitty's make an offer for Hill's? If so, how much should it offer per share?

g. Assume that publicly traded companies in Hill's line of business have stock prices in the range of 5 to 6 times earnings before interest, taxes, depreciation, and amortization (EBITDA). Use the market multiple approach to value the target company.

h. There has been considerable research undertaken to determine whether mergers really create value and, if so, how this value is shared between the parties involved. What are the results of this research?

i. What are the two methods of accounting for mergers?

j. What merger-related activities are undertaken by investment bankers?

k. What is a leveraged buyout (LBO)? What are some of the advantages and disadvantages of going private?
l. What are the major types of divestitures? What motivates firms to divest assets?
m. What are holding companies? What are their advantages and disadvantages?

Selected Additional References and Cases

Considerable empirical investigation has been conducted to determine whether stockholders of acquiring or acquired companies benefit most from corporate mergers. Several excellent studies are

Black, Bernard S., and Joseph A. Grundfest, "Shareholder Gains from Takeovers and Restructurings between 1981 and 1986: $162 Billion Is a Lot of Money," *Journal of Applied Corporate Finance*, Spring 1988, 5–15.

Jarrell, Greg A., and Annettee B. Poulsen, "The Returns to Acquiring Firms in Tender Offers: Evidence from Three Decades," *Financial Management*, Autumn 1989, 12–19.

Mandelker, Gershon, "Risk and Return: The Case of Merging Firms," *Journal of Financial Economics*, December 1974, 303–335.

For some additional insights into merger returns, see

Elgers, Pieter T., and John J. Clark, "Merger Types and Shareholder Returns: Additional Evidence," *Financial Management*, Summer 1980, 66–72.

Mueller, Dennis C., "The Effects of Conglomerate Mergers," *Journal of Banking and Finance*, December 1977, 315–347.

Wansley, James W., William R. Lane, and Ho C. Yang, "Abnormal Returns to Acquired Firms by Type of Acquisition and Method of Payment," *Financial Management*, Autumn 1983, 16–22.

For an interesting test of the existence of synergy in mergers, see

Haugen, Robert A., and Terence C. Langetieg, "An Empirical Test for Synergism in Merger," *Journal of Finance*, September 1975, 1003–1014.

For more insights into the likelihood of acceptance of a cash tender offer, see

Hoffmeister, J. Ronald, and Edward A. Dyl, "Predicting Outcomes of Cash Tender Offers," *Financial Management*, Winter 1981, 50–58.

Some additional works on tender offers include

Dodd, Peter, and Richard Ruback, "Tender Offers and Stockholder Returns," *Journal of Financial Economics*, November 1977, 351–373.

Kummer, Donald R., and J. Ronald Hoffmeister, "Valuation Consequences of Cash Tender Offers," *Journal of Finance*, May 1978, 505–516.

The following articles examine the effect of merger accounting on stock price:

Davis, Michael L., "The Purchase versus Pooling Controversy: How the Stock Market Responds to Goodwill," *Journal of Applied Corporate Finance*, Spring 1996, 51–59.

Hong, Hai, Gershon Mandelker, and R. S. Kaplan, "Pooling versus Purchase: The Effects of Accounting for Mergers on Stock Prices," *Accounting Review*, January 1978, 31–47.

For a selection of articles on LBOs, see the Spring 1989 issue of the Journal of Applied Corporate Finance *and the Spring 1992 issue of* Financial Management.

The Summer 1989 issue of the Journal of Applied Corporate Finance *also focuses on mergers and acquisitions.*

For a selection of articles on LBOs, see the Spring 1989 issue of the Journal of Applied Corporate Finance.

For a very interesting discussion of many of the important merger issues, see

"A Discussion of Mergers and Acquisitions," *Midland Corporate Finance Journal*, Summer 1983, 21–47.

Other recent articles that pertain to this chapter include the following:

Allen, Jay R., "LBOs — The Evolution of Financial Strategies and Structures," *Journal of Applied Corporate Finance,* Winter 1996, 18–29.

Baker, George P., "Beatrice: A Study in the Creation and Destruction of Value," *Journal of Finance,* July 1992, 1081–1119.

Baker, George P., and Karen H. Wruck, "Lessons from a Middle Market LBO: The Case of O. M. Scott," *Journal of Applied Corporate Finance,* Spring 1991, 46–58.

Eckbo, B. Espen, "Mergers and the Value of Antitrust Deterrence," *Journal of Finance,* July 1992, 1005–1029.

Ezzell, John R., H. Christine Hsu, and James A. Miles, "An Analysis of Regulated Rates of Return for Wholly Owned Subsidiaries," *Journal of Financial Research,* Summer 1991, 167–180.

Kaplan, Steven, and Michael S. Weisbach, "The Success of Acquisitions: Evidence from Divestitures," *Journal of Finance,* March 1992, 107–138.

Mitchell, Mark L., and Kenneth Lehn, "Do Bad Bidders Become Good Targets?" *Journal of Applied Corporate Finance,* Summer 1990, 60–69.

Mohan, Nancy, M. Fall Ainina, Daniel Kaufman, and Bernard J. Winger, "Acquisition/Divestiture Valuation Practices in Major U.S. Firms," *Financial Practice and Education,* Spring 1991, 73–81.

Morck, Randall, Andrei Shleifer, and Robert W. Vishny, "Do Managerial Objectives Drive Bad Acquisitions?" *Journal of Finance,* March 1990, 31–48.

Romano, Roberta, "Rethinking Takeover Regulations," *Journal of Applied Corporate Finance,* Fall 1992, 47–57.

Weaver, Samuel C., Robert S. Harris, Daniel W. Bielinski, and Kenneth F. MacKenzie, "Merger and Acquisition Valuation," *Financial Management,* Summer 1991, 85–96.

Wruck, Karen H., "What Really Went Wrong at Revco?" *Journal of Applied Corporate Finance,* Summer 1991, 79–92.

The following cases in the Cases in Financial Management: Dryden Request *series illustrate merger analysis:*

Case 40, "Nina's Fashions, Inc.," Case 40A, "Nero's Pasta, Inc.," and Case 40B, "Computer Concepts/CompuTech," which focus on merger valuation.

MULTINATIONAL FINANCIAL MANAGEMENT*

*F*rom the end of World War II until the 1970s, the United States dominated the world economy. However, that situation no longer exists. Raw materials, finished goods, services, and money flow freely across most national boundaries, as do innovative ideas and new technologies. World-class U.S. companies are making breakthroughs in foreign labs, obtaining capital from foreign investors, and putting foreign employees on the fast track to the top. Dozens of top U.S. manufacturers, including Dow Chemical, Colgate-Palmolive, Gillette, Hewlett-Packard, and Xerox, sell more of their products outside the United States than they do at home. Service firms are not far behind, as Citicorp, Disney, McDonald's, and Time Warner all receive more than 20 percent of their revenues from foreign sales.

The trend is even more pronounced in profits. In recent years, Coca-Cola and many other companies have made more money in the Pacific Rim and Western Europe than in the United States.

As U.S. companies begin to reap half or more of their sales and profits from abroad, they are finding it necessary to blend into the foreign landscape in order to win product acceptance and avoid political problems.

At the same time, foreign-based multinationals are arriving on American shores in ever greater numbers. Sweden's ABB, the Netherlands's Philips, France's Thomson, and Japan's Fujitsu and Honda are all waging campaigns to be identified as American companies that employ Americans, transfer technology to America, and help the U.S. trade balance. Few Americans know or care that Thomson owns the RCA and General Electric names in consumer electronics, or that Philips owns Magnavox.

The emergence of "world companies" raises a host of questions for governments. For example, should domestic firms be favored, or does it make no difference what a company's nationality is as long as it provides domestic jobs? Should a company make an effort to keep jobs in its home country, or should it produce where total production costs are lowest? What nation controls the technology developed by a multinational corporation, particularly if the technology can be used in military applications? Must a multinational company adhere to rules imposed in its home country with respect to its operations outside the home country? And if a U.S. firm such as Xerox produces copiers in Japan and then ships them to the United States, should they be reflected in the trade deficit in the same way as Toshiba copiers imported from Japan? Keep these questions in mind as you read this chapter. When you finish it, you should have a better appreciation of both the problems facing governments and the difficult but profitable opportunities facing managers of multinational companies.

---

*This chapter was coauthored with Professors Roy Crum of the University of Florida and Subu Venkataraman of Northwestern University.

Managers of multinational companies must deal with a wide range of issues that are not present when a company operates in a single country. In this chapter, we highlight the key differences between multinational and domestic corporations, and we discuss the impact these differences have on the financial management of multinational businesses.

MULTINATIONAL, OR GLOBAL, CORPORATIONS

The term **multinational,** or **global, corporation** is used to describe a firm that operates in an integrated fashion in a number of countries. During the past 20 years, a new and fundamentally different form of international commercial activity has developed, and this has greatly increased worldwide economic and political interdependence. Rather than merely buying resources from and selling goods to foreign nations, multinational firms now make direct investments in fully integrated operations, from extraction of raw materials, through the manufacturing process, to distribution to consumers throughout the world. Today, multinational corporate networks control a large and growing share of the world's technological, marketing, and productive resources.

Companies, both U.S. and foreign, go "global" for six primary reasons:

1. **To broaden their markets.** After a company has saturated its home market, growth opportunities are often better in foreign markets. Thus, such homegrown firms as Coca-Cola and McDonald's are aggressively expanding into overseas markets, and foreign firms such as Sony and Toshiba now dominate the U.S. consumer electronics market. Also, as products become more complex, and development becomes more expensive, it is necessary to sell more units to cover overhead costs, so larger markets are critical. Thus, movie companies have "gone global" to get the volume necessary to support pictures such as *Titanic*.

2. **To seek raw materials.** Many U.S. oil companies, such as Exxon, have major subsidiaries around the world to ensure access to the basic resources needed to sustain the companies' primary business line.

3. **To seek new technology.** No single nation holds a commanding advantage in all technologies, so companies are scouring the globe for leading scientific and design ideas. For example, Xerox has introduced more than 80 different office copiers in the United States that were engineered and built by its Japanese joint venture, Fuji Xerox. Similarly, versions of the superconcentrated detergent that Procter & Gamble first formulated in Japan in response to a rival's product are now being marketed in Europe and the United States.

4. **To seek production efficiency.** Companies in high-cost countries are shifting production to low-cost regions. For example, GE has production and assembly plants in Mexico, South Korea, and Singapore, and even Japanese manufacturers are shifting some of their production to lower-cost countries in the Pacific Rim. BMW and Mercedes-Benz, in response to high production costs in Germany, have built assembly plants in the United States. The ability to shift production from country to country has important implications for labor costs in all countries. For example, when Xerox threatened to move its copier rebuilding work to Mexico, its union in Rochester agreed to work rule changes and productivity improvements that kept the operation in the United States. Some multinational companies make decisions almost daily on

where to shift production. When Dow Chemical saw European demand for a certain solvent declining, the company scaled back production at a German plant and shifted its production to another chemical which had previously been imported from the United States. Relying on complex computer models for making such decisions, Dow runs its plants at peak capacity and thus keeps capital costs down.

5. **To avoid political and regulatory hurdles.** The primary reason Japanese auto companies moved production to the United States was to get around U.S. import quotas. Now Honda, Nissan, Toyota, Mazda, and Mitsubishi are all assembling vehicles in the United States. One of the factors that prompted U.S. pharmaceutical maker Smith-Kline and Britain's Beecham to merge was that they wanted to avoid licensing and regulatory delays in their largest markets, Western Europe and the United States. Now SmithKline Beecham can identify itself as an inside player in both Europe and the United States. Similarly, when Germany's BASF launched biotechnology research at home, it confronted legal and political challenges from the environmentally conscious Green movement. In response, BASF shifted its cancer and immune system research to two laboratories in Boston suburbs. This location is attractive not only because of its large number of engineers and scientists but also because the Boston area has resolved controversies involving safety, animal rights, and the environment. "We decided it would be better to have the laboratories located where we have fewer insecurities about what will happen in the future," said Rolf-Dieter Acker, BASF's director of biotechnology research.

6. **To diversify.** By establishing worldwide production facilities and markets, firms can cushion the impact of adverse economic trends in any single country. For example, General Motors softened the blow of poor sales in the United States during the 1990–1991 recession with strong sales by its European subsidiaries. In general, geographic diversification works because the economic ups and downs of different countries are not perfectly correlated. Therefore, companies investing overseas benefit from diversification in the same way that individuals benefit from investing in a broad portfolio of stocks.

Over the past 10 to 15 years, there has been an increasing amount of investment in the United States by foreign corporations, and in foreign nations by U.S. corporations. This trend is shown in Figure 27-1, and it is important because of its implications for eroding the traditional doctrine of independence and self-reliance that has been a hallmark of U.S. policy. Just as U.S. corporations with extensive overseas operations are said to use their economic power to exert substantial economic and political influence over host governments in many parts of the world, it is feared that foreign corporations are gaining similar sway over U.S. policy. These developments suggest an increasing degree of mutual influence and interdependence among business enterprises and nations, to which the United States is not immune.

The world economy is quite fluid. Here are a few of the recent events which have dramatically changed the international financial environment:

1. The disintegration of the former Soviet Union and the movement toward market economies in the newly formed countries have created a vast new market for international commerce.

2. The reunification of Germany, coupled with the collapse of communism in Eastern Europe, has created significant new opportunities for foreign investment.

3. The European Community and the European Free Trade Association have created a "borderless" region where people, capital, goods, and services move freely among

| FIGURE 27-1 | Direct Investment for the United States, 1982–1995 |

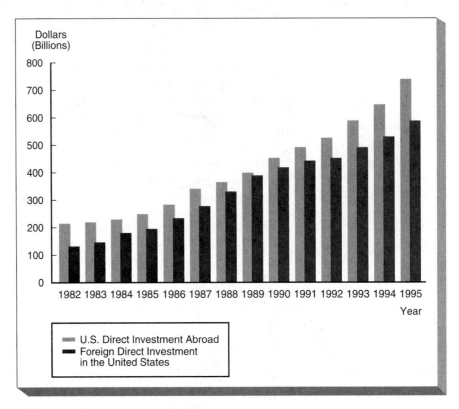

SOURCE: J. Lowe and S. Vargas, "Direct Investment Positions on a Historical Cost Basis," *Survey of Current Business,* July 1996.

The NAFTA (North American Free Trade Agreement) ensures that continued international investment will be made by U.S. corporations. An interesting report about the effect of NAFTA on the U.S. economy can be found on the United States Trade Representative's home page at http://www.ustr.gov/reports/index.html.

the 19 nations without the burden of tariffs. Negotiations are also under way to create a single "Eurocurrency," which would greatly simplify economic exchange among the participating countries.

4. The North American Free Trade Agreement (NAFTA) has moved the economies of the United States, Canada, and Mexico much closer together, and made them more interdependent.

5. U.S. bank regulations have been loosened dramatically. One key deregulatory feature was the removal of interest rate ceilings, thus allowing banks to attract foreign deposits by raising rates. Another key feature was the removal of barriers to entry by foreign banks, which resulted in more cross-border banking transactions. Still, U.S. commercial and investment banks do not have as much freedom as foreign banks, which has led many U.S. banks to establish subsidiaries in Europe that can offer a wider range of services. All this has increased global competition in the financial services industry.

SELF-TEST
QUESTIONS

What is a multinational corporation?

Why do companies "go global"?

MULTINATIONAL VERSUS DOMESTIC FINANCIAL MANAGEMENT

In theory, the concepts and procedures discussed in the first 26 chapters are valid for both domestic and multinational operations. However, six major factors distinguish financial management in firms operating entirely within a single country from firms that operate globally:

1. **Different currency denominations.** Cash flows in various parts of a multinational corporate system will be denominated in different currencies. Hence, an analysis of exchange rates must be included in all financial analyses.

2. **Economic and legal ramifications.** Each country has its own unique economic and legal systems, and these differences can cause significant problems when a corporation tries to coordinate and control its worldwide operations. For example, differences in tax laws among countries can cause a given economic transaction to have strikingly different after-tax consequences, depending on where the transaction occurs. Similarly, differences in legal systems of host nations, such as the Common Law of Great Britain versus the French Civil Law, complicate matters ranging from the simple recording of business transactions to the role played by the judiciary in resolving conflicts. Such differences can restrict multinational corporations' flexibility in deploying resources, and can even make procedures that are required in one part of the company illegal in another part. These differences also make it difficult for executives trained in one country to move easily to another.

3. **Language differences.** The ability to communicate is critical in all business transactions, and here U.S. citizens are often at a disadvantage because we are generally fluent only in English, while European and Japanese businesspeople are usually fluent in several languages, including English. Thus, they can invade our markets more easily than we can penetrate theirs.

4. **Cultural differences.** Even within geographic regions that are considered relatively homogeneous, different countries have unique cultural heritages that shape values and influence the conduct of business. Multinational corporations find that matters such as defining the appropriate goals of the firm, attitudes toward risk, dealings with employees, and the ability to curtail unprofitable operations vary dramatically from one country to the next.

5. **Role of governments.** Most financial models assume the existence of a competitive marketplace in which the terms of trade are determined by the participants. The government, through its power to establish basic ground rules, is involved in the process, but its role is minimal. Thus, the market provides the primary barometer of success, and it gives the best clues about what must be done to remain competitive. This view of the process is reasonably correct for the United States and Western Europe, but it does not accurately describe the situation in most of the world. Frequently, the terms under which companies compete, the actions that must be taken or avoided, and the terms of trade on various transactions are determined not in the marketplace but by direct negotiation between the host government and the multinational corporation. This is essentially a political process, and it must be treated as such. Thus, our traditional financial models have to be recast to include political and other noneconomic aspects of the decision.

6. **Political risk.** A nation is free to place constraints on the transfer of corporate resources and even to expropriate without compensation assets within their boundaries. This is

political risk, and it tends to be largely a given rather than a variable that can be changed by negotiation. Political risk varies from country to country, and it must be addressed explicitly in any financial analysis. Another aspect of political risk is terrorism against U.S. firms or executives. For example, U.S. and Japanese executives have been kidnapped and held for ransom in several South American countries.

These six factors complicate financial management, and they increase the risks faced by multinational firms. However, the prospects for high returns, diversification benefits, and other factors make it worthwhile for firms to accept these risks and learn how to manage them.

SELF-TEST QUESTION

Identify and briefly discuss six major factors that complicate financial management in multinational firms.

EXCHANGE RATES

The Bloomberg World Currency Values site provides up-to-the-minute foreign currency values versus the U.S. dollar, as well as a cross-currency table similar to that found in *The Wall Street Journal* for the world's major currencies. The site can be accessed at http://www.bloomberg.com/markets/fxc.html.

An **exchange rate** specifies the number of units of a given currency that can be purchased with one unit of another currency. Exchange rates appear in the financial sections of newspapers each day. Selected rates from *The Wall Street Journal* are given in Table 27-1. The values shown in Column 1 are the number of U.S. dollars required to purchase one unit of foreign currency; this is called a *direct quotation.* Direct quotations have a dollar sign in their quotation. Thus, the direct U.S. dollar quotation for the German mark is $0.6418, because one German mark could be bought for 64.18 cents. The exchange rates given in Column 2 represent the number of units of foreign currency that can be purchased for one U.S. dollar; these are called *indirect quotations.* Indirect quotations often begin with the foreign currency's equivalent to the dollar sign. Thus, the indirect quotation for the German mark is M1.5581. (The "M" stands for *Mark,* and it is equivalent to the symbol "$.") Normal practice in the United States is to use indirect quotations (Column 2) for all currencies other than British pounds, for which direct quotations are given. Thus, we speak of the pound as "selling at $1.67" but of the mark as "being at 1.56."

It is also a universal convention on the world's foreign currency exchanges to state all exchange rates except British pounds on a "dollar basis"—that is, as the foreign currency price of one U.S. dollar as reported in Column 2 of Table 27-1. Thus, in all currency trading centers, whether in New York, Frankfurt, London, Tokyo, or anywhere else, the exchange rate for the German mark would be displayed as M1.5581. This convention eliminates confusion when comparing quotations from one trading center with those from another.

We can use the data in Table 27-1 to show how one works with exchange rates. Suppose a U.S. tourist on holiday flies from New York to London, then to Paris, then on to Munich, and finally back to New York. When she arrives at London's Heathrow Airport, she goes to the bank to check the foreign exchange listing. The rate she observes for U.S. dollars is $1.6650; this means that £1 will cost her $1.6650. Assume that she exchanges $2,000 for $2,000/$1.6650 = £1,201.20 and enjoys a week's vacation in London, spending £701.20 while there and saving £500.

At the end of the week she travels to Dover to catch the Hovercraft to Calais on the coast of France and realizes that she needs to exchange her 500 remaining British pounds for French francs. However, what she sees on the board is the direct quotation between pounds and dollars ($1.6650) and the indirect quotation between francs and dollars (FF5.2575). (For our purposes, we assume that the exchange rates in effect at

TABLE 27-1	Illustrative Exchange Rates	

	DIRECT QUOTATION: U.S. DOLLARS REQUIRED TO BUY ONE UNIT OF FOREIGN CURRENCY (1)	**INDIRECT QUOTATION: NUMBER OF UNITS OF FOREIGN CURRENCY PER U.S. DOLLAR** (2)
British pound	$1.6650	0.6006
Canadian dollar	0.7315	1.3671
Dutch guilder	0.5736	1.7435
French franc	0.1902	5.2575
German mark	0.6418	1.5581
Italian lira	0.0006523	1,533.0000
Japanese yen	0.008769	114.0400
Mexican peso	0.12726	7.8580
Spanish peseta	0.007634	130.9900
Swiss franc	0.7465	1.3395

NOTE: Column 2 equals 1.0 divided by Column 1. However, rounding differences do occur.
SOURCE: *The Wall Street Journal,* December 20, 1996.

the start of the trip remain in effect throughout our example. This is unrealistic for reasons explained later in this chapter.) The exchange rate between any two currencies is called a *cross rate*. Cross rates are actually calculated on the basis of various currencies relative to the U.S. dollar. For example, the cross rate between British pounds and French francs is computed as follows:

$$\text{Cross rate} = \frac{\text{Dollars}}{\text{Pound}} \times \frac{\text{Francs}}{\text{Dollar}} = \frac{\text{Francs}}{\text{Pound}}$$

$$= 1.6650 \text{ dollars per pound} \times 5.2575 \text{ francs per dollar}$$

$$= 8.7537 \text{ francs per pound.}$$

Therefore, for every British pound she would receive 8.7537 French francs, so she would receive $8.7537 \times 500 = 4,376.87 \approx 4,377$ francs.

When she finishes touring in France and arrives in Germany, she again needs to determine a cross rate, this time between French francs and German marks. The dollar-basis quotes she sees, as shown in Table 27-1, are FF5.2575 per dollar and M1.5581 per dollar. To find the cross rate, she must divide the two dollar-basis rates:

$$\text{Cross rate} = \frac{\dfrac{\text{Marks}}{\text{Dollar}}}{\dfrac{\text{Francs}}{\text{Dollar}}} = \frac{\text{Marks}}{\text{Franc}}$$

$$= \frac{\text{M1.5581 per \$}}{\text{FF5.2575 per \$}} = 0.2964 \text{ marks per franc.}$$

Then, if she had FF3,000 remaining, she could exchange them for $0.2964 \times 3,000 = $ M889.20, or about 889 marks.

Finally, when her vacation ends and she returns to New York, the quotation she sees is M1.5581, which tells her that she can buy 1.5581 marks for a dollar. She now holds 50 marks, so she wants to know how many U.S. dollars she will receive for her marks. First, she must find the reciprocal of the quoted indirect rate,

$$\frac{1}{M1.5581} = \$0.6418,$$

which is the direct quote shown in Table 27-1, Column 1. Then she will end up with

$$\$0.6418 \times 50 = \$32.09.$$

In this example, we made three very strong and generally incorrect assumptions. First, we assumed that our traveler had to calculate all the cross rates. For retail transactions, it is customary to display the cross rates directly instead of a series of dollar rates. Second, we assumed that exchange rates remain constant over time. Actually, exchange rates vary every day, often dramatically. We will have more to say about exchange rate fluctuations in the next section. Finally, we assumed that there were no transactions costs involved in exchanging currencies. In reality, small retail exchange transactions such as those in our example usually involve fixed and/or sliding scale fees that can easily consume 5 or more percent of the transaction amount. However, credit card purchases minimize these fees.

Major business publications such as *The Wall Street Journal* regularly report cross rates among key currencies. A set of cross rates is given in Table 27-2. When examining the table, note the following points:

1. Column 1 gives indirect quotes for dollars, that is, units of a foreign currency that can be bought with one U.S. dollar. Examples: $1 will buy 5.2575 French francs or 1.5581 German marks. Note the consistency with Table 27-1, Column 2.

2. Other columns show number of units of other currencies that can be bought with one pound, one Swiss franc, etc. For example, the D-Mark column shows that 1 D-mark will buy 0.87741 Canadian dollar, 3.3743 French francs, or 0.64181 U.S. dollar.

TABLE 27-2		Key Currency Cross Rates								
	DOLLAR	**POUND**	**SFRANC**	**GUILDER**	**PESO**	**YEN**	**LIRA**	**D-MARK**	**FFRANC**	**CDNDLR**
Canada	1.3671	2.2762	1.0206	0.78411	0.17398	0.01199	0.00089	0.87741	0.26003	—
France	5.2575	8.7537	3.9250	3.0155	0.66906	0.04610	0.00343	3.3743	—	3.8457
Germany	1.5581	2.5942	1.1632	0.89366	0.19828	0.01366	0.00102	—	0.29636	1.1397
Italy	1533.0	2552.4	1144.5	879.27	195.09	13.443	—	983.89	291.58	1121.4
Japan	114.04	189.88	85.136	65.409	14.513	—	0.07439	73.192	21.691	83.417
Mexico	7.8580	13.084	5.8664	4.5070	—	0.06891	0.00513	5.0433	1.4946	5.7479
Netherlands	1.7435	2.9029	1.3016	—	0.22188	0.01529	0.00114	1.1190	0.33162	1.2753
Switzerland	1.3395	2.2303	—	0.76828	0.17046	0.01175	0.00087	0.85970	0.25478	0.97981
United Kingdom	0.60060	—	0.44838	0.34448	0.07643	0.00527	0.00039	0.38547	0.11424	0.43932
United States	—	1.6650	0.74655	0.57356	0.12726	0.00877	0.00065	0.64181	0.19020	0.73148

SOURCE: "Key Currency Cross Rates," *The Wall Street Journal*, December 20, 1996, C17.

3. The rows show direct quotes, that is, number of units of the currency of the country listed in the left column required to buy one unit of the currency listed in the top row. The bottom row is particularly interesting, as it shows the direct quotes for the U.S. dollar. This row is consistent with Column 1 of Table 27-1. Note too that the values on the bottom row are reciprocals of the values in Column 1. Thus, $1/0.6006 = 1.6650$.

4. Now notice, by reading down the FFranc column, that one French franc was worth $0.29636 \approx 0.2964$ German mark. This is the same cross rate that we calculated for the U.S. tourist in our example.

The tie-in with the dollar ensures that all currencies are related to one another in a consistent manner. If this consistency did not exist, currency traders could profit by buying undervalued and selling overvalued currencies. This process, known as arbitrage, works to bring about an equilibrium wherein the same relationship described earlier would exist. Currency traders are constantly operating in the market, seeking small inconsistencies from which they can profit. The traders' existence enables the rest of us to assume that currency markets are in equilibrium and that, at any point in time, cross rates are all internally consistent.

SELF-TEST
QUESTIONS

What is an exchange rate?

Explain the difference between direct and indirect quotations.

What is a cross rate?

THE INTERNATIONAL MONETARY SYSTEM

Every nation has a monetary system and a monetary authority. In the United States, the Federal Reserve is our monetary authority, and its task is to hold down inflation while promoting economic growth and raising our national standard of living. Moreover, if countries are to trade with one another, we must have some sort of system designed to facilitate payments between nations.

From the end of World War II until August 1971, the world was on a **fixed exchange rate system** administered by the International Monetary Fund (IMF). Under this system, the U.S. dollar was linked to gold ($35 per ounce), and other currencies were then tied to the dollar. Exchange rates between other currencies and the dollar were controlled within narrow limits but then adjusted periodically. For example, in 1964 the British pound was adjusted to $2.80 for £1, with a 1 percent permissible fluctuation about this rate.

Fluctuations in exchange rates occur because of changes in the supply of and demand for dollars, pounds, and other currencies. These supply and demand changes have two primary sources. First, changes in the demand for currencies depend on changes in imports and exports of goods and services. For example, U.S. importers must buy British pounds to pay for British goods, whereas British importers must buy U.S. dollars to pay for U.S. goods. If U.S. imports from Great Britain exceeded U.S. exports to Great Britain, there would be a greater demand for pounds than for dollars, and this would drive up the price of the pound relative to that of the dollar. In terms of Table 27-1, the dollar cost of a pound might rise from $1.6650 to $2.0000. The U.S. dollar would be said to be *depreciating*, because a dollar would now be worth fewer pounds, whereas the pound would be *appreciating*. In this example, the root cause of the change would be the U.S. **trade deficit** with Great Britain. Of course, if U.S. exports to Great Britain were greater than U.S. imports from Great Britain, Great Britain would have a trade deficit with the United States.[1]

Changes in the demand for a currency, and the resulting exchange rate fluctuations, also depend on capital movements. For example, suppose interest rates in Great Britain were higher than those in the United States. To take advantage of the high British interest rates, U.S. banks, corporations, and even sophisticated individuals would buy pounds with dollars and then use those pounds to purchase high-yielding British securities. This buying of pounds would tend to drive up their price.[2]

Before August 1971, exchange rate fluctuations were kept within a narrow 1 percent limit by regular intervention of the British government in the market. When the value of the pound was falling, the Bank of England would step in and buy pounds to push up their price, offering gold or foreign currencies in exchange. Conversely, when the pound rate was too high, the Bank of England would sell pounds. The central banks of other countries operated similarly.

Devaluations and **revaluations** occurred only rarely before 1971. They were usually accompanied by severe international financial repercussions, partly because nations tended to postpone needed measures until economic pressures had built up to explosive proportions. For this and other reasons, the old international monetary system came to a dramatic end in the early 1970s, when the U.S. dollar, the foundation upon which all other currencies were anchored, was cut loose from the gold standard and, in effect, allowed to "float."

The United States and other major trading nations currently operate under a system of **floating exchange rates,** whereby currency prices are allowed to seek their own levels without much governmental intervention. However, the central bank of each country does intervene to some extent, buying and selling its currency to smooth out exchange rate fluctuations.

Each central bank would like to keep its average exchange rate at a level deemed desirable by its government's economic policy. This is important, because exchange rates have a profound effect on the levels of imports and exports, which influence the level of domestic employment. For example, if a country is having a problem with unemployment, its central bank might try to lower interest rates, which would cause capital to flee the country to find higher rates, which would lead to the sale of the currency, which would cause a *decline* in the value of the currency. This would cause its goods to be cheaper in world markets and thus stimulate exports, production, and

---

[1]If the dollar value of the pound moved up from $1.67 to $2.00, this increase in the value of the pound would mean that British goods would now be more expensive in the United States. For example, a box of candy costing £1 in England would rise in price in the United States from about $1.67 to $2.00. Conversely, U.S. goods would become cheaper in England. For example, the British could now buy goods worth $2.00 for £1, whereas before the exchange rate change £1 would buy merchandise worth only $1.67. These price changes would, of course, tend to *reduce* British exports and *increase* imports, and this, in turn, would lower the exchange rate, because people in the United States would be buying fewer pounds to pay for English goods.

[2]Such capital inflows would also tend to drive down British interest rates. If British rates were high in the first place because of efforts by the British monetary authorities to curb inflation, these international currency flows would tend to thwart that effort. This is one of the reasons domestic and international economies are so closely linked.

A good example of this occurred during the summer of 1981. In an effort to curb inflation, the Federal Reserve Board helped push U.S. interest rates to record levels. This, in turn, caused a flow of capital from European nations to the United States. The Europeans were suffering from a severe recession and wanted to keep interest rates down in order to stimulate investment, but U.S. policy made this difficult because of international capital flows. Just the opposite occurred in 1992, when the Fed drove short-term rates down to record lows in the United States to promote growth, while Germany and most other European countries pushed their rates higher to combat the inflationary pressures of reunification. Thus, investment in the United States was dampened as investors moved their money overseas to capture higher interest rates.

domestic employment. Conversely, the central bank of a country that is operating at full capacity and experiencing inflation might try to raise the value of its currency to reduce exports and increase imports. Under the current floating rate system, however, such intervention can affect the situation only temporarily, because market forces will prevail in the long run.

Exchange rate fluctuations can have a profound impact on international monetary transactions. For example, in 1985 it cost Honda Motors 2,380,000 yen to build a particular model in Japan and ship it to the United States. The model carried a U.S. sticker price of $12,000. Since the $12,000 sales price was the equivalent of (238 yen per dollar)($12,000) = 2,856,000 yen, which was 20 percent above the 2,380,000 yen cost, the automaker had built a 20 percent markup into the U.S. sales price. However, three years later the dollar had depreciated to 128 yen. Now if the model still sold for $12,000, the yen return to Honda would be only (128 yen per dollar)($12,000) = 1,536,000 yen, and the automaker would be losing about 35 percent on each auto sold. Therefore, the depreciation of the dollar against the yen turned a healthy profit into a huge loss. In fact, for Honda to maintain its 20 percent markup, the model would have to sell in the United States for 2,856,000 yen/128 yen per dollar = $22,312.50. This situation, which grew even worse, led Honda to build its most popular model, the Accord, in Marysville, Ohio.

The inherent volatility of exchange rates under a floating system increases the uncertainty of the cash flows for a multinational corporation. Because these cash flows are generated in many parts of the world, they are denominated in many different currencies. Since exchange rates can change, the dollar-equivalent value of a company's consolidated cash flows can also fluctuate. For example, Toyota estimates that each one-yen drop in the dollar reduces the company's annual net income by about 10 billion yen. This is known as *exchange rate risk,* and it is a major factor differentiating a global company from a purely domestic one.

Concerns about exchange rate risk have led to attempts to stabilize currency movements. In 1979, the *European Monetary System (EMS)* was formed. Participants in the EMS agreed to limit fluctuations in their exchange rates so that rates stayed within a prespecified range. It was felt that this arrangement would prevent the frequent disruptions to international trade and economic health that were caused by the vagaries of a floating foreign exchange market. However, efforts to fix exchange rates rather than letting them float have not met with much success. For example, Britain was forced to withdraw from the exchange rate arrangement of the EMS because of its inability to support the pound. Similarly, Mexico recently attempted to stabilize the peso. However, participants in the foreign exchange market simply sold billions of pesos and forced the Mexican central bank to allow the peso to float.

European nations are now moving toward an alternative to the EMS. Under the *Treaty of Maastricht* (signed in 1991), participants in the *European Monetary Union (EMU)* agreed to take a step beyond merely trying to fix their exchange rates relative to each other. They agreed to move to a common currency, the *Euro,* that will replace the currencies of the member countries. The hope is that such an arrangement will be more successful than past arrangements in terms of creating a stable international economic environment.

Note too that in today's floating exchange rate environment, many countries have chosen to peg their currencies to one or more major currencies. Countries with **pegged exchange rates** establish a fixed exchange rate with some major currency, and then the values of the pegged currencies move together over time. For example, Venezuela pegs its currency to the U.S. dollar at a rate of 0.002107 Bolivar per dollar.

Its reason for pegging its currency to the dollar is that a large portion of its revenues are linked to its oil exports, which are typically traded in dollars, and its trading partners feel more comfortable dealing with contracts that can, in essence, be stated in dollar terms. Similarly, Kuwait pegs its currency to a composite of currencies that roughly represents the mix of currencies used by its trading partners to purchase its oil. In other instances, currencies are pegged because of traditional ties—for example, Chad, a former French colony, still pegs its currency to the French franc.[3]

Before closing our discussion of the international monetary system, we should note that not all currencies are **convertible.** A currency is convertible when the nation which issued it allows it to be traded in the currency markets and is willing to redeem it at market rates. This means that, except for limited central bank influence, the issuing government loses control over the value of its currency. However, a lack of convertibility creates major problems for international trade. For example, consider the situation faced by Pepsico when it wanted to open a chain of Pizza Hut restaurants in the former Soviet Union. The Russian ruble is not convertible, so Pepsico could not take the profits from its restaurants out of the Soviet Union in the form of dollars. There was no mechanism to exchange the rubles it earned in Russia for dollars, so the investment in the Soviet Union was essentially worthless to the U.S. parent. However, Pepsico arranged to use the ruble profit from the restaurants to buy Russian vodka, which it then shipped to the United States and sold for dollars. Pepsico managed to work things out, but lack of convertibility significantly inhibits the ability of a country to attract foreign investment.

SELF-TEST QUESTIONS

What is the difference between a fixed exchange rate system and a floating rate system? Which system is better? Explain.

What are pegged exchange rates?

What does it mean to say that the dollar is depreciating with respect to the British pound? For a U.S. consumer of British goods, would this be good or bad? How could changes in consumption arrest the decline of the dollar?

What is a convertible currency?

Current currency future prices are available directly from the Chicago Mercantile Exchange (CME) on their web site at http://www.cme.com/market/prices/currencies.html. The quotes are updated every ten minutes throughout the trading session. Updated currency spot and forward rates (from 1 to 12 months) are also provided by the Bank of Montreal Treasury Group at http://www.bmo.com/economic/fxrates.htm.

TRADING IN FOREIGN EXCHANGE

Importers, exporters, tourists, and governments buy and sell currencies in the foreign exchange market. For example, when a U.S. trader imports automobiles from Germany, payment will probably be made in German marks. The importer buys marks (through its bank) in the foreign exchange market, much as one buys common stocks on the New York Stock Exchange or pork bellies on the Chicago Mercantile Exchange. However, whereas stock and commodity exchanges have organized trading floors, the foreign exchange market consists of a network of brokers and banks based in New York, London, Tokyo, and other financial centers. Most buy and sell orders are conducted by computer and telephone.[4]

---

[3]The International Monetary Fund reports each year a full listing of exchange rate arrangements in its *International Monetary Statistics.*

[4]For a more detailed explanation of exchange rate determination and operations of the foreign exchange market, see Mark Eaker, Frank Fabozzi, and Dwight Grant, *International Corporate Finance* (Fort Worth, TX: Dryden Press, 1996).

Spot Rates and Forward Rates

The exchange rates shown earlier in Tables 27-1 and 27-2 are known as **spot rates,** which means the rate paid for delivery of the currency "on the spot" or, in reality, no more than two days after the day of the trade. For most of the world's major currencies, it is also possible to buy (or sell) currencies for delivery at some agreed-upon future date, usually 30, 90, or 180 days from the day the transaction is negotiated. This rate is known as the **forward exchange rate.**

For example, suppose a U.S. firm must pay 500 million yen to a Japanese firm in 30 days, and the current spot rate is 114.04 yen per dollar. Unless spot rates change, the U.S. firm will pay the Japanese firm the equivalent of $4.38 million (500 million yen divided by 114.04 yen per dollar) in 30 days. But if the spot rate falls to 105 yen per dollar, for example, the U.S. firm will have to pay the equivalent of $4.76 million. The treasurer of the U.S. firm can avoid this risk by entering into a 30-day forward exchange contract. This contract promises delivery of yen to the U.S. firm in 30 days at a guaranteed price of 113.5 yen per dollar. No cash changes hands at the time the treasurer signs the forward contract, although the U.S. firm might have to put some collateral down as a guarantee against default. Because the firm can use an interest-bearing instrument for the collateral, though, this requirement is not costly. The counterparty to the forward contract must deliver the yen to the U.S. firm in 30 days, and the U.S. firm is obligated to purchase the 500 million yen at the previously agreed-upon rate of 113.5 yen per dollar. Therefore, the treasurer of the U.S. firm is able to lock in a payment equivalent to $4.41 million, no matter what happens to spot rates. This technique, which is called "hedging," was discussed in more detail in Chapter 24.

Forward rates for 30-, 90-, and 180-day delivery, along with the current spot rates for some commonly traded currencies, are given in Table 27-3. If one can obtain *more* of the foreign currency for a dollar in the forward than in the spot market, the forward currency is less valuable than the spot currency, and the forward currency is said to be selling at a **discount.** Thus, because 1 dollar could buy 0.6006 British pound in the spot market but 0.6035 pound in the 180-day forward market, forward pounds sell at a discount as compared with spot pounds. Conversely, since a dollar would buy *fewer* yen and marks in the forward than in the spot market, the forward yen and marks are selling at a **premium.**

TABLE 27-3	Selected Spot and Forward Exchange Rates (Number of Units of Foreign Currency per U.S. Dollar)				

		FORWARD RATES			
	SPOT RATE	**30 DAYS**	**90 DAYS**	**180 DAYS**	**FORWARD RATE AT A PREMIUM OR DISCOUNT**
British pound	0.6006	0.6009	0.6019	0.6035	Discount
Japanese yen	114.0400	113.5000	112.5900	111.1300	Premium
German mark	1.5581	1.5551	1.5493	1.5401	Premium

NOTES:

a. These are representative quotes as provided by a sample of New York banks. Forward rates for other currencies and for other lengths of time can often be negotiated.

b. When it takes more units of a foreign currency to buy one dollar in the future, the value of the foreign currency is less in the forward market than in the spot market, hence the forward rate is at a *discount* to the spot rate.

SOURCE: *The Wall Street Journal,* December 20, 1996.

Differentiate between spot and forward exchange rates.

Explain what it means for a forward currency to sell at a discount, and at a premium.

INTEREST RATE PARITY

Market forces determine whether a currency sells at a forward premium or discount, and the general relationship between spot and forward exchange rates is specified by a concept called interest rate parity.

Interest rate parity holds that investors should earn the same return on security investments in all countries after adjusting for risk. It recognizes that when you invest in a country other than your home country, you are affected by two forces—returns on the investment itself and changes in the exchange rate. It follows that your overall return will be higher than the investment's stated return if the currency your investment is denominated in appreciates relative to your home currency. Likewise, your overall return will be lower if the foreign currency you are holding declines in value.

Interest rate parity is expressed as follows:

$$\frac{\text{Forward exchange rate}}{\text{Spot exchange rate}} = \frac{(1 + k_h)}{(1 + k_f)}.$$

Here both the forward and spot rates are expressed in terms of the amount of home currency received per unit of foreign currency, and k_h and k_f are the periodic interest rates in the home country and the foreign country, respectively. If this relationship does not hold, then currency traders will buy and sell currencies—that is, engage in arbitrage—until it does hold.

To illustrate interest rate parity, consider the case of a U.S. investor who can buy default-free 90-day German bonds that promise a 4 percent nominal return. The 90-day interest rate, k_f, is 4%/4 = 1% because 90 days is 1/4 of a 360-day year. Assume also that the spot exchange rate is $0.6418, which means that you can exchange 0.6418 dollar for one mark, or 1.5581 marks per dollar. Finally, assume that the 90-day forward exchange rate is $0.6455, which means that you can exchange one mark for 0.6455 dollar, or receive 1.5493 marks per dollar exchanged, 90 days from now.

The U.S. investor can receive a 4 percent annualized return denominated in marks, but if he or she ultimately wants to consume goods in the United States, those marks must be converted to dollars. The dollar return on the investment depends, therefore, on what happens to exchange rates over the next three months. However, the investor can lock in the dollar return by selling the foreign currency in the forward market. For example, the investor could simultaneously

- Convert $1,000 to 1,558.1 marks in the spot market.

- Invest the 1,558.1 marks in 90-day German bonds that have a 4 percent annualized return or a 1 percent quarterly return, hence will pay (1,558.1)(1.01) = 1,573.68 marks in 90 days.

- Agree today to exchange these 1,573.68 marks 90 days from now at the 90-day forward exchange rate of 1.5493 marks per dollar, or for a total of $1,015.74.

This investment, therefore, has an expected 90-day return of $15.74/$1,000 = 1.57%, which translates into a nominal return of 4(1.57%) = 6.28%. In this case, 4 percent of the expected 6.28 percent return is coming from the bond itself, and 2.28 percent arises because the market believes the mark will strengthen relative to the dollar. Notice that by locking in the forward rate today, the investor has eliminated any exchange rate risk.

And, since the German bond is assumed to be default-free, the investor is assured of earning a 6.28 percent dollar return.

Interest rate parity implies that an investment in the United States with the same risk as a German bond should have a return of 6.28 percent. Solving for k_h in the parity equation, we indeed find that the predicted interest rate in the United States is 6.28 percent.

Interest rate parity shows why a particular currency might be at a forward premium or discount. Notice that a currency is at a forward premium whenever domestic interest rates are higher than foreign interest rates. Discounts prevail if domestic interest rates are lower than foreign interest rates. If these conditions do not hold, then arbitrage will soon force interest rates back to parity.

SELF-TEST QUESTION | Briefly explain interest rate parity, illustrating with an example.

PURCHASING POWER PARITY

We have discussed exchange rates in some detail, and we have considered the relationship between spot and forward exchange rates. However, we have not yet addressed the fundamental question: What determines the spot level of exchange rates in each country? As it turns out, exchange rates are influenced by a multitude of factors that are difficult to predict, particularly on a day-to-day basis. However, over the long run, market forces work to ensure that similar goods sell for similar prices in different countries after taking exchange rates into account. This relationship is known as purchasing power parity.

Purchasing power parity (PPP), sometimes referred to as the *law of one price,* implies that the level of exchange rates adjusts so that identical goods cost the same amount in different countries. For example, if a pair of tennis shoes costs $150 in the United States and 100 pounds in Britain, PPP implies that the exchange rate be $1.50 per pound. Consumers could purchase the shoes in Britain for 100 pounds, or they could exchange their 100 pounds for $150 and then purchase the same shoes in the United States at the same effective cost, assuming no transaction or transportation costs. Here is the equation for purchasing power parity:

$$P_h = (P_f)(\text{Spot rate}),$$

or

$$\text{Spot rate} = \frac{P_h}{P_f}.$$

Here

P_h = the price of the good in the home country ($150, assuming the United States is the home country).

P_f = the price of the good in the foreign country (100 pounds).

Note that the spot market exchange rate is expressed as the number of units of home currency that can be exchanged for one unit of foreign currency ($1.50 per pound).

PPP assumes that market forces will eliminate situations where the same product sells at a different price overseas. For example, if the shoes cost $140 in the United States, importers/exporters could purchase them in the United States for $140, sell them for 100 pounds in Britain, exchange the 100 pounds for $150 in the foreign exchange market, and earn a profit of $10 on every pair of shoes. Ultimately, this trading

HUNGRY FOR A BIG MAC? GO TO CHINA!

Purchasing power parity (PPP) implies that the same product will sell for the same price in every country after adjusting for current exchange rates. One problem when testing to see if PPP holds is that it assumes that goods consumed in different countries are of the same quality. For example, if you find that a product is more expensive in Italy than it is in Switzerland, one explanation is that PPP fails to hold, but another explanation is that the product sold in Italy is of a higher quality and therefore deserves a higher price.

One way to test for PPP is to find goods that have the same quality worldwide. With this in mind, the *Economist* magazine occasionally compares the prices of a well-known good whose quality is the same in nearly 80 different countries: the McDonald's Big Mac hamburger.

The table on the next page provides information collected during 1995. The first column shows the price of a Big Mac in the local currency. Column 2 calculates the price of the Big Mac in terms of the U.S. dollar — this is obtained by dividing the local price by the actual exchange rate at that time. For example, a Big Mac costs 18.5 French francs in Paris. Given an exchange rate of 4.80 francs per dollar, this implies that the dollar price of a Big Mac is 18.5 francs/4.80 francs per dollar = $3.85.

The third column backs out the implied exchange rate that would hold under PPP. This is obtained by dividing the price of the Big Mac in each local currency by its U.S. price. For example, a Big Mac costs 8,100 rubles in Russia, and $2.32 in the United States. If PPP holds, the exchange rate should be 3,491 rubles per dollar (8,100 rubles/$2.32).

Comparing the implied exchange rate to the actual exchange rate in Column 4, we see the extent to which the local currency is under- or over-valued relative to the dollar. Given that the actual exchange rate at the time was 4,985 rubles per dollar, this implies that the ruble was 30 percent undervalued.

The evidence suggests that strict PPP does not hold, but the Big Mac test may shed some insights about where exchange rates are headed. For example, the Big Mac 1995 test suggests that the yen was highly overvalued relative to the dollar, and since that time the dollar has strengthened roughly 30 percent relative to the yen.

One last benefit of the Big Mac test is that it tells us the cheapest places to find a Big Mac. According to the data, if you are looking for a Big Mac, head to China, and avoid Switzerland.

SOURCE: Excerpted from "Big MacCurrencies," *The Economist,* April 15, 1995, 74. Reprinted by permission from *The Economist.*

activity would increase the demand for shoes in the United States and thus raise P_h, increase the supply of shoes in Britain and thus reduce P_f, and increase the demand for dollars in the foreign exchange market and thus reduce the spot rate. Each of these actions works to restore PPP.

Notice that PPP assumes that there are no transportation or transaction costs, or import restrictions, all of which limit the ability to ship goods between countries. In many cases, these assumptions are incorrect, which explains why PPP is often violated. An additional complication, when empirically testing to see whether PPP holds, is that products in different countries are rarely identical. Frequently, there are real or perceived differences in quality, which can lead to price differences in different countries.

Still, the concepts of interest rate and purchasing power parity are critically important to those engaged in international activities. Companies and investors must anticipate changes in interest rates, inflation, and exchange rates, and they often try to hedge the risks of adverse movements in these factors. The parity relationships are extremely useful when anticipating future conditions.

	BIG MAC PRICES		IMPLIED EXCHANGE RATE BASED ON PPP[a] (3)	ACTUAL $ EXCHANGE RATE 7/4/95 (4)	LOCAL CURRENCY UNDER(−)/OVER(+) VALUATION[b] (%) (5)
	IN LOCAL CURRENCY (1)	IN DOLLARS (2)			
United States[c]	$2.32	2.32	—	—	—
Argentina	Peso3.00	3.00	1.29	1.00	+29
Australia	A$2.45	1.82	1.06	1.35	−22
Britain	£1.74	2.80	1.33[d]	1.61[d]	+21
Canada	C$2.77	1.99	1.19	1.39	−14
China	Yuan9.00	1.05	3.88	8.54	−55
Denmark	DKr26.75	4.92	11.50	5.43	+112
France	FFr18.5	3.85	7.97	4.80	+66
Germany	DM4.80	3.48	2.07	1.38	+50
Hong Kong	HK$9.50	1.23	4.09	7.73	−47
Italy	Lire4,500	2.64	1,940.00	1,702.00	+14
Japan	¥391	4.65	169.00	84.20	+100
Mexico	Peso10.9	1.71	4.70	6.37	−26
Russia	Ruble8,100	1.62	3,491.00	4,985.00	−30
Spain	Ptas355	2.86	153.00	124.00	+23
Switzerland	SFr5.90	5.20	2.54	1.13	+124
Thailand	Baht48.0	1.95	20.70	24.60	−16

NOTES:

[a]Purchasing power parity: local price divided by price in the United States.

[b]Against dollar.

[c]Average of New York, Chicago, San Francisco, and Atlanta.

[d]Dollars per pound.

SOURCE: McDonald's.

SELF-TEST QUESTION | What is meant by purchasing power parity? Illustrate it.

INFLATION, INTEREST RATES, AND EXCHANGE RATES

Relative inflation rates, or the rates of inflation in foreign countries compared with that in the home country, have many implications for multinational financial decisions. Obviously, relative inflation rates will greatly influence future production costs at home and abroad. Equally important, inflation has a dominant influence on relative interest rates and exchange rates. Both of these factors influence the methods chosen by multinational corporations for financing their foreign investments, and both have an important effect on the profitability of foreign investments.

The currencies of countries with higher inflation rates than that of the United States by definition *depreciate* over time against the dollar. Countries where this has occurred include Italy, Mexico, and all the South American nations. On the other hand, the currencies of Germany, Switzerland, and Japan, which have had less inflation than the United States, have *appreciated* against the dollar. *In fact, a foreign currency will, on average, depreciate or appreciate at a percentage rate approximately equal to the amount by which its inflation rate exceeds or is less than our own.*

Relative inflation rates also affect interest rates. The interest rate in any country is largely determined by its inflation rate. Therefore, countries currently experiencing higher rates of inflation than the United States also tend to have higher interest rates. The reverse is true for countries with lower inflation rates.

It is tempting for a multinational corporation to borrow in countries with the lowest interest rates. However, this is not always a good strategy. Suppose, for example, that interest rates in Germany are lower than those in the United States because of Germany's lower inflation rate. A U.S. multinational firm could therefore save interest by borrowing in Germany. However, because of relative inflation rates, the mark will probably appreciate in the future, causing the dollar cost of annual interest and principal payments on German debt to rise over time. Thus, *the lower interest rate could be more than offset by losses from currency appreciation.* Similarly, multinational corporations should not necessarily avoid borrowing in a country such as Brazil, where interest rates have been very high, because future depreciation of the Brazilian cruzeiro could make such borrowing end up being relatively inexpensive.

SELF-TEST QUESTIONS

What effects do relative inflation rates have on relative interest rates?

What happens over time to the currencies of countries with higher inflation rates than that of the United States? To those with lower inflation rates?

Why might a multinational corporation decide to borrow in a country such as Brazil, where interest rates are high, rather than in a country like Germany, where interest rates are low?

INTERNATIONAL MONEY AND CAPITAL MARKETS

One way for U.S. citizens to invest in world markets is to buy the stocks of U.S. multinational corporations that invest directly in foreign countries. Another way is to purchase foreign securities—stocks, bonds, or money market instruments issued by foreign companies. Security investments are known as *portfolio investments,* and they are distinguished from *direct investments* in physical assets by U.S. corporations.

From World War II through the 1960s, the U.S. capital markets dominated world markets. Today, however, the value of U.S. securities represents less than one-fourth the value of all securities. Given this situation, it is important for both corporate managers and investors to have an understanding of international markets. Moreover, these markets often offer better opportunities for raising or investing capital than are available domestically.

Eurodollar Market

A **Eurodollar** is a U.S. dollar deposited in a bank outside the United States. (Although they are called Eurodollars because they originated in Europe, Eurodollars are really any dollars deposited in any part of the world other than the United States.) The bank in which the deposit is made may be a non-U.S. bank, such as Barclay's Bank in London; the foreign branch of a U.S. bank, such as Citibank's Paris branch; or even a foreign branch of a third-country bank, such as Barclay's Munich branch. Most Eurodollar deposits are for $500,000 or more, and they have maturities ranging from overnight to about one year.

The major difference between Eurodollar deposits and regular U.S. time deposits is their geographic locations. The two types of deposits do not involve different currencies — in both cases, dollars are on deposit. However, Eurodollars are outside the direct control of the U.S. monetary authorities, so U.S. banking regulations, including reserve requirements and FDIC insurance premiums, do not apply. The absence of these costs means that the interest rate paid on Eurodollar deposits can be higher than domestic U.S. rates on equivalent instruments.

Although the dollar is the leading international currency, British pounds, German marks, Swiss francs, Japanese yen, and other currencies are also deposited outside their home countries; these *Eurocurrencies* are handled in exactly the same way as Eurodollars.

Eurodollars are borrowed by U.S. and foreign corporations for various purposes, but especially to pay for goods exported from the United States and to invest in U.S. security markets. Also, U.S. dollars are used as an international currency, or international medium of exchange, and many Eurodollars are used for this purpose. It is interesting to note that Eurodollars were actually "invented" by the Soviets in 1946. International merchants did not trust the Soviets or their rubles, so the Soviets bought some dollars (for gold), deposited them in a Paris bank, and then used these dollars to buy goods in the world markets. Others found it convenient to use dollars this same way, and soon the Eurodollar market was in full swing.

Eurodollars are usually held in interest-bearing accounts. The interest rate paid on these deposits depends (1) on the bank's lending rate, as the interest a bank earns on loans determines its willingness and ability to pay interest on deposits, and (2) on rates of return available on U.S. money market instruments. If money market rates in the United States were above Eurodollar deposit rates, these dollars would be sent back and invested in the United States, whereas if Eurodollar deposit rates were significantly above U.S. rates, which is more often the case, more dollars would be sent out of the United States to become Eurodollars. Given the existence of the Eurodollar market and the electronic flow of dollars to and from the United States, it is easy to see why interest rates in the United States cannot be insulated from those in other parts of the world.

Interest rates on Eurodollar deposits (and loans) are tied to a standard rate known by the acronym *LIBOR*, which stands for *London Interbank Offer Rate*. LIBOR is the rate of interest offered by the largest and strongest London banks on dollar deposits of significant size. In December 1997, LIBOR rates were almost half a percentage point above domestic U.S. bank rates on time deposits of the same maturity — 5.31 percent for three-month CDs versus 5.75 percent for LIBOR CDs. The Eurodollar market is essentially a short-term market; most loans and deposits are for less than one year.

International Bond Markets

Any bond sold outside the country of the borrower is called an *international bond*. However, there are two important types of international bonds: foreign bonds and Eurobonds. **Foreign bonds** are bonds sold by a foreign borrower but denominated in the currency of the country in which the issue is sold. For instance, Northern Telcom (a Canadian company) may need U.S. dollars to finance the operations of its subsidiaries in the United States. If it decides to raise the needed capital in the United States, the bond will be underwritten by a syndicate of U.S. investment bankers, denominated in U.S. dollars, and sold to U.S. investors in accordance with SEC and

Current three-month and six-month LIBOR rates can be obtained from a site maintained by Kuhlmann Commercial Capital at http://www.kuhlmann.com. The site also allows the user to view historical charts of LIBOR rates.

applicable state regulations. Except for the foreign origin of the borrower, this bond will be indistinguishable from those issued by equivalent U.S. corporations. Since Northern Telcom is a foreign corporation, however, the bond would be a foreign bond.

The term **Eurobond** is used to designate any bond issued in one country but denominated in the currency of some other country. Examples include a Ford Motor Company issue denominated in dollars and sold in Germany, or a British firm's sale of mark-denominated bonds in Switzerland. The institutional arrangements by which Eurobonds are marketed are different than those for most other bond issues, with the most important distinction being a far lower level of required disclosure than is usually found for bonds issued in domestic markets, particularly in the United States. Governments tend to be less strict when regulating securities denominated in foreign currencies, because the bonds' purchasers are generally more "sophisticated." The lower disclosure requirements result in lower total transaction costs for Eurobonds.

Eurobonds appeal to investors for several reasons. Generally, they are issued in bearer form rather than as registered bonds, so the names and nationalities of investors are not recorded. Individuals who desire anonymity, whether for privacy reasons or for tax avoidance, like Eurobonds. Similarly, most governments do not withhold taxes on interest payments associated with Eurobonds. If the investor requires an effective yield of 10 percent, a Eurobond that is exempt from tax withholding would need a coupon rate of 10 percent. Another type of bond—for instance, a domestic issue subject to a 30 percent withholding tax on interest paid to foreigners—would need a coupon rate of 14.3 percent to yield an after-withholding rate of 10 percent. Investors who desire secrecy would not want to file for a refund of the tax, so they would prefer to hold the Eurobond.

More than half of all Eurobonds are denominated in dollars. Bonds in Japanese yen, German marks, and Dutch guilders account for most of the rest. Although centered in Europe, Eurobonds are truly international. Their underwriting syndicates include investment bankers from all parts of the world, and the bonds are sold to investors not only in Europe but also in such faraway places as Bahrain and Singapore. Up to a few years ago, Eurobonds were issued solely by multinational firms, by international financial institutions, or by national governments. Today, however, the Eurobond market is also being tapped by purely domestic U.S. firms, because they often find that by borrowing overseas they can lower their debt costs.

International Stock Markets

New issues of stock are sold in international markets for a variety of reasons. For example, a non-U.S. firm might sell an equity issue in the United States because it can tap a much larger source of capital than in its home country. Also, a U.S. firm might tap a foreign market because it wants to create an equity market presence to accompany its operations in that country. Large multinational companies also occasionally issue new stock simultaneously in multiple countries. For example, Alcan Aluminum, a Canadian company, recently issued new stock in Canada, Europe, and the United States simultaneously, using different underwriting syndicates in each market.

In addition to new issues, outstanding stocks of large multinational companies are increasingly being listed on multiple international exchanges. For example, Coca-Cola's stock is traded on six stock exchanges in the United States, four stock exchanges in Switzerland, and the Frankfurt stock exchange in Germany. Some 500 foreign stocks are listed in the United States—an example here is Royal Dutch Petroleum, which is listed on the NYSE. U.S. investors can also invest in foreign companies through *American Depository Receipts (ADRs),* which are certificates representing ownership of foreign stock held in trust. About 1,700 ADRs are now available in the United States, with most of them traded on the over-the-counter (OTC) market. However, more and more ADRs are being listed on the New York Stock Exchange, including Germany's Daimler-Benz, England's British Airways, Japan's Honda Motors, and Italy's Fiat Group.

S E L F - T E S T
Q U E S T I O N S

Differentiate between foreign portfolio investments and direct foreign investments.

What are Eurodollars?

Has the development of the Eurodollar market made it easier or more difficult for the Federal Reserve to control U.S. interest rates?

Differentiate between foreign bonds and Eurobonds.

Why do Eurobonds appeal to investors?

MULTINATIONAL CAPITAL BUDGETING

Up to now, we have discussed the general environment in which multinational firms operate. In the remainder of the chapter, we will see how international factors affect key corporate decisions. We begin with capital budgeting. Although the same basic principles of capital budgeting analysis apply to both foreign and domestic operations, there are some key differences. First, cash flow estimation is more complex for overseas investments. Most multinational firms set up separate subsidiaries in each foreign country in which they operate, and the relevant cash flows for the parent company are the dividends and royalties paid by the subsidiaries to the parent. Second, these cash flows must be converted into the parent company's currency, hence they are subject to exchange rate risk. For example, General Motors' German subsidiary may make a profit of 100 million marks in 1999, but the value of this profit to GM will depend on the dollar/mark exchange rate: How many *dollars* will 100 million marks buy?

Dividends and royalties are normally taxed by both foreign and home-country governments. Furthermore, a foreign government may restrict the amount of the cash that may be **repatriated** to the parent company. For example, some governments place a ceiling, stated as a percentage of the company's net worth, on the amount of cash dividends that a subsidiary can pay to its parent. Such restrictions are normally intended to force multinational firms to reinvest earnings in the foreign country, although restrictions are sometimes imposed to prevent large currency outflows, which might disrupt the exchange rate.

Whatever the host country's motivation for blocking repatriation of profits, the result is that the parent corporation cannot use cash flows blocked in the foreign country to pay dividends to its shareholders or to invest elsewhere in the business. Hence, from the perspective of the parent organization, *the cash flows relevant for foreign investment analysis are the cash flows that the subsidiary is actually expected to send back to the parent*. The present value of those cash flows is found by applying an appropriate discount rate, and this present value is then compared with the parent's required investment to determine the project's NPV.

In addition to the complexities of the cash flow analysis, *the cost of capital may be different for a foreign project than for an equivalent domestic project, because foreign projects may be more or less risky*. A higher risk could arise from two primary sources — (1) exchange rate risk and (2) political risk. A lower risk might result from international diversification.

Exchange rate risk relates to the value of the basic cash flows in the parent company's home currency. The foreign currency cash flows to be turned over to the parent must be converted into U.S. dollars by translating them at expected future exchange rates. An analysis should be conducted to ascertain the effects of exchange rate variations, and, on the basis of this analysis, an exchange rate risk premium should be added to the domestic cost of capital to reflect this risk. It is sometimes possible to hedge against exchange rate fluctuations, but it may not be possible to hedge completely, especially on long-term projects. If hedging is used, the costs of doing so must be subtracted from the project's cash flows.

Political risk refers to potential actions by a host government which would reduce the value of a company's investment. It includes at one extreme the expropriation without compensation of the subsidiary's assets, but it also includes less drastic actions that reduce the value of the parent firm's investment in the foreign subsidiary, including higher taxes, tighter repatriation or currency controls, and restrictions on prices charged. The risk of expropriation is small in traditionally friendly and stable countries such as Great Britain or Switzerland. However, in Latin America, Africa, the Far East, and Eastern Europe, the risk may be substantial. Past expropriations include those of ITT and Anaconda Copper in Chile, Gulf Oil in Bolivia, Occidental Petroleum in Libya, Enron Corporation in Peru, and the assets of many companies in Iraq, Iran, and Cuba.

Several organizations rate the political risk of countries. For example, International Business Communications, a London company, publishes the *International Country Risk Guide,* which contains individual ratings for political, financial, and economic risk, along with a composite rating for each country. Table 27-4 contains selected portions of a recent report. The political variable — which is given 50 percent of the weight in the composite rating — includes factors such as government corruption and the gap between economic expectations and reality. The financial rating looks at such things as the likelihood of losses from exchange controls and loan defaults. The economic rating takes into account such factors as inflation and debt-service costs.

The best, or least risky, score is 100 for political factors and 50 each for the financial and economic factors, and the composite risk is a weighted average of the political, financial, and economic factors. The United States is ranked ninth, below Switzerland,

TABLE 27-4	Selected Countries Ranked by Composite Risk				
RANK	**COUNTRY**	**POLITICAL RISK**	**FINANCIAL RISK**	**ECONOMIC RISK**	**COMPOSITE RISK**
1	Switzerland	93.0	50.0	39.5	91.5
9	United States	78.0	49.0	39.5	83.5
10	Canada	81.0	48.0	37.0	83.0
25	Venezuela	75.0	40.0	36.0	75.5
50	Israel	58.0	33.0	34.5	63.0
75	Panama	47.0	24.0	38.0	54.5
100	Peru	45.0	28.0	21.5	47.5
125	Burma	27.0	9.0	22.5	28.5
129	Liberia	10.0	8.0	12.0	15.0

NOTE: A total of 129 countries are ranked, but only 9 are shown here.
SOURCE: *International Country Risk Guide.*

Luxembourg, Norway, Austria, Germany, Netherlands, Brunei, and Japan. Liberia, as shown in Table 27-4, is ranked last.

Note that companies can take several steps to reduce the potential loss from expropriation: (1) finance the subsidiary with local capital, (2) structure operations so that the subsidiary has value only as a part of the integrated corporate system, and (3) obtain insurance against economic losses from expropriation from a source such as the Overseas Private Investment Corporation (OPIC). In the latter case, insurance premiums would have to be added to the project's cost.

<table>
<tr><td>SELF-TEST
QUESTIONS</td><td>List some key differences in capital budgeting as applied to foreign versus domestic operations.

What are the relevant cash flows for an international investment—the cash flow produced by the subsidiary in the country where it operates or the cash flows in dollars that it sends to its parent company?

Why might the cost of capital for a foreign project differ from that of an equivalent domestic project? Could it be lower?

What adjustments might be made to the domestic cost of capital for a foreign investment due to exchange rate risk and political risk?</td></tr>
</table>

INTERNATIONAL CAPITAL STRUCTURES

Companies' capital structures vary among countries. For example, the Organization for Economic Cooperation and Development (OECD) recently reported that, on average, Japanese firms use 85 percent debt to total assets (in book value terms), German firms use 64 percent, and U.S. firms use 55 percent. One problem, however, when interpreting these numbers is that different countries often use very different accounting conventions with regard to (1) reporting assets on a historical- versus a replacement-cost basis, (2) the treatment of leased assets, (3) pension plan funding, and (4) capitalizing versus expensing R&D costs. These differences make it difficult to compare capital structures.

A recent study by Raghuram Rajan and Luigi Zingales of the University of Chicago attempts to control for differences in accounting practices. In their study, Rajan and Zingales used a database which covers fewer firms than the OECD but which provides a more complete breakdown of balance sheet data. They concluded that differences in accounting practices can explain much of the cross-country variation in capital structures.

Rajan and Zingales' results are summarized in Table 27-5. There are a number of different ways to measure capital structure. One measure is the average ratio of total liabilities to total assets—this is similar to the measure used by the OECD, and it is reported in Column 1. Based on this measure, German and Japanese firms appear to be more highly levered than U.S. firms. However, if you look at Column 2, where capital structure is measured by interest-bearing debt to total assets, it appears that German firms use *less* leverage than U.S. and Japanese firms. What explains this difference? Rajan and Zingales argue that much of this difference is explained by the way German firms account for pension liabilities. German firms generally include all pension liabilities (and their offsetting assets) on the balance sheet, whereas firms in other countries (including the United States) generally "net out" pension assets and liabilities on their balance sheets. To see the importance of this difference, consider a firm with $10 million in liabilities (not including pension liabilities) and $20 million in assets (not

TABLE 27-5	Median Capital Structures among Large Industrialized Countries (Measured in Terms of Book Value)				
COUNTRY	TOTAL LIABILITIES TO TOTAL ASSETS (UNADJUSTED FOR DIFFERENCES IN ACCOUNTING DIFFERENCES) (1)	DEBT TO TOTAL ASSETS (UNADJUSTED FOR ACCOUNTING DIFFERENCES) (2)	TOTAL LIABILITIES TO TOTAL ASSETS (ADJUSTED FOR DIFFERENCES IN ACCOUNTING DIFFERENCES) (3)	DEBT TO TOTAL ASSETS (ADJUSTED FOR ACCOUNTING DIFFERENCES) (4)	TIMES INTEREST EARNED (TIE) RATIO (5)
Canada	56%	32%	48%	32%	1.55×
France	71	25	69	18	2.64
Germany	73	16	50	11	3.20
Italy	70	27	68	21	1.81
Japan	69	35	62	21	2.46
United Kingdom	54	18	47	10	4.79
United States	58	27	52	25	2.41
Mean	64%	26%	57%	20%	2.69×
Standard deviation	8%	7%	10%	8%	1.07×

SOURCE: Raghuram Rajan and Luigi Zingales, "What Do We Know about Capital Structure? Some Evidence from International Data," *The Journal of Finance,* Vol. 50, No. 5, December 1995, 1421–1460. Used with permission.

including pension assets). Assume that the firm has $10 million in pension liabilities which are fully funded by $10 million in pension assets. Therefore, net pension liabilities are zero. If this firm were in the United States, it would report a ratio of total liabilities to total assets equal to 50 percent ($10 million/$20 million). By contrast, if this firm operated in Germany, both its pension assets and liabilities would be reported on the balance sheet. The firm would have $20 million in liabilities and $30 million in assets—or a 67 percent ($20 million/$30 million) ratio of total liabilities to total assets. Total debt is the sum of short-term debt and long-term debt and excludes other liabilities including pension liabilities. Therefore, the measure of total debt to total assets provides a more comparable measure of leverage across different countries.

Rajan and Zingales also make a variety of adjustments which attempt to control for other differences in accounting practices. The effect of these adjustments are reported in Columns 3 and 4. Overall, the evidence suggests that companies in Germany and the United Kingdom tend to have less leverage, whereas firms in Canada appear to have more leverage, relative to firms in the United States, France, Italy, and Japan. This conclusion is supported by data in the final column, which shows the average times-interest-earned ratio for firms in a number of different countries. Recall from Chapter 3 that the times-interest-earned ratio is the ratio of operating income (EBIT) to interest expense. This measure indicates how much cash the firm has available to service its interest expense. In general, firms with more leverage have a lower times-interest-earned ratio. The data indicate that this ratio is highest in the United Kingdom and Germany and lowest in Canada.

SELF-TEST
QUESTION

Do international differences in financial leverage exist? Explain.

MULTINATIONAL WORKING CAPITAL MANAGEMENT

Cash Management

The goals of cash management in a multinational corporation are similar to those in a purely domestic corporation: (1) to speed up collections, slow down disbursements, and thus maximize net float; (2) to shift cash as rapidly as possible from those parts of the business where it is not needed to those parts where it is needed; and (3) to maximize the risk-adjusted, after-tax rate of return on temporary cash balances. Multinational companies use the same general procedures for achieving these goals as domestic firms, but because of longer distances and more serious mail delays, such devices as lockbox systems and electronic funds transfers are especially important.

Although multinational and domestic corporations have the same objectives and use similar procedures, multinational corporations face a far more complex task. As noted earlier in our discussion of political risk, foreign governments often place restrictions on transfers of funds out of the country, so although IBM can transfer money from its Salt Lake City office to its New York concentration bank just by pressing a few buttons, a similar transfer from its Buenos Aires office is far more complex. Buenos Aires funds are denominated in australs (Argentina's equivalent of the dollar), so the australs must be converted to dollars before the transfer. If there is a shortage of dollars in Argentina, or if the Argentinean government wants to conserve dollars to purchase strategic materials, then conversion, hence the transfer, may be blocked. Even if no dollar shortage exists in Argentina, the government may still restrict funds outflows if those funds represent profits or depreciation rather than payments for purchased materials or equipment, because many countries, especially those that are less developed, want profits reinvested in the country in order to stimulate economic growth.

Once it has been determined what funds can be transferred, the next task is to get those funds to locations where they will earn the highest returns. Whereas domestic corporations tend to think in terms of domestic securities, multinationals are more likely to be aware of investment opportunities all around the world. Most multinational corporations use one or more global concentration banks, located in money centers such as London, New York, Tokyo, Zurich, or Singapore, and their staffs in those cities, working with international bankers, know of and are able to take advantage of the best rates available anywhere in the world.

Credit Management

Like most other aspects of finance, credit management in the multinational corporation is similar to but more complex than that in a purely domestic business. First, granting credit is more risky in an international context because, in addition to the normal risks of default, the multinational corporation must also worry about exchange rate fluctuations between the time a sale is made and the time a receivable is collected. For example, if IBM sold a computer to a Japanese customer for 90 million yen when the exchange rate was 90 yen to the dollar, IBM would obtain $90,000,000/90 = $1,000,000$ for the computer. However, if it sold the computer on terms of net/6 months, and if the yen fell against the dollar so that one dollar would now buy 112.5 yen, IBM would end up realizing only $90,000,000/112.5 = $800,000$ when it collected the receivable. Hedging can reduce this type of risk, but at a cost.

Offering credit is generally more important for multinational corporations than for purely domestic firms for two reasons. First, much U.S. trade is with poorer, less-developed nations, where granting credit is generally a necessary condition for doing business. Second, and in large part as a result of the first point, developed nations whose economic health depends on exports often help their manufacturing firms compete internationally by granting credit to foreign countries. In Japan, for example, the major manufacturing firms have direct ownership ties with large "trading companies" engaged in international trade, as well as with giant commercial banks. In addition, a government agency, the Ministry of International Trade and Industry (MITI), helps Japanese firms identify potential export markets and also helps potential customers arrange credit for purchases from Japanese firms. In effect, the huge Japanese trade surpluses are used to finance Japanese exports, thus helping to perpetuate their favorable trade balance. The United States has attempted to counter with the Export-Import Bank, which is funded by Congress, but the fact that the United States has a large balance of payments deficit is clear evidence that we have been less successful than others in world markets in recent years.

The huge debt which countries such as Korea and Thailand owe U.S. and other international banks is well known, and this situation illustrates how credit policy (by banks in this case) can go astray. The banks face a particularly sticky problem with these loans, because if a sovereign nation defaults, the banks cannot lay claim to the assets of the country as they could if a corporate customer defaulted. Note too that although the banks' loans to foreign governments often get most of the headlines, many U.S. multinational corporations are also in trouble as a result of granting credit to business customers in the same countries where bank loans to governments are on shaky ground.

By pointing out the risks in granting credit internationally, we are not suggesting that such credit is bad. Quite the contrary, for the potential gains from international operations far outweigh the risks, at least for companies (and banks) that have the necessary expertise.

Inventory Management

As with most other aspects of finance, inventory management in a multinational setting is similar to but more complex than for a purely domestic firm. First, there is the matter of the physical location of inventories. For example, where should Exxon keep its stockpiles of crude oil and refined products? It has refineries and marketing centers located worldwide, and one alternative is to keep items concentrated in a few strategic spots from which they can then be shipped as needs arise. Such a strategy might minimize the total amount of inventories needed and thus might minimize the investment in inventories. Note, though, that consideration will have to be given to potential delays in getting goods from central storage locations to user locations all around the world. Both working stocks and safety stocks would have to be maintained at each user location, as well as at the strategic storage centers. Problems like the Iraqi occupation of Kuwait and the subsequent trade embargo, which brought with it the potential for a shutdown of production of about 25 percent of the world's oil supply, complicate matters further.

Exchange rates also influence inventory policy. If a local currency, say, the Danish krone, were expected to rise in value against the dollar, a U.S. company operating in Denmark would want to increase stocks of local products before the rise in the krone, and vice versa if the krone were expected to fall.

Another factor that must be considered is the possibility of import or export quotas or tariffs. For example, Apple Computer Company was buying certain memory chips from Japanese suppliers at a bargain price. Then U.S. chipmakers accused the Japanese of dumping chips in the U.S. market at prices below cost, so they sought to force the

Japanese to raise prices.[5] That led Apple to increase its chip inventory. Then computer sales slacked off, and Apple ended up with an oversupply of obsolete computer chips. As a result, Apple's profits were hurt and its stock price fell, demonstrating once more the importance of careful inventory management.

As mentioned earlier, another danger in certain countries is the threat of expropriation. If that threat is large, inventory holdings will be minimized, and goods will be brought in only as needed. Similarly, if the operation involves extraction of raw materials such as oil or bauxite, processing plants may be moved offshore rather than located close to the production site.

Taxes have two effects on multinational inventory management. First, countries often impose property taxes on assets, including inventories, and when this is done, the tax is based on holdings as of a specific date, say, January 1 or March 1. Such rules make it advantageous for a multinational firm (1) to schedule production so that inventories are low on the assessment date, and (2) if assessment dates vary among countries in a region, to hold safety stocks in different countries at different times during the year.

Finally, multinational firms may consider the possibility of at-sea storage. Oil, chemical, grain, and other companies that deal in a bulk commodity that must be stored in some type of tank can often buy tankers at a cost not much greater — or perhaps even less, considering land cost — than land-based facilities. Loaded tankers can then be kept at sea or at anchor in some strategic location. This eliminates the danger of expropriation, minimizes the property tax problem, and maximizes flexibility with regard to shipping to areas where needs are greatest or prices highest.

This discussion has only scratched the surface of inventory management in the multinational corporation — the task is much more complex than for a purely domestic firm. However, the greater the degree of complexity, the greater the rewards from superior performance, so if you want challenge along with potentially high rewards, look to the international arena.

SELF-TEST QUESTIONS	What are some factors that make cash management especially complicated in a multinational corporation?
	Why is granting credit especially risky in an international context?
	Why is inventory management especially important for a multinational firm?

---

[5]The term "dumping" warrants explanation, because the practice is so potentially important in international markets. Suppose Japanese chipmakers have excess capacity. A particular chip has a variable cost of $25, and its "fully allocated cost," which is the $25 plus total fixed cost per unit of output, is $40. Now suppose the Japanese firm can sell chips in the United States at $35 per unit, but if it charges $40, it will not make any sales because U.S. chipmakers sell for $35.50. If the Japanese firm sells at $35, it will cover variable cost plus make a contribution to fixed overhead, so selling at $35 makes sense. Continuing, if the Japanese firm can sell in Japan at $40, but U.S. firms are excluded from Japanese markets by import duties or other barriers, the Japanese will have a huge advantage over U.S. manufacturers. This practice of selling goods at lower prices in foreign markets than at home is called "dumping." U.S. firms are required by antitrust laws to offer the same price to all customers and, therefore, cannot engage in dumping.

SUMMARY

This chapter discussed the most important differences between multinational and domestic financial management. Some of the key concepts are listed below:

- **International operations** are becoming increasingly important to individual firms and to the national economy. A **multinational,** or **global, corporation** is a firm that operates in an integrated fashion in a number of countries.

- Companies "go global" for six primary reasons: (1) **to expand their markets,** (2) **to obtain raw materials,** (3) **to seek new technology,** (4) **to lower production costs,** (5) **to avoid trade barriers,** and (6) **to diversify.**

- Six major factors distinguish financial management as practiced by domestic firms from that practiced by multinational corporations: (1) **different currency denominations,** (2) **different economic and legal structures,** (3) **languages,** (4) **cultural differences,** (5) **role of governments,** and (6) **political risk.**

- When discussing **exchange rates,** the number of U.S. dollars required to purchase one unit of a foreign currency is called a **direct quotation,** while the number of units of foreign currency that can be purchased for one U.S. dollar is an **indirect quotation.**

- Financial forecasting is more difficult for multinational firms, because **exchange rate fluctuations** make it difficult to estimate the dollars that overseas operations will produce.

- Prior to August 1971, the world was on a **fixed exchange rate system** whereby the U.S. dollar was linked to gold, and other currencies were then tied to the dollar. After August 1971, the world monetary system changed to a **floating system** under which major world currency rates float with market forces, largely unrestricted by governmental intervention. The central bank of each country does operate in the foreign exchange market, buying and selling currencies to smooth out exchange rate fluctuations, but only to a limited extent.

- **Pegged exchange rates** occur when a country establishes a fixed exchange rate with a major currency. Consequently, the values of pegged currencies move together over time.

- **Spot rates** are the rates paid for delivery of currency "on the spot," while the **forward exchange rate** is the rate paid for delivery at some agreed-upon future date, usually 30, 90, or 180 days from the day the transaction is negotiated. The forward rate can be at either a **premium** or a **discount** to the spot rate.

- **Interest rate parity** holds that investors should expect to earn the same return in all countries after adjusting for risk.

- **Purchasing power parity,** sometimes referred to as the *law of one price,* implies that the level of exchange rates adjusts so that identical goods cost the same in different countries.

- Granting credit is more risky in an international context because, in addition to the normal risks of default, the multinational firm must worry about **exchange rate changes** between the time a sale is made and the time a receivable is collected.

- Credit policy is important for a multinational firm for two reasons: (1) Much trade is with less-developed nations, and in such situations granting credit is a necessary condition for doing business. (2) The governments of nations such as Japan whose economic health depends upon exports often help their firms compete by granting credit to foreign customers.

- Foreign investments are similar to domestic investments, but political risk and exchange rate risk must be considered. **Political risk** is the risk that the foreign government will take some action which will decrease the value of the investment, while **exchange rate risk** is the risk of losses due to fluctuations in the value of the dollar relative to the values of foreign currencies.

- Investments in **international capital projects** expose firms to exchange rate risk and political risk. The relevant cash flows in international capital budgeting are the dollars which can be turned over to the parent company.

- **Eurodollars** are U.S. dollars deposited in banks outside the United States. Interest rates on Eurodollars are tied to **LIBOR,** the London Interbank Offer Rate.

- U.S. firms often find that they can raise long-term capital at a lower cost outside the United States by selling bonds in the **international capital markets.** International bonds may be either **foreign bonds,** which are exactly like regular domestic bonds except that the issuer is a foreign company, or **Eurobonds,** which are bonds sold in a foreign country but denominated in the currency of the issuing company's home country.

Questions

27-1 Define each of the following terms:
a. Multinational corporation
b. Exchange rate
c. Fixed exchange rate system; floating exchange rates
d. Trade deficit
e. Devaluation; revaluation
f. Exchange rate risk; convertible currency
g. Pegged exchange rates
h. Interest rate parity; purchasing power parity
i. Spot rate; forward exchange rate
j. Discount on forward rate; premium on forward rate
k. Repatriation of earnings; political risk
l. Eurodollar; Eurobond; international bond; foreign bond
m. The Euro

27-2 Under the fixed exchange rate system, what was the currency against which all other currency values were defined? Why?

27-3 Exchange rates fluctuate under both the fixed exchange rate and floating exchange rate systems. What, then, is the difference between the two systems?

27-4 If the French franc depreciates against the U.S. dollar, can a dollar buy more or fewer French francs as a result?

27-5 If the United States imports more goods from abroad than it exports, foreigners will tend to have a surplus of U.S. dollars. What will this do to the value of the dollar with respect to foreign currencies? What is the corresponding effect on foreign investments in the United States?

27-6 Why do U.S. corporations build manufacturing plants abroad when they could build them at home?

27-7 Should firms require higher rates of return on foreign projects than on identical projects located at home? Explain.

27-8 What is a Eurodollar? If a French citizen deposits $10,000 in Chase Manhattan Bank in New York, have Eurodollars been created? What if the deposit is made in Barclay's Bank in London? Chase Manhattan's Paris branch? Does the existence of the Eurodollar market make the Federal Reserve's job of controlling U.S. interest rates easier or more difficult? Explain.

27-9 Does interest rate parity imply that interest rates are the same in all countries?

27-10 Why might purchasing power parity fail to hold?

Problems

27-1
Cross Rates

A currency trader observes that in the spot exchange market, 1 U.S. dollar can be exchanged for 1,498.2 Italian lira or for 111.23 Japanese yen. What is the cross-exchange rate between the yen and the lira; that is, how many yen would you receive for every lira exchanged?

27-2
Interest Rate Parity

Six-month T-bills have a nominal rate of 7 percent, while default-free Japanese bonds that mature in 6 months have a nominal rate of 5.5 percent. In the spot exchange market, 1 yen equals $0.009. If interest rate parity holds, what is the 6-month forward exchange rate?

27-3
Purchasing Power Parity

A television set costs $500 in the United States. The same set costs 2,535 French francs. If purchasing power parity holds, what is the spot exchange rate between the franc and the dollar?

27-4
Exchange Rate

If British pounds sell for $1.50 (U.S.) per pound, what should dollars sell for in pounds per dollar?

27-5
Currency Appreciation

Suppose that 1 French franc could be purchased in the foreign exchange market for 20 U.S. cents today. If the franc appreciated 10 percent tomorrow against the dollar, how many francs would a dollar buy tomorrow?

27-6
Cross Exchange Rates

Suppose the exchange rate between U.S. dollars and the French franc was FF5.9 = $1, and the exchange rate between the dollar and the British pound was £1 = $1.50. What was the exchange rate between francs and pounds?

27-7
Cross Exchange Rates

Look up the 3 currencies in Problem 27-6 in the foreign exchange section of a current issue of *The Wall Street Journal*. What is the current exchange rate between francs and pounds?

27-8
Foreign Investment Analysis

After all foreign and U.S. taxes, a U.S. corporation expects to receive 3 pounds of dividends per share from a British subsidiary this year. The exchange rate at the end of the year is expected to be $1.60 per pound, and the pound is expected to depreciate 5 percent against the dollar each year for an indefinite period. The dividend (in pounds) is expected to grow at 10 percent a year indefinitely. The parent U.S. corporation owns 10 million shares of the subsidiary. What is the present value in dollars of its equity ownership of the subsidiary? Assume a cost of equity capital of 15 percent for the subsidiary.

27-9
Exchange Gains and Losses

You are the vice-president of International InfoXchange, headquartered in Chicago, Illinois. All shareholders of the firm live in the United States. Earlier this month, you obtained a loan of 5 million Canadian dollars from a bank in Toronto to finance the construction of a new plant in Montreal. At the time the loan was received, the exchange rate was 75 U.S. cents to the Canadian dollar. By the end of the month, it has unexpectedly dropped to 70 cents. Has your company made a gain or loss as a result, and by how much?

27-10
Exchange Rates

Table 27-1 lists foreign exchange rates for December 19, 1996. On that day, how many dollars would be required to purchase 1,000 units of each of the following: German marks, Italian lira, Japanese yen, Mexican pesos, and Swiss francs?

27-11
Exchange Rates

Look up the 5 currencies in Problem 27-10 in the foreign exchange section of a current issue of *The Wall Street Journal*.
a. What is the current exchange rate for changing dollars into 1,000 units of marks, lira, yen, pesos, and Swiss francs?
b. What is the percentage gain or loss between the December 19, 1996, exchange rate and the current exchange rate for each of the currencies in Part a?

27-12
Results of Exchange
Rate Changes

Early in September 1983, it took 245 Japanese yen to equal $1. More than 13 years later, in December 1996, that exchange rate had fallen to 114 yen to $1. Assume the price of a Japanese-manufactured automobile was $8,000 in September 1983 and that its price changes were in direct relation to exchange rates.
a. Has the price, in dollars, of the automobile increased or decreased during the 13-year period because of changes in the exchange rate?
b. What would the dollar price of the automobile be on December 19, 1996, again assuming that the car's price changes only with exchange rates?

27-13
Spot and Forward Rates

Boisjoly French Imports has agreed to purchase 15,000 cases of French wine for 16 million francs at today's spot rate. The firm's financial manager, James Desreumaux, has noted the following current spot and forward rates:

	U.S. DOLLAR/FRANC	FRANC/U.S. DOLLAR
Spot	0.16933	5.9055
30-day forward	0.16890	5.9207
90-day forward	0.16807	5.9499
180-day forward	0.16719	5.9812

On the same day, Desreumaux agrees to purchase 15,000 more cases of wine in 3 months at the same price of 16 million francs.
a. What is the price of the wine, in U.S. dollars, if it is purchased at today's spot rate?
b. What is the cost, in dollars, of the second 15,000 cases if payment is made in 90 days and the spot rate at that time equals today's 90-day forward rate?
c. If the exchange rate for the French franc is 5.00 to $1 in 90 days, how much will he have to pay for the wine (in dollars)?

27-14
Interest Rate Parity

Assume that interest rate parity holds and that 90-day risk-free securities yield 5 percent in the United States and 5.3 percent in Germany. In the spot market, 1 mark equals 0.63 dollar.
a. Is the 90-day forward rate trading at a premium or discount relative to the spot rate?
b. What is the 90-day forward rate?

27-15
Interest Rate Parity

Assume that interest rate parity holds. In both the spot market and the 90-day forward market 1 Japanese yen equals 0.0086 dollar. The 90-day risk-free securities yield 4.6 percent in Japan. What is the yield on 90-day risk-free securities in the United States?

27-16
Purchasing Power Parity

In the spot market 7.8 pesos can be exchanged for 1 U.S. dollar. A compact disk costs $15 in the United States. If purchasing power parity holds, what should be the price of the same disk in Mexico?

27-17
Purchasing Power Parity

A chair costs 500 French francs. The same chair also costs 10,000 Japanese yen. If purchasing power parity holds, what should be the exchange rate between the yen and the French franc?

MINI CASE

Citrus Products Inc. is a medium-sized producer of citrus juice drinks with groves in Indian River County, Florida. Until now, the company has confined its operations and sales to the United States, but its CEO, George Gaynor, wants to expand into Europe. The first step would be to set up sales subsidiaries in Spain and Portugal, then to set up a production plant in Spain, and, finally, to distribute the product throughout the European common market. The firm's financial manager, Ruth Schmidt, is enthusiastic about the plan, but she is worried about the implications of the foreign expansion on the firm's financial management process. She has asked you, the firm's most recently hired financial analyst, to develop a 1-hour tutorial package that explains the basics of multinational financial management. The tutorial will be presented at the next board of directors meeting. To get you started, Schmidt has supplied you with the following list of questions.
a. What is a multinational corporation? Why do firms expand into other countries?
b. What are the six major factors which distinguish multinational financial management from financial management as practiced by a purely domestic firm?
c. Consider the following illustrative exchange rates.

U.S. DOLLARS REQUIRED TO BUY
ONE UNIT OF FOREIGN CURRENCY

Spanish peseta	0.0075
Portuguese escudo	0.0063

(1) Are these currency prices direct quotations or indirect quotations?
(2) Calculate the indirect quotations for pesetas and escudos.
(3) What is a cross rate? Calculate the two cross rates between pesetas and escudos.
(4) Assume Citrus Products can produce a liter of orange juice and ship it to Spain for $1.75. If the firm wants a 50 percent markup on the product, what should the orange juice sell for in Spain?
(5) Now, assume Citrus Products begins producing the same liter of orange juice in Spain. The product costs 200 pesetas to produce and ship to Portugal, where it can be sold for 400 escudos. What is the dollar profit on the sale?
(6) What is exchange rate risk?
d. Briefly describe the current international monetary system. How does the current system differ from the system that was in place prior to August 1971?
e. What is a convertible currency? What problems arise when a multinational company operates in a country whose currency is not convertible?
f. What is the difference between spot rates and forward rates? When is the forward rate at a premium to the spot rate? At a discount?
g. What is interest rate parity? Currently, you can exchange 1 peseta for 0.0080 dollar in the 30-day forward market, and the risk-free rate on 30-day securities is 4 percent in both Spain and the United States. Does interest rate parity hold? If not, which securities offer the highest expected return?

h. What is purchasing power parity? If grapefruit juice costs $2.00 a liter in the United States and purchasing power parity holds, what should be the price of grapefruit juice in Portugal?
i. What impact does relative inflation have on interest rates and exchange rates?
j. Briefly discuss the international capital markets.
k. To what extent do average capital structures vary across different countries?
l. What is the impact of multinational operations on each of the following financial management topics?
   (1) Cash management.
   (2) Capital budgeting decisions.
   (3) Credit management.
   (4) Inventory management.

Selected Additional References and Cases

Perhaps the best way to obtain more information on multinational financial management is to consult one of the many excellent textbooks on the subject. For example, see

Eaker, Mark R., Frank J. Fabozzi, and Dwight Grant, *International Corporate Finance* (Fort Worth, Tex.: Dryden Press, 1996).

Levi, Maurice, *International Finance* (New York: McGraw-Hill, 1996).

Madura, Jeff, *International Financial Management* (St. Paul: West, 1995).

For some recent articles on multinational financial management, see

Black, Fischer, "Equilibrium Exchange Rate Hedging," *Journal of Finance,* July 1990, 899–907.

Carre, Herve, and Karen H. Johnson, "Progress Toward a European Monetary Union," *Federal Reserve Bulletin,* October 1991, 769–783.

Choi, Jongmoo Jay, and Anita Mehra Prasad, "Exchange Risk Sensitivity and Its Determinants: A Firm and Industry Analysis of U.S. Multinationals," *Financial Management,* Autumn 1995, 77–88.

Frankel, Jeffrey A., "The Japanese Cost of Finance," *Financial Management,* Spring 1991, 95–127.

Hammer, Jerry A., "Hedging Performance and Hedging Objectives: Tests of New Performance Measures in the Foreign Currency Market," *Journal of Financial Research,* Winter 1990, 307–323.

Hunter, William C., and Stephen G. Timme, "A Stochastic Dominance Approach to Evaluating Foreign Exchange Hedging Strategies," *Financial Management,* Autumn 1992, 104–112.

Kester, George W., Rosita P. Chang, and Kai-Chong Tsui, "Corporate Financial Policy in the Pacific Basin: Hong Kong and Singapore," *Financial Practice and Education,* Spring/Summer 1994, 117–127.

Lee, Insup, and Steve B. Wyatt, "The Effects of International Joint Ventures on Shareholder Wealth," *Financial Review,* November 1990.

Mahajan, Arvind, "Pricing Expropriation Risk," *Financial Management,* Winter 1990, 77–86.

Pauls, B. Dianne, "U.S. Exchange Rate Policy: Bretton Woods to Present," *Federal Reserve Bulletin,* November 1990, 891–908.

Two finance journals have devoted entire issues to multinational financial management. See Financial Management, *Winter 1991, and* Journal of Applied Corporate Finance, *Winter 1991, Winter 1994, Fall 1996, and Winter 1997.*

The following case from the Cases in Financial Management: Dryden Request *series focuses on multinational capital budgeting:*

Case 18, "Alaska Oil Corporation."

PENSION PLAN MANAGEMENT*

In 1995, GTE Corporation initiated a strategy that, if adopted by other firms, would have a significant effect on how companies manage their pension plan assets. The $12 billion pension fund organized a contest among some of the biggest money management names on Wall Street. Goldman Sachs, Morgan Stanley, J. P. Morgan, and the Boston firm of Grantham, Mayo, Van Otterloo & Company are each getting $1 billion to invest worldwide as they see fit. At the end of the exercise, which will last three to five years, the best performers will win a larger share of GTE's pension business.

Each manager's results will be measured against a benchmark index consisting of 45 percent U.S. stocks, 25 percent foreign stocks, 20 percent U.S. bonds, 5 percent foreign bonds, and 5 percent money market funds. Further, the managers will be rewarded for good performance beyond mere bragging rights: Those who do well can earn as much as twice the standard fee, while those who perform poorly can lose up to two-thirds of the standard fee.

The GTE contest is unusual because most pension funds make their own broad asset allocation choices and then pick several speciality managers within each category to invest solely within that category. The new approach, which turns over a chunk of the fund to a few broad-based managers with global reach, will reduce the time spent by GTE's staff in choosing and monitoring a large number of individual managers. In addition, it leaves the asset allocation decision (that is, the mix of stocks, bonds, real estate, and so forth, and also the geographic markets), which is by far the most important factor in determining investment performance, to the outside managers.

GTE admits that the new approach is untried. According to GTE's pension fund chief, John Carroll, "If you want to stay ahead of your peers, you've got to do something different, which may or may not be the right thing." But he added, "If these four money managers can't beat the fixed allocation, then I don't think anybody can."

GTE was once known in the pension community for having an unusually large number of money managers—60 just for U.S. stocks in 1984. Since he was hired in 1985, Carroll has whittled the number down and shifted more of the actual stock and bond picking functions to GTE's internal managers. He also began negotiating performance fees for GTE's outside equity managers in 1986. Since his arrival, GTE's results have been excellent, with an average annual return of more than 14 percent for the past decade.

Pension plan management is important both to the employees, who depend on the plan for retirement income, and to the company itself, whose very existence could be threatened by poor pension plan management. Although this chapter cannot make you an expert in pension plans and their management, it can inform you about the key issues that managers and employees must face.

---

*This chapter was coauthored by Professor Jim Bicksler of Rutgers University. Professor Russ Fogler of the University of Florida also provided important contributions.

Pension plans are an important component of the U.S. financial system: (1) In 1998, pension funds had an aggregate market value of more than $6 trillion, and they owned more than 25 percent of all U.S. stocks and more than 40 percent of all corporate bonds. (2) Pension plans provide workers with the majority of their retirement income. (3) Contributions to pension plans are an important component of most compensation plans, and they affect morale, labor productivity, and economic stability. (4) The rate of return on pension plan assets can have a major effect on corporate earnings, employees' retirement incomes, or both. (5) Because pension plans are large and concentrated owners of corporate stocks, their managers play an important role in the direction and control of corporate policy.

In this chapter, we discuss the different types of pension plans, their management and regulation, and their effects on both individuals and firms.

THE ROLE AND SCOPE OF PENSION PLAN MANAGEMENT

Most companies—and practically all government units—have some type of employee pension plan. Typically, the chief financial officer (CFO) administers the plan, and he or she has these three specific responsibilities: (1) deciding on the general nature of the plan, (2) determining the required annual payments into the plan, and (3) managing the plan's assets. Obviously, the company does not have total control over these decisions—employees, often through their unions, have a major say about the plan's structure, and the federal government imposes strict rules on certain aspects of all plans. Still, companies have considerable latitude regarding several key decisions, and these decisions can materially affect the firm's profitability and its employees' welfare.

Although a few firms have provided pensions since the turn of the century, the real start of large-scale pension plans dates from 1949, when the United Steelworkers negotiated a comprehensive retirement plan in their contract with the steel companies. Other industries followed, and the plans grew rapidly thereafter. Under a typical pension plan, the company (or governmental unit) agrees to provide retirement payments to employees. These promised payments constitute a liability, and the employer is required to establish a *pension fund* and place money in it each year in order to have sufficient assets to meet pension payments as they come due.

Pension plan assets represent a large fraction of total assets for many firms. For example, Chrysler has about $60 billion in total assets, of which $15 billion (25 percent) is represented by pension fund assets. If the pension fund is managed well and produces relatively high returns, the firm's required annual additions can be minimized. However, if the fund does not perform well, then the firm will have to increase contributions to the fund, which will lower earnings.

Pension fund management is an important but complex job. Indeed, pension fund administration requires so much specialized technical knowledge that companies typically hire specialized consulting firms to help design, modify, and administer their plans. Still, because the plans are under the general supervision of the financial staff, and because they have such significant implications for the firm as a whole, it is important that financial managers understand the basics of pension plan management.

S E L F - T E S T
Q U E S T I O N

Why is pension fund management important to most firms?

THREE TYPES OF PENSION PLANS

There are three principal types of pension plans: (1) defined contribution plans, (2) defined benefit plans, and (3) profit sharing plans. The key features of these plans are discussed in this section.

Defined Contribution Plan

Under all pension plans, the employer agrees to do something to help employees when they retire. Rather than specifying exactly how much each retiree will receive, companies can agree to make specific payments into a retirement fund and then have retirees receive benefits that depend on the plan's investment success. This type of plan is called a **defined contribution plan.** For example, a trucking firm might agree to make payments equal to 15 percent of all union members' wages each year into a pension fund administered by the Teamsters' Union, and the fund would then dispense benefits to retirees. Such plans do not have to be administered by unions — indeed, today the most common procedure is for the monthly payment applicable to each employee to be turned over to a mutual fund of the employee's choice and credited to the employee's account. Thus, a defined contribution plan is, in effect, a savings plan that is funded by employers, although many plans also permit additional contributions by employees. The firm is obligated, in bad times as well as in good, to make the specified contributions.

There are a number of different types of defined contribution plans, including 401(k) plans and Employee Stock Ownership Plans (ESOPs).[1] Defined contribution plans are not subject to the rules of the Employee Retirement Income Security Act of 1974 (discussed later). Additionally, these plans are portable (also discussed later) in that the assets belong to the employee and can be carried forward whenever he or she changes jobs. Since the sponsoring firm does not guarantee any specific dollar payments to participants upon retirement, participants in a defined contribution plan bear all of the investment risk associated with poor portfolio performance. However, most defined contribution plans allow participants to choose among several investment alternatives, so each individual can accommodate his or her own risk preference.

To illustrate a defined contribution plan, consider the one offered by Merck. Employees can contribute up to 15 percent of their pre-tax salaries into the plan, which is deductible from the employees' taxable income. Further, the company will match an employee's contribution by 50 cents on each dollar up to 5 percent of salary. For example, if an employee making $50,000 per year contributes the maximum $0.15($50,000) =$ $7,500, Merck will chip in an additional $2,500 for a total contribution of $10,000.

In the Merck plan, all contributions from the employee are deducted from the employee's salary before income taxes are paid. This means that the employee does not pay tax on the income that is contributed to the pension plan at the time the contribution is made, nor does the employee pay taxes when any income or capital gains are generated by the retirement account. However, retirees must pay income taxes when they receive retirement benefits. Since contributions to the plan were deducted from taxable income, all benefits received from the plan are fully taxed.

Upon retirement, employees have several options. Although most begin receiving benefits immediately upon retirement, some might choose to leave the funds in the

---

[1]Section 401(k) is part of the federal law which authorized the most widely used defined contribution plan, hence the name "401(k) plan." An ESOP invests in the firm's common stock. In a KASOP, which is a variation of the ESOP, the firm's contribution consists of shares of its common stock, but employee contributions can be invested in other alternatives.

retirement account and perhaps take a job with another company, especially if they are reasonably young. Note that this defers the payment of income taxes. However, they may not leave the funds in the retirement account indefinitely. IRS regulations require that they begin withdrawing funds when they reach a specified age. When retirees do begin receiving benefits, they can choose a lump-sum disbursement, but this would result in a large tax liability. Most retirees choose to "roll over" the retirement account by purchasing an annuity, often sold by an insurance company. A typical lifetime annuity guarantees a monthly payment for as long as the retiree lives. The amount of the payment depends on the amount that was in the retirement account and the age of the retiree. There are many other features available on annuities, such as a surviving spouse option (in which the spouse of the retiree continues to receive payments after the death of the retiree), fixed-term annuities, inflation-linked payments, and an option that guarantees a minimum number of payments to the retiree's heirs should the retiree die soon after the annuity's first payment.

Defined Benefit Plan

Under a **defined benefit plan,** the employer agrees to give retirees a specifically defined benefit, such as $500 per month, 50 percent of his or her average salary over the five years preceding retirement, or 2.5 percent of his or her highest annual salary for each year of employment. The payments could be fixed as of the retirement date, or they could be indexed to increase as the cost of living increases. The key, though, is that *payments to retirees,* not *contributions by* the company, are specified (defined).

Defined benefit plans differ in several important respects from defined contribution plans. Most important, the sponsoring firm, not the participants, bears the risk of poor portfolio performance. The company has a firm obligation to its retirees that must be met regardless of how well or poorly the pension plan assets perform. Note, though, that defined benefit participants still bear purchasing-power risk — that is, the risk that inflation will eat away at the purchasing power of a fixed pension payment.

To illustrate a defined benefit plan, consider the plan offered by Eastman Kodak. Assuming an employee had 30 years of service and a final annual income of $50,000, Kodak's plan promises to pay $19,700 per year at age 65. This is 1.31 percent of the final salary for each year of service. Thus, an employee who started with Kodak at age 21 could quit work at age 51 and begin to collect his or her pension at age 65. Alternatively, full benefits could be collected when the employee's years of service plus age equals 85, so an employee could begin with Kodak at age 25, work to age 55, and collect full benefits. If a vested employee does not meet one of these guidelines for full benefits, he or she can still receive retirement benefits, but at less than the full amount.

Profit Sharing Plan

A third type of plan calls for the employer to make payments into the retirement fund, but with the payments varying with the level of corporate profits; this is a **profit sharing plan.** For example, a computer manufacturer might agree to pay 10 percent of its pre-tax profits into a fund which would then invest the proceeds and pay benefits to employees upon their retirement. These plans are operated like defined contribution plans in the sense that each employee's funds are maintained in a separate account, and benefits depend on the plan's performance. Profit sharing plans can be operated separately or used in conjunction with defined benefit or defined contribution plans. For example, Schering-Plough does not match employee 401(k) contributions, but it funds a separate profit sharing plan with contributions up to 15 percent of each participant's annual salary. As noted above, under most profit sharing plans, a separate account is maintained for each employee, and each employee gets a share of the contribution each year based upon his or her salary. The employee's account builds up over time just as if the employee were putting money into a mutual fund, which may in fact be the case.

S E L F - T E S T
Q U E S T I O N S

Name and define the three principal types of pension plans.

Which type plan is most risky from the standpoint of sponsoring corporations? From the standpoint of beneficiaries?

KEY TERMS AND CONCEPTS

Certain terms and concepts are used frequently in discussions of pension plans, and it is useful to define them at this point.

Vesting

If employees have a right to receive pension benefits even if they leave the company prior to retirement, then their pension rights are said to be **vested.** If the employee loses his or her pension rights by leaving the company prior to retirement, the rights are said to be *nonvested.* Defined contribution and profit sharing plans generally provide immediate vesting (as soon as the employee is eligible to participate in the plan). However, most defined benefit plans have *deferred vesting,* which means that pension rights are nonvested for the first few years, but become fully vested if the employee remains with the company for a prescribed period, say, five years. The costs to the company are clearly lower for plans with deferred vesting, because such plans do not cover employees who leave prior to vesting. Moreover, deferred vesting tends to reduce turnover, which, in turn, lowers training costs. However, it is much easier to recruit employees if the plan offers early vesting. Also, many argue that vesting is socially desirable, and as a result there has been a tendency over time for Congress to require vesting for more and more employees and within a shorter and shorter period of time.

Currently, companies with defined benefit plans are required to vest participants at least as fast as either the five-year rule or the three-to-seven-year rule:

1. **Five-year rule.** Under this rule, participants must be fully vested after five years of service. This is called *cliff vesting*—the participant is either vested or not vested, with no partial vesting.

2. **Three-to-seven-year rule.** Under this rule, participants are partially vested according to the number of years of service:

YEARS OF SERVICE	PERCENT VESTED
3	20%
4	40
5	60
6	80
7	100

Of course, employers may offer plans that vest pension rights more quickly than mandated by these two vesting rules.

Portability

Portable means "capable of being carried," and a **portable pension plan** is one that an employee can carry from one employer to another. Portability is extremely important in occupations such as construction, where workers move from one employer to another fairly frequently. A defined contribution plan is always portable, because the plan's assets are held in the employees' names. However, for a defined benefit plan to be portable, both the old employer and the new employer would have to be part of the same plan—it would simply not be feasible for an IBM employee to leave IBM and go to work for Delta Airlines and take along a share of the IBM plan. (Note, however, that if the employee's rights under the IBM plan were vested, then he or she could receive payments from both Delta and IBM upon retirement.) Where job changes are frequent—as in trucking, construction, and coal mining—union-administered plans are used to make portability possible.

In 1996, Bell Atlantic instituted a novel approach to portability, adding a "cash balance" component to its traditional defined benefit plan. The company uses a simple formula, based on age and years of service, to credit each employee's retirement account with from 4 to 7 percent of his or her salary. The amount in each account earns interest at the T-bill rate. If an employee leaves the company, even prior to vesting, he or she can withdraw the existing cash value. According to Bell Atlantic, its cash balance plan is in response to a changing workforce. By adding portability to the advantages of a traditional defined benefit plan, it can better serve the retirement needs of employees of all ages.

Funding

Under either a defined contribution plan or a profit sharing plan, the company must make annual contributions. However, under a defined benefit plan the company promises to give employees pensions for some unknown number of future years based on their unknown future salaries, and from a fund whose future value is unknown, so its true costs are uncertain. However, pension fund actuaries can estimate the present value of the expected future benefits under a defined benefit plan, and this present value constitutes a liability of the plan. The liability may be measured (1) by the present value of *all projected* benefits accrued by present workers, or (2) by the present value of *vested* benefits earned to date. The vested amount is obviously smaller, and it represents the expected present value of the benefits that would be paid to workers if the firm went out of business today or if all workers resigned today. The value of the fund's assets can be determined: it is the current market value of the fund's assets. If the present value of all expected retirement benefits is equal to assets on hand, then the plan is said to be **fully funded.** If assets exceed the present value of benefits, the plan is **overfunded.** If the present value of benefits exceeds assets, the plan is **underfunded,** and an **unfunded pension liability** exists.

Actuarial Rate of Return

The discount rate used to determine the present value of future benefits under a defined benefit plan is called the **actuarial rate of return.** Often, this rate is the same as the assumed rate of return on the plan's assets.

The actuarial rate of return is a critical element in pension plan management. A higher assumed actuarial rate leads to lower current contribution requirements because (1) the present value of benefits will be lower and (2) the plan's assets will be assumed to earn more, hence to grow at a faster rate. Since the actuarial rate is a forecast of the expected future rate of return on the plan's assets, there is a great deal of room for judgment. Some firms base their actuarial rate on recent plan performance, while others base the rate on long-term historical returns on different asset classes and then apply these historical returns to the plan's current asset mix to get a weighted average. If the estimates are unbiased, errors in actuarial rate assumptions should balance out over time. However, if a firm purposely sets its actuarial rate too high in order to hold down its contributions and thus raise its reported income, its pension plan will build up a large unfunded deficiency.

ERISA

The **Employee Retirement Income Security Act of 1974 (ERISA)** is the basic federal law governing the structure and administration of corporate pension plans. ERISA requires that companies fully fund their defined benefit pension plans, although it gives them up to 30 years to make up for underfunding of past service benefits. For example, if a company agreed in 1998 to double payments to all employees who retire in the future, it would immediately have a large unfunded liability. If the company had to come up with the money to fully fund its plan, it would probably not be able to offer the improved benefits. The phased adjustment period is obviously important in such a situation.

In addition, ERISA has several other provisions which affect the management of defined benefit plans. First, ERISA mandates that pension funds be managed according to the "prudent man" rule, which focuses on diversification as the cornerstone of portfolio management. This has resulted in pension funds diversifying into such investments as real estate, international stocks and bonds, LBOs, and venture capital. Second, ERISA sets the mandatory vesting requirements discussed earlier to prevent situations whereby long-term employees are fired or laid off just before their benefits are vested. Finally, ERISA established the Pension Benefit Guarantee Corporation (PBGC), which we discuss next.

PBGC

The **Pension Benefit Guarantee Corporation (PBGC)** was established by ERISA to insure corporate defined benefit pension funds. The PBGC, which is an agency within the U.S. Department of Labor, steps in and takes over payments to retirees of bankrupt companies with underfunded pension plans. Currently, the PBGC is paying (or will pay when they retire) benefits to some 440,000 retirees from about 2,300 companies, including Pan American Airlines, Eastern Airlines, Allis-Chalmers, Republic Steel, and LTV Corporation.

Funds for the PBGC come from premiums paid by sponsors of defined benefit plans. Currently, the premium is $19 per participant per year, plus an additional fee of $9 per $1,000 of unfunded liabilities, not to exceed a total of $72. However, the ultimate backers of the PBGC are the taxpayers. Just a few years ago, the PBGC was grossly underfunded, with known obligations exceeding assets by some $3 billion. At that time, pundits were predicting that the only thing that would save the PBGC was a large government bailout. However, by 1997, increased collections from sponsoring corporations, coupled with high investment returns and a decline in large bankruptcies, resulted in a PBGC surplus of about $900 million, its first ever.

To help control costs, the PBGC does not cover company-promised health insurance for retirees. Further, PBGC payments to retirees are capped at about $33,000 (in 1997 dollars) per year, which for some highly paid workers is much less than their plan originally promised. Finally, the PBGC does not guarantee pensions that are to be paid by annuities purchased by plans from insurance companies. This feature is important, because in the 1980s, many companies terminated overfunded defined benefit plans, used a portion of the plan's assets to purchase insurance contracts to cover promised benefit payments, and then recovered the excess assets for the stockholders.

Contributions to the Plan

Actuaries calculate annually how much a company must pay into its defined benefit fund in order to keep it fully funded (or to move it toward full funding). These contributions are a tax-deductible expense, just as are wages. Obviously, if a company agrees to an increase in benefits, this increases its required contribution and consequently lowers its reported profits and cash flow to stockholders. Also, if pension benefits are tied to wages, then any wage increase will also require an increase in payments to the pension plan. Payments also depend on the investment performance of the pension fund—if the fund's managers do a good job of investing its assets, then required annual contributions will be reduced, and vice versa if the fund's investment performance is poor.

During the 1990s, as a result of the greatest bull market in history, many corporations' pension plans are overfunded to such an extent that they do not have to make any annual contributions. Indeed, many firms are getting earnings credits. For example, in 1995 GTE reported earnings of $2.5 billion, of which $403 million was a pension fund credit—its fund earned that much more than the required earnings or contribution for the year. Du Pont and GE also had big earnings credits in 1995, and things are looking even better for 1998.[2]

FASB

The *Financial Accounting Standards Board (FASB),* together with the SEC, establishes the rules under which a firm reports its financial condition to stockholders. FASB Statement 87, "Employers' Accounting for Pension Plans," and Statement 35, "Accounting and Reporting by Defined Benefit Plans," provide guidance for reporting pension costs, assets, and liabilities. The reporting of defined contribution plans is relatively straightforward—the annual contribution is shown on the income statement, and a note to the financial statements explains the entry. However, reporting for defined benefit plans is much more complex. Basically, a firm with a defined benefit plan must report in its annual report the plan's overall funding status; the annual pension expense; a full description of the pension plan, including the employee groups covered, type of benefit formula, funding policy, and types of assets held; the actuarial discount rate used, and any justified difference between this rate and the rates used to project the benefit obligation or to project the return on the plan's assets; and the amounts and types of securities issued by the employer and/or related parties that are held by the plan.[3]

SELF-TEST QUESTIONS

Define the following terms:
1. (1) Vested; nonvested; deferred vesting
2. (2) Portability
3. (3) Fully funded; overfunded; underfunded
4. (4) Actuarial rate of return
5. (5) ERISA
6. (6) PBGC
7. (7) Plan contributions

---

[2]Suzanne Woolley, "Corporate America's Clean Little Secret," *Business Week,* March 18, 1996, 104.

[3]FASB Statement 87 is very complex, hence we cannot discuss its provisions in detail in this text.

PENSION FUND MATHEMATICS: DEFINED BENEFIT PLANS

It is clear that the calculation of the present value of expected future benefits is of primary importance for defined benefit pension plans. This calculation determines both the required contribution to the fund for the year and the reported unfunded liability or surplus. Thus, it is essential that financial managers understand the basic mathematics which underly the benefits calculation.

To illustrate the process, let us begin with the following assumptions:

1. A firm has only one employee, age 40, who will retire 25 years from now, at age 65, will die at age 80, and hence will live for 15 years after retirement. There is no uncertainty about these facts.

2. The firm has promised a benefit of $10,000 at the end of each year following retirement until death. For accounting purposes, 1/25 of this $10,000 payment will be vested each year the employee works for the company.

3. No uncertainty regarding the contribution stream exists; that is, the company will definitely make the required payments, in equal annual installments over the next 25 years, in order to build up the fund to the level needed to make the payments of $10,000 per year during the employee's 15-year retirement life.

4. The pension fund will earn 8 percent on its assets; this rate is also known with certainty.

The problem is to find (1) the present value of the future benefits and (2) the company's required annual contributions. We find these values as follows:

Step 1. Find the present value (at retirement) of a 15-year regular annuity of $10,000 per year. Using a financial calculator, enter PMT = 10000[or − 10000], n = 15, and i = 8; then solve for PV = $85,594.79.

Step 2. Find the set of equal annual cash contributions required to accumulate $85,594.79 over 25 years. Using a financial calculator, enter FV = 85594.79 [or −85594.79], n = 25, and i = 8; then solve for PMT = $1,170.83. Thus, the company must contribute $1,170.83 per year to satisfy its pension requirements. If it makes these payments each year, it will be able to report a fully funded position.

A graphical representation of the contributions, benefits, and fund value is presented in Figure 28-1. The "Value of Fund" line is drawn continuously, although in reality it would be a step function. Note also that setting up a pension plan for this worker requires analysis over a 40-year horizon.

The rate of return assumed makes a substantial difference in the annual contribution. If we had assumed a return of 9 percent rather than 8 percent, the annual contributions would have dropped from $1,170.83 to $951.67. Thus, annual contributions would have fallen by 18.7 percent from only a one percentage point change in the assumed investment rate. Conversely, if we had assumed a 7 percent return, the annual contributions would have increased to $1,440.01, a 23 percent increase. Assumptions about how long the worker will live, years before retirement, and, if the payment is based on salary, annual raises will have similarly large effects on the required annual contribution.

S E L F - T E S T
Q U E S T I O N S

Draw a sketch which summarizes the mathematics of pension funding.

How can discounted cash flow (DCF) concepts be used to estimate the annual funding requirement?

FIGURE 28-1 Pension Fund Cash Flows and Value under Certainty

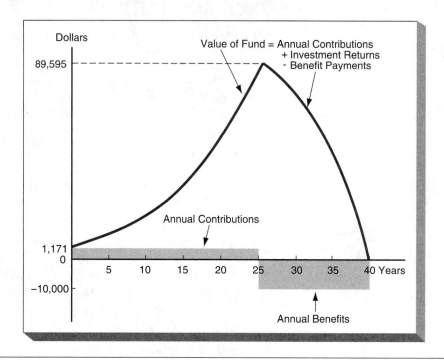

RISKS INHERENT IN PENSION PLANS

Different types of plans differ with regard to the certainty of cash contributions, investment earnings, and promised benefits at retirement. In a *defined contribution plan,* the corporation, or *plan sponsor,* contributes a guaranteed amount which will be invested for eventual payments to the beneficiaries. No guarantee, however, is made about either the rate of return earned on the funds contributed or the final payments. Thus, the beneficiaries assume the risk of fluctuations in the rate of return on the invested money, so they must bear a risk regarding the level of their retirement incomes.

A *profit sharing plan* is similar to a defined contribution plan, except that the sponsor's cash contributions are also uncertain. This uncertainty regarding contributions on top of the uncertainty about the fund's earned rate of return increases the risk to the beneficiaries. The value of the fund at retirement, hence retirees' incomes, could be quite large or quite small, depending on (1) how profitable the corporation is and (2) how well the plan's assets are managed.

Finally, under a *defined benefit plan,* the corporate sponsor guarantees to pay a stated amount from retirement to death, hence the sponsor bears all risks of unexpected variations in rates of return on investment. Note too that the required level of the fund, and the resulting annual contributions, could vary if the defined benefits are based on some average of the final years' salaries, for salaries can grow at a rate different from the assumed level. Thus, the corporation's future cash payment requirements are relatively uncertain. Further, these payments cannot be reduced even if the corporation's profits fall, as they would be under a profit sharing plan.

For all these reasons, a defined benefit plan is by far the riskiest from the standpoint of the sponsoring corporation, but the least risky from the standpoint of the employees.

Large corporations generally use defined benefit plans, while smaller ones typically use profit sharing and/or defined contribution plans. As a result, approximately 75 percent of current pension plans are defined contribution or profit sharing plans, but they include only 35 percent of the total number of employees participating in pension plans. The reason for this situation lies in the relative ability to bear risk. Large firms such as GM, GE, and IBM can assume the risks inherent in defined benefit plans better than their employees. In contrast, many small firms simply do not have the stability required to assume such long-term risks, and consequently both they and their employees are better off under a defined contribution and/or profit sharing plan. However, the high and volatile inflation of the 1970s and early 1980s has motivated even some very large companies to terminate their defined benefit plans in favor of defined contribution plans. So, with new companies opting for defined contribution and/or profit sharing, and older companies switching to such plans, there is a strong trend away from defined benefit plans.

Risks to the Corporation

The allocation of risks inherent in pension plan operations depends on how the plans are structured. Under a defined benefit plan, the risks fall primarily on the corporation. If the plan calls for defined contributions, then risks are shared. Under a profit sharing plan, almost all the risk falls on the beneficiaries. Risk to the corporation under a defined benefit plan can be further subdivided into (1) uncertainty about the annual cash contribution and (2) uncertainty about the firm's obligations in the event it goes bankrupt.

Risks of Annual Cash Contributions.   The *minimum annual cash contribution* is the sum of (1) the amount needed to fund projected future benefit payments that were accrued during the current period, (2) the amount (which could be zero) that must be contributed to make up for not having funded all benefits for service that occurred prior to the current period, and (3) an additional amount (which could be zero or negative) required to offset unexpected deviations from the plan's actuarial assumptions, especially deviations in the earned rate of return and in employee turnover and wage rates.

In our Figure 28-1 illustration of pension fund mathematics, the annual cash contributions were known with certainty. In actual plans, there are three key types of actuarial assumptions which reflect real-world risks: (1) *personnel assumptions,* which allow the actuary to adjust annually for the probability that any employee will leave the company (that is, terminate employment, become disabled, retire, or die); (2) *future salary assumptions,* which take into account expected future average wage increases, which will, of course, affect the final salary and hence defined benefit payments based on the final salary; and (3) *discount rate assumptions,* which explicitly forecast the portfolio's expected future rate of return, which is used both to compound the fund's growth from investment and to discount and thus find the present value of future benefits.

At the end of each year, the assumptions are examined and modified if necessary, and actuaries determine the present value of expected future benefits. Then the deviation between this value and the actual value of the fund's assets is calculated, and it becomes part of an account called "total cumulative actuarial gains and losses." Then the annual cash contribution is adjusted by an amount sufficient to amortize this cumulative amount over a 15-year period. For example, suppose a fund were set up on January 1, 1998, and money were deposited based on a set of actuarial assumptions. Then, at the end of the year, the actual actuarial conditions were examined and compared with the assumed conditions, and the actual value of the fund was compared with the money that would be needed for full funding under the revised actuarial assumptions. Any difference between the actual and required fund balance would be added to the cumulative gains and losses account, and the required annual contribution would be increased or decreased by an amount sufficient to amortize this account's balance over a 15-year period. The same method would be used at the end of 1999; the cumulative gains and losses account would be adjusted, and a new 15-year amortization payment for actuarial gains and losses would be determined. All of this is designed to build the fund up to its required level but, at the same time, to smooth out the required annual cash contribution and thus smooth out the firm's reported profits and cash flows.

Bankruptcy Liens.   Prior to ERISA, employees had no claim against a corporation's assets in the event of bankruptcy. Of course, if a defined benefit plan were fully funded, bankruptcy would present no problem for employees, but bankruptcies did impose serious hardships on members of plans that were not fully funded. Congress changed the bankruptcy statutes to raise the priority of unfunded vested pension liabilities, and today unfunded vested liabilities have a lien with the same priority as federal taxes on up to 30 percent of the stockholders' equity. Thus, the pension fund ranks above the unsecured creditors for up to 30 percent of common and preferred equity, and any unsatisfied pension claims rank on a par with those of the general creditors.[4]

If one of the subsidiaries of a holding company had been operating at a loss, and consequently had a low net worth, and if the subsidiary also had an unfunded pension liability which was greater than its net worth, then the parent company would be better off without the subsidiary than with it. This situation has led companies to spin off or otherwise dispose of subsidiaries. Such spin-offs have a detrimental effect on the PBGC, which in fact sued International Harvester (IH) for selling its Wisconsin Steel subsidiary three years before the subsidiary went bankrupt. The PBGC claimed that the purpose of the divestiture was to rid IH of its subsidiary's underfunded pension liability.

Effects of Pension Plans on Stock Prices.   The value of a firm's stock is obviously affected by its pension plan, but because of the uncertainties inherent in pension plan calculations, devising reasonable accounting procedures for reporting both the annual pension expense and the corporation's pension liabilities has proved to be quite difficult. FASB Statement 87 was designed both to increase the disclosure of information about a pension fund's condition and to mandate more uniformity in choosing the actuarial rate of return used to calculate the present value of benefits. However, because of the vast variety of funding techniques and the great difficulty involved in forecasting future pension liabilities, reported pension plan data must still be viewed with a certain amount of skepticism.[5]

Can investors make sense of pension fund accounting data? To help answer this question, researchers have examined the relationship between corporations' market values and their pension fund liabilities, and they concluded that investors recognize the existence of unfunded pension liabilities and lower the firm's value accordingly.[6]

---

[4]Note that if a company has been suffering losses prior to bankruptcy, which is generally the case, its equity will be low, and 30 percent of a low number is lower yet. Nevertheless, PBGC must still make full payments as specified in the company's plan to all vested pension holders, subject to the limits noted previously.

[5]FASB Statement 87 was passed by a 4–3 vote, which reflects the lack of consensus regarding the proper accounting treatment for pension plans.

[6]For example, see Martin Feldstein and Randall Morck, "Pension Funds and the Value of Equities," *Financial Analysts Journal*, September–October 1983, 29–39.

This and other evidence indicates that investors are well aware of the condition of companies' pension funds, and that unfunded pension liabilities do reduce corporate value.

Risks to Beneficiaries

Although the preceding section might suggest that most of the risks inherent in defined benefit pension plans are borne by the PBGC or the corporate sponsor, this is not entirely true. For example, suppose that in 1998 a corporation went bankrupt and its employees were laid off. It is true that the PBGC will provide the promised retirement payments when the employees actually retire. But suppose an employee is 50 years old now, his or her benefits are $10,000 per year, and retirement, as defined by the plan, is 15 years away. If the firm is in an industry where employment is declining, such as steel or textiles, the worker will have a hard time finding a new job offering comparable wages. Moreover, even if the worker could get another job that provides the same salary and an equivalent pension plan, his or her benefits will still be adversely affected. The benefits under the bankrupt company's plan will be frozen—the past benefits from the now-bankrupt firm will not be increased as a result of pay increases over the worker's remaining employment life, as they probably would have been had the original employer not gone bankrupt. The worker's benefits under his or her new plan, assuming he or she does get a new job, would rise with inflation, but the worker's retirement income will be the sum of payments under the old frozen plan and the new one, hence will almost certainly be lower than they would have been had no bankruptcy occurred. To illustrate, if his or her plan were terminated, a 50-year-old manager with a $100,000 annual salary might rate a yearly pension of $36,000 when he or she reaches age 65, based on a payout of 36 percent of the final year's salary. However, if the manager had been able to continue working at the company, and if salaries had increased by 5 percent annually, then the pension benefit would have come to about $75,000 a year, without even increasing the payout percentage. Thus, bankruptcy definitely imposes hardships on workers, and a realization of this fact has been a major factor in unions' acceptance of reduced wages and benefits in situations where bankruptcy and resulting layoffs would otherwise have occurred.

It should also be recognized (1) that prior to the 1930s most people had to depend on personal savings (and their children) to support them in their old age, (2) that Social Security was put into effect in 1933 to help provide a formalized retirement system for workers, (3) that corporate pension plans did not really "take off" until after World War II, and (4) that even today many workers, especially those employed by smaller firms, have no formal retirement plan other than Social Security. Also, when the Social Security Act was passed in 1933, it was supposed to be based on insurance principles in the sense that each person would pay into the system and then receive benefits which, actuarially, were equivalent to what he or she had paid in. Thus, Social Security was designed to help workers provide for their own future. Today, Social Security has become an income transfer mechanism in that workers with high salaries get less out of the system than they pay in, while low-salaried workers get more out than they pay in. In a sense, the Social Security system, including Medicare, has become a "safety net" for all older Americans, irrespective of their payments into the system. Even so, few people want to be totally dependent on the income provided by Social Security, so private pension plans are a vital part of the American economic scene.

S E L F - T E S T
Q U E S T I O N

Consider the three types of pension plans: (1) defined benefit, (2) defined contribution, and (3) profit sharing. Describe each plan with respect to the risks borne by the corporation and the beneficiaries.

ILLUSTRATION OF A DEFINED BENEFIT VERSUS A DEFINED CONTRIBUTION PLAN

Some corporations and governmental units give their employees a choice between a defined benefit plan and a defined contribution plan. The implications of these plans ought to be understood both by employees and by the agencies responsible for paying the prescribed benefits. Although pension plan status would rarely be the primary factor when choosing a job, it still should be given at least some consideration. Our example does not correspond (to our knowledge) exactly with the plan of any company, but many companies do have plans that are similar to our hypothetical Company DB (for defined benefit), while other companies have plans similar to our hypothetical Company DC (for defined contribution).

Here are the assumptions used in the illustration:

1. It is now 1999.
2. The employee is 30 years old, earns $30,000 per year, and plans to retire in 35 years, at age 65.
3. Both companies provide for immediate vesting. (This is not always the case, especially for defined benefit plans.)
4. The rate of inflation is expected to be 6 percent per year. Salaries will also increase at this same rate.
5. Pension fund assets are expected to earn a return of 10 percent.
6. The employee is expected to live for 15 years past retirement at age 65, or to age 80.

Company DB: Defined Benefit

This firm has a defined benefit plan which offers 2 percent of the average salary paid during the last year the employee works for the company for each year of service at the company. Thus, if the employee worked for one year and then resigned, we would have the following situation:

1. The annual benefit at age 65 would be 0.02($30,000) = $600.
2. The amount needed to establish an annuity of $600 per year for 15 years (assuming payment at the end of each year) would be $4,564.
3. The firm would have to put up $162 today to provide the required annuity 35 years from now.[7] The cost to the firm would have been $4,564 had the employee been 64 years old instead of 30; this helps explain why older workers sometimes have a hard time landing jobs.
4. Given an inflation rate of 6 percent, the real (1999) value of the income for the employee from this pension would be $78 in the first year of retirement:

$$\text{Real income} = \$600/(1.06)^{35} = \$78.$$

If the person remained at Company DB until retirement, and if his or her salary increased with inflation, then the final salary would be $30,000(1.06)^{35} = $230,583 per year, and his or her retirement income would be 0.02(35)($230,583) = $161,408, or 70 percent of the $230,583 final salary. The real (1999 dollar) retirement income would be $21,000, or 70 percent of the 1999 employment income, $30,000.

---

[7]We have assumed that inflation in wages is not built into the funding requirement. If a 6 percent wage inflation were built in, then the cost would rise from $162 to $1,245 (as determined by a simple spreadsheet model).

Company DC: Defined Contribution

This firm has a defined contribution plan under which an amount equal to 6 percent of each employee's salary is put into a pension fund account. The fund keeps track of the dollar amount of the contribution attributable to each employee, just as if the company had put the money into a bank time deposit or mutual fund for the employee. (Indeed, the money probably would go into a mutual fund.) Here is the situation if the employee worked for one year and then resigned:

1. The firm would contribute 0.06($30,000) = $1,800 to the employee's account in the pension fund. This is the firm's cost, and it would be the same irrespective of the employee's age.

2. The fund's assets would earn 10 percent per year, so when the employee retired, the value of his or her share of the fund would be $1,800(1.10)^{35} = $50,584.

3. At a 10 percent rate of return, this $50,584 would provide an annuity of $6,650 per year for 15 years. To get this result, enter N = 15, I = 10, PV = $50,584, and FV = 0, and press PMT to obtain $6,650.

4. The real (1999) retirement income for this person would be $6,650/(1.06)^{35} = $865. If the person remained at Company DC, his or her retirement fund would accumulate to $1,024,444 over the 35-year employment period (we used a spreadsheet model to obtain this amount). This would provide a retirement income of $134,688, or 58 percent of the $230,583 final salary. The real (1999 dollar) retirement income would be $17,524, or 58 percent of the 1999 employment income.

Conclusions

1. A young employee who has a high probability of moving would be better off under a defined contribution plan such as the one offered by Company DC.

2. A worker who planned to spend his or her entire career at one firm would be better off at Company DB, with its defined benefit plan.

3. The economic consequences of changing jobs are much worse under the defined benefit plan because benefits are frozen rather than increased with inflation. Therefore, defined benefit plans contribute to lower employee turnover, other factors held constant.

4. It is much more costly to a company to hire older workers if it operates under a defined benefit plan than if it operates under a defined contribution plan. In our example, the 1999 cost to provide pension benefits to a 30-year-old employee under the defined benefit plan would be $162 versus $4,564 for a 64-year-old employee earning the same salary. The average cost per employee to the firm would depend on the age distribution of employees. However, the cost would be $1,800 per employee, irrespective of age, under the defined contribution plan. Thus, defined benefit plans carry with them an economic incentive to discriminate against older workers in hiring, while defined contribution plans are neutral in this regard. Of course, it is illegal to discriminate on the basis of age, but other reasons could be stated for favoring younger workers.

5. If one were to vary the assumptions, it would be easy to show that employees are generally exposed to more risks under the defined contribution plan, while employers face more risks under the defined benefit plan. In particular, the pension benefits under the defined contribution plan are highly sensitive to changes in the rate of return earned on the pension fund's investments. Likewise, the costs to Company DB would vary greatly depending on investment performance, but Company DC's costs would not vary with respect to changes in investment performance.

6. We could have changed the facts of the example to deal with an "average man" with a life expectancy of 70.6 years and an "average woman" with a 78.2-year life expectancy. Obviously, an average woman would receive benefits over a longer period and thus would need a larger accumulated sum in the plan upon retirement, hence would have a higher actuarial annual required cost to the firm than an average man under the defined benefit plan. Thus, other factors held constant, there is an economic incentive for employers to discriminate against women in their hiring practices if they use defined benefit plans. Defined contribution plans are again neutral in this regard.

SELF-TEST QUESTIONS

Would a young worker with a high probability of changing jobs be better off under a defined contribution or a defined benefit pension plan? Explain.

Would a company with a defined benefit plan or one with a defined contribution plan have more economic incentive to hire younger workers? Explain.

Would a company with a defined benefit plan or one with a defined contribution plan have more economic incentive to hire men? Explain.

DEFINED BENEFIT VERSUS DEFINED CONTRIBUTION PLANS: THE EMPLOYEE CHOICE

Since some large employers offer both defined benefit and defined contribution plans, many employees have to choose between the two types of plans. This is not an easy decision to make, because it depends on both the specifics of the plans and the situation of the individual. Each individual must examine his or her expected cash flows from wages and investments and pick the plan that provides the incremental cash flows (both costs and benefits) that maximize his or her expected utility. Clearly, an employee must consider a vast array of economic variables such as expected work life, potential job changes, vesting provisions, risk of inadequate funding, and inflation. These factors can vary so much among individuals and employers that meaningful generalizations are impossible.

To illustrate the complexity of the decision, consider only one of the relevant factors, inflation. Participants in a defined benefit plan face substantial inflation risk. For example, assume an individual retires at age 65 and receives a fixed pension each year. (Most defined benefit plans promise fixed *nominal* payments, so there is no adjustment for inflation once the worker retires.) If the annual inflation rate is 5 percent, each dollar would buy 78 cents worth of goods and services after 5 years, and only 61 cents after 10 years. If the inflation rate is 10 percent, purchasing power would fall to 62 cents after 5 years and to only 39 cents after 10 years. For individuals who retire before age 65 and hence face 20 or more years of retirement, inflation can easily erode the purchasing power of their pensions to only a small fraction of the original dollar amount.

The inflation factor also increases the complexity of decisions under a defined contribution plan. Here the participant must choose among a number of investment alternatives, including money market funds, fixed income funds, balanced funds, company stock, and stock funds. The ability of the fund to withstand the ravages of inflation depends on the performance of the investments chosen for the portfolio. Many studies have looked at the ability of various portfolio combinations to maintain a stable real return under inflation.[8] Although it is common "wisdom" that stocks are a good hedge

---

[8]For example, see Zvi Bodie, "An Innovation for Stable Real Retirement Income," *Journal of Portfolio Management,* Fall 1980, 5–13.

against inflation, studies show that stock returns and inflation are often negatively correlated—when inflation heats up and the plan's portfolio needs to perform best, stocks do poorly. Some studies have suggested that a portfolio consisting of T-bills and commodity futures can be a good hedge against inflation, but very few defined contribution plan participants would be willing to place their assets in such a portfolio. In recent years, a few financial institutions have offered, as a more realistic alternative, certificates of deposit with returns that are tied to the consumer price index. Better yet are inflation-indexed U.S. Treasury bonds, whose interest rates are adjusted to offset inflation. These securities can be used by investors in defined contribution plans to provide a constant real-dollar pension.

SELF-TEST
QUESTIONS

> What factors should be considered by an employee when choosing between a defined benefit and a defined contribution plan?
>
> Explain how inflation affects payments from a defined benefit plan versus a defined contribution plan.

DEVELOPING A PLAN STRATEGY

When an employer establishes a pension plan, the plan type may be influenced by competitive conditions in the labor market. For example, unions generally seek defined benefit plans to cushion beneficiaries from investment risks inherent in defined contribution and profit sharing plans. Even if a firm has the economic power to resist a defined benefit plan, it may still agree to one on the grounds that such a plan might reduce its turnover rate. Still, there is no universal answer as to whether a defined benefit or a defined contribution plan is better for a particular company.

A defined benefit plan provides tax-planning flexibility, because firms can vary the fund contribution from year to year. Thus, in highly profitable years firms can make large contributions, which decrease taxable income, hence taxes. Defined contribution plans do not afford such flexibility, because the specified contributions must be made each year regardless of the firm's profitability. However, defined contribution plans do not require firms to increase contributions if the fund's investment performance is poor.[9] Defined benefit plans also have higher administrative costs, plus the burden to make promised pension payments regardless of the fund's investment performance. In recent years there has been a tendency for new firms to adopt defined contribution or profit sharing plans. Also, the high administrative costs and the regulatory burdens of ERISA have driven a large number of older firms to replace defined benefit with defined contribution plans.

Assuming a firm has a defined benefit plan, proper strategic planning requires integrating the plan's funding and investment policies into the company's general corporate operations. **Funding strategy** involves two decisions: (1) How fast should any unfunded liability be reduced, and (2) what rate of return should be assumed in the actuarial calculations? **Investment strategy** deals with this question: Given the assumed actuarial rate of return, how should the portfolio be structured?

Pension fund managers use **asset allocation models** when making funding and investment decisions. These models use computer simulation to examine the

[9]The distinction between a pension *plan* and a pension *fund* should be noted. A pension plan is a contract between the participants and the firm which spells out the rights and obligations of each party. A pension fund is the investment portfolio that provides the collateral which secures the plan's contractual benefits.

risk/return characteristics of portfolios with various mixes of stocks, bonds, T-bills, real estate, international assets, and so on, under different economic scenarios. Note first that the very nature of pension funds suggests that safety of principal is a paramount consideration, so pension fund managers ought not to "reach" for the highest possible returns. Also, as we discussed in Chapter 5, for a given level of return, the inclusion of more types of assets generally reduces the portfolio's risk, because returns on different asset types are not perfectly correlated. Choices among the possible portfolios may be limited by the introduction of managerial constraints, such as (1) that the portfolio value should not drop more than 30 percent if a 1930s-level depression occurs, or (2) that the portfolio should earn at least 10 percent if a 1970s level of inflation occurs.

Pension fund managers must also consider the effects of the portfolio mix and actuarial assumptions on required contributions. First, note that the most commonly used measure of a pension plan's cost is the ratio of pension contributions to payroll. Now suppose a young company has no retirees, and salary inflation heats up to 15 percent, causing the company's projected benefit payments under a final pay plan to grow by 15 percent per year for active participants. Here inflation would not affect the percentage of pension costs to payroll costs, because payroll and contributions would rise at the same rate. However, if an older company has a large number of retirees relative to actives, and if the payments to retirees are fixed while the reinvestment rate rises on assets held for retirees (because inflation pushes up interest rates), then pension costs as a percentage of payroll might even decline. On the other hand, in a 1930s-style depression a company with a lot of retirees on defined benefits might be in substantial trouble. For example, suppose production cutbacks caused employees to be laid off, and many of them elected to take early retirement. This would reduce payroll expenses but increase retirement expenses. At the same time, the pension fund, if it had invested heavily in stocks, would decline substantially in value, which, in turn, would lead to higher required contributions. For such a company, pension expenses could lead to bankruptcy.

Asset allocation models generally indicate that portfolios consisting of 25 to 50 percent bonds and 50 to 75 percent stocks provide adequate diversification for safety along with a satisfactory expected return. Additionally, it is now recognized that further benefits can be gained by investing in assets other than stocks and bonds. Indeed, many pension funds invest in at least four asset categories, including international securities and such "hard assets" as real estate, timberland, oil and gas reserves, and precious metals, mainly as inflation hedges.

To illustrate one company's approach to asset allocation, consider Table 28-1, which contains the recent asset allocation of General Electric's pension fund. GE's pension fund is diversified along three lines. First, the fund contains numerous types of securities, including stocks, bonds, real estate, options, and venture capital. Second, the portfolio contains both domestic and international securities. Finally, although it is not apparent from the table, the fund is diversified across maturities so that securities more or less continuously mature, providing cash that can either be paid out to beneficiaries or reinvested in other securities.

SELF-TEST QUESTIONS	What is a plan's funding strategy? What is a plan's investment strategy?
	What are asset allocation models?
	What types of assets are held in pension funds? Why?

TABLE 28-1   General Electric Company: Pension Fund Assets (Millions of Dollars)

ASSET CATEGORY	VALUE	PERCENT OF PORTFOLIO
Cash/short-term equivalents	$ 1,703	5.9%
Common stock:		
GE	$ 184	0.6%
Actively managed domestic portfolios	5,704	19.8
Passive (indexed) domestic portfolios	5,337	18.5
Actively managed international portfolios	1,647	5.7
Passive (indexed) international portfolios	201	0.7
Total equities	$13,073	45.3%
Fixed income:		
Domestic bonds	$ 8,448	29.3%
International bonds	90	0.3
Total fixed income	$ 8,538	29.6%
Real estate:		
Ownership	$ 1,782	6.2%
Mortgages	412	1.4
Total real estate	$ 2,194	7.6%
Specialized investments:		
Guaranteed investment contracts	$ 1,619	5.6%
Options	66	0.2
Venture capital	254	0.9
Private placement	1,387	4.8
Total specialized investments	$ 3,326	11.5%
Total assets	$28,834	100.0%

SOURCE: *Nelson's Directory of Plan Sponsors and Tax Exempt Funds,* updated annually.

PENSION FUND INVESTMENT PERFORMANCE

Three factors have a major influence on pension funds' investments: (1) the dollar amount of assets, (2) the mix of the funds' liabilities between those attributable to active workers and those attributable to retired beneficiaries, and (3) the tax situation facing the corporate sponsor. We now discuss how these characteristics affect funds' investment decisions and performance.

Active Workers vis-à-vis Retirees

Many pension fund managers view pension fund liabilities as consisting of (1) benefits due now to plan participants who are already retired, and (2) benefits due in the future to current employees. Thus, they segregate pension assets into two parts: a "retiree portfolio" that provides income to current retirees and a "worker portfolio" that builds value for current workers.

The retiree portfolio is usually invested in fixed-income securities chosen to produce a cash stream that matches the required retiree pension payments. In managing the retiree portfolio, fund managers often use **immunization** techniques such as **duration** to eliminate, or at least significantly reduce, the risk associated with changing interest rates.[10] Simply put, matching the duration of the portfolio to the duration of the required payments ensures that any loss of market value due to rising interest rates is offset by additional interest income, and vice versa. Matching asset and liability durations balances interest rate and reinvestment rate risks in such a way that the realized return on the portfolio is very close to the targeted actuarial rate of return, regardless of how interest rates vary.

The worker portfolio usually consists of some relatively risky assets such as stocks and real estate, along with some lower-risk assets such as bonds. To reduce the risk inherent in such a portfolio, pension fund managers often use a hedging technique called **portfolio insurance,** which does not appreciably affect upside potential but limits the downside risk. Portfolio insurance involves buying or selling options or futures contracts that would gain about the same amount of value that the portfolio loses if the market takes a sudden fall.

Performance Measurement

Pension fund sponsors generally evaluate the performance of portfolio managers on a regular basis and then use this information when allocating the fund's assets among managers. Suppose a fund's common stock portfolio provided a total return of 16 percent during a recent year—is this good, bad, or average performance? To answer this question, the portfolio's market risk (beta) should be estimated, and then the portfolio's return should be compared with the Security Market Line (SML). Suppose, for example, that the "market" portfolio, say, the S&P 500, returned 15 percent, that 20-year Treasury bonds returned 9 percent, and that our fund's equity portfolio had a beta of 0.9 (that is, it was invested in stocks that had below-average market risk). An SML analysis would lead to the visual comparison shown in Figure 28-2. Here we see that the portfolio did better than expected—it is said to have an *alpha* (α) of 1.6 percentage points. Alpha measures the vertical distance of a portfolio's return above or below the Security Market Line. Looked at another way, alpha is the portfolio's extra return (positive or negative) after adjusting for the portfolio's market risk.[11]

Alpha analysis adds substantially to a pension manager's knowledge about his or her equity portfolio's results, but several shortcomings must be recognized. First, alpha is based on the CAPM, which, as we discussed in Chapters 5 and 6, is an ex ante equilibrium concept which in theory requires that all risky assets be included in the market portfolio (for example, human capital and residential real estate). Therefore, market proxies such as the Standard & Poor's 500 Index result in some degree of measurement

---

[10]Duration is the weighted average time to receipt of cash flows from a bond. For a zero coupon bond, duration equals term to maturity. A coupon bond has a duration that is less than its term to maturity, and the higher the coupon for any given maturity, the shorter its duration. See the Extension to Chapter 24 for an expanded discussion of duration.

[11]The Jensen alpha, so called because this measure was first suggested by Professor Michael Jensen, is popular because of its ease of calculation. Theoretically, its purpose was to measure the performance of a single portfolio versus the market portfolio, after adjusting for the portfolio's beta. However, this measure is not useful in evaluating the performance of portfolios which include real estate and other infrequently traded assets. This fact has led to the development of a number of other portfolio performance measures. For a discussion of these measures, see Jack L. Treynor and Fischer Black, "How to Use Security Analysis to Improve Portfolio Selection," *Journal of Business,* January 1973, 66–86.

FIGURE 28-2   Alpha Analysis

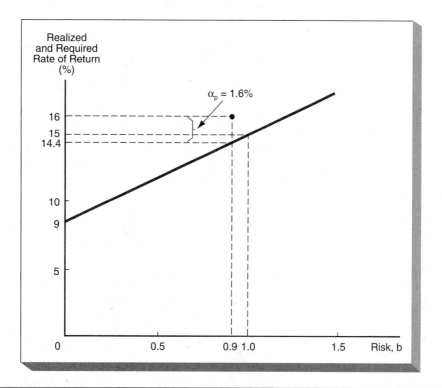

error.[12] Second, the statistical significance of alpha is often too low to make strong statements about the portfolio's relative performance. And third, all of the measurements are based on ex post results which contain both expected returns and unanticipated returns caused by random economic events. Thus, a large positive alpha may indicate good luck rather than good management, and vice versa.

Another way to measure portfolio performance is peer comparison. At the end of each year, managers with similar investment objectives, say, aggressive growth, can be ranked on the basis of total realized return. Managers who are consistently in the top quartile have done a better job than their peers. Unfortunately, though, good past performance is no guarantee of good future performance.

More and more investors, including both pension fund managers and individuals, have been shifting assets from actively managed funds to index funds. Today (1998), there are 126 index mutual funds with a combined $85.4 billion in assets, up from just 85 funds with $27.1 billion in assets three years ago. The reason for this surge in popularity is simple—during the past ten years, only 19 percent of equity funds have bettered the return on the S&P 500 stock index. Equity managers have been quick to point out that large capitalization stocks have significantly outperformed smaller stocks in recent years, and this stacks the performance deck in favor of the index funds, which are dominated by large companies. However, index funds are now available for small

---

[12]Although managerial performance statistics exhibit about 80 to 90 percent correlation regardless of the index used, Richard Roll presents some interesting examples which show how easily rankings can be changed by measurement procedures. See Richard Roll, "Ambiguity When Performance Is Measured by the Securities Market Line," *Journal of Finance*, September 1978, 1051–1069.

and mid-cap companies, and early results tend to confirm that such funds also outperform their managed counterparts. Management fees explain these results.

How is Jensen's alpha used to judge the performance of common stock fund managers? Can you think of any other measures?

What is the difference between active and passive portfolio management?

"TAPPING" PENSION FUND ASSETS

Corporate sponsors administer defined benefit plans with assets running into the hundreds of billions of dollars. To what extent should a corporation be able to invest its fund's assets to the corporation's own advantage? Or, if the plan is overfunded—perhaps because investment results were better than the actuaries had assumed—should the company be able to take assets out of the plan? (Obviously, we are talking about defined benefit plans only; companies are not permitted to touch the assets of defined contribution or profit sharing plans.) Here are some examples of recent actions which have been called into question:

1. When Occidental Petroleum acquired Cities Service, their combined pension plans had assets of $700 million, but the combined vested funding requirement was only $300 million. Occidental terminated the two old defined benefit plans, replaced them with a new defined contribution plan, and took $400 million out of the fund's assets. Similarly, FMC Corporation recently restructured its plan in a way that allowed it to recoup about $325 million. FMC's pension investments had earned an average return of about 16 percent over the past ten years, placing it near the top in performance ratings. FMC used outside advisors and investment funds for its plan, and the vast bulk of the plan's assets were invested in stocks. Recent estimates suggest that, in total, corporate pension funds are overfunded by about $300 billion, so there is a lot of scope for actions such as those of Occidental and FMC.[13]

2. Some cash-short companies have been making required payments to their funds by using their own stock, bonds, and real property rather than cash. This is legal under ERISA provided that a fund has no more than 10 percent of its sponsor's own securities and assets, and provided that the Department of Labor agrees that the transaction is made at a fair price. Thus, Exxon recently contributed a $5.4 million office complex to its plan; Boise Cascade added timberland worth $16 million to its plan; and U.S. Steel, Alcoa, Armco, Reynolds Metals, and Republic Steel all contributed their own newly issued securities rather than cash.

3. Grumman Corporation, Bendix, and others have attempted to use their pension funds to help thwart hostile takeover attempts, or to help the fund's company take over another firm. For example, Grumman's pension fund bought 1.2 million of its shares, paying a 43 percent premium over the pre-bid price, to help fend off a takeover attempt by LTV. The takeover failed, but the fund incurred an immediate $16 million paper loss on these shares.[14] Similarly, Bendix tried (unsuccessfully) to

[13]This type of action can be taken only (1) when approved by the plan's beneficiaries, (2) in conjunction with the establishment of a new pension plan, and (3) after approval by the Labor Department, Internal Revenue Service, and the PBGC if the new plan is a defined benefit plan.

[14]Although the Grumman pension fund eventually made a $13.2 million profit on the Grumman stock it purchased, a lawsuit brought against the plan's trustees resulted in a ruling which held that trustees are liable for actions in using the fund to counter takeover attempts. This ruling sends a clear signal that plan assets must be managed, according to ERISA, for the "sole and exclusive benefit" of beneficiaries.

stop its fund's trustee from tendering 4.5 million shares of its stock to Martin Marietta.

These examples raise some interesting issues: (1) Do the excess assets in a defined benefit plan belong to the sponsoring company or to the employees? Legally, they belong to the company, which de facto contributed more to the plan than was required. However, a number of union leaders have argued that they ought to belong to the workers. (2) Should the PBGC get involved in revisions such as Occidental's? Since Occidental switched from a defined benefit to a defined contribution plan, it left the PBGC's jurisdiction (and also eliminated the $19 annual employee "head tax"), but if it had simply reduced the funding level of a defined benefit plan from overfunded to fully funded, the plan would have been exposed to more risk after assets were removed. (3) Should companies be able to use fund assets to help fight off takeovers?

There are no easy answers to these questions. Obviously, actions which would either violate existing laws or jeopardize the safety of the plan should not be permitted, but many actions are not clear-cut. Given the importance of pension plans, it is safe to assume that the debate will continue.

<table>
<tr><td>S E L F - T E S T
Q U E S T I O N S</td><td>How can companies "tap" excess pension fund assets?

Do pension plan assets belong to the sponsoring company or to the employees?</td></tr>
</table>

RETIREE HEALTH BENEFITS

Most companies offer health care benefits as part of their retirement packages, usually from the time of retirement until the retiree reaches age 65 and becomes eligible for Medicare. The plans typically cover hospitalization, some physicians' fees, and prescription drugs, with employers paying the entire cost of the coverage. Some firms even pay for supplemental coverage after age 65, the so-called Medigap insurance. Until recently, not much attention was paid to such benefits — firms merely paid the benefits each year and, if the cost was material, reported the annual cost as a note to the annual report. Companies were able to overlook retiree health care costs because the number of retirees was small compared with active workers, health care costs were affordable, and many companies didn't even have an idea of the potential liability created by such benefits.

However, with the population aging and health care costs soaring, at many companies the liability of estimated future costs represents 20 to 40 percent of the firm's net worth, and for some smokestack companies, it exceeds net worth. For low-income retirees, health care benefits can cost corporations two to three times more than pension benefits. Now that they realize what is happening, many companies are trying to reduce retiree health care benefits. Thus far, most of the reductions have been minor, such as mandating second opinions and increasing co-payments. However, corporate planners and consultants say that changes are likely to become more prevalent and more profound. Possibilities range from cutting back benefits for retirees, forcing them into managed care plans, or even eliminating retiree health care altogether.

Perhaps the most important factor forcing companies to consider health care benefits is the Financial Accounting Standards Board (FASB) rule that requires companies to set up a reserve for future medical benefits of retirees. Prior to FASB Statement 106, companies merely deducted retiree medical payments from income in the year that they were paid. Now firms must take current write-offs to account for vested future medical benefits, which impacts both the income statement and the balance sheet. The new rule was implemented in 1993, and companies could either take a one-time charge or amortize the write-off over 20 years. Some strong companies, such as General Electric, took the write-off. Its liability totaled $1.8 billion in 1993 (more than $4 billion today), but GE had more than $20 billion of book equity to absorb the charge. Other companies, however, found it impossible to take the one-time charge option. For example, General Motors had a $24 billion liability but only $28 billion in book equity, so a one-time charge would have almost wiped out its net worth. Thus, GM had to amortize its current liability. The rationale behind Statement 106 is clear: retiree health care costs should be reported just like pension costs—at the time the benefits are earned by workers.

S E L F - T E S T   Do retiree health care benefits pose a significant problem for corporations? Explain.
Q U E S T I O N S   What impact has FASB Statement 106 had on the reporting of retiree health benefits?

SUMMARY

This chapter provides an introduction to pension fund management. The key concepts covered are listed below:

- Most companies, and almost all governmental units, have some type of employee pension plan. The management of these plans is important to employees, who use pensions to provide post-retirement income, and to stockholders, who bear the costs of pension plans.

- Pension funds are big business, totaling more than $6 trillion in assets.

- There are three basic types of pension plans: (1) defined contribution plans, (2) defined benefit plans, and (3) profit sharing plans.

- Under a **defined contribution plan,** companies agree to make specific payments into a retirement fund, perhaps 10 percent of an employee's salary, and then retirees receive benefits based on the total amount contributed and the investment performance of the fund.

- Under a **defined benefit plan,** the employer agrees to give retirees a specifically defined benefit, such as $500 per month or 50 percent of their final year's salary.

- In a **profit sharing plan,** companies make contributions into an employee-owned account, but the size of the payments depends on corporate profits.

- If an employee has the right to receive pension benefits even if he or she leaves the company, the benefits are said to be **vested.** Congress has set limits on the amount of time it takes employees to become vested.

- A **portable pension plan** can be carried from one employer to another. Defined contribution plans are portable because the contributions and fund earnings effectively belong to the employee. Also, unions manage the pension funds in some industries, enabling employees with defined benefit plans to move among firms in that industry without losing benefits.

- Under defined contribution or profit sharing plans, the firm's obligations are satisfied when the required contributions are made. However, under a defined benefit plan companies must cover all promised benefits. If the present value of expected retirement benefits equals the assets in the fund, the plan is said to be **fully funded.** If fund assets exceed the present value of expected benefits, the fund is **overfunded.**

If assets are less than the present value of expected benefits, the plan is **underfunded.**

- The discount rate used to determine the present value of future benefits under a defined benefit plan is called the **actuarial rate of return.** This rate is also the expected rate of return on the fund's assets.

- The **Employee Retirement Income Security Act of 1974 (ERISA)** is the basic federal law governing the structure and administration of corporate pension plans.

- The **Pension Benefit Guarantee Corporation (PBGC)** was established by ERISA to insure corporate defined benefit pension funds. Funds used by the PBGC come from fund sponsors, and these funds are used to make payments to retirees whose firms have gone bankrupt with underfunded pension funds. However, taxpayers will have to pay if the PBGC does not have sufficient funds to cover its payments to bankrupt firms' retirees.

- The different types of pension plans have different risks to both firms and employees. In general, a defined benefit plan is the riskiest for the sponsoring organization but the least risky from the standpoint of employees.

- Assuming a company has a defined benefit plan, it must develop the fund's **funding strategy:** (1) How fast should any unfunded liability be reduced, and (2) what actuarial rate of return should be assumed?

- A defined benefit plan's **investment strategy** must answer this question: Given the assumed actuarial rate of return, how should the portfolio be structured so as to minimize the risk of not achieving the target return?

- The performance of pension fund managers can be assessed in two ways: (1) The fund's beta can be estimated, and the return can be plotted on the Security Market Line (SML). (2) The fund's historical performance can be compared with the performance of other funds with similar investment objectives.

- Pension fund managers use **asset allocation models** to help evaluate funding and investment strategies.

- During the major bull market of recent years, many defined benefit plans have become overfunded. Some corporate sponsors have terminated their overfunded plans, used some of the proceeds to buy annuities to cover the plan's liabilities, and then reclaimed the remainder.

- Retiree health benefits have become a major problem for employers for two reasons: (1) these costs are escalating faster than inflation, and (2) a recent Financial Accounting Standards Board (FASB) ruling forced companies to accrue the retiree health care liability rather than merely expense the cash flows as they occur.

Questions

28-1 Define each of the following terms:
a. Defined benefit plan
b. Defined contribution plan
c. Profit sharing plan
d. Vesting
e. Portability
f. Fully funded; overfunded; underfunded
g. Actuarial rate of return
h. Employee Retirement Income Security Act (ERISA)
i. Pension Benefit Guarantee Corporation (PBGC)

    j. FASB reporting requirements
    k. Funding strategy
    l. Investment strategy
    m. Asset allocation models
    n. Jensen alpha
    o. "Tapping" fund assets
    p. Retiree health benefits

28-2   Suppose you just started employment at a large firm that offers both a defined benefit plan and a defined contribution plan. What are some of the factors that you should consider in choosing between the two plans?

28-3   Suppose you formed your own company several years ago and now intend to offer your employees a pension plan. What are the advantages and disadvantages to the firm of both a defined benefit plan and a defined contribution plan?

28-4   Examine the annual report of any large U.S. corporation. Where are the pension fund data located? What effect does this information have on the firm's financial condition?

28-5   A firm's pension fund assets are currently invested only in domestic stocks and bonds. The outside manager recommends that "hard assets" such as precious metals and real estate, and foreign financial assets, be added to the fund. What effect would the addition of these assets have on the fund's risk/return trade-off?

28-6   How does the type of pension fund a company uses influence each of the following:
    a. The likelihood of age discrimination in hiring?
    b. The likelihood of sex discrimination in hiring?
    c. Employee training costs?
    d. The likelihood that union leaders will be "flexible" if a company faces a changed economic environment such as those faced by the airline, steel, and auto industries in recent years?

28-7   Should employers be required to pay the same "head tax" to the PBGC irrespective of the financial condition of their plans?

Problems

28-1
Benefits and Contributions

The Certainty Company (CC) operates in a world of certainty. It has just hired Mr. Jones, age 20, who will retire at age 65, draw retirement benefits for 15 years, and die at age 80. Mr. Jones's salary is $20,000 per year, but wages are expected to increase at the 5 percent annual rate of inflation. CC has a defined benefit plan in which workers receive 1 percent of the final year's wage for each year employed. The retirement benefit, once started, does not have a cost-of-living adjustment. CC earns 10 percent annually on its pension fund assets. Assume that pension contribution and benefit cash flows occur at year-end.
    a. How much will Mr. Jones receive in annual retirement benefits?
    b. What is CC's required annual contribution to fully fund Mr. Jones's retirement benefits?
    c. Assume now that CC hires Mr. Smith at the same $20,000 salary as Mr. Jones. However, Mr. Smith is 45 years old. Repeat the analysis in Parts a and b under the same assumptions used for Mr. Jones. What do the results imply about the costs of hiring older versus younger workers?
    d. Now assume that CC hires Ms. Brown, age 20, at the same time that it hires Mr. Smith. Ms. Brown is expected to retire at age 65 and to live to age 90. What is CC's annual pension cost for Ms. Brown? If Mr. Smith and Ms. Brown are doing the same work, are they truly doing it for the same pay? Would it be "reasonable" for CC to lower Ms. Brown's annual retirement benefit to a level that would mean that she received the same present value as Mr. Smith?

28-2
Performance Measurement

Houston Metals Inc. has a small pension fund which is managed by a professional portfolio manager. All of the fund's assets are invested in corporate equities. Last year, the portfolio manager realized a rate of return of 18 percent. The risk-free rate was 10 percent and the market risk premium was 6 percent. The portfolio's beta was 1.2.
    a. Compute the portfolio's alpha.
    b. What does the portfolio alpha imply about the manager's performance last year?
    c. What can the firm's financial manager conclude about the portfolio manager's performance next year?

28-3
Plan Funding
Consolidated Industries is planning to operate for 10 more years and then cease operations. At that time (in 10 years), it expects to have the following pension benefit obligations:

YEARS	ANNUAL TOTAL PAYMENT
11–15	$2,500,000
16–20	2,000,000
21–25	1,500,000
26–30	1,000,000
31–35	500,000

The current value of the firm's pension fund is $6 million. Assume that all cash flows occur at year-end.
a. Consolidated's actuarial rate of return is 10 percent. What is the present value of the firm's pension fund benefits?
b. Is the plan underfunded or overfunded?

MINI CASE

Southeast Tile Distributors Inc. is a building tile wholesaler that originated in Atlanta but is now considering expansion throughout the region to take advantage of continued strong population growth. The company has been a "mom and pop" operation supplemented by part-time workers, so it currently has no corporate retirement plan. However, the firm's owner, Andy Johnson, believes that it will be necessary to start a corporate pension plan to attract the quality employees needed to make the expansion succeed. Andy has asked you, a recent business school graduate who has just joined the firm, to learn all that you can about pension funds, and then prepare a briefing paper on the subject. To help you get started, he sketched out the following questions:
a. How important are pension funds to the U.S. economy?
b. Define the following pension fund terms:
   (1) Defined benefit plan
   (2) Defined contribution plan
   (3) Profit sharing plan
   (4) Vesting
   (5) Portability
   (6) Fully funded; overfunded; underfunded
   (7) Actuarial rate of return
   (8) Employee Retirement Income Security Act (ERISA)
   (9) Pension Benefit Guarantee Corporation (PBGC)
c. What two organizations provide guidelines for reporting pension fund activities to stockholders? Describe briefly how pension fund data are reported in a firm's financial statements. (Hint: Consider both defined contribution and defined benefit plans.)
d. Assume that an employee joins the firm at age 25, works for 40 years to age 65, and then retires. The employee lives another 15 years, to age 80, and during retirement draws a pension of $20,000 at the end of each year. How much must the firm contribute annually (at year-end) over the employee's working life to fully fund the plan by retirement age if the plan's actuarial rate of return is 10 percent? Draw a graph which shows the value of the employee's pension fund over time. Why is real-world pension fund management much more complex than indicated in this illustration?
e. Discuss the risks to both the plan sponsor and plan beneficiaries under the three types of pension plans.
f. How does the type of pension plan influence decisions in each of the following areas:
   (1) The possibility of age discrimination in hiring?
   (2) The possibility of sex discrimination in hiring?
   (3) Employee training costs?
   (4) The militancy of unions when a company faces financial adversity?
g. What are the two components of a plan's funding strategy? What is the primary goal of a plan's investment strategy?

h. How can a corporate financial manager judge the performance of pension plan managers?
i. What is meant by "tapping" pension fund assets? Why is this action so controversial?
j. What has happened to the cost of retiree health benefits over the last decade? How are retiree health benefits reported to shareholders?

Selected Additional References

For more information on how pension fund management has been affected by the Employee Retirement Income Security Act of 1974 (ERISA), including the establishment of the Pension Benefit Guarantee Corporation (PBGC), see

Treynor, Jack L., W. Priest, and Patrick J. Regan, *The Financial Reality of Pension Funding Under ERISA* (Homewood, Ill.: Dow Jones-Irwin, 1976).

The following articles provide additional insights into the relationship between pension plan funding and capital costs:

Malley, Susan L., "Unfunded Pension Liabilities and the Cost of Equity Capital," *Financial Review,* May 1983, 133–145.

Regan, Patrick J., "Pension Fund Perspective: Credit Ratings and Pension Costs," *Financial Analysts Journal,* September–October 1983, 19–23.

For more information on pension plan terminations, see

Alderson, Michael J., and K. C. Chen, "The Consequences of Terminating the Pension Fund," *Midland Corporate Finance Journal,* Winter 1987, 55–61.

Haw, In-Mu, William Ruland, and Ahmed Hamdallah, "Investor Evaluation of Overfunded Pension Plan Terminations," *Journal of Financial Research,* Spring 1988, 81–88.

Other pertinent works include

Bicksler, James L., and Andrew H. Chen, "The Integration of Insurance and Taxes in Corporate Pension Strategy," *Journal of Finance,* July 1985, 943–957.

Black, Fischer, "The Tax Consequences of Long-Run Pension Policy," *Financial Analysts Journal,* July–August 1980, 25–31.

Bodie, Zvi, "Pension Funds and Financial Innovation," *Financial Management,* Autumn 1990, 11–22.

Bodie, Zvi, and Leslie E. Papke, "Pension Fund Finance," *Pensions and the Economy,* Zvi Bodie and Alicia H. Munnell, eds. (Philadelphia: University of Pennsylvania Press, 1992).

Bodie, Zvi, and J. Shoren, eds., *Financial Aspects of the United States Pension System* (Chicago: University of Chicago Press, 1983).

Bulow, Jeremy I., "What Are Corporate Pension Liabilities?" *Quarterly Journal of Economics,* August 1982, 435–452.

Copeland, Thomas E., "An Economic Approach to Pension Fund Management," *Midland Corporate Finance Journal,* Spring 1984, 26–39.

Datta, Sudip, Mai E. Iskandar-Datta, and Edward J. Zychowicz, "Managerial Self-Interest, Pension Financial Slack and Corporate Pension Funding," *Financial Review,* November 1996, 695–720.

Logue, Dennis E., *Managing Corporate Pension Plans* (New York: HarperCollins, 1991).

Munnell, Alicia H., "Guaranteeing Private Pension Benefits: A Potentially Expensive Business," *New England Economic Review,* March–April 1982, 24–47.

Oldfield, G. S., "Financial Aspects of the Private Pension System," *Journal of Money, Credit and Banking,* February 1977, 48–54.

Roe, Mark J., "The Modern Corporation and Private Pensions: Strong Managers, Weak Owners," *Journal of Applied Corporate Finance,* Summer 1995, 111–119.

Warshawsky, Mark J., "Pension Plans: Funding, Assets, and Regulatory Environment," *Federal Reserve Bulletin,* November 1988, 717–730.

Warshawsky, Mark J., H. Fred Mittelstaedt, and Carrie Cristea, "Recognizing Retiree Health Benefits: The Effect of SFAS 106," *Financial Management,* Summer 1993, 188–199.

For an excellent discussion of the relationship between pension funding policy and the firm's overall financial policy, see

Bodie, Zvi, Jay O. Light, Randall Morck, and Robert A. Taggart, Jr., "Funding and Asset Allocation in Corporate Pension Plans: An Empirical Investigation," National Bureau of Economic Research Working Paper #1315.

The Winter 1994 issue of the Journal of Applied Corporate Finance *contains several articles pertaining to pension plan management.*

Mathematical Tables

TABLE A-1   Present Value of $1 Due at the End of n Periods

Equation: **Financial Calculator Keys:**

$$PVIF_{i,n} = \frac{1}{(1 + i)^n}$$

n   i   0   1.0

[N]   [I]   [PV]   [PMT]   [FV]

TABLE
VALUE

Period	1%	2%	3%	4%	5%	6%	7%	8%	9%	10%
1	.9901	.9804	.9709	.9615	.9524	.9434	.9346	.9259	.9174	.9091
2	.9803	.9612	.9426	.9246	.9070	.8900	.8734	.8573	.8417	.8264
3	.9706	.9423	.9151	.8890	.8638	.8396	.8163	.7938	.7722	.7513
4	.9610	.9238	.8885	.8548	.8227	.7921	.7629	.7350	.7084	.6830
5	.9515	.9057	.8626	.8219	.7835	.7473	.7130	.6806	.6499	.6209
6	.9420	.8880	.8375	.7903	.7462	.7050	.6663	.6302	.5963	.5645
7	.9327	.8706	.8131	.7599	.7107	.6651	.6227	.5835	.5470	.5132
8	.9235	.8535	.7894	.7307	.6768	.6274	.5820	.5403	.5019	.4665
9	.9143	.8368	.7664	.7026	.6446	.5919	.5439	.5002	.4604	.4241
10	.9053	.8203	.7441	.6756	.6139	.5584	.5083	.4632	.4224	.3855
11	.8963	.8043	.7224	.6496	.5847	.5268	.4751	.4289	.3875	.3505
12	.8874	.7885	.7014	.6246	.5568	.4970	.4440	.3971	.3555	.3186
13	.8787	.7730	.6810	.6006	.5303	.4688	.4150	.3677	.3262	.2897
14	.8700	.7579	.6611	.5775	.5051	.4423	.3878	.3405	.2992	.2633
15	.8613	.7430	.6419	.5553	.4810	.4173	.3624	.3152	.2745	.2394
16	.8528	.7284	.6232	.5339	.4581	.3936	.3387	.2919	.2519	.2176
17	.8444	.7142	.6050	.5134	.4363	.3714	.3166	.2703	.2311	.1978
18	.8360	.7002	.5874	.4936	.4155	.3503	.2959	.2502	.2120	.1799
19	.8277	.6864	.5703	.4746	.3957	.3305	.2765	.2317	.1945	.1635
20	.8195	.6730	.5537	.4564	.3769	.3118	.2584	.2145	.1784	.1486
21	.8114	.6598	.5375	.4388	.3589	.2942	.2415	.1987	.1637	.1351
22	.8034	.6468	.5219	.4220	.3418	.2775	.2257	.1839	.1502	.1228
23	.7954	.6342	.5067	.4057	.3256	.2618	.2109	.1703	.1378	.1117
24	.7876	.6217	.4919	.3901	.3101	.2470	.1971	.1577	.1264	.1015
25	.7798	.6095	.4776	.3751	.2953	.2330	.1842	.1460	.1160	.0923
26	.7720	.5976	.4637	.3607	.2812	.2198	.1722	.1352	.1064	.0839
27	.7644	.5859	.4502	.3468	.2678	.2074	.1609	.1252	.0976	.0763
28	.7568	.5744	.4371	.3335	.2551	.1956	.1504	.1159	.0895	.0693
29	.7493	.5631	.4243	.3207	.2429	.1846	.1406	.1073	.0822	.0630
30	.7419	.5521	.4120	.3083	.2314	.1741	.1314	.0994	.0754	.0573
35	.7059	.5000	.3554	.2534	.1813	.1301	.0937	.0676	.0490	.0356
40	.6717	.4529	.3066	.2083	.1420	.0972	.0668	.0460	.0318	.0221
45	.6391	.4102	.2644	.1712	.1113	.0727	.0476	.0313	.0207	.0137
50	.6080	.3715	.2281	.1407	.0872	.0543	.0339	.0213	.0134	.0085
55	.5785	.3365	.1968	.1157	.0683	.0406	.0242	.0145	.0087	.0053

TABLE A-1   *continued*

PERIOD	12%	14%	15%	16%	18%	20%	24%	28%	32%	36%
1	.8929	.8772	.8696	.8621	.8475	.8333	.8065	.7813	.7576	.7353
2	.7972	.7695	.7561	.7432	.7182	.6944	.6504	.6104	.5739	5407
3	.7118	.6750	.6575	.6407	.6086	.5787	.5245	.4768	.4348	.3975
4	.6355	.5921	.5718	.5523	.5158	.4823	.4230	.3725	.3294	.2923
5	.5674	.5194	.4972	.4761	.4371	.4019	.3411	.2910	.2495	.2149
6	.5066	.4556	.4323	.4104	.3704	.3349	.2751	.2274	.1890	.1580
7	.4523	.3996	.3759	.3538	.3139	.2791	.2218	.1776	.1432	.1162
8	.4039	.3506	.3269	.3050	.2660	.2326	.1789	.1388	.1085	.0854
9	.3606	.3075	.2843	.2630	.2255	.1938	.1443	.1084	.0822	.0628
10	.3220	.2697	.2472	.2267	.1911	.1615	.1164	.0847	.0623	.0462
11	.2875	.2366	.2149	.1954	.1619	.1346	.0938	.0662	.0472	.0340
12	.2567	.2076	.1869	.1685	.1372	.1122	.0757	.0517	.0357	.0250
13	.2292	.1821	.1625	.1452	.1163	.0935	.0610	.0404	.0271	.0184
14	.2046	.1597	.1413	.1252	.0985	.0779	.0492	.0316	.0205	.0135
15	.1827	.1401	.1229	.1079	.0835	.0649	.0397	.0247	.0155	.0099
16	.1631	.1229	.1069	.0930	.0708	.0541	.0320	.0193	.0118	.0073
17	.1456	.1078	.0929	.0802	.0600	.0451	.0258	.0150	.0089	.0054
18	.1300	.0946	.0808	.0691	.0508	.0376	.0208	.0118	.0068	.0039
19	.1161	.0829	.0703	.0596	.0431	.0313	.0168	.0092	.0051	.0029
20	.1037	.0728	.0611	.0514	.0365	.0261	.0135	.0072	.0039	.0021
21	.0926	.0638	.0531	.0443	.0309	.0217	.0109	.0056	.0029	.0016
22	.0826	.0560	.0462	.0382	.0262	.0181	.0088	.0044	.0022	.0012
23	.0738	.0491	.0402	.0329	.0222	.0151	.0071	.0034	.0017	.0008
24	.0659	.0431	.0349	.0284	.0188	.0126	.0057	.0027	.0013	.0006
25	.0588	.0378	.0304	.0245	.0160	.0105	.0046	.0021	.0010	.0005
26	.0525	.0331	.0264	.0211	.0135	.0087	.0037	.0016	.0007	.0003
27	.0469	.0291	.0230	.0182	.0115	.0073	.0030	.0013	.0006	.0002
28	.0419	.0255	.0200	.0157	.0097	.0061	.0024	.0010	.0004	.0002
29	.0374	.0224	.0174	.0135	.0082	.0051	.0020	.0008	.0003	.0001
30	.0334	.0196	.0151	.0116	.0070	.0042	.0016	.0006	.0002	.0001
35	.0189	.0102	.0075	.0055	.0030	.0017	.0005	.0002	.0001	*
40	.0107	.0053	.0037	.0026	.0013	.0007	.0002	.0001	*	*
45	.0061	.0027	.0019	.0013	.0006	.0003	.0001	*	*	*
50	.0035	.0014	.0009	.0006	.0003	.0001	*	*	*	*
55	.0020	.0007	.0005	.0003	.0001	*	*	*	*	*

*The factor is zero to four decimal places.

TABLE A-2	Present Value of an Annuity of $1 per Period for **n** Periods

Equation:

$$PVIFA_{i,n} = \sum_{t=1}^{n} \frac{1}{(1+i)^t} = \frac{1 - \frac{1}{(1+i)^n}}{i} = \frac{1}{i} - \frac{1}{i(1+i)^n}$$

Financial Calculator Keys:

n	i	1.0	0
N	I	PV	PMT	FV

TABLE
VALUE

NUMBER OF PERIODS	1%	2%	3%	4%	5%	6%	7%	8%	9%
1	0.9901	0.9804	0.9709	0.9615	0.9524	0.9434	0.9346	0.9259	0.9174
2	1.9704	1.9416	1.9135	1.8861	1.8594	1.8334	1.8080	1.7833	1.7591
3	2.9410	2.8839	2.8286	2.7751	2.7232	2.6730	2.6243	2.5771	2.5313
4	3.9020	3.8077	3.7171	3.6299	3.5460	3.4651	3.3872	3.3121	3.2397
5	4.8534	4.7135	4.5797	4.4518	4.3295	4.2124	4.1002	3.9927	3.8897
6	5.7955	5.6014	5.4172	5.2421	5.0757	4.9173	4.7665	4.6229	4.4859
7	6.7282	6.4720	6.2303	6.0021	5.7864	5.5824	5.3893	5.2064	5.0330
8	7.6517	7.3255	7.0197	6.7327	6.4632	6.2098	5.9713	5.7466	5.5348
9	8.5660	8.1622	7.7861	7.4353	7.1078	6.8017	6.5152	6.2469	5.9952
10	9.4713	8.9826	8.5302	8.1109	7.7217	7.3601	7.0236	6.7101	6.4177
11	10.3676	9.7868	9.2526	8.7605	8.3064	7.8869	7.4987	7.1390	6.8052
12	11.2551	10.5753	9.9540	9.3851	8.8633	8.3838	7.9427	7.5361	7.1607
13	12.1337	11.3484	10.6350	9.9856	9.3936	8.8527	8.3577	7.9038	7.4869
14	13.0037	12.1062	11.2961	10.5631	9.8986	9.2950	8.7455	8.2442	7.7862
15	13.8651	12.8493	11.9379	11.1184	10.3797	9.7122	9.1079	8.5595	8.0607
16	14.7179	13.5777	12.5611	11.6523	10.8378	10.1059	9.4466	8.8514	8.3126
17	15.5623	14.2919	13.1661	12.1657	11.2741	10.4773	9.7632	9.1216	8.5436
18	16.3983	14.9920	13.7535	12.6593	11.6896	10.8276	10.0591	9.3719	8.7556
19	17.2260	15.6785	14.3238	13.1339	12.0853	11.1581	10.3356	9.6036	8.9501
20	18.0456	16.3514	14.8775	13.5903	12.4622	11.4699	10.5940	9.8181	9.1285
21	18.8570	17.0112	15.4150	14.0292	12.8212	11.7641	10.8355	10.0168	9.2922
22	19.6604	17.6580	15.9369	14.4511	13.1630	12.0416	11.0612	10.2007	9.4424
23	20.4558	18.2922	16.4436	14.8568	13.4886	12.3034	11.2722	10.3711	9.5802
24	21.2434	18.9139	16.9355	15.2470	13.7986	12.5504	11.4693	10.5288	9.7066
25	22.0232	19.5235	17.4131	15.6221	14.0939	12.7834	11.6536	10.6748	9.8226
26	22.7952	20.1210	17.8768	15.9828	14.3752	13.0032	11.8258	10.8100	9.9290
27	23.5596	20.7069	18.3270	16.3296	14.6430	13.2105	11.9867	10.9352	10.0266
28	24.3164	21.2813	18.7641	16.6631	14.8981	13.4062	12.1371	11.0511	10.1161
29	25.0658	21.8444	19.1885	16.9837	15.1411	13.5907	12.2777	11.1584	10.1983
30	25.8077	22.3965	19.6004	17.2920	15.3725	13.7648	12.4090	11.2578	10.2737
35	29.4086	24.9986	21.4872	18.6646	16.3742	14.4982	12.9477	11.6546	10.5668
40	32.8347	27.3555	23.1148	19.7928	17.1591	15.0463	13.3317	11.9246	10.7574
45	36.0945	29.4902	24.5187	20.7200	17.7741	15.4558	13.6055	12.1084	10.8812
50	39.1961	31.4236	25.7298	21.4822	18.2559	15.7619	13.8007	12.2335	10.9617
55	42.1472	33.1748	26.7744	22.1086	18.6335	15.9905	13.9399	12.3186	11.0140

TABLE A-2 *continued*

NUMBER OF PERIODS	10%	12%	14%	15%	16%	18%	20%	24%	28%	32%
1	0.9091	0.8929	0.8772	0.8696	0.8621	0.8475	0.8333	0.8065	0.7813	0.7576
2	1.7355	1.6901	1.6467	1.6257	1.6052	1.5656	1.5278	1.4568	1.3916	1.3315
3	2.4869	2.4018	2.3216	2.2832	2.2459	2.1743	2.1065	1.9813	1.8684	1.7663
4	3.1699	3.0373	2.9137	2.8550	2.7982	2.6901	2.5887	2.4043	2.2410	2.0957
5	3.7908	3.6048	3.4331	3.3522	3.2743	3.1272	2.9906	2.7454	2.5320	2.3452
6	4.3553	4.1114	3.8887	3.7845	3.6847	3.4976	3.3255	3.0205	2.7594	2.5342
7	4.8684	4.5638	4.2883	4.1604	4.0386	3.8115	3.6046	3.2423	2.9370	2.6775
8	5.3349	4.9676	4.6389	4.4873	4.3436	4.0776	3.8372	3.4212	3.0758	2.7860
9	5.7590	5.3282	4.9464	4.7716	4.6065	4.3030	4.0310	3.5655	3.1842	2.8681
10	6.1446	5.6502	5.2161	5.0188	4.8332	4.4941	4.1925	3.6819	3.2689	2.9304
11	6.4951	5.9377	5.4527	5.2337	5.0286	4.6560	4.3271	3.7757	3.3351	2.9776
12	6.8137	6.1944	5.6603	5.4206	5.1971	4.7932	4.4392	3.8514	3.3868	3.0133
13	7.1034	6.4235	5.8424	5.5831	5.3423	4.9095	4.5327	3.9124	3.4272	3.0404
14	7.3667	6.6282	6.0021	5.7245	5.4675	5.0081	4.6106	3.9616	3.4587	3.0609
15	7.6061	6.8109	6.1422	5.8474	5.5755	5.0916	4.6755	4.0013	3.4834	3.0764
16	7.8237	6.9740	6.2651	5.9542	5.6685	5.1624	4.7296	4.0333	3.5026	3.0882
17	8.0216	7.1196	6.3729	6.0472	5.7487	5.2223	4.7746	4.0591	3.5177	3.0971
18	8.2014	7.2497	6.4674	6.1280	5.8178	5.2732	4.8122	4.0799	3.5294	3.1039
19	8.3649	7.3658	6.5504	6.1982	5.8775	5.3162	4.8435	4.0967	3.5386	3.1090
20	8.5136	7.4694	6.6231	6.2593	5.9288	5.3527	4.8696	4.1103	3.5458	3.1129
21	8.6487	7.5620	6.6870	6.3125	5.9731	5.3837	4.8913	4.1212	3.5514	3.1158
22	8.7715	7.6446	6.7429	6.3587	6.0113	5.4099	4.9094	4.1300	3.5558	3.1180
23	8.8832	7.7184	6.7921	6.3988	6.0442	5.4321	4.9245	4.1371	3.5592	3.1197
24	8.9847	7.7843	6.8351	6.4338	6.0726	5.4509	4.9371	4.1428	3.5619	3.1210
25	9.0770	7.8431	6.8729	6.4641	6.0971	5.4669	4.9476	4.1474	3.5640	3.1220
26	9.1609	7.8957	6.9061	6.4906	6.1182	5.4804	4.9563	4.1511	3.5656	3.1227
27	9.2372	7.9426	6.9352	6.5135	6.1364	5.4919	4.9636	4.1542	3.5669	3.1233
28	9.3066	7.9844	6.9607	6.5335	6.1520	5.5016	4.9697	4.1566	3.5679	3.1237
29	9.3696	8.0218	6.9830	6.5509	6.1656	5.5098	4.9747	4.1585	3.5687	3.1240
30	9.4269	8.0552	7.0027	6.5660	6.1772	5.5168	4.9789	4.1601	3.5693	3.1242
35	9.6442	8.1755	7.0700	6.6166	6.2153	5.5386	4.9915	4.1644	3.5708	3.1248
40	9.7791	8.2438	7.1050	6.6418	6.2335	5.5482	4.9966	4.1659	3.5712	3.1250
45	9.8628	8.2825	7.1232	6.6543	6.2421	5.5523	4.9986	4.1664	3.5714	3.1250
50	9.9148	8.3045	7.1327	6.6605	6.2463	5.5541	4.9995	4.1666	3.5714	3.1250
55	9.9471	8.3170	7.1376	6.6636	6.2482	5.5549	4.9998	4.1666	3.5714	3.1250

TABLE A-3	Future Value of $1 at the End of **n** Periods

Equation: **Financial Calculator Keys:**

$FVIF_{i,n} = (1 + i)^n$ n   i   1.0   0

[N] [I] [PV] [PMT] [FV]

TABLE
VALUE

PERIOD	1%	2%	3%	4%	5%	6%	7%	8%	9%	10%
1	1.0100	1.0200	1.0300	1.0400	1.0500	1.0600	1.0700	1.0800	1.0900	1.1000
2	1.0201	1.0404	1.0609	1.0816	1.1025	1.1236	1.1449	1.1664	1.1881	1.2100
3	1.0303	1.0612	1.0927	1.1249	1.1576	1.1910	1.2250	1.2597	1.2950	1.3310
4	1.0406	1.0824	1.1255	1.1699	1.2155	1.2625	1.3108	1.3605	1.4116	1.4641
5	1.0510	1.1041	1.1593	1.2167	1.2763	1.3382	1.4026	1.4693	1.5386	1.6105
6	1.0615	1.1262	1.1941	1.2653	1.3401	1.4185	1.5007	1.5869	1.6771	1.7716
7	1.0721	1.1487	1.2299	1.3159	1.4071	1.5036	1.6058	1.7138	1.8280	1.9487
8	1.0829	1.1717	1.2668	1.3686	1.4775	1.5938	1.7182	1.8509	1.9926	2.1436
9	1.0937	1.1951	1.3048	1.4233	1.5513	1.6895	1.8385	1.9990	2.1719	2.3579
10	1.1046	1.2190	1.3439	1.4802	1.6289	1.7908	1.9672	2.1589	2.3674	2.5937
11	1.1157	1.2434	1.3842	1.5395	1.7103	1.8983	2.1049	2.3316	2.5804	2.8531
12	1.1268	1.2682	1.4258	1.6010	1.7959	2.0122	2.2522	2.5182	2.8127	3.1384
13	1.1381	1.2936	1.4685	1.6651	1.8856	2.1329	2.4098	2.7196	3.0658	3.4523
14	1.1495	1.3195	1.5126	1.7317	1.9799	2.2609	2.5785	2.9372	3.3417	3.7975
15	1.1610	1.3459	1.5580	1.8009	2.0789	2.3966	2.7590	3.1722	3.6425	4.1772
16	1.1726	1.3728	1.6047	1.8730	2.1829	2.5404	2.9522	3.4259	3.9703	4.5950
17	1.1843	1.4002	1.6528	1.9479	2.2920	2.6928	3.1588	3.7000	4.3276	5.0545
18	1.1961	1.4282	1.7024	2.0258	2.4066	2.8543	3.3799	3.9960	4.7171	5.5599
19	1.2081	1.4568	1.7535	2.1068	2.5270	3.0256	3.6165	4.3157	5.1417	6.1159
20	1.2202	1.4859	1.8061	2.1911	2.6533	3.2071	3.8697	4.6610	5.6044	6.7275
21	1.2324	1.5157	1.8603	2.2788	2.7860	3.3996	4.1406	5.0338	6.1088	7.4002
22	1.2447	1.5460	1.9161	2.3699	2.9253	3.6035	4.4304	5.4365	6.6586	8.1403
23	1.2572	1.5769	1.9736	2.4647	3.0715	3.8197	4.7405	5.8715	7.2579	8.9543
24	1.2697	1.6084	2.0328	2.5633	3.2251	4.0489	5.0724	6.3412	7.9111	9.8497
25	1.2824	1.6406	2.0938	2.6658	3.3864	4.2919	5.4274	6.8485	8.6231	10.835
26	1.2953	1.6734	2.1566	2.7725	3.5557	4.5494	5.8074	7.3964	9.3992	11.918
27	1.3082	1.7069	2.2213	2.8834	3.7335	4.8223	6.2139	7.9881	10.245	13.110
28	1.3213	1.7410	2.2879	2.9987	3.9201	5.1117	6.6488	8.6271	11.167	14.421
29	1.3345	1.7758	2.3566	3.1187	4.1161	5.4184	7.1143	9.3173	12.172	15.863
30	1.3478	1.8114	2.4273	3.2434	4.3219	5.7435	7.6123	10.063	13.268	17.449
40	1.4889	2.2080	3.2620	4.8010	7.0400	10.286	14.974	21.725	31.409	45.259
50	1.6446	2.6916	4.3839	7.1067	11.467	18.420	29.457	46.902	74.358	117.39
60	1.8167	3.2810	5.8916	10.520	18.679	32.988	57.946	101.26	176.03	304.48

TABLE A-3 *continued*

PERIOD	12%	14%	15%	16%	18%	20%	24%	28%	32%	36%
1	1.1200	1.1400	1.1500	1.1600	1.1800	1.2000	1.2400	1.2800	1.3200	1.3600
2	1.2544	1.2996	1.3225	1.3456	1.3924	1.4400	1.5376	1.6384	1.7424	1.8496
3	1.4049	1.4815	1.5209	1.5609	1.6430	1.7280	1.9066	2.0972	2.3000	2.5155
4	1.5735	1.6890	1.7490	1.8106	1.9388	2.0736	2.3642	2.6844	3.0360	3.4210
5	1.7623	1.9254	2.0114	2.1003	2.2878	2.4883	2.9316	3.4360	4.0075	4.6526
6	1.9738	2.1950	2.3131	2.4364	2.6996	2.9860	3.6352	4.3980	5.2899	6.3275
7	2.2107	2.5023	2.6600	2.8262	3.1855	3.5832	4.5077	5.6295	6.9826	8.6054
8	2.4760	2.8526	3.0590	3.2784	3.7589	4.2998	5.5895	7.2058	9.2170	11.703
9	2.7731	3.2519	3.5179	3.8030	4.4355	5.1598	6.9310	9.2234	12.166	15.917
10	3.1058	3.7072	4.0456	4.4114	5.2338	6.1917	8.5944	11.806	16.060	21.647
11	3.4785	4.2262	4.6524	5.1173	6.1759	7.4301	10.657	15.112	21.199	29.439
12	3.8960	4.8179	5.3503	5.9360	7.2876	8.9161	13.215	19.343	27.983	40.037
13	4.3635	5.4924	6.1528	6.8858	8.5994	10.699	16.386	24.759	36.937	54.451
14	4.8871	6.2613	7.0757	7.9875	10.147	12.839	20.319	31.691	48.757	74.053
15	5.4736	7.1379	8.1371	9.2655	11.974	15.407	25.196	40.565	64.359	100.71
16	6.1304	8.1372	9.3576	10.748	14.129	18.488	31.243	51.923	84.954	136.97
17	6.8660	9.2765	10.761	12.468	16.672	22.186	38.741	66.461	112.14	186.28
18	7.6900	10.575	12.375	14.463	19.673	26.623	48.039	85.071	148.02	253.34
19	8.6128	12.056	14.232	16.777	23.214	31.948	59.568	108.89	195.39	344.54
20	9.6463	13.743	16.367	19.461	27.393	38.338	73.864	139.38	257.92	468.57
21	10.804	15.668	18.822	22.574	32.324	46.005	91.592	178.41	340.45	637.26
22	12.100	17.861	21.645	26.186	38.142	55.206	113.57	228.36	449.39	866.67
23	13.552	20.362	24.891	30.376	45.008	66.247	140.83	292.30	593.20	1178.7
24	15.179	23.212	28.625	35.236	53.109	79.497	174.63	374.14	783.02	1603.0
25	17.000	26.462	32.919	40.874	62.669	95.396	216.54	478.90	1033.6	2180.1
26	19.040	30.167	37.857	47.414	73.949	114.48	268.51	613.00	1364.3	2964.9
27	21.325	34.390	43.535	55.000	87.260	137.37	332.95	784.64	1800.9	4032.3
28	23.884	39.204	50.066	63.800	102.97	164.84	412.86	1004.3	2377.2	5483.9
29	26.750	44.693	57.575	74.009	121.50	197.81	511.95	1285.6	3137.9	7458.1
30	29.960	50.950	66.212	85.850	143.37	237.38	634.82	1645.5	4142.1	10143.
40	93.051	188.88	267.86	378.72	750.38	1469.8	5455.9	19427.	66521.	*
50	289.00	700.23	1083.7	1670.7	3927.4	9100.4	46890.	*	*	*
60	897.60	2595.9	4384.0	7370.2	20555.	56348.	*	*	*	*

*FVIF > 99,999.

TABLE A-4   Future Value of an Annuity of $1 per Period for n Periods

Equation:

Financial Calculator Keys:

$$FVIFA_{i,n} = \sum_{t=1}^{n} (1 + i)^{n-t} = \frac{(1+i)^n - 1}{i}$$

n   i   0   1.0

[N] [I] [PV] [PMT] [FV]

TABLE
VALUE

NUMBER OF PERIODS	1%	2%	3%	4%	5%	6%	7%	8%	9%	10%
1	1.0000	1.0000	1.0000	1.0000	1.0000	1.0000	1.0000	1.0000	1.0000	1.0000
2	2.0100	2.0200	2.0300	2.0400	2.0500	2.0600	2.0700	2.0800	2.0900	2.1000
3	3.0301	3.0604	3.0909	3.1216	3.1525	3.1836	3.2149	3.2464	3.2781	3.3100
4	4.0604	4.1216	4.1836	4.2465	4.3101	4.3746	4.4399	4.5061	4.5731	4.6410
5	5.1010	5.2040	5.3091	5.4163	5.5256	5.6371	5.7507	5.8666	5.9847	6.1051
6	6.1520	6.3081	6.4684	6.6330	6.8019	6.9753	7.1533	7.3359	7.5233	7.7156
7	7.2135	7.4343	7.6625	7.8983	8.1420	8.3938	8.6540	8.9228	9.2004	9.4872
8	8.2857	8.5830	8.8923	9.2142	9.5491	9.8975	10.260	10.637	11.028	11.436
9	9.3685	9.7546	10.159	10.583	11.027	11.491	11.978	12.488	13.021	13.579
10	10.462	10.950	11.464	12.006	12.578	13.181	13.816	14.487	15.193	15.937
11	11.567	12.169	12.808	13.486	14.207	14.972	15.784	16.645	17.560	18.531
12	12.683	13.412	14.192	15.026	15.917	16.870	17.888	18.977	20.141	21.384
13	13.809	14.680	15.618	16.627	17.713	18.882	20.141	21.495	22.953	24.523
14	14.947	15.974	17.086	18.292	19.599	21.015	22.550	24.215	26.019	27.975
15	16.097	17.293	18.599	20.024	21.579	23.276	25.129	27.152	29.361	31.772
16	17.258	18.639	20.157	21.825	23.657	25.673	27.888	30.324	33.003	35.950
17	18.430	20.012	21.762	23.698	25.840	28.213	30.840	33.750	36.974	40.545
18	19.615	21.412	23.414	25.645	28.132	30.906	33.999	37.450	41.301	45.599
19	20.811	22.841	25.117	27.671	30.539	33.760	37.379	41.446	46.018	51.159
20	22.019	24.297	26.870	29.778	33.066	36.786	40.995	45.762	51.160	57.275
21	23.239	25.783	28.676	31.969	35.719	39.993	44.865	50.423	56.765	64.002
22	24.472	27.299	30.537	34.248	38.505	43.392	49.006	55.457	62.873	71.403
23	25.716	28.845	32.453	36.618	41.430	46.996	53.436	60.893	69.532	79.543
24	26.973	30.422	34.426	39.083	44.502	50.816	58.177	66.765	76.790	88.497
25	28.243	32.030	36.459	41.646	47.727	54.865	63.249	73.106	84.701	98.347
26	29.526	33.671	38.553	44.312	51.113	59.156	68.676	79.954	93.324	109.18
27	30.821	35.344	40.710	47.084	54.669	63.706	74.484	87.351	102.72	121.10
28	32.129	37.051	42.931	49.968	58.403	68.528	80.698	95.339	112.97	134.21
29	33.450	38.792	45.219	52.966	62.323	73.640	87.347	103.97	124.14	148.63
30	34.785	40.568	47.575	56.085	66.439	79.058	94.461	113.28	136.31	164.49
40	48.886	60.402	75.401	95.026	120.80	154.76	199.64	259.06	337.88	442.59
50	64.463	84.579	112.80	152.67	209.35	290.34	406.53	573.77	815.08	1163.9
60	81.670	114.05	163.05	237.99	353.58	533.13	813.52	1253.2	1944.8	3034.8

TABLE A-4 *continued*

NUMBER OF PERIODS	12%	14%	15%	16%	18%	20%	24%	28%	32%	36%
1	1.0000	1.0000	1.0000	1.0000	1.0000	1.0000	1.0000	1.0000	1.0000	1.0000
2	2.1200	2.1400	2.1500	2.1600	2.1800	2.2000	2.2400	2.2800	2.3200	2.3600
3	3.3744	3.4396	3.4725	3.5056	3.5724	3.6400	3.7776	3.9184	4.0624	4.2096
4	4.7793	4.9211	4.9934	5.0665	5.2154	5.3680	5.6842	6.0156	6.3624	6.7251
5	6.3528	6.6101	6.7424	6.8771	7.1542	7.4416	8.0484	8.6999	9.3983	10.146
6	8.1152	8.5355	8.7537	8.9775	9.4420	9.9299	10.980	12.136	13.406	14.799
7	10.089	10.730	11.067	11.414	12.142	12.916	14.615	16.534	18.696	21.126
8	12.300	13.233	13.727	14.240	15.327	16.499	19.123	22.163	25.678	29.732
9	14.776	16.085	16.786	17.519	19.086	20.799	24.712	29.369	34.895	41.435
10	17.549	19.337	20.304	21.321	23.521	25.959	31.643	38.593	47.062	57.352
11	20.655	23.045	24.349	25.733	28.755	32.150	40.238	50.398	63.122	78.998
12	24.133	27.271	29.002	30.850	34.931	39.581	50.895	65.510	84.320	108.44
13	28.029	32.089	34.352	36.786	42.219	48.497	64.110	84.853	112.30	148.47
14	32.393	37.581	40.505	43.672	50.818	59.196	80.496	109.61	149.24	202.93
15	37.280	43.842	47.580	51.660	60.965	72.035	100.82	141.30	198.00	276.98
16	42.753	50.980	55.717	60.925	72.939	87.442	126.01	181.87	262.36	377.69
17	48.884	59.118	65.075	71.673	87.068	105.93	157.25	233.79	347.31	514.66
18	55.750	68.394	75.836	84.141	103.74	128.12	195.99	300.25	459.45	700.94
19	63.440	78.969	88.212	98.603	123.41	154.74	244.03	385.32	607.47	954.28
20	72.052	91.025	102.44	115.38	146.63	186.69	303.60	494.21	802.86	1298.8
21	81.699	104.77	118.81	134.84	174.02	225.03	377.46	633.59	1060.8	1767.4
22	92.503	120.44	137.63	157.41	206.34	271.03	469.06	812.00	1401.2	2404.7
23	104.60	138.30	159.28	183.60	244.49	326.24	582.63	1040.4	1850.6	3271.3
24	118.16	158.66	184.17	213.98	289.49	392.48	723.46	1332.7	2443.8	4450.0
25	133.33	181.87	212.79	249.21	342.60	471.98	898.09	1706.8	3226.8	6053.0
26	150.33	208.33	245.71	290.09	405.27	567.38	1114.6	2185.7	4260.4	8233.1
27	169.37	238.50	283.57	337.50	479.22	681.85	1383.1	2798.7	5624.8	11198.0
28	190.70	272.89	327.10	392.50	566.48	819.22	1716.1	3583.3	7425.7	15230.3
29	214.58	312.09	377.17	456.30	669.45	984.07	2129.0	4587.7	9802.9	20714.2
30	241.33	356.79	434.75	530.31	790.95	1181.9	2640.9	5873.2	12941.	28172.3
40	767.09	1342.0	1779.1	2360.8	4163.2	7343.9	22729.	69377.	*	*
50	2400.0	4994.5	7217.7	10436.	21813.	45497.	*	*	*	*
60	7471.6	18535.	29220.	46058.	*	*	*	*	*	*

*FVIF > 99,999.

| TABLE A-5 | | Values of the Areas under the Standard Normal Distribution Function | | | | | | | | |

z	0.00	0.01	0.02	0.03	0.04	0.05	0.06	0.07	0.08	0.09
0.0	.0000	.0040	.0080	.0120	.0160	.0199	.0239	.0279	.0319	.0359
0.1	.0398	.0438	.0478	.0517	.0557	.0596	.0636	.0675	.0714	.0753
0.2	.0793	.0832	.0871	.0910	.0948	.0987	.1026	.1064	.1103	.1141
0.3	.1179	.1217	.1255	.1293	.1331	.1368	.1406	.1443	.1480	.1517
0.4	.1554	.1591	.1628	.1664	.1700	.1736	.1772	.1808	.1844	.1879
0.5	.1915	.1950	.1985	.2019	.2054	.2088	.2123	.2157	.2190	.2224
0.6	.2257	.2291	.2324	.2357	.2389	.2422	.2454	.2486	.2517	.2549
0.7	.2580	.2611	.2642	.2673	.2704	.2734	.2764	.2794	.2823	.2852
0.8	.2881	.2910	.2939	.2967	.2995	.3023	.3051	.3078	.3106	.3133
0.9	.3159	.3186	.3212	.3238	.3264	.3289	.3315	.3340	.3365	.3389
1.0	.3413	.3438	.3461	.3485	.3508	.3531	.3554	.3577	.3599	.3621
1.1	.3643	.3665	.3686	.3708	.3729	.3749	.3770	.3790	.3810	.3830
1.2	.3849	.3869	.3888	.3907	.3925	.3944	.3962	.3980	.3997	.4015
1.3	.4032	.4049	.4066	.4082	.4099	.4115	.4131	.4147	.4162	.4177
1.4	.4192	.4207	.4222	.4236	.4251	.4265	.4279	.4292	.4306	.4319
1.5	.4332	.4345	.4357	.4370	.4382	.4394	.4406	.4418	.4429	.4441
1.6	.4452	.4463	.4474	.4484	.4495	.4505	.4515	.4525	.4535	.4545
1.7	.4554	.4564	.4573	.4582	.4591	.4599	.4608	.4616	.4625	.4633
1.8	.4641	.4649	.4656	.4664	.4671	.4678	.4686	.4693	.4699	.4706
1.9	.4713	.4719	.4726	.4732	.4738	.4744	.4750	.4756	.4761	.4767
2.0	.4773	.4778	.4783	.4788	.4793	.4798	.4803	.4808	.4812	.4817
2.1	.4821	.4826	.4830	.4834	.4838	.4842	.4846	.4850	.4854	.4857
2.2	.4861	.4864	.4868	.4871	.4875	.4878	.4881	.4884	.4887	.4890
2.3	.4893	.4896	.4898	.4901	.4904	.4906	.4909	.4911	.4913	.4916
2.4	.4918	.4920	.4922	.4925	.4927	.4929	.4931	.4932	.4934	.4936
2.5	.4938	.4940	.4941	.4943	.4945	.4946	.4948	.4949	.4951	.4952
2.6	.4953	.4955	.4956	.4957	.4959	.4960	.4961	.4962	.4963	.4964
2.7	.4965	.4966	.4967	.4968	.4969	.4970	.4971	.4972	.4973	.4974
2.8	.4974	.4975	.4976	.4977	.4977	.4978	.4979	.4979	.4980	.4981
2.9	.4981	.4982	.4982	.4982	.4984	.4984	.4985	.4985	.4986	.4986
3.0	.4987	.4987	.4987	.4988	.4988	.4989	.4989	.4989	.4990	.4990

SOLUTIONS TO SELF-TEST PROBLEMS

Chapter 2

ST-1 a.

EBIT	$5,000,000
Interest	1,000,000
EBT	$4,000,000
Taxes (40%)	1,600,000
Net income	$2,400,000

b.
$$NCF = NI + DEP$$
$$= \$2,400,000 + \$1,000,000 = \$3,400,000.$$

c.
$$NOPAT = EBIT (1 - T)$$
$$= \$5,000,000 (0.6)$$
$$= \$3,000,000.$$

d.
$$OCF = EBIT (1 - T) + DEP$$
$$= \$5,000,000 (0.6) + \$1,000,000$$
$$= \$4,000,000.$$

e.
$$FCF = NOPAT - \text{Net investment in operating capital}$$
$$= \$3,000,000 - (\$25,000,000 - \$24,000,000)$$
$$= \$2,000,000.$$

f.
$$EVA = EBIT (1 - T) - (\text{Total capital}) (\text{After-tax cost of capital})$$
$$= \$5,000,000 (0.6) - (\$25,000,000) (0.10)$$
$$= \$3,000,000 - \$2,500,000 = \$500,000.$$

ST-2

	1999	2000	2001
Henderson's Taxes as a Corporation			
Income before salary and taxes	$52,700	$90,000	$150,000
Less: salary	(40,000)	(40,000)	(40,000)
Taxable income, corporate	$12,700	$50,000	$110,000
Total corporate tax	1,905[a]	7,500	26,150
Salary	$40,000	$40,000	$ 40,000
Less exemptions and deductions	(17,650)	(17,650)	(17,650)
Taxable personal income	$22,350	$22,350	$ 22,350
Total personal tax	3,353[b]	3,353	3,353
Combined corporate and personal tax:	$ 5,258	$10,853	$ 29,503

	1999	**2000**	**2001**
Henderson's Taxes as a Proprietorship			
Total Income	$52,700	$90,000	$150,000
Less: exemptions and deductions	(17,650)	(17,650)	(17,650)
Taxable personal income	$35,050	$72,350	$132,350
Tax liability of proprietorship	$ 5,258[c]	$14,902	$ 32,685
Advantage to being a corporation:	$ 0	$ 4,049	$ 3,182

[a]Corporate tax in 1999 = (0.15)($12,700) = $1,905.
[b]Personal tax (if Henderson incorporates) in 1999 = (0.15)($22,350) = $3,353.
[c]Proprietorship tax in 1999 = (0.15)($35,350) = $5,258.

Notice that in 1999, both the corporate form of organization and the proprietorship form have the same tax liability; however, in 2000 and 2001, the corporate form has the lower tax liability. Thus, the corporate form of organization allows Henderson to pay the lowest taxes in each year. Therefore, on the basis of taxes over the 3-year period, Henderson should incorporate her business. However, note that to get additional money out of the corporation so she can spend it, Henderson will have to have the corporation pay dividends, which will be taxed to Henderson, and thus she will, sometime in the future, have to pay additional taxes.

Chapter 3

ST-1   Billingsworth paid $2 in dividends and retained $2 per share. Since total retained earnings rose by $12 million, there must be 6 million shares outstanding. With a book value of $40 per share, total common equity must be $40(6 million) = $240 million. Since Billingsworth has $120 million of debt, its debt ratio must be 33.3 percent:

$$\frac{\text{Debt}}{\text{Assets}} = \frac{\text{Debt}}{\text{Debt} + \text{Equity}} = \frac{\$120 \text{ million}}{\$120 \text{ million} + \$240 \text{ million}}$$

$$= 0.333 = 33.3\%.$$

ST-2   a. In answering questions such as this, always begin by writing down the relevant definitional equations, then start filling in numbers. Note that the extra zeros indicating millions have been deleted in the calculations below.

(1)
$$\text{DSO} = \frac{\text{Accounts receivable}}{\text{Sales}/360}$$

$$40 = \frac{\text{A/R}}{\$1,000/360}$$

$$\text{A/R} = 40(\$2.778) = \$111.1 \text{ million.}$$

(2)
$$\text{Quick ratio} = \frac{\text{Current assets} - \text{Inventories}}{\text{Current liabilities}} = 2.0$$

$$= \frac{\text{Cash and marketable securities} + \text{A/R}}{\text{Current liabilities}} = 2.0$$

$$2.0 = \frac{\$100 + \$111.1}{\text{Current liabilities}}$$

$$\text{Current liabilities} = (\$100 + \$111.1)/2 = \$105.5 \text{ million.}$$

(3)
$$\text{Current ratio} = \frac{\text{Current assets}}{\text{Current liabilities}} = 3.0$$

$$= \frac{\text{Current assets}}{\$105.5} = 3.0$$

$$\text{Current assets} = 3.0(\$105.5) = \$316.50 \text{ million.}$$

(4)   Total assets = Current assets + Fixed assets

$$= \$316.5 + \$283.5 = \$600 \text{ million.}$$

(5)   ROA = Profit margin × Total assets turnover

$$= \frac{\text{Net income}}{\text{Sales}} \times \frac{\text{Sales}}{\text{Total assets}}$$

$$= \frac{\$50}{\$1,000} \times \frac{\$1,000}{\$600}$$

$$= 0.05 \times 1.667 = 0.0833 = 8.33\%.$$

(6)   ROE = ROA × $\frac{\text{Assets}}{\text{Equity}}$

$$12.0\% = 8.33\% \times \frac{\$600}{\text{Equity}}$$

$$\text{Equity} = \frac{(8.33\%)(\$600)}{12.0\%}$$

$$= \$416.50 \text{ million.}$$

(7)   Total assets = Total claims = \$600 million

Current liabilities + Long-term debt + Equity = \$600 million

$$\$105.5 + \text{Long-term debt} + \$416.5 = \$600 \text{ million}$$

$$\text{Long-term debt} = \$600 - \$105.5 - \$416.5 = \$78 \text{ million.}$$

Note: We could have found equity as follows:

$$\text{ROE} = \frac{\text{Net income}}{\text{Equity}}$$

$$12.0\% = \frac{\$50}{\text{Equity}}$$

$$\text{Equity} = \$50/0.12$$

$$= \$416.67 \text{ million (rounding difference).}$$

Then we could have gone on to find current liabilities and long-term debt.

b. Kaiser's average sales per day were $\$1,000/360 = \$2.8$ million. Its DSO was 40, so A/R = $40(\$2.8) = \$111.1$ million. Its new DSO of 30 would cause A/R = $30(\$2.8) = \$83.3$ million. The reduction in receivables would be $\$111.1 - \$83.3 = \$27.8$ million, which would equal the amount of cash generated.

(1)   New equity = Old equity − Stock bought back

$$= \$416.5 - \$27.8$$

$$= \$388.7 \text{ million.}$$

Thus,

$$\text{New ROE} = \frac{\text{Net income}}{\text{New equity}}$$

$$= \frac{\$50}{\$388.7}$$

$$= 12.86\% \text{ (versus old ROE of 12.0\%).}$$

(2)   New ROA = $\dfrac{\text{Net income}}{\text{Total assets} - \text{Reduction in A/R}}$

$$= \frac{\$50}{\$600 - \$27.8}$$

$$= 8.74\% \text{ (versus old ROA of 8.33\%)}.$$

(3) The old debt is the same as the new debt:

$$\text{Debt} = \text{Total claims} - \text{Equity}$$

$$= \$600 - \$416.5 = \$183.5 \text{ million.}$$

$$\text{Old total assets} = \$600 \text{ million.}$$

$$\text{New total assets} = \text{Old total assets} - \text{Reduction in A/R}$$

$$= \$600 - \$27.8$$

$$= \$572.2 \text{ million.}$$

Therefore,

$$\frac{\text{Debt}}{\text{Old total assets}} = \frac{\$183.5}{\$600} = 30.6\%,$$

while

$$\frac{\text{New debt}}{\text{New total assets}} = \frac{\$183.5}{\$572.2} = 32.1\%.$$

Chapter 4

ST-1   a. Average = (4% + 5% + 6% + 7%)/4 = 22%/4 = 5.5%.

b. $k_{\text{T-bond}} = k^* + IP = 2\% + 5.5\% = 7.5\%$.

c. If the 5-year T-bond rate is 8 percent, the inflation rate is expected to average approximately 8% − 2% = 6% during the next 5 years. Thus, the implied Year 5 inflation rate is 8 percent:

$$6\% = (4\% + 5\% + 6\% + 7\% + I_5)/5$$

$$30\% = 22\% + I_5$$

$$I_5 = 8\%.$$

Chapter 5

ST-1   a. The average rate of return for each stock is calculated simply by averaging the returns over the 5-year period. The average return for each stock is 18.90 percent, calculated for Stock A as follows:

$$k_{\text{Avg}} = (-10.00\% + 18.50\% + 38.67\% + 14.33\% + 33.00\%)/5$$

$$= 18.90\%.$$

The realized rate of return on a portfolio made up of Stock A and Stock B would be calculated by finding the average return in each year as k_A(% of Stock A) + k_B(% of Stock B) and then averaging these yearly returns:

YEAR	PORTFOLIO AB'S RETURN, k_{AB}
1994	(6.50%)
1995	19.90
1996	41.46
1997	9.00
1998	30.65
	$k_{\text{Avg}} = 18.90\%$

b. The standard deviation of returns is estimated, using Equation 5-3a, as follows (see Footnote 5):

$$\text{Estimated } \sigma = S = \sqrt{\dfrac{\displaystyle\sum_{t=1}^{n}(\bar{k}_t - \bar{k}_{Avg})^2}{n-1}}.\tag{5-3a}$$

For Stock A, the estimated σ is 19.0 percent:

$$\sigma_A = \sqrt{\dfrac{(-10.00 - 18.9)^2 + (18.50 - 18.9)^2 + \cdots + (33.00 - 18.9)^2}{5-1}}$$

$$= \sqrt{\dfrac{1{,}445.92}{4}} = 19.0\%.$$

The standard deviation of returns for Stock B and for the portfolio are similarly determined, and they are as follows:

	STOCK A	STOCK B	PORTFOLIO AB
Standard deviation	19.0	19.0	18.6

c. Since the risk reduction from diversification is small (σ_{AB} falls only from 19.0 to 18.6 percent), the most likely value of the correlation coefficient is 0.9. If the correlation coefficient were −0.9, the risk reduction would be much larger. In fact, the correlation coefficient between Stocks A and B is 0.92.

d. If more randomly selected stocks were added to a portfolio, σ_p would decline to somewhere in the vicinity of 20 percent; see Figure 5-8. σ_p would remain constant only if the correlation coefficient were +1.0, which is most unlikely. σ_p would decline to zero only if the correlation coefficient, r, were equal to zero and a large number of stocks were added to the portfolio, or if the proper proportions were held in a two-stock portfolio with r = −1.0.

ST-2   a.
$$b = (0.6)(0.70) + (0.25)(0.90) + (0.1)(1.30) + (0.05)(1.50)$$
$$= 0.42 + 0.225 + 0.13 + 0.075 = 0.85.$$

b.
$$k_{RF} = 6\%; \ RP_M = 5\%; \ b = 0.85.$$
$$k = 6\% + (5\%)(0.85)$$
$$= 10.25\%.$$

c.
$$b_N = (0.5)(0.70) + (0.25)(0.09) + (0.1)(1.30) + (0.15)(1.50)$$
$$= 0.35 + 0.225 + 0.13 + 0.225$$
$$= 0.93.$$
$$k = 6\% + (5\%)(0.93)$$
$$= 10.65\%.$$

Chapter 6

ST-1   a. For Security A:

P_A	k_A	$P_A k_A$	$(k_A - \hat{k}_A)$	$(k_A - \hat{k}_A)^2$	$P_A(k_A - \hat{k}_A)^2$
0.1	−10%	−1.0%	−25%	625	62.5
0.2	5	1.0	−10	100	20.0
0.4	15	6.0	0	0	0.0
0.2	25	5.0	10	100	20.0
0.1	40	4.0	25	625	62.5
		$\hat{k}_A = 15\%.$			$\sigma_A = \sqrt{165} = 12.8\%.$

b. $w_A = \dfrac{\sigma_B(\sigma_B - r_{AB}\sigma_A)}{\sigma_A^2 + \sigma_B^2 - 2r_{AB}\sigma_A\sigma_B}$

$= \dfrac{25.7[25.7 - (-0.5)(12.8)]}{(12.8)^2 + (25.7)^2 - 2(-0.5)(12.8)(25.7)}$

$= \dfrac{824.97}{1,153.29} = 0.7153.$

or 71.53% invested in A, 28.47% in B.

c. $\sigma_p = \sqrt{(w_A\sigma_A)^2 + (1 - w_A)^2(\sigma_B)^2 + 2w_A(1 - w_A)r_{AB}\sigma_A\sigma_B}$

$= \sqrt{(0.75)^2(12.8)^2 + (0.25)^2(25.7)^2 + 2(0.75)(0.25)(-0.5)(12.8)(25.7)}$

$= \sqrt{92.16 + 41.28 - 61.68}$

$= \sqrt{71.76} = 8.47\%, \text{ when } w_A = 75\%.$

$\sigma_p = \sqrt{(0.7153)^2(12.8)^2 + (0.2847)^2(25.7)^2 + 2(0.7153)(0.2847)(-0.5)(12.8)(25.7)}$

$= 8.38\%, \text{ when } w_A = 71.53\%. \text{ This is the minimum } \sigma_p.$

$\sigma_p = \sqrt{(0.5)^2(12.8)^2 + (0.5)^2(25.7)^2 + 2(0.5)(0.5)(-0.5)(12.8)(25.7)}$

$= 11.13\%, \text{ when } w_A = 50\%.$

$\sigma_p = \sqrt{(0.25)^2(12.8)^2 + (0.75)^2(25.7)^2 + 2(0.25)(0.75)(-0.5)(12.8)(25.7)}$

$= 17.89\%, \text{ when } w_A = 25\%.$

% IN A	% IN B	$\hat{k}_P$	σ_P
100%	0%	15.00%	12.8%
75	25	16.25	8.5
71.53	28.47	16.42	8.4
50	50	17.50	11.1
25	75	18.75	17.9
0	100	20.00	25.7

Calculations for preceding table:

$\hat{k}_p = w_A(\hat{k}_A) + (1 - w_A)(\hat{k}_B)$

$= 0.75(15) + 0.25(20)$ $= 16.25\%$ when $w_A = 75\%.$

$= 0.7153(15) + 0.2847(20)$ $= 16.42\%$ when $w_A = 71.53\%.$

$= 0.5(15) + 0.5(20)$ $= 17.50\%$ when $w_A = 50\%.$

$= 0.25(15) + 0.75(20)$ $= 18.75\%$ when $w_A = 25\%.$

d.

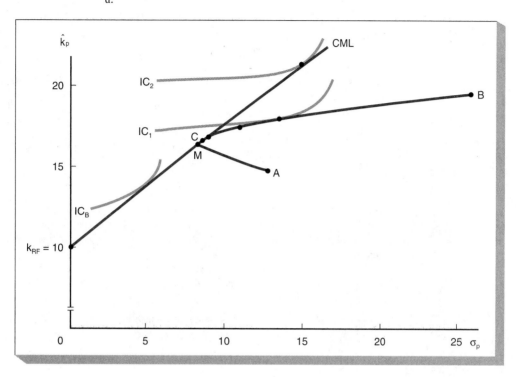

e. See indifference curve IC_1 above. At the point where $\hat{k}_p = 18\%$, $\sigma_p = 13.5\%$.

$$\hat{k}_p = w_A(\hat{k}_A) + (1 - w_A)\,(\hat{k}_B)$$
$$18 = w_A(15) + (1 - w_A)\,(20)$$
$$= 15w_A + 20 - 20w_A$$
$$5w_A = 2$$
$$w_A = 0.4 \text{ or } 40\%.$$

Therefore, to an approximation, your optimal portfolio would have 40 percent in A, 60 percent in B, with $\hat{k}_p = 18\%$ and $\sigma_p = 13.5\%$. (We could get an exact σ_p by using $x = 0.4$ in the equation for σ_p.)

f. The existence of the riskless asset would enable you to go to the CAPM. We would draw in the CML as shown on the graph in Part d. Now you would hold a portfolio of stocks, borrowing on margin to hold more stocks than your net worth, and move to a higher indifference curve, IC_2.

You can put all of your money into the riskless asset, all in A, all in B, or some in each security. The most logical choices are (1) hold a portfolio of A and B plus some of the riskless asset, (2) hold only a portfolio of A and B, or (3) hold a portfolio of A and B and borrow to leverage the portfolio, assuming you can borrow at the riskless rate.

Reading from the graph, we see that your $\hat{k}_p$ at the point of tangency between your IC_2 and the CML is about 22 percent. We can use this information to find out how much you invest in the market portfolio and how much you invest in the riskless asset. (It will turn out that you have a *negative* investment in the riskless asset, which means that you borrow rather than lend at the risk-free rate.

$$\hat{k}_p = w_{RF}(k_{RF}) + (1 - w_{RF})\,(\hat{k}_M)$$
$$22 = w_{RF}(10) + (1 - w_{RF})\,(16.8)$$
$$= 10w_{RF} + 16.8 - 16.8\,w_{RF}$$

$$-6.8 \, w_{RF} = 5.2$$

$$w_{RF} = -0.76 \text{ or } -76\%, \text{ which means that you borrow.}$$

$$1 - w_{RF} = 1.0 - (-0.76)$$

$$= +1.76 \text{ or } 176\% \text{ in the market portfolio.}$$

This investor, with $200,000 of net worth, thus buys stock with a value of $200,000(1.76) = $352,000 and borrows $152,000.

The riskiness of this leveraged portfolio is

$$\sigma_p = \sqrt{(-0.76)^2(0)^2 + (1.76)^2(8.5)^2 + 2(-0.76)(1.76)(0)(8.5)(0)}$$
$$= \sqrt{(1.76)^2(8.5)^2}$$
$$= (1.76)(8.5) = 15\%.$$

Your indifference curve suggests that you are not very risk averse. A risk-averse investor would have a steep indifference curve (visualize a set of steep curves that were tangent to CML to the left of Point C). This investor would hold some of A and B, combined to form portfolio M, and some of the riskless asset.

g. Given your assumed indifference curve, you would, when the riskless asset becomes available, change your portfolio from the one found in Part e (with $\hat{k}_p = 18\%$, $\sigma_p = 13.5\%$) to one with $\hat{k}_p \approx 22.0\%$ and $\sigma_p \approx 15.0\%$.

h.

$$k_A = k_{RF} + (k_M - k_{RF}) \, b_A$$

$$15 = 10 + (16.8 - 10) \, b_A$$

$$= 10 + (6.8) \, b_A.$$

$$b_A = 0.74.$$

$$20 = 10 + (6.8) \, b_B$$

$$b_B = 1.47.$$

Note that the 16.8 percent value for k_M was approximated from the graph. Also, note that this solution *assumes* that you can borrow at $k_{RF} = 10\%$. This is a basic—but questionable—CAPM assumption. If the borrowing rate is *above* k_{RF}, then CML would turn down to the right of Point M.

Chapter 7

ST-1   a.

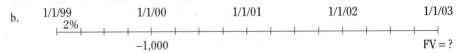

1/1/99	8%	1/1/00		1/1/01		1/1/02		1/1/03
−1,000								FV = ?

$1,000 is being compounded for 3 years, so your balance on January 1, 2003, is $1,259.71:

$$FV_n = PV(1 + i)^n = \$1,000(1 + 0.08)^3 = \$1,259.71.$$

Alternatively, using a financial calculator, input N = 3, I = 8, PV = −1000, PMT = 0, and FV = ? FV = $1,259.71.

b.

1/1/99		1/1/00		1/1/01		1/1/02		1/1/03
2%								
−1,000								FV = ?

Use FVIF for 2%, 3 × 4 = 12 periods:

$$FV_{12} = \$1,000(FVIF_{2\%,12}) = \$1,000(1.2682) = \$1,268.20.$$

Alternatively, using a financial calculator, input N = 12, I = 2, PV = −1000, PMT = 0, and FV = ? FV = $1,268.24. (Note that since the interest factor is carried to only 4 decimal places, a rounding difference occurs.)

c.

	1/1/99	8%	1/1/00	1/1/01	1/1/02	1/1/03
			250	250	250	250
						FV = ?

As you work this problem, keep in mind that the tables assume that payments are made at the end of each period. Therefore, you may solve this problem by finding the future value of an annuity of $250 for 4 years at 8 percent:

$$FVA_4 = PMT(FVIFA_{i,n}) = \$250(4.5061) = \$1,126.53.$$

Alternatively, using a financial calculator, input N = 4, I = 8, PV = 0, PMT = −250, and FV = ? FV = $1,126.53.

d.

	1/1/99	8%	1/1/00	1/1/01	1/1/02	1/1/03
			?	?	?	?
						FV = 1,259.71

N = 4; I = 8; PV = 0; FV = 1259.71; PMT = ?; PMT = $279.56.

$$PMT(FVIFA_{8\%,4}) = FVA_4$$
$$PMT(4.5061) = \$1,259.71$$
$$PMT = \$1,259.71/4.5061 = \$279.56.$$

Therefore, you would have to make 4 payments of $279.56 each to have a balance of $1,259.71 on January 1, 2003.

ST-2   a.   Set up a time line like the one in the preceding problem:

	1/1/99	8%	1/1/00	1/1/01	1/1/02	1/1/03
			PV = ?			1,000

Note that your deposit will grow for 3 years at 8 percent. The fact that it is now January 1, 1999, is irrelevant. The deposit on January 1, 2000, is the PV, and the FV is $1,000. Here is the solution:

N = 3; I = 8; PMT = 0; FV = 1000; PV = ?; PV = $793.83.

$$FV_3(PVIF_{8\%,3}) = PV$$
$$PV = \$1,000(0.7938) = \$793.80 = \text{Initial deposit to accumulate } \$1,000.$$

(Difference due to rounding.)

b.

	1/1/99	8%	1/1/00	1/1/01	1/1/02	1/1/03
			?	?	?	?
						FV = 1,000

Here we are dealing with a 4-year annuity whose first payment occurs 1 year from today, on 1/1/00, and whose future value must equal $1,000. You should modify the time line to help visualize the situation. Here is the solution:

N = 4; I = 8; PV = 0; FV = 1000; PMT = ?; PMT = $221.92.

$$PMT(FVIFA_{8\%,4}) = FVA_4$$
$$PMT = \frac{FVA_4}{(FVIFA_{8\%,4})}$$

$$= \frac{\$1,000}{4.5061} = \$221.92 = \begin{array}{l}\text{Payment necessary} \\ \text{to accumulate \$1,000}\end{array}$$

c. This problem can be approached in several ways. Perhaps the simplest is to ask this question: "If I received $750 on 1/1/00 and deposited it to earn 8 percent, would I have the required $1,000 on 1/1/03?" The answer is no:

1/1/99	8%	1/1/00	1/1/01	1/1/02	1/1/03
		−750			FV = ?

$$FV_3 = \$750(1.08)(1.08)(1.08) = \$944.78.$$

This indicates that you should let your father make the payments rather than accept the lump sum of $750.

You could also compare the $750 with the PV of the payments:

1/1/99	8%	1/1/00	1/1/01	1/1/02	1/1/03
		221.92	221.92	221.92	221.92
		PV = ?			

N = 4; I = 8; PMT = −221.92; FV = 0; PV = ?; PV = $735.03.

$$PMT(PVIFA_{8\%,4}) = PVA_4$$

$$\$221.92(3.3121) = \$735.02 = \begin{array}{l}\text{Present value} \\ \text{of the required payments}\end{array}$$

(Difference due to rounding.)

This is less than the $750 lump sum offer, so your initial reaction might be to accept the lump sum of $750. However, this would be a mistake. The problem is that when you found the $735.02 PV of the annuity, you were finding the value of the annuity *today,* on January 1, 1999. You were comparing $735.02 today with the lump sum of $750 1 year from now. This is, of course, invalid. What you should have done was take the $735.02, recognize that this is the PV of an annuity as of January 1, 1999, multiply $735.02 by 1.08 to get $793.82, and compare $793.82 with the lump sum of $750. You would then take your father's offer to make the payments rather than take the lump sum on January 1, 2000.

d.

1/1/99	i = ?	1/1/00	1/1/01	1/1/02	1/1/03
		−750			1,000

N = 3; PV = −750; PMT = 0; FV = 1000; I = ?; I = 10.0642%.

$$PV(FVIF_{i,3}) = FV$$

$$FVIF_{i,3} = \frac{FV}{PV}$$

$$= \frac{\$1,000}{\$750} = 1.3333.$$

Use the Future Value of $1 table (Table A-3 in Appendix A) for 3 periods to find the interest rate corresponding to an FVIF of 1.3333. Look across the Period 3 row of the table until you come to 1.3333. The closest value is 1.3310, in the 10 percent column. Therefore, you would require an interest rate of approximately 10 percent to achieve your $1,000 goal. The exact rate required, found with a financial calculator, is 10.0642 percent.

e.

1/1/99	i = ?	1/1/00	1/1/01	1/1/02	1/1/03
		186.29	186.29	186.29	186.29
					FV = 1,000

N = 4; PV = 0; PMT = −186.29; FV = 1000; I = ?; I = 19.9997%.

$$PMT(FVIFA_{i,4}) = FVA_4$$

$$\$186.29(\text{FVIFA}_{i,4}) = \$1,000$$

$$\text{FVIFA}_{i,4} = \frac{\$1,000}{\$186.29} = 5.3680.$$

Using Table A-4 in Appendix A, we find that 5.3680 corresponds to a 20 percent interest rate. You might be able to find a borrower willing to offer you a 20 percent interest rate, but there would be some risk involved—he or she might not actually pay you your $1,000!

f.

Find the future value of the original $400 deposit:

$$\text{FV}_6 = \text{PV}(\text{FVIF}_{4\%,6}) = \$400(1.2653) = \$506.12.$$

This means that on January 1, 2003, you need an additional sum of $493.88:

$$\$1,000.00 - \$506.12 = \$493.88.$$

This will be accumulated by making 6 equal payments which earn 8 percent compounded semiannually, or 4 percent each 6 months:

N = 6; I = 4; PV = 0; FV = 493.88; PMT = ?; PMT = $74.46.

$$\text{PMT}(\text{FVIFA}_{4\%,6}) = \text{FVA}_6$$

$$\text{PMT} = \frac{\text{FVA}_6}{(\text{FVIFA}_{4\%,6})}$$

$$= \frac{\$493.88}{6.6330} = \$74.46.$$

Alternatively, using a financial calculator, input N = 6, I = 4, PV = −400, FV = 1000, and PMT = ? PMT = $74.46.

g.

$$\text{Effective annual rate} = \left(1 + \frac{i_{\text{Nom}}}{m}\right)^m - 1.0$$

$$= \left(1 + \frac{0.08}{2}\right)^2 - 1 = (1.04)^2 - 1$$

$$= 1.0816 - 1 = 0.0816 = 8.16\%.$$

h. There is a reinvestment rate risk here because we assumed that funds will earn an 8 percent return in the bank. In fact, if interest rates in the economy fall, the bank will lower its deposit rate because it will be earning less when it lends out the funds you deposited with it. If you buy certificates of deposit (CDs) that mature on the date you need the money (1/1/03), you will avoid the reinvestment risk, but that would work only if you were making the deposit today. Other ways of reducing reinvestment rate risk will be discussed later in the text.

ST-3   Bank A's effective annual rate is 8.24 percent:

$$\text{Effective annual rate} = \left(1 + \frac{0.08}{4}\right)^4 - 1.0$$

$$= (1.02)^4 - 1 = 1.0824 - 1$$

$$= 0.0824 = 8.24\%.$$

Now Bank B must have the same effective annual rate:

$$\left(1 + \frac{i}{12}\right)^{12} - 1.0 = 0.0824$$

$$\left(1 + \frac{i}{12}\right)^{12} = 1.0824$$

$$1 + \frac{i}{12} = (1.0824)^{1/12}$$

$$1 + \frac{i}{12} = 1.00662$$

$$\frac{i}{12} = 0.00662$$

$$i = 0.07944 = 7.94\%.$$

Thus, the two banks have different quoted rates—Bank A's quoted rate is 8 percent, while Bank B's quoted rate is 7.94 percent; however, both banks have the same effective annual rate of 8.24 percent. The difference in their quoted rates is due to the difference in compounding frequency.

Chapter 8

ST-1   a. Pennington's bonds were sold at par; therefore, the original YTM equaled the coupon rate of 12%.

b.

$$V_B = \sum_{t=1}^{50} \frac{\$120/2}{\left(1 + \frac{0.10}{2}\right)^t} + \frac{\$1,000}{\left(1 + \frac{0.10}{2}\right)^{50}}$$

$$= \$60(PVIFA_{5\%,50}) + \$1,000(PVIF_{5\%,50})$$

$$= \$60(18.2559) + \$1,000(0.0872)$$

$$= \$1,095.35 + \$87.20 = \$1,182.55.$$

Alternatively, with a financial calculator, input the following: N = 50, I = 5, PMT = 60, FV = 1000, and PV = ? PV = $1,182.56.

c.

$$\text{Current yield} = \text{Annual coupon payment/Price}$$

$$= \$120/\$1,182.55$$

$$= 0.1015 = 10.15\%.$$

$$\text{Capital gains yield} = \text{Total yield} - \text{Current yield}$$

$$= 10\% - 10.15\% = -0.15\%.$$

d.

$$\$916.42 = \sum_{t=1}^{13} \frac{\$60}{(1 + k_d/2)^t} + \frac{\$1,000}{(1 + k_d/2)^{13}}.$$

Try $k_d = 14\%$:

$$V_B = INT(PVIFA_{7\%,13}) + M(PVIF_{7\%,13})$$

$$\$916.42 = \$60(8.3577) + \$1,000(0.4150)$$

$$= \$501.46 + \$415.00 = \$916.46.$$

Therefore, the YTM on July 1, 1998, was 14 percent. Alternatively, with a financial calculator, input the following: N = 13, PV = −916.42, PMT = 60, FV = 1000, and $k_d/2$ = I = ? Calculator solution = $k_d/2$ = 7.00%; therefore, k_d = 14.00%.

e.

$$\text{Current yield} = \$120/\$916.42 = 13.09\%.$$

$$\text{Capital gains yield} = 14\% - 13.09\% = 0.91\%.$$

f. The following time line illustrates the years to maturity of the bond:

1/1/98	7/1/98	12/31/98	7/1/99	12/31/99	12/31/04

3/1/98

Thus, on March 1, 1998, there were $13\frac{2}{3}$ periods left before the bond matured. Bond traders actually use the following procedure to determine the price of the bond:

(1) Find the price of the bond on the next coupon date, July 1, 1998.

$$V_{B\ 7/1/98} = \$60(PVIFA_{7.75\%,13}) + \$1,000(PVIF_{7.75\%,13})$$
$$= \$60(8.0136) + \$1,000(0.3789)$$
$$= \$859.72.$$

Note that we could use a calculator to solve for $V_{B\ 7/1/98}$ or we could substitute $i = 7.75\%$ and $n = 13$ periods into the equations for PVIFA and PVIF:

$$PVIFA = \frac{1 - \dfrac{1}{(1+i)^n}}{i} = \frac{1 - \dfrac{1}{(1+0.0775)^{13}}}{0.0775} = 8.0136.$$

$$PVIF = \frac{1}{(1+k)^n} = \frac{1}{(1+0.0775)^{13}} = 0.3789.$$

(2) Add the coupon, \$60, to the bond price to get the total value, TV, of the bond on the next interest payment date: TV = \$859.72 + \$60.00 = \$919.72.

(3) Discount this total value back to the purchase date:

$$\text{Value at purchase date (March 1, 1998)} = \$919.72(PVIF_{7.75\%,4/6})$$
$$= \$919.72(0.9515)$$
$$= \$875.11.$$

Here

$$PVIF_{7.75\%,2/3} = \frac{1}{(1+0.0775)^{2/3}} = \frac{1}{1.0510} = 0.9515.$$

(4) Therefore, you would have written a check for \$875.11 to complete the transaction. Of this amount, \$20 = $(\frac{1}{3})(\$60)$ would represent accrued interest and \$855.11 would represent the bond's basic value. This breakdown would affect both your taxes and those of the seller.

(5) This problem could be solved *very* easily using a financial calculator with a bond valuation function, such as the HP-12C or the HP-17B. This is explained in the calculator manual under the heading, "Bond Calculations."

ST-2 a. \$100,000,000/10 = \$10,000,000 per year, or \$5 million each 6 months. Since the \$5 million will be used to retire bonds immediately, no interest will be earned on it.

b. The debt service requirements will decline. As the amount of bonds outstanding declines, so will the interest requirements (amounts given in millions of dollars):

SEMIANNUAL PAYMENT PERIOD (1)	OUTSTANDING BONDS ON WHICH INTEREST IS PAID (2)	INTEREST PAYMENT[a] (3)	SINKING FUND PAYMENT (4)	TOTAL BOND SERVICE (3) + (4) = (5)
1	\$100	\$6.0	\$5	\$11.0
2	95	5.7	5	10.7
3	90	5.4	5	10.4
.	.	.	.	.
.	.	.	.	.
.	.	.	.	.
20	5	0.3	5	5.3

[a]Interest is calculated as $(0.5)(0.12)$(Column 2); for example: interest in Period 2 = $(0.5)(0.12)(\$95)$ = \$5.7.

The company's total cash bond service requirement will be $21.7 million per year for the first year. The requirement will decline by 0.12($10,000,000) = $1,200,000 per year for the remaining years.

c. Here we have a 10-year, 9 percent annuity whose compound value is $100 million, and we are seeking the annual payment, PMT. The solution can be obtained with a financial calculator. Input N = 10, I = 9, PV = 0, and FV = 100000000, and press the PMT key to obtain $6,582,009. We could also find the solution using this equation:

$$\$100,000,000 = \sum_{t=1}^{10} PMT(1 + k)^t$$

$$= PMT(FVIFA_{9\%,10})$$

$$= PMT(15.193)$$

$$PMT = \$6,581,979 = \text{Sinking fund payment.}$$

The difference is due to rounding the FVIFA to 3 decimal places.

d. Annual debt service costs will be $100,000,000(0.12) + $6,582,009 = $18,582,009.

e. If interest rates rose, causing the bonds' price to fall, the company would use open market purchases. This would reduce its debt service requirements.

Chapter 9

ST-1 a. This is not necessarily true. Because G plows back two-thirds of its earnings, its growth rate should exceed that of D, but D pays higher dividends ($6 versus $2). We cannot say which stock should have the higher price.

b. Again, we just do not know which price would be higher.

c. This is false. The changes in k_d and k_s would have a greater effect on G; its price would decline more.

d. The total expected return for D is $\hat{k}_D = D_1/P_0 + g = 15\% + 0\% = 15\%$. The total expected return for G will have D_1/P_0 less than 15 percent and g greater than 0 percent, but $\hat{k}_G$ should be neither greater nor smaller than D's total expected return, 15 percent, because the two stocks are stated to be equally risky.

e. We have eliminated a, b, c, and d, so e should be correct. On the basis of the available information, D and G should sell at about the same price, $40; thus, $\hat{k}_s = 15\%$ for both D and G. G's current dividend yield is $2/$40 = 5%. Therefore, g = 15% − 5% = 10%.

ST-2 The first step is to solve for g, the unknown variable, in the constant growth equation. Since D_1 is unknown but D_0 is known, substitute $D_0(1 + g)$ as follows:

$$\hat{P}_0 = P_0 = \frac{D_1}{k_s - g} = \frac{D_0(1 + g)}{k_s - g}$$

$$\$36 = \frac{\$2.40(1 + g)}{0.12 - g}.$$

Solving for g, we find the growth rate to be 5 percent:

$$\$4.32 - \$36g = \$2.40 + \$2.40g$$

$$\$38.4g = \$1.92$$

$$g = 0.05 = 5\%.$$

The next step is to use the growth rate to project the stock price 5 years hence:

$$\hat{P}_5 = \frac{D_0(1 + g)^6}{k_s - g}$$

$$= \frac{\$2.40(1.05)^6}{0.12 - 0.05}$$

$$= \$45.95.$$

[Alternatively, $\hat{P}_5 = \$36(1.05)^5 = \$45.95$.]

Therefore, Ewald Company's expected stock price 5 years from now, $\hat{P}_5$, is $45.95.

ST-3   a. (1) Calculate the PV of the dividends paid during the supernormal growth period:

$$D_1 = \$1.1500(1.15) = \$1.3225.$$
$$D_2 = \$1.3225(1.15) = \$1.5209.$$
$$D_3 = \$1.5209(1.13) = \$1.7186.$$
$$\text{PV D} = \$1.3225(0.8929) + \$1.5209(0.7972) + \$1.7186(0.7118)$$
$$= \$1.1809 + \$1.2125 + \$1.2233$$
$$= \$3.6167 \approx \$3.62.$$

(2) Find the PV of Snyder's stock price at the end of Year 3:

$$\hat{P}_3 = \frac{D_4}{k_s - g} = \frac{D_3(1 + g)}{k_s - g}$$

$$= \frac{\$1.7186(1.06)}{0.12 - 0.06}$$

$$= \$30.36.$$

$$\text{PV } \hat{P}_3 = \$30.36(0.7118) = \$21.61.$$

(3) Sum the two components to find the value of the stock today:

$$\hat{P}_0 = \$3.62 + \$21.61 = \$25.23.$$

Alternatively, the cash flows can be placed on a time line as follows:

Enter the cash flows into the cash flow register, I = 12, and press the NPV key to obtain $P_0 = \$25.23$.

b. $\hat{P}_1 = \$1.5209(0.8929) + \$1.7186(0.7972) + \$30.36(0.7972)$

$$= \$1.3580 + \$1.3701 + \$24.2030$$
$$= \$26.9311 \approx \$26.93.$$
(Calculator solution: $26.93.)

$\hat{P}_2 = \$1.7186(0.8929) + \$30.36(0.8929)$

$$= \$1.5345 + \$27.1084$$
$$= \$28.6429 \approx \$28.64.$$
(Calculator solution: $28.64.)

c.

YEAR	DIVIDEND YIELD	+	CAPITAL GAINS YIELD	=	TOTAL RETURN
1	$\dfrac{\$1.3225}{\$25.23} \approx 5.24\%$		$\dfrac{\$26.93 - \$25.23}{\$25.23} \approx 6.74\%$		$\approx 12\%$
2	$\dfrac{\$1.5209}{\$26.93} \approx 5.65\%$		$\dfrac{\$28.64 - \$26.93}{\$26.93} \approx 6.35\%$		$\approx 12\%$
3	$\dfrac{\$1.7186}{\$28.64} \approx 6.00\%$		$\dfrac{\$30.36 - \$28.64}{\$28.64} \approx 6.00\%$		$\approx 12\%$

ST-4   a. $V_{Op} = \dfrac{FCF(1+g)}{k_c - g} = \dfrac{\$100,000(1+0.07)}{0.11 - 0.07} = \$2,675,000.$

b.   Total value = Value of operations + Value of nonoperating assets

$$= \$2,675,000 + \$325,000 = \$3,000,000.$$

c.   Value of equity = Total value – Value of debt

$$= \$3,000,000 - \$1,000,000 = \$2,000,000.$$

Chapter 10

ST-1   a.   Component costs are as follows:

Debt at $k_d = 12\%$:

$$k_d(1-T) = 12\%(0.6) = 7.2\%.$$

Preferred with F = 5%:

$$k_{ps} = \frac{\text{Preferred dividend}}{P_n} = \frac{\$11}{\$100(.95)} = 11.6\%.$$

Common with DCF:

$$k_s = \frac{D_1}{P_0} + g = \frac{\$3.924}{\$60} + 9\% = 15.5\%.$$

Common with CAPM:

$$k_s = 11\% + 1.51(14\% - 11\%) = 15.5\%$$

b. $$WACC = w_d k_d(1-T) + w_{ps}k_{ps} + w_e k_s$$
$$= 0.25(12\%)(1-0.4) + 0.15(11.6\%) + 0.60(15.5\%)$$
$$= 12.8\%.$$

Chapter 11

ST-1   a.   *Payback:*
To determine the payback, construct the cumulative cash flows for each project:

	Cumulative Cash Flows	
Year	Project X	Project Y
0	($10,000)	($10,000)
1	(3,500)	(6,500)
2	(500)	(3,000)
3	2,500	500
4	3,500	4,000

$$\text{Payback}_X = 2 + \frac{\$500}{\$3,000} = 2.17 \text{ years.}$$

$$\text{Payback}_Y = 2 + \frac{\$3,000}{\$3,500} = 2.86 \text{ years.}$$

Net present value (NPV):

$$NPV_X = -\$10,000 + \frac{\$6,500}{(1.12)^1} + \frac{\$3,000}{(1.12)^2} + \frac{\$3,000}{(1.12)^3} + \frac{\$1,000}{(1.12)^4}$$

$$= \$966.01.$$

$$NPV_Y = -\$10,000 + \frac{\$3,500}{(1.12)^1} + \frac{\$3,500}{(1.12)^2} + \frac{\$3,500}{(1.12)^3} + \frac{\$3,500}{(1.12)^4}$$

$$= \$630.72.$$

Alternatively, using a financial calculator, input the cash flows into the cash flow register, enter I = 12, and then press the NPV key to obtain $NPV_X = \$966.01$ and $NPV_Y = \$630.72$.

Internal rate of return (IRR):
To solve for each project's IRR, find the discount rates which equate each NPV to zero:

$$IRR_X = 18.0\%.$$
$$IRR_Y = 15.0\%.$$

Modified internal rate of return (MIRR):
To obtain each project's MIRR, begin by finding each project's terminal value (TV) of cash inflows:

$$TV_X = \$6,500(1.12)^3 + \$3,000(1.12)^2$$
$$+ 3,000(1.12)^1 + \$1,000 = \$17,255.23.$$
$$TV_Y = \$3,500(1.12)^3 + \$3,500(1.12)^2$$
$$+ \$3,500(1.12)^1 + \$3,500 = \$16,727.65.$$

Now, each project's MIRR is that discount rate which equates the PV of the TV to each project's cost, $10,000:

$$MIRR_X = 14.61\%.$$
$$MIRR_Y = 13.73\%.$$

b. The following table summarizes the project rankings by each method:

	PROJECT WHICH RANKS HIGHER
Payback	X
NPV	X
IRR	X
MIRR	X

Note that all methods rank Project X over Project Y. In addition, both projects are acceptable under the NPV, IRR, and MIRR criteria. Thus, both projects should be accepted if they are independent.

c. In this case, we would choose the project with the higher NPV at k = 12%, or Project X.

d. To determine the effects of changing the cost of capital, plot the NPV profiles of each project. The crossover rate occurs at about 6 to 7 percent (6.2%). See the graph on the next page.

If the firm's cost of capital is less than 6 percent, a conflict exists because $NPV_Y > NPV_X$, but $IRR_X > IRR_Y$. Therefore, if k were 5 percent, a conflict would exist. Note, however, that when k = 5.0%, $MIRR_X = 10.64\%$ and $MIRR_Y = 10.83\%$; hence, the modified IRR ranks the projects correctly, even if k is to the left of the crossover point.

e. The basic cause of the conflict is differing reinvestment rate assumptions between NPV and IRR. NPV assumes that cash flows can be reinvested at the cost of capital, while IRR assumes reinvestment at the (generally) higher IRR. The high reinvestment rate assumption under IRR makes early cash flows especially valuable, and hence short-term projects look better under IRR.

NPV Profiles for Projects X and Y

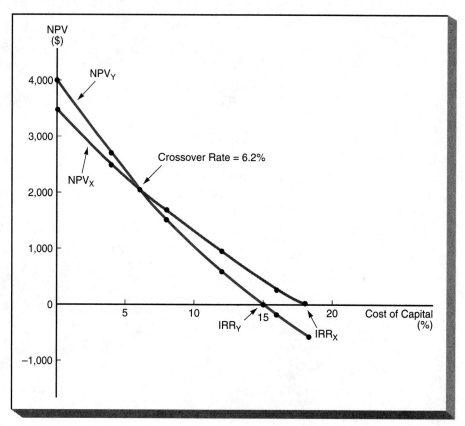

COST OF CAPITAL	NPVₓ	NPVᵧ
0%	$3,500	$4,000
4	2,545	2,705
8	1,707	1,592
12	966	631
16	307	(206)
18	5	(585)

Chapter 12

ST-1   a. *Estimated investment requirements:*

Price	($50,000)
Modification	(10,000)
Change in net working capital	(2,000)
Total investment	($62,000)

b. *Operating cash flows:*

	YEAR 1	YEAR 2	YEAR 3
1. After-tax cost savings[a]	$12,000	$12,000	$12,000
2. Depreciation[b]	19,800	27,000	9,000
3. Depreciation tax savings[c]	7,920	10,800	3,600
Operating cash flow (1 + 3)	$19,920	$22,800	$15,600

[a]$20,000 (1 − T).

[b]Depreciable basis = $60,000; the MACRS percentage allowances are 0.33, 0.45, and 0.15 in Years 1, 2, and 3, respectively; hence, depreciation in Year 1 = 0.33($60,000) = $19,800, and so on. There will remain $4,200, or 7 percent, undepreciated after Year 3; it would normally be taken in Year 4.

[c]Depreciation tax savings = T(Depreciation) = 0.4($19,800) = $7,920 in Year 1, and so on.

c. *Termination cash flow:*

Salvage value	$20,000
Tax on salvage value[a]	(6,320)
Net working capital recovery	2,000
Termination cash flow	$15,680

[a]Sales price	$20,000
Less book value	4,200
Taxable income	$15,800
Tax at 40%	$ 6,320

Book value = Depreciable basis − Accumulated depreciation
= $60,000 − $55,800 = $4,200.

d. *Project NPV:*

$$\text{NPV} = -\$62,000 + \frac{\$19,920}{(1.10)^1} + \frac{\$22,800}{(1.10)^2} + \frac{\$31,280}{(1.10)^3}$$

$$= -\$1,547.$$

Alternatively, using a financial calculator, input the cash flows into the cash flow register, enter I = 10, and then press the NPV key to obtain NPV = −$1,547. Because the earthmover has a negative NPV, it should not be purchased.

ST-2 *First determine the net cash flow at t = 0:*

Purchase price	($8,000)
Sale of old machine	3,000
Tax on sale of old machine	(160)[a]
Change in net working capital	(1,500)[b]
Total investment	($6,660)

[a]The market value is $3,000 − $2,600 = $400 above the book value. Thus, there is a $400 recapture of depreciation, and the company would have to pay 0.40($400) = $160 in taxes.

[b]The change in net working capital is a $2,000 increase in operating current assets minus a $500 increase in operating current liabilities, which totals to $1,500.

Now, examine the operating cash inflows:

Sales increase	$1,000
Cost decrease	1,500
Increase in pre-tax operating revenues	$2,500
After-tax operating revenue increase:	

$$\text{After-tax operating revenue increase:} \quad \$2,500(1 - T) = \$2,500(0.60) = \underline{\underline{\$1,500}}.$$

Depreciation:

YEAR	1	2	3	4	5	6
New[a]	$1,600	$2,560	$1,520	$960	$880	$480
Old	350	350	350	350	350	350
Change	$1,250	$2,210	$1,170	$610	$530	$130
Depreciation						
Tax savings[b]	$ 500	$ 884	$ 468	$244	$212	$ 52

[a]Depreciable basis = $8,000. Depreciation expense in each year equals depreciable basis times the MACRS percentage allowances of 0.20, 0.32, 0.19, 0.12, 0.11, and 0.06 in Years 1–6, respectively.
[b]Depreciation tax savings = $T(\Delta \text{Depreciation}) = 0.4(\Delta \text{Depreciation})$.

Now recognize that at the end of Year 6 the company would recover its net working capital investment of $1,500, and it would also receive $800 from the sale of the replacement machine. However, since the machine would be fully depreciated, the firm must pay 0.40($800) = $320 in taxes on the sale. Also, by undertaking the replacement now, the firm foregoes the right to sell the old machine for $500 in Year 6; thus, this $500 in Year 6 must be considered an opportunity cost in that year. No tax would be due because the $500 salvage value would equal the old machine's Year 6 book value.

Finally, place all the cash flows on a time line:

	0	1	2	3	4	5	6
Net investment	(6,660)						
After-tax revenue increase		1,500	1,500	1,500	1,500	1,500	1,500
Depreciation tax savings		500	884	468	244	212	52
Working capital recovery							1,500
Salvage value of new machine							800
Tax on salvage value of new machine							(320)
Opportunity cost of old machine							(500)
Net cash flows	(6,660)	2,000	2,384	1,968	1,744	1,712	3,032

The net present value of this incremental cash flow stream, when discounted at 15 percent, is $1,335. Thus, the replacement should be made.

Chapter 13

ST-1   a. First, find the expected cash flows:

YEAR	EXPECTED CASH FLOWS			
0	0.2(−$100,000)	+ 0.6(−$100,000)	+ 0.2(−$100,000) = ($100,000)	
1	0.2($20,000)	+ 0.6($30,000)	+ 0.2($40,000) = $30,000	
2			$30,000	
3			$30,000	
4			$30,000	
5			$30,000	
5*	0.2($0)	+ 0.6($20,000)	+ 0.2($30,000) = $18,000	

$$\begin{array}{ccccccc} 0 & 10\% & 1 & 2 & 3 & 4 & 5 \\ \hline -100{,}000 & & 30{,}000 & 30{,}000 & 30{,}000 & 30{,}000 & 48{,}000 \end{array}$$

Next, determine the NPV based on the expected cash flows:

$$NPV = -\$100{,}000 + \frac{\$30{,}000}{(1.10)^1} + \frac{\$30{,}000}{(1.10)^2} + \frac{\$30{,}000}{(1.10)^3}$$

$$+ \frac{\$30{,}000}{(1.10)^4} + \frac{\$48{,}000}{(1.10)^5} = \$24{,}900.$$

Alternatively, using a financial calculator, input the cash flows in the cash flow register, enter I = 10, and then press the NPV key to obtain NPV = $24,900.

b. For the worst case, the cash flow values from the cash flow column farthest on the left are used to calculate NPV:

$$\begin{array}{ccccccc} 0 & 10\% & 1 & 2 & 3 & 4 & 5 \\ \hline -100{,}000 & & 20{,}000 & 20{,}000 & 20{,}000 & 20{,}000 & 20{,}000 \end{array}$$

$$NPV = -\$100{,}000 + \frac{\$20{,}000}{(1.10)^1} + \frac{\$20{,}000}{(1.10)^2} + \frac{\$20{,}000}{(1.10)^3}$$

$$+ \frac{\$20{,}000}{(1.10)^4} + \frac{\$20{,}000}{(1.10)^5} = -\$24{,}184.$$

Similarly, for the best case, use the values from the column farthest on the right. Here the NPV is $70,259.

   If the cash flows are perfectly dependent, then the low cash flow in the first year will mean a low cash flow in every year. Thus, the probability of the worst case occurring is the probability of getting the $20,000 net cash flow in Year 1, or 20 percent. If the cash flows are independent, the cash flow in each year can be low, high, or average, and the probability of getting all low cash flows will be

$$0.2(0.2)(0.2)(0.2)(0.2) = 0.2^5 = 0.00032 = 0.032\%.$$

c. The base-case NPV is found using the most likely cash flows and is equal to $26,142. This value differs from the expected NPV of $24,900 because the Year 5 cash flows are not symmetric. Under these conditions, the NPV distribution is as follows:

P	NPV
0.2	($24,184)
0.6	26,142
0.2	70,259

Thus, the expected NPV is $0.2(-\$24,184) + 0.6(\$26,142) + 0.2(\$70,259) = \$24,900$. As is generally the case, the expected NPV is the same as the NPV of the expected cash flows found in Part a. The standard deviation is $29,904:

$$\sigma^2_{NPV} = 0.2(-\$24,184 - \$24,900)^2 + 0.6(\$26,142 - \$24,900)^2$$
$$+ 0.2(\$70,259 - \$24,900)^2$$
$$= \$894,261,126.$$
$$\sigma_{NPV} = \sqrt{\$894,261,126} = \$29,904.$$

The coefficient of variation, CV, is $\$29,904/\$24,900 = 1.20$.

d. Since the project's coefficient of variation is 1.20, the project is riskier than average, and hence the project's risk-adjusted cost of capital is $10\% + 2\% = 12\%$. The project now should be evaluated by finding the NPV of the expected cash flows, as in Part a, but using a 12 percent discount rate. The risk-adjusted NPV is $18,357, and, therefore, the project, should be accepted.

Chapter 14

ST-1 To solve this problem, we will define ΔS as the change in sales and g as the growth rate in sales, and then we use the three following equations:

$$\Delta S = S_0 g.$$
$$S_1 = S_0(1 + g).$$
$$AFN = (A^*/S_0)(\Delta S) - (L^*/S_0)(\Delta S) - MS_1(1 - d).$$

Set AFN = 0, substitute in known values for A^*/S_0, L^*/S_0, M, d, and S_0, and then solve for g:

$$0 = 1.6(\$100g) - 0.4(\$100g) - 0.10[\$100(1 + g)](0.55)$$
$$= \$160g - \$40g - 0.055(\$100 + \$100g)$$
$$= \$160g - \$40g - \$5.5 - \$5.5g$$
$$\$114.5g = \$5.5$$
$$g = \$5.5/\$114.5 = 0.048 = 4.8\%$$
$$= \text{Maximum growth rate without external financing.}$$

ST-2 Assets consist of cash, marketable securities, receivables, inventories, and fixed assets. Therefore, we can break the A^*/S_0 ratio into its components—cash/sales, inventories/sales, and so forth. Then,

$$\frac{A^*}{S_0} = \frac{A^* - \text{Inventories}}{S_0} + \frac{\text{Inventories}}{S_0} = 1.6.$$

We know that the inventory turnover ratio is sales/inventories = 3 times, so inventories/sales = $1/3 = 0.3333$. Further, if the inventory turnover ratio can be increased to 4 times, then the inventory/sales ratio will fall to $1/4 = 0.25$, a difference of $0.3333 - 0.2500 = 0.0833$. This, in turn, causes the A^*/S_0 ratio to fall from $A^*/S_0 = 1.6$ to $A^*/S_0 = 1.6 - 0.0833 = 1.5167$.

This change has two effects: First, it changes the AFN equation, and second, it means that Weatherford currently has excessive inventories. Because it is costly to hold excess inventories, Weatherford will want to reduce its inventory holdings by not replacing inventories until the excess amounts have been used. We can account for this by setting up the revised AFN equation (using the new A^*/S_0 ratio), estimating the funds that will be needed next year if no excess inventories are currently on hand, and then subtracting out the excess inventories which are currently on hand:

Present conditions:

$$\frac{\text{Sales}}{\text{Inventories}} = \frac{\$100}{\text{Inventories}} = 3,$$

so

$$\text{Inventories} = \$100/3 = \$33.3 \text{ million at present.}$$

New conditions:

$$\frac{\text{Sales}}{\text{Inventories}} = \frac{\$100}{\text{Inventories}} = 4,$$

so

New level of inventories = $100/4 = $25 million.

Therefore,

Excess inventories = $33.3 − $25 = $8.3 million.

Forecast of funds needed, first year;

$$\Delta S \text{ in first year} = 0.2(\$100 \text{ million}) = \$20 \text{ million}.$$
$$AFN = 1.5167(\$20) - 0.4(\$20) - 0.1(0.55)(\$120) - \$8.3$$
$$= \$30.3 - \$8 - \$6.6 - \$8.3$$
$$= \$7.4 \text{ million}.$$

Forecast of funds needed, second year:

$$\Delta S \text{ in second year} = gS_1 = 0.2(\$120 \text{ million}) = \$24 \text{ million}.$$
$$AFN = 1.5167(\$24) - 0.4(\$24) - 0.1(0.55)(\$144)$$
$$= \$36.4 - \$9.6 - \$7.9$$
$$= \$18.9 \text{ million}.$$

ST-3   a.

$$\begin{aligned}\text{Full capacity sales} &= \frac{\text{Current sales}}{\begin{array}{c}\text{Percentage of capacity at which}\\ \text{FA were operated}\end{array}} = \frac{\$36,000}{0.75} = \$48,000.\end{aligned}$$

$$\begin{aligned}\text{Percentage increase} &= \frac{\text{New sales} - \text{Old sales}}{\text{Old sales}} = \frac{\$48,000 - \$36,000}{\$36,000} = 0.33\\ &= 33\%.\end{aligned}$$

Therefore, sales could expand by 33 percent before Van Auken Lumber would need to add fixed assets.

b. Because none of the operating ratios are assumed to change, it is easier to let the appropriate items increase at the sales growth rate.

VAN AUKEN LUMBER: PRO FORMA INCOME STATEMENT FOR DECEMBER 31, 1999 (THOUSANDS OF DOLLARS)

	1998	(1 + g)	PRO FORMA 1999
Sales	$36,000	(1.25)	$45,000
Operating costs	30,783	(1.25)	38,479
EBIT	$ 5,217		$ 6,521
Interest	1,017		1,017
EBT	$ 4,200		$ 5,504
Taxes (40%)	1,680		2,202
Net income	$ 2,520		$ 3,302
Dividends (60%)	$ 1,512		$ 1,981
Addition to RE	$ 1,008		$ 1,321

VAN AUKEN LUMBER: PRO FORMA BALANCE SHEET FOR DECEMBER 31, 1999 (THOUSANDS OF DOLLARS)

	1998	(1 + g)	ADDITIONS	1999	AFN	1999 AFTER AFN
Cash	$ 1,800	(1.25)		$ 2,250		$ 2,250
Receivables	10,800	(1.25)		13,500		13,500
Inventories	12,600	(1.25)		15,750		15,750
Total current assets	$25,200			$31,500		$31,500
Net fixed assets	21,600			21,600[a]		21,600
Total assets	$46,800			$53,100		$53,100
Accounts payable	$ 7,200	(1.25)		$ 9,000		$ 9,000
Notes payable	3,472			3,472	+2,549	6,021
Accruals	2,520	(1.25)		3,150		3,150
Total current liabilities	$13,192			$15,622		$18,171
Mortgage bonds	5,000			5,000		5,000
Common stock	2,000			2,000		2,000
Retained earnings	26,608		1,321[b]	27,929		27,929
Total liabilities and equity	$46,800			$50,551		$53,100
AFN =				$ 2,549		

[a]From Part a we know that sales can increase by 33% before additions to fixed assets are needed.
[b]See income statement.

c.

VAN AUKEN LUMBER: PRO FORMA INCOME STATEMENT FOR DECEMBER 31, 1999 (THOUSANDS OF DOLLARS)

	1ST PASS 1999	FINANCING FEEDBACK	2ND PASS 1999
Sales	$45,000		$45,000
Operating costs	38,479		38,479
EBIT	$ 6,521		$ 6,521
Interest	1,017	+306[a]	1,323
EBT	$ 5,504		$ 5,198
Taxes (40%)	2,202		2,079
Net income	$ 3,302		$ 3,119
Dividends (60%)	$ 1,981		$ 1,871
Addition to RE	$ 1,321		$ 1,248

[a]Δ in interest = $2,549 \times (0.12) = $306.

VAN AUKEN LUMBER: PRO FORMA BALANCE SHEET FOR DECEMBER 31, 1999 (THOUSANDS OF DOLLARS)

	1ST PASS 1999	FINANCING FEEDBACK	2ND PASS 1999
Total assets	$53,100		$53,100
Accounts payable	9,000		$ 9,000
Notes payable	6,021		6,021
Accruals	3,150		3,150
Total current liabilities	$18,171		$18,171
Mortgage bonds	5,000		5,000
Common stock	2,000		2,000
Retained earnings	27,929	−73[a]	27,856
Total liabilities and equity	$53,100		$53,027
AFN =			73

[a]Change in RE addition = $1,248 − $1,321 = −$73.
NOTE: The cumulative AFN for the first 2 passes = $2,549 + $73 = $2,622.

d. The rate of return projected for 1999 under the conditions in Part c is (calculations in thousands):

$$\text{ROE} = \frac{\$3,119}{\$29,856} = 10.45\%.$$

If Van Auken Lumber attained the industry average DSO and inventory turnover ratio, this would mean a reduction in financial requirements of:

$$\text{Receivables:} \frac{\text{New A/R}}{\$45,000/360} = 90$$

$$\text{New A/R} = \$11,250.$$

$$\text{Change in A/R} = \$13,500 − \$11,250 = \$2,250.$$

$$\text{Inventory:} \frac{\$45,000}{I} = 3.33; I = \$13,500.$$

$$\text{Change in Inventory} = \$15,750 − \$13,500 = \$2,250.$$

$$\text{Total Change} = \$2,250 + \$2,250 = \$4,500.$$

If this freed capital was used to reduce equity, the new figures for common equity would be $29,856 − $4,500 = $25,356. Assuming no change in net income, the new ROE would be:

$$\text{ROE} = \frac{\$3,119}{\$25,356} = 12.3\%.$$

One would, in a real analysis, want to consider both the feasibility of maintaining sales if receivables and inventories were reduced and also other possible effects on the profit margin. Also, note that the current ratio was $25,200/$13,192 = 1.91 in 1998. It is projected to decline in Part c to $31,500/$18,244 = 1.73, and the latest change would cause a further reduction to ($31,500 − $4,500)/$18,244 = 1.48. Creditors might not tolerate such a reduction in liquidity and might insist that at least some of the freed capital be used to reduce notes payable. Still, this would reduce interest charges, which would increase the profit margin, which would in turn raise the ROE. Management should always consider the possibility of changing ratios as part of financial projections.

Chapter 15

ST-1   a.

$$S = \frac{(EBIT - k_d D)(1 - T)}{k_s}$$

$$= \frac{[\$4,000,000 - 0.10(\$2,000,000)](0.65)}{0.15} = \$16,466,667.$$

$$P_0 = S/n = \frac{\$16,466,667}{600,000} = \$27.44.$$

$$V = D + S = \$2,000,000 + \$16,466,667 = \$18,466,667.$$

b.

$$WACC = (D/V)(k_d)(1 - T) + (S/V)(k_s)$$

$$= \left(\frac{\$2,000,000}{\$18,466,667}\right)(10\%)(0.65) + \left(\frac{\$16,466,667}{\$18,466,667}\right)(15\%)$$

$$= 14.08\%.$$

c. Under the new capital structure,

$$S = \frac{[\$4,000,000 - 0.12(\$10,000,000)](0.65)}{0.17} = \$10,705,882.$$

$$V = \$10,000,000 + \$10,705,882 = \$20,705,882.$$

The new value of the firm will thus be $20,705,882. This value belongs to the *present* stockholders and bondholders, so we may calculate the new equilibrium price of the stock, P_1:

$$P_1 = \frac{V_1 - D_0}{n_0} = \frac{\$20,705,882 - \$2,000,000}{600,000} = \$31.18.$$

$$\text{Check: Shares repurchased} = \frac{\text{New debt}}{P_1} = \frac{\$8,000,000}{\$31.18} = 256,575.$$

$$P_1 = \frac{S_1}{n_1} = \frac{\$10,705,882}{600,000 - 256,575} \approx \$31.18.$$

$$WACC = \left(\frac{\$10,000,000}{\$20,705,882}\right)(12\%)(0.65) + \left(\frac{\$10,705,882}{\$20,705,882}\right)(17\%) = 12.56\%.$$

Thus, the proposed capital structure change would increase the value of the firm and the price of its stock (from $27.44 to $31.18), and lower its cost of capital. Therefore, the firm should increase its use of financial leverage. Of course, it is possible that some amount of debt other than $10 million would result in an even higher value, but we do not have enough information to make this determination.

Chapter 16

ST-1   a. Value of unleveraged firm, $V_U = EBIT(1 - T)/k_{sU}$:

$$\$12 = \$2(1 - 0.4)/k_{sU}$$

$$\$12 = \$1.2/k_{sU}$$

$$k_{sU} = \$1.2/\$12 = 10.0\%.$$

Therefore, $k_{sU} = WACC = 10.0\%$.

b. Value of leveraged firm according to MM model with taxes:

$$V_L = V_U + TD.$$

As shown in the following table, value increases continuously with debt, and the optimal capital structure consists of 100 percent debt. Note: The table is not necessary to answer this question, but the data (in millions of dollars) are necessary for Part c of this problem.

DEBT, D	V_U	TD	$V_L = V_U + TD$
$ 0	$12.0	$ 0	$12.0
2.5	12.0	1.0	13.0
5.0	12.0	2.0	14.0
7.5	12.0	3.0	15.0
10.0	12.0	4.0	16.0
12.5	12.0	5.0	17.0
15.0	12.0	6.0	18.0
20.0	12.0	8.0	20.0

c. With financial distress costs included in the analysis, the value of the leveraged firm now is

$$V_L = V_U + TD - PC,$$

where

$V_U + TD$ = value according to MM after-tax model.
P = probability of financial distress.
C = present value of distress costs.

D	$V_U + TD$	P	PC = (P)$8	$V_L = V_U + TD - PC$
$ 0	$12.0	0	$ 0	$12.0
2.5	13.0	0	0	13.0
5.0	14.0	0.0125	0.10	13.9
7.5	15.0	0.0250	0.20	14.8
10.0	16.0	0.0625	0.50	15.5
12.5	17.0	0.1250	1.00	16.0
15.0	18.0	0.3125	2.50	15.5
20.0	20.0	0.7500	6.00	14.0

NOTE: All dollar amounts in table are in millions.

Optimal debt level: D = $12.5 million.
Maximum value of firm: V = $16.0 million.
Optimal debt/value ratio: D/V = $12.5/$16 = 78%.

d. The value of the firm versus debt value with and without financial distress costs is plotted next (millions of dollars):

V_L = Value without financial distress costs.
V_B = Value with financial distress costs.

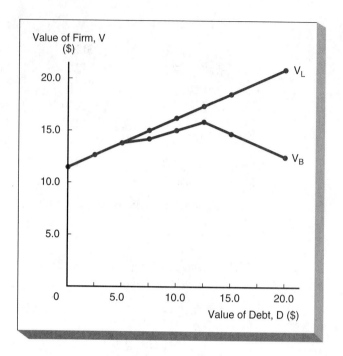

Chapter 17

ST-1   a.

Projected net income	$2,000,000
Less projected capital investments	800,000
Available residual	$1,200,000
Shares outstanding	200,000

$$\text{DPS} = \$1,200,000/200,000 \text{ shares} = \$6 = D_1.$$

b.   EPS = $2,000,000/200,000 shares = $10.

Payout ratio = DPS/EPS = $6/$10 = 60%, or

Total dividends/NI = $1,200,000/$2,000,000 = 60%.

c. $$\text{Currently, } P_0 = \frac{D_1}{k_s - g} = \frac{\$6}{0.14 - 0.05} = \frac{\$6}{0.09} = \$66.67.$$

Under the former circumstances, D_1 would be based on a 20 percent payout on $10 EPS, or $2. With $k_s = 14\%$ and $g = 12\%$, we solve for P_0:

$$P_0 = \frac{D_1}{k_s - g} = \frac{\$2}{0.14 - 0.12} = \frac{\$2}{0.02} = \$100.$$

Although CMC has suffered a severe setback, its existing assets will continue to provide a good income stream. More of these earnings should now be passed on to the shareholders, as the slowed internal growth has reduced the need for funds. However, the net result is a 33 percent decrease in the value of the shares.

d. If the payout ratio were continued at 20 percent, even after internal investment opportunities had declined, the price of the stock would drop to $2/(0.14 − 0.06) = $25 rather than to $66.67. Thus, an increase in the dividend payout is consistent with maximizing shareholder wealth.

Because of the diminishing nature of profitable investment opportunities, the greater the firm's level of investment, the lower the average ROE. Thus, the more money CMC retains and invests, the lower its average ROE will be. We can determine the average ROE under different conditions as follows:

Old situation (with founder active and a 20 percent payout):

$$g = (1.0 - \text{Payout ratio})(\text{Average ROE})$$

$$12\% = (1.0 - 0.2)(\text{Average ROE})$$

$$\text{Average ROE} = 12\%/0.8 = 15\% > k_s = 14\%.$$

Note that the *average* ROE is 15 percent, whereas the *marginal* ROE is presumably equal to 14 percent.

New situation (with founder retired and a 60 percent payout):

$$g = 6\% = (1.0 - 0.6)(\text{ROE})$$

$$\text{ROE} = 6\%/0.4 = 15\% > k_s = 14\%.$$

This suggests that the new payout is appropriate and that the firm is taking on investments down to the point at which marginal returns are equal to the cost of capital. Note that if the 20 percent payout was maintained, the *average* ROE would be only 7.5 percent, which would imply a marginal ROE far below the 14 percent cost of capital.

Chapter 19

ST-1 a. *Cost of leasing:*

	YEAR 0	YEAR 1	YEAR 2	YEAR 3	YEAR 4
Lease payment	($10,000)	($10,000)	($10,000)	($10,000)	$0
Payment tax savings	4,000	4,000	4,000	4,000	0
Net cash flow	($ 6,000)	($ 6,000)	($ 6,000)	($ 6,000)	$0

PV cost of owning @ 6% = ($22,038)

b. *Cost of owning:*

In our solution, we will consider the $40,000 cost as a Year 0 outflow rather than including all the financing cash flows. The net effect is the same since the PV of the financing flows, when discounted at the after-tax cost of debt, is the cost of the asset.

	YEAR 0	YEAR 1	YEAR 2	YEAR 3	YEAR 4
Net purchase price	($40,000)				
Maintenance cost		($1,000)	($1,000)	($1,000)	($1,000)
Maintenance tax savings		400	400	400	400
Depreciation tax savings		5,280	7,200	2,400	1,120
Residual value					10,000
Residual value tax			$6,600		(4,000)
Net cash flow	($40,000)	$4,680	$6,600	$1,800	$6,520

PV cost of owning @ 6% = ($23,035)

Since the present value of the cost of leasing is less than the present value of the cost of owning, the truck should be leased. Specifically, the NAL is $23,035 – $22,038 = $997.

c. Use the cost of debt because most cash flows are fixed by contract and consequently are relatively certain; thus lease cash flows have about the same risk as the firm's debt. Also, leasing is considered as a substitute for debt. Use an after-tax cost rate to account for interest tax deductibility.

d. The firm could increase the discount rate on the residual value cash flow. Note that since the firm plans to replace the truck after 4 years, the residual value is treated as an inflow in the cost of owning analysis. This makes it reasonable to raise the discount rate for analysis purposes. However, had the firm planned to continue using the truck, then we would have had to place the estimated residual value as an additional Year 4 outflow in the leasing section, but without a tax adjustment. Then, higher risk would have been reflected in a *lower* discount rate. This is all very ad hoc, which is why analysts often prefer to use one discount rate throughout the analysis.

Chapter 21

ST-1   THE CALGARY COMPANY: ALTERNATIVE BALANCE SHEETS

	RESTRICTED (40%)	MODERATE (50%)	RELAXED (60%)
Current assets	$1,200,000	$1,500,000	$1,800,000
Fixed assets	600,000	600,000	600,000
Total assets	$1,800,000	$2,100,000	$2,400,000
Debt	$ 900,000	$1,050,000	$1,200,000
Equity	900,000	1,050,000	1,200,000
Total liabilities and equity	$1,800,000	$2,100,000	$2,400,000

THE CALGARY COMPANY: ALTERNATIVE INCOME STATEMENTS

	RESTRICTED	MODERATE	RELAXED
Sales	$3,000,000	$3,000,000	$3,000,000
EBIT	450,000	450,000	450,000
Interest (10%)	90,000	105,000	120,000
Earnings before taxes	$ 360,000	$ 345,000	$ 330,000
Taxes (40%)	144,000	138,000	132,000
Net income	$ 216,000	$ 207,000	$ 198,000
ROE	24.0%	19.7%	16.5%

ST-2   a. First, determine the balance on the firm's checkbook and the bank's records as follows:

	FIRM'S CHECKBOOK	BANK'S RECORDS
Day 1: Deposit $500,000; write check for $1,000,000	($500,000)	$500,000
Day 2: Write check for $1,000,000	($1,500,000)	$500,000
Day 3: Write check for $1,000,000	($2,500,000)	$500,000
Day 4: Write check for $1,000,000; deposit $1,000,000	($2,500,000)	$500,000

After Upton has reached a steady state, it must deposit $1,000,000 each day to cover the checks written 3 days earlier.

b. The firm has 3 days of float; not until Day 4 does the firm have to make any additional deposits.

c. As shown above, Upton should try to maintain a balance on the bank's records of $500,000. On its own books it will have a balance of *minus* $2,500,000.

Chapter 22

ST-1 a. and b.

INCOME STATEMENTS FOR YEAR ENDED DECEMBER 31, 1998 (THOUSANDS OF DOLLARS)

	VANDERHEIDEN PRESS		HERRENHOUSE PUBLISHING	
	a	b	a	b
EBIT	$ 30,000	$ 30,000	$ 30,000	$ 30,000
Interest	12,400	14,400	10,600	18,600
Taxable income	$ 17,600	$ 15,600	$ 19,400	$ 11,400
Taxes (40%)	7,040	6,240	7,760	4,560
Net income	$ 10,560	$ 9,360	$ 11,640	$ 6,840
Equity	$100,000	$100,000	$100,000	$100,000
Return on equity	10.56%	9.36%	11.64%	6.84%

The Vanderheiden Press has a higher ROE when short-term interest rates are high, whereas Herrenhouse Publishing does better when rates are lower.

c. Herrenhouse's position is riskier. First, its profits and return on equity are much more volatile than Vanderheiden's. Second, Herrenhouse must renew its large short-term loan every year, and if the renewal comes up at a time when money is very tight, when its business is depressed, or both, then Herrenhouse could be denied credit, which could put it out of business.

Chapter 23

ST-1 Under the current credit policy, the firm has no discounts, collection expenses of $50,000, bad debt losses of $(0.02)($10,000,000) = $200,000$, and average accounts receivable of (DSO)(Average sales per day) = $(30)($10,000,000/360) = $833,333$. The firm's cost of carrying these receivables is (Variable cost ratio)(A/R)(Cost of capital) = $(0.80)($833,333)(0.16) = $106,667$. It is necessary to multiply by the variable cost ratio because the actual *investment* in receivables is less than the dollar amount of the receivables.

Proposal 1: Lengthen the credit period such that
1. Sales increase by $1 million.
2. Discounts = $0.
3. Bad debt losses = $(0.02)($10,000,000) + (0.04)($1,000,000)$

$$= \$200,000 + \$40,000$$

$$= \$240,000.$$

4. DSO = 45 days on all sales.
5. New average receivables = $(45)($11,000,000/360)$

$$= \$1,375,000.$$

6. Cost of carrying receivables = (v)(k)(Average accounts receivable)

$$= (0.80)(0.16)(\$1,375,000)$$

$$= \$176,000.$$

7. Change in cost of carrying receivables = $176,000 – $106,667

$$= \$69,333.$$

8. Collection expenses = $50,000.

Analysis of proposed change:

	INCOME STATEMENT UNDER CURRENT POLICY	EFFECT OF CHANGE	INCOME STATEMENT UNDER NEW POLICY
Gross sales	$10,000,000	+ $1,000,000	$11,000,000
Less discounts	0	+ 0	0
Net sales	$10,000,000	+ $1,000,000	$11,000,000
Variable costs (80%)	8,000,000	+ 800,000	8,800,000
Profit before credit costs and taxes	$ 2,000,000	+ $ 200,000	$ 2,200,000
Credit-related costs:			
Cost of carrying receivables	106,667	+ 69,333	176,000
Collection expenses	50,000	+ 0	50,000
Bad debt losses	200,000	+ 40,000	240,000
Profit before taxes	$ 1,643,333	+ $ 90,667	$ 1,734,000
Taxes (50%)	821,666	+ 45,333	867,000
Net income	$ 821,667	+ 45,334	$ 867,000

The proposed change appears to be a good one, if the assumptions are correct.

Proposal 2: Shorten the credit period to net 20 such that
1. Sales decrease by $1 million.

2. Discount = $0.

3. Bad debt losses = (0.01)($9,000,000)

$$= \$90,000.$$

4. DSO = 22 days.

5. New average receivables = (22)($9,000,000/360)

$$= \$550,000.$$

6. Cost of carrying receivables = (v)(k)(Average accounts receivable)

$$= (0.80)(0.16)(\$550,000)$$

$$= \$70,400.$$

7. Collection expenses = $50,000.

Analysis of proposed change:

	INCOME STATEMENT UNDER CURRENT POLICY	EFFECT OF CHANGE	INCOME STATEMENT UNDER NEW POLICY
Gross sales	$10,000,000	−$1,000,000	$9,000,000
Less discounts	0	0	0
Net sales	$10,000,000	−$1,000,000	$9,000,000
Variable costs (80%)	8,000,000	− 800,000	7,200,000
Profit before credit costs and taxes	$ 2,000,000	−$ 200,000	$1,800,000
Credit-related costs:			
Cost of carrying receivables	106,667	− 36,267	70,400
Collection expenses	50,000	0	50,000
Bad debt losses	200,000	− 110,000	90,000
Profit before taxes	$ 1,643,333	−$ 53,733	$1,589,600
Taxes (50%)	821,666	− 26,866	794,800
Net income	$ 821,667	−$ 26,867	794,800

This change reduces net income, so it should be rejected. The firm will increase profits by accepting Proposal 1 to lengthen the credit period from 25 days to 30 days, if all assumptions are correct. This may or may not be the *optimal,* or profit-maximizing, credit policy, but it does appear to be a movement in the right direction. However, before a final decision is made, the riskiness of the change must be considered.

ST-2   a.

$$EOQ = \sqrt{\frac{2(F)(S)}{(C)(P)}}$$

$$= \sqrt{\frac{(2)(\$5,000)(2,600,000)}{(0.02)(\$5.00)}}$$

$$= 509,902 \text{ bushels.}$$

Since the firm must order in multiples of 2,000 bushels, it should order in quantities of 510,000 bushels.

b.
$$\text{Average weekly sales} = 2,600,000/52$$
$$= 50,000 \text{ bushels.}$$
$$\text{Reorder point} = 6 \text{ weeks' sales} + \text{Safety stock}$$
$$= 6(50,000) + 200,000$$
$$= 300,000 + 200,000$$
$$= 500,000 \text{ bushels.}$$

c. Total inventory costs:

$$TIC = CP\left(\frac{Q}{2}\right) + F\left(\frac{S}{Q}\right) + CP(\text{Safety stock})$$

$$= (0.02)(\$5)\left(\frac{510,000}{2}\right) + (\$5,000)\left(\frac{2,600,000}{510,000}\right) + (0.02)(\$5)(200,000)$$

$$= \$25,500 + \$25,490.20 + \$20,000$$

$$= \$70,990.20.$$

d. By ordering 650,000 bushels at a time, ordering costs would be reduced to $1,500, so total inventory costs would be:

$$\text{TIC} = (0.02)(\$5)\left(\frac{650,000}{2}\right) + (\$1,500)\left(\frac{2,600,000}{650,000}\right) + (0.02)(\$5)(200,000)$$

$$= \$32,500 + \$6,000 + \$20,000$$

$$= \$58,500.$$

Since the firm can reduce its total inventory costs by ordering 650,000 bushels at a time, it should accept the offer and place larger orders. (Incidentally, this same type of analysis is used to consider any quantity discount offer.)

Chapter 24

ST-1 a. Exercise value = Current stock price − Strike price
$$= \$30 - \$25 = \$5.$$

b. Premium = Option price − Exercise value
$$= \$7 - \$5 = \$2.$$

ST-2 a. An increase in stock price increases the value of a call option because it increases the size of the profit should the option be exercised.

b. An increase in volatility means that the stock price might become much higher or much lower than the strike price. Stock prices higher than the strike price lead to high exercise values, but the exercise value will never be less than zero, no matter how low the stock price. So volatility increases the upside potential without increasing the downside risk. Therefore, volatility increases the value of a call option.

c. As the risk-free rate increases, the present value of the cost of exercising the option in the future decreases, which causes the value of the call option to increase.

d. A decrease in the time remaining until expiration reduces the chance that the stock price will go up very much. Therefore, a decrease in time reduces the value of a call option.

Answers to End-of-Chapter Problems

We present here some intermediate steps and final answers to selected end-of-chapter problems. Please note that your answer may differ slightly from ours due to rounding differences. Also, although we hope not, some of the problems may have more than one correct solution, depending upon what assumptions are made in working the problem. Finally, many of the problems involve some verbal discussion as well as numerical calculations; this verbal material is not presented here.

2-1 $1,000,000.

2-2 $3,600,000.

2-3 5.76%.

2-4 $21,804.

2-5 25%.

2-6 Tax = $107,855; NI = $222,145; Marginal tax rate = 39%; Average tax rate = 33.8%.

2-7 a. Tax = $3,575,000.
b. Tax = $350,000.
c. Tax = $105,000.

2-8 AT&T preferred stock = 5.37%.

2-9 Municipal bond; yield = 7%.

2-10 NI = $450,000; NCF = $650,000; OCF = $650,000.

2-11 a.

2-12 a. $584.
c. $1,520.

2-13 a. $2,400,000.

2-14 $2,500,000.

2-15 a. NOPAT = $90,000,000.
b. $NOWC_{97}$ = $210,000,000;
   $NOWC_{98}$ = $192,000,000.
c. Operating $capital_{97}$ = $460,000,000;
   Operating $capital_{98}$ = $492,000,000.
d. FCF = $58,000,000.

2-17 Tax_{1999} = $0; Tax_{2000} = $0; Tax_{2001} = $12,000,000; Tax_{2002} = $32,000,000; Tax_{2003} = $0 and receive refund of $44,000,000 for 2001 and 2002 taxes.

2-18 a. 1999 advantage as a corporation = $1,248; 2000 advantage = $4,498; 2001 advantage = $5,648.

2-19 a. Personal tax = $26,262.50.
b. Marginal rate = 31%; average rate = 24.9%.
c. Disney yield = 5.52%; choose FLA bonds.
d. 25%.

3-1 CL = $2,000,000; Inv = $1,000,000.

3-2 AR = $800,000.

3-3 D/A = 58.33%.

3-4 TATO = 5; EM = 1.5.

3-5 $\dfrac{NI}{S}$ = 2%; $\dfrac{D}{A}$ = 40%.

3-6 $262,500; 1.19×.

3-7 Sales = $2,592,000; DSO = 36 days.

3-8 TIE = 3.86×.

3-9 ROE = 23.1%.

3-10 7.2%.

3-11 a.

3-12 a. +5.54%.
b(2). + 3.21%.
(3). + 2.50%.

3-13 a. Current ratio = 1.98×; DSO = 75 days; Total assets turnover = 1.7×; Debt ratio = 61.9%.

3-14 A/P = $90,000; Inv = $90,000; FA = $138,000.

3-16 a. Quick ratio = 0.8×; DSO = 37 days; ROE = 13.1%; Debt ratio = 54.8%.

4-1 6%; 6.33%.

4-2 1.5%.

4-3 5.5%.

4-4 0.2%.

4-5 6.4%.

4-6 8.5%.

4-7 6.8%.

4-8 a. k_1 in Year 2 = 6%.

4-9 k_1 in Year 2 = 9%; Year 2 inflation = 7%.

4-10 1.5%.

4-11 6.0%.

4-12 a. $k_1 = 9.20\%$; $k_5 = 7.20\%$.

4-14 a. 8.20%.
    b. 10.20%.
    c. $k_5 = 10.70\%$.

5-1 $\hat{k} = 11.40\%$; $\sigma = 26.69\%$; $CV = 2.34$.

5-2 $b = 1.12$.

5-3 $k_M = 11\%$; $k = 12.2\%$.

5-4 $k = 10.90\%$.

5-5 a. $\hat{k}_M = 13.5\%$; $\hat{k}_j = 11.6\%$.
    b. $\sigma_M = 3.85\%$; $\sigma_j = 6.22\%$.
    c. $CV_M = 0.29$; $CV_j = 0.54$.

5-6 a. $\hat{k}_Y = 14\%$.
    b. $\sigma_X = 12.20\%$.

5-7 a. $b_A = 1.40$.
    b. $k_A = 15\%$.

5-8 a. $k_i = 15.5\%$.
    b(1). $k_M = 15\%$; $k_i = 16.5\%$.
    (2). $k_M = 13\%$; $k_i = 14.5\%$.
    c(1). $k_i = 18.1\%$.
    (2). $k_i = 14.2\%$.

5-9 $b_N = 1.16$.

5-10 $b_p = 0.7625$; $k_p = 12.1\%$.

5-11 $b_N = 1.1250$.

5-12 4.5%.

5-13 a. $0.5 million.

5-14 a. $k_i = 6\% + (5\%)b_i$.
    b. 15%.
    c. Indifference rate = 16%.

5-15 a. $\bar{k}_A = 11.30\%$.
    c. $\sigma_A = 20.8\%$; $\sigma_p = 20.1\%$.

5-16 a. $b_X = 1.3471$; $b_Y = 0.6508$.
    b. $k_X = 12.7355\%$; $k_Y = 9.254\%$.
    c. $k_p = 12.04\%$.

6-1 b. X: 10.6%; 13.1%.
    M: 12.1%; 22.6%.
    c. 8.6%.

7-1 a. $530.
    b. $561.80.
    c. $471.70.
    d. $445.00.

7-2 a. $895.40.
    b. $1,552.90.
    c. $279.20.
    d. $i = 12\%$; $500.03.
    $i = 6\%$; $867.14.

7-3 a. $n \approx 10$ years.
    b. $n \approx 7$ years.
    c. $n \approx 4$ years.
    d. $n \approx 1$ year.

7-4 a. $6,374.96.
    b. $1,105.12.
    c. $2,000.00.
    d(1). $7,012.46.
    (2). $1,160.38.
    (3). $2,000.00.

7-5 a. $2,457.84.
    b. $865.90.
    c. $2,000.00.
    d(1). $2,703.62.
    (2). $909.20.
    (3). $2,000.00.

7-6 a. $PV_A = \$1,251.21$.
    $PV_B = \$1,300.27$.
    b. $PV_A = \$1,600$.
    $PV_B = \$1,600$.

7-7 a. 7%.
    b. 7%.
    c. 9%.
    d. 15%.

7-8 a. $881.15.
    b. $895.40.
    c. $903.05.
    d. $908.35.

7-9 a. $279.20.
    b. $276.85.
    c. $443.70.

7-10 a. $5,272.32.
    b. $5,374.07.

7-12 b. $13,189.87.
    c. $8,137.27.

7-13 a. $I_z = 9\%$; $I_B = 8\%$.

7-14 a. $61,203.
    b. $11,020.
    c. $6,841.

7-15 $1,000 today.

7-16 a. $i \approx 15\%$.

7-17 $i = 7.18\%$.

7-18 $i = 12\%$.

7-19 $i = 9\%$.

7-20 a. $33,872.00.
    b(1). $26,243.04.
    (2). $0.

7-21   15 years.

7-22   6 years; $1,106.01.

7-23   (1). $1,428.57.
       (2). $714.29.

7-24 $893.26.

7-25 $984.88.

7-26   57.18%.

7-27   a. $1,432.02.
       b. $93.07.

7-28 $i_{Nom} = 15.19\%$.

7-29   PMT = $36,949.61.

8-1 $935.82.
8-2   12.48%.

8-3   YTM = 6.62%;   YTC = 6.49%.

8-4   8.55%.

8-5 $1,028.60.

8-6   a. V_L at 5 percent = $1,518.97; V_L at 8 percent =
       $1,171.15; V_L at 12 percent = $863.79.

8-7   a. YTM at $829 $\approx$ 15%.

8-8   15.03%.

8-9   a. 10.37%.
       b. 10.91%.
       c. −0.54%.
       d. 10.15%.

8-10   8.65%.

8-11   10.78%.

8-12   YTC = 6.47%.

8-13   a. $1,251.26.
       b. $898.90.

8-15   a. YTM = 3.4%.
       b. YTM $\approx$ 7%.
       c. $934.91.

8-16   a. YTM = 8%;   YTC = 6.1%.

8-17   10-year, 10% coupon = 6.75%;
       10-year zero = 9.75%;
       5-year zero = 4.76%;
       30-year zero = 32.19%;
       $100 perpetuity = 14.29%.

8-18   a. $C_0 = \$1,012.79$; $Z_0 = \$693.04$;
       $C_1 = \$1,010.02$; $Z_1 = \$759.57$;
       $C_2 = \$1,006.98$; $Z_2 = \$832.49$;
       $C_3 = \$1,003.65$; $Z_3 = \$912.41$;
       $C_4 = \$1,000.00$; $Z_4 = \$1,000.00$.

9-1 $D_1 = \$1.5750$; $D_3 = \$1.7364$; $D_5 = \$2.1011$.

9-2 $P_0 = \$6.25$.

9-3 $P_1 = \$22.00$; $k_s = 15.50\%$.

9-4 $k_{ps} = 8.33\%$.

9-5 $V_{op} = \$6,000,000$.

9-6 $50.50.

9-7 $g = 9\%$.

9-8 $\hat{P}_3 = \$27.32$.

9-9   a. 13.3%.
       b. 10%.
       c. 8%.
       d. 5.7%.

9-10 $23.75.

9-11   a. $k_C = 10.6\%$; $k_D = 7\%$.

9-12 $25.03.

9-13 $P_0 = \$19.89$.

9-14   a. $V_{op2} = \$2,700,000$.
       b. $2,303,571.43.

9-15   a. $125.
       b. $83.33.

9-16   b. PV = $5.29.
       d. $30.01.

9-17   a. 7%.
       b. 5%.
       c. 12%.

9-18   a(1). $9.50.
       (2). $13.33.
       b(1). Undefined.

9-20   a. Dividend 2001 = $2.66.
       b. $P_0 = \$39.42$.
       c. Dividend yield 1999 = 5.10%; 2004 = 7.00%.

9-21   a. $P_0 = \$54.11$.

9-22   FCF = $37.0.

9-23   a. $713.33.
       b. $527.89.
       c. $43.79.

9-24   a. $P_0 = \$21.43$.
       b. $P_0 = \$26.47$.
       d. $P_0 = \$40.54$.

9-25   a. New price = $31.34.
       b. beta = 0.49865.

10-1 $k_s = 13\%$.

10-2 $k_{ps} = 8\%$.

10-3 $k_s = 15\%$.

10-4 a. 13%.
b. 10.4%.
c. 8.45%.

10-5 7.80%.

10-6 11.94%.

10-7 7.2%.

10-8 a. 16.3%.
b. 15.4%.
c. 16%.

10-9 a. 8%.
b. $2.81.
c. 15.81%.

10-10 a. $g = 3\%$.
b. $EPS_1 = \$5.562$.

10-11 a. $15,000,000.
b. 8.4%.

10-12 a. 4.8%; 12.3%.
b. 10.05%.

10-13 Short-term debt = 11.14%.
Long-term debt = 22.03%.
Common equity = 66.83%.

10-15 $w_{d(Short)} = 0\%$; $w_{d(Long)} = 20\%$; $w_{ps} = 4\%$; $w_{ce} = 76\%$.
k_d (After-tax) = 7.2%; $k_{ps} = 11.6\%$; $k_s \approx 17.5\%$.

11-1 4.34 years.

11-2 NPV = $7,486.20.

11-3 IRR = 16%.

11-4 DPP = 6.51 years.

11-5 MIRR = 13.89%.

11-6 5%: $NPV_A = \$16,108,952$; $NPV_B = \$18,300,939$.
15%: $NPV_A = \$10,059,587$; $NPV_B = \$13,897,838$.

11-7 NPV = $174.90.

11-8 $NPV_T = \$409$; $IRR_T = 15\%$; $MIRR_T = 14.54\%$; Accept;
$NPV_P = \$3,318$; $IRR_P = 20\%$; $MIRR_P = 17.19\%$;
Accept.

11-9 $NPV_E = \$3,861$; $IRR_E = 18\%$; $NPV_G = \$3,057$; $IRR_G = 18\%$; Purchase electric-powered forklift; it has a higher NPV.

11-10 $NPV_S = \$814.33$; $NPV_L = \$1,675.34$; $IRR_S = 15.24\%$;
$IRR_L = 14.67\%$; $MIRR_S = 13.77\%$; $MIRR_L = 13.46\%$;
$PI_S = 1.081$; $PI_L = 1.067$.

11-11 b. $PV_C = -\$556,717$; $PV_F = -\$493,407$; Forklift should be chosen.

11-12 $MIRR_X = 13.59\%$.

11-13 $IRR_L = 11.74\%$.

11-14 MIRR = 10.93%.

11-15 a. NPV = $136,578; IRR = 19.22%.

11-16 a. Payback = 0.33 year; NPV = $81,062.35; IRR = 261.90%.

11-17 a. No; $PV_{Old} = -\$89,910.08$; $PV_{New} = -\$94,611.45$.
b. $2,470.80.
c. 22.94%.

11-18 b. $IRR_A = 18.1\%$; $IRR_B = 24.0\%$.
d(1). $MIRR_A = 15.10\%$; $MIRR_B = 17.03\%$.
(2). $MIRR_A = 18.05\%$; $MIRR_B = 20.49\%$.

11-19 a. $0; −$10,250,000; $1,750,000.
b. 16.07%.

11-20 a. $NPV_A = \$18,108,510$; $NPV_B = \$13,946,117$;
$IRR_A = 15.03\%$; $IRR_B = 22.26\%$.
b. $NPV_\Delta = \$4,162,393$; $IRR_\Delta = 11.71\%$.

11-21 d. 7.61%; 15.58%.

11-23 a. Undefined.
b. $PV_C = -\$911,067$; $PV_F = -\$838,834$.

11-24 a. A = 2.67 years; B = 1.5 years.
b. A = 3.07 years; B = 1.825 years.
d. $NPV_A = \$18,243,813$; choose A.
e. $NPV_B = \$8,643,390$; choose B.
f. 13.53%.
g. $MIRR_A = 21.93\%$; $MIRR_B = 20.96\%$.

12-1 $12,000,000.

12-2 $2,600,000.

12-3 $4,600,000.

12-4 NPV = $15,301; Buy the new machine.

12-5 NPV = $22,329; Replace the old machine.

12-6 Extended $NPV_A = \$12.76$ million.

12-7 Machine A; Extended $NPV_A = \$4.51$ million; $EAA_A = \$0.845$ million.

12-8 a. −$126,000.
b. $42,518; $47,579; $34,926.
c. $50,702.
d. NPV = $10,841; Purchase.

12-10 a. $89,000.
b. $26,220; $30,300; $20,100.
c. $24,380.

12-11 a. $88,400.
b. $46,770; $52,890; $37,590; $33,510; $29,940.
c. −$10,000.
d. $46,051.

12-13 a. 3 years.
b. No.

12-14 a. NPV = $106,537.

13-1 E(NPV) = $3 million; σ_{NPV} = $23.622 million; CV_{NPV} = 7.874.

13-2 k_p = 8.5%; $b_{F,\ New}$ = 1.26; $k_{F,\ New}$ = 11.3%.

13-3 a. 16%.
b. NPV = $411; Accept.

13-4 a. 15%.
b. 1.48; 15.4%; 17%.

13-5 a. Expected CF_A = $6,750; Expected CF_B = $7,650; CV_A = 0.0703.
b. NPV_A = $10,037; NPV_B = $11,624.

13-7 a. $117,779.
b. σ_{NPV} = $445,060; CV_{NPV} = 3.78.

13-8 a. 16.5%.

13-9 a. E(IRR) ≈ 15.3%.
b. $38,589.

14-1 AFN = $410,000.

14-2 AFN = $610,000.

14-3 AFN = $200,000.

14-4 ΔS = $68,965.52.

14-5 a. $13.44 million.
b. Notes payable = $31.44 million.
c. Current ratio = 2.00×; ROE = 14.2%.
d(1). −$14.28 million.
(2). Total assets = $147 million; Notes payable = $3.72 million.
(3). Current ratio = 4.25×; ROE = 10.84%.

14-6 a. Total assets = $33,534; AFN = $2,128.
b. Notes payable = $4,228; AFN = $70; ΔInterest = $213.

14-7 a. AFN = $128,783.
b. Notes payable = $220,392; ΔInterest = $8,371; AFN = $8,028.
c. 3.45%.

14-8 a. AFN = $667.
b. Increase in notes payable = $51; Increase in common stock = $368.

14-9 a. $480,000.
b. $18,750.

14-10 AFN = $360.

15-1 a. ROI = 21.25% > WACC = 15%.
b(1). OL_{Old} = 44.44%; OL_{New} = 47.17%.
(2). $Q_{BE_{Old}}$ = 40; $Q_{BE_{New}}$ = 45.45.

15-2 a. ROE_C = 15%; σ_C = 11%.

15-3 b. $2 million.
c. $20.28; $17.96.

15-4 a. V = $3,283,636.
b. $16.42.
c. $1.81.

15-5 a. 14.0%.
c. $38.85.

16-1 a. b_U = 1.13.
b. k_{sU} = 15.65%; 5.65%.
c. 1%; 2.42%; 4.62%.
d. 4.62%.

16-2 a. V_U = V_L = $20 million.
b. k_{sU} = 10%; k_{sL} = 15%.
c. S_L = $10 million.
d. $WACC_U$ = 10%; $WACC_L$ = 10%.

16-3 a. V_U = $12 million; V_L = $16 million.
b. k_{sU} = 10%; k_{sL} = 15%.
c. S_L = $6 million.
d. $WACC_U$ = 10%; $WACC_L$ = 7.5%.

16-4 a. V_U = 9.6 million.
b. V_L = $12.93 million.
c. $3.33 million versus $4 million.
d. V_L = $20 million; $0.
e. V_L = $16 million; $4 million.
f. V_L = $12.64 million; $4 million.

16-5 a. V_U = V_L = $14,545,455.
b. At D = $6 million: k_{sL} = 14.51%; WACC = 11.0%.
c. V_U = $8,727,273; V_L = $11,127,273.
d. At D = $6 million: k_{sL} = 14.51%; WACC = 8.63%.
e. D = V = $14,545,455.

16-6 a. A: $32.5 million; B: $30.0 million.
b. Project B.

16-7 a. Harris: $10.0 million;
Broske: $10.0 million.

17-1 Payout = 55%.

17-2 P_0 = $60.

17-3 P_0 = $40.

17-4 $3,250,000.

17-5 Payout = 20%.

17-6 Payout = 52%.

17-7 D_0 = $3.44.

17-8 Payout = 31.39%.

17-9 a(1). $3,960,000.
  (2). $4,800,000.
  (3). $9,360,000.
  (4). Regular = $3,960,000; Extra = $5,400,000.
 c. 15%.
 d. 15%.

17-10 a. $6,000,000.
 b. DPS = $2.00; Payout = 25%.
 c. $5,000,000.
 d. No.
 e. 50%.
 f. $1,000,000.
 g. $8,333,333.

18-1 a. $700,000.
 b. $3,700,000.
 c. −$2,300,000.

18-2 964,115.

18-3 a. 1998: $12,000; $6,000; $90,000.
 b. Edelman: g_{EPS} = 8.0%; g_{DPS} = 7.4%.
 e. 1998: $3.00; $1.50; $22.50.
 f. Kennedy: 15.00%; Strasburg: 13.64%.
 g. 1998: Kennedy: 50%; Strasburg: 50%.
 h. Kennedy: 43%; Strasburg: 37%.
 i. Kennedy: 8×; Strasburg: 8.67×.

19-1 a(1). 50%.
  (2). 60%.
  (3). 50%.

19-2 Cost of owning = −$127; cost of leasing = −$128.

19-3 a. NAL = $37,206.

20-1 $196.36.

20-2 25 shares.

20-3 a(1). −$5, or $0.
  (2). $0.
  (3). $5.
  (4). $75.
 d. 10%; $100.

20-5 a. 14.1%.
 b. $12 million before tax.

20-6 b. Plan 1: 49%; Plan 2: 53%; Plan 3: 53%.
 c. Plan 1: $0.59; Plan 2: $0.64; Plan 3: $0.88.
 d. Plan 1: 19%; Plan 2: 19%; Plan 3: 50%.

20-7 b. 11.65%.

21-1 $10,000.

21-2 $3,000,000.

21-3 A/R = $59,500.

21-4 a. $103,350.
 b. $97,500.

21-5 a. DSO = 28 days.
 b. A/R = $70,000.

21-6 a. ROE_T = 11.75%; ROE_M = 10.80%; ROE_R = 9.16%.

21-7 a. $1,600,000.
 c. Bank = $1,200,000; Books = −$5,200,000.

21-8 b. $420,000.
 c. $35,000.

21-9 a. Feb. surplus = $2,000.

21-10 a. Oct. loan = $22,800.

22-1 k_{Nom} = 74.23%; EAR = 107.72%.

22-2 EAR = 8.37%.

22-3 $7,500,000.

22-4 $233.56.

22-5 EAR = 21.60%.

22-6 b. 14.69%.
 d. 20.99%.

22-7 a. 44.54%.

22-8 a. k_d = 12%.
 b. k_d = 11.25%.
 c. k_d = 11.48%.
 d. k_d = 14.47%. Alternative b has lowest interest rate.

22-9 Nominal cost = 14.69%; Effective cost = 15.66%.

22-10 Bank loan = 13.64%.

22-11 d. 8.3723%.

22-12 a. $100,000.
 c(1). $300,000.
  (2). Nominal cost = 36.73%; Effective cost = 43.86%.

22-14 a. $300,000.

22-15 a. 11.73%.
 b. 12.09%.
 c. 13.45%.

22-16 b. $384,615.
 c. Cash = $126.90; NP = $434.60.

22-17 a(1). $27,500.
  (3). $25,833.

23-1 a. 83 days.
 c. 4.8×.

23-2 ΔNI = −$3,450.

23-3 a. 3,000 bags.
b. 4,000 bags.
c. 2,500 bags.
d. Every 12 days.

23-4 $\Delta NI = + \$28,115$.

23-5 a. March: $146,000; June: $198,000.
b. Q1: ADS = $3,000; DSO = 48.7 days; Q2: ADS = $4,500; DSO = 44.0 days; Cumulative: ADS = $3,750; DSO = 52.8 days.
c. 0–30 days: 65%; 31–60 days: 35%.
d. Receivables/Sales = 130%.

23-6 b. $22,500.
c. 100.

24-1 $1.82.

24-2 $27.00; $37.00.

24-3 $k_d = 7.95\%$; $91,227.97.

24-4 b. Futures = +$2,165,343; Bond = –$1,101,851; Net = +$1,063,492.

25-1 a. Total assets: $327 million.
b. Income: $7 million.
c. Before: $15.6 million.
After: $13.0 million.
d. Before: 35.7%.
After: 64.2%.

25-2 a. $0.
b. First mortgage holders: $300,000.
Second mortgage holders: $100,000.
c. Trustee's expenses: $50,000.
Wages due: $30,000.
Taxes due: $40,000.

25-3 b. AP = 24%; NP = 100%; WP = 100%; TP = 100%; Mortgage = 85%.
Subordinated debentures = 9%; Trustee = 100%.

26-1 $P_0 = \$37.04$.

26-2 $P_0 = \$43.48$.

26-3 $37.04 to $43.48.

26-4 a. 17%.
b. V = $14.65 million.

26-5 NPV = –$6,747.71; Do not purchase.

26-6 a. 14%.
b. TV = $1,143.4; V = $877.2.

27-1 0.07425 yen per lira.

27-2 $f_t = \$0.00907$.

27-3 1 FF = $0.19724 or $1 = 5.07 FF.

27-4 0.6667 pound per dollar.

27-5 4.5455 FF.

27-6 8.85 francs per pound.

27-8 $480,000,000.

27-9 +$250,000.

27-10

	DOLLARS PER 1,000 UNITS OF:			
MARKS	LIRA	YEN	PESOS	SWISS FRANCS
$641.80	$0.65	$8.77	$127.26	$746.50

27-12 b. $17,192.80.

27-13 a. $2,709,339.
b. $2,689,121.
c. $3,200,000.

27-14 b. $f_t = \$0.6295$.

27-15 $k_{\text{Nom-U.S.}} = 4.6\%$.

27-16 117 pesos.

27-17 $e_0 = 20$ yen per 1 FF, or 0.05 FF per 1 yen.

28-1 a. $80,865.
b. $856.
c. $10,613; $1,409.
d. $1,021.

28-2 a. 0.8%.

28-3 a. $6,772,460.

Selected Equations and Data

Chapter 2

Net operating working capital = All current assets that do not pay interest − All current liabilities that do not charge interest.

= Operating current assets − operating current liabilities.

Operating capital = (Net operating working capital) + (Net plant and equipment).

NOPAT = EBIT(1 − Tax rate).

Operating cash flow = NOPAT + Depreciation.

$$\text{Equivalent pre-tax yield on taxable bond} = \frac{\text{Yield on muni}}{1 - \text{Marginal tax rate}}.$$

Free cash flow (FCF) = Operating cash flow − Gross investment in operating capital.

= NOPAT − Net investment in operating capital.

MVA = Market value of equity − Equity capital supplied by shareholders

= (Shares outstanding)(Stock price) − Total common equity.

EVA = After-tax operating profit, or NOPAT − After-tax dollar cost of capital used to support operations.

= EBIT(1 − Tax rate) − (After-tax percentage cost of capital)(Operating capital).

INDIVIDUAL TAX RATES FOR APRIL 1997

Single Individuals

IF YOUR TAXABLE INCOME IS	YOU PAY THIS AMOUNT ON THE BASE OF THE BRACKET	PLUS THIS PERCENTAGE ON THE EXCESS OVER THE BASE	AVERAGE TAX RATE AT TOP OF BRACKET
Up to $24,650	$ 0	15.0%	15.0%
$24,650–$59,750	3,697.50	28.0	22.6
$59,750–$124,650	13,525.50	31.0	27.0
$124,650–$271,050	33,644.50	36.0	31.9
Over $271,050	86,348.50	39.6	39.6

Married Couples Filing Joint Returns

IF YOUR TAXABLE INCOME IS	YOU PAY THIS AMOUNT ON THE BASE OF THE BRACKET	PLUS THIS PERCENTAGE ON THE EXCESS OVER THE BASE	AVERAGE TAX RATE AT TOP OF BRACKET
Up to $41,200	$ 0	15.0%	15.0%
$41,200–$99,600	6,180.00	28.0	22.6
$99,600–$151,750	22,532.00	31.0	25.5
$151,750–$271,050	38,698.50	36.0	30.1
Over $271,050	81,646.50	39.6	39.6

CORPORATE TAX RATES

IF A CORPORATION'S TAXABLE INCOME IS	IT PAYS THIS AMOUNT ON THE BASE OF THE BRACKET	PLUS THIS PERCENTAGE ON THE EXCESS OVER THE BASE	AVERAGE TAX RATE AT TOP OF BRACKET
Up to $50,000	$ 0	15%	15.0%
$50,000–$75,000	7,500	25	18.3
$75,000–$100,000	13,750	34	22.3
$100,000–$335,000	22,250	39	34.0
$335,000–$10,000,000	113,900	34	34.0
$10,000,000–$15,000,000	3,400,000	35	34.3
$15,000,000–$18,333,333	5,150,000	38	35.0
Over $18,333,333	6,416,667	35	35.0

Chapter 3

$$\text{Current ratio} = \frac{\text{Current assets}}{\text{Current liabilities}}.$$

$$\text{Quick, or acid test, ratio} = \frac{\text{Current assets} - \text{Inventories}}{\text{Current liabilities}}.$$

$$\text{Inventory turnover ratio} = \frac{\text{Sales}}{\text{Inventories}}.$$

$$\text{DSO} = \begin{matrix}\text{Days}\\\text{sales}\\\text{outstanding}\end{matrix} = \frac{\text{Receivables}}{\text{Average sales per day}} = \frac{\text{Receivables}}{\text{Annual sales}/360}.$$

$$\text{Fixed assets turnover ratio} = \frac{\text{Sales}}{\text{Net fixed assets}}.$$

$$\text{Total assets turnover ratio} = \frac{\text{Sales}}{\text{Total assets}}.$$

$$\text{Operating capital requirement ratio} = \frac{\text{Operating capital}}{\text{Sales}}.$$

$$\text{Debt ratio} = \frac{\text{Total debt}}{\text{Total assets}}.$$

$$\text{D/E} = \frac{\text{D/A}}{1 - \text{D/A}}, \text{ and D/A} = \frac{\text{D/E}}{1 + \text{D/E}}.$$

$$\text{Equity multiplier} = \frac{\text{Total assets}}{\text{Equity}} = \frac{A}{E}.$$

$$\text{Debt ratio} = 1 - \frac{1}{\text{Equity multiplier}}.$$

$$\text{Times-interest-earned (TIE) ratio} = \frac{\text{EBIT}}{\text{Interest charges}}.$$

$$\begin{matrix}\text{Fixed charge}\\\text{coverage ratio}\end{matrix} = \frac{\text{EBIT} + \text{Lease payments}}{\text{Interest charges} + \text{Lease payments} + \frac{\text{Sinking fund payments}}{(1 - \text{Tax rate})}}.$$

$$\text{Profit margin on sales} = \frac{\text{Net income available to common stockholders}}{\text{Sales}}.$$

$$\text{Operating profit margin after taxes} = \frac{\text{NOPAT}}{\text{Sales}}.$$

$$\text{Basic earning power ratio} = \frac{\text{EBIT}}{\text{Total assets}}.$$

$$\text{Return on total assets (ROA)} = \frac{\text{Net income available to common stockholders}}{\text{Total assets}}.$$

$$\text{ROA} = \left(\begin{array}{c}\text{Profit} \\ \text{margin}\end{array}\right)(\text{Total assets turnover})$$

$$= \frac{\text{Net income}}{\text{Sales}} \times \frac{\text{Sales}}{\text{Total assets}}.$$

$$\text{Return on common equity (ROE)} = \frac{\text{Net income available to common stockholders}}{\text{Common equity}}.$$

$$\text{Price/earnings (P/E) ratio} = \frac{\text{Price per share}}{\text{Earnings per share}}.$$

$$\text{Book value per share} = \frac{\text{Common equity}}{\text{Shares outstanding}}.$$

$$\text{Market/book (M/B) ratio} = \frac{\text{Market price per share}}{\text{Book value per share}}.$$

$$\text{ROE} = \text{ROA} \times \text{Equity multiplier}$$

$$= \left(\begin{array}{c}\text{Profit} \\ \text{margin}\end{array}\right)\left(\begin{array}{c}\text{Total assets} \\ \text{turnover}\end{array}\right)\left(\begin{array}{c}\text{Equity} \\ \text{multiplier}\end{array}\right)$$

$$= \left(\frac{\text{Net income}}{\text{Sales}}\right)\left(\frac{\text{Sales}}{\text{Total assets}}\right)\left(\frac{\text{Total assets}}{\text{Common equity}}\right)$$

$$= \frac{\text{Net income}}{\text{Common equity}}.$$

Chapter 4

Quoted interest rate = $k = k^* + IP + DRP + LP + MRP$.

$k_{\text{T-bill}} = k_{RF} = k^* + IP$.

$$IP_n = \frac{I_1 + I_2 + \ldots + I_n}{n}.$$

Chapter 5

$$\text{Rate of return} = \frac{\text{Amount received} - \text{Amount invested}}{\text{Amount invested}}.$$

$$\text{Expected rate of return} = \hat{k} = \sum_{i=1}^{n} P_i k_i.$$

$$\text{Variance} = \sigma^2 = \sum_{i=1}^{n} (k_i - \hat{k})^2 P_i.$$

$$\text{Standard deviation} = \sigma = \sqrt{\sum_{i=1}^{n} (k_i - \hat{k})^2 P_i}.$$

$$CV = \frac{\sigma}{\hat{k}}.$$

$$\hat{k}_p = \sum_{i=1}^{n} x_i \hat{k}_i.$$

$$\sigma_p = \sqrt{\sum_{i=1}^{n} (k_{pi} - \hat{k}_p)^2 P_i}.$$

$$b_p = \sum_{i=1}^{n} w_i b_i.$$

Expected return on stock market $= \hat{k}_m$.

Market risk premium $= \hat{k}_m - k_{RF}$.

$$RP_i = (k_M - k_{RF})b_i = (RP_M)b_i.$$

SML: $k_i = k_{RF} + (k_M - k_{RF})b_i$.

$$b = \frac{Y_2 - Y_1}{X_2 - X_1} = \text{slope coefficient in } \bar{k}_{it} = a + b\,\bar{k}_{Mt} + e_t.$$

Chapter 6

$$\sigma_p = \sqrt{\sum_{i=1}^{n} (k_{pi} - \hat{k}_p)^2 P_i}.$$

$$Cov(AB) = \sum_{i=1}^{n} (k_{Ai} - \hat{k}_A)(k_{Bi} - \hat{k}_B)P_i.$$

$$r_{AB} = \frac{Cov(AB)}{\sigma_A \sigma_B}.$$

$$\sigma_p = \sqrt{x^2 \sigma_A^2 + (1-x)^2 \sigma_B^2 + 2x(1-x)r_{AB}\sigma_A\sigma_B}.$$

$$\hat{k}_p = x\hat{k}_A + (1-x)\hat{k}_B.$$

$$\text{Minimum risk portfolio: } x = \frac{\sigma_B(\sigma_B - r_{AB}\sigma_A)}{\sigma_A^2 + \sigma_B^2 - 2r_{AB}\sigma_A\sigma_B}.$$

$$\text{Capital Market Line (CML): } \hat{k}_p = k_{RF} + \left(\frac{\hat{k}_M - k_{RF}}{\sigma_M}\right)\sigma_p.$$

Security Market Line (SML): $k_i = k_{RF} + (k_M - k_{RF})b_i$.

$$b_p = \sum_{i=1}^{n} x_i b_i.$$

$$b_i = \frac{Cov(\bar{k}_i, \bar{k}_M)}{\sigma_M^2} = \frac{r_{iM}\sigma_i\sigma_M}{\sigma_M^2} = r_{iM}\left(\frac{\sigma_i}{\sigma_M}\right).$$

Predicted future rate of return $= \hat{k}_j = a_j + b_j\hat{k}_M + e_j$.

$\sigma_i^2 = b_i^2\sigma_M^2 + \sigma_{e_i}^2$.

$k_i = k_{RF} + (k_1 - k_{RF})b_{i1} + \cdots + (k_j - k_{RF})b_{ij}$.

Chapter 7

$FV_n = PV(1 + i)^n = PV(FVIF_{i,n})$.

$PV = FV_n\left(\dfrac{1}{1 + i}\right)^n = FV_n(1 + i)^{-n} = FV_n(PVIF_{i,n})$.

$PVIF_{i,n} = \dfrac{1}{FVIF_{i,n}}$.

$FVIFA_{i,n} = \displaystyle\sum_{t=1}^{n}(1 + i)^{n-t} = \dfrac{(1 + i)^n - 1}{i}$.

$PVIFA_{i,n} = \displaystyle\sum_{t=1}^{n}\dfrac{1}{(1 + i)^t} = \dfrac{1 - \dfrac{1}{(1 + i)^n}}{i} = \dfrac{1}{i} - \dfrac{1}{i(1 + i)^n}$.

$FVA_n = PMT(FVIFA_{i,n})$.

FVA_n (Annuity due) $= PMT(FVIFA_{i,n})(1 + i)$.

$PVA_n = PMT(PVIFA_{i,n})$.

PVA_n (Annuity due) $= PMT(PVIFA_{i,n})(1 + i)$.

PV (Perpetuity) $= \dfrac{\text{Payment}}{\text{Interest rate}} = \dfrac{PMT}{i}$.

$PV_{\text{Uneven stream}} = \displaystyle\sum_{t=1}^{n} CF_t\left(\dfrac{1}{1 + i}\right)^t = \sum_{t=1}^{n} CF_t(PVIF_{i,t})$.

$FV_{\text{Uneven stream}} = \displaystyle\sum_{t=1}^{n} CF_t(1 + i)^{n-t} = \sum_{t=1}^{n} CF_t(FVIF_{i,n-t})$.

$FV_n = PV\left(1 + \dfrac{i_{Nom}}{m}\right)^{mn}$.

Effective annual rate $= \left(1 + \dfrac{i_{Nom}}{m}\right)^m - 1.0$.

Periodic rate $= i_{Nom}/m$.

$i_{Nom} = APR = (\text{Periodic rate})(m)$.

$FV_n = PVe^{in}$.

$PV = FV_ne^{-in}$.

Chapter 8

$V_B = \displaystyle\sum_{t=1}^{N}\dfrac{INT}{(1 + k_d)^t} + \dfrac{M}{(1 + k_d)^N}$

$= INT(PVIFA_{k_d,N}) + M(PVIF_{k_d,N})$.

$$V_B = \sum_{t=1}^{2N} \frac{INT/2}{(1 + k_d/2)^t} + \frac{M}{(1 + k_d/2)^{2N}} = \frac{INT}{2}(PVIFA_{k_d/2,2N}) + M(PVIF_{k_d/2,2N}).$$

$$\text{Price of callable bond} = \sum_{t=1}^{N} \frac{INT}{(1 + k_d)^t} + \frac{\text{Call price}}{(1 + k_d)^N}.$$

Accrued value at end of Year n = Issue price $\times (1 + k_d)^n$.

Interest in Year n = Accrued value$_n$ − Accrued value$_{n-1}$.

Tax savings = (Interest deduction)(T).

Chapter 9

$$\hat{P}_0 = \text{PV of expected future dividends} = \sum_{t=1}^{\infty} \frac{D_t}{(1 + k_s)^t}.$$

$$\hat{P}_0 = \frac{D_0(1 + g)}{k_s - g} = \frac{D_1}{k_s - g}.$$

$$\hat{k}_s = \frac{D_1}{P_0} + g.$$

$\bar{k}_s$ = Actual dividend yield + Actual capital gains yield.

$$V_{ps} = \frac{D_{ps}}{k_{ps}}.$$

$$k_{ps} = \frac{D_{ps}}{V_{ps}}.$$

V_{op} = Value of operations

= PV of expected future free cash flows

$$= \sum_{t=1}^{\infty} \frac{FCF_t}{(1 + k_c)^t}.$$

Chapter 10

After-tax component cost of debt = $k_d(1 - T)$.

$$\text{Component cost of preferred stock} = k_{ps} = \frac{D_{ps}}{P_n}.$$

$k_s = \hat{k}_s = k_{RF} + RP = D_1/P_0 + \text{expected } g.$

$k_s = k_{RF} + (k_M - k_{RF})b_i.$

k_s = Bond yield + Risk premium.

g = (Retention rate)(ROE) = (1.0 − Payout rate)(ROE) = b(ROE).

WACC = $w_d k_d(1 - T) + w_{ps}k_{ps} + w_{ce}k_s$.

Chapter 11

$$\text{Payback period} = \text{Year before full recovery} + \frac{\text{Unrecovered cost at start of year}}{\text{Cash flow during year}}.$$

$$NPV = CF_0 + \frac{CF_1}{(1+k)^1} + \frac{CF_2}{(1+k)^2} + \cdots + \frac{CF_n}{(1+k)^n}$$

$$= \sum_{t=0}^{n} \frac{CF_t}{(1+k)^t}.$$

$$\text{IRR: } CF_0 + \frac{CF_1}{(1+IRR)^1} + \frac{CF_2}{(1+IRR)^2} + \cdots + \frac{CF_n}{(1+IRR)^n} = 0.$$

$$\sum_{t=0}^{n} \frac{CF_t}{(1+IRR)^t} = 0.$$

$$\text{MIRR: PV costs} = \sum_{t=0}^{n} \frac{COF_t}{(1+k)^t} = \frac{\sum_{t=0}^{n} CIF_t(1+k)^{n-t}}{(1+MIRR)^n} = \frac{TV}{(1+MIRR)^n}.$$

$$PI = \frac{\text{PV benefits}}{\text{PV costs}} = \frac{\sum_{t=0}^{n} \dfrac{CIF_t}{(1+k)^t}}{\sum_{t=0}^{n} \dfrac{COF_t}{(1+k)^t}}.$$

Chapter 12

Recovery Allowance Percentage for Personal Property

OWNERSHIP YEAR	CLASS OF INVESTMENT			
	3-YEAR	5-YEAR	7-YEAR	10-YEAR
1	33%	20%	14%	10%
2	45	32	25	18
3	15	19	17	14
4	7	12	13	12
5		11	9	9
6		6	9	7
7			9	7
8			4	7
9				7
10				6
11				3
	100%	100%	100%	100%

$$\text{NPV(no inflation)} = \sum_{t=0}^{n} \frac{RCF_t}{(1+k_r)^t} = \sum_{t=0}^{n} \frac{NCF_t}{(1+k_n)^t}.$$

$$\text{NPV(with inflation)} = \sum_{t=0}^{n} \frac{NCF_t}{(1+k_n)^t} = \sum_{t=0}^{n} \frac{RCF_t(1+i)^t}{(1+k_r)^t(1+i)^t}.$$

Chapter 13

$$\sigma_{NPV} = \sqrt{\sum_{i=1}^{n} P_i[NPV_i - E(NPV)]^2}.$$

$$CV_{NPV} = \frac{\sigma_{NPV}}{E(NPV)}.$$

$$k_p = k_{RF} + (k_M - k_{RF})b_p.$$

Chapter 14

$$AFN = (A^*/S_0)\Delta S - (L^*/S_0)\Delta S - MS_1(1 - d).$$

$$\text{Full capacity sales} = \frac{\text{Actual sales}}{\text{Percentage of capacity at which fixed assets were operated}}.$$

$$\text{Target FA/Sales ratio} = \frac{\text{Actual fixed assets}}{\text{Full capacity sales}}.$$

$$\text{Required level of FA} = (\text{Target FA/Sales ratio})\,(\text{Projected sales}).$$

Chapter 15

$$EBIT = PQ - VQ - F.$$

$$Q_{BE} = \frac{F}{P - V}.$$

$$\text{Total risk} = \sigma_{ROE}.$$

$$\text{Business risk} = \sigma_{ROE(U)}.$$

$$\text{Financial risk} = \sigma_{ROE} - \sigma_{ROE(U)}.$$

$$S = \frac{(EBIT - k_dD)(1 - T)}{k_s} = \frac{\text{Dividend}}{k_s}.$$

$$V = D + S.$$

$$V = \frac{EBIT(1 - T)}{WACC}.$$

$$V = \frac{(EBIT - k_dD)(1 - T)}{k_s}.$$

$$WACC = \left(\frac{D}{V}\right)k_d(1 - T) + \left(\frac{S}{V}\right)k_s.$$

$$EPS = \frac{(EBIT - k_dD)(1 - T)}{\text{Original shares} - \text{Debt/Price}}.$$

Chapter 16

$$V_L = V_U = \frac{EBIT}{WACC} = \frac{EBIT}{k_{sU}}.$$

$$k_{sL} = k_{sU} + (k_{sU} - k_d)(D/S).$$

$V_L = V_U + TD.$

$V_U = \dfrac{EBIT(1 - T)}{k_{sU}}.$

$k_{sL} = k_{sU} + (k_{sU} - k_d)(1 - T)(D/S).$

$V_L = V_U + TD - \left(\begin{array}{c} \text{PV of} \\ \text{expected} \\ \text{financial distress} \\ \text{costs} \end{array} \right) - \left(\begin{array}{c} \text{PV of} \\ \text{agency} \\ \text{costs} \end{array} \right).$

$CF_L = (EBIT - I)(1 - T_c)(1 - T_s) + I\,(1 - T_d).$

$V_L = V_U + \left[1 - \dfrac{(1 - T_c)(1 - T_s)}{(1 - T_d)} \right] D.$

$V_U = \dfrac{EBIT\,(1 - T_c)(1 - T_s)}{k_{sU}}.$

Hamada equation: $k_{sL} = k_{RF} + (k_M - k_{RF})b_U + (k_M - k_{RF})b_U(1 - T)(D/S).$

$b = b_U[1 + (1 - T)(D/S)].$

$b = b_U + b_U\,(P/S) + b_U\,(1 - T)(D/S).$

Chapter 19

NAL = PV cost of owning − PV cost of leasing.

Chapter 20

$\begin{array}{c} \text{Price paid for} \\ \text{bond with warrants} \end{array} = \begin{array}{c} \text{Straight-debt} \\ \text{value of bonds} \end{array} + \begin{array}{c} \text{Value of} \\ \text{warrants.} \end{array}$

$\text{Conversion price} = P_c = \dfrac{\text{Par value of bond given up}}{\text{Shares received}}$

$\qquad\qquad\qquad = \dfrac{\text{Par value of bond given up}}{CR}.$

$\text{Conversion ratio} = CR = \dfrac{\text{Par value of bond given up}}{P_c}.$

Chapter 21

$A/R = \begin{array}{c} \text{Credit sales} \\ \text{per day} \end{array} \times \begin{array}{c} \text{Length of} \\ \text{collection period} \end{array}.$

$ADS = \text{Annual sales}/360 = \dfrac{(\text{Units sold})(\text{Sales price})}{360}.$

Receivables = (ADS)(DSO).

Chapter 22

$$\text{Nominal cost of payables} = \frac{\text{Discount percent}}{100 - \dfrac{\text{Discount}}{\text{percent}}} \times \frac{360}{\dfrac{\text{Days credit is}}{\text{outstanding}} - \dfrac{\text{Discount}}{\text{period}}}.$$

$$\text{Simple interest rate per day} = \frac{\text{Nominal rate}}{\text{Days in year}}.$$

Simple interest charge for period = (Days in period)(Rate per day)(Amount of loan).

$$\text{Face value}_{\text{Discount}} = \frac{\text{Funds received}}{1.0 - \text{Nominal rate (decimal)}}.$$

APR = (Periods per year)(Rate per period).

Chapter 23

$$\frac{\text{Inventory conversion}}{\text{period}} = \frac{\text{Inventory}}{\text{Sales}/360}.$$

$$\frac{\text{Receivables collection}}{\text{period}} = \text{DSO} = \frac{\text{Receivables}}{\text{Sales}/360}.$$

Payables deferral period = Payables/Credit purchases per day

$$= \text{Payables}/(\text{Cost of goods sold}/360).$$

$$\begin{matrix} \text{Inventory} \\ \text{conversion} \\ \text{period} \end{matrix} + \begin{matrix} \text{Receivables} \\ \text{collection} \\ \text{period} \end{matrix} - \begin{matrix} \text{Payables} \\ \text{deferral} \\ \text{period} \end{matrix} = \begin{matrix} \text{Cash} \\ \text{conversion} \\ \text{cycle} \end{matrix}.$$

Total costs = Holding costs + Transaction costs

$$= \frac{C}{2}(k) + \frac{T}{C}(F).$$

$$C^* = \sqrt{\frac{2(F)(T)}{k}}.$$

$$A = \frac{\text{Units per order}}{2} = \frac{S/N}{2}.$$

$$\text{TCC} = (C)(P)(A).$$

$$\text{TOC} = (F)(N) = F(S/2A).$$

$$\text{TIC} = \text{TCC} + \text{TOC}$$

$$= (C)(P)(A) + F(S/2A)$$

$$= (C)(P)(Q/2) + (F)(S/Q).$$

$$\text{EOQ} = \sqrt{\frac{2(F)(S)}{(C)(P)}}.$$

$$\text{Cost of carrying receivables} = (\text{DSO})\left(\begin{matrix} \text{Sales} \\ \text{per} \\ \text{day} \end{matrix}\right)\left(\begin{matrix} \text{Variable} \\ \text{cost} \\ \text{ratio} \end{matrix}\right)\left(\begin{matrix} \text{Cost} \\ \text{of} \\ \text{funds} \end{matrix}\right).$$

$$\text{Opportunity cost} = \left(\frac{\text{Old sales}}{360}\right)(\Delta\text{DSO})(1 - v)(k).$$

Chapter 24

$$\text{Exercise value} = \begin{array}{c}\text{Current price}\\\text{of stock}\end{array} - \text{Strike price.}$$

$$V = P[N(d_1)] - Xe^{-k_{RF}t}[N(d_2)].$$

$$d_1 = \frac{\ln(P/X) + [k_{RF} + (\sigma^2/2)]t}{\sigma\sqrt{t}}.$$

$$d_2 = d_1 - \sigma\sqrt{t}.$$

Chapter 27

$$\frac{\text{Forward exchange rate}}{\text{Spot exchange rate}} = \frac{(1 + k_h)}{(1 + k_f)}.$$

$$P_h = (P_f)(\text{Spot rate}).$$

$$\text{Spot rate} = \frac{P_h}{P_f}.$$

Abandonment option, 478, **484**
Abandonment value, 482–484
"Abnormal," or inverted, yield curve, 140
Absolute priority doctrine, 961
Accelerated Cost Recovery System (ACRS), (See also Modified Accelerated Cost Recovery System [MACRS]), 465–467
Accounting beta method, 392
Accounting for inventory, 876–877
Accounting income vs. cash flow, 45
Accounting profit, 45
Accounts payable (See also Current asset financing and Short-term financing), **43**
Accounts receivable (See also Receivables management and Current asset management), **814**
  credit policy, 818–819
  factoring, 862
  financing, 862–864
  pledging, 862
Accruals, 839–840
Accrued wages and taxes, 43
Acid test, 74, 792
Acquiring company, 991
Actual (realized) rate of return ($\bar{k}_s$), 172, 331
Actuarial rate of return, 1064–1065
Additional funds needed (AFN), 554
Add-on interest, 851
Adjustable rate preferred stock, 786
Adjustment bureau, 955–956
Agency costs, 21
Agency problem, 21
Agency relationships, 20–25
Agent, 20, 700
Aging schedule, 817
Alternative forms of business organization, 9–12
American Stock Exchange (AMEX), 123
Amortization schedule, 271
Amortized loans, 269–271
Annual compounding, 261
Annual percentage rate (APR), 264, 852
Annual report, 33
Annuity, 250–257
  annuity due, 250, 252–254, 256–257
  ordinary (deferred), 250–252, 254–256
Arbitrage, 1009–1010
Arbitrage Pricing Theory (APT), 223–226
Arrearages, 764
Asked price, 124

Asset allocation models, 1075–1076
Asset-backed securities, 718
Asset beta, 507
Asset management ratios (See also Financial ratios), **74–77**
  days sales outstanding, 75–76
  fixed assets turnover ratio, 76
  inventory turnover ratio, 74–75
  total assets turnover ratio, 76–77
Asset securitization, 718
Assignee, 957
Assignment, 957
Asymmetric information theory, 592–593 (See also Signaling theory)
Automatic stay, 959
Average collection period (ACP), 75
Average daily sales (ADS), 816
Average loss, 945
Average-risk stock, 180
Average tax rate, 51

Bailee, 946
Bailments, 946
Balance sheet (See also Financial statements), 34–36
Bank loans, 845–852
  add-on interest, 851
  annual percentage rate (APR), 264, 852
  choosing, 852–853
  commercial paper, 854
  compensating balance, 846
  cost, 848–852
  discount interest, 846, 849–851
  installment, 845
  line of credit, 847
  prime rate, 848
  promissory note, 845–846
  regular, or simple, interest, 848–849
  revolving credit agreement, 847
  secured, 854–855
  short-term, 845–847
  simple interest, 848–849
Bankruptcy (See also Reorganization), 951–972
  absolute priority doctrine, 961
  adjustment bureau, 955–956
  assignee, 957
  assignment, 957
  automatic stay, 959
  common pool problem, 959

Bankruptcy *continued*
   composition, 955
   cramdown, 960
   debtor-in-possession (DIP) financing, 961
   extension, 955
   fairness/feasibility, 961
   federal laws, 958
   holdout problem, 960
   insolvent, 962
   liquidation, 957, 967–970
   other motivations for, 971
   prepackaged, 965
   relative priority doctrine, 961
   reorganization in, 959–967
   restructuring, 955
   some criticisms of laws, 971–972
   trustee, 957, 958
   voluntary/involuntary, 958
   workouts, 955
Base case, 499
Base-case NPV, 498
Basic earning power ratio, 82
Baumol model, 874
Benchmarking, 91
Best-case scenario, 499
Beta coefficient (See also Capital Asset Pricing
   Model), **180–184, 188**
   calculating, 180
   changes in, 180
   fundamental, 415
   historical, 415
   portfolio, 183–184
   risk, 180–184, 387, 496, 505–509
   techniques for measuring risk, 391–392
Bid price, 124
Bird-in-the-hand theory, 661
Black-Scholes option pricing model, 920–924
Blanket lien, 864
Bond ratings, 308–310
Bonds, 285, 286–315
   assessing riskiness, 302–305
   call provision, 289–290
   convertible, 291
   corporate, 287
   coupon interest rate, 287–288
   coupon payment, 287–288
   current yield, 300–301
   debenture, 307
   default risk, 306–313
   development (pollution control), 308
   discount, 296, 298
   duration, 302, 948
   floating rate, 288
   foreign, 287
   income, 291
   indenture, 306
   indexed (purchasing power), 288, 291
   immunization, 948
   interest rate risk, 302–305
   investment grade, 308–309
   junk, 309, 310–314
   key characteristics, 287–291
   markets, 314–315
   maturity date, 288
   mortgage, 307
   municipal, 287
   new issue, 295
   original issue discount, 288, 713–716
   original maturity, 288
   outstanding, 295
   par value, 287
   premium, 296, 298
   rebalanced, 949
   redeemable at par, 289
   reinvestment rate risk, 305
   restrictive covenants, 306
   seasoned issue, 295
   sinking fund provision, 290–291
   subordinated debenture, 307–308
   tax-exempt bonds, 308
   treasury, 286–287
   valuation, 291–298
   warrant, 291, 767–772
   who issues, 286–287
   yields, 298–301
   yield to call, 299–300
   yield to maturity, 298–299
   zero coupon, 288, 713–716
Bond valuation (See also Valuation),
   291–298
   semiannual coupons, 301–302
Bond-yield-plus-risk-premium approach, 380
Book value per share, 84
Bracket creep, 51
Breakpoint, 409
Breakup value, 988
Business activity, 145
Business and financial risk, 580–588
   business risk, 580–585, 608
   financial risk, 585–588
Business ethics, 18–19
Business ethics and social responsibility, 18–20

Business organization, 9–12
Bylaws, 11

Call option, 767, 913
Call premium, 289
Call provision, 289–290
Cannibalization, 463
Capital, 374
Capital assets, 53
Capital Asset Pricing Model (CAPM), 178, 212
  approach, 379–380
  assumptions, 212
  beta coefficients, 180–183
  Capital Market Line, 213–215
  empirical tests, 220–223
  market risk premium, 185
  portfolio beta coefficients, 183–184
  required rate of return on equity (k_s), 331
  risk-free rate, 132
  Security Market Line, 186
Capital budgeting, 374, 422
  basics, 421–449
  business practices, 444–445
  cannibalization, 463
  capital rationing, 522–523
  cash flow estimation, 460–461
  changes in net working capital, 462
  combining the MCC and IOS schedules,
    537–538
  comparing projects with unequal lives, 479–482
  comparison of NPV and IRR methods, 433–439
  conclusions on capital budgeting methods,
    442–444
  crossover rate, 435
  dealing with inflation, 484–486
  decision rules, 426–433
  depreciation, 464–467
  discounted cash flow (DCF) techniques, 429
  discounted payback period, 427–429
  **equivalent annual annuity (EAA) method,
    481–482**
  establishing in practice, 523–524
  evaluating capital budgeting projects, 468
  expansion project, 468–472
  externalities, 463
  feedback effect, 760–761
  generating ideas for, 423
  hurdle rate, 433
  identifying relevant cash flows, 461–464
  importance of, 422–423
  in the small firm, 446–447

incremental cash flow, 461, 462–463
independent projects, 427, 436
internal rate of return (IRR) method, 431–439
**investment opportunity schedule (IOS), 411,
  536**
IRR, 431–433
linear programming, 523
marginal cost of capital schedule, 537
modified IRR, 440–441
multinational, 1047–1049
multiple IRRs, 437–439
mutually exclusive projects, 427, 436–437
net present value (NPV) method, 429–431
net present value profile, 434–435
opportunity cost, 374
optimal capital budget, 521–523, 536–537
payback period, 426–429
post-audit, 445–448
project classifications, 424–425
reinvestment rate assumption, 437
relevant cash flows, 461–464
replacement project analysis, 473–476
**replacement chain (common life) approach,
  480–481**
risk-adjusted discount rate, 509
salvage value, 467
similarities with security valuation, 425
strategic business plan, 423
sunk cost, 462–463
using capital budgeting techniques in other
  contexts, 448–449
Capital component, 374
Capital gain/loss, 53, 330
Capital gains yield, 296, 332
Capital intensity ratio, 561
Capital lease, 737
Capital markets, 115
Capital rationing, 522–523
Capital structure, 579–612, 621–651
  additional insights, 611–612
  agency costs, 638–639
  **asymmetric information, 592–593, 641,
    642–645**
  book weights versus market weights, 649–651
  business risk, 580–585, 608
  business and financial risk, 580–588
  considerations, 605–609
  control, 608
  criticisms of the MM and Miller models,
    635–636
  degree of operating leverage, 582, **583–585**

Capital structure *continued*
  effect of bankruptcy costs, 590–591
  effect of taxes, 589–590
  financial distress, 636–638
  financial leverage, 600–603
  financial risk, 580, 585–588
  financing flexibility, 607–608
  Hamada equation, 630–632
  homogeneous expectations, 622
  homogeneous risk class, 622
  illustration of the MM models, 626–630
  Miller model, 632–**633,** 634
  Modigliani-Miller models, 622–630
  MM's arbitrage proof, 623–625
  MM with corporate taxes, 626
  MM without taxes, 622–623
  operating leverage, 582, 583–585
  optimal, 382
  pecking order of financing, 641–642
  perfect capital market, 622
  reserve borrowing capacity, 593
  setting the target, 595–604
  signaling theory, 592–593, 641, **642–645**
  tax shelter benefits, 591
  theory, 589–594
  trade-off models, 636–641
  trade-off theory, 591–592
  variations among firms, 647–649
  view of capital structure theory, 645–647
Capitalizing the lease, 740
Career opportunities in finance, 4–5
Carry-back/forward, 57
Carve-out, 1014
Cash budget, 792, 798–803
Cash conversion cycle, 868–870
Cash discount, 820–821
Cash flow, 258
  depreciation, 464–467
  estimation bias, 476–477
  free, 45, 345, 461
  incremental, 461, **462–463**
  net, 40, 468
  operating, 45
  relevant, 461–464
  synchronized, 804
Cash flow statement, 39, 40–42
Cash management, 796–798
  cash budget, 792, 798–803
  check clearing, 804
  collections float, 804
  compensating balance, 797

  disbursement float, 804
  float, 804
  kiting, 805
  lockbox plan, 805
  net float, 804
  precautionary balance, 797
  speculative balance, 797
  synchronized cash flows, 804
  target cash balance, 799, 871–875
  techniques, 803–806
  trade discount, 798
  transactions balance, 799
Certainty equivalent, 509, 534
Changes in net working capital, 462
Characteristic line, 218
Charter, 10
Classified stock, 325–326
Clientele effect, 665–666
Cliff vesting, 1063
Closely held corporation, 326
Coefficient of variation (CV), 166–167
Collateralized Mortgage Obligations (CMOs), 927–928
Collection policy, 820
Collections float, 804
Combination lease, 737–738
Commercial bank loans (See also Bank loans), 845–852
  cost, 848–852
Commercial banks, 120
Commercial paper, 854
Commodity futures, 933
Common equity, 36
Common pool problem, 959
Common size analysis, 86, 109
Common stock, 323–361
  actual (realized) rate of return ($\bar{k}_s$), 172, 331
  actual stock prices and returns, 355–359
  advantages and disadvantages, 704–705
  book value per share, 84
  capital gains yield, 296, 332
  classified, 325–326
  constant growth model, 335–337
  constant growth, 335–337
  cost of, 378–382
  dividend yield, 331
  efficient markets hypothesis, 352–353
  equilibrium, 349–352
  expected rate of return ($\hat{k}_s$), 331
  expected total return, 332

flotation cost, 406
founders' shares, 326
going public, 328, 698–700
growth rate (g), 331
horizon value, 346
initial public offering (IPO) market, 328–329
intrinsic value ($\hat{P}_0$), 331
legal rights and privileges, 324–325
listing, 700–701
marginal investor, 350
market equilibrium, 349–355
market for, 326–330
market price (P_0), 331
nonconstant growth, 339–342
normal (constant) growth, 335–337
organized security exchange, 123, 326
oversubscribed, 328
over-the-counter market, 124, 326
perpetuity, 257–258
preemptive right, 325, 701
primary markets, 115, 327
procedures for selling new, 701–704
proxy, 324
proxy fight, 324
public offering, 701
publicly owned corporation, 326
required rate of return (k_s), 331
right, 701
rights offering, 701
secondary markets, 115, 327
supernormal (nonconstant) growth,
    339–342
takeover, 324
terminal value, 346
types, 325–326
valuation, 330–342
zero growth stock, 333–334
Common stockholders' equity, 35
Company-specific risk (See also Risk), 219
Comparative ratios and "benchmarking," 91–93
Comparison of CAPM, Risk premium, and DCF
    methods, 382
Comparison of types of interest rates, 266–268
Compensating balances, 797, 846
Competitive advantage period, 549
Competitive bid, 706
Component cost, 374
Composition, 955
Compounding, 237, 261–266
    annual, 261
    semiannual, 261–266

Computerized financial planning models, 567–568
Computerized inventory control system, 811
Concerns about beta and the CAPM, 190–191
Congeneric merger, 989
Conglomerate merger, 989
Consol, 257
Constant growth model, 335–337
Constant ratio method of forecasting, 549
Consumer credit markets, 115
Continuous compounding and discounting, 282
    continuous compounding, 282
    continuous discounting, 282
Continuous probability distribution, 231–234
Conversion price (P_c), 773
Conversion ratio (CR), 773
Conversion value (C_t), 776
Convertible bond, 291
Convertible currency, 1038
Convertible securities, 773–779
    comparison with warrants, 779–780
Corporate alliances, 1011–1012
Corporate bond, 287
Corporate income taxes, 632–634
Corporate objectives, 543–544
Corporate purpose, 542–543
Corporate scope, 543
Corporate strategies, 544
Corporate valuation model, 342–349
Corporate (within-firm) risk, 387, 496–497, 505
Corporation, 10–11
Correlation, 172–175
Correlation coefficient (r), 172–175, 204
Cost of capital, 373–419
    after-tax cost of debt, $k_d(1 - T)$, 376–377, 745
    beta, 180–184, 188
    bond-yield-plus-risk-premium approach, 380
    break point (BP), 409
    capital component, 374
    CAPM approach, 379
    composite, or weighted average, cost of capital,
        WACC, 374–375, 382–383
    cost of common stock, k_s, 378–382
    cost of debt, 376–377
    cost of equity for small firms, 394
    cost of new common equity (k_e), 406
    cost of preferred stock (k_{ps}), 377–378
    DCF approach, 380–382
    divisional, 506
    factors affecting, 383–385
    flotation cost (F), 406
    investment opportunity schedule (IOS), 411

Cost of capital *continued*
  marginal cost of capital, 408
  marginal cost of capital (MCC) schedule, 408
  market risk premium, 185–187, 215, 413
  opportunity cost, 374
  problem areas in cost of capital, 395
  project (k_p), 390
  target (optimal) capital structure, 375
  weighted average cost of capital (WACC), 374–375, 382–383
Cost of money, 126–127
Costly trade credit, 843
Country risk, 137
Coupon interest rate, 287–288
Coupon payment, 287–288
Covariance, 203
Coverage ratios, 605–607 (See also Financial ratios)
Cramdown, 960
Credit (See also Trade credit), 840–844
  line of, 847
  revolving, 847
Credit policy, 818–819
  analyzing proposed changes, 893–895
  cash discount, 820–821
  collection policy, 820
  five Cs of credit, 820
  other factors influencing, 821
  period, 819
  seasonal dating, 820
  standards, 819
  terms, 819
Credit unions, 121
Cross rate, 1033
Crossover rate, 435
Cumulative, 764
Cumulative voting, 324
Currency swap, 927
Current asset financing, 835–855
  accounts payable (trade credit), 840–844
  advantages and disadvantages of short-term, 838–839
  alternative financing policies, 835–838
  choosing a bank, 852–853
  commercial paper, 854
  cost of bank loans, 848–852
  short-term bank loans, 845–847
  sources of short-term, 839–840
  trade credit, 840–844

  use of security in short-term financing, 854–855, 862–865
Current asset management, 791–821
  alternative investment policies, 793–795
  cash budget, 792, 798–803
  cash conversion cycle, 868–870
  cash discounts, 820–821
  cash management, 796–798
  cash management techniques, 803–806
  concept of zero working capital, 795–796
  credit policy, 818–819
  inventory, 807–809
  inventory control systems, 810–814
  inventory costs, 809–810
  marketable securities, 806–807
  moderate investment policy, 794
  other factors influencing credit policy, 821
  receivables management, 814–818
  relaxed investment policy, 793
  restricted investment policy, 794
  setting collection policy, 820
  setting credit period and standards, 819–820
  working capital terminology, 792–793
Current assets, 791–821, 835–855, 868–870
  financing, 835–855
  managing, 791–821
  permanent, 835
  temporary, 836
Current ratio, 73–74, 792
Current yield, 300–301

Days sales outstanding, 75–76, 816
Dealer, 700
Debenture, 307
Debt (See also Bonds; Current asset financing; Short-term financing), 285–315
  advantages and disadvantages of long-term, 719
  bonds, 285, 286–315
  cost of, 376–377
  floating rate debt, 288
  ratio, 79–80
Debt capacity, 509
Debt management ratios (See also Financial ratios), 77–81
  debt ratio, 79–80
  fixed charge coverage ratio, 80–81
  times-interest-earned (TIE) ratio, 80
Debtor-in-possession (DIP) financing, 961
Decision node, 515
Decision tree, 514–515, 516

branch, **515**
Declaration date, 674
Default risk, 306–313
Default risk premium, 134
Defensive merger, 988
Deferred (ordinary) annuity, 250–252
Deferred call, 289
Deferred vesting, 1063
Defined benefit vs. defined contribution, 1072–1074
Defined benefit plan, 122, 1062, 1068
Defined contribution plan, 122, 1061, 1068
Demand-based management, 796
Demand flow management, 796
Depreciable basis, 465–467
Depreciation, 59, 464–467
  effect on cash flows, 464
  tax depreciation calculations, 465–467
Detachable warrant, 769
Derivatives and risk management, 907–939, 944–949
  background on, 910–913
  Black-Scholes option pricing model, 920–924
  call option, 767, 913
  Collateralized Mortgage Obligations (CMOs), 927–928
  commodity futures, 933
  currency swap, 927
  derivatives, 114, 116, 910
  exercise value, 915
  financial futures, 933
  forward contract, 924–925
  fundamentals of risk management, 929–932
  futures contract, 924–925
  hedging, 936
  interest rate futures, 925
  interest rate swap, 926
  intro to option pricing models, 918–920
  inverse floater, 928–929
  large losses in, 932
  long hedges, 936
  long-term equity anticipation security (LEAPS), 914–915
  natural hedges, 911
  notional principal, 926
  options, 913–918
  Orange County blues, 912
  other types, 924–929
  perfect hedge, 936
  put option, 913
  risk management, 929
  riskless hedge, 918
  short hedges, 936
  side payment, 926
  speculation, 936
  strike (exercise) price, 913
  stripping, 927
  structured note, 927–928
  swap, 925–927
  using to reduce risks, 933–939
Determinants of market interest rates, 131–136
Determinants of shape of yield curve, 140–143
  expectations theory, 140–142
  liquidity preference theory, 142–143
Devaluation, 1036
Developing a strategy, 1075–1076
Direct losses, 945
Direct quotation, 1032
Direct transfers, 119
Discount bond, 296, 298
Discount interest, 849–851
Discount on forward rate, 1039
Discounted cash flow analysis (See also Time value of money), **995**
Discounted cash flow techniques, 380–382, 429
Discounted payback period, 427–429
Discounting, 245
Diversifiable risk, 175–178, 179–180, 219
Divestitures, 1013
  carve-out, 1014
  liquidation, 1014
  sale to another firm, 1013
  spin-off, 1013
Dividend policy, 660–666
  bird-in-the-hand theory, 661
  changing, 675–676
  clientele effect, 665–666
  decision, 16
  declaration date, 674
  establishing in practice, 668–675
  ex-dividend date, 674
  holder-of-record date, 674
  information content (or signaling) hypothesis, 664–665
  irrelevance theory, 660–661
  low regular dividend plus extras, 672
  optimal, 660
  other issues, 664–666
  overview of decision, 679–681
  payment date, 675
  reinvestment plans, 676–677

Dividend policy *continued*
  residual dividend model, 668–672
  stability, 666–667
  stock dividends and splits, 681–683
  stock repurchases, 683–**687**
  summary of factors influencing, 678–679
  target payout ratio, 660
  tax preference theory, 661–662
  versus capital gains, 660–664
Dividend reinvestment plans, 676–**677**
Dividends, 332–333
  basis for stock values, 332–333
  stock dividends, 681–**682**
  stock repurchases, 683–**687**
  stock splits, 681
Dividend yield, 331
Divisional beta, 506
Divisional cost of equity, 506
Divisional WACC, 506
Double taxation, 52
Du Pont chart, 86
Du Pont equation, 88
Due diligence, 997
Duration, 948, 1078

Earnings per share (EPS), 16–**17**
  does it make sense to maximize, 16–17
Economic ordering quantity model (EOQ),
    877–**883**
Economic life, 483
Economic perils, 945
Economic Value Added (EVA), 22–23, **47**
Economies of scale, 563
Effective annual rate (EAR), 263–266, **268**
Efficient frontier, 209
Efficient Markets Hypothesis (EMH),
    352–353
Efficient portfolio, 206–**208**
Employee choice: benefit vs. contribution,
    1074–1075
Employee Retirement Income Security Act of
    1974 (ERISA), 1065
Employee Stock Ownership Plan (ESOP),
    702–**704**
EOQ model extensions, 883–888
Equilibrium, 245, 350
Equilibrium price, 711
Equity (See also Common stock), 323–361
  cost of common stock, k_s, 378–382
Equity beta, 507
Equity multiplier, 89

Equity residual method, 996
Equivalent annual annuity (EAA) method,
    481–**482**
Ethics, 18–**19**
Eurobond, 1046
Eurodollar, 1044
EVA and working capital, 795
event risk, 290
Exchange rates, 1032–**1035**
Exchange rate risk, 137, 1037, **1047**–1048
Ex-dividend date, 674
Executive stock option, 22
Exercise price, 767
Exercise value, 915
Expansion project, 468–472
Expectations theory, 140–142
Expected rate of return ($\hat{k}$), 161–164, **331**
Expected return on a portfolio ($\hat{k}_p$), 170–**172**
Expected total return, 332, 338–339
Explicit forecast period, 549
Extended Du Pont equation, 90
Extension, 955
Externalities, 463

Factor analysis, 225–**226**
Factoring, 862
Factors of long-term financing decisions, 719–722
Factors that influence interest rate levels,
    144–146
Fair (equilibrium) value, 245
Fairness/feasibility, 961
FASB #13, 740
Federal bankruptcy laws (See also Bankruptcy and
    Reorganization), 951–972
Federal deficits, 144
Federal income tax system, 50–59
Federal Reserve policy, 144
Feedback effect, 760–761
Field warehouse, 864
Finance in the organizational structure of the
    firm, 12
Financial Accounting Standards Board (FASB),
    1066
Financial analysis in the small firm, 96
Financial asset markets, 114
Financial distress, 636–638
  and its consequences, 952–954
  issues facing a firm, 954–955
Financial environment, 113–154
Financial forecasting, 546–568
  additional funds needed, 554

AFN formula, 559–562
capital intensity ratio, 561
computerized financial planning models, 567–568
constant ratio method, 549
lumpy assets, 563–564
other techniques, 565–567
sales forecast, 546–548
spontaneously generated funds, 553
when balance sheet ratios change, 563–565
Financial futures, 933
Financial institutions, 118–123
Financial instruments, 114
Financial intermediaries, 119–**120**
Financial lease, 737
Financial leverage, 77–79
Financial management, 4
Financial management overview, 3–27
Financial management in the 1990s, 6–8
Financial markets, 114–118
Financial merger, 995
Financial ratios (See also the specific type of ratios), 72–97
  asset management, 74
  debt management, 77–81
  liquidity, 72–**73**, 74
  market value, 84–85
  profitability, 81–83
Financial risk (See also Risk), **580, 585**–588
Financial service corporation, 123
Financial staff's responsibilities, 8
Financial statements, 31–70
  analysis, 71–111
  annual report, 33
  balance sheet, 34–36
  depreciation, 59, 464–467
  Du Pont chart, 86
  forecasting, 549–559
  history, 32–33
  income statement, 36–38
  ratio analysis, 72
  statement of cash flows, 39, 40–42
  statement of retained earnings, 38
Financial statements and reports, 33–34
Financing feedbacks, 554
Financing flexibility, 607–608
Financing policies (current assets), 835–838
  aggressive approach, 836

conservative approach, 836
  maturity matching, 836
Fixed assets turnover ratio, 76
Fixed charge coverage (FCC) ratio, 80–81, **606**
Fixed exchange rate system, 1035
Flexibility option, 519
Float, 804
  collections, 804
  disbursement, 804
  net, 804
Floating exchange rates, 1036
Floating rate debt, 288
Floor price, 776
Flotation cost, 406
Forecast horizon, 549
Forecasting financial requirements when the balance sheet ratios are subject to change, 563–565
Forecasting financial statement variables, 565–567
Foreign bond, 287, 1045
Foreign trade deficit, 145
Formula method for forecasting AFN, 559–562
Forward contract, 924–925
Forward exchange rate, 1039
Founders' shares, 326
401(k) plan, 122
Fractional time periods, 268–269
Free cash flow, 45, 345, 461
Free trade credit, 843
Friendly merger, 991
Fully funded, 1064
Fundamental beta coefficient, 415
Funding strategy, 1075
Futures contract, 924–925
Futures markets, 115
Future value (See also Time value of money), **237**–244
  annuity (FVA$_n$), 250–254
  annuity due, 250, 252–254
  interest factor, 239–241
  interest factor for an annuity, 251–252
  ordinary (deferred) annuity, 250–252
  uneven cash flow stream, 260–261

General partners, 11
Global corporations, 1028–1030
Globalization of business, 6–7
Goals of the corporation, 13–18
Going public, 328, 698–700
Golden parachutes, 1008

Goodwill, 1004
Gordon/Lintner, 661
Gross investment in operating capital, 46
Growth, 331
    constant (normal), 335–337
    nonconstant (supernormal), 339–342
    zero, 333–334
Growth rate (g), 331
Guideline (tax-oriented) lease, 738–739

Hedging, 118, 936
Historical beta coefficient, 415
History of accounting and financial statements,
    32–33
Holdout problem, 960
Holder-of-record date, 674
Holding companies, 1016–1019
Horizon value, 260–261, 346
Horizontal merger, 989
Hostile merger, 992
Hostile takeover, 24
Hurdle rate, 433
Hybrid, 764

Immunization, 948, 1078
Improper accumulation, 58
Improper actions, 947
Income bond, 291
Income statement (See also Financial
    statements), 36–38
Incremental cash flow, 461, 462–463
Indenture, 306
Independent projects, 427, 436
Indexed (purchasing power) bond, 291
Indifference curve, 210
Indirect losses, 945
Indirect quotation, 1032
Inflation, 126–127, 187, 484–486
Inflation premium, 133–134
Inflow, 236
Information content (signaling) hypothesis,
    664–665
Initial public offering (IPO) market, 328–329
Insiders, 705
Insolvent, 962
Installment loans, 851–852
Interest (See also Bank loans), 845–852
    add-on, 851
    discount, 849–851
    simple, 848–849
    yield, 300–301

Interest rate levels, 127–131
Interest rate parity, 1040–1041
Interest rate swap, 926
Interest rates, 126–148
    business activity, 145
    business decisions affected by, 146–148
    comparison of types, 266–268
    default risk premium, 134
    determinants of market, 131–136
    effective annual (EAR), 263–266, 268
    federal deficits, 144
    Federal Reserve policy, 144
    inflation premium, 133–134
    international factors, 145
    levels, 127–131
    levels and stock prices, 146
    liquidity premium, 134
    maturity risk premium, 134–136
    nominal, 132–133, 263–266
    nominal risk-free rate, 132–133
    other factors that influence, 144–146
    real risk-free rate, 132
    reinvestment rate risk, 136
    risk, 136, 302–305, 947
    solving for, 247–249
    term structure, 137–140
    yield curve, 138–140
Internal rate of return (IRR) method, 431–439
    comparison with NPV, 433
    IRR, 431–433
    modified IRR, 440–441
    multiple, 437–439
    rationale for, 433
    reinvestment rate assumption, 437
Interstate public offerings, 705
Intrinsic value ($\hat{P}_0$), 331
Inventory, 807–809
    accounting for, 876–877
    computerized control systems, 811
    conversion period, 868
    control systems, 810–814
    costs, 809–810
    Economic ordering quantity model (EOQ),
        877–883
    finished goods, 807
    First-in, first-out, (FIFO), 876
    just-in-time system, 811–812
    keeping lean, 812–813
    Last-in, first-out, (LIFO), 876
    outsourcing, 812–813
    red-line method, 810–811

turnover ratio, **74**–75
two-bin method, 811
weighted average, 876
work-in-process, 807
Inventory financing, 864–865
   blanket lien, 864
   field warehouse, 864
   public warehouse, 864
   trust receipt, 864
   warehouse receipt, 864
Inverse floater, 928–**929**
Inverted (abnormal) yield curve, 140
Investing overseas, 137
Investment banking house, 119–**120**
Investment grade bonds, 308–309
Investment opportunity schedule (IOS), 411, 536
Investment performance, 1077–1080
Investment returns, 158–160
Investment strategy, 1075
Investments, 4
Investor-supplied capital, 43
Investors, 43
Irrelevance theory, 660–661

Joint venture, 1011
Junk bonds, 309, 310–314
Just-in-time system, 16, 811–812

Kiting, 805

Lead underwriter, 711
Leasing, 735–753
   capitalizing, 740
   combination, 737–**738**
   evaluation by lessee, 742–746
   evaluation by lessor, 746–749
   FASB #13, 740
   financial capital, 737
   financial statement effects, 740–741
   guideline (tax-oriented), 738–739
   lessee, 736
   lessor, 736
   leveraged, 748
   non-tax oriented, 739
   net advantage to (NAL), 745–746
   off balance sheet financing, 740
   operating, 736–737
   other issues in analysis, 749–751
   payments, 736
   residual value, 744
   sale and leaseback, 737

   service, 736
   tax effects, 738–739
   types of, 736–738
Lessee, 736
Lessor, 736
Leverage, 77–79, 582–588
   financial, 77–79
   operating, 582, 583–585
Leveraged buyout (LBO), 1012–1013
Liability, 946
Liability loss exposure, 946–947
   bailee, 946
   bailments, 946
   improper actions, 947
   liability, 946
   nuisance, 946
   patent and copyright infringement, 946
   product liability, 946
   professional liability, 947
   unfair trade practices, 946
Life insurance companies, 121
Limited liability company, 11
Limited liability partnership, 11–12
Limited partnership, 11
Line of credit, 847
Linear programming, 523
Liquid asset, 72
Liquidation, 957, 1014
Liquidity, 11
Liquidity preference theory, 142–143
Liquidity premium, 134
Liquidity ratios, 72–**73**, 74
   current ratio, 73–74
   quick, or acid test, ratio, 74
Liquidity (marketability) risk (See also Risk),
   134
Listing stock, 700–701
Loans (See also Bank loans), 845–852,
   854–855
   bank, 845–852
   secured, 854–**855**, 862–865
Lockbox plan, 805
Long hedges, 936
Long-term equity anticipation security (LEAPS),
   914–915
Long-term sustainable growth, 549
Loss frequency, 945
Loss severity, 945
Lumpy assets, 563

Maintenance margin, 935

Managerial options, 514
Margin, 935
Margin calls, 706
Margin requirements, 706
Marginal cost of capital (MCC) (See also Cost of capital), 408
  break point (BP), 409
  schedule, 408
Marginal investor, 350
Marginal tax rate, 51
Marketable securities, 806–807
Market/book ratio, 84–85
Market multiple analysis, 998
Market portfolio, 177–178
Market price (P₀), 331
Market risk (See also Risk), 178–180, 219, 387, 496, 505–509, 630
Market risk and divisional betas, 505–509
Market risk premium, 185–187, 215, 413
Market segmentation theory, 143
Market Value Added (MVA), 46–47, 48–50
Market value ratios, 84–85
  market/book ratio, 84–85
  price/earnings ratio, 84
Marketable securities, 806–807
Mathematics: defined plans, 1065
Maturity date, 288
Maturity matching, 836
Maturity risk premium, 134–136
Maximum loss, 945
Mergers, 986
  accounting treatment, 1002–1005
  acquiring company, 991
  analysis for "true consolidation", 1006
  analysis, 995–1001
  breakup value, 988
  combining more than just financial statements, 1001
  congeneric, 989
  conglomerate, 989
  defensive, 988
  due diligence, 997
  financial, 995
  friendly, 991
  horizontal, 989
  hostile, 992
  hostile versus friendly takeovers, 991–993
  level of activity, 989–991
  market multiple analysis, 998
  means of exiting closely held business, 1018
  operating, 995

  pooling of interests, 1003
  proxy fight, 324, 992
  rationale for, 986–988
  regulation, 993–994
  role of investment bankers, 1007–1010
  structuring takeover bid, 1001–1002
  synergy, 986–987
  target company, 991
  tender offer, 992
  types, 989
  vertical, 989
  who wins: the empirical evidence, 1010–1011
Mission statement, 542
Moderate current asset investment policy, 794
Modified Accelerated Cost Recovery System (MACRS), 465–467.
Modified internal rate of return (MIRR), 440–441
Modifying accounting data for managerial decisions, 42
Modigliani-Miller model, 622–628
Money market fund, 121
Money market preferred stock, 786
Money markets, 4, 115
Monte Carlo simulation, 501–504
Mortgage bonds, 307
Mortgage markets, 115
Multinational corporations, 1028–1030
Multinational financial management, 1027–1053
  accounting differences, 82
  benefits of diversifying overseas, 179
  capital budgeting, 1047–1049
  capital structures, 1049–1050
  convertible currency, 1038
  cross rate, 1033
  devaluation, 1036
  discount on forward rate, 1039
  eurobond, 1046
  eurodollar, 1044
  exchange rates, 1032–1035
  exchange rate risk, 137, 1037, 1047–1048
  fixed exchange rate system, 1035
  floating exchange rate, 1036
  foreign bond, 1045
  forward exchange rate, 1039
  inflation, interest rates, and exchange rates, 1043–1044
  international capital structures, 1049–1050
  international monetary system, 1035–1038
  international money and capital markets, 1044–1047
  interest rate parity, 1040–1041

investing in emerging markets, 358
measuring country risk, 138
multinational, or global, corporations,
     1028–1030
pegged exchange rate, 1037
political risk, 1031–1032, **1048**
premium on forward rate, 1039
purchasing power parity, 1041–1042
repatriation of earnings, 1047
revaluation, 1036
spot rate, 1039
trade deficit, 1035–1036
trading in foreign exchange, 1038–1039
versus domestic financial management,
     1031–1032
working capital management, 1051–1053
Multiple internal rates of return, 437–439
Municipal bonds or "munis," 53, 287
Mutual funds, 121
Mutually exclusive projects, 436–**427**, 437
Mutual savings banks, 121
MVA, 47
MVA and EVA, 46–50

National Association of Securities Dealers, 125,
     706
Natural hedges, 911
Negotiated deals, 706
Net advantage to leasing (NAL), 745–**746**
Net asset value, 1004
Net cash flow, 40
Net float, 804
Net investment in operating capital, 45
Net operating profit after taxes, 44
Net present value (NPV), 429–**431**
     comparison with IRR, 433–439
     profiles, 434–**435**
     rationale for, 431
     reinvestment rate assumption, 437
Net working capital, 43
Net worth, 35
New product options, 520
New York Stock Exchange (NYSE), 123
Nominal (quoted) interest rate, 132–**133,**
     263–**265, 266**–**268**
Nominal (quoted) risk-free interest rate,
     132–133
Nonconstant growth, 339–**342**
Nondiversifiable risk, 219
Nonoperating assets, 42
Non-tax oriented lease, 739

Normal distribution, 231
Normal, or constant, growth, 335–339
Normal profits/rates of return, 19
Normal yield curve, 140
Notional principal, 926
Nuisance, 946

Off balance sheet financing, 740
Operating assets, 42
Operating capital requirement ratio, 77
Operating cash flow, 45
Operating company, 1017
Operating lease, 736–**737**
Operating leverage, 582, 583–**585**
Operating merger, 995
Operating plans, 544–545
Operating profit margin after taxes, 82–83
Opportunity cost, 47, 378, 463
Opportunity cost of capital, 374
Opportunity cost rate, 244
Optimal capital budget, 521
Optimal capital budget in practice, 523–524
Optimal dividend policy, 660
Option value, 477–**478**, 479
Options, 478–479, 913–918
     real (determining the value of), **514**, 517–519
Ordinary (deferred) annuity, 250–252, 254–256
Organized security exchanges, 123, 326
Original maturity, 288
Outflow, 236
Out-sourcing, 812–813
Over-the-counter (OTC) market, 124, 326

Parent company, 1017
Partnership, 9–10
Par value, 287
Patent and copyright infringement, 946
Payables deferral period, 869
Payback period, 426–**429**
     discounted payback period, 427–**429**
Payment (PMT), 258
Payment date, 675
Payments pattern approach, 888, 889–**893**
Payoff matrix, 161–162
Pegged exchange rate, 1037
Pension Benefit Guarantee Corporation (PBGC),
     1065–1066
Pension funds, 122, 1060
Pension plan management,1059–1082
     actuarial rate of return, 1064–**1065**
     asset allocation models, 1075–1076

Pension plan management *continued*
   cliff vesting, 1063
   deferred vesting, 1063
   defined benefit vs. defined contribution,
      1072–1074
   defined benefit plan, 1062, 1068
   defined contribution plan, 1061, 1068
   developing a strategy, 1075–1076
   duration, 1078
   employee choice: benefit vs. contribution,
      1074–1075
   **Employee Retirement Income Security Act of
      1974 (ERISA), 1065**
   fully funded, 1064
   funding strategy, 1075
   immunization, 1078
   investment performance, 1077–1080
   investment strategy, 1075
   key terms and concepts, 1063–1066
   mathematics: defined plans, 1067
   **Pension Benefit Guarantee Corporation
      (PBGC), 1065**–1066
   plan sponsor, 1068
   portable pension plan, 1064
   portfolio insurance, 1078
   profit sharing plan, 1062, 1068
   retiree health benefits, 1081–1082
   risks, 1068–1071
   role and scope, 1060
   tapping assets, 1080–1081
   three types of plans, 1061–1063
   unfunded pension liability, 1064
   vesting, 1063
Percent change analysis, 86, 109
Percent of sales, 549–559
Perfect hedge, 936
Performance shares, 22
Periodic interest rate, 262, **266–268**
Permanent current assets, 835
Perpetuities, 257–258
Personal property, 945
Personal taxes, 632
Physical asset markets, 114
Physical assets versus securities, 189–190
Physical life, 483
Physical perils, 945
Plan sponsor, 1068
Plant and equipment, 42
Pledging, 862
Poison pills, 1008
Political risk, 1031–1032, **1048**

Pooling of interests, 1003
Portable pension plan, 1064
Portfolio, 158, 169–183
   choosing optimal, 209–212
   efficient, 206–208
Portfolio beta coefficients, 183–184
Portfolio insurance, 1078
Portfolio risk (See also Risk), 172–175
   correlation coefficient (r), 172–175
   expected return on a portfolio ($\hat{k}_p$), 170–172
   measuring, 202–206
   negative correlation, 172
   positive correlation, 172
   realized rate of return ($\bar{k}$), 172
   relevant risk, 178
Post-audit, 445–448
Precautionary balance, 797
Preemptive right, 325
Preferred stock, 361–362, 377–378, 764–767
   adjustable rate, 786
   arrearages, 764
   cost of, 377–378
   cumulative, 764
   money market, 786
   valuation, 360–361
Premium bond, 296, 298
Premium on forward rate, 1039
Present value (See also Time value of money),
      244–247
   annuity (PVA_n), 254–257
   annuity due, 256–257
   interest factor, 245–246
   interest factor for an annuity, 245
   ordinary annuities, 254–256
   uneven cash flow stream, 258–260
Price/earnings ratio, 84
Primary markets, 115, 327
Prime rate, 848
Principal, 20
Private markets, 115
Private placement, 702
Pro forma (projected) financial statements, 542
Probability distributions, 160–161
   continuous, 231–234
   normal, 231
   triangular, 231
   uniform, 231
Product liability, 946
Production opportunities, 126
Professional association, 12
Professional corporation, 12

Professional liability, 947
Profitability index (PI), 442
Profitability ratios (See also Financial ratios), 81–83
  basic earning power ratio, 82
  profit margin on sales, 81–82
  return on common equity (ROE), 83
  return on total assets (ROA), 83
Profit margin on sales, 81–82
Profit maximization, 16
Profit sharing plan, 1062, 1068
Progressive tax, 51
Project cost of capital (k_p), 390
Project financing, 716–717
Projects with unequal lives, 479–482
Promissory note, 845–846
Proprietorship, 9
Prospectus, 705
Proxy, 324
Proxy fight, 324, 992
Public offering, 701
Public markets, 115
Public warehouse, 864
Publicly owned corporation, 326
Purchasing power parity, 1041–1042
Pure play method, 391–392, **507–509**
Put option, 913

Quantity discount, 885–887
Quick ratio, 74, 792
Quoted interest rate, 131

Rate of return, 159
Ratio analysis (See also Financial ratios), 72, 94–97
  looking beyond the numbers, 95–97
  uses and limitations of, 94–95
Real options, 514
Real property, 945
Real risk-free rate of interest (k^*), 132
Realized rate of return ($\bar{k}$), 172, 331
Rebalanced bonds, 949
Receivables collection period, 868–869
Receivables management (See also Accounts receivable and Current asset management), 814–818
  account receivable, 814
  aging schedule, 817
  credit policy, 818–819
  days sales outstanding, 75–76, 816
Recent innovations in bond financing, 713–718

Recovery allowance percentages, 465–467
Red herring, 705
Red-line method, 810–811
Refunding operations, 723–728
Registration statement, 705
Regression line or equation, 218
Regular, or simple, interest, 848–849
Reinvestment rate assumption, 437
Reinvestment rate risk, 136, 305, 947
Relationship investing, 118
Relative priority doctrine, 961
Relaxed current asset investment policy, 794
Relevant cash flows, 461–464
Relevant risk, 178
Rental payments, 736
Replicating portfolio, 520
Reorganization (See also Bankruptcy), 959–967
  federal bankruptcy laws, 958
  standard of fairness, 961
  standard of feasibility, 961
Repatriation of earnings, 1047
Replacement project analysis, 473–476
Replacement chain approach, 480–481
Required rate of return, 374
Required rate of return on equity (k_s), 331
Residual dividend model, 668–672
Residual value, 744
Restricted current asset investment policy, 794
Restrictive covenants, 306
Restructuring, 955
Retained earnings, 35
  breakpoint, 409
  cost of, 378–382
  statement of, 38
Retention growth model, 418
Retiree health benefits, 1081–1082
Return on common equity (ROE), 83
Return on total assets (ROA), 83
Revaluation, 1036
Revolving credit agreement, 847
Right, 701
Rights offering, 701
Risk, 126–127, 157–**160,** 161–200, 1068–1071
  accounting beta method, 392
  adjusted discount rate, 509, 534
  analysis and real options, 495–524
  and rates of return, 184–189
  arbitrage, 1009–1010
  average loss, 945
  aversion, 168–169, 187–188, **210**
  best-case scenario, 499

Risk *continued*
    beta, 180–184, **387**, **496**, 505–509
    business, 580–582
    Capital Asset Pricing Model (CAPM), 178
    cash outflows, 512–513
    certainty equivalent, 509, 534
    coefficient of variation, 166–**167**
    company-specific, 219
    corporate (within-firm), **387**, **496**, **505**
    country, 137
    decision trees, 514–**515**, 516
    default, 306–313
    default premium, 134
    diversifiable, 175–**178**, 179–180, **219**
    efficient portfolios, 206–208
    estimating project, 387–388
    event, 290
    exchange rate, 137
    financial, 580, 585–588
    homogeneous risk class, 622
    identification and measurement, 944–947
    indifference curve, 210
    inflation, 133–134, 187
    interest rate, 136, 302–305, **947**
    introduction to project risk analysis, 496–497
    liquidity (marketability), 134
    loss frequency, 945
    loss severity, 945
    management, 929
    market, 178–180, **219**, **387**, **496**, 505–509, **630**
    market premium, 185
    maximum loss, 945
    measuring risk, 164–167
    Monte Carlo simulation, 501–504
    nondiversifiable, 219
    political, 1031–1032, 1048
    portfolio, 202–206
    portfolio context, 169–184
    premium, 169, 210
    price, 136, 302–305, 947
    probability distributions, 160–161
    project, 496–497
    pure play method, 391–392, **507**–509
    reasons to manage, 908–910
    reinvestment rate, 136, **305**, **947**
    relationship between, and rates of return, 184–189
    relevant, 178
    scenario analysis, 499–501
    Security Market Line, 186
    sensitivity analysis, 497–499
    should firms diversify to reduce corporate, 505

    stand-alone, 160–169, **387**, **496**–504, **580**
    standard deviation, 164–166
    systematic, 178
    techniques for measuring beta, 391–392
    techniques for measuring stand-alone, 497–504
    unsystematic, 178
    variance, 165
    versus volatility, 191
    within-firm, 387, 496, 505
    worst-case scenario, 499
Risk and return extensions, 201–234
Risk aversion, 168–169, 187–188, **210**
Riskless hedge, 918
Riskless Treasury bonds, 135
Risky cash outflows, 512–513

S corporation, 12, 59
Safety stock, 883–885
Sale and leaseback, 737
Sales forecasts, 546–548
Salvage value, 467
Savings and loan associations (S&Ls), 120
Scenario analysis, 499–501
Seasonal dating, 820
Seasoned issue, 295
Secondary markets, 115, 327
Secured loan, 854–855
Secured short-term financing, 862–865
Securities and Exchange Commission (SEC), 705–706
Securities regulation and investment banking, 705–712
Securitization, 717–718
    asset, 718
Security, 717
    asset-backed, 718
Security Market Line (SML), 186
Security markets, 114–118
    efficient markets hypothesis, 352–353
    equilibrium, 245, 350
    trends in trading procedures, 125–126
Semiannual compounding, 261–266
Sensitivity analysis, 497–499
Service lease, 736
Settlements without formal bankruptcy, 955–957
Shelf registration, 712
Short hedges, 936
Short-term bank loans (See also Bank loans), 845–847
Short-term financing (See also Bank loans), 835–855, 862–865

accounts payable, **43**
accruals, **839**–840
advantages and disadvantages, 838–839
commercial paper, 854
compensating balances, 846
line of credit, 847
promissory note, 845–846
revolving credit agreement, 847
secured loans, 854–**855**
sources, 839–840
trade credit, 840
use of security, 854–855
Side payment, **926**
Signaling theory, 592–593, 641, **642**–645
Simple interest, **848**–849
Sinking fund provision, **290**–291
Social perils, **945**
Social responsibility, **19**–20
Sole proprietorship, **9**
Solving for interest rate and time, 247–250
Specific identification, **876**
Speculation, **936**
Speculative balance, **797**
Spin-off, **1013**
Spontaneously generated funds, **553**
Spot markets, 115
Spot rate, **1039**
Spread, 124
Stakeholders, 25
Stand-alone risk, **160**–169, **387**, **496**–504, **580**
techniques for measuring, 164–167, 497–504
Standard deviation, **164**–166
Statement of cash flows, **39**, **40**–42
Statement of retained earnings, **38**
Stepped-up exercise price, **770**
Stock dividends, 332–333, **681**–682
Stock exchanges, 123–126
Stockholders' equity, **35**
Stockholder wealth maximization, **13**
Stock market, 123–126
Stock market equilibrium, 349–355
Stock market reporting, 358–359
Stock price maximization and social welfare,
    14–15
Stock repurchases, **683**–687
an easy way to boost stock price, 685
less common overseas, 687
Stocks (See individual entries, such as Common
    stock; Preferred stock)
Stock splits, **681**
Stock values with zero growth, 333–334

Straight line depreciation method, 464
Strategic business plan, 423
Strategic options, 514
Strategic plans, 542–544
Stretching accounts payable, 842
Strike (exercise) price, 913
Stripping, 927
Structured note, 927–928
Subordinated debenture, 307–308
Sunk cost, 462–463
Super poison put, 290
Supernormal (nonconstant) growth, 339–342
Swap, 925–927
Symmetric information, 592–593
Synchronized cash flows, 804
Synergy, 986–987
Systematic risk, 178

Takeover, **324**
Tapping assets, 1080–1081
Target cash balance, **799**, 871–875
Target (optimal) capital structure, **375**
Target company, **991**
Target payout ratio, **660**
Taxable income, **51**
Taxes, 50–59
    corporate, 54–58
    individual, 51–54
    progressive, 51
    small business, 58–59
Tax havens, 58
Tax loss carry-back and carry-forward, **57**
Temporary current assets, **836**
Tender offer, **992**
Terminal value, **260**–261, **346**
Term structure of interest rates, **137**–140
Time lines, **236**–237
Time preferences for consumption, **126**–127
Times-interest-earned (TIE) ratio, **80**, **606**
Time value of money, 235–282
    amortization schedule, 271
    amortized loans, 269–271
    annuity, 250–257
    annuity due, 250, 252–254, 256–257
    comparison of different types of interest rates,
        266–268
    compounding, 237
    compounding periods, 261–266
    consol, 257
    discounting, 245
    effective annual rate (EAR), 263–266, 268

Time value of money *continued*
  fractional time periods, 268–269
  future value (FV), 237–244
  future value interest factor, 239–241
  **future value interest factor for an annuity,
      251–252**
  future value of an annuity, 250–254
  nominal interest rate, 263–266
  ordinary (deferred) annuity, 250–252, 254–256
  periodic interest rate, 266–268
  perpetuities, 257–258
  present value (PV), 244–247
  present value interest factor, 245–246
  **present value interest factor for an annuity,
      245**
  present value of an annuity, 254–257
  solving for time and interest rates, 247–250
  uneven cash flow streams, 258–261
Timing options, 479, **520**
Total assets turnover ratio, 76–77
Trade credit, 840
  costly, 843–844
  free, 843–844
  stretching accounts payable, 842
Trade deficit, 1035–1036
Trade discount, 798
Trade-off between risk and return, 170
Trade-off theory, 591–592
Transactions balance, 797
Treasury stock, 683
Trend analysis, 85–86
Triangular distribution, 231
Trust receipt, 864
Trustee, 306, 957–958
Two-bin method, 811
Tying the ratios together: the Du Pont chart and
      equation, 86–91

Underwriting syndicates, 711
Uneven cash flow streams, 258–261
Unfair trade practices, 946
Unfunded pension liability, 1064
Uniform distribution, 231
Unsyndicated stock offering, 712
Unsystematic risk, 178
Uses and limitations of ratio analysis, 94–95

Valuation, 285–315, 323–361
  bond valuation, 291–298, 301–302
  common stock valuation, 330–342
  preferred stock valuation, 360–361
  zero bonds, 291–295
Value-based management, 559
Variance, 165
Vertical merger, 989
Vesting, 1063
Volatility versus risk, 191

Warehouse receipt, 864
Warrant, 291, 767–772
  comparison with convertibles, 779–780
  detachable, 769
Weighted average cost of capital (WACC),
      374–375, 382–383
  factors that affect, 383–385
White knight, 1007
White squire, 992
Within-firm risk, 387, 496, 505
Window dressing techniques, 94
Working capital (See also Current assets), 42,
      792
  cash conversion cycle, 868–870
  financing policies, 835–838
  investment policies, 793–795
  management, 792
  multinational, 1051–1053
  net, 43, 792
  operating, 43, 792
  permanent current assets, 835
  policy, 792
  temporary current assets, 836
  terminology, 792–793
  zero, 795
Workouts, 955
Worst-case scenario, 499

Yield curve, 138–140
  determinants of its shape, 140–143
Yield to call, 299–300
Yield to maturity, 298–299

Zero coupon bonds, 288, 713–716
Zero growth stock, 333–334